A HISTORY OF
MACEDONIA

N. G. L. Hammond has been Fellow of Clare
College, Cambridge (1920-54), Headmaster,
Clifton College (1954-62), and Professor of
Greek, University of Bristol (1962-73).

HAMMOND, Nicholas Geoffrey Lemprière. A history of Macedonia. v.2: 550–336 B.C., by N. G. L. Hammond and G. T. Griffith. Oxford, 1979. 755p ill maps bibl index 73-154748. 65.00 ISBN 0-19-814814-3. C.I.P.

Recent years have seen a rebirth of interest in the history of pre-hellenistic Macedon. In v.1 of *A history of Macedonia* (CHOICE, Jul-Aug. 1973) Hammond provided a masterful synthesis of the evidence for the prehistory and historical geography of Macedonia. Volume 2 is a worthy successor to that now indispensable research tool. In a lucid and sometimes witty style Hammond and G. T. Griffith recount in abundant detail the history of the first two centuries of the Macedonian monarchy from the accession about 550 B.C. of Amyntas I, the first historical king of Macedon, to the death of Philip II in 336 B.C. The core of the book is Griffith's 443-page study of the reign of Philip II, the fullest available in any language. Much that is familiar does not survive Griffith's acute criticism, such as Philip's regency in 359 or his supposed alliance with Persia in the late 340s. Historical revision, however, is not Griffith's main contribution but rather his richly documented and thorough narrative of Philip's consolidation of the Macedonian monarchy and the acquisition of its Balkan empire. It is this that will make v.2 of *A history of Macedonia* mandatory reading for all students not only of Macedonian but of Greek history in general. Except for the lack of a good bibliography, the reference features—index, notes, and maps—of the volume are excellent. Highly recommended for purchase by libraries of institutions with programs in classics and ancient history.

CHOICE   OCT. '79
History, Geography &
Travel
Ancient (Incl.
Archaeology)

Also
v. 1
DR
701
M2
H22

670

Travel
Ancient (Incl.
Archaeology)

A HISTORY OF
MACEDONIA

VOLUME II
550–336 B.C.

N. G. L. HAMMOND
Hon. Fellow of Clare College, Cambridge

AND

G. T. GRIFFITH
Fellow of Gonville and Caius College, Cambridge

OXFORD
AT THE CLARENDON PRESS
1979

Oxford University Press, Walton Street, Oxford OX2 6DP

OXFORD LONDON GLASGOW
NEW YORK TORONTO MELBOURNE WELLINGTON
KUALA LUMPUR SINGAPORE JAKARTA HONG KONG TOKYO
DELHI BOMBAY CALCUTTA MADRAS KARACHI
NAIROBI DAR ES SALAAM CAPE TOWN

© *Oxford University Press 1979*

British Library Cataloguing in Publication Data
Hammond, Nicholas Geoffrey Lemprière
A history of Macedonia.
Vol. 2: 550–336 B.C.
1. Macedonia – History – to 168 B.C.
2. Macedonia – History – 168 B.C.–1453 A.D.
I. Title II. Griffith, Guy Thompson
938'.1 DF261.M2 77-30205
ISBN 0-19-814814-3

*Printed in Great Britain
at the University Press, Oxford
by Eric Buckley
Printer to the University*

PREFACE

CHAPTERS I TO IV AND XX are from the pen of N. G. L. Hammond, who had the good fortune to be appointed Visiting Johnson Professor at the Institute for Research in the Humanities, at the University of Wisconsin, for the academic year 1973–4. These chapters were written under ideal conditions there. His colleagues at the Institute were a constant inspiration, and above all he owes a debt of special gratitude to Professor C. F. Edson of the University of Wisconsin, who placed at his disposal a profound knowledge of Macedonia, discussed innumerable problems, and read the typescript with a sympathetic eye. His enthusiasm and his insights have added much to these chapters. The same may be said of his co-author G. T. Griffith, who has made valuable comments on many points. Many friends and colleagues in America have helped with particular subjects and matters of detail, and mention should be made especially of Professors E. Bennett, H. J. Dell, R. Drews, P. Ducrey, L. Gunderson, P. A. MacKay, D. G. Mitten, W. Moon, and H. Thompson. The typing was done with scrupulous care by Mrs. Wanda Schultz of the Institute for Research in the Humanities.

In September 1972 N. G. L. Hammond was invited to attend the First Colloquium on the Illyrians at Tirana and travelled up the Shkumbi valley and then to Pogradec, Koritsa, and Tren. He received every kindness and much help from his Albanian colleagues, especially Frano Prendi, Dhimosten Budina, Zhaneta Andrea, Neritan Ceka, and Gjerak Karaiskaj. In August 1973 he was invited to attend the Second Conference on Macedonia at the Institute for Macedonian Studies in Salonica, and received much help and encouragement from his Greek colleagues, especially Professors Andronikos and Petsas. He benefited greatly also from attending the Third International Colloquium on Aegean Prehistory, held at Sheffield in April 1973. He is particularly grateful to Professors M. Garašanin and F. Papazoglou in Yugoslavia and to Professors C. Danov and G. Mihailov in Bulgaria for their kindness in sending him copies of their books and offprints; to Mrs. Sigrid Jalkotzy-Deger in Austria and Professor J. Bouzek likewise; and to Professor S. I. Dakaris and Mrs. Julia Vokotopoulou for keeping him abreast of discoveries in Epirus. One advantage of undertaking a regional study of this kind is that it brings an author into contact with so many delightful and helpful people.

N. G. L. Hammond's part was completed in August 1974. A few

additions were made later, when he heard of the Asyut hoard from Dr. C. M. Kraay and was given information most kindly by Dr. M. J. Price, who is to publish the catalogue of the hoard. Work published between August 1974 and October 1975 has not been taken into account.

N. G. L. H.

G. T. Griffith writes: My first thanks are to Hammond for having honoured me by the invitation to join him in this volume, but also for a wealth of constructive criticism and discussion of my chapters, and for much patience in bearing with my indecisions. Inevitably there are a few things on which in the end we do not agree, and I have called attention to this where it has seemed necessary. In the spelling of names I have followed the lines mentioned in the Preface of Volume I, except that I have not used the Latinized forms of a few Greek names which seem not to take kindly to it.

The age of Philip (and Demosthenes) has long attracted able workers and writers. Schaefer's great work is still indispensable. Among the more recent writers I have gained most from Beloch and Momigliano, and then from Wüst and Geyer, Bengtson and Hampl. To all of these, and perhaps to others, I owe more, certainly, than the sum of my references to them for particular points or topics (and especially as one tends to refer sometimes in order to disagree). G. L. Cawkwell, too, on Demosthenes, and Marta Sordi on Thessaly leave me greatly in their debt; and a younger generation of English-writing scholars working on this period have done much good work in recent years which has been a great help to me and sometimes an inspiration.

My thanks are due to Dr. A. H. Jackson for kind permission to refer to his unpublished dissertation (Cambridge, 1970). Dr. R. D. Dawe, Professor Charles F. Edson, Dr. C. M. Kraay, Professor D. J. Mosley, Sir Denys Page, Professor H. W. Parke, the late Sir Edward Robinson, and Professor E. G. Turner have been kind enough to advise me on particular points or problems. I have profited greatly from the discussions and criticism of Mr. J. R. Hamilton, Dr. D. H. Kelly, Professor R. D. Milns, Dr. T. T. B. Ryder, and Mr. A. G. Woodhead, all of whom have found time to read drafts of certain chapters or sections; and I thank Mr. Woodhead also for much good advice about inscriptions. Professor P. A. Brunt did me the singular kindness of offering the loan of his own lecture notes, a stimulus and a source of enjoyment as well as of practical assistance. For all these offices of friendship I am grateful indeed.

The typing of my sometimes untidy material has been done beauti-
fully by (first) Miss Margaret Webb and later by Mrs. Patricia
McCullagh, and I thank them both. Finally I owe most of all to the
two main supports of my existence, my College, and my wife; to
whom and to our family I offer my portion of this book.

Both authors join in special thanks to Mrs. Sonia Argyle of the
Oxford University Press.

G. T. G.

Addendum: Our best thanks are due to Professor M. Andronikos for his
kind permission to reproduce on the jacket the photograph of the small
ivory head from the royal tomb at Vergina (Aegeae).

CONTENTS

LIST OF MAPS

LIST OF PLATES

(at end)

ABBREVIATIONS AND
SELECT BIBLIOGRAPHY

Not every title mentioned in notes or text is listed here.

ABBREVIATIONS are those listed in LSJ[9] except as follows:

Abel	O. Abel, *Makedonien vor König Philipp* (Leipzig, 1847)
AD	Ἀρχαιολογικὸν Δελτίον
AE	Ἀρχαιολογικὴ Ἐφημερίς
AHR	*American Historical Review*
AI	*Archaeologia Iugoslavica*
AM	*APXAIA MAKEΔONIA* etc. = *Ancient Macedonia: Papers read at the First International Symposium . . . August 1968* (Institute of Balkan Studies, Thessaloniki, 1970)
Anderson	J. K. Anderson, *Military Theory and Practice in the age of Xenophon* (Berkeley and Los Angeles, 1970)
ANS Mus N	*American Numismatic Society Museum Notes*
Arch. Anz.	*Archäologischer Anzeiger* in *JDAI* (q.v.)
ASI	*Ancient Society and Institutions: Studies presented to Victor Ehrenberg* (Blackwell, Oxford, 1966)
ATL	B. D. Meritt, H. T. Wade-Gery, and M. F. McGregor, *The Athenian Tribute Lists* (Harvard, 1939–53)
Badian	E. Badian, 'The death of Philip II', *Phoenix* 17 (1963) 244 ff.
Bellinger, 'Philippi'	A. R. Bellinger, 'Philippi in Macedonia', *American Numismatic Society Museum Notes* 11 (1964) 29 ff.
Bellinger, 'Thessaly'	A. R. Bellinger, 'The Thessaly Hoard of 1938', *Congresso internazionale di numismatica*, Rome, 1971, 2 (*Atti*) 57–60
Beloch	K. J. Beloch, *Griechische Geschichte*, 2nd edition, vol. 3. 1 and 2 (Berlin and Leipzig, 1922–3)
Bengtson, *GG*[2]	H. Bengtson, *Griechische Geschichte*, 2nd edition (Munich, 1960)
Bengtson, *Staatsv.*	H. Bengtson, *Die Staatsverträge des Altertums:* ii *Die Verträge der griechisch-römischen Welt von 700 bis 338 v. Chr.* (Munich and Berlin, 1962)
Bengtson, *Strategie*	H. Bengtson, *Die Strategie in der hellenistischen Zeit* (Munich, 1937–52)
Berve	H. Berve, *Das Alexanderreich auf prosopographischer Grundlage*, vols. 1 and 2 (Munich, 1926)
Best	J. G. P. Best, *Thracian Peltasts and their Influence on Greek Warfare* (Groningen, 1969)
BMC	*Catalogue of Coins in the British Museum*
Bosworth, 'Asth.'	A. B. Bosworth, 'ΑΣΘΕΤΑΙΡΟΙ', *CQ* N.S. 23 (1973) 245 ff.

Bosworth, 'PUM'   A. B. Bosworth, 'Philip II and Upper Macedonia', *CQ* N.S. 21 (1971) 93 ff.

Briant   P. Briant, *Antigone le Borgne* (Paris, 1973)

Brunt   P. A. Brunt, 'Euboea in the time of Philip II', *CQ* N.S. 19 (1969) 245 ff.

BS   *Balkan Studies*

BUST   *Buletin i Universitetit Shtetëror të Tiranës, Seria Shkencat Shoqërore* (Tirane)

BVSA   *Berichte über die Verhandlungen der Sächsischen Akademie, phil.-hist. Klasse*

CAH   *Cambridge Ancient History*, vol. 6 (Cambridge, 1927)

Casson   S. Casson, *Macedonia, Thrace and Illyria* (Oxford, 1926)

Cawkwell, 'Demosthenes'   G. L. Cawkwell, 'Demosthenes' Policy after the Peace of Philocrates', *CQ* N.S. 13 (1963) 120 ff. and 200 ff.

Cawkwell, 'Olynthus'   G. L. Cawkwell, 'The defence of Olynthus', *CQ* N.S. 12 (1962) 122 ff.

Cawkwell, 'Peace'   G. L. Cawkwell, 'Aeschines and the Peace of Philocrates', *REG* 73 (1960) 416 ff.

Chroust   A.-H. Chroust, *Aristotle* 1 (London, 1973)

Cloché   P. Cloché, *Histoire de la Macédoine jusqu'à l'avènement d'Alexandre le Grand* (Paris, 1960)

Cloché, *FE*   P. Cloché, *Un Fondateur d'empire: Philippe II roi de Macédoine* (Saint-Étienne, 1956)

Cloché, *PEA*   P. Cloché, *La Politique étrangère d'Athènes de 404 à 338 avant J.-C.* (Paris, 1934)

Collart   P. Collart, *Philippes, ville de Macédoine* (Paris, 1937)

CP   *Classical Philology*

Crum   R. H. Crum, *Philip II of Macedon and the City-State*, Diss. Columbia, 1966 (not seen)

Daux   G. Daux, 'Remarques sur la composition du conseil amphictionique', *BCH* 81 (1957) 95 ff.

Dindorf 8, 9   W. Dindorf (ed.), *Demosthenes*, vols. 8 and 9, *Scholia graeca ex codicibus aucta et emendata* (Oxford, 1851)

Dobesch   G. Dobesch, *Der panhellenische Gedanke in 4. Jh. v. Chr. und der 'Philippos' des Isokrates* (Vienna, 1968)

Ellis   J. R. Ellis, 'Amyntas Perdikka, Philip II and Alexander the Great', *JHS* 91 (1971) 15 ff.

Ellis, *PT*   J. R. Ellis, 'Population-transplants under Philip II', *Mak* 9 (1969), 9 ff.

Ellis and Milns   J. R. Ellis and R. D. Milns, *The Spectre of Philip* (Sydney, 1970)

J. R. Ellis, *Philip II and Macedonian Imperialism* (London, 1976) was not available for our use, unfortunately

Epirus   N. G. L. Hammond, *Epirus* (Oxford, 1967)

Errington	R. M. Errington, 'Macedonian "Royal Style" and its historical significance', *JHS* 94 (1974) 20 ff.
FGrH	F. Jacoby, *Die Fragmente der griechischen Historiker* (Berlin, 1923–30; Leiden, 1940–58)
Focke	F. Focke, *Demosthenesstudien*; Tübinger Beiträge zur Altertumswissenschaft 5 (1929)
R. L. Fox	Robin Lane Fox, *Alexander the Great* (London, 1973)
Franke	P. R. Franke, 'Geschichte, Politik und Münzprägung im frühen Makedonien' *Jahrb. f. Num. u. Geldgesch.* 314 (1952) 99 ff.
Gaebler *and* G.	H. Gaebler, *Die antiken Münzen Nord-Griechenlands* 3, *Makedonia und Paionia* 2 (Berlin, 1935)
Geyer	F. Geyer, *Makedonien bis zur Thronbesteigung Philipps II* (Oldenburg, 1930 = *Historische Zeitschrift*, Beiheft 19)
Geyer, *RE Mak.*	F. Geyer, 'Makedonia' in *RE* 14.1 (1928) 638–771
Geyer, *RE Phil.*	F. Geyer, 'Philippos' in *RE* 19 (1938) 2266–303
GGM	C. Müller, *Geographi Graeci Minores* (Paris, 1855–61)
Glotz	G. Glotz and R. Cohen, *Histoire grecque* 1–3 (Paris, 1925–36)
Gomme	A. W. Gomme, A. Andrewes, and K. J. Dover, *A Historical Commentary on Thucydides* (Oxford, 1945–70)
G & R	*Greece & Rome*
GRBS	*Greek, Roman and Byzantine Studies*
Griffith, *Mercenaries*	G. T. Griffith, *The Mercenaries of the Hellenistic World* (Cambridge, 1935)
Griffith, 'Thessaly'	G. T. Griffith, 'Philip of Macedon's early interventions in Thessaly (358–352 B.C.)', *CQ* N.S. 20 (1970) 67 ff.
Grote	G. B. Grote, *History of Greece* (London, 1846–56)
Gutschmid	A. Gutschmid, *Kleine Schriften* (Leipzig, 1889–94)
Hamilton	J. R. Hamilton, *Plutarch, Alexander; a Commentary* (Oxford, 1969)
Hammond, 'DSW'	N. G. L. Hammond, 'Diodorus' narrative of the Sacred War', *JHS* 57 (1937) 44 ff.
Hammond, 'SD'	N. G. L. Hammond, 'The sources of Diodorus XVI: part one', *CQ* 31 (1937) 79 ff.
HG²	N. G. L. Hammond, *A History of Greece to 322 B.C.*, 2nd edition (Oxford, 1967)
Hampl	F. Hampl, *Der König der Makedonen* (Diss. Leipzig, 1934)
Hampl, *GS*	F. Hampl, *Die griechische Staatsverträge des 4. Jahrhunderts v. Christi Geb.* (Leipzig, 1938)
HBNum	*Hamburger Beiträge zur Numismatik*
Head *and* H.	B. V. Head, *Historia Numorum*, 2nd edition (Oxford, 1911)
Hesp.	*Hesperia*

Hoffmann *and* H.   O. Hoffmann, *Die Makedonen, ihre Sprache und ihr Volkstum* (Göttingen, 1906)

Hogarth   D. G. Hogarth, *Philip and Alexander of Macedon* (London, 1897)

IGBR   G. Mihailov, *Inscriptiones Graecae in Bulgaria repertae*, 1–4 (Sofia, 1961–70)

JDAI   *Jahrbuch des Deutschen archäologischen Instituts*

JIAN   *Journal international de l'archéologie numismatique*

Kalléris *and* K.   J. N. Kalléris, *Les Anciens Macédoniens* i (Athens, 1954)

Kienast   D. Kienast, *Philipp II von Makedonien und das Reich der Achaimeniden* (Munich, 1973)

Kromayer, *AS*   J. Kromayer and G. Veith (edd.), *Antike Schlachtfelder in Griechenland* (Berlin, 1903–31)

Larsen, *GFS*   J. A. O. Larsen, *Greek Federal States* (Oxford, 1968)

Larsen, *RG*   J. A. O. Larsen, *Representative Government in Greek and Roman History* (Berkeley and Los Angeles, 1955)

Launey   M. Launey, *Recherches sur les armées hellénistiques*, 1 and 2 (Paris, 1949–50)

Le Rider   'Trésor de monnaies trouvé à Thasos', *BCH* 80 (1956) 1 ff.

Mak   Μακεδονικά

Markle   M. M. Markle III, *The Peace of Philocrates*, Diss. Princeton, 1970 (not seen)
                id., 'The strategy of Philip in 346 B.C.', *CQ* N.S. 24 (1974) 253 ff.

May, *Abdera*   J. M. F. May, *The Coinage of Abdera* (London, 1966)

May, *Ainos*   J. M. F. May, *Ainos; History and Coinage* (Oxford, 1950)

May, *Damastion*   J. M. F. May, *The Coinage of Damastion* (Oxford, 1939)

Mikulčić   I. Mikulčić, *Pelagonija* (Skopje, 1966)

Milns   R. D. Milns, 'Philip II and the Hypaspists', *Historia* 16 (1967) 509 ff.

Milns, *AAG*   *Entretiens Hardt 22, Alexandre le Grand* (Geneva, 1976), 'The army of Alexander the Great', 87 ff.

M–L, *GHI*   R. Meiggs and D. M. Lewis, *Greek Historical Inscriptions* (Oxford, 1969)

Momigliano, *FM*   A. Momigliano, *Filippo il Macedone* (Florence, 1934)

Momigliano, *QC*   A. Momigliano, *Quarto contributo — etc.* (Rome, 1969) 225 ff.

Momigliano, *TC*   A. Momigliano, *Terzo contributo alla storia degli studi classici e del mondo antico* (Rome, 1966)

NC   *Numismatic Chronicle*

Nock, *Essays*   A. D. Nock, *Essays on Religion and the Ancient World*, 1 and 2 (Oxford, 1972)

PAE   Πρακτικὰ τῆς ἐν Ἀθήναις Ἀρχαιολογικῆς Ἑταιρείας

Parke   H. W. Parke, *Greek Mercenary Soldiers* (Oxford, 1933)

Parke and Wormell	H. W. Parke and D. E. W. Wormell, *The Delphic Oracle* 1 and 2 (Blackwell, Oxford, 1956)
PCPhS	*Proceedings of the Cambridge Philological Society*
Perlman, 'Coins'	S. Perlman, 'The coins of Philip II and Alexander the Great and their Pan-Hellenic propaganda', *NC* s. 7. 5 (1965) 57 ff.
Perlman, *PA*	S. Perlman (ed.), *Philip and Athens* (Heffer, Cambridge, 1973)
Petsas	Ph. M. Petsas, 'Pella: literary tradition and archaeological research', *BS* 1 (1960) 113 ff.
Pokorny	E. Pokorny, *Studien zur griechischen Geschichte im sechsten und fünften Jahrzehnt des vierten Jahrhunderts v. Chr.*, Diss. Greifswald 1913
Pomponas *and* P.	I. K. Pomponas, Ἡ συγγένεια Μακεδονικῆς καὶ Μυκηναϊκῆς διαλέκτου καὶ ἡ Πανελληνικὴ καταγωγὴ τῶν Μακεδόνων (Athens, 1973)
PP	*La parola del passato*
Pritchett, *GSW*	W. K. Pritchett, *The Greek State at War* (Univ. of California, 1971–4)
Raymond *and* R.	D. Raymond, *Macedonian Royal Coinage to 413 B.C.* (New York, 1953)
RE	Pauly–Wissowa, *Realencyclopädie*
REA	*Revue des études anciennes*
REG	*Revue des études grecques*
Rev. arch.	*Revue archéologique*
Rev. belge de num.	*Revue belge de numismatique*
Rev. num.	*Revue numismatique*
RFIC	*Rivista di filologia e di istruzione classica*
RIL	*Rendiconti dell'Istituto Lombardo, Classe di Lettere, Scienze morali e storiche*
Robert, *Études*	L. Robert, *Études épigraphiques et philologiques* (Paris, 1938)
Robert, *Hellenica*	L. Robert, *Hellenica. Recueil d'épigraphie de numismatique et d'antiquités grecques* (Limoges and Paris, 1940–65)
Robinson, *Olynthus*	D. M. Robinson (and others), *Excavations at Olynthus* (Baltimore, 1930–52: Johns Hopkins University Studies in Archaeology)
Roebuck	Carl Roebuck, 'The settlements of Philip II with the Greek states in 338 B.C.', *CP* 43 (1948) 73 ff.
RPh	*Revue de philologie*
Ryder, *KE*	T. T. B. Ryder, *Koine Eirene* (University of Hull Publications, Oxford, 1965)
SA	*Studia Albanica*
SAWW	*Sitzungsberichte der Akademie der Wissenschaften in Wien, philos.-hist. Klasse*
Schaefer	A. Schaefer, *Demosthenes und seine Zeit*, 2nd edition, 3 vols. (Leipzig, 1885–7)

Schmitt, *Staatsv.*   H. Schmitt, *Die Staatsverträge des Altertums*, 3 (Munich and Berlin, 1969)

Schwahn   W. Schwahn, *Heeresmatrikel und Landfriede Philipps von Makedonien*, *Klio* Beiheft 21 (Leipzig, 1930)

SDAW   *Sitzungsberichte der deutschen Akademie der Wissenschaften zu Berlin, Klasse für Philosophie, Geschichte*, etc.

Sealey   R. Sealey, 'Dionysius of Halicarnassus and some Demosthenic Dates', *REG* 68 (1955) 77 ff.

SEG   *Supplementum Epigraphicum Graecum*

Snodgrass   A. M. Snodgrass, *Arms and Armour of the Greeks* (London, 1967)

Sordi, *LT*   M. Sordi, *La lega tessala fino ad Alessandro Magno* (Rome, 1958)

Sordi, 'Naopes'   M. Sordi, 'La fondation du collège des naopes et le renouveau politique de l'amphictionie au IVe siècle', *BCH* 81 (1957) 38 ff.

Spomenik   Српска Академија наука споменик (Belgrade)

Ste. Croix   G. E. M. de Ste. Croix, 'The alleged secret pact between Athens and Philip II', *CQ* N.S. 13 (1963) 110 ff.

StGH   N. G. L. Hammond, *Studies in Greek History* (Oxford, 1973)

Svoronos *and* S.   J. N. Svoronos, *L'Hellénisme primitif de la Macédoine* (Paris and Athens, 1914) = *JIAN* 1919. 1–265

*Syll.*³   W. Dittenberger, *Sylloge Inscriptionum Graecarum*, 3rd edition, 1 (Leipzig, 1915)

TAPA   *Transactions and Proceedings of the American Philological Association*

Tarn   W. W. Tarn, *Alexander the Great*, 2 *Sources and Studies* (Cambridge, 1948)

Tod *and* Tod, *GHI*   M. N. Tod, *Greek Historical Inscriptions* vol. 1, 2nd edition (Oxford, 1946); vol. 2 (Oxford, 1948). Citations are by number of inscription.

Walbank, *Commentary*   F. W. Walbank, *A Historical Commentary on Polybius* (Oxford, 1957–   )

Wescher   C. Wescher, *ΠΟΛΙΟΡΚΗΤΙΚΑ* ... etc. *Poliorcétique des Grecs* (Paris, 1867)

West, *CL*   A. B. West, *The History of the Chalcidic League* (Madison, Wisconsin, 1918)

West, *NC*   A. B. West, 'The early diplomacy of Philip II of Macedonia, as illustrated by his Coins', *NC* s. 5. 3 (1923) 169 ff.

Westlake   H. D. Westlake, *Thessaly in the Fourth Century B.C.* (London, 1935)

Wüst   F. R. Wüst, *Philipp II von Makedonien und Griechenland 346–338* (Munich, 1938)

ZA   *Ziva Antika*

Zahrnt   M. Zahrnt, *Olynth und die Chalkidier* (Munich, 1971)

ZfN   *Zeitschrift für Numismatik*

PART ONE

THE DEVELOPMENT OF THE
MACEDONIAN STATE AND THE
STRUGGLE FOR SURVIVAL

I

THE TRADITIONS AND THE LANGUAGES
OF EARLY MACEDONIA

1. *The Royal House of the Macedones*

THE claim of the Macedonian royal house to ancient descent is more surely attested than the claim of any royal house in Greece. When one of the kings, Alexander I, competed as a young man in the Olympic Games *c.* 500 B.C., his qualifications for entry were checked; he proved that he was an Argive, and so was pronounced by the Hellanodicae to be Greek (Hdt. 5. 22). That 'the descendants of Perdiccas were Greeks' is stated with unusual emphasis by Herodotus; 'this', he said, 'is what they say themselves and I myself happen to know it is so.' Evidently Herodotus had visited Macedonia, as we may infer also from other citations of 'what the Macedonians say' (7. 73 and 8. 138. 3), and he had spoken with some of the descendants of Perdiccas. It was from them that he learnt how the descendants of Temenus founded the royal house. Thucydides must also have visited Macedonia, as he owned property close to Macedonia (4. 105. 1) and began his period of exile in the vicinity, and he stated twice that the Macedonian kings were 'Temenidae from Argos' (2. 99. 3; 5. 80. 2). Moreover, as Temenus, king of Argos, was himself descended from Heracles, son of Zeus, the kings of Macedon as Temenidae were descended from Heracles, son of Zeus, no less than, for instance, the contemporary kings of Sparta. Thus the kings were Argive Greeks ruling over Macedones. Just as the Spartan king Cleomenes spoke of himself as an Achaean ruling over Dorian Spartans (Hdt. 5. 72. 3), so Alexander I was represented as a Greek ruling over Macedones ἀνὴρ Ἕλλην Μακεδόνων ὕπαρχος (Hdt. 5. 20. 4).[1]

---

[1] The fact that there was another Argos in Macedonia (in fact there were two others) seems to have hypnotized scholars since the time of Abel into supposing that the kings came from Macedonian and not Peloponnesian Argos and so were not Temenidae at all. What Gutschmid 4. 54 wrote is typical (cf. Geyer 37): 'den Nachweis Abels [*Makedonien* 95], dass das orestische Argos die Heimath der Makedonier ist, dem erst später der grösseren Berühmtheit halber das peloponnesische substituirt habe, halte ich für durchaus gelungen.' This is misplaced ingenuity. The Hellanodicae were convinced; Herodotus and Thucydides had no doubts in the matter; and it was easy to check in the list of Olympic victors that Alexander won the stadion, a foot-race of some 200 yards, in a particular year. He was admitted to the race as a Greek. There are no grounds for doubting the story in Herodotus that his qualifications were challenged by fellow competitors and upheld by the judges; presumably Alexander spoke Greek, probably of the Doric dialect, and the attestation of his genealogy was given

The uniqueness of this royal family within continental Macedonia was extremely important. No pretender to the Macedonian throne had a strong claim unless he was of the stock of Heracles, and no member of the family could think of himself as anything but a Greek and a descendant of Heracles. As a Greek the king had a natural relationship with the Greeks who visited his court and with the Greek settlers on his coast. He looked both ways, to the Macedones and to the Greeks.

Both Herodotus and Thucydides gave the number of kings down to Perdiccas II inclusive as eight (Hdt. 8. 137. 1; Thuc. 2. 100. 2). Herodotus went on to give the names as Perdiccas, Argaeus, Philippus, Aëropus, Alcetas, Amyntas, Alexander, and Perdiccas II (Hdt. 8. 139). He was giving the official king-list as it was cited to him in Macedonia in the mid-fifth century. There is no reason to question its authenticity, especially as the names are Greek, appropriate to an Argive family, and recurrent in later generations of the royal family. The founder of the dynasty is stated by Herodotus to have been Perdiccas ὁ κτησάμενος ... τὴν τυραννίδα and ὁ κτησάμενος τὴν ἀρχήν (8. 137. 1 and 8. 139). Neither Herodotus nor Thucydides dated the coming of Perdiccas to Macedonia except with the vague term τὸ ἀρχαῖον which implied the sixth century or earlier[1] (Hdt. 9. 45. 2; Thuc. 2. 99. 3), but we shall not be far out if we allow thirty years for the span of the average generation and place the beginning of the dynasty about 650 B.C., reckoning as adult Archelaus *c.* 413, Perdiccas *c.* 443, Alexander *c.* 473, Amyntas *c.* 503, Alcetas *c.* 533, Aëropus *c.* 563, Philippus *c.* 593, Argaeus *c.* 623, and Perdiccas I *c.* 653.[2]

---

inter alios by members of the Argive branch of the Temenidae. Once Abel and others fell into this error, they failed to differentiate the traditions of the Temenid house from the traditions of the Macedones.

[1] See T. J. Dunbabin, *The Western Greeks* 57, n. 4, for such a term referring to the seventh or sixth centuries usually in Aristotle, *Politics*.

[2] I differ here from Beloch, *GG*² 3. 2. 52, who seems to have been followed by later scholars without question. Accepting the tradition that Amyntas I was on the throne when the Peisistratidae were expelled from Athens *c.* 510, he reckoned backwards at three generations to a century and arrived at Perdiccas' accession to the throne at the beginning of the seventh century. This is simply a miscalculation; for Amyntas *c.* 510, Alcetas *c.* 543, Aëropus *c.* 576, Philippus *c.* 609, Argaeus *c.* 642, and Perdiccas *c.* 675 falls a generation short of 700. He went on to mention the chronographers' use of generations of 33 years and 35 years respectively, as if that justified his own assumption of three generations to a century; Gutschmid 4. 52 took a generation at 33$\frac{9}{11}$ths! Beloch dismissed Herodotus' statement that son followed father in the succession from Perdiccas to Alexander on the ground that in the fourth century the succession was contested and son did not follow father in each case. But this argument runs counter to his chronology; for he himself gives 11 reigns for 77 years of the fourth century, an average of only 7 years and not an average of 33 years as he assumes for the earlier period. There is no ground, of course, for supposing that the conditions of the fourth century obtained in the preceding centuries; indeed we have only four reigns between 510 at the latest and 399, and there is no reason to question the statements that each was the son of his predecessor (Hdt. 8. 139; Thuc. 1. 57. 2; Thuc. 2. 100. 2). In the fourth century intervention

Additions to the royal line, sometimes of as many as three kings preceding Perdiccas I, were recorded by authors later than Herodotus and Thucydides. These additions are certainly to be regarded as unhistorical and unauthentic; for the authoritative statements of Herodotus and Thucydides cannot be called in question on any reasonable grounds. Nevertheless, it is desirable to note the additions because they are of historiographical interest and of some historical relevance.

The first addition, that of Caranus as the first king, was recorded in an oracle which has come down to us.[1] He was told that 'he and all his offspring[2] must dwell' at the place where he first saw the goats (*aigas*), that is at Aegeae. Now this oracle must have been worded in this way before the royal dwelling-place was moved from Aegeae to Pella by Archelaus (it is presumed), who reigned from *c.* 413 to 399 B.C.[3] The first bearer of the name in the royal house as far as we know was a son of Philip II called Caranus (Justin 11. 2. 3), and one of Alexander's hipparchs had that name (Arrian 4. 5. 7).

The second addition appears in a fragment of Euripides' play *Archelaus*, which was produced in Macedonia in the year 408/7.[4] There Archelaus figures as the son of Temenus, hitherto childless, and it is clear from the summary of the play in Hyginus, *Fab.* 219, that this Archelaus was represented as the founder of the royal line in Macedonia. There is no doubt that with his usual freedom in the use of myth Euripides has simply invented a variation of the traditional theme in order to pay honour to his host, Archelaus, as homonymous with the supposed founder. It is thus not surprising that an Archelaus does not appear in any of the genealogies of either the Argive royal house or the Macedonian royal house for the early period.

How and when was the first addition made? We may be confident that it was made officially, that is with the support of a king, because Caranus was firmly ensconced in the official genealogy by the middle of the fourth century, as we shall see. The time of the addition was certainly after the recording of the genealogy by Herodotus in mid-fifth century (or a bit later), and most probably after the statement which was made by Thucydides at 2. 100. 2, that Archelaus had eight predecessors.

by outside powers helped to upset the succession; in the fifth century this was less so, and in the sixth still less. Accordingly we should take the fifth century, not the fourth century, as our model, and take a succession from father to son with an average generation gap of 30 years.

[1] D.S. 7. 16. See H. W. Parke and D. E. W. Wormell, *The Delphic Oracle* (Oxford, 1956) 1. 63 and 2. 93 no. 226.

[2] For this meaning of *genea* in oracles see ibid. 2 nos. 35, 43, 111, 334, and 357.

[3] Parke and Wormell made this important point, ibid. 1. 64; for the move to Pella see p. 139 below.

[4] See C. Austin, *Nova Fragmenta Euripidea in papyris reperta* (Berlin, 1968) frs. 1 and 2.

I say most probably, because we cannot exclude the possibility that Thucydides knew of, and disbelieved, a rival version which Archelaus had put out. When did Thucydides write the words at 2. 100. 2? They form a subsequent addition to a text which was probably composed before the outbreak of the Decelean War, and they have to be dated well within the reign of Archelaus because the building of forts and roads must have taken some years; so we may say after 408/7. The presumed move of the capital from Aegeae to Pella then came late in that reign, when the reputation of Archelaus stood very high. Thus the addition of Caranus may be placed most probably within the years *c.* 407–*c.* 400.

The story attached to Perdiccas I is and no doubt was in antiquity one of the best-known stories in Herodotus' history, comparable in its simplicity to the story of Alfred burning the cakes. It goes as follows.

This Alexander was seventh in descent from Perdiccas who acquired the kingship of the Macedones in the following manner. Three exiles from Argos came to the Illyrians—three brothers they were of the line of Temenus, named Gauanes, Aëropus, and Perdiccas—and from the Illyrians they crossed over into Upper Macedonia and they came to a town Lebaea. There they served for wages as thralls in the king's household, one tending horses, another oxen, and the youngest of them, Perdiccas, the lesser stock. The king's wife cooked their food herself; for in olden days the royal families among men and not the common people only were lacking in money. Whenever she baked bread, the loaf of the thrall Perdiccas rose to twice its size. Seeing that it always happened so, she told her husband; and as soon as he heard that, it struck him that it was a portent and signified something important. So he sent for the thralls and bade them leave his territory. But they said they had a right to be given their wages before they departed. When the king heard them speak of wages, as the sun was shining into the house through the smoke-vent, he said 'That's the wage you deserve and that's what I give you', indicating the sunlight; for he was crazed by a god. Gauanes and Aëropus, who were the older, stood horrified on hearing that; but the boy, happening to have a knife on him, said 'We accept what you give, O king' and drew a line around the sunlight on the floor with his knife; which done, he gathered up the sunlight into the fold of his garment three times and went away, he and his companions.

So they departed, but one of the king's advisers explained what it was that the boy had done and how it was with intent that the youngest had accepted the proffered gift. On hearing this the king was enraged, and he sent some horsemen after them to kill them. Now there is a river in that land to which the descendants of these men from Argos make sacrifice as their deliverer. This river, when the Temenidae had crossed over, rose in such a spate that the horsemen could not cross through it. The brothers came to another land in Macedonia and lived close to the gardens, as they are called, of Midas, son of Gordius, in which roses grow of their own accord, each one with sixty petals, and they surpass all other roses in fragrance. In these gardens too the

Silenus was caught, so it is said by the Macedones; above the gardens stands a mountain called Bermium, impassable in wintry weather. When they had acquired[1] possession of this land, they issued forth from it and began to subdue the rest of Macedonia as well.

On hearing this story any child will ask questions: what happened to the wicked king? did Perdiccas get the crown? how did he get the gardens of Midas? It is obvious that Herodotus had to cut himself short and return to Alexander delivering the message of Mardonius at Athens. But he told us enough for it to be certain that the kernel of the story is a piece of folk-lore, derived very probably from Persia, and not peculiar to Macedonia. As H. Kleinknecht has observed,[2] 'mehr noch als im Sonne-Schöpfen spiegelt sich in der Rettung der Brüder durch den plötzlich anschwellenden Strom noch ein klassisches Stück alt-iranischer, vorzarathustrischer chvareno-Mythologie'. But we should notice the features which derive from its Macedonian setting: Perdiccas tending the lesser stock, by which goats and sheep are meant; the king's advisers; the river as the frontier between the two kingdoms (that of the Macedones and that of the Briges at one time, as we have heard at 7. 73); the worship of the river god as deliverer; the gardens of Midas, the Silenus and Mt. Bermium; and the stages of expansion of Perdiccas' kingdom (the acquisition of which has dropped out of Herodotus' narrative).

If Herodotus had been able to give the full story, we should have seen that Perdiccas' tending of the lesser flocks led him to the site of his new capital, not Lebaea but Aegeae; and the oracle which we shall mention shortly would have been included.[3] As I argued in Volume I. 434 when I gave the locations of the two kingdoms, the river god was Beres, who was included as a son of Macedon in the local genealogy,[4] and the river is now the river of Verria. The conquests by Perdiccas were evidently represented in three stages: acquiring the kingdom of the Macedones, increasing that kingdom by acquiring the kingdom within which the gardens lay, and lastly beginning the conquest of the rest of Macedonia.

Some of these points become significant when we turn to the oracle which was attached to the name of Perdiccas. 'Perdiccas wishing to increase his own kingdom asked at Delphi' wrote Diodorus Siculus 7. 16; and this is turned into Latin in Eusebius, *Chron.* 1. p. 227 (Schoene) 'hic regnum suum adaugere volebat ac propterea Delphos misit'. The oracle is as follows.

> ἔστι κράτος βασίλειον ἀγαυοῖς Τημενίδαισι
> γαίης πλουτοφόροιο· δίδωσι γὰρ αἰγίοχος Ζεύς.

[1] The aorist tense is to be contrasted with the imperfect tense of *katestrephonto*.

[2] 'Herodot und die Makedonische Urgeschichte', *Hermes* 94 (1966) 142.

[3] F. Jacoby, for instance, noted the connection between 'the lesser flocks' and the oracle, in *FGrH* II B p. 401. [4] St. Byz. s.v. *Mieza*.

ἀλλ' ἴθ' ἐπειγόμενος Βουτηΐδα πρὸς πολύμηλον·
ἔνθα δ' ἂν ἀργικέρωτας ἴδῃς χιονώδεας αἶγας
εὐνηθέντας ὕπνῳ, κείνης χθονὸς ἐν δαπέδοισι
θῦε θεοῖς μακάρεσσι καὶ ἄστυ κτίζε πόληος.

The noble Temenidae have royal rule over a wealth-producing land;[1] for it is the gift of aegis-bearing Zeus.[2] But go in haste to the Bouteïd[3] land of many flocks, and wherever you see gleaming-horned, snow-white goats sunk in sleep, sacrifice to the gods and found the city of your state on the level ground of that land.[4]

The word 'wealth-bearing' was probably chosen as the epithet of 'the heavenly goat', a symbol of fertility,[5] rather than with reference to the mine of Alexander I, which was mentioned by Herodotus (5. 17. 2). For the goat-motif is all-pervading: the aegis, the flocks (*polumelon* being the lesser flocks of goats and sheep), and the sight of the goats, *aigas*, where the new capital of the increased kingdom is to be established, *Aigeai*. While the oracle was composed *post eventum* to incorporate an explanation of the name Aegeae, the goat had a great importance of its own; for it was the mascot of the kings, it was placed upon the coinage of Alexander I, and it played a part in ceremonial,[6] perhaps as it used to do in leading a parade of the Welch Regiment. When, then, Herodotus wrote of Perdiccas tending the lesser flocks, there is every likelihood that he had this very oracle in mind.

The mention of the king's advisers (*paredroi*) suggests that Herodotus knew or was told of the Macedonian king's Hetairoi. The gardens of Midas were probably in the region of Mieza, near the modern Naoussa (see Volume I. 163 f.). The stages of expansion, which emerge from the last sentence of Herodotus' abbreviated version, suggest again that either he knew or his narrator knew of the oracle and the tradition that there were three or more stages of conquest. The same tradition no doubt supplied Thucydides with the basis for his account at 2. 99. 3–6.

The oracle which was attached to the name of Caranus is also preserved. It is introduced in the following way by the scholiast to Clem. Alex. *Protr.* 2. 11.

[1] The oracle begins with ἐστι which means a present, not a future situation (as in other oracles, e.g. nos. 33, 163, and 381 in Parke and Wormell, op. cit. 2); that is why the ancient commentators, such as Diodorus, spoke of Perdiccas *increasing* the (already existing) kingdom.
[2] So Tyrtaeus 2. 2 claimed that Zeus gave Sparta to the kings.
[3] The manuscripts have this reading; Parke and Wormell give the emended version *Botteida*, not attested elsewhere (see Volume I. 435 n. 1). For Boutis see St. Byz. s.v. *Pella*.
[4] Parke and Wormell, op. cit. I. 63, seem to me to give an incorrect translation. They do not bring out the implication of ἐστι, translate ἔνθα δ' ἂν as 'there if' which would need a long alpha in ἄν, and fail to translate κείνης χθονός as marking the beginning of the main sentence. This form of oracle with ἔνθα is common (see nos. 71, 225, 228, and 374. 11).
[5] See LSJ[9] s.v. αἴξ, citing *Com. Adesp.* 8; the proverb was current in the fifth century, e.g. in Cratinus (T. Kock, *CAF* I. 244).   [6] See Just. 7. I. 9, cited p. 12 below.

When Caranus, the son of Poeanthes, intended to leave Argos and make a colonial settlement in Macedonia, he came to Delphi and received this response from Apollo:

φράζεο, δῖε Καρανέ, νόῳ δ' ἐμὸν ἔνθεο μῦθον·
ἐκπρολιπὼν Ἄργος τε καὶ Ἑλλάδα καλλιγύναικα
χώρει πρὸς πηγὰς Ἁλιάκμονος· ἔνθα δ' ἂν αἶγας
βοσκομένας ἐσίδῃς πρῶτον, τότε τοι χρεών ἐστιν
ζηλωτὸν ναίειν αὐτὸν γενεάν τε πρόπασαν.

Attend, noble Caranus, and set my words in your mind. Forsake Argos and Hellas of the fair women and go to the waters of Haliacmon, and wherever you first see goats grazing, then you are to dwell in happiness, you and all your offspring.[1]

This oracle is different in meaning from that attached to Perdiccas.[2] Caranus is to leave Argos for Macedonia, seeking a new home, whereas Perdiccas is founding a new capital for his kingdom which already exists. The idea of a colonial settlement (*apoikia*) in this oracle was elaborated later as 'Caranus cum magna multitudine Graecorum sedes in Macedonia responso oraculi iussus quaerere' (Just. 7. 1. 7) and 'with settlers from Argos and the rest of the Peloponnese' (Syncellus 373 ed. Dindorf). The elaboration may have been made by Theopompus in the fourth century, because he was used by Pompeius Trogus, whom Justin is here epitomizing,[3] and the supposed colony resembles those of Timoleon in Sicily which attracted settlers from the Peloponnese.

The account attached to Caranus by Syncellus[4] has reference to a different oracle from that given by the scholiast. Caranus and his force arrived 'in the regions by Macedonia'. He made an alliance with the king of the Orestae against the Eordani, a neighbouring people, and received half of the new-won territory because of the alliance; he then took over 'Macedonia' and founded a city in it 'according to an oracle', and setting out from it he formed the Macedonian kingdom which his descendants in succession inherited. It is evident that this account is in part an elaboration of points in Herodotus' story; for 'the regions by Macedonia' correspond with his Illyrians, the Orestae with his Upper Macedonia, and the final stage 'setting out (*hormomenos*) he formed the

---

[1] Parke and Wormell, op. cit. 1. 63 and 2. 92 no. 225. The word πηγαί in Homeric or pseudo-Homeric oracular Greek means 'water' and not 'sources'; see LSJ⁹ s.v. πηγή. The point is missed by Parke and Wormell in their translation.

[2] Modern commentators have fallen into the error of regarding the oracles as alternative versions; so Abel and Gutschmid in their general approach 'die Karanossage die ich in noch höherem Grade wie Abel als blosse Verdoppelung der Perdikkassage auffassen zu müssen glaube' (Gutschmid 4. 54), and Parke and Wormell, op. cit. 1. 63 'an alternative version' and 'two versions of the Delphic oracle are extant.'

[3] The 7th book of Pompeius Trogus contained 'origines Macedonicae, regesque a conditore gentis Carano usque ad magnum Philippum'.

[4] Syncellus 373 ed. Dindorf in *Corpus Scriptorum Historiae Byzantinae* 1.

Macedonian kingdom' with his 'setting out (*hormomenoi*) they began to conquer the rest of Macedonia'. The founding of the city in accordance with an oracle refers to Perdiccas' oracle and not to Caranus' oracle.

A similar but not identical account is given in the Armenian version of Euseb. *Chron*. p. 169 (cited in the Loeb edition of Diodorus Siculus 7. 15). 'Before the first Olympiad' Caranus collected troops from Argos and other parts of Peloponnese and undertook an expedition into 'the territory of the Macedones', but he was deflected by answering the request of the king of the Orestae for help. This king was at war with his neighbours, the Eordaei, and offered half his kingdom to Caranus in the event of success. All went well, the king kept his promise, and Caranus got 'that region'. He ruled there for thirty years, was succeeded by Coenus, and he by Tyrimmas. Perdiccas ruled for forty-two years. Being anxious to extend his kingdom, he sent an embassy to Delphi. In this account[1] there are some obscurities which seem to arise from abbreviation of the original; for the relationship of 'the territory of the Macedones' to the kingdom of the Orestae is not stated, and 'the region' which Caranus got seems later to be the kingdom which Perdiccas wished to extend. Once again we see an attempt to fit together the activities of Caranus and those of Perdiccas in fulfilment of the oracle.

Euripides attached two oracles to Archelaus. Temenus being childless consulted Dodona, and the priest of Dione replied that he would be given a child by Zeus and that the child should be called Archelaus.[2] This is entirely fictitious, as we have noted already. The second oracle appears in the summary of the play by Hyginus, *Fab*. 219. Archelaus, being exiled from Argos, went to Thrace[3] where he had to serve a king Cisseus, who plotted to kill him; so Archelaus killed Cisseus and fled into Macedonia 'ex responso Apollinis . . . capra duce oppidumque ex nomine caprae Aegeas constituit'. Euripides evidently took Cisseus from *Iliad* 11. 223, probably connected the name with Mt. Cissus (now Mt. Khortiatis) near the head of the Thermaic Gulf, and gave his own version of the oracle connecting Aegeae and goats. It is possible that Euripides' goat leading the way inspired Theopompus to make up the fuller account, complete with weather conditions, which appears in Justin 7. 1. 7.

If my interpretation of the oracles and the narratives is correct, the sequence of events was more or less as follows. In the middle of the seventh century some exiles from Argos, led by Perdiccas, a member of the Temenid house, went to Illyris as adventurers or mercenaries and raided

---

[1] Other stories about Caranus and his son Coenus are in Paus. 9. 40. 8–9 and *FGrH* 135/6 (Marsyas) F 14.

[2] C. Austin, op. cit. fr. 2. 23 f.

[3] The emendation of 'Thraciam' to 'Macedoniam' which C. Robert has suggested is out of sense; for the story goes on to say that 'Archelaus profugit . . . in Macedoniam'. Everything east of the Axius was in Thrace at the time to which the oracle referred.

with Illyrians into south-western Macedonia, where Perdiccas managed to set himself up as king of the Argeadae Macedones. His realm then was in the hill country of northern Pieria (see Volume I. 147), and he enlarged it first by acquiring the edge of the plain, where he made his capital at Aegeae, and later by annexing the district of Mieza and Naoussa. His successors enlarged the kingdom further by stages, the crown remaining within his family.

The genealogy of the royal house was approved by the judges at the Olympic Games *c.* 500 B.C. During the Persian period Macedonia became prominent and Alexander I well known, and he or perhaps one of his predecessors obtained from Delphi an oracle which gave approval to the Temenid kingdom and celebrated the founding of the capital at Aegeae. When Herodotus visited the court and made inquiries, he was informed of this oracle, a story about Gauanes, Aëropus, and Perdiccas (which was more respectable than an Illyrian raid),[1] and the gradual growth of the kingdom in several stages. In his narrative (8. 137–8) the story took pride of place. When Thucydides wrote his account of Macedonia, probably in the first part of the Peloponnesian War, he accepted the Temenid genealogy and he mentioned areas rather than stages of expansion, obtaining his information in Macedonia.

When Euripides visited the court of Archelaus, a most enterprising king in Thucydides' opinion (2. 100. 2), he wrote and produced in 408/7 a play about the early days of the royal house. He worked into it three oracles—the famous one about the monocular mule of the Dorian invasion,[2] a new one about Temenus' childlessness, and a variant of the local one about the founding of Aegeae. As a compliment to his host he replaced the traditional founder Perdiccas with an ancestral Archelaus. This Archelaus was never accepted, but Euripides' *jeu d'esprit* may have inspired Archelaus to seek a more impressive account of the origins of the Macedonian kingdom than that contained in the brilliant and only too memorable story told by Herodotus. Enlisting the aid of Delphi, he introduced Caranus as the founding father who came direct from Peloponnesian Argos to make a new home at Aegeae in Macedonia. The name may have been chosen because it had the ring of that authority with which the Great King invested Cyrus as *karanos* in 407 (X. *HG*

---

[1] I made this point also in Volume I. 433.

[2] C. Austin, op. cit. p. 12, and Parke and Wormell, op. cit. 2. 120 no. 293. Caranus was a good Dorian name (at Sparta, Hdt. 7. 173. 2; in Crete, *Inscr. Cret.* 4 no. 182), and it was chosen rather for connection with Dorian Argos than for any association with the violent Lapiths of mythical times, such as Abel 101 f. and Hoffmann 124 f. have suggested, equating Κάρανος with Κόρωνος and using Hesych. s.v. Κόρανος· βασιλεὺς Μακεδονίας to bridge the gap. The Macedonian form Κάρανος is clearly given by Marsyas (*FGrH* 135/6 F 14). For the meaning 'goat' see Hesych. s.v. *karannos* and Schol. Clem. Alex. *Strom.* 4 p. 96. I am grateful to Mr. Stewart Karren of the University of Wisconsin, who helped me with this note.

1. 4. 3), or because the words *karano* and *karannos* in some dialects meant a goat or kid;[1] for the familiar theme of goats grazing was included in the new oracle which purported to be the answer to an inquiry by Caranus. The oracle was so worded that it did not clash with the older oracle which Herodotus had known; and it was made up before the capital was moved to Pella, an event which must therefore be placed late in the reign of Archelaus.

Caranus appeared at different places in the extended genealogy: just before Perdiccas (Just. 7. 2. 1), or with two others (Coenus and Tyrimmas) coming between him and Perdiccas. Sometimes he was the son of Poeanthes or Poeas, and sometimes the son or the brother of the Argive king Pheidon, son of Aristodamidas. As a late arrival in the genealogical tables he was at first something of a floater.[2] But from the mid-fourth century onwards Caranus was a fixture. 'One thing which is completely accepted' wrote Plutarch in his *Life* of Alexander the Great 'is Alexander's descent on his father's side from Caranus as a Heraclid and on his mother's side from Neoptolemus as an Aeacid.'

The canonized version has survived in an abbreviated form in Justin 7. 1. 7–12, which is derived via Pompeius Trogus from Theopompus, *Philippika*.

Caranus with his large company of Greeks came to Emathia [direct to the central plain][3] in accordance with the oracle which had ordered him to seek a place of settlement in Macedonia [the oracle cited on p. 9 above], and following a flock of goats which were running away from the rain, for there was a tremendous downpour and thick mist, he seized the town of Edessa without the townsfolk being aware of his approach. And being reminded of the oracle in which he had been ordered 'to seek a realm where goats lead' he made it the capital of his kingdom. And he scrupulously maintained the practice thereafter of keeping the same she-goats in front of his standard whenever his army was on the march, so that they should be leaders of his undertakings, just as they had been the authors of his kingdom. In memory of their service he named the town Edessa 'Aegeae' and the people 'Aegeadae' [probably not an error for Argeadae]. Next he drove out Midas, for Midas held a part of Macedonia,[4] and he drove out other kings, and he replaced them all; and he was the first to unite the tribes of various peoples and make Macedonia, as it were, one body; and his kingdom grew, he laid strong foundations for growth. After him reigned Perdiccas.

All that was left to recount about Perdiccas was his dying words which fulfilled an oracle. He showed his son Argaeus where his bones and those

---

[1] See LSJ[9] s.vv.

[2] There is a convenient table of the lists in Jacoby, *FGrH* II B 401–2.

[3] For the geographical meaning of Emathia see Volume I. 153 f.

[4] This is based on a conflation of Hdt. 7. 73 and 8. 138. 2–3, but Herodotus implied that the Briges left Macedonia for Asia of their own volition; see Volume I. 412 f.

of his successors were to be buried, and he prophesied that the kingdom would remain in his family as long as the remains of his posterity were buried there. While this version was composed for the greater glory of Macedonia, it is clear that in the last few words of our quotation Theopompus attributed to the founder the achievements which he associated with Philip II in his own lifetime.[1]

The canonized version of the genealogy, as it was known in the Hellenistic period, was given by Satyrus, writing about the demes of Alexandria in Egypt.[2] The line began with Dionysus and Zeus, as Deianeira, daughter of Dionysus, was the mother and Heracles, son of Zeus, was the father of Hyllus, from whom the third in direct descent was Temenus and the ninth was Caranus. Then came Coenus, Tyrimmas, Perdiccas, etc. In some cases the mothers were given. We know of Peridea, mother of Temenus,[3] Dor— mother of Ceisus, Lan— (probably Lanice),[4] mother of Coenus, Cleonice, mother of Perdiccas, Cleopatra, mother of Argaeus, Prothoe, mother of Philippus, and Niconoë, mother of Aëropus. They were no doubt projections of names used in the fifth and fourth centuries in the royal house.

We are left with a point of geography, the location of Aegeae, which we discussed in Volume I. 156 f. and 435, deferring until now consideration of the Macedones' own traditions. These indicate that Aegeae was the capital from the time of Perdiccas (or Caranus, if that version is followed) down to the late fifth century, and that all the kings were buried there until Alexander the Great. Everyone knew then where Aegeae was, and the oracles and stories were designed to lead the founder to it. The starting-point for Perdiccas was the original 'Macedonis', i.e. the hill country of northern Pieria, and he was told to go to the lowland pastures of Bouteïs and found a city on 'the level ground of that land'. The name 'Bouteïs' does not help us; it was evidently associated with the capital because Pella in Syria was called ἡ Βουτίς. The oracle to Caranus supplies the clue we need. His starting-point was Argos, and he came to the coastal plain 'Emathia', presumably by sea. 'Forsake Argos and Hellas of the fair women and go to the waters of Haliacmon.' Thus Aegeae was beside the Haliacmon; moreover as we saw from the oracle to Perdiccas, it was on level ground below the hill country of northern Pieria. It is a fair description of the site of Palatitsa–Vergina, where the so-called palace is built on the level terrace and the great cemetery of 300 tumuli lies on the edge of the plain between the terrace and the river Haliacmon. The next stage in the expansion of the kingdom (e.g. in

---

[1] Thus Justin 9. 8. 21 used of Philip the phrase 'orbis imperii fundamenta iecit', recalling 7. 1. 12 'valida incrementorum fundamenta constituit'.

[2] *FGrH* 630 (Satyrus) F 1 and *Oxyr. Pap.* 27 (1962) 2465 pp. 121 f.

[3] Schol. Lyc. *Alex.* 804.   [4] See Arr. *An.* 4. 9. 3.

Just. 7. 1. 11) was the conquest of the adjacent region of Naoussa, in which the gardens of Midas were traditionally situated, and of the classical city of Edessa.

Even when Caranus had been grafted on to the line of kings, it seems that the credit for acquiring the kingdom in an enlarged form was still accorded to Perdiccas. For the phrases of Herodotus 8. 137. 1 Περδίκκης ὁ κτησάμενος . . . τὴν τυραννίδα and 139 Περδίκκης ὁ κτησάμενος τὴν ἀρχήν were repeated by Isocrates in 346 in his appeal to Philip, when he mentioned the founder as τὸν κτησάμενον τὴν βασιλείαν and ὅ τε κτησάμενος τὴν ἀρχήν (*Philippus* 105–6), and it is probable that Isocrates had the name of Perdiccas in mind and expected Philip to have it in mind too. Aristotle also accepted the general tradition about the founding and the growth of the Macedonian monarchy, when he gave the kings of the Macedones as an example of kings who were honoured for establishing and extending a kingdom (ἢ κτίσαντες ἢ κτησάμενοι χώραν, *Politics* 1310^b39).

2. *The Royal Houses of Upper Macedonia and Adjacent Areas*
(See Map 9)

In discussing the tribal peoples of northern Epirus and Upper Macedonia Strabo made the comment that they were ruled by dynasties of native stock except in three cases: the Enchelii, the Molossi, and the Lyncestae (Str. 7 C 326). For most of his description Strabo was drawing upon the work of Hecataeus,[1] but his source for the kings of the *Lyncestae* is likely to have been Theopompus.[2] These kings claimed descent from Bacchis, king of Corinth, and thus belonged to the clan of the Bacchiadae who were expelled from Corinth *c.* 650 B.C. Members of this clan took refuge then in Corcyra (*FGrH* 90 (Nic. Dam.) F 57, 7), and they may have become established in Illyria through participating in the colonization of Apollonia Illyrica or Epidamnus; in any case it is very probable that they seized power in Lyncus with the help of the Illyrians. The claim of the Lyncestid royal house was made in the middle of the fifth century; it must have rested upon demonstrable evidence of descent and it was very far from being derived from a myth of the remote past.

Strabo gave the name of the founder as Arrhabaeus and added a piece of Bacchiad genealogy: 'Eurydice, the mother of Philip, son of Amyntas, was Arrhabaeus' daughter's daughter and the daughter of Sirras.' If we reckon thirty years to a generation, we can then put Arrhabaeus' floruit *c.* 445 and equate him with the Arrhabaeus, son of Bromerus,

---

[1] See *Epirus* 463 f.

[2] *FGrH* 115 (Theopompus) F 29 shows that he dealt with Philip's genealogical relationships in the first book of the *Philippika*.

against whom Perdiccas and Brasidas fought in 423 (Thuc. 4. 83. 1); on that occasion the Illyrians came to the aid of Arrhabaeus. We hear of another Arrhabaeus in Aristotle, *Politics* 1311ᵇ13: Archelaus (king of Macedon *c.* 413–399) was hard pressed in a war against Sirras and Arrhabaeus, when he gave his elder daughter in marriage to the king of Elimea. As it was customary not to name father and son alike but to give the grandfather's name to a grandson, we may infer that Arrhabaeus II was the grandson of Arrhabaeus I and was therefore a minor in the years before 399. Sirras then was regent; he was a member of the royal house who was chosen to marry a daughter of the founder, and it was a characteristic of the Bacchiadae that they practised endogamy,[1] as indeed many royal houses did. Thus Strabo mentioned the names of Eurydice and Sirras as members of the Bacchiad family (Str. 7 C 326).

Some scholars have argued that Sirras was a member of another royal family, e.g. of Orestis or Elimea or a supposed Illyrian dynasty.[2] If that were so, his daughter would have been in that royal family (for the bride went to the husband's family), and her daughter, Eurydice, would have been a princess in that family. Thus neither Sirras nor Eurydice would have been members of the Bacchiad house; yet it was in connection with this house that Strabo mentioned them. There is also a further complication; for, if Sirras was a member of another royal house, Arrhabaeus II must have been an active king before 399, as Archelaus was at war with Sirras and Arrhabaeus. In other words, Arrhabaeus II has to be not the grandson but the son of Arrhabaeus I; this Beloch postulated, but as I have said it was not the practice to name father and son alike in these dynasties.

Three brothers were believed to have been involved in the assassination of Philip II, and one of them was referred to as ὁ Λυγκηστὴς Ἀλέξαν-δρος (D.S. 17. 80. 2; cf. Curt. 7. 1. 5, Just. 11. 2. 2 and 12. 14. 1). They were thus members of the Lyncestid royal house: Arrhabaeus, Heromenes, and Alexander, sons of Aëropus (Arr. *An.* 1. 7. 6), and Alexander was married to the daughter of Antipater, a leading Macedonian. It is then probable that these brothers were in the line of succession and their father had been king of the Lyncestae at the time when Philip II became king of Macedon.

The stemma of the Lyncestid royal house[3] may then be reconstructed as follows:

[1] Hdt. 5. 92. b 1.
[2] Beloch, *GG²* 3. 2. 74; Geyer 81; Cloché 86; and F. Papazoglou in *Historia* 14 (1965) 151.
[3] See my article in *BSA* 61 (1966) 243 f. In a paper at the Macedonian Conference in August 1973 C. Habicht agreed with my article on most points but he differed in making Arrhabaeus II a son of Arrhabaeus I, which is unlikely on chronological grounds and on the succession of the name, normally from grandfather.

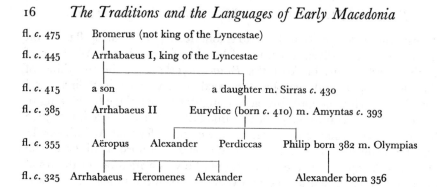

fl. c. 475   Bromerus (not king of the Lyncestae)

fl. c. 445   Arrhabaeus I, king of the Lyncestae

fl. c. 415   a son   a daughter m. Sirras c. 430

fl. c. 385   Arrhabaeus II   Eurydice (born c. 410) m. Amyntas c. 393

fl. c. 355   Aëropus   Alexander   Perdiccas   Philip born 382 m. Olympias

fl. c. 325   Arrhabaeus   Heromenes   Alexander   Alexander born 356

The line of succession ran on from Arrhabaeus and not from Eurydice, who joined the family of Amyntas and was the mother of Macedonian, not Lyncestid kings.

The names may have been spelt in more than one way. Arrhabaeus is the form in *IG* I².71 (line 76, Ἀρραβαῖοι) and Arrhibaeus in the manuscripts of Thucydides. Sirras is found in Aristotle and Irras in Strabo; and a dedication to the Muses by Eurydice has come down with the form Irras, if we accept an emendation by Wilamowitz-Moellendorff.[1] There is no doubt that Arrhabaeus and his successors spoke Greek, presumably in the Dorian dialect of Corinth. As the Bacchiadae were descended from Heracles,[2] they, like the Temenidae, were Heraclids and the two royal houses of the Lyncestae and the Macedones were thus closely related to one another. We should not be misled by the abusive way in which Eurydice was described no doubt by Attic orators and through them by sensational writers as 'an Illyrian, thrice barbarous', and a mother who passed off as her own sons children who were of other origins.[3] Rather the Lyncestid and Macedonian royal houses were particularly bound together, and that is probably the reason why Leonnatus, who was of the Lyncestid royal family through his relationship with Eurydice (on my interpretation that she and Sirras were of that family) and had been brought up with Alexander the Great, was regarded as being of 'royal' Macedonian 'descent' in the period after Alexander's death.[4]

---

[1] In *Hermes* 54 (1919) 71, accepted by Beloch, loc. cit. 78. The emendation is not even mentioned in the Loeb edition of Plu. *Mor.* 14 B (*De educ. puer.*), but it is hardly possible to escape the inference from the abusive description of Eurydice in the preceding words that she is the famous Eurydice, mother of Alexander, Perdiccas, and Philip, and that an emendation is needed on the lines suggested by Wilamowitz-Moellendorff.

[2] See Gutschmid 4. 14 f.

[3] The allegations are in Plu. *Mor.* 4 B, Suid. s.v. *Karanos*, and Libanius, *Arg. D.* 9; Theopompus may well have been an intermediary source.

[4] Suid. s.v. *Leonnatus*; *FGrH* 156 (Arrian) F 178 Λεόννατος, στρατηγὸς Μακεδονίας, κατὰ γένος προσήκων Φιλίππου μητρί, συντραφεὶς δὲ Ἀλεξάνδρῳ; Curt. 10. 7. 8 'stirpe regia genitus'. Beloch, *GG*² 3. 2. 78 argued that Leonnatus belonged to the royal house of the Orestae.

The importance which was attached to the ancestry of these royal houses—the Temenidae and the Bacchiadae—has been shown by a new papyrus fragment of Satyrus,[1] which is concerned with the names of the demes in Ptolemaic Alexandria. There the Bacchiad genealogy is traced backwards from Bacchis, king of Corinth, through Prymnis, Agelas, and Anaxion to Aletes, who won Corinth 'together with the Heracleidae', and from Aletes through Hippotes, and Phylas to Antiochus. This Antiochus appears elsewhere as a son of Heracles.[2] The mother of Antiochus was Deianeira, who was the daughter of Dionysus and Althaea. It was because of this lineage that two demes of Alexandria were named Deianeiris and Althaeis, and the Ptolemies traced their descent from Dionysus (*FGrH* 631 (Satyrus) F 1, lines 16 and 19–22).

In the papyrus fragment of Satyrus there is a lacuna after Antiochus. We should adopt one of the suggestions which the editors have made,[3] namely to restore as follows:

line 17　ὁ δ' Ἀλήτης υἱὸς μὲν *ν Ἱππ[ότου τοῦ Φύ-]
λαντος. ὁ δὲ Ἀν[τί]οχος [υἱὸς ὢν Ἡρακλέους]
θυγατέρα Πυραίχ[μου γήμας ἐγέννη-]
σεν Φύλαντα τὸν ['Ιππότου πατέρα.]

The number of letters varies generally between 28 and 32 to a whole line, and the restorations give lines of 29, 32, 28, and 26, the last line ending with a full stop (as in line 11). The Bacchiadae thus traced their line back to Heracles and so to Dionysus. This seems to be the reference in fragment 11 of the papyrus if we accept the authors' restoration:

το]ῦ γένους ἀ[ρ]χηγέτου Δι-
[ονύσου]

Thus Dionysus was the founder of the Bacchiad family, whereas the Temenids stressed Zeus or Heracles as the founder of their family (e.g. Isoc. *Philippus* 105 τὸν τοῦ γένους ἀρχηγόν).

For *the royal house of the Orestae* we have only one name, Antiochus, who was king in 429 (Thuc. 2. 80. 6) and entrusted 1,000 Orestae to the command of Oroedus, king of the Parauaei. The name is that of the son of Heracles who figured in the Bacchiad genealogy; however, it seems here to be indigenous to the native dynasty of the Orestae. When Alexander the Great died, one of those who belonged to the royal stock (of the Macedones) was Perdiccas, son of Orontes, who came 'from Orestis'.[4] The best explanation seems to be that, as with Leonnatus, the

---

[1] *Oxyr. Pap.* 27 (1962) 2465 p. 127.
[2] Paus. 2. 4. 3; Apollod. 2. 8. 3. See Gutschmid 4. 14 and 20.
[3] Their other suggestion on p. 128 is to make Antiochus the husband of a daughter of Hyllus called Pyraechme; this would mean that Antiochus was not a Heraclid and his descendants were not Heraclids either, which conflicts with other evidence.
[4] Arr. *An.* 6. 28. 4 and *Ind.* 18. 5.

mother of Perdiccas was a member of the Temenid house and had married into the royal house of the Orestae, where Orontes was king. If this Perdiccas, presumably so named from his mother's ancestral Perdiccas, was a man of forty in 326, he was born *c.* 366 and at that time Orontes was king of the Orestae.

The first named *king of Elimea* is Derdas 'the ruler of Elimea' (X. *HG* 5. 2. 38, Δέρδαν τὸν Ἐλιμίας ἄρχοντα). In 382 Teleutias, the Spartan commander, sent messages to both Amyntas and Derdas, thus treating them as independent kings, and Derdas came to his aid with 400 cavalry, a force which represented a considerable kingdom.

In the treaty between Athens and Perdiccas II there is a King Derdas, but his realm is not preserved in the inscription. Earlier in the treaty 'the kings with Perdiccas' (*IG* I². 71, line 27, τὸς βασιλέας τὸς μετὰ Περδίκκο) are mentioned, and then 'kings' appeared individually as signatories to the treaty: one is [Δέ]ρδας βασι[λεύς] in line 86. He was no doubt king of Elimea and the grandfather of Xenophon's Derdas. This Derdas, Derdas I we may call him, helped Athens against Perdiccas in 432 (Thuc. 1. 57. 3), and the scholiast added a note that 'Derdas was son of Arrhidaeus and cousin of Perdiccas and Philip'. As 'cousin' is probably first cousin, Arrhidaeus was connected by marriage with Alexander I, father of Perdiccas and Philip; but we do not know whether Arrhidaeus married Alexander's sister or Alexander Arrhidaeus' sister.[1]

In the first part of the campaign of 432 the Athenians fought in Macedonia against Perdiccas and co-operated 'with Philip and the brothers of Derdas who had invaded [Lower Macedonia] with an army from Upper Macedonia' (Thuc. 1. 59. 2, ἄνωθεν). In the second part of the campaign, when they advanced towards Potidaea, the Athenians had their own infantry and 'of Macedonians 600 cavalry with Philip and Pausanias' (1. 61. 4, τοῖς μετὰ Φιλίππου καὶ Παυσανίου); Perdiccas, having left a deputy to defend his kingdom, was in Potidaea with a force of 200 cavalry. It seems clear that if Pausanias was a brother of Philip, the two of them could not have raised so many cavalry, and we must conclude that Pausanias was in command of the cavalry of Elimea. At this point the scholiast comments 'according to some this Pausanias was a son of Derdas, according to others a brother'. Since it is unlikely that the command dropped a generation in a few months, it is better to suppose that Pausanias was a brother of Derdas I.[2]

We learn from Aristotle, *Politics* 1311ᵇ14 that Archelaus gave his elder daughter in marriage to 'the king of Elimea' when he was hard pressed in a war against Sirras and Arrhabaeus, i.e. against the royal house of Lyncus, as have seen (p. 15 above). As this point was men-

---

[1] Beloch, *GG²* 3. 2. 74 assumes the former and does not mention the latter alternative.
[2] See Gomme 1. 203, 212, and 218.

tioned in connection with the assassination of Archelaus, the marriage was just before 399; let us say *c.* 400 for convenience. We should attribute the marriage to the king who reigned between Derdas I and Derdas II, but not as his first marriage, because he was at least in his forties in 400.

Early in his reign Philip II married Phila, 'sister of Derdas and Machatas' (Athen. 13. 557 c, citing Satyrus). It was presumably the same Derdas who was captured at the fall of Olynthus to Philip in 348 (*FGrH* 115 (Theopompus) F 143). He is likely in view of the dates to have been a son of Derdas II rather than a grandson, and he was of importance as the heir apparent of the royal house of Elimea.

Finally there was a Derdas who killed Amyntas the Little (Ar. *Pol.* 1311ᵇ3). He was a young boy at the Macedonian court *c.* 390, and he was most likely a member of the Macedonian royal family or of a leading family of Lower Macedonia.

These conclusions are summarized in the following stemma for the royal house of Elimea:

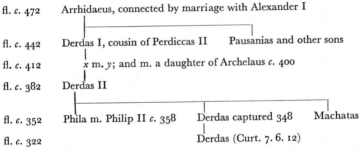

fl. *c.* 472   Arrhidaeus, connected by marriage with Alexander I

fl. *c.* 442   Derdas I, cousin of Perdiccas II   Pausanias and other sons

fl. *c.* 412   *x* m. *y*; and m. a daughter of Archelaus *c.* 400

fl. *c.* 382   Derdas II

fl. *c.* 352   Phila m. Philip II *c.* 358   Derdas captured 348   Machatas

fl. *c.* 322   Derdas (Curt. 7. 6. 12)

Our literary sources do not mention a *king of the Pelagones* specifically, but it is likely that Thucydides had one in mind when he wrote of the monarchies of the Lyncestae, Elimeotae, and 'other tribes up inland' (2. 99. 2). In fact a 'king of the Pelagones' has been convincingly restored in an inscription of 365/4 (*IG* ii². 190; dated by W. S. Ferguson in *Klio* 14. 393) in which the Athenians recorded as their proxenus and benefactor Π[. . . . . . τὸν Πε]λαγόνων βα[σιλέα]. Although we cannot restore P's name,[1] the existence of a king of the Pelagones is most probable.

In 362 another Pelagonian benefactor of Athens was honoured (*IG* ii². 110=Tod, *GHI* no. 143). The heading of the stone is [Μ]ενέλαος Πελαγὼν εὐεργέτη[ς] and he is mentioned in the text as Μενέλαον τὸν Πελαγόνα. It is stated that 'the ancestors of Menelaus' were benefactors of the Athenian people, and we shall surely be right if we suppose that some at least of them were kings and that the proposer had in mind the king P

---

[1] As we find a Pyraechmes and a Pelegon in the mythical genealogy of this region, it is possible that our king P had one of these names.

who (most probably) had been named a benefactor two or three years earlier. But Menelaus was certainly not himself a king; if he had been he would have been accorded the title which P had received. His services and his position seem to be personal rather than official in the decree. 'Since Timotheus the general declares that Menelaus the Pelagon both fought in person together with Timotheus and provided money for the war against Chalcidice and Amphipolis', he should be complimented for his services and the generals 'around Macedonia' should take care of him in case he needs anything. These words fit a captain of a mercenary band or an adventurer with strong backing rather than a head of state or a general.

For this reason it seems likely that Menelaus the Pelagonian is the man who was honoured *c.* 359 by Ilium as 'Menelaus, son of Arrhabaeus, citizen of Athens' for his services in the cause of freedom (*Syll.*[3] 188; Tod no. 148). If so, he had abandoned his Pelagonian citizenship or been deprived of it by banishment, and he had been given Athenian citizenship in the interim between 362 and 359. It was probably this same Menelaus who was mentioned by Demosthenes in the *First Philippic* 27, delivered *c.* 350, as an Athenian commander of cavalry who was fighting for the possessions of Athens against Philip II.

Beloch, *GG*[2] 3. 2. 76 f., equated Menelaus the Pelagon and Menelaus, son of Arrhabaeus, citizen of Athens. He then seized upon the name Arrhabaeus and concluded that Menelaus was the son of Arrhabaeus, king of the Lyncestae, and grandson of Arrhabaeus, first king of the Lyncestae *c.* 450, and that he was therefore a 'sovereign or half-sovereign prince of Lyncestis'. Beloch's view has been followed by other scholars (e.g. Tod, *GHI* 143 'Menelaus appears to have been a king of the Lyncestians'). It is, however, an improbable view. Menelaus was a Pelagonian and not a Lyncestian at all. We have in our texts $\Pi[\ldots\ldots\tau\grave{o}\nu \ \Pi\epsilon]\lambda\alpha$-$\gamma\acute{o}\nu\omega\nu \ \beta\alpha[\sigma\iota\lambda\acute{e}\alpha]$ and $\textit{Ἀρραβαῖον} \ldots \Lambda\upsilon\gamma\kappa\eta\sigma\tau\hat{\omega}\nu \ M\alpha\kappa\epsilon\delta\acute{o}\nu\omega\nu \ \beta\alpha\sigma\iota\lambda\acute{e}\alpha$ (Thuc. 4. 83. 1). To suppose that 'Pelagonian' and 'Lyncestian' were alternatives and that kings of Lyncus and Pelagonia were interchangeable is as absurd as to suppose that kings of France and Prussia were interchangeable. What misled Beloch was the name Arrhabaeus; but we should recognize that by the middle of the fourth century such names were not the monopoly of one royal house but had become common coin through the effects of inter-dynastic marriages. For example, we find an Arrhabaeus in Orestis (*SEG* 24. 485 from Nestorion near Kastoria), and another at Amphipolis *c.* 300 B.C. (*AD* 24. 1969. B2. 354).

The tribes which were neighbours of Macedonia were in general ruled by kings. Polyperchon, son of Simmias, commanded the regiment of *Tymphaei* in Alexander's army and brought the son of Alexander and

Barsine, Heracles, to his 'ancestral kingdom', evidently Tymphaea (Arr. *An.* 2. 12. 2; D.S. 17. 57. 2; 20. 28. 1). His kingdom may have included the Aethices, who were neighbours of the Tymphaei (Lyc. *Alex.* 802 δράκων Τυμφαῖος . . . Αἰθίκων πρόμος). His father, Simmias, had been king of the Tymphaei *c.* 370. While Tymphaea lay to the south of Orestis in Upper Macedonia, Parauaea lay to the south-west of it.[1] Here too there was a monarchy; Oroedus was king of the Parauaei in 429 (Thuc. 2. 80. 6). Further afield the royal house of the Molossi traced its line back to Neoptolemus, son of Achilles, and that of the Chaones to the Trojan Helenus, son of Priam; these claims were accepted in antiquity.[2] The Molossian royal house, called the Aeacidae after the grandfather of Achilles, Aeacus, was particularly close to the royal house of the Macedones, the Temenidae, because their ancestors went back to the period before the Trojan War and they were distinct from the people over whom they ruled.

The neighbouring tribes which did not speak Greek were similarly ruled by kings.[3] The Illyrian Taulantii were ruled by a King Galaurus in the latter part of the seventh century (Polyaen. 4. 1, though the story is apocryphal) and by Glaucias in the latter part of the fourth century (Arr. *An.* 1. 5. 1). The *Enchelii* were ruled by descendants of Cadmus and Harmonia (Str. 7 C 326), and Cadmus was claimed as the founder of Lychnidus (*Greek Anthology* 697, 6 ed. Loeb). In the time of Philip II, the *Grabaei* were ruled by Grabus, the *Ardiaei* by Pleuratus, the *Autariatae* probably by Pleurias, and the *Dardanii* by Bardylis—names which recurred later in each dynasty. The *Paeonians* were ruled by Agis (D.S. 16. 4. 2) and later by Lycceus or Lyppeus (Tod, *GHI* no. 157), and the Thracians who were closest to Macedonia (D.S. 16. 22. 3) by Cetriporis (Tod, ibid.).

I give the stemmata for the royal house of the Ardiaei and for the house of Bardylis who seized power among the Dardanii, as I have argued in *BSA* 61 (1966) 239 f.

We can thus see that monarchy, exercised on the hereditary principle within a royal house, was characteristic of all the tribes in the central Balkan region, whether the language of the tribe was Greek, Illyrian, Paeonian, or Thracian. In many royal houses there were one or more dynastic names which ran from grandfather to grandson. Intermarriage between the dynasties was common enough in the fourth and third centuries, again without distinction of linguistic groups, and it probably had been in earlier centuries. As a result of this a name typical of one dynasty might be found in another dynasty: for example, an Alcetas

---

[1] For these regions see *Epirus* 681 f. and Map 11 in Volume 1. 112.

[2] For this house see *Epirus* 384 f.

[3] See my article in *BSA* 61 (1966) 239 f. with a map.

and an Alexander in both the Molossian royal house and the Macedonian royal house, an Arrhidaeus in both Elimea and Macedonia, a Monunius in western Thrace and in Dardania, and so on. Their institutions too were similar in many respects. For example, when Derdas, king of Elimea, was absent, 'the brothers of Derdas' commanded his forces; in the treaty between Perdiccas II and Athens *c.* 415 the signatories after the king were brothers of the king; and in the treaty of alliance between Cetriporis and Athens the alliance was expressly made with 'Cetriporis the Thracian and his brothers'.

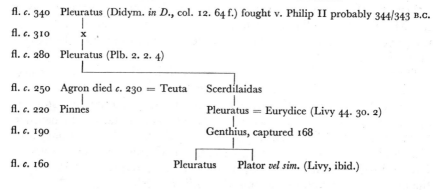

THE ROYAL HOUSE OF THE ARDIAEI

fl. *c.* 340   Pleuratus (Didym. *in D.*, col. 12. 64 f.) fought v. Philip II probably 344/343 B.C.

fl. *c.* 310   x

fl. *c.* 280   Pleuratus (Plb. 2. 2. 4)

fl. *c.* 250   Agron died *c.* 230 = Teuta   Scerdilaidas

fl. *c.* 220   Pinnes   Pleuratus = Eurydice (Livy 44. 30. 2)

fl. *c.* 190   Genthius, captured 168

fl. *c.* 160   Pleuratus   Plator *vel sim.* (Livy, ibid.)

THE FAMILY OF BARDYLIS

fl. *c.* 385   Bardylis, but born *c.* 448, died *c.* 358
fl. *c.* 355   Cleitus, expelled in 335
fl. *c.* 325   Bardylis
fl. *c.* 295   Birkenna = Pyrrhus *c.* 295

3. *The Tribal Systems of the Macedones and their Neighbours*
(See Map 9)

In northern Greece and in the central Balkan area the basic unit of organized life was the small tribe, and it seems to have maintained its identity by the practice of endogamy. A number of these small tribes were named in ancient literature, especially by Hecataeus and in some areas by Rhianus, who was drawing on information of the sixth or even the seventh century.[1] For example the Imphees were one tribe in the cluster known as the Perrhaebi (*FGrH* 1 (Hecataeus) F 137), the Dexari one tribe in the cluster known as the Chaones (F 103), and the Abri one tribe in the cluster known as the Taulantii (F 103; cf. St. Byz. s.v. *Dyrrachion*). Rhianus recorded a large number of small tribes in Epirus,

---

[1] See *Epirus* 702.

and many more are now known from inscriptions which date from the fourth century B.C. onwards. Similarly in the area of Mt. Pangaeum Herodotus gave the names of small tribes: the Doberes and Paeoples belonging to the Paeones, and the Pieres, Odomanti, and Satrae to the Thrakes (Hdt. 7. 112–13; cf. Hecataeus F 157). To the north of these there were 'tribes of Maedi' (St. Byz. s.v. *Odones*). Some small tribes are known from inscriptions only: for instance, the Dostoneis, the Geneatai, and the Argestaei belonging to the Pelagones (see Volume I. 88). Again the Battynaei and the Triclari belonged to the Orestae (see Volume I. 111 f.). There is good reason to suppose that the Macedones too were originally made up of small tribes, and it may be that we have the name of one of them in the Argeadae Macedones, whom we shall investigate shortly.

The economic background to the tribal system was originally and often continuously pastoral, with stock-raising and hunting taking priority over agriculture and arboriculture. In such an economy the transhumance of sheep was practised extensively. Sometimes a whole tribe moved with the sheep (as Vlach tribes did early last century), and always a part of the tribe—mainly men—did so. In such tribes the hunters and the herdsmen were held in honour and the workers of the soil in dishonour. As Herodotus remarked, with the scorn perhaps of a civilized man, among the Thracians 'the agricultural worker is least esteemed, and the idler most esteemed; for to live by war and rapine is the most honourable of all' (Hdt. 5. 6. 2; cf. 2. 167. 1, where he applied this generalization to 'most barbarians'). The old custom among the Macedones that a man wore a halter round his waist until he had killed an enemy was typical of that stage of civilization.

In the sixth century some of the tribes in northern Greece were still fully nomadic. Thus the western Perrhaebi were nomadic (μετανάσται Str. 9 C 434), whereas the eastern Perrhaebi by Mt. Olympus were settled. Sometimes a tribe split in two when it took to a settled life; thus there were Talares on both sides of the Pindus range, and they both belonged to the Molossian group (Τάλαρες, Μολοττικὸν φῦλον, τῶν περὶ τὸν Τόμαρον ἀπόσπασμα).[1] Their men probably met every summer on the Pindus pastures. In Macedonia it is clear that pastoralism and the transhumance of sheep were predominant in the life of the peoples especially of Upper Macedonia until the accession of Philip in 359. For Alexander said to the Macedonians at Opis 'Philip found you nomadic, impoverished, most of you in your cloaks herding a few sheep on the mountain pastures' (Arr. *An.* 7. 9. 2). When Justin, drawing ultimately on Theopompus, the contemporary of Philip, compared Philip's moving of peoples and cities to the shepherd's moving of his flocks from the

---

[1] A similar scorn underlies Achilles' use of the word *metanastes* in *Iliad* 9. 648.

winter to the summer pastures (8. 5. 7), he may have had the practice of Macedonian shepherds in mind.

In such a way of life a tribe can move relatively easily from one area to another. Thucydides was probably drawing on his knowledge of conditions in Thrace and Macedonia in his own day when he wrote his brilliant account of early times in the Greek peninsula.

> In early times migrations were common, and each tribe readily left its own land when it was under pressure from a more numerous people. . . . They developed their soil only so far as to obtain a bare living, had no reserve of wealth and planted no trees, because no one knew when an invader might come and spoil them, especially as they had no walled fortifications. (1. 2. 1–2)

Even at the time of Sitalces' invasion in 429 the Macedonians had few such fortifications and relied on escape into the mountain fastnesses (Thuc. 2. 100. 1); and the same point was made in the speech of Alexander at Opis (Arr. *An.* 7. 9. 2). Thus the Macedones were able to move readily, and they displaced other tribes such as the Almopes and Edoni which found habitats elsewhere (Thuc. 2. 99. 3).

The early migrations of the Macedones were discussed in Volume I. 309 f. The tentative conclusions were as follows. The Orestae, a Molossian tribe, lay west of the Balkan range at some time in the Late Bronze Age, and they moved into the upper Haliacmon valley early in the period of the great migrations, which was marked by the incursion of the Phrygians into Macedonia and southern Illyria and the movement southwards of the Dorians from Epirus and west-central Greece.[1] Before the coming of the Orestae the area of the upper Haliacmon was called 'Maceta' (*FGrH* 135/6 Marsyas F 10),[2] and the southern side at least of the middle Haliacmon valley was called 'Macednia', both words meaning 'highland'. This name was adapted by their successors to 'Orestis', 'mountain-land'. The corresponding ethnics were Macetai and Macednoi. The arrival of the Orestae caused a shift of the Macetai and Macednoi down the Haliacmon valley and into the hill country of Pieria. In the latter part of the sixth century the Macedones, their name having developed out of Macetai and Macednoi, were centred in 'the Makedonikon mountain' (the Pierian range north of Olympus), which with its outliers and a part of the coastal plain was 'the land

---

[1] Str. 9 C 434; see *Epirus* 462.

[2] The correct form is Maceta and a variant is Macetta. The manuscripts of Marsyas give the former form, which Dindorf wrongly emended to 'Maketia', and Hesychius s.v. the latter form; St. Byz. s.v. *Makedonia* gives both forms. See Volume I. 309 for further references. The ethnic termination of Mak-etai is not paralleled in Epirus, where a very large number of tribal ethnics are known (excluding 'Zeus Etheton' as not an ethnic; see *Epirus* 550), and the only personal names with such a termination in Epirus are Alcetas, a Macedonian name, given to one of the early Temenid kings, and Glaucetas. The ethnic Μακέτας is attested in *GDI* 2082, 2–3, of 194 B.C.

Macedonis' (Hdt. 7. 127, 128. 1, and 131 ἡ Μακεδονὶς γῆ; see Volume 1. 146 f.).

The 'Tymphaei', who, like the Orestae and the Pelagones, were regarded as a Molossian or Epirotic tribe came into the high country south-west of the bend of the Haliacmon from their earlier home in the headwaters of the river Arachthus by Mt. 'Tymphe' (the area of Metsovon).[1] The Elimiotae, another Molossian or Epirotic tribe (Str. 9 C 434), came into the rich country of the middle Haliacmon basin, and they pushed the Macedones on their way into Pieria. We have an interesting analogy to the movements of the Macedones in those of the Molossi during the same period; for they moved from the lower Aous valley into the hill country of the upper Aous (by Konitsa) and then into the central plain of Epirus, and later they extended their realm to the Gulf of Ambracia.

There are some traditions which are attached to particular places on the general route taken by the Macedones. One, associating Orestes, son or grandson of Agamemnon, with the naming of Orestis and Orestikon Argos, was dismissed as unhistorical in Volume 1. 311. Another was concerned with the founding of three cities in Elimeotis: Aeane, Elimea, and Ilium. Aeanus, son of Elymus, king of the Tyrreni, founded Aeane (St. Byz. s.v. *Aiane*). 'Elymus the hero, or Helenus (son of Priam), or Elymas, king of Tyrreni' founded Elimea (St. Byz. s.v. *Elimia*). Ilium was founded by Helenus (St. Byz. s.v. "Ιλιον . . . τρίτη Μακεδονίας, Ἐλένου κτίσμα). The founding of these cities was linked to the story of Aeneas and his followers, including Elymus the Trojan ('the hero' in St. Byz.), who 'some say took up their abode around Makedonikos Olympus' (Str. 13 C 608) and who were believed to have founded Aenea on the eastern coast of the Thermaic Gulf (*FGrH* 4 (Hellanicus) F 31). In Volume 1. 300 f. it was argued that there may well be a historical basis to the tradition of migrations by Trojans and Tyrreni from the Thermaic Gulf to the Adriatic coast via the Tsangon pass. However, the linking of this tradition to the founding of particular cities will have to be considered later.

A link between 'Maceta' as an early name and the migration by the Tyrreni is probably to be seen in a fragment from the first book of Cleidemus, *Atthis*, which was concerned with the early traditions of Attica. After mentioning that Marsyas gave Maceta as the name of a part of Macedonia, the text proceeds ἀλλὰ καὶ τὴν ὅλην Μακεδονίαν Μακετίαν οἶδεν ὀνομαζομένην Κλείδημος ἐν πρώτῳ Ἀτθίδος· "καὶ ἐξῳκίσθησαν ὑπὲρ τὸν Αἰγιαλὸν ἄνω τῆς καλουμένης Μακετίας" (*FGrH* 323 F 3 = Const. Porphyr. *De Them.* 2 p. 48, 9). The only people who are known both to have been expelled from early Attica and to have settled

---

[1] See *Epirus* 477 and 680.

traditionally in the region of the Thermaic Gulf are the Tyrseni (Thuc. 4. 109. 4 and Hdt. 1. 57. 1; see Volume I. 302), and there can be little doubt that Cleidemus was writing of them. Within Macedonia in the middle of the fourth century, when Cleidemus was writing, there were two places associated with the Tyrreni: Elimeotis and Crestonia. But it is unlikely that Crestonia, east of the Axius, would have been regarded by Cleidemus as belonging to Macedonia rather than to Thrace or Paeonia in legendary times. The case is stronger for Elimeotis.

The next problem is the location of 'Aigialos'. Jacoby thought it might be the Aigialos by the mouth of the Strymon which Hecataeus mentioned (*FGrH* III Suppl. B p. 64); but this is too far east. What we want for Elimeotis is something in Pieria or below Beroea. I suggest that we amend Αἰγιαλόν to Αἰγίδιον or Αἰγύδιον, a city in Pieria (Pliny, *NH* 4. 33; see Volume I. 139 n. 1), and translate 'they migrated perforce beyond Aegidium inland into part of Maketia so called'. Alternatively, one could read Αἰγαῖον and translate 'they migrated perforce over the Aegean sea inland into part of Macetia so called'. But the former translation is more specific and appropriate. If it is accepted, the area called Macetia was the Haliacmon valley inland. The term may or may not have been extended later to the whole of Macedonia; for it does not necessarily ensue from the words of Cleidemus which Porphyrogenitus has quoted.

During the long period when the Macedones were an unimportant tribe or tribal cluster living in the hilly country of northern Pieria, they seem to have abandoned the names Macetai and Macetia. The next events in their history were the seizure of the throne by the Temenidae and then the expansion which was led by the Argeadae. Who were these Argeadae? They are mentioned twice in an historical context. Fragment 11 of Strabo's 7th book gives the locations of the various tribes in Macedonia before the expansion by the Macedones and then continues: 'but all these fell under the sway of the so-called Argeadae and the Chalcidians of Euboea.' The reference in time is to the period of Macedonian expansion and Chalcidian colonization, that is to the seventh and sixth centuries. Fragment 25 of the same book contains a geographical description which ends with the Homeric Amydon, located at a strong place on the Axius called Abydon; the fragment adds the note that 'the place was destroyed by the Argeadae'. As the place is probably to be identified with Vardarophtsa on the left bank of the river (see Volume I. 177), the destruction is likely to have occurred in the third phase of expansion, when the Macedones acquired territory east of the Axius, but we cannot exclude the possibility that a sortie was made across the river during the second phase when Macedonian sway reached the right bank of the river. In both fragments we are given information from an account of early Macedonia which was drawn upon directly or indirectly by

Herodotus. This account was almost certainly that of Hecataeus; for he was used by Herodotus for the description of Crousis (see Volume 1. 188 f.), and Strabo made considerable use of Hecataeus for his description of Epirus and Macedonia (see Volume 1. 146 f., 310 f., and 415 f., and *Epirus* 447 f.). Thus the Argeadae led the expansion which spread into the plain *c.* 650 and which crossed the Axius considerably later.

That the Argeadae were Macedones is clear from some small items of information. Appian, *Syr.* 63, having occasion to list some of the places called Argos, appended details to two of them; one was Ἄργος τὸ ἐν Ὀρεστείᾳ ὅθεν οἱ Ἀργεάδαι Μακεδόνες, 'the Argos in Orestis whence the Argeadae Macedones'.[1] Other informants are Stephanus Byzantinus who mentions twice a small island 'Argeou', i.e. 'of Argeas', by the western mouth of the Nile near Canobus (s.v. *Argeou* and s.v. *Argaïs*), and Ps.-Callisthenes 1. 31. 10 mentioning a river Argeos at Alexandria and a shrine 'Argeion'. As the Macedonians transferred names from their homeland to places with similar features abroad, we may infer that there was an island of Argeas in Macedonia, probably on the western side of the delta of the Haliacmon or the Axius. Stephanus adds in the entry s.v. *Argeou* that the island was called 'after Argeas, son of Macedon, and after him are [the] Argeadae [so named]' (ἀπὸ Ἀργέου τοῦ Μακεδόνος ἀφ' οὗ Ἀργεάδαι). Thus the Argeadae Macedones had an eponymous ancestor, a son of Macedon, Argeas. He should take his place alongside Pierus, Amathus, and Brousis in the genealogy, which was recorded by Marsyas Macedon (see below, pp. 35 f.).

The meaning of the word Argeadae is not open to doubt. As a normal patronymic in Greek, it means 'descendants of Argeas', as already in *Iliad* 16. 417. Such patronymics were used to describe the members of a clan, such as the Boutadae or Aethalidae in Attica and the Temenidae in Argos and Macedonia; or to describe the hereditary members of a deme, such as the Boutadae again in Attica (for a number of demes had patronymic names, as Stephanus observed s.v. *Boutadae*); or to describe a tribe or people, such as one of the old Ionic tribes, the Argadeis (St. Byz. s.v. *Aigikoreos*), the Argives in prehistoric times being Ἀργειάδαι (St. Byz. s. v. *Argos*), and the Halicarnassians being called 'Antheadae... after the most distinguished persons among them' (Ἀνθεάδαι . . . ἀπὸ τῶν διασημοτάτων παρ' αὐτοῖς). Thus the Argeadae were the members of a clan or a tribe or a people. When we find the words 'Argeadae Macedones', we must take the Argeadae to have been a part of the group known as 'the Macedones', just as 'Boutadae Athenaioi' were a part of

---

[1] The words 'whence the Argeadae Macedones' are sometimes bracketed as a gloss. If this is done, we should also bracket the information given about the Argos in the Ionian Gulf in the following sentence; but it is not possible to do so for grammatical reasons. It is more sensible to retain both as part of Appian's text. So Geyer, *RE* 699.

the Athenian people. It should be emphasized that the name Argeadae is patronymic and not local. It does not mean 'people from Argos';[1] as Stephanus pointed out, the people from the numerous towns called Argos were all called Ἀργεῖοι (St. Byz. s.v. *Argos*).

When Thucydides described the expansion of the Macedonians, he made a distinction between the Macedones of Upper Macedonia— Lyncestae (more fully 'Lyncestae Macedones' at 4. 83. 1), Elimiotae, and others—and 'these Macedones' (2. 99. 6) who were the conquerors of Lower Macedonia and the immediate subjects of Perdiccas II in 429, the year of Sitalces' invasion, which Thucydides was describing. As we have seen in Volume I. 439, the tribes of Upper Macedonia were called Molossian by Hecataeus (*FGrH* I F 107 Ὀρέσται· Μολοσσικὸν ἔθνος), or Epirotic by later authors. It follows that the name Macedones was reserved by Hecataeus for the people of Lower Macedonia. It follows then that, if he used the expression 'Argeadae Macedones', as we have argued, he meant thereby a part of the Macedones, that is one tribe among a group of tribes known to him as the Macedones. As this tribe formed the spearhead of the expansion, it was presumably the leading or royal tribe in the group, the tribe over which the indigenous royal house ruled before it was displaced by the Temenid usurper, Perdiccas I, *c.* 650.[2]

Our conclusion, then, is that the Argeadae Macedones were the leading tribe of the group of tribes called the Macedones. Originally, i.e. at the beginning of the Early Iron Age, this tribe lived in Maceta, the territory which later came to be called Orestis. Other tribes of the same stock were in this high area of country on the north-east side of the Pindus range. When they moved down into Pieria, these tribes cohered as a group under the leadership of the Argeadae whose indigenous royal house perhaps was called 'the Argeadae'. When the Temenidae displaced the indigenous royal house, the kings led the Argeadae and their related tribes down into the plain and conquered the area west of the Axius. One of the most important achievements of the Temenid kings was to abolish the old tribal system and fuse the people into one group, the Macedones, which was now settled over a much wider area of country. During the latter part of the reign of Alexander I the name Argeadae seems to have been no longer in use as a political term; it lived on mainly in ritual and perhaps in ceremonial.[3]

---

[1] As, e.g., is suggested by H. L. Jones in the Loeb edition of Strabo: 'the name appears to have been derived from the Macedonian Argos.'

[2] In citing examples of the word Argeadae I have not used Just. 7. 1. 10, where Caranus, having founded his capital, called the city Aegeae and the people Aegeidae (because goats, *aiges*, had led him there). The text is usually emended to read Argeadae for Aegeidae; but this loses the goatiness and there is little to be said in favour of the Greek Caranus giving the name Argeadae to the tribe, if Argeas was not one of Caranus' ancestors.

[3] It occurred as the personal name of a citizen of Larissa in the third century B.C. and as

It is necessary at this point to note that 'Argeadae' seems always to have been interpreted by historians as the Macedonian royal house of classical times, 'das Argeadenhaus', as Beloch called it.[1] The classical authors are not ambivalent in the matter: the members of the royal house were Temenidae (Hdt. 8. 137. 1 and 138. 2; Thuc. 2. 99. 3), descended not from Argeas but from Temenus. If Beloch were correct, the eponymous ancestor Argeas would have figured in the genealogy of the Temenids. He does not do so, although we have that genealogy back to Zeus. To suppose that the royal house was called concurrently both Temenidae and Argeadae is even more improbable than to suppose that their capital was called concurrently both Aegeae and Edessa. I propose then to maintain the distinction between an indigenous royal house, ruling over the Argeadae and perhaps itself called by that name, a house which traced its origin geographically to Maceta (later called Orestis), and a Greek royal house, the Temenidae, which came from Peloponnesian Argos and regarded itself as Macedonian only by right of rule, as a branch of the Hanoverian house has come to regard itself as English.

The Temenid house of Macedonia died with the son of Alexander the Great. The Antigonids succeeded, and they traced their descent from an indigenous noble family. When that line too came to an end with the conquest by Rome and the partition of the country, an *oraculum post eventum* was made up in which a contrast was drawn between the successes of Philip II (a Temenid) and the failures of Philip V (an Antigonid). The oracle is cited in two forms, both beginning with the following two lines:

αὐχοῦντες βασιλεῦσι Μακηδόνες Ἀργεάδῃσιν,
ὑμῖν κοιρανέων ἀγαθὸν καὶ πῆμα Φίλιππος.

O Macedonians boastful of your Argead kings, a Philip's rule will be a blessing and a disaster for you' (Paus. 7. 8. 9 and App. *Mac.* fr. 2).

The word Argead was used here to cover both dynasties; it was an archaic word, appropriate to the style of a Sibylline oracle, and particularly appropriate if the word was the traditional one for the original Macedonian monarchy. For what the Sibylline oracle had in mind was the end of the Macedonian monarchy and the victory of Rome.[2]

a patronymic of Menedemus, priest at Dodona within the period 168–148 B.C. (P. R. Franke, *Die antiken Münzen von Epirus* (Wiesbaden, 1961) 39 f.). The use of the term in ritual in G. Kroll, *Historia Alex. Magni* (Berlin, 1958) 141 and perhaps in Athen. 14. 659 will be discussed in Volume III.

[1] *GG*[2] 3. 2. 72; cf. Kaerst, s.v. *Argeadae* in *RE*, Franke, loc. cit., Geyer, Hoffmann 121, Kalléris 7, Glotz 3. 212, Cloché 29. Raymond 3 n. 12 thought that Argeadae was the name of the tribe 'to which the kings belonged', but the note is confused.

[2] In Appian the oracle is introduced as encouraging the Romans to attack Macedonia; it was evidently composed to please Roman ears after 167 B.C.

When Herodotus retailed the story of the Temenids displacing the indigenous kings of the Argeadae Macedones, as we may now call them, he said that Perdiccas, the acquirer of the throne, had two brothers Gauanes and Aëropus. In the folk-tale the loaf of Perdiccas was the one which grew double its original size, but the brothers also received a loaf each. If Herodotus had had time to tell the sequel, it seems that Gauanes and Aëropus would each have received a kingdom or the promise of one. Their names are therefore significant. Gauanes may be a dialectal version of Gaianes, because one finds Auos as a variant of Aias and the people Parauaei meaning those beside the Auos (or Aias) river.[1] Gaianes comes close to Aianos, the founder of Aiane, in St. Byz. s.v. *Aiane*. If so, Gauanes was to have the next best kingdom, that of Elimeotis. Aëropus is free from doubt. The name occurs as that of a king of the Lyncestae. As we shall see below (p. 37), the Aëropes were a distinguished family in Macedonia, and they perhaps claimed to have been kings of Lyncus before the usurpation by the Bacchiadae. In other words the claims of the three brothers were to become the kings of three peoples—the Macedones proper (the Argeadae Macedones and related tribes), the Elimiotae, and the Lyncestae. If the story was told to Herodotus late in the reign of Alexander I or soon after his death, it may reflect a contemporary claim by the Temenid kings to hold sway over Upper Macedonia; for it was probably in the time of Alexander I that the Elimiotae and the Lyncestae ceased to be called Molossian tribes and became known as Macedonian tribes.

At the other end of the time scale we have two stories in Syncellus and Eusebius in which Caranus makes alliance with the Orestae against the Eordani or Eordaei, both erroneous names for the early people called Eordi. Neither story has any claim to be considered historical.[2] They were built upon the early traditions, in which the Macedones were once in Maceta and later founded a city at Aegeae on the edge of the coastal plain by the waters of the Haliacmon.

When Perdiccas I had established himself at Aegeae, he and his successors led the Argeadae Macedones and the related tribes of Macedones to the conquest of further areas, from which they expelled the existing inhabitants, the Pieres from southern Pieria, the Almopes from Almopia, and the Bottiaei from Bottiaea. The subjects of the Temenid kings now occupied the coastal lands west of the Axius river and their immediate hinterland. If an eponymous genealogy existed at this time, the sons of Macedon may well have been Argeas, Pierus, and Amathus, which represented the original kingdom as the homeland of the Argeadae Macedones, the rich land of Pieria and the sandy plain, Amathia or

---

[1] See *Epirus* 699.
[2] These stories are narrated on p. 9 above.

Emathis.[1] But the important development was that the Macedones had no substratum of subject peoples, they apparently abandoned the old tribal differentiations within the group of Macedones, and they all derived their citizenship or their membership of the enlarged Macedonian state by receiving land from the king.

Some of the institutions which we associate with the Macedonian monarchy of the classical period may have existed before the usurpation of the throne by the Greek Temenidae. For example, the Companions or advisers of the king were included in the pre-Temenid phase of the story told by Herodotus, and such Companions were typical of the Homeric type of monarchy. The concept of the king as owner and dispenser of land, commander of the men-at-arms, judge in many cases, and conductor of sacrifices for the community, may well have been traditional to the tribal community of Macedones, as it was to many tribal states of northern Greece, Macedonia, and neighbouring territories. What was to be significant for the future was the adaptation of such institutions by the Greek kings, the Temenidae, who, having had experience in the Peloponnese, managed to free the Macedones from tribal jealousies and divisions and make them into a united kingdom, in which all men were free.

4. *Legends and Genealogies Invented by Hellenistic Writers*

It is necessary first to discuss the date which should be given to the 'Macedonian Traditions' of Theagenes (Μακεδονικὰ πάτρια, *FGrH* 774). In one of the fragments of this work Theagenes was concerned with the famous battle of the Gods and the Giants at Phlegra (e.g. as in Pindar, *Nemean* 1. 67) and its possible location. A writer of the late fourth century, Hegesippus of Mecyberna in the peninsula of Pallene, had identified Phlegra with Pallene, had put the Giants there, and had located the battle of the Gods and the Giants there (*FGrH* 391 (Hegesippus) F 1). This view was criticized by Theagenes, as we learn from Stephanus Byzantinus s.v. *Pallene* who gave first Hegesippus' identification and then continued as follows.

Theagenes, *Makedonika*. Here the story about Pallene does not stand [i.e. breaks down].[2] The story is [literally 'they say'] that this land was called 'Phlegra' and the inhabitants of it 'Giants', whose outrageous misanthropy horrified Heracles when he put in; and when they began a battle, Heracles took up his usual weapons and pursued them vigorously, killing those who had given him war as a gift of welcome on his coming to their country by sea;

---

[1] Perhaps another son, Brousus, may have represented Almopia (the modern Moglena; see Map 1 in Volume 1).

[2] See LSJ⁹ ἵστημι B 11 2. Or the meaning may be 'it is not here that the story about Pallene is set.'

and in the battle there were thunderbolts and hurricanes which were mythologized into the battle of the Gods against the Giants (ἀφ' ὧν ἡ τῶν θεῶν μάχη
πρὸς αὐτοὺς μεμυθολόγηται).

There is some scorn in the word 'mythologized'. An echo of this controversy appears in a fragment of Strabo's 7th book, fragment 25, which
is an abbreviation of the original text. 'The mythologizers (οἱ μὲν
μυθολογοῦντες) say that the Giants lived here [in Pallene] and the land
was called Phlegra, but those who give a more credible account declare
that a savage and impious race occupied the place and was destroyed by
Heracles when he came by sea.'

It seems to be almost certain that Strabo was drawing directly on the
work of Theagenes and adopted his version of the events, a rationalized
one which excluded the battle of the Gods and the Giants. Moreover,
Conon (*FGrH* 26 F 1 xxxii 3) adopted the same or a similar version, when
having located Proteus in Pallene he continued: 'his sons were not like
himself but cruel and impious, and Heracles destroyed them because
he hated villainy.' Parthenius, *Narr. Am.* 6 (cited as *FGrH* 391 (Hegesippus) F 2) gave the entry: 'On Pallene the story of Diogenes and
Hegesippus in *Palleniaka*.' The story which follows came obviously from
Hegesippus. The name Diogenes is clearly incorrect. It has been convincingly emended to Theagenes by Gale; the emendation was adopted
by Jacoby in *FGrH* iii B p. 273, but not in iii C p. 770.

As Strabo, Conon, and Parthenius were writing towards the close of
the first century B.C., Theagenes must be placed in the Hellenistic
period if my inferences are correct. Jacoby, however, in iii C p. 770
placed him with a question-mark in the third or fourth century A.D.,
but there seems to be nothing to support his view. He belongs rather to
the period of local historians and topographers; he attacks Hegesippus
in a way which suggests he was not seven centuries later in time. We
may be able to date him more closely by considering his account of
Orestes.

In F 10 = St. Byz. s.v. *Orestai* Theagenes says that when Orestes was
freed from his madness, he went into exile because of his sense of shame
and came with Hermione to this land and had a child Orestes, who
assumed the rule and they were called Orestae; and Orestes himself
(viz. the older) died in Arcadia etc. Theagenes' story is evidently the
source of Solinus 9. 3 f. who explained the origin of the name of the
'peoples' called Orestae as follows.

Orestes being in exile from Mycenae after killing his mother chose to go
rather a long way away, and when he had a baby boy born to him in Emathia
by Hermione, his constant companion in all tribulations, he ordered that the
baby should be hidden. The boy grew up in the spirit of his royal blood,
bearing the name of his father, gained control of the whole area from the

Macedonian [Thermaic] Gulf to the Adriatic Sea, and called the land over which he had ruled 'Orestis'.

This story[1] far outdoes the story of Perdiccas, the founder of the kingdom of the Macedones, and was clearly composed to outdo it. Orestes came from Achaean Mycenae, the rival of Dorian Argos, and he conquered not just a bit near Pieria but a vast area. The motive and the occasion for floating such a claim came with the independence of Orestis and the fall of Macedon. Theagenes, then, wrote very probably in the middle of the second century B.C.

All fifteen fragments of Theagenes and one which Jacoby considered doubtful came from Stephanus Byzantinus. There is no doubt that Theagenes was Stephanus' main source for Macedonia, just as Rhianus, a Hellenistic writer of the third century, was his main source for Epirus. In that case we may be justified in attributing to Theagenes those Macedonian names and persons whom Stephanus mentions without acknowledging his source.[2] Photius too made reference to Theagenes, for in *Bibl.* 161 b 13 he says that Sopater the Sophist used for his tenth book the *Makedonika Patria* of Theagenes and some of Plutarch's *Lives*.

We can now return to the foundation stories of Aeane, Elimea, and Ilium. In the tribal and pastoral stage of development there were a few cities in Lower Macedonia and very few in Upper Macedonia. In the fourth century the number and the importance of the cities increased greatly, and the provision of foundation stories for such cities as Aeane, Elimea, and Ilium in Elimeotis was a feature of the Hellenistic period. We may then attribute these stories at the latest to Theagenes, especially as they were recorded by Stephanus Byzantinus. Together with them we may note other foundation stories of cities which not only were recorded by Stephanus Byzantinus but also were said by him to have come from Theagenes: Acesamenae, foundation of Acesamenus, one of the kings in Pieria (F 1); Lete, named after the near-by shrine founded in honour of Leto (F 6); Mieza, named from Mieza, daughter of Beres, son of Macedon, and Beroea, named from another daughter of Beres (F 7); Parthenopolis founded by Grastus, son of Mygdon, and named after his daughters (F 12); Tirsae, named after Tirse, one of the daughters[3] of Grastus, son of Mygdon (F 13).

We may note the following in Stephanus Byzantinus without acknowledgement of source. Atintania, named after Atintan, son of Macedon;

---

[1] A shorter version is given in Martianus Capella 6. 665. An oracular shrine of Hermione in Macedonia is mentioned in Tertullian, *De Anima* 46. 11.

[2] e.g. Marsyas of Pella and Marsyas of Philippi are cited only once by Stephanus and that for Aethicia, which was not in Macedonia.

[3] The text has 'wives', but we know from F 12 that Grastus had several daughters, so that emendation seems desirable.

Azorus, founded by a certain Azorus; Aenea, founded by Aeneas; Almopia, named after the Giant Almops, son of Poseidon and Helle, the daughter of Athamas; Anthemous, named after Anthemous; Beres, a city of Thrace, named after Beres, son of Macedon; Bisaltia, named after Bisaltes, son of Helius and Ge; Briges, a Thracian tribe, named after Brigus who founded their settlement in Macedonia; Brousis, named after Brousus, son of Emathius; Chalastra, named after Chalastre; Crousis, a part of Mygdonia, named after Crousis, son of Mygdon; Eordaeae, named after a certain Eordus; Europus, named after Europus, son of Macedon and Oreithyia, daughter of Cecrops; Galadrae, named after Galadrus, son of Emathius, 'but some say that Galadrus founded the city'; Grestonia, a region of Thrace, named after a certain Grastus; Dicaea, a city of Thrace, named after Dicaeus, son of Poseidon; Lyncus, a city of Epirus (a part of Macedonia as St. Byz. cites Strabo), named after Lynceus; Mygdonia, a part of Macedonia, named after Mygdon; Olynthus, a city of Thrace, named after Olynthus, son of Heracles; Oropus, named after Oropus, son of Macedon, son of Lycaon; Pella, named after its founder, Pellas; Pelagonia, assumed to be named after 'the hero Pelegon'; and Xaurus, named after a certain Xaurus.

When we compare the entries where Theagenes is named as the source with those entries for which no source is given, we can see that we may reasonably attribute to Theagenes the following. By the analogy of his first one (Acesamenae, foundation of Acesamenus) the entries for Atintania, Azorus, Chalastra, Eordaeae, Lyncus, Mygdonia, Pella, and Pelagonia. By the analogy of the second, in which the shrine of Leto is given, the entry for Gazorus, where we are told of a local Artemis Gazoria, and a point under Ichnae's ethnic Ἰχναία ἡ Θέμις. By the analogy of the third and fourth, where we have part of the genealogy of Macedon, the entries for Beres, Europus, and Oropus. By the analogy of the fifth and sixth, where we have part of the genealogy of Mygdon, the entries for Crousis, Grestonia, and Mygdonia.

The genealogy of Macedon, as it appeared in Theagenes, may then have been Lycaon, father of Macedon, who had a son Beres, blessed with two daughters Mieza and Beroea; a son Europus by his wife Oreithyia daughter of Cecrops; and two other sons, Atintan and Oropus. There were, however, two more sons in the family if we turn to Marsyas (*FGrH* 135/6 F 13), namely Pierus and Amathus, after whom the cities Pieria and Amathia were named. But it is unlikely that they were in Theagenes' version, because Stephanus has entries for Pieria and Emathia which lack any mention of a namesake or founder.

The genealogy of Mygdon in Theagenes may have been as follows. Mygdon has three brothers, Edonus, Odomantus, and Biston, all apparently sons of Ares and Callirrhoe, daughter of Nestus (St. Byz.

s.vv. *Bistonia, Edonoi*); Mygdon's sons are Crousis and Grastus, the latter having several daughters, of whom one is Tirse. This genealogy is entirely different from that of the Homeric Mygdon of Asiatic Phrygia.[1] It was designed for the area between the Axius and the Nestus; and it stressed the Thracian connection of the Mygdones. There were rival versions; some regarded the Mygdonian group as Paeonian (St. Byz. s.v. *Bistonia* and Pliny, *NH* 4. 35) and others as Illyrian (St. Byz. s.v. *Mygdonia*).[2]

Two writers by the name of Marsyas wrote about Macedonia (*FGrH* 135/6). The older was a 'Macedon' of Pella, who was of a leading family; he was brought up with Alexander the Great, was a brother of Antigonus Monophthalmus, and commanded a flotilla at Salamis in 307. He wrote a history of Macedonia from 'the first king of the Macedones', probably Caranus,[3] down to 331; it was in ten books and was entitled 'Macedonica'. The younger Marsyas was a citizen of Philippi; we do not know whether he was a 'Macedon', he may have lived in the third century B.C.,[4] and his work too was called 'Macedonica' or 'Macedonicae Historiae' (F 7). The fragments which were not assigned by ancient authors to one or the other (F 10–25) may remain unassigned at present except that F 16 should be attributed to the elder Marsyas as the citation is 'Marsyas Macedon' and F 17 should go with it, both being in Didymus and both concerning Philip losing an eye at Methone, and except that F 12 should be attributed to the younger Marsyas, because Harpocration evidently made use of him (as in F 5 and 6).

One or other Marsyas gave a genealogy of Macedon which differed from that given by Theagenes. Macedon, son of Zeus and Thyia (F 13), seized the land which was part of Thrace and named it Macedonia after himself, and marrying a local girl had two sons, Pierus and Amathus, after whom two cities in Macedonia were named Pieria and Amathia (F 13). This parentage of Macedon agrees with the oldest account, that of Hesiod, but it disagrees with that given by Theagenes and also with

---

[1] See *RE* 16. 997 'Mygdon (2)'.

[2] The reading, however, is doubtful. Meineke read 'Maidous' but the manuscripts' is 'Mardous', which might be an error for 'Mardonas' (St. Byz. s.v. *Mardones*).

[3] F 14 tells of Caranus and gives an antecedent for the Macedonian name Coenus; this fragment seems to be appropriate to Marsyas Macedon. It is probable too that we should read Καράνου in place of καί in T 1, the passage from Suidas which describes the contents of his *Makedonika*. The passage will then read ἤρξατο δὲ ἀπὸ τοῦ πρώτου βασιλεύσαντος Μακεδόνων Καράνου μέχρι τῆς Ἀλεξάνδρου τοῦ Φιλίππου ἐπὶ τὴν Συρίαν ἐφόδου μετὰ τὴν Ἀλεξανδρείας κτίσιν. That Caranus was the first king was the official view in the fourth century, and later chronographers, e.g. Malalas 161, wrote πρῶτος ἐβασίλευσεν ὁ Κάρανος.

[4] On general impression from the matters which interested him, e.g. in F 4 and F 8. There is less to go on than might appear from Jacoby, *FGrH* 135/6 T 2, which conceals the fact that Suidas listed three historians called Marsyas, the third writing about Tabae in Caria, 'his own country', in which Marsyas was a traditional name from the time of the founder (see Tabae in *RE*).

that given by Hellanicus, for whom Aeolus was the father of Macedon
(*FGrH* 4 F 74). Amathus and Amathia, usually in the Attic form Emathus
and Emathia, are much found in later authors. Thus St. Byz. s.v. *Brousis*
derived the name from Brousus, son of Emathius, and again s.v. *Galadrai*,
a city in Pieria, from Galadrus, son of Emathius; St. Byz. s.v. *Emathia* and
s.v. *Oisyme* equated Emathia with 'the present Macedonia', and Hesychius did likewise and mentioned 'Emathus the hero' (s.vv. *Emathia* and
emathoentos). These instances may be compatible with the genealogy
put forward by Marsyas, for whom Macedon was the eponymous
progenitor of the country and its salient features. On the other hand the
accounts in Justin and Solinus are incompatible with it, because the
Macedon–Emathius bond is severed and Emathius precedes Macedon.
The clearer account is in Solinus,[1] writing in the third century A.D.
Emathius was the first to acquire power in the area and was indigenous
to it. The land was called 'Emathia' (after him) until the rise of 'Macedo',
maternal grandson of Deucalion (i.e. son of Thyia), and he changed the
country's name to 'Macedonia' (9. 10). In the period before Macedo
there were 'Edonii olim populi, Mygdonia terra, Pierium solum vel
Emathium'.

We have already seen that Solinus drew his account of Orestes and
Hermione at 9. 3 f. from Theagenes, and it is evident that he got the new
order of Emathius and Macedo and also the importance of Mygdon and
his genealogy from Theagenes. Justin 7. 1. 1, like Solinus, has 'Emathion'
first, giving the name 'Emathia' to the country; but the names of the
people of that period are different and Macedo dropped out of the story,
perhaps because Justin cut the account short in epitomizing the work of
Pompeius Trogus.

The change of Macedon's father from Zeus to Lycaon, which we have
argued was due to Theagenes, is found also in Aelian, *NA* 10. 48:
'Lycaon, king of Emathia, has a son Macedon, from whom the land has
been called, no longer retaining its ancient name.' Here too Emathia,
deriving doubtless from Emathio, comes before Lycaon and Macedon.
A folk-story about Pindus, son of Macedon, which is related to a river
Pindus, is then told. In a version by Tzetzes, *Chil.* 4. 329 f., Lycaon is
father of Macedon and Pindus is the mountain. The whole thing may
have been lifted from Theagenes, *Makedonika Patria*. Macedon in the
form 'Makednos' figured in the list of Lycaon's fifty sons in Apollodorus
3. 8. 1.

The name 'Emathio' occurs in the one and only fragment of Melisseus,
Delphica, which comes from the scholia to Tzetzes *Chil.* 6. 931 f. (*FGrH*
402 F 1). Jacoby prints the passage as if it all comes from Melisseus, but
I think the citation should be limited to one sentence. The contextual

---

[1] A similar account in Martianus Capella 6 C 655, who abridged the work of Solinus.

passage within which the citation lies is concerned with Pieria and Helicon as mountains and cities of Boeotia. The first sentence with μέν explains the origins of Boeotian Pieria, and the second with δέ that of Boeotian Cithaeron. Pieria was 'formerly' (it says) called Pieria, because it was founded by Pierus, brother of Methone and father of Linus (or 'Linus was his father' as in *Certamen Hom. et Hes.* 314 fin., where Linus was father and Methone wife of Pierus; the setting of the contest and the cult of Linus lay in Boeotia and Chalcis), and 'subsequently' it was called Lyncus, over which Aëropus, the oldest of the sons of Emathio, took power, as Melisseus, the author of *Delphica*, says. What has happened is a confusion by the scholiast between a Lyncus in Boeotia[1] and the Lyncus in Macedonia, and the name has triggered off the citation from Melisseus. The actual fragment should then be ἧς [τῆς Λύγκου] καὶ τὴν ἀρχὴν ἔσχεν Ἀέροπος, ὁ πρεσβύτατος τῶν 'Ημαθίωνος παίδων: 'which [Lyncus] was ruled by Aëropus, eldest son of Emathio'. Nothing is known of Melisseus, but he presumably drew on Theagenes for the genealogy of Emathion and the mythical eponymous hero Aëropus.

Theagenes too may underlie the note in Hesychius Ἀέροπες ἔθνος Τροιζῆνα κατοικοῦντες καὶ ἐν Μακεδονίᾳ γένος τι καὶ ὀρνεά τινα: 'Aëropes a race inhabiting Troezen, and a clan in Macedonia, and certain birds.' The aim of Theagenes in providing a first ruler of Lyncus was no doubt to have a legitimate dynasty before the usurpation of the throne by the Bacchiadae *c.* 450; indeed it is possible that there was still in the second century a family which claimed descent from such an Aëropus. The name occurred of course in the Temenid line of the Macedonian kings, in Herodotus' story as a brother of Perdiccas, and in the Bacchiad house of Lyncus in the middle of the fourth century.

The younger Marsyas, citizen of Philippi, seems to have been primarily a local historian, since three of the six named fragments are concerned with the area east of the Axius, and since F 12, being about Amphipolis, should probably be ascribed to him. In F 5 = Harpocration s.v. *Galepsus*, Galepsus was said to have been named after Galepsus, son of Thasus and Telephe; the same information recurs in St. Byz. s.v. and *EM* 219, 45, and therefore comes ultimately from Marsyas the younger. Equally we may ascribe to him St. Byz. s.v. *Dardanus* where Telephae is the first wife of Cadmus and s.v. *Thasus* where Telephe, daughter of Europe, dies in the island, and the statement in Conon (*FGrH* 26 F 1, 37) that Thasus, brother of Cadmus, gave his name to the island. Marsyas himself drew evidently upon Hegesippus of Mecyberna, writing *c.* 350–300, where Telephae, mother of Europe, came to —— (the name is corrupt

---

[1] This is the Lyncus of St. Byz. s.v., derived from Lynkeus and having an ethnic Lynkios or Lynkeus, whereas the ethnic of Macedonian Lyncus was Lyncestes. Lynceus occurs as an ethnic in Sicyonia (*SEG* 11. 255).

but should be Thasus),[1] and crossed to the mainland opposite on learning that Europe was ruling in Thrace. This Europe, said Hegesippus, was not the wife of Phoenix[2] but a local woman, who gave her name to 'Europe, all the land north of Thrace'.

We may now put the local historians of Macedonia into a chronological framework. (1) Marsyas Macedon of Pella, born *c.* 356, developed the traditional account of Macedon, son of Zeus and Thyia, daughter of Deucalion, which was mentioned by Hesiod, and made Macedon give his own name to the country Maceta, which later was renamed Orestis. Macedon's sons provided eponyms for Pieria, Emathia, Brusis, and probably other places in Lower Macedonia west of the Axius. (2) Marsyas of Philippi, writing probably in the third century, dealt mainly with the country east of the Axius; he drew on Hegesippus of Mecyberna, and he attached much importance to Thasus. (3) In the second century, when Macedonia was conquered and partitioned by Rome and Orestis was declared free, the chance to redraw the legendary picture of the area was seized by Theagenes, who wrote probably *c.* 150. He cut Macedon down to size by making him not a son of Zeus but a son of Lycaon, who fathered many eponyms including Thesprotus. He then made Emathius not a son but a forerunner of Macedon and gave to Emathius the credit of being the founder (*ktistes*) of the country. The land was still called Emathia when Orestes and Hermione arrived; their son gave his name to Orestis, which was the centre of his empire, spanning as it did the Balkan peninsula. Macedon appeared later. He gave his name to the land, and his sons gave their names to some cities in Lower Macedonia west of the Axius and also to such remote places as Atintania.[3] He gave a record too of many traditional foundation legends and perhaps emphasized those which preceded the coming of Macedon, e.g. at Aeane, Elimea, and Ilium; even Heracles, so dear to the royal

---

[1] *FGrH* 391 F 3. The suggestions of 'Athens', 'Pallene', and 'Athos' in Jacoby's apparatus seem to be inept; 'Thasus' is not mentioned, but the association of Cadmus and Thasus in the other references I have cited makes it an almost certain correction. For the corrupt text ἐπίει περὶ Ἀθήνας I suggest ἔπλει περὶ τὴν Θάσον.

[2] As she is in Moschus 2. 7. 42. In Hegesippus' scheme and that of Marsyas the stemma runs Thasus brother of Cadmus m. Telephae

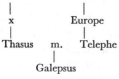

```
   x            Europe
   |              |
Thasus   m.   Telephe
         |
      Galepsus
```

Galepsus was a Greek city, a colony of Thasus (e.g. Harpocrat. s.v. *Stryme*).

[3] This is the Atintania north, north-east, and north-west of Lake Lychnitis (see Volume I. 36 and 76, and *Epirus* 599 f.). It was annexed to Macedonia probably by Philip II, and it was ceded by the Romans to Philip V; part of it stayed in Macedonia on the Roman partition of Macedonia.

house, appeared now as the father of Olynthus,[1] the eponymous hero of the city Philip II had destroyed. For the area east of the Axius Theagenes developed the legend of Mygdon, which emphasized the Thracian influence in the area. He touched upon Chalcidice, rationalizing the legends about Phlegra and Pallene. It was the work of Theagenes which had most influence on later writers. He was widely used, for instance, by Strabo,[2] Conon,[3] Parthenius, and Stephanus Byzantinus, and his influence is apparent in Justin's epitome of Pompeius Trogus[4] for the legendary period, upon which Theopompus had probably not written.

5. *The languages of the Macedones and of other peoples in early times*

The most thorough work on the problem of the language spoken by the *Macedones* was published by O. Hoffmann in 1906[5] and summarized by him in *RE* 14. 681–97 in 1928. His approach was that of the comparative

---

[1] So too in Athenaeus 8. 334 e, where a shrine by the river of Olynthus is mentioned. The orthodox legend made Olynthus a son of the Thracian king Strymon (*FGrH* 26 (Conon) F 1, 4); his brothers were Brangas and Rhesus, and the city was named by Brangas when Olynthus was killed by a lion.

[2] As we argued on p. 32 above with reference to the battle of Gods and Giants. In fr. 11 of book 7 we find the sequence which is familiar from our consideration of Theagenes: Emathia as the name for what became later Macedonia, and a city Emathia near the sea (cf. St. Byz. s.v. *Emathia*); Bottiaei derived from Crete in the time of Minos (6 C 279, 6 C 282, 7 frs. 11 and 11a); then Macedon giving to the country its current name. In 7 frs. 38 and 39 Pelegon, father of Asteropaeus, is associated with Paeonia. The story of Orestes coming to Orestis occurs at 7 C 326; it is told very briefly, and Orestes 'leaves the country named after himself' (rather than after Orestes' son, Orestes, as in Theagenes) and 'founds a city, Argos Orestikon'. The matter was probably all in Theagenes, but Strabo may have obtained it through an intermediate source and compressed it. Some of it too was or may have been in writers earlier than Theagenes.

[3] As we pointed out with regard to the battle of Gods and Giants (p. 32 above). Cretans of Minos coming to Bottiaea in Macedonia occur in *FGrH* 26 F 1, 26.

[4] Just. 7. 1 differs from Solinus 9. 1 in giving different people for the period before the arrival of Macedon. They are Pelasgi, who may have been linked with the Tyrseni and Pelasgi of Thuc. 4. 109. 4 (see p. 26 above); the region Bottia, which may have been linked with the tradition of Botton bringing the Bottiaei from Crete and ruling most of what became Macedonia; Paeonia, where we are given the Trojan War heroes (see Volume 1. 296 f.; Telegonus in Justin should be changed to Pelegon, the correct father of Asteropaeus); and Europus had a kingdom in 'Europa' 'ex alio latere' (probably by the Axius rather than in Almopia, this being made clear in the longer version by adding 'on the other side'; see Volume 1. 168). I think the ultimate source is again Theagenes, as for Solinus, but Justin has chosen different parts to epitomize.

The tangled skein of genealogies for Macedon, which I have tried to unravel, is given in its complexity by the scholia to Eustathius on Dion. Perieg. 427. The following relationships are mentioned: Macedon son of Zeus, Macedon one of the ten sons of Aeolus, Emathion son of Zeus and Electra preceding the birth of Macedon son of Aeacus (an error probably for Lycaon), and the country being named Emathia and later Macedonia.

[5] *Die Makedonen, ihre Sprache und ihr Volkstum* (Göttingen, 1906). He owed much to the work of his predecessors, especially O. Abel, A. Flick, G. Hatzidakis, Felix Solmsen, and P. Kretschmer.

philologist, and his aim was to reconstruct the Macedonian dialect from the many names of prominent Macedonians and the relatively small number of Macedonian words which have been transmitted in inscriptions and in literature. For Hoffmann, as for his predecessors, 'the decisive word in the Macedonian question is accorded to the remains of the Macedonian language.'[1] It was therefore a critical matter to decide whether the name Perdiccas came from πέρδιξ, a partridge, or was a form of Περιδίκαιος 'overly just'; and whether the entry in Hesychius γοτάν· ῦν. Μακεδόνες should be regarded as simply the local name for a grunter or as an indication that γοτ- in Macedonian equalled ὐ- in normal Greek, 'Laut für Laut', as Hoffmann argued.[2] In order to make as much evidence available as possible there was a tendency to dismiss other considerations. Thus Hoffmann argued that the claim of the royal house to be descended from Temenus and to have come from Argos in the Peloponnese was fictitious and that the names of the royal family were therefore 'echtmakedonisch'.[3]

On the other hand he misapplied the passage in Herodotus (1. 56. 3), where the *Dorian* group is said to have moved away from north-east Thessaly and settled in Pindus and been called 'Makednon', for he assumed that the *Macedones* also moved from north-east Thessaly into what became southern Macedonia.[4] This interpretation encouraged him to look particularly for Thessalian features in the Macedonian words which have survived.[5] He had a simple view of the racial situation within Macedonia; for he argued that the inhabitants of all cities in Philip II's kingdom up to and beyond the Strymon were called 'Macedones', and that any strange word in the Macedonian language could be ascribed to those outside Macedonia who were 'Reichsangehörige'.[6]

The influence of Hoffmann on Macedonian studies has been very strong. It is apparent still in the important work of J. N. Kalléris, *Les Anciens Macédoniens* 1 (Athens, 1954); for although his approach was wider and more practical than that of Hoffmann, he too placed the onus of proof upon the fragments of the Macedonian language. The work of Kalléris and his successors has been used by I. K. Pomponas, who has made a comparison between the Macedonian dialect as he reconstructs it

---

[1] Op. cit. iii, in the preface.   [2] pp. 131 and 44.
[3] p. 121; he called the royal house 'das Herrscherhaus der Argeaden', which is a misnomer in my opinion.
[4] p. 258 and his conclusion on p. 259 'die Makedonen gehörten zu einer Gruppe griechischer Stämme, die an den Abhängen des Pindos im nordwestlichen Thessalien wohnten und sich entlang dem oberen Laufe des Haliakmon bis gegen das illyrische Gebiet hinaufschoben.'
[5] e.g. pp. 114–15. He also dismissed certain words which did not fit his theory: e.g. because he assumed that Macedonian had no initial theta in names, he rejected two cult names, 'Thaulos' and 'Thourides'.
[6] pp. 116–17.

and the Mycenaean form of Greek which has been revealed by the decipherment of Linear B script. Although Pomponas and I arrive at similar conclusions, our paths are separate; for I do not think that the remains of 'Macedonian' are sufficient to support such a comparison in any conclusive manner.

My approach is based upon more general considerations, because I have studied the prehistory and the tribal organization of the territory before tackling the problem of the Macedonian language—a problem which, in my opinion, cannot be resolved conclusively by the study solely of the linguistic fragments now at our disposal. It is important, for instance, to decide who precisely the Macedones were. Thus we have already seen that the Pelagones, Lyncestae, Orestae, Elimiotae, and Tymphaei were related to the Molossians of Epirus, and we have inferred from this that they spoke a form of West Greek. On the other hand, the Macedones were a tribe apart from these, and they remained apart in that it was they who conquered extensive areas and imposed their own language in matters at least of administration. So too in the fourth century the possessors of Macedonian citizenship—those who called themselves Μακεδόνες—were only one element of the population in the cities and within the extensive domains of Philip II. Thus the Macedonian language, in as far as it was spoken in the fourth century, was specific to this élite, and it was their special words which were recorded, for instance, by Marsyas Macedon in the latter part of the fourth century and by Amerias Macedon in the third century. Thereafter, once the power of Macedon was broken by Rome, it is doubtful whether the Macedonian language lingered on or whether anyone would have been interested to record it. Thus the odds are high that words ascribed to the Macedones by Hesychius (who preserves most of them) were taken from the works of these Macedonian writers and similar ones,[1] and that they are genuine, at least if uncorrupted in transmission.

The names of the noble houses within the territory which we call Macedonia were certainly Greek. This is natural, because the royal house of the Macedones came from Argos and that of the Lyncestae from Corinth, and the indigenous royal houses of the Pelagones, Orestae, Elimiotae, and Tymphaei were speakers of West Greek; but it does not prove that the Macedones themselves were Greek-speaking,[2] any more than the Greek names of the Philaïdae in the Chersonese prove that the Dolonci were Greek-speaking. The early names give some signs of external relations: thus distinctive names of the royal houses of Upper

[1] e.g. Zoilus Macedon, mentioned by Pliny, *NH* 1. 12. 13, as a source alongside Marsyas Macedon; he wrote in the latter part of the fourth century, probably about Amphipolis rather than western Macedonia (*FGrH* 71 T 1 and T 4).

[2] *Pace* Hoffmann 230 f. who went on from the Greekness of these names to claim the Greekness of the Macedones as a people.

Macedonia are found also in Epirus, e.g. Derdas, Pausanias, and Machatas of the Elimiote house, Antiochus of the Orestid house, Simmias of the Tymphaean house, and Aëropus of the perhaps pre-Bacchiad Lyncestid house.[1] But through intermarriage the names of the royal houses within Macedonia and later of the nobles when they were absorbed into the Macedonian state became almost common coin, and the only light they may throw on the language of the Macedones comes from dialectal forms, such as Iollas for Iolaos. In general, then, the names of the nobles will not be brought into the present discussion.[2]

The number of place-names which may be definitely attributed to the Macedones is very small. For it is to be assumed that the peoples of Upper Macedonia used the names which they had either taken over from their predecessors or had themselves invented, and in Lower Macedonia on both sides of the Axius the names are likely to have been given by any one of the predecessors of the Macedones. There are some place-names in the homeland of the Macedones in Pieria which I have taken into account, and in a more detailed study it might be possible to identify certain names which the Macedones carried with them into their territories outside Macedonia and could therefore be thought *a priori* to be their own names.

After these prolegomena I describe the situation in Macedonia today, as it may provide an analogy to the situation in ancient Macedonia. Many languages are spoken in the geographical area which we have defined in Volume I as Macedonia: purist (or Atticized) Greek, peasant Greek with local dialect and diction (e.g. affinities with Zagori in Epirus are noticeable in Voïon, part of ancient Orestis), imported Greek of an altogether different dialect (from Asia Minor, known as Lazika), Vlach, Bulgarian, Serbo-Croatian, and Albanian. Moreover, past invasions and occupations of Macedonia have left linguistic traces throughout the country, especially in place-names, except where they have been changed by governmental decrees. We find a similar situation when we turn to ancient Macedonia.

In Upper Macedonia *Illyrian* was spoken by the Penestae, who lived in the westernmost headwaters of the Axius; and at one period in the Early Iron Age Illyrian-speaking conquerors held part of the coastal plain and in particular Vergina, where they were immediate neighbours of the Macedones (see Volume I. 420 f.). *Paeonian* was probably a separate language, brought perhaps by the Early Bronze Age invaders into the coastal plain. At any rate Herodotus regarded the Paeonians as

---

[1] See the Onomastikon Epeirotikon in *Epirus* 795–817. On the other hand the names in the Bacchiad house of the Lyncestae—Bromerus, Arrhabaeus, and Heromenes—are not found in Epirus; for the name Aëropus as perhaps that of an earlier dynasty in Lyncestis see above, p. 37.

[2] K. 289 f. gives a list of such names and discusses their significance.

an offshoot of the Teucrians of Troy who had settled in Macedonia before the time of the Trojan War (5. 13. 2; 7. 20. 2); other invaders at that time were the Mysi, and they may have been neighbours of the Macedones as Hellanicus asserted (*FGrH* 4 F 74).[1] The 'Paeonian tribes'—the Agrianes, Laeaei, and others—were distinguished from the Thracian tribes by Thucydides at the time of Sitalces' invasion in 429 (2. 96. 1–2).[2] *Greek* was spoken by the Derriopes, Pelagones, Lyncestae, Orestae, Elimiotae, and Tymphaei.[3] Their dialect was akin to that spoken in Epirus, probably a form of *West Greek*, and we learn from Strabo 7 C 326 fin., that the whole of the mountainous area which included Upper Macedonia, northern Epirus, and a part of southern Illyris was regarded 'by some authors' as a single cultural area with similar dialect, tonsure, and short cloak (*chlamys*), except that 'some are bilingual'. The 'some authors' were writing probably after the fall of Macedon,[4] when the Orestae and other tribes of 'Free Macedonia' preferred to associate themselves with Epirus rather than with the Macedones. The *Eordi*, who were expelled from their old territory and settled at Physca (Thuc. 2. 99. 5), probably spoke a pre-Hellenic language of their own.[5]

In the south the Greek-speaking Magnetes held the coastal part of Pieria in the Late Bronze Age. When they migrated into Thessaly (see Volume I. 298) they spoke *Aeolic Greek*. This happened before the Trojan War, when their place was taken by Thracian invaders who settled in southern Pieria. Thracians also held the central plain for a time. These people spoke an early dialect of *Thracian*. On the western side of Mt. Olympus the Perrhaebi spoke *Achaean Greek*;[6] they stayed in their territory from the Late Bronze Age down to classical times. We shall leave the language of the Macedones for later consideration. But in their own homeland in northern Pieria the Macedones were at various times neighbours of peoples who spoke not only Aeolic Greek, Achaean Greek, and Thracian but also *Doric Greek* (Hdt. 1. 56. 3 and 8. 43), *Mysian* (Hdt. 7. 20. 2 and Hellanicus in *FGrH* 4 F 74), *Phrygian* (Hdt. 7. 73), and *Illyrian* (Str. 7 fr. 11; especially at Vergina).[7] They were also in contact

[1] This fragment is discussed below, p. 47. For the Paeonians see also Volume I. 296 and 418.

[2] *Pace* Gomme 2. 243 'Paeonian Thracians'; Thucydides distinguishes carefully between three groups, the Thracians and Getae of the Odrysian kingdom, the independent Thracians, and the Paeonian tribes, and his repetition of the verb ἀνίστημι stresses this distinction.

[3] See *Epirus* 422 f. and 460 f. and Volume I. 89 f.

[4] During their period of power the Macedones distinguished themselves from the Epirotes. In the following sentence Strabo speaks of subjection to Rome. The passage is discussed by Hoffmann 151 f.

[5] For these people and their distinctive burial practices see Volume I. 414 f.

[6] See *RE* 19. 907 s.v.

[7] See Volume I. 420 f.

with the Bottiaei of the coastal plain, who claimed descent from Crete and may therefore have spoken a *Cretan* language.[1]

To the east of the Axius *Phrygian* and later dialects of *Thracian* were spoken in Mygdonia and adjacent areas. The Crousaei, for instance, probably spoke Phrygian in early times, because their eponymous ancestor was connected with Mygdon. *Paeonians* had also held this area at one time (Str. 7 fr. 41). When the *Bottiaei* came *c.* 650 to occupy the base of the Chalcidic peninsula, they were presumably still speaking their own language. The two western prongs of Chalcidice were occupied by *Greeks* of various dialects. The promontory ending in Mt. Athos had a small Chalcidic element and small groups of 'bilingual barbarians' (Thuc. 4. 109. 4; cf. D.S. 12. 68. 5); among the latter there were Tyrseni, speaking their form of *Etruscan*, Bisaltae (Hdt. 8. 116. 1) and Edones speaking *Thracian*, and *Crestonaei* speaking perhaps a separate language (see Volume I. 181).

Within the classical period the two languages which were gaining ground in Macedonia and Chalcidice respectively were Macedonian and Greek. When the Macedones expelled the existing populations from Pieria, Bottiaea, Almopia, and Eordaea, they brought their own language, whatever that language was, into their new territories. When they acquired control of the lands east of the Axius, they employed Macedonian as the language of administration. There is no indication, for instance, that the Macedonians ever adopted Illyrian or Thracian as their language. Indeed Perseus sent a bilingual Illyrian and not a bilingual Macedonian to act as interpreter in negotiations with the Illyrian Genthius, presumably because such Macedonians did not exist; for it is always safer to use one's own nationals as interpreters. No one ever suggested that the Macedones spoke Thracian, although Demosthenes and others would have been only too glad to have done so. On the other hand Greek spread outwards from the colonies of the Chalcidic peninsula. Its use can be seen among the 'bilingual barbarians' on the promontory of Mt. Athos (a most remote place, as it is today), and can be assumed in the case of the Crousaei and Bottiaei, who were in much closer commercial contact with the Greek colonists than the bilingual barbarians had ever been. But that is as far as the spread of Greek is likely to have gone, because relations with the Macedones of the coastal plain and of Mygdonia seem generally to have been hostile. Across the Thermaic Gulf, on the coast of Macedonia west and south of the Axius, there were only two Greek cities, Pydna and Methone, which were close together. Their influence is likely to have extended only to their immediate neighbours.

We are better informed for the western side of the Pindus than we are

[1] Volume I. 153 and 295 f.; no one can say which Cretan language Botton and his followers may have spoken.

for Macedonia. This is because inscriptions of the early fourth century have been found. They show that the members of the Thesprotian and Molossian tribes spoke Greek, had Greek names, and used Greek constitutional terms. As a language cannot be adopted overnight, it is certain that these tribes spoke Greek throughout the fifth century and probably before that date.[1] These inscriptions have shown conclusively what Thucydides meant when he called these and other tribes in Epirus 'barbaroi'. He referred not to language but to civilization: those who did not participate in the world and the ideas of the Greek city-state were 'barbaroi', and all tribal societies, all ἔθνη as Thucydides and Aristotle called them, were barbarian by definition.[2] Now in one of the passages in which Epirote tribes were called 'barbarians', there was mention also of 2,000 Macedones sent by Perdiccas (2. 80. 5–7) and these Macedones were part of the 'barbarian' force (e.g. 2. 81. 6). Again at 4. 124. 1 the Hellenes and the barbarians were contrasted in the army which Brasidas and Perdiccas led against Arrhabaeus, and these barbarians included 'the Macedonian cavalry . . . and *the rest* of the large company of the barbarians' (4. 124. 1 ἱππῆς . . . Μακεδόνων . . . καὶ ἄλλος ὅμιλος τῶν βαρβάρων πολύς). The distinction between Greek and barbarian in Macedonia was a distinction not of language but of civilization. So too when the Thessalians were contrasted with the Macedonians as 'Greeks with barbarians' c. 400 (Ἀρχελάῳ δουλεύσομεν Ἕλληνες ὄντες βαρβάρῳ). On the same basis Demosthenes called Philip 'the barbarian at Pella' at the time when Isocrates was appealing to Philip as a Greek whose 'fatherland is Argos' (*Phil.* 32 Ἄργος μὲν γάρ ἐστί σοι πατρίς). The question of language was entirely separate.

On the western side of Pindus we have some tribes which were also 'bilingual'. When Strabo was describing the whole area north of Amphilochia up to 'the country which joins the Illyrian mountains' (they began north of the Via Egnatia, i.e. north of Lake Ochrid), he contrasted with the Epirotic tribes of this area (e.g. the Orestae) the Illyrian tribes 'which were intermingled with them', namely Bylliones, Taulantii, Parthini, and Brygi.[3] It was these latter tribes or some of them which were bilingual, speaking Greek in addition to a native language. Just as the bilingual peoples of the Athos promontory were on the fringe of the Greek-speaking peoples in the fifth century, so the bilingual peoples of the area inland of the Ionian Gulf were on the fringe of the Greek-speaking peoples in the fourth century or perhaps later (Str. 7 C 326–7; the source of the final sentence 'some too are bilingual' is not clear).[4]

---

[1] See *Epirus* 423 and 525 f.   [2] Ibid. 419 f.   [3] Ibid. 466 f.

[4] Strabo's use of the present tense, coming between two past tenses, suggests that he is referring to a time after the Roman conquest and that he may be thinking in terms of the contemporary situation, in the time of Augustus.

They represent the high-water-mark of Greek speech in the Balkan peninsula.

What language, then, did the *Macedones* speak? The answer is to be derived first from a consideration of the position in the fourth century. When Alexander trained 30,000 young Persians for incorporation into the Macedonian army, he arranged that they should 'learn Greek letters and be brought up in Macedonian weapons' (Plu. *Alex.* 47. 3 γράμματά τε μανθάνειν Ἑλληνικὰ καὶ Μακεδονικοῖς ὅπλοις ἐντρέφεσθαι). The 'Greek letters' were to express the Greek language, and the Macedonian weapons were to be used in fighting alongside Macedonians. Further, when Alexander returned from India, he made each infantry section consist of four Macedonians and twelve Persians (Arr. *An.* 7. 23. 3–4). In an army organized in this way a common language was a practical necessity, and that was why the Persians were taught Greek in the first place. It follows that the language of the Macedonian soldiers was Greek.[1] There is a further indication that the speech of the Macedonian army was Greek in the affair of Cleitus, when Alexander, fearing an attempt on himself in the uproar, called out to his guardsmen 'in Macedonian, as this was the watchword[2] for a serious disturbance' (Plu. *Alex.* 51. 4 Μακεδονιστὶ καλῶν τοὺς ὑπασπιστάς, τοῦτο δὲ ἦν σύμβολον θορύβου μεγάλου). The use of Macedonian made this order unique, used by the king only in such a crisis, because all other orders were in Greek. It follows that the ordinary language of the Macedonian soldiers was Greek. If, then, the Macedones of the fourth century spoke Greek as their language, we must conclude that they were speaking it in the fifth century, when Thucydides described them as barbarians, and probably earlier when they were winning lands on both sides of the Axius river.

The meaning of Μακεδονιστὶ thus becomes clear. 'Macedonian' was not a non-Greek language but a dialect of the Greek language in which Alexander spoke for a special purpose; and in the case of his order the vocabulary, as well as the pronunciation, was probably particular to this dialect. On a later occasion the Macedonian soldiers gave a special welcome to Eumenes by greeting him Μακεδονιστὶ τῇ φωνῇ, i.e. by calling out in the Macedonian dialect (Plu. *Eum.* 14. 5); it was perhaps even more of a compliment to Eumenes because he was a Greek and not a Macedonian by origin.

[1] The same assumption underlies the historically worthless words of Philotas in Curt. 6. 9. 35. We had an interesting parallel in the army of British India, when Sikhs and Ghurkas learnt English. Members of the French Foreign Legion learnt French in the same way. To suppose that the Persians were taught Greek and the Macedonians spoke a non-Greek language would be as absurd as to suppose that the Sikhs were taught French when the English spoke English.

[2] The use of Macedonian language was an indication of a civil commotion for which military intervention was needed; the word σύμβολον had a general sense, as in Aesch. *Agam.* 8, and a particular meaning in the context, 'watchword'.

There is a further indication that to 'speak Macedonian' was not to speak a separate language but to speak a dialect of Greek. Plutarch (*Ant.* 27) tells us that some of the Ptolemies not only made no effort to learn Egyptian but even gave up 'speaking Macedonian', τὸ Μακεδονίζειν (i.e. on special occasions as the standard language was ordinary Greek). The implication is that others of the Ptolemies maintained the use of Macedonian. This becomes credible if Macedonian was a dialect of Greek but not if Macedonian was a separate language. Again, when there was contact between Macedonia and Greece, many Attic writers wrote 'Macedonian' (Athen. 3. 122 a), this being a matter of dialect and not of a non-Greek language.

The conclusion that the Macedones of the fourth century spoke ordinary standard Greek and also on special occasions a Macedonian dialect of Greek will not surprise us, if we turn back to consider the early traditions about them. The fragment of Hesiod, *Eoeae*, in which Magnes and Macedon are sons of Zeus and Thyia, daughter of Deucalion, and therefore cousins of Hellen's sons, Dorus, Xouthus, and Aeolus, can only mean that the Macedones were regarded as Greek and not, say, as Thracian or Illyrian; and to be Greek was to speak Greek, and in this case, as the Magnetes spoke Aeolic Greek, presumably to speak Aeolic Greek. A different version of Greek genealogy in the mythical period was preserved in the record of the priestesses of Argos, the city from which the royal house of Macedon came, and the part which concerned Macedon was cited by Hellanicus in his first book about them, published not long after 423, when Macedonia and its people were fairly well known to the Greek world. The passage as Jacoby prints it (*FGrH* 4 F 74) is as follows:

STEPH. BYZ. (CONSTANT. PORPH. De them. II p. 48 Bonn.) s. Μακεδονία· ἡ χώρα, ἀπὸ Μακεδόνος τοῦ Διὸς καὶ Θυίας τῆς Δευκαλίωνος, ὥς φησιν Ἡσίοδος (F 5) . . . ἄλλοι δ' ἀπὸ Μακεδόνος τοῦ Αἰόλου, ὡς Ἑλλάνικος Ἱερειῶν πρώτηι τῶν ἐν Ἄργει· "καὶ Μακεδόνος ⟨τοῦ⟩ Αἰόλου, ⟨ἀφ'⟩ οὗ νῦν Μακεδόνες καλοῦνται, μόνοι μετὰ Μυσῶν τότε οἰκοῦντες".

The words which precede the quotation make the meaning clear. As a son of Aeolus Macedon was worked into the direct line of descent from Hellen, instead of being in a collateral branch. The time of Macedon's appearance was tied to the invasion of the Mysi, which was put by Herodotus 'before the Trojan War' (7. 20. 2) and by Hellanicus in probably the third generation before that war.[1] The transference of Macedon to the direct line was no doubt due to the influence of a Temenid king of Macedon with the Argive priestesses, whether Alexander I or Perdiccas or Archelaus, who, we have argued, introduced Caranus into the royal

---

[1] As with F 75 from the same book; see Jacoby's comment, *FGrH* I a 454.

line.[1] But the interesting thing is the choice of Aeolus rather than Dorus or Xouthus. The reason for the choice was presumably that the Macedones spoke an Aeolic form of Greek—and were known to speak it at the time when Hellanicus published his book, after 423.

Only a small number of words can be confidently associated with the Macedones in the pre-classical period of their existence. Of these the tribal and clan names are Μακεδνός, Μακέται, Ἀργεάδαι, Ἀέροπες.[2] The place-names are Μακεδνία, Μάκετα, Λεβαία, Βέρης, Ἁλιάκμων, Πιερία, Ἑλικών, Ὄλυμπος, Λείβηθρα, perhaps Αἰγίδιον.[3] The names of months are Ἀπελλαῖος, Ἀρτεμίσιος, Δῖος, Πάναμος, Δαίσιος, Λώιος, Δύστρος, Ξανδικός, Περίτιος, Ὑπερβερεταῖος, Αὐδναῖος, Γορπιαῖος.[4] Cult names are Δῖα, Ἑταιρίδια, Θαῦλος, Ὀλύμπια, Ψευδάνωρ, Ἀραντίδες, Δάρρων, Θουρίδες.[5] There is no doubt that these words are overwhelmingly, and probably without exception, Greek. They have no affinities at all with what is known of Illyrian and Thracian.

A few inferences can be made from these words, and also from other Macedonian words of whatever date which are certainly Greek. They are not in the Ionic (or Attic) dialect. This indicates that they were not derived from nor even influenced by the Ionic-speaking settlements at Methone, Dicaea, and in the Chalcidic peninsula, and further that they were not introduced into the country by settlers or traders from the Aegean basin. Nor are there any distinctively Doric features. Thus the vocabulary of the Macedones was not affected by the presence of two Doric-speaking royal houses in the country nor by the powerful Dorian colony, Potidaea. There are, however, some features of the Aeolic dialect, namely the use of omicron occasionally for alpha and the doubling of some consonants;[6] and there are features which Macedonian shares with Thessalian, itself a mixture of Aeolic and other dialects, namely ou for omega, syncopation of certain prepositions, doubling of some consonants, and the patronymic form ending in *-ios*.[7] (Hoffmann added a genitive

---

[1] The scholia to Eustathius on Dion. Perieg. 427, which gives a summary of the various genealogies (see p. 39 n. 4, above), mention the descent from Aeolus. As it is not known elsewhere, the scholiast may have got the information from Hellanicus.

[2] Hdt. 1. 56. 3; St. Byz. s.v. *Makedonia*; Str. 7 fr. 11; Hesych. s.v. *Aeropes*.

[3] Volume I. 309; *FGrH* 135/6 (Marsyas) F 10 and *FGrH* 323 (Cleidemus) F 3; Hdt. 8. 137. 1; for Beres see Volume I. 434, and for Aegidium above, p. 26.

[4] These are given in *RE* 14. 690. A variant form Αἰδοναῖος in *AD* 20 (1965) 2. 411.

[5] *RE* ibid. 690–1. The first, second, and fourth are associated with Zeus, the third with Ares, the fifth with Dionysus, the sixth with the Erinyes, the seventh with a god of healing, and the last with Nymphs and Muses. The Magnetes also celebrated a Hetairidia and the Thessalians had a famous cult of Zeus Thaulios. 'Darron' may be a loan word from Paeonian (see p. 75 below on ΔΕΡΡΟΝΑΙΟΣ) and not a form of θαρρῶν, as Hoffmann supposed.

[6] Hoffmann 48 κόμμαραι for κάμμαροι, 'lobsters' and P. 14; names such as Simmias, Perdiccas, and words such as δάρυλλος, ἄππα, ματτύη.

[7] Hoffmann 43 κυνουπεύς from κνωπ-; ἄσπιλοι from ἀπό and σπίλος (39); the patronymic form is inferred from city-names, Alexandreia, Antigoneia, etc. (See also P. 21.)

form in -*oi*, explaining the place-name Philippoi as '(the city) of Philip',[1] but I doubt his explanation.) Finally, there are characteristics particular to Macedonian words, and these are the mark of a strong dialect: the uses of beta for phi,[2] delta for theta,[3] gamma for kappa,[4] *au* for *ao*,[5] and words which are closer to Homeric forms than to classical forms.[6] Thus there are strong reasons for concluding that the Macedonian dialect of Greek belonged to the Aeolic group; that it developed more or less in isolation from the beginning at least of the Early Iron Age, and that it owed its affinities with Thessalian Aeolic and mixed Aeolic more to a common origin than to any shared development or to continuous contact.

When we put together all the arguments which we have adduced from archaeology, modern analogy, comparison with a similar area west of Pindus, the practical problem of Alexander's army, the traditions about Macedon and the Macedones, and the form of early and specific Macedonian words, we come to the firm conclusion that the Macedones spoke their own distinctive dialect of Aeolic Greek. This dialect was affected very little by the dialects of Greek which were spoken by their neighbours in the 'Greek cities' of the Pierian coast and the Chalcidic peninsula. Rather the Macedones carried their own dialect into the territories which they acquired on both sides of the river Axius before the death of Alexander I.

Towards the end of the fifth century and rapidly during the fourth century local dialects declined and a standard Greek, known later as the *koine*, came into use throughout most Greek-speaking lands. Macedonia was no exception. Indeed, under the leadership of a Greek royal house which sought to introduce the arts and culture of southern Greece into the kingdom, the standard Greek became the general language of the people and the army by the middle of the century at the latest. The Macedonian dialect still survived as a local idiom, used only in special circumstances and regarded by scholars as an interesting survival. Words were therefore recorded from the dialect, not because they were ordinary words or words close to Greek in other dialects but because

[1] Hoffmann 251 and again in *RE* 14. 696; the inscription on the coins is **ΦΙΛΙΠΠΩΝ** and Philip founded a Philipp*ou*polis in Thrace.

[2] Noted by St. Byz. p. 165, 1 (ed. Meineke), as characteristic of the Macedonians' πατρῴα φωνή e.g. Phryges to Briges, p. 186. 13; see P. 17.

[3] As in Δάρρων (95) and ἀδραιά for αἰθρία (37); see P. 56.

[4] As γώπας for σκῶπες (47). The word meant 'jackdaw' in Macedonia and 'screech-owl' elsewhere; it is onomatopoeic, with a hard *g* close to a *k* and ω pronounced as *au* for the jackdaw's caw. So too γοτάν for a pig in Macedonia is probably onomatopoeic, like the modern Greek 'gourouni', for the grunt of a pig; the explanation of the word which Hoffmann 44 gives seems to me far-fetched and unconvincing.

[5] As σαυτορία for σωτηρία (11).

[6] As ἀδραιά and αἴθρη (37), νίβα and νίφα (37), ὑέτης and οἰετέης (66). See P. 13 and 56.

they were rare words or words unlike Greek in other dialects.[1] But after the conquest by Rome interest in the special qualities of the Macedones died, and it was only occasionally in the court of a Macedonian king abroad that dialect words were used for special occasions.[2]

Armed with these general conclusions we may consider some words which are of particular interest. In religious matters we may be sure that early vocabulary and local dialect were retained for a long period, just as Byzantine Greek is used in the liturgy of the Greek Orthodox Church. Amerias Macedon has recorded σαυάδαι· σαῦδοι as the Macedonian name for the Sileni, and σαυτορία as the Macedonian word for σωτηρία. Both have the characteristic αυ, which served to express au and omega in the local brogue. As we learn from Herodotus, it was in connection with the presence of the Phrygian Briges below Mt. Bermion that the Silenus was captured in the gardens of Midas, 'so it is said by the Macedones' (Hdt. 8. 138. 3), and the Briges were immediate neighbours of the Macedones before the former moved eastwards (7. 73), that is before c. 800.[3] The explanation of σαυάδαι is apparent from Demosthenes, *De Corona* 260, and the comments of Strabo 10 C 471, where Demosthenes derided Aeschines for leading the Phrygian rites and crying εὐοῖ σαβοῖ, as Strabo says 'in honour of Σαβάζιος and the Mother'; for *sauadai* is clearly derived from the same root as Sauazius (in the Attic form Sabazius).[4] *Sautoria* may have been used in the same context.

Two other Macedonian words may also pertain to this cult. Demosthenes 18. 260 mentions garlands of white poplar (*leuke*) and Hesychius preserves the Macedonian name ἄλιζα· ἡ λεύκη τῶν δένδρων. Μακεδόνες. Kalléris paraded seven different explanations of this word as Greek, and no doubt others could be added, if the arm of derivation was stretched yet further;[5] but it is more likely that it is the Macedonian version of a loan-word from Phrygian. Demosthenes mentioned too a special mixture of bran and loam, and Hesychius gives us ἄδισκον· κυκεῶνα. Μακεδόνες (*kukeon* being a mixture of meal and other stuff for religious or magical purposes). This word is more likely to be the Macedonian form of a Phrygian word than a word of Greek origin, whether corrupted from ἄδιστον in the view of Kalléris or a diminutive of ἄδος, an unattested word, in the view of Fick.[6] The gardens of Midas were famous for wild roses, and roses were used in the cult of the dead.[7] Hesychius gives the Macedonian word for roses: ἄβαγνα· ῥόδα. Μακε-

---

[1] See the excellent remarks of Kalléris p. 58.

[2] e.g. at the court of some of the Ptolemies (Plu. *Ant.* 27).

[3] See Volume I. 410 f.

[4] It was also a loan-word in Illyrian, where it took the form *Deuadai* (Hesych. s.v.). For discussion of *Sauadai* see B. 80, H. 6, K. n. 139, and P. 52.

[5] K. no. 19 pp. 90–4.   [6] K. no. 12; H. 72.

[7] Hdt. 8. 138. 2; *Anacreontea* 55, 25–7 and other references in K. 72 notes 3 and 4.

δόνες. The interpretation is complicated by a floating word ἀμαράντων, which does not fit the preceding entry of Hesychius and may have belonged to the original form of this entry. Kalléris cites four derivations and then adds his own, meaning 'roses with tender thorns'.[1] But it may be doubted whether *abagna* is an epithet rather than a name, and I should be inclined to suggest that the origin of the word may be Phrygian rather than Greek.

In connection with the worship of the originally Thracian god Dionysus two Macedonian words have been preserved: Κλώδωνες or Κλώδονες, superseded in the reign of Argaeus (fl. *c.* 623) by Μιμαλλόνες. These were the names of women worshippers, usually called in Greece the Mainades and in Thrace the Bassarai or Bassarides. The proposed derivations of these words from Greek seem to be very dubious.[2] As we know that the Macedones were immediate neighbours of the Thracians in Pieria, it is likely that they adopted the terms together with the worship from these Thracians, who were themselves distinct from the later group of Thracians who occupied the eastern part of the plain and used the term Bassarai. The alleged early date of the change, advanced probably by Callimachus, would fit with this view,[3] although the story and explanation attached to the word Mimallones belong to folk-lore.[4] Again, a local name for Aphrodite was 'Zeirene' (Hesychius s.v.), and this too was probably Thracian.[5]

Phrygian influence accounts also for the Macedonian use of the word βέδυ in ritual. As Clement of Alexandria stated, this was the Phrygian word for water, and it formed the root of the two town-names Edessa (one replaced by Aegeae, and the other the classical Edessa). It was used also in the Orphic religion. Clement gave examples of the word being used with this meaning in a Greek context, and then went on to give two examples where it meant air, one of these being in the prayers of priests of the Macedones. We should accept the two uses of the word as two sources of life rather than look for a separate derivation of the term.[6]

On the other hand Marsyas Macedon has preserved some words of the Macedonian dialect which seem to be of Greek derivation. One is κοριναῖος the son of an unmarried girl (*FGrH* 135/6 F 24), and linked to it is κύρνος, given the same meaning by Photius s.v. in the usage of the

---

[1] K. no. 1 pp. 66–73; also pp. 42 f. His explanation of *abaru* as heavy incense from origanum seems very convincing with its Greek derivation; see K. no. 3 and p. 75 n. 1 where I propose to read Μακεδονιστί for Μακεδονίσια.

[2] See K. 210–17.　　　　　　　　　　　　　　　　　[3] *EM* and Polyaen. 4. 1.

[4] Polyaen. 4. 1. and Schol. Pers. 1. 100. The Illyrian soldiers were frightened away by a crowd of Mimallones whom they supposed to be troops; a similar story is told today of Napoleon's Frenchmen who landed in Wales being frightened away by a lot of Welsh women.

[5] K. no. 79 p. 179.

[6] Clem. Al. *Strom.* 5. 8. 6; K. no. 43 pp. 118–30 and P. 48 f.

Macedones. Five other words of family relationships may perhaps come from the same source: three for a female child ἀκραία, ἀκρέα, and ἀμαλή, and two used respectfully for an older member of a family ἄππα and πέλιος (cf. πελιγάν). All five are certainly of Greek derivation.[1] Marsyas has also given us a sword-dance of the Macedones, called τελεσιάς (F 11; cf. Hesych. s.v. *telesias*), and he is probably the source of another Macedonian war-dance, καρπαία or καρπέα (Hesych. s.v.).[2] Again we owe to Marsyas the name of a ritual goblet, used by the kings of Macedon on entering 'the city' (? Pella), γυάλα, and the name of a wooden cup, such as is made nowadays by nomad shepherds, κύπελλον (F 21 and 22).[3] Both are clearly Greek. Lastly, as Pliny mentioned Marsyas Macedon as one of his sources on timber, we may assume that Marsyas was the chief source for local words on this topic. One is in Hesychius ἄξος· ὕλη παρὰ Μακεδόσιν, where the meaning is probably cut or rather split wood,[4] where the woodman used an axe, and it is possible that the river Axios owed its name to its use for floating prepared timber down to the sea. Others are in Hesychius δάρυλλος· ἡ δρῦς ὑπὸ Μακεδόνων, which is again clearly a Greek word; ἄδδαι· ῥυμοί. Μακεδόνες, which means probably dried wood and is a dialect form of ἄζα 'dryness' or 'dry stuff';[5] and ἴλαξ· ἡ πρῖνος 'the holm-oak'.

Finally one may note three interesting words. Hoffmann emended the text of Hesychius to read ἀβαρκνᾷ· κομᾷ(τε). Μακεδόνες and explained it as a dialect form of ἁβροκομᾷ 'wears his hair long'.[6] This hair-style was characteristically Macedonian, and it is interesting that hair-rings for men as well as for women were so very common in burials in Macedonia, especially at Vergina (where I place Aegeae) in the Early Iron Age.[7] The Suda gave as names for spears among the Macedones σιγύνη καὶ σιγύννους, words which we know from a fragment of Ennius were the names of Illyrian weapons written with beta instead of gamma, evidently hunting spears. No doubt the Macedones adopted the weapon and the

---

[1] See *EM* s.v. *akraia, amale,* and *appa,* Hesych. s.v. *akrea,* Str. 7 fr. 2, Hesych. *peliganes,* and K. nos. 17, 22, 27, and 125 b, and P. 13 and 37.

[2] H. 90 f., mentioning that the Magnetes (once the neighbours of the Macedones), the Aenianes, and the Thracians had similar dances.

[3] K. no. 53; H. 71; it is likely to be Marsyas of Pella and not Marsyas of Amphipolis because an old custom seems to be being described, and the old capital may be meant. Other Macedonian words for cups were ἄλεισον and κύλιξ according to Marsyas (*FGrH* 136/6 F 23); Kaibel's suggested addition to the text is unacceptable because alternatives to *kotule* are being cited.

[4] The same word, *axos,* was used in Cretan for the Attic *agmos,* meaning a 'fracture' or split in medical terminology. For the numerous large axes found in Macedonia see references in the Index of Volume 1.

[5] Well explained by K. no. 10; see P. 54 f. During the war I tried to learn some of the technical terms for timber in western Macedonia; they are very specialized.

[6] H. 54 f., supported by K. no. 2.

[7] See Volume 1. 331 f. and 398.

name from their neighbours either in the period overlapping the Late Bronze Age and the Early Iron Age[1] or in the eighth century when Illyrians held Vergina (see Volume I. 420 f.) ; for at both periods warriors were buried often with two spears and many of these were for throwing, as their small heads indicate. The Suda gives also ἄργελλα· οἴκημα Μακεδονικόν, ὅπερ θερμαίνοντες λούονται. This, we learn from Ephorus (*FGrH* 70 F 134), was the name of underground buildings, called ἄργιλλαι by the Cimmerians. Now, although he was writing of Cimmerians who had settled in South Italy, this word was doubtless used by the Cimmerians of South Russia, and the word in Macedonia was a legacy of the Cimmerian raids of *c.* 700–650 (see Volume I. 427), which have left archaeological traces in Macedonia and Epirus.[2] Thus the Cimmerian bath, like the Turkish bath, came to stay.

Kalléris listed 153 words as surviving from the Macedonian language. We have already discussed seventy-one. We may omit some thirty military terms, because they were invented or adopted from standard Greek to describe the new features of Philip's specialized army, and another six terms which are associated with places outside the home-land of Macedonian speech (Bloureitis, Edessaios, Gazoreitis, Ichnaia, Pasikrata, Tauropolos). There are six names of animals and birds which are clearly Greek (αἰγίποψ, ἀργίπους, δρῆγες, κυνουπεύς, παραός, χάρων). Of the remaining forty words some are dialectal forms of Greek words (e.g. δάνος, δανῶν, δώραξ, δαίτας, ζέρεθρον, ἰδνέα, κεβαλή) and some are standard Greek, whereas others are corrupt and others are not explicable.[3]

When we call to mind the movements of the tribal group known as the Macedones and the contacts which they had with Mysians, Phrygians, Thracians, Illyrians, Cimmerians, and various Greek-speaking peoples, the fragments of their language which have survived, partly through choice of the eccentric words, are very much what we should expect. The chief impression is that the dominant element is Greek. Then there are indications of a strong dialect, developed early and more akin to Homeric Greek than fifth-century Greek. Finally, we find a considerable

[1] When the Macedones were in what became known as Orestis; for javelins in northern Epirus see *Epirus* 338 f.; many javelin-heads, especially of the faceted type, have been found in Albania and were on show, for instance, in Koritsa museum in 1972 when I visited it. See P. 40 for a different explanation of *sigune*. Hesychius explained the form συμβίνης as a 'pig-sticker'.

[2] Hoffmann 59 f. was the first to explain the word *argella* on these lines. His explanation has been rejected by K. no. 29, who prefers to derive it from the Greek word for clay, *argilos*. It is a good example of the fact that almost any foreign word transliterated into Greek with a little licence can be provided with a plausible Greek derivation; yet why should 'the clay one' come to mean an underground heated building for washing?

[3] Those words which I have not mentioned and come under these last categories are K. nos. 4, 5, 7, 8, 11, 18, 20, 25, 31, 33, 35, 36, 39, 40, 46, 49, 50, 61, 68, 72, 74, 75, 76, 84, 95, 98, 100, 102, 105, 109, 110, 135, 136, 137.

number of loan-words, some assignable to a specific people and others not. All in all, the language of the Macedones was a distinct and particular form of Greek, resistant to outside influences and conservative in pronunciation. It remained so until the fourth century when it was almost totally submerged by the flood tide of standardized Greek.

II

THE GROWTH OF THE MACEDONIAN STATE AND ECONOMIC DEVELOPMENTS

FROM *c.* 550 TO *c.* 480

1. *The historical events and the movements of peoples*

(See Map 9)

IN Volume I it was maintained that by 550 the Argeadae Macedones had gained control of Pieria, Bottiaea, and Almopia,[1] expelling such of the existing populations as they did not kill (Thuc. 2. 99. 3 and 5; cf. Hdt. 8. 127). Thus they held a readily defensible block of territory, except that it was exposed to attack from the east. There the Thracians who had moved westwards after the seventh-century Cimmerian migrations were still in possession of the lands from the Axius to the Strymon, and the discovery of mouthpieces of gold plaque in burials at Chauchitsa in Amphaxitis and at Zeitenlik near Salonica of the mid-sixth century shows that Thracians then held Amphaxitis, probably the crossing of the Axius with a footing on the west bank,[2] and the north-eastern coast of the Thermaic Gulf as well as Mygdonia, parts of Chalcidice, and the Strymon basin. It was from this time that the area east of the Axius and Chalcidice too were regarded as part of Thrace, for instance by Hecataeus (see Volume I. 427 f.).

After 550 the Paeonians emerged as the most powerful people in the area. Whereas they had been confined to the hinterland of the Axius and Strymon valleys with the capital of the kings at Astibus (Štip) in the Bregalnitsa valley, they now broke through to the coast, occupying Amphaxitis and the coastal strip by Pella and Ichnae (Thuc. 2. 99. 4 and Str. 7 fr. 11 Παίονες δὲ περὶ τὸν Ἀξιὸν ποταμὸν καὶ τὴν καλουμένην διὰ τοῦτο Ἀμφαξῖτιν), Crestonia and all Mygdonia (Str. 7 fr. 41 καὶ Κρηστωνίαν καὶ Μυγδονίδα πᾶσαν), and the lowlands of the Strymon basin (ibid.). Two powerful Paeonian tribes were the Siriopaeones in the region of the modern city Serres and the Paeones of Lake Prasias, now Lake Butkova (see Volume I. 194). They came probably from the valleys of the Strumitsa and the upper Strymon, because the Agrianes, who were normally

---

[1] I mentioned Eordaea also but reserve it now for discussion.

[2] This narrow strip of coast, as it then was (see Volume I Map 15), went with the possession of Amphaxitis.

associated with the headwaters of the Strymon, were mentioned as holding lands in the Strymon basin by Herodotus (5. 16. 1)[1] and Strabo (7 fr. 41, a somewhat confused passage).[2] During these changes the Bisaltae may have maintained their independence in the valleys of Mt. Dysoron, inland of Mygdonia, as their territory is not in Strabo's list. It was during this period of Paeonian power that the Paeonians made an attack on Perinthus on the northern shore of the Propontis, marching successfully through the whole length of southern Thrace (Hdt. 5. 1 and Str. 7 fr. 41).

The information about this period which has survived in the fragments of Strabo's 7th book was almost certainly recorded by Hecataeus. As I have argued in *Epirus* 451 f., Strabo's ultimate source for his general account of Epirus, Illyris, and Western Macedonia was Hecataeus, who wrote *c.* 500 and knew the position as it was before the final stages of Macedonian expansion. So too Str. 7 fr. 11, giving the position in Macedonia *before* the Argeadae conquered such tribes as the Paeones, Edoni, and Bisaltae, can only have come ultimately from Hecataeus. There are probably echoes of Hecataeus in the similarities of the phrasing in Herodotus 7. 123. 3 τὸ παρὰ θάλασσαν, στεινὸν χωρίον, πόλιες Ἴχναι καὶ Πέλλα[3] and Thucydides 2. 99. 4 στενήν τινα καθήκουσαν ἄνωθεν μέχρι Πέλλης καὶ θαλάσσης. Certainly Herodotus used Hecataeus for his description of the cities of Crousis, as we noted in Volume I. 188 f.

The period of Paeonian power lasted until the arrival of the Persians. The lack of success which attended Darius' invasion of Scythia *c.* 513 has often caused historians to underestimate his achievement in the Balkans. His fleet sailed two days' journey up the Danube and bridged the river, and his army subdued the Getae, the strongest tribe in northern Thrace (Hdt. 4. 93). Probably in 512 his army under the command of Megabazus reduced 'every city and every tribe of the inhabitants' as he marched through Thrace (Hdt. 5. 2. 2). No one achieved anything similar until Philip II of Macedon, and then only after almost twenty years of campaigning. The Persian conquest reorientated the trade of Thrace, encouraging the inland tribes to look across the wide and fertile plains of central Thrace towards the Black Sea and the markets of Asia Minor and the Persian Empire. Nor did the Thracian tribes prove rebellious; indeed the influence of Persia on their culture seems to have extended well beyond the withdrawal of Persia from Europe. The turn of the Paeonians came next, not because their women were handsome

---

[1] Stein's bracketing of the Doberes, Agrianes, and Odomanti, which is accepted in the Oxford Classical Text, should be rejected; for the Agrianes appear in the vicinity of Mt. Pangaeum in Strabo 7 fr. 41 which refers to Paeonia's period of power.

[2] The fragments of the epitome are often rendered obscure by compression, but the first sentence was concerned with the period which Herodotus was describing at 5. 1.

[3] Hecataeus probably mentioned Pella in *FGrH* 1 F 144; see Volume I. 147.

and industrious as Herodotus tells us so charmingly (5. 12–13),[1] but because they were the leading power in the path of imperial expansion. Darius' orders to Megabazus were to deport the Paeonians—men, women, and children—from their territory (Hdt. 5. 14. 1).

Probably in 511 the Paeonians concentrated their forces on the defence of the coastal route, expecting the Persian army to march south of Mt. Pangaeum and reach the Strymon at Eïon and Nine Ways (Ennea Hodoi, later Amphipolis). However, the Persians turned the enemy's positions by marching inland via Gazorus into the Strymon valley (see Volume I. 197 and Map 17 on p. 180), took the unmanned cities of the Paeonians in the Strymon basin, and deported the Paeonians of the plain between Lake Butkova and the sea, namely the Siriopaeones, the Paeoplae and other Paeonian tribes. Here the back of Paeonian power was broken irretrievably. A few tribes survived in the hills and in the pile-settlements of Lake Prasias (Hdt. 5. 16. 1 and 7. 113); there were Paeonians 'near Mt. Pangaeum, near the Doberes (in the lower Strumitsa), near the Agrianes (perhaps by the Rupel pass, where the Strymon enters the plain) and near the Odomanti' (north of Mt. Pangaeum probably; see Hdt. 7. 112), and a Paeonian block of territory in the Kumli valley which extended down to Lake Prasias (Butkova). This last was called rather pathetically ἡ Παιονική (Hdt. 7. 124) or ἡ Παιονία (Str. 7 fr. 36).

The Thracians, favoured by Persia as loyal subjects, evidently took part in the next stage of the advance which drove the Paeonians out of Mygdonia. The Thracians who now ruled over areas liberated from the Paeonians were generally called Edoni (Str. 7 fr. 11), but they were known by region as the Edones (mainly on the eastern side of the Strymon basin), the Mygdones in Mygdonia (from the pass of Rendina to the mouth of the Axius), and the Sithones (in central Chalcidice). The royal tribe of this group was evidently the Edones. It is likely that the Thracians took over the mine by Lake Prasias, because, when the envoys of Megabazus went that way to meet Amyntas, king of Macedon (Hdt. 5. 17), it lay evidently in Persian territory. They acquired too the territory of Crestonia, where the name of the Gallikos river became 'Edonos' (*EM.* s.v. *Echeidoros*). As we shall see when we consider Aeschylus, *Persae* 492 f., the Thracian tribes dominated the area between the Axius and the Strymon from 510 to 480 but not entirely throughout that time.

The Bisaltae must have made their peace with Persia. At some later date the Bisaltae grew in power at the expense of the Thracian Mygdones, because they extended their territory south-eastwards down to Argilus on the coast of the Strymonic Gulf and took over the territory as far as

---

[1] The element of folk-lore in the story is emphasized by E. Will, 'Hérodote et la jeune Péonienne', *REG* 80 (1967) 176 f.

Heraclea, that was up to the Strymon, including control of the mine by Lake Prasias (Hdt. 7. 115. 1; Str. 7 fr. 36 ὑπὲρ δὲ τῆς Ἀμφιπόλεως Βισάλται καὶ μέχρι πόλεως Ἡρακλείας, ἔχοντες αὐλῶνα εὔκαρπον, ὃν διαιρεῖ ὁ Στρυμών). Thus they were as favoured as the Edoni. As Strabo 7 fr. 11 expressed it, *before* the Argeadae became masters, 'the Edoni and the Bisaltae held the rest of the country as far as the Strymon.' This was so in 480 (Hdt. 7. 115. 1). As the Bisaltic realm ran across the line of communication between Mygdonia and the eastern Edones, the Bisaltic advance may have taken place at some time after 500 and perhaps by agreement, since the king 'of the Bisaltae and Crestonian territory' in 480 was a Thracian (Hdt. 8. 116).

The Macedones too took advantage of the overthrow of the Paeonians. They seized Amphaxitis, probably when the Bisaltae seized Crestone; for Amphaxitis was part of 'Macedonia' when Megabazus opened negotiations with Amyntas (see Map 4). Probably in 510[1] Megabazus demanded the submission of Amyntas, king of the Macedones. His envoys, seven noble Persians and their entourage, took the route which Herodotus described as 'the short route'. Starting from Lake Prasias (Butkova) they passed the mine close to it 'which at a time later than this' (ὕστερον τούτων)[2] yielded Alexander a talent of silver a day, crossed over Mt. Dysoron and 'were in Macedonia' (5. 17. 2). There is no doubt about the route, which was used later by the army of Xerxes (Hdt. 7. 124 ἐπορεύετο διὰ τῆς Παιονικῆς καὶ Κρηστωνικῆς ἐπὶ ποταμὸν Ἐχείδωρον). It ascended the Kumli valley, crossed a spur of Mt. Krousia, and descended via the headwaters of the Gallikos (Echedorus) into the plain of Amphaxitis, then held by the Macedones. In fact the route was the shortest between the Strymon basin and the Axius plain, and it was also the driest; for the Mygdonian basin was swampy (A. *Persae* 494). Nor is there any doubt about the time: it was anterior to the advance of the Macedones into Bisaltia, an advance foreshadowed by Thuc. 2. 99. 6 and Str. 7 fr. 11, and it was when Amyntas was on the throne. Thus 'Macedonia' *c.* 510 began with Amphaxitis.

The result of Megabazus' demand is not in doubt either, whatever one may think of Herodotus' story about the fate of the first envoys (Hdt. 5. 18–20, discussed below): Amyntas submitted, the Macedones became

---

[1] The chronology of Persian moves in the Balkans is uncertain. The conquest of Central Thrace, undertaken firmly after Darius' return from Scythia in 513, must have involved at least one year of campaigning. It is unlikely that the Persians demanded the submission of the Macedones, until their own position in Thrace was thoroughly secure. I. L. Merker, 'The ancient kingdom of Paionia', BS 6 (1965) 35 f., treated the Paeonian deportation in isolation.

[2] Geyer 45 translates 'In der Zeit nach den Perserkriegen'; this can only be an oversight. See Hdt. 9. 75 for the same phrase and its meaning. I am not persuaded by M. Papageorgiou in *Mak.* 10 (1970) 1–22, who argues that Herodotus referred to two mines and equates Dysoron with Paiko.

subjects of Persia (Hdt. 5. 18. 21), and Amyntas gave his daughter in marriage to Bubares as a Persian overlord (Hdt. 5. 21. 2; Just. 7. 3. 9). He was confirmed in possession of the territories which he held at that time, and he was probably given the westernmost part of Mygdonia. For when Sparta failed to persuade her allies to invade Attica and restore Hippias as tyrant, probably in 505, Amyntas offered Anthemus to Hippias (Hdt. 5. 94. 1).[1] In fact Hippias declined and Amyntas retained Anthemus, perhaps as a royal domain or preserve. But the implication is clearly that he had access to Anthemus as ruler of the lowlands round the north-eastern part of the Thermaic Gulf.

The territorial gains of Amyntas were considerable. He had added the area which must be regarded as a strategic unit, namely Amphaxitis, Pella, and Ichnae on the western side of the Axius outflow into the sea, and westernmost Mygdonia which covered the coastland of the Thermaic Gulf east of the Axius as far as the outlet of the long valley of Anthemus. Any power which holds this area is able to defend in depth the all-important crossing of the Axius by Ichnae. As long as Amyntas was loyal, it suited Persia's policy to have the control of this crossing in his hands. It was, however, difficult for Amyntas to hold the relatively narrow strip of coastland in westernmost Mygdonia, and that is why he would have been glad to have had the wealthy and well-connected Hippias in occupation of his frontier zone, Anthemus. It is also to be noted that Amyntas inaugurated a new policy. Whereas his predecessors had exterminated or ejected the existing populations of Pieria, Bottiaea, and Almopia, Amyntas incorporated the local populations—apart from the Paeonian rulers—into his enlarged kingdom (Thuc. 2. 99. 4 and 6).

The bond between Macedon and Persia which was created by Bubares was under-emphasized by Herodotus, probably through his sympathy for Alexander, but there is no doubt that it was very important. Herodotus mentions later that Bubares was a son of Megabazus (7. 22. 2) and that Amyntas, son of Bubares and Gygaea, was given by the Great King the wealthy city of Alabanda (8. 136. 1). Thus Bubares was of the highest rank and, as such, was effectively in charge of Macedonia, perhaps for a decade after *c.* 510, and his relationship with Amyntas and Alexander was stated by Justin 7. 4. 1 to have produced peace and friendship between the two countries under both Darius and Xerxes. Indeed his period of residence was so important in the Macedonian tradition that the death of Amyntas was dated in relation to the departure of Bubares by Justin 7. 5. 1, 'post discessum Bubaris Amyntas rex decedit.' There is no doubt, in view of Justin's statement, that Macedonia was included in the satrapy which the Persians named 'Skudra', most probably

---

[1] The region, not the city, which is unlikely to have existed at that date. Geyer 41 assumed that it was the city.

a Phrygian word, reminiscent of the Phrygian occupation of the region round Edessa before the migration to Asia (7. 73 and 8. 138. 3; J. B. Pritchard, *Ancient Near Eastern Texts*[2] (1955) 316).

The departure of Bubares, whether as governor or adviser to the governor of the satrapy, may have been due to the Ionian Revolt early in 498, and the death of Amyntas then came a year or two later. This is compatible with the athletic activities of Alexander, who competed not only in the foot-race but also in the pentathlon at the Olympic Games (Just. 7. 2. 14 'Olympio certamine vario ludicrorum genere contenderet'). A fragment of a Pindaric ode in honour of Alexander has been dated to the middle 490s and will therefore have celebrated the pentathlon, for which a man is likely to have been heavier in build than he was as a sprinter. Now it is unlikely that Alexander competed as king of Macedon, because the prestige of his kingdom might have been involved. If Gygaea was twenty years old when she was married to Bubares *c.* 510 and was older than Alexander, he would have been in his teens for the alleged killing of the Persian envoys and nearing thirty *c.* 496. As we shall see when we work backwards to the accession of Alexander, the death of Amyntas should be placed *c.* 495.

The Ionian Revolt of 498–493 proved to have little effect on the Persian satrapy in Europe. The Greek cities on the coast which rose in sympathy with their fellow Greeks were soon subjugated, and the defection of the Dolonci under Miltiades in the Chersonese was on the periphery of the satrapy. The Thracians and the Macedones made no move. In 492, when Mardonius brought a large army and navy from the east and marched along the coast of Thrace and Macedonia, he met with no resistance at first; for, as Herodotus expressed it (6. 44. 1), 'all the nations that side of the Macedones had already become subject to Persia.' We should probably make no exception of the Macedones. Herodotus, it is true, said that at this time Mardonius reduced the Macedones to subjection (ibid.).[1] But there is no indication that they had ever thrown off the Persian yoke, and, as we have just seen, Justin 7. 4. 1 emphasized the friendly relations of Macedon and Persia under Amyntas and Alexander. What did happen was a disaster to the Persian fleet off Mt. Athos in a storm and a night attack by 'Thracian Brygi', when the army was encamped 'in Macedonia' (6. 45. 1). These Brygi were soon reduced to obedience, and they served in the army of Xerxes some ten years later (Hdt. 7. 185).

These 'Thracian Brygi' are something of a mystery. Herodotus clearly distinguished them from the 'Briges' whom he described as having moved

---

[1] I discuss Herodotus' statement below (p. 99). Geyer 43 held that Alexander rebelled from Persia and later submitted to Persia; he relied on this passage and on Syncellus 500 (ed. Dindorf). Edson, *AM* 25, shares my opinion that Alexander remained loyal to Persia.

away from Macedonia to Phrygia in Asia long before this time and whom he evidently regarded as Phrygian Briges (7. 73). We too should keep his 'Thracian Brygi' separate. In 492 they were evidently adjacent to the realm of the Macedones (not within it, as we see when we read Thuc. 2. 99), that is to the realm as it was in 492. It follows more or less, as the Mygdones and the Bisaltae neighboured the Macedones to the east, that the Thracian Brygi were their neighbours to the north-east, that is between Lake Doiran and the Strumitsa valley on the slopes of Mt. Orbelus. We know in fact from Herodotus (5. 3. 2 and 5) that there were Thracians living to the north of Crestonia, and that they had idiosyncratic customs. The term itself Βρύγοι Θρήικες is reminiscent of the terminology used by Hecataeus, for instance in the verbatim citation Θέρμη πόλις Ἑλλήνων Θρηίκων (*FGrH* 1 F 146) and again less clearly in Γαληψός· πόλις Θραίκης καὶ Παιόνων (F 152). It may mean that they were in a Thracian-controlled area rather than that the Brygi were Thracian by race.[1]

When Herodotus described the march of Xerxes' army in 480, he mentioned where Macedonia ended (7. 131, at the frontier with Perrhaebia; and 7. 173, at Tempe), but not where Macedonia began. He assumed probably that his readers would realize there had been no change since the reign of Amyntas, Alexander being now on the throne. However, we learn the situation more clearly from Aeschylus, *Persae*, of which the production date was 472 and the dramatic date was 480. The Messenger described the return of Xerxes that winter as follows.

> Μαγνητικὴν δὲ γαῖαν ἔς τε Μακεδόνων
> χώραν ἀφικόμεσθ', ἐπ' Ἀξιοῦ πόρον,
> Βόλβης θ' ἕλειον δόνακα, Πάγγαιόν τ' ὄρος,
> Ἠδωνίδ' αἶαν· νυκτὶ δ' ἐν ταύτῃ θεὸς
> χειμῶν' ἄωρον ὦρσε, πήγνυσιν δὲ πᾶν
> ῥέεθρον ἁγνοῦ Στρυμόνος.
>
> A. *Persae* 492–7

I have not added any punctuation to lines 492–4 in case I seem to prejudge the answer to the question: what makes up the Edonian land? I translate in prose, supplementing to clarify the sense. 'We came to the land of the Magnetes [by Tempe] and [we came to] the land of the Macedones [on our way] to the ford of the Axius, and [we came to] the reedy marshland of Bolbe and the mountain Pangaeum, [these being] the Edonian land. And in this [Edonian land] at night[2] a god brought on winter before its time and freezes the entire flow of Strymon's pure waters.' It seems to me that 'the mountain Pangaeum' alone cannot

---

[1] See also Volume 1. 303.

[2] The Loeb edition translates 'on that night'; but νυκτί alone means 'at night', and ταύτῃ 'this' looks back not to any previously mentioned night but to Ἠδωνίδ' αἶαν.

be the Edonian land, because the scene of the disaster at the crossing of the Strymon was not in 'the mountain Pangaeum' at all. Rather it was 'the reedy marshland of Bolbe and the mountain Pangaeum' together and the route between them which belonged to the Edoni (as we saw above, p. 57).[1] Having three territories in mind, Aeschylus used τε to mark the beginning of two territories, Macedonia and Edonis, and added an important feature at the other end of each territory, the ford of the Axius in the one and the mountain Pangaeum in the other. Aeschylus, like Herodotus (7. 114), allocated the crossing of the Strymon to the sphere of the Edoni.

Thus the realm of Alexander in late 480 was the same as that of Amyntas had been *c.* 509, at least towards the east; for it stopped short of the basin of Mygdonia, i.e. short of Lete. The Bisaltae were a separate people in 480, their Thracian king even refusing to co-operate with Xerxes (Hdt. 8. 116. 1); Crestonia was then part of the Bisaltic kingdom. It was thus at some time after 480 that Alexander and the Macedones went on to annex Crestonia and Bisaltia and Mygdonia and also land up to the Strymon, from which they expelled the Edones (distinct from but included among the Edoni); these annexations were mentioned in Thucydides 2. 99. 4 and 6, a passage which is arranged not chronologically but geographically (see Volume 1. 437). It is to be noted that Alexander reverted to the practice of Amyntas' predecessors; for he expelled the Edones and also some of the Bisaltae and Crestones (Thuc. 2. 99. 4; 4. 109. 4; Str. 7 fr. 36). Most of them settled east of the Strymon (Str. 7 fr. 36 and Hdt. 9. 75); a few took refuge in the Athos peninsula of Chalcidice (Thuc. 4. 109. 4).

Before we summarize the stages of Macedonian expansion, it is advisable to mention the Eordi. When we turn shortly to the hinterland of Macedonia, we shall suggest that Strabo's description of peoples in Upper Macedonia was derived ultimately from Hecataeus. It is marked by two unusual names: 'Eordi', and not Eordaei as the inhabitants were called after the Macedonian conquest, and 'Eratyra', a name of a district which is never mentioned again in extant literature or inscriptions. If Hecataeus described the situation as it was in the latter half of the sixth century, the Eordi had not been expelled by 550, the date which I suggested in Volume 1. 438. On the other hand, they must have been expelled before 480 because the survivors settled at Physca in Mygdonia, named an area there 'Eordaea',[2] and served in the army of Xerxes (Hdt.

---

[1] H. D. Broadhead, *The Persae of Aeschylus* (Cambridge, 1960) 138, limits Edonian territory to that which 'lies between the southern end of the Strymon and the southern tip of the range'. No wonder that he then finds Aeschylus confusing.

[2] Ptolemy 3. 13. 6 named Physcae a city of Mygdonis, and St. Byz. ᾽Εορδαῖαι δύο χῶραι Μυγδονίας [?καὶ Μακεδονίας], which may well have come from Hecataeus who wrote not long after the resettlement of the surviving Eordi.

7. 185. 2). To settle at Physca would have been sensible in the Paeonian period of power before *c.* 509, but very hazardous thereafter, when the Macedones were so close to Lete. On balance I think the conquest of Eordaea and the expulsion of the small number who were not exterminated (Thuc. 2. 99. 5) took place *c.* 520–510.

Of the situation in Upper Macedonia during the period 550–480 we know relatively little. When Paeonia was at the height of her power, it is likely that she extended her control westwards of the Axius into Pelagonia and Lyncus; for she was involved in the commerce in silver bullion mined in the region of Resen, which is further to the west. There a strong power arose in the basin north of Lake Ochrid, resulting apparently from the fusion of two royal houses, that of the indigenous Encheleae, as Hecataeus called them (*FGrH* 1 F 103), and that of the Peresadyes, if a corrupt passage in Strabo, 7 C 326, is so restored.[1] The royal tombs at Trebenishte show that it flourished in the last decades of the sixth century and in the first half of the fifth century, and that goods reached it from the Corinthian colonies on the Ionic Gulf, Apollonia and Epidamnus, and from the Corinthian colony on the Thermaic Gulf, Potidaea, which were now becoming strong themselves.

When Macedon gained possession of Eordaea, probably in the decade 520–510, it served as a strong bastion of defence against the peoples of Upper Macedonia, because it closed the main route of entry to Lower Macedonia through the pass of Kara Burun (see Volume I. 51 and 106), and being ringed round with mountains it could be held by itself. But any advance from Eordaea made it necessary to conquer the whole of Upper Macedonia, because any one canton, such as Lyncus, was open to attack from two neighbouring cantons. At the time of which Hecataeus wrote, *c.* 500 B.C., the Orestae were for him a Molossian tribe (*FGrH* 1 F 107); and the Elimiotae, Orestae, Tymphaei, and Pelagones were described as Epirotic tribes by Strabo (7 C 326 and 9 C 434), who was drawing probably on an account by Hecataeus.[2] That these tribes became 'Macedones' in a political sense before the time of the Peloponnesian War is clear from the account of Thucydides (2. 99), but he does not indicate when and how the change came about.

The only clue is in Justin 7. 4. 1, who states that after the death of Amyntas the tie of kinship formed between Alexander and Bubares not only secured peaceful relations in the reign of Darius but also made Xerxes so friendly that 'when a storm of trouble swooped down on Greece, he presented Alexander with the rule of the whole region between Olympus and Haemus'. Because we think of Haemus as the Stara Planina between Plovdiv and the Danube in Central Bulgaria,

---

[1] See *Epirus* 466 f. and Volume I. 93.
[2] See Volume I. 439 and references there to *Epirus*.

this passage has been regarded as a rhetorical folly. But in antiquity, as we see from Strabo, Haemus was used also in a different sense. Haemus and Rhodope were thought of as two long ranges roughly parallel to the Aegean coast and extending from the Black Sea (Str. 7 C 319) almost to the Adriatic sea—ranges pierced by great rivers such as the Axius and the Strymon. We see this most clearly in Strabo 7 fr. 36 'As you go northwards from Heraclea to the narrows of the Strymon [the Rupel pass] and keep the river on your right, you have on your left Paeonia and the regions round Doberus, Rhodope and the Haemus range τὸν Αἷμον ὄρος, and on your right the region round the Haemus.' Thus, while Doberus is the basin of the Strumitsa and Rhodope is Mt. Plaskovitsa, the Haemus range runs from Mt. Osogov to Šar Planina, the ancient Scardus (cf. 7 fr. 10, where the northern boundary of Macedonia is formed by a mountainous line including Scardus). Justin's phrase is then a grandiose expression but represents no more than the inclusion of Upper Macedonia in the kingdom of Alexander within the period between Darius' death in 486 and Xerxes' retreat in 480. Bubares, the patron clearly of Alexander, was in charge of the building of the canal through the neck of the Athos peninsula in the years 483–481, and Alexander's conquest of Upper Macedonia should be dated around that time.

We are apt to forget that Persia held her European satrapy for some thirty years and that Darius saw strategic problems in depth. As his conquest of Thrace involved sailing up the Danube and conquering far inland, so his advance into Macedonia seems to have involved the conquest of the Paeonians not just in the Strymon basin but also in the middle Axius valley. When an advance by land into Greece was contemplated by Xerxes, the defence in depth of his line of communications through Lower Macedonia would be enhanced by the reduction of the peoples of the hinterland. It was probably with Persian aid and as a Persian vassal that Alexander established his suzerainty over those peoples and named the region for the first time 'Upper [literally "inland"] Macedonia' and the various peoples—Elimiotae, Tymphaei, Orestae, Lyncestae, and Pelagones—'Macedones'.

The stages of Macedonian expansion, as illustrated in Maps 1–3, may be summarized as follows.[1] (i) By 550 South Pieria and Bottiaea. (ii) Soon after 550 Almopia. (iii) About 520–510 Eordaea. (iv) About 510–505 Amphaxitis, the narrow coastal strip including Ichnae and Pella, the north-east coast of the Thermaic Gulf, and Anthemus.

---

[1] Geyer 39 f. made what seems to me an arbitrary list of stages on the basis not of the literary evidence but of what he thought geographically probable; even so he seems mistaken in holding that Xerxes used the Volustana pass and therefore made Elimiotis subject to Alexander (see p. 100 n. 2). Casson 161 is no better.

(v) Probably in 483–480 the cantons of Upper Macedonia. (vi) After 480 Crestonia, Bisaltia, Mygdonia, and the western part of the lower Strymon basin. The policy of extermination and expulsion was employed in stages (i), (ii), (iii), and to a limited extent only in (vi).

Native cities grew up in this period, if not earlier. Thus Aegeae and Dium were Macedonian cities, and Pydna and Methone were Greek

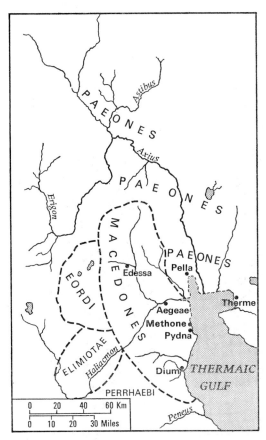

MAP I. THE MACEDONES AND THEIR NEIGHBOURS SOON AFTER 550

cities on the west coast of the Thermaic Gulf. Ichnae and Pella were πόλιες in Hdt. 7. 123, and passed under the control of Thracians, Paeonians, and Macedones successively. Chalastra and Therme on the coast east of the Axius mouth, Aenea and the cities of Crousis, and then the Greek colonies of the Chalcidic peninsula, and Olynthus, a city of the Bottiaei in Chalcidice, were all engaged in trade which passed through the waters of the Thermaic Gulf. In Mygdonia Lete was an important native city, as we know from its coins. The Paeonians had many cities in the basin of the Strymon (Hdt. 5. 13. 2 and 15. 2), and the Greek cities of eastern Chalcidice and of the Strymonian 'shore' (*aigialos*) such as Argilus (Hdt. 7. 115. 1) engaged in trade which passed through the waters of the Strymonic Gulf. Further east native cities such as Galepsus (*FGrH* 1 F 152) and Greek cities such as Neapolis traded with the island of Thasos, the richest and strongest sea power in the northern Aegean.

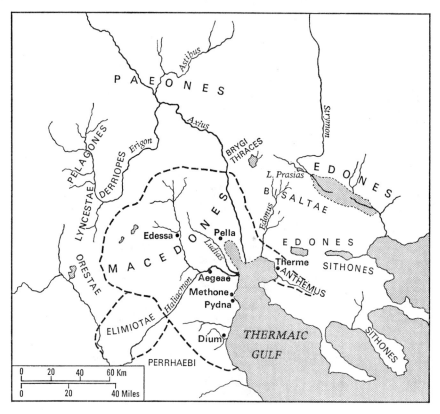

MAP 2. THE MACEDONES AND THEIR NEIGHBOURS C. 508

The native peoples worshipped gods or heroes whom the Greeks identified with their own deities, whatever the native names may have been. Thus the Bisaltae honoured Rhesus. The Paeonians worshipped the sun, which was represented as a small disc at the top of a long pole; they also had a god of healing, whom scholars have identified with Apollo when he appeared on coins.[1] The Crestonaeans worshipped

---

[1] Str. 7 fr. 36 (Rhesus); Max. Tyr. 8. 8 (sun). When the Muse prophesies that Rhesus shall lie deified as an '*anthropodaimon* in a cave of this silver-veined land', just as the seer

a god Candaon, whom the Greeks identified as Ares, and they had a
famous precinct of Dionysus.[1] The Thracian royal houses worshipped
a god whom the Greeks identified as Hermes, and the Thracian commoners worshipped gods whom the Greeks identified as Ares, Dionysus,
and Artemis (Hdt. 5. 7). The worship of Dionysus was a feature of
Philippi, for instance, and the Satrae had a cult of Dionysus (Hdt. 7. 111).

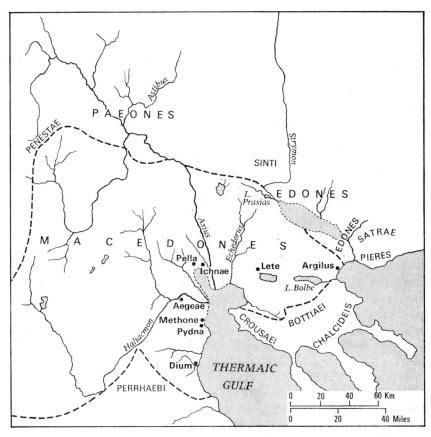

MAP 3. THE MACEDONES AND THEIR NEIGHBOURS SOON AFTER 478

The native peoples and the Greeks alike seem to have adopted and
assimilated the gods of the people with whom they came into contact,
whether by conquest or by commerce. Hecataeus and Herodotus showed

of Dionysus had lived on Mt. Pangaeum (E. *Rhes.* 970 f.), the reference is to the worship of
Rhesus among the Bisaltae and the parallel is taken from the seer of Dionysus' famous
oracle on Mt. Pangaeum. 'The god' of Hdt. 5. 1. 2 may have been an oracular god of the
Bisaltic area. I think Casson 63 is wrong to refer both to Mt. Pangaeum.

[1] Lyc. *Alex.* 937 and Tzetz. ad loc.; Arist. *Mir.* 122; see Volume I. 181.

an interest in and sometimes a respect for the customs of the native peoples of the area. One fragment of Hecataeus about the Paeonians serves to remind us that Hecataeus gave a full description of the traditions and the characteristics of the Balkan peoples. 'The Paeonians make beer from barley and *parabie* ("over-strength") from millet and fleabane, and anoint themselves with an oil extracted from milk' (*FGrH* 1 F 154).[1]

The rapid development of trade between the Thraco-Macedonian area and the Aegean and Asia drew the attention of Greek adventurers. Peisistratus of Athens formed a settlement on the high table-land, called Rhaecalus, which overlooks the plain of Sedhes, when he was driven out of Athens *c.* 555. Here on a promontory jutting into the Thermaic Gulf he was well placed to engage in or interfere with trade. Later he moved to the region of Mt. Pangaeum, where he made money and hired soldiers for the *coup d'état* at Athens in 546. During these years the Thracians were the leading people in these areas, and he evidently collaborated with them.[2] In both places he was attracted, we may assume, by the trade in gold and silver. At Rhaecalus he may have anticipated the role of Aenea, his immediate neighbour, as an intermediary in this trade (see below, p. 79). Another Athenian nobleman, Miltiades, established himself in a similar way among the Thracian Dolonci in the Chersonese *c.* 556.[3] When the Milesian Histiaeus was offered a reward by Darius, he chose and was granted possession of an 'Edonian city, Myrcinus',[4] which lay on the east side of the Strymon and near the coast, ideally situated to tap the trade in silver and ship-building timber, as Herodotus made Megabazus point out (5. 11 and 23). Histiaeus attracted further settlers to Myrcinus and began to fortify the city, but Darius recalled him soon afterwards. In 496 and 495 his son-in-law, Aristagoras, seized Myrcinus in Edonis once again, but he and his army were destroyed when they were engaged in trying to subjugate a neighbouring Thracian city (Hdt. 5. 124–6).

Macedonia and Thrace had particular importance for the Aegean world at this time, because they exported ship-building timber, as Megabazus remarked to Darius. As Persia advanced westwards, fewer areas were free to export this timber, and this was particularly so in 483–480, when the Persian fleet controlled the coast of Thrace from the Chersonese to Mt. Athos, where a canal was being dug. The only coast

---

[1] Not so much butter, as LSJ[9], as cream, such as Cleopatra is supposed to have bathed in.

[2] Arist. *Ath. Pol.* 15. 2; for the date see my arguments in *CQ* 6 (1956) 51. Cloché 32 and Geyer 41 think that the king of Macedon helped Peisistratus both at Rhaecalus and at Mt. Pangaeum; this is both untestified and inherently unlikely at such a date. L. R. Laing, *Coins and Archaeology* (London, 1969) 96, believes that Athens obtained silver from the Thraco-Macedonian area before 500.

[3] See *CQ* 6 (1956) 113 f.

[4] As the city was not Paeonian but Edonian, Histiaeus obtained it after 509, the year probably in which the Paeonians were deported by Megabazus.

on the northern Aegean not under their immediate surveillance was that of Macedonia, where Alexander 'a Greek ruling over Macedones' was not only in sympathy with the Greek cause but also 'a *proxenus*, benefactor, and friend of Athens', to which he claimed to have rendered service before 480.[1] It is a likely conjecture that he had, unknown to the Persians, supplied timber for the building of the 100 triremes which were to win the day at Salamis.[2] Another important export was minerals in which the area was rich. We turn to this in the next section.

2. *The coinages of tribes, cities, and kings* c. 550–480

(See Plate I)

The so-called 'tribal coinages of the Thraco-Macedonian area'— a misnomer as some are issued by cities and others by kings—have been studied intensively by numismatists but almost entirely in a vacuum.[3] No attempt has been made to relate the coinages to the centres of mineral ore or to the historical events which I have described in the last section or to the geographical conditions. Given such an approach, it is not surprising that datings for the beginning of these coinages have ranged from soon after 600 to 500, and that there has been a tendency to lump all the coinages together within whatever bracket of dates has been chosen. In what follows a new view of these coinages is being advanced.

The early appearance of coinage in the Thraco-Macedonian area was due to an abundance of minerals, the presence of Greek colonies on and off the Thraco-Macedonian coast, and a demand for silver which arose within the Persian empire in Asia and also in Egypt.[4] While the richest mineral deposits were in the district of Mt. Pangaeum to the east of the Strymon, there were many deposits in the region between the Axius and

[1] Hdt. 5. 20. 4; 7. 173. 3; 8. 136. 1; 8. 140 b 1; 8. 143. 3; Arist. *Ath. Pol.* 22. 7.

[2] Arist. *Ath. Pol.* 22. 7; dates as in *HG*[2] 222. If he conquered Upper Macedonia at this time, as I have suggested, he had access to unlimited timber. Edson, *AM* 25 f., suggested that Alexander supplied Athens with timber in these years.

[3] The pioneer in this field was J. N. Svoronos, *L'Hellénisme primitif de la Macédoine* (Paris and Athens, 1919) = *JIAN* 1919. 1–265. His work was carried further by H. Gaebler, *Die antiken Münzen Nord-Griechenlands* 3, *Makedonia und Paionia* 2 (Berlin, 1935). A new insight was given by Doris Raymond, *Macedonian Royal Coinage to 413 B.C.* (New York, 1953); her work was reviewed in *NC* 1953. 166 f. by J. M. F. May, who carried the inquiry a stage further in his *Coinage of Abdera* (London, 1966) 8 f. Raymond's conclusions in regard to numismatics were accepted in general by P. R. Franke; but he put forward a different view of the nature of the Macedonian state in early times. Cloché 50 f. follows Gaebler.

[4] Most of the heaviest coins have been found in hoards buried in Asia and Egypt—e.g. coins of the Tynteni and Acanthus in Afghanistan (*Rev. Num.* 11 (1969) 7), and coins of the Bisaltae, Lete, Tynteni, and 'Aegae' in Jordania (*Rev. Num.* 10 (1968) 183), and coins of Acanthus and the Bisaltae in Syria (ibid. 211). On the other hand, two of the Tynteni coins were first reported in a collection at Kavalla (*Rev. Num.* 1903. 315–16), and another is thought to have come from the neighbourhood of Salonica (*ZfN* 3 (1876) 132 n. 1 'in der Nähe von Thessalonich').

the Strymon and considerable deposits far inland. I shall avoid the labels 'Macedonian' and 'Thracian' because their meaning changed within the period under consideration.

The mineral resources of the area have been fully recorded in the years after 1940. They were shown on Map 1 and described on pp. 12 f. of Volume 1, and I give here a summary of gold and silver by regions (see also Map 8, below):

(i) Between the lower Axius and the lower Strymon:

Gold in the rivers of Crestonia, especially in the Gallikos (ancient Echedorus); near Lete in Mygdonia; at Stratoniki between Stagirus and Acanthus; and above Nigrita on the easternmost side of Bisaltia.

Silver at Stratoniki between Stagirus and Acanthus.

(ii) East of the lower Strymon:

Gold at Akhladhokhori in Paroreia; and at Mt. Pangaeum.
Silver in the same two districts.

(iii) In the inland areas:

Gold in Metohija and Kossovo, which were partly in Illyris and partly in Dardania; at Kratovo (ancient Tranupara) in Paeonia; and at Kjustendil (ancient Pautalia) in the territory of the Paeonian Laeaei on the western side of the upper Strymon.

Silver near Resen in eastern Illyris;[1] at Tetovo in Polog, which was an area often in dispute between the Penestae and the Dardanii; in Metohija and Kossovo, which were partly in Illyris and partly in Dardania; at Kratovo (ancient Tranupara) and at other sites in the valleys of the Pecinj and the Bregalnitsa, which flow from the east into the Axius, all being in Paeonia; and at Kjustendil (ancient Pautalia) in the territory of the Laeaei, a Paeonian tribe on the western side of the upper Strymon.

The exploitation of these minerals has a long history. At different times in the Bronze Age gold was obtained from the district of Kilkis and from the vicinity of Lete (see Volume 1. 312 f.). Gold from the former district was worked at Vardarophtsa very early in the Iron Age. Copper and lead were mined and worked in the Amphaxitis district in the Late

---

[1] Known from the ancient workings; see *ŽA* 3 (1953) 261, cited in Volume 1. 93, 'officinae antiquissimae, quae ad effodiendum ac elaborandum plumbum cum argento pertinent, inventae sunt.' The ancient workings of another silver mine were reported by Ami Boué as having been seen in 1839 (see *Archäol-epigr. Mitt.* 10 (1886) 84 n. 65 and 205); they were in the district of Divra 'on Sar Planina', which is very vague, and they are probably too far north to be identifiable with the ancient mines of Damastium. Philippson, *RE Damastion* and Casson 60 missed these references. Silver mines in the Sanjak of Ochrid were reported by Haci Halfa in the seventeenth century, and Turkish workings at Gümüş Çeşme to the north-west of Resen were reported by O. Davies, *Roman Mines in Europe* 249 with Map VI. It is possible that both reports refer to the workings mentioned in *Živa Antika*.

Bronze Age. The use of iron, of which there were large deposits, began relatively early in Macedonia. A mould for making copper and bronze axe-heads, which was found in Pelagonia and belongs to the period *c.* 1250–1150, and the peculiar features of short swords and faceted javelin heads[1] in this region, which belong to the end of the Bronze Age and the early centuries of the Iron Age, suggest that there was some metallurgical skill in the areas of Kratovo, Kjustendil, and the Mati valley of central Albania, where there were large deposits of copper. The working of these mines accounts for the abundance of silver in the late-sixth-century graves at Trebenishte, the tumulus burials of the Mati valley and dedications of the period at Dodona. Their gold came from Metohija and Kossovo. The remains of a bronze-working shop have been found at Anchialos (Inglis), dating to the ninth or eighth century, and a mould for making bronze plaques at Saratse, dating to the Early Iron Age (*AD* 20 (1965) 2. 241 and Pl. 472, 3; *PM* 108 and fig. 112*b*).

That gold and silver were being obtained during the sixth century is clear from the literary evidence. The silver mines at Damastium are mentioned in Strabo 7 C 326 in the context of a sixth-century dynasty in which Encheleae and probably Peresadyes combined, in the vicinity of Lake Lychnitis (Ochrid); this information, as we have seen, stems from Hecataeus. Some fragments of Strabo's 7th book—all that has survived for the Thraco-Macedonian area—mention gold and silver mines. Fr. 33 'Daton has excellent fruitful soil, shipyards, and gold mines.' Fr. 34 'There are very many gold mines at Crenides, where Philippi is now situated as a city, near Mt. Pangaeum. Pangaeum itself has gold and silver mines, and so has the country beyond and the country this side[2] of the Strymon up to Paeonia; and they say that those who cultivate the Paeonian land find nuggets of gold.'[3] Fr. 36 'By the sea-coast of the Strymon and of the Dateni there are a city Neapolis and Daton itself, possessing fertile plains, a lake,[4] rivers, shipyards, and profitable gold mines.'

These fragments leave no doubt that for Strabo Datum and Crenides are different places; indeed Strabo makes it clearer still by saying that Crenides was the name of Philippi 'in ancient times' (fr. 42). Indeed anyone who has visited Philippi can see that shipyards are not in place and never were in place at Philippi.[5] We must remember that there have

[1] *BSA* 66 (1971) 234 f.; *StGH* 42; and A. F. Harding in *SA* 1972. 2. 216 f.

[2] As in fr. 36 ἐντός is used to mean west of the Strymon.   [3] So too Arist. *Mir.* 45.

[4] Needlessly emended from λίμνην to λιμένα by Tafel and C. Müller.

[5] Casson, who rejected the emendation to λιμένα, tried to overcome the difficulty by saying (67 n. 1) 'Philippi was on a lake after all'; yes but on an inland lake, distant some 44 miles from the Strymon river, and separated from it by a plain (App. *BC* 4. 105). At the same time he also suggested in his text on that page that 'the harbour' (which he had apparently rejected), being Antisara (Steph. Byz. Ἀντίσαρα ἐπίνειον Δατίνων), could be identified, as it was by Svoronos, with Kavalla. In fact, however, an ἐπίνειον on the coast is not the same

been great changes not only in the Thermaic Gulf but also in the Strymonic Gulf since antiquity. Ships sailed up the river to Nine Ways, later Amphipolis, and beyond into the lake or lakes of the Strymon as far as Berge, some 25 miles above Amphipolis (fr. 36; 200 stades). I take it that Datum was on the eastern side of the Strymonic lakes, in 'the country beyond the Strymon' (fr. 34), and near the Odomanti (fr. 36). Now the phrases 'up to Paeonia' and 'Paeonian land' give us a chronological clue, because Strabo cannot be referring to the Paeonia of the middle Axius valley but must be referring (as in fr. 34) to the 'Paeonia this side of the Strymon', that is to 'the Paeonian land' by Lake Prasias, near which Herodotus said there was a silver mine (5. 17. 2; 7. 124; 8. 115. 3). This interpretation fits the fact that all three fragments were concerned with the Strymon basin. Once again it seems that Strabo's source was Hecataeus, because this was a sixth-century use of 'Paeonia'. Some fragments of Hecataeus survive which reveal his knowledge of the Strymon basin: F 152 Galepsus, a city of Thrace and Paeonians (belonging to the Paeonian period of power) and F 155 Aegialus of Thrace alongside the Strymon.

Herodotus mentioned several mines in our area. First, the gold mines at 'Datum of the Edoni' (9. 75); second, the gold and silver mines on Mt. Pangaeum which the Pieres, the Odomanti, and especially the Satrae possess (7. 112);[1] and third, the gold mines at Scapte Hyle on the mainland opposite Thasos, from which the Thasians derived 80 talents a year (6. 46. 2); and fourth, the silver mine just west or northwest of Lake Prasias, from which Alexander subsequently obtained a talent a day (5. 17. 2). He saw with his own eyes the mines on Thasos which yielded less revenue than those at Scapte Hyle; we may infer that he had not seen the others which he mentioned. He certainly distinguished Datum from the mines of Mt. Pangaeum because the former was worked, he says, by the Edoni, and the others by three separate tribes. Thus both Datum and the Edoni must lie further up the Strymon valley. The famous gold and silver mines of Pangaeum were probably within Phyllis,

---

thing as Datum having shipyards; and it was Neapolis, the colony of Thasos, which was at Kavalla. The equation Crenides = Datum = Philippi was due to Appian (*BC* 4. 105), but it runs counter to Strabo and to Herodotus who attributes Datum to the Edoni, and Appian is inferior to either as an authority for the situation *c.* 500 B.C. J. Schmidt, *RE* 19. 2212, follows Casson and many others in putting Datum after Crenides and before Philippi and all at the same place. P. Collart, *Philippes* (Paris, 1937) 1. 45 and 48, following L. Heuzey, saw that Daton was the name of 'une assez vaste région, comprenant des montagnes, une plaine, un littoral'; we differ in that I think the name applied in the archaic period particularly to the district north of the river Angites. Later, when a mining colony was founded by Callistratus and called Datum (see pp. 197–8 below), the name was used more of the district south of the Angites.

[1] Herodotus seems to include in the Pangaeum range the mountainous interior where the Odomanti were (5. 16; cf. Str. 7 fr. 36 fin.).

as Herodotus 7. 113. 2 named the Pangaeum region proper, that was to the south-east of the river Angites. The gold mines at Scapte Hyle were not on Mt. Pangaeum proper, as they yielded revenue to Thasos in and before 491; they were no doubt in the area where the mines of Crenides lay, that was on the range north-east of Pangaeum and inland of the Thasian colony Neapolis (ἀντικρὺ Θάσου, St. Byz. s.v.). The silver mine near Lake Prasias lay in the territory which Herodotus elsewhere called 'Paeonia'. It was worked probably from c. 510 by the Edones but at some time after 500 by the king of the Bisaltae and at a later date by Alexander of Macedon.

When we put together our knowledge of events, modern mineral discoveries,[1] and the mines of the ancient period c. 550–480, we obtain the following picture:

Modern name	Resen S	Kratovo G+S	Kilkis G²
Ancient name	Damastium	—	Crestonia
Users or neighbours	Atintani, close to late VI/early Vth dynasty of the Trebenishte area	Derrones, the royal Paeonian tribe at Štip	c. 540–511 Paeonians c. 510–480 Bisaltae
	Lete G	Theodoraki S (now lead)	Nigrita G
	Lete	'Near L. Prasias'	—
	c. 550–540 Thracians c. 540–511 Paeonians c. 510–480 Edones	c. 540–511 Paeonians c. 510–500 Edones c. 500–480 Bisaltae	c. 540–509 Paeonians c. 510–500 Thracians c. 500–480 Bisaltae
	Akhladhokhori G+S	Pangaeum G+S	Philippi G+S
	Datum	Pangaeum	Asyla, Scapte Hyle, Crenides
	c. 550–540 Thracians c. 540–511 Sirio-paeones c. 510–480 Edoni	c. 550–480 Satrae, Odomantes, Pieres	?–480 Neapolis and Thasos
	Stratoniki G+S		
	—		
	c. 550–480 Acanthus and Stagirus		

[1] To these we should add the evidence of ancient workings for gold and silver to the north of Pontolivadho opposite Thasos, as reported by Ch. Chrysanthaki in *Ath. AA* 6 (1973) 238. I have not discussed the views, for instance, of Casson 59 f. which were advanced when there was no modern geological map (see Volume I. 10 n. 1 for such a map, published in 1954). His own knowledge of Balkan geography was of the weakest: for instance on p. 60 'Strabo says that among the Ceraunian mountains [on the east side of the Strait of Taranto], before you get to the region of the modern town of Monastir [in southern Yugoslavia near the Cerna Reka], there are the silver mines of Damastium . . . in all probability somewhere behind Mount Bermios [overlooking coastal Macedonia].' He thought it undesirable to classify the mines 'as being either of gold or silver' (p. 60).

[2] For gold-washing in the Echedorus (Gallikos), which is additional to the deposits at Kilkis, see *EM* s.v. *Echeidoros*; the Germans washed gold in the river during their occupation of Greece in the last war.

In many of the coinages there were very heavy silver pieces. The discovery of such pieces in hoards in Syria, Jordania, Egypt, Iraq, Afghanistan, and elsewhere in the East has made it clear that they were an acceptable form of exported bullion and that the Persian Empire provided the most profitable market. Electrum too may have been exported in the same way; but as most writers except Svoronos and recently Raymond have denied this, I have mentioned only a few electrum coins in this discussion. Gold certainly was exported but not in the form of coin, and it is possible that silver travelled also in the form of ingots.[1] Some only of the coins, and those mainly heavy ones, carry inscriptions in Greek, written from left to right and from right to left indifferently; the great majority are uninscribed. We may infer that the issuers were illiterate, as the inscribers for any one issue frequently used more than one alphabetic script; and that they were not selling primarily to Greek purchasers.

Gaebler's collection of the coins is that most cited, and I use it here; but he was unduly quick to see forgery at work and he omits unaccountably quite a number of coins published by his predecessor, the pioneer Svoronos. I have brought some of Svoronos's coins back into the picture. Recently Raymond has made a special study of the coins she attributes to kings of the Macedones. In particular she has put forward a new system of weights, supported by May; these are three in number, the stater or standard coin for each being for A 9·82 gr, B 3·27 (drachma), and C 3·68 (drachma). Raymond and May held that the three parallel systems of weights were interconnected and in contemporaneous use during the second half of the sixth century and the earlier decades of the fifth. I advocate a different view later on.[2]

Coins inscribed **TYNTENON** (a genitive plural) were dismissed as forgeries by Gaebler, although they were accepted by Svoronos (G. 211 nos. 41–6, XXIV. 40, 41, XXXIX. 8–11; S. 46 f., IV. 20). Two more such coins, which

---

[1] Gold ingots from Scapte Hyle figure in the Athenian Tribute Lists (see also *IG* I². 301 B 103 f.), and fourth-century silver coins of Damastium have the ingot as a device, no doubt advertising a local product (Casson fig. 17, 1). On electrum see May's comments in *NC* 1953. 167. Silver ingots have been found in hoards in Asia and Egypt which contained sixth-century Thraco-Macedonian silver coins.

[2] J. M. F. May, *The Coinage of Abdera* 8 n. 4, from which I reproduce the system.

Series A		Series B		Series C	
triple stater	29·46 gr	octadrachm	26·18 gr	octadrachm	29·46 gr
double stater	19·64	tetradrachm	13·09	tetradrachm	14·73
stater	9·82	octobol	4·36	didrachm	7·36
hemi-stater	4·91	drachm	3·27	octobol	4·91
trite	3·27	tetrobol	2·18	drachm	3·68
hecte	1·64	triobol	1·64	tetrobol	2·45
hemi-hecton	0·82	diobol	1·09	triobol	1·83
		obol	0·545	obol	0·61

Not all of these are attested by actual coins.

were found one in a hoard buried in the fifth century B.C. in Jordania and the other in Afghanistan, prove Gaebler wrong and Svoronos right.[1] They vary from 29·83 gr (a generous triple stater of series A) to 5·97 gr which fits no series; but three coins are A staters. The devices are in common with those of the Ichnaei, who had a more prolific coinage: a man holding a prancing horse / a wheel with reinforced spoking within an incuse square, and (on the heaviest coin) a bearded man between two oxen / a wheel etc. as above. The Tynteni have not hitherto been identified, but there is little doubt that the inscription, being in Ionic dialect, refers to the Atintani in whose territory the silver mine near Resen lay (see *Epirus* 600 and Volume I. 76 and 93 f. and Map 6), and probably other silver mines which were called collectively 'the mines at Damastium'. In the phonetic spelling of 'Atintenon' the initial A has dropped out. The shared devices are explained by the fact that the best route for export from Resen to the East was down the Axius valley to Ichnae on the coast until *c.* 509. Thereafter it may have been better to send coins to the area of the Strymon; for three of the TYNTENON coins were said by Perdrizet (*Rev. Num.* 1903. 315 f.) to have been found in the area of Pangaeum, two being in a collection at Kavalla (ancient Neapolis). The nonconformist coins may be explained on the grounds that the Atintani were far away from the centre, or that they catered also for other customers. The letter forms, e.g. of N, in the inscriptions vary.

Coins inscribed ΔΕΡΡΟΝΙΚΟΣ *vel sim.* are very heavy pieces *sui generis*, weighing from 41·21 gr to 34·70 gr, and a few tetrobols of series B. It follows that the Derrones were far inland and owned a silver mine, from which they made huge pieces for bullion export. The clue to the position of the Derrones is provided by a fourth-century coin of Lykkeios,[2] a Paeonian king, whose capital in the time of Philip II of Macedon was at or near Astibus (Štip) in the Bregalnitsa valley below the rich mine of Kratovo:[3] ΔΕΡΡΩΝΑΙΟΣ head of 'Apollo' (so modern scholars) / ΛΥΚΚΕΙΟΥ Heracles and a lion. The word ΔΕΡΡΩΝΑΙΟΣ defined the god of the Derrones, and he was known to the Macedones as ΔΑΡΡΩΝ, a god of healing (after whom, I suppose, the Derrones were named).[4] Our early coins were no doubt minted there. Indeed one in the British Museum came from Štip, and Svoronos reported several such in a hoard found at Štip.[5] However, Svoronos placed the Derrones much further south-east

---

[1] *Rev. Num.* 1968. 182 and 1969. 7; cf. C. M. Kraay, *Greek Coins and History* (London, 1969) 47.

[2] For the coin see *Rev. Num.* 1897. 122 f. and *ZfN* 37 (1927) 228, 4, XI. 3. The name was also spelt ΛΥΚΠΕΙΟΣ in an inscription of the period (*GHI* 157).

[3] See Volume I. 202 with n. 5.

[4] Δάρρων, Μακεδονικὸς δαίμων, ᾧ ὑπὲρ τῶν νοσούντων εὔχονται (Hsch.). See Kalléris 147 for a discussion of the word.

[5] The coins from this hoard, not having passed into museums, seem to have been dis-

because he thought Doiran (the modern name of a lake) was a survival of Derron (S. 9 f. and the map at the end). Franke put them in 'east Macedonia' (op. cit. 103).

The inscriptions on these coins ΔEPPONIKOΣ (probably sc. *basileus*), and ΔEPPONIKON (probably a genitive plural), as with Bisaltikos and Bisaltikon, and the abbreviations ΔEPPONI and ΔEPPO, all on very heavy pieces, were written with more than one form of rho, and the omicron is not that of the Thasian alphabet.[1] The devices were an ox-drawn car or wagon, sometimes unaccompanied, sometimes with a god walking or riding / incuse square quadripartite or a triskeles (G. 55 f. nos. 1–7, I 11, xxv. 12, 14–18, 208 nos. 15–18, xxv. 13, xxxix. 16–18; S. 5 f.). Svoronos reported two coins from the hoard found at Štip and a third in private hands which had the names of kings: EYEPΓETE, EX (rather than XE), and EKΓO . . . (probably EKΓONOY), the genitive apparently being used as with some coins of Edonian kings. The coinage, then, may have overlapped three reigns at least. On the Paeonian kings' coins Ɔ in retrograde expressed gamma, and there were two kinds of epsilon (S. 9–10, 11. 5 and 6).

Of the coins inscribed IXNAON, IXNAIΩN, IXNAI . . ., some have the same form of chi as occurred in the name EX of a Paeonian king, and others have two different forms of chi. Here again different alphabets were used by the inscribers, so that we may infer that Ichnae was not a Greek-speaking city, and that it obtained inscribers from different Greek cities. Ichnae minted very heavy coins of 29·20 to 27·85 gr with a bearded man between two oxen / a four-spoked wheel inside an incuse square (G. 63 f., I. 20, xiv. 7, xxvii. 30; S. 40 f., iv. 5 and 6). One came from a hoard near Antioch, which contained a very heavy coin of Getas. Another was struck twice; according to Gaebler 64 no. 3 the second striking had a barely legible inscription which he read as [ΓETA B]AΣIΛ[EΩΣ H]ΔONA[N]; but Svoronos 46 no. 3, iv. 19 had read not AΣIΛ but NAIO (which seems to be confirmed by his illustration), and he did not mention any restriking. It seems that the coin carried signs of both inscriptions [IX]NAIO[N] and [H]ΔONA[N]; and it is impossible in this case to say which was the earlier inscription. Another very heavy coin of Ichnaean type was overstruck with the name ΛITA, definitely added later (G. 66 no. 12, I. 22; S. 45 no. 1, iv. 16). Two diobols of series B with ΛITP (S. 45 no. 2, iv. 17–18) may give a variant spelling of his name with early letter forms.

regarded by later writers, but Svoronos's illustrations leave little doubt that they are genuine. Another hoard was found at Velitchkovo north-west of Plovdiv in Bulgaria (*NC* 1938. 80 f. and *SchwMBU* 1952. 1 f.).

[1] The alphabet on the Thraco-Macedonian coins is discussed by M. L. Jeffery, *The Local Scripts of Archaic Greece* (Oxford, 1961) 364–5, and all comments on the alphabet which follow are taken from her discussion.

The other coins inscribed IXNAON are the normal staters of the A series, weighing between 9·48 and 9·20 gr, and one such lacks an inscription (G. 65 nos. 10 and 11; S. 43, IV. 13–15). The devices are a bearded warrior holding a prancing horse / a wheel with reinforced spoking inside an incuse square (as on coins of the Tynteni), or the same / a four-spoked wheel within an incuse square. The lighter coins, a hemi-stater and some hemi-hectae of series A, carry no inscription and are recognized by the devices: a bull rising from a kneeling position with head back-turned / four-spoked wheel or wheel with reinforced spoking in an incuse square. Two coins have a dolphin, and one has imprints of two feet, ἴχνη punning in Greek on the name Ἴχναι (S. 44 no. 14) in accordance with a legend preserved by Stephanus Byzantinus.[1] The rest of the coins attributed to Lete are recognized by their devices; they are very numerous. They portray an ithyphallic Silenus and a Nymph in different attitudes / a quadripartite incuse square, or a kneeling Centaur with a Nymph in his arms / Corinthian helmet in an incuse square (these are the inscribed coins); see G. 67 f. nos. 1, 3–7, 9–12, 15, 18–21, 26–7, XIV. 16 f., and the Danish *Sylloge Num. Gr.* 1 no. 188. Svoronos attributed to Lete two A staters with a bearded Centaur looking back and holding a stone / incuse square divided into four triangular parts, and three coins with Λ above the head of the Centaur, as above but holding a *cantharus* / the same; these weighing from 1·07 to 0·89 gr are diobols probably of the B series (S. 38 nos. 1–2, VI. 1; one stater being found in Macedonia). There are also overweight staters, hemi-staters, and hectae of the A series. The nearest port serving Lete was Therme on the Thermaic Gulf.

The inscriptions ΒΙΣΑΛΤΙΚΟΣ, ΒΙΣΑΛΤΙΚΟΝ, and ΒΙΣΑΛΤΙΚΩΝ are found on most of the very heavy coins issued by the Bisaltae (G. 48 nos. 1–7; S. 106 has many more); I take the issuing agents to be respectively the *basileus* and the people (the second being also a genitive plural).[2] These coins weigh between 34·10 and 25·67 gr, and more than one alphabet was used with that of Thasos prominent, e.g. for beta, which suggests that the bullion coins were exported from the Strymonic Gulf. Fragments of three more very heavy coins have been found recently in hoards buried in Jordania and Syria.[3] The devices are a naked warrior with two spears beside a horse / a quadripartite incuse square. The warrior, it is generally agreed, represents Rhesus, who was worshipped by the Bisaltae in a cave of this 'silver-veined land' (E. *Rhes.* 970; Str. 7 fr. 36; Polyaen. 6. 53). There are a considerable number of octobols of

---

[1] St. Byz. s.v. *Ichnai*.

[2] Gaebler and others have suggested supplying the words ἀργύριον, ἄργυρος, χαρακτήρ, and even μετάλλων ἄργυρος (G. 48 no. 3 note), but the inscriptions were used to define the issuing agent, whether an ἔθνος or a βασιλεύς, and not the material of the coin, which must have been self-evident.   [3] *Rev. Num.* 1968. 182 and 211.

series B (G. 49 nos. 8–10, XII. 8–10; 207 f. nos. 8–9, XII. 7 and 11; S. 107 f. nos. 9–15, XI. 9–17); these portray a warrior with two spears beside a horse / incuse square quadripartite or divided into four triangular parts. One of these octobols carries on the crupper of the horse the symbol $\&$ (G. 49 no. 8, XII. 8). Four very heavy coins, uninscribed of the Rhesus type, carry on the crupper a part of a caduceus,[1] the symbol **8**, an α (?), and a C having the value of a beta (S. 108–9).

A very heavy coin of 27·06 gr carries the inscription ΓΕΤΑΣ ΗΔΟΝΕΟΝ ΒΑΣΙΛΕΥΣ round a quadripartite incuse square and on the obverse a man between a pair of oxen. On other coins of the same weight and devices the inscriptions are ΓΕΤΑ ΒΑΣΙΛΕΩΣ ΗΔΩΝΑΝ and ΓΕΤΑ ΒΑΣΙΛΕΥ ΗΔΩΝΕΩΝ (two examples). We noted the possible restoration of another Getas inscription on a coin of Ichnae, weighing 29·20 gr. The inscribers of Greek came from more than one Greek city, Potidaea being probably among them for the Doric form, and the perpetrator of the genitive ΒΑΣΙΛΕΥ was presumably not a Greek at all. All Getas coins are very heavy, and three were found in Iraq. See G. 144 no. 1, XXVII. 29–30, and 64 no. 3; 214 no. 60, I. 19; S. 51 f., IV. 1–4.

Coins inscribed ΟΡΡΕΣΚΙΟΝ, ΟΡΗΣΚΙΟΝ, and ΩΡΗΣΚΙΩΝ (all genitive plurals) and light coins inscribed ΟΡΡ, ΟΡΡΗ, and ΗΡΟ are found in a large number of denominations. The heaviest weigh 28·52 to 27·29 gr (S. 55 f., VI; G. 89 nos. 1–2, 210 no. 30, XVIII. 1–3); next come A staters between 9·91 and 9·48 gr (G. 91 nos. 15–18, XVIII. 12–13, 19–20; S. 57 nos. 15–20 and 22, V. 14 f; Danish *Sylloge Num. Gr.* 1 no. 252). The devices on these are respectively a naked man between a pair of oxen / an incuse square quadripartite, and a bearded clothed man leading a prancing horse / an incuse square divided into four triangular parts, or a Centaur and a Nymph / two other types of incuse square and also a Corinthian helmet (as on the inscribed coins of Lete). The lighter coins are hemi-staters of series A and diobols and obols probably of series B (G. 90–1; Danish *Sylloge Num. Gr.* 1. 250–1); these show a kneeling ox, the protome of a kneeling ox, and the protome of a running ox with a variety of incuse squares. Again, the inscribers came from different cities, as the letters vary. The dolphin figures on some coins, indicating that the Orrescii, like the Ichnaei, were close to the sea (*pace* Franke, who put them in the upper Strymon valley). A heavy coin of gold or electrum with the Centaur and Nymph / incuse square quadripartite should be attributed to the Orrescii (H. 174).

Other rare inscribed coins should be noted. Two heavy coins with devices of the Orrescii last mentioned have one ΖΑΙΕΛΕΩΝ and the

---

[1] See Volume I. 335, 398, and fig. 17 *t* for a caduceus-pendant from a tumulus burial at Vergina, perhaps of the ninth century; its use may have been associated by the Greeks with the 'Hermes', whom the Thracian kings but not the commons worshipped (Hdt. 5. 7).

other NAIΩ (G. 133 no. 2, 212 n. 49; H. 174–5; S. 58 f., VI. 11 and 13);
they are A staters. Svoronos alone recorded two A staters inscribed
ΔIONY Centaur and Nymph / roughly divided incuse square (S. 68, VI. 5),
and seven A staters inscribed ΣIPINON Silenus and Nymph / incuse
square quadripartite (S. 76, 82, VIII. 18 f.).

Among Greek cities on the fringe of our area Aenea, situated at the
entry to the inner part of the Thermaic Gulf, had a small part in the
bullion trade, if we may judge by a much-slashed coin, weighing 17·12
gr, which portrays the flight of Aeneas and members of his family from
Troy and is inscribed AINEAΣ, the city's name in the genitive (H. 189;
G. 20, V. 33). Acanthus coined freely on the Euboic standard from the
ores of Stratoniki, and Stagirus followed her example; both cities faced
the Strymonic Gulf (G. 23 f. and 110 f.). Neapolis, a colony of Thasos,
situated on the coast south-east of Mt. Pangaeum, issued A staters and
hemi-staters, and lighter coins of series B; its characteristic device, the
Gorgoneion, was not found on the so-called tribal coinages (H. 175;
G. 79–83).

Last we should mention two coins of 32·08 and 31·94 gr, both very
badly preserved, which have the inscription ΛAIAI between the feet of
an ox drawing a car on which a driver sits—exactly as on a coin of the
Derrones— / Pegasus with furled wings, walking; the letters are clearly
visible in S. 22, III. 7 and 9, and the coins were accepted as genuine by
him, Head and Gardner. But Gaebler (56 no. 7, XXV. 18, and 20 no. 16)
and Babelon rejected them, Gaebler calling them 'eine barbarische
Nachprägung', if not a 'phantasy-product' of modern times. As one of
the coins was found in Egypt together with a Bisaltic coin, its genuineness
is practically certain, because the realization that so many coins of this
type were buried in hoards in the East is quite a recent one. They are
barbaric indeed, but as they are clearly the coins of the Laeaei that is
not surprising.

The identification and the localization of these coinages may now be
attempted. (1) The *Tynteni* = Atintani in the district of Resen by the
silver mines named Damastium. (2) The *Derrones* near Štip by the gold
and silver mines of Kratovo, situated in the centre of the main Paeonian
state. (3) The *Ichnaei* (near Koufalia), west of the Axius, near the then
coast of the head of the Thermaic Gulf; it had no mines in its vicinity but
served as an entrepôt and a mint for the ores of the Tynteni and the
Derrones, and perhaps the Laeaei. (4) *Aenea*, a Greek city, on the east
side of the entry to the inner Thermaic Gulf. (5) The *Letaei* in Mygdonia,
possessing gold nearby; Lete minted silver from elsewhere (as Ichnae did),
and probably exported it from Therme. (6) The *Bisaltae* possessing a silver
mine (perhaps near Theodoraki) and obtaining gold from the area
inland of Lake Prasias and from Nigrita. (7) The *Edones*, holding the

eastern side of the Strymon basin, where the famous mine of Datum lay and where gold and silver are now found at Akhladhokhori. (8) The *Orrescii*, near the coast, most active in trade and prolific coiners, owned the richest mines on Mt. Pangaeum. (9) The *Sirines*, the people of Siris (or Sirris)[1] in Paeonia, where Xerxes left his sacred chariot (Hdt. 8. 114. 3), situated in the north-eastern part of the Strymon basin, where we have located the mine of Datum. (10) The *Zaieleis* and the —*naei*, using the devices of the Orrescii, were probably tribes of the Mt. Pangaeum area. (11) The *Diony[?sii]*, using the same devices but perhaps situated just east of Philippi, where there were mines of gold and silver by the mountain named 'the hill of Dionysus', having a gold-mine 'Asyla' (Appian *BC* 4. 106). (12) The *Laeaei* of the middle Strymon valley, owning the rich gold and silver mines of Kjustendil; a Paeonian tribe geographically close to the Derrones and using the same devices as they. (13) *Acanthus* and *Stagirus*, Greek cities facing the Strymonic Gulf from the west, by the gold and silver mines of Stratoniki. (14) *Neapolis*, a colony of Thasos, exploiting the gold and silver mines by Philippi, and engaging in the bullion trade in silver with its issue of A staters.

We shall consider next the interrelationship of these coinages and some of the unassigned coinages. The classes of coins by weight of the various states are given in alphabetical order (the asterisks refer to coins which will shortly be attributed):

	Overweights	A×3	A×2	A	½A	Lesser A	B: octobol	Drachma	Tetrobol	Diobol	Obol	½ obol
Aenea			x									
Bisaltae		x		*			x			*	*	
Derrones	x								x			
Diony(?sii)				x								
Edones		x					*	*		*	*	
Ichnaei[2]		x		x	x	x				x		x
Laeaei	x											
Letaei				x	x	x				x		
Neapolis				x	x			x				
Orrescii			x	x						x	x	
Sirines				x								
Tynteni		x		x								
Zaieleis				x								
—naei				x								

It is obvious from this table (excluding the asterisks) that the Bisaltae and the Edones are short, because they possessed rich mines and were

[1] So epigraphically.
[2] The hemiobol is published by Svoronos only (S. 44 no. 14 a); it depends on the amount of wear whether the two half-staters should be considered as such or as octobols of the B series.

well placed to engage in trade, having access to the sea in their hands. In particular, unlike the majority of the states, they lack the A stater. On the other hand, the Derrones and the Laeaei, being far inland and issuing only the largest bullion coins, might reasonably be short of smaller pieces.

In fact a link between the Bisaltic coinage and one of the unassigned coinages is provided by the symbol Æ, found on the horse's crupper on a Bisaltic B octobol and on several of the late group of 'goat' A staters (G. 49 no. 8; S. 7 no. 6, I. 15; G. 19 no. 6, v. 29; R. 52, I. 5–6; S. 6 no. 5, I. 4–5). The link is certain; no other coins have a ligatured pair of letters. Svoronos correctly attributed both lots of coins to one state; but because he held that Æ stood for Derrones he attributed them to the Derrones (S. 6 no. 5, and 7 no. 6). Gaebler incorrectly separated them; he attributed the horse with the symbol to the Bisaltae and the goats with the same symbol to the Macedones. The weakness of Svoronos's attribution was that the horse is not a Derronian emblem at all, and that it is precisely the emblem employed by the Bisaltae, that of Rhesus; indeed it is proved to be so by its appearance on a triple stater of the A series inscribed ΒΙΣΑΛΤΙΚΟΝ. In fact Svoronos himself attributed to the Bisaltae every coin bearing this emblem *except* the one with Æ (S. 106 f., xi, and xii. 1–8). The correct course is clearly to attribute to the Bisaltae both the B octobol with the symbol Æ on the horse's crupper (noting that five other Bisaltic coins have a symbol in that position; S. 108 no. 16 a, b, g, and 109 no. 17 a, b) and the 'goat' staters of the A series with the symbol Æ. We can now add to the Bisaltae on our chart stater A, diobol B, and obol B.

The Strymon basin was famous for its lakes and water-birds. A crane appears on a coin of the Bisaltae, who were near Lake Prasias. The magnificent 'goose' coins, some having also a frog or a salamander, should be given to the Edones as the owners of the mine at Datum, a city which had its own lake (Str. 7 fr. 36). The electrum coins with the goose (S. 186, ix. 4; G. 141 init.) should probably also go to the Edones. But leaving them aside we can add to the Edones on our chart octobol B, drachma B, diobol B, and obol B (G. 139–41).

In a general way the so-called tribal coinages have many points either in common with or overlapping one another, and this phenomenon has led to the suggestion that 'there was a monetary convention among the issuing agents', that this became 'a military alliance' *c.* 492, and that the Macedones (whom we still have to consider) participated 'in the alliance' (R. 47 and 59, supported by Franke, op. cit. 99 and 106). This seems entirely fanciful. The truth lies rather with Justin 7. 2. 6 'sed Macedonibus adsidua certamina cum Thracibus et Illyriis.' The relations of the Balkan tribes with one another were marked by war and deportation, as anyone can see who reads the words of Thucydides 2. 99, and there was no trace of any alliance or combined operation against Persia when she smashed and deported the Paeonians of the Strymon basin or punished the 'Brygi' for their successful night-attack on the Persian army. The demand for bullion silver in the form of coins, the use of Greek engravers, and above all the stock of religious ideas shared by so many tribes, whether Paeonian or Thracian or Bisaltic or Crestonaean, account for the general resemblances in these coinages without invoking a system of military alliance or a more sophisticated form of monetary alliance.

Let us keep closer to the historical facts, as we have described them in the preceding section. The Paeonian period of power *c.* 540–511 is surely reflected in the coinages of the Derrones, the Laeaei, the Tynteni, and the Ichnaei; for coins of the first two have the same obverse showing the ox-drawn car with its driver and a helmet above, and the coins of the second two used the same obverses showing a man between two oxen or a warrior holding a prancing horse / the wheel with reinforced spoking. No doubt the driver was a Paeonian god; the oxen of Paeonia were most famous, and the kings may have paraded in full armour in an ox-drawn chariot. The sun, which the Paeonians worshipped in particular, figured very prominently above the oxen drawing the car. Sacred cars have been found further north at Dupljaja (*AI* 3. 41); and a child's grave of the fifth century at Mikhalitsi near Preveza in Epirus had a miniature car of bronze with an iron axle (*AthAA* 6 (1973) 223 fig. 15). The reinforced spoking is of a central-European kind, as Dr. P. Ducrey has kindly informed me.

As we see on the chart of weights, the Ichnaei used more denominations of the A series than anyone else, and they were perhaps its originators. Thus the central core of Paeonian power extended from the Laeaei, exploiting the gold and silver of Kjustendil, to the royal Paeonian tribe, the Derrones, controlling the gold and silver mines of Kratovo and other sites in the Pecinj and Bregalnitsa valleys, and even beyond to some form of controlled trade in silver with the Tynteni or Atintani of the Resen area. The export of silver and presumably of gold also was channelled down the Axius valley to Ichnae, the Paeonian chief city on the coast of the Thermaic Gulf and the possessor of the most active mint. Ichnae itself, of course, had no silver mines nor access to any in its vicinity. Its coinage ceased soon after it was captured by the Macedones.

The other sphere of Paeonian power was in Mygdonia and the Strymon basin, stopping short of Mt. Pangaeum. The Siriopaeones controlled the mines of gold and silver at Akhladhokhori, and their coins ΣΙΡΙΝΩΝ were those of their capital city, Siris. On the western side of the river Strymon the Paeonians controlled the mines of gold and silver by Lake Prasias and at Theodoraki and the gold mines by Nigrita, and also the gold near Lete in Mygdonia. It is evident that the mint for this area was at Lete, which had convenient access to the Thermaic Gulf at Therme, and the silver was brought from inland to Lete, as in the case of Ichnae. It seems that the Paeonians organized their empire closely on Ichnae and Lete as their chief centres, while the tribes east of the Strymon were grouped round Siris (now Serres). In this sphere the worship of Dionysus was particularly strong. There were famous sanctuaries of the god and his associates in Crestonia in the west, and the oracle of Dionysus on Mt. Pangaeum in the east. Silenus and a Nymph and Centaur and a Nymph as concomitants of Dionysus became the emblems of the coinage of Lete, which was coining not so much for itself as for the western part of the Strymon basin, Mygdonia and Crestonia. Both groups, headed by the Siriopaeones and the Letaei, coined on the A series of weights, and the Letaei came close to the Ichnaei in the number of A denominations of coinage and eventually surpassed them in output. The Paeonians exported their silver mainly from the Thermaic Gulf.

When Persia overthrew the power of the Paeonians, the Edones led the advance of the Thracians as far as the Axius and perhaps for a time beyond the river to Ichnae, because triple staters of the Ichnae mint were overstruck by Litas and later Getas as kings of the Edones. But Ichnae and Amphaxitis passed to the Macedones, and Ichnae ceased to coin by 509. While the Thracian tribes held the mines by Theodoraki, Lake Prasias, and Nigrita, from approximately 510 to some time after 500, they coined freely at Lete, using the already popular devices of the ithyphallic Silenus and the Nymph which became more licentious as the Nymph ceased to protest and accepted courtship, and of the Centaur with a Nymph. These issues carried no inscription, and the Corinthian helmet on the reverse of the earlier inscribed coins was no longer used. The central mint of the Thracians east of the Strymon was near the gold and silver mines of Akhladhokhori, probably at 'Datum of the Edones' (Hdt. 9. 75), and from there Getas, king of the Edones, issued his triple staters of the A series. The Edones sent their goods down the Strymon past their stronghold at Nine Ways (later Amphipolis) into the Strymonic Gulf and their trade was mainly with Thasos, as they used for the 'goose' coins almost all denominations of the B series.

The Bisaltae entered the field as coiners probably at some time after 500. Then they had the ores of the mines by Theodoraki, Lake Prasias, and Nigrita, and their territory extended down to Argilus on the coast west of the Strymon. Thus they sent their goods into the Strymonic Gulf and traded with Acanthus and Thasos. The 'Rhesus' coins now appeared as he was the hero of the Bisaltae, and the 'goat' coins emphasized another aspect of the worship of Dionysus, revered in Crestonia. Being so rich in ore, the Bisaltae issued many triple staters of the A series, and they employed the B octobol (as Neapolis did) and lesser B coins, probably for trade with the Greek cities. They had their name inscribed on some only of their coins.

The Pangaeum group of tribes was independent in both periods, i.e. from *c.* 540 to *c.* 480; for the chief exploiters of the mines, the Satrae, were never subject to anyone according to Herodotus (7. 112). Thus the Orrescii, a constituent tribe of the group known as the Satrae, probably began to coin as soon as the bullion trade in silver got under way. They issued triple staters and hemi-staters of the A series, and they added to these diobols and obols of the B series later. The Orrescian coins portraying a man between two oxen (G. xviii. 1–3) may be the earliest, as oxen figure most in the Paeonian period of influence; those showing a warrior leading a prancing horse may represent a Thracian favourite, Ares (xviii. 12); and those showing a Centaur and a Nymph were connected probably with the cult of Dionysus and the local oracle of Dionysus. The coins of the Zaieleis and the —naei have the Centaur and the Nymph probably for the same reason. Of these the former is the later, as it has the straight-barred alpha (see p. 110 below).

In the area just east of Philippi, where gold and silver were mined, a hill with a gold mine called Asyla was named 'the hill of Dionysus' (Appian *BC* 4. 106). It is possible that the Diony(?sii) were the first to exploit the silver there and to issue A staters with the Centaur and the Nymph in honour of Dionysus. The Thasian colony Neapolis may have entered the field later, displacing the Diony(?sii). She issued A staters and later octobols of the B series; the fact that she did not issue smaller units in either the A or the B series suggests that Thasos kept the local trade in her own hands.

Soon after 480 Alexander led his Macedones as far as the Strymon. He acquired the mine of the Bisaltae, whose king had flouted Persia in 480, and began to issue the first Macedonian coinage by taking over the current issues: the kneeling goat with back-turned head but substituting the first two letters of his own name AΛ for the symbol $\mathcal{E}$ (see G. v. 25 and 29), and the man with a walking horse[1] / a quadripartite square but substituting for the inscription ΒΙΣΑΛΤΙΚΟΝ round the square his own inscription ΑΛΕΞΑΝΔΡΟ, which is also a genitive (G. xii. 11 and G. xxviii. 2 and 1, an octadrachm; R. 68, vi–vii). Alexander produced a new type showing a mounted man with two spears but having the old reverse except that ΒΙΣΑΛΤΙΚΟΝ was replaced by ΑΛΕΞΑΝΔΡΟ (R. 68, iii); later the reverse changed to a new one, showing the head of a goat

---

[1] As Desneux put it, 'les chevaux des Bisaltes repris par Alexandre I après 500' (*Les Tetradrachmes d'Acanthos = Rev. belge de num.* 1949. 5–122).

(R. 69, IV). Of these coins the kneeling goat was still an A stater, but the others were on the B and the C series of weights. For a new era was dawning in which Athens and not Persia became the strongest customer in the Aegean.

If our interpretations are correct, the A series of weights began c. 540,[1] when the Persian Empire became a market for the silver bullion, and it lasted until the withdrawal of Persia soon after 480. The B series of weights was introduced around 510 for trade in the Strymonic area, where Thasos was now becoming important.[2] The C series was introduced by Alexander after 480 when a new market was developing. There is no evidence to support the view of Raymond and May that all three series were used contemporaneously[3] (a daunting thought with some twenty-five denominations for the workers), but rather series A overlapped with series B in the latter part of the period and series B overlapped with series C after 480.

Our general conclusions may be summarized in chronological form.

(1) c. 540–c. 511 trade in bullion coins and some smaller denominations of the A series, including overweight and nonconformist coins, by Tynteni, Derrones, Ichnaei, Letaei, Laeaei, and Siriopaeones during the Paeonian period of power; and from the independent Thracian tribes of Mt. Pangaeum—the Orrescii and others—and from perhaps the Diony(?sii) of the Philippi area, and sometime afterwards[4] from Neapolis, the colony of Thasos, which exploited the mines of the Philippi area.

(2) c. 510–c. 480 trade in bullion coins of the A series and in the smaller denominations of the B series by Thracians at Lete, Edones, Orrescii, Zaieleis, —naei, and Neapolis. The Ichnaei issued some small coins of the B series, probably when the Thracians first held the area, but they ceased to coin by 509, when it fell into the hands of the Macedones.

(3) At some time after 500 the Bisaltae expanded. They coined from then until 480, both in bullion coins and in smaller denominations.

(4) After 480 Alexander of Macedon captured the Bisaltic mines and produced at first Bisaltic types but with the first two letters of his name, and then his own new type. The goat staters of the A series continued

---

[1] May gave 540/35 for the beginning of coinage at Abdera, and J. Desneux started the coinage of Acanthus c. 530; on the other hand, Raymond started the latter c. 560.

[2] J. Pouilloux, *Recherches sur l'histoire et les cultes de Thasos* (Paris, 1954) 1. 49, commented on the lack of close contact between the Thraco-Macedonian area and Thasos in the archaic period; it was only towards the end of the sixth century that Thasian coins of the Satyr and the protesting Nymph were reaching the East (ibid. 54).

[3] May wrote of Raymond's 'ingenious and elaborate reconstruction of the three parallel series of weights, and their inter-connexion, as used by both Greek cities and native tribes during the second half of the sixth century and the earlier decades of the fifth' (*Abdera* 8).

[4] If the influence of Thasos came late in the sixth century (as Pouilloux, n. 2 above), it is unlikely that Neapolis was active in the mining world much earlier. The engravers of the Acanthus coins had more influence on mainland styles (see G. VI. 12 and I. 20, XII. 5 and XIV. 13).

only for a short time; for his other issues he used the B and C series of weights.

In the past the goat coins have been attributed to the Macedones by all writers[1] except Svoronos, who assumed that ⚿ was short for 'Derrones'. The argument was that the goat was revered specially by the Macedones because of the two oracles saying that goats would lead the founders of Aegeae to the site; but we have shown that one of these was not earlier than *c.* 400 and that the other, though known to Herodotus, was probably not current in the sixth century. In any case the coins of Alexander do not support the argument; for he reduced the magnificent kneeling goat to a mere protome on the reverse of a short-lived issue of tetra-drachms (R. gave the issue only two years of life). The horse and the helmet were the particular marks of Alexander's coinage. The goat was not; rather it was important in the cult of Dionysus, as any student of Greek tragedy knows, and his cult was widespread from Crestonia to Pangaeum but not practised particularly by the Macedones at this time, as far as we know. The next argument was that ⚿ should be read retrogressively and be short for 'Edessa' (or 'Edessaei'), a city on the upper Lydias; that this city was renamed Aegeae; and that the coins were therefore attributable to Aegeae (as in G. 18 f.). We have shown that Edessa of the upper Lydias and Aegeae were not one and the same city but two cities, and that Edessa was not the seat of the Macedonian kings.[2] But again we should learn from the known Macedonian coins: they carry the name of the king and not that of Aegeae, which was the capital. For the king owned the mines and coined in his own name. So too did the Paeonian kings—Euergetes, Ecgonus, and Ech— and the Thracian kings Getas and Litas and a Bisaltic king De—.

The modern Geological Map of Greece has no indication of lead, let alone of gold and silver, in the territories west of the lower Axius. Callisthenes alone mentioned the existence of mines by Mt. Bermium 'providing the wealth of Midas', whose Phrygian Briges left for Asia *c.* 800 (*FGrH* 124 F 54; see Volume I. 411). He did not speak of that remote period from knowledge, but it may be held that the existence of some mines there made his story plausible. There are deposits of chrome, iron, and iron pyrites by Mt. Bermium (see Map 1 of Volume I), and the Phrygians may well have made their wealth by exploiting and exporting iron at a relatively early date. Certainly the striking thing about the burials in the great cemetery of tumuli at Vergina near Mt. Bermium is the extraordinary amount of bronze and iron[3] and the

---

[1] R. 49, citing Head, Babelon, and Gaebler, to whom all recent writers may be added.

[2] See Volume I. 156 f.

[3] A point emphasized by A. M. Snodgrass, *The Dark Age of Greece* (Edinburgh, 1971) 253 f. M. Andronikos, *Vergina* 1. 224 listed more than 1,000 pieces from his excavations alone.

absence of silver. When we realize that the Macedones did not get their hands on any silver mine until they entered Bisaltia, we shall not be surprised that they did not coin in silver until soon after 480.[1]

Persia may have taken her tribute partly in bullion and she seems to have left the tribes free to issue coinage. It was apparently the Persian arrival on the Aegean coast about 546 which stimulated the demand for silver, and markets for silver became available as Persia conquered area after area, first Mesopotamia and Syria, then after 525 Egypt where the satrap Aryandes made silver coinage of the most pure silver (Hdt. 4. 166. 2). Darius (522–486) issued gold darics and silver shekels, which were both renowned for their purity. Thus Balkan silver, being particularly pure, was increasingly in demand and spread into one area after another. It was exported most commonly in the form of A staters, and seems often to have been melted down. Schaeffer, for instance, describes a silversmith's workshop at Ras Shamra on the Syrian coast, where many coins had been melted and thirty-nine silver staters, averaging 9·62 gr, were about to be melted, when the whole collection was buried; almost all the staters were from our area, and analysis showed the silver of the Lete coins to be 99·80 per cent pure.[2]

Relations with Persia went through different phases. When the Persian domain stopped at the Greek cities of Asia Minor and some offshore islands, *c.* 540–514, much of the silver passed through Greek hands on the Asiatic coast and it was sensible to label the coins with inscriptions in Greek script. From 513 to 498 the silver of the Thraco-Macedonian area went direct into Persian hands, and there was no point in adding labels in a language which was alien to exporter and importer; that is why the great bulk of Thraco-Macedonian coins have no inscriptions. Between 498 and 480 economic conditions were altered by the Ionian Revolt and the expeditions of Darius and Xerxes; once again Greek traders were involved and Greek inscriptions were used on later coinages, e.g. those of the Bisaltae. One may guess that the peak periods for the movement of silver eastwards were *c.* 512–498, and *c.* 485–480, when Persian armies came to and returned from the Balkans. If these periods were reflected in the hoards, we shall obtain some clues to the dating of particular issues. I give a list of contents of the main hoards, including one at Taranto as silver was exported also to Italy,

---

[1] The only story of gold in 'Pieria of Macedonia' is not of mining but of hoarding and is not such as to carry conviction: 'they say that the ancient kings dug some uncoined gold into the ground in four holes and one piece sprouted a span high from one of the holes' (Arist. *Mir.* 47).

[2] C. F. A. Schaeffer, 'Une trouvaille de monnaies archaïques grecques à Ras Shamra' in *Mélanges syriens offerts à R. Dussaud* 1. 461 f. The hoards found at Taranto, at Myt-Rahineh, and in Jordania, for instance, contained bits of ingots and lumps of silver and were a silversmith's working lot; that at Ras Shamra included an 'undispersed consignment' from our area (C. M. Kraay, *Greek Coins and History* 45).

but not a recently discovered hoard at Asyut, to which I shall refer later.

	Approximate date of burial	Abdera	Acanthus	Bisaltae	Derrones	'Goat'	Lete	Mac. King	Neapolis	Orrescii	Potidaea	Stagirus	Thasos	Tynteni
Afghanistan:														
Kabul			2										1	
Oxus			2											
Persia:														
Malayer	380		8	2				3						
Jordania	450–425	1	3	2	1		2	1		1			1	1
Syria:														
Massyaf	425		1	1									1	
Ras Shamra	500	1					12					4		
Egypt:														
Benha	485	2	4				6		2	3			2	
Demanhûr	end of 6th c.		1				17		4	1		9	12	
Delta	500						1		1				1	
Myt-Rahineh						1	1							
Sakha	500–490		1				4		1				1	
Zagazig	450–425		5	2							4		1	
Italy:														
Taranto	510–508		4				2					3	2	
Totals		4	31	5	2	2	45	4	8	5	7	13	22	1

The main hoards with Thraco-Macedonian and neighbouring coins[1]

An interesting feature of this list is the very poor representation for the period of Paeonian power *c.* 540–511. There are no gross overweights, no coins of Ichnaei, Sirines, and Laeaei, only one of the Tynteni and two of the Derrones, both of whom may well have found a means of export through the Thracian area after the loss of Ichnae (see p. 75 above). As we know of an Ichnae coin and an overweight Getas coin being found

[1] The references for the hoards are as follows (with a number in brackets giving the hoard number in S. P. Noe, *A Bibliography of Greek Coin Hoards*[2], American Numismatic Society, *Numismatic Notes and Monographs* no. 78 (1937), where mentioned): D. Schlumberger, *Trésors monétaires d'Afghanistan* 33 (Kabul), 48 (Oxus); ibid. 51 and *ANSMusN* 15 (1969) 15 (Malayer); *Rev. Num.* 1968. 182 f. (Jordania); *Rev. Num.* 1968. 211 f. (Massyaf); *NC* 1930. 93 f. (Benha, Noe 143); *ZfN* 37 (1927) 103 (Demanhûr, Noe 323); *NC* 1890. 1 f. (Delta, Noe 362); *Rev. Num.* 1861. 414 (Myt-Rahineh, Noe 722); *ZfN* 22 (1900) 231 f. (Sakha, Noe 888); *ZfN* 37 (1927) 137 (summary) (Zagazig, Noe 1178); P. Wuilleumier, *Tarente* 223 f. and *Rev. Num.* 1912. 1 f. (Taranto, Noe 1052). *ANSMusN* 15 (1969) 1 f. adds coins of Lete, Acanthus, probably Stagirus, and Dicaea which were probably in a hoard found at Balkh in Afghanistan.

before 1898 in a small hoard at Antioch,[1] the conclusion we can draw from this list is that the coinages of these peoples did indeed fall in the earliest period of coinage and were not in production, at least heavily, when exchange with Persia livened up after *c.* 512. Equally the inscribed coins of Lete are also absent.[2] Another point to note is that in two of the hoards which were buried latest, those at Malayer and in Jordania, there are inscribed coins of the Bisaltae and of Alexander I, and in the latter there is also an uninscribed 'goat' coin; as we argued that the inscribed coins of the Bisaltae and some of the goats were immediately prior to the first coinage of Alexander I, our view receives considerable support, especially as Alexander's coins are absent from all other hoards.

The Lete coins top the list, but all forty-five of them are uninscribed. This confirms our view that the earliest coins of Lete were the heavy inscribed pieces, contemporary with the coins of the Ichnaei, which are also absent from the list. That Lete coins should be so very numerous is not surprising, if we are right in having maintained that Lete coined early under the Paeonians, continued as the chief mint in the Thracian period *c.* 510 to soon after 500, and then coined alongside the Bisaltae until 480. It has been suggested by Schaeffer and others that the Lete coins can be divided into two groups, the earlier when the Nymph runs away from the Silenus, and the later when she receives some courting. This is confirmed by the list. For the specimens in the Ras Shamra hoard belong to the former class, and those in the Benha hoard to the latter group (as the ithyphallic Satyr in the kneeling position on the Benha coins is also held to be late). The two Lete staters in the Taranto hoard belong to the later type. As the Taranto hoard was buried *c.* 510/8, we can conclude that the earlier type evolved during the Paeonian period of power, *c.* 540–511.

The importance of Lete is made even clearer, if we take the four earliest hoards, laid down *c.* 510–500, viz. Demanhûr, Ras Shamra, Delta, and Taranto. In these Lete had 32 coins, Thasos 15, Stagirus 13, Acanthus 5, Neapolis 5, Potidaea 3, Orrescii 1, and Abdera 1. If we may take *c.* 500 as a general base for the burial of the hoards and allow say a fifteen-year run for the coins generally,[3] then Lete was coining

---

[1] Noe 55; together with coins of Acanthus and Mende.

[2] As I pointed out on p. 87 above, the inscribed coins seem to have been the earliest. The inscription ΛΕΤΑΙΟΝ was found on staters showing a Centaur with a Nymph in his arms/helmet in an incuse square, and the helmet itself seems to have been a feature of the early issues only (e.g. *Danish Sylloge Num. Gr.* 1 no. 188 and no. 196), as well as of the Paeonian coins of the Derrones and the Laeaei.

[3] Some coins may date further back, as in the case of the coins of Evelthon, king of Salamis in Cyprus *c.* 560–525, which were found in the Ras Shamra hoard. For features common to the Demanhûr and Ras Shamra hoards such as the Lete coins with a Silenus offering a myrtle branch to the Nymph, inscribed coins of Stagirus, and upright griffins on Abdera coins see Schaeffer, loc. cit., for Ras Shamra.

most prolifically *c.* 515–500, at which time Persia was taking most coin back to the East.

The next group, laid down *c.* 500–475, was represented only by Sakha and Benha until recently, when a large hoard was found at Asyut in Egypt, deposited *c.* 475. Some information about this hoard has been given to me most generously by Dr. M. J. Price of the British Museum, who will be publishing the contents of the hoard shortly. In the Table I have kept Sakha–Benha separate from Asyut, because the building of the canal and the expedition of Xerxes came between them. The last group is less informative, because the hoards had only a few Thraco-Macedonian coins and were spread over a period from 450/425 to 380.

Time of deposit	Abdera	Acanthus	Bisaltae	Derrones	Dicaea	Goat-coins	Ichnaei	Lete	Maced. Kings	Neapolis	Orrescii	Potidaea	Stagirus	Thasos	Tynteni
c. 510–500	1	5	—	—	—	—	—	32	—	5	1	3	13	15	—
c. 500–485	2	5	—	—	—	—	—	10	—	3	3	—	—	3	—
c. 475	15	38	—	15	4	4	6	29	1	—	37	6	2	—	—
c. 450–380	3	26	5	2	—	2	—	13	4	—	4	4	4	7	1

Deductions from hoards are obviously hazardous, because we do not know the habits of hoarders and in particular the length of time during which a coin may have been kept or worn as bullion, even as gold napoleons were worn in Albania until quite recently. The six coins of the Ichnaei provide an example; for one might deduce that they were first coined after *c.* 485, but Ichnae fell to the Macedones and ceased to coin by 509, as we have seen. These very heavy coins were survivors of the Paeonian period. So too, at an even later date, was the only coin of the Tynteni found in these hoards. But the large numbers and the changes in their relationships may be more informative. Thus Stagirus was ousted by its neighbour Acanthus after *c.* 485; Lete remained very strong down to *c.* 475 and declined only gradually thereafter; Abdera gained ground and Neapolis and Thasos lost ground after *c.* 485; the Derrones and the Orrescii became prominent after *c.* 485; and the Orrescii in particular, being on my interpretation exploiters of Mt. Pangaeum, came up as Neapolis and Thasos went down.[1] Where numbers are small, *argumenta ex silentio* should be avoided. The absence, for instance, of Bisaltae coins until after the Asyut hoard of *c.* 475 does not in itself demonstrate that the Bisaltae coined first after *c.* 475; for we happen to know that the king of the Bisaltae was a determined enemy of Xerxes (Hdt. 8. 116),

---

[1] The decline of Thasos was no doubt connected with the action Darius took against her in 491 (Hdt. 6. 46–7), while Acanthus was close to the labour force which made the canal through the neck of the Athos peninsula in 483–481.

and that his territory included a rich mine (Hdt. 5. 17. 2), which is likely to have been worked at that time of mining activity.

The larger number of tribal states and city-states from the north-east Aegean area represented in the Asyut hoard shows that they were literally cashing in on the huge demand provided by the Persian forces of Xerxes and his subordinates. As these forces moved along the coast, the coastal peoples especially in Chalcidice were particularly well placed, and from inland it was only bullion-coiners, like the Derrones with their outsize pieces, who could make their way into the market. In relation to the Greek world generally the Thraco-Macedonian area held a strong position in the Persian period, *c.* 515–480; but after 479, when Athens and her Allies were taking the place of Persia in the Aegean world, the Greek states went ahead. For instance, in the Benha hoard the proportion of coins from the Thraco-Macedonian area was more than a half, but it became a quarter in the Zagazig hoard and a seventh in the hoard in Jordania.[1] We shall consider that situation in a later chapter.

3. *The Archaeological Evidence for 550–480*

(See Maps of Volume 1 as cited under each name in the Index of Volume 1)

The most impressive site of the period was at Trebenishte, north of Lake Ochrid, where ten warriors were buried each with his own iron sword, spears and helmet and dress-pins and ornaments, and three women with their pins and ornaments, and many dedications in addition.[2] As we see from the wealth in gold and silver, and especially from the gold death-masks so reminiscent of those at Mycenae, the gold gloves and gold sandals, the dead were the rulers of this region from *c.* 540, the date of the earliest 'royal' burial, to *c.* 480 or 470. Their gold came probably from the cantons of Metohija and Kossovo or from further north, and the silver from 'Damastium' (which included a mine west of Resen and probably others further north) and from Tetovo, Metohija, and Kossovo. Fine bronzes of a marked Corinthian style, eight black-figured vases, and other imported objects show that Trebenishte was in trade with the Greek cities of the Ionian Gulf and the Thermaic Gulf, and there was evidently some movement of commerce across the peninsula, taking the route north of Lake Ochrid which became known later as the Via

---

[1] So C. M. Kraay in *Rev. Num.* 1968. 182 f.

[2] The original publication was by B. Filow, *Die archaische Nekropole von Trebenischte* (Berlin, 1927); subsequent excavations were reported in *Arch. Anz.* 45 (1930) 276 f.; 48 (1933) 459 f.; *Rev. Arch.* 34. 26 f.; *OeJ* 27 (1932) 1 f. and 28 (1933) 164 f. See also L. Popović, *Katalog nalaza iz nekropole kod Trebeništa* (Belgrade, 1956), V. Lahtov and J. Kastelić, *Lihnid* 1. 5–54; VII. 27–8; XVIII. 10 f.; and V. Lahtov, *Problem trebeniške kulture* (Ochrid, 1965). Similar remains were found in excavations at Radolište near Strouga; see L. Popović, *Radolište, Zbornik radova Narodnog muzeja* 1 (1938) 75 f. There is a useful summary of Lahtov's results in *AI* 5 (1964) 72 f. by M. Paravić-Pešikan for both Trebenishte and Radolište.

Egnatia.[1] Thus the silver coins of the Tynteni and perhaps silver ingots travelled to Macedonia and Neapolis, and silver coins of Lete, Potidaea, Acanthus, and Mende were found in a hoard at Taranto in South Italy. Northern influences are apparent in the dress-pins and double-shanked hairpins, the death-masks and various forms of decoration. Northerners themselves, the rulers of Trebenishte seem to have been in close contact with Dodona,[2] but on present evidence not with Lower Macedonia. Their relations were more probably with the Paeonians on the eastern side of the watershed, and the prominence of the helmet on Paeonian coinages may mean that they were more often warlike. A fine Illyrian helmet, inscribed 'I belong to Paeon', which is in the Canellopoulos Collection, has been dated *c.* 550 and came probably from Macedonia (P. Amandry in *BCH* 95 (1971) 589 f.); the inscription is in the Corinthian alphabet.

Situated at the edge of the plain, Trebenishte is at the very exit of the main route from the north.[3] The high country north and east of it is heavily forested. No dynasty would have sited its cemetery there, unless it ruled the northern territories, which extend through Kitsevo and Tetovo towards Kossovo, and also the area immediately to the east. The resources of a kingdom based on Trebenishte were certainly drawn from the plain and the fisheries north of Ochrid town, and it is probable that its power extended throughout the Ochrid basin, which is an economic unit. Further south a belt of hill country is easily crossed, and one traverses the rich flat plains of Malik and Koritsa, from which passes lead into the Haliacmon valley of Macedonia and into North Epirus.[4] The holder of the Ochrid plain thus stands at the cross-roads of the southern Balkans in a long sink between parallel mountain ranges, from which egress is easier towards the south-west than the south-east.[5]

The natural centre of the Ochrid basin was at Lychnidus (Ochrid), a city traditionally founded by Phoenician Cadmus in the territory ruled by the Encheleae (Str. 7 C 326), whom Hecataeus described as adjacent to the 'Dexari', i.e. the later 'Dassaretae' of the Malik–Koritsa plain (*FGrH* 1 F 103). The rulers of Trebenishte and of Lychnidus are likely to have been in league, and this was evidently stated to be so in

[1] I. Mikulčić, *Pelagonija* (Skopje, 1966) 41 f. and 92 (in the German summary) stresses the influence and trade of the Chalcidian colonies, rightly but rather to the exclusion of the western colonies, Apollonia and Dyrrachium. See *Rev. Arch.* 1973. 1. 39 f. for imported Greek pottery at Trebenishte and at Radolište; for sixth-century Apollonia see *BUST* 1960. 1. 51 f. The finds at Radolište, which included bronze vessels, ear-rings and a 'greco-illyrian helmet', were dated all to the second half of the sixth century in *AI* 5. 75.

[2] See *Epirus* 437 f.

[3] See Volume I. 43 for a geographical description. I visited Trebenishte in 1968 and walked up to the Trebenishte 'kale', a walled site of the fourth century B.C. (V. Lahtov, *Lihnid* II (1959) Pl. 5; *AI* 5. 76).

[4] For this area, which I visited in 1972, see *JHS* 94 (1974) 66 f.   [5] See Volume I. 45.

a corrupt passage in Strabo 7 C 326. As I read the passage, 'the Peresadyes joined the dynasty of the Encheleae'. The Peresadyes, then, were the rulers of Trebenishte, and Hecataeus wrote of them when they were at the height of their power.[1] It is likely, as we have seen, that they came from the north; they may have been Dardanii, forerunners of the fourth-century dynasty of Bardylis, and they had contact with the Thracians, because the use of gold death-masks probably has Thracian associations.[2] Later the inhabitants of the land north of Lake Ochrid were the Atintani, and in the sixth century the 'Tynteni' of the coins were evidently the same people; wherever the Peresadyes came from, they were clearly the ruling house among the Atintani and were in league with the Encheleae. The rise of this strong tribal state, under an able monarchy, extending from Tetovo at least and including the Ochrid basin, is a parallel to the rise of the tribal state of the Paeonians, again under an able monarchy, extending to the basins of the Axius and the Strymon. It continued to exist after the overthrow of the Paeonians by Persia and after the rise in their place of the Edones, led by their kings.

The cemetery of a royal dynasty in Derriopus has been excavated at Saraj, near Brod, beside the Cerna river (Erigon). The latest burials in it were towards the end of the sixth century or the beginning of the fifth century, as indicated for instance by a pyramid-shaped ear-ring.[3] The latest burials in the tumuli of Visoï on the western side of the plain, midway between Heraclea Lyncou and Styberra, were made well within the sixth century, but some slight changes in burial practices were already appearing. The new development in the latter part of the sixth century was the formation of small settlements on the edge of the plain, each with its own cemetery at a distance of some 200 or 300 m, in which the dead of the community were buried in cist-graves without any tumulus, close together, and occasionally having a funerary *stele*.[4] These developments show a weakening in the pastoral way of life which had prevailed since late in the Late Bronze Age, and which left few traces except the tumulus-burials of the chieftains, and the beginning of agricultural settlements, which developed with continuity into 'the cities of the Derriopes all by the Erigon' (Str. 7 C 327). One of the cemeteries has been excavated by the leading scholar of this region, Ivan Mikulčić, at Crkvište Beranci which is just north of Visoï. Both inhumation

---

[1] See *Epirus* 466 f. Bronze vessels and other offerings like those at Trebenishte have been found at Visoï II near Monastir and at Gorno Selo near Štip (see *AI* 5. 74 f.).

[2] The use of gold mouth-pieces at Chauchitsa, Ayios Vasilios, Zeitenlik, and Kalamaria showed the spread of Thracians as a ruling people in the area east of the lower Axius *c.* 550 (see Volume I. 428 f.); two of these, intact with their strings, were found in the excavations of tumuli at Kuç i zi near Koritsa, which is still under way (*Iliria* I (1971) 350, a report by Zhaneta Andrea who showed me some of her discoveries). The tumuli belonged to a dynasty, controlling the Malik–Koritsa area from *c.* 800 on to at least 550.

[3] See Volume I. 338, and Mikulčić 90 with Pls. IX h and XI h.   [4] Mikulčić 90 f.

and incineration were practised in the late sixth century; pyramid-shaped ear-rings, double-shanked hairpins, mushroom- and disc-topped dress-pins, rings and bracelets, and iron spearheads had much in common with the past, but their possession was no longer limited to the ruling family.[1]

Another change which took place at that time in the Pelagonian plain was the dying away of the 'North-western Geometric style' of pottery, which had been in vogue since late in the Late Bronze Age,[2] and the appearance of a wheel-made pottery imitating the shapes often of archaic Greek pottery, the ware being fired grey or having a brown slip. The Hellenizing influences which reached Pelagonia came from Ionia—transmitted probably through the Persian advance into Europe—and from Chalcidice and Corinth. Black-figured vases were found at Bela Tsarkva-Brod where the Erigon leaves the plain. It is likely that the main route of trade came up the Axius valley through Paeonian territory as far as Gradsko (Stobi),[3] and branched from there up the Bregalnitsa valley to Štip, up the Axius valley to Skopje and the Kačanik pass, and via Prilep into the Pelagonian plain and thence via Monastir to the Ochrid basin. At the end of the sixth century the growing towns of Derriopus and the royal house of the Pelagones were the immediate neighbours of the rulers of Trebenishte to the west and of the Paeonian kings to the east.

Two tumuli from a group of ten have been excavated at Orlova Čuka on the southern side of the Bregalnitsa valley above Štip.[4] One of them had a peribolos, consisting of a loose stone wall, 0·80 m wide, and it contained five burials (some in cists of slabs, and others bounded by rough stones), which were aligned towards the larger central burial, roughly rectangular but with apsidal ends. These tumuli resemble some at Ayios Pandeleëmon in Eordaea and those at Visoï in Pelagonia both in the manner of burial and in the objects with the dead.[5] The latest burial was just before or just after 600, so that we may date to the turn of the century the withdrawal of Illyrian control and the advance of the

[1] *Starinar* 21 (1970) 139 f. and Pl. 1 for the late-sixth-century tombs.

[2] For the 'North-western Geometric style' see Volume 1. 281 f.; Mikulčić ibid.; D. Vučković-Todorović, 'La Céramique grecque et hellénistique dans l'est de la Yougoslavie', *Rev. Arch.* 1973. 1. 39 f.; *Starinar* 15–16 (1966) 220.

[3] A black-figured vase in the Titov Veles Museum is said to have come from Doiran (*Rev. Arch.* 1973. 1. 40); bronzes of the archaic period were found in the vicinity of Stobi (J. Wiseman, *Stobi: a Guide to the Excavations*); Ionian goods came via the Danube to northern Yugoslavia (*AI* 6. 14 f.).

[4] I. Mikulčić in *Zbornik na Arheol. muzej* (Skopje) 2 (1960–1); R. Pasić-Vinčić in *Starinar* 21 (1970) 129 f.

[5] Objects illustrated in *Starinar* 21 Pls. III–IV are an iron sword with a haft, fragments of bronze hair-coil (as in Volume 1 fig. 17 a), a bronze two-springed fibula with catch-plate (ibid. fig. 18 j), a biconical bronze bead, a bronze cap-button, and an ear-ring of silver, which suggests that the local silver ore at Kratovo was being mined. For Visoï see Volume 1. 336 f.

Paeonians, who established their capital probably at Astibus (Štip). We do not know whether a city existed at Astibus before the end of the sixth century. Yet the strength of the Paeonian kingdom and the use of city-centres in the basins of the Axius and the Strymon suggest that the magnificent oxen of the Derrones belonged to agricultural communities and that towns were developing in the Bregalnitsa valley, as in Pelagonia.

Some remarkable burial groups at Karaorman near Štip, dated to the late sixth century and the fifth century by I. Mikulčić in *Starinar* 13 (1962) 197 f., were probably those of Paeonian kings or at least resembled those of Paeonian kings, because sacrifice was made for decades after the interment of the dead. For each group walls of large stones, rising to 1·10 m and one block thick, marked off an area of e.g. 5·00×4·60 m, within which there were rough graves surrounded by loose stones and containing incinerated remains. At a subsequent date a rectangular enclosure, consisting of well-built walls of squared masonry and measuring e.g. 8·40×8·20 m, was constructed round the original walls of large stones. The graves themselves were covered with masses of loose stones, in which the remains of many vases used in sacrifice were found, and the later enclosure walls were banked on the outer side with gravel, in which the remains of vases used in sacrifice were also found. Offerings included double-shanked pins, fibulae of Blinkenberg's class XII, beads of amber and of coloured glass, an ornamental plaque, and a silver coin attributable to Doki(?mos).

The cantons of Lyncus, Orestis, and Elimea have yielded practically nothing of this period, although Keramopoullos and other Greek scholars explored the areas and made small excavations. The explanation is that western Macedonia was a backwater, in which the primitive conditions of pastoral life continued as they had done since late in the Bronze Age; for a strong and probably hostile power held Eordaea and cut the interior off from the main route into the central plain of Lower Macedonia, and the main artery of trade ran east of the lower Axius and then through Pelagonia to Ochrid. The latest burials in the great cemetery at Ayios Pandeleëmon (Pateli) in Eordaea may well have fallen in the sixth century;[1] at any rate we have argued on other grounds that it was *c.* 520–510 that the Macedones exterminated or drove out the Eordi and their rulers, who had been powerful for several centuries and were so idiosyncratic in their burial practices. Even after this date, when settlements such as that at Pharangi were made, Eordaea has yielded nothing of archaeological interest for the decades down to 480.

The one exception is at Kozani, where a group of six graves has been excavated.[2] Two gold bracelets, ending in snake's heads, and a silver phiale are typical of the latter part of the sixth century, and a bronze

[1] See Volume I. 340 f., 344 n. 2, and 369.   [2] *AE* 1948/9 85 f.

dress-pin is probably of that period; it seems that these remain from burials which were earlier than the other contents of the graves. The silver phiale has an inscription in archaic letters ΑΘΑΝΑΙΑΣ ΙΑΡΑ ΤΑΣ ΜhΕΓΑΡΟΙ, and it has been held that it had travelled from Megara in the Peloponnese to Kozani (? as loot, with the original inscription undeleted, or in the hands of a refugee).[1] Another explanation is possible; for A. S. Arvanitopoulos reported an inscription including the word ΜΕΓΑΡΟΙΣ on a stone in the old Turkish cemetery at Dortali, midway between Kozani and Verria, and it is evident that the Macedonian Megara by a river (Plu. *Pyrrh.* 2. 2–3) was situated somewhere by the river Tripotamos.[2] Was the phiale dedicated to a local Athena and was the owner a devotee of a local Athena? The Kozani museum has a black-figured alabastron, dating late in the archaic period.[3]

There are two routes from western Macedonia to the coastal plain, one from Kozani over the pass of Zoödokos Pege to Verria,[4] and the other from Lake Ostrovo to Edessa (the route of the Via Egnatia). When the Eordi controlled the latter, any traffic between Lyncus–Orestis–Elimea and the Macedones followed the former route, and this was particularly convenient when the centre of the kingdom was at Vergina–Palatitsa. The only black-figured pottery of our period in the plain west of the Axius has been found just north of Verria in some tile-covered graves of the late archaic period and at Vergina–Palatitsa where some stray finds included four fine black-figured vases of *c.* 500, clearly imported.[5] At that time the head of the Thermaic Gulf was as on Map 15 of Volume I; the Greek cities Methone and Pydna were on the coast to the south and Alorus, a Macedonian town, was on the westernmost side of the Gulf (probably in Hecataeus' terms),[6] being by the delta of the Haliacmon, which may have been navigable for some way inland. Aegeae, at Vergina–Palatitsa, held a strong position on the routes from these ports leading inland.

More important than any of these in the Paeonian period of power was Ichnae, to which Pella was ancillary; for Ichnae issued silver coinage, controlled the passage of timber by the Axius to the Gulf, and held the ford over the Axius which was used by traffic between west and east

---

[1] Kallipolitis cites a similar dedication in *IG* VII. 35 and A. Wilhelm, *ÖJ* 2 (1899) 240 n. 51 of the period *c.* 500–475; and the hoard of bronze vessels, including one with an inscription referring to probably Heracles at Thespiae in Boeotia, which was found at Voutonosi (*Epirus* 440), would provide a parallel for a sixth-century piece from the south surviving to a late date in the north.

[2] *PAE* 1912. 241. St. Byz. gives several towns called Megara but not one in Macedonia. As I mentioned in *Epirus* 809, the Megara in Molossis is different from the Megara in Macedonia.

[3] *AD* 17 (1961–2) 2. 216, Pl. 256 b.   [4] See Volume I. 158–9.

[5] *Mak.* 2 (1940–50) 39; *AD* 17 (1961–2) 218, Pl. 262, 3–4. For other imported pieces at Vergina see *AD* 25 (1970) B 2. 386.

[6] See Volume I. 133; the source of the phrase in Str. 7 fr. 20 is probably Hecataeus.

Macedonia. Pella, Ichnae and Amydon were Paeonian cities before they were acquired *c.* 510–505 by the Macedones, who raised Pella to importance, because it was closer to their homeland, and destroyed Amydon, which was on the east bank of the river (Str. 7 fr. 20 fin.).[1] It is uncertain whether the 'archaic megaron' at Pella reported in *AJA* 77 (1973) was built in the Paeonian or the Macedonian period of the city. When the Macedones gained possession of the head of the Thermaic Gulf as far east as the valley of Anthemus, they controlled the natural outlet for the trade of the Axius catchment area; but it is doubtful whether good relations existed between the Paeonians of the immediate hinterland and the Macedones, and there are signs that the Derrones and other Paeonian tribes preferred to bypass the Macedones and send their silver to the ports of the Strymon basin.

There were many cities at the head of the Thermaic Gulf and on its east coast: Chalastra, Sindus, Therme, Aenea, the cities of Crousis known to Hecataeus and Herodotus, and the Greek colonies from Potidaea onwards. The character of the area was very different from that of the Macedonian homeland and that of Lyncus–Orestis–Elimea. Commerce and coinage attracted Greek settlers and adventurers, and there was a large import of Greek goods in this and earlier periods. Therme, a Greek city by Mikro Karaburnu, was a leading port, as excavations have shown, and gold jewellery and fine pottery from graves at Nea Sillata in southernmost Crousis give an indication of the prosperity of this area in the archaic period.[2] Traffic went both ways. For the painter Brygus came to Athens from Macedonia, and the representation of Aeneas escaping from Troy on a coin of Aenea was inspired by a painting on a vase at Athens, or vice versa (G. 20, V. 33). An archaic marble *kouros* has been found at Europus (*Mak.* 9 (1969) 179). The Greek cities of Chalcidice too flourished at this time, as we can see from the distribution of the coins of Potidaea and Acanthus, for example, and in the interior Lete was a city of importance and the Paeonians had developed many cities in the Strymon basin. The coast of the Strymonic Gulf was perhaps even more attractive to Greek adventurers than the delta of the Axius, because its riches were better developed and the Gulf had its inner seaway.[3] During the period of Persian domination the area of the southern Strymon was one of the richest areas in the satrapy.

[1] See Volume I. 176 f.

[2] *Epitymbion Tsounta* (1941) 358 f.; *Antike Kunst*, Beiheft 1 (1963) 30 f.; and *AD* 19 (1964) 1. 84 f.

[3] Imported Greek pottery has been found in considerable quantities near Aëdhonokhori = Tragilus (*AD* 24. B. 2. 355; sixth-century Corinthian); at Berge (*AD* 22. B. 2. 425; fifth century); at Hill 133, north of Amphipolis (Geometric, Subgeometric, Archaic, Attic BF and RF; *PAE* 1964. 37 and *Ergon* 1965. 28); and further east at Kalamitsa = Antisara (*PAE* 1935. 29 f.; *AD* 25. B 2. 397), Kavalla = Neapolis (*PAE* 1937. 59 f.; *AE* 1938. 106 f.), and N. Karvale = Acontisma (*AD* 22. B 2. 420 f.; sub-Geometric and Attic BF).

III

THE EVENTS OF 479 TO 399 AND
THE INSTITUTIONS OF MACEDON

1. *Alexander Extends and Defends his Kingdom, 479–452*

HERODOTUS tells us that he visited the mines on Thasos, and it was presumably on this visit that he learnt of Thasos and the Phoenicians having colonized the island first (6. 47. 1). It is probable that he made a trip by sea as far as Lake Prasias, touching at Eïon and Nine Ways; for it is only of these places that he adds the vivid details which suggest seeing and hearing things on the spot: Boges throwing all the gold and silver of Eïon from the walls into the Strymon (7. 107. 2), Xerxes sailing off from Eïon in a Strymonian blizzard and his Persian chiefs doing obeisance before they jumped into the sea (8. 119–20),[1] the resources of near-by Myrcinus and the fate there later of Aristagoras (5. 23 and 126), and the pile-settlement on Lake Prasias, described with the vivid details of an eye-witness (5. 16, e.g. little children tied by the ankle lest they fall in, and native words for two kinds of fish).[2] On the other hand, nothing suggests a visit by him to the head of the Thermaic Gulf or to coastal Macedonia; indeed it is clear that Herodotus drew directly upon Hecataeus for his description of Crousis and western Mygdonia (see Volume I. 146 and 188 f.).

There can be little doubt that Herodotus met Alexander, whether at Eïon or in Greece. There are stories which Alexander himself is likely to have told him: the challenge to Alexander at the Olympic Games and its sequel (5. 22), the assassination of the Persian envoys by Alexander and six other striplings (5. 19–21, especially the point that it was Alexander and not Amyntas who tricked the second lot of envoys, although the latter was still king at 5. 94. 1), the secret message to the Greeks at Tempe (7. 173. 3), the Boeotian cities saved by Alexander sending Macedonians south (8. 34),[3] the details of Alexander's relations in Persia (8. 136. 1), Alexander's citation of the Great King's orders to

---

[1] Even Herodotus rejected this absurd story, which he surely heard at Eïon.

[2] Another later episode in this area which Herodotus mentions at 9. 75 was the death of Sophanes at Datum, in 465.

[3] The purpose of this operation is not clear in Herodotus. The appointments to control certain Boeotian towns must have been made in the first place by Xerxes or a Persian officer, and not by Alexander whose contingent of Macedonian troops rated very low.

Mardonius, Mardonius' orders to Alexander, and Alexander's own advice to the Athenians (8. 140), Alexander's visit at the dead of night to the Greek lines, and his speech to the Athenian generals at Plataea (9. 44–5, attached to a non-event). The picture of Alexander is always flattering: he is innocent of evil (5. 19), clever (5. 21), a good and loyal counsellor (7. 173. 3), a benefactor of Athens (8. 136. 1 and 140 b 1), concerned for Greece and eager for liberation himself (9. 45). If I am correct in supposing that Alexander was the informant, we can see that Alexander charmed Herodotus into accepting his versions of how Perdiccas won the Macedonian throne (8. 137–9), how Alexander killed and tricked the Persian officials at the Macedonian court—surely unhistorical as Macedonia was favoured by Persia thereafter—and how Alexander's heroic words and acts were in the interest of the Greeks.

As we have argued above, there is no ground for supposing that Macedon ever rebelled and broke away from Persia and was subsequently reduced by Mardonius (as is implied in Hdt. 6. 44. 1); for Persia gave short shrift to rebels, and Xerxes would not have extended the realm of Alexander (Just. 7. 4. 1), if Alexander had been a rebel. The truth lies rather with Justin: 'cognatio Bubaris . . . Darei . . . temporibus pacem praestitit.' This is not to deny the ability of Alexander. He played a double game with great skill, serving Persians and Greeks alike, acquiring credit with the Persian command and with the medizing Boeotians, and at the same time keeping contact with the Greeks and in particular with the Athenians. Whichever side won, he stood to gain. When Persia failed, Alexander seems not entirely to have lost favour with them; for his relations in Persian territory were specially favoured.

The entry of Persia into Europe was a blessing for the kingdom of the Macedones. Darius' destruction of Paeonian power and Amyntas' ready submission made it possible for Macedon to expand beyond the Axius and acquire Anthemus; the royal house made contacts with the outside world, and the country obtained trade from both Persia and Greece; and Xerxes helped Alexander to acquire control of Upper Macedonia. The kingdom was much enlarged territorially by 480. But it had small resources; for it issued no coinage, its produce alone was insufficient to feed the Persian army on its march (7. 25. 2), and its troops were treated as light-armed skirmishers like the upland Thessalians (9. 31. 5; compare the Thessalians proper in a preceding sentence). There is no mention of Macedonian cavalry in the account of Herodotus. But when Persia withdrew, Alexander filled the gap, conquering and annexing Crestonia, Bisaltia,[1] Mygdonia, and the Strymon basin as far as and including Nine Ways. Taking over the Bisaltic mines of silver and

---

[1] Here too Alexander may have been helped by some recent Persian action; for the king of the Bisaltae rebelled and fled. On his return he blinded his own sons (Hdt. 8. 116).

gold, he coined for the first time and surpassed his Balkan neighbours in the amount of his coinage.

Persia opened up the overland communications of Macedonia. It is clear that Xerxes was extending the royal-road system into northern Greece during his campaign. His three army columns, marching between Doriscus and Acanthus one on the coast, another inland, and the third further inland (7. 121), were not only building a main road on a scale which impressed the Thracians (7. 115. 3) but also clearing subsidiary routes. Some of the work had been done in the preceding years; for the Strymon had been bridged at Nine Ways (7. 114. 1) and dumps of supplies had been laid down at various points on the coast, particularly at Eïon and 'in Macedonia' (7. 25. 2). The main route was that which Xerxes usually took. As the details were discussed in Volume I, it is sufficient to show this route on Map 4, together with the subsidiary land-routes and the voyage of the fleet.

Herodotus himself writes in a confused manner, which indicates his lack of geographical knowledge. For instance, he makes Xerxes march from Acanthus via 'Paionike' and 'Crestonike' to Therme; but he seems to have regarded this as a 'short' route (5. 17. 2 and 7. 121. 1, a passage which appears to have a lacuna). At this point in the advance there were three routes: Acanthus–Olynthus–Aenea–Therme for the army accompanying the fleet, Argilus–Apollonia–Therme for the central force, and Siris–Lake Prasias–Upper Echedorus–Strepsa–Therme for the column furthest inland. As Herodotus tells us, Xerxes accompanied the last column in this instance; thus he and his entourage made a long detour, as they started from Acanthus.[1] The road-building was undertaken by the troops, who felled trees and laid a track for wheeled vehicles. Thus when it was decided not to use the narrow defile of Tempe as the main route but to go over the shoulder of the Pierian range into Perrhaebia, this being the 'safest' route (7. 128. 1), one-third of the entire army felled trees on a line through 'the Macedonian mountain' and prepared a road for immediate use. This took 'many days' (7. 131).[2]

The Persians recruited troops from their subjects as they advanced. Xerxes' army included infantry from the Thracians, Paeones, Eordi, Bottiaei, Chalcidians, Brygi, Pieres, Macedones, Perrhaebi, Aenianes,

---

[1] In point of fact Xerxes took the longest route from Acanthus, the shortest being the second one. But if he had started from Philippi, the route via Lake Prasias and Stena Dov Tepe (see Volume I. 194) would have led him directly into upper Amphaxitis.

[2] There was room for little more than a pack-horse in the narrowest part of the Tempe pass in the time of Polybius (see Volume I. 134 n. 2). The road for Xerxes was built through the Petra pass (Volume I. 123 and Map 12). Geyer 46, followed by Gomme (Volume I. 430 n. 2), misunderstood the situation; he proposed to send an army up the Haliacmon—'den Haliakmon aufwärts'—and so into Elimea and over the Volustana pass into Perrhaebia; this long detour would begin with the Haliacmon gorge which is impassable for an army, as I know, having walked through it.

Dolopes, Magnetes, Achaei, and inhabitants of coastal Thrace—all being *ethne* (Hdt. 7. 185. 2). This list is not in geographical order, because the Bottiaei of Olynthus, for instance (8. 127), lay west of the Pieres, who lived to the south of Mt. Pangaeum (7. 112). The Eordi were evidently those in Mygdonia near Physca (Thuc. 2. 99. 5), and the Brygi those who had been reduced by Mardonius (Hdt. 6. 45). Some of these peoples figured in the army of Mardonius at Plataea: the Macedones were arrayed with 'the dwellers round Thessaly' (Perrhaebi, Aenianes, Dolopes, Magnetes, Achaei—all light-armed skirmishers), and a motley force included Paeones, Thracians, and 'the rest', whoever they were (Hdt. 9. 31–2). For the first time the Macedones and their neighbours had the experience of entering Greece, and in the case of some leading Macedones of being concerned with the administration of Greek cities in Boeotia (Hdt. 8. 34).

When the Persian armies retreated, there was no sign of any attack by the Macedones, at least in the account of Herodotus.[1] Xerxes' own force was escorted to the Hellespont by 60,000 men under Artabazus (8. 126). On his return Artabazus destroyed the Bottiaei of Olynthus, who had revolted from Xerxes; he handed the city over to the Chalcidians. Potidaea, which had also revolted, survived a siege of three months (8. 129). Meanwhile Mardonius and the main army wintered in Thessaly and Macedonia (8. 126. 2). The account of Xerxes' flight which Aeschylus gave in the *Persae* was impressionistic; one event in it which presumably did take place was the loss to the army at Nine Ways when the ice on the Strymon collapsed through the act of the river god (*Persae* 495 f.). In 479, when Artabazus at the head of 40,000 men withdrew after the defeat at Plataea, 'he marched his army rapidly through Thessaly and Macedonia straight for Thrace, being really in haste and taking the inland route of the journey' (9. 66. 2; 70. 5; 89. 4) that was through 'Paionike' and Siris;[2] and he lost many men to attacks by the Thracians (9. 89. 4). There is no mention of Alexander attacking either Xerxes or Artabazus; indeed his own forces would have been entirely inadequate for the purpose. If he was given the name 'Philhellene',[3] it was due to his warnings to the Greeks rather than to any damage he did to Persia during Xerxes' invasion, and his particular services to Athens earned him certain privileges but probably not Athenian citizenship immediately after the campaigns of Plataea and Mycale.[4]

---

[1] *Pace* Geyer 45 'nach dem Siege hat er allem Anschein nach durch sein Land zurückziehenden Persern nach Kräften Abbruch getan'.

[2] τὴν μεσογαίαν τάμνων τῆς ὁδοῦ, the same phrase as at 7. 124.

[3] All the evidence for this epithet is late. I am inclined to think that it came into use to distinguish Alexander from his greater successor of the same name; it was in fact a characteristic of the Hellenistic period to add an epithet to homonymous kings. See Harp. s.v. *Alexandros*; Schol. Thuc. 1. 57. 2; Dio Chrys. 2. 23; D.H. *De D. dict.* 26; Bekker *Anecd. Gr.* 375. 19; Schol. D. *Oly.* 3. 35. 7 (Dind.). Cloché 37 regarded the epithet as contemporary.

[4] He was *proxenus* and *euergetes* of Athens already before 480. The *ateleia* of [D.] 13. 24 and

Alexander and the Chalcidians gained most from the withdrawal of Persia. Their gains were primarily at the expense of the Thracians (Str. 7 fr. 11); for Alexander reduced the Thracians of Mygdonia and the western Strymon basin. The Chalcidians overran the Sithones in the central peninsula and they were given Olynthus, a most important site facing Potidaea. At some point Alexander attacked the Persians, because he dedicated gold statues of himself at Delphi and at Olympia (Herodotus referring only to the former) as a 'firstfruit of spoils from captive Medes'.[1] The so-called Letter of Philip ([D.] 12. 21) alone connects the dedication of the statue with Alexander being the first to seize the region where Amphipolis was founded later, and this Letter, whether genuine or not, seems to have been based on sound information. Alexander's capture of Nine Ways would then precede the siege of Boges at Eïon by the Athenians under Cimon (Hdt. 7. 107); for if the Persians had held Nine Ways, they would have come to the relief of Boges. Thus I put Alexander's capture of Nine Ways between 478 and the Attic year 476/5, within which year Cimon captured Eïon from the Persians and an Athenian force suffered losses from the Thracians further inland.[2]

These two events—the capture of Nine Ways by Alexander and the capture of Eïon by Athens—were rival attempts to control the exit of the Strymon basin. Thenceforth Alexander and Athens were certainly at enmity, and later in the 470s when Themistocles was on the run from Athens and Sparta Alexander gave him sanctuary at Pydna, a Greek town then held by him (Thuc. 1. 137. 1; Plu. *Them.* 25. 2). In the eyes of the Macedones Athens replaced Persia as a threat to the liberty of their country. Moreover, Athens was likely to be more harmful, if she should gain control, because her aim was to seize capital resources and carry off slaves, as the nearby Thracians knew only too well. In 465, when Athens landed 10,000 'colonists' in the region of Nine Ways, Alexander

the *politeia* of D. 23. 200 refer to 479 or later. These two passages form part of a long commonplace; both have the same mistake, naming Perdiccas instead of Alexander, and both have the same wording, except that D. 23. 200 omits ἀπὸ τῆς ἥττης. I do not consider the timing to be dependable, and I distrust the catch phrase 'completing the disaster for the Great King' as an absurd exaggeration. If Alexander had done so, Herodotus would not have passed it over in silence. After 479 it was not easy to gain honours for Alexander; his visit to Athens as the emissary of Mardonius had aroused some suspicion, although Lyc. *C. Leocr.* 71 exaggerates, and his seizure of Nine Ways soon after 479 did not recommend him to the Athenians. A grant of citizenship is unlikely, as no other writer refers to it, although such citizenship would have been of topical interest in the time of Philip and Alexander.

[1] Hdt. 7. 121. 2 ὁ Μακεδὼν Ἀλέξανδρος ὁ χρύσεος. The words of the so-called Letter of Philip, [D.] 12. 21, τῶν αἰχμαλώτων Μήδων ἀπαρχήν, probably echo the words of the dedication. It is clear from Plu. *Cimon* 7. 1–2 that the Persian headquarters was situated in this area, and Alexander's prisoners may have included 'kinsmen of the King', for whom a high ransom was obtainable.

[2] Schol. Aeschin. 2. 31 (Dodson p. 97, 6) dates the capture to the archonship of Phaedon = 476/5 (D.S. 11. 48); Plu. *Cimon* 7; D.S. 11. 60. 2 (in a condensed narrative under a later year).

no longer held the site, which was in the hands of the Edoni (Thuc. 1. 100. 3); and all the attacks the Athenians and their collaborators made inland were against the Thracians and in particular against the Edones, who destroyed them at Drabescus.[1] But the Athenian plan was also to 'cut off a large part of Macedonian territory'; for Cimon, the Athenian general in charge of operations, was prosecuted in 462 for failing to do so, the charge being that he had been bribed by Alexander.[2] One objective was no doubt the Bisaltic mines. At that time there may still have been Persian forces at Doriscus; and it was significant of the attitude of the Balkan tribes that the coastal Thracians at least supported the Persians against the Athenians.[3]

Alexander had close contacts at one time or another not only with Athens and Sparta but also with the medizing states in Boeotia and with Argos, where his own family had originated. When he dedicated the statue of himself at Olympia, he is likely to have visited Argos. It was probably in agreement with Argos that he gave a home in Macedonia in 468 to the bulk of the people of Mycenae, when they were forced by Argos and her allies to capitulate (Paus. 7. 25. 6). Pindar wrote an ode in his honour, perhaps *c.* 490, and addressed him as 'bold-scheming son of Amyntas'; he is said to have visited the court of Alexander, who encouraged lyric writers and gave lavish entertainment (Solin. 9. 13). There was certainly an air of heroic, perhaps barbaric, splendour about Alexander's dedications to Apollo and Zeus of statues of himself in gold, if we compare them with the bronze statue of Zeus and the golden tripod on a bronze serpent which the victorious Greek states dedicated after the battle of Plataea (Paus. 5. 23. 1; 10. 13. 9). These must have been among the earliest portrait sculptures at any Greek shrine. Alexander certainly deserved the place of distinction which Thucydides gave him in the creation of the greater Macedonian kingdom by singling him out among the predecessors of Perdiccas (2. 99. 3). He was the first example of a brilliant 'Greek ruling Macedonians' (ἀνὴρ Ἕλλην Μακεδόνων ὕπαρχος), who was able to extend his Macedonian realm and to benefit the Greek world of city-states.

The date of Alexander's death, whether by assassination or in war,[4] is uncertain. We have to reckon back from the accession of Archelaus between 414 and 411 (Thuc. 7. 9. 1; D.S. 13. 49. 1), say in 413, because Syncellus p. 494 and p. 500 allotted him a reign of 14 years and he died in 400/399 (D.S. 14. 37. 6). Now Athenaeus (5. 217 e) has preserved variants for the length of the reign of Perdiccas, son of Alexander and father of Archelaus: 41 years according to Nicomedes of Acanthus =

---

[1] Thuc. 1. 100. 3; 4. 102; Hdt. 9. 75; D.S. 11. 70. 5; 12. 68. 2; Paus. 1. 29. 4.
[2] Plu. *Cimon* 14. 2.   [3] e.g. Plu. *Cimon* 7. 2 and 14. 1; for Doriscus see Hdt. 7. 106.
[4] Curt. 6. 11. 26 in the speech of Philotas.

FGrH 772 F 2 (also 41 in the Marmor Parium = 239 A 58), 40 Anaximenes = 72 F 27, 35 Theopompus = 115 F 279, 28 Hieronymus = 154 F 1, 23 both Marsyas = 135/6 F 15 and Philochorus = 328 F 126. It is clear that there were two ways of reckoning the length of Perdiccas' reign, the longer in the time of Philip II and shorter ones in the time of Alexander (Hieronymus of Cardia and Marsyas Macedon,[1] followed by Philochorus). If we drop Theopompus out of the count as a headstrong individualist,[2] we have for the first way *c.* 452 to *c.* 413 being 40 years on inclusive reckoning and for the second way *c.* 435 to *c.* 413 being 23 years on inclusive reckoning (one chronographic tradition also giving 23 years, and another 28 years).[3] The best explanation of the period *c.* 452 to *c.* 435 (or to *c.* 440 if we prefer Hieronymus) is that the throne was divided or disputed between the sons of Alexander in the opinion of the Alexander historians. In any case the death of Alexander should be put *c.* 452.

This date is compatible with the giving in marriage of a daughter of Alexander, Stratonice, to Seuthes in 429 (Thuc. 2. 101. 6); for she should not have been beyond her middle twenties. Herodotus too could have met Alexander before 452 and included Alexander's colourful stories in the recital which he gave at Athens probably in 445. Taking the year of Alexander's death as 452, we can adopt the 44 or 43 years given by the late chronographers (based presumably on dates given by historians of Philip II) as the length of his reign. He ascended the throne then *c.* 495. This is compatible with the date we advanced when we worked forward from Amyntas (p. 60 above).

2. *The Coinage of Alexander and other Balkan Kings*
(See Plates I and II)

On the interpretation which I have given above (p. 84) the first coinage of Alexander was issued late in the winter of 479/8 when he took over the Bisaltic mines of gold and silver. He was now able to dedicate two gold statues of himself, and as he drew a talent of silver a day from a mine by

---

[1] Rather than Marsyas of Philippi, who was not a 'Macedon' and was concerned more with local history (see p. 37 above).

[2] Beloch, *GG*[2] 3. 2. 53, was equally headstrong; emending Anaximenes' number to 30, he put the death of Alexander at 440, a year which fits Hieronymus alone among the sources as transmitted and one chronographic source. It seems a better method to accept the earlier tradition as seen in writers of Philip's reign—Anaximenes, Nicomedes, and with a personal aberration Theopompus—and to suppose a revision by Alexander historians which may reflect contemporary conditions.

[3] These traditions are listed conveniently in Beloch, *GG*[2] 3. 2. 50. As they are derived from Marsyas, Philochorus and Hieronymus respectively, they have no independent authority, but they do show that the text of Athenaeus is not corrupt for these entries.

Lake Prasias (Hdt. 5. 17. 2), he emulated the Bisaltae in minting large coins as a form of bullion silver. In her special study, *Macedonian Regal Coinage*, Raymond has overthrown the views of Gaebler in many respects,[1] but her own conclusions are not devoid of improbabilities. I give first a summary of the three Groups into which she has divided the coinage of Alexander, but I have grafted on to the first Group a few transitional coins which she had referred to her pre-Groups era, i.e. pre-480/79 on her chronology (R. 52). Group I then has the following issues (R. 78–85).

1. Bisaltic goat coins with ΛΑ replacing ⟨, being staters of series A (9·82 gr).

2. Bisaltic goat diobols with the addition of ΛΑ, being of series B (1·09 gr).

3. Bisaltic Rhesus coins (walking horse and man alongside, holding two spears), with ΑΛΕΞΑΝΔΡΟ (G. 153, xxviii. 2) replacing ΒΙΣΑΛΤΙΚΟΝ (G. 48, xii. 2; cf. 208, xii. 11) on the reverse; they are triple staters of series A = octadrachms of series C (both being 29·46 gr).

4. Bisaltic Rhesus octobols with ⟨ occurring only once on a horse's crupper, and then ΑΛΕΞΑΝΔΡΟ on the reverse took its place (G. 49 no. 8 and 153 n. 32); being of series B (4·36 gr).

5. A new obverse, showing a mounted man with two spears, and a reverse of Bisaltic type, with ΑΛΕΞΑΝΔΡΟ replacing ΒΙΣΑΛΤΙΚΟΝ. These coins are triple staters of series A = octadrachms of series C (both being 29·46 gr).

6. The new obverse but a new reverse, being either a goat's head or a crested helmet in an incuse square; they are tetradrachms of series C (14·73 gr).

7. The new obverse but a different new reverse, being the forepart or head of a lion in an incuse square; being tetrobols of series C (2·45 gr).

8. A different new type of obverse, showing a horse unattended, and reverses as in 6. Of these one carries the letters ΛΑ. They are tetrobols, some apparently of series B and others of series C (2·18 and 2·45 gr respectively).

We can see that in this first period Alexander was moving towards the adoption of a new weight series, 'C', not used hitherto in the Thraco-Macedonian coinages. 'C' included within itself the triple stater of series A as an octadrachm, which was now the largest piece coined for bullion exchange. Raymond (p. 97) has explained that one purpose of some of Alexander's weight systems was ease of trade with Athens. Thus Alexander's tetradrachms of series B were exchangeable with

---

[1] For instance, R. disagrees with G. 148, who held that the octadrachms and the tetradrachms were issued only in the latter part of Alexander's reign. The fact that some are found in hoards supports R. against G.

Attic tetradrachms at four to three, and the light tetrobols of series B with Attic triobols. On the other hand the octadrachms of series C, not being readily exchangeable with any Greek coinage, were no doubt intended for a non-Greek market. A tetrobol of series C together with a tetradrachm of series B equalled a Chian–Rhodian tetradrachm (15·52 gr); perhaps he hoped to reach the bullion market in Asia and Egypt via Chios and Rhodes. He tried out some new types of his own (5–8). Raymond (p. 99) attributes some obols with a horse's head to this period, but it is not possible to decide to which series of weights they belong.

Her Group II has the following issues. Octadrachms continue as in 3, being of series C. Tetradrachms change to series B (13·09 gr) and otherwise continue as in 6, except that the goat's head alone is used on the reverse. Rhesus octobols continue as in 4, being of series B (4·36 gr). There are two classes of tetrobols: one, carrying the letter A, is predominantly of series B (2·18 gr) but a few coins seem to be of series C (2·45 gr; e.g. R. 105, 82b, 85, and 86a); the other, carrying the letter H, is entirely of series B. The earlier devices which do not appear in this period are the Bisaltic kneeling goat and the forepart or head of a lion. The change in the weight of the tetradrachm eased exchange with Athens by making it equal to three Attic drachms (R. 109); but as he did not issue many tetrobols of series C, there was little trade with Chios and Rhodes. The artistic level of the engraving was higher than in the preceding period. There were a few small coins down to the obol, but they are not clearly assignable to a specific series (R. 123 f.).

Her Group III has four main issues. Of these three portray the mounted man with two spears: octadrachms as in 3, tetradrachms as in the preceding period, and heavier tetrobols of series C. The forepart of a lion—absent from the preceding period—was reintroduced on the reverse of these tetrobols. On the fourth issue, light tetrobols of series B, the same devices were used as in the preceding period, except that the crested helmet lacked a nose piece. Neither issue of tetrobols carried any inscription. The rider was often accompanied by a dog, perhaps a Molossian hound, on the larger coins, and the caduceus appeared quite frequently, sometimes on the horse's crupper. There were again a few small coins, not assignable to any series. Raymond noted a marked deterioration in the engraving of the light tetrobols of series B, which in her opinion continued to be coined when the other issues had been suspended.

The dates which Raymond gives for her Groups are 480/79–477/6, 476/5–*c.* 460, and *c.* 460–451. The distribution of coins over these periods may be expressed as follows (she herself did not make this analysis):

	Octadrachms	Tetradrachms	Octobols	Tetrobols B	Tetrobols C	Totals	Anvil dies
Group I 480/79–477/6	6	26	—	22	21	75	38
Group II 476/5–*c.* 460	15	18	24	44	—	101	50
Group III *c.* 460–451	4	13	—	9	7	33	21
Totals	25	57	24	75	28	209	109

The surprising feature of this distribution is that more than one-third of all the anvil dies of the whole twenty-seven years of minting were produced within the two and a half years of Group I (since it was started in fact in 478). Or to put it in another way, if Alexander had coined at the same rate after 476 as he had done in 478 to 476, he would have completed his production by 471. Thus the chronological equation which Raymond gave to her Groups seems to be unacceptable. The odds are rather that the output of the mines was regular, as Herodotus implied (5. 17. 2), and so was the output of his coins, as long as he was in possession of the mines. I shall propose a redistribution later.

The next oddity is that Raymond has two series of light tetrobols, in her Group II, one with A on the coins and the other with H on the coins, both of B weight and both having the same devices on both obverse and reverse. Why this change of letter? There are other peculiar features about the H series (R. 107 nos. 96–107, IX). No other Alexander coin has an H, or a horse of such slight short-barrelled build (as R. 114 remarks), or a crested helmet of the odd kind appearing on one H coin (R. 113 nos. 107, IX), or such poor technique, especially when the technique of the A series of the same Group is the most advanced (compare R. IX with R. VIII). These peculiarities can be explained only by concluding that series H is not Macedonian at all.[1]

That H stands for HΔONEON, the tribal name on the coins of Getas, for instance, is an obvious and perhaps obviously correct suggestion. We have already attributed the goose coins to the Edones on other grounds, and two of them had H upon them (G. 140. 41 and *Arch. Anz.* 1967. 76 no. 71); these are the only instances of H being used except on the H series of light tetrobols. The Edones were the immediate neighbours of Alexander, and they were very powerful in 464 when they destroyed the Athenian

[1] Gaebler 151 and others have given the coins to Alexander without comment or question. Giesecke, *HBNum* 3 (1949), attributed the A coins to Alcetas, brother of Perdiccas, but the position of Alcetas is uncertain.

force at Drabescus. That there were ebbs and flows of war between Macedones and Edones is almost certain, if we think of other periods of their history, and in some years after 464 it is likely enough that the Edones captured and held for a time the silver mine by Lake Prasias. They then produced coins of the locally known types but of inferior workmanship, and carrying H instead of A. A nice thing is that we have two antithetic instances: an A appears on a goose diobol,[1] which we have attributed on other grounds to the Edones, and an A appears on a few Silenus and Nymph coins, which were minted usually by Thracians of the Strymon basin (S. 98, 21, x. 27). Alexander had his moment of triumph too, when he captured and held—but for a short time only within 467–460, when he used this abbreviation most—the gold and silver mines of the Edones near Datum, i.e. by Akhladhokhori, and perhaps some Thracian mines on Mt. Pangaeum.

The situation on the coast of the Strymon basin was overshadowed by the power of Athens from 476/5 until 460, when she turned her attention towards the Peloponnese and Egypt. The years of greatest pressure were 465 to 461. It seems probable that the Edones engaged in war with Alexander after 461 rather than before 461. I should then suggest the following chronological arrangement for Alexander's coins, from which the fifteen coins of the H series have been withdrawn.

SUMMARY OF CONCLUSIONS ON THE COINAGE OF ALEXANDER I

Device	Goat	Goat	Rhesus	Rhesus	Mounted	Mounted	Mounted	Mounted	Horse
Denomination	Stater	Diobol	3-stater	Octobol	Octadr.	Tetradr.	Tetradr.	Tetrobol	Tetrobol
Weight series	A	B	A+C	B	A+C	C	B	C	B(some C)
Transition 478–476	+	+	+	+					
Group I 475–468					+	+		+	+
Group II 467–460				+	+		+		+
Group III 459–452					+	+		+	+

The number of coins which have survived from these Groups of equal duration are from I to III respectively 75, 86, and 33 (a total of 194, apart from small pieces not here taken into account). The figure for Group III expresses the decline when the Edones held the Lake Prasias mine and issued their version of the popular horse tetrobol. After the period of transition Alexander favoured in Group I the C series of weights, which implies a trade with many states and not predominantly Athens, i.e. from 475 to 468. After the battle of the Eurymedon c. 467 the trade of Athens and her Allies dominated the Aegean and in particular from 465 to 461 large forces of Athens and her Allies provided a demand in the area. During this period Alexander concentrated in Group II on the B series of weights, which facilitated trade with Athens. In the last

---

[1] G. 140 no. 38, xxvii. 19; he does not comment on the significance of the letter.

period, when the presence of Athens and her Allies near Thasos was no longer so strong a factor, he turned back in Group III to series C. In all periods the octadrachm was intended for a non-Greek market. It should not be taken into the consideration of his policies when one looks at the changes in weight.

In the transitional period Alexander recorded himself as the issuing agent of the coins in the form ΛA, being retrograde for the first two letters of his name, on staters and diobols. In Group I he put AΛEΞANΔPO (not retrograde), a genitive, round the incuse square (as the Bisaltae had put their name), but only on octadrachms; one tetrobol of series C has AΛEΞANΔPO, and five tetrobols of series B have ΛA, which places them closest to the transitional period. In Group II AΛEΞANΔPO occurs again on all octadrachms and octobols, round the incuse square in each case, and A appears for the first time as an abbreviation on some tetradrachms and on more than half of the tetrobols. In Group III AΛEΞANΔPO occurs again on all octadrachms but nowhere else; A and AΛE occur on the reverse of two tetradrachms; and the tetrobols have no letters at all. Octadrachms, being for a non-Greek market, had to have the full name throughout, no doubt as a recognizable feature of authenticity. His practice as regards abbreviation was consistent within Group I and Group II, different as between Group I and Group II, and inconsistent and very rare within Group III. No other letter occurs, what looks like a Φ being probably a religious emblem (G. 149 no. 8, a diobol).

The preferred device of Alexander was the mounted man with two spears, sitting with his knees high and well forward on a long-barrelled and relatively large horse, these features being more noticeable in Groups II and III than in Group I. He was not armed for war; he wore a soft hat (*kausia*), and his spears were presumably for hunting. Coins of Groups II and III come closer than those of Group I to consistency and portraiture. I infer that the man is Alexander himself, who did not scruple to dedicate statues of his own person to the gods of Delphi and Olympia. Clean shaven, he wears a cloak (*chlamys*), a flat, wide-brimmed hat, and a band (comparable with a diadem) with its ends hanging behind his neck (G. 152 no. 30, XXVIII. 4 with the caduceus on the horse's crupper). The large horse, so important for the cavalryman, was specially bred in Macedonia, probably from Persian stock,[1] which had been evolved to carry a heavy-armed cuirassier. It is itself, running free, the favoured device of the lighter tetrobol.

The Rhesus device which Alexander resumed in Group II was of religious significance and local importance. The devices on the reverse of his coins were probably also of religious significance: the head of

---

[1] The famous Nesaean horses of Hdt. 7. 40. 2; 9. 20; Arr. *An.* 7. 13. 1. For the band on the *kausia* see Athen. 12. 536 a and 537 e, and Franke, op. cit. 108.

a goat, which had led the founder to Aegeae and was a mascot in war; the crested helmet, associated evidently with a Macedonian god of war; and the forepart of a lion, associated with Heracles, an ancestor of the royal house. The crested helmet was not peculiar to Macedon; it featured on coins of the Derrones (G. 56 nos. 5–7 and 208 nos. 15–16), the Laeaei (S. III. 7 and 9), Bastares (G. 147 no. 16), and Doki[?mos] (G. 144 nos. 2–7), and we may infer that it was associated with the local god or goddess of war, as the helmets of Athens and Corinth were in the Greek states. The helmet itself was of a distinctive, presumably local type.

Lesser emblems were the frog, certainly worshipped in prehistoric times, which was represented also on a goose tetrobol, here attributed tentatively to the Edones (R. 78 no. 4 = G. 152 no. 29 and G. 139 no. 33); the vine or ivy leaf, both sacred to Dionysus and both found on coins of Acanthus (R. 81 no. 15, G. 149 no. 7, 25 no. 20, 26 no. 24), while the ivy leaf figured also on a goose coin and a Mosses coin (G. 140 no. 41, 146 no. 7; a bunch of grapes on a Mosses coin, S. 115, 5); the caduceus, associated with a local god, who was equated with Hermes by the Greeks, found occasionally on coins of the Bisaltae and Neapolis (G. 49 no. 7 and 82 no. 18); the waning moon, connected with the cult of Artemis, found also on a coin of the —naei and one of Mende (R. 101 nos. 54–7, being octadrachms; G. 74. 14, 133. 3);[1] and a hound, represented also on a coin of Ichnae which was re-struck by Litas (G. 66 no. 12) and on an unattributed coin showing Pegasus (G. 116 no. 4).

Thus we may conclude that the devices and the lesser emblems on Alexander's coinage were overwhelmingly of religious significance. Many of them were not prerogatives of the Macedones alone but came from cults which were widespread among the tribes of the Thraco-Macedonian area. On the other hand, if the mounted man with two spears was a portrayal of Alexander I, it was without parallel; but then so was the dedication of two golden statues of the king by the king. Yet the portrayal was not purely secular. Alexander the king represented the state, and both king and state were set within a religious aura.

Turning to the coinages of other kings, we may note a point to which Raymond drew attention, namely that the slanting-barred alpha was displaced by the straight-barred alpha 'shortly after 479' (R. 118). If this is correct in general, our conclusions so far conform with such a chronological distinction. The coins of Aenea (overweight), Ichnae,

---

[1] Raymond 120 comments on the waning moon as follows. 'This I take to be Alexander's way of making known his sentiments to the Athenians, who were at Thasos conducting a siege. It was the symbol they had used to mark their defeat of the Persians, interlopers into their world. Alexander used their own symbol to mark their defeat (at Drabescus) as interlopers into his world.' This interpretation, like others she has advanced, seems to me too far-fetched to be credible. Franke 109 f. disagrees with R. and thinks the moon means a close tie with Athens.

Lete, Bisaltae, Stagirus, and —naei have the slanting-barred alpha; the coins of Getas have some the slanting-barred and some the straight-barred alpha and one has examples of both;[1] and Alexander's coins in the transitional period *c.* 478–476 have some one and some the other. On the other hand, almost all the coins of Groups I–III have only the straight-barred variety, the exceptions being on a set of five tetrobols in Group I (R. 84 no. 38). In fact, then, both forms of alpha were in use *c.* 478 to *c.* 470; the slanting-barred alpha may have been distinctive of the pre-480 period; and the straight-barred alpha was characteristic of the period after *c.* 470. Thus the coins of the Zaieleis, having the straight-barred alpha, may be dated in or after the 470s. We conclude that the Pangaean tribes were issuing coins with Centaur and Nymph as on the Zaieleis coins, and also with Silenus and Nymph which were so very popular (the so-called 'Lete' coins) after 480 for some decades.

Coins of *Bastares*, inscribed with the straight-barred alpha, carry the devices of a crested helmet and a tossing bull (G. 147). Erratic in weight, they may be tetradrachms of series B, which were in fashion with Alexander *c.* 467–460. As the crested helmet was associated early with the Paeonian tribes—Derrones and Laeaei—as one of the Bastares coins was found at Kjustendil in Laeaean territory, and as a town Basteira was in Thrace, we may regard Bastares as king of the Laeaei, exploiting the gold and silver mines of Kjustendil with a *floruit c.* 465. The tetrobols and diobols of *Doki*[?*mos*], being of series C in weight, have the devices of the kneeling ox and the crested helmet (G. 144 f.). The kneeling ox is very close in style to that on tetrobols of the Derrones (G. 57 nos. 8 and 9), especially with the flower above (compare G. xxvii. 26 and 34). We may then regard him as a king of the Derrones, exploiting the gold and silver mines of Kratovo, in the period after 480, and this is supported by the discovery of one of his coins in a burial at Karaorman near Štip (see p. 95 above). The coins of *Mosses* do not conform to any of the weight series we have mentioned (3·96 to 3·48 gr; G. 145 f.). His devices are a warrior with two spears beside a horse, i.e. the Rhesus type of Bisaltic coins, and his name runs round the outside of a quadripartite incuse square, which is later in style than the incuse square of Alexander's coins. His name may well be related to the place 'Mossynon of Thrace' where cattle were fed on fish (Athen. 8. 345 e), namely on or by Lake Prasias in Bisaltia where cattle were so fed (Hdt. 5. 16. 4).[2] It seems

---

[1] When she made her conclusion about the straight-barred alpha, she did not mention the example of it on a goat coin (G. 20 no. 16). The distinction is not hard and fast; for, as Dr. Price has pointed out, Abdera used a straight-barred alpha on a coin to be dated *c.* 490 at the latest.

[2] The word 'mossynoi' was used to describe wooden houses in northern Asia Minor (Schol. Ap. Rh. 2. 379); it may have been the term for the wooden houses on piles in Lake Prasias. See W. Tomaschek, *Thraker* 2. 2. 67.

then that Mosses held the Bisaltic mines, probably after the **death** of Alexander, and presumably as an independent Bisaltic king and not a vassal king as Franke 106 n. 53 suggested. An octobol, probably of series B, has the name *Demetrios* above an unattended horse and on the reverse a woman's head; Gaebler dated the coin to the latest years of Alexander or to the time of his successor (G. 146), and the dull-spirited horse resembles one on the H tetrobols, which we ascribed to the Edones (G. xxxvi. 20 and R. ix. 100). Perhaps Demetrios was a king of the Edones overlapping with Perdiccas II.

On the coast of the Thermaic Gulf a single tetrobol of Aenea with a straight-barred alpha was ascribed to *c.* 450 by Gaebler, and the incuse square is certainly of the same type as that of Mosses' coins (compare G. v. 37 and xxvii. 41). Potidaea continued to issue tetradrachms, tetrobols, and diobols showing Poseidon Hippios (G. 103 f.), as she had done before 480. Capsa in Crousis issued tetrobols which have the device of Mende, an ithyphallic donkey, and in addition used the very die which served Mende also (G. 66 and 74 no. 9). Scithae, in the vicinity of Nea Sillata, where rich burials of the archaic period have been found, issued didrachms and tetrobols of series C with a lion and the forepart of a lion as its devices (G. 110). Sermylia, mentioned by Hecataeus (*FGrH* 1 F 151), situated at the head of the Toronaic Gulf, issued tetradrachms, didrachms, and tetrobols with an armed rider brandishing a spear; they are not of any of the series of weights which we have mentioned. One of the tetradrachms was overstruck on a coin of Mende (G. 107 note to no. 1), and the incuse square of another resembles very closely that on a coin of Scithae (G. 107 note to no. 3).

Inscriptions on the coins of Capsa, Scithae, and Sermylia have the slanting-barred alpha only, so that they may be dated provisionally *c.* 478–476 and earlier. The explanation of this group, unique and short-lived as it was, is that the cities lay on the route of the Persian fleet and of the accompanying army in 480. Mende in particular was glad to provide the expertise and perhaps some of the silver to Capsa and Sermylia, because she herself was less well placed to tap this moving market. Scithae was perhaps the outlet of the Bottiaei on this route, because its near neighbour Olynthus was a Bottiaean city until early in 479; it alone used weights current in the Thraco-Macedonian area. Of the Chalcidian cities Mende, Scione, and Torone continued to issue their own coinages throughout this period. On the east side of Chalcidice Acanthus continued to coin freely and apparently forced Stagirus out of the field; when it added its name in full to its coins, 'after 480' according to Desneux, it used the straight-barred alpha. It was the place where Xerxes' coastal army and his fleet met in 480.

There are a number of unattributed coinages of this period, as of the preceding one. One issue, dated *c.* 500 by Gaebler, was attributed with a question-mark to Therme. As the Macedonian king held this part of Mygdonia from *c.* 510 onwards, the attribution can be confidently discarded; for there is no doubt that he had a monopoly of coining within his realm. There are other reasons too for rejecting the attribution. The weights of the tetradrachms do not conform with any of the weight series used either by Alexander or in the Thraco-Macedonian area generally; on the other hand the tetrobols and obols seem to be of series C, which came into use after the date suggested by Gaebler. The style is far inferior to that of the earliest coins of Alexander; and the Pegasus is not of the Greek type which we find on coins of Corinthian colonies but wears harness of an unusual kind (G. XXVI. 23, 27, 30). However, the connection of this walking Pegasus with its furled wings is clearly with the coins of the Laeaei which showed such a Pegasus on the reverse (see p. 79 above, and compare G. XXV. 19 and XXVI. 21). Then again the awkward Pegasus with its forelegs almost striking its muzzle on the tetrobols (G. XXVI. 25) resembles the awkward horse on the tetrobols which we have attributed to the Edones (G. XXVIII. 35). We may, then, with some confidence assign the Pegasus coins to the Laeaei and date them on both sides of 480. The lesser devices were a palmette common to the Derrones, an acanthus flower common to the Derrones, Ichnaei, Orrescii, and Sermylaei, and a hound common to the Ichnaei and others. These are compatible with the attribution of the coinage to the Laeaei, a Paeonian tribe.

The Persian occupation which had imposed peace and provided opportunity for economic growth for a generation did not end abruptly but tapered off gradually east of the Strymon. A period of wars and some economic decline followed. Small cities, such as Capsa, Scithae, and Sermylia ceased coining in the late 470s. The Chalcidians conquered the Thracians in Sithonia, Alexander overran Crestonia, Bisaltia, and Mygdonia and captured the Persian garrison at Nine Ways. Athens captured Eïon and gave an example of her methods in warfare by killing all males and enslaving the women and children, as she did soon afterwards at Scyros (Thuc. 1. 98. 1–2). The power of Thasos extended beyond Philippi on the mainland, but Thracian tribes, including the Zaieleis, still worked the mines of Pangaeum in the decades after 480. The Edones, who had lost ground to Alexander and to Athens, recovered in the 460s and inflicted a severe defeat on Athens and her supporters at Drabescus in 464; but Athens still succeeded in subjugating Thasos and acquiring her mines on the mainland.

These events were reflected to some extent in the coinage. The mines at Damastium seem to have traded with Epidamnus and Apollonia, when the eastern market for silver bullion became inaccessible. The mines at Kratovo and other places in Paeonia were exploited by a king of the Derrones, Doki(?mos), in the decades after 480, and those of Kjustendil by the Laeaei and then by Bastares, one of their kings, who was active probably until 450 or so. It is probable that they exported their silver and produce through the ports of the Thermaic gulf in the kingdom of Alexander, because a number of the crude Pegasus coins which we have attributed to the Laeaei were found in the region of Salonica (S. 120 f.). The mines at Theodoraki near Lake Prasias supplied the silver for Alexander's fine coinage, but it is probable that he lost them to the Edones for some years after *c.* 460. The Strymon basin was the scene of much fighting between Athenians, Macedones, and Edones. The ruler of the last was Getas in the years before and after 470, but it is possible that he had no immediate successor; for the coins of the 450s carried the first letter of the tribal name only, at a time when the mines at Theodoraki were in the hands of the Edones. The mines at Akhla-dhokhori, near the ancient Datum, were in the possession of the Edones, who thwarted the attempt of Athens to acquire them. Finally Thracian tribes worked the mines of Mt. Pangaeum, and those near Philippi were under the control first of Thasos and then of Athens.

In this troubled period Alexander's Macedon was the strongest state on the Thraco-Macedonian mainland, keeping control of the Axius basin and the head of the Thermaic Gulf, and capable of resisting the Chalcidians, the Edones, and the Athenians, who had designs upon his possessions. He probably established trading relations with the kings of the Derrones and the Laeaei, offering them access to the Aegean Sea through his ports, and he deliberately orientated his own trade towards Athens in the years *c.* 467–460, when her forces were operating in his vicinity. Whereas the power of Persia had been of economic assistance to this area, that of Athens was damaging, because the aim of the Athenian people was to cause disunity among the Balkan tribes and 'cut off' pro-fitable areas, especially those with mineral resources and ship-building timber. In the 450s the kingdom of Alexander declined in strength, and the loss of the Bisaltic mines to the Edones for some years was a serious blow to its economy.

Alexander emerges as the first personality in the history of Macedon. A fine athlete, physically strong and nimble, daring in hunting and in war, a strong and enterprising leader of his people, the creator of an enlarged kingdom, a man of Greek outlook and Panhellenic spirit when it suited his book, he was a worthy forerunner in many respects of Philip and Alexander. But the bulk of his people led a pastoral life and the economy of the country was primitive, as compared with that of a city-state such as Athens. The excellence of his cavalry, to which his coins are indirectly a testimony, and the lack of heavy-armed infantry show that the organization of society in Macedonia was still at the feudal stage when he died a violent death *c.* 452.

3. *The Events of the Reign of Perdiccas c. 452–413*

The death of Alexander by violence, whether through assassination or in war,[1] was followed by a period of weakness during which the kingdom was divided within itself and territories were lost. As we have seen, the hypothesis which best explains the discrepant traditions about the length of Perdiccas' reign is that his throne was insecure and disputed from *c.* 452 to *c.* 435 but fully recognized thereafter until his death *c.* 413. Other evidence supports this interpretation. Of his four brothers Philip had a principality of some kind which included the strategically important district of Amphaxitis (Thuc. 2. 100. 3, and Volume I. 169 f.), and Alcetas too had one of which Perdiccas 'deprived' him (Pl. *Gorg.* 471 b). It is probable that they were older than Perdiccas and staked their claim on the fact. As Alexander died unexpectedly, it is most unlikely that he had suggested a division of the kingdom before his death, and we must suppose that it came about through dissension between the brothers and a decision by the Macedonian assembly.[2] The Bisaltic mine by Lake Prasias had been lost for a time and then regained by Alexander, probably in the 450s, and after his death Bisaltia itself was lost to Mosses, who set himself up as an independent king. To the east the Edones, whose king was probably named Demetrios, held the Strymon basin, and in central Thrace a greater power than Alexander's Macedon arose in the form of the Odrysian kingdom, founded by Teres in the 440s.[3] The dissension in the Macedonian kingdom was probably exploited by the principalities of Upper Macedonia, which *c.* 483–481 had been brought firmly within Alexander's realm but after his death were often independent and only nominally 'allied' to Macedon.

Athens too was a formidable power in the 440s. Her hand rested securely on the eastern side of the outer Thermaic Gulf. 'The citizens of Dicaea, colonists of the Eretrians'—as distinct from those 'by Abdera'—

---

[1] Curt. 6. 11. 26 (speech of Philotas), implies that the deaths of Alexander, Archelaus and Perdiccas III were avenged. As Archelaus was murdered and Perdiccas was killed in battle, we can say only that Alexander died a violent death.

[2] Syncellus p. 500 (Dind.) adds that Amyntas lived throughout as a private person; there is no evidence either way about Menelaus. They may be mentioned in Ael. *VH* 2. 41 and 12. 43. Abel 167 and Droysen, *Hellenismus* I. 1². 71 f. have speculated on the ages of the brothers and possible principalities; there is no firm evidence as Geyer 51 points out.

[3] As Sitalces was at the height of his power *c.* 429, Teres *floruit c.* 460. As Herodotus mentions the Odrysians as one among other Thracian tribes (4. 92), through whose territory Darius marched, and as he emphasized the divisiveness of the Thracian tribes (5. 3), Teres cannot have formed the greater kingdom until after 450.

appear on the earliest surviving record of the Tribute Lists, being assessed in 453 to pay 4 talents. The neighbouring city, Aenea, does not appear in this list. However, in 434 Dicaea paid 1 talent and Aenea 3 talents. It is therefore most probable that Dicaea and Aenea were assessed together in 453 for 4 talents, the entry being in the name of the former as she had become a member of the Athenian Alliance earlier; for her mother city, Eretria, having fought as an ally of Athens in 490, is likely to have joined the Alliance in 477 and carried her colonies with her. Aenea was presumably an early member, whether willingly or perforce, because she occupied so strategic a position on the coast at Megalo Karaburnu.[1] The small cities on the coast of Crousis—Smila, Gigonus, and Haisa—and 'Kithas' between Crousis and Potidaea (see Volume 1. 189) appeared on the list of 433 for the sum of 3,000 drachmae, being in the category of states proposed by individuals (as restored by the editors of *ATL*). There is no evidence that they had been members earlier, but it is in itself probable. Potidaea was assessed regularly for 6 talents from 444 (perhaps from 445) until 432, when 15 talents was entered. Potidaea was no doubt an early member of the Alliance, having survived the Persian siege in the winter of 480/79, but she may have ceased to pay at some time in the First Peloponnesian War, when her mother city was at war with Athens. The states of Chalcidice, extending on the east to Acanthus and Stagirus, paid a large sum in total. All these cities probably joined in the 470s.

The entries Στρεψαῖοι and Σερμαῖοι need special consideration. The former were assessed for 1 talent in 453, 449, 445, 443/2, and 435–432, and similar entries for some intervening years have been plausibly restored by the editors of *ATL*. In 446 Strepsa was assessed for 5 talents, when it was apparently paying on behalf of Aenea and Dicaea, which do not figure on this—an imperfect—list but regularly paid 3 talents and 1 talent. If so, the three cities were not far apart. As we argued in Volume 1. 183 f., Strepsa should be identified with Inglis (now Ankhialos), which was close to the coast or on the coast in the fifth century and probably lay by the navigable mouth of the river Gallikos (Echedorus).[2] The people of Serme were assessed for 500 drachmae in 449, 447, 444/3, 439, and 434–431. The city then was tiny, comparable to Aeoleion, the lowest contributor in Chalcidice, which also paid 500 drachmae. The editors of *ATL*, followed most recently by R. Meiggs, have proposed to

---

[1] So too *ATL* 4. 221, but not including Dicaea among the original members. For the site see Volume 1. 186 f. and C. F. Edson, 'Notes on the Thracian Phoros', *CP* 42 (1947) 88 f., and *ATL* 2. 84 and 3. 318 n. 73, accepting his view on Mt. Cissus (see Volume 1. 189 n. 2).

[2] Gomme 1. 217 argued against an identification with any place north of Therme, and Edson, op. cit. 105 n. 125, recorded his support of Gomme; *ATL* 3. 220 n. 122, 318 n. 76 maintains its earlier view that Strepsa was north of Therme. H. B. Mattingly in *CQ* 16 (1966) 178 put it east of the head of the Thermaic Gulf.

identify Serme with Therme.[1] Now that an English-speaker should confuse Serme and Therme may be plausible; but it is unacceptable for a Greek stone-cutter or rather a series of stone-cutters, for whom Therme had an everyday meaning whereas Serme had none. Moreover, Therme gave its name to the Thermaic Gulf, well known to Athenians and called not the Sermaic Gulf but 'the Thermaic Gulf' in *IG* i². 302. 68. Nor was there any aversion to writing 'Thermaioi'; it occurred on the Tribute Lists for the people of Therme in Icaros. Nor would 500 drachmae have been enough for Athens to have taken from Therme as a large— probably the largest—port on the Gulf (Hdt. 7. 121. 1 and 124. 1). Let us keep Σερμαῖοι at its face value and place Serme among the numerous small cities in Chalcidice.[2]

On the eastward side of Chalcidice Argilus appeared on the list of 453 with an entry 'implying a payment of 10½ talents' which was amended by the editors of *ATL* to one of 1½ talents, because it paid 1 talent in 445–442 and 437. Next, Berge appeared on the list of 451 for 2,880 drachmae, 446 for 3,240 drachmae, and again 434, 432, and 431 for 3,120 drachmae. Berge was situated 'among the Bisaltae as you sail up the river Strymon, being a village distant from Amphipolis by some 200 stades' (Str. 7 fr. 36); thus the seaway led some 25 miles inland to Berge, which was on the west side of the river in Bisaltia.[3] As Amphipolis was not founded until 437/6, the Athenians had a remarkable success in bringing Berge into the Alliance by 451 at the latest. Her success becomes more understandable when we note that Athens sent 1,000 settlers 'to live with Bisaltae' (Plu. *Pericles* 11. 5). At that time, in 451 at the latest according to the Tribute Lists, whether the settlers were at or near Berge, the Bisaltae were an independent people, as the wording of Plutarch implies, and as we have argued from the coinage of Mosses and other considerations. Indeed, it was precisely because the Bisaltae were independent and no doubt were threatened by the Macedones on one side and the Edones on the other, that they welcomed the support of Athenian settlers and let Berge enter the Athenian Alliance.

The supposition of *ATL* that the mason made an error in the tribute of Argilus and that the error went for ever uncorrected, X being erroneously cut for H, is almost a counsel of despair; for one is dealing not with a transmitted text or a private document but a state record of financial

---

[1] *ATL* 4. 220 n. 123 resisting the arguments of Gomme 1. 214 and Edson, op. cit. 100 f., that Serme is not Therme; R. Meiggs, *The Athenian Empire* (1972) 49 and Map I (III), although neither Serme nor Therme figures in his Index to the Tribute Tables.

[2] For the colonization of this area see *HG*² 116. Edson, op. cit. 92 f., argued eloquently against associating the Haisonioi with the river Aeson in Pieria, and Gomme 214 thought *ATL*'s placing of the Haesonioi 'quite uncertain'. Meiggs follows *ATL* on his Map I (III).

[3] For its position see also Edson, op. cit. 94 f., where he reports the occurrence of the 'Bergaoi' in an inscription recording a pentapolis, which included Sirrae, Gazorus, and Berge. He thought of the Bisaltae as being subject to the king of Macedon, 'their suzerain'.

details which must have been checked.[1] I take the 10½ talents to be
correct. Now if Argilus entered the Athenian Alliance before Berge did,
which is consistent with the evidence of the Tribute Lists, Argilus
obtained from Athens the opportunity to export overseas the produce
of the western side of the Strymon basin and in particular the gold and
the silver bullion from the Bisaltic mines; or to put it more bluntly
Argilus had to pay a heavy price for freedom to export into the Athenian
mare clausum. The next step of Athens was to obtain a footing inland at
Berge but still on the seaway, and in addition to plant a settlement with
the Bisaltae in order to secure her interests.[2] No doubt the land for the
1,000 settlers was not bought by Athens, but its value was offset against
the tribute payable by two centres of export, Argilus and Berge; in
consequence Argilus paid only 1 talent in 445 and Berge 3,240 drachmae
in 446. It is possible too that the ownership of the Bisaltic mines changed
hands between 453 and 446/5.

Another problem is presented by the name *ḥαισονες* or *Αἰσόνιοι*,
appearing also in abbreviated form. The authors of *ATL* connected the
word with the small river Aeson in Pieria, but there is no indication that
the river-name was also a place-name, such a coincidence being extremely
rare. The place *Αἶσα* in Crousis offers a better connection; for while the
Haesonioi could not be citizens of Haesa, they could well be inhabitants
of a region Haison of which Haesa was a synoecized centre. If this is so,
we find the Haesonioi paying tribute of 1,500 drachmae from 450
onwards, and their exposed position on the open, gently shelving coast
between Aenea and Potidaea makes it very likely that they had been
members from the early days of the Alliance. On the other hand, the
region of the river Aeson offers no harbour for a sea power until you
reach either Pydna or Methone to the north, and Athens obtained access
to only the latter and then only later, c. 431; it is inconceivable that
Athens controlled a plain so central to the Macedonian kingdom without
having a port at her disposal.[3] I conclude then that the Haesonioi were
the people of Crousis in the vicinity of Haesa; that they paid as a group
before and after 450; and that in 433–431 they appeared as sponsored
by individuals but as cities, namely Haesa, Gigonus, and Smila,[4] if we
accept the editors' proposal for a lacuna.

---

[1] Meiggs, op. cit. 159 n. 3, 'this is not a natural mistake for the cutter to make', puts the
matter too mildly.

[2] The cleruchy of Brea was separate from the joint settlement of Bisaltae and Athenians
(cf. *HG*² 313; *contra* Gomme 1. 373 and Meiggs, ibid.). Thurii also, mentioned in the same
sentence in Plu. *Pericles* 11. 5, was not a cleruchy but a joint settlement.

[3] See the arguments too of Edson, op. cit. 92 f., supported by H. B. Mattingly in *CQ*
16 (1966) 184. 'Haisonioi' in the full list of 443/2, so that one should not enter 'absent'
against the individual cities, as in Meiggs, op. cit. 548. I have not included the highly conjectural entry in *ATL* 1 A 10 v 41 [πολε]s [Κροσσι]δος; it does not clash with my views, if it
is accepted.   [4] Not including Kithae, which lay outside Crousis; see Volume 1. 189 n. 2.

To summarize our deductions, Athens and her Allies enrolled no members from the coast west of the river Axius before *c.* 431. They did enroll Strepsa, assessed for 1 talent in 453 and probably in years before 453, but not Therme. This is very striking, because Strepsa occupied a strategic position both on the main trade routes and on military communications, and Athens can have acquired and kept the alliance with Strepsa only by reaching a *modus vivendi* with the king of Macedon. This was no doubt accomplished by threat of *force majeure*; for Athens could use her seapower to raid shipping, intercept trade, make men slaves, and destroy cities by slaughtering and enslaving as she had done at Eïon, and it may have suited Alexander and his successors to safeguard their own trade and their own coast by letting Strepsa enter the Athenian Alliance and pay tribute. However, they kept Therme within their own hands. The position could be expressed, as it was in [D.] 7. 12 by an Athenian writer (cf. [D.] 11. 16 and Arr. *An.* 7. 9. 4), 'Macedonia was under us, and they paid us tribute, and there was more mutual trade between us then than now' or more aggressively by Demosthenes himself, 'the king of this land was subject to us, as a barbarian should be to Greeks' (3. 24).

Similar arrangements were made by Athens in 453–451, first with Argilus and then with Berge, but behind them in fact with the power in control of the rich mines of gold and silver, perhaps Alexander in 453 and after that Mosses, an independent king of the Bisaltae, who permitted a joint settlement of Athenians and Bisaltae to be formed. The coastal cities between Aenea on the west and Stagirus on the east were probably from early days members of the Alliance, which then offered them many advantages. The position in the Strymon basin was altered by the founding of Amphipolis at Nine Ways, from which the Edones were expelled in 436, and the recruiting of a large population to defend this strongly walled city in its position of great natural strength. The Athenian element was very small, and there were settlers from near-by Argilus, who later betrayed the place to Brasidas (Thuc. 4. 102–3). The possessor of Amphipolis was thenceforth able to control the egress of all trade from the lower Strymon basin by sea and the passage of armies and goods along the land route between coastal Thrace and coastal Macedonia.

The coinage of Perdiccas (see Plate II) shows that he was short of silver ore; for he struck nothing larger than a tetrobol—'an almost incredible performance', as Raymond remarks; and indeed it would be if he had had control of the Bisaltic mines throughout his reign. Early in his reign at least he obtained his silver rather by trade with the Paeonians and the Atintani. Raymond has arranged in four series the tetrobols of weight B, which facilitated trade with Athens; in her chronology they covered the years *c.* 452–434 and then *c.* 415–413. The tetrobols of weight C which aimed for trade elsewhere were issued in the period 445 to 424. There was no coinage at all between 424 and 415. The only years in which both heavy and light tetrobols were coined, according to R.'s classification and chronology, were 445/4 to 435/4. We may deduce with confidence that Perdiccas did not control the Bisaltic mines from (*very approximately*) 452 to 445—at which time we suggested on other grounds that they were being exploited by Mosses—and from 434/3 to 415. On the other hand he may have owned the mines from 445/4 to 435/4; and this may account for the absence of Berge from the Tribute List of 443/2. If so, he coined in smaller denominations than Mosses had done. I say *very approximately* because, although the series are fixed by linking dies and the excavations at Olynthus afford some control for the later period, the actual years are fluid.

Although Alexander had put his name in full or in abbreviation on most of his coins, the first occurrences of any name thereafter were *c.* 438/7 on tetrobols of weight C, namely ΠΕΡ and Π (R. 142 no. 194 and no. 216). This is understandable because, as we argued on other grounds, Perdiccas did not come into full recognition as king until *c.* 435, and it was only then that he was able to put his royal mark on the coinage. He employed ΠΕΡΔΙΚ on coins of the latest period only. During Alexander's last years the coinage had been mainly of weight C, but after his death the coinage switched to weight B, which aimed at trade with Athens and continued so until *c.* 434; but meanwhile from *c.* 445 onwards coins of weight C were issued also, so that the realm looked for trade also outside the Athenian orbit. The break with Athens was complete from *c.* 434 to *c.* 424. The devices were inherited: horse unattended / helmet in incuse square, and mounted man with two spears / forepart of a lion. Additional emblems until *c.* 415 were added only on the tetrobols and one obol of weight C (letters of Perdiccas' name, a flowering plant, a dog, a plant without a flower, and a caduceus), and being traditional within the Thraco-Macedonian area they were designed to encourage local trade with the Balkan tribes.[1] Fractional pieces of weight B showed an unattended horse / quadripartite incuse square, the same / forepart of a lion with ΠΕΡ (these being dated within 443/2–432/1 by R. 164), head of Heracles / bow and club with ΠΕΡ, and horse galloping / forepart of a boar, club, and ΠΕΡ (R. 163 f., xi d–g; G 154, I. 21, and xxix. 9).

Although R. claims that coins with the last two devices 'must have been struck near the end of Perdiccas' life, when he was striking only light tetrobols', viz. R.'s 415–413, it should be noted that the abbreviation on these coins is ΠΕΡ and on the last tetrobols it is always ΠΕΡΔΙΚ.

---

[1] R. 140, xiv–xv; G. 153 f., xxviii–xxix. The mounted man is not the same as that on Alexander's coins and may represent Perdiccas; it is only on tetrobols of weight C.

Moreover, the stress on the connection between the royal house, Heracles, and Argos was particularly in place during the Peace of Nicias, when it became politically effective (Thuc. 5. 80. 2 and 83. 4). I prefer to place them in 417/16.[1] His worst years were perhaps in 416/15, when at least one tetrobol was of copper plated with silver, and the reference to a Perdiccas using such coins when he was making war may well have applied to Perdiccas' last war against Athens (Polyaen. 4. 102, see p. 133 below).[2]

The drachmae issued after 452 by Mosses as king of the Bisaltae have one point in common with the earliest tetrobols of weight C of Perdiccas, namely the petasus worn low on the nape of the neck; as these tetrobols were issued c. 445/4–438/7, we may assume either that there was an overlap between Mosses and Perdiccas at that time, or that on taking over the Bisaltic mines from Mosses c. 445/4 Perdiccas continued to use this happy feature.[3] The octobol of Demetrios, whom we have tentatively identified as a king of the Edones, was issued early in the period of Perdiccas and followed on after the octobols with H for 'Edoneon'.[4] Coins of 3·95 to 3·43 gr showing a kneeling Silenus and Nymph / incuse square, typical of the Thracian issues based originally on Lete, were issued by Thracians of the Strymon basin for some decades after 480. One of these coins has the inscription ΒΕΡΓΑΙ on the obverse, and four others have ΒΕΡΓΑΙΟΥ on the reverse (S. 99 f., x. 32); they correspond probably to the two periods when Berge appeared on the Tribute Lists, i.e. c. 451 and c. 434–431. If Berge was in fact a mixed settlement of Athenians and Bisaltae ΒΕΡΓΑΙΟΥ may be explained as Βεργαίου συνοικισμοῦ. Another city west of the Strymon, which issued silver coins of small denominations c. 450–400 (G. 131, XXIV. 32–9), was Traïlos which evidently had access to the gold mines at Nigrita; but it managed to stay outside the Athenian Alliance until 425/4.[5]

The attitude of Macedon to Athens was inevitably one of suspicion and fear. When the Euboeans came to terms 'by agreement' with Athens in 446 (Thuc. 1. 114. 3), one article in the agreement was evidently that the people of Hestiaea be given safe conduct to Macedonia (*FGrH* 115 = Theopompus F 387).[6] There, as refugees bitterly hostile to Athens, they

---

[1] See p. 133 below.

[2] So R. 154 no. 16: 'there is no way of knowing the reason for his lack of silver; perhaps his enemies got possession of his source of supply in the interior.'

[3] As pointed out by R. 155 n. 17; she assumes that Mosses' coins were earlier, which would support my second suggestion.

[4] G. 146 n. to no. 14 remarked that the horse resembled in style the horse on the H tetrobol, his. XXVIII 34.

[5] Both Berge and Tragilos appear in St. Byz. as 'near the Cherronesus', which was the term used by Hecataeus for the peninsula of Chalcidice. They were native cities of Bisaltic people c. 500. The inscription on the coins of the latter is ΤΡΑΙ or ΤΡΑΙΛΙΟΝ.

[6] Thucydides and Theopompus mention ὁμολογία and ὁμολογίαι respectively, referring

were resettled by Perdiccas[1] and became his loyal subjects. Soon after this Perdiccas seems to have regained possession of the Bisaltic silver mine by Lake Prasias; this was no doubt resented by Athens which had her mixed settlement not far off at Berge. At the same time Perdiccas was adept at playing both friend and enemy towards his powerful neighbour; for probably in the period *c.* 452–446, when his coins show the closest trade relations, he was 'ally and friend' to Athens, terms which imply a formal decree by the Athenian demos (Thuc. 1. 57. 3). The event which caused widespread alarm was the establishment of the Athenian settlement at Amphipolis in 436; for it was a very powerful base, dominating an area rich in ship-timber, minerals, and cereals, from which attacks could be launched against neighbouring peoples, whether Thracian, Macedonian, or Chalcidian. He lost control of the Bisaltic silver mine soon afterwards, no doubt to Athens and her settlement at Berge, and he ceased to issue coins suitable for trade with Athens *c.* 434.

Certainly in late 434 he was at war with Athens, which had made an alliance with his enemies, Philip (his brother) and Derdas, king of Elimea (Thuc. 1. 57. 3). A fragment of such an alliance with Philip, probably the very one, survives in *IG* 1². 53. Athens and her Allies undertake to become the enemies of anyone attacking the territory of Philip and to abstain from harbouring pirates or engaging themselves in plundering or campaigning together with Philip's enemies against Philip or against his allies.[2] As Philip's realm was Amphaxitis at least (Thuc. 2. 100. 3) and the inscription shows he had access to the sea, i.e. at the head of the Thermaic Gulf, we can see that Perdiccas was in danger of being driven back into the original homeland. He countered in 432 by encouraging Sparta to start a general war against Athens, Corinth to bring Potidaea into revolt from Athens, and the Chalcidians and the Bottiaeans of Bottice to join together in revolting from Athens (Thuc. 1. 57). Meanwhile the Athenians acted, sending thirty ships and 1,000 hoplites in early summer 432 to Macedonia, where in collusion with the forces of Derdas and Philip they captured Therme and probably the surrounding territory in order to cut Perdiccas off from Chalcidice, where trouble had already started. For Potidaea, the Chalcidians and the Bottiaeans had risen in concert with Perdiccas, who had persuaded

doubtless to the recorded terms which 'stretched the Euboeans on the rack'; the Hestiaeans had killed the crew of an Athenian ship (see *HG*² 313). Geyer 53 no. 1, 'καθ' ὁμολογίας bezieht sich natürlich nicht auf Athen', has a different interpretation, apparently supposing 'the agreements' to have been between Perdiccas and the Hestiaeans, which is not a point worth stating at all.

[1] Perhaps at Euboea, inland of Edessa, which had legendary connections with the Abantes of Euboea (see Volume I. 165 and 301).

[2] So E. Schweigert in *Hesp.* 8 (1939) 170 f.

the Chalcidians to abandon some coastal sites and concentrate at Olynthus, creating a single strong state, and had offered to their non-combatant and surplus population lands of his own by Lake Bolbe in Macedonia (1. 58. 2). The Athenians then switched their attack to Pydna, close to Perdiccas' capital (1. 61. 2–3), and reinforcements of forty ships and 2,000 Athenian hoplites joined them there. But the news that a force of Peloponnesians under Aristeus had reached Potidaea distracted them, and they made an agreement and an alliance 'under compulsion'[1] with Perdiccas (1. 61. 3 ξυμμαχίαν ἀναγκαίαν).

The army of 3,000 Athenian hoplites, protected by the agreement and also by the 600 cavalrymen of Derdas and Philip, marched round the coast of the Gulf[2] via Beroea and Strepsa, which they tried unsuccessfully to capture *en route*. Strepsa had been assessed to pay a talent of tribute in 432 but had thrown in its lot with Perdiccas. The whole armament met apparently at Strepsa, advanced slowly (κατ᾽ ὀλίγον προϊόντες), and on the third day after leaving Strepsa made camp at Gigonus in Crousis.[3] However, Perdiccas had moved with speed. Having made Iolaus regent at Aegeae, he was already at Potidaea with 200 Macedonian cavalry and had been appointed to command the confederate cavalry force against Athens (1. 62. 2). In the ensuing battle neither the cavalry of Perdiccas nor that of Derdas and Philip went into action. Potidaea was invested; and Chalcidice and Bottice were ravaged by the Athenians in the latter part of 432.

In summer 431 Perdiccas joined Athens (Thuc. 1. 65. 2 and 2. 29. 6). This new alignment was due to Nymphodorus, a Greek whose sister was married to Sitalces, the Odrysian king, and an arrangement he made with the Athenians, whose aim was to subdue both the Chalcidian area and Perdiccas (treacherously) with the help of Sitalces (Thuc. 2. 29. 4). While Nymphodorus arranged an alliance between Athens and Sitalces and promised to get Sitalces to send a Thracian army of cavalry and peltasts, he also negotiated an agreement between Athens and Perdiccas,

---

[1] The compulsion, of course, was on Athens as is indicated by Thucydides' next sentence: 'since Potidaea and Aristeus' arrival were pressing'.

[2] See Volume 1. 183 for this march and the emendation of the text. Geyer 58 rejected the emendation but failed to notice κατ᾽ ὀλίγον προϊόντες in Thucydides' text. J. A. Alexander gave a summary of views and his own view in *AJPhil* 83 (1962) 265 f.; add H. B. Mattingly in *CQ* 16 (1966) 172 f.

[3] 'The third day' has to be related to the place last mentioned, i.e. Strepsa. The city was then either on the coast or reachable by river. For Gigonus see Volume 1. 188. The distance from Strepsa to Gigonus was some 70 klm (or on *ATL*'s identification of Gigonus 85 klm). Gomme 1. 217, 'they went by sea the shortest way to Chalcidice, landing probably near or at the town of Aenea . . . and went by slow stages to Gigonus', loses track of Thucydides' words ἐπορεύοντο κατὰ γῆν, supposes that the fleet of 70 warships could have transported the army of 3,000 Athenian hoplites, 'many' hoplites of the Allies (at least 3,000), and the 600 cavalry of 1. 61. 4, and gives the army three days to cover 20 klm, which is rather absurd.

whereby Athens 'restored' Therme to Perdiccas[1] and Perdiccas joined the Athenian forces in their campaign against Chalcidice. Needless to say, there was no love or faith lost between Athens and Perdiccas, but the arrangement paid both of them for the moment.

Sitalces too had his own plans; for we learn later that he had extracted certain promises from Perdiccas, which were dependent upon Sitalces reconciling Perdiccas and Athens (which he did) and not supporting Philip as a rival to the throne. In 429, when Sitalces moved, Perdiccas had not fulfilled his promises, but then Sitalces had Amyntas, son of Philip, at his court (Thuc. 2. 95).

Potidaea fell in the winter of 430/29 and was occupied by Athenian settlers (2. 70. 4; D.S. 12. 46. 7, 1,000 settlers; M–L *GHI* 66). Perdiccas does not figure in Thucydides' narrative of the siege or of the subsequent campaign near Spartolus (2. 79), but shortly after the latter he sent 1,000 Macedonians 'without the knowledge of Athens' (still his ally) to help the Spartan Cnemus in a campaign against Acarnania *c.* July 429 (2. 80. 7). In fact they arrived late. In autumn 429 Sitalces and the Athenian commander, Hagnon, set out to attack Perdiccas and the Chalcidians, whatever the formal treaty relations may have been between the various parties at the time (2. 95). Before we describe the course of that campaign, we must turn aside to consider the situation of Methone.

Four Athenian decrees concerning Methone (possibly more) were inscribed at Athens on one block in 423, and of these there are preserved the first two, of which the second was passed originally in midsummer 426. The date of the first is disputed.[2] In it Methone was a member of the Athenian Alliance and had been since at least 'the preceding Panathenaea', which fell either in 430 or in 434, depending on our dating of the current decree. In the past the attempts to reach a date have been made with little or no consideration of the situation in Macedonia. Let us bear that situation in mind and consider the difficulties inherent in the earlier date. Methone, having never figured in any earlier list, was not recorded in the full list of 434. If it was a member in 432, it is very surprising that Thucydides did not mention it in his account of the campaign of 432; for the object of trying to capture Pydna (1. 61. 2) was clearly to establish a base on the Pierian coast, from which the powerful Athenian army could attack the heart of the Macedonian state at Aegeae, and there would have been no need to attack Pydna at all if Methone had been already Athenian, being only 5 miles from Pydna and closer to Aegeae and the head of the Thermaic Gulf. The best

---

[1] The implication of the word is that Perdiccas had always held Therme and not that Athens had had it in her Alliance.

[2] Tod, *GHI* no. 61; M–L *GHI* no. 65; *ATL* 2 D 3–6, 3. 133; *CQ* 11 (1961) 154 f., 16 (1966) 183.

explanation of the Athenian decision to lay siege to Pydna is that Methone was in the hands of Perdiccas and Pydna was easier to capture, as we may infer incidentally from Archelaus' decision later to move the city to a site inland (D.S. 13. 49. 2).[1]

When then after May or so, 432, did Perdiccas lose Methone? We are told by Thucydides at 2. 95. 2, that the promise of Perdiccas to Sitalces was dependent upon two things, Sitalces reconciling Athens and Perdiccas who 'was at the beginning hard pressed by the war', and Sitalces not restoring Philip as a claimant to the throne. Thus at some time after the investment of Potidaea c. June 432 when the pressure was on Chalcidice (1. 65. 2) and before the negotiations with Sitalces which Thucydides mentioned just after the lunar eclipse of 3 August 431, Perdiccas had been hard pressed, although he had evidently succeeded in driving Philip out of Amphaxitis and eastern Macedonia into the arms of Sitalces. The most likely suggestion to account for the pressure on Perdiccas and his desire for reconciliation with Athens was that in this interim c. June 432–c. August 431[2] Methone joined the Athenian Alliance and was being used as a base against the heart of the kingdom. Moreover, if Athens held Methone, we can see why she was willing late in 431 to hand back Therme (2. 29. 6), which was of less value strategically and less easily defended than Methone.

If Methone first joined the Athenian Alliance between June 432 and c. August 431, we can understand the absence of Methone from the list of 434 and its non-occurrence in the lists of 433 and 432, and we can take the option of restoring its name and a payment of 3 talents in the spring list of 431.[3] 'The preceding Panathenaea' mentioned in the decree itself (line 31) fell then in 430. 'The soldiers in Potidaea' whose reports will influence Athens' attitude towards Perdiccas (line 27) were then the garrison soldiers of the Athenian settlement, as in Thuc. 4. 7 τῶν στρατιωτῶν, and not the hoplites of a field army, as in 1. 61. 4, for which the generals would have had to make report; and this means that the decree should be dated *after* the withdrawal of the army in summer 429, when all the generals were killed (2. 79. 7). Thereafter Athenian operations in this theatre were trivial (4. 7), and garrison troops only were in a position to report.

At the time of the decree Athens and Perdiccas were in diplomatic relations, not at war but in an uneasy peace. This first became so in late summer 431 (2. 29. 6) and remained so even after the one-month invasion by Sitalces of autumn 429, when Perdiccas and Athens were both on friendly terms with the Thracian (2. 101. 6). So this situation does not

---

[1] For the two sites see Volume I. 128 f. and Map 12.
[2] Using the chronology of Gomme 1. 425 and 2. 89.
[3] So *ATL* and Meiggs, *The Athenian Empire*, 546.

lead us to any restricted date. As the decree provides for envoys to visit Macedonia and then, if they are not successful, for envoys of Macedonia and Methone to visit Athens 'at the Dionysia', i.e. in April or so, it is clear that negotiations were envisaged as proceeding late in the winter.[1] The urgency for a decision (αὐτίκα line 5, αὐτίκα μάλα lines 6–7) indicates that the time for Methone to make a payment at the time of the Dionysia was within sight. Finally, the decree ended with a note of the people's decision that Methone should pay the quota only. In Tribute List 26 = *IG* I². 216/17+231 Methone was recorded as paying the quota only, so that the *a priori* probability is that the decree was passed in the winter preceding Tribute List 26. Unfortunately the dating of this List is disputed as between spring 429 and spring 428, with the balance of recent opinion in favour of the latter. From the inferences which we have made it is better to place the decree in the late winter of 429/8, the provision for further negotiations in reference to the Dionysia *c*. April 428, the recorded decision of the people early in 428, the recorded payment of the quota in Tribute List 26 *c*. April 428, and 'the preceding Panathenaea' in 430.

Our study of the situation in the Macedonian theatre of the war and of the internal evidence of the decree has led us to a date which differs from that advanced, for instance, by Meiggs, being 430, and by Mattingly, being 426, some months in each case before a Panathenaic Festival, which came at a four-yearly interval. The tying of the decree to the year of the Festival arises from the view in *ATL*, accepted by Meiggs and Mattingly,[2] that τοῖς προτέροις Παναθηναίοις implies a contrast 'between two strictly comparable occasions', and therefore a Panathenaea is immediately impending. I believe that this is fallacious. Of course a former Panathenaea implies a latter Panathenaea, but the comparison is one of time between προτέροις and ὑστέροις; for the Greek comparative προτέροις is used for contrast with an expressed or supposed Greek comparative which follows.[3] Thus in Thucydides, to give an example from Greek more or less contemporary with the decree, we have τῇ μὲν προτέρᾳ (ἐκκλησίᾳ) . . . ἐν δὲ τῇ ὑστεραίᾳ (1. 44. 1) and καταλαμβάνουσι τοὺς προτέρους χιλίους, where the subject is the '2,000 Athenian hoplites' who formed the subsequent expedition (1. 61. 2). Thus 'the preceding

---

[1] *ATL* 1. 135 n. 1 'the ambassadors (elderly men, over fifty) are probably not expected to travel in winter' seems to me little short of absurd. In ancient society men of over fifty served in the armed forces, and there are plenty of examples of diplomatic missions in the winter. To suppose that diplomacy ceased from November to March is extraordinary.

[2] *ATL* 3. 134 f., followed by M–L *GHI* 179, Mattingly in *CQ* 11 (1961) 162 and Meiggs, *The Athenian Empire* 535. On the other hand Tod *GHI* 1. 131 saw no difficulty in placing the first decree in 429 immediately after a Panathenaic year or in 428.

[3] As so frequently in Thucydides, e.g. 1. 72. 1 τοῖς τε πρεσβυτέροις . . . . . καὶ τοῖς νεωτέροις, words which mean not older than the old and younger than the young, but old in contrast to young with comparatives of contrast.

Panathenaea', as LSJ⁹ correctly translates the phrase, is contrasted in the mind with τοῖς ὑστέροις Παναθηναίοις 'the succeeding Panathenaea'. The timing of the succeeding event may be either now (7. 11. 1), or some time in the future (7. 17. 3 τὴν προτέραν πέμψιν, the actuality ensuing some months later at 7. 19. 4), as in English to say 'last winter was severe' may be said either in the spring with a coming winter in mind or in fact in the course of the ensuing winter. So too at Athens one could use in say January 428 the words τοῖς προτέροις Παναθηναίοις (i.e. of 430) and have in mind a coming Panathenaea (i.e. of 426); there is no cogency in the argument that these words can be used only in say January or a subsequent month of 426.¹

The interest of the first Methone decree is that the city had clearly been over-assessed and had fallen into debt, a situation which had been aggravated by Perdiccas having restricted both the movements of Methonaean or Methone-bound shipping and the trade inland which Methone had enjoyed 'hitherto' (καθάπερ τέως). Athens defended the full autonomy of Methone *vis-à-vis* Perdiccas, who was not to march troops through Methonaean territory without Methone's permission (as he presumably had done before she joined the Athenian Alliance), and she treated him with some *hauteur* in requiring him to send envoys to Athens and expecting him to accept the decision of the *boule* and the *demos*. The second decree, of midsummer 426, showed Methone still in difficulties: she was to be allowed to import grain up to a specified amount annually from Byzantium, notice being given duly to the Hellespontophylakes; she was not necessarily to be subject to general rules about 'the cities'; and she would be fulfilling her obligations if she preserved her own territory. Her complaints of aggression by Perdiccas were to be considered when the two sets of Athenian ambassadors already absent from Athens reported back to the people. Neither Methone nor Athens was getting much joy from the situation, but Athens was eager to retain her base for operations against Perdiccas.

In fact Athens might have used Methone to devastating effect in autumn 429 when Sitalces 'campaigned against Perdiccas and the Chalcidians'. He intended in the latter case to fulfil his undertaking to his ally Athens; but although Athenian envoys accompanied him and the Athenian Hagnon was accorded a position of command, the Athenians did not honour their undertaking to send a fleet and the largest possible army against the Chalcidians (2. 95. 3 and 101. 1). For the campaign against Perdiccas he brought Amyntas, son of Philip, intending to put

¹ Indeed how otherwise would one refer in, say, late 428 to the Panathenaea of 430? *ATL*'s alternative suggestions (ibid.) do not work, namely τοῖς πέρυσι Παναθηναίοις which applies only to the Attic year 429/8, and τοῖς Παναθηναίοις τοῖς μεγάλοις which adds nothing, because for assessment purposes the only relevant Panathenaea was the Great Panathenaea.

him in the place of Perdiccas; and the Athenians, although in alliance with Perdiccas, were eager to join Sitalces in disposing of Perdiccas (2. 29. 4 and 7). The realm of Sitalces extended from the Black Sea to the Strymon river and in its upper reaches to the Laeaei and Agrianes, and from the Aegean coast to the Danube as far as the Getae, Treres, and Tilataei (2. 96; cf. D.S. 12. 50). The total forces of the Empire were estimated at 120,000 infantry and 50,000 cavalry, and on this occasion

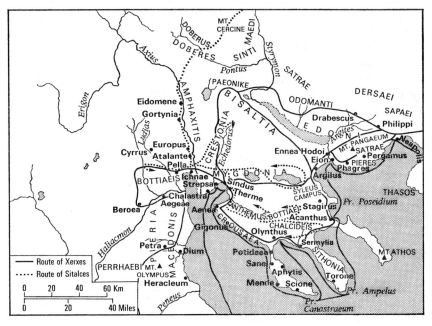

MAP 4. THE ROUTES USED BY THE FORCES OF XERXES AND BY THOSE OF SITALCES

he 'is said' to have brought 150,000 men, a huge army by the standards of Perdiccas, Chalcidice, and Athens.

Sitalces marched through Mt. Cercine (Mt. Ograzden), taking a road he had cut through the forest (see Map 4), and came down into Paeonian Doberus, where the Strumitsa valley bends (2. 98. 1–2; see Volume I. 197 and 200). From there he took the pass by Valandovo and invaded 'Lower Macedonia from the top', entering Amphaxitis and capturing its leading cities except Europus which withstood a siege;[1] most of them came over through affection for Amyntas. When his army came down to the coast he swung west into the plain below Pella and Cyrrus (2. 100. 4).

[1] See Volume I. 169. He took Eidomene by storm (2. 100. 3); it is evidently referred to as 'the first fortification' by Diodorus (12. 50. 6), which would mean that Idomenae at Marvinci had no walls at that time. See Volume I. 140 Map 14.

From here he could have joined hands with an Athenian army based on Methone and their joint forces would certainly have driven Perdiccas into the hills; but the Athenians had not come. Sitalces then turned to the east, overrunning Mygdonia, Crestonia, and Anthemus and sending troops to pin down the Bottiaeans and the Chalcidians in their towns and ravage their country (2. 101. 1). Systematic pillaging and ravaging followed. While the army was still in Macedonia Perdiccas showed his usual skill. Getting into touch secretly with Seuthes, an influential brother of Sitalces, and offering him the hand of his sister and money in dower, he won him over. Seuthes then persuaded Sitalces to return home, evidently via Valandovo,[1] after a campaign of thirty days in all. Perdiccas kept his promise; his sister Stratonice married Seuthes, who succeeded to the Odrysian throne in 424.

Sparta and Perdiccas were in communication during the war. Agents travelled overland from the Peloponnese to Macedonia and went on as far as Persia (e.g. 2. 67. 1 and 4. 50. 1). In 424 agents from Perdiccas and the Chalcidians, both those in revolt and those subject to Athens, invited Sparta to send an army north which they would maintain at their expense, in order to increase the area in revolt from Athens (4. 79. 2; 80. 1; and 83. 4). Perdiccas hoped also to use such an army against Arrhabaeus, king of the Lyncestae. For their part the Chalcidians requested that Brasidas should be chosen to command the force, which proved to be 700 Helots armed as hoplites and 1,000 Peloponnesian hoplites on pay. The passage of the army through Thessaly was skilfully managed by friends and agents of the Chalcidians at Pharsalus and of Perdiccas at Larissa (4. 78. 1–2); they were evidently leaders of the ruling oligarchies (78. 3). Brasidas went next through Perrhaebia to Dium via the Petra pass. Learning of his arrival, the Athenians cancelled their existing alliance with Perdiccas and increased their garrison forces in the Chalcidian towns (4. 82; cf. 4. 7).

Perdiccas at once led Brasidas off to the Kirli Dirven pass, leading from Eordaea into Lyncus (see Volume I. 104), where Arrhabaeus opened negotiations and offered to accept Brasidas as arbiter. Perdiccas demanded military action; Brasidas refused, partly because he wanted to bring Arrhabaeus into alliance with Sparta and partly because representatives of the Chalcidians were advising him not to strengthen Perdiccas and so make him a free agent. A quarrel ensued. Brasidas then heard the case of Arrhabaeus, accepted its justice, and withdrew his army; whereupon Perdiccas cut down to a third his contribution to the maintenance of Brasidas' army, which had been a half (4. 83). Later in

---

[1] Because he did not go through Bisaltia or the upper part of the Strymon basin, where some tribes feared that he might come (2. 101, 3). I discuss the military arrangements of Perdiccas below, p. 147.

424, having won over Acanthus and Stagirus, Brasidas advanced on Amphipolis, where partisans of Perdiccas and also partisans of the Chalcidians—particularly those transplanted from Argilus by the Athenians—betrayed the outer part of the city to him before dawn. By clever diplomacy Brasidas won over the inner city, but Thucydides reinforced Eïon before Brasidas could reach it (4. 106. 4). Perdiccas arrived on the scene when Amphipolis fell, and he helped Brasidas to win over Myrcinus, Galepsus, and Oesyme. The first of these, an Edonian city, came over more readily because the king of the Edones, Pittacus, had just been killed by 'the sons of Goaxis and Brauro, his wife' (4. 107. 3); he had probably succeeded Demetrios (see p. 112 above).[1] There is no indication that Perdiccas gained any direct advantage from the successes of Brasidas either in the Strymon basin or later in the year on the Athos peninsula and at Torone; indeed we have argued on other grounds that he did not gain control even of the Bisaltic mines at this time.

In 423 the armistice made between Athens and the Peloponnesians was broken in the north by the coming over of Scione and Mende to Brasidas, who reinforced them with Peloponnesian and Chalcidian troops but no Macedonians. What Perdiccas wanted was a combined attack on Arrhabaeus, and he got his way, although Thucydides does not say by what means. Invading Lyncus, Perdiccas and Brasidas found the forces of Arrhabaeus in a chosen position, their infantry on a hill (or ridge) and their cavalry beside a plain below it. The confederate infantry took up a position on a hill (or ridge) opposite, and a cavalry battle ensued in the plain. The Lyncestian hoplites came down first to join the fight, and the confederate infantry then entered the plain, engaged and routed the hoplites, of whom many were killed. As I explained in Volume I. 107 the battle was fought probably just north-west of Monastir, near the exit of the Diavat pass. The enemy took refuge on neighbouring heights and the Greeks set up a *tropaion*.[2] The confederates waited two or three days for the arrival of some Illyrian troops whom Perdiccas had hired, but when they did not appear Perdiccas and Brasidas quarrelled, the former wishing to advance and attack the villages of Arrhabaeus' realm, and the latter being reluctant and preferring to retreat.

During their dispute the Illyrians arrived but joined Arrhabaeus, breaking their agreement with Perdiccas, and this made Perdiccas and Brasidas both favour retreat. But being still at odds and encamped far apart, they did not agree on a course of action, and during the night

---

[1] If our deductions from the coins are correct, the kings of the Edones were Litas (*floruit c.* 510) and Getas (*fl. c.* 480); then a period followed when no king's name figured on the coins (*c.* 460–455); then Demetrius (*fl. c.* 450) and Pittacus (ob. late in 424).

[2] It was not a Macedonian custom to do so.

'the Macedones and the mass of barbarians' panicked and fled, forcing Perdiccas to go with them, without informing Brasidas. At dawn Brasidas found himself deserted and exposed to the attacks of the Illyrians and Arrhabaeus. His masterly retreat for some 27 miles and his capture of the ridge by the Kirli Dirven pass have been described in Volume I. 104–8. His Greeks reached safety in Macedonian territory at Arnisa (probably Petres), killing any draught-oxen and confiscating any lost baggage of the Macedonians which they found. From then on Perdiccas regarded Brasidas as his enemy and was bent on getting rid of him, although it was in his natural interest to use Brasidas against the Athenians, as Thucydides pointed out (4. 128. 5).

During the campaign in Lyncus an Athenian expedition entered the Thermaic Gulf.[1] When it went on to capture Mende and blockade Scione, Perdiccas made an agreement with Athens (4. 128. 5; 132. 1). Meanwhile Brasidas allied himself with the Edones. In order to show his friendliness to Athens, Perdiccas prevented reinforcements for Brasidas from passing through Thessaly, where his high-ranking friends closed the routes, and only a few Spartan officers got through to Chalcidice (4. 132). The action of Perdiccas put an end to the plans of Brasidas. In 422 Cleon moved the main Athenian force to Eïon. He sent envoys to Perdiccas, asking him to present himself for the expedition in accordance with his alliance, and to the king of the Odomanti, Polles, where Cleon hoped to hire Thracian mercenaries (5. 6. 2). But he did not wait for a response. During a reconnaissance of Amphipolis he was killed and Brasidas fell in the engagement.[2]

The Peace of Nicias did not bring an end to hostilities in Chalcidice. The terms of the first treaty between Sparta and Athens provided for the autonomy, subject to the payment to Athens of tribute on the basis of Aristides' original assessment, of Argilus, Stagirus, Acanthus, Scolus, Olynthus, and Spartolus; for the return of Amphipolis to Athens; for the independence (probably from Acanthus and Olynthus) of Sane, Singus, and Mecyberna;[3] and for Athens to treat Scione, Torone, Sermylia, and 'any other city they hold' as they liked (5. 18. 5–6 and 8). The meaning of the last clause was clear enough when Athens captured Scione: she killed the adult men and sold the rest of the population into slavery (5. 32. 1). The Chalcidian states refused to accept such terms,

[1] It evidently called at Methone to pick up troops; for 120 light-armed Methonaeans served in an attack outside Mende (4. 129. 4).

[2] Brasidas had reinforced his garrison at Amphipolis with 1,000 peltasts who were Myrcinians (i.e. Edones of Myrcinus) and Chalcidians. He had sent for 1,500 Thracian mercenaries and 'all the Edones' (with whom he presumably had an alliance), both being peltasts and cavalry (5. 6. 4), but they did not arrive in time for the battle.

[3] Following Gomme 3. 673, especially in view of 5. 39. 1, where Olynthus took Mecyberna which had an Athenian garrison in it.

and the Corinthians in particular accused Sparta of betraying their interests (5. 30. 2). The Chalcidians and the Corinthians went into an alliance with Argos and then into abortive negotiations with Boeotia (5. 31. 6 and 38. 1); and after the battle of Mantinea in 418 they entered the coalition headed by Sparta and Argos (5. 80. 2).

For some years Perdiccas maintained his alliance with Athens. But he was drawn into the diplomatic game in 418, when Sparta and Argos invited him to join their coalition, alongside the Chalcidians (5. 80. 2). He accepted and took the oaths. At this point Thucydides added the comments that Perdiccas was originally from Argos—we have seen evidence of his strong attachment to Argos in his coinage (p. 121 above)— and 'intended' to follow the example of Argos in breaking away from Athens. But he did not break away from Athens at once (οὐ μέντοι εὐθύς γε ἀπέστη τῶν Ἀθηναίων). On the other hand, Athens was not inactive in view of the Sparta–Argos coalition; for there is evidence that she paid money twice for operations in the Thraco-Macedonian area in the Attic year 418/17, first at about the time in 418 when the Sparta– Argos coalition was formed and again in late spring 417, when Nicias was to lead an expedition to the north (M–L *GHI* no. 77 p. 235). In fact the expedition never sailed, largely because Perdiccas broke away from Athens at this point (5. 83. 4 reading ἐκείνου ἀποστάντος for ἀπάραντος as indicated by the use of ἀπέστη at 5. 80. 2),[1] and Athens took revenge by instituting a blockade of the ports of the Macedones in the winter of 417/16 (5. 83. 4 reading κατέκλῃσαν δὲ τοῦ αὐτοῦ χειμῶνος καὶ Μακεδόνας Ἀθηναῖοι and Περδίκκᾳ in accordance with the sense given by the scholiast).[2] Such a blockade in winter could have been carried out only if Athens held some of the Macedonian harbours and was able to patrol the Thermaic Gulf from them.

We must consider now what the nature of Perdiccas' relationship to Athens was from summer 423 until spring 417. Having broken with Brasidas and thus with the Chalcidians and Bottiaeans, Perdiccas was in great need of help; for Brasidas, having shown himself able to win over Arrhabaeus in the past, now won over the Edones and might well support a rival to the Macedonian throne as Athens had done in the past. For once Perdiccas was wooing Athens to give him protection, and we can be sure her price was a high one. She held Methone already, and she added as members of the Athenian Alliance two cities which appeared first in the assessment of 421/20, Heracleum and Bormiscus (*ATL* 1. A 10 v 21 f.).[3] Of these Heracleum controlled the entry from Thessaly into

---

[1] Discussed in Gomme–Andrewes–Dover 4. 154, but without noticing the preceding use of the word, which is absolute.

[2] Ibid. 153; the case of Samos (1. 117 ταῖς ναυσὶ κατεκλῄσθησαν) is analogous, because it has a coast-line of comparable length.

[3] *ATL* 1 A 9 IV 108, restores these two names and others for the list of 425/4, because

Macedonia via the Tempe pass, and the latter the entry from the Strymon basin into Macedonia via the Rendina pass; they were of the greatest strategic value to Perdiccas and also to Athens, especially as both were on the coast.[1] Traïlus too appeared first in the assessment of 421/20; and it only became possible for Athens to include it in her Alliance because she held the adjacent port of Bormiscus. Heracleum and Bormiscus were to pay a mere 1,000 drachmae each, whereas Traïlus was assessed for 1 talent. As Athens did not hold Amphipolis and the Chalcidians were strong in 421/20, Athens must have had the active support of Perdiccas in Mygdonia to hold Traïlus.

The treaty which Perdiccas made with Athens in 423 imposed an obligation on him to support an Athenian expedition, evidently under Athenian command (as in 5. 6. 2), and this makes it very probable that Macedon was to all intents and purposes a member of the Athenian ἀρχή. In that case we see why Thucydides used the word ἀπέστη: Perdiccas 'revolted'.[2] Another requirement of the alliance would certainly be that Perdiccas should export timber for naval construction to Athens, which was desperately in need of it after the loss of Amphipolis (4. 108. 1). It is likely too that Athens deprived him of the right to issue coins; for there is no other plausible explanation for his failure to coin c. 424–416 in R.'s chronology, or rather, as we now see, between late 423 and spring 417, whereafter he issued small denominations celebrating his alliance with Argos. Once again (see p. 119 above), the king of Macedon could be described as subject to Athens.

Now at war with Perdiccas, the Athenians were able to use the ports of Heracleum, Methone, and Bormiscus as well as Potidaea in the winter of 417/16 and impose a blockade. In the following winter they brought a force of cavalry by sea to Methone and ravaged the territory of Perdiccas, the cavalry being in part Athenian and in part provided by the refugees from Macedonia whom they were harbouring (6. 7. 3). As Perdiccas had abandoned Athens for Sparta and Argos, his only hope now was Sparta (for Argos had recently joined Athens), and Sparta did indeed order the Chalcidians to go to his aid; but they were unwilling. During these desperate years Perdiccas coined again but some of the coins were plated.[3] Isolated as he was, Perdiccas yielded to necessity. In summer 414 we find him serving with the Athenian general Euetion, who had a large number of Thracians, in a campaign against Amphipolis (7. 9). He had fallen back into the position which he had held

the figures for payment correspond; but there are no mentions in Thucydides of any Athenian operations in that theatre in 425/4, except for a defeat in a trivial operation (4. 7). Attractive though the restoration is, the historical situation is entirely against it.

[1] See Volume I. 135 and 186; and Edson in *CP* 42 (1947) 96 f. and 98 f.

[2] His regular word in this connection, from 1. 98. 4 onwards; he used it of Perdiccas in 432 (1. 62. 2).   [3] Polyaen. 4. 102; see p. 121 above.

between 423 and 417, and he probably ceased to coin. In the following year, 413, he died a natural death. In duplicity he had been the equal of Athens and Sparta, and he could fill his ships with lies as well as timber, as Hermippus wrote in *Phormophoroi*. On the whole he succeeded remarkably well in playing one side off against the other and so maintaining his independence. But Thucydides was correct to censure him for breaking with Sparta through his anger against Brasidas (4. 128. 5; 132. 1); for from then on he had no one to employ against Athens, and he was foolish to suppose that Argos would be able to help him. In effect he put himself twice at the mercy of Athens, and he left his country impoverished and probably divided.

It remains to date a very important treaty between Athens and Perdiccas, which is known from an inscription, found on the Acropolis of Athens. The earliest date has been advanced by *ATL* 3. 313 n. 61 as 'before 432', the alliance being that implied in 1. 57. 2, 'Perdiccas being formerly an ally and friend of Athens'. The strongest argument for this date lies in the restoration of two persons in the list of those taking the oath to the treaty, 'Philippos Alexandro, Amyntas Philippo', their names corresponding to the lacuna in the length of the line in the inscription, if it is assumed to have 100 letters. The inscription then reads: 'Perdiccas Alexandro, Alcetas Alexandro, Archelas P[erdicco, Philippos Alexandro, Amyntas Philippo], Menelaus Alexandro, Agelaus A[9 letters] —yrus Alceto etc.'

But there are serious objections. In the period before 432 Philip had his own ἀρχή and was an ally of Athens (see p. 122 above), and Alcetas too was holder of an ἀρχή at some time before 432. Why then does it happen that 'Archelas P[erdicco]' comes between them in what is clearly an order of court precedence? The position of Archelaus shows clearly that he was the intended heir or regent in the next generation. It seems difficult, if not impossible, to accept this in the years before 432, since it was Iolaus and not Archelaus who was left as acting king in 432 (1. 62. 2). Moreover, even if we attach no importance to Plato, *Gorgias* 471 A, where Archelaus was represented as son of Perdiccas by a slave woman, he is most unlikely to have been elevated to such a position in the court in the years before 432, when he was presumably in his teens (see p. 141 below). Finally we must note that in the lines preceding the list of names there is mention of 'Perdiccas and the sons of Perdiccas', if we accept the practically certain restoration Περδικκαν και το[ς παιδ]ας το[ς Περδικκο]. The lacuna after 'Archelas Perdicco' should surely be filled by the names of another son or of other sons of Perdiccas.

The next date to be considered is 423/2, when Perdiccas deserted Brasidas and turned to Athens, making a ὁμολογίαν (4. 132. 1), the precursor no doubt of an alliance (5. 6. 2). This date was accepted until

ATL proposed some time 'before 432'; and it has been advocated since then by Gomme 3. 621, Bengtson, *Staatsverträge* 186, and Mattingly in *BCH* 92 (1968) 472 f.[1] But it is doubtful if this date suits the internal situation in Macedonia. As we have seen, the power of Perdiccas was at almost its lowest ebb in 423/2: his army had run away ignominiously, he probably ceded Heracleum and Bormiscus to Athens, and he lost his current allies—the Chalcidians and the Bottiaeans. It seems unlikely not only that Arrhabaeus would want alliance with Athens rather than with Brasidas, who had a strong army and position in the north, had shown himself sympathetic to Arrhabaeus' claims (4. 83. 6), and was now at odds with Perdiccas, but also that the kings of the states of Upper Macedonia would choose this time to show compliance with the wishes of Perdiccas and Athens; it was rather a moment when they had a good chance of asserting their independence and pursuing their own aims. The advocates of the 423/2 date usually accept the restoration of 'Philippos Alexandro'. However, this is unacceptable because he was evidently dead by 429, when Sitalces proposed to restore not Philip but Philip's son to the throne of Macedon (Thuc. 2. 95. 3; 2. 100. 3).

The course of events in Macedonia supports in my opinion a later date than 423/2. Here the statements in Plato, *Gorgias* 471, are important. Archelaus killed (1) his uncle Alcetas, (2) his cousin Alexander, a son of Alcetas 'almost his contemporary', and (3) his seven-year-old half-brother who was a son of Perdiccas and Cleopatra. Alcetas was said to have had the first claim to the throne, and his son after him; when they were killed, Archelaus should have brought up the seven-year-old boy and given him the throne to which he was justly entitled. The situation which the story implies as existing in the years before 413 is reflected in the list of names: the senior member is Alcetas, second to Alcetas is Archelaus (having precedence over Menelaus, son of Alexander), and then there is room in the lacuna either for two other sons of Perdiccas or for one son of Perdiccas and someone else.

Whatever the truth of the matter, this story became proverbial. It was alluded to by Aelius Aristides, and a commentary on it was written by the scholiast (Aristid. 46. 120, 2, ed. Dindorf vol. 3). He is well informed, giving correctly the relationships between the participants, and he cites his unnamed source as saying that the boy was called Alcetas or Meropos; τοῦτον δὲ ἐπικεκλῆσθαί φησιν Ἀλκέταν ἢ Μέρωπον. There were evidently two sons of Perdiccas, and the source gave both names, not knowing which had been the victim. The second name has generally been emended to Aëropos, because Meropos is not a known name in the royal house.

---

[1] Meiggs, *The Athenian Empire* 428 f., having reviewed the earlier discussions, has expressed himself as undecided between pre-432 and 423/2; 'purely epigraphic arguments', he writes, '. . . favour the later date, but not decisively'.

I propose then to take Alcetas as the name of the seven-year-old boy, who being even younger at the time would not have sworn to the treaty, and Aëropus as the name of an elder brother, who was a signatory. As the names have the same number of letters, one could reverse them; but considerations which will appear later (p. 170 below) favour what I am proposing.

If then we place Ἀεροπος Περδικκο next in the lacuna, we are left with space for seventeen letters, and this space is taken up exactly by the names Ἀλεχσανδρος Ἀλκετο. Now we are able to account for the fact that it was not this son of Alcetas but another son (evidently younger as we should expect from Plato's remarks), called —yrus, who follows later in the list. Indeed I should be inclined to enter two sons of Alcetas there. The opening of this part of the treaty would then read as follows:

ομνυον ηγεμον]ες Μακεδ[ονο]ν Περδικκας [Αλεχσανδρο] Αλκετες
Αλεχσανδρο Αρχελας Π[ερδικκο Αεροπος Περδικκο Αλεχσανδρος Αλκετο]
Μενελαος Αλεχσα[νδρ]ο Αγελαος Α[λκετο . . . .]υρος Αλκετο Βυργινος Κραστονο[ς

Thus they are all members of the royal line until we come to Byrginus, son of Craston, and they are in order of precedence. Philip and his son Amyntas and any other sons he may have had do not appear; no doubt when Perdiccas made his alliance with Sitalces, he captured them and they were all killed as traitors in accordance with Macedonian custom. The position in Upper Macedonia which the treaty implies is that Arrhabaeus was independent, his position being confirmed, since we find the phrases Π]ερδικκαι και τοις χ[συμμαχοις +10 letters] και Αρ[ραβα]ιοι και τοις χσυμ[μαχοις]. There are also 'kings' of Upper Macedonian districts: [De]rdas, evidently of Elimea (see p. 122 above), Antiochus, evidently of Orestis (Thuc. 2. 80. 6; see p. 17 above), and at least one other, because part of the title survives; these kings are mentioned in the text of the treaty as τος βασιλεας τος μετα Περδικκο, and they are clearly regarded not as vassals but as associated kings.

During the years after 423, when Perdiccas went with Athens perforce, he was at peace and trade flowed well between his kingdom and the Greek world, even if the main ports were controlled by Athens. There is thus no reason to expect in the last years of that period, i.e. in 420–418, a formal treaty of such fullness between all the parties. After that he broke away. He returned perforce to the Athenian fold at some time between winter 416/15 and summer 414 (see p. 133 above), and it was on that occasion that the treaty between Athens, Perdiccas, and Arrhabaeus was concluded, as I think *c.* 415 B.C.[1]

---

[1] The treaty was clearly not of Perdiccas' choosing; he had always wanted to subjugate Arrhabaeus, and he had no love for Derdas who had supported Athens against him in the past. It was Athens which dictated the arrangements at this time, and one of them may have been to restore to thrones in Upper Macedonia those who had been 'refugees' and had helped

4. The Events of the Reign of Archelaus c. 413–399

Whatever the truth which lies behind the story in Plato, *Gorgias*,[1] Archelaus had an ability which Thucydides evidently admired.

> There were not many fortified points, but later Archelaus, the son of Perdiccas, being made king, built the fortified points there now are in the country and cut straight roads and made the rest of the arrangements of military importance—in cavalry and hoplites and the other forms of armament, which became stronger—more so than all the eight preceding kings put together (2. 100. 2).

It is evident that Thucydides wrote from personal knowledge of Macedonia and probably of Archelaus, whose court was hospitable to many leading Greeks. Indeed his statement of the motives of Perdiccas (1. 57. 3–5; 4. 79. 2; 4. 128. 5; 4. 132. 1) implies conversations also with Perdiccas, because Thucydides was scrupulous in not giving to a character his own conception of what might be a probable motive; and this implication is surely confirmed by his mention of details where Perdiccas played a part (1. 62. 2; 4. 103. 3; 4. 107. 3), of Perdiccas' 'secret' negotiations (2. 80. 7; 2. 101. 5), of Perdiccas' remarks to Brasidas (4. 83. 5) and of what looks like an attempt by Perdiccas to justify his leaving Brasidas in the lurch unwarned (4. 125. 1 fin.). If Thucydides knew Perdiccas personally, there is considerable humour in the dry comment at 2. 101. 6, when Perdiccas actually kept a secret promise: 'as indeed he promised'.

Archelaus was helped greatly by the decline of the Greek powers. He escaped from the pressures which had pinned Macedon down since 477 and had split the kingdom of Perdiccas by political intrigue, and he was able to free his country from the economic stranglehold of Athenian sea power. This came about largely through the defeat of Athens at Syracuse, because with Amphipolis free and hostile she had desperate need of Macedonian ship-timber to reconstitute her fleet. Macedon could now call the tune, and it was for this reason that Theramenes in command of twenty ships helped Archelaus early in 410 to blockade and capture Pydna, a Greek city which Athens had previously coveted as a base against the king of Macedon (D.S. 13. 49. 1–2; X. *HG* 1. 1. 12). Secure in his own realm, he was able to maintain neutrality in the final stages of the conflict between Athens and Sparta (Ps.-Herod. *Peri Politeias* 19), and he was fortunate in that Thessaly was torn with internal strife, Chalcidice

the Athenians to carry out cavalry raids into Macedonia from Methone in 416–415 (6. 7. 3); perhaps Derdas and his sons were among the 'refugees' in Athenian service. The rhetorical question which Meiggs asked, op. cit. 430, 'would he [Derdas] have been trusted by Perdiccas?', may not be apposite to the situation *c.* 415.

[1] There have been numerous speculations, summarized by Geyer 84; it would be uncritical to accept the details in Plato's story.

ceased to be a storm-centre, and Amphipolis was a single independent state and not the base of an imperialist power.

There is no doubt that he gained control of the Bisaltic mines; for the debased small coinage of Perdiccas was succeeded by issues of didrachms, tetrobols, diobols, obols, and hemiobols of good silver, with the full name ΑΡΧΕΛΑΟ (in the genitive) or an abbreviation of it (G. 155 f., XXIX. 10–19 and 21–2; see Plate II). The devices on the didrachms were a mounted man with two spears on a cantering horse, an unattended horse walking (both as on the coins of Perdiccas), a young male head with short hair bound by a band (a new device), and the forepart of a goat with back-turned head (as on coins of Alexander I). Is the male head a portrait of the king, young at first and then in middle age (G. XXIX. 11 and 12)? It seems possible, as there is no sign of any divine attribute, but improbable, because subsequent kings put the same head on their coins.[1] The revival of the goat motif was probably due to the promotion of the foundation legend of Aegeae by Archelaus (see p. 11 above). Of the devices on the tetrobols, diobols, and obols the unattended horse and the crested helmet were traditional; a standing eagle with back-turned head and raised wings was a new device; and the head of Heracles and the associated lion's head, club, and wolf-head show that Archelaus was anxious to emphasize the connection of the royal house of Macedon with Heracles and Argos, which was promoted also by Euripides in his play *Archelaus*, produced in Macedonia in 408/7.

The tetrobols of 2·10 to 1·83 gr, diobols of 1·00 gr, and obols of 0·47 gr were on the B series of weight which favoured trade with Athens; for she was still the chief trading state in the northern Aegean, where her fleets kept some control until nearly the end of the war. The so-called didrachms of 10·73 to 9·76 gr were based not on any of the standard weights used by Archelaus' predecessors but on the contemporary Persian standard. Thus Archelaus and his successors found a new market for their larger coins in the East. He coined for the first time in copper in small denominations with the head of a lion / a running boar and a running ox (G. 156, XXIX. 21 and 22). It is probable that he was exploiting the deposits of copper in western Macedonia, particularly in the territories of Orestis and Tymphaea (see Volume I Map I).[2]

The changed relationship between a prosperous Macedon and a weakened Athens is illustrated by a decree of 407/6, in which the Athenian people congratulated Archelaus on his good and zealous services and his benefactions to the city and recorded him and his sons

[1] G. 215 no. 73, XL. 7 noted a fine example in gold and another in silver; he rated both as forgeries, but he may be mistaken, as in other cases.

[2] Also at Verria, near Kilkis and by the Bisaltic mine at Theodoraki; there are copper mines in use at Kratovo in Paeonia. For slag from copper working at Avdhella in Tymphaea see *Epirus* 266, and at other places in the Pindus range *AE* 1932. 112 f.

as *proxenoi* and *euergetai* of Athens (M–L *GHI* 91 p. 277 = *IG* 1². 105). What Archelaus had done was to let Athens have timber, oars, and other materials for ship-building, and (if Meritt's restorations are accepted) he allowed shipwrights from Athens to build trireme hulls in his ports, as Brasidas had planned to do on the Strymon after capturing Amphipolis (Thuc. 4. 108. 6). These hulls were then towed to Athens, where the ships were fitted out and sent overseas. The fulsome expression of gratitude is very different from the imposition of the oath on Perdiccas not to export oars 'except to the Athenians' (*IG* 1². 71. 22 f., which we have dated *c*. 415). Archelaus was the benefactor too of his Athenian friend Andocides; for he allowed him to cut locally and export as many oars as he wanted for the fleet at Samos in 411 (Andocides 2. 11).

Towards the end of his reign Archelaus was able to intervene in the affairs of north Thessaly. This can have been practicable only when he had control over Elimea, Tymphaea and Orestis.[1] As we have seen, the Derdas who was king of Elimea *c*. 415 was probably the old enemy of Perdiccas, but Archelaus gave his elder daughter in marriage *c*. 400 to 'the ruler of Elimea', evidently the son of Derdas (see p. 18 above), which means that they were on good terms with one another. At that time he was hard pressed in war by Arrhabaeus II and Sirras (the son-in-law of Arrhabaeus I, as we have argued),[2] who were then the rulers of Lyncus (Arist. *Pol.* 1311ᵇ14). Thus he ended up no stronger in relation to the dynasts of Lyncus than Perdiccas had been. On the other hand he made a very important acquisition in the northern part of his kingdom by gaining control of the northern entry to the Demir Kapu and establishing in the southern part of Kavadarci (Tikvetch) a settlement of Macedonians which is known only from excavation (see Volume I. 174). In the north-eastern sector he regained control of Bisaltia, an area which Perdiccas seems to have held only for some ten years *c*. 445–435, and he freed Bormiscus from the grip of Athens; for it was a Macedonian town when Euripides was torn to death by sheep-dogs there (St. Byz. s.v. *Bormiskos*). Equally in the south of his realm we may assume that he gained possession again of Heracleum, essential to his military frontier with northern Thessaly. There is no information concerning Methone. It is generally assumed that Archelaus moved his capital from Aegeae to Pella, now central to his extended kingdom; for in 382 it was described as 'the greatest of the cities in Macedonia' (X. *HG* 5. 2. 13). If the

---

[1] As the pass of Tempe was then so narrow that it could readily be blocked (see Volume I. 134 n. 2), any Macedonian king operating in Thessaly needed to have control of the two passes which lead into Perrhaebia—the Petra pass from Pieria and the Volustana pass from Elimea. Even so, he could not afford to have his lines of communication enfiladed from Tymphaea and Orestis if they were hostile to him.

[2] See p. 15 above; if Sirras had been the ruler of Orestis (as some have held), I do not think that Archelaus could have intervened in Thessaly in this year.

assumption is correct, the move was made near the end of his reign (see p. 6 above).

When Thucydides says that Archelaus 'cut straight roads' (2. 100. 2), he is using a variant of the phrase he employed at 2. 98. 1, where Sitalces 'made a road by cutting the forest' on Mt. Cercine. Thus the roads which Archelaus made were not the well-worn roads in the plains of Lower Macedonia, for instance Bormiscus–Lete–Strepsa–Ichnae–Pella–Beroea–Aegeae, where the land was under some form of cultivation and there were cities of some size; rather they opened up new, direct routes through forested country, which were important for the rapid movement of armies and had particular value in relation to the cantons of Upper Macedonia. At that time all the cantons except the area of Derriopus had a primarily pastoral way of life and the forest cover probably extended into some of the cantonal plains. Archelaus was the creator of the *viae militares* or *viae regiae* (Livy 44. 43. 1, translating Macedon's ὁδοὶ βασιλικαί). One ran through the Pierian forest from Aegeae direct to Pydna; others no doubt from Beroea via the Zoödokos Pege into Elimea and from Edessa via Kara Burun into Eordaea. He certainly made one important road, that through the Demir Kapu where it was necessary to cut away some rock in order to create an adequate passage on the right bank of the river Axius (see Volume 1. 173); for without this road it would have been impossible to plant and maintain the settlement of Macedones on the northern side of Demir Kapu, 'the Iron Gates'. Of course these roads operated both ways; one cut them only if one expected to be stronger than the occupants of the adjacent territories. Thus in the case of the last road Archelaus was confident of holding the Demir Kapu against the Paeonians, who no doubt had been severely weakened by the invasions of the Odrysians (one was mentioned in Thuc. 2. 98. 1). I discuss the 'fortified points' and the military developments under Archelaus in the next section.

For his improved forces Archelaus needed weapons, made from bronze for body-armour, and from iron for spear and javelin heads. They may well have been made on the spot; for both copper and iron were mined earlier in Macedonia, and the expertise of manufacturing armour could be developed, as it had been at Amphipolis. Then too he learnt from the Athenian shipwrights how to build triremes; but the fitting out of these may have been beyond his financial power. 'The other forms of armament' included missile weapons, cavalry gear, and the stocking of supply depots with grain and fodder, as Brasidas had arranged at Amphipolis (D.S. 12. 68. 5).

It was when Archelaus had reached this level of preparedness for war that he was invited to intervene *c.* 400 in Thessaly in support of the ruling oligarchs, the Aleuadae, led by Aristippus. The moderates turned to Lycophron of Pherae and to Sparta, the leading power in Greece. However, Archelaus went ahead. His army captured Larissa after a hard struggle, he placed the oligarchs in power, and he was rewarded with the citizenship of the city. A territory recently acquired by Larissa was then ceded to him. This was probably Perrhaebia which was strategically essential, if he was to have access to the Thessalian plain and Larissa, as he intended. Sparta reacted to the initiative of Archelaus with a declaration of hostility. But he and Sparta never came to blows, for Archelaus was assassinated in 399 under circumstances which we shall consider later. In that year he was probably between forty-five and fifty years of age, because his elder daughter was given in marriage *c.* 400 at the age of twenty or so.

The collapse of the Athenian Empire after 413, as again after 357, gave Macedon the chance to rise and grow strong. Archelaus seized the chance and made a plan for growth, which resembled in some ways the plan actualized by his great successor Philip II. He showed himself to be a man of energy, enterprise, and vision; he was ambitious to bring Macedon into the arena of Greek politics; but the fact that he had not conquered Lyncus when he invaded Thessaly was an indication that, unlike Philip II, he advanced into danger before his base of operations was properly consolidated.

5. *The Archaeological Background and the Influence of Greek Culture, 480–399*

(See maps of Volume I as cited under each name in the Index of Volume I)

In the Balkan area the Persian period was more prosperous than that which succeeded it. The royal graves at Trebenishte were followed after *c.* 470 by a separate group of so-called 'poor graves', situated also alongside the Ochrid–Kitsevo road. As the manner of interment was the same, there was no indication of a change of dynasty, but the offerings were now of local pottery and there was hardly any imported Greek pottery. The settlement near by at Radolište came to an end early in the fifth century. Writing generally of southern Yugoslavia, M. Garašanin noted that the closest contacts of the area with the Greek world were in the last third of the sixth century; thereafter intercourse slackened and almost came to an end in the period 450–400.[1] We have seen the same curve towards impoverishment in the state of Macedon not only in coinage but also in military and commercial strength. The most conspicuous Greek export was the so-called 'Illyrian' helmet, made probably at Corinth and sent to barbarian areas, where the Illyrians of Central

[1] *AI* 5 (1964) 72 f. (Trebenishte); 75 (Radolište); 78 (Garašanin).

Albania and Ochrid, and the aristocrats of Paeonia, Pelagonia, and Macedonia were leading customers. Any wearer of such a fine helmet was evidently a cavalryman; he was buried usually with two spears and sometimes with a knife also.[1] Indeed, on coins Balkan kings or heroes were often shown with two spears, whether on horseback or on foot; and the 'Illyrian' helmet was an emblem on coins of the Derrones, the Laeaei, Alexander I, and (much later) Bastares. A similar decline in Greek imports was noticeable further north. For instance, at Atenica near Čačak, when imports came from the Greek colonies of the Black Sea coast via the Danube, the period of the royal burials under a tumulus ran from the middle of the sixth century to the early decades of the fifth century.[2]

The decline in prosperity was due to a number of factors. Persia had imposed a long period of peace. It had been her policy to support and even strengthen the dynasties which collaborated with her, such as that of Macedon, and her empire had supplied a market for silver and other produce of the Balkan area. When Athens replaced Persia as the imperial power on the northern Aegean coast, her policy was to promote war among the local dynasts and to impose her control by weakening others. For instance, in the course of the fifth century the kingdom of Macedon was split between rivals and overrun by Sitalces at the prompting of Athens. The Bottiaei and the Chalcidians were ravaged and weakened. Potidaea, which had supplied 300 hoplites against Persia at Plataea (Hdt. 9. 28. 3), was totally destroyed; Eïon, Scione, and Torone were victims of andrapodization by Athens, and the power of the Edoni was undermined by the Athenian colonization of Amphipolis.[3]

Nor were Athens' activities limited to the litoral. She promoted strife in the interior, making alliances for instance with Grabus, king of the Grabaei like his fourth-century namesake, and with Sitalces, king of the Odrysae. The Balkans became a welter of warring tribes. The words which Herodotus applied to the Thracians might have been designed as a motto for them all: 'to live by war and rapine was their ideal' (5. 6. 2). But these words applied mainly to the aristocrats of the tribes, those who were buried with helmet, spears, and knife in fine tombs, and had their womenfolk tattooed. While they fought and looted, the unfortunate

[1] e.g. at Kačanj near Sarajevo four Illyrian warriors of the late sixth century were buried each with helmet, spears, and curving knife (*AI* 5 (1964) 66). A cavalryman was portrayed on the cheekpiece of a helmet from Trebenishte. Helmets have been found in tumulus-burials at Kukës, Mati, Scodra, Durrazzo, Tirana and Elbasan in Albania (*Les Illyriens et le genèse des Albanais* (Tirana, 1971), published by the University of Tirana, 95 with Pl. II, 4).

[2] *AI* 6 (1965) 14 f. Tumulus II, for instance, measuring 70 m in diameter, was raised up above a levelled area on which a dog, two wild boars, and three wild oxen were first sacrificed.

[3] In this part of the world Athens was regarded with hatred and fear, whatever the attitude of the islanders may have been towards her immediate rule.

peasants were butchered or enslaved,[1] so that 'the worker of the soil became the most despised member of society.' It is not surprising that such unsettled conditions led to impoverishment during the course of the fifth century.

In the wide plain of Pelagonia towns continued to develop beside the river Erigon, and it is clear that the Derriopes were the most advanced people of Upper Macedonia. An important site at Bučin, guarding the 'Pelagoniae fauces' (see Volume I. 60), has yielded silver and bronze fibulae of Blinkenberg's Class XII and pottery of the classical period (*Sbornik* 1961–6 (Skopje) 1–21). A few pieces of imported Attic pottery have been found at and near Bukri (*Rev. Arch.* 1973. 1. 41) and a helmet came from Bukri (Mikulčić, *Pelagonija* Pl. 19a). The cantons south of Derriopus seem still to have been pursuing a pastoral way of life. There is no evidence of towns or even of village settlements, for instance at a site near Florina in Lyncus which was excavated by Keramopoullos (*PAE* 1931. 55 f.; 1933. 58 f.; 1934. 98 f.), and two tombs at Sianitsi near Tsotyli in Orestis, which were attributed to the fifth century, were those of a warrior with two spearheads and a broad-backed knife, all of iron, and a piece of gold diadem, and of a woman with vessels of bronze and of pottery (*PAE* 1934. 74 f.). 'Illyrian' helmets and a bronze shield-boss were found near Neapolis in Orestis (*AE* 1932. 130 f.) and a helmet came from a burial at Akrini in Eordaea (*PAE* 1934. 87). The site of Pharangi, south-east of Lake Ostrovo in Eordaea, yielded some imported Attic pottery (*AD* 17. 2. 216, Pl. 253, 8–9).

As in the preceding period Kozani in Elimea was a place of importance on the route from Upper Macedonia to Aegeae via Beroea. Imported Attic pottery of the fifth century has been found there (*AD* 17. 2. 216, Pl. 256b; *AE* 1948–9. 87); and a number of tombs have been excavated in the ancient cemetery. Conditions here in the fifth century were much as elsewhere in Upper Macedonia; for the men were buried with two iron-headed spears, one larger than the other, a curving iron knife, sometimes an iron scraper, a spectacle-fibula of bronze, a bead of clay or bronze, sometimes a bronze pendant, and a pair of pots (*PAE* 1950. 283 f., Tombs XII and XIII), and the women were buried with bronze pendants, double-shanked bronze pins or long iron pins with a spherical head, a spectacle-fibula of bronze, and some pottery (ibid., Tombs XIV–XVI). It seems that the knife was supplanting the sword: for earlier in the fifth century a warrior had had a bronze sword and two iron spearheads (*PAE* 1958. 96 f., Tomb XVII). Two 'Illyrian' helmets

---

[1] Hdt. 5. 6. 1, where people sold their own children as slaves—evidently peasants in distress; the destruction wrought by Thracian mercenaries at Mycalessus was not untypical (Thuc. 7. 29. 4–5 ὅμοια τοῖς μάλιστα τοῦ βαρβαρικοῦ), and victorious tribes reduced their victims to serfdom, if we may generalize from the Dardanii and an Illyrian tribe, the Autariatae (*FGrH* 86 Agatharchides F 17 and 115 Theopompus F 40).

from Kozani were of the sixth or fifth century (*PAE* 1934. 83; *AE* 1948–9. 102). High up in Tymphaea a fifth-century bronze *lebes* was found at Perivoli. It contained a warrior's arms: an iron spearhead 0·66 m long, another 0·45 m long, a spear-butt spike 0·13 m long, and an iron short sword 0·49 m long (*AD* 20 B 3. 438). Some of the pottery in Upper Macedonian tombs was still decorated in the 'North-western Geometric style', which had lapsed earlier in Derriopus.

Moving to the edge of the coastal plain, we find evidence of imported pottery at Verria, which is built on top of the ancient town of Beroea (*AD* 20 B 3. 424). Within the area of the plain, from Palatitsa–Vergina (Aegeae) to Liti (Lete), there is no doubt that Greek pottery was imported, although relatively little has been found, excavators having concentrated mainly on prehistoric mounds or Hellenistic tombs. Very rich offerings were found in a tomb in the Stavropolis district of Salonica, dated *c.* 425: magnificent gold-plated bronze vessels of the finest workmanship, pieces of gold plaque of which two show a lion about to spring and a lion-head facing, a double-shanked gold pin, gold lotus-leaves on a gold wire, and an Attic RF lekythos (*AD* 20 B 2. 411). In general, however, the best imported pottery which reached the Museum of Salonica came rather from Chalcidice and the Strymon basin (*Mak.* 9 (1969) 132 and 146 f.). A silver hydria of the late fifth century came from Gephyra on the east side of the Axius crossing, where also a fifth-century coin of Thebes was picked up (*AD* 21 B 2, Pl. 361; *Mak.* 9. 145). The 'Illyrian' helmet was worn in Lower Macedonia during the sixth and the fifth centuries (cf. E. A. Snodgrass, *Early Greek Armour* 20 and n. 75); four fine specimens of the later form were found at Mikro Karaburnu and Zeitenlik (*Bericht. über d. Ausgrab. in Olympia* 6. 138 f.), and another at Mandaron in Emathia (*AD* 21 B 2. 341). Helmets of a different kind were found at Mikro Karaburnu and at Nea Sillata (*Bericht.* 8. 148 f.; *BCH* 95 (1971) 599). From Mikro Karaburnu, where I put the citadel of Therme, came a bronze hydria which was a prize awarded by Athens to a winner in the games held probably in 479 in honour of those who had fallen in the war against Persia (*Epitymb. Chr. Tsounta* (Athens, 1941) 358 f.; *AJA* 45. 631 f.; *AD* 24 A 3; *BCH* 95 (1971) 608).

Proceeding inland beside the Axius, we find imported pottery of the fifth century at Europus and in its vicinity a *kouros* in reddish marble, a provincial piece in the island tradition, which came probably from a tomb of the late archaic period (*AD* 23 B 2. 338; *Mak.* 9, Pls. 85–6). On the northern side of the Demir Kapu Yugoslav excavators have made exciting discoveries which include a wide range of excellent Attic pottery manufactured after 440 and predominantly in the period 425–400 (*Starinar* 12 (1961) 229–69 with fig. 30 and figs. 65–9). The finest piece is a hydria by the painter Meidias, unsigned, which portrays Dionysus with the thyrsus, seven Maenads, two Erotes, and three deer in a Bacchic scene; it may be dated with Beazley *c.* 420–410 or with the excavators *c.* 420–400.[1] A gold ear-ring with fine granulation was also found. As the excavators said, this was evidently a colony founded within the period 425–400 at the northern end of the narrows through which a road was made along the right bank of the Axius. The rather thin wall of a two-storied secular building, which dated to the foundation of the colony, was excavated on the slope above the road, and a stretch of the road was traced, 1·45 m wide including ruts, each 10 cm wide, and cut into the rock in places (ibid. figs. 7 and 8; see also Volume I. 174 f.). To the north of the colony the area Kavadarci, remarkable for its yellow soil, was called Emathia by the Macedonians (Plb. 24. 8).

How far did cities develop in the course of the fifth century? Dium was described by Thucydides 4. 78. 6 as a *polisma* or insignificant town (cf. 1. 10. 1 and 4. 54. 4), when Brasidas came to it in 424, and its excavator, G. Bakalakis, has concluded that the western and southern walls of the city dated first from the middle of the fourth century.[2] When I visited Edessa and saw the walls and gateway there, I attributed them tentatively to the mid fourth century. In 429, when Sitalces invaded Lower Macedonia, Europus withstood a siege (Thuc. 2. 100. 3) and was therefore walled or at least had a walled citadel. Such an acropolis has been identified by N. Kotzias on the ridge above the right bank of the Axius, lying 'to the south-west of the modern village' (*Mak.* 9. 178). Extensive remains of the ancient town are also reported to be on that ridge. As we noted above (p. 137), Thucydides wrote not of fortified towns but of τὰ καρτερὰ καὶ τὰ τείχη '[naturally] strong places and fortified points, as many as there were in the country'—'and there were not many'—into which the Macedonians removed (2. 100. 1). Attempts to find such points were made by Keramopoullos after the First World War. He reckoned the fort of Palatitsa to be an early example; otherwise his discoveries were of hill forts on high places which served for refugees in time of war but were not in themselves datable.[3] It is probable from the words of Thucydides that such high places, being τὰ καρτερά, were not fortified in 429. There were evidently a few walled fortresses, attached probably to open towns, as at Palatitsa (Aegeae), Europus, and Strepsa (Thuc. 1. 61. 4), and perhaps at Ayios Elevtherios near Kozani in

---

[1] The vase is described by D. Vučković-Todorović in *AI* (1956) 31; J. D. Beazley, *Etruscan Vase-Painting* (Oxford, 1947) 3. The earliest coin from the site was a bronze piece from Amphipolis of the end of the fifth century (*AI* 5 (1964) 76).

[2] *AD* 21 B 2. 346; also reported verbally at the Conference at Salonica in August 1973.

[3] *AE* 1932. 97 f. and 111 (Palatitsa fort). The different type of fortification in e.g. Perrhaebia and in Macedonia may be seen if one compares *PAE* 1914. 188 f. and 1930. 78 or 1933. 60 f. I visited a site of the latter type at Sut Burun (see Volume I. 53 f.).

Elimea (*Ergon* 1965. 17 f., although evidence of the town is only of the third century, *PAE* 1965. 241).

Subsequently Archelaus built a number of fortified points. We see one by Demir Kapu, which Nevenka Petrović has described as Markove Kule, 'the towers of Marko' (see Map 5). It stands on the rocky top of the hill opposite the ancient settlement (this hill is pierced by the modern

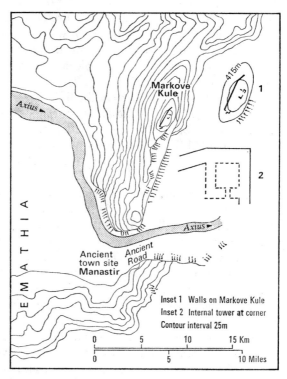

MAP 5. DEMIR KAPU AND MARKOVE KULE

highway's tunnel), and there are remains of the enceinte some 520 m in length and a quadrangular tower (see Inset 2). The latter is built of well-squared blocks laid in an almost regular ashlar style. This tower is dated to the end of the fifth century by Petrović, who makes comparison with masonry styles at Lissus and Medun on the Adriatic coast.[1] The curtain wall and the inner wall of the tower are some 2 m wide. No doubt the fortification was made when the colony was planted on the open site. Similar complexes were probably being developed in Macedonia at this

---

[1] *Starinar* 12 (1961) 217 f. with figs. 11, 12, and 14 (enceinte) and 10 (tower); I should arrive at the same period for the tower on a comparison with fortifications in Epirus (see *Epirus* 713).

period. There is a second fortress on the hill to the south of the open site, but it was probably added later.

The archaeological evidence enables us to draw a fairly clear picture of conditions in Macedonia before the reign of Archelaus. Throughout the Balkans the rulers were relatively few in number and they fought as armoured cavalrymen in the plains; they could also fight as armoured infantrymen on rocky ground. They wore the 'Illyrian helmet', carried a light shield, two spears, and a short sword or a curving knife (*makhaira*), and in action they probably hurled their smaller spear and wielded their heavier one at close quarters. The spiked spear-butt was used to stand up one spear, while you threw the other. Armament and tactics were the same whether the rulers were Illyrian, Paeonian, Thracian, or Upper Macedonian. Only the cavalry of advanced cantons of Upper Macedonia such as Elimea and of the Macedones proper was superior; for, to use the phrase of Thucydides in 429, they were 'good horsemen and cuirassiers' (ἱππέας τε ἀγαθοὺς καὶ τεθωρακισμένους), and they had no match among the 50,000 or so cavalrymen who were serving with Sitalces. Even by Athenian standards they were formidable. On the other hand the ordinary infantrymen of the Balkans were second rate. They did not fight in a tight formation like the Greek hoplites (Thuc. 4. 126. 5 the Illyrians οὔτε τάξιν ἔχοντες), but each man acted for himself (ibid. αὐτοκράτωρ μάχη). In terms of Greek warfare they were written off as a useless mob and proved to be so during Brasidas' retreat (4. 124. 1 ἄλλος ὅμιλος τῶν βαρβάρων πολύς). Yet they were dangerous to one another, not so much through their battle-cries and waving of weapons (Thuc. 4. 126. 5; cf. Arr. *An.* 1. 6. 2–4) as in their numbers and ruthlessness. Sitalces brought 100,000 or so, and Thracians, professionally trained, showed the merciless nature of Balkan warfare at Mycalessus (Thuc. 7. 29. 4).

Balkan armies fought for slaughter and for loot of all kinds, as Thucydides showed in his description of Sitalces' invasion of Macedonia, Bottiaea, and Chalcidice. When the enemy came in superior strength, the population of Macedonia took to the hills and any defeated infantrymen did likewise (4. 124. 3 πρὸς τὰ μετέωρα); the cavalry alone stayed in the plains and they could always gallop away. There were exceptions. In 423 the Lyncestae had hoplites (4. 124. 3) and Perdiccas commanded a force of 3,000 hoplites, these being drawn from Greeks resident in his kingdom (4. 124. 1). It was in this direction that Archelaus made his reforms, achieving more than his eight predecessors in the matter of 'cavalry, hoplites, and the other forms of armament' (2. 100. 2 ἵπποις καὶ ὅπλοις καὶ τῇ ἄλλῃ παρασκευῇ).[1] When he began to develop some

---

[1] For the meaning compare the same phrase in Thuc. 1. 80. 3, where cavalry and hoplites were intended.

Macedonian hoplites, as contrasted with Greek hoplites resident in his kingdom, he drew the men doubtless from urban centres such as Pella, just as the Lyncestae drew their hoplites—unique at that time in Macedonia—from the urban settlements of Derriopus (see p. 94 above). Archelaus' hoplites were for use against hoplites, whether in Lyncus, Chalcidice, or Thessaly. But he needed differently trained infantrymen for the Balkan theatre. There the Thracian peltast set the standard, and it was Thracian peltasts as well as cavalry that Athens hoped to recruit in 431 (2. 29. 5). Armed with a light shield, spears, and a large knife or short sword, and professionally trained, the peltasts of 'the knife-carrying Thracians' held their own in 413 against the fine Theban cavalry by 'dashing out and closing ranks in the formation adopted by their countrymen' (7. 30. 2). It is probable that Archelaus began the training of infantrymen on similar lines; for the recurrent menace came not from the Greek states but from the Balkan peoples.

Generally speaking, the Balkan peoples were divisible into the rulers and the ruled. As Thucydides made Brasidas say of the Lyncestae and the Illyrians, 'the rulers, so few among so many, have obtained their dynastic power simply because they are stronger in war' (4. 126. 2). That was the heyday of the cavalryman. In 432 all Macedonia, peopled probably by a million souls, had little more than 1,000 cavalrymen (1. 61. 4 and 62. 3); on the other hand there was no infantry worthy of the name, apart from local Greeks. Such a system arose from a structure of society in which the entourage of the king was immensely richer than the rest of the population. But under Archelaus a modification began. The creation of a reputable infantry group was concomitant with the growth of urban centres and the emergence of a native Macedonian middle class in the towns. This went, of course, hand in hand with the growth of commerce and prosperity, which became possible only when the repressive forces of Athenian imperialism had died away and Macedonia's produce was exported freely. In particular the planting of a Macedonian city at the north end of the Demir Kapu defile[1] set an important precedent in the use of this new class for the advancement of commerce and the military strengthening of the realm.

Hellenism had a long history in Lower Macedonia. The 3,000 Greek hoplites of Perdiccas in 423 came from Greek cities which were in his realm at that date and from the descendants of naturalized Greeks who had migrated for instance from Mycenae and Hestiaea; but these Greeks maintained the particularism of the Greek *polis* only if they were able to maintain their independence *vis-à-vis* the king, as the Methonaeans did for long periods. The importance of the Greeks-in-Macedonia was that

---

[1] N. Petrović thought the name of the city was probably Stenae, but the station Stenas on the Roman road was at the southern end of the defile (see Volume 1. 172 f.).

they practised and encouraged in others commerce, capitalism, agriculture, literacy, and enlightenment. Moreover, the Macedonian kings, being Greeks by descent, led the way in the worship of Greek gods and in the patronage of Greek art. For instance, Perdiccas II entertained a dithyrambic poet Melanippides and the famous doctor Hippocrates of Cos. Thus it was no new thing for Archelaus to attract to his court Greek artists, such as Zeuxis, musicians, such as Timotheus of Miletus, writers of epic, such as Choerilus, and writers of tragedy, such as Euripides and Agathon.[1] In this respect the Macedonian court was an extension of the Greek world. Moreover, the kings were as generous to their clients as the Sicilian monarchs had been to Pindar.[2]

By the end of the fifth century Hellenism was both an indigenous growth and a naturalized plant; for the worship of the Greek gods and the practice of athletic contests were certainly as old as the royal house, if not older, and the assimilation of the Greek immigrants was complete and unquestioned. Thus it was to be expected that when Archelaus planted a colony of Macedonians at Demir Kapu the town should have the outward form and the artistic crockery of a contemporary city in the Greek world, and that when Euripides produced his *Archelaus* and probably his *Bacchae*[3] in Macedonia his audience would be attuned to contemporary developments in Greek drama. Indeed at that time Greeks and Macedones had much to learn from one another. The gulf between the disillusioned war plays of Euripides and the fervour of his *Bacchae* is explicable only by what Euripides saw and learnt during his stay in Macedonia from 408 until his death at the beginning of 406, and there is no doubt that the Macedones found much to admire in the achievements of Athens in art and literature.

It is a mistake to suppose, as Geyer and others have done, that Archelaus aimed to convert the state of Macedon into a little Greece, thinking like a Greek state and entering the Aegean world like a Greek state.[4] What made Macedon strong in relation to its constantly dangerous Balkan neighbours and the sometimes ambitious Greek powers was not its likeness to the Greeks but its essential difference in political structure,

---

[1] Ael. *VH* 14. 17; Plu. *Apophth. Archelaou* = *Mor.* 177; Athen. 8. 345 d; Suid. s.v. *Choerilus*; Ael. *VH* 2. 21; 13. 4; Schol. Ar. *Frogs* 85; Suid. s.v. *Agathon*; Plu. *Amator* 24. Socrates too may have been invited to the court (D. Chr. 13. 30; D.L. 2. 25).

[2] As in the story that Euripides was given a golden cup at a banquet (Plu.*Mor.* 177 and 531).

[3] In *Frogs* 100 and 311, produced in 405, Aristophanes mocks Euripides' expression 'the foot of time'. The scholiast refers the phrase to the *Alexandros*, produced in 415, but the joke would be more topical if it referred to *Bacchae* 889, which would then have been produced in Macedonia in 407 and known as a text from then onwards.

[4] Geyer 98, supposing Archelaus to have thought that Macedon could only enter the Aegean world as a great power 'wenn es den Anschluss an die Kultur der Stammesbrüder im Süden gewann. Sein ganzes Volk sollte und musste griechisch denken und fühlen lernen.' So too Hogarth 9, 'the Macedonian came to learn that he must cultivate the Hellene and identify himself and his interest with the south.'

social layering, and economic development. When Archelaus captured the Greek city of Pydna, he removed it inland and placed it $2\frac{1}{2}$ miles away from the sea (D.S. 13. 49. 2), because he intended to re-establish it on the Macedonian model and include its Greek population within the Macedonian system. When he planted a colony at Demir Kapu, its people may have included Greeks but its status and purpose were purely Macedonian. When he founded a dramatic festival at Dium, he dedicated it to the local Macedonian gods, namely Zeus of Olympus and the nine Muses of Pieria, and he probably included in it the Macedonian sacrifices and other features which Alexander the Great observed in 335/4 (D.S. 17. 16. 3–4; Arr. *An.* 1. 11. 1); for he was building on to native festivals which had been established in the past in honour of Olympian Zeus and the Muses and were celebrated at Aegeae (Arr. ibid.).[1] If he moved the capital from Aegeae to Pella near the end of his reign (as is usually assumed), he did so not because it was suited to be 'the centre of a Reich looking towards the Aegean',[2] as Geyer supposed, but because the strategic and commercial centre of his continental kingdom lay by the river Axius, when he had gained firm control of Demir Kapu and eastern Macedonia as far as the Strymon. What he wanted in his dealings with the Greek states was security, as in capturing Pydna, and territorial gains, as in Perrhaebia. At the same time, as a Greek, he wished to establish the fame of himself and his house by winning the most prestigious event, the four-horse-chariot race, at the Olympic and the Pythian Games[3] and by obtaining from Euripides and Delphi a more impressive version of his family's coming to Macedonia.[4]

6. *The Institutions of the Macedones and their Neighbours*

Most of the historians who described the exploits of Alexander the Great did not concern themselves with the historical background of the Macedonian people. Arrian, for instance, very rarely referred to earlier events at all. One case where he does so is illuminating. His sources, Ptolemy and Aristobulus, as he has told us, evidently supplied the information that the sacrifice made by Alexander to Zeus Olympios had been established by Archelaus and that Alexander held the Olympian games at Aegeae (1. 11. 1). Arrian then indicated that another source reported a contest in honour of the Muses (i.e. at Dium). The version of this other source appears in D.S. 17. 16. 3–4: the contests in honour of Zeus and the Muses ἐν Δίῳ τῆς Μακεδονίας were attributed to Archelaus

---

[1] Geyer 100, 'Arrian . . Dion mit Aigai verwechselt', creates unnecessary confusion. What was attributed to Archelaus was only the dramatic festival at Dium and the sacrifice to Zeus of Olympus and the Muses at this festival (D.S. 17. 16. 3 places 'at Dium in Macedonia' between the two objects because it is common to both). The Aegeae festival was different and presumably older.

[2] Geyer 98.   [3] As he did according to Solin. 9. 16.   [4] See p. 11 above.

(οὓς Ἀρχέλαος ὁ προβασιλεύσας πρῶτος κατέδειξε) and the festival lasted nine days, each day being called after a Muse. This other source was used also by the Scholia to Dem. 19. 401, 13 (ed. Dindorf): τὰ Ὀλύμπια δὲ πρῶτος Ἀρχέλαος ἐν Δίῳ τῆς Μακεδονίας κατέδειξεν, ἤγετο δὲ ἐπ' ἐννέα ἡμέρας ἰσαρίθμους ταῖς Μούσαις. Thus there was an author, writing about Alexander (for Diodorus was not likely to have used anyone else), who was more interested in the details of earlier festivals in Macedonia than Ptolemy and Aristobulus. When we turn to the account of Curtius we find many examples of Macedonian customs. These came probably from the same source.

Who might this author have been? Surely a Macedonian who knew his country's customs and was concerned to preserve them. If so, there is only one firm candidate—Marsyas of Pella, who wrote a *Makedonika* from the first king down to Alexander's march into Syria in 331. He was brought up together with Alexander and held a high position (see p. 35 above); for instance, he was 'the priest of Heracles' (F 21), presumably at his own town, Pella, where we know Heracles was worshipped.[1] In one of his fragments we are told of a Macedonian custom: 'Whenever the king enters the city, he is met by someone bearing a *gualas* full of wine, and the king takes it and makes a libation' (F 21). Such a ceremony in Hellenistic times is recorded in *Pap. Gourob* 2. 23 f. and 3. 20 f. This is just the sort of custom we find in Curtius; e.g. 'the king marked out the circuit of the new city with peeled barley as is the custom of the Macedones' (4. 8. 6; misunderstood by Arrian *An.* 3. 2. 1), and 'the king was ashamed to leave the soldiers unburied, the custom having been transmitted that hardly any military duty is as sacred as that of burying the dead' (5. 4. 3).

In what follows I take it that the report of these customs rests on good authority and may be accepted. We are concerned here with the institutions of the Macedones proper, those who inhabited the homeland of Pieria and spread out from there.[2]

---

[1] Two unpublished inscriptions record dedications to Heracles at Pella; one was made by a man who had acted as a priest of Heracles in the third or second century B.C. (*AJA* 77 (1973) 69). As the sense of Marsyas F 21 is entirely clear, there is no need to follow Wilamowitz in his proposal to excise the words 'the priests of Heracles' on the ground that they might once have been a gloss on τινα and then entered the text. Nor need we follow P. Collart, *Philippes* 183 n. 1, in supposing the fragment is from Marsyas of Philippi and refers to the king entering Philippi, in some respects an autonomous city. Dionysus and Heracles were 'ancestral gods' of Philippi, from its foundation evidently, whereas the association of the king with *Heracles patroos* had its roots in the distant past.

[2] Earlier work on the subject in German especially has been very well summarized and discussed by F. Granier, *Die makedonische Heeresversammlung* (Munich, 1931). It was vitiated by three assumptions, that the Companion cavalry came from a tribal nobility, that all freemen in the Macedonian homeland were either noble or non-noble, and that all of them were 'Macedones'. Moreover, Granier supported the view that there was a revolutionizing army reform which created alongside the *Reiterheer* a new *Fussheer* and gave to it a political

(a) The King

The central institution of the Macedones was the monarchy. The central fact in its history was that it was legitimately held only by members of one family and only in the male line from *c.* 650 to *c.* 310. That family, the Temenidae, tracing its descent through Temenus from Heracles, son of Zeus, was not Macedonian but Greek; more specifically, it was Dorian Greek from Argos in the Peloponnese. Consequently its members were known in Greece and competed in the Greek games at Olympia and elsewhere not as Macedones but as Hellenes.[1] Within its original realm the royal family was unique in being Greek and in being descended from Heracles; no indigenous family of the Macedones could claim a comparable status. In consequence the Temenidae were not involved in any traditional rivalries of family, clan, or tribe which may have existed among the Macedones. This was a great advantage. For in a feudal society ruled by an indigenous family, such rivalries may disrupt the kingdom. To the Macedonian peasant the Temenidae were a family apart, invested with a religious aura and highly regarded for their achievements; indeed the cohesion of the Macedonian state was due primarily to what Curtius 3. 6. 17 called 'the people's inborn reverence for their kings' ('ingenita illi genti erga reges suos veneratio'). In the one known case, when the state fell apart, the regions were awarded only to sons of the previous king, Alexander I.

The monopoly of royal power by the men of this family does not seem to have made them arrogant or aloof. The traditional name of their entourage 'the Companions' was well found in a social sense, for the kings drank, hunted, and fought alongside their contemporaries. The recorded instances of the soldiers speaking frankly to their king are

power which was voiced in the *Heeresversammlung*. Personally I see rather an evolution in the growth of infantry forces and no sudden political change. P. R. Franke in *Jahrb. f. Num. u. Geldgesch.* 3–4 (1952) 99 f. made an advance by relating the growth of the Macedonian state to the coinage and the geographical conditions; but we disagree over the so-called 'Aegae coinage', and his idea that the Ichnaei, Derrones, Edoni, Orrescii, etc., living like nomad Vlachs in the archaic period, later made up the 'makedonischer Stamm' does not deal with the literary and other evidence. As history has shown, when the nomad Vlachs grow prosperous, their centres are in the high Pindus where they meet each summer on the great pastures and not on the coastal plains where they are dispersed in penny packets. Franke was resisting the view of F. Hampl, *Der König der Makedonen* (Diss., Leipzig, 1934), who saw the Macedonian state in terms only of an 'Army-king' and an 'Army-assembly'. The views of Granier were challenged by P. De Francisci, *Arcana Imperii* 2 (Milan, 1947) 343 f. and by A. Aymard, 'Sur l'assemblée macédonienne', *REA* 52 (1950) 115 f., but they too did not define who the Macedones were exactly. The criticisms of A. Aymard have been carried further by P. Briant, *Antigone le Borgne; les débuts de sa carrière et les problèmes de l'assemblée macédonienne* (Paris, 1973), who has made important contributions to the subject. He too has a 'nobility'—'les nobles et le *vulgus*'—and his application of conclusions derived from the Hellenistic period to early Macedonia is sometimes unconvincing.

[1] Hdt. 5. 20. 4; 5. 22; Isoc. *Philippus* 32 Ἄργος μὲν γάρ ἐστί σοι πατρίς; Arr. *An.* 4. 11. 6.

typical of the independent spirit of a people, which, as Curtius remarked (4. 7. 31), 'was accustomed to the rule of a king but lived with a greater sense of freedom than any others subject to a monarchy'.

When the king died, the succession was determined by the Assembly of the Macedones. The choice might be obvious, as it was when Alexander I followed Amyntas or when Alexander III followed Philip II; or it might be contested, as it evidently was after the death of Alexander I; or, if the choice fell on a minor, a regent had to be appointed, usually from the royal family, as in the case of Aëropus. The Assembly's right was inalienable. Even in Asia, when the generals were engaged in intrigues, it was the Assembly which appointed as Alexander's successor Arrhidaeus 'brother of the departed king, closest in kinship, and associated with him in sacrifices and ceremonies' (10. 7. 2). Expressing their opinion by acclamation (as at Sparta), the members of the Assembly declared on that day, as they must have done on many days through three centuries, that they would accept as king 'only one who had been born to that hope' (10. 7. 6). On election the king put on the royal dress and received the royal signet-ring. The Royal Guard moved to his side, and the Assembly indicated, by clashing their spears upon their shields, that they would fight to the death against any of the king's enemies (10. 7. 14). He was the head of the state in every aspect of its activities from that day until his death, unless he was deposed by the body which had created him king, the Assembly of the Macedones.

An important duty of the king was to beget heirs: not one but several, because the princes were foremost in the hunt and in battle, and casualties among them were frequent. For this reason polygamy was desirable, though not statutory;[1] thus Philip II took many wives and had many sons, but only two sons outlived him (Just. 9. 8. 3 'habuit et multos alios filios ex variis matrimoniis regio more susceptos, qui partim fato, partim ferro periere'). The king chose his wives himself, generally as Satyrus put it[2] with an eye to war and politics but not exclusively, one trusts; and for reasons of diplomacy, if for none other, he treated them all as royal consorts. The sons were all legitimate ('regio more suscepti', Just. 9. 8. 3, cf. 11. 2. 3). He gave his sisters or his daughters in marriage with war and politics generally in view. Thus Amyntas gave a daughter to the Persian Bubares, Perdiccas gave one to the Thracian Seuthes, and Archelaus gave one to the ruler of Elimea. The male members of the royal family attended on the king, they participated with him in everything he did in public, and they fought alongside him in war. They came first in the order of precedence at court; thus in the treaty

---

[1] Polygamy was practised in some noble families of Attica in the sixth century (see my article in *CQ* 6 (1956) 120 n. 3); it was preferable to the methods of Henry VIII.

[2] *HG* 3. 161 fr. 4.

between Perdiccas and Athens the male members of the royal family swore the oath after the king and before the commoners.

The women of the royal family played no part in ceremonial, public life or social festivities. Thus when the Persian ambassadors were entertained at the court of Amyntas I, they missed the company of ladies, but Herodotus expressed the historical truth when he put into the mouth of Amyntas the words 'our custom is that the men and the women are separate.'[1] The women of the royal household performed the same duties as those of a commoner household—making clothes from homespun wool for the men, grinding corn, and baking bread (Curt. 5. 2. 20; Aristides 45. 55 ed. Dindorf; Hdt. 8. 137. 2). There is no evidence of household slaves in Macedonia, even at the court. Those who waited on the king, for instance if he was ill, were his 'Friends', a select group of the 'Companions', and they alone had immediate access to him;[2] and those who served him at table or tasted his drink first were the sons of his relations and friends. These, the Royal Pages, as we may call them, carried out duties which were similar to those carried out in other societies by slaves, as Curtius remarked (8. 6. 2 'munia haud multum servilibus ministeriis abhorrentia'); moreover, if one of them committed an offence, he was beaten by the king or at his order (Curt. 8. 8. 3), a form of punishment acceptable in some closed communities but regarded in a Greek state as appropriate only for a slave. If the king wanted a sexual adventure, he was more apt to find it with his pages than with Macedonian women, who were kept apart from men in society; for there was certainly no taboo on homosexuality which was practised as readily as and not to the exclusion of heterosexuality. In this way Archelaus fell victim to a pages' conspiracy; for he had been familiar with two boys and had had a third beaten for being rude to the aged Euripides (Arist. *Pol.* 1311^b8–35).

Some aspects of the Macedonian monarchy were not fully understood, or were deliberately misrepresented, by Greeks who were accustomed to the exploitation of slaves and the independence of freemen in a city-state. Thus Theopompus (*FGrH* 115 F 27) thought of Philip's wives and Hyperides' slave-girl mistresses as equally a sign of incontinence. Being monogamous, Greek writers thought of one royal consort as queen and regarded the others as concubines. Hence they called the sons of the latter 'illegitimate'. It was probably in this sense that Menelaus, son of Alexander I, was rated among 'the bastard sons' (εἰς τοὺς νόθους ἐτέλει), and that Simiche, one of Alcetas' wives, was written off as

---

[1] This was still the case in the villages of Epirus and Western Macedonia in and before 1939–45; Hdt. 5. 18. 3.

[2] Curt. 6. 7. 17 'Cebalinus . . . opperiens aliquem ex prima cohorte amicorum, a quo introduceretur ad regem.'

a slave.[1] In the same way some Greek writers thought of the Royal Pages in terms of a normal Greek household. Thus a member of the royal house who waited upon the king was 'a waiter and a slave'; he attended upon a 'master', the term for a slave's owner;[2] and he might be punished in a manner which to a Greek eye was appropriate for a slave only.

Of particular importance to the royal family was the worship of their ancestor Heracles at the royal seat, Aegeae. A recent excavation has uncovered three marble blocks, bearing the words HPAKΛHI ΠΑΤΡΩΙΩΙ. which lay close to the Tholos of the 'palace' at Palatitsa–Vergina, identified as Aegeae in Volume I. The Temenidae evidently worshipped Heracles Patroüs, as Athenians worshipped Apollo Patroüs; when the court moved to Pella, a similar worship was no doubt established there.[3]

The chief function of the king was to conduct relations with the gods. This he did daily in person (Just. 9. 4. 1 'solita sacra'); for there was no professionally established priesthood. Even in his final illness Alexander III carried out 'the prescribed sacrifices' daily until he passed beyond speech and movement (Arr. *An.* 7. 25. 3–6). The king's day began with sacrifice (Plu. *Alex.* 23. 2). He worshipped the traditional state gods but also had his own chosen deities; Philip II, for instance, honoured 'The Twelve Gods' by naming the months at Philippi after them and associated himself with them towards the end of his life (D.S. 16. 92. 5 and 95. 1; cf. Just. 11. 5. 4). The king was accompanied in the sacrifices by those who were in the line of succession (Curt. 10. 7. 2), and it is probable that special attendants read the omens or gave interpretations, although our earliest evidence is from the time of Alexander III. On set occasions the king conducted sacred festivals. For example, Philip II held sacrifices and contests at the wedding of his daughter Cleopatra, and Alexander III conducted the sacrifice to Olympian Zeus as it had been 'established by Archelaus' (D.S. 16. 91. 4; Arr. *An.* 1. 11. 1). Above all in time of war it was the presence of the king which, even if he was a baby, obtained the favour of the gods (Just. 7. 2. 9–12).

One of the royal cults was in honour of Heracles Cynagidas, the god of hunting;[4] for the king and his entourage devoted themselves to hunting,

---

[1] Ael. *VH* 12. 43; Archelaus was, of course, illegitimate in a different way according to the Greek tradition that Perdiccas got him on his brother's wife.

[2] Ibid. ὑπηρέτης Ἀερόπου καὶ δοῦλος. The system was not initiated but finally formalized by Philip II (Arr. 4. 13. 1).

[3] *AD* 25 (1970) B 2. 394 (reported without comment); the Tholos was of the fourth century (*AJA* 77. 1973. 70). As two unpublished inscriptions from Pella were in honour of Heracles and Heracles Phylacus, T. H. Price has suggested that he was worshipped in the small tholoi attached to the Tholos (*AJA* ibid.).

[4] Worshipped throughout Macedonia, as we see from inscriptions, for instance in *PAE* 1912. 240, 267; *BSA* 1911/12. 134, 368; *Spomenik* 71 (1931) no. 503; *AE* 1925/26. 77, 82; 1933. 40 f.; 1936 Chron. 4 with further references; *BCH* 1923. 291; *REG* 1930. 361, 368; *Syll.*³ 459. See also Edson in *Harv. Cl. St.* 51 (1940) 125 f.

and details of the chase were reported in the court diaries, known as the *Ephemerides*, in the time of Alexander III (Plu. *Alex.* 23. 3). Royal parks were maintained by the king as game preserves throughout the kingdom. Strict etiquette was practised in the making of the kill; thus one of the Royal Pages was beaten for anticipating the king in giving the *coup de grâce* to a wild boar (Curt. 7. 6. 7). Hunting was close to warfare, in that the same skills and weapons were used, and the Assembly of the Macedones required the king to hunt on horseback and to be accompanied by his leading Companions.[1] The magnificent octadrachms of Alexander I show a horseman, probably the king himself, riding to the hunt and accompanied by a hunting dog.

The king (or in practice the regent, if the king was a minor) commanded the army of the Macedones, who individually owed loyalty, obedience, and service to him (Just. 11. 1. 10). His command was absolute; it was only at his discretion that he called a meeting of an advisory council on a campaign. His orders were obeyed to the letter; indeed in the time of Alexander III the orders of the day were apparently recorded in the *Ephemerides*, whether they were executed or not.[2] Discipline was strict, and the king had the right to sentence a soldier to flogging or execution (Arr. *An.* 7. 8. 3). Charges of high treason, however, were tried before the Assembly of the Macedones and the king himself acted on occasion as prosecutor, as Alexander III did in the trial of Philotas (Curt. 6. 8. 25 f.). In battle the king led the foremost troops, whether cavalry or infantry, and was always in the thick of action. His immediate entourage tried to protect him, laying down their lives for him, as Pausanias did for Philip II (D.S. 16. 93. 6). But the king himself was likely to be an impetuous fighter; for the Temenids were brought up in a tradition of epic heroism, they fought and hunted in boyhood as Royal Pages, and they often held subordinate command before they were elected to the throne by the Macedones, who were themselves experienced judges of kingly prowess in war. As elsewhere in the Balkans the kings of Macedon were primarily warrior kings.

Whether the king owned all land within the kingdom is not clear. What is clear is that he owned all 'spear-won' land from the time of the expansion beyond the homeland of 'Macedonis', and that he sequestered very considerable areas of land for his own estate. Thus Amyntas I was able to offer the district Anthemus to Hippias, and his successors kept it as a royal fief (D. 6. 20); Perdiccas gave some of 'his own land' by Lake Bolbe to Chalcidian evacuees (Thuc. 1. 58. 2). In war the king took the spoil of the opposing king; thus the soldiers kept the tent of Darius intact

---

[1] Curt. 8. 1. 18 (keeping the reading of A 'scivere gentis suae morem') 'the Macedones affirmed the traditional order, to the effect that the king etc.'

[2] See my article in *JHS* 94 (1974) 77–8.

for Alexander, 'tradito more ut victorem victi regis tabernaculo exciperent' (Curt. 3. 11. 23). He owned the natural wealth inherent in the land; this was represented by the mines of gold, silver, copper, and iron, by the quarries, and by the vast forests which provided the best ship-timber in the Aegean world and immense quantities of lumber. The king sold or gave these possessions to whomsoever he pleased.[1] In some cases at law he acted as sole judge (Plu. *Alex.* 42. 2).

When the king died, purificatory ceremonies were carried out by the state, that was by the people in arms, as after the death of Alexander III a 'lustratio castrorum propter mortem regis' (Just. 13. 4. 7). The corpse lay in state for a traditional number of days. Then it was embalmed,[2] placed in a coffin, and carried in a wagon to the royal tombs, οἱ βασιλικοὶ τάφοι, in which every king from Perdiccas to Philip II was laid to rest in obedience to an oracle (Just. 7. 2. 2–3). In the grave the king's weapons and various rich offerings were laid beside the coffin,[3] in accordance with an old tradition (D.S. 22 fr. 12), and a tumulus of soil was raised over the spot. In the latter part of the fourth century the grave developed into the built tomb, which resembled a shrine; it was, of course, covered with the traditional tumulus of soil.

All the royal tombs were at Aegeae before the death of Alexander III, as our sources say repeatedly. As yet only one demonstrably royal tomb has been found, namely one of the late fourth century containing a magnificent marble throne. This tomb is, of course, on the slope between the 'palace' of Palatitsa and the cemetery of tumuli called Vergina. It shows decisively that Aegeae is at Palatitsa–Vergina, and that the royal tombs of the fourth and later centuries were in the tradition of the tumulus burials of the Vergina cemetery (see Volume I. 329 f.). When the funeral was performed, there were ritual sacrifices and funerary games.[4] In the case of Philip II, the corpse of the assassin was cremated on the tumulus and those privy to the conspiracy were also sacrificed on the spot.[5] Thereafter sacrifices were paid to the king 'as a hero' in perpetuity.[6] There is no doubt that all these rites were very similar to rites

---

[1] e.g. *IG* 1². 71. 22 f., Andoc. 2. 11, and M–L *GHI* no. 91. 25 f. For gifts to Hetairoi see Ps.-Aeschines, *Letter* 12, and Plu. *Alex.* 15. 2.

[2] Curt. 10. 10. 9, lying in state for probably seven days; for embalming see Curt. ibid. and the views of Keramopoullos in *AE* 1927–8. 99 f.

[3] The description of the coffin etc. of Alexander III marks the extreme of splendour; it mentions his weapons (D.S. 18. 26–8).

[4] D.S. 18. 28. 4 θυσίαις ἡρωικαῖς καὶ ἀγῶσι μεγαλοπρεπέσι.

[5] Just. 9. 7. 11 and 11. 2. 1 'caedis conscios ad tumulum patris occidi iussit.'

[6] As in the preceding note, and Just. 9. 7. 11 'parentarique eidem quotannis incussa populo superstitione curavit' (sc. Olympias for Philip II). Alexander gave Hephaestion a royal burial under a tumulus and had him honoured not as a god, 'ut deum' (Just. 12. 12. 12) but as 'a hero' (Arr. *An.* 7. 14. 7 ἐναγίζειν . . . ἀεὶ ὡς ἥρωι); for him too there was a period of official mourning, a state wagon carrying the coffin, and lavish funerary games and musical-literary contests (7. 14. 10). The image of the hero was carried before the military unit he

performed in the Balkans in honour, for instance, of the kings at Trebenishte in Illyria and the kings at Karaorman in Paeonia with their evidence of continuing sacrifices.[1] To a contemporary Greek they appeared to be barbarous and ostentatious.

The Macedonian monarchy was an example of what Thucydides called 'hereditary monarchies with stated rights' (1. 13. 1). Those rights were very wide but not absolute (Arr. *An.* 4. 11. 6). Thus the Assembly chose who was to be king. Once he was chosen, he governed by consent; but if he lost that consent he was deposed by the body which had created him king. So Amyntas III 'was expelled by [the] Macedones' (see p. 175 below). If treason against the king was alleged, the case was tried by the Assembly and the sentence was passed by the Assembly.[2] In everything else the king was a free agent, conducting all affairs as he thought fit and not subject to approval by any organ of what we might call 'government'. Indeed he was the government. The fortune of the state depended upon his personal ability. Because the life of the state and the life of the king were so tightly intertwined, any step which was taken to protect the life of the king was held to be justified.[3]

(b) The Council

If I am correct in supposing that Alexander I or someone in a position of authority gave to Herodotus the story of Gauanes, Aëropus, and Perdiccas, it follows that there was a form of Council in the early fifth century; for the story contains the advice given to the king by 'one of the Councillors' (Hdt. 8. 138. 1 τῷ δὲ βασιλέϊ σημαίνει τις τῶν παρέδρων). The word παρέδρων is general; for it was used of the Councillors of Xerxes and the Ephors at Sparta by Herodotus (7. 147. 2 and 6. 65. 4). The particular name of the Councillors of the king of Macedon in the early fifth century was no doubt 'the Companions', οἱ ἑταῖροι, because the word was already traditional when it was used in the fourth century and because the worship of Zeus Hetaireios implied its early existence. Indeed the fact that the Magnetes and the Macedones both celebrated

had commanded, just as the statues of the Aeacidae attended the Aeginetan fleet before the battle of Salamis.

[1] Similarly in Thrace, although the evidence is later; there was worship of a dead man as 'a hero', e.g. at Kepia near Kavalla (*AD* 24 (1969) A 248). In Paeonia, when the king was first enthroned, there were purificatory rights and then feasting at the royal table in the traditional manner (Polyaen. 4. 12. 3).

[2] e.g. Arr. *An.* 3. 27. 2 and Curt. 8. 2. 12; when Amyntas and his brothers were acquitted, it was carried by the 'una vox' of the Assembly and Alexander added his personal 'sententia' only to show that he was in agreement. If we accept the restoration of Hedicke, the procedure is made clear by Curt. 6. 8. 25 'de capitalibus rebus vetusto Macedonum modo inquirebat ⟨rex, iudicabat⟩ exercitus.'

[3] And any failure to take such a step was punishable by death, as in the case of Philotas; the motto of the state might have been 'salus regis suprema lex esto.'

a festival called 'Hetairideia' suggests that it existed already in the Bronze Age when they were together by Olympus (see Volume 1. 276). In any case the word 'Hetairoi' in *Iliad* 1. 179 was used of Achilles' companions in war, and the Companions of the Macedonian king fought alongside him as cavalrymen. This was implicit in the story of Gauanes, Aëropus, and Perdiccas; for cavalrymen immediately pursued the fugitives (8. 138. 1).[1]

The name 'Companions' is itself a pointer. Whereas the term Gerontes implies the elders or heads of familial groups and the term Bouleutai implies regular Counsellors, Companions simply means those chosen to accompany the king in war. Having regard to the powers of the monarchy, we may add that they were chosen by the king in the time of Alexander I as well as in that of Alexander III. What determined the king's choice was clearly their ability to fight well at his side as cavalrymen. It was from this corps of cavalry Companions that he selected those best fitted to advise him, οἱ πάρεδροι in Herodotus, those who formed the 'consilium' in Curtius (e.g. 4. 11. 1), but properly described by Arrian, *An.* 1. 25. 4–5, as friends of Alexander called to counsel him and giving advice as 'Companions' (συναγαγὼν δὲ τοὺς φίλους βουλὴν προύτίθη ὅ τι χρὴ ὑπὲρ Ἀλεξάνδρου γνῶναι. καὶ ἐδόκει τοῖς ἑταίροις . . .). The decision whether or not to take their advice lay with the king alone.

In the historians of Alexander III we find two names for those who were called upon to advise the king: 'friends' which stresses the fact that the choice of them was made by the king for personal reasons, and 'commanders', ἡγεμόνες, which indicates a function, possessed in common by the king as commander-in-chief and by those to whom he deputes command. It was when the army was already mutinous and he wanted it to go further in India that Alexander summoned τοὺς ἡγεμόνας τῶν τάξεων (Arr. *An.* 5. 25. 2 and 28. 1), no doubt because such a council could be expected to carry most weight; again at Opis he brought about a change of heart in the army when he made Persians ἡγεμόνας καὶ τούτους προῆγεν ἐπὶ τὸ πρωτεῖον (D.S. 17. 109. 3), because it was an official promotion to the highest rank. This term may have been used in the fifth century, because it seems likely that we should restore in the treaty between Athens and Perdiccas ὄμνυον ἡγεμόν]ες before the list of names running from the king himself down to the last of what was evidently a considerable number of persons, all taking the oath apparently on behalf of the Macedonian state.

Because Macedonia was constantly open to attack on all sides, no

---

[1] It was implicit also in the word πεζέταιρος because the contrast of the 'foot-companion' was with the 'cavalry-companion', called simply ἑταῖρος. For the term ἑταιρεία in archaic Dorian states see *SEG* 9. 3 and R. F. Willetts, *Aristocratic Society in Ancient Crete* (London, 1955) 13 f.

distinction was made between times of peace and times of war.[1] The Companions were always on a war footing. It was a secondary and tertiary meaning of the word that they also accompanied the king in hunting by ancient statute (Curt. 8. 1. 18) and in feasting at his invitation. The earliest mention of feasting is in Aelian *VH* 13. 4; 'Archelaus prepared a rich feast for the Companions', at which Euripides drank too much and kissed Agathon. One might dismiss the setting as a later invention, were it not for an epigram which records honours paid posthumously to Euripides by the 'hetaireia of Archelaus' at Arethusa, where he was killed.[2] There is then no doubt that Archelaus had made Euripides a Companion; he was present at the feast as such, and he received honours as such after death. Probably all Companions were so honoured.

(c) *The Assembly*

The first mention of the Assembly may be that which refers to the time of Amyntas III: 'after reigning one year he was expelled by the Macedones' *c.* 393 (Porphyr. fr. 1, *FHG* 3. 691 ὑπὸ Μακεδόνων ἐξεβλήθη);[3] for the expression οἱ Μακεδόνες or Μακεδόνες was certainly used to denote the body which elected or deposed a king and was convened to listen to the king or judge a case of treason (D.S. 16. 3. 1 of Philip II τοὺς Μακεδόνας ἐν συνεχέσι ἐκκλησίαις συνέχων; Arr. *An.* 3. 26. 2 quoting Ptolemy and 3. 27. 2). We do not know whether the technical term for a meeting of the body was ἐκκλησία (as in D.S. 16. 3. 1 and often). The

---

[1] A contrast between peace and war is made in Curt. 6. 8. 25. 'De capitalibus rebus vetusto Macedonum modo inquirebat exercitus—in pace erat vulgi—et nihil potestas regum valebat, nisi prius valuisset auctoritas.' 'In the matter of capital charges, in accordance with the ancient practice of the Macedones, the inquiry was conducted by the army—in peace it [the army] was part of the people—and the legal power of the kings was of no avail, unless their influence had had some force before the event.' The manuscript makes good sense and there is no need to add with Hedicke 'rex, iudicabat' between 'inquirebat' and 'exercitus'. The aside is difficult to understand. In Macedonia one imagines that a trial for treason was conducted by the same body, whether the state was at war or at peace, say, with Athens. My own opinion is that Curtius was drawing a contrast between what happened in Asia and what happened in Macedonia and expressed himself awkwardly. The actual army on service in Drangiana conducted the inquiry in 330; if the trial had been in Macedonia, this particular army would have been only a part of the total assembly of Macedones (for there were other Macedones with Antipater). This explanation fits best the request of Olympias in D.S. 19. 51. 1–4, where the contrast seems to have been between the Macedones with Cassander at Pydna and an assembly of 'all Macedones'. See P. Briant, *Antigone le Borgne* (Paris, 1973) 297 f. and 339 f. for a full discussion of these passages; Hampl 15 did not realize their importance.

[2] *Anth. Pal.* 7. 5. 1, by the Macedonian Adaeus; A. Gellius, *AN* 15. 20. 10 also records the honouring of the grave of Euripides in Macedonia. The 'hetaireia' of the king is a technical term, as in Athen. 11. 508 d–e.

[3] Geyer 115 n. 4 rejected the passage as erroneous; Aymard in *REA* 52. 128 did not make the inference that it was done by the Assembly, but he wrote 'l'assemblée existe néanmoins comme organe traditionnel.' We have an analogy in the deposition of Aeacides, king of the Molossi, in D.S. 19. 36. 4.

Macedones met under arms, whatever the circumstances and the purpose of the meeting. For instance the king summoned a meeting of 'omnes armati' for the trial of Philotas on a charge of treason (Curt. 6. 8. 23). No doubt this was an old custom; for there was no danger of an attack. The fact that they met under arms indicates that those bearing arms in the king's forces were 'the Macedones'. No one else was entitled to attend.[1] On a similar occasion Callisthenes, being a Greek, hitherto high in the king's favour, was excluded as he was not a 'Macedon' (Curt. 8. 8. 19 'Olynthio non idem iuris est'). In the earliest instances which are known to us 'the Macedones' were convened by the king; but it is clear that if the Macedones wished to depose a king they could convene themselves. So too the king dismissed or adjourned a meeting. In this sense he may be said to have presided. But every Macedon had the same right to speak as the king: εἶχον γὰρ ἀεὶ τὴν τοιαύτην ἰσηγορίαν Μακεδόνες (Plb. 5. 27. 6). The verdict of the Assembly was expressed by acclamation (Curt. 7. 2. 7). When it found a man guilty of treason, it decided how he should be put to death, whether by javelins, stones, or crucifixion, and in the first instance acted at once, because they were armed. During

---

[1] Although the discussion about the trial of Philotas will be in Volume III, it is advisable to comment briefly on the view of P. Briant, *Antigone le Borgne* 341 f., that this Assembly was composed only of infantrymen (his phalanx-assembly) and civilians (p. 343). As Briant accepts Curtius' account, his first point is disproved by the opening words of 6. 9. 1, which show that on entering the Assembly the king and his 'amici' wore gloomy expressions (see also 6. 11. 9); the 'amici' were of course Companions of the king, and as such usually cavalry-men. The 'somatophylakes' were also present (6. 11. 8). His suggestion that Alexander was trading on the dislike of the phalanx for the cavalry is not supported by the remark of Alexander that the cavalry was 'the best part of the army' (6. 9. 21). In fact Alexander is represented always as addressing the 'milites' in general; Philotas was a traitor to 'the army' and he was killed without exciting the anger of 'the whole army' ('milites' *vel sim.*, Curt. 6. 9. 2, 3, 6, 19 (*bis*), 24 and 10. 8; 'exercitus', 6. 9. 30 and 6. 11. 39; see also 7. 1. 1 and 7. 1. 4). The 'contio' was clearly a gathering of cavalry and infantry alike, namely 'the Macedones', 'omnes armati'. On the second point, that civilians were present, Briant has in mind the 'turba lixarum calonumque', 'the mob of hangers-on and batmen', who were represented by Curtius 6. 8. 23 as filling up the parade-ground when some 6,000 'milites' had come in response to the edict of Alexander 'omnes armati coirent', which I take to be that 'all should come together under arms'. The camp-followers were obviously separate from the 'armati' and the 'milites', and Alexander never mentions them; I take it that they were not summoned at all but were, true to their nature, 'hangers-on'. In what I should regard as a fictitious speech by Philotas, he does address them as well as the soldiers, but as 'non-Macedones' at 6. 9. 35. 'Praeter Macedonas plerique adsunt quos etc.' Such people were of low quality in Greek and Latin diction, civilians indeed as opposed to soldiers but not 'cives' or in this case 'Macedones'. The parallel account in Arrian, *An.* 3. 26. 1–3, makes it clear that Philotas was called before and shot down by the (armed) Macedones; so too D.S. 17. 79. 6–80. 2. The 'lixae calonesque' may have carried a knife, but they were not 'armati', not what we call 'the armed forces', nor the time-expired or disabled 'Macedones' who were settled in Alexandria Eschate, as Hampl 12 n. 1 suggested (Arr. *An.* 4. 1. 1). The different methods of execution were shooting down with javelins, which was immediate and in a sense a soldier's death, and stoning, which was a slow form of death and ignominious; the former was carried out in the case of Philotas, although most of Alexander's 'amici' wanted the latter (Curt. 6. 11. 10).

the trial the defendant was entitled to call witnesses and relatives (Curt. 6. 10. 30), and the king as prosecutor also called witnesses. In earlier times certainly the relatives (probably the males only) of a man condemned for treason were also executed (Curt. 8. 6. 28 'Macedonum more'); indeed it is doubtful whether Alexander III annulled this practice.[1]

That the state was the Macedones under arms is clear also from certain ritual acts which had become formalized long before the fourth century. Thus at Ephesus Alexander III followed a sacrifice to Artemis with a procession of the army under arms in battle array (Arr. *An.* 1. 18. 2) and again at Tyre a sacrifice to Heracles (2. 24. 6). A state funeral was carried out with the whole army in battle array (2. 12. 1). When Alexander died, the army under arms was purified by a solemn ceremony in 'the traditional manner' (Curt. 10. 9. 11 f. 'patrio more'; cf. Livy 40. 6). The infantry of the fifth century may have been a rabble by the standards of a Thucydides (4. 124. 1), but they were none the less the majority of the Macedones and carried out the traditional procedures.

One decision of the Assembly of Macedones in the last years of the fifth century has been recorded by A. Gellius, *AN* 15. 20. 10. When Euripides died and was buried at Arethusa, the Athenians sent an embassy to ask that his remains should be brought to Athens, and 'the Macedones with general agreement persisted in their refusal' ('maximo consensu in ea re deneganda perstiterunt'). The terms are those used of an assembly, whether acting by vote or by acclamation. We have already seen that the tradition of Euripides being buried at Arethusa is confirmed by an epigram; there is thus every reason to suppose that the Athenians did make such a request and received such an answer. It is probable that Aelian, *VH* 13. 4 (cited on p. 160), and A. Gellius drew on an accurate source about the life and death of Euripides. Another activity of the Assembly of the Macedones was the appointing of *proxenoi* in other states. Thus in 335, when Thebes was destroyed, an exception was made in favour of the representatives of the Macedones in Thebes (ὅσοι πρόξενοι Μακεδόνων ἐγένοντο Arr. *An.* 1. 9. 9), who, unlike the personal friends of Philip and Alexander in the same passage, had evidently been accredited by some resolution of the Macedones. We may assume that it was the same in the fifth century.

(d) *The structure and the ideas of society*

There is a complete absence of any tribal nobility in the Macedonian state of the fourth century. Whereas the Persian king Darius had his 'kindred' cavalrymen, recruited by ties of kinship (D.S. 17. 59. 2), the

---

[1] That he did so is stated only in a speech in Curt. 8. 8. 18, which is a rhetorical exercise and may not rest on fact.

king of Macedon had his 'Companion' cavalrymen, chosen on grounds of personal merit. As we have seen (above, p. 27), the Macedones proper had originally been a cluster of small tribes, one being called the 'Argeadae', but after the expansion of the state by Alexander I the tribal system disappeared, no doubt on the initiative of Alexander himself. A new system of organization took its place.[1] It was designed to solve the problems which arose from the conquest and annexation of the coastal area up to the Strymon. It seems that the subjects of the king were now registered as members of a city, e.g. 'Pellaios', or of an area, e.g. 'Eordaios', each having its own citizenship and therefore its own form of local government. A number of persons selected by the king without consideration of tribal or even racial origins were made 'Macedones', thus obtaining a second and superior citizenship. They served in the king's army and they were the state in that they alone elected and deposed a king, judged cases of treason, and carried out ritual acts of state. The evidence for this system of organization will be discussed later (pp. 647 f. below).

As the kingdom of Macedon grew larger, the king secured his control of new territory by founding cities in which he placed a population of his own choosing. Alexander I used the people of Mycenae and Perdiccas the people of Hestiaea in this way. The first example known through archaeology is the city at the northern exit of the Axius defile, known as the Demir Kapu, which was founded by Archelaus between 413 and 400; but it is most likely that Alexander I had also planted cities in order to secure control of the rich lands east of the Axius up to Bormiscus. We shall discuss the significance of these cities when we come to the reign of Philip II.

It is unlikely that any king of Macedon in the fifth century absorbed the peoples of Upper Macedonia into his own state. As I argued in Volume I. 439 f., those peoples were called Lyncestae Macedones or Elimiotae Macedones because they became associated politically with the king of Macedon, but the manner and the degree of association varied with the circumstances of the time. We have an analogy in the rule exercised by the Spartan kings over 'the Lacedaemonians', a term which included both the Spartiatae and the Perioeci, although only the former enjoyed the élitist citizenship. The king of Macedon ruled over two groups, the Macedones proper and the Macedones of Upper Macedonia, but only the former constituted the state of Macedon. So the

---

[1] A parallel development took place in archaic Crete where 'the aristocratic system progressed from a tribal association based on kinship to a firmly-knit privileged corporation based on narrow political rights of citizenship' (R. F. Willetts, *Aristocratic Society in Ancient Crete* (London, 1955) 85). There too the corporation was a 'hetaireia' and worshipped 'Zeus Hetaireios'; there are numerous points of similarity, which it is not appropriate to develop in this book.

treaty between Athens and the Macedonian area *c.* 415 distinguished quite clearly three separate entities: the leaders of the Macedones, the associated kings of Upper Macedonia, and the totally independent state formed by Arrhabaeus and his allies.

Thus the Macedones proper were an élite group of men, trained for war and chosen by the king for their prowess in war and dependability in his service, a small proportion only of all his subjects. The position of men within this élite depended entirely upon the king's favour; he alone promoted a man to be a Companion or to attend upon his person, and he alone could expel a man from membership of the élite. Thus the social values of the Macedones were centred upon the king and not upon any consideration of family lineage, beyond the fact that the son of a Companion was likely to enter the service of the king as a Royal Page. What united the state was loyalty to the king, and what preserved the state was the king's leadership of his warriors against the enemies who ringed them round.

In Macedonian society the male element was dominant to an unusual degree. War, hunting, and administration were respected above all other activities, and the male friendships and male love-affairs which gained publicity when they led to conspiracies at the court were probably a feature of ordinary life among the Macedones. It does not follow that they were a brutal or irreligious people. Rather the reverse, they were more humane in war than their neighbours whether Thracian or Greek; for they did not massacre, enslave, or reduce to serfdom, as far as the evidence goes. They were certainly very religious in the sense that they practised many cults themselves and they expected their king to enlist the aid of the gods by regular sacrifices and ritual acts. The list of cults of all periods and in all parts of Macedonia which was compiled by Baege[1] and to which many additions can now be made is very long and testifies to the religiosity of the peoples of the land.

The chief god of the Macedonian state was Zeus the Highest, the ruler of Olympus, the progenitor of Macedon, the god of the Hetairoi, and the special centres of his cult were at Aegeae and Dium.[2] Because the royal family was the centre of the Macedonian state, the cult of their ancestor Heracles was very prominent, especially at Aegeae and Pella. He was worshipped under various aspects: Heracles Patroüs

---

[1] W. Baege, *De Macedonum sacris* (Halle, 1913).

[2] Zeus the Highest (Ζεὺς Ὕψιστος) was worshipped also in Elimea at Aeane (*AD* 24 B 2. 332) and at Ayios Elevtherios near Kozani (*PAE* 1965. 26); in Eordaea at Akrini (*AE* 1936 Chronica 4 f. no. 9); at Edessa (*AD* 14. parartema 33); and by the Strymon (*PAE* 1936. 67). For Zeus Olympius see *SEG* 24. 408–10. Other cult titles of Zeus were Zeus Cronides at Ayios Elevtherios near Kozani (*PAE* 1965. 26) and Zeus Ctesius at Ptolemaïdha in Eordaea (*AD* 14. 33 f. no. 8). See *SEG* 24. 480–2. These inscriptions are of the Hellenistic and Roman periods.

(ancestor of the royal family), Heracles Cynagidas (god of hunting) Heracles Phylacus (guardian), Heracles Propylaeus (protector of the gates).[1] It seems that the war-spirit to whom the Macedones appealed was a hero and not a deity, namely Xanthus; for every year in the spring in the month Xanthicus a festival of 'the Macedones' was held with the making of sacrifices and the parade of the armed forces. As the illustrious arms of all the kings from the very beginnings of Macedon were carried in the procession, it was believed to have been celebrated since the days of the founder, Caranus. A mock fight was conducted by the army which, as in the purification ceremony after the death of Alexander III, marched between the severed parts of a dog.[2] Beside these male gods and heroes the goddesses held a less prominent position. Thus Artemis Cynagus was worshipped far off in Pelagonia (*Spomenik* 94. no. 354), and other worships of her seem to have been of local significance.[3] The protectress of the state in war was Athena Alcidemus, of whom we hear only from Livy 42. 51. 2, referring to the year 171.

(e) The neighbouring peoples

The Greek-speaking peoples of Tymphaea, Elimea, Orestis, and parts of Lyncus and Pelagonia were still organized as tribal groups and lived primarily as hunters and pastoralists. We have seen this from the archaeological remains and the lack of towns. They had certain points in common: they wanted access to the winter pastures of Lower Macedonia for their sheep, they met to some extent in the summer pastures of Pindus, and they feared the raiding Illyrians. But this did not stop them from fighting one against the other and also against the king of Macedon. The exceptions were in Elimea, where there were town centres, at Aeane, near Kozani and at Palaeogratsiano, and here Derdas was in command of a strong cavalry force; and in northern Lyncus where the towns of Derriopus were able to provide hoplites at the time of Brasidas' invasion. The royal houses in the several cantons were indigenous except in Lyncus. There the Bacchiadae, descended from Heracles through the branch at Corinth, were a foreign dynasty which, like the Temenidae, came from the Peloponnese and was acknowledged to be Greek.

To the west of Pindus the tribal groups which made up the Molossi and the Parauaei were indistinguishable from the Orestae etc. in their way of life and their interests. Sometimes they acted together. The Molossian

---

[1] *AD* 25 B 2. 394 (at Vergina, viz. Aegeae, as Patroüs); *AJA* 77. 69 (at Pella as Phylacus); *Ergon* 1965. 17 (at Ayios Elevtherios near Kozani as Propylaeus). For Cynagidas see p. 155 n. 4 above.

[2] Hsch. s.v. *Xanthika*; Suid. s.v. *enagizon* and s.v. *diadromai*; Livy 40. 6. See Granier 22 f. For the word Xanthika at Beroea see *SEG* 24. 502.

[3] See Volume I. 67 n. 1, 159, 164 and now *AD* 24 B 2. 333 (Artemis Epone near Tsotyli in Orestis).

royal house, like those of Macedon and Lyncus, was not indigenous; it claimed descent from Aeacus, the grandfather of Achilles, and this claim was recognized by the Greek states. To the north-west the Illyrians were organized again in tribal groups, which might coalesce and become powerful, as we see from the remains at Trebenishte, and as happened with the Taulantii. Generally they were engaged in fighting one another; sometimes they combined to raid a canton of Upper Macedonia or join in a war on that side of the Pindus range. Dardanians, Paeonians, and Thracians fell into the same pattern of tribal life and of intertribal warfare, practised often for plunder. In all these Balkan areas the warriors were armed alike and fought in the same manner; the monarchies were comparable in kind; and the élite troops were formed around the king (e.g. Arr. *An.* 1. 5. 2), as in the state of Macedon. They were all essentially military states. When Aristotle made his category in *Politics* 1324[b] 10–23 of expansionist tribal states (*ethne*) which rated military prowess and power most highly, he gave examples from Scythians, Thracians, and Macedonians in the Balkans. A man who had not killed an enemy in war was not allowed to drink from the loving cup in Scythia, and he had to wear a halter instead of a belt at one time in Macedonia. The institutions and the worships of these tribal states too had much in common, the cult of Dionysus for instance spreading from Thrace through Lower Macedonia.

The Greek city-states of Chalcidice and those which traded with the ports of the Thermaic Gulf were entirely different from what they called the *ethne* of the Balkan area, Macedon and Molossia included. To them monarchy was tantamount to despotism, and tribalism was the mark of a savage society. If individual Greeks chose to settle at the court of a Balkan king, they were attracted by the hope of financial gain and not by any idea that they would find there a comparable way of life. The same contrast existed between Macedonia and the city-states of Thessaly. There was however a link between Aegeae and Larissa in that the Temenidae and the Aleuadae both claimed descent from Heracles. It gave Archelaus an opening for diplomacy, but the real difference between Greek and Macedonian ways of life was expressed by the polemical words of Thrasymachus in his speech *For the Larissaeans*

Ἀρχελάῳ δουλεύσομεν, Ἕλληνες ὄντες βαρβάρῳ;

Shall we, being Greeks, be the slaves of the savage, Archelaus?

IV

A PERIOD OF INSTABILITY
399–359

1. *Problems of the succession to the throne, 399–393*

THE killer of Archelaus was named as Craterus, Crateas, Crataeus, and Crateuas, of which we may adopt the last. The sources agree that Crateuas was 'the beloved' of Archelaus. One version, transmitted perhaps through Marsyas Macedon, made the killing of the king by Crateuas an accident during a hunting expedition (D.S. 14. 37. 6 ἀκουσίως). The other version, appearing first in Aristotle *Politics* 1311ᵇ8–35, made Crateuas commit a *crime passionnel*, his love affair with the king having gone wrong; but it included other details which suggested a conspiracy, led by one Decamnichus and involving Hellanocrates of Larissa. It is evident that Crateuas and Decamnichus were Royal Pages and that Hellanocrates was associated with them; for that was why Crateuas was at the hunt, Decamnichus was flogged and Hellanocrates was exposed to the lust of the king, who moreover had promised to restore him to Larissa but had not done so. The story was filled out with further explanations: Crateuas had been promised the hand of a daughter of the king but she had been given to another, and Decamnichus had enraged Euripides by commenting on his foul breath and so had been handed over to Euripides to get a flogging. The story was almost too good to be true. It was picked up by the unknown authors of [Plato] *Alcibiades* 2. 141 D and [Plu.] *Amatorius* 23 and by Aelian *VH* 8. 9 and received the additional embellishment that Crateuas, whose love of power rivalled Archelaus' love of him, occupied the throne for three or four days and was then put down either by (the) others (ἑτέρων τινῶν), implying a rival set of conspirators, or by some Companions (emending the text to ἑταίρων τινῶν, as Professor Edson has suggested to me). Everything from halitosis to rough justice!

We may conclude from these accounts that Archelaus was killed by the javelin of Crateuas on a hunting expedition, and that Crateuas was put on trial. The result of the trial was either that Crateuas, Decamnichus, and Hellanocrates were suspected of a plot but the case was not proven, or that Crateuas was acquitted on the ground that it was an accident.[1]

---

[1] I omit the alternative of conviction by the Assembly of the Macedones, because it would then have been impossible for Marsyas Macedon (or whoever it was) to assert that the death was accidental.

I prefer the former interpretation, because the authority of Aristotle probably outweighs that of Marsyas Macedon or whoever reported the death as accidental. The mention of Hellanocrates is interesting; he was no doubt the son of a leading member of the Aleuadae of Larissa, and Archelaus, like Philip and Alexander later, used association with the system of the Royal Pages to further diplomatic alliances. The suggestion that Crateuas occupied the throne is obviously absurd.[1]

Between the death of Archelaus in 400/399 and the accession of Amyntas III in 394/3, if we follow the chronological data of Diodorus 14. 37. 6, 84. 6, 89. 2, and 15. 60. 3, the throne was held by Orestes, Aëropus, and Pausanias; and when we consult the chronographic lists we find another Amyntas (i.e. Amyntas II) as king between Aëropus and Pausanias. When we remember that the official Macedonian year differed from the year or years of various Greek chronographers, it is not surprising that we have different periods of rule attributed to these kings. The nearest we can get to probability is that Orestes was king but a minor within the years 400/399 to 398/7, Aëropus having been regent became king and ruled within the years 398/7 to 395/4, and Amyntas II and Pausanias fitted into 394/3 as well as Amyntas III. The point which is best attested is that Aëropus died of disease in 395/4 (D.S. 14. 84. 6), and right at the end of that year because he was outwitted by Agesilaus a month or two before the eclipse of the sun on 14 August 394 (Polyaen. 2. 1. 17 and 4. 4. 3; X. *HG* 4. 3. 10). The adherents of Amyntas II and Pausanias cited the year 394/3 as the year of each, and indeed the only way of recording their reigns was in units of a year.[2]

Although no source says so, it may be assumed that Orestes was a son of Archelaus because, although a minor, he was elected king (D.S. 14. 37. 6). Later he was replaced by Aëropus, though whether he was killed by Aëropus (as in D.S. loc. cit.) or died in some other way must remain

---

[1] If I am correct in my interpretation, the system of Royal Pages existed from the time of Archelaus at least, and the passage in Arr. *An.* 4. 13. 1 was either incorrect or has been misinterpreted by those who maintain that Philip II invented the system. As in other matters, Philip II may have extended or redefined an already existing system. The whole affair has been treated by Geyer 103 f., citing the earlier literature, and he accepted a conspiracy and gave Crateuas some days on the throne. Cloché 89 and others have held that Hellanocrates was not a member of the Aleuadae.

[2] The chronological data were best discussed by Beloch, *GG* 3². 2. 55 f., his conclusions differing from mine. Geyer 109 criticized Beloch's views. The chronographic lists of Syncellus, Eusebius, and others do not help as they are inconsistent. The error of Beloch was to reckon exclusively in year-units. For example, if Archelaus died in 400/399 and Aëropus died in 395/4, Beloch reckoned for Aëropus a 'fünfjährige Herrschaft' and thought this incompatible with Diodorus giving him six years of rule; but if we count inclusively and make 400/399 common to Archelaus and Aëropus, then six years is correct, as in D.S. 14. 37. 6 and 14. 84. 6. The passage of Agesilaus through Macedonia (X. *HG* 4. 3. 3) can hardly have been earlier than July 394, even if his speed of a month in all was exaggerated as it probably was in X. *Ages.* 2. 1. The tradition of two Amyntases led to the erroneous entries 'Archelaus alius' in Exc. Barb. and Syncellus 494 and 500; it should be 'Amyntas alius'.

uncertain. Next, what were the origins of Amyntas II? We are helped by the list of kings and tyrants who were overthrown in Aristotle, *Politics* 1311ᵇ3–15. In this short passage Aristotle introduces 'Amyntas the Little' in his list as a king, and then naturally resumes him just as 'Amyntas'; in other words the Amyntas of line 3 and the Amyntas of line 14 are one and the same.[1] The reading in line 14 is disputed as between Ἀμύντα, Ἀμύντῳ, and Ἀμύντᾳ, and the genitive seems more likely. The sense too is better with a genitive. The situation is that Archelaus, having a very young son as heir, gave one of his daughters in marriage to the son of Amyntas (i.e. the Little), thinking thereby that a dispute would then be least likely to arise between him (Amyntas) and his (Archelaus') son by Cleopatra. Thus Archelaus hoped to bring to his side an Amyntas who was at least as old as himself and perhaps older.[2] In fact this Amyntas succeeded Aëropus as Amyntas II, probably under circumstances which could be regarded as suspicious because Amyntas figured in Aelian's gallery of disreputable kings or members of the royal house of Macedon: Archelaus son of a slave woman, Menelaus a bastard, and Menelaus' son, Amyntas, who 'had been trusted as a slave and an attendant of Aëropus' (*VH* 12. 43). In fact this means that as a Royal Page Amyntas had waited on Aëropus, then an older member of the royal family, and later (as alleged by Aelian's source) betrayed that trust by doing something detrimental to Aëropus. Aelian says in the same passage that Menelaus was the grandfather of Philip. We can put this in the form of a stemma:

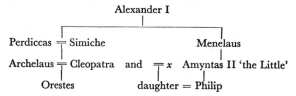

When the Assembly of Macedones appointed Aëropus regent, it is to be presumed that Aëropus stood higher in the succession than Amyntas the Little. We have inferred already that Aëropus was older, and we must now infer that he was another grandson of Alexander I in the male line. We shall return to that relationship later.

[1] So too Beloch, *GG* 3². 2. 56, and Geyer 108, countering the views of Gutschmid 36 and E. Meyer, *GdA* 5. 303.

[2] Here I disagree with Beloch, Geyer, and others, who read a dative; they then take Amyntas the Little to be a son of Archelaus, and the result is that Archelaus married off his son to his daughter. Beloch also had Archelaus marry his step-mother, Cleopatra, and get Orestes by her. An unparalleled and unlikely set of relationships, which ends up with a pointless marriage, as far as I can see. Cleopatra was a favourite name for girls in Macedonia, and there is no need to assume that because the wife of Perdiccas and the wife of Archelaus were both called Cleopatra they were one and the same woman.

Amyntas the Little was killed by Derdas, because he had taunted Derdas with his youthfulness according to Aristotle (*Pol.* 1311^{b}4); thus Derdas evidently was a Royal Page. Next on the throne came Pausanias, son of Aëropus according to D.S. 14. 84. 6, a passage which overlooks the Amyntas II episode altogether. It is evident then that the Assembly chose not to appoint Philip, son of Amyntas II, but to go back to a son of Aëropus. But Pausanias died soon afterwards, 'being disposed of by Amyntas by a trick' according to D.S. 14. 89. 2, which probably rests on nothing more than suspicion. In any case this Amyntas, who became Amyntas III, came from a different branch of the stemma, being descended from Amyntas, son of Alexander I.

Who then was Aëropus? He was chosen to be regent presumably because he was next of kin among adults to the young king, just as Philip in 359 was appointed regent as next of kin to Amyntas IV. Moreover, if Aëropus ranked so high in the royal house in 399, he was likely to have been one of those who swore to the treaty of *c.* 415, and that is where we find him on the restoration which I have proposed: 'Aëropus, son of Perdiccas'. Now we know that Perdiccas had a son by Cleopatra, who was said to have been disposed of when he was seven years old by Archelaus *c.* 413 (see p. 135 above); it is possible that Aëropus was an elder brother of that boy, or he may have been a half-brother by another wife.[1] We show the full stemma of Alexander's sons' descendants facing p. 176 below.

We can now see that the dynastic struggles of 400–394 were at first between the line of Perdiccas and that of Menelaus. The former had Archelaus, Orestes, Aëropus, and Pausanias as kings, and tried to win over Amyntas the Little by the marriage of *c.* 400; but the line of Menelaus came into power when Amyntas the Little became king as Amyntas II. Meanwhile the lines of Alcetas and Philippus had died out, the former having been removed probably by Archelaus and the latter probably by Perdiccas and Sitalces. One line was left, that of Amyntas, son of Alexander I; and in 394/3 his grandson came to the throne as Amyntas III. But there must still have been those who thought the lines of Perdiccas and Menelaus had better claims to the position.

We can see too that the source behind Diodorus' list of kings supported the house of Perdiccas and disregarded that of Menelaus: it ran Archelaus, Orestes, Aëropus, Pausanias. The comments too are in the same vein: Archelaus was killed accidentally, Aëropus was regent before he disposed of the minor Orestes and became king (14. 37. 6), Aëropus died 'of illness' and his son Pausanias succeeded (14. 84. 6). It was represented

---

[1] Geyer 107 and 111 rightly rejects the views of Abel, Droysen, Swoboda, and Kaerst that Aëropus was a member of the Lyncestid house. Cloché 106 regards him as next of kin to Orestes in the Macedonian royal house.

as a straightforward line of succession. Amyntas II was omitted altogether and Amyntas III was greeted with an adverse note: 'Pausanias, the king of the Macedones, being disposed of by Amyntas by a trick' (14. 89. 2). If the source was Marsyas Macedon, his sympathies lay with the house of Perdiccas. Justin, however, favoured Amyntas III, but he confused him with Amyntas II as 'the son of Menelaus' (7. 4. 3). On the other hand, we have hostile comments in Aelian and elsewhere, and we may attribute them ultimately to a Greek writer such as Theopompus who was critical of any branch of the Macedonian royal house.

During this troubled period coins were issued by Aëropus, Amyntas II, Pausanias, and Amyntas III (see Plate II). The link in coinage between Archelaus, Aëropus, and Pausanias is clear; for they used the same style, standard, and emblems, e.g. the silver didrachm with young male head with band in hair / unattended horse walking right.[1] Aëropus and Pausanias placed the forepart of a springing lion on their bronze coins. The only new type was that of Pausanias with the forepart of a running boar, which revived a type used by Archelaus in bronze.[2] On the other hand Amyntas II introduced a head of Pan, the forepart of a wolf, and a Corinthian helmet,[3] and Amyntas III turned to a head of Heracles, an eagle, and a man riding.[4] The names were recorded all in the genitive.

In 399–394 Sparta was the leading power in the Greek world. She was hostile to the ambitions of Archelaus in northern Thessaly, and it is likely that Aëropus withdrew from that area. When she became committed to war against Persia, her forces used the land route through Thessaly and Macedonia probably with or without the leave of Aëropus. When the Corinthian War started, Aëropus revealed his sympathy with the insurgents by trying to hold up the army of Agesilaus; but he was outsmarted and made a treaty with Sparta (Polyaen. 2. 1. 17).[5] The Thessalians, however, harassed the army on its way south. So Aëropus and they were of one mind in their attitude to Agesilaus (X. *HG* 4. 3. 3–8); it is probable that they had been brought together by Ismenias, the Theban leader, and the Argives, who had operated in Thessaly in the winter of 395/4. It may have been as a tribute to Argos that Aëropus placed the springing lion on his coins; for Perdiccas had marked his friendship with Argos *c.* 417–416 in the same way (see pp. 120–1 above). The struggle for power within the royal house in 394/3 was carried out

---

[1] G. 157. 1, XXIX. 23; 157, 2 and 158. 1 and 2, XXXIX. 31 and 33.
[2] G. 159. 6 and 7, XXIX. 34, 35; and G. 156. 12, XXIX. 21.
[3] G. 158. 2–4, in bronze; G. 157. 1, a silver didrachm being an Aëropus type but with the name of Amyntas.
[4] G. 159 f.
[5] The actual stratagem, adding mules and asses to a cavalry group to make it look impressive, is the silly stratagem which was attached to three different generals by Polyaenus; it is unhistorical, but the historical setting may be genuine.

while the Greek states were at war with one another near the Isthmus. There is no indication that it enabled the Illyrians or the peoples of Upper Macedonia to weaken the kingdom.[1]

2. *The reign of Amyntas III 393–370/69*

The motto of Amyntas' reign was given aptly by Justin 7. 4. 6: 'cum Illyriis deinde et cum Olynthiis gravia bella gessit.' It was probably around the turn of the century that Bardylis usurped the position of king of the Dardanii and organized a formidable state in the agricultural area of Kossovo, which is rich in minerals.[2] He expanded southwards at the expense evidently of the declining dynasty at Trebenishte where the 'poor graves' of the last phase petered out towards 400. It is evident that he conquered and probably annexed the fertile territories round the lakes of Ochrid, Prespa, and Malik; for he was able to invade both Molossis and Macedonia. This large and aggressive state was at its height in the period *c.* 395 to 358. The first great raid into Macedonia was in 393/2 according to Diodorus 14. 92. 3, who was drawing probably on Ephorus. The Illyrians drove Amyntas out of his kingdom; in other words they occupied Lower Macedonia and reached the Thermaic Gulf, as they had done in the Early Iron Age (see Volume I. 422). Amyntas gave 'to the Olynthians the territory near at hand' (τὴν σύνεγγυς χώραν); this was probably, as in 432, the area round Lete and Lake Bolbe. It appears from Diodorus' account that there was no official successor to Amyntas in the Macedonian tradition but that the Illyrians put in a puppet king, called Argaeus, who held power for part of 393/2–392/1, a 'two-year period'.

At that time, when the Greek states were locked in conflict round the Isthmus, Amyntas had no one in eastern Macedonia to help him except the Chalcidian League, which had grown in power with the collapse of Athens and had switched its alliance from Sparta to Boeotia and Argos in 395/4. To deposit rich territory with this League, led by 'the Olynthians' in the phrase of Diodorus, was a matter of Hobson's choice. As an exile Amyntas turned to a traditional friend of Macedon, the Aleuadae of Larissa. There Medius, the leader of the clan, was in a powerful position. He had used help from Boeotia and Argos to drive out Spartan garrisons and had then extended his own power in 394 (D.S. 14. 82. 5–6), bringing Crannon, Scotoussa, and Pharsalus into his orbit (X. *HG* 4. 3. 3), so that he controlled the central plain and gave the army of Agesilaus rough treatment in 394 (X. *HG* 4. 3. 3–8; D.S. 14. 83. 4). In 391 Amyntas was 'restored by the Thessali' (D.S. 14. 92.

[1] Geyer 112 and others assume the opposite: 'sie haben dabei teils Unterstützung bei den Barbaren, teils bei den obermakedonischen Vasallen und bei unzufriedenen Elementen unter dem Adel gefunden.'
[2] See my article in *BSA* 61 (1966) 243 and 248.

3), of whom Medius was probably the leader, as in 394 (D.S. 14. 82. 5 and X. *HG* 4. 3. 3 naming Larissa first).

A treaty between Amyntas and the Chalcidian League has survived (Tod, *GHI* no. 111). It probably regulated the relations between the two states *c.* 391, when Amyntas had regained his throne and received back his territory round Lake Bolbe *c.* 391. The first fragment of the stone, which was found at Olynthus, records a defensive alliance for fifty years between 'the Chalcidians and Amyntas son of Errhidaeus', each agreeing to help the other if their territory is invaded. On the reverse of this fragment there are regulations permitting the Chalcidians to export pitch, all forms of constructional timber, and only such shipbuilding timber of fir as the Chalcidian state needs. The Chalcidian state is free to export these forms of timber if they tell Amyntas in advance, on payment of the recorded dues. As regards all other commodities there are equal rights of export and transit between the two parties on payment of dues. Neither party is to enter separately into relations of friendship with Amphipolis, the Bottiaeans, Acanthus, and Mende, but only jointly if both parties think fit. The oath of alliance is then stated. It begins with help to Amyntas if his territory is invaded. The fragment then breaks off.[1]

The next attack by the Illyrians was directed against Molossis in 385/4. Dionysius, the tyrant of Syracuse, supporting the claims of an exiled king of the Molossians, Alcetas, sent troops and equipment to the Illyrians, who invaded Epirus and intended to put Alcetas on the throne as their puppet king. They defeated the Molossians in battle and killed more than 15,000 of them. In this crisis, Sparta sent an army north and drove out the Illyrians (D.S. 15. 13. 2–3).[2] These events showed the strength of the Illyrian forces.

In 383/2 they invaded Macedonia and defeated Amyntas in battle (D.S. 15. 19. 2; Isoc. 6. 46). Despairing of this situation, Amyntas gave a large amount of 'the neighbouring land to the people of Olynthus' (τῆς ὁμόρου χώρας). Once again it was Hobson's choice for Amyntas. But this time the people of Olynthus, who led the Chalcidian League, were much stronger than they had been at the time of the treaty with Amyntas. It is clear from the account in Xenophon, *HG* 5. 2. 11 f., that they had acquired much of the base of the peninsula, cutting off the Bottiaei from the sea and incorporating Crousis; for only so could their territory come to march with that of Amyntas, e.g. at Anthemus, which was no doubt part of 'the neighbouring territory' which he entrusted to them.[3] At the same time they threatened the independence of Acanthus and Apollonia

---

[1] The treaty is discussed by Geyer 112 and by J. R. Ellis in *Mak.* 9 (1969) 3.

[2] See *Epirus* 278, 524, and 533.

[3] The word used by Diodorus here and at 14. 92. 3 was ἐδωρήσατο; but the land was given evidently for use and not for outright possession, and Amyntas asked for it back at 15. 19. 2 fin.

(the latter being some 10 miles from Olynthus, i.e. not the Apollonia in Mygdonia). The Olynthians enjoyed the revenues of Amyntas' land for a time, but Amyntas then made an unexpected recovery and won all his kingdom back (D.S. 15. 19. 2). We learn more detail from Isocrates, who tells us that Amyntas thought better of his first decision to leave the country; 'he seized a small place, summoned help from there, and got possession of all Macedonia in three months, and spent the rest of his life on the throne' (Isoc. 6. 46). Isocrates, writing to Archidamus *c.* 366, was referring to the events of 383/2, after which the throne of Amyntas was secure.

It was at one time a fashion in scholarship to seek out 'doublets', i.e. two accounts of one and the same incident, and choose one only as an actual event. This has been done by Beloch, *GG* 3². 2. 57 f., and others with reference to Diodorus' two Illyrian invasions of Macedonia, which they either cut down to one or modify in various ways.[1] While I have argued in the past against this manner of approach to events in Diodorus,[2] it is necessary now to defend my attitude to these two invasions in particular. In the first place, as they are recounted by Diodorus, the two invasions are not the same. In 393/2 the Illyrians invaded and drove Amyntas out of the country; but the Thessalians restored him and he won back the kingdom 'after a short time . . . some say two years'. In 383/2 Amyntas was defeated by the Illyrians (Isocrates added μάχῃ in his account) but later recovered himself unexpectedly and won back the whole kingdom (Isocrates gave details which remind one of Thrasybulus' unexpected success from Phyle). The points of difference between D.S. 14. 92. 3–4 and D.S. 15. 19. 2 are obvious: in one case the Illyrian occupation was complete and lasted up to two years, and it was the Thessalians who put Amyntas on his feet; in the second a disastrous defeat in battle was followed fairly soon afterwards by Amyntas unaided recovering himself in an unexpected way (Isocrates adding the point that within three months he regained all Macedonia). The theory, then, that Diodorus repeated himself inadvertently or that he described the same incident twice from different sources, does not stand. On the other hand the superficial similarities—Illyrians, giving land to Olynthus, and Amyntas despairing—arise from the geographical setting which was the same on both occasions.

---

[1] Beloch was followed by Swoboda in *Arch-epigr. Mitteil. a. Österr.* 7. 14 f. and Costanzi in *Klio* 6. 298 with various modifications, and Geyer 113 f. had his own version. Their views have been generally accepted, e.g. in Tod, *GHI* 2. 32 f. Recently in *Mak.* 9 (1969) 1–8 J. R. Ellis has brought very strong arguments to bear against the theory of Beloch and others. His article, 'Amyntas III, Illyria, and Olynthos 393/2–380/79', gives a sequence of events which is different from mine; for instance, he put the alliance between Amyntas and the Chalcidians in 393/2 before the Illyrian invasion, and the rule of Argaeus in 385–3.

[2] See *StGH* 486 f. = *JHS* 57 (1937) 44 f.

One of Beloch's arguments concerned the data in our sources for the length of Amyntas' reign. As I see it, Diodorus gave Amyntas twenty-four years from 394/3 at 14. 89. 2; at 14. 92. 3, when writing of the restoration; and at 15. 60. 3, when recording his death in 370/369. Diodorus' chief source therefore gave Amyntas a continuous reign from 394/3 to 370/369 as lawful king, whether he was in Macedonia or in exile. On the other hand, Diodorus used a second source who inserted for Argaeus a two-year period, namely 393/2 and 392/1; this source regarded Argaeus as lawful king (as in Euseb. *Chron.* 200. 11). There is support for this source in Porphyr. fr. 1, *FHG* 3. 691, which says that after reigning one year (viz. 394/3) Amyntas was expelled by the Macedones (ὑπὸ Μακεδόνων ἐξεβλήθη); in other words he was formally deposed by the Assembly and Argaeus no doubt was elected king in his place. There is a distorted echo too in Schol. Aeschines 2. 26, where Amyntas was said to have been expelled from the kingship by the Thessalians (ἐκβληθέντα . . . ἐκ τῆς βασιλείας). We have seen a similar instance of two sources being used by Diodorus, one giving the succession as Orestes–Aëropus–Pausanias, and the other inserting Amyntas the Little as lawful king (see p. 170 above). In the present case, at 14. 92. 4, Diodorus cited his second source anonymously in the words ἔνιοι δέ φασι. What Beloch did was to take the two mentions of the twenty-four years at 14. 89. 2 and 14. 92. 3, and argue that Diodorus had repeated himself and committed a 'Duplikat'. But once again the contexts are entirely different; and in the second passage Diodorus reaffirmed the twenty-four years precisely because he went on to mention a different tradition. I see no reason to reject either passage.

Who was Argaeus? The name was a revered one in the royal family, because a son of Temenus and the first successor of Perdiccas I had been so called (Paus. 2. 28. 3; Hdt. 8. 139). The clue is provided by a fragment of Theopompus (*FGrH* 115 F 29), preserved in Harpocration s.v. *Argaios*, which referred to two pretenders to the throne in 359, Argaeus and Pausanias: περὶ τούτου καὶ Θεόπομπος ἐν τῷ αʹ τῶν Φιλιππικῶν λέγει· τὸν Ἀρχέλαον καλοῦσι καὶ Ἀργαῖον καὶ Παυσανίαν (MSS: B, AC). Even as emended, the passage is absurd;[1] for it is impossible that both Argaeus and Pausanias were called 'Archelaus'. Now, Harpocration was identifying Argaeus, and he used a passage in which Theopompus had identified Argaeus and Pausanias. I suggest an obvious emendation τὸν Ἀρχελάου καλοῦσι, and I then translate 'they call both Argaeus and Pausanias the son of Archelaus.' In the case of Pausanias we know from

---

[1] As Jacoby remarks 'die Gleichsetzung der Namen ist ausgeschlossen.' In an article, 'The step-brothers of Philip II', *Historia* 22 (1973) 350–4, J. R. Ellis discussed this passage and took the Archelaus in it to be the eldest son of Amyntas III and Gygaea; but this does not make the passage any clearer.

Diodorus 16. 2. 6 that he was a member of the royal family (τῆς βασιλικῆς συγγενείας κοινωνῶν); and this means in effect that he was decended from either Archelaus or Aëropus, if we have been correct in supposing that the lines of Philippus and Alcetas had been cut off respectively *c.* 429 and *c.* 413. If the emendation is accepted, Archelaus had three sons named Orestes, Argaeus, and Pausanias, of whom the oldest was a minor in 399, the second was adult *c.* 392 and active still in 359 (i.e. born *c.* 410 at the latest), and the third was active in 359. The relationships are shown on the accompanying stemma.

Having won back his kingdom with his own military resources in Macedonia in the course of 383, Amyntas asked the Chalcidian League to return his land to him, but the Olynthians had no intention of complying (D.S. 15. 19. 2 fin.). The ambitions of the League and its achievements at the expense of Amyntas, with whom it now went to war, were described by envoys from Acanthus and Apollonia in a speech which seems to be based on reliable information (X. *HG* 5. 2. 12 f.). The Chalcidians, representing themselves as 'liberators', had acquired the Macedonian cities nearest to them and then moved against those which were further away and incidentally larger; at the time of the envoys' departure, in autumn 383, the Chalcidian League had captured Pella, 'the largest of the Macedonian cities'. The envoys represented Amyntas with little exaggeration as 'only not expelled entirely from all Macedonia'. Indeed, he was in a desperate position; for he was confined to the western part of Lower Macedonia and the Chalcidians held the crossing of the Axius and eastern Macedonia, as well as his capital. But the Chalcidians had ambitions also of expanding eastwards. There 'the neighbouring Thracians, those without a king', were friendly and might join the Chalcidian Alliance; if so, they would help the Chalcidians to lay hands on the gold mines of Mt. Pangaeum. These Thracians were no doubt the Bisaltae, then independent of Macedon, and some of the tribes of Mt. Orbelus, which were hostile to the Edoni and the Odrysians. As the Chalcidian League had something like 800 excellent cavalry, 8,000 hoplites, and 'a much larger number of peltasts', i.e. infantry trained in the Thracian manner, these ambitions were to be taken seriously.[1]

Amyntas had little chance of surviving unaided. It was probably at this time, as Geyer 118 f. suggested, that Amyntas made common cause

---

[1] The cavalry had particular prestige with the Balkan peoples. Acanthus and Apollonia had some cavalry, which if added to those of the Chalcidian League would have made a total of over 1,000; and we hear of a Chalcidian cavalry force of 600 operating some 11 miles away from Olynthus (X. *HG* 5. 3. 1). The figure for the hoplites in X. *HG* 5. 2. 14 is 800, probably a corruption of 8,000, because this army was able to face and defeat the army of Teleutias which set out from Greece with more than 10,000 soldiers, predominantly hoplites (D.S. 15. 19. 3). Crousis had peltast infantry in 429 (Thuc. 2. 79. 4).

with Cotys, king of the Odrysians, and perhaps received the help of some Thracian troops under the command of Iphicrates, who was then in the service of Cotys and had married his daughter. For we learn later that Amyntas adopted Iphicrates as his son, no doubt in gratitude for some outstanding service.[1] But the main appeal of Amyntas was addressed to Sparta, then the leading power in the Greek world and the constant opponent of federalism. His request in the autumn or winter of 382 came more or less at the same time as that of the envoys from Acanthus and Apollonia (D.S. 15. 19. 3; X. *HG* 5. 2. 11–20).[2]

Sparta and her Allies answered the appeals with alacrity. Eudamidas led an advance force of 3,000 hoplites north in spring 382 and won over the all-important base, Potidaea, from which he could threaten Olynthus, some 8 miles away (D.S. 15. 20. 3; X. *HG* 5. 2. 24). He put garrisons into allied cities, such as Acanthus and Apollonia, and awaited the arrival of the main force, which took possession of Thebes on its way north. The new commander, Teleutias, sent instructions ahead to Amyntas, asking him 'to hire mercenaries and give money to the nearby kings in the hope of gaining their alliance, if he wanted to win back his kingdom' (X. *HG* 5. 2. 38). Clearly Teleutias thought little of any infantry Amyntas could offer; Teleutias wanted Thracian mercenaries above all, just as Brasidas had done, and Amyntas may have obtained some through the offices of Iphicrates.[3] The kings whom Teleutias had in mind were the kings of Upper Macedonia and perhaps the king of the Paeonians. At the same time he sent to one of the former, Derdas, 'the ruler of Elimea' (X. *HG* 5. 2. 38), pointing out that 'the lesser realm' of Derdas was in danger of being swallowed up by the Olynthians, who had already subdued 'the greater realm of Macedonia', i.e. the realm of Amyntas.

In the campaigns which followed the most conspicuous services were rendered not by 'as many of the Macedonian cavalry as were present' in summer 382—in fact they were part of a confederate force which was defeated by the Chalcidian cavalry—but by the cavalry squadrons of Derdas, which twice inflicted heavy losses on the Chalcidian cavalry. The troopers of Derdas were fully armed and well mounted, and they had been trained to manœuvre and fight in close formation (X. *HG* 5. 2. 42 and 5. 3. 1). But the campaigns of 382 and summer 381 ended disastrously for Teleutias outside the walls of Olynthus, when he sent his peltasts into action against the Chalcidian cavalry and then committed

---

[1] Aeschines 2. 28; the marriage of Iphicrates with the daughter of Cotys was *c.* 386 (see U. Kahrstedt in *RE* 9. 2019).

[2] I am following the chronology of G. E. Underhill, *A Commentary on the Hellenica of Xenophon* (Oxford, 1900) lix f.

[3] According to D.S. 15. 19. 3 Amyntas got together 'a personal force' ἰδίαν τε δύναμιν, as opposed to a public or national force; the implication is that apart from his cavalrymen he had to rely mainly on mercenaries.

his whole force within range of the defenders of the walls (X. *HG* 5. 3. 3–6; D.S. 15. 21. 2–3). But Sparta sent out another large force under one of the kings, Agesipolis, who enlisted the help of Amyntas and Derdas and also of the Thessalian cavalry. During the blockade of Olynthus and its capitulation in 379 we hear no more of Amyntas and Derdas. It is clear that Sparta made terms which suited herself: the dissolution of the Chalcidian League, and the dependence of Olynthus and other states in Chalcidice on Sparta for all matters of foreign policy (X. *HG* 5. 3. 26; D.S. 15. 23. 3). Amyntas rejoiced to see the destruction of his most formidable neighbour at so small a cost to himself, and he doubtless resumed control of the cities of the plain and Anthemus.[1] Even if Sparta demanded his obedience to her in matters of her foreign policy, as she most probably did, it was a small price to pay.

With the decline of Sparta which followed the liberation of Thebes and the rise of Athens as the leader of a growing Alliance Amyntas was quick to reorientate his foreign policy. Most of the last part of an alliance between Amyntas and Athens is preserved on two fragments of a *stele* at Athens, praising Amyntas and his envoys Ptolemy, Antenor, and .. sōn and recording the taking of oaths from Amyntas, son of Arrhidaeus, and Alexander, son of Amyntas—the four last names being in larger letters.[2] The date is in dispute; but the position of Alexander suggests that he was an adult and first in the line of succession. As Alexander was the oldest son of Eurydice who married Amyntas *c.* 393 (see p. 16 above), Alexander became eighteen probably *c.* 373. At that time the Second Athenian Alliance was firmly established in the northern Aegean, and in 373 the Athenian commander Timotheus brought many new members from there into the Alliance (D.S. 15. 47. 2–4). Amyntas had sold much ship-timber to Athens for the reconstitution of her fleet between 377 and 373 (X. *HG* 6. 1. 11 Μακεδονίαν ἔνθεν καὶ Ἀθηναῖοι τὰ ξύλα ἄγονται); also it suited him to be on good terms with her, because the Chalcidian cities were hostile to her as well as to himself.

It was probably in the last years of his reign that Amyntas arbitrated between the city of Doliche in northern Perrhaebia and Elimea in a dispute concerning their mutual frontier. There is no reason to suppose that Amyntas held any authority in either area; rather he was chosen as an impartial observer by both parties in the dispute.[3] In Thessaly itself

---

[1] As Isocrates pointed out in *Panegyricus* 126, Sparta was in fact assisting Amyntas to make his kingdom as large as possible. A reference to such assistance may be contained in the confused remarks of the scholiast to Aeschines 2. 26.

[2] Tod, *GHI* no. 129, bracketing it between 375 and 373; Geyer 123 f. favoured 375/4. It is an alliance between Athens and Amyntas, not between Athens and her Allies and Amyntas. The friendship between the two states at this period was emphasized by Aeschines. 2. 26 and 28 fin.

[3] *BSA* 17 (1910–11) 193 f.; see Volume I. 117 f. Geyer 125 assumed that Derdas, king of Elimea, recognized 'die Oberhoheit des Königs', and Rosenberg in *Hermes* 51 (1916) 499 f.

Jason, the tyrant of Pherae, became ruler of all Thessaly, subjecting the Aleuadae of Larissa, with whom Amyntas had had ties of friendship. But it suited Amyntas rather to make alliance with Jason as the strongest power in northern Greece (D.S. 15. 60. 2). Soon afterwards in 371 Athens and Sparta called a conference to discuss terms for a general peace. According to Aeschines 2. 32 Amyntas sent a deputy who attended the conference and Amyntas exercised 'a vote in his own right' (τῆς καθ' αὑτὸν ψήφου κύριος ὤν); not only that, but his deputy recognized the claim of Athens to possess Amphipolis and voted with the rest of the Greeks to help Athens recover it. It is surprising to find Amyntas at a conference of Greek states at all, because Macedon was not regarded as a Greek state, and it is also surprising to find him voting Amphipolis to Athens. Perhaps the two are to be connected. Athens may have arranged with Sparta that Amyntas should attend as an ally of Athens, and Athens' object was to use Amyntas as a stalking horse for her claim to Amphipolis; it is an indication of Amyntas' dependence on Athens that he was prepared to play this part.[1]

In the course of 370/69, probably in the latter half of 370, Amyntas died at an advanced age (D.S. 15. 60. 3; Just. 7. 4. 8; Isoc. 6. 46).[2] The kingdom which he left was weaker than that which he had inherited. Two Illyrian invasions and a period of Illyrian suzerainty had impoverished the country, because rapine and looting were the specialities of Illyrian warriors (e.g. Frontinus, *Strat.* 2. 5. 19), and this was followed by the loss of the eastern part of the central plain as far as Pella to the Chalcidians, who doubtless looted before they fell back during the campaigns against the Spartan armies. The forces of Amyntas at that time were inferior to those of Derdas, the king of Elimea, and he himself was little more than a vassal of Sparta. It is doubtful whether his kingdom recovered much in the 370s. The whole of Chalcidice and the adjacent districts had been looted and ravaged by both sides, which cut down the olive trees in particular (X. *HG* 5. 2. 43, 5. 3. 1, and 5. 3. 3); that area did not regain full prosperity until a generation later, *c.* 350. The revival of Athens as a relatively strong power was not necessarily to his advantage; for Athens too was in severe financial distress by 373, and she was

thought that Amyntas had intervened as 'Oberherr'; but in either case the people of Doliche would have been most foolish to accept an interested party as arbitrator. Cloché 119 is of the same opinion as Geyer.

[1] Aeschines wanted to represent Amyntas as a free agent; therefore he may have misstated that aspect of the situation. However, Aeschines' statement that he produced oral and written evidence of Amyntas' vote must surely mean that such a vote was in fact cast. Geyer 126 believed that Macedon was taking its place at the conference as a state on a par with, and equal in rights with the Greek powers; this seems to me unlikely.

[2] Diodorus differs here from the *Marmor Parium* (*FGrH* 239 A 72), which gives 371/0, as restored by Jacoby.

unlikely to pay for anything she could obtain by *force majeure*. Both Methone and Pydna were independent of his rule.

When Elimea was a separate state, indeed stronger than Macedon *c.* 382, it is clear that Tymphaea and Orestis were out of the reach of Amyntas, and it is most unlikely that he had any influence in Lyncus and Pelagonia which were close to the great power headed by Bardylis. Late in his reign Amyntas was defeated by the Illyrians and was forced to pay tribute to Bardylis (D.S. 16. 2. 2). Equally Amyntas had no control over the easternmost part of Macedonia. There the Bisaltae sided in the 380s with the Chalcidians, and it is doubtful whether Amyntas was able to assert his authority over them for more than a short time. His coinage was at first underweight in silver, and more coins survive in bronze than in silver; indeed his successor, Alexander II, coined in bronze only. The signs of impoverishment are clear.

The emblems on the coins of Amyntas III stress the claim of the new line of the royal family to be descended from Heracles: his head, his club, and the wild boar he slew figure most prominently. An eagle standing on and striking a snake is a new emblem; it occurred also at Pydna and Aphytis. A standing horse unattended continues the earlier tradition.[1] There is a fine full-weight didrachm of silver, on the two sides of which a hunting scene was apparently portrayed: a rider on a prancing horse, with a spear raised to strike downwards / a lion biting and pawing a spear. The horse carried a caduceus brand on its crupper; such a brand occurred on coins of the Bisaltae and then of Alexander I.[2] It may be that Amyntas gained possession of the silver mines in Bisaltic territory towards the end of his reign; and perhaps it was then that he was willing to support Athens against Amphipolis.

Amyntas showed remarkable courage, tenacity, and resilience.[3] But the power and the ambition of his neighbours, in both Illyria and Chalcidice, pinned him down in a struggle for survival; indeed it was almost a miracle that he and his kingdom did survive. Neither he nor his people seem to have made any innovations during his long reign. Cavalry alone was redoubtable. Infantry and the class which provided it were negligible factors in war and in politics.

3. *Alexander, Ptolemy, and Perdiccas*

Amyntas left three sons and a daughter by his marriage to Eurydice, namely Alexander, Perdiccas, Philip, and Eurynoë, and three sons by his marriage to Gygaea, namely Archelaus, Arrhidaeus, and Menelaus

---

[1] G. 159 f., xxx. 1–11.   [2] G. 160 no. 6, xxx. 6; 49 no. 7; 152 no. 30.
[3] Just. 7. 4. 4 summed him up as 'insignis industria et omnibus imperatoriis virtutibus instructus'. For the 'Amynteum' at Pydna, see p. 693.

(Just. 7. 4. 5). The people elected the eldest son, Alexander, to the throne (Just. 7. 4. 8 'regno maximo ex filiis Alexandro tradito'; Aeschines 2. 26; D.S. 15. 60. 3). Threatened by the Illyrians he paid a danegeld and gave them his younger brother, Philip, as a hostage (Just. 7. 5. 1, preferable to D.S. 16. 2. 2). Soon after his accession he was approached by the Aleuadae of Larissa, who wished to make themselves independent of the power of Pherae. There Jason had been assassinated and his successor had been poisoned. The tyrant of the moment, Alexander of Pherae, knew the plans of the Aleuadae and prepared to invade Macedonia. But Alexander of Macedon moved first, bringing the Aleuadae to Larissa, where he gained control of the city (apart from the citadel which he took by siege later). Crannon in central Thessaly came over to him, when he promised to entrust the government of the cities to the Thessalians; but he went back on his word and occupied the cities with his own garrisons. It was a shortsighted action. Thessaly was the centre of conflicting interests, and Alexander had insufficient strength to hold by force what he had gained through goodwill.

In 368 Pelopidas at the head of a Boeotian army intervened at the invitation of the Thessalians, liberated Larissa from Macedonian control, and confined Alexander of Pherae to his own city. He then entered Macedonia, where Alexander was at war with 'Ptolemy of Alorus', no doubt the Macedonian who had headed the embassy to Athens *c.* 373 (see p. 178 above). At their request he arbitrated between them. It seems that he reconciled Ptolemy to the rule of Alexander and persuaded Alexander to restore some persons he had exiled; for the final result was that he entered into an alliance with Alexander as king. But it was an alliance made under compulsion, because Alexander surrendered into the hands of Pelopidas his youngest brother Philip (now restored by the Illyrians) and thirty sons of leading men. On his return to Thessaly Pelopidas formed the Thessalian League, and later in 368 he placed Philip, then aged thirteen or fourteen, in the house of Pammenes at Thebes, where he was destined to live for three years.[1]

The settlement in Macedonia was short-lived. The king was assassinated during a festival at which a war-dance, the *telesias*, was performed, late in 368 or early in 367.[2] The earliest authority for the killing is Marsyas Macedon fr. 3 (*FGrH* 135/6 writing of this dance) ἧ χρησάμενοι οἱ περὶ

[1] Plu. *Pelop.* 26; D.S. 15. 67. Both passages derive probably from Ephorus. For the chronology see *HG²* 663, and below p. 186 n. 1. A. Aymard, 'Philippe de Macédoine otage à Thèbes', *REA* 56 (1954) 15 f., argued in favour of 369.

[2] D.S. 15. 71. 1 under the year 368/7. If the war-dance was part of the Xanthica festival, held in the spring, the killing was in spring 367. This date fits better with the entry at 15. 77. 5 under 365/4, where Ptolemy was credited with three years of rule, viz. 367/6, 366/5, and 365/4; for spring comes close to the beginning of the Attic year 367/6. The same year, 368/7, was given in the *Marmor Parium* (*FGrH* 239 A 74), where the restoration of the text by Jacoby carries conviction.

Πτολέμαιον Ἀλέξανδρον τὸν Φιλίππου ἀδελφὸν ἀνεῖλον, ὡς ἱστορεῖ Μαρσύας ἐν τρίτῳ Μακεδονικῶν. The faction of Ptolemy was believed by Marsyas to have been responsible for the death of the king; but this became the work of Ptolemy himself in other sources, e.g. in D.S. 15. 71. 1 ἐπὶ δὲ τούτων Πτολεμαῖος ὁ Ἀλωρίτης ὁ Ἀμύντου υἱὸς ἐδολοφόνησεν Ἀλέξανδρον τὸν ἀδελφόν.

Who was this Ptolemy? We have suggested that Diodorus drew on Marsyas Macedon for his official list of Macedonian kings. Certainly in this case he drew on someone familiar with the technical terminology of Macedon, because he found in his source the phrase 'the Alorite', i.e. a citizen of Alorus,[1] and the presumption is that the source was a Macedonian, namely Marsyas Macedon. The next phrase 'the son of Amyntas' cannot refer to Amyntas III, whose six sons were named by Justin, but does most probably refer to Amyntas II the Little. If this is so, we see why Amyntas III married off his daughter to Ptolemy, the senior claimant in the line of Menelaus; his action was exactly analogous to that of Archelaus in marrying off his daughter to Philip, son of Amyntas the Little, *c.* 400 (see p. 169 above). In both cases it was an attempt to link the two lines of descent.

Ptolemy then being probably a younger brother of Philip, son of Amyntas II, may have been born *c.* 418 and so was a man of around fifty years of age *c.* 368. We see now why he headed the envoys to Athens *c.* 373 (see p. 178 above). In that treaty Amyntas and Alexander took the oaths; Ptolemy, next in precedence among the adult males of the royal house, held the next senior position. Finally, after describing the killing of Alexander, Diodorus added the words 'his brother',[2] which is non-sensical because Diodorus had already named Alexander's brothers as Perdiccas and Philip at 15. 60. 3. If he was using Marsyas, as we have suggested, we can see that he took the words out of Marsyas τὸν Φιλίππου ἀδελφόν, saw that he was anticipating the accession of Philip, removed Φιλίππου but left τὸν ἀδελφόν.[3]

A sensational account of the intrigues of Eurydice has come down to us in two places. Justin 7. 4. 7–7. 5. 8 gave it special prominence.

---

[1] As Geyer 102 f. and 129 argued convincingly against the view of J. L. F. Flathe, *Geschichte Makedoniens* (Leipzig, 1832–4) i. 38, that Ptolemy held a separate principality centred on Alorus, which was close to Aegeae.

[2] Repeated at D.S. 15. 77. 5. The word means strictly sons of the same mother and so was correctly used by Marsyas. It cannot mean 'brother-in-law' (i.e. through Ptolemy's marriage with Eurynoë), as C. L. Sherman in the Loeb edition, vol. 7 p. 148 n. 1, and others have suggested.

[3] Beloch, *GG* 3². 2. 67 and Geyer 125 assumed too readily that Ptolemy did not belong to the royal family at all. If so, his position as regent would be unique and contrary to Macedonian insistence upon the position being held by members of that house. The only support for their view is in Syncellus p. 500 (ed. Dindorf) ἀλλότριος τοῦ γένους, a late source not preferable to Diodorus; A. Aymard in *REA* 56 (1954) 31 agrees with Beloch and Geyer.

Eurydice, having arranged the marriage of her daughter [Eurynoë] to her son-in-law [Ptolemy] made an undertaking with her paramour [Ptolemy] to murder her husband and hand over the throne to him, and Amyntas would have been caught in his wife's plot, if the daughter [Eurynoë] had not revealed her mother's adultery and the criminal design . . . Not long afterwards Alexander fell a victim to the plot of his mother Eurydice, who had been caught in crime before but had been spared by Amyntas on account of the children he and she shared; for Amyntas did not know that she would be the cause of their death one day. His brother too, Perdiccas, was caught by a plot of equal treachery. It was indeed a dreadful thing that these children were deprived of life by their own mother in her lust, a mother who had already been released from the punishment her crimes merited by the thought of the children. The killing of Perdiccas was all the more dreadful because even his little, little son did not arouse compassion in the breast of that mother.

A further horror is added by the scholia to Aeschines 2. 29, which make Eurydice marry Ptolemy Alorites.

That this account is absurd need hardly be more than stated. Who knew what Eurydice and Ptolemy plotted against Amyntas? How did Eurynoë find out? If Amyntas knew the plot, why did he not get rid of Ptolemy? Would he really have forgiven Eurydice and let the wicked pair go on plotting? The elaboration that Perdiccas too was killed by his mother is of course false; Perdiccas met his death in battle against the Illyrians. The whole story is poppycock; it bears no relation to the procedure in the Assembly of the Macedones against those who were detected in a treasonable plot. We can dismiss it as a malicious and invented piece of scandal, not unlike other passages we have considered, and we shall discuss later who composed it.[1]

When Alexander was killed during the war-dance, one at least of 'the killers' was executed (D. 19. 194 δολοφονηθεὶς ἐτελεύτησε), Apollophanes of Pella, a married man with children and so not a Royal Page. The Assembly must have met to investigate the killing of the king and to decide on the succession. Ptolemy was appointed regent for Perdiccas, who was still a minor, and any coins which were minted during the next three years bore the name of Perdiccas and not of Ptolemy. Our sources, using non-technical language, call Ptolemy both regent and king,[2] e.g. scholia to Aeschines 2. 29 ἐπιτροπεύσας Περδίκκου καὶ Φιλίππου παίδων ὄντων ἐβασίλευσεν ἔτη ε'. The fact that he was appointed to this position of trust indicates that he was not believed by the Assembly to

---

[1] Aeschines 2. 26, speaking near the time, used the word for a natural death τετελευτηκότος. Plutarch and Diodorus have no plot by Eurydice. But Beloch, Geyer, Cloché, and others have accepted it almost *in toto*; so too G. H. Macurdy in *AJPhil* 48 (1927) 201 f. Geyer 132 n. 3 asked rather plaintively, when recounting the marriage of Eurydice and Ptolemy, 'Was wurde aus der Königstochter Eurynoë?'

[2] Regent in Plu. *Pelop.* 27. 3 and Aeschin. 2. 29; king in D.S. 15. 71. 1 and 77. 5, *Marmor Parium* (*FGrH* 239 A 74), and other chronographic lists.

have been responsible for the death of Alexander; had he been, no one would have trusted Perdiccas and Philip to him.[1]

A pretender came forward in the person of Pausanias, 'an exile, who enjoyed much support in Macedonia, where those who were thought to be friends of Eurydice betrayed her' (Aeschines 2. 27). He had been exiled by Amyntas III (Suid. s.v. *Karanos*). He was, of course, a member of the royal house, as D.S. 16. 2. 6 and Schol. Aeschines 2. 27 say, and he was described by the latter at 2. 26 as 'related to the supporters of Philip' συγγενὴς τῶν περὶ Φίλιππον. This Pausanias was evidently the son of Archelaus mentioned by Theopompus, if we emend τὸν Ἀρχέλαον to τὸν Ἀρχελάου (see p. 175 above). He was, then, descended from Perdiccas, and he was the brother-in-law of Philip, the son of Amyntas the Little, descended from Menelaus. Thus it seems that the men of both lines were combining against the descendants of Amyntas, and they were known as οἱ περὶ Φίλιππον. The fact that Philip and Ptolemy were brothers or more probably half-brothers did not deter the supporters of Philip and Pausanias, because Ptolemy had joined the rival camp.[2]

Pausanias entered Macedonia early in 367 with a force of Greek soldiers, recruited probably in Chalcidice, and captured Anthemus, Therme, Strepsa, and some other places (Aeschines 2. 27). Meanwhile Ptolemy obtained help from Iphicrates, the Athenian commander, who was operating with a small fleet against Amphipolis and may have used his influence with Cotys to bring aid from Thrace. According to Aeschines 2. 29, who was anxious to paint Athenian aid in the brightest of colours, 'Iphicrates drove Pausanias out of Macedonia and saved the dynasty for you [i.e. Philip II].' A similar picture was given by Nepos, *Iphicrates* 3. 2. In both passages Eurydice cut a pitiful figure as the mother of the two young princes (in fact already teenagers).[3] In Suidas s.v. *Karanos* she ejected Pausanias with the help of an Athenian general.

---

[1] Even though he accepted it as true, Geyer 134 admitted his surprise: 'Man muss sich überhaupt wundern, dass zwei so skrupellose Menschen wie Ptolemaios und Eurydike den jungen König nicht ebenfalls beseitigt haben.'

[2] Geyer 132 thought that the scholiast was referring to the future king, Philip II; but this is to read the situation backwards. In 367 Philip was aged fourteen and a hostage at Thebes. Beloch, *GG* 3². 2. 65, made the conjecture that Pausanias was a son of the Pausanias who followed Amyntas II on the throne; but names passed more frequently from grandfather to grandson, and the connection of that Pausanias with either Philip is not particularly close. When the scholiast comments on the opportune moment which favoured Pausanias in his attempt to return from exile (Aeschines 2. 27 τῷ καιρῷ δ' ἰσχύοντος), he remarks as follows: ἀντὶ τοῦ "τῇ εὐκαιρίᾳ θαρροῦντος", καθ' ὃ κατὰ νέων τὴν ἡλικίαν ἐπεχείρει κατὰ τῶν περὶ Φίλιππον. He explains that the age of the young princes Perdiccas and Philip favoured the attempt (repeating what Aeschines said at 2. 26 fin.), and then the next words seem to be corrupt. When the verb means 'to make an attack', it can be followed by some prepositions but not by κατά. Perhaps we should read κάθοδον for κατά and translate 'he was attempting the recall of the supporters of Philip'.

[3] This pathetic passage was obviously worked up by Aeschines, perhaps after the delivery of the speech; one thinks of Themistocles' appeal to Admetus as a parallel (Thuc. 1. 136. 3). The

The intervention of Athens was a challenge to Thebes as the dominant power in Thessaly. When the friends of the dead king, Alexander, evidently those who were thought to be friends of Eurydice, appealed to Pelopidas in spring 367, he enlisted a force of mercenaries and invaded Macedonia. Ptolemy won over the mercenaries with bribes, but he came to terms with Pelopidas; for he knew that he had no chance against the power of Thebes. The terms were an offensive and defensive alliance with Thebes, and the provision of hostages. Ptolemy handed over his son Philoxenus and fifty of the Companions, and they were sent to Thebes, where they joined the earlier group of hostages (Plu. *Pelop.* 27. 2–4). The policy of Thebes was clearly to support Perdiccas as the legitimate king; the taking of Philoxenus was a guarantee against Ptolemy seizing the throne, and the fifty Companions may have been those who had betrayed their friendship to Eurydice and intrigued with Pausanias. For Ptolemy the terms were humiliating: Macedon was a satellite of Thebes, tied to her foreign policy (as in Arr. *An.* 7. 9. 4). Ptolemy conformed by reinforcing the resistance of Amphipolis to Athens, the enemy of Thebes (Aeschines 2. 29).

It was probably at this time of weakness, *c.* 370–365, that the Orestae joined the Molossian state, which was more likely to help them against the dreaded Illyrians. Our knowledge of this is due to an inscription found at Dodona in which one of the fifteen *synarchontes* of the Molossian state was Phrynus with his ethnic 'Orestes' (*SEG* 23. 471, 13; see *Epirus* 527 f.). Four other tribes situated in the highlands of the Pindus range entered the Molossian state at the same time as the Orestae. Thus the Orestae became 'Orestae Molossi' as they had been in the sixth century (see Volume I. 111 and 439), and they cast off the nominal suzerainty of Macedon, under which they had been described as 'Orestae Macedones'.

We hear no more of Ptolemy until his death in 365 (D.S. 15. 77. 5, under 365/4; 16. 2. 4). Diodorus says that Perdiccas assassinated him; the Scholiast to Aeschines 2. 29 says that he was disposed of by a plot which Perdiccas himself organized against him. If either is true, it is more likely to be the latter. As Philip was born in 382 and Perdiccas was his predecessor in the family, he was born at the latest in 383; if so, he came of age at eighteen in 365. It is possible that he became king first and then disposed of Ptolemy.

fact that Philip was a hostage in Thebes at the time would not have deterred Aeschines, who was addressing an Athenian jury twenty-four years after the event. I have therefore not followed Geyer 133 n. 4 in deferring the removal of Philip to Thebes until after this episode in 367. It has been customary to see a doublet in the cases of hostages being taken by Pelopidas (Plu. *Pelop.* 26. 4 and 27. 3) and bunch them together at the later date; but this is unwise, because there were certainly two interventions by Pelopidas, different persons were taken hostage on each occasion, and the objects in view were different. I am generally in agreement with A. Aymard, 'Philippe de Macédoine otage à Thèbes', *REA* 56 (1954) 15 f.; except that I put Pelopidas' first intervention in 368.

Perdiccas reaffirmed his alliance with Thebes and obtained the release of Philip, who returned home in 365 at the age of sixteen or seventeen.[1] At that time Perdiccas was probably supplying timber for the building of the fleet which Epaminondas intended to launch in 363. However, in 364 the Athenian fleet under Timotheus operated in the Thermaic Gulf, winning possession of Pydna, Methone, and Potidaea (D. 4. 4) and later Torone (D.S. 15. 81. 6) and using these as bases from which to threaten both Perdiccas and the Chalcidian League. We learn from Demosthenes, *The First Philippic* 4–5, that Athens made 'all the territory around this [i.e. the three cities] her own' and that 'many of the tribes (*ethne*) which later were aligned with Philip were then free and independent and sided rather with Athens', whereas Perdiccas was devoid of allies. It is probable that Athens obtained some base at the head of the Thermaic Gulf, as she had done in the fifth century (see p. 119 above), and that she was also in league with some of the kings of the tribes in Upper Macedonia which Thucydides 2. 99. 2 had described as *ethne*. Indeed we have evidence of the latter point. Orestis, as we have seen, had joined the Molossian state, then a member of the Athenian Alliance (see *Epirus* 524). An Athenian decree of 365/4 recorded a king of the Pelagones as a proxenus and benefactor of Athens, if the restoration cited on p. 19 above is accepted (*IG* II². 190). Another Athenian decree of the year 362 honoured Menelaus the Pelagonian for his special services in fighting on Athens' side and providing money in the war against the Chalcidian League and Amphipolis; it went on to describe him and his ancestors as benefactors of the Athenian people (Tod, *GHI* no. 143).[2] There is little doubt that the king of the Pelagones was one of those ancestors. But Menelaus was not himself a king; rather he seems to have been a leader of mercenaries or an adventurer, because the decree goes on to recommend that help be given to him by the generals 'around Macedonia' (see p. 20 above). It is probable that Timotheus used other inland princes too against Perdiccas.

Late in 364 or early in 363 Perdiccas was compelled to accept the terms which Athens dictated. Timotheus used Perdiccas' forces against Olynthus; since Demosthenes described the contribution of 'the Macedonian power and kingdom' as considerable, it is likely that the Macedonian cavalry acquitted itself well against the Chalcidian cavalry, of which Timotheus was afraid (D. 2. 14; Polyaen. 3. 10. 7). During his operations with Perdiccas in Chalcidice Timotheus debased some Macedonian silver coinage, mixing it with poor copper from Cyprus,

---

[1] He was a hostage for three years at Thebes (Just. 7. 5. 3 'triennio Thebis obses'). Aymard, op. cit., accepted the three years but dated the return to 367, when Philip was fourteen or fifteen. Diodorus 16. 2. 5 implied that Philip escaped from Thebes just before he became king; more exciting but untrue.

[2] Discussed on p. 19 above.

so that only a quarter was silver (Polyaen. 3. 10. 14), and he himself coined in bronze, promising to redeem it (Ps.-Arist. *Oec.* 2. 23). However, even with the help of Perdiccas, Timotheus was still unable to take Amphipolis, which was being supported by the Thracians and the Chalcidians. In summer 363 one of the Athenian generals, Alcimachus, surrendered to the Thracians at Amphipolis (Aeschines 2. 30, and Schol. to 31).

It was probably[1] in 363 that Perdiccas broke away from Athens, encouraged perhaps by the naval expedition of Epaminondas in that year. Athens attacked him in 362. This time he was beaten to his knees and asked for an armistice, which was granted by the Athenian general Callisthenes (κρατοῦντες τῷ πολέμῳ Περδίκκαν Καλλισθένους ἡγουμένου ἀνοχὰς πρὸς αὐτὸν ἐποιήσασθε, Aeschines 2. 30). Later Callisthenes was executed at Athens. Perdiccas indeed showed no gratitude, as Aeschines went on to point out; for he sent troops to help Amphipolis against Athens.[2] In 360 Timotheus operated with success against the Chalcidian League,[3] but he failed completely at Amphipolis, having to burn his fleet before he slipped away (Polyaen. 3. 10. 8).

In 361/60 an able Athenian statesman, Callistratus, who had been condemned to death, escaped to Methone and later went to Thasos. In Ps.-Arist. *Oec.* 2. 22 he is said to have doubled the value of the harbour-dues in Macedonia which had previously been sold for 20 talents, and to have done so by reducing the deposit, so that the purchase (of the contract) was not confined to the richest persons. As Methone was in the hands of Athens, Callistratus cannot have stayed there, and it follows that the harbour-dues 'in Macedonia' were those of the kingdom of Perdiccas, then at war with Athens. Since the purchase-money went presumably to the king, like other revenues of state, Callistratus was employed on this task by Perdiccas, who had broken the grip on his ports in the Thermaic Gulf which Athens had had in 364.[4]

While Callistratus was at Thasos, he prompted the Thasians to found a colony on the mainland north of their early colony Neapolis, in order to exploit the gold mines there (Isoc. 8. 24; Zenob. 4. 34). While its coins were issued in the name of 'the mainland of the Thasians' (see p. 193 below), it was called Crenides in the year 356/5 (Tod, *GHI* no. 157 line 46; so too D.S. 16. 3. 7). The later attribution of yet another name,

[1] The chronology of these events is uncertain. I follow the sequence as it is given by Aeschines 2. 29 f.; F. H. Marshall, *The Second Athenian Confederacy* (Cambridge, 1905) 99 n. 1, departs from it.
[2] A Macedonian garrison was at Amphipolis in 359 (D.S. 16. 3. 3).
[3] Isoc. 15. 113 and Nepos, *Timotheus* 1. 2 with some exaggeration.
[4] The suggestion of Geyer 137, that 'in Macedonia' means in Amphipolis where Perdiccas had a garrison, is not acceptable because Amphipolis was outside the Macedonia of 360 and was at that time beleaguered by Timotheus and had few if any harbour-dues.

Datum, to this colony by Appian, *BC* 4. 105, who supposed the sequence of names to have been Crenides–Datum–Philippi, should probably be discarded as erroneous. As we have seen above (p. 72), Datum seems to have been a region facing the Strymon basin and the Datos which is said to have been founded by Callistratus (Ps.-Scylax 67) and is named in the inscription of the Epidaurian Thearodoci late in the 360s, may have been a mining town on this side of the Strymon basin, distinct from Crenides–Philippi (Eustath. *ad Dion. Perieg.* 517 = *GGM* 2. 315 'on the coast of the Strymon').

In a letter of Speusippus to Philip, which is discussed below (p. 207), the Platonic philosopher Euphraeus is said to have persuaded Perdiccas to assign a territory in Macedonia to his brother Philip, who was able to maintain a force there. One is reminded of the territories held by some of the sons of Alexander I (see p. 115 above), but there is no indication that there was any hostility between Perdiccas and Philip. Rather it is probable that Perdiccas was glad to have Philip protect some vital area during these years, when he was under pressure from many sides. The influence of Euphraeus on Perdiccas was probably exaggerated by Speusippus, and there may be more truth in a fragment of Carystius (*FHG* 4. 356 F 1) which says that the lectures of Euphraeus cast a chill over 'the Hetairia of the king'.

Meanwhile a greater danger threatened in the west. The kingdom of Bardylis had again become very powerful and prosperous (*FGrH* 115 Theopompus F 286), and the Illyrians made a raid into Epirus in search of loot *c.* 360. The Molossian king, Arybbas, sent the non-combatant population to Aetolia and laid ambushes in his own kingdom, which were successful when the Illyrians hurried on to seize the spoil (Frontin. *Strat.* 2. 5. 19). But the fact remained that the Molossian army was not willing to risk a set battle.[1] The rule of Bardylis extended at this time from the borders of Molossis to those of Macedonia (*FGrH* 124 Callisthenes F 27), so that he held the wide belt of lakeland which stretches from Lake Ochrid to the plain of Poloskë. There had already been an earlier clash between Bardylis and Perdiccas, of which we know only from Polyaenus 4. 10. 1, a passage which shows that the Illyrians either killed their prisoners or held them to ransom. Early in 359 a pitched battle was fought between the Illyrians and the Macedonians. Perdiccas was killed, more than 4,000 of his men were lost (D.S. 16. 2. 4–5), and the Illyrians carried their raids far and wide. This terrible disaster exposed the kingdom to attack by all its neighbours—Illyrians, Paeonians, Thracians, Chalcidians, and Athenians alike. The state was on the verge of collapse.

---

[1] For Bardylis' kingdom see my article in *BSA* 61 (1966) 248 f.; for the operations in Molossis see *Epirus* 533 and 553.

4. *Archaeological evidence and relations with Greece 399–359*

(See Maps of Volume I as cited under each name in the Index of Volume I)

Early in the fourth century, *c.* 395, the 'Damastini' began to produce a fine silver coinage (see Plate II).[1] They were evidently the tribe which owned 'the silver mines at Damastium', mentioned by Strabo 7 C 326 and located in the district west and north-west of Resen, as we saw above.[2] In the sixth century some at least of these mines had been worked to produce the silver for the coinage of the Tynteni or Atintani, which had been exported as a form of bullion to the Persian Empire, and had owed its artistic inspiration to Ichnae and ultimately to Chalcidice. So now the earliest coins of the Damastini were certainly inspired by the magnificent silver tetradrachms of the Chalcidian League, which had first been produced *c.* 410. The Damastine standard too was taken from Chalcidice but was a lighter version of the Chalcidian one, and it is most probable that the first coins were made by Chalcidian artists who came to Damastium.[3] Later the Greek influence declined, and locally trained cutters of less artistic ability took over. The first phase of the coinage, covering May's Groups I to V, is to be dated to the period *c.* 395–*c.* 380, within which falls the acme of the Chalcidian League. The influence of Larissa also appeared in the earliest silver drachmae of the Damastini; it was strong but short-lived, and it was due no doubt to visits by die-cutters from Larissa.[4]

The tetradrachms with an average weight of some 13·50 gr were very much more common than the smaller denominations. Throughout our present period they had the head of Apollo laureate on the obverse, and a tripod on the reverse, both adopted from coins of the Chalcidian League. The drachmae had the head of a female deity, adopted from the head on coins of Larissa, on the obverse, and a portable ingot—a local emblem— on the reverse; and the tetrobols had the same head of Apollo on the obverse and a tripod on the reverse. No doubt the Damastini had their own names for the male god and the female deity, but they are not known to us. The one local emblem shows that Damastium was a mining town, which exported ore in ingot form as well as in coinage.[5] In issues after 359 the miner's pick was sometimes added as an emblem.

[1] See the excellent study by J. M. F. May, *The Coinage of Damastion* (Oxford, 1939).

[2] Volume I. 93 f. and *Epirus* 466 and 541.

[3] See May, *Damastion* 17 f., 31, and 56 for the influence of Chalcidice. His connection of the Damastine coinage with 'the old Abderite standard' of the sixth century (14 f.) seems to be a matter of academic interest only; for the Damastini were concerned with contemporary trade.

[4] Ibid. 18 f., 31, and 66. The Larissaean cutter may have left his monogram NE on the earliest specimen of this coinage in May 65 no. 1.

[5] Ibid. 37, although May seems to understate the case in saying 'Damastion's export trade [in silver] . . . was not based solely on her coinage.'

It is interesting that the same designs for each denomination were used throughout this period, and the inference is that the coins circulated in non-Greek areas where a consistently recognizable type was desirable. The distribution of the coins, whether as single finds or in hoards, shows that this was so. They were most common in the region of the upper Vardar valley and its eastern tributaries (at Stobi, Skopje, west of Karatovo, and Kumanovo) and in the Metohija (at Prizren, Ipek, etc.). They have been found to the north-east in the Morava valley at Vranje and Kutina near Leskovać, in Bulgaria, and even in Rumania. They have been found also at Scodra, from where they travelled on probably by sea; for hoards have turned up at Risan (Rhizon) on the bay of Kotor and at Sinj, inland of Split.[1] On the other hand few, if any, have been found in central and southern Albania, and in Epirus only one at Dodona;[2] and they were not current in Greece generally. Thus we are dealing with a coinage issued for trade in the Balkan area, which was channelled along fairly clear routes: north-westwards along the Drin to Scodra and the Dalmatian coast, northwards and north-eastwards via the Kačanik, Preševo, and Kjustendil passes into the central Balkan area; and south-eastwards into the area of the upper and middle Vardar, which was mainly Paeonian but extended to the border of Macedon at Demir Kapu. The standard tells the same story; for it was used in the Thraco-Macedonian area and in Chalcidice but not in the west or to the south.[3]

As Garašanin pointed out,[4] this part of the fourth century saw a steep decline and almost a cessation of Greek objects imported from the south into the central Balkans. It seems that an almost separate trade *koine* was developing within the central Balkans which looked more towards central Europe and the Black Sea, using its internal land routes and as waterways the northern part of the Adriatic sea as well as the Danube. Dionysius of Syracuse sought to tap the western part of it, when he planted colonies in the Adriatic region, and the Cnidian colony at Korčula (Corcyra Nigra) at the beginning of the fourth century was situated off the main waterway inland up the Narenta (Naro) valley towards Sarajevo. Theopompus and Arist. *Mir. Ausc.* 839[b] referred to the meeting of the trade-routes from the Adriatic and from the Black Sea in the central Balkans: amphorae (of olive oil probably) from Corcyra came up the former and amphorae (of wine certainly) from Thasos, Lesbos, and Chios travelled via the Black Sea and the Danube to an inland

---

[1] May, *Damastion*, 7 f.

[2] See *Epirus* 717 f.; the coin from Damastium is listed on p. 726. The negative evidence in Epirus is based on a considerable collection of coins.

[3] I am writing of coins only; silver ingots may have been exported, for instance, to Epidamnus in the west, which had a most prolific coinage at this time (see *Epirus* 541).

[4] *AI* 5 (1964) 79.

emporion.[1] Transport from Thasos was evidently safer on that route than overland through Macedonia.

A most important development at the start of the fourth century was the rise of Bardylis, who built up the kingdom of the Dardanii in the rich areas of Kossovo and Metohija and then expanded southwards to include first the country of the Penestae, and then the basins of Ochrid and Resen.[2] This kingdom controlled the chief routes between Macedonia–Paeonia and central Yugoslavia, and again between Macedonia–Paeonia and the Adriatic sea at Scodra. He was well placed to exploit the trade which passed through these areas, and it is certain that the mint at Damastium came quickly under his control. When we compare the prolific coinage of Damastium and its pattern of distribution with the restricted coinage of the kings of Macedon, partly in silver and partly in bronze, we can see that the Illyrians had considerably greater resources at their disposal. At other times too powerful states have grown up in this area, for instance the prehistoric settlement at Malik, the first Bulgarian empire and the economic centre of the Vlachs. In all cases they have traded within the central Balkans and towards Central Europe. The great wealth of Bardylis was proverbial. Theopompus described him as 'an Illyrian robber who divided the loot honourably' (*FGrH* 115 F 286), but Bardylis must have had qualities of statesmanship and leadership which the censorious Theopompus was reluctant to praise in a barbarian. In particular, it is probable that he developed the rich agricultural lands and the fisheries in the basins of Ochrid, Prespa, and Korcë. Here there were some urban settlements such as Lychnidus and Pelium, and it is probable that they were fortified with walls in the time of Bardylis.[3]

Two silver coins bearing the inscription ΔΑΠΑΡΡΙΑ and having the same types and standard as the coins of Damastium have been dated by J. M. F. May to the years *c.* 365–360. As the portable ingot appears on a later coin of this series, which extends over some forty years, it is likely that the Daparria coinage was that of a mining centre in the same general area. To the north of Damastium there were deposits of silver at Tetovo and in Metohija–Kossovo. As I shall argue later that Pelagia, which issued coins after *c.* 360, is to be placed at Tetovo, I should suggest that Daparria was a mining town in Metohija–Kossovo in the realm of Bardylis.[4]

[1] Theopompus in Str. 7 C 317 indicates the importance of the Naro valley, where there was a *koine agora* or *emporion*.

[2] See my article in *BSA* 61 (1966) 248 f.

[3] For Pelium see Arr. *An.* 1. 5. 5 and 8, and my article in *JHS* 94 (1974) 71–76.

[4] May, *Damastion* 164 f. I disagree with his view that the coins of Daparria were struck at Damastion on silver mined at Damastium (168 n. 1). That might be so if the inscription on the coins was that of a dynast. But being that of a town, like Damastium, I think it was a separate mining centre.

It is to be assumed that the mines of gold and silver in Illyria which we have mentioned and also those in Paeonia near Kratovo and Kumanovo were worked during the fifth and the fourth centuries. The precious metal was traded only in ingot form. The fact that the coinages of the archaic period were discontinued, is perhaps an indication of a political decline which lasted in the north-west until the rise of Bardylis and continued in Paeonia until the rise of Lycceus in the 350s.

Between 370/69 and 360/59 Alexander II coined in bronze only and Perdiccas III issued some silver didrachms on the Persian standard and more coins in bronze (see Plate II).[1] The absence of coins bearing the name of Ptolemy is clear evidence that he was regent and not king; the coinage of Perdiccas III should be regarded as covering the years from 368 to 359. Alexander used one type only, a young male head, clean shaven / a rider on a prancing horse, and he added a thunderbolt as an emblem. Thus he abandoned the emphasis which his father Amyntas III had laid on Heracles, and he introduced a new emblem into the royal coinage, perhaps from Aphytis where a shrine of Zeus Ammon was commemorated on contemporary coins. Perdiccas returned to the tradition of his father and put the head of a young Heracles on all his coins; the reverse carried a horse unattended, a lion teasing a spear, a butting bull, or an eagle with closed wings. The butting bull appeared for the first time on the royal coinage; it resembled the bull on the coinage of Aenea.[2] It is apparent from the nature of this coinage that the kingdom of Macedon was poorer than it had been in the time even of Amyntas III, and that it had far less precious metal than the kingdom of Bardylis.

On the Macedonian coast Pydna issued a bronze coinage with the head of a young Heracles / an eagle standing on a snake, which were types used in the contemporary coinage of Amyntas III *c.* 381 to *c.* 369. The city had clearly regained its independence since the time of Archelaus, and it gained in prosperity during and after the short reign of Argaeus. It adopted a new type of its own sometime in the 360s, head of a nymph / owl on an olive twig, which emphasized the city's friendship with Athens, then the chief maritime power in the Thermaic Gulf.[3] Methone too issued a bronze coinage, which is rarer than that of Pydna; it showed a female head / a lion biting a spear, the latter being a device of Amyntas III and Perdiccas III.[4] Methone was evidently independent, like Pydna, from at least 381 to 359. On the east side of the Thermaic Gulf the first city south of the kingdom, Aenea, showed its independence too by issuing a bronze coinage with the head of the young Aeneas / a butting bull. Its neighbour Dicaea issued coins in bronze with the same reverse and the head of a nymph on the obverse. Inland to the east

---

[1] G. 161 f., xxx. 12–17 and xxxi. 28.   [2] G. xxx. 16 and vi. 3–4.
[3] G. 105 f., sometimes with the name spelt Pyndnaion.   [4] G. 78 f.

Apollonia in Mygdonia issued a bronze coinage during the period *c.* 400–375. It is evident that from the time when Amyntas III entrusted part of Mygdonia to the Chalcidian League *c.* 393/2 Apollonia was able to maintain its independence and act as the commercial centre for the region. Her coins had the head of Apollo / a marsh-bird or a fish, the local products of Lake Bolbe.[1]

The wealthiest coinages in the area were provided by the Chalcidian League, which issued gold coins, silver tetradrachms, and small denominations, and a few bronze pieces throughout this period; by Acanthus which issued silver tetradrachms and smaller denominations until *c.* 380; and further east by Amphipolis which issued gold coins, silver tetradrachms, and small denominations, and some bronze pieces.[2] It is clear that they had access to deposits of gold and silver. The Bisaltic silver mines may have been exploited mainly by the Bisaltae during this period, probably exporting their bullion through Amphipolis; for Tragilus ceased to coin around 400. Further to the east Neapolis on the coast opposite Thasos coined throughout this period in silver and in bronze, and *c.* 360 there appeared for the first time the gold staters and bronze coins of the mining town Crenides with the inscription ΘΑΣΙΟΝ ΗΠΕΙΡΟ which marked the Thasian control of the mainland.[3]

We gain an important insight into the situation in Macedonia from the list of the Epidaurian Thearodoci, that is of the states and their representatives which offered hospitality to sacred missions. The list for Macedonia was inscribed in the latter part of the 360s,[4] and the entries in *IG* IV². 95, II lines 6–20 are as follows:

Homolion: Dorieus. Pydna: Damatrios. Methona: Polyphantos. Makedonia: Perdiccas. Aineia: Euboulos. Dikaia: Nymphodorus. Poteidaia: Callicrates. Kalindoia: Pausanias. Olynthus: Archon. Apollonia: Epixenos. Arethusa: Bolon. Arkilos: Onesandros. Amphipolis: Hiarax. Berga: Antiphanes. Tragila: Peisies.

While Homolion was the last city of Magnesia in Thessaly, the realm of Perdiccas was indicated by 'Macedonia', so that Heracleum, for instance, was comprehended within it. On the other hand, Pydna, Methone, Aenea, and Dicaea (that it is the Dicaea of the Thermaic Gulf seems likely from its position in the list)[5] were independent states. Olynthus stood for the Chalcidian League. Outside it were Potidaea, occupied by

---

[1] G. 22 (Aenea); 59 ('Dikaiopoliton'); 46 (Apollonia). The similarity of type with Aenea and the Bottiaeans shows that the coinage is of this Dicaea and not of the Dicaea by Abdera.

[2] G. 85 f. (Chalcidian League); 27 f. (Acanthus); 30 f. (Amphipolis). After *c.* 380 Acanthus coined in bronze only, presumably because the Chalcidian League on its revival took over the gold and silver mines at Stratoniki.

[3] G. 100.

[4] The entries for Epirus refer to the same period; see *Epirus* 517 f.

[5] Despite the comment to the contrary in *IG*.

Athenian cleruchs, and Kalindoia, a Bottiaean city,[1] of which the representative was Pausanias, probably the pretender to the throne of Macedon, who had been defeated in 367. Apollonia was not the Chalcidian city of that name, cities of the League being represented by Olynthus alone, but the Apollonia of Mygdonia.[2] Arethusa, which controlled the pass from Mygdonia into the Strymon basin, was independent. And in that basin itself Berga, near the Bisaltic mines, and Argilus and Tragila near the coast were independent both of the Chalcidian League and of the Thracian dynasts. Amphipolis, strengthened as it was by a Macedonian garrison, was also an independent city. Many of these independent cities, as we have seen, were issuing their own coins.

We find similar information in the work of Ps.-Scylax 66, which was written between 338 and 335, but often refers only to an earlier period. He introduces the Macedones as a nation (*ethnos*) 'after the Peneus'. He gives Heracleum as the first city of Macedonia; then Dium, Pydna a Greek city, Methone a Greek city, the river Haliacmon, Alorus a city, the river Lydias, Pella a city and a palace in it and a waterway up the Lydias to it; the river Axius, the river Echedorus, Therme a city, Aenea a Greek city, Cape Pallene. After Chalcidice has been described, he mentions Arethusa a Greek city, Lake Bolbe, Apollonia a Greek city, and continues 'there are also many other cities of Macedonia in the interior (ἐν μεσογείᾳ), and after Macedonia there is the river Strymon, which is the boundary between Macedonia and Thrace.' Again we see

---

[1] Mentioned at the end of the treaty between Athens and the Bottiaeans in *IG* I². 90.

[2] The geographical sequence in which the names are listed shows that it lay between Olynthus (standing for the Chalcidian League) and Arethusa in easternmost Mygdonia. For other views see the commentary in *IG*. As I understand, there were three Apollonias: (1) 10 miles from Olynthus (X. *HG* 5. 3. 2) and on the Thermaic Gulf side of the mountains in Chalcidice (Str. 7 fr. 21); (2) south of Lake Bolbe in Mygdonia, on the inland side of the Chalcidian mountains, probably located at Kalamoto, where inscriptions have been found (see Volume I. 186 and 196); (3) east of Amphipolis on the Thracian coast (Str. 7 fr. 35 fin.). It was the last of these which was destroyed by Philip II ([D.] 7. 28 and D. 9. 26, picked up by Str. 7 fr. 35 fin.). The first fought against the Chalcidian League in 382 (X. *HG* 5. 2. 11) and probably came over to Philip in 349 or 348; but it was incorporated later into Cassandrea as one of 'the cities of Crousis and the cities facing the Thermaic Gulf' (Str. 7 fr. 21). The richest of the three was the second one, which exploited the fisheries (*FHG* 4. 420, Hegesander fr. 40) and the fertile swampy lands of Lake Bolbe; in the first half of the fourth century it issued bronze coins with fish and marsh-birds as emblems advertising their fisheries (G. 46, 1. 5–6). The territory in which it lay was loaned to the Chalcidians by Perdiccas II and then by Amyntas III; its prosperity had been shown earlier by the prolific coinage of Lete. The squadron of Companion Cavalry 'from Apollonia' (Arr. *An.* 1. 12. 7) came evidently from this 'Mygdonian' Apollonia, as Ptolemy called it, when it was a station on the Via Egnatia (see Volume I. 196). Of the named squadrons of Alexander's cavalry four came from areas with marshy plains, appropriate for the raising of fine horses: Bottiaea in the coastal area of Lower Macedonia, Anthemus inland of Therme, Mygdonian Apollonia by Lake Bolbe, and Amphipolis by Lake Cercinitis. I see no reason to follow Hampl 32 f., who confused Bottiaea and Bottice, conflated my first and second Apollonias into one and the same, and argued that Philip raised his cavalry from the Macedonians whom he planted on land acquired by his own conquests (his pp. 73 f.).

a number of independent Greek cities (here contrasted with the Macedonian cities, namely Heracleum, Dium, Alorus, Pella, and Therme),
which were all on the coast or reachable by water. The cities 'in the
interior' were no doubt those of Lower Macedonia. The period to which
this description applies best is that of the 360s.[1] When he put the Strymon
as the frontier between 'Macedonia' and 'Thrace', he was using the
words as geographical terms.

Ps.-Scymnus 618 f.:

The land of the Macedones is beyond Tempe, lying alongside Olympus, of
which the king they say was earth-born Macedon; and [there is] the nation
(*ethnos*) of Lyncestae and [that of] the Pelagones, who are situated in that
direction alongside the Axius,[2] and [that] of Botteatae, and that of those
round the Strymon. And in the interior there are many cities, and Pella and
Beroea are the most distinguished, and on the coast are Thessalonice and
Pydna.

The interest of Ps.-Scymnus was in the traditional mythology of the area:
hence Macedon, ruling over the original Macedonis by Olympus; the
Pelagones and the Axius, both having connections with Homeric epic;
and the Botteatae, who were mythologically descendants of a Cretan
Botton. Perhaps the Lyncestae came in because of their connection
with the Bacchiadae. There is little of geographical interest, and the
entry of Thessalonice dates the passage to after the period which we
are now considering.

While Bardylis became the head of a strong state in the north-west,
Cotys gained control of the Odrysian realm and exercised his rule over
the whole of inland Thrace. In the 380s he reunited the parts of the
Odrysian empire of Sitalces, which were split between Seuthes II,
Amadocus I, and Hebryzelmis, with all of whom Athens tried to maintain uneasy alliances,[3] and he emerged as a sole ruler *c.* 384. During his
reign he made much use of Greek mercenaries, especially in his dealings
with the Greek states, and his son-in-law, the Athenian mercenary
captain, Iphicrates, was held in high esteem by him.[4] Cotys, as well as
Iphicrates, was interested in the succession to the throne of Macedon in
367 and again, according to D.S. 16. 2. 6, 360/59. He was also concerned
to prevent the Athenians from capturing Amphipolis. At first made an
Athenian citizen, he became their hated enemy in the 360s,[5] when he
began to break their hold on the Bosporus and the Hellespont. In 360/59

---

[1] See *Epirus* 511 for the dating of the entries for Epirus, which are comparable.
[2] He probably means the area west of the middle Axius valley as the habitat of the Pelagones. As always the Lyncestae are separate from the Pelagones.
[3] e.g. Tod, *GHI* no. 117.
[4] The marriage was *c.* 387, when Cotys was on the way to power.
[5] D. 23. 114–18.

he was assassinated by two Greeks of Aenus, whom Athens made Athenian citizens and crowned with golden crowns as benefactors of the city.[1]

Greek writers such as Theopompus and a writer of Attic comedy Anaxandrides mocked Cotys as a pleasure-loving drunkard, a perverter of religion, and a brutal sadist, and they ridiculed the ostentatious wealth and unsophisticated tastes of his court.[2] But his achievement was very remarkable. He held his kingdom secure against strong neighbours such as the Triballi who in 376/5 descended from their lands near Niš to pillage and almost destroy the Greek city of Abdera.[3] He issued a good coinage in silver and bronze, and he employed Greek specialists in his armed forces. His power was based upon the development of trade within the Balkan area, in which the richest single area was that of the central Thracian plain, extending from Plovdiv to the Black Sea; here the centre of his realm was situated. Nor was this trade all in the hands of the Greeks on his coasts; for it looked also towards central Europe and the Black Sea coasts.

In comparison with its Balkan neighbours the kingdom of Macedon was weak in the 360s. The most advanced part of north-western Macedonia, Derriopus, which had some urban settlements and some trade with the kingdom of Bardylis, was evidently independent of Macedon; indeed the kings of the Pelagones intrigued with Athens, probably against Macedon. Even there life was at a low level. Excavation at Tsepicovo, the ancient Styberra, yielded only an occasional coin which might have been deposited before 359.[4] The Macedonian city at the northern end of Demir Kapu on the Axius, though small, was better. It had its citadel; it imported good Attic pottery in the first half of the fourth century, and in that respect it resembled Olynthus. Some silver jewellery and bronze fibulae of Class XII were in the tombs, but there were surprisingly few coins.[5] In Lyncus and the western cantons of Upper Macedonia there seem to have been no new developments; even at Ayios Elevtherios by Kozani there are no conclusive indications of a town before the third century.[6] In general these areas were still engaged primarily in pastoral life.

In Lower Macedonia the native cities seem to have developed slowly in the period 399–359. The excavators of Dium have found some imported

[1] D.S. 23. 119.

[2] *FGrH* 115 Theopompus F 31; Athen. 4. 131 'at the banquet were your butter-eating, shock-haired, swarming gentry . . . Cotys himself wearing an apron brought on the soup in a golden bowl and tasted the wines so liberally that he was drunk before his guests.'

[3] D.S. 15. 36; Aen. Tact. 15. 8. 9. Their territory is defined in Str. 7 C 318 init.

[4] *AI* 4 (1963) 89. Cemeteries at Crkvište Beranci (*Starinar* 21 (1970) 139 f.) and Treskavac by Prilep (*AI* 5 (1964) 77) show some concentrations of population but in open settlements.

[5] *Starinar* 12 (1961) 229 f.; 21 (1970) 135 f.; *AI* 5 (1964) 76.

[6] *PAE* 1965. 24 f.

fourth-century pottery and the earliest coin was one of Amyntas III, dated to the first part of his reign.[1] Pella was the largest city (X. *HG* 5. 2. 13); it was the seat of the palace (Ps.-Scylax 66 βασίλειον) and the treasury (Str. 7 fr. 20 ἐνταῦθα ἦν πάλαι τὸ τῆς Μακεδονίας χρηματιστήριον). A preliminary report[2] has been made on a large and apparently unroofed Tholos, 30 m in diameter, which was of the classical period, and on three small Tholoi abutting on to it. Similarly there is a Tholos of the fourth century at Vergina–Palatitsa, that is Aegeae. It is likely that each was a part of the palace buildings of the kings; for worship of Heracles Patroüs at Aegeae and of Heracles Phylacus at Pella is attested by inscriptions, that at Aegeae being found on the site of the Tholos. T. H. Price suggested that the Assembly of the Macedones may have met in the Tholos; but this is physically impossible as they numbered some thousands. Rather the Council was convened there by the king, as was the case in 171 (Livy 42. 51. 1 'Pellae in vetere regia Macedonum hoc consilium erat').[3] But even Pella was small when compared with a Greek city; 'it was a small city when Philip grew up in it, and it was he who enlarged it' (Str. 7 fr. 20 ηὔξησε τὴν πόλιν ἐκ μικρᾶς Φίλιππος, τραφεὶς ἐν αὐτῇ).

The top of Mt. Khortiatis was fortified with a wall some 2 m wide, built of long, thin blocks (e.g. 1·00×0·30 m) laid in a roughly ashlar style, and some 600 m in length; two towers projected only a short distance from the curtain wall (see Map 6 and inset). The earliest imported pottery inside the fortifications was of 375–350. The excavator, G. Bakalakis, dated the fortification to the middle of the fourth century, but he noted that such a fortification was hard to justify at that time. Rightly so; for we should surely date it to the troubled period between 375 and 360, when Athens was exerting pressure in the Thermaic Gulf and Illyrians raided into Upper Macedonia. A considerable number of arrow-heads, spear-heads, and spear-butts were found during the excavation, and these suggest that the small fort was garrisoned by troops when danger threatened. The scale of the fort is like that above Demir Kapu. If it was the acropolis of Cissus, as was suggested in Volume 1. 187, the 'town' consisted of several small villages, such as have been noted by Bakalakis at Panorama. The view is magnificent. This fort is much smaller and simpler than the fortifications of contemporary Greek cities in Chalcidice (*Mak.* 3. 353 f.; *BSA* 23. 57).

The distinction between the Macedonian city and the Greek city was firmly drawn by a number of writers and decisively by Ps.-Scylax

---

[1] *AD* 24 (1969) B. 2. 340–2.
[2] By T. H. Price in her article in *AJA* 77 (1973) 66 f.
[3] The Council met in the Royal Tent where the throne was set up, when Alexander III was in Asia. See Plu. *Eum.* 13. 3.

writing of the 360s. They were totally different in population, status, and institutions. A shared language did not begin to bridge the gap. Macedonian cities at that time were generally unwalled and the population did not have a slave basis;[1] the city was an administrative unit, like a borough or municipium within a kingdom, and not independent; and the distinctions in citizenship between a 'Pellaios' and a 'Macedon

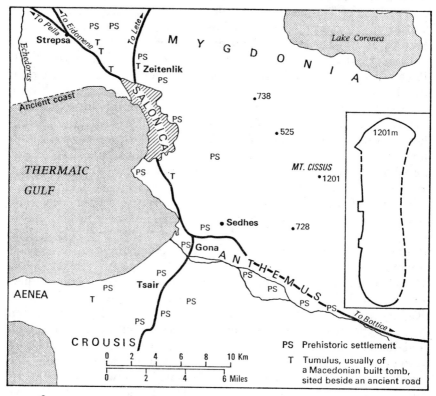

MAP 6. THE HEAD OF THE THERMAIC GULF AND THE FORT ON MT. CISSUS (*inset*)

of Pella' were alien to Greek thinking (see p. 163 above). A native city could never had been called πόλις Ἑλληνίς, nor did the citizens want it to be called such; they preferred their form of independence to enforced incorporation by the Chalcidian League of Greek cities.[2] For their part the Greeks regarded the Macedones as unGreek, because their institutions were those of an *ethnos* and they submitted to the almost absolute rule of a monarch. They regarded the Macedones as more on a par with

[1] For the extent of slavery in Greek cities see *HG*² 524 f. For slaves at Torone, for instance, see Polyaen. 3. 10. 15.

[2] Though this was misrepresented in the speech of Cleigenes in X. *HG* 5. 2. 12.

the Illyrians and the Thracians; for they carried them off into slavery too and managed to capture their seaboard towns. When Plato wrote the *Gorgias c.* 390, he showed complete ignorance of the Macedonian court and its customs. To him the mother of Archelaus was 'a slave' in the Greek sense of the word, and Archelaus should have been 'the slave' of Alcetas in the same sense. He then told two stories about Archelaus, to which there were no witnesses whatever, and made up a fictitious picture of the child chasing a goose and falling into the well. It is on the same level of acceptability as Anaxandrides' picture of Cotys wearing an apron or Theopompus' picture of Bardylis the robber presiding over the sharing of the loot. The Greeks associated the barbarians of the Balkans with drunkenness; so Archelaus made his victims drunk first, and Cotys got drunk before his guests. Although the father of Aristotle served as physician at the court, Aristotle himself preferred the more sensational explanation for the killing of Archelaus. It had to be a *crime passionel* of paederasty, a matter of ἀφροδισιαστικὴ χάρις, rather than a conspiracy organized by young men of thwarted aspirations and ambitions, although Aristotle is honest enough to hint at the latter. Some writers were less scrupulous. The portrait of Eurydice as an Illyrian, thrice barbarous, fobbing off bastard children as her own, plotting to murder her husband in order to put her lover on the throne, and all the rest[1] had no more claim to historical accuracy than any smear campaign against the leaders of a hated state, especially when the targets are monarchs or their consorts.

It is against this sort of background that we should think of Hellenizing influences entering Macedonia and other Balkan states. They were particularly economic, in that they developed trade and created a middle class and capital resources, for instance at Therme, a Macedonian city on the Thermaic Gulf. They were frequently technical, when a skilled financier like Callistratus or a professional soldier like Iphicrates hired out his services to a Perdiccas or a Cotys. They were artistic and cultural, when die-cutters went to Damastium or one of Plato's disciples, Euphraeus of Oreus, lectured at Pella. The kings themselves had the desire as well as the wealth to attract to their court many of the finest artists and thinkers of the Greek world. But that was not to say that they wished Macedon to enter the Greek world or the Greeks to take over Macedon.

In the opening chapters of his history Thucydides defined the obstacles which prevent the growth of any significant degree of power: unsettled population, political instability, lack of capital resources, and limited range. In 399–359 Macedon failed to surmount these obstacles. The peoples of Upper Macedonia were mainly nomadic pastoralists, and the cities of Lower Macedonia were still at an early stage of development.

[1] Plu. *Mor.* 4 B; Suid. s.v. *Karanos*; Libanius *Arg. D.* 9; Just. 7. 4. 7; 7. 5. 4–8.

The monarchy in which lay the whole security of the state was repeatedly shaken by the struggle for power, the *stasis* between the descendants of the sons of Alexander I, of whom no less than ten sat on the throne as king or as regent within these forty years. The economy of the country was hand-to-mouth as long as it was subject to invasions by Illyrians, Chalcidians, and Boeotians, and it had lost access to all sources of precious metals. The Orestae had defected to the Molossian state, and the royal house of the Pelagones was in league with the enemy of Macedon. Its range by 359 was parochial. The kingdom had shrunk almost into its original confines, and the people did not look beyond their immediate neighbours, whom they viewed with terror and despair (D.S. 16. 2. 5 οἱ δὲ λοιποὶ καταπεπληγμένοι τὰς τῶν Ἰλλυριῶν δυνάμεις περίφοβοι καθεστήκεισαν καὶ πρὸς τὸ διαπολεμεῖν ἀθύμως εἶχον). Few can have seen in 359 the qualities of greatness which would make Macedon the leading power in the world within the next forty years.

PART TWO

THE REIGN OF
PHILIP THE SECOND

V

THE ACCESSION OF PHILIP

THE history of Macedonia so far has been a study in survival, and there have been times (the end of Perdiccas III is one of them) when the margin seems not particularly wide. It was no great king or kingdom that in the 360s was being pushed around by the Thebans, patronized by Plato, reorganized as to its finances by the expert Callistratus. When Callistratus had doubled the revenues from foreign trade, they still came to only 40 talents, quite a small fraction of the revenues of Athens, for example, from comparable sources.[1] When Plato had finished handing out advice to Perdiccas, and even an adviser to represent him as resident political consultant, one cannot truly feel that the future of Perdiccas is now fully insured. Plato and Euphraeus of Oreus will have told him about principles and practice of monarchy, and even at the level of local personalities and details (below); but foreign policy held no interest for Plato, and Euphraeus is unlikely to have contributed anything useful about Illyrians, or even about Boeotians or Athenians in this connection.

Yet if Perdiccas had not died in battle against the Illyrians, to judge by the recent form he would have lived making the best he could of it all, between the power of Thebes and the power of Athens (above, pp. 186 f.). So far the clues to Macedonian growth and greatness have not appeared. The seeds of it germinate only now, and they germinate so fast that in thirty years the whole face of the civilized world has been changed; yet so unobtrusively that the whole thing can almost seem to be due to a couple of kings and a goldmine. With due respect for the Common Man and with due suspicion for the personality cult, we ignore at our peril the testimony of Theopompus, that there was something quite new here: never before had Europe produced a man such as Philip the son of Amyntas.[2] Theopompus came to know him well through residence at his court in the 340s, and though he can be thought of in a sense as an 'official' historian in the employ of Philip, yet he wrote of him on occasion with a candour or a malice that scandalized Polybius while to us it comes as something not wholly uncongenial just because it is equivocal.[3]

---

[1] [Arist.] *Econ.* 2. 22. 1350ᵃ. [2] Theopomp. *FGrH* no. 115 F 27.
[3] Plb. 8. 10. 7 ff. (= Theopomp. ibid. T 19). For Theopompus in general, see A. Momigliano, 'Teopompo', *TC* 367 ff.; K. von Fritz, 'The historian Theopompus', *AHR*

Unfortunately no ancient *Life* of Philip has survived; only the longish excerpt (which we owe to Athenaeus) from the *Life* by Satyrus, the piece about all his marriages.[1] Plutarch's collection of *Apophthegmata* make up a little of what we have lost;[2] but gone beyond recall, it may be said, is Philip's boyhood. He was born in either 383 or 382,[3] and he was only twelve or thirteen years old when his father Amyntas III died and his eldest brother Alexander II became king. From now on, his life is part of an adventure story, its principal characters the members of this royal household (above, pp. 180 f.). In the light of the queen mother Eurydice's alleged murder of her son Alexander II (but see pp. 181 ff. above) especially interesting is the vignette of the united family in high politics which Aeschines once happens to give us. Aeschines as ambassador in 346 reminded Philip (so he says) of the occasion of his meeting in 368 with the famous Athenian general Iphicrates, when Eurydice had put the young Perdiccas in the general's arms, and set the younger Philip at his knees.[4] Even an Attic orator, when describing a scene which he never witnessed himself to those who were present at it, would see the need to get the main facts approximately right; and this visit of Iphicrates (in 368) ought to be the one reliable way of dating the only important event that we know of Philip's early years, the visit to Thebes.[5] Of the two interventions of Pelopidas in Macedonia the second followed quickly on that of Iphicrates, and his taking of hostages on the second occasion was in this same year or in 367. Though the historians (Diodorus, Justin, Plutarch, a long Suda entry) set Philip's going to Thebes in the reign of Alexander II (or even earlier), Aeschines clearly is to be preferred as to this, and Plutarch shows clearly that hostages (different

1941. 765 ff.; W. R. Connor, 'History without heroes: Theopompus' treatment of Philip of Macedon', *GRBS* 8 (1967) 133 f.; I. A. F. Bruce, 'Theopompus and classical Greek historiography', *History and Theory*, 9 (1970) 86 ff.; R. L. Fox, 49, 412 ff.

[1] Satyrus *FHG* 3. 161 F 5 ap. Athen. 13. 557.   [2] Plu. *Mor.* 177 c–179 d.

[3] 383, Just. 9. 8. 1; 382, Paus. 8. 7. 6; cf. Suid. s.v. *Karanos*. I see no basis for a preference.

[4] Aeschin. 2. 26–9. There is no need to undermine the credibility of Aeschines by translating Περδίκκαν μὲν τὸν ἀδελφὸν τὸν σὸν καταστήσασα εἰς τὰς χεῖρας τὰς 'Ιφικράτους, σὲ δὲ εἰς τὰ γόνατα τὰ ἐκείνου θεῖσα παιδίον ὄντα ... as (e.g.) 'she put your brother Perdiccas into the arms of Iphicrates and set you *upon* his knees—for you were a little boy ...' (my italics). Philip is fourteen or fifteen now, Perdiccas a year or two older. Eurydice is virtually a suppliant here and εἰς τὰ γόνατα alludes to this (cf. Soph. *OC* 1607). Παιδίον is an exaggeration certainly, but I do not believe that Aeschines ever reminded Philip of a day when the seated Iphicrates was half-smothered with royal babies.

[5] So Beloch 3². 1. 182. *Contra* A. Aymard, 'Philippe de Macédoine otage à Thèbes', *Études d'histoire ancienne* 1967. 418 f. (= *REA* 56 (1954) 15–36). In this, surely one of his least happy papers, Aymard argued that Aeschines was capable of describing to Philip how he (Philip) met Iphicrates twenty-two years ago, when really Philip had never met Iphicrates, because he was at Thebes already at that time. But see p. 184 n. 3 above.

Whether Philip was also a hostage with an Illyrian king before he went to Thebes (D.S. 16. 2. 2; Just. 7. 5. 1) is (to me) unclear. I see no way of disproving it; but the story would carry more weight if it named the Illyrian king, and not just 'the Illyrians'.

hostages) were taken by Pelopidas twice, first from Alexander II (369), later (above) from Ptolemy of Alorus and Eurydice.[1] The purpose of taking hostages in the first place was to ensure that Alexander did not try to repeat his move into Thessaly. In 368 (or 7) Pelopidas was now concerned to ensure that Ptolemy and Eurydice renewed the undertakings of Alexander and stuck to them. They had disturbed his settlement of affairs by supplanting Alexander, and it was in their power to wipe out the sons of Amyntas one by one.[2] To take as hostages now Philip (the date follows from Aeschines), as well as the son of Ptolemy and fifty Macedonian *Hetairoi* (so Plutarch), left with the Thebans the material for intervening again in Macedonia and setting up an alternative government, if it should prove that any harm came to Perdiccas, or that Ptolemy and Eurydice were unsatisfactory.

The length of Philip's stay at Thebes may be accepted as Justin's *triennio*, 368 (or 7) to 365 (rather than Aymard's 369–367).[3] It may be accepted too that he lived, as Plutarch tells us, in the house of Pammenes.[4] In this context we expect to be told (and we are) that Pammenes became his lover; and in this context most probably the tale is true.[5] It was Philip's fortune to spend these years in the city where the two most famous living generals of the Greeks were to be found, where too there was a famous corps of infantry (the Sacred Band), and cavalry far above the Greek average. Pelopidas he had met already, at home, and Epaminondas he is sure to have met now. These formative years were giving something (who can doubt it?) towards the future *hegemon* of the Greeks. If he had spent these same years as a hostage in Athens instead of in Thebes, free to be a pupil of Plato or of Isocrates, as well as to study a Greek polis in action at its most sophisticated, should we perhaps have seen a king more serious and more enlightened than the one whom we do see presently? It almost seems as if the Greek literary tradition noticed wistfully all the things that Philip missed, and tried to make it up to him in ineptitudes which make him fellow pupil with Epaminondas of a Pythagorean philosopher in Thebes.[6] Plutarch however, though he brings the two together of course, writes sensibly that Philip learned a lot from Epaminondas—a lot about war. As for *arete* and the qualities that made up the *arete* of that great man, Philip was incapable of profiting from the association.[7] A hard word, this, and perhaps an impatient one. But no one who reviews the course of Philip's life in all its devotion to war will doubt that three years in the Thebes of Epaminondas might

---

[1] Plu. *Pelop.* 26. 5–8; 27. 3 f.; D.S. 15. 67. 4; 16. 2. 2; Just. 6. 9. 7; 7. 5. 2–3; Suid. s.v. *Karanos*.

[2] For the murder of Alexander, Schol. Aeschin. 2. 29 etc.

[3] Just. 6. 9. 7; 7. 5. 3; Aymard, loc. cit. 424 ff.   [4] Plu. *Pelop.* 26. 5.

[5] Suid. s.v. *Karanos*.   [6] D.S. 16. 2. 2 f.

[7] Plu. *Pelop.* 26. 5.

well have been his own choice of how and where to spend this time (below, p. 214).

Meanwhile he was at least safe in Thebes from his mother (and his brother). And though Thebes was not Athens, for the eloquence or elegance of its orators and self-confident elaboration of a machinery of self-government, still it was the most powerful city of Greece at this time, the city where met a *synedrion* of the allies of the Boeotians, and where the federal democracy of the Boeotians conducted its affairs in primary assembly and in law courts in a way which suited the Thebans (ἐπιτηδείως τοῖς Θηβαίοις δημοκρατούμενοι, as Thucydides might have written).[1] For a young student of Greek politics Thebes was a serviceable enough working model of the democracy which had settled upon most of the cities of Greece by now, even on those which were mainly or wholly agricultural. It is probably not fanciful to think that the young prince whose talents were to lie no less in diplomacy than in war was gladly absorbed in noting the point and counterpoint through which these people came to make up their minds, and in learning the unstraight-forward language compounded of self-preservation, self-deception, and self-esteem which led to political decisions.

His return to Macedonia will have been in 365 when his brother Perdiccas managed to rid himself of Ptolemy his guardian and regent (and of his mother). Interesting—and equivocal—is the glimpse that we are given of life at the court of Perdiccas III. It was Perdiccas evidently who was the philosopher and intellectual of the family. Plato's former pupil, Euphraeus of Oreus, gained a strong influence over him, so much so that he was able to dictate the character of the company and conversation at dinner and after. 'Accordingly, when Philip had become king, Parmenion when he captured Euphraeus in Oreus, put him to death.'[2] The amusing inaccuracy of Carystius here (the capture of Oreus being about eighteen years later at least) implies a rare unpopularity of Euphraeus among the leading Macedonians. Philip himself, whatever the truth about his Pythagorean studies in Thebes, was no great Platonist probably. The tone of the symposium in the heyday of Euphraeus ('Let no man ungeometered enter here!') is quite unlike what we hear of Philip's parties later. Nor do we ever hear of Euphraeus himself as still present in Macedonia after Philip came to the throne. Yet there is a story that Euphraeus once had done Philip a good turn (and a very strange story it is).

Speusippus, the nephew of Plato who succeeded him as head of the

---

[1] For *synedrion*, Tod, *GHI* 160, 11 and 24; X. *HG* 7. 3. 11. For Assembly and Courts, especially D.S. 15. 52. 1 f.; 71. 7; 72. 2; 78. 4; 79. 5; 80. 2; Plu. *Pelop.* 25. 1 f.; ibid. 7.

[2] Caryst. Perg. *FHG* 4. 356 F 2 (*ap.* Ath. 11. 508d). According to Demosthenes (9. 62) Euphraeus committed suicide.

Academy, found occasion to write to Philip early in the year 342. In a section of the Letter directed against Theopompus, who was in Pella at the time, and whose denigration of Plato had been reported back to Athens, Speusippus reminded Philip that it was to Plato that he owed the beginning of his career as a ruler, and that Plato always 'took it greatly to heart if anything uncivilized or unbrotherly happened between you'.[1] The scholar Carystius of Pergamum alludes to this letter and elucidates the reference to 'the beginning of his career as a ruler': 'For Plato sent to Perdiccas Euphraeus of Oreus, who persuaded him to assign some territory to Philip (ὃς ἔπεισε ἀπομερίσαι τινὰ χώραν Φιλίππῳ). There he maintained a force, and when Perdiccas met his death having the force in readiness plunged in and took charge (ἐπέπεσε τοῖς πράγμασι).'[2] The explanation is a little mysterious, because Macedonia at this time had no internal provinces to which governors or generals were appointed regularly. A prince of the royal house could expect to be given a part of the royal estates to live on, one supposes, and it is not easy to see just what *more* than this 'assigning some territory to Philip' could possibly mean, or just what, in the way of a private army, Philip could maintain without becoming positively an object of suspicion. Perdiccas was an enterprising ruler, as his acquisition of Amphipolis shows; and he may have had some warning of the coming Illyrian invasion. His 'assigning territory' to Philip may have been part of his preparations and precautions, and the training of an army. Perhaps the 'assigning' concerned Pelagonia, where Menelaus of the ruling house had shown more independence than was good (above, pp. 186, 188). Or is it possible even that the 'assigning territory' has an element of euphemism, and means really that Philip was allowed to live on a royal estate instead of being arrested or chased into exile?

This sinister suggestion of course is inspired by the remark of Speusippus (above), about Plato's distress when these brothers quarrelled. 'If anything uncivilized or unbrotherly happened between you' is unmistakably the tactful way of alluding to the fact that they *had* quarrelled. As younger brother of a philosopher king Philip in the earliest twenties of his age (one can see it) may well have seemed a little wild. If this was so, and if the brothers did not get on well together, the dreaded Euphraeus did well to advise Perdiccas as he did, in a way designed to avoid the doing of anything rash, and with the effect of at least keeping Philip in

---

[1] Speusippus *Epist. Socrat.* 30 12 (R. Hercher, *Epistologr. graeci*). On this letter, see p. 514 below.

[2] Caryst. Perg. F 1. *FHG* 4. 356 (*ap.* Athen. 11. 506 e). Plato's *Fifth Letter* (Pl. 321 c–322 B) is addressed to Perdiccas, and introduces or recommends Euphraeus to him. I do not know that anyone claims it as a genuine letter of Plato, and to me Hackforth's grounds for rejecting it seem not merely good but decisive (R. Hackforth, *The Authorship of the Platonic Epistles* (1913) 73–5; cf. also H. Leisegang, *RE* 20. 4 (1950) 2529 s.v. *Platon*).

the country and on the ration strength. When the Illyrians came Philip must surely have been there, for everything that we hear of him later makes nonsense of the notion that a great battle was going to take place on Macedonian soil without this dedicated soldier having a hand in it.

The death of Perdiccas had brought Macedonia to a crisis.[1] With Bardylis gathering his forces to overrun the whole kingdom, it may seem surprising that there was as much competition for the throne as evidently there was. Besides Philip himself and the boy Amyntas (son of Perdiccas), three men associated with the Royal House thought of themselves as claimants. The two most formidable, Pausanias and Argaeus, were supported by foreign powers, by Berisades, king of the western Odrysians, and by Athens. But they were pressing their claims in Thrace and in Athens respectively; Philip was on the spot. He was able at some time to arrest and execute Archelaus, his half-brother, the other active claimant who was present (his two younger brothers escaped, and are heard of later at Olynthus).[2]

For the moment the throne lay between him and his nephew, the young Amyntas. The army no doubt was mobilized for defence, and to elect or acclaim the new king. The issue can never have been seriously in doubt. The possibility of a regency may well have been discussed; but it is hard to see why it should have been discussed for long. That Philip aged twenty-three or twenty-four should have given no inkling of his qualities seems out of the question. This was the moment for a man, and not for a collection of court cliques or factions scheming round a boy-king. To appoint Philip regent for the boy-king might seem a fair compromise. But was this the time for compromise? Ephorus (if he was the source of Diodorus here) knew nothing of any regency, or if he knew of something he rejected it.[3] The source of Pompeius Trogus (Theopompus?) perhaps did know something of a regency, and Justin's epitome is usually interpreted as recording that Philip was appointed regent for Amyntas; but this in a context and in terms which cast the gravest doubts on his veracity. Justin obviously has got the death of Perdiccas all wrong here (in his previous sentence), by leaving out the Illyrians altogether. J. R. Ellis has argued recently that he has got Philip's regency wrong too, if that is what he meant to record.[4] This seems probable.

---

[1] D.S. 16. 2. 4 ff.

[2] Just. 7. 4. 5; 8. 3. 10. Theopomp. *FGrH* no. 115, F 27; cf. Beloch 3². 1. 225; 2. 66 f. I have assumed that Archelaus, first named by Justin, was the eldest brother (as at p. 176, stemma). From Justin's allusion, à propos the Olynthian war of 349, *back* to the execution of Archelaus, it is impossible to know its date. But no date seems more probable than one very close to Philip's accession. See further p. 700 below.

[3] For Ephorus as probable source of Diodorus here, Hammond, *CQ* 31 (1937) 79 ff.

[4] Just. 7. 5. 6–10. Justin makes no mention of the Illyrian invasion, and makes Perdiccas the victim of conspiracy initiated by Eurydice, the queen mother. Then—'Itaque Philippus

A regency was discussed, very likely; but it was never brought into being, for the reasons mentioned above. Philip was acclaimed as king.[1] His reign of twenty-four years (as Diodorus gives it in this context) begins now.[2] The young Amyntas might be thought to be in a position of great personal danger now; but he comes to no harm, we find. He is destined to grow up at court, to marry his first cousin, a daughter of Philip, to live a quiet life in security, thanks to his own quiet personality which Philip never came to misjudge (below, p. 702).

To decide this question the army had been summoned to assemble according to the Macedonian practice. Which of the Macedonians really did assemble on these occasions we can only surmise. In normal times the princes and chief men from the whole kingdom, presumably, came to show their acceptance of the new king (if they did accept him): many of the smaller landowning gentry too no doubt; but not, one must

diu non regem sed tutorem pupilli egit. At ubi graviora bella imminebant serumque auxilium in expectatione infantis erat, compulsus a populo regnum suscepit.'

The difficulties raised by *diu* and *graviora bella* are obvious, for no *bella* of Philip's whole career were *graviora* than those of the next twelve months or so. (See my next note.)

For a full discussion, see J. R. Ellis, 'Amyntas Perdikka, Philip II and Alexander the Great', *JHS* 91 (1971) 15–25. Ellis argues that the well-known inscription of Lebadeia (below, Appendix 2) recording this Amyntas as the king of the Macedonians belongs to the year 336/5 after Philip's death. Though this cannot be right, I agree with Ellis in rejecting Justin as evidence for a regency of Philip.

[1] To try to interpret what Justin thought he was saying and meant to say is an unenviable task. His words which follow the last words of the quotation (see previous footnote), *regnum suscepit*, are (7. 6. 1) 'Ut est ingressus imperium . . .' and he proceeds to write of the desperate situation of Macedonia in 359/8, and of Philip's acts to meet it. Here imperium can refer to the regency, if we believe in a regency. But equally the phrase can mean 'Having become king . . .'. Justin could not write *regnum* here because he had written it only five words before.

The words of the quoted passage cannot be interpreted to make sense if they are related to a period of some years in which Philip *was* regent (because of *diu*, and *graviora bella*). It seems possible to me that they can be thought to make sense if they are referring to a period of *some weeks* immediately after the death of Perdiccas and while the question of a regency was still open. In this case *diu* would mean 'for the whole of this period of a few weeks or most of it': *non regem, sed tutorem pupilli egit* would mean 'He did not claim to be king, but guardian of his ward': *ubi graviora bella imminebant* would mean that the news from the frontiers and beyond was alarming—the Illyrians, Paeonians, and Odrysians could all be expected to close in, and Athens had decided to support Argaeus. This is the best I can do. (This interpretation is fairly close to that of D. G. Hogarth, *Philip and Alexander of Macedon* 42 n. 1.)

[2] D.S. 16. 1. 3; 2. 1. See Beloch 3². 2. 49 ff. on the surviving king-lists of Eusebius and others, with a table at p. 51, and discussion pp. 60 f. Taking the twenty-four-year reign of Diodorus as correct, for an accession in 360/59 (archonship of Callimedes), we find Philip assigned a shorter reign, allowing for a year or years of regency first, only by Syncellus (twenty-three years) and by Satyrus F5, *FHG* 3. 161 ff. (twenty-two years). (Beloch is mistaken in emending the numeral of Satyrus so as to make him conform to twenty-four.) Even Justin, who is said to be telling us of a regency, gives twenty-five years as the length of the reign (9. 8. 1).

This view of Philip's accession is unorthodox. Most modern interpreters think that Amyntas was elected king now, and Philip was regent; and naturally there are some good reasons for thinking this. The reasons against it seem to me to be the stronger. For further discussion, see Appendix 2, p. 702. For a different view, p. 651.

suppose, the smallholders and shepherds from the principalities of Upper Macedonia, except for some few who might accompany great men as their retainers. The small people of the Thermaic plainland and Pieria, of the lower Axios valley, and of Eordaea this side of Mt. Bermion, could stream in to make up an assembly of some thousands (as 'representative' as the five or six thousands of an Athenian Ecclesia, anyway). But on this occasion their numbers were not a matter of academic interest only. Whoever they were, these people, and however many (or few), it was they who when they had acclaimed the new king, became immediately the soldiers who for the moment were the only army he had. At this moment Macedonia was looking ominously like a free-for-all, a prize for the nearest, the quickest, the strongest to divide and plunder.

Invasion could be expected from four separate quarters; from the Illyrians of Bardylis occupying parts of the kingdom in the north-west, from the Paeonians on the northern frontier, from beyond the Strymon to the east where the Thracian king Berisades entertained the pretender Pausanias, and from the sea when the Athenians implemented their decision to restore Argaeus to the throne. Viewed as a purely military problem, Philip's immediate future looked nearly hopeless. To view it with a wider vision was necessary in order to survive.

Men, money, and time he needed, these three; and especially time. Buying time has always been a primary function of diplomacy, and diplomacy was destined to be Philip's favourite field of action. No début was ever more electrifying. The practitioner who could talk his way steadily through, round, over, under, and out of this mess need never fear the future. The Paeonian king, he judged, and the Thracian Berisades might be bought off or bribed. They were, however, kings, not seedy characters of an underworld, happy to take 20 or 30 talents to slit a pretender's throat. In terms of mere cash one would think of at least 100 or 200 talents apiece as the sort of money which might induce these kings to change their minds in this matter of policy where their interests obviously were very well served by not changing them. How or where Philip could raise that sort of money in a hurry is not obvious.[1] One is tempted to think that these transactions must have been as much diplomatic as financial. The small sums of money (the 20 or 30 talents) could have been offered acceptably perhaps if they were accompanied by undertakings to continue paying small sums regularly. 'Danegeld' or 'tribute', both words could suggest themselves in the context, each with implications concerning the status of Philip and the Macedonians *vis-à-vis*

---

[1] I judge it an impossibility. To raise 200 or 300 talents in a few weeks needed something abnormal. Confiscation of estates? Those of Pausanias doubtless had been confiscated long since. Even if the estates of Archelaus were taken now, and were worth 200–300 talents, who was able to pay for them on that scale quickly?

these two kings. A little money and a lot of talk, this is probably what Philip's ambassadors carried with them to Paeonia and to Thrace, the talk no doubt including promises, promises which would have been a great disgrace if they had ever been kept.[1] Meanwhile, better to be disgraced than dead, or a fugitive from the kingdom.

Yet the fears of what might have come from Paeonia or Thrace were as nothing compared with the fear of what the Illyrians might do. The inactivity of Bardylis is an enigma, due in part very likely to Illyrian affairs of which we can know nothing. Bardylis was old, too, and we see him a year later negotiating with Philip with what seems a prudent moderation, as of one who knows how much better the half is than the whole (below, p. 213). But this was when something had been seen already of Philip and his capacity: in these first months it surely must have seemed to Bardylis that he could move in for the kill, if only not to be forestalled. And he did begin (as Diodorus writes) to collect a great army and prepare to invade Macedonia.[2] It might be expected that Philip should have tried to bring the war with the Illyrians formally to an end by a peace treaty, even on very bad terms—and it will be recalled that his father Amyntas twice had had to pay for an Illyrian disaster by abandoning some territory (pp. 172 f. above). Certainly no treaty was made now, but it would be surprising if there were no negotiations, and if Philip did not do everything in his power to spin them out in the hope of being able to negotiate from greater strength later. However that may be, the failure to follow up his great victory with speed and decision was to cost Bardylis very dear.

Meanwhile Philip cultivated the men who had acclaimed him king, the army. Now began that long time of training and innovation which, though its first results are quickly seen, must be thought of as a continuing process spread over many years (below, pp. 418 ff.). The army was low, and thanked God it was not marching against Illyrians again this summer. The first campaign of the new regime was ideal for its purpose. It was the pretender Argaeus landing at Methone supported by an Athenian admiral and 3,000 Greek mercenary hoplites who first gave the Macedonians some confidence in their new general and king who had taken their training so firmly in hand, and (what they needed most of all) who gave them a new confidence in themselves.

The attempt of Argaeus was a small affair in itself, and in its military details merits small attention.[3] Argaeus was misinformed as to the reception he would find. From Methone he marched the few hours to

---

[1] Of the Paeonians Diodorus wrote (16. 3. 4) 'Some of them he bribed, others by promises he persuaded to keep the peace.' I have presumed that the decision of the king Agis was what mattered most, as was that of the Thracian king (ibid.). For Agis, ibid. 4. 2.

[2] D.S. 16. 2. 6.　　　　　　　　　　　　　　　　　　　　[3] D.S. 16. 3. 5f.

Aegeae,[1] where he expected evidently to be admitted and to be able to begin to organize there a Macedonian rising in his favour. But the people of Aegeae had taken note of Philip and preferred him to Argaeus: there was no rising. Argaeus could only march back to the sea. He did not make it, however. Philip had collected the troops he could raise quickly, and raced to the relief of Aegeae.[2] His strength is not known, but if he had only a few dozen cavalry besides some Macedonian infantry the advantage could have been decisive against hoplites or peltasts unsupported. The mercenaries were roughly handled, and when they broke the survivors including Argaeus and his staff were surrounded on the hill to which they had fled; and there they surrendered. What became of Argaeus we are not told, but we can guess.

This military picnic was spoiled only by Philip's decision not to ransom or sell the prisoners but to give them back gratis to the Athenians at once. The money from them would have been a good windfall for the treasury, even if some of it had been given to the troops to cheer them up still more. Philip's act of self-denial underlines the importance of the Argaeus incident in providing the opportunity of coming to a good understanding with Athens. The real key to this however was Amphipolis (below, p. 236).

The treaty with Athens, concluded now in the second half of the year 359, must be counted on the short term an important diplomatic success, even though it abandoned the traditional Macedonian policy of opposition to any extension of Athenian power in the neighbourhood. But the short term was still paramount, and Philip's assessment of the priorities was correct. A second military intervention by the Athenians was something that he could not allow to happen before he had done more to build up the army, and especially before he had achieved some security in the north and the north-west. Meanwhile he continued to work on the army as much as he could, probably in the autumn of 359 and again in spring 358: and probably some rearming was done over this winter (below, p. 421). The time for action came with the good news from the north of the death of Agis the Paeonian king. Philip invaded Paeonia and won what was evidently a decisive victory, enabling him to impose a treaty of alliance on the new king and to wipe out the discreditable memory of his 'money and promises' of a few months earlier.[3] He was

---

[1] On the site of Aegeae, see Hammond, Volume I. 155–8.

[2] Hammond (*HG²* 537) has surmised that he refrained deliberately from moving on Aegeae more quickly, to demonstrate that he could rely on the loyalty of his own people there. This is certainly possible. But if (as is likely) he knew of the Athenian expedition's approach, and had the army mobilized in readiness in a central position at or near Pella, until the point of landing was known he was not able to move. Argaeus' march from Methone to Aegeae needed a few hours only. For the news of the landing to reach Pella and for Philip to march from there to Aegeae took perhaps two days.

[3] D.S. 16. 4. 2 καὶ παρατάξει τοὺς βαρβάρους νικήσας ἠνάγκασε τὸ ἔθνος πειθαρχεῖν τοῖς Μακεδόσιν.

able to do this, it seems, without interference or fear of interference by Bardylis and his Illyrians.

The army was doing well now, for the Paeonians could fight, and had good light cavalry.[1] The Macedonian cavalry must have come up to scratch, and the infantry will have needed to move fast to get to grips with an enemy mostly mobile and light-armed. Philip felt strong enough to challenge Bardylis. From what we see later of his methods, it would be in character here if he gave Bardylis the opportunity of withdrawing without a trial of strength. Bardylis offered peace on terms which confirmed him in possession of those regions of Macedonia which he occupied.[2] To sacrifice Amphipolis to Athens was diplomacy, but to cede important parts of the kingdom itself to the Illyrians was folly, a writing off of capital, material and moral, which he could not contemplate. He marched, with the fullest levy of the Macedonians that he could muster, and sought out the Illyrians probably in Lyncestis, where Bardylis (as we see from what follows) was confident that what had been good enough for Perdiccas would be good enough for Philip.

Both commanders wanted battle, which was fought therefore in open country, and between armies nearly equal in numbers.[3] Though Diodorus' account of it is brief enough, it comes evidently from a well-informed source (Ephorus?), and it allows us to see or to infer what really happened here, a thing rare enough in the military record of Philip's reign.[4] There is something paradoxical in the strategy of Bardylis, for though he is described as confident because of the past and its victories, and though this confidence is confirmed by his failure to provide for a safe withdrawal in the event of a reverse, yet his actual dispositions on the day were defensive, his army drawn up in the form of a square. It seems possible that it was not till he saw the Macedonians, their sarissas displayed now for the first time, that he realized that this would be no mere encore of the previous action, and that he needed to be careful now. The square formation was his way of being careful.

Philip's performance looks remarkably mature. Though his cavalry only slightly outnumbered the Illyrian (600–500), he counted on its superiority, and its ability to dispose of the enemy cavalry and ultimately to break up the defensive square once it had been prized open somewhere. He did not lead the cavalry himself however, but 'the best of the Macedonians' (the Foot Guards?) on the right wing, next to the cavalry outside them.[5] He intended to make sure that the square was prized open somewhere, and he led the Foot Guards against (presumably) an

---

[1] For the Paeonian cavalry with Alexander, later, see below, p. 432.

[2] D.S. 16. 4. 4.

[3] Ibid. 3 and 5. Philip had 10,000 infantry, 600 cavalry; Bardylis had 10,000 infantry, 500 cavalry.

[4] Ibid. 5–7; cf. Hammond, *CQ* 31 (1937) 79 f.   [5] D.S. 16. 4. 5.

angle of the square, in order to offer to the cavalry their best attack
'on flanks and rear' of the enemy, as their orders ran.[1] The Illyrian
infantry were not Greek hoplites and they were not Macedonians of the
new style, but they had thrashed the Macedonians of the old style, and
there was fierce fighting before Philip was able to make the opening for
the cavalry to come in. Then it was quickly over. The rout and the long
pursuit were unusually lethal. Seven thousand of the Illyrians (nearly
three-quarters of the whole army) are said to have been killed, and even
if the figure is an exaggeration, it must still be thought to represent
something never or seldom seen in Greek battles up to now.[2] This
general looks suspiciously like a master. This army too, already, looks
a formidable proposition indeed. Victory by cavalry opens a new vista.
The old is represented by that concentrated attack by infantry on one
sector of a front, reminiscent of the Theban method. The co-ordination
of the two arms, preserved in Diodorus' account of Philip's orders to the
cavalry, might pass nearly unnoticed on a Lyncestian upland. But there
would be other days.

It would be hard to overestimate, probably, the importance of this
day's work. It stands out now as a landmark in Macedonian history.
For the Macedonians then and their neighbours its effect may have been
something like the impact of Leuctra on Greece, especially in its paradox
of the victim victorious: instead of being carved up finally now, it is
the victim who emerges holding the knife. The Illyrian disaster of
Perdiccas had not been an isolated piece of misfortune. At the time it
might almost have been thought the penultimate stage in a process of
disintegration; for it will be recalled that one of the Molossian inscriptions of 370–368 records the Orestae as forming then one of the constituent
tribes of the Molossian tribal state; the Orestae whose place in the
fifth century had been with Macedonia, and who of course are to be
found again presently making up one of the divisions of the Macedonian
phalanx.[3]

One of the signs of success and the status it conferred may be seen in
Philip's early marriages, which Satyrus (who listed them) called marriages
κατὰ πόλεμον, 'in the course of war', a particular refinement of what in
general we call marriages of state or policy.[4] The first in the list (and
probably in time) was to Phila, sister of Derdas of Elimea, renewing the
link by marriage with this Upper Macedonian principality which went
back through Archelaus to Alexander I.[5] Next, the Illyrian princess
Audata came to him presumably as part of the settlement by which

---

[1] D.S. 16. 5–6.   [2] Ibid. 7.

[3] For the Orestae, above, pp. 185 ff.; below, 426 ff. The best text of the Molossian inscription is at Hammond, *Epirus* 530 f. (the Orestian magistrate at line 14).

[4] Satyrus, *FHG* 3. 161 F 5.

[5] Above, pp. 18, 139; A. B. Bosworth, *CQ* N.S. 21 (1971) 100 f.

a peace with Bardylis was made. The two kings were on equal terms now, with the occupied parts of Macedonia restored. Audata, however, though she became the mother of a future queen, is hardly heard of again. (Phila, too, disappears from the story, and no children of hers are recorded.) It was only a year to eighteen months after the victory over Bardylis when Philip married again. Olympias was the granddaughter of Alcetas I king of the Molossians, daughter of King Neoptolemus (now dead), and niece of the reigning King Arybbas. The royal houses of Macedonia and Epirus were much alike; so were their peoples, in language, race, and culture (indeed the Orestae, we have just seen, could pass from one state to the other and be integrated easily into either). A Molossian princess was not really a foreign queen among the Macedonians.[1] This was a good marriage of policy, for Arybbas was as much concerned as Philip in having the Illyrians kept in their place.[2] Though nothing is heard of co-operation between them recently against Bardylis, their co-operation in the future undoubtedly was the best foundation for security, as each will have seen. There was, true, the little matter of the Orestae outstanding between them still. When the Orestae left the Molossian organization and became part again of the Macedonian kingdom, we are never told. To suggest that Orestis may have been the dowry of Olympias in 357 is a guess, no more, but a reasonable one perhaps.[3] Olympias herself in the succession of Philip's wives was evidently seen by Satyrus as in some sense an official queen, to whom later wives were 'introduced'.[4] There is no sign of any attempt to keep a monogamous household with only one wife at a time, and even the final withdrawal of Olympias in 337 was no protest at a new wife but a consequence of events which look undesigned. Besides the wives already mentioned the two Thessalian wives, also, were married 'in the course of war', probably the one in 358 and the other in 352. One purpose of all this marrying (above, p. 153), was to rear plenty of sons so as to secure the succession: this was only partly achieved.

[1] *Contra*, Bosworth, loc. cit. 102.

[2] Satyrus loc. cit. 'he gained the kingdom of the Molottians by marrying Olympias', oversimplifies–of course. The tradition preserved by Plutarch (*Alex.* 2. 2) that this was a love match of a very young couple seems ruled out by chronological improbability (H. Strasburger, *RE* 18. 1 (1939) 178).

[3] Topographically, Tymphaea might be thought likely to go with Orestis in any centrifugal movements of the outer-Macedonian *ethne*. Tymphaea may have broken away too, but there is no evidence connecting it with the Molossian organization.

[4] Satyrus loc. cit., of both Meda and Cleopatra (γήμας δὲ καὶ ταύτην ἐπεισήγαγεν τῇ Ὀλυμπιάδι; and καὶ ταύτην ἐπεισάγων τῇ Ὀλυμπιάδι).

VI

THE FIRST ADVENTURES ABROAD
(358–355)

WITH the defeat of Bardylis Philip regained control of those parts of Upper Macedonia which had been occupied by the Illyrians. The kingdom was reunited and immediate dangers of invasion were over. The modern reader of his story is struck by the speed with which now he seems to pass to the offensive and to plans of expansion. A precise chronology is not possible, but it may be only a matter of weeks, it seems, or months at the most, before he made his first intervention in Thessaly; and his attack on Amphipolis can hardly have been delayed more than nine months after the ending of the Illyrian campaign. The impression of opportunism, and of an ambition which can hardly wait to expand, is hard to resist. Resisted it must be, however, for even if it contains truth it certainly does not comprise the whole truth: as a historical interpretation it suffers from the fact that our own knowledge of where Thessaly and Amphipolis were to lead Philip was not shared by Philip himself at this time. His own approach to Thessaly and to Amphipolis was based necessarily on the past, and especially the recent past.[1]

But first a word about Greece in general terms. The weakness and the divisions of the city-states in the fourth century are a commonplace, and one which needs no long analysis here. The great power concentrations of the fifth century and the 390s and the wars to which they gave rise had decided one thing only, that no single city had the resources to enable it to impose its rule on the rest. Imperialism on that scale and at that pitch dug its own grave. The reactions and the resistances to it produced a new principle as the basis of the inter-state relations of the Greeks from the time of the King's Peace on (386), autonomy for all cities great and small. Since this was really a return, broadly speaking, to the way in which the Greeks had lived before Athens, and then Sparta, had tried to impose their own rule, the principle needs no explanation: it explains itself. But some new rules were introduced now into the treaty arrangements and obligations, for which a new name also was found, *koine eirene* (Common Peace):

first . . . their principal clause laid down that all Greek states should be free and autonomous; second, that the treaties were made between all the Greeks,

[1] Above, pp. 181, 184–7.

that is to say that they were not bilateral agreements limited to the two sides fighting a war, but were agreements of a general nature applicable to all Greeks equally, whether or not they had taken part in the preceding war.[1]

Rules are a start; but the realist could ask 'How many hoplites has the Book of Rules?' The victims (and the perpetrators) of the recent imperialisms recognized that genuine security could not be gained in isolation. This truth had for long been underlined by the permanent associations in federal groups of clusters of cities which had affinities both ethnical and geographical (in Thessaly, Phocis, Locris, Boeotia, Aetolia, Acarnania, Achaea, and elsewhere). The federal group still at this time has before it a long and interesting part to play in Greek history (as the new development in Arcadia of the 360s well shows). But naturally the day of the more widely flung grouping by means of alliance was not over. When even the leading cities such as Athens and Thebes knew that they were insecure without allies, *a fortiori* many smaller cities needed the alliance of a stronger one (a *hegemon*) for protection. The Second Athenian Confederacy was a success for some years because it served this need of both the stronger and the weaker. In this way if the new rule about freedom and autonomy was observed (and now none of the leading cities was pre-eminent enough in power to be able to ignore it), a reconciliation was possible between the two ancient incompatibles of the fifth century; *res olim dissociabiles*, freedom and hegemony. Now, however, the hegemonies are localized, their limits imposed by the limited power of the leaders. Correspondingly the wars of these alliances give an impression of being on a lower pitch of intensity, wars for advantage rather than for survival.

Though Xenophon wrote gloomily enough about the state of Greece after the battle of Mantinea in 362, it does not seem wholly necessary to agree with him. The battle which all men had expected to settle everything gave no clear victory to either side and consequently settled nothing. 'The state of Greece was still more evenly balanced and disturbed after it than before it.'[2] This was perhaps true; but more questionable is the opinion that a victory for either side *would* have opened the way to a hegemony over most of Greece (as Xenophon implies). And there remains the fact (which he does not mention) that all the Greeks now except Sparta agreed to join in a *koine eirene* accepting the present situation with all its imperfections.[3] In one sense this low-keyed realism can be seen as something more promising for the future than any new attempt by a victor to impose a hegemony wider or tighter than others would tolerate or than the victor could sustain. Either way, there would be wars again, some day. Meanwhile as it was, hardly any Greeks

[1] Ryder, *KE* xvi.   [2] X. *HG* 7. 5. 26 f.   [3] D.S. 15. 89. 1; Plu. *Ages.* 35. 3 f.

could complain of being 'enslaved' (*douleia*), and even Sparta, isolated because she refused to subscribe to this *koine eirene*, still was not molested.[1] True, Greece had its sensitive areas now, one of them the Peloponnese where Sparta would never accept the liberation of Messenia; another of them Thessaly, deeply split by the tyranny at Pherae. In both these places trouble was to be expected; but not necessarily trouble which need involve the leading powers in wars to the death or nearly. In short the state of Greece after Mantinea, viewed in isolation, was uninspiring certainly and untidy, but it was not fraught with doom.

Viewed in the context of the wider world, too, the signs were not ill omened. Persia, especially, which had been able to lean heavily on the Greeks to produce 'the King's Peace' of 386, and occasionally since then, was weakened now by revolt among the satraps of Asia Minor.[2] The Greek peace-conference of 362, it is thought, expressed itself and its policy towards the Great King in terms correct indeed but of a refreshing independence.[3] In the north, a great Thracian kingdom of the Odrysians united under Cotys II gave some problems to Athens with her interests in the Chersonese and the sea-route to the granary of South Russia, but presented no danger to Greece. Macedonia was still a kingdom of no real weight in the world and one to be used and exploited, economically for its wealth in timber especially, politically by whichever of the Greek leaders, now Sparta now Thebes now Athens, had the power at the time for action to further its own interests in this peripheral part of the world. Philip's sojourn as a hostage at Thebes was a symptom of Macedonian weakness in a time of trouble. The kingdom had not always been weak, and need not always be weak now; but even in a time of strength no Greek south of Larissa in Thessaly had ever needed to worry about it. So at the time of Philip's accession no Greek politician without the power of second sight can have included Macedonia among the factors that might make an impact on Greece itself in the foreseeable future.

1. *Thessaly*

Philip's father Amyntas III had owed something to Thessalian support for the recovery of his throne (? 384), and later had had reason to fear the territorial ambitions of Jason of Pherae (? 373). It had been the merest prudence, therefore, on the part of Philip's eldest brother Alexander II

---

[1] For Sparta's refusal to recognize the independence of Messene, see (besides the references of the previous footnote) Plb. 4. 33. 8 f.

[2] For the King's Peace, and Persian influence on renewals of *koine eirene* in general, Ryder 25 ff., 58, 80 ff., 137 ff., with bibliography.

[3] The undated inscription from Argos (Tod, *GHI* 145) which records the reply of 'the Greeks' to an approach from 'the Satraps', though its date and occasion has been the subject of much controversy, now is commonly attributed (rightly, no doubt) to the peace conference after Mantinea (362). Cf. Bengtson, *Staatsv.* no. 292, with bibliography.

to accede to a request for help from the Aleuadae of Larissa in their struggle to free themselves from the grip of Alexander of Pherae (369): this was breaking up the union of Thessaly under a *tagos* from Pherae, the menace which had threatened earlier. Any more ambitious hopes that Alexander II may have had, of acquisitions in Thessaly, were removed by the Theban intervention under Pelopidas which followed swiftly.[1] The 360s were the years of Boeotian ascendancy over Thessaly, the years, too, in which Macedonia itself twice experienced Theban interventions in her own succession wars, and in which the young Philip himself was transferred to Thebes for three years as a hostage.[2] To Philip now newly in power in Macedonia and still intent on securing his position, Thessaly represented one more potential threat, whether from the Thessalians themselves should they be reunited or from those Boeotians in the background, whom he had learned to know in Thebes and to respect. To use any friends that he had in Thessaly, and to make more, was a matter of preventive diplomacy and of insurance against contingencies. His motives for going into Thessaly early in his reign were probably much like those of his brother Alexander more than ten years before.

One intriguing question which puts itself from time to time as we try to follow Philip's movements is, how many operations on different fronts can we believe that he undertook in the space of a single campaigning year? Occasionally he seems to have too many things on his hands, too close together.[3] Two factors, which may be taken as constants, may be useful here. (1) It is not necessary to think of him as calling out the full military levy of Macedonia for every campaign recorded. As we shall see, there is good reason to think that the full levy or something approaching it was mobilized comparatively seldom. If we think of him as working often with relatively small forces, and those sometimes including mercenaries, we shall probably have a truer understanding of what was possible for him, and what was tolerable for his people, in terms of campaigns on different fronts in rapid succession. (2) The interior lines which were so great an asset to his defensive strategy in 359–358 (see above, p. 210) will still operate in his favour when he acts on the offensive abroad: and this will be particularly true of the early years, when the attacks are being launched at objectives still not far removed from the heart of Macedonia itself. Indeed as late as 352 we can see a remarkable transfer of effort, from Thessaly in the summer where he was really heavily committed, to Thrace in the autumn where that long, deep

---

[1] See above, pp. 181, 185.
[2] D.S. 15. 61. 3 ff.; Plu. *Pel.* 26; Just. 6. 9. 6 f.; 7. 5. 2 ff.; cf. Sordi, *LT* 193 ff.; Westlake 129 ff.
[3] The year 356 is a good example.

probe as far as Heraion Teichos knocked out the strongest of the Thracian kings and threatened for the first time the Athenian interests in the Thracian Chersonese. In 358 his arena is still a small one, and it is not difficult to accept that he can have acted on three different fronts all in the space of (say) six months. The defeats inflicted on the Paeonians and the Illyrians carried the weight probably of the full strength of Macedonia at that time, in the summer of 358 (see above, p. 213). With all frontiers secured now, an entry into Thessaly that same autumn seems feasible, more particularly if we think of it as a reconnaissance in force, with the greater part of his Macedonians dispersed to their homes for the winter. There was nothing rash or irresponsible in such a move, and recent history warned not to neglect an opportunity here, if one offered. Nevertheless since not all modern interpreters have accepted the ancient evidence supporting this Thessalian move by Philip at this time, some further discussion of it will be in place.

Chronology of Philip's interventions in Thessaly

The narrative of Diodorus Siculus, who selected and condensed from the much fuller narratives of historians contemporary with the events or more nearly so than himself, and Justin's much slighter epitome of the *Philippic Histories* of Pompeius Trogus, present many problems, some of which are considered elsewhere. But the chronological problem of the stages by which Philip's interventions in Thessaly led to his being elected *archon* of the Thessalian League, though it may seem more properly a subject for an Appendix, really is so fundamental to the interpretation of his policy that it seems necessary to summarize it here.

When was Philip elected *archon* of the Thessalian League?[1] That he was so elected we know, from the fact that Alexander the Great on his accession as king was elected by the Thessalians as their own head of state in succession to Philip.[2] But neither Diodorus nor any other of our sources records an occasion when Philip himself achieved this position. Many modern interpreters have turned to the years 344–342 as the likeliest time, because they provide good evidence for Philip's having tightened his grip then on Thessaly in several ways. The only alternative to this seems to be the year 352, year of his great victory over the Phocian leader Onomarchus as a result of which the tyrants of Pherae capitulated, Pherae and Pagasae were taken, and Thessaly was reunited. This is the date proposed in the most recent detailed study of Thessalian

---

[1] We do not know the character of the federal Assembly of the Thessalian League at this period, whether it was a 'direct' Assembly or one of representatives from the cities. But it will be agreed, I hope, that *an* Assembly (or Council of representatives) there must have been. For discussion, see Sordi, *LT* 329 ff.; Larsen, *GFS* 19, 23 f.

[2] D.S. 17. 4. 1; Just. 11. 3. 2.

history, by M. Sordi, with very full discussions which carry conviction.[1] The three main reasons which seem to favour the year 352 decisively are these:

(1) A pasage of Demosthenes (below, p. 222) suggests rather strongly that when these words were spoken, in 349, Philip was *archon* of Thessaly already. Allusions to Thessaly by Isocrates and Justin may be thought to point in the same direction.

(2) The election of a foreign king by a League of Greek cities as their head of state is something so extraordinary that really it requires some 'special occasion' to explain it. Once stated, this needs no elaboration, probably; but it does need to be stated, because it has not always received the consideration that it deserves. The year 352 contains the special occasion, the great victory, bringing the reunification of Thessaly. It was the glory and the euphoria from all this, it is suggested, that helped to carry the architect and hero of the victory through the ethnic barrier and into the office of *archon*, for life.

No other year besides 352 can serve this purpose. For glory and euphoria, 346 *might* do: the year when Philip led an Amphictyonic army through Thermopylae, freed Delphi from the Phocians, and was elected himself to the Amphictyony with votes on its Council. But in 346 Demosthenes (and others) were well aware of Thessaly and its importance, and Philip's election *then* as *archon* could not possibly have escaped notice and comment.[2]

(3) If the election did not take place in 352, how could it take place in 344–342 without a war? In 344–342 we hear of Philip 'disciplining' the Thessalians in several ways (below, pp. 523 ff.). But in what capacity? If in 344 he was still only their powerful ally and no more, why did no Thessalians appeal to other Greek states for help, to Thebes for example, or to Athens, as the Olynthians had appealed for help in 349? The 'discipline' applied in 344–342 makes sense if it is the *archon* who is applying it (with a majority of the League cities concurring, presumably); but if it was really a matter of intervention by a foreign ally, it is much harder to explain. And this atmosphere of 'discipline' seems far from conducive to the extraordinary 'break-through' by which the foreign king *then* (we must suppose) was elected *archon*.

The election, then, must have been, it seems, in 352, its immediate motivation supplied by the Phocian war, which still needed to be carried through to its end. In this way and at this time Philip gained the grip on Thessaly which he never relinquished, and which he certainly

---

[1] Sordi, *LT* 249 ff.; cf. Griffith, 'Thessaly' 67 ff.

[2] D. 5. 20 and 23, spoken in September 346 when the Amphictyons were still in session at Delphi, alludes to the Thessalians and their equivocal attitude to Philip then. D. may misrepresent their attitude, but he could not have been silent on election as *archon*, recent or impending, if anything had been known of it.

tightened in 344–342. This interpretation may be thought to meet an objection provided by an allusion to Thessaly by Polybius, who certainly thought of Philip's control as dating from *after* the Olynthian War (348).[1] Polybius was not normally either ignorant or inaccurate in his allusions to past history, and it cannot be denied that for him an obvious landmark by which to date Philip's control would have been the date of his election as *archon*, if he knew it. Perhaps he did not know it; or perhaps he chose as landmark 346 the great year at Delphi when Philip's control of Thessaly was displayed in the Amphictyony and its settlement of affairs; or even the years 344–342 the years of 'discipline'. In any case the view of Polybius cannot override here the evidence of the contemporary Demosthenes, which must be considered briefly now.

In the *First Olynthiac* (349) Demosthenes encouraged the Athenians by telling them that Philip was having trouble in Thessaly.

Thessalian politics have always had their pitfalls for all men, and now most certainly they have for him. They have voted to demand Pagasae back from him, and to tell him not to build forts in Magnesia. And my information is that they are going to stop the taxation of their harbours and markets being allocated to him for his use; they claim that these should be used for the administration of Thessaly and not for Philip to appropriate. If he loses those funds he will certainly be in difficulties for the pay and upkeep of his mercenaries.[2]

The authenticity (or not) of Demosthenes' information need not concern us here, because it is enough to be sure (and we can) that he was telling the Athenians things which they knew to be possible and which contained nothing new or surprising (otherwise he would have needed to explain them). Pagasae and Magnesia do not help us here, because they could have been in dispute between Philip and the Thessalians as allies. A dispute about taxes, however, suggests a new dimension. Greek allies did not allocate specific taxes for each other's use.[3] They agreed upon fixed sums as war-contributions, and where the money came from was a matter for the contributor. For the Thessalians to assign their harbour and market revenues to Philip suggests very strongly that he is no longer an external ally now but their own executive officer; and the nature of their complaints (as reported) bears the traditional stamp of complaints against 'the Government' of every age and place—that money is being misapplied to purposes other than those for which it was voted.

Justin included the taxes of Thessaly in his very brief record of the

---

[1] Plb. 9. 28. 2 f. Walbank, *Commentary* 2, ad loc., describes the allusion to Thessaly as 'a simplification'.

[2] D. 1. 21–2.

[3] The Athenian 'allies' in 413 were subjects, and were obeying orders when they paid the *eikostē* instead of the *phoros* (Thuc. 7. 28. 4).

occasion when Alexander was elected *archon* on Philip's death.[1] Indeed Justin writes of Philip and Thessaly (and Thebes) in the year 352 in words which we could perhaps recognize as his way of saying that the Thessalians elected him *archon* of their League, if we are thinking of the election in 352 as possible or probable.[2] An allusion of Isocrates in 346 to Philip and Thessaly can be seen as equivocal, but rightly interpreted it can be seen as a rather graceful compliment to Philip on his position as *archon*—this for a public which knew the facts and could take the allusion. 'There was a time when the Thessalians were overlords in Macedonia. But now, see how closely he has attached them to himself, each group of them putting more trust in him than in their own fellow citizens.'[3] The remark is a fair, loose fit if it means 'They trust their ally more than they trust each other'; but it is an exact fit if it means 'each group of them has preferred to elect him as *archon* rather than elect a leader from another group'. It is hard to see this fit as accidental. It should be allowed to reinforce the impression received already from Demosthenes (1. 21–2).

This conclusion has important consequences for our interpretation of the evidence on Philip's relations with Thessaly in the years before 352. Briefly, the consequence is that this evidence, consisting of a few brief allusions, ought not to be minimized, and indeed needs to be

---

[1] Just. 11. 3. 2 'exemplo patris dux universae gentis creatus est et vectigalia omnia reditusque suos ei tradiderant.'

[2] Just. 8. 2. 1 'adversus quem [sc. Onomarchum] Thebani Thessalique non ex civibus suis, ne victores potentiam ferre non possent, sed Philippum Macedoniae regem ducem eligunt; et externae dominationi, quam in suis timuerunt, sponte succedunt.' If Justin intended to record here election as general merely, for the war, his remark about foreign domination, in its application to Thebes, looks forward as far as 338. This is not uncharacteristic of Justin, and it may represent his intention. But another possibility is that the Thebans are included here merely as principals in the war, but that the 'foreign domination' is applied to the Thessalians only, and that Justin is recording here the election as *archon*.

[3] Isoc. 5. 20 οὐ Θετταλοὺς μὲν τοὺς πρότερον ἐπάρχοντας Μακεδονίας οὕτως οἰκείως πρὸς αὑτὸν διακεῖσθαι πεποίηκεν ὥσθ' ἑκάστους αὐτῶν μᾶλλον ἐκείνῳ πιστεύειν ἢ τοῖς συμπολιτευομένοις; τῶν δὲ πόλεων τῶν περὶ τὸν τόπον ἐκεῖνον τὰς μὲν ταῖς εὐεργεσίαις πρὸς τὴν αὑτοῦ συμμαχίαν προσῆκται, τὰς δὲ σφόδρα λυπούσας αὐτὸν ἀναστάτους πεποίηκεν; It is necessary to print the second sentence here, because it has been taken often to refer to Thessaly (not unnaturally, in a sense). But it refers, I am sure, to the cities in the neighbourhood of *Macedonia*; and Isocrates (I suggest) avoided ambiguity, which he could not afford not to avoid in this rather delicate context, by writing περὶ τὸν τόπον ἐκεῖνον = 'the locality I mentioned *before* I mentioned the Thessalians'. (This passage in five consecutive rhetorical questions deals with different areas controlled by Philip: (1) Thessaly, (2) (here) cities in the neighbourhood of Macedonia, (3) Magnesia, Perrhaebia, and Paeonia, (4) Illyria, (5) Thrace.)

In the section cited here, the remark about the cities ('some . . . allies, others . . . wiped out') is exactly appropriate to the Greek-city-neighbours of Macedonia, especially in Chalcidice. Applied to cities of Thessaly or its *perioikis*, it makes us wonder which cities Philip had destroyed, and why in this case the Thessalians loved him and trusted him so well; and of course if the surviving cities are now his allies, this means that he has not yet been elected *archon*. This second sentence is a valuable contribution to our knowledge of the final status of some cities in Chalcidice (where we badly need it—below, pp. 365 ff.).

maximized, if it is to carry conviction; if the paradox of his election to the archonship so early as 352 is to be adequately explained.[1]

It may be taken as certain that Philip made two large-scale military interventions in Thessaly, in successive years 353 and 352, the first ending in disaster, the second in triumph.[2] In addition most modern interpreters bring him into Thessaly in 354, for the capture of the important Pagasae, port of Pherae. But this depends on a laconic entry of Diodorus in which the taking of Pagasae is linked with that of Methone (certainly in 354), and in which the name Pagasae appears in our text only by emendation (of unidentified Pagae). This has been questioned recently by C. Ehrhardt, rightly as it seems. Grote and Schaefer refused to accept a capture of Pagasae at a time when Pherae was still undefeated, and Ehrhardt's statement of the objections, especially on the military grounds, is altogether convincing.[3] Pagasae was taken after Pherae, as Demosthenes does tell us;[4] the date, 352. Before 353 Diodorus and Justin allow Philip each only one Thessalian adventure. Diodorus places his first entry into Thessaly, invited by the Aleuadae of Larissa, considerably later than the death of Alexander of Pherae (early 357 at latest).[5] Justin makes him enter Thessaly earlier, after the victory over the Illyrians (358) but before his marriage to Olympias,[6] which can hardly have been later than November 357 and may have been months earlier: Justin's 'date for Thessaly' here in fact is late 358 or early 357: Diodorus' date (we shall see) is 356 or later still. Interpretation of the two historians is not made easier by the fact that both of them include in these remarks on Thessaly a summary of some of Philip's future actions there, not confining themselves to the year or the occasion at which they start their entry.

M. Sordi in her excellent analysis of this question pointed out that the manuscripts' reading of Diodorus here οὗτος δ' ἐπανελθὼν εἰς τὴν

---

[1] Sordi, *LT* 252 ff., arguing for 352 as the date of Philip's election, adduces also his dealings in 352 or soon after with Thessalian *perioikoi* and with some cities of the League itself. I would agree that all those things are consistent with the supposition that Philip acted then as *archon*. But, equally, he could have acted in the same way if he had still been merely the ally and the architect of the victory over Onomarchus, exploiting a *de facto* position of power partly for his own advantage (Pagasae, Magnesia etc.) and partly for that of his allies the Thessalians (coercing cities that had been recalcitrant).

On these events, see below, pp. 285 ff.

[2] For the chronology of the Sacred War, of which these operations of Philip made a part, I rely on the conclusions of Hammond (*JHS* 57 (1937) 44 ff.), which have won a wide acceptance, though naturally there are dissenters.

[3] D.S. 16. 31. 6. C. Ehrhardt, *CQ* N.S. 17 (1967) 298 ff.; Grote 11. 64 n. 2, 98 f.; Schaefer, 1. 509 n. 2. The manuscripts give Πάγας (Παγὰς) δὲ χειρωσάμενος ἠνάγκασεν ὑποταγῆναι, where ὑποταγῆναι suggests a barbarian people rather than a Greek city. Παίονας seems possible. (See below, pp. 251, 264 n. 2.)

[4] D. 1. 12–13 τὸ πρῶτον Ἀμφίπολιν λαβών, μετὰ ταῦτα Πύδναν, πάλιν Ποτείδαιαν, Μεθώνην αὖθις, εἶτα Θετταλίας ἐπέβη· μετὰ ταῦτα Φεράς, Παγασάς, Μαγνησίαν . . .

[5] D.S. 16. 14. 1 f., discussed below, p. 225; cf. C. Ehrhardt, art. cit. (at n. 3 above).

[6] Just. 7. 6. 8.

Θετταλίαν is perhaps to be preferred to the emended text now commonly printed, οὗτος δὲ παρελθὼν etc.[1] If this were accepted, it would mean that Diodorus' source here knew of a previous entry into Thessaly by Philip and alluded to it, and that Diodorus preserved the allusion, in ἐπανελθών, though he had omitted the previous entry himself from his condensed narrative. I accept this as probable, and as support for the view that Justin's record of an entry by Philip into Thessaly in 358/7 is historical, even though his details attached to it are incredible. It is supported, too, by the allusions in early books of Theopompus, and by the sequence of Philip's marriages as recorded by Satyrus.[2]

Though the economy of the *Philippic History* of Theopompus cannot be reconstructed securely enough for events to be dated firmly by the number of the book in which he refers to them, it is presumably not without significance that in his Book I he chose to enlarge on Cineas of Larissa, one of those whose co-operation helped Philip ultimately to win control of Thessaly.[3] The connection with Larissa is found again in the story of Philip's marriages. Philinna of Larissa, one of two Thessalian brides with whom he is credited, comes fourth in Satyrus' list of his marriages, which seems meant to be in chronological order (Olympias, whom he married late in 357 probably, comes fifth).[4] Philip's son from Philinna, Philip Arrhidaeus, was old enough in 337 to be considered marriageable, and was therefore more likely to have been born about 357 than two or three years later.[5] Philinna is described by Justin as *saltatrix* (9. 8. 2) and *scortum* (13. 2. 11), and if she was really a *hetaira* there would be no need to think that Philip must have met her in Larissa. But Satyrus counted this as in some sense a 'marriage', and Arrhidaeus the son (the future Philip III) was evidently brought up as a royal prince at court.[6] The likelihood, therefore, is that Philinna came of a good family in Larissa, and that it was there that Philip did meet her—late in 358 or very early in 357.[7]

[1] D.S. 16. 14. 2; Sordi, *LT* 349. Cf., too, μετακληθείς at D.S. 16. 35. 1.

[2] For discussion of Philip's marriages, see Beloch 3². 2. 68 ff. It seems most probable that Satyrus derived his material on this topic partly if not wholly from Theopompus, who will have enjoyed dilating on it. (Cf. also *CQ* n.s. 20 (1970) 69 ff.)

For the view that Theopompus was also an important source used by Pompeius Trogus (summarized by Justin), see especially A. Momigliano, *RIL* 66 (1933) 983 ff.; M. Gigante, *PP* 1 (1946) 127 ff.; O. Seel, *Die Praefatio des Pompeius Trogus* (Erlangen, 1955) 31 ff.

[3] Theopomp. F 35 (*FGrH* 115), = Harpocration s.v. Κινέας· . . . ὡμολόγηται καὶ παρὰ τοῖς ἱστορικοῖς, ὅτι Κινέας εἷς ἦν τῶν προιεμένων Φιλίππῳ τὰ Θετταλῶν πράγματα, καὶ μάλιστα Θεοπόμπῳ ἐν ᾱ, ἅμα καὶ διεξερχομένῳ τὰ περὶ τὸν ἄνδρα.

Cf. also F 34 and F 48 (Bk. III), for operations in the territory of Larissa, though in these Fragments Philip is not named as taking part in them.

[4] Satyrus, F 5, *FHG* 3. 161 (ap. Athen. 13. 557).   [5] Plu. *Alex.* 10. 1 ff.

[6] Ibid.

[7] The siege of Amphipolis (below, pp. 237 ff.) seems to have occupied Philip from the spring of 357 into the summer. And, as Beloch justly pointed out, he is unlikely to have married Philinna only a few weeks before his marriage to Olympias (autumn 357 at latest).

The actual details recorded by Justin of the Thessalian adventure are highly unsatisfactory.

Post hos [sc. Athenienses] bello in Illyrios translato multa milia hostium caedit, urbem nobilissimam Larissam capit. Hinc Thessaliam non praedae cupiditate, sed quod exercitui suo robur Thessalorum equitum adiungere gestiebat, nihil minus quam bellum metuentem inprovisus expugnat, unumque corpus equitum pedestriumque copiarum invicti exercitus fecit.[1]

In this tale the motive, the circumstances and the results of the expedition all seem incredible, unless as a tale told by an idiot, who knew what was to happen some years later and chose to allude to it all here.[2] We can be certain from what did happen later that Philip did not take Larissa or conquer Thessaly in 358; and though we are not entitled to say that at this time he cannot have thought how good it would be to have the Thessalian cavalry under his command, we can safely rule it out as one of his objectives for the immediate or near future. Yet in spite of all this, neither Justin nor Pompeius Trogus can have invented a whole Thessalian 'incident' at this point. It is here because Trogus found something about Thessaly in his source or sources, after the Illyrian victory and before the Olympias marriage. We may allow ourselves to doubt whether Philip really mounted an unprovoked invasion or raid into Thessaly now. The allusions of Theopompus and Satyrus to Larissa, and indeed that of Justin himself here (crazy though it is as it stands in our text)[3] make it more probable that this move followed the pattern of those earlier moves by Macedonian kings, supporting friends in Larissa against an enemy, and most likely by invitation.[4]

This indeed is just the move that Diodorus does give to Philip in his record, though he does not make clear to which year he assigns it.[5] Briefly, Diodorus makes it clear that Philip intervened in Thessaly on this occasion not only after the death of Alexander, tyrant of Pherae, but some considerable time after: the interval was not one of weeks, but of months certainly, and more likely of a year or two at least.[6] The

---

[1] Just. 7. 6. 8 f.

[2] This same habit is exemplified in his next incident (P.'s marriage with Olympias), where the fate of Arybbas king of the Molossians is foreshadowed, fifteen years in advance (ibid. 10–12).

[3] Sordi (*LT* 349 n. 3) repunctuates, with full-stop after *caedit*. This eases out the geographical muddle; but still the sense remains preposterous. Better to suppose (with Westlake 167 n. 2) that *Larissam* is corrupt. Perhaps Justin himself wrote *Larissa* here by mistake for another name, because *Larissa* appeared a little later in the text of Trogus.

[4] Cf. Sordi, *LT* 231 ff., who ingeniously uses the anecdote in Theopomp. F 352 to show that Crannon (only 12 miles from Larissa) was held at this time by 'friends' of Alexander of Pherae, a fact which, if true, was certainly cause for alarm to the Aleuadae of Larissa.

[5] D.S. 16. 14. 1 f.

[6] D.S. ibid. κατὰ δὲ τὴν Ἑλλάδα Ἀλέξανδρος ὁ Φερῶν τύραννος ὑπὸ τῆς ἰδίας γυναικὸς Θήβης καὶ τῶν ταύτης ἀδελφῶν Λυκόφρονος καὶ Τισιφόνου ἐδολοφονήθη. οὗτοι δὲ τὸ μὲν πρῶτον

precise date of Alexander's death is unknown. It was earlier than early summer 357, when it was Tisiphonus of Pherae (the elder of his murderers) who supported Thebes against Athens in Euboea.[1] But Alexander's murder was followed by an interval of 'good' or constitutional rule in Pherae, long enough for Diodorus to use the words τὸ μὲν πρῶτον . . . μεγάλης ἐτύγχανον ἀποδοχῆς, ὕστερον δὲ μετανοήσαντες . . . ἀνέδειξαν ἑαυτοὺς τυράννους etc. In this interval the 'liberators' are most unlikely to have undertaken aggressive war against Larissa, for obvious reasons. Therefore, as Sordi showed, Philip's move into Thessaly late in 358 must have been to counter Alexander himself, and cannot be identical with the move against his successors which Diodorus records.

Sordi, in her analysis of the events in Thessaly in and after 358, shows good reason for believing that there was peace between Pherae and the Thessalian League (including Larissa) in the period of constitutional government at Pherae after Alexander's death: she believes, however, that this peace lasted while Tisiphonus remained in control of Pherae, and was broken only when he was succeeded by his younger brothers Peitholaus and Lycophron (354) and that Diodorus' first record of an intervention in Thessaly by Philip (above) belongs really to a campaign late in 354 after his capture of Methone.

The Thessalian 'peace' of 357 is entirely acceptable; but there are difficulties in the way of believing that it lasted unbroken for the three years that Sordi desiderates. (1) The delay of eighteen months between the seizure of Delphi by the Phocians (spring 356) and the Amphictyonic declaration of a Sacred War against them (autumn 355) is very difficult to explain satisfactorily except on the lines that during that interval it was not possible to muster a majority in favour of declaring war, *because the Thessalian voting power was not united.*[2] That the Thebans, leaders in the anti-Phocian moves in the Amphictyony from the start, both wanted and needed first the votes and next the armies of Thessaly at the earliest possible moment, must be self-evident:[3] and there was no tradition of

---

ὡς τυραννοκτόνοι μεγάλης ἐτύγχανον ἀποδοχῆς, ὕστερον δὲ μετανοήσαντες . . . ἀνέδειξαν ἑαυτοὺς τυράννους . . . κατασκευασάμενοι δὲ τὴν δύναμιν ἀξιόλογον βίᾳ κατεῖχον τὴν ἀρχήν. οἱ δ' Ἀλευάδαι καλούμενοι παρὰ τοῖς Θετταλοῖς . . . ἀντεπράττοντο τοῖς τυράννοις. οὐκ ὄντες δὲ καθ' ἑαυτοὺς ἀξιόμαχοι προσελάβοντο Φίλιππον σύμμαχον τὸν Μακεδόνων βασιλέα. Cf. Sordi, *LT* 232 n. 2, and 239 ff., especially 242 and n. 1.

[1] Schol. Aristid. *Panath.* 179. 6. For chronology, cf. R. Sealey, *REG* 68 (1955) 111 f. A probable date for Alexander's death seems to be winter 358/7, since the Euboean campaign began certainly before the end of that archon-year.

[2] For the chronology, Hammond, *JHS* 57 (1937) 44 ff. For the votes in the Amphictyonic Council, Theopomp. *FGrH* 115 F 63; Aeschin. 2. 116; Paus. 10. 8. 2; cf. Daux 95 ff.

[3] Cf. Hammond, loc. cit. 72 and n. 116. Sordi (*LT* 237 f.), believing Thessaly 'united' during the whole of these relevant eighteen months, argues that Thebes could no longer influence the Thessalians as in the days of Pelopidas and Epaminondas, and was obliged therefore to try to 'go it alone'. This is good sense of course, but it still does not carry conviction, because the Thessalians too had an obligation to restore order at Delphi (D.S. 16.

friendship for Phocis in Thessaly.[1] There may have been reasons of which we know nothing why some Thessalian cities which controlled the votes were averse from war in 356 and early 355; but much the most obvious reason, in the light of recent Thessalian history, is that the old split had reopened, so that neither the 'League' cities nor Pherae dared to undertake war outside Thessaly, each group for fear of the other. On this interpretation the rapprochement of Pherae under Tisiphonus and the League cities will have lasted a year or more, till after the spring 356 Amphictyonic meeting, but will then have broken down.[2]

(2) Even the evidence of Diodorus recording the ultimate support from Thessaly for the Amphictyonic war, which appears to show Thessaly 'united' in autumn 355, is robbed of much of its weight by the evidence of Diodorus recording the first actual operation undertaken by the Thessalians in the war. The Thessalian army, including their *perioikoi* allies, defeated by the Phocians in eastern Locris (probably summer 354), was only 6,000 strong, a figure which suggests a divided rather than a united Thessaly. Whether the 'Thessalian' support for declaration of the Sacred War the previous autumn had included that of Pherae, or not, is problematical.[3] But a genuinely united Thessaly, in which all cities including Pherae were prepared to implement the declaration of war seems ruled out by the smallness of this Thessalian army next year.

(3) It is not self-evident that Diodorus under the archon-year 357/6 would have added to his brief account of the death of Alexander of Pherae and what then happened in Thessaly, an allusion there to an intervention by Philip, if in reality it was not till three years later that

23. 2 f.; cf. Sordi, *BCH* 81 (1957) 49 ff.), and they had no love for the Phocians in any case (see next note for references).

[1] Aeschin. 2. 140 διὰ τὴν . . . πρὸς Φωκέας ἔχθραν, ἣ προϋπῆρχε Θετταλοῖς ἐκ παλαιῶν χρόνων . . .; Paus. 10. 2. 1. Cf. Sordi, *LT* 238.

[2] There is no need to assume, with Sordi (*LT* 236), that because Tisiphonus alone ruled Pherae in 357 (aiding Thebes in Euboea, Schol. Aristid. 298, Dindorf), therefore he remained sole ruler till his death (355/4?), and that the change of front at Pherae, from good to bad relations with Larissa, coincides with the succession to power of T.'s younger brothers Lycophron and Peitholaus after his death. The addressing of a letter by Isocrates 'To the Sons of Jason' is much more appropriate to three brothers than to two, and suggests that there was a time when all three ruled together (Isoc. *Epist.* 6; Sordi, *LT* 242 n. 1, discusses its date). In any case Tisiphonus, with or without his brothers, was capable no doubt of changing his mind to suit an opportunity, like any other politician.

[3] D.S. 16. 29. 1 σχιζομένης δὲ τῆς τῶν ἐθνῶν καὶ πόλεων αἱρέσεως τῷ μὲν ἱερῷ βοηθεῖν ἔγνωσαν Βοιωτοὶ καὶ Λοκροὶ καὶ Θετταλοὶ καὶ Περραιβοί, πρὸς δὲ τούτοις Δωριεῖς καὶ Δόλοπες, ἔτι δὲ Ἀθαμᾶνες καὶ Ἀχαιοὶ Φθιῶται καὶ Μάγνητες, ἔτι δὲ Αἰνιᾶνες καί τινες ἕτεροι, τοῖς δὲ Φωκεῦσι συνεμάχουν Ἀθηναῖοι καὶ Λακεδαιμόνιοι καί τινες ἕτεροι τῶν Πελοποννησίων.

D.S. 16. 29. 4 for the figure 6,000. For the paper-strength of the army of united Thessaly (ὅταν ταγεύηται Θετταλία), see the figures for Jason's army, without the mercenaries (X. *HG* 6. 1. 8 f.): cavalry 6,000, hoplites more than 10,000, peltasts supplied by the *perioikoi*. Westlake (170 f.) writes shrewdly 'However, even if the neighbouring tribes supplied only a thousand men in all, this army [sc. of 354] does not represent the full fighting strength of Thessaly, and large reserves must have been left to watch any movement by the tyrants.'

Philip did intervene. Diodorus certainly anticipates events by mentioning here the decisive intervention culminating in the expulsion of the tyrants from Pherae (in 352), which he narrates later (16. 35. 1 ff.). But this need not exclude the possibility of indecisive interventions in the interval, even though Diodorus did not narrate them. It seems more probable, in fact, that the peace in Thessaly did break down earlier, and that we should look for an appeal from Larissa to Philip and an intervention by him in the year 356/5; not indeed in 356 when Crenides and Potidaea and the coalition of the three kings occupied him sufficiently (see below, pp. 246 ff.), but in the first half of 355. On the Macedonian side, there seems nothing to prevent this. On the Thessalian side, it seems to make good sense. Since spring 356 the Amphictyons had been under an obligation to expel the Phocians from Delphi, and the Boeotians and Locrians had taken the field against them; but the Thessalians, who together with their *perioikoi* commanded the majority of Amphictyonic votes, are not recorded in action in 356, and the autumn Amphictyonic meeting (and that of spring 355) passed with no declaration of an Amphictyonic war.

If (as is suggested) the Thessalians in this interval were at war or on the point of war among themselves, the League cities could not count on Boeotian help against Pherae, because the Boeotians were sufficiently preoccupied with the Phocians in Delphi, and indeed the movement of a Boeotian army into Thessaly in these conditions was perhaps not a good military risk: if it got there safely it might not be able to return safely, exposed *en route* to an attack from the Phocians on ground of their choosing. These were the conditions perhaps in which Philip was called in to support Larissa against Pherae, in early summer 355. The results were indecisive in the sense that Pherae and her tyrants remained, able to give trouble to their neighbours next year. But they have had the effect of enabling the Thessalians to take up their Amphictyonic obligations in the autumn of 355 by declaring the Sacred War. Whether Pherae joined in this Amphictyonic move, or whether (as seems more likely) she abstained, but the League cities felt themselves strong enough to go forward and ignore her, is something that cannot be known in the present state of our evidence.[1]

To sum up, Philip's earliest experiences in Thessaly were essentially exploratory, motivated at first by aims which were primarily defensive

---

[1] This well-known problem is discussed by Sordi (*LT* 239, cf. also 220, with bibliography). The naming of the Magnetes among those who were for war is not decisive in favour of Pherae, too, being of that number (on the ground that the Magnetes, or the southern Magnetes, were normally controlled by Pherae); D.S. 16. 29. 1. They normally were so, yet these relationships were not immutable (cf. e.g. Sordi, loc. cit. 220 and n. 2), and we cannot know that these Magnetes had not been 'freed' from Pherae, for example in a clash between Pherae and Larissa in which Pherae came off worst (see below).

or preventive, and with the Boeotians most in view. They were probably not undertaken in great strength: anything like a 'great battle' would presumably have found a place in Diodorus' synopsis,[1] and we should not have been left to grope our way into a chronological setting that seems to fit the evidence. It is worth noting, however, that the well-known *Stratagem* of Polyaenus, rare in its genre because it tells a tale not of one occasion but of a series which led to Philip's 'winning Thessaly', itself supports a view that his interventions were numerous, and hence that these 'early' ones ought to be given their full place in the record.[2] The first move to the aid of Larissa, late in 358, led to no quick developments, because the death of Alexander of Pherae next spring relaxed the tension in Thessaly: Pherae under the 'liberators' may well have seemed ripe for rejoining the League and living at peace with her neighbours. But Philip's first visit had not been wasted. He and his Macedonians in their ordinary way of life had more in common with high society in Larissa than they would have had in most Greek cities outside Thessaly. Wine, women, and horses draw those who are used to them together, and make them good companions. Philinna did not become queen, but her family probably became Philip's men from now on. These contacts were renewed when Philip returned in 355: and the charm which later was felt by Aeschines will have found its targets across the dining tables in a society where the owner of the winning *keles* at Olympia the year before was automatically 'one of us'.

2. *Amphipolis*

As we have seen already, Amphipolis, prosperous, independent, and isolationist for choice, yet by her situation holding a key which greater powers could hope to use for far-reaching ends could they only possess it, in the past dozen years had become of importance again in the power politics of the North Aegean. Already Macedonian kings since Perdiccas II, and Athenian generals since Thucydides the historian, had had cause to wonder perhaps whether this name might not be found graven, however lightly, on their hearts.[3] Yet Amphipolis meant very different things to different people. To the Amphipolitans themselves she was a strong

[1] Diodorus occasionally makes a double record of the same event, the first entry (brief) from a chronographic source, it is thought, the second (fuller) from a narrative source. A good example is the siege and capture of Methone (16. 31. 6; 35 f.), in successive archon-years. But to think of a double record here for Thessaly, is implausible, because 16. 14. 1 f. and 16. 35. 1 ff. are too widely separated, and because 14. 2 clearly represents not a 'chronographic' entry but D.'s own 'anticipation' of the end of the story which he begins at 14. 1.

[2] Polyaen. 4. 2. 19 (discussed below, pp. 286, 288), ἀεὶ προσεβοήθει τοῖς καλοῦσι. Westlake (167 f.) saw 'more than one expeditionary force into Thessaly' as probable, in the years 358–356.

[3] See above, pp. 184 ff.; J. Papastavru, *Amphipolis: Geschichte und Prosopographie, Klio* Beiheft 37 (Leipzig, 1936) 24–31.

mother city and their own. Increased by new citizens from Chalcidice, and with a democratic government reachieved by a revolution which had overturned an oligarchy, they had kept the independence brought to them by Brasidas, with remarkable success for more than sixty years.[1] To the Chalcidians their nearest Greek neighbours, she was a highly desirable acquisition as an ally, and one which did briefly come their way; and to acquire her as a permanent member of their League was perhaps not out of the question, if common dangers were to dictate it. Yet they had lived without Amphipolis for most of their League's existence and lived well, and it would seem an over-estimate of the power or the pretensions of the Chalcidians to attribute to them plans to use Amphipolis for conquests or expansion in Thrace.[2] We may presume that on general principles they would always rather see her independent than occupied or controlled by Athens: and also that the Macedonian protection and the garrison installed by Perdiccas had been unwelcome to them (above, p. 187).

To the Athenians, it remains a little of a mystery to know exactly what Amphipolis was. A valuable possession, as a loyal colony or ally no doubt, as Thucydides remarked, for its export of timber for ship-building and for the revenue it brought them.[3] Yet, though this revenue (along with others) was lost now, it is hard to believe that the Amphipolitans independent, however much they disliked Athenians, can have refused to trade with them in time of peace: and the site of the city as strategic key to an interior seems far beyond the powers of Athens to exploit at any time in the fourth century. Part of the truth may be that to the Athenians the name Amphipolis still brought emotion as well as calculation into their deliberations. The Peace of Nicias had given Amphipolis back to them, and in a sense they were being cheated of it ever since.[4] The independence of Amphipolis was a standing affront, a little comparable to the trauma of Alsace–Lorraine on the French psyche during more than forty years. Whether the Athenians had been claiming Amphipolis as 'theirs' whenever occasion arose in the years since the revival of 395 seems doubtful: we could hardly have failed to be informed of the claim (whether it was admitted or not) in connection with the King's Peace of 386. It seems likely that they reawoke to the situation in the 370s, and that the reawakening was due to the success of the new Confederacy, in two ways. By enlisting as members of the Confederacy cities adjacent to Amphipolis they became more nearly interested again in 'the parts towards Thrace' and their potential, and the knife was turned in the old

---

[1] For new citizens, Arist. *Pol.* 1303[b]: for the revolution, ibid. 1306[a].

[2] The speech of the Acanthians at Sparta in 383, recorded by Xenophon, is to be discounted as deliberately alarmist (X. *HG* 5. 2. 17).

[3] Thuc. 4. 108. 1 ὠφέλιμος ξύλων τε ναυπηγησίμων πομπῇ καὶ χρημάτων προσόδῳ.

[4] Thuc. 5. 18. 5.

wound. But also as successful leaders of the new Confederacy they felt again an itch of imperialism. To gratify it at the expense of their League members was ruled out by the terms of the charter, reinforced by a salutary sense of what was possible. What *was* possible, for example, was to revive the practice of establishing Athenian cleruchies abroad on the fifth-century model, provided that it was done on territory not taken from a member of the Confederacy.[1] And another thing possible was to revive the claim to Amphipolis, 'theirs' by a prescriptive right of a by now respectable antiquity.

Precisely in what sense Amphipolis was 'theirs' is a theme which abler pens have pursued (and occasionally into some strange by-ways).[2] To reargue the matter here would be tedious, and not even necessary. My own opinion is that the Athenians had two legal *bases* for the claim. The first was the clause in the Peace of Nicias by which Amphipolis was 'given back' by Sparta to Athens.[3] The second was the fact that Amphipolis was an *apoikia* of Athens:[4] before her 'revolt' in 423 she had conformed to the theory of the duty and subservience of colony to metropolis which fifth-century Athens (and Corinth) had been strong enough often to enforce.[5] For the present purpose, however, the exact legal basis of the Athenian claim, whether it was good law or bad law or good in parts, matters very little. It does matter, though, that the claim had been admitted as valid by something recognizable as a Panhellenic congress, and also by the Great King in the presence of representatives from other Greek cities.[6] Though autonomy for all cities great or small by now had become the accepted first principle of inter-city relations in Greece, circumstances could still alter cases. Sparta could still object that the principle of autonomy could not apply to Messene, and could dissociate herself from any Panhellenic congress or agreement which decided that it did. Athens maintained that autonomy was not for Amphipolis (any more than for Lemnos, Imbros, Scyros, or Samos and

---

[1] Potidaea, Chersonese, Samos. (For the charter, Tod *GHI* 123, especially 11. 15 ff., 35 ff.)

[2] The best treatment of this question now is by A. J. Graham, *Colony and Mother City in Ancient Greece* (Manchester U.P., 1964) 199 ff., 245 ff., with bibliography.

[3] Thuc. 5. 18. 5 ἀποδόντων δὲ Ἀθηναίοις Λακεδαιμόνιοι καὶ ξύμμαχοι Ἀμφίπολιν. I understand this to mean 'give back' to be 'theirs' politically, not 'theirs' in the sense that its territory was Athenian property (on this, Graham, op. cit. 201 ff.).

[4] The fact that Amphipolis had repudiated the relationship (Thuc. 5. 11. 1) does not mean, naturally, that the Athenians recognized their right to repudiate it, then or ever.

[5] The theory is summarized in the speech of the Corinthian ambassadors at Athens in Thucydides (1. 38. 2 f., cf. 1. 25. 3 f.) ἡμεῖς δὲ οὐδ' αὐτοί φαμεν ἐπὶ τῷ ὑπὸ τούτων ὑβρίζεσθαι κατοικίσαι, ἀλλ' ἐπὶ τῷ ἡγεμόνες τε εἶναι καὶ τὰ εἰκότα θαυμάζεσθαι. αἱ γοῦν ἄλλαι ἀποικίαι τιμῶσιν ἡμᾶς, καὶ μάλιστα ὑπὸ ἀποίκων στεργόμεθα. See in general Graham, op. cit. *passim*.
That Amphipolis did conform is proved by the fact that she had financial obligations to Athens (Thuc. 4. 108. 2; cf. Graham, 200).

[6] Aeschin. 2. 32; D. 19. 253; [D.] 7. 29. The date of these two acts of recognition, the former of which has been much in dispute, is well discussed by Ryder, *KE* 128 ff., 136, 138 f. (with bibliography). I agree with him in preferring the Congress of 370/69.

her other 'possessions'): and to this proposition the Greek world and the Great King had given formal assent, though no Greek (and certainly no Persian) was going to take any trouble in support of the Athenian claim unless it should be in their own interests also.

Thus stood the 'Amphipolis question' in the eyes of the world in the year 358. There remains the Macedonian viewpoint. It is really not an over-simplification to say that each Macedonian king was liable ultimately to be faced with a choice: which was the more important to him, the friendship of Athens, or to gain possession of Amphipolis? It is important to think of this choice in the light of the Macedonian experience *before* Philip. Seen in this light, Amphipolis was desirable of course, for its revenues and for its value as a splendid fortress defending the eastern-frontier region which marched with Thrace. But as the base and bridgehead for invasions of Thrace eastwards, it must seem very doubtful whether this aspect can have been much considered by Amyntas Philip's father; for Macedonia, no more than the Chalcidian League or indeed fourth-century Athens, had developed military power and reserves yet on a scale sufficient to implement plans like these.

Amyntas publicly recognized the Athenian claim as valid, probably at the Congress held in Athens in winter 370/69;[1] his choice, though not necessarily irrevocable, was plain at that moment. Ptolemy of Alorus, though he owed his place to Iphicrates, evidently changed his attitude to Athens so far as to negotiate an alliance with Thebes with an eye to Amphipolis (if Aeschines is to be believed),[2] but his death seems to have forestalled any developments. Perdiccas III began by supporting Timotheus in his operations against the Chalcidian League,[3] when he must have known that they would be extended against Amphipolis if the opportunity came; and indeed they were (in 363).[4] The Athenian defeat on this occasion, and presumably a calculation that he could dispense with the alliance with Athens and had nothing to fear from her enmity, tempted him to the vital change of front. By means entirely unknown to us he succeeded in detaching Amphipolis from her Chalcidian alliance, and installing a Macedonian garrison in the city.[5] It seems possible (though there is no evidence) that he took advantage of a *stasis* in which a broad line of division may have been that between the 'old' Amphipolitans and the new (Chalcidian) settlers. This would justify the

---

[1] See previous note.   [2] Aeschin. 2. 29.   [3] D. 2. 14.

[4] Schol. Aeschin. 2. 31 (of 364/3 B.C.). Cf. Tod 143, ll. 7 ff. (early 362), εἰς τὸν πόλεμον τὸν πρὸς Χαλκιδέας καὶ πρὸς Ἀμφίπολιν.

[5] To infer that Amphipolis remained technically autonomous (e.g. Bengtson, *GG*² 299 n. 4), from the fact that she was one of the states recorded at Epidaurus among the *thearodokoi* of 360/59, seems correct (*IG* ɪᴠ². 1. 94. 18). Yet the 'charter' of the Second Athenian Confederacy shows clearly that a garrison was one of the things held to be incompatible with a state of freedom and autonomy (Tod 123, 20 ff.). By consent, perhaps? (Tod 114, 13 ff., etc.)

entry of the Macedonian troops in the eyes of the winners, who for the time being may even have welcomed their having come to stay.

An intriguing question here is, how far is Perdiccas' policy to be explained by a conventional, opportunistic reaction to changes in a local balance-of-power, so as to take advantage of temporary weaknesses shown by the other participants (both Athenians and Chalcidians)? Or how much weight ought we to give to the influence of a new factor, the mining venture which, we know, was launched publicly a year or two later about 40 miles east of Amphipolis, and which we may safely presume to have been based on some reliable foreknowledge which justified the risks of launching it then? To seize Amphipolis in the years 362–360 was to invite the hostility of both Athens and the Chalcidian League. Perdiccas seems to have been an energetic and sanguine ruler; but the Illyrian invasion which ended his reign and life (360/59) showed up the limitations of his real strength.[1] And if the year before it came (or two years before) he had some reason to fear its coming (as to this we have no information), any risk that he chose to take elsewhere at that time must be judged a greater risk still. Does it need a greater prize to explain why it was taken? Where so little is known the historian will not be expected to build without foundations. But it seems possible (no more) that Perdiccas was tempted to seize Amphipolis because it could be seen now already (in 362 or 361) also as the gateway to an important new source of wealth from the gold and silver mines of Mt. Pangaeum.

The previous history of this interesting region is well enough known not to need retelling here.[2] The precious metals of this and other parts of Thrace had not escaped the notice of Greek enterprise or of the Thracian princes who owned it. No Greek power, however, had ever succeeded in dominating any area of the interior of Thrace. It seems likely from the later developments themselves that what happened in these years which we are considering was that prospectors or local inhabitants struck gold as well as silver, in places where it could be got at, near the north-eastern end of the Pangaeum range, only some ten miles from the sea as the crow flies, and easily accessible by a route inland from the Greek city of Neapolis (the modern Kavalla), situated on the coast a little westwards of the island of Thasos. That Greek settlers, sponsored by Thasos, could be sent to the place (probably in 360) argues that already before then either mine-workings were in production, or at least the ground had been sufficiently explored to satisfy the Thasians that production was a certainty in the future.[3] The new foundation was called variously by two

---

[1] See above, p. 188.   [2] See especially Collart 39 ff.

[3] This aspect is well seen by J. Pouilloux, *Recherches sur l'histoire et les cultes de Thasos* (Paris, 1954) 1. 219 n. 5, who evidently envisages some haphazard settlement before the formal 'foundation' of the new city organized by Thasos.

names, but there is no reason for any doubt whatever that they refer to the same place.[1] Datos (or Daton) derives from the district in which the city was founded, and is the name used in a document dating probably to the year of its foundation, and also by the contemporary historians Ephorus and Theopompus.[2] The name Crenides came from certain little springs rising near the foot of its acropolis, and so described the exact spot.[3] The document just mentioned, the well-known inscription of Epidaurus recording states which had entertained her envoys, dates the city's foundation securely before the death of King Perdiccas early in 359.[4] Since the name of Callistratus is linked with the act of foundation (see below), the year of his exile from Athens (361) gives a *terminus post quem*, so that Diodorus may well be right in placing it in the archon-year 360/59.[5] Any preliminary developments leading up to this settlement were going on, therefore, at the time when Perdiccas saw an opportunity to seize Amphipolis, and seized it, probably in 360. News of any gold strike in the Pangaeum area will not have been long in reaching Macedonia.

The actual initiator of the Thasian settlement is said to have been the great Athenian Callistratus, now an exile.[6] He had already, it seems, visited Macedonia since leaving Athens, and it may have been in Macedonia that he learned of the gold strike of Pangaeum. He moved on to Thasos. Though Callistratus had made himself useful to Perdiccas by improving the yield from the import and export duties of the kingdom, it seems certainly mistaken to implicate him in any way with Macedonian policy *vis-à-vis* Thrace.[7] His own actions were motivated surely by a hope

---

[1] Collart, loc. cit., for a good exposition of the nomenclature, with all the texts.

[2] *IG* iv². 1. 94. 1(b). 32 (the Epidaurus *thearodokoi* inscription); Ephorus F 37 (*FGrH* 70); Theopomp. F 43 (*FGrH* 115).

[3] Appian, *BC* 4. 105 (439): on the topography, Collart, loc. cit.

[4] *IG* iv². 1. 9.   [5] D.S. 16. 3. 7.

[6] [Scylax] 67 (C. Müller, *GGM* 1, pp. 54 f.); cf. Isoc. 8. 24 (also Zenobius 4. 34; Himerius 40. 2).

[7] [Aristot.] *Econ.* 2. 2. 22. 1350ᵃ; cf. B. A. van Groningen, *Aristote, le second livre de l'Économique* (Leyden, 1933) 148.

There is no certain proof that Callistratus' work as financial consultant in Macedonia is to be dated at this point in his exile rather than later. He was exiled in 361 and returned to Athens in 355. He is reported meanwhile first at Methone ([D.] 50. 46 ff.), next at Thasos (360/59), then at Byzantium (Schol. ad Aeschin. 2. 124). He could have spent time in Macedonia after the founding of Crenides (360/59): indeed some writers have seen his influence behind the Macedonian–Athenian *entente* of Philip's early years (359–357): cf. especially, A. B. West, *NC* 3. 1923, 183 ff.; P. Cloché, *REA* 25 (1923) 5–32, id. *Pol. étrangère* 134 ff. Yet Philip in 359 did not need Callistratus to show him what was as plain as a pike-staff; and personally I see as an insuperable objection to this proposed connection the fact that no ancient author who survives has mentioned it, a reticence very surprising where two such famous men are concerned, if they did in truth ever collaborate. For this reason I think it most probable that it was Perdiccas with whom Callistratus collaborated and not Philip. (So van Groningen, loc. cit.; F. Geyer, *RE* s.v. Perdikkas (3) 603.) The evidence is well set out by Collart 133 ff., 149 ff.; cf. H. Swoboda, *RE* 1734 f. s.v. Kallistratos (1).

to procure his recall to Athens; and the taking of Amphipolis by Perdiccas, with whom he had had dealings, can have done those hopes no good. It is even possible that his initiative at Thasos which linked his name with the founding of the colony was inspired in part by the knowledge that Perdiccas in possession of Amphipolis had access to Pangaeum second only to that of Thasos via Neapolis: to stake the claim quickly may have seemed important now.

When Philip took over control in Macedonia, his action over Amphipolis is a measure of the extreme pressures to which he was being subjected.[1] To buy time was the first priority. In some quarters he paid for it in cash (to the Paeonians, and to the Thracian king Berisades who supported the pretender Pausanias).[2] Of the Athenians he bought time with Amphipolis. It seems right to assume that the Athenian support of Argaeus in his bid for the Macedonian throne was conditional on an undertaking by Argaeus to restore Amphipolis to Athens.[3] For Mantias with his mercenaries to replace the Macedonian garrison there by agreement represented the best chance Athens had ever had of recovering the place in reality and not merely on paper. Philip in turn, even after defeating the mercenaries, conscious of the Illyrians still to reckon with, can hardly have hesitated to try to make his peace with Athens by showing himself no less compliant than Argaeus. If Diodorus is to be trusted in the order of his narrative, he had already withdrawn the garrison from Amphipolis in the hope of averting the Athenian intervention altogether. After the defeat of the mercenaries he still sent to Athens a letter offering alliance and a renewal of the hereditary friendship, and an embassy with assurances that he had renounced all claim to Amphipolis.[4] A treaty

---

[1] See above, pp. 210 ff.

[2] D.S. 16. 3. 4; cf. Beloch 3. 1. 224 f. (for Berisades).

[3] D.S. ibid. seems to imply this; but we could assume it without the implication.

[4] D. 23. 121 (the letter); D.S. 16. 3. 3; 4. 1 (the embassy); Polyaen. 4. 2. 17. G. E. M. de Ste. Croix (*CQ* N.S. 13 (1963) 111 f.) is rightly critical of those who have too easily accepted statements of Demosthenes and Hegesippus about messages of Philip to Athens during the siege in 357, to the effect that he recognized the Athenian claim to Amphipolis (D. 2. 6; 23. 116; [D.] 7. 27 f.). But this statement of Diodorus (4. 1) that in 359 Philip abandoned his own claim seems eminently probable, because Philip was at this time the weaker party, as Momigliano well showed (*FM* 45 f., cited with approval by de Ste. Croix, art. cit. 111 n. 1). That Polyaenus wrote, of the same occasion, οὐκ ἀπέδωκεν ἀλλ' ἀφῆκεν ἐλευθέραν has no juridical significance whatever. P., who needs to give his *Stratagems* each a background in a condensed précis form, is mainly concerned to show why, as a matter of practical politics, it was possible for Philip to reoccupy Amphipolis once he had withdrawn from it. Nor is the silence of Aeschines on any renunciation of claim by Philip of any value here (Aeschin. 2. 25 ff., where he recounted his own remarks addressed to Philip as ambassador in 346 on the subject of Amphipolis): eight other ambassadors (besides Demosthenes) spoke on the same occasion, and the same points could not be made by all of them (one trusts). That Philip really did renounce any claim to Amphipolis in 359 is not open to reasonable doubt, and I cannot follow de Ste. Croix in his scepticism here. This information derives from no orator but from Diodorus (16. 4. 1) ἐπὶ δὲ τούτων ὁ Φίλιππος πρέσβεις ἐκπέμψας εἰς Ἀθήνας ἔπεισε τὸν δῆμον εἰρήνην πρὸς αὐτὸν συνθέσθαι διὰ τὸ μηδὲν ἔτι προσποιεῖσθαι τὴν

of peace and alliance was agreed.[1] For Philip in 359 the present was so demanding that he was prepared to mortgage the future if it could serve. But he still remembered (one guesses) that the Spartans more than sixty years ago had withdrawn a garrison from Amphipolis; that more recently his father Amyntas and 'the Greeks' and the Great King had recognized publicly the Athenian claim—but still the Athenians could never actually occupy the place.

In 358 they had their last chance, ever, of occupying it, while Philip was securing his kingdom by his Paeonian and Illyrian campaigns. They did not take their chance, and by next year it was too late. Philip reopened with Amphipolis itself the question of its status. We are told that 'the Amphipolitans were unfriendly to him and had given him provocation'; and what this means we are left to guess.[2] It may be suggested that Philip, knowing the Athenians to be much preoccupied with Euboea and the Chersonese, decided that it was time to recover Amphipolis, and first invited the Amphipolitans to return voluntarily to the position of two years earlier, and admit a Macedonian garrison. Their refusal was 'provocation', and Philip led his army, with siege engines, against the city. The place was strong, and did not fall easily. But after a resistance lasting some weeks or more probably months, the city wall was breached with rams, and the Macedonians forced their way in.[3]

There had been time for help to reach Amphipolis before it fell; but no help came. Philip's Illyrian victory the year before was doubtless recognized by his immediate neighbours for what it was, the biggest military thing in the north for very many years. Amphipolis doubtless (though we are not told so) sought help from the nearest source, Olynthus and the Chalcidian League. She certainly turned now—and this is the mark of her fears—to the ancient enemy Athens. Before the Macedonian army marched, and in the hope of averting the march, Amphipolitan

---

Ἀμφίπολιν ... (though de Ste. Croix seems to overlook this in his verdict—art. cit. 112— 'The only facts of which we can be confident are those given by Diodorus 16. 3. 3 and 16. 4. 1, and Polyaenus 4. 2. 17: Philip in 359–358, withdrawing his garrison from Amphipolis, allowed it to regain its independence, and made peace with Athens'). The fact that Diodorus wrote this does not make it true; but what does make it true is the reflection (again) that Athens was the stronger party here, and would not have agreed to make peace without this assurance, formally and officially given, and incorporated in the oath which Philip was required to swear on this occasion.

[1] Though Diodorus (16. 4. 1) is silent on alliance, it seems almost certain that an alliance was made now between Philip and Athens, unless the statements of the orators later, that Potidaea was the ally of Philip when attacked by him in 356, are pure invention ([D.] 7. 10; D. 2. 7). Potidaea with its Athenian cleruchs can only have become an ally of Philip if Athens also had done so. Cf. Tod 146 (361); *IG* ii². 118 for Athens and Potidaea.

The inclusion in this agreement of a bargain about Amphipolis and Pydna (so, most recently, Bengtson, *Staatsv.* 2 no. 298 pp. 266 ff.) is inadmissible. It belongs to the negotiations of 357, after Philip's capture of Amphipolis (below, pp. 238 ff.).

[2] D.S. 16. 8. 2. [3] Ibid.

ambassadors Hierax and Stratocles were in Athens offering to put Amphipolis in Athenian hands.[1] The Athenian inaction was due mainly perhaps to the other military commitments at this moment; but they may have relied, too, on a diplomatic warning to Philip now, though we hear of none. We do hear however that Philip while actually besieging Amphipolis sent a Note to Athens explaining his actions: he intended to hand the city over, when it fell, to Athens the rightful owner.[2] It certainly seems that when Amphipolis did fall the Athenians still did not realize the truth; they still thought that they could do business with Philip over Amphipolis, to recover it for themselves. Ambassadors were sent to him for this very purpose.[3]

De Ste. Croix has done good service by demolishing for ever the myth that a secret agreement was arrived at, by which Athens was to receive Amphipolis from Philip, and give him Pydna in exchange.[4] No valid secret agreement could be made with any Greek democracy, because it needed the public vote (at Athens of the *demos*) to make it valid, as Philip well knew. But that some curious negotiations did take place now between Philip and the Athenian ambassadors is certain.[5] They evidently delayed the day when the Athenian people came to realize that they were not going to get Amphipolis back from Philip; and one

---

[1] D. 1. 8 κελεύοντες ἡμᾶς πλεῖν καὶ παραλαμβάνειν τὴν πόλιν. The physical difficulty for the Athenians of 'taking over the city' once it was invested by Philip is obvious. It would have been more obvious still to Demosthenes' audience, aware more vividly than we of what a siege was like; and therefore I doubt if this phrase is a mere orator's flourish, used of a city which really was already invested at the moment when the offer was made: in that case its dishonesty would have been so transparent as to be damaging.

[2] [D.] 7. 27 (cf. D. 2. 6; 23. 116) ἔφη γὰρ ἐκπολιορκήσας ὑμῖν ἀποδώσειν, ὡς οὖσαν ὑμετέραν καὶ οὐ τῶν ἐχόντων. This summary by Hegesippus 14 years after the event (like the two allusions of Demosthenes, 8 and 5 years after it respectively) could well be falsified or slanted to suit his purpose (cf. de Ste. Croix, art. cit. at p. 236 n. 4 above). Yet reflection suggests that Philip probably did write or convey something of this sort. What else could he write or say, if he communicated at all? He could not justify himself legally for attacking a city which he had formally recognized as belonging to Athens (see above, loc. cit.). All he could offer was the practical justification that he was doing it for the benefit of Athens. He did think it important, no doubt, that Athens should not intervene before Amphipolis was taken.

[3] Theopomp. F 30 A (*FGrH* 115) Τί ἐστι τὸ ἐν τοῖς Δημοσθένους Φιλιππικοῖς 'καὶ τὸ θρυλούμενόν ποτε ἀπόρρητον ἐκεῖνο', Θεόπομπος ἐν [λ]α´ δεδήλωκε. φησὶ γάρ· 'καὶ πέμπει πρὸς τὸν Φίλιππον πρεσβευτὰς Ἀντιφῶντα καὶ Χαρίδημον . . .'

[4] Art. cit. at p. 236 n. 4. Momigliano had reached the same conclusion in a brief but cogent passage (*FM* 45 ff.).

[5] Theopomp. F 30 A and B: 30 A (see end of n. 3 above) continues: καὶ πέμπει πρὸς τὸν Φίλιππον πρεσβευτὰς Ἀντιφῶντα καὶ Χαρίδημον πράξοντας καὶ περὶ φιλίας, οἳ παραγενόμενοι συμπείθειν αὐτὸν ἐπεχείρουν ἐν ἀπορρήτῳ συμπράττειν Ἀθηναίοις, ὅπως ἂν λάβωσιν Ἀμφίπολιν, ὑπισχνούμενοι Πύδναν. οἱ δὲ πρέσβεις οἱ τῶν Ἀθηναίων εἰς μὲν τὸν δῆμον οὐδὲν ἀπήγγελλον, βουλόμενοι λανθάνειν τοὺς Πυδναίους ἐκδιδόναι μέλλοντες ἐκείνους, ἐν ἀπορρήτῳ δὲ μετὰ τῆς βουλῆς ἔπραττον. B Schol. D. 2. 6 διὰ τί ἐν ἀπορρήτῳ; ἵνα μὴ ἑκάτεροι μαθόντες φυλάξωνται, οἵ τε Ποτιδαιᾶται καὶ οἱ Πυδναῖοι. Θεόπομπος δέ φησιν ὅτι περὶ Πύδνης μόνον καὶ Φιλίππου, ἵνα δῷ αὐτὸς μὲν Ἀθηναίοις Ἀμφίπολιν, δέξηται δὲ παρ' αὐτῶν τὴν Πύδναν αὐτοῦ οὖσαν. καὶ τὸ ἀπόρρητον δέ, ἵνα μὴ μαθόντες οἱ Πυδναῖοι φυλάξωνται· οὐ γὰρ ἐβούλοντο εἶναι ὑπὸ τὸν Φίλιππον.

effect of this perhaps was to lead them to miss an opportunity of making an alliance with the Chalcidian League, the only chance open to them of doing Philip some real damage once he was recognized as their enemy.[1] The negotiations had their importance, then, and the 'secret that everyone talked about' to which they gave rise.

This 'secret', which perforce has been discussed by all modern writers who have considered these events, was alluded to by Demosthenes (in 349) in the following terms:

I, too, gentlemen, should most certainly be thinking Philip a formidable figure, if I saw that his success had been due to his fair dealing. But, as it is, all my researches show me that our own simplicity in the beginning, when certain of our politicians would not listen to the Olynthians who were here and desirous of negotiating with you, was won over by his saying that he would surrender Amphipolis and by his manufacturing that famous secret that everyone once talked about . . . [and the Olynthians and Thessalians later were 'won over' by other things].[2]

It has been suggested that the 'famous secret' may not have been concerned with Amphipolis at all, but with something quite different and now unidentifiable by us.[3] But the context in Demosthenes rules this out. It is spoken eight years after the event, when nobody present could be expected to understand the allusion without being reminded what the 'famous secret' was about. Demosthenes reminded them here that it was about Amphipolis; this is certain.

To say that the Athenians still thought they could do business with Philip over Amphipolis, is not just to accept without question the evidence of Theopompus and the scholiast concerning some alleged bargaining between the two parties.[4] Rather, it is an inference based on a recognition of the fact that Philip's capture of the city changed the situation in an important way, *and that the Athenians themselves must have realized this*, firm though they stood in their assumption that Amphipolis belonged to them and that Philip should now hand it over. The braver and more realistic of the orators at Athens will not have failed to point out to the *demos* that a friendly king who has succeeded in taking after a longish siege a city which has defied all efforts of the Athenians to regain it for sixty years and more, is entitled to a *quid pro quo* when he puts it into Athenian hands. The ambassadors will not have been dispatched to Philip without being

---

[1] D. 2. 6.   [2] Ibid.   [3] Momigliano, *FM* 45 ff.; de Ste. Croix, art. cit. 118.

[4] De Ste. Croix (art. cit. 114) writes that 'any unsupported statement of this very unreliable historian should be examined with special vigilance'. If a statement of T. contains any judgement, I would concur, for clearly he was a writer of vast prejudices, and in this sense is unreliable. But to think of him as a habitual liar when narrating seems certainly wrong. There is no such suggestion in any of the numerous *Testimonia* collected by Jacoby (*FGrH* no. 115); indeed Dionysius of Halicarnassus and others suggest very much the opposite (Jacoby, *FGrH* 115 T 20, especially 2; T 28 (a) and (b) φιλαλήθης ἐν οἷς ἔγραψεν.

briefed, at the very least, to find out exactly what he would take in exchange, not exactly for Amphipolis, but for the outlay and the performance of taking it. The Greek world was nearly unshockable in such matters, and there is no need for us to shy away from the notion that in the Athenian Assembly on this occasion names of places and territories were mentioned as possible articles of exchange. These Athenians were the grandsons and great-grandsons of the *demos* that had applauded Alcibiades and voted for him after he had displayed to them the prospects of conquering Syracuse and all Sicily, this in time of peace and with no ground for war against any Siceliot city. To suppose that they boggled now at hearing Pydna mentioned in this present connection, and probably Potidaea and Methone likewise, is to endow them with the ethical enlightenment and pretensions of the twentieth century A.D. Indiscreet talk, no doubt; but the Greeks were used to hearing the reports of indiscretions uttered in other people's public meetings: sometimes the wild talk became fact, more often not, but in any case this was what public meetings were for. Pydnaeans who heard reports now, or Methonaeans or Potidaeans, will have been disquieted and probably angry, but they will not have been shocked, or surprised.

There is no reason, then, to disbelieve Theopompus when he writes that the Athenian ambassadors Antiphon and Charidemus, sent to Philip 'to negotiate about friendly relations also, tried to persuade him in secret to give up Amphipolis to them, promising him Pydna'.[1] It is quite possible that they did do just that. If they did, they promised him Pydna because it was the least among the cities in some sense under Athenian control, which Philip might accept in exchange (and also the one most suitable, as having been a Macedonian possession in the past): and they promised it to him in secret because now the 'indiscreet talk' of the Assembly was developing into an actual operation, and one which it was hoped to achieve peaceably and not as an operation of war. It was better to give up Pydna than Methone, and, especially, better than Potidaea, a much more important city which contained Athenian cleruchs and was in some sense a possession of Athens and not merely an ally.[2]

As for Philip, the one thing certain is that he did not intend to give up Amphipolis now or ever, though it always remained possible for him to do so if some unforeseeable reversal of fortune should make it necessary. Why then did he spend time (now when the place was in his hands and Athens in no condition to take it from him by force), talking and listening

---

[1] Theopomp. F 30 A, quoted above, p. 238 n. 5. The singular subject of πέμπει is presumably ὁ δῆμος.

[2] The scholiast's reference to Potidaea in association with Pydna (above, loc. cit., B) was not necessarily so wayward as has been assumed. Clearly he alluded here to the version of another historian, one who in his account did bring Potidaea into the discussion

and appearing to be disposed to bargain about it, and above all still allowing the Athenians to believe that they would get it back from him? A little is owing here, perhaps, to the *ethos* of the age. Negotiations were not then the grinding and unmitigated bore that they have become for us. Negotiators listened then, and with no cause for intellectual distaste; good speakers could actually entertain. Moreover the young king of the Macedonians (he was only twenty-five), though he had proved himself already in the field, will not have wanted to appear less civilized or cultivated than the Athenian protagonists in these conversations. These social factors had some influence. But obviously the main motives behind Philip's diplomacy now must be sought in his own reactions to this political situation, in his ability now to relate the Amphipolis question to the politics of the whole Aegean world and to the long years stretching ahead in which Athens would still be always one of the neighbours to be lived with. Politeness costs nothing, a serviceable lubricant in the relations of enemies no less than of friends: for in inter-state politics the winner is he who sees in the enemy of today the friend of tomorrow. Moreover, negotiations if protracted long enough can obscure even the clearest issues, ethical or legal. And if Athens seemed now to be negotiating from a position of weakness, the indications were that, given a little more time, she would be doing it from greater weakness still.

Philip did, then, succeed in making or letting the Athenian ambassadors believe that a bargain could be struck; for it was the 'secret that everyone was talking about', according to Demosthenes,[1] that influenced the Athenian Assembly to reject the overtures from Olynthus at this time. Such a situation is explained by supposing that the ambassadors on their return to Athens communicated their results to the Council in secret session but not immediately to the Assembly (as Theopompus indeed suggests),[2] and that it was in this interval that the 'secret' spread outwards from the 500 Councillors. It seems almost certain that Philip must have intended to find further reasons for not putting the exchange into effect, if the Athenian Assembly agreed to it: and if this is so, it follows that his reasons for negotiating thus at length must have been concerned mainly with the gaining of time. Unfortunately our knowledge of the

---

[1] D. 2. 6.

[2] Theopomp. F 30 A. See *Hell. Oxy.* 6. 1 (Bartoletti), for the interesting occasion in 396 when Demaenetus took a trireme from Piraeus for an important purpose, with no authority to take it, 'but having consulted the Council in secret, as it is said'. But no question here of this 'consultation' (if it happened) being accepted as valid authority. The incident immediately roused a storm, and the Council denied all knowledge of it.

The Council's denial may have been the truth; but the fact that 'it was said' that there had been the secret consultation proves that such a 'secret' was possible, for a short interim period (a few days at most) until the thing was reported to the Assembly. For a good discussion of secret sessions in general and the Council's limited scope for independent action, see now P. J. Rhodes, *The Athenian Boule* (Oxford, 1972) 40 ff.

chronology of the year 357 does not allow of exact explanations. We do not know how far advanced in late summer or autumn were the movements in the Athenian Confederacy which developed into the secession of important members and the 'War of the Allies':[1] Philip may have been awaiting a moment when he could know that he could break with Athens with impunity. Or again, the attitude of the Chalcidian League may have caused him to play for time. Neutral in his war against Amphipolis, but alarmed by its result, the Chalcidians (we have seen) did try now to negotiate with Athens: and it would be surprising if Philip on his side did not try to negotiate with them. Their rebuff at Athens was so fortunate for Philip that it is difficult not to think that he himself must have worked for it, and that this may have been a principal motive for the charade of 'the secret that everyone talked about', which lasted long enough at least to serve this purpose for the moment.

At Athens itself, one must presume, the 'secret' was eventually disclosed to the Assembly: for Athenian ambassadors could not return home and simply omit to make any report to the *demos*.[2] Whether the Assembly ever voted to exchange Pydna for Amphipolis we are never told; but this does not necessarily mean that it did not happen, for Diodorus here on Athenian history is very brief, and the orators in their allusions years later to these events could easily pass over this one if it existed, so little creditable to all concerned, and with so little influence on the future. For the 'secret' had served its purpose. Within a few weeks or months Philip had decided that now there was nothing to fear from Athens. News arrived from the north that he was attacking Pydna. And the next news was that he had taken it.[3]

Pydna was for Philip at this moment a *parergon*, and his choosing to settle with it now (probably late 357) was perhaps decided by some local factors (for example, a party inside) that we shall never know about. Speaking generally, it was good to eliminate any potential base on his coastline which the Athenians might use when they again should become able to make war against him: and a city with revenues brought under his direct control meant presumably an increase in his own revenues.[4]

---

[1] On the chronology, see Sealey 111 ff.

[2] The casual attitude of the actor Aristodemus towards this duty was untypical, and gave offence. He was a busy man with his professional engagements, and had to be sent for, to report (Aeschin. 2. 16 f. See below, p. 335 n. 5).

[3] D. 1. 9, and schol.; D.S. 16. 8. 3. The inference from these texts is that there was a siege of Pydna, but not a long one. Diodorus mentions none (εὐθὺ γὰρ τὴν μὲν Πύδναν ἐχειρώσατο . . .): Demosthenes here includes Pydna in a list of besieged places which Athens had had time to save if she had acted promptly. But in another passage (4. 35) he lists only Methone, Pagasae, and Potidaea, omitting Pydna. The siege of Pydna may have been cut short by treachery (D. 20. 63).

Nepos (*Timoth.* 3. 1 ff.) seems to imply that Chares did actually command a force against Philip at this time, but was then switched to Samos and reinforced to deal with the war in the east Aegean. Cf. Cloché *PEA* 159.   [4] See below, p. 357.

But strategically there were more important things than Pydna, both for the security of Macedonia and for the future of its expansion, now that he had acquired Amphipolis. His own access to Amphipolis was flanked by the territory of the Chalcidian League, which was doubtless always willing to acquire Amphipolis itself. When deciding to force the issue with Amphipolis he must have calculated that the army which had defeated the Illyrians, greatly strengthened now that Macedonia was reunited, was capable of seeing the Chalcidians home should they try either to relieve Amphipolis or to invade Macedonia while the siege was on. (A nice division of his forces must have been needed, for these contingencies.) The Chalcidians, we may be sure, had been 'willing to wound, but yet afraid to strike'. Very recently they had entered into a defensive alliance with Grabus, king of the Illyrian Grabaei, the neighbours (to the north) of Bardylis and (to the north-west) of Macedonian Lyncestis.[1] They had seen the victor over Bardylis capture by siege the city which Athens had never been able to take. Was even Olynthus (of their own cities) more impregnable than Amphipolis? They, sooner than Athens, realized that their local balance of power had changed decisively. They saw only the one means of restoring it, by the alliance of Athens if it could be achieved. The danger for them was an affair near the heart. For Athens it was a matter of importance, but peripheral: the Athenians had rejected the overtures from Olynthus, misjudging still the man with whom they were dealing. It must have come as great news to Philip when he heard it, for these two powers acting together could still at this time have made him fight seriously. A really strong expeditionary force from Athens joined to the Chalcidian army, well led and wisely used, could have taxed the Macedonians to their utmost.

It was presumably the attack on Pydna which stripped the Athenians of their last illusions, and left them with no choice but to declare war on Philip (late 357).[2] For him, it was the merest prudence now to try to win the Chalcidians to a friendly neutrality or to co-operation by alliance. Yet Philip was a young general in the flush of victory. The conqueror of Amphipolis, and now of Pydna, may have been tempted to forgo the velvet glove and rely on intimidation as the best diplomacy, particularly when Athens now (winter 357/6) for the next year or two years looked sure to be tied down in the war with her own Allies. Few of his decisions

[1] D. M. Robinson, *TAPA* 69 (1938) 44 ff. no. 2 = Bengtson, *Staatsv.* 2 no. 307.

The peculiarities of the stone (the inscription incomplete), and its discovery in a river-bed, persuaded Robinson that this treaty must have become out of date very soon indeed after it was made, by reason of the Chalcidian treaty with Philip himself (below). If this is right (and it ought to be), the initiative for making it will have come probably from the Chalcidian side, since they (more than Grabus) were disturbed by Philip's attack on Amphipolis.

For the Grabaei, Hammond, *BSA* 61 (1966) 244.

[2] Aeschin. 2. 70, Amphipolis as *casus belli* (cf. 2. 21 and 72; id. 3. 54; Isoc. 5. 2), shows that thirteen years later it was possible to think of this war and the 'War of the Allies' as one.

show better the qualities characteristic of his statesmanship: the cool head thinking beyond the crest of the present wave, the judgement which saw the long-term advantages of the safer, less spectacular choice, the patience which did not boggle at committing itself to a difficult association with a reluctant ally, and the constructive instinct which sought a means to bind the ally to him by a real community of interest. The Chalcidians feared him, with good reason. He perhaps had the power now, while Athens was heavily engaged, to put military pressure on them sufficient, by an invasion of their territories and capture of some of the smaller and weaker cities, to deter Olynthus from a fight to the finish and coerce her into accepting an alliance with him (for what that was worth). But instead he chose to bribe the Chalcidians with something really worth while to them. He offered to cede to them the Macedonian territory of Anthemus on their north-western frontier; and he offered them Potidaea, when they should have taken it together. In this way he did what he could towards ensuring that the Chalcidians and Athens would never come together again in friendship, while Potidaea lay between them as a cause of enmity.[1] This alliance in fact was directed against Athens, and one of its clauses was that neither party should make a separate peace with her.[2]

The interesting but incomplete inscription found near Olynthus (see previous note) unfortunately preserves no details of the actual terms of the alliance (except that they were subject to amendment by consent of the high contracting parties). Its details concern the oath itself (who was to swear it, and by what gods) and the arrangements for preserving copies of the treaty at Olynthus, at Dium in Macedonia, and at Delphi. The negotiations which resulted in this agreement may well have been protracted in any case, and they were drawn out still further by a delay between the reaching of agreement on the text ([τὰ ὡμο]λογημένα of line 13) and the swearing of the oath, while Delphi was consulted:[3] only after the god had answered to the Chalcidians and to Philip that it was meeter and better that they be friends and allies on the terms agreed (lines 12–13), was the alliance formally concluded. The full

---

[1] For the prehistory, especially Timotheus in Chalcidice (364–362), see J. Papastavru, *Amphipolis* 27 ff., J. A. Anderson, *Potidaea; its history and remains* (Athens, Ga., 1963), 85 ff. Important is that the Athenian cleruchs of 362/1 were sent at Potidaea's request (Tod no. 146). The main motive for the request must have been for security, against Olynthus and the League.

[2] Tod no. 158; D.S. 16. 8. 3 f.: D. 23. 107; 2. 7 and 14; 6. 20; 1. Hypoth. 2 (Libanius). Philip and Athens, therefore, were already at war when this alliance was concluded. Demosthenes thus described the Potidaeates accurately as τοὺς . . . πρότερον συμμάχους (of Philip) when he attacked them (D. 2. 7).

[3] Papastavru, *Amphipolis* 37, comments on this interval, and thinks that ὡμολογημένα refers to an agreement reached between Philip and the Chalcidians even before Amphipolis fell.

implications of the response for Delphian sympathies at this time escape
us;[1] but in general the Delphians are sure to have been anti-Athenian
still (after a recent quarrel), and this perhaps is enough to account for
their line here.[2] More intriguing is the question why the oracle was
consulted at all about this, and on whose initiative. In the Persian War
period and earlier, we hear continually of states consulting Delphi on
questions of foreign policy which include sometimes the making of
alliances.[3] But not so in the fourth century, it seems: Delphi now is
consulted 'for victory' on the great occasions,[4] but for the great decisions
of foreign policy the god was not consulted regularly, or perhaps even
occasionally (since we hear of it not at all). In 368 a peace conference
was held in Delphi itself, but without the god being consulted, as Xenophon reports.[5]

The very fact that this treaty of Philip and the Chalcidians is (for us)
unique in this period, in its clause about Delphi, invites us to think of
Philip as responsible, and to conjecture that this marks some important
development in his public relations; but second thoughts counsel
circumspection. If Philip had had some policy which included the
consulting of Delphi when negotiating treaties of alliance, this would
have made him a sort of fourth-century Croesus-figure, and we should
infallibly have heard more of it in the next few years (after 346). For
this reason it seems likely that on this occasion the consultation was
prompted by some purely tactical grounds, whether on the initiative of
Philip or of the Chalcidians.[6] If the consultation delayed final ratification
of the treaty, this might perhaps explain it, and in this case it can only
have been the Chalcidians who may have dragged their feet. Philip
wanted this treaty and needed it; but at Olynthus a strong group must
have known that really their right place was with Athens now. They
feared Philip still *et dona ferentem*. The delay while the mission journeyed
to Delphi and did its business there in due season and returned gave
time for better news to come of Athens and her difficulties in the
Aegean: the god could be relied on to be up to date with the news, and

[1] Parke and Wormell 1. 234; 2. 105 no. 260. Cf. A. D. Nock, *Essays* 2. 534 n. 2.

[2] *Syll*³. 175. 15 ff. (363/2). In these years the Delphians were loyal co-operators with the
Boeotians in the Amphictyony.

[3] e.g. Hdt. 1. 53. 1 Croesus; 1. 66. 1 Sparta; 5. 63. 1 Sparta; 5. 79. 1 Aegina; 5. 89. 2
Athens; 6. 76. 1 cf. 80 Cleomenes I of Sparta; 7. 140. 1 and 141. 1 Athens; 7. 148. 2 Argos;
7. 169. 1 the Cretans; 7. 178. 1 the Delphians; 7. 220. 3 Sparta; Paus 8. 39. 3 Phigaleia and
Onesthasium, for alliance.

[4] See Parke and Wormell 2 no. 253 and 255 Thebes and Sparta for Leuctra; no. 261
Philomelus 356; no. 265 the Amphictyons 339; nos. 266 and 267 Philip 336; no. 268 Philip,
occasion unknown.

[5] X. *HG* 7. 1. 27.

[6] Nock, loc. cit., assumed that the initiative was Philip's and for reasons of importance
(... 'an exceptional and deliberate use of the oracle, with an eye on Greek public opinion').
Cf. also Bengtson, *Staatsv.* 281.

interpretation of it.[1] There was reason to hope that Philip's inland neighbours were no less alarmed by him than the Chalcidians themselves.
Here was the material for a coalition; but that Athens should be able
and willing to join it as a serviceable member was vital. If these were the
hopes, they were disappointed. No good news came. The god's response
came, and the Chalcidians found no choice but to take his word for it that
it was indeed meeter and better for them to be friends and allies of
Philip; receiving Anthemus and Potidaea (Athenian Potidaea) for their
trouble. All this they accepted, with some misgivings some of them, and
we may presume with some private reservations.[2]

The year 356, then, offered Philip the prospect of the move against
Potidaea, necessary to implement the agreement with the Chalcidians.
But this was not the only action in prospect, indeed this year is the first in
which we can see him engaged for certain on more than one front
simultaneously, and delegating one important command to the later
famous Parmenion. This was the year of the coalition of the three kings
against him (Illyrian, Paeonian, and Thracian), a coalition which Athens
eventually supported with her alliance (end of July). It was also the year
of his seizure of Crenides. Though the sequence in time of some of these
events can be established, Philip's personal priorities which he allotted
to them need more discussion.

The order of these events in the narrative of Diodorus cannot be
correct.[3] The dated text of the Athenian treaty of alliance with the three
kings shows, almost for certain, that already at this date (July 26) the
three kings were in alliance with each other,[4] and that Philip already was
in possession of Crenides.[5] Potidaea, however, was not yet in Philip's
hands, if we are to trust the synchronism, reported by Plutarch, by which
its capture was not long ($\mathring{a}\rho\tau\iota$) before the news reached him of the victory
at Olympia with his racehorse: allowing for the time needed for this
message to make the journey, Potidaea will have fallen not much before
mid-August, after a considerable siege.[6] Moreover a victory won by
Parmenion over the Illyrians was reported to him at this same time:[7]
while he himself besieged Potidaea, a part of the Macedonian army was

---

[1] For the 'due season', Parke and Wormell 30 f.

[2] Once the god had pronounced, it was difficult no doubt not to act accordingly. Perhaps
this consultation of Delphi is a sign of near-deadlock in the counsels of the League, when the
situation in the Aegean was fluid, and even the latest facts could not easily be known at
Olynthus for certain.

[3] D.'s order is (1) P.'s alliance with Olynthus (16. 8. 3–4), (2) Capture of Potidaea (8. 5),
(3) Capture of Crenides ($\mu\epsilon\tau\grave{a}$ $\delta\grave{\epsilon}$ $\tau\alpha\hat{v}\tau\alpha$ . . . 8. 6–7), (4) Coalition of the three kings against
P. (22. 3—in D.'s next-but-one archon year).

D. does indicate (8. 3) that the rest of that chapter is an anticipatory digression, to illustrate
the justice of his remarks about the importance of Amphipolis to Philip.

[4] Tod, *GHI* no. 157, 1–6.　　　　　　　　　　　　　　　　　　　[5] Ibid., 46.

[6] Plu. *Alex.* 3. 8, and J. R. Hamilton's note on 3. 5 (*Commentary*, p. 7).

[7] Ibid.

defending the kingdom, whether by repelling an invasion or by a preventive action, against the most westerly of the kings of the coalition. And meanwhile earlier in this same summer Philip himself had found time to push forward more than 40 miles east of Amphipolis, 60 miles east of Potidaea, to take possession of Crenides.

Clearly this is not the summer that Philip would have planned for himself if he had been left free to plan without interference or interruption. The new war with the Illyrians was a plain nuisance, and none of his choice. All the same, it seems fair to suppose that, in view of the scale and seriousness of the previous Illyrian war (of 358), Philip would have commanded in person on this occasion too if he had not been committed to another important operation himself already. Either the campaign against Potidaea or that against Crenides had already begun, Philip commanding, when the news from the Illyrian frontier made him detach Parmenion with a force from his own army, or (much more probably) made Parmenion, left behind in Macedonia for such a contingency, mobilize the reserve and take the field. Philip, then, early in the year had decided to take Potidaea or Crenides. But which? Or which first? As we have seen, it was Crenides that actually fell into his hands first. And certainly it was Crenides that was the better and bigger prize, not only because if he took it, it was his and not destined for the Chalcidian League, but also because it promised some important addition to his revenues, even though he could not know at this moment just how rich this prize was going to be. On the other hand, the advantage of dealing with Potidaea immediately was obvious, and may even be thought overwhelming. The attraction of taking this Athenian possession, containing Athenian cleruchs, while Athens was still heavily engaged in a losing war against her rebellious allies was more than a temptation, it was a satisfaction of every sound strategic and political instinct. It seems very highly probable that Philip's plan for this season was to give first priority to Potidaea, and that he may even have taken the field himself against Potidaea when envoys reached him from Crenides with news that an attack by Thracians was expected there, and with appeals for his help.[1]

It seems clear, then, that the timing of Philip's campaign by which he took Crenides was not of his own choosing. Though no one will doubt that the place stood high on his list of places for investigation and annexation, it is equally plain that this is no instance (as Amphipolis was) of a contrived occasion for an intervention with or without the help of a party inside. It is hardly conceivable that Philip was able to engineer this Thracian attack by persuading or bribing Cetriporis, the king ruling the most westerly (between Strymon and Nestus) of the three kingdoms

---

[1] St. Byz. s.v. Φίλιπποι ... τοῖς δὲ Κρηνίταις πολιορκουμένοις ὑπὸ Θρᾳκῶν βοηθήσας ὁ Φίλιππος Φιλίππους ὠνόμασεν.

into which the great Thracian kingdom of Cotys had been divided when he died.[1] The settlement of Crenides in 360 could never have been made at all except by agreement with the father of Cetriporis, Berisades,[2] who no doubt counted on receiving a *phoros* from the ceded territory just as the Thracian kings got it from Greek cities in the Chersonese:[3] and we may guess that a clause about the mining royalties will have been part of the original agreement too. In any case it has been shown beyond doubt that it was not Cetriporis who attacked or threatened Crenides now, but the more formidable Cersobleptes,[4] ruler of the most easterly of the three kingdoms, who, though capable without doubt of co-operating with Philip at this time for his own advantage, is exceedingly unlikely to have done so in order to leave Philip with the prize. Cersobleptes now was attacking the other two Thracian kings with the object of reuniting the kingdom of Cotys.[5] The settlers at Crenides, already producing some gold,[6] must have had reason to think that if they fell into the hands of Cersobleptes they could not expect the same favourable treatment as hitherto, and might even join the number of those earlier Greek settlements inland which ended in being wiped out by Thracians. Since they could hardly count on remaining fully independent if they called Philip in, it must have been a crisis of survival that made them do so, when they realized there was no hope of protection either from Cetriporis, or from Thasos the mother city, or from Athens not yet disengaged from her own naval war.

For Philip, as we have seen, the appeal came at a busy time. If he had not yet invested Potidaea, it will have been necessary to postpone the investment by some weeks while he hastened to Crenides. More likely, the siege of Potidaea had already begun. It is not too much to assume that Philip knew, whether from *akoē* or from reading Thucydides, that it had once cost Athens more than two years and 2,000 talents to capture this city. Allowing that Amphipolis had given him reason for confidence in his siege train, it was still common sense not to risk being overtaken by winter still besieging, and to begin the siege as early in the year as he possibly could. If he had begun already, he had the choice now of abandoning it temporarily, or of dividing his forces yet again. If he had 10,000 Macedonians in the field, he could withdraw half or more of them for the march to Crenides, and reinforce the remainder at Potidaea by

[1] Cetriporis, who had an Athenian minister and general Athenodorus, had good and close relations with Athens even before the treaty of alliance of July 356 (D. 23. 170 ff.): see on this Collart 152 ff.

[2] See above, p. 208.   [3] Tod, *GHI* no. 151, 10 ff. (357); D. 23. 177.

[4] Collart ibid. This was first seen, perhaps, by A. W. Pickard-Cambridge (*CAH* 6. 208), though he gave no reasons.

[5] D. 23. 9 f. and 179 f. alludes to an occasion when Cersobleptes attacked the other two kings.

[6] See below, p. 358.

insisting that the Chalcidians add to the number of the troops they had supplied already.[1] In this way the siege could be maintained, if not pressed home in his absence.[2] This seems perhaps the most probable reconstruction: not a planner's dream operation obviously, but an opportunist's best answer to an opportunity arriving unforeseen and when he was not quite ready for it.

If this is how it was, what followed can be imagined. Philip with his Macedonians will have reached Crenides in three days. Whether he found Cersobleptes or his general Charidemus already attacking we cannot know, but we are probably safe in thinking that if he did, his arrival caused the Thracians to draw off: a battle here and now between these two important powers would probably not have been passed over by our literary sources entirely.[3] Five or six thousand Macedonians with the names Bardylis, Amphipolis, Pydna, among their trophies were probably more than Cersobleptes or Charidemus was prepared to argue with, without special preparation. Philip entered Crenides now, and made it clear to the people there that his protection, so effectively exercised before their eyes, was theirs for all time. A strong garrison was doubtless installed of perhaps two or three thousand Macedonians; enough certainly to carry the conviction to Cersobleptes or any other attacker in the future that he would get nothing but a bloody nose for his trouble. Whatever Philip's arrangements now for defence, they were effective. Though Cetriporis and Thasos and Neapolis (as well as Cersobleptes) had the strongest direct interest, and though Athens had a very strong indirect interest, in undoing this day's work, Κρηνίδας συνεξαιρήσω (the words in the Athenian oath to Cetriporis later in this same summer) remained no more than a statement of good intentions. Surprisingly (astonishingly, even), we do not know for certain that Philip ever had to fight for Crenides again.[4] In the immediate future a problem of supply will have faced him. The existing population may well have been able to feed themselves from their very fertile upland plain, but the extra supplies for a strong garrison may have had to be hauled overland from Amphipolis 40 miles; both Cetriporis and Neapolis (outlet and intake port for Crenides) being now at war with Philip. But this was a small logistical price to pay for an opportunism which had succeeded brilliantly. For the next months the garrison stood on guard

[1] It may be taken as certain that a Chalcidian force must have co-operated in the siege from the start.

[2] Who commanded in Philip's absence, Parmenion being probably absent too? (See above, p. 247.) We can only guess, and the obvious guess is Antipater (aged now forty-two: Suidas, s.v. *Antipatros*, cf. Berve 2 no. 44).

[3] Especially by Demosthenes in his speech (23) *Against Aristocrates*, which contains so many allusions to the events in Thrace since Cersobleptes' accession, for the necessary information of Athenian jurymen in the year (probably) 352.

[4] But see below, pp. 281 f.

while the miners mined and the field-workers harvested and the mules in convoy from Amphipolis made up any shortfall in supplies. But before long Philip would return, to reorganize the city for its future, and to inaugurate a new era in her young history.

And so, back to Potidaea. That it was besieged we know, but not for how long, or how it fell. Only this we can infer, that the siege was not exactly short. There was time for the news to reach Athens, and for the Athenians, their resources strained to the utmost by their war in the Aegean, nevertheless to vote (not easily, we may judge) that a force be sent to relieve it: and the implication is that the force was in fact mobilized or being mobilized, if it did not actually embark.[1] But in truth Potidaea was beyond the power of Athens to save, now. An army on the scale of the great Sicilian expedition would have been needed, and even if this had existed it would have been unwise to risk it. It was the fate of Athens to be at war now with an opponent whom she was totally unable to hurt in any serious way, because she had not the troops to fight it out with the Macedonian army.[2] She was like a very mobile boxer who can do everything in the ring, except punch. Potidaea, then, fell and was handed over to the Chalcidians, the city and its territory. Of the inhabitants, the Athenian cleruchs were allowed to depart free and unransomed, though they could have been killed or sold into slavery: an act of humanity and policy, this, not without significance.[3] The remaining population, however, was sold into slavery, or most of it, though it has been suggested (implausibly) that some picked survivors were spared to become colonists of the enlarged Crenides in the immediate future.[4] The proceeds of the sales will have gone towards meeting the

---

[1] D. 4. 35 καίτοι τί δήποτ' . . . τοὺς δ' ἀποστόλους πάντας ὑμῖν ὑστερίζειν τῶν καιρῶν, τὸν εἰς Μεθώνην, τὸν εἰς Παγασάς, τὸν εἰς Ποτείδαιαν; Whether the trenchant words that follow (36 f.), about the Athenians laboriously *getting* ready (instead of *being* ready) when news arrived in wartime, can refer specifically to Potidaea, seems doubtful. In the desperate circumstances of this year, the Assembly could perhaps have met the bad news from Potidaea by optimistically voting for a squadron already in commission to be transferred thither as soon as possible. If so, it never was possible.

[2] This was seen later by Demosthenes in (probably) 351: D. 4. 23 ὅτι οὐκ ἔνι νῦν ἡμῖν πορίσασθαι δύναμιν τὴν ἐκείνῳ παραταξομένην, ἀλλὰ λῃστεύειν ἀνάγκη καὶ τούτῳ τῷ τρόπῳ τοῦ πολέμου χρῆσθαι τὴν πρώτην.

[3] D.S. 16. 8. 5.

[4] Ibid., accepting the emended text, τὴν δὲ πόλιν ἐξανδραποδισάμενος παρέδωκε τοῖς Ὀλυνθίοις, for the unacceptable τὴν δὲ Πύδναν . . . etc. The preceding μὲν clause refers to Potidaea, and so must this clause.

For colonists from Potidaea at Crenides–Philippi, I know of no evidence except the inscription published by S. Mertizides in 1897 quoted by Collart 178 n. 2, and pronounced a forgery by L. Robert (see below, p. 360). It is a list of ephebes of Philippi, headed by the names of six officials, one of them Athenodorus son of Gorgias, of Potidaea.

The attraction in making Potidaea supply some of the new settlers to Crenides is more apparent than real: surplus Potidaeates, and (simultaneously) new settlers needed for Crenides. But the important Crenides needed *reliable* new settlers; if Greeks, preferably volunteers. At this moment the Chalcidian League cities would seem by far the best source.

costs (in soldiers' pay) of this very active campaigning season. Loot may have cheered the army too.

Meanwhile, what of the coalition of the three kings? Grabus the Illyrian (we have seen) suffered defeat in July or August at the hands of Parmenion, but the history of this coalition is given to us only in the briefest summary.[1] It would seem the merest prudence that the Illyrians and Lyppeius king of the Paeonians should draw what advantage they could from their geographical position, by acting together.[2] Yet Paeonians are not mentioned in the allusions by Plutarch to Parmenion's victory, and Diodorus gives the general impression that Philip was able to deal with the three kings separately and in detail, and perhaps before they were ready.[3] If Parmenion in fact had moved to anticipate a junction between Illyrians and Paeonians, and caught Grabus alone, we are left quite in the dark as to how and when retribution overtook Lyppeius. In 349 Demosthenes could allude to 'the Paeonian and the Illyrian and generally speaking all that lot' as vassal peoples and no longer autonomous and free.[4] For the Illyrians (and the Thracians too) the issue is not a simple one, for more than one people and king were concerned, and there was more campaigning in the interval between 356 and 349. But the Paeonians so far as we know were united at this time, and in the absence of any notice of wars after this date, it seems likely that Lyppeius was disciplined now, and reduced to a vassal status. Whether or not he was in action against Parmenion in 356, probably an invasion of Paeonia or a military demonstration by Philip himself when he was at leisure (in 355?), brought him finally to terms.[5]

Cetriporis, the third member of the coalition, had already suffered a severe blow by the capture of Crenides. He had been at war with Cersobleptes (above), and though his eastern neighbour Amadocus was friendly, he too was threatened by Cersobleptes and had his hands full. Athens, though she had joined the coalition, was at this time a broken reed. For Philip, there was everything to be gained by settling with Cetriporis quickly. If Crenides was being partly supplied by overland convoys from Amphipolis, these occasions may well have invited attacks from the Thracians, on a scale not beyond their powers yet with something worth while to be gained. It was not a situation to be endured longer than

[1] D.S. 16. 22. 3.

[2] The kingdom of Grabus, described as 'having a common frontier with the Macedonians' (D.S. ibid.), must have been north-west of Lake Lychnitis, as Hammond shows (*BSA* 61 (1966) 244). It was probably separated from the Paeonians by the kingdom of Bardylis.

[3] Plu. *Alex.* 3. 8 (cf. Just. 12. 16. 6); D.S. 16. 22. 3 ἀθροιζόντων τὰς δυνάμεις ἐπιφανεὶς ἀσυντάκτοις etc.

[4] D. 1. 23.

[5] But see p. 224 n. 3 above, for the tentative suggestion to restore Παίονας for Παγασάς (MSS. Πάγας) at D.S. 16. 31. 6. If accepted this would point to (probably) 354 for the final subjection of Paeonia.

necessary: and especially (one must think) not through the winter if it could be avoided. It certainly seems right to read Diodorus' summary of the coalition and its fate as alluding to campaigns either all in this same year or at any rate with no long delay. On all counts, to settle with Cetriporis ought to have been the very next thing that Philip did, once he was free from Potidaea. The last campaign of this year (autumn 356) may well have been a demonstration in force with the army released from Potidaea (the Chalcidians now excused). A long march eastwards, over the Strymon at Amphipolis, then either by the road leading direct to Neapolis, past the city itself (now an enemy) and on by the coast road to the river Nestus near its mouth: or up the Strymon's tributary river Angites and following the route of the modern railway past Drama to the Nestus some 25 miles inland. It was this strip of territory, jutting east from Amphipolis some 60 miles with a depth of 30–35 miles inland, that Philip needed to bring under control immediately. This made Crenides secure. As he moved into it on this occasion, and about it, there was no question, for Cetriporis, of disputing possession by giving battle to the Macedonians. The question was, to elude now and indefinitely, closing in to continue a war of nuisance when this army had retired for the winter, and so on again next year: or to seek for an accommodation with Philip or accept an invitation to discussions if one was offered.

That an accommodation was reached now seems probable. On the subsequent history of Cetriporis and how he ended, we have no details at all. But he evidently had quite a long life and reign after this, since his name could be used by Aristotle and others to define this region of Thrace, a situation more likely the outcome of an early and peaceful submission to Philip than of a more protracted struggle and his deposition after a few years.[1] It seems clear that Cetriporis was still alive and reigning in 352, when Demosthenes could include him among certain 'friends abroad, who may do us some service': and of course by his treaty of alliance with Athens (above) he was presumably still bound to do just that.[2] But in the same speech Demosthenes is significantly silent about Cetriporis when mentioning military operations on the Thracian coast (belonging probably to the previous year): it was Amadocus alone of the kings who resisted Philip on that occasion.[3] Perhaps it was not beyond the optimism of Demosthenes to count Cetriporis still a friend and a possible helper, even if he had been constrained already to become Philip's vassal. He will have been obliged now to give up all claim to

---

[1] Arist. *HA* 9. 36. 620ᵃ ἐν δὲ Θράκῃ τῇ καλουμένῃ ποτὲ Κεδρειπόλιος ἐν τῷ ἕλει θηρεύουσιν οἱ ἄνθρωποι τὰ ὀρνίθια κοινῇ μετὰ τῶν ἱεράκων. Cf. Beloch 3². 1. 222 n. 3.

[2] D. 23. 189. It might be thought that Philip might have wished Cetriporis to dismiss his Athenian adviser Athenodorus. Perhaps he did wish, but was not quite in the position yet to insist. Or perhaps he knew his Athenodorus.

[3] D. 23. 183.

Crenides and recognize Philip in possession. Philip's access to Crenides, and the city's future safety must have been guaranteed by some provisions concerning this coastal strip of Cetriporis' kingdom between the Nestus and the Strymon; but whether this western piece of his kingdom was formally ceded to Philip and became part of Macedonia now seems very doubtful. It cannot have been a full year yet since Cetriporis had come to the throne in succession to Berisades his father: if he really lost this part of the kingdom to Macedonia in the first year of his reign, it seems incredible that a Peripatetic writer writing at least a generation later could describe Cetriporis' kingdom as 'that part of Thrace which is beyond Amphipolis'.[1] Much more probably Philip, having clarified by treaty the position of Crenides, as to ownership and rights of access and defence, imposed on Cetriporis the obligations of a vassal king. He will have become liable to supply some troops on demand in time of war (as we see later under Alexander both Thracians and Paeonians—and others—serving in this capacity).[2] And he will have been assessed to pay some tribute annually.

That Demosthenes (quoted above, p. 251) called 'the Paeonian and the Illyrian and all that lot' *douloi* ('subjects') does not absolutely require that we think of the kings who became in some sense vassals of Philip as paying tribute to him. But all the same the many and ancient associations of that word in this sort of context, with Persia, with Athens and her fifth-century empire via Thucydides, with Sparta and her harmost-ridden subjects, do seem to make it probable that Demosthenes and his audience were assuming without question the paying of tribute among the other disabilities of these *douloi* of Philip, and that we should regard the paying of tribute as a certainty, for Cetriporis now and for those others. The beauty of tribute, for an 'overlord'—apart from the actual cash, which in the world of Greek politics had its own beauty too—was that it enabled him to know exactly where he was with these neighbours year by year. If a *phoros* did not come in at the appointed time and there were no explanations, something was wrong: if it did not come in but explanations came instead, something was probably wrong. There was really no excuse (except weakness) for letting anybody get away with anything, once this comfortable relationship had been established. Cetriporis, then, probably paid his *phoros* regularly from now on, and so left his name to be attached by Aristotle and others for convenience to 'his' piece of Thrace. Incidentally, he was freed too from the fear of

[1] [Arist.] *Mir.* 118, 841ᵇ15 ἡ Θρᾴκη ἡ ὑπὲρ Ἀμφίπολιν; the identification of this with 'Cetriporis' part of Thrace' is made by the recurrence here of the allusion to hawking (p. 252 n. 1 above). On Cetriporis' accession, see Tod, no. 151. 5 etc., which shows Berisades still reigning. (The extant part of this Athenian decree contains no date, but the résumé of these events in D. 23. 173 (with ibid. 8 ff.) seems to put this treaty securely in 357.)

[2] See below, pp. 432 ff.

being driven from his kingdom by Cersobleptes: this *douleia* had its grounds for resentment and anguish for him (we cannot doubt it), but it was not without its compensations.

It had been a great year for Philip, this. The armies had worked hard, and had done well. He (and Parmenion) had done well directing them, and the political gains of the year had been, on a sober estimate, something more than solid. Further abroad and at a less exalted level, there had been a flash of glory on a Greek racecourse, and where it mattered most, at Olympia.[1] His name (and the name of his horse, one hopes) was spread through the cities by this victory, and lodged especially with those families who still thought horses important. These were the houses that were going to send sons in some dozens before many years were past, to the north to the court of this ruler with lands, and soon with money, for the enrichment of the right sort of young men prepared to make a career with him and be numbered among his Companions.[2] His own house, too, had been gladdened by the birth of Alexander (mid July). The story goes that the seers foretold the baby invincible, born in the hour of three fresh victories.[3] The story is true, for any seer who threw away this particular line would have been a disgrace to his profession, asking to be replaced. The birth was the occasion for rejoicing and celebration as was proper, we need not doubt. For the time being the most important thing about Alexander may have been that he was a boy and not a girl. That a man so prone to marriage as Philip can ever have doubted his ability to procreate heirs seems an absurdity (indeed he probably owned already a son from Philinna). But the arrival of a son and heir presented to him by the royal Olympias was a fitting garland for this year of victories.

3. *Epilogue: Methone*

Isocrates, if he got nothing else right in his remarks about Amphipolis in his *Philip* and his *Peace*, was certainly right in naming it as the proximate cause of the war between Philip and Athens ('since I saw the war which broke out between you and my city about Amphipolis . . .').[4] The taking of Amphipolis, as we have seen, led on directly to an immense strengthening of Philip's position in the 'parts towards Thrace', which the Athenians, embarrassed by their war in the Aegean simultaneously,

---

[1] Plu. *Alex.* 3. 8.   [2] See below pp. 375, 400.

[3] Plu. *Alex.* 3. 9; Hamilton, *Commentary*, ad 3. 5. Though such synchronisms as this are always suspect, and the Olympic date here is thought more likely to be late August than late July, it still seems improbable that this whole combination, with the seers' comment based on it, is fictitious.

[4] Isoc. 5. 2. His advice on the subject to Philip in 346 (5. 1–7), and to his own people in 355 (8. 22) seems strangely remote from the facts of life.

were quite unable to prevent and scarcely able even to oppose with some token acts of resistance. The war, however, was still on. By summer of 355 the Athenians were freed of their other great commitment by a peace disastrous indeed but at least offering the opportunity to recoup and recover, and to organize themselves against further losses at Philip's hands, or even, if their resilience went so far, for counter-attack to recover what they had lost to him already.

It is a sign and a measure of the Athenian demoralization at this time that the first twelve months after their Peace of 355 brought them nothing except one more reverse in the north, a repetition, it seems, of those they had had already: Philip's attack on their ally Methone, which he took after a long siege, and which Demosthenes counts later among the places where Athenian action had come too little and too late.[1] The timing of the attack is not without interest. It was probably late in the year. Methone was under siege, probably by December 355, and its fall must have been either in spring 354 or perhaps well on into that summer.[2] Philip could not know for certain in advance that Athens would do little to help or save Methone, and it seems surprising, therefore, that he did not attack early in the year while the Athenians were still at war elsewhere. Methone was the one base remaining to Athens on the Macedonian coastline. To take it was not a matter of absolute urgency in the sense that its continued existence was a deadly danger; but it was obviously a good thing to take it, and from all points of view the sooner the better.

The explanation for the delay is most likely the simple one that Philip moved against Methone just as soon as he was free to move. We have seen already that the momentous and eventful year 356 seemed to contain even more than its share of events, and that some overspill into 355 seems probable. The final reckoning with the Paeonians, and the refounding of Crenides as Philippi with the new colonization, occupied each of them perhaps some weeks, even months, of Philip's personal attention in the first half of 355.[3] Especially Neapolis, the natural indeed the only port which could serve Crenides–Philippi, must have advanced high now in his list of priorities, both for the economic life of Philippi in the long term, and for the strategy of the present war. If Athens were ever going to be able to counter-attack in strength, a thrust based on

---

[1] D. 4. 35; cf. 1. 9.

[2] *IG* ii². 1. 130. This Athenian decree (of the 5th prytany) honours with *proxenia* a Lachares of Apollonia 'because . . . he sent his son to Methone', implying clearly that the siege was on, or imminent, in December. (Cf. U. Kahrstedt, *Forschungen zur Geschichte des ausgehenden fünften und des vierten Jahrhunderts* (Berlin, 1910) 42.)

The siege was not a short one (D. 16. 34. 5 μέχρι μέν τινος οἱ Μεθωναῖοι διεκαρτέρουν). Diodorus records it twice (16. 31. 6 and 34. 5), a fact which may be (but need not be) due to its duration spreading into a second archon-year.

[3] See above, p. 251.

Neapolis inland to Philippi offered much more promise than one based on Methone into Lower Macedonia itself. Though our record of the embassy of Neapolis to Athens in May 355 falls short of telling us what Neapolis was asking or proposing then, and exactly what had made her ask or propose it, it would not be surprising if some pressure exerted by Philip lay behind it.[1] Neapolis presumably was losing much of her normal livelihood (from trade with the interior) by being at war with Philip now, and though he may have hesitated to besiege a city which could so easily be supplied and reinforced from Thasos as well as by Athens, he may well have thought it good policy to invade her territory and devastate the grain harvest in May or June, and so tighten the screw.

However this may be, a third theatre of operations also claimed Philip's presence in the summer of 355—Thessaly. It was now, most probably, that he intervened on behalf of the Thessalian League and against Pherae, and with effect enough perhaps to enable the League to vote for the declaration of the Sacred War against the Phocians at the autumn Amphictyonic meeting, and to join actively in the war next year.[2] How much of Philip's time this intervention consumed we can only guess; but, again, 'some weeks perhaps even months' seems the fair estimate. It cannot have been an easy choice, between the definite job at home (Methone) that needed doing and was best done quickly, and the seductive invitation abroad with its opportunities of renewing and strengthening the contacts made nearly three years ago, for making himself as necessary as possible to as many as possible of the leading men of Larissa and the League cities; in short for not wasting or losing any of the immense potential that this stasis-ridden country showed him. Some part of the summer, then, he spent in Thessaly. He can have left instructions, without doubt, that all was to be ready for the attack on Methone to begin at short notice when he returned. Methone of course cannot possibly have been unprepared. She had watched the siege and fall of Pydna from the front row of the stalls: the two cities were no more than 6 miles apart.[3] Since that time as an ally of Athens she had been technically at war with Philip, who for all we know may have devastated either or both of her next two harvests to put pressure on her to change sides.[4] Methone was not a great city, and the inducement to come to terms with Philip peacefully, avoiding the agonies of a siege against great odds, must have been very real; advocates of this course inside the city cannot have been wanting. Nevertheless Methone is not one of the places where we hear of treachery inside, or of a pro-Macedonian party. She resisted stoutly through this winter. An assault on the walls by the Macedonians with

---

[1] Tod, no. 159.   [2] See above, pp. 227 ff.   [3] Str. 7 F 20.
[4] The harvests of 356 and 355. He must have had a small garrison in Pydna now, and no great army was needed to devastate the countryside of Methone.

scaling-ladders was beaten off.[1] Philip himself suffered the worst wound of his life here while directing the siege works within bowshot of the defenders. He lost his right eye.[2] The future of the infant Alexander the Great came now, we must suppose, within some fraction of an inch of being snuffed out.

The inspiration of their resistance must have been the hope, even the expectation, that Athens would save them; for her circumstances were quite changed now from those which had prevented her from doing anything effective for Pydna and Potidaea. Nor are we quite entitled to say that she did nothing now for Methone. Demosthenes (4. 35) implied this perhaps in his allusion made three years or more after the events, but what he actually said was that she had acted too slowly to succeed in saving the place: and indeed the decree honouring Lachares (p. 225 n. 2) shows that before midwinter somebody at any rate had been doing something. Whatever was done, however, was not enough. The Methonaeans exacted their appalling price from Philip personally, but Philip soldiered on. He was not the only soldier, we may be sure, to lose an eye in these campaigns, and doubtless he had a better doctor than most. But he was the only soldier obliged to continue in command while under torture. Perhaps it is not altogether fanciful to read something of this horrible experience into the ending itself of this passage of arms. Methone was never stormed, but capitulated on terms only acceptable to defenders exhausted and perhaps on the verge of famine.[3] If any city ever staked with Philip a claim to be stormed and sacked, the citizens to be put to the sword or sold as slaves, it was Methone. The capitulation may show Philip's magnanimity,[4] but more likely it shows a failure of will, his rejection of a risk that the siege might be prolonged for weeks or months if relief from Athens should arrive, a craving to be finished with this ghastly place for ever: let vengeance go, 'so to interpose a little ease'.

The lesson of Methone went deep for contemporaries well read in the history of their past, if there were any such. The fifth-century miracle of the liberation of the Greek cities of Asia Minor had been based ultimately on the calculation, justified in the event, that Athenian sea power

---

[1] Polyaenus (4. 2. 15) records a narrow escape of being stormed. Though Polyaenus leaves us to suppose that this attempt succeeded, in reality it must have failed, for there is no reason to doubt the plain statement of Diodorus (16. 34. 5) that in the end Methone capitulated on terms. (So, too, Just. 7. 6. 15 ff.)

[2] Theopomp. F 52 (*FGrH* 115); Marsyas F 16 (*FGrH* 135, 136); D.S. 16. 34. 5; Just. 7. 6. 14; Str. 7. F 22; Duris F 36 (*FGrH* 76).

The details of Theopompus and Marsyas are likely to be right (his right eye, and by an arrow). Strabo's detail (of source unknown) that the wound was from a catapult bolt is interesting but implausible, for Philip would have been less likely to survive this.

[3] D.S. 16. 34. 5, 'to depart with nothing but the clothes they wore'.

[4] So Just. 7. 6. 15 f. 'Quo vulnere nec segnior in bellum nec iracundior adversus hostem factus est etc.'

could keep them free. Great Persian armies might march up to their walls; but there they could stay, provided that the citizens kept stout hearts and put their trust in the Athenian navy to bring in supplies and reinforcements as needed. All this now was gone. This continental aggressor was more determined and resourceful, better equipped to deal with city walls. The naval power was there still, but the will that decided on its use was more hesitant, more divided in its aims in life, less concentrated on the self-preservation and self-help which sea power could serve so well: and the Athenians were short of money now, for naval expeditions.[1] If Methone was lost, Athens being free to save her, who then should be saved? Which Athenians, if any, asked this question, we do not know. But Philip is likely to have bethought himself to ask it, while he learned to live without his right eye.

---

[1] It does not need demonstrating (one hopes) that, speaking in material terms, it was the tribute from the Empire that had enabled the Athenians to conduct an enterprising foreign policy without taxing themselves severely. This does not rule out psychological factors also which were not directly dependent on the material terms.

VII

THESSALY AND THRACE
(353–352)

1. *The alternatives*

THE taking of Methone freed Macedonia finally from foreign encroach-
ments and from the threat of attacks or nuisances based on a strong
point occupied by an enemy on her own coast line. While the
Chalcidian alliance stayed firm, neither the Athenians nor any other
Greeks could mount force enough to invade from the sea. Inland, the
invaders from the north and north-west had been disciplined twice. The
revenues of the kingdom were improved already by territorial gains and
especially by the output of the mining based on Crenides–Philippi. This
summer (354), if it gave Philip a space for convalescence, will have given
him too some opportunity for planning how best, where next, to direct
the military potential which was the manpower of Macedonia, seasoned
already by exposure to these campaigns which had given it even now,
we must judge, some name in the world.

The easy going must have been seen to lie to the east. Here spread
Thrace, its three Odrysian kings divided by some mutual animosities
and by the inordinate ambition of one of them (Cersobleptes): of the
two others one (Cetriporis) was in Philip's power already. Only a combination of the three, with Athens putting her full weight behind, would
be enough to offer real hazards if he launched himself into Thrace. So
far neither the combination nor the Athenian weight had shown signs
of being mobilized seriously against him. As for the rewards of Thrace,
they were not spectacular perhaps in the short term, but they were worth
having. More Thracian territory would bring in more revenue and scope
for more colonization if that should seem called for; and even the military
power of Macedonia could be increased by expansion here. No one will
suppose that any Thracians were going to be willing subjects of a foreign
king; but Philip was near enough and strong enough to be perpetually
intimidating, and the balance between the gain from claiming Thracian
levies and the loss from having to reckon with unreliable or intransigent
subjects is likely to have seemed securely on the credit side. East Thrace
might be another matter, with its great distances (from Macedonia), its
important Greek cities, its seaway vital to Athens and by long tradition a

scene of Athenian colonization. The prizes here were bigger, so were the difficulties. But these things were not for this year, or next year. Some time?

Meanwhile it was impossible, always, to forget the south—Thessaly was a land of diversions whether social or political, as he had learned already. But how serious a place was it, for a dedicated statesman? The past suggested that no Macedonian king concerned with the defence of his own realm could afford not to pick up anything that was dropped in Thessaly.[1] The question was, how far to follow opportunities here when they offered, or to seek new ones? Jason's towering figure had thrown its shadow across Greece for a year or two. (The sixth book of Xenophon's *Hellenica* was completed now these twelve months perhaps.[2] Was Philip among its readers? Whether or not, in Larissa he had met and talked with men who remembered Jason and the glories and discomforts of a Thessaly united under a great *tagos*.) The hated Pherae could be counted on still, it seems, not to let old acquaintance be forgot. Moreover, the Sacred War now raging brought Thessaly into the whirlpool of Central Greece and beyond in a quite unusual way. While Philip besieged Methone the Thessalians (without Pherae?) had mixed it with the Phocians and their mercenaries for the first time, and had taken a beating.[3] How much did these things concern Philip? What was there in all this for a king of the Macedonians?

To cast a shadow across Greece himself, to make great allies—and great enemies—to become committed to policies and expenditures which outdistanced the defence of his own realm and its requirements, was this to act as a statesman still, and not as some busy *polypragmon* snatching any chestnuts out of any fire without too much considering whether he wants chestnuts and whether they are good for him anyway? The difficult thing (but it needs to be attempted) is to recapture what was the impact of the world of Greek politics on the most efficient king of the Macedonians there had been as yet. In Thessaly he had seen a lot, yet Thessaly was not Greece; not quite. In Thebes as a boy in the house of Pammenes he had been close to the centre, old enough then to see now in retrospect (if not altogether at the time) how power worked in one of the greatest Greek cities, what set it working and what set the limits to what it could do. Thebes had been nearly destroyed by Sparta just

---

[1] Above, pp. 181, 218 f.

[2] On Jason, X. *HG* 6. 1. 4 ff. On the date of composition of Book 6, E. Delebecque, *La Vie de Xénophon* (Paris, 1957), 300 ff., 434 ff., 450 ff. If, as seems likely, Book 7 was completed by the beginning of 355, we still do not know when the two books were published, whether separately or together. Delebecque in his table of dates (op. cit. 509) assigns the composition of Book 6 to '357 (*fin*)', but he warns that the dates proposed for X.'s works are '*simplement possibles*', and indeed his own arguments concerning Iphicrates and Timotheus (450 ff.) seem to recommend a date one year later (for completion of Book 6).

[3] D.S. 16. 30. 4; cf. 16. 31. 6 (Methone—ἅμα δὲ τούτοις πραττομένοις). For Pherae in this connection, above, pp. 226–9.

before her great revival in the 370s. Domination had become necessary to avert being destroyed, or at least avert becoming *douloi* of people whom their history had taught them to distrust. The same seemed true of all the Greeks who made pretensions to power: the alternative to domination was, at best (as a great expert had put it), survival in subjection.[1] This situation, multiplied, and complicated by the number of smaller units too weak to dominate but still determined to survive, made up the world of Greek politics. In this highly competitive existence a wealth of Greek talent was incessantly employed. The arts and skills of self-government, painfully evolved, were subordinated continually to the imperative needs of survival or of gaining some advantage over a neighbour, while many of the best virtues and characteristics of the race were expended in a process which tended to weaken the race as a whole. For these Greeks this made sense, because all intended to survive, and by as good a margin as they could get.

But what sense did it make to the king of the Macedonians, once none of these people could threaten Macedonia any more? One thing must be clear—Philip can never have thought of going into Greece for the money. Any notion of conquering and annexing parts of Greece and exacting tribute from it was a proposition unsound financially, to say nothing of any other criterion. True, the Greek cities had some money, but it did not amount to very much, and the citizens objected very strongly to parting with any proportion of it regularly in taxation to any government even their own; to any other government much more so. The cost of collecting it (with garrisons to intimidate the citizens) would have left nothing worth while for the Treasury. The whole taxable capital available to Athens (the wealthiest city of Greece) after 378 was a little less than 6,000 talents.[2] The problems of interpreting this figure are notorious,[3] but if (as seems probable) the actual capital in existence greatly exceeded 6,000 T., this merely proves (for our present purpose) that the Athenian *demos* realized that to set a target for taxation which was realistic by our own modern standards was for them impracticable: people would not pay.[4] *A fortiori* they would not pay heavy taxes to a foreign government unless they were terrorized. Nor would they pay any taxes to a foreign government without recognizing them as a sign of 'subjection'.

Even the firmest believers in the popularity of the Athenian Empire in the fifth century must find it hard to convince even themselves that the *phoros* was popular. Granted that in the subject cities it was the few (rich) and not the many (poor) who paid this tax, yet it must be a mistake, in

---

[1] Thuc. 2. 63. 3 (ἀσφαλῶς δουλεύειν).

[2] Plb. 2. 62. 7. D. 14. 19 names the round figure 6,000 (speaking in and of 354/3).

[3] Cf. (e.g.) A. H. M. Jones, *The Athenian Democracy* 23 ff., 84 f.; A. M. Andreades, *A History of Greek Public Finance* (trans. Carroll N. Brown, Harvard U.P. 1933) 1. 334 ff.

[4] Cf. D. 14. 27.

this context as in others, to underrate the intelligence of the poor, who know better than anybody else that the one thing you cannot do with money is to spend the same money twice. The money that went to Athens as *phoros* was not available to be gently redistributed among the poorer citizens at home in the way which became a characteristic of radical democracy;[1] and this must have meant that the rich sometimes were taxed twice, once for the *phoros* and once for their own democracy, with results that are well known (though not always well interpreted). In the new dispensation of the Second Athenian Confederacy, one of the named attributes of being 'free and autonomous' was to be immune from *phoros*.[2] The financial contribution of an allied city now was called not *phoros* but *suntaxis*: and though the name was longer the money was less (*much* less than *phoros* on the Cleonian standard of taxation). This cannot be demonstrated by Athenian Syntaxis Lists, but it is shown on almost every page of the Confederacy's history, by the chronic inability of Athens to pay properly for any campaign she undertook.[3] (What Cleon would have thought of it all we cannot know; but we can guess.)

It may be objected that Jason of Pherae is reported as having made light of the revenues of the Athenian maritime empire in comparison with the potential revenues of a Greek land empire which he proposed to create and to finance by imposing taxation on those whom he compelled to belong to it.[4] It must be concluded that though he had better opportunities than we for knowing what money could be screwed out of Greece by taxation, if he really ever did say this Jason undoubtedly was talking through his hat, and if he believed it he got what he deserved. He was assassinated (it will be recalled) some four years after this report of his words was given at Sparta, and at a time when his 'land empire' still had not developed beyond Thessaly itself and its *perioikis*. The determination of the Thessalians of the League not to be dominated again by the tyrants of Pherae who came after him is sufficient comment on what some Thessalians at any rate thought of this kind of imperialism (which needed of course to begin at home, by uniting Thessaly itself, willy-nilly). The noble and the powerful in many cities opposed it naturally; but it is probably sound to think that there was much 'built-in' support for their opposition from taxpayers in general, who were also the most valuable citizens as soldiers, and on whom the brunt of imperialism would be imposed: a fire-eating *tagos* asked merely for their money *and* their lives.

---

[1] 'Gently' in comparison with Marxist precept and practice of redistribution, accepted now as normal in most modern states.

[2] Tod, *GHI* no. 123, l. 23, μήτε φόρον φέροντι . . .; see above, pp. 216 f.

[3] Cf. S. Accame, *La lega ateniese del sec. IV A.C.* (Rome, 1941) 134 ff.

[4] X. *HG* 6. 1. 12. There is no reason to doubt that Xenophon was well informed of what the Pharsalian Polydamas said of Jason at Sparta on this occasion, though it does not follow that all he said was true. Cf. Delebecque, op. cit. 300, 436.

The whole climate of opinion, then, in the cities of Greece was unfavourable to high taxation except in the acutest emergencies of war, and to any regular system of taxation which could be thought of as the paying of tribute to an imperialist power. Such a system could only be imposed and maintained by a formidable and continuing military operation.[1] It cannot have been as a source of wealth that the Greek cities attracted Philip if they did. The only rational explanation (which does not exclude others that might be wholly or partly irrational) is that they attracted him as a source of power.

Power for its own sake or power as a means to ends? Perhaps the answer to the question, if we could know it, would contain a qualified affirmative to both of its parts. The function of the king of a military people, when he has proved his talent for leadership in war and self-advancement in inter-state politics, is to use the talent and go on using it almost instinctively, unless he is subject to restraints of principle or to some external pressures that prohibit. Which of us does not enjoy doing that which he knows he does well? It seems entirely possible that Philip, when he began to be drawn further and deeper into Greek affairs than Macedonia required him to be drawn, was moved less by calculation than by the working of his own *phusis*. To gain control of all Greece, to yoke a new source of power to the power of Macedonia and drive the team towards some goal outside and beyond the Aegean altogether, this was to be rational, to distinguish end from means; and the time was to come, we can see, when this was done. But at present, if Philip thought in those terms, we might be right to characterize it as a dream rather than a plan. Meanwhile his *phusis*, rather, impelled him towards the south, and he could think of some excellent reasons in support, if anybody wanted reasons. Thus, already he was at war with one of the three leading Greek powers, Athens. Though the Athenians had shown no ability to injure or even inconvenience Macedonia as yet, and it was hard to see now how they could do so in the future, still, on general principles it was sensible to acquire friends in Greece who were enemies or potential enemies of Athens. Such were the Boeotians, heavily engaged now in their Sacred War against the Phocians holding Delphi. Such were his friends in the Thessalian League, for though they had formed an alliance with Athens in 361–360, their more recent co-operation with the Boeotians and involvement in the Phocian war made the present alignment plain.

When, then, at some time in the summer of 354 the campaign at Methone was over, Philip may well have felt obliged to weigh south

[1] The anecdote at Plu. *Mor.* 177 D (*Apophth. Phil.* 4) shows Philip in 338 or later rejecting proposals to hold Greece down by garrisons, on ethical grounds. While there is no need to doubt his genuine concern for his own reputation (see also ibid. 7 and 11), it seems safe to say that the practical reasons will have been no less in his mind.

against east, east against south. But as it chanced, this same summer brought a development in the south that seemed to withdraw for the present the opportunity of intervening there; the defeat and death of the Phocian leader Philomelus in the battle of Neon, which persuaded the winners that a victorious end to the Sacred War was within their grasp now.[1] For Philip, some diplomatic exchanges with the victorious Boeotians were not ruled out; but the next military objectives now had better be in Thrace.[2]

2. *Interlude in Thrace: spring 353*

The most probable reconstruction of the known events brings Philip into Thrace in the early months of 353; but the date of this Thracian move has been so much discussed that it seems well to give in full the three pieces of ancient evidence bearing on it. It will be observed that it is only the connection with the Theban general Pammenes at Maroneia that allows this affair to be put in any chronological setting at all with anything approaching probability.[3]

1. Diodorus 16. 34. 1. 'In the same year Artabazus, the satrap in revolt from the Great King . . . persuaded the Thebans to send him a reinforcement. The Thebans appointed Pammenes to command and gave him 5,000 men and sent him on his way to Asia.'

The archon year, according to Diodorus, was 353/2. But this Theban decision, characterized by Diodorus as 'remarkable' (ibid.), is plain incredible unless it was taken in the one period, after the death of Philomelus, when there was reason to think that the Phocian War was over, bar mopping up. This means in the winter 354/3 (above), so that Pammenes can have set out in very early spring of 353. His route lay overland (we shall see), through Thessaly, Macedonia, and Thrace.

---

[1] D.S. 16. 34. 1 f.; 32. 1; cf. Hammond, *JHS* 57 (1937) 58 ff.

[2] The chronological connection in Diodorus (16. 31. 6) between Philip's capture of Methone and his capture of Pagasae the port of Pherae depends on a textual emendation which supplies Παγασάς for the unidentifiable Πάγας or Παγάς. Though this has become generally accepted (with capture of Pagasae 354/3, consequently), recently C. Ehrhardt has argued against it convincingly (*CQ* N.s. 17 (1967) 298 ff.). In brief, there was evidently a siege of Pagasae (D. 1. 9; 4. 35), and this seems feasible only after Pherae itself has fallen, in 352 (so Pickard-Cambridge, *Demosthenes* 177). Demosthenes at 1. 12–13 gives the correct order of the events: 'First he took Amphipolis, then Pydna, then Potidaea, then Methone and then he invaded Thessaly; then Pherae, Pagasae, Magnesia, the lot, he fixed to suit himself; and so he went off to Thrace . . .'.

As to the true reading at D.S. 16. 31. 6, Ehrhardt rightly pointed out that 'Diodorus' phrase Πάγας δὲ χειρωσάμενος ἠνάγκασεν ὑποταγῆναι would also seem better applicable to an independent tribe or people, rather than to a town with no political status'. Παίονας comes to mind; but I know of no Paeonian war in 354 or 353.

[3] It depends therefore on the dating of the battle of Neon to 354 (Schaefer's date, 1. 442), on which the arguments of Hammond (*JHS* 57 (1937) 44 ff., esp. 56–60) still seem to me conclusive.

Philip's consent was needed to march through Macedonia, and doubtless was given ungrudgingly, with an eye both to past favours and to the future, since the enemies of Thebes (Pherae and Phocis) were his enemies too.

2. Demosthenes 23. 183. 'For when Philip had come to Maroneia he [sc. Cersobleptes] sent Apollonides to him, offering guarantees to Philip and to Pammenes: and if Amadocus, whose territory this was, had not forbidden Philip to advance, there would have been nothing to stop our being at war straight away with Cardia and with Cersobleptes.'

3. Polyaenus 4. 2. 22. 'Philip having laid waste the territory of Maroneia and of Abdera was on his way back:[1] he had a large squadron of ships, and an army on shore. Chares in command of twenty ships was lying in wait off Neapolis. . . .' (Philip's successful stratagem, which follows, was to send in advance his four best ships to decoy Chares in a chase out to sea, in the course of which Philip's squadron slipped past Neapolis safely.)

Demosthenes (above) tells us about the route taken by Pammenes. Not only did Philip grant him leave, it seems, to march through Macedonia, he also helped him on his way through Thrace. The passage implies that both the Thracian kings had been asked by Philip for a safe conduct for Pammenes through their territories.[2] Amadocus (loyal to the Athenian alliance and rightly fearing Philip) had refused, and put up a resistance when his country was invaded. Cersobleptes, we see, agreed; and the cryptic sentence which ends the quotation suggests that he accepted now a treaty containing a bargain which Philip had proposed. Demosthenes does not say 'If Amadocus had not stood firm Philip himself would have been able to come through and attack the Chersonese', but merely that Cersobleptes supported by Cardia would have gone to war with Athens. The bargain, therefore, was that Philip was to have a free hand to deal with Amadocus, while Cersobleptes was to have a free hand with the Chersonese.

The Polyaenus passage fills in the picture a little, for there is no known Thracian campaign of Philip to which it can possibly refer, except this. Whatever its objectives, its achievements were limited: Polyaenus in his introductory *mise-en-scène* would not have named the territories of Abdera and Maroneia if there had been more important victims, or if

---

[1] Reading τὴν Ἀβδηριτῶν καὶ Μαρωνιτῶν καταδραμὼν ἐπανῄει. The MS. καταλαβὼν is plainly unsatisfactory (applied to the territory of cities, and not to the cities themselves), and καταδραμὼν (Hertlein) is printed by Melber (Teubner, 1937). And see p. 266 n. 2 below.

[2] Demosthenes' phrase at 23. 183, πίστεις δοὺς ἐκείνῳ καὶ Παμμένει, excludes the possibility that this incident belongs to Pammenes' return journey from Asia (as Cloché, *PEA* 191 f., etc.). Pammenes needed no agreements with Cersobleptes then (and if he had needed one he could have made it while passing through Cersobleptes' territory to Maroneia on his way back).

Philip had really penetrated beyond the Hebrus on this occasion.[1] Philip's 'many ships' may have been designed to act against Abdera and Maroneia, or even against Thasos and Neapolis, if opportunity served (all were Athenian allies); or they may have been designed as a protection for the army on this coastal march in the event of a descent by an Athenian squadron; though Philip's extreme precaution (described here) in face of the twenty ships of Chares seems rather to discount this possibility. The truth may be that some of the 'many ships' were cargo ships carrying supplies for an army which originally (counting the 5,000 of Pammenes) cannot have been less than 10,000 strong. Anyhow, they got home safely, and the short campaign had demonstrated Macedonian power to Amadocus and had done some damage to the two Greek cities.[2]

It remains pertinent to ask, however, whether this was worth the trouble and the time that had been given to it. There may have been some local reasons, of which we know nothing, for applying some pressure now on Amadocus: and certainly there was always good reason for putting pressure on Neapolis (see above, pp. 255 f.), where now we find Chares standing guard.[3] But what is obscure is the importance in Philip's calculations of the good relations with the Boeotians which we see as something established, and in operation here for the first time. The political advantages of an alliance with the Boeotians have been suggested already (above); and it seems most probable that this was the occasion when the alliance was entered into, and probably by an initiative from Thebes, when the decision to send Pammenes to Asia was taken there.[4]

---

[1] Beloch was thus not justified in attaching this incident to the campaign of 347 beyond the Hebrus (3². 1. 500 f.; 2. 282 f.), arguing that Philip would not have had a fleet in 354 (*sic*). Yet, as I have tried to suggest in my text (above), a fleet which he was afraid to expose to a squadron of twenty Athenian triremes need not be taken too seriously.

[2] There is no question of either city's falling into Philip's hands now, as is sometimes stated. Maroneia, we know, was still an ally of Athens in 340 ([D]. 12. 17), as Accame rightly recognized (*Lega ateniese* 198 and n. 7). For Abdera, *IG* ii². 1. 218, cf. Beloch 3. 2. 283: and below, p. 379.

[3] The selection of Neapolis by Chares as his base may have been due to some specific instructions from Athens, if Neapolis had already suffered at Philip's hands in the previous year (see above, pp. 255 f.).

[4] The occasion when Philip and the Boeotians became allies is nowhere recorded, though Pausanias (writing casually) thought of it evidently as coming between the battle of Neon and the Crocus Plain battle (Paus. 10. 2. 5). Bengtson (*Staatsv.* no. 327, with bibliography) correctly cites D.S. 16. 58. 2 as evidence for the alliance in existence in 347, but cites D. 4. 48 incorrectly as evidence that it does not exist yet in 351 (date of *First Philippic*). Demosthenes spoke here of rumours about Philip. 'Some of us go round telling the tale that he is working with the Spartans to overthrow Thebes and dissolve the federations [?—πολιτείας—two more rumours follow] . . . in short we each make up our own piece of fiction and circulate it' (οἱ δὲ λόγους πλάττοντες ἕκαστος περιερχόμεθα). No one will suppose that the existence of an alliance between Philip and 'Thebes' would have stopped Athenians from starting or passing on this rumour (their own experience of Philip as 'ally' had not been happy in 359–357).

If the alliance was made after 351 but before 347, Philip made no move to implement it till 346. If it was made in the winter 354/3 (as I propose), the years 353 and 352 show him

On a long view Philip's interest in Thessaly, manifested already, was not going to commend him to the Boeotians once their Phocian troubles were over. But meanwhile they could use him here; and he on his side was content to combine some service to the new ally with his own immediate plans in Thrace. And even while he acted in Thrace between the Nestus and the Hebrus, events in the south had not stood still. Whatever his plans really were, it seems possible that they were curtailed, by news and messages that took priority.

3. The decision in Thessaly

It must have been early summer, and it may have been later than this, when Philip moved into Thessaly again. The march of Pammenes from Thebes to Macedonia, their joint march to Maroneia and presumably beyond to the Hebrus, the spoliation of the territories of Abdera and Maroneia by the Macedonians, and the return to Macedonia will have occupied not less than two months of the spring; after which this army may well have been sent home. The month Daisios could well intervene at this point, the month (May/June) when it was 'not customary' to call out the Macedonians on campaign (Plu. *Alex.* 16. 2). Philip can hardly have expected all along that this year later would see him in Thessaly. We can only guess how early in that year it may have been that the Boeotians (and then others) realized that the Sacred War was not safely over and done with. Onomarchus the new general did rally the Phocians, did hire a new army, and did know what to do with it when hired. In a matter of months (but it did take months, obviously) this war which had nearly died grew into life again. In Thessaly no doubt Pherae revived and the enemies of the Phocians were in trouble. Philip's opportunity was here again. Our evidence however is merely that on this occasion too 'the Thessalians' appealed to him for reinforcements, to enable them to withstand Lycophron of Pherae.[1]

Diodorus has placed the whole career of Onomarchus as commander-in-chief of the Phocians in the single archon-year 353/2, an arrangement which no modern historian has accepted, or indeed could accept, since the year contains apparently an invasion by Onomarchus of Ozolian Locris and of Doris, an invasion of Boeotia,[2] an invasion of Thessaly by his brother Phayllus (and this is where Philip first comes in), and finally three battles in Thessaly (another invasion of Boeotia intervening) between Onomarchus and Philip, the last of them fatal to Onomarchus

not merely supporting Pammenes in Thrace but also undertaking the two great campaigns against the Phocians in Thessaly.

[1] D.S. 16. 35. 1 ($\mu\epsilon\tau\alpha\kappa\lambda\eta\theta\epsilon\grave{\iota}s$ . . .).
[2] D.S. 16. 33. 3–4.

　　　　K

but the second of them obviously a very severe defeat for Philip himself.[1]
Clearly two summers are needed for all this, and equally clearly the
winter between them must come after Philip's great defeat forcing him
to withdraw from Thessaly. In this way Onomarchus' second invasion of
Boeotia, and his final campaign in Thessaly against Philip, belong to
352. The year 353 remains eventful enough; but the command of
Phayllus in Thessaly shows that the Phocian armies here are divided
(with Onomarchus in Boeotia, presumably), so that the first duel of
Onomarchus and Philip falls in the late summer and autumn of this
year.

It is a great effort that the Phocians make in Thessaly at this time. The
aim to keep the Thessalian League immobilized in its local war with
Pherae and incapable of joining forces with the Boeotians may be taken
as certain. Even while Onomarchus was first securing his position in
Phocis and collecting his great army (winter 354/3), we hear that he
trained the diplomatic and financial weapon on politicians in Thessaly
as well as elsewhere, using the treasures of Delphi. With Philip too an
adept at this game, any Thessalian politicians who were for sale found
themselves enjoying now, enviably if briefly, a sellers' market. Onomarchus had his successes, 'even in Thessaly', we learn.[2] But evidently he
could not buy Thessalian neutrality altogether. In the spring of 353
Pherae could not crush entirely the League's will to resist, and when
Philip entered Thessaly, Lycophron too needed reinforcement. That it
was given is not surprising; but interesting is the extent to which Onomarchus was (or became) prepared to commit himself in support of Pherae,
till in the end he lost his whole army and his life. We can see that he can
have come to recognize in these two campaigning seasons how essential
it was, for him, to get Philip out of Thessaly and keep him out, and we
cannot know (for lack of evidence) what elements in his own temperament may have disposed him not to shrink from even the ultimate
hazards of increasing stakes.

For what actually happened in Thessaly this summer, we are desperately short of details, and have no chance of seeing with any exactitude
what the commanders planned to do. It would seem that, left to themselves, the forces of the League and of Lycophron of Pherae were not ill
matched, since the League needed to summon Philip to gain superiority.[3]
If we are to include a siege of Pherae among Philip's military failures,
then it must belong to this summer, whether before or after the opera-

---

[1] D.S. 16. 35. 1 ff., cf. Hammond, 'DSW' 57 f.: Beloch (3². 2. 267 f.) also saw the necessity
of allocating these events to two years, though he made the years 354 and 353 instead of
353 and 352.

[2] D.S. 16. 33. 2–3 καὶ γὰρ τοὺς Θετταλοὺς μέγιστον ἔχοντας τῶν συμμάχων ἀξίωμα δωροδο-
κήσας ἔπεισε τὴν ἡσυχίαν ἔχειν. For a different explanation, Sordi, *LT* 241.

[3] D.S. 16. 35. 1.

tions in support of Lycophron commanded by Phayllus.[1] Lycophron's appeal for help cannot have been welcome to Onomarchus who was probably in Boeotia now, where his invasion went well, the important city of Orchomenus having fallen into his hands. He detached his brother Phayllus with 7,000 men, all he could spare. For himself in Boeotia, it was too many to lose, but for Thessaly it proved too few. Phayllus was defeated by Philip, and driven out of Thessaly.[2]

That Onomarchus could not or would not accept this reverse is striking in its implications. Though the division of forces had probably spoiled his own Boeotian campaign (he was defeated now by the Boeotians),[3] he reacted with the utmost resilience, by invading Thessaly with an army probably in the region of 20,000 strong when Lycophron's troops had joined up with him. His superiority in numbers over Philip (recorded by Diodorus, 35. 2) cannot have been very great, since it looks as if both generals hoped to win a decision in this campaign.[4] Two battles were fought, and both are described as victories for Onomarchus; but the first must have been indecisive. The second however was not, and since a description of it contains an interesting clue, I give it here:

Onomarchus preparing to give battle to the Macedonians chose a position in front of a crescent-shaped mountain. On the high ground on each flank he concealed stone-throwing catapults and the ammunition for them. Then he advanced on to the level ground below. When the Macedonians came to meet them and opened fire with their missiles, the Phocians made a show of fleeing towards the recess of the mountain. The Macedonians charged in pursuit, but the men posted on the hilltops opened fire with the artillery and began to punish the Macedonian phalanx. And then Onomarchus gave the trumpet-call to the Phocians to turn and charge. With this charge at their backs as they tried to withdraw, and with the stones from up above still coming down on them, the Macedonians had all they could do to escape and make their retreat.[5]

Diodorus, who gives no details of the campaign itself, does tell us that as a result of it Philip's situation was desperate: his men were badly shaken and turned against him, and he had a job to restore their morale and discipline.[6] Diodorus writes of all such things like a bad journalist,

---

[1] Polyaen. 4. 2. 20 Φίλιππος πολιορκῶν χρόνῳ μακρῷ †Κάρας† ἐχυρὸν χωρίον, ἑλεῖν τ᾽ οὐχ οἷος ὤν, ἀποχωρῆσαι βουλόμενος ἀσφαλῶς . . . etc.

Καρδίαν Blume, Φεράς Woelfflin. (Κάρας is unknown.)

Personally I think the description ἐχυρὸν χωρίον much more likely to have been given to some barbarian stronghold than to a famous Greek city. (Cf. 4. 2. 18 Φαρκήδονα πόλιν Θετταλικήν.)

[2] D.S. 16. 33. 4; 35. 1.   [3] D.S. 16. 33. 4.

[4] D.S. 16. 35. 2. Diodorus' ἀναλαβὼν πᾶσαν τὴν δύναμιν, however, is probably not strictly true, since he cannot have left Delphi and Phocis defenceless, to say nothing of garrisons in Boeotia and elsewhere.   [5] Polyaen. 2. 38. 2.

[6] D.S. 16. 35. 2 Φίλιππος δ᾽ εἰς τοὺς ἐσχάτους κινδύνους περικλεισθεὶς καὶ τῶν στρατιωτῶν διὰ τὴν ἀθυμίαν καταλιπόντων αὐτὸν παραθαρσύνας τὸ πλῆθος μόγις ἐποίησεν αὐτοὺς εὐπειθεῖς.

with an idiom that makes the very most of the ups and downs of life. But allowance made for this, there is no mistaking the story of this battle for anything but a comprehensive defeat for the Macedonians, their first since the Illyrian disaster more than six years ago and their worst in the open field (as it turned out) during the whole of Philip's reign. They had been outfought because they had been out-generalled, and this sours the best of soldiers, because they know there is not much they themselves can do about it: they can only hope, but they can never feel sure, that nothing like this is going to happen again. Meanwhile Philip withdrew now from Thessaly; and doubtless in the winter that came on more soldierly bad language was heard in the Macedonian homesteads than for many a long day.

The significant detail, however, of this story I take to be the presence of artillery, for Onomarchus to use. To suppose that he had brought it specially in order to use against Philip in the field is probably wrong. Because the machines could not be assembled and tuned for action quickly enough (and likewise were liable to be overrun by an enemy before they could be got away), the Greeks never did develop a regular field artillery.[1] We hear of its effective use occasionally by way of improvisations, of generals who saw an opportunity in conditions that were favourable. Here for Onomarchus, as we see, the element of surprise was complete. But his purpose in bringing his artillery into Thessaly is more likely to have been in order to attack walled cities. There is evidence that Onomarchus now may have gained possession of certain places which were members of the Thessalian League itself, places perhaps in which his bribes had taken some root.[2] The only city of which this seems reasonably certain is Crannon (less than 15 miles south-west of Larissa), if we accept the restoration $K\rho\alpha[\nu\nu\acute{\omega}\nu\iota o\iota]$ in a list of subscribers to the 'rebuilding fund' of the Delphic temple, this in the period when the Naopoioi have been reconstituted by the Phocians (Onomarchus), and when no official or subscriber concerned can be anything but a friend of the Phocians.[3]

A second city which can be called a 'possible' as a Phocian adherent in this connection is Pelinna in Hestiaeotis, about 10 miles west of Pharcedon. The evidence here is that 'stratagem' of Polyaenus which consists of Philip's general method in Thessaly over a period of time and in a number of places, and the account of it begins 'When the Pelinnaeans

---

[1] See on this E. W. Marsden, *Greek and Roman Artillery: Historical Development* (1969) 59, 164–8.

[2] See p. 268 above.

[3] *Fouilles de Delphes* 3. 5. 5, line 11. See, on the date, M. Bourguet, ibid. p. 47, Sordi, *LT* 247 and n. 1. The tyranny at Crannon of Deinias, a Pheraean, is unlikely to have begun now (Polyaen. 2. 34), because the likeliest reason for his having settled in Crannon originally must be that he was an enemy of the tyrants of Pherae (so Sordi, *LT* 231 and 247).

were at war with the Pharsalians and the Pheraeans with the Larissaeans, and the rest formed groups in support, he always reinforced those who asked him.'[1] It seems likely that if Pharsalus had ever joined up with Pherae at this time we should have heard of it, and therefore that it is Pelinna, here, that is acting outside the League. But only support from Pherae or Phocis, or both, would enable Pelinna to survive against Pharsalus and the League.[2] In fact only in this period (353–352) of Phocian involvement in Thessaly does a reinforcement of Pharsalus by Philip in this context seem to make good sense.

The suggestion that Pelinna may have gone over to the Phocians after this defeat of Philip in 353 is strengthened by the fact that without doubt something unfortunate befell two other of the small cities of this western plain of Thessaly (Hestiaeotis), and most probably at this time. They are Pharcedon and Trikka. Of Pharcedon we have the story (from Polyaenus) of its surrender to Philip after a siege, and we know that Theopompus mentioned it in his 9th book (but unfortunately not what he said about it, only the detail that he called it Pharkadon).[3] Other allusions to Thessaly, however, in the 9th book make it probable that this book treated of the years 353 and 352.[4] Pharcedon and Trikka suffered the condign punishment of being made *anastatoi*;[5] and though we do not know when this happened, we are certainly entitled to wonder why it happened. To bring them, too, inside the scope of Onomarchus' activities in late 353 seems attractive. One is left with a picture of Onomarchus going home for the winter with limited but definite gains in Thessaly to show for his great victory. He had made a distinct impression on the small and peripheral cities of Hestiaeotis, and also had one more central success at Crannon to his credit. Diodorus imputed to him the belief that in this campaign he would 'conquer all Thessaly'.[6] The gains I have mentioned would show him having made a start on doing just this, while still leaving intact the main body of the League. And this body

---

[1] Polyaen. 4. 2. 19.

[2] For a different view, based on acceptance of the emendation (of Melber) Φαρκηδονίοις for Φαρσαλίοις, see Westlake 177 f. The topographical attraction of the emendation is beyond doubt (the two cities being neighbours), but Sordi's arguments against accepting it seem to me right (*LT* 256 and n. 1). Her own tentative suggestion that Πελινναίων in the text may be corrupt, and that Ἀλέων might be preferred, is not acceptable, because the well-known dispute between Pharsalus and Halus (settled by Philip in 346) seems too far removed in time from the Larissa/Pherae dispute to be combined with it here in a phrase which is intended to 'date' this stratagem. It is unfortunate that we do not know the background of a dispute between Pharsalus and Pelinna; but in view of our ignorance in general of internal politics in Thessaly it is not surprising.

[3] Polyaen. 4. 2. 18; Theopomp. *FGrH* no. 115 82.

[4] Theopomp. F 78–81.

[5] D.S. 18. 56. 5; cf. Sordi, *LT* 254, for discussion.

[6] D.S. 16. 35. 2 νομίζων ὅλης τῆς Θετταλίας κυριεύσειν: cf. 16. 35. 4 οὗτος (Lycophron) ... μετεπέμψατο συμμαχίαν παρὰ Φωκέων, ἐπαγγελλόμενος συγκατασκευάσειν αὐτοῖς τὰ κατὰ τὴν Θετταλίαν.

has got to be intact, still, to throw its weight against him and under Philip's command next year (352), the year of decision.

Sordi was right, it seems, to seek a really ambitious Phocian policy for Onomarchus, consonant with the renewed activity of a Board of Naopoioi at Delphi (already mentioned).[1] By a combination of bribery and military power applied in Thessaly, it evidently came to seem possible to him now to bring the Sacred War to an end by winning over Thessaly and its *perioikis*, and so commanding a majority of votes on the Council of the Amphictyony. In some circumstances this could be no more than a victory on paper, to be disregarded by those who did not like it. But if meanwhile he could impress the Boeotians themselves with his military superiority, there was a chance that they would be satisfied not to pursue the war alone: and this situation was on the way to being achieved, with his capture of Orchomenus in 353 and his successful campaign in Boeotia in spring 352, in which Coronea fell into his hands and a Boeotian army was defeated.[2] It remained now to make the final move into Thessaly, where the League unsupported by Philip could certainly not have opposed him effectively now, and would have been obliged to come to terms with him. But it was his misfortune to have found an antagonist who, though in general very far from being a war-to-the-death fighter who on principle or by instinct never let go, nevertheless here and now had evidently come to a firm conclusion that this was not an occasion for accepting two defeats and cutting some losses: Thessaly, it seems, was not one of the places which Philip at this time felt that he could afford to be thrown out of.

In that story of Philip's great defeat in the previous year, Polyaenus ends by recording a remark of Philip himself at the time, 'In that retreat they say that Philip the king of the Macedonians commented "I did not run away, I came back like the rams; I walk back in order to charge again, harder".'[3] Whether or not the remark is authentic, certainly it is *ben trovato*. It does give the picture we need of Philip's reaction to the defeat, and we can surmise that even the setting of the remark is right, in the moment of defeat and retreat itself. We can see that the simile of the ram is apposite: next year Philip did come back with a greater army. But what seems clear is that if Philip did react in this way to the second defeat, then he must have given his intentions all the publicity that he could, for the sake of his allies in Thessaly. This had been a bad year for them, and it was absolutely necessary that he should find them still there, when he did come back in the spring. The remark about the rams sounds like someone whistling to keep up the courage; but it is plain whose courage is being kept up. It looks as if Philip has become really

---

[1] Sordi, *LT* 244 ff.: and in *BCH* 81 (1957) 56.   [2] D.S. 16. 35. 3.
[3] Polyaen. 2. 38. 2.

deeply involved in Thessaly in a way which seems susceptible of explanation only in terms of the politics and policies of the Thessalian League cities themselves. It is they who keep summoning him into the country; but of course he is not their lackey, and he need not come. After two defeats he is not obliged to increase the stakes and throw once more, perhaps with an uncomfortable amount of his resources committed. It seems very probable that what brings Philip back is the knowledge, arrived at in his intimate dealings with these allies in this last year, that there was some real chance now that this Thessalian League might choose him as its titular head and thereby deliver the control of the country into his hands. This was a real prize: its greatness ruled out mere indifference, though it will not have put an end to calculation. And conversely the abandoning of Thessaly to Phocian control, an unattractive enough policy on general grounds anyway, became a policy of painful loss once it had become a question of great hopes and not merely of some foreign cities being abandoned.

Philip will have talked long with those Thessalian leaders whom he could trust before he left the country for the winter. During the winter he may have kept writing letters to them, for there was at least one big practical thing he needed from them, and to make sure of getting it, and on the right scale, there was nothing like nagging, early, late, and often. Onomarchus, too, had his hopes of important help from abroad, from as far afield as Athens, and may even have tried to concert some plan which would include an Athenian squadron operating in the gulf of Pagasae. It may have been partly to give the Athenians more time, or partly or entirely to suit his own view of the priorities, that he made his first campaign of the new year a new invasion of Boeotia, with results that were excellent (above). But consequently in Thessaly it was Philip who showed the flag first. It is not likely to have been now that a siege of Pherae (referred to earlier) will have been begun, to be broken off when time ran out:[1] operations perhaps against those smaller cities which had shown themselves disloyal to the League. The combined army was large, and for a time could be fed more easily while divided: over 20,000 infantry, which may mean up to 15,000 of the Macedonian phalanx: cavalry 3,000. This last would seem to be Philip's answer to the unpleasant lessons of the year before. He had provided himself with the certainty of being able to deliver a knock-out blow, always provided that the enemy would meet him on cavalry ground. In the few words which Diodorus devotes to the battle itself he names 'the Thessalian cavalry' as

---

[1] D.S. 16. 35. 3 makes Philip operate 'against Pherae' before the arrival of Onomarchus. All the same, I do not believe in a siege of Pherae now, for a big siege was among the most exhausting of operations, and an abortive one was poor encouragement for the army at a critical time. The disloyal smaller cities were allies of Pherae now, of course.

having decided the day by their numbers and their valour.[1] Though it would be surprising if Philip, with a cavalry battle in mind, had not brought at least 1,000 of his Macedonians along, there is no reason to doubt that he pressed his Thessalian friends to raise every horseman that the League could raise—and perhaps that the Greek source of Diodorus, if he did not much like Macedonians anyway, wrote this the way he liked it better.

The battle of the Crocus Plain, as it is often called, was fought in a coastal plain of Achaea Phthiotis, between Phthiotic Thebes and Halus. Beloch was probably right in putting Philip where Onomarchus needed to go through or round him in order to make a junction with Lycophron of Pherae. This, and perhaps some thought to a rendezvous with an Athenian fleet, and perhaps (dare we guess?) a comfortable feeling that this general at all events had no terrors for him, induced Onomarchus to fight on Philip's ground; flat ground, not far from the sea. The sea indeed may have guarded one of his flanks. But who or what would guard the other flank, when the Macedonian and Thessalian cavalry numbered in all 3,000 to his own 500? The Phocians suffered very heavily when they broke and ran for the seashore; 6,000 killed and 3,000 taken prisoner, and some had tried first to swim out to the large Athenian squadron under Chares which 'happened' to be cruising offshore. Philip treated the defeated as temple-robbers now: there should be no funeral rites for these hierosules.[2]

This act of retribution or vengeance needs explaining, especially as it is orthodox to understand it as applying to the living (prisoners) as well as to the dead; and indeed the text of Diodorus seems unequivocal on this, until one begins to have second thoughts about it. But (first), this act is a sort of propaganda, and clearly linked with what we are told of Philip's attempt to make this campaign present the appearance of a kind of crusade. Before the battle he had ordered his men to wear laurel wreaths, proclaiming that they were soldiers of Apollo on this occasion, fighting against the sacrilegious sinners who had taken Phocian pay.[3] To whom, then, was this charade addressed? And why had the same thing not been done the year before, when the cause and the enemy had been precisely the same?[4] First, the notion that this was a propaganda addressed to the Greeks, to any Greeks, seems very highly improbable. Everybody in Greece knew that the 'sacredness' of the Sacred War was a ramp, that the Phocians had only become 'impious' because the Boeotians had practically forced them to, and even had become 'temple-robbers' only

---

[1] D.S. 16. 35. 4-5.　　　　[2] D.S. 16. 5-6.　　　　[3] Just. 8. 2. 3.

[4] That it had not been done seems certain, for two reasons. (1) If it had, we should probably have heard of it, in the striking context of Philip's two defeats. (2) If it had been done then, after the two defeats Philip would not be repeating it now!

when they really had no other means of surviving. People who had suffered from the Phocians, like the Boeotians, Locrians, Thessalians and others, were no doubt delighted when Philip did something nasty to them, while the Athenians and Spartans and other friends of Phocis thought it disgusting. But a neutral, unpolitical public opinion of ordinary people who were genuinely shocked by the 'impiety' of the Phocians probably did not exist. This is shown by the ease with which the Phocian generals could raise army after army of mercenaries, while their sacred money lasted. It seems much more likely that the charade was for the benefit of the Macedonians. They knew the real facts presumably much less (perhaps hardly at all); but they knew of Apollo of Delphi, and they could be genuinely impressed by the idea of fighting with the god directly engaged on their side. Above all, perhaps they needed this, badly. If the defeated troops of last year had been really seriously shaken, there was nothing like the god for restoring their confidence. The Thessalians in this army knew they had been fighting for the god for some years now, off and on, and a fat lot of good it had done them: they may have put on laurel now reckoning that it might do some good and anyway could do no harm. Only the Macedonians, one may think, had the psyche of the nearly virgin soil, the approach to this war uncomplicated by any knowledge of what it was really about, the determination to win because they were used to winning and because it was for the losers that these battlefields became really dangerous places, and finally the knowledge that last year something had gone wrong, and a great readiness to believe their king (whom they mostly trusted) when he told them that Apollo's laurel was the thing that was going to make quite, quite sure that nothing would go wrong this time. They knew what 3,000 cavalry could do, given the chance. Apollo (who better?) could take away the wits of this general who had made them run twice last year: Apollo might give the cavalry their chance.

The victory confirmed the glory of the god, and it can have done no harm to the glory of the king of the Macedonians.[1] But what is it, exactly,

---

[1] Justin's report of the victory combines ('contaminates'?) scepticism with piety in a strange way. On the one hand (8. 2. 3) 'Igitur Philippus, quasi sacrilegii, non Thebanorum ultor esset, omnes milites coronas laureas sumere iubet . . .' On the other hand (8. 2. 4–5) '. . . Phocenses insignibus dei conspectis conscientia delictorum territi abiectis armis fugam capessunt. . . . Incredibile quantum ea res apud omnes nationes Philippo gloriae dedit; illum vindicem sacrilegii, illum ultorem religionum . . . Dignum itaque qui a diis proximus habeatur, per quem deorum maiestas vindicata sit.' And the defence of Thermopylae by the Athenians which follows (8. 2. 8 ff.), is compared unfavourably, for its motives, with the defence against the Persians. If this account derives from one Greek source (Theopompus?), it looks as if that writer had abandoned himself to rhetorical claptrap here, but still could not refrain from indicating the truth, surviving in 'quasi sacrilegii, non Thebanorum ultor esset'. Polybius criticized an inconsistency of Theopompus in his treatment of Philip (Plb. 8. 9. 1 f.; 10. 1 f.; 11. 1 f. = Theopomp. T. 19, *FGrH* no. 115), now favourable now hostile; though Polybius selected as favourable the *prooimion* to the *Philippica* in contrast to instances of

that Diodorus is saying here about Philip's treatment of the defeated? 'In the end more than 6,000 of the Phocians and mercenaries were killed, including their general [Onomarchus], and 3,000 or more were taken prisoner. Onomarchus Philip hanged; the rest he threw into the sea as temple-robbers (τὸν μὲν Ὀνόμαρχον ἐκρέμασε, τοὺς δ' ἄλλους ὡς ἱεροσύλους κατεπόντισεν).'[1] Onomarchus was dead when Philip hanged him, on a cross or gibbet, this is clear;[2] a bad way to use a general and a man of family, but he had earned it (in this context), a hierosule. And 'the others' (hierosules), 6,000 of them dead, 3,000 still alive as prisoners of war? Which of them is Diodorus telling us that Philip threw in the sea? The corpses? The prisoners? Both? To take his words literally, they ought to mean both, no doubt. The modern reader instinctively rejects this, and takes them to mean the prisoners only.[3] But can this be right? The ancient Greek reader, I suspect, when he had just been told what became of the corpse of the general, would have taken τοὺς ἄλλους to mean the other corpses, only. I suspect that he would never even have thought of including the prisoners in this, partly because to him the corpses mattered more; but also because of the extreme difficulty, in practice, of drowning 3,000 men.[4] Though *muthos* and *logos* were full of drowning stories, they knew nothing of mass-drownings: and personally I do not believe in this one here.[5] The Boeotians already had found it impractical to kill their 'Phocian' prisoners as sacrilegious criminals, because the Phocians killed

hostility on particular aspects or topics later. Whether this dichotomy could be observed in greater detail throughout the work, we do not know.

[1] D.S. 16. 35. 6.

[2] D.S. 16. 61. 2 confirms, μετὰ τῶν . . . Φωκέων καὶ μισθοφόρων κατακοπεὶς ἐσταυρώθη, cf. D. 19. 319. According to Pausanias 10. 2. 5, he was killed by his own men.

[3] P. Ducrey, *Le Traitement des prisonniers de guerre dans la Grèce antique*, (Paris, 1968) 69 and 323. I have not noticed any modern account that does not make Philip drown the prisoners.

[4] To 'shoot' prisoners down was practicable, even 3,000 of them no doubt (cf. D.S. 16. 31. 1–2, ἅπαντας κατηκόντισαν . . . ἅπαντας . . . κατηκόντισε, where the numbers would be a few dozen probably). But there could be no question of drowning 3,000 men by embarking them on ships and throwing them overboard (only thalassocrats might think of that). I think that some hundreds of armed Macedonians would have needed to herd and edge the 3,000 disarmed prisoners over a pre-selected cliff into deep water from which there was no getting out.

[5] See P. Ducrey 202 n. 3; Schulthess, *RE* 10. 2 (1919) 2480 f. s.v. καταποντισμός; G. Glotz, Daremberg, and Saglio 3. 1 (1889) 808–10, s.v. *Katapontismos*. The many instances, both mythological and historical, invariably concern individuals or small groups such as a family. The nearest I can find to a possible mass drowning is the execution of the two ships' crews taken prisoner by the Athenian general Philocles (X. *HG* 2. 1. 31–2 where κατακρημνίσειαν, κατεκρήμνισε, may really mean 'threw overboard', cf. LSJ[9] s.v.). *Katapontismos* was never a matter of Law, but of lynch law; it was not *nomos*, but a survival of *themis*. As Glotz wrote, victims of it were in the nature of an offering to the gods, for them to take or to spare. In the fourth century it was used occasionally by tyrants, it seems—and against tyrants. (By Hicetas, against the wife of Dion, Plu. *Dion* 58; *Timol.* 33. By the Locrians, against the wife and children of Dionysius II, Athen. 12. 541 e. By Cleomenes tyrant of Methymna, Athen. 10. 443 a. By Alexander the Great, against the leaders of the mutineers, Curt. Ruf. 10. 4. 2. By Ptolemy II, against a poet! Athen. 14. 621 a.)

their own prisoners by the same methods, for being Boeotians.[1] Philip knew this, obviously. Consequently we can believe in his drowning 3,000 prisoners only by believing, too, that he counted on this being the end of the war, with no danger of Macedonians or Thessalians being prisoners of the Phocians, ever. But he did not count on this, clearly. If he had, he would have marched now straight on Thermopylae, instead of allowing the Athenians and their allies to occupy it while he himself was busy with something else that he reckoned more important (below).

Both Isocrates and Demosthenes, as it happens, mention *katapontismos* in a way that shows their opinion of it. Isocrates counted it among the crimes and horrors of the age which peopled Greek mythology and filled the tragic stage from year to year.[2] Demosthenes described a recent instance of it in a way that made it discreditable to the perpetrators (enemies of Athens, the Cardians).[3] It was not really a civilized practice, and if Philip really had this unique mass-performance of it to his discredit, one could have expected it to leave more mark on the tradition. These prisoners, in short, were not drowned at all. What became of them now we do not know. But meanwhile to deny burial rites to the enemy was a good weapon for Apollo's soldiers and general now that they had won. The Locrians had tried this earlier; indeed the Amphictyons may have made a standing order to this effect at the start of this war.[4] This again invited reprisals (as the Locrians found). But these reprisals (the refusal of burial in return) did first require that the enemy too had some corpses in his power.[5] He needed to have killed somebody and to have won a victory. On all this Philip felt much more confident than the Locrians that he could dictate about corpses and not be dictated to. To be able to do this was impressive at the time, and when the war was over and the Phocians were down, it even invited praise from the more odious kinds of historian.[6] For the present, there were things nearer at hand that mattered more to him at this moment. In the Crocus Plain campaign he had evidently acted as commander of the Thessalian League army as well as his own,[7] and the fruits of the campaign were on no account to be neglected. Especially Pherae, the arch-collaborator with the Phocians, now genuinely was isolated, unless the Athenians were prepared to

---

[1] D.S. 16. 31. 1–2 (cf. 25. 2–3 for similar reprisals in the matter of returning the dead for burial).

[2] Isoc. 12. 122.

[3] D. 23. 169–70. The oligarchs who slew Hyperbolus at Samos (μοχθηρὸν ἄνθρωπον, Thuc. 8. 73. 3) put his body in a sack and threw it in the sea (Theopomp. F 96, a and b).

[4] D.S. 16. 25. 2 οἱ δὲ Λοκροὶ τὴν ἀναίρεσιν αὐτῶν οὐ συγχωροῦντες ἀπόκρισιν ἔδωκαν ὅτι παρὰ πᾶσι τοῖς Ἕλλησι κοινὸς νόμος ἐστὶν ἀτάφους ῥίπτεσθαι τοὺς ἱεροσύλους.

[5] D.S. 16. 25. 3.

[6] For Justin, p. 275 n. 1 above: for the fatuous digression of Diodorus on the bad ends that the sacrilegious Phocians and their soldiers came to, D.S. 16. 61–4.

[7] D.S. 16. 35. 4; cf. Sordi, *LT* 248.

undertake a major campaign on land on her behalf in Thessaly (they were not, of course). The tyrants of Pherae, Lycophron and Peitholaus, recognized their position, and came to terms with Philip, handing over the city to him in return for a safe retreat for themselves and their mercenaries.[1]

Pagasae, however, did resist still, though briefly. It was another of the places (Demosthenes could say later) which the Athenians might have saved if they had acted more promptly.[2] The geographical situation of Pherae and Pagasae was like that of Argos and Nauplia: they were nearly 10 miles apart.[3] Pagasae itself was a very considerable city to invest, with a circumference greater than that of the walls of Athens before the building of the Long Walls.[4] This modern work of fortification was almost certainly that of Alexander of Pherae.[5] It enclosed an area partly unoccupied by buildings, doubtless in order to use topographical advantages given by low hills as well as by the Kastro-Acropolis on its north-eastern salient, though this scheme did include also some obvious weak places where the wall crossed valleys or depressions between the hills. For the besieged now help from Phocis was out of the question. But with an Athenian squadron in the area, supplies by sea were not in danger; and, given time, a reinforcement from Athens could probably be expected. Nevertheless Pagasae fell, whether by assault or by treachery (or by a combination) we do not know. Though the Thessalian League forces no doubt will have co-operated in the siege, Philip kept the place in his own hands for the time being, and doubtless installed a garrison.[6] If it was now, as seems probable (above, p. 220) that he was elected *archon* by the Thessalian League, there were things to be done in Thessaly.[7]

To take advantage of being popular abroad was not an opportunity of every day, and Philip is not likely to have wasted it. It certainly seems most probable that this summer witnessed his 'marriage' to Nikesipolis of Pherae, a beauty and a niece of Jason. No doubt it was much easier for Philip to be magnanimous to Pherae than for the Thessalians of the League, but in making this gesture of reconciliation Philip was doing his best for the future of Thessaly as well as for himself. Like the earlier marriage to Philinna of Larissa (p. 225), though it did not make the bride a queen, it cannot have been a mere association devoid of all honour

---

[1] D.S. 16. 37. 3; 38. 1.

[2] D. 1. 9. On the chronology, p. 224 above.

[3] Cf. Theopomp. F 53 (*FGrH* no. 115), ἐπίνειον Φεραίων.

[4] On the topography, see (briefly) Ernst Meyer, *RE* 18. 2 (1942) cols. 2299 ff. (with a Plan, ibid. 2287 ff.); and (fully) F. Stählin and Ernst Meyer, *Pagasai und Demetrias* (Berlin and Leipzig, 1934) 8 ff.

[5] Ernst Meyer, *RE* ibid. 2307.   [6] Below, p. 287.

[7] See below, pp. 285 ff.; cf. Sordi, *LT* 249 ff.

or status, since the daughter was evidently brought up at court, and eventually became queen herself, via her marriage to Cassander in 316.[1]

It may be (though it need not be) during this summer that the punitive acts against cities which had gone over to Onomarchus were carried out.[2] What is certain is that any operations of this sort must have been brief, because the League army was on the march again, with bigger things in view, long before the summer was over. 'After his defeat of Onomarchus in a great battle, when he had put an end to the tyranny at Pherae and had settled the affairs of Thessaly in general, he advanced on Thermopylae in order to attack the Phocians.'[3] Though Diodorus places this move in the archon-year following that in which Onomarchus had met his end (and no doubt rightly), there is no need to think of the two events as being separated by more than a few weeks; indeed there is some need not to, in view of all that this autumn has in store for Philip still. In this interval, whatever its length, Phayllus the Phocian general had hired more mercenaries, besides receiving the reinforcements from abroad already mentioned, and had invaded Boeotia, where the Boeotians defeated him in three engagements.[4] The most likely reconstruction of what follows would seem to be that now the Boeotians called on the Thessalians and on Philip to join them in carrying the war into Phocis, or at least in liberating the Boeotian cities still in Phocian hands.[5] It would be surprising indeed if the two principal military powers of the Amphictyonic coalition were not in close rapport now that the chances of achieving something had been so signally improved by the great Thessalian victory. Topographically, the two powers were effectively divided by Phocis itself with its armies, and indeed they had never yet in this war, so far as we know, succeeded in joining forces for an attack. This was their best chance yet of gaining the upper hand.[6]

The upshot is well known. Philip marched on Thermopylae, beyond which either route into Boeotia would be open to him, and he found the pass held by a strong force including the Athenians under Nausicles and others of the Phocian allies.[7] Philip came, saw, and retired; one of

---

[1] Satyrus, *FHG* 161. 5 *ap.* Athen. 13. 557 d. Cf. Beloch 3². 2. 69 on the marriage, and St. Byz. s.v. Θεσσαλονίκη on Nikesipolis (and her daughter). For polygamy see p. 153 above.

[2] See above, pp. 269 ff.   [3] D.S. 16. 38. 1.   [4] D.S. 16. 37.

[5] Schol. D. 6. 13.

[6] The presence in Thessaly of the hostile Pherae had prevented the Thessalians from campaigning abroad except for the one occasion in 354. But also, the main road north–south from Thessaly into Boeotia ran right through eastern Phocis (at Elatea). The much longer coast road through the territory of the friendly (when free) eastern Locrians was presumably not safe to use while the Phocians still had a great army which could defeat either Thessalians or Boeotians separately. In this summer their ability to do this became doubtful.

[7] D.S. 16. 38. 1; cf. 37. 3 (1,000 Spartans were sent, and 2,000 Achaeans, and 5,000 Athenian infantry with 400 cavalry). Only the Athenians are actually named at Thermopylae (by D.S. 37. 3; Just. 8. 2. 8; D. 19. 319): it is possible that only the Athenians had arrived in time, as Cawkwell suggests (*CQ* 12 (1962) 138).

the entertaining decisions of his life. In interpreting it, we are hampered, on the purely military plane, by not knowing exactly the strength of the forces concerned. If, for example, Philip's army was really greatly superior, we are probably safe in explaining his decision on mainly political grounds.[1] Whether any weight should be given to a reluctance on Philip's part to become involved in war with new enemies from the Peloponnese, especially with Sparta, seems very doubtful. Though the Athenian force here was sent no doubt mainly because the Athenians realized that a penetration by Philip into Central Greece could be a very dangerous thing for them, the Spartan and Achaean motives will have been concerned primarily not with Philip at all but with Boeotia: a determination that Thebes should not end the Sacred War and so become free to operate in strength in the Peloponnese once more. But though Philip and Sparta had no quarrel as yet, there was no need really for Philip to let a great opportunity go in order to avoid a quarrel, and it must remain very doubtful whether the presence of Spartan troops as such at Thermopylae can have had much influence on his decision not to attack. The decision was based probably on more practical considerations. In those conditions (assuming a great superiority) he could have found a passage if he were prepared to take some risks, but he preferred not to, presumably because he did not greatly care whether the Sacred War ended now or later: 'Wear both sides down', the advice of one unscrupulous man to another in 411, was good advice for a patient man to give to himself when he felt sure that time was on his side.[2]

In this decision considerations of prestige came in too, no doubt; but they did not prevail. And in practical terms the prime losers by the decision were neither Philip himself nor his friends in Thessaly but the Boeotians, disappointed now of a quick end to this war and its burdens. Thessaly itself, now reunited, had nothing more to fear from the Phocians and could afford to wait for their overthrow. Finally the check at Thermopylae need never have happened, presumably, if Philip had followed up the great victory immediately or with only brief delay. At that time he had chosen to settle first with Pherae, then Pagasae. It was in these weeks, most probably, that the whole future of Thessaly was decided, with his election as *archon* of the Thessalian League. In these great events the Phocians took second place. The march on Thermopylae was delayed. And when he did march, and found the Athenians holding the

---

[1] 10,000 men may be reckoned a maximum figure for the allied forces at Thermopylae (see previous note). Philip's 'more than 20,000 infantry and 3,000 cavalry' of the Crocus Plain battle (D.S. 16. 35. 4) presumably were still available (though Phocis, the objective, was no country for cavalry). A 2 : 1 superiority gave him the margin for the taking of risks, perhaps by dividing his army and invading by the mountain route exploited by Xerxes. It was these or other risks that he refused when he withdrew.

[2] Thuc. 8. 56. 2.

pass, he accepted the situation. Thermopylae would not run away. It was the Athenians and their friends who would not be there always. As for the Phocians, even the treasures of Delphi were not inexhaustible, and the Phocians next year, some year soon, would be weaker than they were now.[1]

Meanwhile for most people the 'year' was drawing to an end. The Olympic Truce was proclaimed; the Athenians under Nausicles went back home. For everyone in Greece except some mercenaries of the Phocians and some few Boeotians, campaigning was over till next year. Philip for his part returned to his own country, and no doubt did whatever was necessary there. But he had not finished for the year. A new levy of Macedonians was called out now (this seems likely, though we are not told it), and the new assignment lay to the east.

4. *Thrace again: the autumn campaign of 352*

The advantage which Philip held over many of his adversaries in the concentration in his own headpiece of all responsibility for making decisions was noticed by Demosthenes, and it was a very real one.[2] This year exemplifies it well. While he was in Thessaly exploiting the great victory, some news (we do not know what) reached him from Thrace; he was needed there also. The need was not so great (we may presume) to make him forgo the opportunity of entering Central Greece and co-operating with the Boeotians to end finally the Phocian resistance. But when he found Thermopylae held and barred, the Thracian news may have helped him to make his decision without hesitation, and his own temperament, not given to procrastination and not shrinking from more long days in the saddle, impelled him to start now on the 300-mile journey to the eastern extremity of his kingdom.

Our only clue to what may have been happening in Thrace since the spring of the year before seems to be the fragment of Theopompus which alludes to a victory by the Athenian general Chares over mercenaries of Philip commanded by Adaeus ('the Cock').[3] The victory was celebrated in Athens by a public feast at Chares' expense, out of money from Delphi given to him by Onomarchus. Since Onomarchus did not begin to use the temple treasure till late 354 and died in early summer 352, and since Chares is known to have commanded a force at Neapolis in spring 353 (p. 265), it seems right to think that his victory was won in that summer, after Philip himself had retired from this front and gone to

---

[1] As to what made the Athenians decide to send the hoplites to Thermopylae, we are in ignorance. A relief force to Pagasae may have been discussed, even decided. But news that Philip virtually controlled all Thessaly, if it came now, will have opened their eyes to the prospect of his advancing on Phocis, to say nothing of the danger to Euboea and Attica.

[2] D. 1. 4.   [3] Theopomp. *FGrH* no. 115 F 249.

Thessaly. Though the scene of the battle is not named, the proximity to Neapolis of Crenides, and its great importance to Philip, encourage one to think that Chares may have been applying some pressure to this sensitive spot. Adaeus may have been the general in command of its garrison, which for the same reasons must have been a strong one; but not strong enough, evidently, (if this reconstruction is sound) to beat Chares in the field. The consequences were not disastrous, for inevitably we must have heard of it if Crenides had even been besieged by an Athenian force. But the success ought to have encouraged Amadocus in his loyalty to Athens and hostility to Philip (p. 265), which may have expressed itself in attacks on Cetriporis in the period (late summer 353 and early summer 352) when Philip was fully engaged in Thessaly. In 352, also, Cersobleptes, who had co-operated with Philip and Pammenes the previous spring (p. 265), was intimidated by the Athenian capture and recolonization of Sestus in the Chersonese, and perhaps too by a realization that he had much to fear from Philip, into renewing his friendship and alliance with Athens; with the optimistic undertaking that he would help her to recover Amphipolis.[1] We do not know just what acts of either or both of the Thracian princes produced from Philip the drastic reaction of a Thracian campaign in the autumn of 352 on top of the Thessalian exertions. But we can see that the general situation in Thrace, with its bearing on the precious Crenides, needed his attention: and Philip judged there was no time like the present.

The details, again, of what followed escape us almost entirely. Philip's operations, what we hear of them, were directed not against Amadocus but against Cersobleptes who, unable to expand now at the expense of Athens, had perhaps committed acts of aggression against the Greek cities Byzantium and Perinthus and also against Amadocus himself. At all events now, if a scholiast on Aeschines is to be believed, he was engaged in a war with these three opponents 'about disputed territory', a war in which Philip intervened with decisive effect.[2] The change in the relations of Philip and Amadocus here seems startling by any standards. Since we learn that there were two kings Amadocus, father and son, and that the son did 'go to fight as Philip's ally in the war against Cersobleptes',[3] it seems possible that the father, who had resisted

---

[1] D. 23. 14. D.S. 16. 34. 3 records the Athenian recovery of Sestus in the year 353/2, and *IG* ii². 1613, 297 shows that Athenian cleruchs have already been sent to Sestus before midsummer 352.

[2] Schol. Aeschin. 2. 81.

[3] Harpokrat. s.v. *Amadocus* (= Theopomp. F 101), δύο γεγόνασι οὗτοι, πατὴρ καὶ υἱός, ὃς καὶ Φιλίππῳ συμμαχήσων ἦλθεν εἰς τὸν πρὸς Κερσοβλέπτην πόλεμον. It may be thought that the lexicographer's comment does not accord particularly well with the scholiast's record (see previous note) of a war against Cersobleptes in which it was Philip who joined as the newcomer; and it is always possible that the comment refers to the later war, of 347/6. If so, and if it was Amadocus *père* with whom Philip co-operated in 352, how they had made

Philip staunchly eighteen months earlier, either had died in the interval, or even was attacked and deposed now by Philip and replaced by his son, who became his ally and vassal.[1] The new alliance paid a quick dividend, both to Amadocus and to the Greek cities. This war ended with Cersobleptes compelled to relinquish the disputed lands.[2] But of the military means and measures by which Philip brought this about we know no details. We know only that in November he was besieging Heraion Teichos,[3] on or near the coast of the Sea of Marmora, and not very far from the Chersonese itself.

Philip had struck deep into this Thracian kingdom, and the blow brought Cersobleptes to his knees. He obtained peace from Philip now, but on hard terms. Not only the territories in dispute were to be ceded, but also his own liberty of action. He became Philip's vassal, a subject ally paying tribute: this seems a safe inference from our information that his son was taken as a hostage to Macedonia (where he was encountered by Aeschines and the other Athenian ambassadors nearly six years later).[4] But in this campaign Cersobleptes was not the only possible objective; indeed it could be suggested that he was not even the principal one. He was the ally of Athens, and now was being forcibly detached from that alliance, a development damaging to the Athenians. Moreover Philip's control of this Thracian kingdom from henceforward, and even more his personal and immediate presence with an army at Heraion Teichos, was a direct threat to the security of the sea route which was a vital interest to them because so much of their food supply passed through it.[5] The Athenians reacted to the news of Heraion Teichos in a way which leaves no room for doubt that they were alarmed by it.

You remember, about three years ago now, when Philip in Thrace was reported to be besieging Heraion Teichos. That was in the month of November and the Assembly met, many speeches were made, and there was great excitement. You voted a decree to launch forty triremes: citizens up to the age of forty-five were to man them: a war tax of 60 talents was declared.[6]

This was a crisis. It was not for fun or from pique that the Athenians (or anybody else) launched triremes in November, for the long haul to

---

peace and become allies must remain unknown. Presumably it would be best explained by the Athenian *rapprochement* to Cersobleptes (D. 23, *passim*), which could have left Amadocus, distrusting Cersobleptes, isolated and aggrieved, and even with no choice but to make his peace with Philip. Demosthenes (23) however, knows nothing of this in the speech, delivered probably in 352 but certainly before the autumn when this campaign was on. See also next note, however.

[1] This possibility is strengthened by D. 1. 13, alluding very briefly to this campaign: μετὰ ταῦτα . . . ᾤχετ᾽ εἰς Θρᾴκην· εἶτ᾽ ἐκεῖ τοὺς μὲν ἐκβαλὼν τοὺς δὲ καταστήσας τῶν βασιλέων ἠσθένησε.

[2] Schol. Aeschin. 2. 81. [3] D. 3. 4 f. [4] Aeschin. 2. 81 and Schol.
[5] D. 20. 31 ff.; cf. Tod 167 lines 12 ff. [6] D. 3. 4.

the inhospitable north-east. It seems established that in the years since 355 the *demos* was relying for its advice on foreign policy mainly on Eubulus and his group, who worked for financial and economic recovery, and who had a realistic estimate of what proportion of their resources the latter-day Athenians were prepared to spend on wars abroad. These resources they conserved for the really essential operations. Two of them had been mounted with success in the past year, the recovery of Sestus and the defence of Thermopylae. The relief of Heraion Teichos, or more probably the reinforcement of the Athenian position in the Chersonese against an expected attack now, was a third.

In the event the Athenian triremes never sailed. Philip was reported now ill (which was true), now dead (which was not).[1] From what follows, or more properly speaking from the fact that nothing follows, we must infer that Philip did really fall ill,[2] so ill probably that he was obliged to break off and leave this campaign unfinished, impose his terms on Cersobleptes, and go home to winter and recover. It was not till about nine months later (August–September 351) that the Athenians did send ten ships, and in the meantime no more is heard of Philip in this theatre of war.[3] This interruption of his plan of operations in 352 leaves us inevitably in the dark as to what the plan really had been, and in particular, how far he was intending a real offensive against Athens herself. His march on Thermopylae could be interpreted as that (Eubulus and his friends did so interpret it); but its aim could have been confined to the immediate task of settling with the Phocians. So, too, with this campaign in Thrace. The immediate objective was Cersobleptes; but was there an ulterior design on the Chersonese now? Was it, even, in the nature of a deliberate retort to the Athenian defence of Thermopylae, a spectacular demonstration of how the interior lines enabled him to change direction at will and still threaten the worst? The only answer to this (and that inconclusive, obviously) is one based on Philip's actions in the years that immediately follow. He did not return to Heraion Teichos or the vicinity, so far as we know, for five years after this. Although he remained at war with the Athenians till 346, he was not concerned evidently to squeeze them by threatening the Chersonese again, and this though his successes of 352 had laid a good foundation. It was from now, we may presume, that his alliance dated with Cardia, on the neck of the Chersonese and an old enemy of Athens. Byzantium and Perinthus had become his allies too (p. 282).[4] The material was here for making the Athenian corn-route exceedingly insecure, if Philip had chosen to con-

---

[1] D. 3. 5. [2] So D. 1. 13.

[3] D. 3. 5. I am not convinced by J. R. Ellis's interpretation (*REG* 79 (1966) 636–9) which sees Philip's illness as having occurred not in November 352 but in August 351, giving him a year or more in Thrace for this campaign instead of three or four months only.

[4] D. 18. 183, for hostility of Cardia to Athens in 352.

centrate on it. Instead, his preoccupations in these next few years were to lie elsewhere.

5. *The first settlement in Thessaly: 352 and the years after*

The acquisition of Thessaly was one of the decisive steps of Philip's career, and I have sought to show that it was in 352 that he actually became titular head of the Thessalian League. In the present state of the evidence it seems probable that there will always be some who remain unconvinced about this, preferring to think of the years 344–342 as the time when he obtained the title as well as a *de facto* control. However that may be, it is important not to be in doubt that the *de facto* control does date from 352.

The most important evidence for this is the information from Demosthenes (speaking in 349) about the taxes from harbours and markets.[1] When discussing it above (p. 222) I left open the question whether or not the information was true. But it is confirmed by Justin that control over taxation was among the powers conferred on Philip *at some time* as 'leader' of Thessaly,[2] and there is no real reason to doubt Demosthenes when he said in 349 that this had already been done. Justin confirms also that in the years after 352 Philip acted in Thessaly very much as the man in control. In a passage of hectic rhetorical colouring he outlines how Philip attacked, seized, and destroyed cities which quite recently (*paulo ante*) had fought victoriously under his own auspices as general.[3] It has been suggested, and probably rightly, that this presentation derives ultimately from Theopompus, who did undoubtedly know the facts exactly—and who combined the industry and devotion of the first-rate historian with the flair of the second-rate journalist for misrepresentation by hyperbole.[4] We do not know in what terms exactly Theopompus described or commented on Philip's treatment of his Thessalian allies, and we are not entitled to apply an extravagant generalization, of which Polybius complained, to this particular Thessalian situation especially.[5] We are entitled to conclude, however, that Justin's picture is grossly overdrawn, whether the fault goes back to Theopompus or whether it was supplied mainly by Pompeius Trogus (or by Justin himself). The evidence of two other contemporaries does not support it.

[1] D. 1. 22.

[2] Just. 11. 3. 2 (writing of Alexander): 'Cupide haec Thessalis audientibus exemplo patris dux universae gentis creatus est et vestigalia omnia reditusque suos ei tradiderant.'

[3] Id. 8. 3. 1.

[4] e.g. Theopomp. F 27 (on Philip's personal vices); 224–5 (on the Companions); 99–100 (on Eubulus and Athens).

[5] Id. F 27, ap. Plb. 8. 1. 1 ff. ἀδικώτατον δὲ καὶ κακοπραγμονέστατον περὶ τὰς τῶν φίλων καὶ συμμάχων κατασκευάς, πλείστας δὲ πόλεις ἐξηνδραποδισμένον καὶ πεπραξικοπηκότα μετὰ δόλου καὶ βίας . . .

Isocrates, though he was anxious to commend himself to Philip when he wrote in 346, would have been making himself ridiculous by the glowing terms in which he referred to Philip's relations with the Thessalians, if in reality his taking over control in Thessaly had been signalized by a blood-bath in which a number of the cities had been destroyed.[1] Demosthenes, writing in 349 and wanting to make the most of Philip's difficulties in Thessaly then, knew (he said) of disputes about taxes and about the possession of places, but he knew nothing of a major and scandalous double-crossing by Philip of his Thessalian allies ending in the destruction of cities.[2] The silence of Demosthenes here does seem to make it quite certain that no such things had happened in the years 352-349. Indeed the silence of Demosthenes on this topic through all the years of his exhaustive criticism of Philip's behaviour in every walk of life seems to make it certain that no such thing ever did happen in Thessaly. This view is supported also by the source or sources summarized by Polyaenus in his *Stratagem* 'How Philip won Thessaly': 'in victory he did not destroy the cities of the vanquished, nor disarm them, nor dismantle their walls. . . .'[3] Philip's 'control', in and after 352, though it was real enough, needs to be stated in more sober terms.

We have seen already that certain cities of Hestiaeotis, as well as Crannon close to Larissa, probably defected from the Thessalian League in 353 under pressure of the Phocian victories. Pharcedon and Trikka, we know, were punished for something at some time, though we are never told the cause or the date. It seems probable (though incapable of proof) that the occasion was the recovery of Hestiaeotis after the Phocian defeat of 352, and that this punishment of the two cities forms the basis for the sensational account of Philip in Thessaly which survives in Justin. These two places, it seems, were destroyed, whether now or later.[4] What happened to Pelinna, which also probably had gone over to the enemy, is not known.[5] Crannon, another probable delinquent, survived, like the principal delinquent Pherae (both had been under tyrants, and hence not responsible).[6] The small city of Gomphi in Hestiaeotis assumes about this time the name Philippopolis:[7] this argues some reorganization in this region, and perhaps some transfer of population, but it can hardly be included among the punishments. In short, so far as we know, the punishments were few in number and the victims

---

[1] Isoc. 5. 20: see above, p. 223 and n. 3, where I have given reasons for believing that the following sentence—τῶν δὲ πόλεων τῶν περὶ τὸν τόπον ἐκεῖνον τὰς μὲν ταῖς εὐεργεσίαις πρὸς τὴν αὑτοῦ συμμαχίαν προσῆκται, τὰς δὲ σφόδρα λυπούσας αὐτὸν ἀναστάτους πεποίηκεν—refers not to Thessaly but to the Greek cities of Macedonia, Chalcidice, and Thrace.

[2] D. 1. 22.   [3] Polyaen. 4. 2. 19.

[4] D.S. 18. 56. 5; Polyaen. 4. 2. 18. Cf. Sordi, *LT* 255 and n. 5 however, for reservations in the case of Trikka (based on *Syll.*³ 250 D 46).

[5] See above, p. 270.   [6] Cf. Sordi, loc. cit.

[7] Steph. Byz. s.v. Philippi; West, *NC* (1923) 176; Head 294 f.

small: and above all they were done, we must presume, by the vote and
with the approbation of the Thessalian League cities themselves.[1] Where
free institutions are operating (as here) under the shadow of a superior
military power, inevitably the doubt arises as to how 'free' we are to
think of them as being at this moment. Yet Demosthenes knew of no
recriminations on this score when he spoke about Thessaly in 349.

What the Thessalians did complain about then (apart from the taxes)
was that Philip still occupied Pagasae, and also parts of Magnesia,
where he had either built some forts or was known to be intending to
build them.[2] The acquisitions of Philip had their origin in the war
against Pherae. Pagasae he had taken by siege, and though Thessalian
troops probably did assist at the taking, it was primarily a Macedonian
feat of arms; and we may guess that it never crossed Philip's mind not to
treat it as his own possession. For Thessalians in general, once the war
was over, Pagasae was a problem: for though the unpopular Pherae was
the first and obvious loser by Philip's retaining it, no Thessalians could
be unaware of the implications of a Macedonian garrison permanently
occupying this important place. Demosthenes may well have been
reporting accurately, that in the years after 352 this question was raised
in the Councils of the League, and that Philip was asked to surrender it.
He never did surrender it, so far as we know, and we may believe that
neither his friends nor his enemies in Thessaly can have been surprised.

Magnesia, too, can be thought of as part of the spoils of the war
against Pherae. If (as seemed likely) the Magnetes in 354 had acted
independently of Pherae in declaring war on the Phocians,[3] it seems very
probable that the victories of Onomarchus in 353 enabled the tyrants of
Pherae to reassert control over the Magnetes. In 352 the tyrants made
their capitulation to Philip personally.[4] Whether by this time he had
already been elected head of the League, we do not know. If he had not,
then his claim to occupy Magnesia (if he could) will not have been
materially different from his claim to occupy Pagasae. He had 'won it by
the spear', and he might well have claimed it as part of the terms on
which the tyrants were allowed to leave Pherae with their troops. If
however he was already head of the League when the tyrants capitulated,
his claim to take control of Magnesia (or of any other of the *perioikoi*
allies) obviously was not so simple; though clearly any complexity in
this situation was not a novelty, or peculiar to Philip as leader, but must
have been experienced by all previous *tagoi* or leaders in the same way.

This question we will return to presently. In practice now, Philip did
undoubtedly assume control of Magnesia or part of it, and though we
do not hear of this (from Demosthenes) till 349, presumably it dates

---

[1] This point is well made by Sordi, *LT* 254.   [2] D. 1. 22; cf. 2. 11.
[3] See above, p. 229 n. 3.   [4] D. 16. 38. 1.

back to 352. In the same way the Perrhaebi, the *perioikoi* of the northern frontier region of Thessaly, began to be administered by an agent appointed by Philip. This appointment of Agathocles, mentioned by Theopompus in his 9th book, ought to belong therefore to the year 352, though this dating cannot be regarded as certain (and indeed it raises difficulties for Philip's relations with Larissa at this time—below, p. 292).[1] But certainly this control by Philip of Perrhaebia does come, and fairly soon, since Isocrates in 346 wrote of the Magnetes, Perrhaebians, and Paeonians as being his subjects (ὑπήκοοι).[2] For the other peoples traditionally *perioikoi* and subjects of the Thessalians there is no evidence at this time.

Though we hear that Philip made important changes in the institutions and administration of Thessaly later (344–342), we hear of no such changes now, and on the whole it seems right to think that this is not due merely to our lack of information in general. Not only does the silence of Demosthenes count for something here (innovations would have made good grounds of complaint when he alluded to these matters in the *First* and *Second Olynthiacs*), but both Isocrates and Polyaenus describe his early rule in Thessaly in terms suggesting that he took trouble not to give grounds of complaint but to make himself agreeable. The Isocrates allusion has been considered above (pp. 223, 286). Polyaenus, in his 'How Philip won Thessaly' stratagem, after describing his entry by accepting invitations from cities engaged in their civil war, and his clemency to the vanquished (above, p. 286), goes on: 'their class war in the cities he encouraged rather than ended, he supported the weak and put down the strong, he was the friend of the populace in the cities, and he cultivated their leaders. It was by these stratagems that Philip won Thessaly, not by arms.'[3] The impression is of a diplomatist and politician talking to the city politicians in their own language. Like Jason the last *tagos* before him, Philip would never have been elected *archon* without the power of his army behind him; but also like Jason he meant to rule by consent.[4] His early years in power, we may suppose, produced nothing to shock Thessalian susceptibilities. The *tagos* of more recent times had been an elected officer for life, and with no hereditary succession.[5] Though Alexander sixteen years later claimed the succession as of right (τὴν πατροπαράδοτον ἡγεμονίαν),[6] it seems safe to think that in 352 nothing

---

[1] Theopomp. F 81.   [2] Isoc. 5. 20 f.   [3] Polyaen. 4. 2. 19.

[4] For Jason, X. *HG* 6. 1. 7. Rather surprisingly, Philip's title as head of the Thessalian League is uncertain. In the Athenian document of 361 (Tod, *GHI* 147. 23 and 34) Agelaus is described as *archon*, no doubt correctly. If *archon* here is an innovation designed to open a new chapter after the *tagia* recently associated with Pherae, it seems unlikely that Philip having defeated Pherae would revive the title *tagos*. Probably he became *archon*. (*Contra*, Sordi *LT* 335–6.)

[5] Sordi, *LT* 336.   [6] D.S. 17. 4. 1.

was said or done about this; Philip was merely elected for life like his immediate predecessors in the office. The election of a *tagos* was the sign of Thessaly united, and his first function was to keep it so: the weakness of the reconstructed League of 369 had been that the central government (without a *tagos*) could not retain the co-operation of Pherae in particular. The individual cities were autonomous; but their foreign policy was decided in common by the central Assembly or Council of the League. These decisions, when they led to wars, were to be supported by the cities[1] which each supplied its quota of the League's forces in the field, under the command of the *archon* when there was one. These forces needed to be fed and paid, and this meant taxation. The man who was powerful enough to be elected *archon* by the cities was powerful enough to ensure that the central government took a share of the taxation of the country sufficient for him to carry out the policies decided. This would seem to be, in essence, the practical thing which Philip was required to manage in his early years as head of the League: we have noticed already glimpses of his managing it, and of some Thessalian reactions.[1]

The financial resources of Thessaly came from two sources, (1) the taxes levied by the cities on their own citizens and residents and on foreigners trading into their harbours and markets; (2) tribute (*phoros*) levied on neighbouring peoples (*perioikoi*). Whether it was laid down by law or custom that a *tagos* (*archon*) had a claim on certain taxes, or on a proportion of some taxes or all, we have no means of knowing. We can be certain however that every *archon* needed money, and we may suspect that what money he got from taxation depended partly on the needs of the time and even more on his own power and prestige.

We hear of only two regular taxes raised by cities in Thessaly, and though it is unlikely that they were the only two (taxes on *metoikoi*, on slaves, or on manumissions are others that come to mind), it would be surprising if these were not the two most important ones, bringing in most of the regular annual income. The one was the tax on turnover in harbours and markets, which has been noticed already. The other was a tithe (*dekatē*), alluded to (at Crannon) as if it were a regular thing needing no explanation:[2] a 10 per cent tax on produce of the land, and though we hear of it at Crannon only, and that by chance, it is probably right to think of it as regular in all these cities. The land must have been by far the most important source of wealth in Thessaly, and this *dekatē*, a tax on income, was the alternative to an *eisphora*, a tax on capital raised occasionally and not (ideally) every year, such as we see it at Athens. To compare Thessaly with what we know of Athens is natural,

---

[1] See above, pp. 222 f., 285 f.
[2] Polyaen. 2. 34 (τῆς δὲ πόλεως τὴν τοῦ σίτου δεκάτην ἀπομισθούσης ... etc.).

but one needs to expect some differences. The economy of Athens was more varied, and the income from indirect taxes, especially from the import and export dues at the Piraeus, will far have exceeded what could be expected from Pagasae or from the harbours and markets of all Thessaly. (It was thus that the Athenians could forgo a regular income tax on land produce, and rely instead on the occasional *eisphora* levied on capital in whatever form.) When we are told, then, (and there is no reason to doubt it) that the Thessalians had voted to make over to Philip the taxes from their harbours and markets, we should think of this probably as being a significant sum, but by no means the major part of the annual income of the cities: what proportion of the total one can only guess, but probably it was very much less than half, and perhaps less than a quarter. It may not be right, either, to think of this as an automatic prerogative of every *tagos* (*archon*). It may have been a war measure, for the duration of the Phocian War, since a year or two later (if Demosthenes is telling the truth) they could find some cause for complaint about how it was being spent[1]—and, as it happened, in those intervening years (late 352 to 349) Philip so far as we know had not exerted himself in any way in the Phocian War. The fact that Alexander in 336 could have the right of levying taxes conferred on him as part of his powers in Thessaly is not necessarily a sure guide to the rights of Philip in 352. Philip (we can see) had strengthened his position and tightened his hold in the interim,[2] and Alexander had the benefit of that.

More substantial, it would seem, than the proceeds from the harbour and market taxation of Thessaly was the *phoros* which could be levied from the *perioikoi*. This appears clearly in the information about Jason in Xenophon. Not only was the amount, when at its greatest, very considerable, but it took a *tagos* to bring it to its greatest, with an implication almost of 'no *tagos*, no *phoros*'.[3] It would be wrong, most probably, to suppose any legal or constitutional basis for this, e.g. that the right of levying this *phoros* was peculiar to the office of *tagos*. This was a practical matter, not a matter of law; a question of what was possible. A *tagos* mobilizing the whole strength of Thessaly could impose his will on the *perioikoi*. In time of *atagia*, the individual cities, and even the *koinon* of the Thessalian League, lacked this power or possessed it only intermittently, for reasons easy to supply. Sometimes the cities were actually fighting each other, and even when they were not it must have been always difficult to achieve unity of decision and action from the *koinon*, when the effect of coercing this or that particular *ethnos* of the *perioikoi*

---

[1] D. 1. 22 τὰ γὰρ κοινὰ τὰ Θετταλῶν ἀπὸ τούτων δέοι διοικεῖν, οὐ Φίλιππον λαμβάνειν.

[2] See below, pp. 541 ff.

[3] X. *HG* 6. 1. 12 πάντα γὰρ δήπου τὰ κύκλῳ φόρον φέρει, ὅταν ταγεύηται τὰ κατὰ Θετταλίαν. Cf. 6. 1. 8 for the same condition (ὅταν ταγεύηται Θετταλία) applied to the military resources.

was going to benefit this or that individual city rather than the others. For there seems no doubt that, historically, the subject status of *perioikoi* had often been in relation to an individual city and not to the League as a whole.[1] The strong cities had made subjects, whenever they could, of those *perioikoi* whom they could most easily lay their hands on.

Thus, the Magnetes were normally subject to Pherae, though the relationship was not immutable as we have seen.[2] The Perrhaebi were traditionally subject to Larissa, and the Phthiotic Achaeans probably to Pharsalus.[3] This goes far back, perhaps to the sixth century, and Sordi (p. 343) even advanced a theory that in some way the situation was juridically regular and satisfactory, as between the individual cities and the Thessalian League, if the cities took the tribute while recognizing that the subject Perioeci were subject not to them but to the League: 'only when a city asserted absolute sovereignty over one of the *perioikoi* peoples, as Pherae did with Magnesia under the tyranny of the sons of Jason, then the League protested officially and complained of the usurpation.' Though this cannot be disproved, it can be said that, if it was really so, the Thessalians must have been a race of men unlike any other we have heard of, if they were content that tribute money which legally was due to the *koinon* (from subjects who were subjects of the *koinon*) should be appropriated by Larissa or Pherae or Pharsalus, thereby increasing the financial burden of those member cities who were not so fortunate as to receive tribute payments from any *perioikoi*. I am not disputing that Larissa and the others did so appropriate it, and by very ancient custom, but I question whether the issue of sovereignty can be separated from the receiving of the tribute. For the *perioikoi*, I suggest, where their treasure went, there went their oath of loyalty also.

Such a situation was too serious to be settled by lawyers, even if there had been any: it affected the pockets of every tax-paying citizen in Thessaly, and perhaps it helps to account for the endemic absence of peace and stability in the country, except when they could be imposed by a *tagos*. A *tagos* was only acceptable, one supposes, to the cities other than that which had produced him, because he could promise peace instead of civil war. If electing a *tagos* meant, for Larissa, automatically surrendering to him (representing the *koinon*) her sovereignty over the Perrhaebi, it is even less surprising that *tagoi* had been comparatively few and far between. More likely this question of the *perioikoi* (or these questions, since there could be several, involving several cities and their subject peoples) was resolved by the individual *tagos* as a matter of practical politics rather than of constitutional law. Every *tagos* was strong by definition

---

[1] Cf. Sordi, *LT* 340 ff.   [2] Above, p. 229 n. 1.

[3] Perrhaebi, Str. 9. 5. 19 (440); Arist. *Pol.* 2. 6. 3. 1269; cf. Sordi, *LT* 340 ff. Phthiotic Achaeans, Arist., ibid.; Sordi, *LT* 340 ff. and 362 f.; and references at p. 292 n. 4 below.

(or he would never have been elected). But not every *tagos* need always have felt himself strong enough to assert that all the *perioikoi* were subjects of the *koinon* and henceforward must pay their *phoros* to him and not to Larissa or Pharsalus. That Jason did this ultimately can be taken as certain (this is implicit in all Xenophon's account of his resources[1]—and how else could he pay a standing army of 6,000 mercenaries, costing at least 400 talents a year?). But Jason was the strongest *tagos* there had ever been. For Philip taking up office in 352 it was, most likely, a matter not of issuing a ukase about the *perioikoi* and their overlords, but of considering cases.

The Magnetes (as we saw) presented no problem. He had received the capitulation of the tyrants of Pherae personally, and no doubt considered himself entitled to dispose of the Magnetes as his personal possession now. The complaint of the Thessalians about Magnesia, mentioned by Demosthenes, does not refer to its ownership, but the use that it was being put to.[2] Some Thessalians in the *koinon* were able to carry a vote that the *archon* should not build forts there. To all Thessalians it may have seemed an improper thing for a *tagos* (*archon*) to do; but we do not know the rights and wrongs of this matter. More difficult is (perhaps *was*) the case of the Perrhaebi, who according to Isocrates had become Philip's subjects by 346.[3] The Perrhaebi were normally subjects of Larissa, and Larissa had been the city through which, or through his noble friends there, he had levered his way into Thessaly. To suppose that he simply forced Larissa, presumably by a vote of the *koinon*, to surrender her rights over the Perrhaebi to him, is to suppose that he presented the Larissaeans thus early with a moment of truth, which would not be lost on the rest of Thessaly. An alternative is, that in the wars and disorders of 354–352 the Perrhaebi had succeeded in freeing themselves from Larissa, and that Philip now reduced them to subjection, and made them tributary to himself. This would not be popular in Larissa, but at least it would be something which people could understand and accept if they had to, without regarding the new *archon* as positively treacherous or tyrannical.

Finally, (to look forward) the Phthiotic Achaeans, subject to Pharsalus. In 346 their city of Halus was in revolt. Philip not only reduced Halus by siege to subjection (delegating the command to Parmenion), but restored it when taken to Pharsalus.[4] This in 346, when he was at the height of his glory with the Phocian War concluded and the peace with Athens made. This incident underlines painfully our ignorance of what went on in Thessaly, most of the time. It seems best to infer that Pharsalus earlier had succeeded in keeping her *perioikoi* of

[1] X. *HG* 6. 1. 19; cf. 6. 1. 9 and 12.   [2] D. 1. 22 (cf. 2. 11).   [3] Isoc. 5. 20.
[4] D. 19, 2 Hypoth. 7; ibid. 163 and 174; [D.] 11. 1; cf. Sordi, *LT* 362 f.

Achaea Phthiotis in subjection, or recovering them unaided in 352 if they had revolted. But the revolt of Halus in 346 obviously offered Philip the opportunity of taking over these *perioikoi* himself like the Perrhaebi and Magnetes, if he had cared to. Why he treated Pharsalus in 346 so much more favourably than he had treated Larissa in 352 or a little later, we do not know.

Philip's new responsibilities in Thessaly as *archon* were no small matter, indeed we shall probably be right to think of them as causing some appreciable change in the tempo of his whole life, and particularly in these first years after 352. Lamentably ill informed though we are on the institutions of the Thessalian League and their working, no one will doubt that there must have been at any rate one statutory meeting in Thessaly each year at which the principal business was the election of its annual officers. Most likely there were some few regular meetings of a Council of representatives as well.[1] And since by far the most important function of the League was to regulate the foreign policy of its members, including when necessary their relations with each other, extraordinary meetings of its Council could be expected, to meet the problems and crises of foreign affairs which seldom conform to any timetable that can be prearranged. To suppose that Philip can have taken these duties less than seriously, or as something that called for his presence only if he had nothing better to do, would be disastrous failure of interpretation, we may be almost sure.

Though to us Thessaly means perhaps less than it ought, to Philip it was the greatest single acquisition that he had made as yet, this land of a size, population, and productivity which, added to those of Macedonia, made up a power formidable beyond anything yet seen. To have achieved the election as *archon* was a mark of the impact made on the Thessalians by Philip's military prowess and political address, and presumably by the attractions of his personality in general. Now he was the hero of the hour. Yet all that he had heard of Thessaly before his own time, and all that he had seen himself of the Thessalians in their civil war just ended, must have warned him of the difficulties ahead. To control Thessaly and to keep on controlling it was nobody's parergon, least of all a foreigner's as *archon*.[2] His election to the office had been popular when it happened, no doubt. But either by an autocratic bearing, or by mere neglect if he became a habitual absentee, he could have devalued his status quickly in the eyes of the Thessalians into an unpopular foreign rule. To avoid this needed his presence and application, so as to know and be known in

---

[1] Sordi, *LT* 329 ff., for discussion of the *koinon*, with the tentative conclusion (with which I agree) that there was no primary Assembly, and no Council corresponding to the 500 at Athens, but a single Council of representatives from the cities.

[2] Cf. Isoc. *Epist.* 2. 20 (343 B.C.) on the difficult character of the Thessalians in general. (D. 1. 22 concurred.)

at any rate the leading cities of Thessaly. 'Make the men of influence in the cities your friends, both the good men and the knaves: then make use of these, and get rid of those.'[1] This saying, attributed by Plutarch to Philip without a context, could be given no more appropriate context than in Thessaly. This must have been the time above all others when (as Polyaenus described it) he 'encouraged their internal discords rather than put a stop to them, supported the weaker and put down the stronger, showed himself the friend of the populace in the cities and cultivated their leaders'.[2] This was getting to know and be known in Thessaly, and it took trouble and time. The years 351 and 350, more than any others in Philip's reign, seem to be years of inactivity, when (as we shall see) very little is known of his movements. It seems highly probable that Thessaly should be held partly accountable for this. Not to spend necessary time and trouble on this great acquisition would have been inexcusable.

When all is said and done, it seems right to recognize this election of Philip to the head of affairs in Thessaly as an event unique in Greek history, and very remarkable. The particularism of the Greek communities has been much emphasized by nearly all modern writers of all generations; but it has not been over-emphasized. The escalation of that admirable careerist Aratus of Sicyon seems to display everything that could be done by such a character, keeping to the normal Greek rules. (A 'foreigner' by birth, only becoming an Achaean when his city joined their League: then annually elected General as often as the rules permitted.) To go beyond this hitherto had been, merely, to become head of other people's cities by some form of conquest or autocracy. So, for example, the Syracusan tyrants, Gelon, Hieron, and the Dionysii: Gelon of Gela, if we knew more precisely how he became tyrant of Syracuse, would give perhaps the nearest approach to Philip's *tour de force* in Thessaly, in the sense that it looks as if Gelon must have made himself acceptable before the event to at any rate one class of the Syracusan citizens.

So Philip, one must suspect, commended himself in the first place to one class, an aristocracy, and perhaps, initially, in one city only (Larissa). It may have been they who in a sense talked him into power.[3] But power was not won, much less held, by talk. It was the political experience of

---

[1] Plu. *Mor.* 178 c (= *Apophthegm. Philippi* 17), οἷς μὲν χρῆσθαι οἷς δ' ἀποχρῆσθαι. Since ἀποχρῆσθαι c. dat. may mean either 'use to the full' or 'misuse', the sense of the epigram is elusive. My translation 'get rid of them' stands for 'misuse'. (So LSJ⁹ s.v. ἀποχράω B2, comparing Plu. *Comp. Alc. Cor.* 2, ἀποχρωμένων μᾶλλον ἢ χρωμένων αὐτῷ.) The alternative makes the speaker advise cynically 'Make use of the good ones and make full use of the knaves.' The alternative cannot be ruled out, I suppose.

[2] Polyaen. 4. 2. 19.

[3] So, it seems, Sordi, *LT* 258 ff. Cf. D. 18. 48, for Eudikos and Simus of Larissa, named among those Greeks who by their collaboration had aided Philip in an important way.

the Thessalian citizens (of all cities) in the past twenty years or more that made the thing feasible. First, the deep rift in Thessalian affairs occasioned by the tyrant house of Pherae: then the stresses and confusion brought to Thessaly by the Boeotian alliance against the Phocians, will have enabled aristocracies and middle classes alike, those who had something greater or smaller to lose, to appreciate that peace abroad and freedom from *stasis* among their own cities were worth almost any price that was within their means to pay. A Macedonian king of Heraclid descent was particularly acceptable perhaps to a few dozen high hats who still were in some cities the people who mattered most. But to the average Thessalian cavalryman or hoplite the conqueror of Onomarchus and the tamer of Pherae (their own commander moreover in both these exploits), since he seemed to be liked and trusted by the men at the top and to be one who was at home 'in the grand Thessalian style',[1] may have commanded now, we must think, a good deal of confidence both in his good faith and in his ability to preserve the country from foreign invasion; and (above all) to anticipate and prevent the inter-city *stasis* which had become endemic. In so far as the motive of this *stasis* had been the leadership of Thessaly, Philip as leader for life relegated this motive to a memory of things past. Pagasae, the *perioikoi*, taxes, rights, claims, and counterclaims might still (would still—for these were Greeks) fill the agenda of Thessalian League assemblies for the foreseeable future; but peace, the peace of the strong arm at home and abroad, was a fact of life which made the difference for the Thessalian thousands between an existence punctuated by miseries and one which became worth living. The Heraclid talked into power (if he was) by the handful of noble families would not have stayed in power so easily if the common man had not recognized his value to themselves.

[1] X. *HG* 6. 1. 3 (of Polydamas of Pharsalus), φιλόξενός τε καὶ μεγαλοπρεπὴς τὸν Θετταλικὸν τρόπον.

VIII

THE OLYNTHIAN WAR
(352-348)

1. *The Olynthian crisis of 352-351*

THE years 351 and 350 mark something of a pause in Macedonia's great phase of expansion. The term however is relative, applied to so dynamic a king as Philip. True, Thessaly saw him in these years as *archon* 'playing himself in', and not pressing home as yet the logical demand of Thessalian foreign policy for a decision in the Phocian war; and Thrace (we can be almost sure) in 351 at any rate saw him not at all.[1] One big campaign in the West, however, must belong now. And the crisis which exploded over Chalcidice in 349 had a strenuous pre-history in which war came near to Olynthus on one occasion before the final assault was delivered. The timing of these developments is impossible to fix exactly; or indeed even approximately without first assigning a date to the *First Philippic* speech of Demosthenes which contains brief allusions to them.

It was, no doubt, this very allusion to Olynthus which most of all inspired the scepticism which found cause to reject the traditional date of this speech (archon-year 352/1) and propose a date in 349:[2] an actual military threat to Olynthus, it was thought, comparable in seriousness to Philip's march on Thermopylae and his campaign in Thrace in 352,[3] since we know of no earlier occasion for it, must really refer to the first operations of the war which did begin in 349. This view, which was an obstacle to our understanding particularly of Demosthenes and the development of his foreign policy, has been refuted now, one hopes, by G. L. Cawkwell in a treatment of admirable lucidity and brevity combined.[4] A date in 349 for the *First Philippic* is shown to be impossible.

---

[1] See above, p. 284.

[2] D. 4. 17; cf. Dion. Hal. *ad Amm.* 725 and 736. By 'traditional date' I mean the date assigned to it by Dionysius, who was not immune from error, but who did have access to all the literary sources now lost and especially to the Atthidographers. For a useful study of his method and its results, R. Sealey, *REG* 68 (1955) 77 ff.

[3] D. 4. 17 ταῦτα μὲν οἶμαι δεῖν ὑπάρχειν ἐπὶ τὰς ἐξαίφνης ταύτας ἀπὸ τῆς οἰκείας χώρας αὐτοῦ στρατείας εἰς Πύλας καὶ Χερρόνησον καὶ Ὄλυνθον καὶ ὅποι βούλεται.

[4] Cawkwell, 'Olynthus' 122 ff., with essential bibliography; M. Zahrnt, *Olynth* 110 (briefly).

A date in 350 cannot be ruled out.[1] But a date in the summer of 351 seems distinctly the most probable.[2] This accepted, it follows that the allusions in the speech to Philip's very recent activities (to be discussed below), including the allusion to Olynthus, refer to activities most probably in the first half of the year 351.

Once the notion has been rejected that an allusion to an attack on Olynthus must be referring to the attack in 349 which ended in the destruction of the city, we are at liberty to recall that an attack in 351 is not (for us) a bolt from the blue: we have been enabled, as it happens, to see it coming. In the speech *Against Aristocrates*, belonging probably to 352 and certainly earlier than the campaign in Thrace which finished up at Heraion Teichos in November, Demosthenes throws a sharp, though narrow, beam of light on the relations of Philip and his Chalcidian allies.[3] Their alliance in 357/6 had been directed against Athens, and we must suppose (bearing in mind Potidaea) that its survival and success would depend in great part on the ability of the Chalcidians to 'hate those whom they had injured'. Demosthenes chooses to compare the Olynthians in their relation to Philip to the Athenians in their relation to Cersobleptes: not altogether aptly in most ways, it must be confessed, and for the present purpose the comparison may be left out of account.

You had as an example our friends the Olynthians: what did Philip do for them, and how do they treat him? Philip gave the Olynthians Potidaea . . . Though he was at war with you and had spent a lot of money, when he had taken it and could have kept it for himself, if he had chosen, he handed it over and never even tried to do otherwise. Yet see *their* reaction. For a time, while they saw Philip of a size that they could trust, they were his allies and through him were at war with you. But when they saw him too great to be trusted . . . they turned to you . . . and have made you their friends, and say that they will make you their allies as well. Do the Olynthians, then, know how to foresee the future, while you, Athenians though you are, will not do likewise? It is scandalous if you, with your reputation for knowing the world and deliberating on that basis, are obviously less successful than the Olynthians at knowing what is good for you.[4]

---

[1] F. Focke, *Demosthenesstudien* in *Tübinger Beiträge zur Altertumswissenschaft* 5 (1929) 21 ff. But the attempt of J. R. Ellis, *REG* 79 (1966) 636 ff., to use D. 3. 4–5 to date Philip's illness in Thrace to September or October 351 is unacceptable. For Ellis it follows that the date of the *First Philippic*, because it alludes to Philip's move against Olynthus which came after his illness, must be later than 351 (he dates it to 'about January 350', R. D. Milns and J. R. Ellis, *The Spectre of Philip* (Sydney, 1970) 13–14).

[2] Cawkwell, 'Olynthus' 125 ff., who supports the identification (Focke, op. cit. 21 ff.) of the expedition alluded to in the speech (4. 43 ff.) with the expedition of Charidemus in October 351 (D. 3. 4), but argues ingeniously that this allusion in the speech is to an expedition already voted but not yet dispatched.

[3] For the date of Philip's presence at Heraion Teichos, Hammond, *JHS* 57 (1937) 57.

[4] D. 23. 107–9.

To the Athenians hearing them, these remarks about Olynthus were no more than a reminder which could be used by Demosthenes as illustration. To us they give information that is new, of two sorts: they tell us something of what the Olynthians actually did and something of their reasons for doing it. After a time, says Demosthenes, the Olynthians at war with Athens became our friends; which can only mean that already before this date (autumn 352 at latest) a treaty of peace had been made between Athens and Olynthus. Though Demosthenes gives no direct indication of how long this treaty had been in existence at this moment, his reference to the possibility of the peace becoming an actual alliance does seem to give fairly strong ground for thinking that it had been made only quite recently.

A passing allusion in the *Third Olynthiac* (more than three years later) to their making of peace gives no help towards dating it.[1] But Libanius in his Hypothesis to the *First Olynthiac* does add the useful detail that the Olynthians waited for a time when Philip was abroad, to send ambassadors to Athens and make peace, in defiance of their treaty with Philip himself, which had bound both parties not to make a separate peace.[2] For Philip to be 'abroad' (ἀποδημοῦντα) in this context means probably that he had to have gone south, west, or north from his kingdom, since his going east meant his passing by the front door of the Olynthians with an army on his way home, a contingency which might be held to be putting too much temptation in his way. It seems that Philip's strong preoccupation in Thessaly in the summer of 353, and again in the summer of 352, offers the best opportunity for the hole-and-corner diplomacy of the Olynthians: and in particular the argument for the peace being recent when Demosthenes spoke, and also the Olynthian fear of Philip because he had grown too great (see below), seem to point to 352, when he came into full control of Thessaly, as the occasion for the Olynthian move.

If this is correct, Philip's first reaction to the Olynthian breach of faith must have been diplomatic and not military. Though he did march east from Pella in the autumn of 352 after his return from Thessaly, it was not to invade Chalcidice but the kingdom of Cersobleptes (see above, pp. 282 f.). To many in Chalcidice hardly less than in Athens the news of his illness, and even of his death, in East Thrace will have been welcome enough. Their disappointment followed. Philip did not die, and it was probably in the spring of 351 (and not very long before the *First Philippic* was written) that he did put military pressure on the Olynthians, by an actual invasion of their territory.[3] But we must presume that

---

[1] D. 3. 7.   [2] D. 1, Hypoth. 2

[3] D. 4. 17, 'these sudden expeditions (στρατείας) from Macedonia to Thermopylae and the Chersonese and Olynthus and wherever he wants'. At D. 1. 13 (written in 349) the

even when the army moved on this occasion negotiations between him and the League were never allowed to break down irrevocably, and that diplomatic contact of some kind was maintained: the invasion is to be seen as Philip's final argument in persuasion rather than as a sign that he had abandoned persuasion and meant to settle with the Olynthians by war. This we can infer from the fact that he himself made an important concession when matters were finally settled between them now. He did not insist on the Athenian–Olynthian peace treaty's being revoked.[1] He must have obtained, however, assurances that the proposed Olynthian alliance with Athens would not be made, and probably he had good reasons for believing that he could still count on his friends and agents in Olynthus to see that any assurances given now could be relied on. He evidently turned a blind eye to his legitimate grievance of the separate peace, while not abstaining from threats and fulminations against those political leaders of the Olynthians who had brought it about.[2] This seems the likeliest occasion for the exile of Apollonides and a temporary eclipse of the anti-Macedonian faction.[3]

It seems likely that Olynthus and the Chalcidian League at this time, if we could know the full facts, would give us almost the classical picture of the Greek state torn several ways on several issues, not all of them purely political. It suited Demosthenes later to say that the Olynthian politicians who were pro-Macedonian were traitors who had been bribed,[4] and of some of them it may even have been true; but this cannot go far towards telling us the whole truth. Harder to evaluate is his explanation (quoted earlier, p. 297) in terms of what is really balance-of-power foreign politics: while Philip was not too big they could trust him, but he became too big to be trusted.[5] The temptation is great to dismiss this as merely naïve, or at least as too grossly oversimplified to contain more than a modicum of the truth. But what compels us to take Demosthenes more seriously on this is the suspicion, which becomes stronger the more we consider the facts that are known, that really the Chalcidian League had done extremely well out of the Macedonian alliance, and that its material prosperity now was bound up with Macedonia as never before. From

recital of Philip's movements seems to call for no long interval between the Thracian expedition (to Heraion Teichos) and this attack on Olynthus: as soon as he recovered from his illness, 'immediately' he attacked the Olynthians.

[1] This is implicit in the allusion to it by Demosthenes in the *Third Olynthiac* (3. 7).

[2] The obscure allusion in Theopompus F 127 (*FGrH* 115) presumably belongs here (so Jacoby ad loc.): . . . καὶ ἐν τῇ εἰκοστῇ Θεοπόμπου τῶν Φιλιππικῶν ὁ [sc. μῦθος] τοῦ πολέμου καὶ τῆς ὕβρεως, ὃν ὁ Φίλιππος διεξέρχεται πρὸς τοὺς αὐτοκράτορας τῶν Χαλκιδέων (where the antecedent of ὅν is μῦθος). Since Books 22, 23 and 24 of the *Philippica* were concerned with the war of 349/8 (F 140 f., 143, 147 ff.) it is likely that this reference in Book 20 is to an earlier occasion.

[3] D. 9. 56 and 66; [D.] 59. 91; Zahrnt 110.   [4] D. 19. 265 ff.; cf. 9. 56, 63 ff.

[5] D. 23. 108.

this point of view, to pick a quarrel with Philip, or to give him clear grounds for picking one with them, seems almost like an act of madness, and is certainly an act requiring some very positive grounds to outweigh the material advantages which it was sacrificing.

Of these something more needs to be said. The advantage of receiving the territory of Potidaea without the embarrassment of the Potidaeates living on it needs no explanation in itself, though it would be a great help to us to know which Chalcidians precisely did benefit from it. Though the League was probably not a democracy as the Athenians would have understood it, and though there is perhaps some ground to think of it as resembling the Boeotia of the 390s described by the Oxyrhynchus historian, with the active citizenship reserved to the hoplite class, yet at this date it seems improbable that a big distribution of land (the territory of Potidaea) could have been made on any basis other than that of giving land to citizens who had been landless hitherto.[1] If this is granted, it follows that an increase in the active citizen body may have had some political side-effects of which we are told nothing. It may not be necessary to think that 'new' citizens with land at Potidaea must have been pro-Macedonian because they were grateful to Philip: five years is a long time for anyone to stay grateful to anybody for anything. But the provision of land on this scale to poorer citizens must have made the community more prosperous, and politically is likely to have had the effect, temporarily, of greatly increasing the prestige of the political leaders who had advocated the Macedonian alliance in 357/6.

Nor was this the only material gain. It has long been recognized that Philip's change of standard for his silver currency, to the so-called Phoenician standard which was traditionally that of the Chalcidian cities also, was designed not only to benefit Macedonia but also to be of some attraction to the Chalcidians, since the change must belong, it seems, to the time when the alliance was either contemplated or recently made.[2] To compare its effects, as has been done, with those of a modern *Zollverein*, is probably to overstate it seriously.[3] Coin-finds at most Greek sites, and notably at Olynthus itself, include almost invariably many coins of weight-standards differing from the local one.[4] And common sense forces us to suppose that the ancient Greeks no less than the nationalities of today were perfectly prepared to undergo some simple mental arithmetic if necessary in order to sell or buy something they wanted abroad or in dealings with foreigners. Philip's change of standard, then, from this point of view was a convenience and perhaps a gesture,

[1] *Hell. Oxy.* 16 (Bartoletti), for Boeotia.
[2] There are no silver coins of Philip himself on any standard other than the Phoenician; but we do not know in what year he first issued coins bearing his own name.
[3] West. *NC* 205.
[4] For Olynthus, Robinson and P. A. Clement, *Olynthus* 9 Section 2 (summary, 363 ff.).

and will have been of some small aid at any rate in the trading relations of the two neighbours.

Much more important than this, however, was the fact that when this alliance was made the Athenians already were excluded from Macedonia by the state of war recently declared, and likely to remain excluded for some years at least—until, indeed, they could either regain Amphipolis or reconcile themselves to the fact of having lost it, and make peace on one basis or the other. Both Athenians and Chalcidians in the past had been interested in buying timber for shipbuilding and indeed for building in general: this may be taken to be the most important Macedonian export commodity.[1] To think of them as competing for a commodity that was scarce or monopolized, except perhaps on some occasions when they were at war with each other, would probably be a mistake. But a more likely field of competition was between shipowners. The volume of the whole overseas trade of Macedonia cannot have been vast even by ancient standards, but it was not negligible.[2] The carrying of the exports and imports may well have given room for competition in which the Chalcidian shipowners had the advantage of proximity, but the Athenians the greater advantage still, at those times when the cities of the Macedonian littoral itself were either in their possession or members of their confederacy. Political vicissitudes will have affected their trade always, when they occurred: and now the war with Athens will have put the trade securely for some years in the hands of the Chalcidians. One does not mean by this, of course, that the Chalcidians themselves began to buy for their own consumption more from Macedonia than they had ever bought before (they could only consume what they could pay for). It was a question, presumably, of their becoming now the carrying and marketing link between Macedonia and the Aegean world in general.[3]

That this will have been profitable goes without saying, and the profits

---

[1] See above, pp. 139, 157, 173.

[2] [Arist.] *Econ.* 2. 22. 1350[a] (revenue from import and export dues raised by Callistratus' reorganization from 20 to 40 talents).

[3] It may be thought dangerous to assume that there were no Macedonians capable of profiting from the carrying trade. My reasons for assuming it are (1) Because we never hear of any such, either in Philip's reign or in Alexander's: (2) because an allusion of Demosthenes in 349 to a 'closure of the trading stations in Macedonia owing to the war' seems to support the assumption. I translate 'trading stations' rather than 'markets', because ἐμπόριον by its etymology means a place for trade by travel (not just a local market), and usually by travel overseas (LSJ⁹ s.v. ἐμπορεύομαι (1) and ἐμπορία (1)): though LSJ⁹ (s.v. ἐμπόριον 1 b) gives 'market centre for district which had no πόλις', in Macedonia, third century A.D. (*SIG* 880. 22), this meaning is excluded in this instance, because 'the war' had done nothing to interrupt the local trade of market towns inside Macedonia. If the ἐμπόρια were closed in 349, it looks as if it must have been because now Chalcidian merchants, as well as Athenian, were enemy aliens and unable to get to them. West (*NC* 202) by his interpretation of this passage seems to concur in thinking that ἐμπορίων here must refer to overseas trade.

will have increased as Macedonia became able to spend some of the revenue from the mines on more imports from abroad. The volume of silver output by the Chalcidian mint at Olynthus in the years 357–352 and especially towards the end of that period (in the magistracy of Ariston) may be presumed to reflect in some way the benefits of the Macedonian alliance at the time when it was most beneficial.[1] But who made the profits? There is obvious danger in an arbitrary classification of (for example) Chalcidian merchants and shipowners as distinct from Chalcidian landed proprietors, to provide pro-Macedonian and anti-Macedonian nuclei among the citizens of the League. For shipowners needed to be men of capital, and nothing is more likely than that some landed proprietors with capital to spare took the unusual opportunity. The big profits fell presumably to a relatively small number of Chalcidian citizens; but the shipping activity promoted by them will have provided more employment in this field than usual, and many citizens concerned in the working or the equipping or the supplying of ships will have felt the benefit. There was thus, we must conclude, a solid and effective basis of material gain to be counted up and expounded by the pro-Macedonian politicians on those occasions at Olynthus when foreign policy and the Macedonian alliance were debated.[2]

And who had lost by the alliance? In material terms nobody, so far as we can tell. The objections to it must have been on other grounds, and those presumably political (using the word in a wide sense). We have no right, most likely, to think that the Athenian *demos* was the only political audience in Greece before which a speaker could judge it to his advantage (as Demosthenes clearly did from time to time) to evoke racial prejudice against the Macedonians, as back-of-beyond barbarians presuming to meet Greeks on equal terms and even confer favours on them.[3] True, most Chalcidians (unlike some Athenians) must have seen a Macedonian some time in their lives and knew that they did not have tails. But there is no need for them to have liked what they had seen. And what business had these people to be a success, anyway? These somewhat primitive feelings and revulsions are not to be discounted. More interesting, though, is the probability (which becomes 'probable' because without it one does not see alternatives of weight enough to explain the actual behaviour of the Chalcidians), that the change in their sentiments towards Philip, by which they moved from a state of alliance to one of war with him, was really brought about most of all by the rational consideration which Demosthenes named at the time:

---

[1] *Olynthus* 9 Section 1B, 160 f. (with 133 ff.).

[2] West, *NC* 201 ff., draws a useful picture of the commercial advantages to the Chalcidians of the alliance in general.

[3] D. 4. 10; 3. 24 cf. 3. 16 f.; 19. 305, 308, 327.

Philip had grown too great to be trusted any longer.[1] Demosthenes is not imputing to Philip in this context any personal untrustworthiness of character, though we may be sure that the omission was due to lack of occasion rather than of conviction. The Chalcidians themselves cannot have been blind to Philip's duplicity in gaining Amphipolis, even though it had worked to their own advantage. And they will have known more details than we know of how he had acquired his extraordinary position as *archon* in Thessaly, to say nothing of his dealings with the kings of Thrace and others of his neighbours. Nor will it have increased their confidence in him if they had reason to think that he was bribing some of their own politicians.[2] Yet it does seem probable that it was not so much his personality but, as Demosthenes said, the great increase of his power that was the decisive factor. Though we have no evidence that any Greek ever thought of 'the balance of power' in those or equivalent words, we have the whole of Greek history as evidence that in every Greek state men knew the realities summarized in that phrase, and habitually acted on them. For the free Greek city intending to stay free, it was good to have strong allies, but it was a deadly danger to have an ally so overwhelmingly strong that only his good will and good faith stood between the weaker ally and subjection.[3] A king was the extreme example. A king of Philip's gifts might even convince of his own good faith and goodwill; but next week he might be dead. What of the next king? It is no wonder if not all Olynthians from the start were captivated by the Macedonian alliance, and if even some who had benefited directly from it could not shut their eyes as time went on to the fact that the political situation to be avoided at all costs was exactly theirs now.

Philip's intervention, then, in 351 was not decisive. It stopped the rot, and perhaps it brought about the exile of Apollonides then, but it did not convince all the Chalcidians for all time that their place in the world henceforward was to be the obedient ally of Philip, strong though he was and terribly close at hand. Those of their politicians who preached loyalty to the alliance did believe in just this, and there is no reason to feel sure that they all must have been in Philip's pay, though some no doubt were. Even these however may well have taken money for saying what their own convictions would have made them say in any case (and what also happened to be true), that Philip was so strong now that there was no feasible alternative to trusting him: there was no real chance now of surviving indefinitely as Philip's enemies, and it was

---

[1] D. 23. 108.

[2] D. 19. 265 (a piece of highly coloured rhetoric, but presumably not a tissue of lies).

[3] The allies of Athens in the Delian Confederacy are a set of examples in series, of course. But an interesting awareness of how the Peloponnese might go the same way can be seen in a reported speech of the Corinthians reacting to the alliance of Sparta with Athens in 421 (οὐκ ἐπ' ἀγαθῷ, ἀλλ' ἐπὶ καταδουλώσει τῆς Πελοποννήσου—Thuc. 5. 27. 2).

even better (they may have reckoned, though this they will not have dared to say) to survive as Philip's subjects if he so insisted, to enjoy the benefits and stomach the disgrace of some form of integration in the Macedonian kingdom, rather than be destroyed fighting to be free. Their opponents in the political struggle inside Olynthus were not choosing, of course, to be destroyed with their eyes open.[1] For whatever reasons, they hated subjection more than their rivals hated it (and partly because their rivals hated it less); and they persuaded themselves and strove to persuade their citizens that the odds against them were only great, when really they were overwhelming. *Possunt qui posse videntur* is true in politics and war, but there comes the situation when it ceases to be true. This was it. It was the geography of this matter that was decisive. If Chalcidice had been a peninsula at an extremity of Philip's empire, where to be tied up in sieges for a year or two years or three would be intolerable to him, war might have been a good prospect, as a Perinthus and a Byzantium showed later, or an Aetolia much later still. But located where they were the Chalcidians were almost in the lion's den, and it was too late in the day to start pretending that they were the lion-tamer.

So the struggle in Olynthus continued for two years yet, its fluctuations concealed from us for the most part by the deficiencies of our sources, its course influenced no doubt by Philip's own movements meanwhile, on which we are almost equally uninformed. But what we know of these, or think we know, comes next in the story.

2. *Philip in the West: the Illyrians and Epirus*

When Demosthenes spoke the *First Philippic* there was evidently uncertainty at Athens both as to what exactly Philip was doing at the moment and where exactly he was doing it: this in the summer of 351 probably, though a date later in the year or even in 350 remains possible (above). One of the rumours (mentioned by Demosthenes) was that he was 'fortifying cities in the land of the Illyrians':[2] and though in the context and in itself Demosthenes' remark about it could be deliberately far-fetched, as an example of the wildness of contemporary Athenian gossip, yet the very lack of definite news about him, which made the rumours possible, does suggest that for some weeks he had been beyond reach of the normal terminals of communications linking up with Athens. A long absence in the interior does seem probable. And an allusion in the *First Olynthiac* confirms the Illyrian rumour up to this point, that he did at any rate make a campaign against the Illyrians at this time.[3]

---

[1] For the two parties, D. 9. 56.　　　　　　　　　　　　　　　　[2] D. 4. 48.

[3] D. 1. 13, where he enumerates the campaigns in which Philip had risen to greatness by his own exertions. Thus—Amphipolis, Pydna, Potidaea, Methone, Thessaly: Pherae,

The passage in the *First Olynthiac* which refers to this Illyrian campaign of Philip couples with it campaigns against the Paeonians and against Arybbas.[1] Of operations in Paeonia at this time nothing whatever is known. But a campaign in Epirus has been reasonably connected with that against the Illyrians as part of one fairly lengthy expedition in the West;[2] more likely as the second part than the first, one would think, since the Illyrians were the more dangerous opponents and more likely to move out to join Arybbas than he to join them. Of reasons for Philip's descent now upon his uncle by marriage we are told nothing: and as to the influence (if any) of Olympias on these events, it seems idle to speculate. The recent family history of the Molossian royal house may well have offered a standing invitation to Philip to intervene and cause trouble, if trouble was what he was looking for. Neoptolemus, the father of Olympias, had been elder and not younger brother of Arybbas, he had been associated in some way with their father Alcetas in the kingship as early as 375, and he was sole king in 370–368, before he and Arybbas became joint rulers after civil war.[3] After his death Arybbas ruled alone, and no doubt was recognized as king by Philip in 357 when he married Olympias.[4] But the young son of Neoptolemus, Alexander, the brother of Olympias, could always be seen as having a good claim to the throne or to a partnership in it.

In size the ethnic combination in which the central Molossian *ethnos* predominated was not much smaller than the Macedonia of the years before Philip.[5] The marriage of Philip and Olympias in 357 was a linking of two royal houses which could still be thought of as equals, and which

---

Pagasae, Magnesia, Thrace: then he fell ill (= late 352): having recovered ... immediately. Olynthus (= 351): τὰς δ' ἐπ' Ἰλλυρριοὺς καὶ Παίονας αὐτοῦ καὶ πρὸς Ἀρύββαν καὶ ὅποι τις ἂν εἴποι παραλείπω στρατείας. In the sentence quoted he could be referring to the Illyrian and Paeonian campaigns of 356 (above, pp. 246, 251); but much more likely to recent campaigns between Olynthus 351 and Olynthus 349. To argue (as Beloch, 3². 2. 282) that Philip's 'fortifying cities' (D. 4. 48) means that he had completed the campaign and was in possession, is to ignore entirely the ironical element in this passage, which ends οἱ δ' ἐν Ἰλλυριοῖς πόλεις τειχίζειν [sc. φασί], οἱ δὲ λόγους πλάττοντες ἕκαστος περιερχόμεθα. On these 'cities', see below, pp. 652 ff.

[1] D. 1. 13.

[2] e.g. by Beloch 3². 1. 490 f.; 3². 2. 282; J. Kaerst *RE* 2. 2 (1896) 1495 ff.

[3] Tod, *GHI* no. 123. 109–10 (Alcetas and Neoptolemus). For Neoptolemus as sole king, see the three inscriptions of which the texts are given by Hammond, *Epirus* 525–6, 530–1. For Neoptolemus and Arybbas joint rulers, Paus. 1. 11. 3.

[4] Both Diodorus (16. 72. 1) and Justin (8. 6. 5) give him the title, for what this is worth. Diodorus in the same sentence records his death mistakenly in 342 (when he was exiled); but that does not make his βασιλέα wrong too, and of course both he and Justin (Trogus) used sources that ought to have been able to get it right. Tod (on *GHI* no. 173 p. 216) comments on the absence of the title βασιλεύς from the Athenian decree of 342 concerned with the recently exiled king, even from that sentence of it which referred to restoring him to his office (ἀρχήν, not βασιλείαν); but he does not explain it.

[5] For the expansion of the Molossian state in the years before 360, see Hammond, *Epirus* 531–3.

had a common interest in warding off the Illyrians, from whom each had suffered in the past.[1] By 352 however Philip had outgrown Arybbas (no less than Olynthus). Whether Arybbas had acted already too independently or in some way contrary to Macedonian interests, or whether Philip merely meant to remind him now never to do so, the object and the effect of this intervention were obviously disciplinary. Beloch's skilful argument that it was now (rather than in 342 when Arybbas was deposed) that the Parauaei were detached from the Molossians and incorporated in Macedonia, is probably good.[2] They were the most northerly *ethnos* of Epirus, and to annex Parauaea drove a territorial wedge between Arybbas and the Illyrians, besides giving command of an invasion route from Illyria up the valley of the upper Aoos.

More radical (for the future of Arybbas and his office) was Philip's removal from his charge of the ten-year-old Alexander. From now on he resided at the Macedonian court, where Philip (inevitably, for he was a beautiful boy) is reported to have grown very much too fond of him.[3] Whatever the truth about this, a more necessary speculation is, what precisely Arybbas was given to understand by this removal, and its implications for his own future. Something nasty, it cannot be doubted. Yet it seems hardly possible that Philip can have let him know plainly that he could consider himself henceforward as merely regent of the Molossians till Alexander should be of an age to rule.[4] That would have been a simple invitation to Arybbas to become Philip's enemy from that moment, by stealth at present and by war at the first good opportunity. This, surely, was not Philip's way. The diplomatist leaves doors open until the time has arrived for them to be closed. If Philip put the fear of God into Arybbas now, with the knowledge that God's instrument could well prove to be the young Alexander, it was still politic not to deprive him of all hope, or all belief in honesty as the best policy for himself. Short of some unforeseeable alternative, Alexander would return; but it could be left an open question whether he would return to rule jointly with Arybbas, or to rule alone.

As to the status of Arybbas as a result of this intervention by Philip, there must be some doubt. Were they still equal allies as they had been since the royal marriage of 357? Or was Arybbas reduced now to vassal

---

[1] Frontin. *Strat.* 2. 5. 19 records an invasion of Epirus by Bardylis, repelled by Arybbas.

[2] Beloch 3². 2. 179 ff. So Hammond, *Epirus* 534. P. Treves, *AJP* 63 (1942) 146 n. 42, preferred to leave the dating open.

[3] Just. 8. 6. 5 ff.

[4] This seems implied by Beloch 3². 1. 491 (cf. Momigliano, *FM* 109); and indeed by Justin (8. 6. 5 'Arybbam regem Epiri . . . pellere regno statuit atque Alexandrum . . . in Macedoniam . . . arcessit . . .'). Either the Greek source of Trogus or (more likely?) Justin himself committed here the unhistorical blunder of using prematurely his own knowledge of how this story ended. Treves (art. cit. 145 n. 38) recognized rightly that any agreement on this kind of basis can be ruled out.

status? There is some suggestion, arising from the coinages of the Molossians themselves and others of the Epirot tribes, of a period of Macedonian influence, which may have its relevance here. The Molossian coinage had its first beginning in the first half of the fourth century, probably soon after 375 when Alcetas and the Molossians entered the Second Athenian Confederacy.[1] The silver coinage is too exiguous to offer anything to the historian; but the bronze, which lasted down to 330–325 was fairly copious, and was studied carefully by P. R. Franke, who found two groups, the second larger than the first. Significant is a distinct stylistic break which he saw in the middle of the first group, and which he interpreted in terms of an interval of time during which the minting of coins was interrupted. (The Molossian coins, it should be said, were issued by the *koinon*, 'the Molossians', and bore no name or mark of the king.)

Linked, perhaps, with this break in the Molossian bronze coinage may be an interesting phenomenon in the bronze coinages of the independent Epirote tribes the Cassopaei and the Eleaei, neighbours just north of the Ambracian Gulf, who coined in this period (ending 330–325).[2] When the coins of the Eleaei began, is not known. But the Cassopaei began minting very likely in 342, when the eclipse of the four Greek cities of their coastal area and their subjection to Alexander and the Molossians (below, p. 507) gave this *ethnos* an unaccustomed opportunity for self-assertion. All specimens of the first group of their coins are overstruck on bronze coins of Philip, and many specimens of the second group too. Moreover the second and third groups of the Eleaean bronze coins are overstruck on Philip coins of the same type, the 'young rider' type which is thought to commemorate the Olympic racehorse victory of 356. Clearly, some special reason accounts for this. A flood of Macedonian bronze money brought in by an army, presumably with Philip in 342?[3] Very unlikely. (These were Macedonian soldiers, not twentieth-century Americans.) Improbable, too, that Philip deliberately supplied these people with a lot of small change so that they could overstrike it with their own names and emblems. He had other things to do, and this would have been an oddly tedious way of financing them if he wanted to finance them, for bronze was not a commodity really hard to come by, for anyone able to pay for it. Much the more likely explanation, as Hammond proposed, is that by 342, when Philip did intervene in these parts, a lot of Philip's money was circulating in Epirus already, in place of the

[1] So Hammond, *Epirus* 543 f., refuting the earlier dating of P. R. Franke, *Alt-Epirus und das Königtum der Molosser* (Erlangen, 1954) 91 and 259, who put it at 390 and 380. The Athena Parthenos head on the first group of bronze suggests the connection, which needs to belong to a time when Athens was strong, and active in the north-west.

[2] P. R. Franke, *Die antiken Münzen von Epirus* 56 f., 44 f.; Hammond, *Epirus* 542 f.

[3] So Franke: *contra*, Hammond.

Molossian currency which had been suspended.[1] The break in the Molossian coinage perhaps is to be explained in this way. If so, the break will have begun most probably in 350, and will last down to 342.[2]

If this is accepted, the implications, for Arybbas, are unmistakable. Generally speaking, the right to coin was a sign of a free king or state, and its denial a sign of subjection. Though one can find the client king who continues to coin even though he seems clearly 'client' (Lyppeius in Paeonia comes to mind, in Philip's time) the converse of this, a king prohibited from coining who still considers himself free and equal, is what one would never expect to find. If we accept that this happened to Arybbas, it must follow that Arybbas has suffered a fall in status and has become client now.[3] If that is correct he was spared some loss of face in that the coinage prohibited was officially that of the Molossians and not (like that of Lyppeius and of course of Philip himself) his own personal issue. But the heavy truth remained; and his future was left ambiguous and at the best insecure.[4]

---

[1] Hammond, *Epirus* 545.

[2] Such reservations as I have are prompted by the question, which only numismatists can answer, How long a break can the stylistic change in the first group of bronze coins be held responsible for? The break of eight years demanded here seems to me probably rather more than enough. Of course Philip's closing down of the mint(s) need not be in 350, it could be in (say) 347, or 346, or 345, and for reasons which we might appreciate if we knew them. But if the shorter period is better for the Molossian 'break', the longer period is better for explaining the plethora of bronze coins of Philip available for overstriking by the Casso-paeans and Eleaeans in 342 and after. This is the stronger of the two requirements, obviously. If the Molossian coins will not bear the eight-year break, then that interpretation of it must be abandoned. In that case, the break, a shorter one, is due to internal Molossian reasons of which we know nothing. But it will remain true that from 350 the Philip coins circulated in large numbers.

[3] The interesting view of R. M. Errington in his recent article 'Arybbas the Molossian' (*GRBS* 16 (1975) 41–50), that it was at this time (before 349) that Arybbas was expelled, does not persuade me. At Trogus, *Prol.* 8, the clause which states that the Olynthian War was concurrent with part of the Phocian War ('interiectumque huic bellum quod Philippus cum Chalcidicis urbibus gessit etc.') ought to mean that the events and topics which follow were not concurrent but subsequent ('Ut Illyrici reges ab eo victi sunt, et Thracia atque Thessalia subactae, et rex Epiro datus Alexander eiecto Arybba, et frustra Perinthos oppugnata'). Errington rightly reminds us that Diodorus under archon-year 342/1 records not the expulsion of Arybbas but his death, adding that he reigned 10 years, and that Alexander the brother of Olympias succeeded to his throne with the co-operation of Philip (D.S. 16. 72. 1). Though Alexander was certainly in possession a year earlier than this (343/2, [D.] 7. 32), the Diodorus notice is not reconcilable with an accession-date of 349 or earlier—except indeed for the 'ten-year reign' (Arybbas was certainly on the throne as early as 357 and probably several years before that). But decisive really is the fact that for Diodorus the death of a king in exile was a non-event; the event was the end of his reign and the beginning of the new one, and it is this that he records here, inaccurately, by writing of Arybbas' death instead of his flight to Athens (below, p. 505).

[4] There is no evidence, either from before 351 or after it, showing Molossian or other Epirote troops fighting as allies in any of Philip's campaigns. But there are so few details of any kind about his armies (even Thessalians are mentioned only rarely, and Chalcidians never; see below, pp. 434 ff.) that this particular gap cannot be thought significant.

3. *Philip and Athens*

Returning again to rumours at Athens current (*First Philippic*) while Philip was still absent in the west; 'some of us', claimed Demosthenes, 'are going round saying that Philip is fixing with the Spartans the downfall of Thebes and the tearing apart of the constitutions, others of us that he has sent ambassadors to the Great King, and others again . . .' (about Illyria etc., above).[1] That there should be rumours about Sparta and Philip is not particularly surprising in itself. The Spartans and Thebans did actually meet in battle (indecisively) in the Argolid in this same summer (351), and Sparta never ceased to pursue her end of bringing back good order and discipline to the Peloponnese.[2] It is not out of the question that the Spartans may have tried to detach Philip from Thebes, either before the campaign or after it, though the omens cannot have been favourable (they themselves were the Phocians' closest allies, and had sent a force to Thermopylae the year before). But the rumour as Demosthenes reports it smells so distinctly of an Athenian pipe-dream that one is discouraged from taking it seriously as based on something that was going to influence effectively the actual political situation of 351 (or 350).

With Persia, the same objections do not prevail (though there are others). The traditional good relations of Persia and Thebes were restored by now.[3] The Great King (Artaxerxes Ochus), with Egypt, Phoenicia, and Cyprus still in revolt, and with much unrest still in the western satrapies, was certainly not indifferent to any military potential across the Aegean that might help him. Philip on his side was no less receptive of new ideas about alliances with those who had something to offer (as well as with those who merely needed him badly): and Artaxerxes of recent years had no cause to love Athens. A specific point of contact at this time may have been the distinguished refugee Artabazus, if indeed his unsuccessful revolt while satrap of Hellespontine Phrygia had failed already, and if his first refuge in flight (as well as his final one) was Macedonia.[4] An embassy from Pella to Persia now is by no means impossible, and the Athenians certainly did well to be exercised by it if it existed, even if (and this must have been so) the intention

---

[1] D. 4. 48.

[2] D.S. 16. 34. 3; 39; cf. Paus. 8. 27. 9 f. I am assuming here that the *First Philippic* belongs to 351.

[3] D.S. 16. 40. 1 f.

[4] D.S. 16. 54. 3. There is no dating either Artabazus' flight from Asia or his arrival in Macedonia, though it is often assumed that he went straight to Macedonia, because we are never told of his going anywhere else (but why should we be told? His going to Macedonia 'made a story'; but there are other places he could have gone to first, without anyone's bothering to record it).

behind it can have been no more than exploratory and may even have been a little less than that.[1]

So much for rumours. More down to earth were letters of Philip, copies of which could be read aloud to the Athenian Assembly, letters addressed 'to the Euboeans'.[2] This is one of the allusions in the *First Philippic* that have been thought to support a date in 349 for the speech. Euboea did of course leave the Athenian alliance in winter 349/8 in circumstances favourable for Philip and more than inconvenient for Athens.[3] Yet there is obviously nothing impossible in the idea that in 351 Philip could have made overtures to the Euboeans which were ineffective. This is presumably what did happen. Since we know of no *koinon* of the Euboean cities at this time to which a single letter could have been addressed, he must have sent identical or similar letters to more than one city. The contents are not preserved, but the nature of a part of them can be inferred from Demosthenes' remarks which follow the reading, in which he makes a kind of apology for having introduced unpleasant truths to the ears of his audience, and then leads on to the famous comparison of Athens fighting Philip with a barbarian boxing, clapping his hands always to the place where he has just been hit, too dim to use his fists and his eyes to protect himself.[4] Philip had evidently included in his letter to the Euboeans some reminder of the Athenian record in the past six years of inability to protect allies who had counted on her. Philip was in a position to offer an alliance which would guarantee the Euboeans from subservience to either of their more powerful neighbours (for the Boeotians were no more popular in Euboea than the Athenians, as the events of 357 had shown). This was diplomatic pressure of a constructive kind, even though it brought no immediate or quick results. And it made unwelcome, even sinister, hearing for the Athenians, to whom Macedonian bases in Euboea would have meant something uncomfortably near to the end.

The other means by which Philip was able at this time to keep up some pressure on Athens without exerting himself unduly was by activity at sea. One of our most trying deficiencies is the lack of evidence on development of a Macedonian navy. All the triremes in the world were growing on hillsides of Macedonian mountains. The money, too, was not lacking for building ships and paying crews, which did not need to be exclusively or even mainly of Macedonians, who were unlikely to become skilled seafarers in a year or two even if they applied themselves to it.[5] Amphipolis quite early in Philip's reign, and Pagasae by 352, were the two

---

[1] See below, pp. 484 f., for Philip's relations with Persia.   [2] D. 4. 37.
[3] See below, pp. 318 f.   [4] D. 4. 40.
[5] For some thoughts on this theme (in connection with the Peloponnesians), Thuc. 1. 142. 9.

important places which had brought into his hands Greek populations with the habit and the skills of navigation. Each of them must have been capable of producing and maintaining a squadron, provided that somebody else paid for it; and it is to them, most likely, that we should look for the bases of Philip's naval power, whatever that may really have been. The small but useful fleet (based on Pagasae) with which Alexander of Pherae had tormented Athens, rather than Jason's big dream-navy, was probably the scale on which Philip worked at this stage.[1]

Early in 353 the fleet which accompanied Philip on his Thracian expedition, though it is reported to us as 'large', was not large enough or good enough to engage a squadron of twenty Athenian triremes under Chares waiting for it on its way home.[2] In the interval there had been time to reinforce it, and a glimpse which we get of it in action in 352/1 suggests at first sight that this had been done. Attacks on merchant shipping in the Aegean, serious enough to enable Demosthenes to say (no doubt with some exaggeration) that Philip was paying for the war from the Athenian allies: successful raids taking Athenian prisoners from Lemnos and Imbros and rich booty from a merchant fleet at Geraestus in Euboea: most recently a descent on Marathon which captured the 'sacred trireme'.[3] It sounds like Alexander of Pherae over again, and maybe a little worse. When Demosthenes earlier in the same speech advocated a standing force of troops using forward bases to carry the war to Philip, he explained 'He has a navy; so we must have a picked squadron too, so that our force can use the sea in safety.'[4] And how strong is the picked squadron to be? Of ten ships. It is this that puts Philip's navy in a proper perspective. Granted that there is over-optimism in the details of these proposals in general (especially in the financial ones, for the pay and maintenance of the force), Demosthenes still could not name a figure here for the ships which all the *demos* knew to be absurd. Phormio could take on odds of 4 to 1 and still win; but nobody can have mistaken Chares for another Phormio, and also Phormio's mission had been purely destructive (he was not responsible for the safety of troop-carrying ships simultaneously). It ought to follow really that Demosthenes was not expecting his picked squadron of ten ships to be even outnumbered. If they could be outnumbered by 2 to 1 he was proposing an undue risk. Probably therefore Philip's naval raids had been carried out by very

---

[1] For Jason, X. *HG* 6. 1. 10 f. For Philip and Pagasae, Grote 11. 425.

[2] Polyaen. 4. 2. 22: see above, pp. 265 f.

[3] D. 4. 34. *Pace* Cawkwell ('Olynthus' 124 n. 4) and others, there seems really no reason to doubt that τὰ τελευταῖα (adverbial), of the Marathon incident, means 'most recently'. Cawkwell (ibid. 123 f.) demonstrates admirably that these incidents referred to in the *First Philippic* do nothing to prevent our dating the speech in 351. Androtion F 24 (*FGrH* no. 324), from Androtion's 6th book, is decisive, since his 7th book dealt with the year 350/49 and perhaps an earlier year too. Philochorus F 47 (*FGrH* no. 328), which records the incident, does not help with the date. [4] D. 4. 22.

small squadrons of two or three triremes, and his effective naval strength still did not exceed about twenty triremes altogether.[1]

However, even if these raids really were only pinpricks, it still remains true that nobody enjoys being pricked by pins, even if he is doing very well in every other way. Just how well the Athenians were doing at this time was a matter of opinion. A defensive strategist at Athens (a Eubulus, for instance) could count '352' as a very good year: Sestus taken, Thermopylae held, Philip taken ill at Heraion Teichos. A more realistic strategist (such as Demosthenes in the *First Philippic*) could count this as not good enough, while the initiative in the war lay always still with Philip.[2] And of course there were many who felt (rather than thought?) that the 'war for Amphipolis' ought certainly to be reducing Philip (by means which they must have found hard to name) to the state of being prepared to surrender Amphipolis to Athens.[3] But perhaps no citizen, whatever his personal view of the war, could be quite free from anxiety at the 'pinpricks' from Philip's triremes, for fear of a time when a blunter instrument might have come into his hands. It is easy to think that Philip, drastic by nature and by now a professional in waging war, believed that the essence of war was to harass an enemy whom he could not cripple, unless there was some good reason for leaving him alone. Checked at Thermopylae by Athens, and in east Thrace by his own illness, now when his plans took him away from the Aegean for some months into the West, with his raiders he could still give the Athenians something to remember him by.

This may have been his instinct, and from the *First Philippic* we can see that it provided at the least a talking-point in Athens. But it remains to see (and this is not easy) why the policy was not kept up, beyond the year 351 and into 350 and 349. Allowing that Philip's campaign into Illyria and Epirus may have taken up most of the summer of 351, and that his final war with Olynthus began in the summer of 349, there is a gap of at least eighteen months when we know nothing whatever of his doings, whether in his own person or through subordinates.[4] Sea raids against

---

[1] By 'effective naval strength' I mean the number which really could be put to sea at one time. Athens in these years possessed more than 350 warships, but could not pay the crews of even one-third of that number for more than a month or two. For Philip the limiting factor will have been a lack of trained crews available, probably. Certainly these could have been hired from all over the Aegean, but this would have been an extravagance unless they were sure of being fully and intensively used; unless, in fact, Philip had decided to challenge the Athenian sea power with a view to breaking it decisively.

[2] D. 4. 5 f., 31, 40 f.

[3] The war which began in 357/6 had achieved this name as early as 346. Since in 347 there were still advocates of a policy for continuing the war, *a fortiori* in 351 many must have thought that the losses could still be regained: see below, pp. 329 ff. Demosthenes in 351 (4. 12) does allude to Amphipolis in a way that implies that it was the prize of the war.

[4] Diodorus has no entry concerning Philip between Thermopylae in 352 and the start of the Olynthian War, which he puts in the year 349/8.

Athens may have gone on, but more likely not, for if they had we should probably have found some reference to them in one or other of the *Olynthiac* speeches. It seems almost certain that there was here a genuine pause in Philip's progress, and presumably one dictated by policy. The preoccupation offered by Thessaly has already been mentioned. There may have been others in Macedonia itself; in 349 we find Olynthus harbouring Arrhidaeus and Menelaus, Philip's half-brothers and hence possible pretenders to the throne of Macedonia.[1] There may have been too, urgent needs for reorganization inside Macedonia, of which also we hear nothing.[2] The fact remains that Philip, still at war with two important adversaries, leaves them both, it seems, to their own devices. The Phocians he has left alone since the late summer of 352, for them and the Boeotians to exhaust each other if they chose: and the state of Thessaly was perhaps such as to call for a spell of peace and quiet now, rather than a renewal of the stresses and efforts of forcing the great Phocian fortress in and round Parnassus. Here, it was certainly good policy to wait if waiting would enable him later to take the Phocians easily and with no risk or strain. But what motives can have dictated his inactivity in the Athenian theatre, if he really was totally inactive (and so it seems)?

Since any argument based on hypothetical strains and stresses hardly applies here (if the naval harassing of Athens probably made no demands except financial on the resources of Macedonia itself), it seems right to ask whether Philip may not have decided, even so early as this, to conciliate Athens with a view to ending this war by a negotiated peace. It is common knowledge that in 348 the peace negotiations were initiated not by Athens but by Philip, and this in the hour (indeed before the hour) of final victory over Olynthus.[3] This in itself does not entitle us to think that he must have wanted peace two years earlier. But there must have been a moment when he began to want peace: and it is certainly relevant that his acquisition of Thessaly had given him grounds for changing his view of the war with Athens. It was expected of him now (and his own ambitions claimed it) that one day he would put an end to the Phocian war by invading Central Greece;[4] the move which the Athenians, alone or with others, had helped the Phocians to thwart in 352. It was still open to the Athenians to thwart him in the same way if he repeated the same move.[5] His quick threat to the Chersonese in

[1] Just. 8. 3. 10 (cf. 7. 4. 5). See below, p. 699.

[2] The great building programme mentioned obliquely by Justin (8. 3. 7 f.) is the only notice in his narrative between the end of 352 and the start of the Olynthian war (349). Though Justin maliciously suggests that the whole programme came to nothing, by his own account it reached at any rate the planning stage at this time.

[3] Aeschin. 2. 12 ff. etc.: cf. below, pp. 329 ff.

[4] This perhaps, partly, lay behind the Thessalian grievances reported in 349 (D. 1. 22; 2. 7).

[5] Demosthenes in 343 maintained that this was still so in 346, but probably wrongly (see below, pp. 322 f.).

November 352 may have been intended to bring extreme pressure on Athens, and the naval raids of 351 to keep up some pressure while he was occupied elsewhere. But it seems just possible that his information from Athens led him to think that he might achieve more by relaxing the pressure now. He certainly knew something (and Demosthenes at this time maintained that he knew everything) of what went on in Athens.[1] This was probably overrating his intelligence (deliberately and for effect), but there is no reason to doubt that he knew of the *First Philippic* and its failure (so far as we know, it effected nothing). He would know, too, that in the year 351/50 the Athenians could contemplate helping Rhodes against Persia, and perhaps actually did embark on some obscure dealings with the rebel Persian satrap Orontes.[2] Demosthenes himself conceded (in order to score a debating point) that there were some in Athens who 'thought Philip himself of no account and often pooh-poohed him'.[3] The traditional date of this speech is 351/50. Though it would be wrong to build too much on this reference (which was not important to Demosthenes or his hearers, really, except as a sort of sleeping-partner in a contrived antithesis), still two inferences from it seem sound. (1) At this moment Philip was not active in any way that was hurting the Athenians (even the pinprick raids, had they been still on or recent, would have devalued the allusion pretty seriously). (2) Since those who thought Philip insignificant (*phaulon*) cannot possibly have maintained at this date that he was *phaulos* in general, they can only have meant that all his great successes, even those at the expense of Athens, concerned things or places that were 'expendable', for the Athenians. If Philip had been led to believe that these people predominated (a belief which the failure of the *First Philippic* may have encouraged), he may have reckoned that it was worth while to leave well alone for the time being: this, rather than irritating or even intimidating them, might be the best way to ensure that, first, the Athenians did not intervene in a war with Olynthus, if it should come to that, and that (taking a longer view) they might be induced to accept a peace on the condition of each side keeping what it held now. And meanwhile there was at any rate one area (Euboea)

---

[1] D. 4. 18 εἴσεται γὰρ ἀκριβῶς· εἰσὶ γάρ, εἰσὶν οἱ πάντ' ἐξαγγέλλοντες ἐκείνῳ παρ' ἡμῶν αὐτῶν πλείους τοῦ δέοντος. Though it seems incredible that Athenian citizens should be in communication with Philip in time of war, this is what the Greek (παρ' ἡμῶν αὐτῶν) most naturally means. If D. did mean this, it may be a piece of cheap sensationalism (or it may not); but in any case neutrals who could visit both Athens and Macedonia could easily inform him accurately of what the Athenians were doing, and could give him their impressions of what they were thinking. Nor is it likely that Philip left this side of things to chance.

[2] *IG* II². 207.

[3] D. 15 ('Rhodians'). 24. ὁρῶ δ' ὑμῶν ἐνίους Φιλίππου μὲν ὡς ἄρ' οὐδενὸς ἀξίου πολλάκις ὀλιγωροῦντας, βασιλέα δ' ὡς ἰσχυρὸν ἐχθρὸν οἷς ἂν προέληται φοβουμένους. (The argument concludes, 'But if we do not resist Philip because he is insignificant, and give up everything to the Great King because he is formidable, whom shall we ever stand up to?')

where he may have pursued still a concealed diplomatic mission, with the aim of setting a trap which might be sprung if and when he hoped to make the Athenians defend a vital interest and refrain from intervening in the north.[1]

4. *The War of 349*

The proximate cause of the Olynthian War in 349 was the harbouring at Olynthus of the half-brothers of Philip, Arridaeus and Menelaus, whose elder brother Archelaus Philip already had put to death.[2] But the arrival of the two exiles in Olynthus must certainly have been recent, more recent (for example) than the time of the strained relations of 351 (above, pp. 296 ff.), because their presence there in 351 would have been just as unwelcome to Philip as in 349, and he would not have ceased his military action then without their being surrendered to him.[3] This surrender of the brothers was his demand on the Chalcidian League now. It was neither a trivial matter, nor the mere trumped-up pretext of an imperialist embarking on a war of conquest, for the brothers were his enemies now in an important way—and the Chalcidians were his allies. If in any case he had come to think of the League as an untrustworthy ally (as now it undoubtedly was), there was no need any longer to put up with it. A limited intervention in Chalcidice could break up the League, isolate and so weaken Olynthus, and annex some territory which the Macedonians could use. Or the conquest could include Olynthus itself. The paper-strength of the League was greater now than it had ever been,[4] but its internal weaknesses must have been well known to Philip. Though we are not informed of it, it would be surprising if there was not in the smaller cities an opposition to Olynthus corresponding to the opposition to Thebes in other cities of Boeotia. And in Olynthus itself (we have seen) there were certainly Macedonian sympathizers, and almost certainly some leading men who were in Macedonian pay.[5]

Our doubts now about the extent of Philip's aims at the start of this war, and about the ability and the will of the Olynthians to resist them,

[1] For Euboea, below, pp. 318 f.

[2] Justin (8. 3. 10; 7. 4. 5) names the three presumably with the eldest first (Archelaus). See in general J. R. Ellis, 'The step-brothers of Philip II', *Historia* 22 (1973) 350–4. On Archelaus and his death, below, pp. 699 ff.

[3] This point is overlooked by Ellis, who dates the flight of the brothers from Macedonia 'from perhaps 352 onwards' (loc. cit. 353), and who thinks it improbable that they fled first to anywhere other than Olynthus (loc. cit. 352). This last possibility seems a very real one, however.

[4] D. 19. 266 and 230: 1,000 cavalry, more than 10,000 hoplites, more than twice its strength in 383/2 when it was attacked by Sparta (19. 263). For some discussion of its territories and membership at this time, Zahrnt 107–10.

[5] See above, p. 303. For the traitors, D. 19. 265–7, 342; 8. 40; D.S. 16. 53. 2. Demosthenes as a witness, though his hostility is obvious, cannot be discredited entirely.

were shared (we can see) in Athens at the very time, and no doubt everywhere in Greece.[1] Nor ought we to think that what he ended up by doing must have been what he meant to do from the beginning. His uncompromising treatment of Olynthus at the finish may owe something to the course of the war itself, if he was provoked or (more probably) persuaded by events into making the great example. The war itself however has no military history to speak of, because no adequate account of it has survived. Only a bare outline can be reconstructed of what actually happened: and some few of the almost random details we possess are interesting for their political implications. It cannot be doubted that Philip, who had chosen his own moment to strike, had it in his power to launch an immediate attack on Olynthus itself, which was certainly not more difficult to take than Potidaea or Amphipolis. Though the Chalcidian League army strength was of 10,000 hoplites and 1,000 cavalry, less than half of these were Olynthians, and the other cities would have been obliged to think of their own defence besides, for Philip had the troops to form a field army as well as the army investing Olynthus. Though Athens could be counted on to send some help, and her reinforcements (as well as all supplies) could get in so long as the Olynthians held the harbour of Mecyberna, Philip by now had taken enough cities which Athens had wanted to save, to be pardoned if he assumed that on this occasion too the Athenians would not do enough to stop him. A siege begun about midsummer should stand a fair chance of succeeding before winter set in, especially if his friends inside the city could earn their money now. In short, if Philip from the start intended to destroy Olynthus, it is hard indeed to see what deterred him from a direct attack with the strongest force he could command.

In actual fact however he proceeded very differently. He invaded Chalcidice soon after midsummer, and began to dismember the League by addressing himself to the weaker members.[2] The Chalcidian cities

---

[1] D. 1. 3–4 (in the first weeks of the war) sees a danger (to Athens) of a negotiated settlement between Philip (who wanted it) and Olynthus, whereas at 1. 5 he argues that the Olynthians must know now that they are fighting with destruction and slavery as the issues. There is some rhetorical manœuvring underlying this partial contradiction, but no doubt Demosthenes was genuinely uncertain as to Philip's intentions. D. 2. 1 allows for both possibilities: a negotiated peace with Philip would be fatal to the Olynthians (and they know it), but it is still a thing that might be open to them. (This, too, spoken very early in the war.)

IG ii². 210+259 (cf. E. Schweigert, *Hesperia* 6 (1937) 329 ff., no. 6) heavily restored, concerns Athenian negotiations (alliance?), perhaps at this time, with Acanthus and Dium, cities of Acte the eastern promontory of Chalcidice. Schweigert (loc. cit.) assumes that they had been up to now Philip's allies as members of the Chalcidian League; but their separate negotiations here suggest rather that they were not members of the League at all (its foreign policy conducted, we must think, by its federal government). They may still have been Philip's allies, however. But I am not convinced that this incident, whatever it amounted to, must belong to this occasion in 349. Zahrnt 108 accepts it, and places it here.

[2] D.S. 16. 52. 9. Philochorus, *FGrH* no. 328, F 49, records the first Athenian expedition to Olynthus as the first event of his archon-year 349/8 (cf. Jacoby, op. cit. p. 532, ad loc.),

were very numerous, and many of them very small. None of them could resist a Macedonian attack for long, unless the whole League army supported them, and this risk evidently its generals declined in the present campaign. Most of these places had really no option but to surrender, indeed we hear of only one that resisted and was destroyed (κατέσκαψε), its name unfortunately denied to us by a corruption of the text of Diodorus.[1] If other important ones had fared likewise, Diodorus would probably have mentioned it here. One name only is known of a place that probably surrendered when threatened by Philip, Chytropolis, its site unknown, but recorded as a colony of Aphytis the Chalcidian League city of the Pallene promontory.[2] But Diodorus tells us that 'some' did so, and this is confirmed by some details of a campaign in the following spring, when the Athenian general Charidemus led his mercenaries and Athenian cavalry reinforced by some of the League troops 'into Pallene and Bottiaea and laid waste the land there':[3] since this territory (comprising the south-western quarter, or so, of the whole Chalcidice peninsula) belonged to cities which normally were League members, it follows that they must have defected to Philip in the first campaign. Philip's terms to them cannot have been so severe on them as to stiffen resistance elsewhere, and a contemporary remark of Demosthenes about 'enslavement of Greek cities' in the first campaign is to be interpreted as his notion of what was possible or probable and not as a factual report.[4]

The campaign of 349, then, showed good progress in the dismembering of the League and the isolating of Olynthus, but it did not bring the Olynthians to heel, if that was the intention. The Athenian alliance and the reinforcements under Chares which reached them (late summer) did not give them any real chance of counter-attack or of defeating Philip in

i.e. perhaps August 349, as soon as the etesian winds allowed. The Olynthian appeal for reinforcement came no doubt as soon as Philip attacked. For a good discussion of these events of the war and their timing, see Cawkwell, 'Olynthus' 130 ff. (For Euboea, ibid. 127 ff.)

[1] D.S. 16. 52. 9 (summarizing the whole campaign in one sentence). Fischer's Stageira for the corrupt Geira or Zeira of the manuscripts would be attractive of course, if this place were not described here as φρούριον. Stageirus (-a) was a 300-year-old polis, and became well known as the city of Aristotle. Zereia is a much more likely restoration (by West, *CL* 127 n. 3), printed now in the Loeb text. For Zeira, *ATL* 1. 488 (its site unknown). That Stageira itself was destroyed by Philip is certain (Plu. *Alex.* 7. 3; *Mor.* 1126 F, D.L. 5. 4, etc.); and presumably in this war, but of the circumstances nothing is known. F. Focke (*Demosthenesstudien* 10–12) assigned this D.S. 16. 52. 9 notice to Philip's earlier attack on Olynthus in 350 (*sic*), and included the sack of Stageira in it, but unconvincingly.

[2] Theopomp. *FGrH* no. 115, F 141. Theopompus mentioned Therme and Thestorus as 'Thracian' cities in the same book (22), in which, as we know from F 139, he did pay attention to the Chalcidian League and its affairs in this war. Cf. Zahrnt 110 f., 254.

[3] D.S. 16. 52. 9; Philoch. F 50 (*FGrH* no. 328); for the date, Cawkwell, 'Olynthus' 130 f.

[4] The context shows that the reference is to Philip's operations of that moment, not to the past. For the date of the *Third Olynthiac*, which has been in dispute, see now Cawkwell, 'Olynthus', especially 133 ff., who dates it (and I agree) not later than autumn 349.

battle, but no doubt they did good to their morale and helped them to feel that they could fight a defensive war and survive.[1] Philip will not have overrated any threat from Athens probably, but he was too good a professional to leave anything to chance, and a diversion which divided the energies of the Athenians now could not be other than favourable to his own plans. The revolt of Euboea (winter 349/8) fulfilled just this function, and though Philip's responsibility for it cannot be proved, it would be surprising if he had no hand in it.[2] That the leader of the movement

---

[1] For the first Athenian reinforcement under Chares, Philoch. F 49 (*FGrH* no. 328).

[2] Plu. *Phoc.* 12–14; Aeschin. 3. 84 ff.; 2. 169; D. 21. 162; 39. 16; [D.] 59. 4. Cf. Pokorny, 132–4. Cawkwell, 'Olynthus' 127 ff., has a good account and discussion of the whole episode, with bibliography. P. A. Brunt in his good article 'Euboea in the time of Philip II', *CQ* N.S. 19 (1969), 245 ff., agrees with Cawkwell's conclusion on this, that Philip was not concerned in this movement, either before or after it began, despite Aeschines 3. 87 and Plu. *Phoc.* 12. 1. So, too, J. M. Carter, 'Athens, Euboea, and Olynthus', *Historia* 20 (1971) 418 ff. As to whether Philip helped to start it, there is no direct evidence either way: it is simply a matter of probability. As to his help after it had started, the text of Aeschines has παρὰ Φιλίππου δύναμιν μεταπεμψάμενος, of Callias and Chalcis; and Plutarch introducing his account of the Euboean campaign of Phocion wrote παραδυομένου δὲ εἰς τὴν Εὔβοιαν τοῦ Φιλίππου καὶ δύναμιν ἐκ Μακεδονίας διαβιβάζοντος. We are invited, however, to emend Φιλίππου to Φαλαίκου in the text of Aeschines, because the scholiast (ad 3. 86) wrote, of Clitarchus of Eretria not of Callias, λαβὼν παρὰ Φαλαίκου τοῦ Φωκέων τυράννου δύναμιν, and because Aeschines goes on immediately to say that Callias' brother Taurosthenes 'brought across the Phocian mercenaries' (τοὺς Φωκικοὺς ξένους διαβιβάσας), before the pair of them attacked the Athenians at Tamynae. The emendation has its attractions (though it is not easy to see why a scribe miscopied Phalaikou as Philippou when it is about forty lines earlier that the name of Philip last appears in the text). The emended text in isolation gives excellent sense: Callias had sent for 'Phocian mercenaries', from Phalaecus, his brother Taurosthenes had actually brought them. But seen in context, the emended text seems implausible, perhaps even impossible. The tone and the detail of this passage emphasize the dangerous situation of the Athenian army in Euboea (Aeschines one of them). To this the unemended text contributes substantially, with its two reinforcements to the Euboeans, the one sent for (from Philip), the other already there ('the Phocian mercenaries'). The emended text, because it is giving us the same reinforcement twice, some of its details unnecessary and for the main purpose useless, is very unlikely to be right.

As for Plutarch (above), he had a source which recorded Philip's sending troops to Euboea, and the source may be Aeschines whether at first or second hand (cf. Beloch 3². 1. 495 n. 1, who saw confirmation here of the manuscripts reading at Aeschin. 3. 87). To say that Plutarch simply anticipated here the conditions in Euboea of some years later, when Philip certainly did have troops there, is unconvincing. In short, if either Aeschines or Plutarch were telling us something inherently improbable, it might be right to emend the one or disbelieve the other, or both. As it is, we remind ourselves that these Euboeans did not know at the start that they were going to win quickly: if they were wise, they asked for reinforcements of all who might send them, including Philip, who had intrigued, we know, in Euboea two years before, and most likely had not ceased then. If he was asked for troops now, he probably sent some: clearly he was on excellent terms with these Euboeans a few months later (below, p. 329 n. 2).

Cawkwell makes the point ('Olynthus' 129–30) that Demosthenes 'was both opposed to the expedition and proud of having been so': how could he 'pride himself on opposing an expedition against troops sent by Philip'? Though the whole question of Demosthenes and Euboea is notoriously complex, I do not really see Cawkwell's (and Brunt's) difficulty here. This expedition after all was a failure (as Brunt, 291, rightly emphasized). Any politician who had opposed it was in a strong position, and had a right to be pleased with himself. (But see also Carter, art. cit. 429.)

Callias of Chalcis sent to Philip for help when the revolt had begun may be taken as certain, though it has been denied. Philip had intrigued with the Euboeans in 351 with no results: now in 349/8 results came, and at a time most opportune for him. To suppose that he had nothing whatever to do with it until after it had started seems to put a greater strain on credulity than to suppose the opposite. This revolt succeeded. Euboea became free of the Athenian alliance, and though the fighting there this winter (February–March) probably did not affect the fate of Olynthus decisively, its loss was a serious undermining of the Athenian position, if Philip were to invade Central Greece and threaten Attica. This contingency cannot have failed to influence Athenian decisions on the scale of their commitments in Chalcidice in 348. Demosthenes had used the threat of invasion of Attica by Philip as an argument for maximum support of the Olynthians now.[1] But any who doubted the possibility of saving Olynthus will have used the same argument in reverse. The existence in Olynthus of pro-Macedonians cannot have been unknown in Athens, and one of the vital decisions needed now was, how much of Athenian strength to commit to Chalcidice in support of allies who might collapse, when clearly, if they did collapse, all the strength might be needed at home very soon.[2]

Philip too, however, had his own difficulties during this winter; and difficulties which, we must conclude, he had not foreseen. It cannot have been according to plan (his plan) that the first operations in Chalcidice of spring 348 were initiated by the enemy, that invasion led by Charidemus of the territories (or part of them) which had submitted to Philip the year before (above). It was bad policy on Philip's part to allow these friends to suffer for having joined him. But the Macedonians evidently were not yet there in force. Philip himself (though this is a question which unfortunately needs discussion) was probably in Thessaly, and notably at Pherae.

Diodorus 16. 52. 9 inevitably has exercised the attention of all who have undertaken to study these events seriously.[3] This section, containing the whole of the material concerning mainland Greece in this archon-year (349/8), consists of two sentences. The first summarizes Philip's campaign (summer and autumn 349) in Chalcidice, and has been considered already (above, pp. 316 f.): the second reads 'Then he moved on to Pherae in Thessaly, and expelled Peitholaus the ruler of the city.' Diodorus has recorded previously (under his year 352/1) that 'Lycophron

---

[1] D. 3. 8 f.

[2] This decision was in some respects very like some which the British Government had to take during the battle of France in early summer 1940. For an excellent discussion of the strategic situation of Athens, Cawkwell, 'Olynthus' 134 ff.

[3] Cf. especially the good Appendix V of Sordi, *LT* (358 ff.), with bibliography; also ibid. 262 ff.

and Peitholaus the tyrants of Pherae, isolated as they were after the death of Onomarchus, surrendered Pherae to Philip, and themselves departed under terms of truce with the mercenaries numbering 2,000, sought refuge with Phayllus, and joined the Phocians.'[1] Modern interpreters may be forgiven for concluding (as some have) that Diodorus has made here one of his occasional and characteristic messes, recording the same event twice in two different years, by using two sources, one a narrative source the other a chronographical one.[2] But this particular mess is uncharacteristic, because his presumed 'chronographic' entry (brief) is made here after the more detailed entry presumed to be from the narrative source.[3] To record 'chronographically' in one year, and then re-record with more detail in a later year seems a method inconvenient and misleading enough. But to reverse the order of two such entries seems to be so stupid as to be impossible; and the gap of three years between the two entries makes the 'doublet' explanation implausible here, too.[4]

If this is accepted, then Diodorus is not re-recording here the expulsion of Lycophron and Peitholaus in 352, but is recording for the first (and only) time a different event at Pherae which he found in his sources and judged important enough not to be omitted. We do know from the allusions of Demosthenes a few months earlier that Philip had been thought to be having trouble now in Thessaly, and since Thessalian claims were said to refer not only to taxes but also to Pagasae and Magnesia, former possessions of Pherae, it is easy to see that dissatisfaction and unrest was likely to be stronger at Pherae than anywhere else.[5] Theopompus, too, lends support to the notion that Diodorus did not invent happenings in Thessaly now which really happened at some other time. Of the six surviving fragments named as from his 22nd book, four refer to Chalcidice, the other two to place-names in Thessaly: and his 23rd book dealt with (*inter alia*) Charidemus at Olynthus in spring 348.[6] Justin, too, records an intervention in Thessaly by Philip, but after (not before) the fall of Olynthus.[7]

The real objection to this notice of Diodorus about Philip, Pherae, and Peitholaus, is to the name Peitholaus. Pherae was to give trouble

---

[1] D.S. 16. 37. 3 (cf. 39. 3).

[2] Westlake, 183 and n. 3 rightly refused to see a double entry here, but his reason (the absence of Lycophron from the second notice) is not decisive.

[3] Contrast the double entries at 16. 31. 6; 34. 4–5 (Methone), and 16. 31. 3; 39. 1–7 (Orneae etc.).

[4] If Momigliano's (*FM* 140) reference to an 'attempt to return by the tyrant Peitholaus', in 344, is based on the text under discussion, it is still harder to see how or why Diodorus, who did record expulsions of tyrants in Thessaly in 344/3 without naming either Pherae or Peitholaus (16. 69. 8), could have so misplaced this entry about Peitholaus, in isolation in 349/8, if it really belonged to 344/3.   [5] D. 1. 22; 2. 11: see above, pp. 222 ff.

[6] Theopompus, *FGrH* 115, F 137–8 (Thessaly); 139–42 (Chalcidice); 143 (Charidemus at Olynthus). For the date of Charidemus' expedition, Cawkwell, 'Olynthus' 131.

[7] Just. 8. 3. 12.

later, and had some reasons for giving trouble now; but Peitholaus in control again there is almost impossible to accept. With Pagasae the port of Pherae in Philip's hands and with most of Thessaly hostile to Peitholaus as an ally of the Phocians, he had no way of returning to Pherae to take charge there. On the other hand, for a popular leader inside Pherae to achieve supreme power (δυναστεύοντα), by shouting the loudest for Pagasae and Magnesia, seems not impossible; for Pherae had these special grievances and Philip perhaps had a special unpopularity there. Perhaps the mistake of Diodorus in this vexed passage was to write the name Peitholaus (which at any rate he knew) in place of the name of a new Pheraean leader which meant nothing to him.[1] What seems certain is that Peitholaus here is unacceptable; but 'trouble at Pherae' in itself is not unacceptable, and may help to explain the slow start to Philip's Chalcidian campaign of 348.[2]

5. *Olynthus: the end*

The spring campaign, it seems, opened with the initiative in the hands of the Olynthians, Philip not yet having reached Chalcidice, and whatever forces he had there being presumably inferior to the enemy, who could still put an army of more than 10,000 in the field, including the reinforcements from Athens.[3] For a Greek army they were unusually

---

[1] As it happens, only a few lines later (16. 53. 2) Diodorus located Olynthus and other Chalcidian cities on the Hellespont. He was not, just here, right at the very top of his form. Diodorus wrote . . . Φίλιππος μὲν σπεύδων τὰς ἐφ' Ἑλλησπόντῳ πόλεις χειρώσασθαι Μηκύβερναν μὲν καὶ Τορώνην . . . παρέλαβεν, ἐπὶ δὲ τὴν μεγίστην . . . Ὄλυνθον στρατεύσας . . . etc. The aberration passes unremarked by Sordi in the *Commentary* of her *Diodorus* XVI p. 94, who thinks that the brief notice at 52. 9 of Philip's attacking 'the Chalcidian cities' is probably from Diodorus' chronographical source, while this at 53. 2 is certainly from his narrative source. This may be true, but 'Hellespont' does nothing to support it. That mistake should never have been made by any literate Aegean Greek of any period, and perhaps was Diodorus' own.

[2] Sordi (*LT* 358) confronts our Diodorus passage with a remark of Demosthenes which, she writes, 'explicitly excludes' any possibility that Pherae in 349 was not firmly in Philip's control. D. 19. 320, alluding to 346, wrote 'when Philip was having great trouble with the Thessalians, and Pherae for the first time refused to follow him . . .' ἡνίκ' ἐστασίαζε μὲν αὐτῷ τὰ Θετταλῶν, καὶ Φεραῖοι πρῶτον οὐ συνηκολούθουν. But Sordi's inference from this remark is incorrect, as her own interpretation of it on an earlier page shows clearly. There (*LT* 282), she comments very justly that ἀκολουθεῖν was used by Xenophon of the military duty of Spartan allies to supply troops for the *hegemon*'s campaigns (X. *HG* 5. 3. 26; 6. 3. 7; 5. 1). Agreed; but there is no suggestion that Pherae was required to march in 349/8, of course. With complaints about Pagasae and Magnesia, and about the funds from Thessalian League taxes being used for non-League purposes, implying that they were meant to be used for the war (Phocian) which interested the Thessalians, any notion that Philip in 349 ever contemplated calling on any Thessalian troops for the war in Chalcidice would be preposterous. Neither Pherae nor any other Thessalian city 'refused to follow', because they were never asked to 'follow'. But if there are other grounds for thinking that Pherae was disaffected in 349/8, or out of Philip's control, this remark of Demosthenes is no obstacle.

[3] See p. 322 and n. 1 below.

strong in cavalry: even after the defections of 348 they must still have had nearly 1,000 horse, including 150 Athenians.[1] The numerical superiority, presently, of the Macedonian cavalry need not have been overwhelming, and this explains perhaps why, when Philip himself had arrived in Chalcidice with the main army, it was possible for two battles to be fought; Macedonian victories.[2] While their cavalry still enabled them to move about without the certainty of being cut to pieces by the Macedonians, the enemy generals probably judged that move they must, and if necessary engage, in the hope of forestalling attempts to detach their remaining League cities individually, and perhaps too to prevent the Macedonians from closing in on Olynthus itself and investing it.

What details we have of these last weeks of Olynthus are almost all concerned with acts of treachery.[3] Some of these we learn of from Demosthenes at his least impartial, but it is difficult not to agree with his estimate of their significance. Without them, Olynthus was not sure to have survived; but with them, *certa mori*, by the choice and decision of some among her own citizens. That Philip should take the important League city of Torone by treachery from within was bad enough. That Mecyberna, the harbour of Olynthus, was betrayed in the same way was disastrous.[4] Meanwhile they suffered the two defeats in the field, and city after city opened its gates. At some stage in this tale of woe the Olynthians pressed Athens urgently for more help (and got it, though

---

[1] For the Chalcidian military strength, D. 19. 266 and 230 is to be used with some reserves, obviously. According to D. the Olynthians themselves had 1,000 cavalry, and were more than 10,000 strong: all the neighbouring states were their allies, and Athens had sent 10,000 mercenaries and 4,000 citizen troops and 50 triremes. D. is concerned, however, to make the point that no state, however strong, can survive the corruption of its own leaders, and that Olynthus had been very strong.

D.'s figures for the Athenian aid are 'corrected' by Philochorus (*FGrH* 328 F 49–51), whose 6,000 mercenaries, 150 cavalry for the first two Athenian reinforcements are generally accepted, no doubt rightly. The third reinforcement (2,000 Athenian hoplites, 300 cavalry) arrived too late. The figures of Philochorus for Athenian triremes add up to 73, as against the 50 of Demosthenes: perhaps ships of the first squadron were to be withdrawn when others arrived (*diadochoi*)? (For some discussion, Cawkwell, 'Olynthus' 131.)

For the Chalcidian army, D.'s exaggeration lies in his giving the impression that Olynthus itself had 1,000 cavalry and an army total of more than 10,000, and in addition the troops of her allies (= Chalcidian League members—'all the neighbouring states were their allies'). As a total for the army of the League, 1,000 cavalry and about 10,000 infantry is not unreasonably high.

[2] D.S. 16. 53. 2.

[3] The source of Diodorus here was probably the Athenian Diyllus (*FGrH* 73); cf. Hammond, 'SD' 89 ff.; M. Sordi, *Diodorus* xvi, note ad 53. 2, and pp. xxx ff., who sees this emphasis on treachery as the work of an anti-Macedonian source (Philip himself might have taken it as a compliment, however). The source is certainly 'Demosthenic' in its attitude, making the most of treachery where it found it. But in the conditions prevailing in Chalcidice in 348 neither Demosthenes nor another need be thought to have invented instances of treachery. The Chalcidians were collapsing now as France collapsed in 1940, and what was treachery for Demosthenes was survival for the people concerned; inglorious but unsurprising.

[4] D.S. 16. 53. 2.

the help arrived too late).[1] But when Philip threatened Olynthus itself they decided, at last, to send to him saying 'Enough': what were his terms? His answer, of an almost oracular solemnity more chilling even than the famous allegory of Cyrus pronounced to the Ionians in a like situation, robbed the Olynthians in a few well-chosen words of their last ally, hope. 'There is not room for us both, for you in Olynthus and me in Macedonia.'[2] The Olynthians fought on.

The war had become a siege, and the siege a nightmare, for a mass of the Olynthian knights had surrendered to the Macedonians, whether by the treachery of their commanders or their own collaboration, or by these two things in some way combined. Demosthenes calls this a record in military terms, and no doubt it was.[3] At what stage in the war it happened is not clear, but it may well have been this that brought the Olynthians to seek terms from Philip (above).[4] (The big cavalry formation of this incident will have been operating in the field still, and not under siege conditions.) Demosthenes spoke of it later as the act of treachery which decided the city's fate.[5] The leaders Euthycrates and Lasthenes, named by Demosthenes as Philip's agents before the war, are named by Diodorus as responsible for the fall of Olynthus.[6] And Lasthenes was *hipparch*, certainly one of the 'commanders' who 'betrayed' the cavalry.[7] The scandal of the cavalry can be seen as evidence of a social disintegration, and in this sense an omen for all Greece; the *beltistoi*, the élite of the city, saving themselves, the city abandoned to its fate. This was not really the cowardice that will do anything to save its skin, for utter cowards appear (like heroes) by ones and twos and not in hundreds. It was, more, a kind of sophisticated prudence, of men who having taken thought had concluded that what they were fighting for was (for them) not so wonderfully good, or the alternative (life under Philip) not so unbearably bad. The effect of the surrender on the mass of the citizens can be imagined. But when they failed to get reasonable terms

---

[1] Philoch. *FGrH* 328, F 51.

[2] D. 9. 11 . . . Ὀλυνθίοις, τετταράκοντ' ἀπέχων τῆς πόλεως στάδια, εἶπεν ὅτι δεῖ δυοῖν θάτερον, ἢ ἐκείνους ἐν Ὀλύνθῳ μὴ οἰκεῖν ἢ αὑτὸν ἐν Μακεδονίᾳ, πάντα τὸν ἄλλον χρόνον. This seems to bear the mark of direct quotation, words which none of those who heard them spoken and reported will have forgotten easily. (For Cyrus, Hdt. 1. 141. 1 ff.)

[3] D. 19. 267 πεντακοσίους δ' ἱππέας προδοθέντας ὑπ' αὐτῶν τῶν ἡγουμένων ἔλαβεν αὐτοῖς ὅπλοις ὁ Φίλιππος, ὅσους οὐδεὶς πώποτ' ἄλλος ἀνθρώπων. Whether D.'s figure of 500 is trustworthy must be very doubtful. But for 100 cavalry to surrender in a body with arms intact is a thing inexplicable in military terms and requiring a political explanation.

[4] The surrender of the knights must surely have come later than the final appeal of the Olynthians to Athens, because the news of treachery on this scale would have warned the Athenians that Olynthus was doomed, and would have deterred them from voting their third and last expedition in (probably) June 348 (Philoch. *FGrH* 328, F 51; cf. Cawkwell, 'Olynthus', 131).

[5] D. 9. 56.   [6] D. 19. 265; D.S. 16. 53. 2; cf. Suidas s.v. *Karanos*.

[7] D. 9. 66; 19. 267.

from Philip they put their trust in Athens still, and made determined resistance under siege.[1] How the end came, whether by more treachery, or by an unconditional surrender or by a storming of the city, is unknown. The war from start to end was over in less than a year, or not much more.[2]

Unfortunately for the Olynthians and for his own good name, Philip had meant what he said. When the city had been sacked, the inhabitants were sold as slaves. Olynthus ceased to exist.[3] That this treatment came as a shock to the rest of Greece need not be doubted. To end the life of a city was repugnant to the ethical standards of the time. Nor were the Greeks impervious to pity for the victims of war: even in a rage they knew that it was 'a savage decision and no light matter, to wipe out a whole city rather than fail to wipe out the guilty'.[4] Yet certain Greeks could accept Olynthian captives as presents from Philip: and if this was possible it seems certain that Greeks, as well as Macedonians and others, bought

[1] D.S. 16. 53. 2 'Philip attacked continually and lost many men in the fighting at the walls.' The excavator of Olynthus reported 247 arrow-heads among the finds, and he associated very many of them with this final siege, with some inferences which seem adventurous (Robinson, *Olynthus* 10, pp. 378, 382, 388, 392, 398, 405). Five of the arrow-heads however bear an inscription, ΦΙΛΙΠΠΟ ; which confirms that there really was siege warfare before the city fell (ibid. p. 383 nos. 1907–11, and Pl. 120). About 500 sling-bullets were found at Olynthus and Mecyberna, more than 100 of them inscribed. Of these, thirteen bear the name of Philip (three of them found at Mecyberna). The name Hipponicus appears on sixteen, and an identification seems possible with the Hipponicus who is reported as commanding 1,000 mercenaries of Philip in Euboea in 343 (D. 9. 58). (See Robinson, ibid. pp. 431–3 nos. 2228–40 and Pl. 132, for 'Philip'; and ibid. pp. 424–6 nos 2186–201, and Pl. 131, for 'Hipponicus'.) The 'Cleobulus' on fifteen bullets is unidentified (ibid. pp. 427–8 nos. 2202–16).

The presence of sling-bullets in this quantity seems conclusive confirmation of the τειχομαχία of Diodorus (above).

[2] D. 19. 266. Olynthus fell probably towards the end of September, not long before the Macedonian Olympia (see p. 327 n. 4).

Perhaps I should mention that I reject [Callisthenes] F 57 (*FGrH* 124) as ungenuine. (*Contra*, it seems, Robinson, *Olynthus* 10. 382.) This writer transfers from Methone to Olynthus the story of Philip's losing his eye, and develops it into a near parallel to the Horatius Cocles story which ends with his swimming the river to safety. But the well-attested story of Philip's entertaining a great assemblage of guests a few days after the fall of Olynthus (below, p. 327 and n. 4) proves that he had not lost an eye recently but was in good health. And from internal evidence Callisthenes could not have been responsible for this version, which is the work not of a native Olynthian with good information enabling him to correct Theopompus and Marsyas of Pella (above, p. 257), but of someone who for some reason used a remark of Demosthenes as his context for this story. D. 9. 26 Ὄλυνθον μὲν δὴ καὶ Μεθώνην καὶ Ἀπολλωνίαν καὶ δύο καὶ τριάκοντα πόλεις ἐπὶ Θράκης ἐῶ . . . etc. [Callisth.] F 57 ap. Plu. *Mor.* 307 D = Stob. 3. 7. 67: Καλλισθένους ἐν τρίτῳ Μακεδονικῶν. Φίλιππος ὁ Μακεδόνων βασιλεὺς δύο καὶ τριάκοντα Χαλκιδικὰς πόλεις τοῖς ἰδίοις ὑποτάξας σκήπτροις Μεθωναίους καὶ ᾿Ολυνθίους λεηλατεῖν ἤρξατο . . . etc. What the author of this curious work (*Parallela Graeca et Romana*) thought he was doing here (or elsewhere), need not concern us now. What he was not doing was quoting Callisthenes of Olynthus.

[3] D.S. 16. 53. 3; D. 9. 26; Just. 8. 3. 11; Str. 10. 447. The literary tradition is confirmed by the excavations. Especially the evidence of the nearly 4,000 coins found on the site shows plainly that it ceased to be inhabited now.

[4] Thuc. 3. 36. 4 (of Mytilene).

the captives who were put up for sale.[1] As for Philip, though the fate of Olynthus might make people afraid of him, they need not positively execrate him for it, or even think of him as peculiarly barbarous. Had not Thebes destroyed Plataea and Thespiae, in the memory of most living adults in Greece? Would not Sparta put an end to Messene tomorrow, if she got the chance? Athens would not be in existence at this moment if the Boeotians and Corinthians had had their way in 404. And what had the Athenians themselves done at Sestus only five years ago? 'Chares the Athenian general led a squadron to the Hellespont and captured the city of Sestus: he put the men of military age to death, and the rest of the population he sold into slavery.'[2] Though it was ethically wrong to destroy cities, it was only really horrible when it happened to friends; and most horrible when it happened to you.

This last thought may have been the one that stayed on when the rest had been put aside. Life had always been hard in Greece for small cities, and there was always the chance that a small city sooner or later might go to the wall. But the really nasty thing, here in Chalcidice, was that Olynthus was a big city, and one which in recent years had succeeded in dominating its immediate neighbours. The Chalcidian League by Greek standards had been a really strong combination, well able to look after itself now that both Athens and Sparta had declined. This swift, efficient conquest by Philip had shown that the victories in Thessaly and elsewhere had not been by a series of lucky accidents. Macedonia undoubtedly was a great power now, and was here to be lived with. But how many combinations in Greece were strong enough to live with it? This was the question to be faced, by Philip's friends as well as his enemies.

The other question, for us, is what led Philip to so uncompromising a solution to the Chalcidian question, if it can be called that? For after all, even if the Chalcidians seemed no longer tolerable as allies, it was possible to annex Chalcidice to Macedonia, to impose a tribute, to garrison Olynthus if it seemed best, to disarm Olynthus and any other city by demolishing the walls and defences, all without destroying any cities or harming their populations. The answer to this seems almost sure to be not quite a simple one. More considerations than one are likely to have contributed to the decision; but there are some motives that probably can be ruled out. Security was one, for surely in these ten years he must have recognized that even untrustworthy allies in Chalcidice, even if they joined forces with Athens, were unable to be a real threat to Macedonia now.[3] Nor was this an act of sheer irritation at being put to

---

[1] D. 19. 196 f.; 229; 305 f.; 309. Allegations of Demosthenes on this topic may not have been true, but he would not have made them if they were impossible and absurd.

The 'refugees from Philip's siege' whom we see being legislated for at Athens (*IG* ii². 211) are presumably Olynthians, though the name appears in the printed text only by restoration.

[2] D.S. 16. 34. 3.   [3] Demosthenes realized this in 351, it seems (D. 4. 43).

trouble, or even righteous indignation at being double-crossed by allies who had been well paid to be faithful: for in general there is no sign that Philip in his political decisions was apt to be ruled by emotion, and the presumption must be that he arrived at this one by calculation. The material advantages of doing what he did are obvious. Booty from Olynthus and other cities, and the sale of captives, no doubt paid for this war; and (more important) it was good to acquire much good land for distribution in estates to Macedonians.[1] (Athens had not been above doing this in Lesbos in her 'lenient' settlement with Mytilene in 427.) In this age winners of wars did not expect to be out of pocket after it, and if the circumstances allowed a victor to help himself to something really worth while, no consideration for the vanquished would stop him (Athens at Samos in 365 is an example). The sheer material gain, then, of annexation in this form most probably weighed quite heavily with Philip.

Terrorization was another factor.[2] Since by his position in Thessaly and his alliance with the Boeotians Philip was committed already to intervening some day soon in central Greece and helping to bring the Sacred War to an end, obviously there was something to be said, on general principles, for his giving the Greeks cause to shake in their shoes; one stern example now might save a deal of bother and bloodshed later. This counted for something perhaps, though it may be thought to be at variance with the very profitable diplomatic methods of his early dealings in Thessaly, and with the Chalcidians themselves: Philip the impressive, the eloquent, the genial and congenial, the pro-Athenian even, and 'absolutely Greek':[3] this was an image not to be tossed away lightly, especially by one who seems to have loved diplomacy just as much as he loved war, and who came to believe that there was almost no one whom money could not buy, or at least that there was nowhere where there was not someone who could be bought.[4]

Terrorization was a two-edged weapon, then; enough so to throw doubt on this as a motive for the blotting out of Olynthus in a gesture addressed to 'the Greeks' indiscriminately. It would be different perhaps if it could be shown that addressed to certain Greeks in particular, just at this moment and in this situation, a terrorizing gesture might seem to him likely to do a power of good. And this is not out of the question. Athens, for example? It is absolutely certain that even before the Olynthian War ended he had decided to make peace with Athens, provided that the Athenians would agree to his terms. Though the war with Athens had done Macedonia no great harm, the Athenians had once (at Thermopylae) stopped him from invading Phocis, and they

---

[1] D.S. 16. 53. 3.   [2] Ibid.   [3] D. 19. 308; Aeschin. 2. 42; 47 f.; 51 f.
[4] D.S. 16. 53. 3 and 54. 3; D. 18. 19 etc.

might perhaps be able to do this again; to say nothing of the complications in the longer term, when the Sacred War one day should be over, and the Amphictyons (Athens one of them) be due to settle the affairs of central Greece. If he judged it really important to make the peace with Athens now (and this seems likely),[1] he may have seen the fall of Olynthus as his opportunity of warning the Athenians not to miss this chance: now they could have peace, not without loss but without disaster. Let them not fight on refusing to cut their losses without first contemplating what disaster meant: the exemplar was Olynthus. A little crude, perhaps; but Philip had no alternative means of persuasion as yet. Up to now, he had had no opportunity to make any politicians in Athens his friends, he had bribed nobody, and had no political 'lobby' that he could count on.[2] The alternative was to make the facts of life and the realities of power clear beyond mistake, and to rely on the Athenian people's instinct for self-preservation.

The other possible target for this demonstration (if it was that) was in Thessaly, and specifically at Pherae (above, pp. 319 ff.). Anything that Philip could do to Olynthus he could do more easily to Pherae. Polybius saw this treatment of Olynthus as 'an example' which helped him not only to become master of the cities of the north ('Thrace') but also to get control of Thessaly 'by intimidation' (διὰ τὸν φόβον).[3] Polybius evidently thought of his 'control of Thessaly' as beginning only after the Olynthian war and not before it; but the fate of Olynthus as 'an example' can still be seen to make sense at whatever stage in the winning of 'control of Thessaly' he had arrived in 348. Obstructors in Thessaly and particularly in Pherae could take warning now. An element of intimidation can hardly be ruled out from all this; but from the whole Chalcidian story from its beginning to its end perhaps the 'example' that Philip hoped most to present was of himself as the good friend and the bad foe. Can a glimpse of this, even, be read between the lines of that long anecdote about the actor Satyrus at the Macedonian festival of Zeus Olympios celebrated by Philip very shortly after the fall of Olynthus, when the victors relaxed with games and feasting, the leading actors of the day having been engaged for the dramatic contests?[4] Satyrus, fresh from a professional triumph and pressed repeatedly to name his boon for the

---

[1] Aeschin. 2. 12 ff. See below, pp. 329 ff.

[2] In nearly ten years of war there had been no contacts, and even Demosthenes makes no suggestions of corruption antedating the first Athenian embassy to Macedonia in 346.

[3] Plb. 9. 28. 3.

[4] D. 19. 192 ff. (cf. D.S. 16. 55). Cawkwell ('Olynthus' 130 and n. 4) uses D.'s opening words ἐπειδὴ γὰρ εἷλεν Ὄλυνθον Φίλιππος, Ὀλύμπι' ἐποίει . . . to date the fall itself inside the period of the Macedonian Olympia (probably October, it seems, from Arr. *An.* 1. 10. 2; 11. 1), but this seems unnecessary and indeed improbable. Translate 'When Philip had taken Olynthus, he was celebrating his Olympic festival . . .'. (D.S. 55. 1 correctly, μετὰ δὲ τὴν ἅλωσιν τῆς Ὀλύνθου Ὀλύμπια ποιήσας . . .)

king to grant, named in the end the daughters of a man now dead (his *xenos*) who were among the Olynthian captives. One sees some 'intimidation' here (*phobos*)—Satyrus had to nerve himself to ask for what he wanted. But when he had spoken the assembled guests, including the professionals from Greece, were unable to contain themselves and burst into applause. Hired here by the king, and hoping no doubt to be hired again, they had had enough to drink to show where their sympathies lay. Is it fanciful to see some success here for Philip in his presentation of 'the good friend'? His guests were not totally intimidated. Indeed even Demosthenes telling the story does not disguise that Philip took this very well: 'he was moved, and he granted the boon.'

Behind the celebrations however the business of state moved on. Of the actors present two others were to act as Philip's diplomatic agents in a matter of the first importance.[1]

[1] See p. 330, for Aristodemus and Neoptolemus. I assume that as distinguished artists (for the 'engagements' of Aristodemus, Aeschin. 2. 19) they were not absent from this important occasion.

IX

THE PEACE OF 346

THE fall of Olynthus meant, as it turned out, the end of the war with Athens, the war which Athenians themselves had come to call 'the war for Amphipolis'.[1] The name is instructive, because it shows well an Athenian capacity for wishful thinking: at the end of the war Athenians as intelligent and well informed as Isocrates and Aeschines really believed they had been fighting for Amphipolis for ten years or more, when in reality they had not been fighting at all, in any sense of the word that would have made sense to a man of war who knew what fighting meant. To Philip for example. It is necessary to make this point because it helps probably to explain why these combatants took such an inordinate time to make peace, once the first informal overtures had been made: at the outset they were not talking about peace in the same language. Philip had not been given the smallest cause for anxiety about Amphipolis since he had taken it nearly ten years ago, and he regarded it in the sphere of international relations (we may suspect) as no more now than a piece of ancient history which nobody could possibly expect to discuss except those who lived in the past or in some world of fantasy of their own. Amphipolis was a city of Macedonia.

It was not, then, in order to make opportunities to discuss the future status of Amphipolis that Philip, even before Olynthus fell, twice or thrice made informal overtures to Athens, to the effect that he would be glad to make peace.[2] Then, after the fall of Olynthus, he released the Athenian prisoner of war, Iatrocles, to carry the same message to Athens again.[3] By these repeated messages he clearly meant business, and there is no reason to doubt his disappointment when he learned of the prosecution at Athens of Philocrates for some illegality concerned with his proposal that Philip should be invited to send ambassadors to Athens to discuss peace (late in 348). That Philocrates was acquitted, and that so convinced an anti-Macedonian as Demosthenes spoke in his defence, was more encouraging for the future of these exchanges;[4] but the

---

[1] So described in 346 by Isocrates (5. 2), in 343 by Aeschines (2. 70).

[2] Aeschin. 2. 12 ff. 'The Euboeans' who conveyed the first message will have been in Athens presumably before midsummer 348, if they were making their own peace after the recent successful rising. The message conveyed by Ctesiphon on his return to Athens, from negotiations about the ransom money of Phrynon (see p. 474 below) will have been in autumn 348 (Phrynon having been captured in July/August).

[3] Aeschin. 2. 15–16.   [4] Aeschin. 2. 13–14.

Athenians, Philip must have learned now, were still some way from recognizing the true facts of their situation and nerving themselves to cut their losses. The fate of Olynthus presumably was felt in Athens as a severe shock, provoking both indignation at the barbarous treatment of allies and alarm as to what Philip might do next. And the occasion was evidently seen as one for rousing Greece as a whole to an awareness of the danger from the north. A great diplomatic effort was set in hand now, to promote a coalition of Greek states in alliance with Athens, and so to continue the war (winter 348/7).[1]

Philip's reaction was itself diplomatic and not military; and this fact is important if it enables us to see into his motives for originating peace feelers and for continuing on the same course in the face of these early rebuffs. For clearly it was open to him, if the Athenians were not interested in peace, to give them war, and war where they wanted it least, either in the Chersonese or in central Greece, or both. (Demosthenes had seen this coming even before the Olynthian war had reached its crisis.[2]) But throughout the year 347 Philip held his hand. His support of a faction in Arcadia was disquieting certainly, in a general way, but at this time more directly so to Sparta than to Athens.[3] We may presume that he had his informants (the actors Neoptolemus and Aristodemus, and no doubt others) who could advise him on the state of feeling in Athens, and from whose reports he perhaps concluded that if he made the Athenians fight for their lives now, they probably would do just that.[4] His agents and *xenoi* up and down Greece, too, must have led him to conclude that he had nothing to fear from a Greek coalition against him: in the Peloponnese especially the fact that Sparta was already committed against him as an ally of the Phocians guaranteed the neutrality (if no more) of most of the other states. It was in Athens and in Thebes, the

---

[1] Aeschin. 2. 79; D. 19. 10; ibid. 303 ff. From these passages it seems clear that the embassies to the Greeks recalled here by both Aeschines and Demosthenes in 343, including that on which Aeschines figured prominently in Arcadia, were before, and probably long before the Athenians decided to send the first embassy to Philip about peace in 346; and therefore that they are not to be confused with the 'embassies to the Greeks' whose return was still awaited at Athens in April 346 when Philip's terms (brought back from Macedonia by the 'first embassy') were under discussion (Aeschin. 2. 57 ff.; 3. 67, 70: and see below, p. 340). In particular (as Schaefer saw, 2². 173), D. 19. 305–6 shows that Aeschines was in Arcadia only a matter of weeks or months, not more, after the fall of Olynthus; that is, in winter 348/7. Aeschines met there a party of about thirty Olynthian women and children arriving from Macedonia, a gift of Philip to the Arcadian Atrestidas. Largesse on this scale to individuals must have dispersed very quickly all the Olynthian captives who had not been put up for sale; and to think of this gift as being made a year or more after the event is out of the question. Cawkwell ('Peace' 421) seems to take too little account of this in his argument designed to prove that the only embassies of Athens 'to the Greeks' were those of early 346.

[2] D. 1. 25 f.   [3] D. 19. 10.

[4] Aeschin. 2. 72. For the important role of Neoptolemus and Aristodemus as intermediaries, D. 19. 12 and 315; 5. 6; Aeschin. 2. 16–19.

cities which already had experienced at close quarters (for ill and for good) what the new Macedonian power could accomplish, that the advisers of the people had the best chance of realizing that the whole balance of power in Greece had changed irrevocably already. In the smaller states, and especially in the Peloponnese, even those who saw this truth could persuade themselves too easily that, if they played their hand with care, the repercussions of the change need never reach them: perhaps.

No great military move, then, came out of Macedonia in 347, but only a renewal of the harassing operations by sea, which caused Aeschines to speak later (in 343) of a threat to the advanced bases of Athens in the north, Lemnos, Imbros, and Scyros, while even Philip's inactivity (relatively speaking), whatever its intention, took on something of the character of a 'war of nerves', in which some Athenian settlers quitted the Chersonese and went back home because of their fears.[1] All this may have been good tactics by Philip (it was justified in the event); but what was the policy behind it? Assuming (as seems right) that he had decided now not to press home attacks which would force Athens into a fight for her existence, what were his reasons for forbearing?

Demosthenes alleged later (as he had once alleged before) that the war had brought Macedonian trade to a standstill, and that Philip was anxious for peace (in 347/6) for this reason.[2] Though Demosthenes was concerned in the *Embassy* speech to represent Philip as weaker and Athens as stronger when peace negotiations began than they really had been, it would be wrong to disregard entirely what he says here. More particularly, if the Chalcidians in the years of their alliance with Philip (357–349) had taken over the trading activities in Macedonian harbours which normally had been in Athenian hands, the treatment of Chalcidice in 348 must certainly have brought this to an end or nearly, and Macedonian trade may well have been reduced temporarily to a trickle of local exchange with Thessaly and only a very few other places. The effect of this on the revenues will have been bad, but not catastrophic, the revenues from duties on trade amounting to only a small fraction of the total revenue of Macedonia now. If Macedonia (like Athens) had needed to import cereals and export the wherewithal to pay for them, in order to survive, it would be necessary to agree with Demosthenes that by 347 Philip was really anxious for peace (ἐπιθυμῶν), because he really needed it. But all that we know of the country suggests that Macedonia could feed herself except perhaps for olives, which grew only in the

---

[1] Aeschin. 2. 72–3.

[2] D. 19. 315 τὸ μὲν γὰρ ἀπ' ἀρχῆς τῆς εἰρήνης ἐπιθυμῶν, διαφορουμένης αὐτοῦ τῆς χώρας ὑπὸ τῶν λῃστῶν καὶ κεκλειμένων τῶν ἐμπορίων, ὥστ' ἀνόνητον ἐκεῖνον ἁπάντων εἶναι τῶν ἀγαθῶν . . . Cf. D. 2. 16 (349) κεκλειμένων τῶν ἐμπορίων τῶν ἐν τῇ χώρᾳ διὰ τὸν πόλεμον.

milder coastal areas.[1] We do hear that in these years Macedonia had bought arms and gear for warships from abroad (ὅπλα . . . ἢ σκεύη τριηρικά), and (astoundingly) from Athens with whom she was at war;[2] and it is easy to believe that Philip's expanding army did set up a demand for shields, helmets, and the like, beyond the capacity of local armourers to satisfy, and that the seafaring cities under his control, especially if this happened after the disruption of Chalcidice, could not meet all the requirements of his fleet. A stoppage of supply from Athens, and a difficulty in importing from elsewhere because of Athenian squadrons cruising off Macedonia and Thrace for much of the summer, may well have been an inconvenience, perhaps even a serious one; but one cannot believe that it was more. Altogether, it seems that a resumption of normal trade would be a great gain at this time certainly, but not so great that Macedonia could not live well and fight well without it, or that Philip can have needed to forgo political objectives in order to obtain it.

The immediate political objective, no doubt, was Phocis. He was presumably committed to the Thessalians, and had been for some years, to bring the Sacred War to an end; and to do this, when it could be done without a desperate military struggle for what may be called the Phocian fortress zone from Thermopylae through to Delphi, would bring him into a commanding position in central Greece. His Boeotian allies too, whatever they might think of his advancement in the long term, immediately would be glad of peace, and relieved to have back the three cities of northern Boeotia still in Phocian hands. The writer of the Hypothesis to the speech of Demosthenes *On the Peace* puts these points clearly, stating unequivocally that Philip's reason for wanting peace was in order to end the Phocian War. He adds 'And this was impossible for him while the Athenians were at war with him': and he refers back to the Athenian defence of Thermopylae in 352.[3] But this is only valid if all the antagonists were of the same strength now as in 352. Of Athens this may be thought doubtful, for though her material strength had not been greatly impaired meanwhile, her will to resist probably had been weakened by the Olynthian débâcle, as is suggested by her ultimate agreement to make peace when the alternative was to continue the war alone or nearly alone.[4] But it is the Phocians who

[1] That olives were very important needs no emphasizing. One might think that entrepreneurs based on Pagasae and the Euboean cities could have organized a supply to meet this known emergency, if it was there, and that the final stage of importing into Macedonia could have been by a coastal traffic, via Pagasae, which the Athenians could not hope to stop.
[2] D. 19. 286 f., a decree of Timarchus prohibiting export of arms or naval gear to Philip in time of war; presumably because it had been found that these things had been exported to Philip. [3] D. 5, Hypoth. 1; cf. D. 19. 318 f.
[4] So D. 5, Hypoth. 1 εἰρήνης ἐπεθύμησαν ὅ τε Φίλιππος καὶ οἱ Ἀθηναῖοι, οἱ μὲν Ἀθηναῖοι κακῶς ἐν τῷ πολέμῳ φερόμενοι . . . But see below, p. 333, on the readiness of the Athenians to assume responsibility for the defence of Thermopylae in February 346.

represent the really weak link in this chain of reasoning. Demosthenes speaking in 343 of the Phocians as they were in 347/6 is not to be trusted without verification, because he is concerned to suggest (among other things) that they would and could have held out, and the Athenians could have saved them, if they had not been misled by bad advisers.[1] He conceals however the fact that the Phocians by now were very short of money: and he says nothing of their internal dissensions which in 347 threw some real doubt on their value as allies. We owe our information on these things mainly to Aeschines, who naturally was concerned to show that the Phocians were not reliable or strong, but whose evidence is supported in part by the narrative of Diodorus, and most signally by the way in which Phalaecus did finally reach his agreement with Philip (below).[2]

Although in the campaigns of 347 against the Boeotians the Phocians something more than held their own, the dismissal of Phalaecus from office and his replacement by a board of three generals (who instituted a financial inquiry and accounting) looks like an attempt to set up a government of moderates, in recognition of the fact that their eleventh hour had come. It was these generals who proposed to put into the hands of the Athenians the forts which commanded Thermopylae (Alponus, Thronion, Nicaea are named by Aeschines), a proposal accepted by the Athenians, who prepared a strong force with a fleet under Proxenus to occupy the positions. But meanwhile Phalaecus and the extremists had intervened; they disarmed (indeed imprisoned) the ambassadors of the Phocians who had negotiated with Athens, gave a hostile reception to Athenian religious envoys (*spondophoroi*), and refused to hand over Thermopylae (February 346).[3] At the same time (probably) they refused also to hand over Thermopylae to the Spartan king Archidamus, who according to Aeschines had been ready to take over that responsibility.[4]

---

[1] D. 19. 84, 317 ff., and 153.

[2] Aeschin. 2. 131 κατελύθησαν δ' ἀπορίᾳ χρημάτων, ἐπειδὴ κατεμισθοφόρησαν τὰ ὑπάρχοντα. The account in Diodorus (16. 56. 3 ff.) of how the Phocians instituted a judicial inquiry into where the money had gone, presupposes (among other things) that it had gone, most of it (D. records the inquiry in the year before the surrender).

[3] Aeschin. 2. 132–5. Aeschines himself was able to make it quite clear to the jury from a dated dispatch of Proxenus in the archives that all this happened before the Athenians decided to negotiate with Philip and elected their ten ambassadors: ibid. 135 ἀκούετε . . . τῶν χρόνων παραναγιγνωσκομένων ἐκ τῶν δημοσίων γραμμάτων, . . . ὅτι πρὶν ἐμὲ χειροτονηθῆναι πρεσβευτήν, Φάλαικος ὁ τῶν Φωκέων τύραννος ἡμῖν μὲν καὶ Λακεδαιμονίοις ἠπίστει, Φιλίππῳ δ' ἐπίστευεν. For the chronology and identification of the Eleusinian truce of Aeschin. 2. 133, with that of February–March 346 (Lesser or City Dionysia), cf. P. Cloché, *Étude chronologique sur la IIIme guerre sacrée* (Paris, 1915) 110 f. and 119 ff.; Cawkwell, 'Peace' 416 ff., especially 428 ff. Cawkwell's very good and full discussion establishes that for the Athenians the Phocian development was decisive. The view of R. Sealey ('Proxenos and the Peace of Philocrates', *WS* 68 (1955) 145 ff.), that the news of Phalaecus' defection did not reach Athens till after the Athenian decision to treat with Philip and decided them then to accept his terms, seems untenable. (For Cawkwell's views on Athenian embassies 'to the Greeks', with which I cannot agree, see above, p. 330 n. 1.) [4] Aeschin. 2. 133.

It was presumably this blow, as Cawkwell has shown, which brought the Athenians to a quick decision to negotiate with Philip. As for Phalaecus himself, his action is really only explicable by the motive of self-preservation. He realized that it was much too late for any Phocian government now to try to make itself look respectable, and that of all the Phocians still alive there was none who looked or was less respectable than himself. The time was in sight now when there would be no more pay for the mercenaries. The Phocian leaders had just one trump card left, Thermopylae. To hand this to Athens, or to Archidamus, or to anyone else, was equivalent to throwing in their hand, unless they could be quite sure that Athens or Archidamus, or both together, could hold Thermopylae not just next week or next month, but for the rest of their natural lives. How could they possibly be sure of this? If the mercenary army did dissolve this year, next year, because it could not be paid, the Phocians alone could not even prevent the Boeotians from marching on Thermopylae from the south while Philip marched from the north:[1] and what would the Athenians and Archidamus do then? (Evacuate by sea, if they could.)

Whether Philip himself meanwhile had exact information of what went on in Phocis or in Phalaecus' head, may be doubted, though he may have got reports via Athens from seafarers, news not very fresh and perhaps not very accurate. But Philip had lived long enough to suspect that an experienced and unprincipled general with nothing left to sell except the pass would not feel insulted at receiving an offer, especially when the pass was Thermopylae. Whether Philip and Phalaecus were in communication already in 347, we can only guess. All that we are told is that the Boeotians appealed to Philip in this year for reinforcement, and that he sent them only a token force, 'observing with pleasure their humiliation, and intending to deflate the Leuctric airs they gave themselves'.[2] Τρίβειν ἀμφοτέρους still, to the very bitter end? The artist's compulsion to 'let the ball do the work', and not to start running about while still it rolled so well? Maybe. But this (and the bit of malice towards the Boeotians too, if that is authentic) would not exclude an exchange of messages with Phalaecus, perhaps even a long exchange, for a bargain like this was not one to be struck in the dark. Philip, we know, loved buying fortresses better than storming them, and no fortress yet had ever been worth more to him. Yet by the time Phalaecus was back in control early in 346, Philip knew that this was a forced sale. If Phalaecus (as for his credit we may hope) tried to exact as part of his price immunity

---

[1] This contingency is once mentioned by Aeschines, 2. 138.

[2] D.S. 16. 58. 3 ὁ δὲ βασιλεὺς ἡδέως ὁρῶν τὴν ταπείνωσιν αὐτῶν καὶ βουλόμενος τὰ Λευκτρικὰ φρονήματα συστεῖλαι τῶν Βοιωτῶν ὀλίγους ἀπέστειλε στρατιώτας, αὐτὸ μόνον φυλαττόμενος τὸ δοκεῖν μὴ περιορᾶν τὸ μαντεῖον σεσυλημένον.

for the Phocian people, he asked too much; for Philip could not forgo the glory and advantage of avenging Apollo and being seen to do so. It seems possible (one cannot say more) that Philip's delay till after midsummer in this year before he moved on Thermopylae was due to a protracted and secret bargaining with Phalaecus, till in the end (and nearly twelve months later) Phalaecus found himself confronted with the superior army itself, and was reduced to selling Thermopylae for his own skin and the skins of his mercenaries and nothing more.[1]

This is to look ahead. Meanwhile in 347 Philip waited and watched and exercised patience. In Central Greece the long struggle had reached a stalemate; not for the first time, but this time the stalemate of genuine exhaustion:[2] he could expect the Boeotian appeal for reinforcement to be renewed next year, and it became the general expectation that this time he would come in full force.[3] The Athenian plan for an anti-Macedonian coalition seemed to present no greater dangers now than a year before. The chances of Athens repeating the 352 defence of Thermopylae, should the occasion arise, seemed problematical to say the least. Athens needed peace, for her war effort in the 'war of Amphipolis', though in reality it was nugatory, seemed a lot, evidently, to this generation of Athenians.[4] Let them wonder, then, about Thermopylae and the consequences if it should fall to Philip, about the Chersonese too if he should mount a major attack on it; and meanwhile let them suffer the raids on their shipping as a reminder of the inconvenience of being at war. They might yet decide to 'make words about peace' rather than face the new campaigning season. And so it proved, when the news came to Athens from Proxenus that Phalaecus had refused to surrender Thermopylae. Meanwhile Philip had used the actor Aristodemus to convey to the Athenians that he still wanted to make peace, and indeed hoped for an alliance with them.[5]

---

[1] Sealey (art. cit. 145 ff.) suggested that Phalaecus had already made his bargain with Philip when he rebuffed the Athenians (and Archidamus). This is always possible; but it does seem reasonable to think that in a bargain at this earlier stage he ought to have got a better price. What he did get in the end looks like a bare minimum, when the only alternative was to stand like Leonidas and be killed.

[2] D.S. 16. 58. 2.

[3] Aeschines 2. 132 ἡ μὲν γὰρ Θετταλῶν καὶ Φιλίππου στρατεία πρόδηλος ἦν . . . etc.

[4] Both Demosthenes in 349 (3. 28) and Aeschines in 343 (2. 71) mentioned the sum of 1,500 talents in this connection, though Aeschines is talking so vaguely that it would be wrong to use this figure as his calculated total for expenditure on the whole war against Philip. Both however named the figure as representing a lot of money, as indeed it was, to the Athenians they addressed, even though it amounted to only an average of about 200 talents a year (for D.'s eight-year period, 357–349). To Periclean Athens this was chickenfeed: 1,500 talents or a little more was somewhere near the average annual expenditure on the Archidamian War.

[5] Aeschin. 2. 17. The time-scale of the events recapitulated by Aeschines here (15–18) is hard indeed to recapture. First, the fall of Olynthus (15, September 348); last, the Athenian decision to send the first embassy (18, March 346). Between, a protracted mission of

It was probably early in March 346 when the Athenian *demos* did finally reach the decision, to send ten ambassadors to negotiate peace with Philip and discuss matters of common interest to him and to Athens.[1] The last words were evidently in acknowledgement of Philip's message concerning an alliance: these instructions to the ambassadors were not closing that door. This board of ambassadors on their two missions to Macedonia became the most famous embassy known to us in ancient history. The speeches of Demosthenes and of Aeschines which alluded to it later give many details of its story, some of them unreliable because each orator hoped to dissociate himself as much as possible from the treaty resulting from it, which was unpopular at Athens when it was made, and hardly less so three years later when the trial of Aeschines for misconduct as an ambassador came on. What was never stated by the orators, but what can be inferred, is that the Athenian people, though it wanted peace now, still did not realize how badly it needed it, and that in reality it had not kept pace with the events themselves and their consequences, and may even have thought there was some chance of successfully reclaiming from Philip in these negotiations Amphipolis and perhaps some others of the places that had been lost.

Philip received the embassy at Pella in the spring, at a time when his preparations were on foot for an expedition into Thrace.[2] He had also a preoccupation in Thessaly, where Pharsalus was in dispute with the Phthiotic Achaean city of Halus, which no doubt was trying to assert its independence in some way. Philip supported Pharsalus in military action against Halus; but he was able to delegate the command to Parmenion, who was actually besieging Halus when the Athenian ambassadors landed nearby on their way north.[3] Philip made leisure to devote to these Athenians on their important mission; and leisure he needed, for each of the ten spoke in turn and with all the conventional gambits of Greek oratory, not excluding the excursus into mythology.[4] (There is no

---

Aristodemus to Philip to negotiate the release of some prisoners of war. Though the mission began, it seems, not too long after the fall of Olynthus (say, spring 347?), the final report of Aristodemus to the Assembly, including the message from Philip, is related by Aeschines (18, ῥηθέντων δὲ τούτων) as immediately before the proposal of Philocrates to send the embassy which actually was sent. This may well be inaccurate; but since there is no obvious reason for falsification, perhaps it is right to think that Philip's message really did come not long before the Athenians made their decision.

(I think that Aeschines 'telescoped' his account of these things, and that Aristodemus perhaps visited Macedonia more than once in these twelve months.)

[1] Aeschin. 2. 18 οἵτινες διαλέξονται Φιλίππῳ περὶ εἰρήνης καὶ τῶν κοινῇ συμφερόντων Ἀθηναίοις καὶ Φιλίππῳ. Aeschines here presumably is either quoting the words of the decree of Philocrates or reporting the gist of them very closely. For the date, see especially Sealey, art. cit. (*WS* 68 (1955) 149 f.)

[2] Aeschin. 2. 82.   [3] D. 19. 163.

[4] For a full account, see, e.g., A. W. Pickard-Cambridge, *Demosthenes* 140 ff.; Schaefer 2². 200 ff.

need to disbelieve Aeschines when he told a jury three years later that he had recounted the Athenian claim to Amphipolis in full.)[1] If Philip felt surprise, he concealed it. He did not lose patience. He was polite, he was charming even; and eventually he paid the Athenians the compliment of replying at some length, answering the points raised by each, and in a style that marked him as a speaker himself of much more than mere competence.[2] No doubt it was partly the technical interest of the performance, and the need which he imposed on himself to meet them on their own ground with something of an oratorical *tour de force*, which enabled him to spend all this time in this way, on an exercise which as a contribution to practical statecraft was of singularly little value in itself, as he must have realized. It was only the good relations with these men that were of consequence.

He will have had his curiosity, too, about these Athenians, four of them known to him already (Aristodemus, Phrynon, Iatrocles, and Ctesiphon).[3] Good company, or even new company, meant much in a society which, with far fewer social and intellectual diversions than our own, had to make its own entertainment most days and most evenings; and Philip was a sociable man. But, more, he did want to make peace (and alliance) with Athens now, and the formal proceedings of the embassy (if only the speech of Aeschines about Amphipolis) will have reminded him (if it was needed) that he really did badly need to make as many of these ten ambassadors as possible his friends. Somebody, some day soon, was going to have to convince the Athenian *demos* that the time had come to stop making-believe about Amphipolis and the rest, and forget about them. His own Macedonian envoys—Antipater or another—might tell them this, and even in some way not offensive; but it would be the eloquent Aeschines, the anti-Macedonian Demosthenes, the handsome and histrionic Aristodemus, who might best get them to believe it. It will have been in these days that Philip made up his mind which of the Athenian ambassadors was for sale, and bought them; Philocrates for certain, Phrynon and Aeschines perhaps.[4] 'He has no contempt for Athens, but he has been told by these people that the *demos* is the most unstable and fickle of things on earth. . . . He must have

---

[1] Aeschin. 2. 31 ff. The statement of Demosthenes in 343 (19. 253) that Aeschines had never mentioned Amphipolis on this occasion is most implausible.

[2] Ibid. 38 f. (P.'s replies): 41 f.; 47; 51 f. (his charm, and skill as a speaker).

[3] Ibid. 12 f.; 15.

[4] The guilt of Philocrates seems to follow from his quitting Athens rather than face the charges which eventually were laid against him. (He was condemned in his absence.)

Aeschines, powerfully supported at his trial by Eubulus and others, was given the benefit of the doubt by the jury—by thirty votes. Obviously he had the opportunity to be bribed by Philip, and Philip had the motive. The voice of Demosthenes on this is probably worthless, though D. 19. 145 is specific (property in Chalcidice which brought in 30 minas a year).

For Phrynon, D. 19. 230 is suggestive.

certain friends to "fix" and manage each thing at Athens, like Aeschines here. If that is arranged, everything will be plain sailing with the *demos*.'[1] This picture, half-falsified and designed to irritate the representatives of the *demos* to whom it was given, and not least by its elements of truth, does give us a view, however distorted, of what Philip needed to do now. He needed his 'agents' in Athens, and some of them might be bought. But what he needed most of all was Athenians who would be his agents from conviction, because they really believed that he meant well by Athens, that he could be trusted to keep to any bargain he made, and that the best interests of Athens would be served from now on by co-operating with him even in the further advancement and expansion of his power. For the future, alliance, with all that that implied: for the present, a recognition of the facts as they were, including the fact that Philip had offered and was offering peace and alliance in spite of the advantage, to all appearance decisive, that he held in the war: for the past, to forget it, and all the ill feeling that a contemplation of it invited. These were the things that the clear-headed and well-disposed among the ambassadors might be expected to understand, and to communicate in due course to the *demos* at Athens. Only if the *demos* understood these things could it become a reasonable 'prospect', as an ally.

It remained to communicate to Athens, *via* these ambassadors, the terms on which peace and alliance would be acceptable to him. (1) The basis of the peace was that each party to it should recognize the right of the other to the territories actually held at that moment.[2] Athens thus was required to recognize the permanency of Philip's conquests at her expense, including Amphipolis. Philip might be represented, in the then state of the war, as conceding something in return, by recognizing the Athenian right to remain in occupation of the Chersonese, except for the city of Cardia (already his ally).[3] We need not doubt that these Athenian ambassadors realized that Amphipolis and the rest were lost, and that no amount of talking would change Philip's mind about them. But the fact that they had talked about Amphipolis, presumably to make sure that they could go on record as having done so, suggests strongly that the Athenian people as a whole was by no means reconciled to the loss; and this becomes clear too from the fact that they went on talking and thinking about Amphipolis for years after this Peace was made.[4]

---

[1] D. 19. 135 f.

[2] [D.] 7. 26; schol. ad 7. 18 and 24.

No ancient source lists the clauses. What we know of them is from the allusions of the orators later. These (with references to many of the attendant circumstances also) are collected by Bengtson, *Staatsv.* 2. 312–18, with essential bibliography. Cf. too the discussions of Hampl, *GS* 56 ff., 111 ff.

[3] D. 19. 78. (For Cardia, 5. 25; 19. 174.)

[4] Cf. [D.] 7. 26 etc.; 12. 20 ff.

(2) There was to be alliance, as well as peace, between Philip and the Athenians, and with no time limitation.¹

(3) The alliance was to be a defensive alliance; the form, this, that was normal between two parties who negotiated an alliance as equals.²

(4) The Peace and alliance was to be binding on the allies of each party.³ This was normal procedure; but some difficulties could be foreseen in some individual cases at this moment. Cardia was one, for Philip meant to insist (with every reason) that she be included among his allies. Halus was another, recently in revolt and under Athenian protection (nominally) as a new ally: this could not be allowed. Most serious, the Phocians, old allies of Athens, and highly valued now for their control of Thermopylae, as well as for all the damage they had managed to do to the Boeotians in the last ten years. But Philip meant to deal with the Phocians now, and they must be excluded from the Peace, along with Halus. This was to give trouble.

(5) The treaty was to contain a clause about the safety of the seas, both parties (with their allies) binding themselves not to comfort and support pirates, and probably undertaking to act against them in common if need be.⁴

This clause, to all appearance unexceptionable, found disfavour nevertheless later with the Athenian politician Hegesippus, who could maintain that it was designed to enable Philip to assert himself in naval operations and tamper with the loyalty of the Athenian allies in the Aegean.⁵ Hegesippus may have been right; but he need not have been. Piracy was a curse to all civilized people, and Macedonia, with a coast line stretching now *de facto* from south of Pagasae to the Nestus, was quite civilized enough to have a legitimate interest. Athens as the leading sea power really held the key to this problem, if she would use it.

These are the clauses which are known to us to have been put before the Assembly at Athens about a fortnight after the arrival of the ambassadors back from the north. When they had left Philip he had been on the point of starting out on a campaign in Thrace, a region concerning which the Athenians were naturally sensitive. He gave assurances to the ambassadors that he would not touch the Chersonese.⁶ He sent also a Note to be communicated to the *demos*, but of its contents we know nothing except one sentence: 'I should have set down expressly the ways in which I shall help you, if I knew for certain that our alliance too [sc. as well as peace] would be concluded.'⁷ This seems a rather obvious and not strikingly effective piece of bargaining. But it was friendly, and

¹ D. 19. 48 τὴν εἰρήνην εἶναι τὴν αὐτὴν ἥνπερ Φιλίππῳ καὶ τοῖς ἐκγόνοις, καὶ τὴν συμμαχίαν. Cf. [D.] 12. 22.　　　　² D. 19. 143; cf. Hampl, *GS* 59A.
³ For the swearing of the oaths by the allies, see below, pp. 341, 344 and n. 4.
⁴ [D.] 12. 2; 7. 14. For some discussion, Wüst 178–80.　　　　⁵ [D.] 7. ibid.
⁶ Aeschin. 2. 82; D. 19. 78.　　　　⁷ D. 19. 40.

it was non-committal; and this we may judge to have been the tone of the Note in general, which for obvious reasons cannot have contained discussion of the proposals to be put before the Assembly, or alternatives to them if any should be unwelcome. High-ranking ambassadors (Antipater, Parmenion, and Eurylochus) were present in Athens to say anything that needed to be said.[1] But it appears from the event that Philip had allowed them little room for manœuvre in the direction of concessions to meet Athenian objections to the terms proposed. It was the Athenians who needed this treaty, though they did not want it: Philip wanted it, but he needed it much less, for his objectives in the short term. And his more distant objectives were not yet public property.

When the actual terms were put before the Assembly for debate (on 18 Elaphebolion—15 April), they had been considered already by the Council of the Confederacy of Athenian allies, which had agreed on proposals for a course of action, which the Assembly needed now to keep in mind. The gist of this δόγμα συμμάχων was that the Assembly should deliberate about peace, with no mention of the proffered alliance with Philip; and that when peace was agreed on, it should be open to all of the Greeks who so wished within three months to become a party to it:[2] that is, that this peace should be a *koine eirene*. It is undeniable that these proposals represented an adroit policy, both to meet an immediate problem and to provide a basis for Athens in the coming years. The immediate problem was the future of the Phocians and of Halus: the 'three months' clause would enable them to participate in a *koine eirene*. In the longer term, the future of Athens and her Confederacy could be thought of as more secure if 'the Greeks' in general were to be sharing in the same *koine eirene*, freeing her thus from the danger of isolation, provided that she did not mismanage her foreign policy in some disastrous way. The only thing wrong indeed with these proposals of the allies was that they were made in fairyland: in the hard, cold world of reality there was no chance that Philip would agree to peace on these terms.

Though both Demosthenes and Aeschines spoke in favour of the policy of the Allies,[3] and probably others too of the ten Athenian ambassadors who were the experts of the moment, one of them, Philocrates, evidently had a better notion of what sort of treaty Philip would agree to. His original motion before the Assembly included the words 'except the Phocians and Halus' in the phrase defining the allies of Athens. This was unacceptable to the Assembly, and these words were struck out; but Philocrates was able to insert a clause to the effect that

---

[1] D. 19. 69; ibid. 2 Hypoth. 5.

[2] Aeschin. 3. 69 f. This summary may be accepted as accurate, because the actual text of the *dogma* was to be read aloud to the dicasts a minute or two later (ibid. 70).

[3] Aeschin. 3. 71.

the Phocians were to surrender the Temple to the Amphictyons, failing which the Athenians themselves would join in coercing them.[1] On the question of alliance, the Macedonian ambassadors when consulted made it clear that peace without alliance was not acceptable to Philip.[2] In this way the policy stroke of the Allies was cut down to size, exposed indeed for the wishful thinking that it was. The peace which the Athenians, and they, were to swear to, if they wanted peace, was not to be a *koine eirene* in which the Phocians and Halus were to find their refuge, but a bilateral treaty of peace and alliance, and one which bound Athens and her allies to co-operate in coercing the Phocians if they refused to surrender the Temple to the Amphictyons. To agree to this treaty was a disillusioning experience for which the Athenians were really not properly prepared; it required the intervention of Eubulus reminding them of the alternative (a war for survival, and one which they could not pay for without some quite unusual sacrifices) to bring them to agreement.[3] They were also influenced by optimistic forecasts made by Philocrates and Aeschines and perhaps others of their ambassadors of the benefits that would accrue from the alliance with Philip, who intended neither to destroy the Phocians nor to allow Thebes to regain its former strength.[4] Despite a plain and public statement by the Macedonian ambassadors that Philip did not accept the Phocians as allies (with the clear implication that they were not included in the peace either, since the two things were obviously inseparable in this treaty), the *demos* must have believed its own advisers instead: it was cosier that way.[5]

They did agree to the terms on 19 Elaphebolion (16 April). The oath was taken, and was administered to the representatives of the allies. An attempt to include Cersobleptes among the allies of Athens was defeated;[6] and the same ten ambassadors journeyed once more to Macedonia to administer the oath to Philip and his allies, to arrange for the repatriation of Athenians who were prisoners, 'and to negotiate any other serviceable matter that they can'.[7]

Philip was still absent in Thrace; but since the embassy awaited him in Pella instead of following him there it seems clear that his plans at any rate were known, and that this campaign was expected all along to be a matter of weeks and not of months.[8] Moreover it must have become generally known in Greece that his next move would be an attempt to

---

[1] D. 19. 159; ibid. 49 'ἐὰν δὲ μὴ ποιῶσι Φωκεῖς ἃ δεῖ καὶ παραδιδῶσι τοῖς Ἀμφικτύοσι τὸ ἱερόν, ὅτι βοηθήσει ὁ δῆμος ὁ Ἀθηναίων ἐπὶ τοὺς διακωλύοντας ταῦτα γίγνεσθαι.' The clause seems to be drafted so as to make a distinction between the Phocian people and an irresponsible Phocian government (Phalaecus and his group).

[2] Aeschin. 3. 72.   [3] D. 19. 291.   [4] D. 19. 42 and 321.   [5] D. 19. 321.

[6] Aeschin. 2. 82 ff.; 3. 73 ff. Cf. Pickard-Cambridge, *Demosthenes* 256, 263.

[7] Aeschin. 2. 104, quoting from the decree of the people which gave the ambassadors their instructions.

[8] Demosthenes' grumble (19. 155 f.) about this was not fair criticism really.

invade central Greece and end the Phocian War. Embassies from many Greek states had gathered to meet him.[1] Though Philip had no intention of using this occasion, or the end of the war when it came, as the opportunity for inaugurating a new *koine eirene* in Greece, nevertheless it was something resembling an international congress that he arrived back to, and one in which considerable tensions had developed in the weeks of waiting for him to return, and more waiting till he was ready to give audience after he had returned. It was evidently not thought to be a foregone conclusion even now that the Sacred War would end in the annihilation of the Phocians and the triumph of Thebes. Of the representatives of the great powers, if Aeschines is to be believed, only the Thessalians seemed confident. The Spartans as well as the Athenians were still not without hope of deflecting Philip from the course to which his existing alliances seemed to commit him. The Thebans were correspondingly uneasy. A typical attitude of the small states is preserved in the reported remark of a representative of one of them 'We of the small cities are scared by the secret diplomacy of the great powers.'[2]

Some secret diplomacy certainly there must have been. But the most surprising thing about these discussions is that the formal arrangements were those actually of a peace conference, and not of exchanges in private between Philip and the embassies of the states individually. This no doubt will have saved Philip some time and trouble, a saving that will seem not unimportant when it is remembered that these exercises in diplomacy were being sandwiched between two campaigns, and were competing with the ordinary business of the kingdom, not to mention Thessaly. This method of diplomacy by open conference may have been chosen because it enabled Philip to avoid some awkward confrontations. He presumably did not want to discuss the Phocian question in detail with the Athenians face to face, or the balance of power in the Peloponnese with the Spartans.[3] Set speeches in the hearing of all the ambassadors present allowed the states to make known their points of view, and we can see that some speakers at any rate, if they knew of any corns easily accessible, did not lose this opportunity of treading on them.[4] But Philip could listen and observe, and perhaps on this occasion was able to avoid committing himself to any formal reply in public.[5]

---

[1] Aeschin. 2. 112 παρόντων τῶν πρεσβέων ὡς ἔπος εἰπεῖν ἐξ ἁπάσης τῆς Ἑλλάδος . . . (with some exaggeration, no doubt).

[2] Aeschin. 2. 120 τοὺς γὰρ μικροπολίτας [sc. ἔφη] . . . φοβεῖν τὰ τῶν μειζόνων ἀπόρρητα. (The speaker was Cleochares of Chalcis.) Cf. ibid. 136 f. for the Spartans, Thebans, and Thessalians.

[3] Demosthenes and Aeschines made their speeches to the full conference (Aeschin. 2. 108 ff., especially 112). A quarrel of the Spartans and the Thebans evidently happened in public (ibid. 136).

[4] Aeschin. (2. 117) included in his speech an attack on the Thebans: for the Thebans and Spartans, see n. 3 above.

[5] No speech from Philip is reported or mentioned by Aeschines or Demosthenes.

Though our information on these things comes all from Athenian sources, and gives an impression, naturally, that only Athens mattered, in reality the Athenians, though they will have seemed important to Philip of course, were not the most important of the people he was dealing with. Within a few weeks he was to lead an army on Thermopylae. It was essential that he should be able to count on the support of the leading Amphictyonic powers, Thessaly and Thebes, for what could still be a big military operation if the worst came to the worst. And then when the Phocians had surrendered, the Amphictyons must be seen to be acting in unison, and in unity with himself their champion in the field. For these reasons the Thessalians and the Theban ambassadors came first among those whom he needed to cultivate personally.[1] To the Thessalians, or some of them, he could speak as to old friends. The Thebans he could reassure, for there was nothing to be gained by keeping them guessing any longer as to his intentions: both he and they wanted to settle with the Phocians now, and each needed the other's fullest co-operation. The future of the Phocians, and a reorganization of the Amphictyony, no doubt were agreed upon at this time, or were confirmed if it had been agreed in principle during the previous winter.

Secondly (or to be precise, even firstly), Phalaecus needed to be bought, and at a price which would not estrange the Thebans (especially) and Thessalians, who were not going to be satisfied with anything less than the political extinction of the Phocian state. It would be surprising if Phalaecus and Philip were not in communication at this time. If so, Phalaecus continued tough as a bargainer, perhaps in the slender hope that Athens might even yet intervene to reinforce him.[2] Philip on his side will have recognized that this meant that the armies were going to be used; Macedonians and Thessalians, with the Boeotians to invade Phocis from the south. But the big question still remained: could they be used as the final argument in the bargaining, and not to batter a way through or round Thermopylae?

As for the Athenians, what really was important was that they should not go back on the peace and alliance which they had just sworn, and should not send, after all, their men and their ships to Thermopylae. They must not forestall the bloodless victory which was Philip's plan. The *demos* of Athens would not be restrained by any mere care for appearances, from tearing up a peace treaty which looked like producing consequences

[1] D. 19. 138 ff. expatiates on the incorruptibility of the Theban ambassadors, and reports what one of them (Philon) said to Philip, not on a public occasion but after a dinner party. Obviously this does not automatically rank high as evidence; but since the Thebans were unpopular with an Athenian jury in 343, it seems unlikely that D. invented this story to their credit: more probably the story really had reached him through his Theban contacts, and he used it because it pointed a good moral for his purpose.

[2] A last embassy from the Phocians, seeking help, was in Athens as Philip moved south from Thessaly to Thermopylae (D. 19. 58): see below, pp. 345 f.

which were unanticipated. This had happened in 374; and those who knew their *demos* best can scarcely have ruled out all possibility of its happening again now, if they knew that the *demos* still had really no inkling that the Phocians were going to be exterminated politically. The Athenian reaction later to the news of this when it did happen does suggest that it came as a great shock to them—but too late for a repudiation of the treaty then to hurt anybody but themselves.[1] Those of the ambassadors who already had led the *demos* to hope for good things from Philip that were not in the text of the treaty (see above, p. 341) must quite certainly have left him in no doubt that the *demos* had not made this peace and alliance in order to see the Phocians destroyed and the Thebans made victorious and strong: they will have told Philip this, not so much for his sake as for their own, because their necks might easily depend on his realizing it, and on his doing some of the things they hoped for. On this question some secret diplomacy, in the form of private talks, was a necessity, and must surely have taken place.[2] Whatever individual ambassadors may have said or done, we know that their own purpose was not served: the Phocians were ruined and Thebes did triumph unequivocally. But all the same, talks such as these may have served Philip's purpose well, and may have affected his timing in an important way. He still encouraged these ambassadors to believe (those of them that could believe it, because they wanted to) that he had good things in store for Athens and something nasty for Thebes.[3] He put off moreover the swearing of the oath to the treaty by his allies till they had all reached Pherae on the southward march of the army; and he found a good reason for delaying the voyage home of the ambassadors till he was on the point of marching on Thermopylae.[4] And he sent them home then still in ignorance of his

[1] D. 19. 86 and 125.

[2] Private interviews between individual ambassadors and Philip were forbidden by the instructions of the Athenian Assembly (D. 19. 268)—which were disobeyed, Demosthenes alleged (ibid. 167, 175 f.). Whatever the truth of that, Aeschines (2. 104) was justified no doubt in claiming later that the vague clause in their brief—'and to negotiate any other serviceable matter that they can' (πράττειν δὲ τοὺς πρέσβεις καὶ ἄλλ' ὅ τι ἂν δύνωνται ἀγαθόν) was designed with this in view, that they should do their best to influence Philip to make the decisions which the Athenians hoped for, about Thebes and the Phocians.

[3] Aeschin. 2. 136 f.

[4] For the oath of the allies, D. 19. 158. Philip himself had taken the oath at Pella (D. 18. 32). Bengtson, *Staatsv.* 316 accepts the less reliable record of D. 19, 2 Hypoth. 7 (which has Philip himself taking the oath at Pherae), while omitting all mention of D. 18. 32. So, too, D. J. Mosley, 'Oaths at Pherae', *Philologus* 116 (1972) 145 ff. (Cf. Shaefer, 2². 263 n. 2 correctly.) Though Demosthenes uses Philip's oath at Pella in support of his allegation that he bribed some of the Athenian ambassadors not to hurry home but to stay on in Macedonia, he did not invent the oath at Pella, we may be certain. If Philip himself had delayed his own oath for many days, the ambassadors would have had reason to doubt his good faith, and D. would have found occasion to mention this. D.'s point about the purpose of his keeping the ambassadors in Macedonia seems valid, whatever the means by which this was done. (Cf. D. 19. 322 etc.)

Philip in his Note sent to Athens on this occasion explained that he had 'kept the ambassa-

true plans for the Phocians and for Thebes, and still prepared, some of them, to mislead the Athenians with false hopes.[1]

Of actual duplicity in the conduct of the formal exchanges with the *demos* Philip must certainly be acquitted: Demosthenes himself acquitted him.[2] At some point in the negotiations he certainly sent to Athens a Note in which he called on the Athenians to implement their alliance with him by sending a force to join in the attack on Thermopylae and Phocis, though it is not clear that he allowed them sufficient time actually to send a force.[3] In the Note which he sent to Athens with this second embassy when it returned, by which time he was himself before Thermopylae with his army, he made a polite remark about doing some service to the Athenians, but he did not actually do any service, nor did he make any positive suggestion, still less any undertaking or promise.[4] The positive encouragements were given by those of the ambassadors who had become his agents whether wittingly or not, for it does not seem unjust to call

dors to help him in reconciling Halus and Pharsalus' (D. 18. 36), and there is no need to dismiss this as pure effrontery or prevarication. Halus was a point at issue between Philip and Athens, and if the Athenian dissatisfaction could have been removed by persuading Halus to surrender on honourable terms, it would have been a conciliatory gesture by Philip. If the attempt was genuinely made, it did not succeed.

[1] D. 5. 9 f. (reliable, because spoken in 346, only about three months later: for the many other references from the later speeches, Shaefer, 2². 272 f.). Wüst 5 ff. summarizes this situation well.

On this see now M. M. Markle, 'The strategy of Philip in 346 B.C.', *CQ* N.S. 24 (1974) 253–68. With Markle's view of Philip's aims in general I mostly agree, but not with regard to Thebes. Markle, like Wüst and Beloch earlier, explains the promises of Athenian ambassadors that Philip would deal severely with Thebes, as corresponding to Philip's own intentions, and he ingeniously makes Philip's execution of the intentions dependent on the degree of support he could get from Athens: when the Athenians sent no troops on demand, he abandoned this plan, and followed the alternative course of 'giving the Thebans a free hand', in Boeotia and (up to a point) in Phocis.

On a short view the attraction for Philip of weakening Thebes by making Boeotian cities independent, and so improving his own capacity to dominate central Greece, is undeniable. But this could only be done by force or intimidation, and a longer view will have shown Philip the disadvantages. The permanent enmity of Thebes could be counted on, and even if he had adroitly passed Oropus now from Thebes back to Athens, Athens herself quite clearly could not be counted on as a loyal ally yet, and the chances must have seemed high that a disgruntled Thebes and a dissatisfied Athens in time would come together, Oropus or no Oropus.

Not to mention treaty obligations (D. 19. 318 εἰ μὲν γὰρ προσδέξαιτο Φωκέας συμμάχους καὶ μεθ' ὑμῶν τοὺς ὅρκους αὐτοῖς ἀποδοίη, τοὺς πρὸς Θετταλοὺς καὶ Θηβαίους ὅρκους παραβαίνειν εὐθὺς ἀναγκαῖον ἦν, ὧν τοῖς μὲν τὴν Βοιωτίαν συνεξαιρήσειν ὠμωμόκει, τοῖς δὲ τὴν πυλαίαν συγκαταστήσειν: cf. D. 18. 19), to end the Sacred War now and punish the Phocians was a genuine and solid benefaction, to Thebes especially, and one which offered some prospect of good relations through the Amphictyony. The Phocians had to be put down, for the sake of Philip's position in Thessaly (Markle ignores Thessaly in all this; but Philip could not afford to ignore it; D. 19. 320, and see p. 343). Wüst (p. 6) is sceptical about the 'oaths' of D. 19. 318 above, but it seems safe to believe in a treaty of Philip and Thebes, whatever its terms.

[2] D. 19. 68 and 38 f.   [3] Aeschin. 2. 137.

[4] D. 19. 40 and 48 (ibid. 34 and 58 for Thermopylae).

them this.[1] Whether from conviction, or for money, or from despair and fear of the possible consequences to themselves if they were to tell nothing but the truth, they still fed the optimism of the *demos* up to the very moment, it seems, when the news came from the north that Phalaecus had surrendered Thermopylae and that Philip 'had given the Thebans a free hand'.[2]

Demosthenes claimed later that the deception practised by Aeschines on the Athenians had deceived the Phocians too into optimism, which led them to surrender to Philip believing that they would be well treated and not left to the mercy of the Thebans.[3] This seems unlikely. Aeschines was probably justified in putting the blame on Phalaecus, for Diodorus states clearly that Phalaecus surrendered the Thermopylae forts to Philip in return for freedom for himself and his army there to withdraw to the Peloponnese, and that he was brought to this by his assessment of the military situation.[4] When Phalaecus had gone the Phocians had no choice but to surrender, their only choice was, to whom; and naturally they chose to surrender to Philip personally, in the hope that he might decide on their future personally and without recourse to the Boeotians and Thessalians.[5] But this can have been only a hope, not a calculation. In the event Philip decided to act correctly and to gratify his allies simultaneously, by referring the decision on the future of the Phocians to the Amphictyons.[6] To do otherwise would have been to spoil a beautiful friendship with the Thebans, and would have made him very unpopular in Thessaly: this decision does not look like one which can have caused him any doubts or hesitations. In the same way he prudently refrained from coming between the Thebans and those Boeotian cities (Orchomenus the most important) who had virtually seceded to the Phocians in recent years: Thebes destroyed them now and enslaved the inhabitants.[7] To pronounce judgement on the Phocians fell to the Amphictyons.[8]

All this was done without the co-operation of Philip's newest ally, the Athenians. Athens had sent no force to join in the operation against Phocis, and indeed had come near to repudiating the alliance and taking up an attitude of self-defence.[9] Philip no doubt was justified in seizing

[1] See pp. 337 f. above.

[2] D. 19. 60 ὅτι πάντα τὰ πράγματ' ἐγκεχείρικε Θηβαίοις ὁ Φίλιππος.

[3] D. 19. 53, 56, 77.

[4] Aeschin. 2. 140 (132 ff.); D.S. 16. 59. 3; cf. D. 19. 62. The Spartan force at Thermopylae had already withdrawn on Philip's approach (D. 19. 77). Its size is unknown.

[5] D.S. 16. 59. 3; D. 19. 62.   [6] D.S. 16. 59. 4; D. 19. 63. See p. 451.

[7] Aeschin. 2. 141 (cf. 2. 104).   [8] D. 19. 63.

[9] D. 19. 86 f. and 125; Aeschin. 2. 139 etc. Many refugees both from Phocis and from the Boeotian cities were received at Athens (D. 5. 18; 19. 80; Aeschin. 2. 142). The third embassy of Athens to Philip was voted and had set out before the bad news arrived (D. 19. 121 f.; 124; Aeschin. 2. 94; 139 ff.; 162).

on this reaction as a sign of bad faith, had he been so inclined. That he did not, may be taken as the first of the many clear signs of the next three or four years that he had no wish to pick a new quarrel with the Athenians, but rather to lay the old one to rest, and to develop the alliance into something really serviceable. Meanwhile and for this present moment, he was very content not to press the Athenians hard, and to allow the dust to settle. Their military presence in Phocis was not necessary in any practical sense. Their diplomatic presence, if they had sent their representatives to the Amphictyonic session deliberating on the fate of the Phocians, could easily have become a positive embarrassment. Any Athenian hieromnemons or ambassadors at this time would have been bound to take up in public a minority position on the Council of Amphictyons, and in private besides would have been continually pressing him to do things which he could not reasonably consider doing, and indeed would not if he could. The Athenian absence, though Philip noted it as calling for official protest, may really have been welcomed by him as one of those small mercies which a busy man feels entitled to expect from time to time, without forgetting to be thankful when they actually come. Sociable man though he was, and good talkers though any Athenian representatives most likely would have been, Philip this once, one guesses, preferred their room to their company.[1]

---

[1] I write here in the belief that at Delphi at this moment it was Philip's decision that decided everything. On the Amphictyonic context (illuminated by Demosthenes 5 *On the Peace*), below, pp. 455 f. An Amphictyonic war on Athens was possible, as Demosthenes pointed out (D. 5. 14; 17; 25). The Athenians were required now to signify approval of the Amphictyonic decisions just taken in their absence. An ultimatum? (τὰ κελευόμεν', D. 5. 24). Perhaps; but on matters that did not affect their vital interests (the Phocians; Philip's election to the Amphictyons). This was not like the issue (for Thebes) of the dissolution of the Boeotian League in 386 and 371, or (for Sparta) of the independence of Messenia in 362. Demosthenes realistically reminded them to distinguish between substance and shadow, and counselled them 'not to go to war about the shadow in Delphi' (5. 25). They took his advice, evidently.

X

GREEK CITIES OF THE NORTH

ONE of the problems of government which claimed Philip's attention from time to time in the years when he expanded the frontiers of Macedonia itself by conquests to the east and on its seaboard of the Thermaic Gulf was, what status to give to the Greek cities which he annexed or came in some way to control. There is no need to assume that he gave the same status to each; indeed, his treatment of them could vary at the very moment of their annexation, as can be seen from those extreme instances in which we know that his first act was to put an end to the city as a Greek *polis* (e.g. Methone, Olynthus) and to get rid of its Greek population. At the other extreme may be named Crenides, where his first act (or certainly a very early one) was to refound it with new settlers and give it his own name, under which (Philippi) it proceeded to issue a coinage for some years, during which it seems difficult not to think of it as a free and independent *polis*.[1] This shows that there can have been nothing either practically or juridically intolerable in the proposition of having even this inland city forming an enclave of free and independent territory inside the kingdom of Macedonia. On the other hand, it is equally relevant to keep in mind that Crenides–Philippi, even in its years of freedom and independence, was no less in Philip's power and at his disposal in practice, even to the point of military occupation, than if it had had its constitution revoked and replaced by a Macedonian governor taking his orders direct from Pella. Philippi from 356 to 346 was in the front line of the war against Athens, with the hostile Neapolis (Athenian ally) less than 10 miles to the south; this, and the importance of the mining, made a permanent Macedonian garrison in these years merely the most elementary prudence. Nothing could better illustrate how unimportant in practice the exact juridical status of a Greek city in, or near, Macedonia may have seemed in many ways to Philip himself, though that is not to say that it is of no interest to us, or that it did not interest its inhabitants at the time. But since obviously there is almost infinite scope for anomaly in the treatment and status of the individual cities, clearly it is as individuals that they are best considered, and best (again) in the chronological order of their annexation or other relationship, so far as that can be known.

First, however, one general observation may properly be made, on

[1] See below, p. 358.

their coinages. It might be thought that numismatic evidence could help us in a really valuable way, if it could be demonstrated that city coinages identified and dated to the fourth century cease (or do not cease) when a city comes under Philip's control, or that they cease in some instances but continue in others. Unfortunately there seems to be hardly any instance in which the end of a city's coinage (unless the city itself has ended, like Olynthus) can be dated reliably on numismatic or archaeological grounds alone and independently of the literary evidence concerned with Philip's own actions. The tendency has been to assume that a coinage ended at the date when the literary evidence suggests there is an opportunity for it to end, namely when Philip assumed control of the city in question.[1] In default of other evidence this may be a reasonable assumption, and very likely a correct one often. But it does not take account of the clear example of Crenides–Philippi (above), which seems to leave open the possibility that particular cities for particular reasons might continue to issue coins after Philip had taken them over in some way. In trying to establish the status of cities after they have become associated with Philip, it has seemed best to leave the numismatic evidence out of account, except for Philippi, Abdera, and Aenus where series of coins can be dated securely enough, and for Mecyberna where some evidence in contrast to the closely neighbouring Olynthus is obviously significant (below).

There are other general propositions which affect this question whether all or some of these cities (besides Philippi) did keep the status of free and (in theory) independent allies of Philip, however much in reality they may have lacked the power to act in any way that displeased him. This view has been widely maintained in the past, and if it were true it would oblige us to reckon with a number of cities which stood to Philip in a relationship not so very different from (say) that of the allies of Athens who were members of the Confederacy: they would be free and autonomous, but would have no corporate means of self-expression corresponding to (e.g.) the *sunedrion* of the Confederacy. They would have, however, in theory the right to conduct a foreign policy of their own, provided that it did not override the terms of their alliance with Philip, and they could be expected to be seen participating as nominally independent allies in (for example) treaties entered into by Philip in which the high contracting powers were 'Philip and his allies' and (e.g.) 'the Athenians and their allies'. They could also be expected to appear (like the Thessalians) as members later of the 'League of Corinth'. This last possibility unfortunately is defeated by the fragmentary nature

---

[1] e.g. at Ambracia, in 338/7, when Philip installed a garrison there. Yet Corinth, where he installed a garrison simultaneously, in the succeeding years was particularly prolific in its issues of coinage. And for Orthagoria near Maroneia, see below p. 665.

of the stone from Athens which preserves the names of some but not all of the League members. The word 'Thrace' surviving between two lacunae gives scope for conjectural restoration, but not for any certainty as to which cities of Thrace the list included, though it is something to know that it included one or more.[1]

The other opportunity for seeing something of the truth about this matter comes with the Peace of Philocrates, which we do know to have been a peace concluded between Athens and her allies and Philip and his allies. The evidence about it, allusions in speeches of Demosthenes and Aeschines, is (predictably) tantalizing. Both orators allude in passing to the procedure of administering the oath to the allies of Philip, but there was no need for either to list those allies, and neither of them did. Demosthenes however does purport to quote words of the Athenian Assembly's *psephisma* which instructed the ambassadors 'to administer the oath to the magistrates in the cities'; and he adds that the instruction was not obeyed literally.[2] Aeschines, concerned to rebut any charge of having failed to obey the instructions, purports to quote from a Note of Philip which reached Athens simultaneously with the Athenian ambassadors returning from the oath-administering mission. In the Note Philip is said to have named those of his allies who had been present and had sworn the oath, and added that 'he would send to Athens those of them who had been prevented by absence from doing so'.[3] These two pieces of information, incomplete as they are, are still very suggestive. From Aeschines it appears that the allies of Philip concerned in taking this oath must have been quite numerous (and some of them, probably, geographically rather remote). From Demosthenes it appears that the Athenians when addressing themselves to think about Philip's allies, thought of them primarily as cities. And Philip's list of his own allies, according to Aeschines, was a list mainly of cities. His allies must have included, besides the two leagues of Thessaly and Boeotia, also several kings (Molossian, Paeonian, Illyrian, Thracian), so that a list in which most of the names were of cities must have contained at least a dozen cities, and perhaps many more than a dozen.[4] The general observation of Isocrates (in 346) on Philip's relations with his neighbours does nothing to discredit this notion.[5]

---

[1] Tod, *GHI* no. 177, 31–2. See below, p. 637 n. 5.

[2] D. 19. 278 οὐ τὸ μὲν ψήφισμα "τοὺς ἄρχοντας ὀρκοῦν τοὺς ἐν ταῖς πόλεσιν", οὗτοι δ', οὓς Φίλιππος αὐτοῖς προσέπεμψε, τούτους ὤρκισαν; (cf. 19. 159 and 204 for vaguer indications that there was irregularity in administering—or not administering—the oath).

[3] Aeschin. 2. 129 καὶ τῶν συμμάχων τῶν ἑαυτοῦ τοὺς παραγενομένους κατ' ὄνομα γέγραφε, καὶ αὐτοὺς καὶ τὰς πόλεις αὐτῶν, τοὺς δ' ὑστερήσαντας τῶν συμμάχων ἀποστελεῖν φησι πρὸς ὑμᾶς.

[4] Thessaly and Boeotia would be 'sworn' each at one time and in one place, and not by Thessalian and Boeotian cities individually. (For the oaths in the Athens/Thessaly alliance of 361, Tod, *GHI* no. 147, 20 ff.)

[5] Isoc. 5. 20 τῶν δὲ πόλεων τῶν περὶ τὸν τόπον ἐκεῖνον τὰς μὲν ταῖς εὐεργεσίαις πρὸς τὴν

Finally (in this connection), no help can be gained from looking at procedure on the occasion of Alexander's accession. Though our sources tell us explicitly of his recognition as Philip's successor by the Macedonians themselves, by the Thessalians, by the Amphictyons, by the Athenians (perhaps gratuitously), and by the members of the 'League of Corinth' in session, they say nothing of his allies, whether kings or cities, in the neighbourhood of Macedonia and Thrace.[1] But it cannot be argued from this that by 336 there were no free Greek city allies in that area, if only because the possibility cannot be excluded that any such allies were now members of the League of Corinth, as indeed the word 'Thrace' occurring in the fragmentary inscription (Tod no. 177) strongly suggests, of some of them.[2]

1. *Amphipolis*

Though we are told that Philip, when he captured Amphipolis, exiled the anti-Macedonian citizens, an act which may have removed quite a large number, yet the well-known decree of the *demos* of the Amphipolitans by which was enacted the exile of the prominent Stratocles (and Philon) shows the city government still functioning after the surrender to Philip, and even with its democracy unimpaired.[3] This decree however belongs clearly to the earliest days (perhaps literally) of Macedonian occupation, and by no means justifies any assumption that Amphipolis remained permanently a free and autonomous city: indeed one interpretation has described the Stratocles decree as 'le dernier acte peut-être de sa liberté'.[4] The course of war and politics in the next years, and the whole political geography of this area, practically ruled out any notion of *otium cum dignitate* as a possible destiny for this city. She was bound to be garrisoned from the start, and though this did not disqualify a city from the status of free and autonomous ally,[5] her bridgehead over the Strymon, developing within a year into the most vital link with Crenides–Philippi and Thrace up to the Nestus, must have conferred on her almost immediately the character (if not the

αὐτοῦ συμμαχίαν προσῆκται, τὰς δὲ σφόδρα λυπούσας αὐτὸν ἀναστάτους πεποίηκεν; See above, p. 223 n. 3 for identification of τὸν τόπον ἐκεῖνον with Macedonia.

[1] D.S. 17. 4 most fully; with Arr. *An.* 1. 1–3.

[2] See p. 350 n. 1 above. Thasos was certainly a member (Tod, *GHI* no. 147 line 28).

[3] D.S. 16. 8. 2; Tod, *GHI* no. 150. The Athenian grave-inscriptions yield no trace of refugee Amphipolitans (*pace* Hampl 25). *IG* II–III². 3. 8076–87 show 13 names, but not one of fourth-century date. Contrast the 12 or 13 Olynthians of this period (*IG* ibid. 10018–20; 10022–5; 10027–8).

[4] P. Perdrizet, *BCH* 21 (1897) 110 f.; followed by Hampl 27.

[5] e.g. (most obviously perhaps) Ambracia in 338, Tod, *GHI* no. 177, 30: for the garrison, D.S. 17. 3. 3.

official status) of capital city of a new province of eastern Macedonia. This will have brought some economic gains (though the continuing war with Athens may have delayed the full advantage from them); but politically it must have done something to tighten the Macedonian grip on the place by mere usage and traffic, and irrespective of any set policy. Some antipathy to the Macedonians is certainly to be reckoned with, and may have contributed in time to bad relations which turned to the city's disadvantage.

The evidence seems clear that Amphipolis was reduced to an inferior status as time went on.[1] Though Isocrates talked of its 'revenues' in 346, he clearly thought of Philip (and not the Amphipolitans) as having the benefit from them.[2] In 349 Demosthenes had alluded, though cryptically, to developments unwelcome to the pro-Macedonians there;[3] and in 343 Aeschines alluded to Amphipolis in a phrase from which it has been inferred not only that the city was no longer free and autonomous but that its land or some of it had been confiscated for the benefit of somebody else.[4]

This question of the territory of Amphipolis assumes a crucial importance when considered in relation to the fact that one of Alexander's eight squadrons ($\emph{ἴλαι}$) of Companion cavalry in Asia later was known as the squadron 'of Amphipolis'.[5] Some modern writers, recognizing that two out of the four identifiable names of these squadrons advertise a Greek (not Macedonian) place of origin, have thought to explain this by supposing that the cavalry of Greek cities (Amphipolis one of them) was incorporated into the Companions alongside the Macedonian squires and the Greek aristocrats who had joined Philip individually.[6] Hampl however argued rightly that this was grossly improbable in itself, and more so when it is recalled that Theopompus does imply that the Companions or some of them became richly endowed with land granted to them by Philip, land which can only have been conquered territory because 'old' Macedonia could not supply it on this scale. Amphipolis and its territory, it is suggested, is one of the 'conquests' to be used in this

---

[1] Cf. D. 1. 5 (349), quoted at n. 3 below.

[2] Isoc. 5. 5. He may not have known the exact truth about the πρόσοδοι themselves, but his evidence is still of value as showing that he considered A.'s status as that of a subject and not a free and equal ally of Philip.

[3] D. 1. 5 καὶ ἴσασιν ἅ τ' Ἀμφιπολιτῶν ἐποίησε τοὺς παραδόντας αὐτῷ τὴν πόλιν . . .

[4] Aeschin. 2. 27, referring back to events in 368/7, Ἀμφιπολιτῶν αὐτῶν ἐχόντων τότε τὴν πόλιν καὶ τὴν χώραν καρπουμένων. Aeschines is recapitulating however what he said to Philip when he was ambassador in 346. Cf. Hampl 24 f., and below, p. 353, for criticism of his extreme view.

[5] Arr. *An.* 1. 2. 5 with 3. 11. 8; cf. Berve 1. 105.

[6] For the composition of the Companions, Theopomp. *FGrH* no. 115 F 224 and 225(a) (written with an ethical bias which is obvious, but which does not invalidate the plain facts, such as they are, about provenance). For further discussion of the squadrons (in connection with Chalcidice), pp. 367 ff. below, and more generally, 409 ff.

way.¹ Three of Alexander's Greek Companions are described by Arrian (on their appointment as trierarchs of the Indus fleet) as 'from Amphipolis', though in each case their original and true Greek provenance is known.² Two Macedonians with Alexander also are described as 'from Amphipolis', and a 'Macedonian from Amphipolis' receives 'proxeny' honours at Delphi.³ The suggestion is that this had become the correct official designation of Macedonians (or Greeks) who had received an estate from the King in the area of which Amphipolis was the administrative centre.⁴

If the territory of Amphipolis became subject to a development of this kind, it is easy to see how Aeschines could think of the Amphipolitans as being in some sense no longer in possession of their city and no longer enjoying the fruits of their land.⁵ The strength of Alexander's squadrons in Asia was at least 200 men each, and 200 seems a possible number for the estates required to form the basis of a squadron 'of Amphipolis'. The Companions lived well, and had big estates, and 200 of them would take in the land of at least 2,000 or 3,000 hoplite-farmers, if these estates were produced by confiscating the land owned by citizens.⁶ It would have taken up a great part, perhaps the greatest part, of all the original city land of Amphipolis, and the farming population would have been reduced to working as hired labour or as tenants on lands which some of them had formerly owned. This seems to be the picture as Hampl saw it, in fact.

In reality however that picture may be overdrawn. Though some city land inevitably will have been confiscated, when political misdemeanours of anti-Macedonian citizens led to their being exiled, it seems likely that, if only for reasons of self-interest, Philip probably stopped short of impoverishing a whole population by confiscations. The country between Amphipolis and Crenides–Philippi was conquered not long after Amphipolis itself. At some time the small Greek cities of Galepsus and Apollonia (near Galepsus) were conquered and destroyed.⁷ There was scope here for increasing, far beyond the original city land of Amphipolis itself, the area of which Amphipolis now could become the administrative centre. It would be possible to grant up to 200 estates mainly out of this larger area without taking more of the city land than the confiscated lands of men who were exiled. It is in this way, probably, that the squadron 'of Amphipolis' came into being, at a date which cannot be determined,

---

¹ *FGrH* 115 F 225(b); Hampl 22 ff.
² Arr. *Ind.* 18. 4.   ³ *Syll.*³ 268 F.
⁴ For other examples, with other localities named, p. 359 below.
⁵ Aeschin. 2. 27 (see p. 352 n. 4 above).
⁶ For further discussion, below pp. 409 ff. D. 19. 235 ἑώρων αὐτοὺς καὶ ἐπὶ τοῖς τοιούτοις ἐκεῖ σεμνυνομένους ὡς εὐδαίμονας καὶ λαμπρούς . . .
⁷ See above, pp. 251 ff. Cf. Hampl 25; U. Köhler, *SDAW* (1891) 485, for Galepsus and Apollonia.

but which may be presumed to be earlier than the date (343) when Aeschines made his remark.[1]

Aeschines at that time implied a contrast between the freedom of the Amphipolitans in 368/7 (Ἀμφιπολιτῶν αὐτῶν ἐχόντων τότε τὴν πόλιν), and a lack of freedom now. He also said that they had had then the full fruits of their territory, with the implication that they have them no longer. Is it necessary then to think that he meant to imply that in 343 they were getting no fruits whatever from their territory? Or that if he meant this, it was also literally true? To think anything of the kind would seem to be a negation of the critical faculty. This allusion to a past Amphipolis was certainly intended to convey a reminder about the Amphipolis of the present; and it seems right to accept the reminder that Amphipolis was no longer a free city, and to accept that this was justified by the real situation in 343. But the second clause, about the land, may really have been little more than decorative detail introduced to corroborate the first clause; and to use it to reconstruct the actual situation on the land in 343 (or in 347/6) seems hazardous. It could be referring to a land-tax, if the Amphipolitans now paid a tithe to Philip, as seems not improbable. Or it could be an exaggerated way of alluding to the fact that some city land had been confiscated for the benefit of Macedonians. But to use it as evidence that all the city land had been expropriated seems to go far beyond what is justified.

Equally misguided, on general grounds, seems the suggestion that before the end of Philip's reign he probably removed most of the original inhabitants of Amphipolis to settlements inland in the region of northern Macedonia known as Parorbelia and in Thrace.[2] Philip no doubt was responsible for Philippopolis, and perhaps for the other settlements. But for us to people them with Amphipolitans seems an indiscretion of which Philip himself is not likely to have been guilty; for these were in

---

[1] Aeschines, 2.27, Ἀμφιπολιτῶν αὐτῶν ἐχόντων τότε τὴν πόλιν, recalls here in 343 things that he had said to Philip in 346. Whether in truth he had found it necessary on that occasion to remind Philip of the political and agricultural freedom of Amphipolis twenty years earlier as a 'point' very slightly reinforcing his general theme, that Macedonia had no historical claim to Amphipolis and that Amyntas III had publicly recognized the Athenian claim to it (ibid. 32 f. especially), does not greatly matter. It seems likely that the important τότε etc. of this clause represents Aeschines' thought in 343 rather than in 346; a gloss not absolutely necessary for any specific rhetorical purpose, but offering interesting thoughts on a variety of themes—e.g. what could happen to people like the Amphipolitans who would not admit how lucky they were to be claimed as the property of Athens.

[2] The suggestion of U. Köhler, *SDAW* (1891) 485 f., inspired by the four Greek place-names mentioned by Strabo (7. 331 F 36), Callipolis, Orthopolis, Philippopolis, and Garescus. On Parorbelia, see Volume I. 199.

At [D.] 7. 28 'the former inhabitants of Amphipolis' (οἱ πρότερον ἐν Ἀμφιπόλει οἰκοῦντες) should not be interpreted to imply that the population had been removed by 342 (date of speech). As the context shows, the orator's point here is concerned with the title to possession of Amphipolis: it is that which Philip had changed, and the phrase 'former inhabitants' arrives in a sense accidentally, as part of the description of the former status.

the nature of frontier places, and they needed as inhabitants loyal subjects and not dispossessed and disgruntled Greeks liable to make friends with any Thracian, Agrianian or Paeonian they could find, provided he disliked the Macedonians enough. Nor does a wholesale removal of population from Amphipolis commend itself as good policy in relation to the future of the city itself. Amphipolis must always have been a 'centre' of its neighbourhood, performing the functions which that implies, in trade particularly. The development of Crenides–Philippi (which for years lacked direct access to the sea at Neapolis), and the annexation of the territory between the Strymon and the Nestus, cannot possibly have diminished Amphipolis as a 'centre', and most likely increased it greatly. Amphipolis contained several thousand people (its citizens) who knew how to 'make it work', as a centre. To remove those people, to make a solitude and call it a Macedonian garrison town, would seem as inept a move as could easily be imagined, and certainly the least profitable economically. Had it been done, the city land of Amphipolis could have been taken over and worked by Macedonian farmers (though there is no evidence that it was). But Macedonian farmers are unlikely to have been able to take over the multifarious and not uncomplicated services of an entrepôt; and we know of no other Macedonians who did go in for that kind of thing.

By 343 then (and probably earlier) Amphipolis had become in effect a Macedonian provincial capital with a population still predominantly Greek, prosperous from its trade overseas now that peace was restored, and also no doubt from its Macedonian and other milords with estates in the countryside east of the Strymon and with plenty of money to spend. (Silver and gold, too, flowed into it from Philippi and the Pangaeum region, for it became the site of Philip's second main mint; but not much of this can have stuck.[1]) Only independence, maintained in defiance of Athens for nearly seventy years, was gone now. No doubt the institutions of the city still functioned, for it needed an administration, which Council and magistrates and the rest could supply. (Whether the Assembly still met, there is no evidence later than the decrees about Stratocles, above.) But there was no foreign policy. Not only was it not open to the Amphipolitans to make or terminate alliances, but when foreign states made peace or alliance with 'Philip and his allies', Amphipolis would not be counted in that number. The installation of a garrison in the citadel, or of a Royal Mint, was doubtless now a matter for Philip's decision expressed as a statement of what he decided, and not a matter for

[1] The presence of a royal mint is no indication in itself that the city containing it is no longer 'free' or an ally. Coins of Alexander were minted at Sicyon throughout his reign (cf. S. P. Noe, *The Alexander Coinage of Sicyon arranged from Notes of Edward T. Newell*, ANS Num. Stud. 6 (New York, 1950)).

discussion in the assembly or council of the city. And presumably taxes were paid to the Macedonian treasury, whether as a lump sum (_phoros_) or in detail. Materially however the consequences of having become a city of Macedonia seem unlikely to have been severe, and more likely to have shown a balance of advantage, even a handsome one.

It has seemed worth while to consider Amphipolis with some care, because some of the factors which operate here may be found to be present in other cases to be considered later, and especially in cities of Chalcidice which were involved in the fall of Olynthus in 348 (below, pp. 375 ff.).

2. _Pydna_

Pydna was taken by Philip probably late in 357 soon after Amphipolis was taken, and like Amphipolis it was betrayed to him after a siege.[1] Its treatment up to a point followed the pattern of Amphipolis rather closely. It was neither destroyed nor totally depopulated, but a part of its population was treated severely, even enslaved.[2] By this we are probably to think of reprisals against prominent anti-Macedonians and their adherents, in which Philip will have been helped by those who had betrayed the city to him. It may have been the lands expropriated in this process which supplied the estates which we must presume to have been conferred at some time on a number of distinguished Macedonians or Greek members of the Companion class; for Pydna, though it does not supply one of the five names of Companion cavalry squadrons that are known, does supply individual Macedonians with the description 'from Pydna' attached to them.[3]

Like Amphipolis Pydna must have been garrisoned from the start, for Methone, an ally of Athens, lay only 5 miles away. It was in the same breath with Amphipolis, too, that Demosthenes in 349 alluded to developments at Pydna extremely unfavourable to the pro-Macedonians who had admitted Philip; but he does not tell us what they were.[4]

---

[1] Above, p. 242. In general, see _RE Suppl._ 10 (1965) 838–9.

[2] D. 1. 5. Pydna's survival as a Greek _polis_ is proved by D. 20. 61, εἴ τινες νυνὶ τῶν ἐχόντων Πύδναν . . ., where a close reading of the context (from ibid. 58 ff.) shows that 'those who hold Pydna' have got to be people comparable with those Thasians who brought Thasos over to Athens, and with those Byzantines who brought Byzantium over to Athens. 'Those who hold Pydna', that is, must be native Pydnaeans, and not Macedonians, because the notion that Macedonians installed in Pydna (its Greek population having been dispersed) could have been used by Demosthenes for his hypothetical comparison with the Thasian and Byzantine friends of Athens, is quite out of the question.

[3] Arr. _Ind._ 18. 5, Metron and Nicarchides, Macedonians ἐκ Πύδνης (cf. Berve 2 nos. 519 and 562–3); Arr. _An._ 3. 5. 3, Pantaleon a Companion, appointed _phrourarch_ at Memphis (Berve 2 no. 306); D.S. 17. 64. 5; Curt. 5. 1. 43, Agathon τῷ Πυδναίῳ appointed _phrourarch_ at Babylon (Berve 2 no. 9).

[4] D. 1. 5 δῆλον γάρ ἐστι τοῖς Ὀλυνθίοις ὅτι νῦν οὐ περὶ δόξης οὐδ' ὑπὲρ μέρους χώρας πολεμοῦσιν, ἀλλ' ἀναστάσεως καὶ ἀνδραποδισμοῦ τῆς πατρίδος, καὶ ἴσασιν ἅ τ' Ἀμφιπολιτῶν ἐποίησε τοὺς παραδόντας αὐτῷ τὴν πόλιν καὶ Πυδναίων τοὺς ὑποδεξαμένους.

We know that neither Amphipolis nor Pydna was destroyed, and that only part of the population of Pydna can have been enslaved (above, p. 356 n. 2); and there is certainly some temptation here to think that there may be not a word of truth behind the alarming picture which obviously it suited Demosthenes to draw. More likely, however, he is giving us exaggeration, and not total lies. Something nasty probably had happened at Pydna, and something which was generally known. If we conjecture that the city had not been left free and autonomous (and was controlled by the 'philippizers' of 357) we shall probably be not far wrong. Even earlier (in the speech *Against Leptines* 355/4) Demosthenes had included Pydna among places which he called 'subject to Philip', though demonstrably he is talking inexactly here and not as a constitutional lawyer weighing his words.[1] One point of interest is that there seems to have been no disarmament by large-scale dismantling of city-walls or citadel. Olympias in 317/16 was able to stand a long siege in Pydna, which suggests that its fortifications had been left intact.[2] For the first two years or more after Philip took it it was (like Amphipolis) in the front line of the war against Athens, Methone being so near. And even after Methone had been taken, it would have been imprudent to create an 'open city', in case of Athenian descents from the sea. When peace came in 346, it probably seemed not worth the bother, to pull down walls at Pydna. No doubt some of its citizens hated Macedonia and would have been glad to hand over the city to an enemy of Philip. But to what enemy? And how? If Athens could be left a few years later with walls and fleet intact, Philip was not going to lose any sleep over Pydna, or its walls.

Summing up, Pydna probably became, like Amphipolis, a city of Macedonia with a predominantly Greek population, retaining its institutions of a *polis*, but losing the power of conducting (even nominally) its own foreign policy; subject to some form of Macedonian taxation, and not to be counted among the free allies of Philip. In 354 it may have become perhaps the administrative centre for the territory of Methone nearby, when the Methonaeans were expelled and the land was 'distributed to the Macedonians' (below, p. 361). And in 337 Philip seems to have selected Pydna to be in some sense an administrative centre for his management of the affairs of Greece through the 'League of Corinth', (below, pp. 640, 643).[3]

---

[1] D. 20. 61. 'Pydna or Potidaea or one of the other places which are subject to Philip and hostile to you.' Potidaea had been handed over by Philip to the Chalcidian League when he took it. (See above, p. 250.)

[2] D.S. 19. 36. 1; 49. 1 ff.; Polyaen. 4. 2. 3. It is possible that the city could have been refortified by or for Antipater in 322, against the danger of a Greek invasion of Macedonia in the Lamian War; but this seems unlikely.

[3] Tod, *GHI* no. 183, 13 ff.

3. *Crenides–Philippi*

This city, excavated by the French with results which were described and discussed in great detail by P. Collart, gives us the rare advantage of a coinage which can be dated, if not exactly at least closely enough to be of value. The view that the series of coins inscribed ΘΑΣΙΩΝ ΗΠΕΙΡΟΥ were issued by and at the new foundation Crenides in the years 359–356 seems established by a continuity of type and style overlapping the last year of the coins with this inscription and the coins of subsequent years bearing the inscription ΦΙΛΙΠΠΩΝ.[1] The earlier inscription does raise legitimate doubts as to whether Crenides had achieved a truly independent status by the time Philip took it, or whether it was not in some sense a dependency of Thasos.[2] But the minting of coins (including gold) at Crenides under Philip, with types unchanged and only the new name indicating a change of status, suggests strongly that Philip when he refounded it with new settlers and renamed it, did recognize it as an independent Greek city. Moreover this coinage of Philippi, though its surviving examples in gold and silver are not exactly numerous, yet shows a sufficient number of different issues to suggest that the city continued to produce its gold probably till the end of Philip's reign, and its silver probably down to 346.[3] An earlier view which sought to connect the end of Philippi's coinage with the beginning of Philip's own issues of gold,[4] though it had some obvious attractions, cannot survive the re-examination of the coins themselves, or indeed some practical considerations as to what purposes the mint of Philippi was fulfilling on the spot. This was a royal foundation now, a place of real strategic and economic importance, and (especially) a place of great developments, where for years the government needed a supply of money for the things that were being done;[5] for enlarging and adorning the city, for exploiting the mines of the area, for draining the extensive marsh lands of the plain, for paying the troops in the years when a garrison was needed. To dig

---

[1] G. le Rider, 'Trésor de monnaies trouvé à Thasos', *BCH* 80 (1956) 1 ff., especially 16 ff. This, what may be called the traditional view (cf. Collart 135 f.; 162 ff., West, *NC* 3 (1923) 169 ff.), had been contested by J. Pouilloux, *Recherches sur l'histoire et les cultes de Thasos* (Paris, 1954) 1. 218 f.

[2] Cf. the guarded comment of A. J. Graham, *Colony and Mother City* (Manchester, 1964) 88.

[3] A. R. Bellinger, 'Philippi in Macedonia', *ANS MusN* 11 (1964) 29 ff.; cf. C. M. Kraay, *Greek Coins and History* (London, 1969) 17. Bellinger was able to distinguish a 'First Series' and a 'Second Series' in both gold and silver, and to name 348 as probably the year of transition (the occasion being provided by the end of the Chalcidian League coinage). Why Philippi, in the 'Second Series', continued its gold for perhaps a decade or more longer than its silver, remains still a mystery.

[4] Collart 164 f., West, *NC* 176 f. (with Bellinger's remarks, loc. cit. 37 n. 8).

[5] Cf. O. Davies, 'Ancient mines in Southern Macedonia', *Journ. R. Anthropol. Inst.* 62 (1932) 145–62 (esp. 155–9 for the neighbourhood of Philippi), reporting the very numerous slag remains which he found, indicative of ancient workings for gold.

gold and silver from the earth near Philippi, carry it to Amphipolis or Pella to be minted, and then carry some of it back again to Philippi seems an exercise in sophisticated bureaucracy improbable at this time and place. There is no evidence that the mint of Philippi was used for Philip's own issues, except for bronze.[1] The city's issues, then, supplied the gold and silver currency that was needed on the spot.

The evidence of the coinage in favour of Philippi's having continued throughout Philip's reign as a free city is neither contradicted nor confirmed conclusively by the other evidence, such as it is. An unpublished inscription of Philippi reveals the city in negotiation with Alexander the Great; but neither the subject of the negotiation (territorial) nor its method (by an embassy) allows us to see whether Philippi was or was not fully independent at the time.[2] Nor is there any positive evidence of Macedonian settlers. Admittedly, it is not essential to know of some Macedonian inhabitants in order to recognize a city as a 'city of Macedonia': some of the small Chalcidian cities (for example) may have come into this category after 348 with no change in their population (see below, p. 376).[3] But at Philippi, refounded and renamed by Philip and given settlers by him, we might have expected to hear of the individuals described as 'Macedonians from Philippi', corresponding to the 'Macedonians from Pella' of a fourth-century Delphian proxeny decree, the Macedonians 'from Amphipolis' and 'from Pydna' mentioned by Arrian, the 'Macedonians from Amphipolis' at Delphi (proxeny), and the 'Macedonian from Arethusa' of a similar Delphian inscription.[4] But on the contrary the only Delphian proxeny decree honouring Philippians of this period records the five sons of Timander as Φιλιππεῦσι, merely.[5]

It may be said (with truth) that there is good reason to identify this Timander with the Timander known as *thearodokos* at Daton in 359, and hence probably a prominent Thasian by origin, one of the original colonists of Crenides: and if this were so his sons would not be ethnically

---

[1] For the bronze issues, both of Philip and of Philippi, see Bellinger, loc. cit. 37 ff., with conclusions 50 f.

[2] Collart 179, wrote of the inscription as if its publication was to be expected shortly, but I have been unable to find it. My best thanks are due to C. F. Edson (who tells me that he too is not aware of its having been published), for having most kindly sent me his transcription of it, taken from his epigraphical notebooks of the year 1938.

[3] There is an interesting suggestion that a century later Philippi perhaps considered itself a Greek city still, in a way that Amphipolis and Cassandreia, equally Greek as to their original population, did not. In 242, at a time when all three cities alike were incorporated in the kingdom of Macedonia, they each on the same occasion passed complimentary decrees for the temple of Asklepios at Cos. Each decree refers to the past friendship shown by Cos towards 'King Antigonus and the Macedonians'; but the decree of Philippi names 'King Antigonus *and the Greeks besides* and the Macedonians' (καὶ πρὸς τοὺς ἄλλους Ἕλληνας). *SEG* 12. 373; cf. ibid. 374 (Pella).

[4] See pp. 353, 356; *Syll.*³ 269K.   [5] *Syll.*³ 267A (dated 'post a. 347/6').

Macedonians at all. It does seem likely that in the time of Philip and Alexander all the individuals described as 'Macedonian from (e.g.) Amphipolis or Pydna'—always men of some importance—were either Macedonians by birth or were privileged Greek Companions on whom the Macedonian citizenship had been conferred (a clear example, Nearchus).[1] Conversely, it is not clear that the Greek citizens of Amphipolis or Pydna or Philippi, if they lost their freedom and became subject to Philip, thereupon became 'Macedonians' and must have been called by that name. If we find inhabitants of Philippi described as Philippians, then, we are not entitled to infer that Philippi must be a free city still. A list of (probably) mercenary soldiers from Athens, naming the men in groups headed by their place of origin, has simply 'Cassandreians', 'Philippians'; but it would be hazardous to use this as evidence for the status of Cassandreia or Philippi at this date (about 300).[2] Other sources of information fail us.[3] But about sixty years later it seems clear that Philippi had become a 'city of Macedonia' indistinguishable in status from Pella, Amphipolis, and others.[4]

There is something equivocal, one must admit, in the sum of the evidence about Philippi and its implications. On the one hand, the continuance of the city's own coinage speaks strongly for its independence, with the status of a free ally. On the other hand the most obvious practical needs of the time and place seem to dictate that Philip himself should be in control here. For defence, self-evidently (with a garrison, for years). But for the whole development of the area too, both its mines and its great potential for fertility, only Philip could direct on the scale that was needed. Who but Philip was to decide how much of the gold and silver year by year Philippi should take for its own issues of coinage? Perhaps his role as founder led to a special relationship. The very name Philippi contained something 'special'; for no one in the Greek world had ever before given his own name to the city of which he was *oikistes*. A notable act of advertisement certainly; but just what was it advertising (apart from himself)?[5] If Philip's new settlers were nearly all Greeks, volun-

---

[1] Arr. *Ind.* 18. 3–4 and 6 puts Nearchus in the group of Macedonians (as opposed to Greeks) whom Alexander appointed trierarchs at the Indus in 326; but ibid. 10 'The admiral set over them was Nearchus . . ., by birth a Cretan, but his place of residence was Amphipolis.' [2] *IG* ii². 1956; Collart 178.

[3] The List of Ephebes in an 'inscription of Philippi' published by S. Mertzides, Οἱ Φίλιπποι, Ἔρευναι καὶ μελεταὶ χωρογραφικαί (Constantinople, 1897) no. 9, is pronounced a fake by L. Robert, *Hellenica*, v. 'Inscriptions de Philippes publiées par Mertzides', *RPh* 3rd ser. 13 (1939) 136–50. The list contains a number of well-known names, including some interesting combinations ('Philip son of Demosthenes', 'Niceratus son of Alcibiades'). I have not seen this book myself. Of its inscriptions, Robert thought only no. 14 to be genuine.

[4] *SEG* 12. 373, 23 ff. (Amphipolis), 36 ff. (Philippi); 374 (Pella): the date is 242.

[5] Bellinger (loc. cit. 50 n. 11) makes the interesting suggestion that Philip designed Philippi as his capital city perhaps. Personally I would not think this possible. The situation of Pella, central for every contingency, was too valuable to be abandoned.

teers perhaps drawn from his allies of the Chalcidian League and joining now the old settlers, Thasians predominantly, to whom he had come not as a conqueror but as a saviour and at their invitation, this would give a Greek population uniquely well disposed to him, and predisposed perhaps to accept a special relationship and allow it to work. If they were declared now free and autonomous, the *oikistes* who was also their defender and provider need not be seen as a foreign tyrant when he reviewed the troops of the garrison or allocated the ingots for the mint. For Philip, Philippi could become (among other things) a kind of show-place, politically, the Greek city which was 'free in a way that suited' him[1]—and liked it. Meanwhile the city grew and flourished, a credit to its founder and an important contributor to the strength of his greater Macedonia.

4. *Potidaea, Methone*

Diodorus states that in 356 Philip sent the Athenian cleruchs home to Athens, and gave Potidaea to the Olynthians together with all the pro-perties in its territory, having sold its population into slavery (τὴν δὲ πόλιν ἐξανδραποδισάμενος παρέδωκε . . .).[2] Demosthenes in 355 alluded to Potidaea as still in existence, one of the places (Pydna another) subject now to Philip and hostile to Athens; and he confirms in a later allusion (344) that the Olynthians had indeed enjoyed the use and benefit of its territory.[3] Nothing more is heard of the Potideiates themselves. It seems most probable that they were 'enslaved' in 356, and that settlers came in from Olynthus to form a new citizen population. In 348 Potidaea fell again into Philip's hands, and its citizens need not necessarily have shared the fate of Olynthus. It is never mentioned as a place 'destroyed' by Philip (for example by Demosthenes when he spoke of the '32 cities', naming Olynthus, Methone, and Apollonia).[4] Potidaea was still there in 316 when it was incorporated with others in the new foundation Cassandreia.[5] As to its status in the years after 348, Greek ally or 'city of Macedonia', there is no further evidence.[6]

When Philip took Methone in 354 (above, pp. 256 ff.) the Metho-naeans were allowed to leave unharmed, and the city itself was in some sense 'destroyed' (κατέσκαψε): its territory he 'distributed among the Macedonians' (διένειμε τοῖς Μακεδόσιν).[7] As I have suggested elsewhere, this phrase certainly implies a distribution *viritim*, to a large number of

---

[1] (Like the Peloponnesian allies in their relationship to Sparta, Thuc. 1. 19 and 144. 2.)
[2] D.S. 16. 8. 5; so Paus. 5. 23; schol. D. 6. 20.   [3] D. 20. 61; 6. 20 f.
[4] D. 9. 26.   [5] D.S. 19. 52. 2.
[6] See in general J. A. Alexander, *Potidaea* (1963) 88–91. A relief sculpture found at Nea Potidaea and published recently is dated on stylistic grounds in the 330s (Th. Stephanides, *Mak.* 13 (1973) 106–16).
[7] D.S. 16. 34. 5.

Macedonians, and consequently in relatively small holdings, rather than the giving of large estates to Companions and the like, though the two scales are not mutually exclusive.[1] This is the only record we possess of the Macedonian people (as distinct from important individuals) being given land from conquered territory, though obviously the same thing could have happened at Crenides–Philippi (above), and also perhaps in Chalcidice and in the eastern Pieria (below). These four localities together might account for not less than 10,000–15,000 grants of land, and if this were true the number would not be excessive. To reward the 'hoplite class' for its services, and to encourage its increase by raising its standard of life, was self-evidently good policy.[2]

That Methone lost its entire Greek population now seems quite clear. But when we are told that Philip 'destroyed' the place itself (above), it seems likely that we ought to think of him as dismantling city-walls, citadel, and naval harbour (such as it was), rather than denying the use of houses and public buildings to the Macedonian settlers who were given land in the city's territory. If Pydna remained as a fortified place with a garrison while the war with Athens lasted (above, p. 336), it was near enough to serve as a centre for both military and civil administration of Methone too, since the remotest farm on Methone's land could be no more than about 10 miles from Pydna itself. Methone can never have ceased to be an inhabited place, (*pace* D. 9. 26!), though we hear no more of it till the time of Strabo, who alluded to it as a *polis* and without reference (in the excerpts that survive) to any destruction by Philip, though an allusion to the siege is preserved.[3] Methone evidently became a city of Macedonia like Pella or Dium, but whether this happened at once, when Philip's Macedonians settled in, or later, there is no means of knowing for sure. The first seems the more likely.

5. *Cities of the eastern Pieria*

The Pieria in question is the country inhabited by the Thracian Pierians after their expulsion at a very early date from the region in the extreme south of Macedonia (between Pydna and Mt. Olympus) which continued to bear their name.[4] 'Thracian' or eastern Pieria extended east from Amphipolis some 25 miles, between Mt. Pangaeum and the sea,

---

[1] *G & R* 12 (1965) 135. No 'Macedonians ἐκ Μεθώνης' are known. The territory of Methone could well have been joined to the neighbouring Pydna as its new administrative centre.

[2] For increase of population in Macedonia in Philip's reign, *G & R* 12 (1965) 129 ff. What the system of land-tenure was in Macedonia, we do not know. But in agricultural societies obviously the problem was, how the *kleroi* (whether or not they were called that) were to support more than one son and their families. It was this problem, met earlier in Greece often by colonization overseas, which would be met now in Macedonia by grants of conquered land in these peripheral regions.

[3] Str. 7 F 22. [4] Thuc. 2. 99. 3; cf. Volume I 417 f.

and its Greek cities were (from west to east) Galepsus, Apollonia, and Oesyme. Of Galepsus and Apollonia we are told by Strabo that Philip destroyed them.[1] Of Oesyme we hear nothing except that, significantly, it became known before Roman times as Emathia.[2] Our only direct clue to the date of these developments is the *terminus ante quem* of 341 for the destruction of Apollonia, if the Apollonia mentioned by Demosthenes then as having been destroyed by Philip can be identified with Apollonia in Pieria which according to Strabo was so destroyed.[3] Most modern writers however put the destruction of Galepsus and Apollonia very close in date to the capture of Crenides, and this seems certainly right. Not only was it important for Philip in a general way to take control of the country between Amphipolis and Crenides (above, p. 252), but in particular it was important then for him to deny to the Athenians a choice of possible bases if and when they might be able to use their naval strength against him.

Of Oesyme Scymnus wrote (*c.* 150):

> Μετ' Ἀμφίπολιν δ' ἡ πρότερον Οἰσύμη πόλις
> Θασίων γενομένη, μετὰ δὲ ταῦτα Μακεδόνων,
> ἀπὸ τῆς Μακέσσης Ἠμαθίας τε λεγομένη.

This suggests that at this date Galepsus and Apollonia had still not been resettled as cities, since their sites lay certainly between Amphipolis and Oesyme.[4] For Oesyme itself Scymnus is recording, it seems, a second foundation, or at least a second 'colonization', by Macedonians, but it might well be a mistake to infer from this that Oesyme too was depopulated (like Methone) when the Macedonians moved in. And when was that? Though a Macedonian colonization at some later time cannot be disproved, it remains obviously true that the reign of Philip must be by far the most probable time, because from the moment of Alexander's invading Asia there ceased to be any surplus Macedonians; and so far as we know there never were any again. It would seem a reasonable hypothesis that Oesyme was occupied and garrisoned soon after the capture of Crenides, because of its superb citadel and position commanding the coast eastwards to Neapolis (ally of Athens), and westwards to Apollonia and on to the Strymon and Amphipolis. The fate of its original citizens will have depended on the immediate prehistory: the fact that they were Thasians by descent does not necessitate that the city

---

[1] Str. 7 F 33 and 35.

[2] Scymnus, 656 ff. (= *GGM* 1 p. 221): cf. Liv. 43. 7. 10; 44. 44. 5 f.; St. Byz. s.vv. Ἠμαθία and Οἰσύμη.

[3] D. 9. 26; Str. 7 F 33. On the Apollonias, pp. 368 f. below. Since there is no evidence that any Apollonia in Chalcidice was destroyed by Philip, it seems best to identify the A. of Demosthenes with that of Strabo. So St. Byz. s.v. Ἀπολλωνία has only two in Greater Macedonia (his γ, Μακεδονίας; and κβ τῶν ἐπὶ Θρᾴκης Ἰώνων ἦν Δημοσθένης φησίν).

[4] Cf. Collart, 81 ff.

must have been predominantly anti-Macedonian, though Thasos itself certainly was that because of its vested interest in Crenides. Attempts by Thasos to dominate her colonies on the mainland (and the earliest coins of Crenides with their inscription Θασίων ἠπείρου do suggest just such an attempt)[1] are sure to have aroused resistance as well as co-operation, and it seems by no means impossible that Philip could have used such a situation to occupy Oesyme with the consent of a group of the citizens temporarily in control, and while Thasos and Neapolis still held to their alliance with Athens. This would explain the absence of any tradition of a 'destruction' of Oesyme, while leaving open the fate of its citizens in the years that followed. But a considerable influx of Macedonian settlers, perhaps to the number of some thousands, does seem required to explain the emergence of the new name Emathia for the city. If this immigration happened in Philip's reign, as seems likely, the status of the place, even if it had begun by entering into an alliance with Philip, is likely to have become that of a 'Macedonian' city before the end of the reign.

6. *Neapolis*

It is a natural inference from Strabo's remarks about the eastern frontier of Macedonia that at some time in his reign Philip officially moved this frontier forward from the Strymon to the Nestus, annexing thereby the lands between, which formerly had been counted part of Thrace.[2] There is no way, so far as I know, of establishing the date at which this was done. But though this is unfortunate, it does not carry serious consequences for an attempt to establish the status of Greek cities in this area, because there is really no reason to be sure that an independent city could not survive as such even when completely surrounded by territory technically Macedonian. Many years of Methone's history had been passed in just this situation; and it seems quite possible that Neapolis, the ally of Athens, had the same experience now. Though her latest known independent act is no later than 355,[3] she may even have remained an Athenian ally to the end (338). What seems more to the point is to suggest that no city can have remained free and independent after the date when it had received (if it did) Macedonian settlers, for practical reasons. It seems impossible to believe that Philip could have been prepared to 'lose' Macedonians by allowing them to become citizens

---

[1] For the coins, see p. 358: for Thasos and her colonies, A. J. Graham, *Colony and Mother City* (Manchester, 1964) 81–90.

[2] Str. 7 F 33 εἶτα τὸ Νέστου στόμα τοῦ διορίζοντος Μακεδονίαν καὶ Θρᾴκην, ὡς Φίλιππος καὶ Ἀλέξανδρος ὁ τούτου παῖς διώριζον ἐν τοῖς κατ' αὐτοὺς χρόνοις. Cf. ibid. F 35. [Scylax] 66 (*GGM* I p. 53 μετὰ δὲ Μακεδονίαν Στρυμὼν ποταμός· οὗτος ὁρίζει Μακεδονίαν καὶ Θρᾴκην, cf. ibid. 67) writes presumably of a time before Philip's annexation.

[3] Tod *GHI* no. 159.

of free Greek cities: and on the other hand if Macedonian settlers remained subjects of their king and not citizens of the Greek city, the city itself was put in the difficult position of harbouring settlers over whom it had no jurisdiction. To think of them as permanent and privileged *metoikoi* or something like it may be possible juridically, but it would seem to invite complications which no Macedonian king at this date would sow for himself when he did not need to.[1] If this reasoning is sound, then it follows that new (Macedonian) Methone was never independent, and that Oesyme–Emathia, Amphipolis, and Pydna, and those cities in Chalcidice which got settlers from Macedonia, will have lost their independence when the settlers came, if not before, and that thereafter they are to be counted as 'cities of Macedonia'.

7. *Cities of Chalcidice*

The fate of Olynthus is not in dispute; the city's existence ended in 348 (p. 324 above). But concerning the Chalcidice peninsula as a whole, the territory of perhaps up to eighty cities, many though not all of them members of the Chalcidian League, there are some real doubts as to the treatment they received, and the relations of them and their territories to Macedonia hereafter. Demosthenes, speaking seven years later and comparing the 'crimes of Philip against the Greeks' with those in earlier years of the Spartans and the Athenians themselves, mentions 'Olynthus and Methone and Apollonia and thirty-two cities of the Thracian shore (ἐπὶ Θρᾴκης), all of which he has destroyed so brutally that a visitor there now can hardly tell if they ever existed'.[2] This, though it does not exclude cities further east (like the Apollonia which he mentions), is taken (no doubt rightly) to refer primarily to Chalcidice, and the reference contains plainly some exaggeration;[3] but the real question is, does Demosthenes exaggerate the whole thing grossly, including the figure thirty-two, and the general impression that a great crime has been done here?

No literary tradition contradicts Demosthenes on this, and Strabo seems to have accepted it.[4] The fragmentary inscription which records

[1] Later, in Asia, more complicated situations could call for less simple solutions, as we see (e.g.) at Magnesia ad Sipylum (*OGIS* 1. 229. 34 ff.), where the relations of Greek city (Smyrna) and Seleucid soldiers and settlers present a challenge to our ingenuity as interpreters (see now B. Bar Kochva, *The Seleucid Army* (Cambridge, 1976) 21 ff., 38 ff., 57 f.).

[2] D. 9. 26; see above, p. 363 n. 3. The Apollonia here mentioned is presumably the one near Galepsus between the Strymon and Neapolis, recorded by Strabo (7 F 36) as destroyed by Philip.

[3] The Chalcidic cities were commonly called 'Thracian', evidently, by Greeks of this generation (e.g. Theopompus, *FGrH* no. 115 F 139, 141, 144, 152, who calls even Therme (near Salonika) Thracian, F 140), just as the Athenian Empire earlier had included them in its Thracian Tribute District (*ATL* 1. 491; cf. e.g. Ar. *V.* 288).

[4] Str. 10. 447, 8. The most recent discussion of the whole question is by Zahrnt 112 ff.

(besides the oath) also the names of some of the Greek states which took the oath to Philip in 337 cannot be made to throw light on the survival (or not) of former Chalcidian League members.[1] Even if it is right to restore Χαλκιδέων in line 31, the restoration is almost useless to us because the numeral which follows the name needs to be restored also. If Schwahn's conjectural Ι Ι Ι (=3) could be supported by some independent evidence, it would tell us that a good part of the former Chalcidian League still existed and that the cities had a free status presumably as allies of Philip.[2] But in reality the missing numeral could just as well be Ι (= 1): and if it were Ι we might be justified in taking it to represent probably the cities of Acte including Acanthus, which most likely had not been Chalcidian League members at all. This is a fair enough conjecture in itself; but the fact remains that 'Thrace' is the only place-name which can actually be read here, and we must allow for the possibility that the lost entries in these lines referred to places east of Chalcidice, cities which had never been overcome in war but had become allies of Philip by agreement and had kept their free status.

Linked to the question of the Greek cities, how many of them were destroyed, is the question of Macedonian settlers. There is evidence for thinking that Chalcidice became now an area containing many estates held in gift from Philip by prominent Greeks and Macedonians. The view that this was so has been orthodox for many years, but the basis for it will bear a brief restatement[3] The practice of Philip and Alexander of giving estates to Greeks and Macedonians is well enough attested in general terms.[4] For individual cases, there are three known examples of estates given to Macedonians by Philip (and one, in Asia, by Alexander).[5] The fewness of the known individual cases, and the fact that Philip's three cases survive for us in a single inscription, is not in itself a good reason

---

[1] Tod, *GHI* no. 177 (= *IG* ii². 236). Lines 31–2 were restored by W. Schwahn, *Heeresmatrikel und Landfriede Philipps von Makedonien* (*Klio* Beiheft xxi) 2:

[Χαλκιδέων: *III*: ἀ]πὸ Θράικης καὶ
[Χερρονήσου: *Γ*:] Φωκέων: *III*: Λοκρῶν: *III*

The restoration was not accepted by Tod (rightly, I would think).

[2] Cf. Tod, ibid., where Phocians (3), Locrians (3), a firm entry in this list, provide a yardstick of some value when conjectural restorations are under consideration.

[3] Cf. especially Hampl 22 ff., 28 ff.; West, *CL* 130 f., 133, 135; Zahrnt 114 f., 157, 178.

[4] Theopomp. *FGrH* no. 115 F 225b; Plu. *Alex.* 15. 3; Just. 11. 5. 5; D. 19. 145 (see next note).

[5] *Syll.*³ 1. 332 and 302. I leave out of account here D. 19. 145, where Demosthenes in 343 alleged that Philocrates and Aeschines had been lavishly rewarded with 'properties and farms in the territory of our allies who came to ruin', which in the context can only mean in Chalcidice. The value of this, I take it, is as contemporary evidence showing that it was common knowledge or belief that Philip had the lands available in Chalcidice for such grants, and already had made great use of them. The information about Aeschines and Philocrates may be true, but it cannot be verified. Aeschines in his defence did not allude to it, though he went to some trouble to rebut a charge of having illtreated an Olynthian woman who was a captive (Aeschin. 2. 4 and 153 ff.).

for thinking of these cases as rare or in some way exceptional. Probably the only exceptional thing about them is their survival in the record, because the nature of this transaction (gift by king to individual) carried with it no reason whatever why the thing should automatically be recorded on stone. These were title-deeds, entries for a record office or registry (and for the individual), they were not honorific or commemorative compliments to be displayed. The single stone that has survived is a piece of good luck for us, and Perdiccas the son of Coenus (or the Registry at Cassandreia), presumably had some special reason for recording a later king's confirmation of his title-deeds in stone.[1] Presumably there were some hundreds of such title-deeds in the records, on paper. This is implied by the significant number of individual Macedonians described as 'from Amphipolis' or 'from Pydna' (conquered Greek cities), and by some oddities in the names that we find attached to the units of the most distinguished arm of the Macedonian army, the Companion cavalry.[2]

The Companion cavalry which invaded Asia later with Alexander was organized in eight squadrons raised, it seems, on a regional basis, except probably for the Guards (the so-called 'Royal' squadron). Of the other squadrons five happened to be 'named' at some time in our sources. They are 'from Leugaia' (unidentified), 'from Anthemus', 'from Apollonia', 'from Bottiaea', 'from Amphipolis'.[3] One squadron, then, (Amphipolis) bore the name of a conquered Greek city (above, p. 352), and another (Anthemus) the name of a region historically Macedonian but intermittently in Chalcidian hands (most recently, Philip retook it now from the Chalcidians after ceding it to them in 357). The other two names suffer from that plurality in nomenclature which (here) is a real obstacle to identification. Which Apollonia? Which Bottiaea? In each case one of the two possible alternatives offers a squadron named from a conquered city or region inside Chalcidice, analogous to the squadron of Amphipolis. One should add that Chalcidian 'Bottiaea' and Chalcidian Apollonia topographically are very close to each other, which makes it unlikely (though not impossible) that *both* these places are giving their names to a squadron now.

---

[1] *Syll.*[3] 1. 332. This stone was found on the site of Potidaea (Cassandreia).

[2] For Amphipolis and Pydna in this connection, see above, pp. 352, 356.

The Macedonian Polydamas of Arethusa (*Syll.*[3] 1. 296κ; cf. Berve 2 no. 648) is a possible candidate for this category. But Arethusa, near Apollonia of Mygdonia, became Macedonian under Alexander I (above, p. 102), though intermittently independent of Macedonia later (in 360, *IG* IV². 94. 16). We cannot be sure whether Polydamas was an old-established Macedonian there, or a new arrival of Philip's reign. The latter seems the more likely perhaps. In the same way the well-known Nicanor of Stagira (Berve 2 no. 557), if his Macedonian provenance 'of Mieza' is acceptable (St. Byz. s.v. Μίεζα), will have received lands at Stagira after the city was destroyed by Philip (p. 317 n. 1).

[3] See p. 411 n. 5 for references.

About Bottiaea the decision ought to be the easier, because the Chalcidian region was properly called *Bottike*, it seems. Bottiaea (or -is) was always the name of coastal Macedonia, the seaboard strip running from the Axius westwards to the northern boundary of Pieria and including Alorus and Pella.[1] From this the Bottiaeans had been expelled by the Macedonians in the sixth century, when they found a new home in Chalcidice to which also they gave their name. *Bottike* was the interior region of Chalcidice itself, south of the mountain range separating it from eastern Mygdonia.[2] Though the Chalcidians encroached at their expense, there were still 'the Bottiaeans' in *c.* 393 (at war with the Chalcidians as was proper)—and presumably they were still there in 348.[3] Does this fact (of 'the Bottiaeans') make it possible for a squadron to be named 'from Bottiaea' rather than 'from *Bottike*', if it was a squadron based on this region in Chalcidice? The naming of a squadron in or after 348 will have been descriptive (as of Amphipolis, and Anthemus), not allusive. The name chosen ought to be a name in current use, not a name of interest mainly to antiquarians (and one incidentally which was also in current use when attached to a different locality). The name ought to be 'from *Bottike*', not 'from Bottiaea'. The only two known and identifiable estates given by Philip to individual Macedonians are in *Bottike* (at Spartolus and at Sinus).[4] But this still ought not to make us think that Philip, if he were naming a squadron based on *Bottike*, would have given it the name which he and everybody else used every day to mean coastal Macedonia. In short, the squadron 'of Bottiaea' was based on coastal Macedonia, we may be reasonably sure.[5]

For the squadron of Apollonia, the choice lies between the Mygdonian Apollonia close to the lake Bolbe, and the Apollonia of Chalcidice proper, 'about 90 stades' (11 miles) from Olynthus.[6] Mygdonia, rather

[1] For discussion, *ATL* 3. 317 and n. 72; and see Volume I. 154, with Map 16.

[2] See Volume I. 191–2, with Map 17: *SEG* 2 no. 408 (a boundary stone of *c.* 400) seems decisive: cf. B. D. Meritt, 'Inscriptional and archaeological evidence for the site of Spartolus', *AJA* 27 (1923) 334–9.

[3] Tod, *GHI* no. 111, 17–18 (Hdt. 7. 128, for Chalcidian encroachment in 480/79).

[4] *Syll.*[3] 332. Of the three estates mentioned there, one is unidentified ('at Trapezus'). For Sinus, see C. F. Edson, 'Notes on the Thracian "Phoros" ', *CP* 42 (1947) 104 f., who shows convincingly that Sinus of the fifth-century tribute lists must be a city of Bottike, and cannot be identified with the Sindus of Herodotus 7. 123. 3 (as suggested at *ATL* 1. 406 f., 548 f.).

[5] So Berve 1. 105, rightly. *Contra*, West, *CL* 130 f.; Hampl 31 f.; Zahrnt 177 f.

[6] X. *HG* 5. 3. 1 f. (90 stades). For a good discussion, Zahrnt 156, arguing against the existence of a Chalcidic Apollonia and one so close to Olynthus in a neighbourhood where no ancient site has been found yet. (Certainly the 'Chalcidic Apollonia' of Athenaeus 8. 334 E, quoting Hegesander, is a red herring in this connection, and refers to the Mygdonian Apollonia.) But Xenophon's '90 stades' is likely to be accurate here. There is no reason to suspect a textual corruption, either in the numeral or in anything else. And Xenophon himself was keenly interested in this numeral because he was describing here the length of a notable pursuit by Macedonian cavalry of Olynthian cavalry, starting from the gates of

like Anthemus, was a region historically Macedonian since Alexander I but occasionally in Chalcidian hands. Its abundance of flat, moist grazing made it a good country for horses. This Apollonia was a fairly important place, and it continued in existence after 348 for many generations. The Chalcidic Apollonia certainly survived Philip's annexation in 348 intact. (It disappears from history after 316 in the synoecism of cities to form Cassander's new foundation Thessalonica.[1]) The suppression of Olynthus may have increased its importance, by creating an administrative vacuum in this heartland of the former Chalcidian League. The League itself had produced 1,000 cavalry, and evidently the country could rear and support the horses.[2] The land of Olynthus and Potidaea was at Philip's disposal in 348 (to say nothing of other Chalcidian territory). All this invites us to think of this Apollonia as another Amphipolis, chosen to be the administrative centre of a squadron of the Macedonian cavalry. Only the suppression of this Apollonia by Cassander seems to suggest that it perhaps was not an important centre of this kind in 316; and even this suggestion, persuasive on a first view, may not survive a second and a closer one. For the other new foundation Cassandreia was flourishing by now, distant only some 20 miles from Apollonia. For a ruler with big ideas and an eye to self-advertisement, to move a record office 20 miles and to rename the squadron of Apollonia (if it still existed) the squadron of Cassandreia would have been no trouble at all. On balance, and especially because of its proximity to the lands vacant in 348, it seems best to identify this Apollonia, rather than the Mygdonian, as the eponymous city of the cavalry squadron.

If this is right, the upshot of this digression on the names of the two squadrons is, that one of the five named squadrons was based on Chalcidice proper (and another of the five on Anthemus, which in this context may be thought to require an area larger than Anthemus itself and stretching to Therme (Salonica) in the north, and eastwards from there into Mygdonia south of Lake Bolbe).[3] Now to consider the local implications. A. B. West, concluding his whole survey, wrote 'Thus the whole of the Chalcidian territory was made part of Macedonia, inhabited in large part by Macedonians . . .'.[4] The 'squadron of Apollonia' by itself would not seem to justify this, if we were to think of some 200 Chalcidian estates being conferred on Macedonians to form the basis of the squadron.[5]

Apollonia and ending at the city-wall of Olynthus. Moreover, the Olynthians had arrived in the Apolloniate territory 'at midday' (Xen. loc. cit.), and were fresh enough to scatter for plunder immediately—as they would, after a ride of less than 11 miles, but not after 20+ miles (28 miles is the distance to the Mygdonian Apollonia).

[1] It is only this disappearance that tells us that the synoecized Apollonia is this one and not the Mygdonian. For the synoecism, Str. 7 F 21.
[2] D. 19. 266; X. *HG* 5. 2. 14.   [3] See Map 4.   [4] West, *CL* 135.
[5] For the strength of the squadrons (200 or more), p. 411. I am not suggesting that there

Even to take account here of the squadron 'of Anthemus' does not help matters enough, since it would be based on territory mostly Macedonian originally. (It is possible of course that one or more of the 'unnamed' Companion squadrons was based on Chalcidice too.) West himself clearly had in mind mainly the remark of Theopompus to the effect that 800 Companions enjoyed the use of as much land as 10,000 of the richest Greeks. But Theopompus himself did not relate the remark specifically to Chalcidice, and in any case Chalcidice did not contain enough land to endow Macedonians without limit.[1] The Chalcidian League, to be more precise, had had enough land to support about 10,000 hoplites and 1,000 knights, assuming (what is unlikely) that they all were living from the land and from nothing else.[2] Perhaps as an approximation one could think of the productive land of the League as having belonged in sum more or less equally to knights and hoplites. In that case 200 estates granted to Companions, if their average size was twice that of the estates of Chalcidian knights, would have taken about two-fifths of the knights' land, and about one-fifth of all the productive land there was. The territories of Olynthus and Potidaea themselves, which were available for distribution in 348, could well have been sufficient to supply land for grants on this scale, for the 200 estates of one Companion squadron ('of Apollonia').

Beyond this it seems hazardous to surmise, in the state of the evidence. For any mass immigration of Macedonians into Chalcidice there is no positive evidence. But the former territories of Olynthus and Potidaea will not have been let go to waste, and the estates of Companions will have been kept up in full productivity. If each Companion brought in

was a fixed legal obligation for each estate to supply one operational horseman to the Companion cavalry on demand, year in year out; but that taking an average over the years, one could expect 200 estates to be able to supply 200 operational horsemen, with some margin of reserve. (Some few estates might supply none for a time, if a Companion, e.g., died leaving sons not yet of age. But others could supply two or more sons of an older Companion simultaneously. For the incidence of brothers, see p. 402 n. 1.)

[1] *FGrH* no. 115 F 225B, from Book 49 of Theopompus, who seems to have written of the events of 349/8 in Books 22–5. The application of F 225B to the annexations in Chalcidice was stressed by U. Koehler, 'Philipp II und die chalkidische Städte' *SPAW* (1891) 473 ff. Theopompus wrote that the 800 (then) Companions 'were richer in lands than 10,000 of the biggest and most prosperous landowners of the Greeks' (οὐκ ἐλάττω καρπίζεσθαι γῆν ἢ μυρίους τῶν Ἑλλήνων τοὺς τὴν ἀρίστην καὶ πλείστην γῆν κεκτημένους) : and Demosthenes had alluded to the citizen strength of the Olynthians (= Chalcidians) as having been 'more than 10,000' (D. 19. 266). But to suppose that Theopompus here had the Chalcidians in mind is not only arbitrary, but it can only be done at all by mistranslating τοὺς . . . κεκτημένους (= 'who *do* possess') as 'who *did* possess'. Theopompus is merely saying in a rhetorically large and loose way that the 800 got very big estates.

[2] D. 19. 266; X. *HG* 5. 2. 14. Demosthenes uses Olynthus here as exemplar of the strong state that fell by its own corruption, 'though they had 1,000 cavalry, and were more than 10,000 strong'. I follow West (*CL* 149 f.) in interpreting this as the strength of the Chalcidian League citizen body, which was also the Chalcidian hoplite strength (with of course the cavalry). So Larsen, *GFS* 76 f. (for 'oligarchic' characteristics of the League).

a dozen or two of his own people from Macedonia, a total of some thousands of immigrants would result. This is possible, though obviously it is not the only way in which the land could have been exploited. In some other places (where no city had been destroyed, no population removed), gifts of estates to Macedonians could have resulted in changes of land-ownership without changing the local population at all.[1] Perhaps the estate at Spartolus granted by Philip to Ptolemaeus may be seen in this light.[2] West took this particular grant as an indication that Spartolus, like its near neighbour Olynthus, was among the cities destroyed.[3] But the fact that this land was identified still in the reign of Cassander (306–296) as 'the estate in Spartolus' suggests rather that Spartolus had not been destroyed but was one of the cities that survived.

This brings us back to the 'thirty-two cities' of Demosthenes. West examined carefully and in detail the evidence for survival-or-destruction of all the Chalcidic places known to him. To repeat the process now is unnecessary, but his results may be summarized, and how he arrived at them. Positive evidence of destruction (places named as having been destroyed) he found to be very scarce; positive evidence of survival much more frequent, and this (apart from a few isolated names) relating to places in certain areas easily defined (below). He found also a significant number of places (thirty-six) of which the existence in the fourth century before 348 is either attested directly or can be assumed with probability, and which are never heard of again after 348. It is from these that the 'thirty-two cities' of Demosthenes could be made up, and West concluded that this probably does explain them. 'The exaggeration is probably not in the number but in the importance of the places described by the term πόλεις. Many of them could have been more accurately called πολίσματα or towns.'[4] West's inquiry was conducted with an impeccable objectivity and modesty: 'This list is offered only by way of suggestion, and no finality is claimed for it; for the evidence on which it is based is largely negative and therefore inconclusive.'[5] But one needs to remember that West, accepting the 'squadron from Bottiaea' as based on Chalcidic *Bottike*, was working on an assumption that Chalcidice proper (not counting Anthemus and the north) was accommodating two squadrons of Macedonian landlords. An interpretation that allows for only one such squadron ('of Apollonia') is liable to view the negative evidence for destruction of cities with more scepticism. With this in mind, there is room for some further brief comment, including one or two things which either (writing in 1912) West could not know or which did not occur to him.

[1] e.g. estates formed from properties of prominent anti-Macedonians.
[2] *Syll.*[3] 1. 332.   [3] West, *CL* 133.   [4] Ibid. 130.
[5] Ibid. 134 n. 37.

(1) The number of places in Chalcidice which we actually know by name to have been destroyed by Philip in 348 is only three (perhaps only two): Olynthus, 'Zeira' or 'Geira', and Stagira.[1] If a list of the cities destroyed included some names which would have meant as much to an Athenian audience as Methone and Apollonia which Demosthenes did name, it would have been more effective for him to have named two or three more and reduce his 'group number' thirty-two to twenty-nine or thirty. Names such as Mende, Scione, Torone, Acanthus, come to mind.[2]

(2) As the Olynthian War was fought, with Philip attacking Olynthus itself only after preliminary campaigns in which he partly or wholly stripped it of its League allies, we can see that in the campaign of 349 at least he has won over some of these allies (in Bottike and Pallene), whose lands were invaded by the Olynthians in 348.[3] These places obviously had not been 'destroyed' by Philip, and it was in his interests to gain all such allies of Olynthus unresisting if possible. Cities which yielded without resisting cannot have been destroyed at the time; and even to destroy them later when the war was over, if they had surrendered on terms, would have been extremely unprincipled: not absolutely impossible, but for obvious and sound practical reasons very unlikely.

(3) West found that there are in reality several groups of cities in specific areas which certainly did survive 348. Quite certainly the twenty-six cities which according to Strabo were concerned in Cassander's synoecism of Thessalonica (316?) cannot all have been destroyed by Philip in 348 and restored meanwhile, and there is no positive evidence that any one of them was. Of the five which are named (Therme, Aenea, Garescus, Cissus, and Apollonia) the first four were all in northern or north-western Chalcidice, the area nearest to Thessalonica.[4] Though we do not know definitely that any of them belonged to the Chalcidian League in 349, it would be surprising if none of them did; but those that

---

[1] D.S. 16. 52. 9 (see above, p. 317 n. 1). Plu. *Alex.* 7. 3 (Stagira). For those who accept the emendation Stagira in the cited text of Diodorus, the number of named places is reduced to two. For 'Zeira', see above, ibid.

[2] Potidaea, no doubt, he would have named if he could; so presumably he could not. Philip undoubtedly had ended its existence as a city in 356 (D.S. 16. 8). But in the hands of the Chalcidians, who must have occupied and farmed its territory, it must have continued to be an inhabited place, perhaps incorporated now in Olynthus itself. And even after the fall of Olynthus, the new occupants of the land of Potidaea will have kept in existence what was the natural market and centre for the area.

[3] See above, p. 317.

[4] Str. 7. 330, 21 and 24. This Apollonia is certainly not that of Mygdonia (*RE* 2. 1 (1895) 114 s.v. Apollonia (3)), but that of Bottike, near Olynthus (ibid. s.v. Apollonia (4)), which is never heard of again after the foundation of Thessalonica.

West, following Beloch and others, recognized the existence of only one Apollonia in this region (the Mygdonian); but this view is unacceptable in the light of X. *HG* 5. 3. 1 f.

were members would be the first to encounter a Macedonian invasion, and they may well have come to terms easily.[1]

Other groups of cities which seem to have survived 348 are those on the three promontories of Chalcidice, Pallene (the most westerly, south of Potidaea on its neck), Sithonia (in the middle), and Acte (the most easterly, containing Athos, and with Acanthus nearly on its neck). The cities of Acte may not all have been members, just as Acanthus stood outside the League in *c.* 393.[2] Sane, however, the close neighbour of Acanthus, may have been the city of that name which Philip is recorded to have attacked and taken with the help of treachery.[3] Pallene is one of the two areas already discussed which seem likely to have come to terms with Philip in 349. The fact that its principal cities are found surviving later encourages the view.[4]

Finally in Sithonia, Torone (near its tip) is found in existence later, and West seems justified in including southern Sithonia among the areas which escaped Philip's destruction.[5] Interesting here, however, is that Torone warns us not to count on the destruction of all cities which did not submit without resistance. Torone evidently did resist, but only briefly, and was captured in 348 with the help of traitors inside.[6] More surprising still is the survival of Mecyberna, the port of Olynthus itself. The literary tradition records its capture (again, with treachery) but not its after-treatment, and on its survival it is equivocal; West was fully justified on general grounds in concluding 'We may assume that Mecyperna was destroyed.'[7] But the excavations there in 1934 do not confirm this. 'The answer is, on the basis of the numismatic evidence so far revealed, that Mecyberna was not destroyed in 348 when Philip captured it, but remained inhabited until the founding of Cassandreia' (in 316).[8] If the coins are rightly attributed and dated, this conclusion seems

---

[1] Therme was mentioned by Theopompus (*FGrH* no. 115 F 140) in his Book 22 (see above, p. 299 n. 2). This does not prove (as West was inclined to assume) that it and other Chalcidic places named by Theopompus (F 142, 144, 147, 152) must have been League cities which Philip attacked or captured. Therme was very near the site of Thessalonica, and hence not truly a Chalcidic city at all (but nor was Amphipolis, and she had once been a League member for a short time). If Therme was a League city in 357, Philip will have been content to leave it so while his alliance with the League survived.

[2] Tod, *GHI* no. 111, 19; X. *HG* 5. 2. 11. Cf. Zahrnt 148 ff.

[3] Frontinus, *Strat.* 3. 3. 5. But Zahrnt 220 warns of the insecurity of Saniorum in the text here (and cf. Frontin. 3. 2. 11).

[4] Mende, Scione, Aphytis. That one or other of them could have been destroyed in 348 and restored later (like Methone) would be possible; but that all of them had this experience can be excluded.

[5] Zahrnt 250–1; West, *CL* 131 n. 37: if Torone was destroyed by Philip (and rose again), Demosthenes might well have named it as destroyed in the passage already discussed (9. 26).

[6] D.S. 16. 53. 2.

[7] West, *CL* 131 n. 37; D.S. 16. 53. 2 (its capture); Mela 2. 3. 34 (its survival); Scymnus, 640 f. (its non-survival).

[8] D. M. Robinson, *Olynthus* 9. 372 ff.

inescapable, surprising though it is. Mecyberna and its citizens, if anybody, we might expect to have shared the fate of Olynthus and the
Olynthians. It is of course possible that the Mecybernians did share it,
and that new inhabitants were put in, though it is not easy to see reasons
for artificially repopulating the capital city's port after first removing
the capital city from the map. Mecyberna remains a problem. It is
helpful to remember, though, that the territory of Olynthus had not been
wiped out along with the city, and that it cannot possibly have been part
of any plan that this territory should lie idle and wasted. It must certainly have been farmed still, and most probably by or on behalf of
new Macedonian occupants. If, as seems likely, much of it now was
given to Companions of Philip in large estates, some administrative
centre will have been needed for this region, and a local marketing
centre will have been convenient, to say no more. A possibility is that
Mecyberna was allowed to remain, to supply that centre; and if so it
seems probable that the Mecybernians were allowed to remain too, to
supply some of the necessary labour on the land as well as such services
of market and harbour as were still needed.

(4) An interesting area for speculation is the Chalcidian upper class
and its treatment by Philip in 348. At a late stage in the siege of Olynthus
the Chalcidian cavalry had disgraced itself by a mass surrender, and
most likely it was in this class that a willingness to compromise and to
live with a Macedonian domination was strongest (above, p. 323).
Is it possible that Philip's quid pro quo was to leave Chalcidian knights
who were prepared to become good Macedonians in possession of their
lands, and perhaps even to add them to his Companion cavalry? Were
the squadrons of Apollonia and of Anthemus in fact to be mixed in their
composition, partly of new Macedonian landlords and partly of upper-
class Chalcidians including of course some Olynthians themselves spared
from the general fate of enslavement? That some individual Olynthians
were spared, we are reminded by the names of Callisthenes, the historians
Strattis and Ephippus, Ophellas the general later of Ptolemy I, and some
others.[1] But the generals Lasthenes and Euthycrates who commanded
the cavalry in 348 and were held responsible for betraying Olynthus to
Philip did themselves no great good by it, it seems.[2] As for a hypothetical

---

[1] See Zahrnt 115–16, and the *Prosopographia Olynthia* (pp. 39 ff.) in M. Gude, *A History
of Olynthus* (Baltimore, 1933) nos. 4, 18, 41, 50 (Euthycrates), 55 (Ephippus), 60, 74 (Callisthenes), 83 (Lasthenes), 102 (Ophellas), 110, 112 (Strattis). I do not include here the fairly
numerous Olynthian refugees at Athens (see p. 351 n. 3).

[2] D. 8. 40 (341) . . . πάντων κάκιστ' ἀπολώλασιν. But contrast Hyperides, F 76 (after
338), from which it appears that Euthycrates was active in the Macedonian interest in
about 345, and was present at Chaeronea in 338. Both orators disliked Euthycrates equally,
no doubt, and Hyperides may be no more reliable than Demosthenes on what E. did on
those occasions; but that he was there and able to do something may be accepted. The truth
may be that Lasthenes really did come to a bad end, as Demosthenes says, while Euthycrates

Chalcidian element in the Companion squadrons from Apollonia and from Anthemus, an argument from silence here must be fairly strong. Some sign or hint of Greeks among the Companion cavalry is to be expected, one would think, somewhere in the Alexander-story, if they had been there. And among the Companions of Alexander's retinue the complete absence of Chalcidians is rather striking: of the nineteen names of Greeks known to have belonged to this select category, though the provenance is known of all except two, not a single Chalcidian is to be found.[1] This from an area that could be thought second only to Thessaly as a pool of Greek talent which could be exploited, if (as in Thessaly) domination could be with a certain consensus and especially with co-operation from the ruling class.[2] Though the Chalcidian upper class presumably still survived in those cities that survived, to postulate for it a new and splendid era under Philip's annexation would be guesswork unsupported by any positive evidence and discouraged by the negative evidence mentioned here.

The Chalcidian League as a league did not survive the destruction of Olynthus, we may be almost sure. Unlike the Leagues of Boeotia, Achaea, and Aetolia after Chaeronea, it is never heard of again. The Chalcidian cities that survived survived as individuals, and it will have been as individuals that Philip disposed of them in 348. Some he destroyed, and the number we assign to these will depend on our view of the value of Demosthenes when he said there were 'thirty-two cities in Thrace destroyed'.[3] The figure is well chosen: it sounds as if someone had been counting. But the context does not inspire confidence. His very next words are 'And I say nothing of the entire Phocian people which he has destroyed', using the same uncompromising verb ($\dot{\alpha}\nu\dot{\eta}\rho\eta\kappa\epsilon\nu$ . . .

---

survived and flourished, perhaps as a *hetairos* of Philip. He was an important enough man for Demades to propose proxeny privileges for him at Athens in the period after 338. (Hyperid. F 76.)

[1] Berve 2. 31 has a list of sixty-one Companions of this high status, including thirteen Greeks, whose provenance (where known) he gives in the Prosopography. To these thirteen I add the six Greeks who were trierarchs in 325 (Arr. *Ind.* 18. 7 f.), whom he agrees to have been almost certainly Companions of the retinue, though not attested as such (ibid.); also Onesicritus, and Androsthenes of Thasos (and Amphipolis) (ibid.).

(To correct any impression that as many as one-third of the Companions of the retinue were Greeks, it is to be remembered that Berve's sixty-one include only those whose status is actually attested in our sources. To them must be added the Macedonian trierarchs of 325, several of the Bodyguards, and all the satraps and high-ranking generals (including men as eminent as Parmenion, Antigonus, and Antipater) who do not happen to be attested. The total of sixty-one will rise to about a hundred, and the proportion of Greeks will fall to about one-fifth.)

[2] The same nineteen names include four from Thessaly. The importance of the Thessalian cavalry in the army of Philip and Alexander is well known (pp. 435 ff.). The Thessalian League still flourished, Philip its *archon*. The leading Thessalians had their political role, especially through the Delphic Amphictyony (p. 539).

[3] D. 9. 26.

ἀνῃρημένον). The Phocians, we know, were *not* destroyed, they were only disintegrated politically: they were not wiped out or removed from Phocis (and a few years after this they are restored politically also). Of the 'thirty-two cities of Thrace', Demosthenes had added that they were 'destroyed so savagely that a tourist would find it hard to say whether they had ever been inhabited'; and of Olynthus, Methone, and the Apollonia which he names, this may have been nearly true and known to be true. But of the rest? It is difficult not to have grave doubts about this emotive phrase, concerning which (as for his other emotive phrase about the traitors Lasthenes and Euthycrates and their 'bad end') the true facts of the matter were not easily accessible to his audience at that moment (in 341). In Chalcidice Olynthus was destroyed, in the full sense of Demosthenes, and so was Stagira; but we actually know of no others. Olynthus, dominant in the League and its capital city, may well have come to incorporate a number of the small cities, as Thebes did in Boeotia in a similar situation, and if so 'Olynthus' could contain a number of city-sites 'destroyed' in Demosthenes' sense.[1] But further than this it might be unwise to go in search of these total destructions, with only Demosthenes as guide.

At the more matter-of-fact level, where 'destruction' is recognized as orator's licence for 'political disintegration' (as of the Phocians), Demosthenes may be thought to carry more conviction. Undeniably Chalcidice was disintegrated now politically, its League broken up and its surviving members reduced to some status in which they recognized Philip's hegemony. But to what status precisely? Do they become now Philip's allies, free and autonomous technically though his dependants in reality? Or are they formally annexed so as to become mere municipalities of Macedonia, like Pella or (as suggested above) Amphipolis? It is by no means necessary of course to assume that all were treated identically; Apollonia, for example, giving its name to a cavalry squadron of the Macedonian army, could be thought a good candidate for municipalization.[2] But allowing for the occasional anomaly there are still two things that invite us to think of these Chalcidian cities as broadly speaking in one category, though unfortunately the two signposts here point in opposite directions. The first of them is the allusion of Isocrates in 346 to the surviving cities as 'allies':[3] the second is the great synoecizing programme of Cassander in 316 to found Cassandreia (and to a lesser

---

[1] For Thebes (in 395), *Hell. Oxy.* 16. 3 (Bartoletti).

[2] [D]. 7. 28 supports—οὐδ' Ὄλυνθόν γε οὐδ' Ἀπολλωνίαν οὐδὲ Παλλήνην, οὐκ ἀλλοτρίας ἀλλὰ τὰς ἑαυτοῦ χώρας κέκτηται. These places are named here as being in the same category as Amphipolis, places which Philip counted as his own possessions. For Pallene, Potidaea on its isthmus certainly belonged to this category. Whether to accept this remark as evidence that the cities of the promontory belonged to it too, I am in doubt.

[3] Isoc. 5. 20.

degree at Thessalonica shortly after), where plainly Cassander, who was
not even king at the time, treated the synoecized cities as subjects. It is
tempting to see this subject status of Chalcidian cities in 316/15 as the
status assigned to them by Philip in 348, since there has been no occasion
for a change of status meanwhile. Probably however the temptation
should be resisted; for though nothing in Chalcidice specifically had
changed, the whole situation in Greece had been changed by the
Lamian War and its outcome. The 'League of Corinth' was defunct, and
the principles on which it had been based were discredited for a time in
Macedonian ruling circles. To Cassander in 316 it was no longer an
axiom that Greek cities were free and autonomous, and of all Greek
cities those of Chalcidice were the most vulnerable to his big ideas and
his strong arm. In short, what Cassander chose to do in 316 is not good
evidence for the nature of Philip's arrangements in 348.

Isocrates in 346 is a different matter. He knew just what Philip had
done two years before; but of course Philip (whom he is addressing)
knew it too, so Isocrates merely alludes to it in the briefest possible way,
and taking good care to be innocuous. 'And of the cities in that part of
the world some he has befriended and in this way has gained them as
allies, others under extreme provocation he has destroyed.'[1] Of Greek
cities 'in that part of the world' Chalcidice contained by far the greatest
and most important concentration, obviously. And Isocrates, when
allowance is made for his extreme brevity and his lack of concern here
with any individual anomalies, thinks of them in two categories: either
they were dead, or they were allies of Philip now. It is not easy to ignore
this evidence, in spite of its limitations. Probably it ought to rule out
any notion that most of the Chalcidian cities at this time had been
annexed and had become municipalities of Macedonia. But 'allies' was
a word of infinite variety in terms of status. The subject cities of the
Athenian empire had been 'the allies'. In 346, however, with a generation or more of *koine eirene* precept and practice in his head, Isocrates
ought to have meant by 'allies' cities which were technically free and
autonomous. It seems best to think of this as the status of most of these
surviving Chalcidian cities by Philip's settlement of 348, and to think
of them as among the allies of Philip who took the oath to the treaty
with Athens in 346. But if they were 'free' to conduct their own foreign
policy still, this did not give them the power *de facto* to act independently
of Philip their *hegemon*. With Olynthus gone, they had no potential for
collective strength, and they were in Philip's grip as firmly as if they had
been formally annexed. A few years later the Athenians could still send
ambassadors to Thessaly in the hope of making some trouble there; but

---

[1] Ibid. 'That part of the world' (τῶν δὲ πόλεων τῶν περὶ τὸν τόπον ἐκεῖνον) means in the
Macedonian area, not in Thessaly as it is often misinterpreted. See above, p. 223 and n. 2.

they sent no ambassadors to Chalcidice.[1] It would have been a waste of time.

In this way, then, the Chalcidian cities (and not only thirty-two of them) were 'destroyed', in the sense that genuine freedom was at an end. The interesting and effective federal institutions, their response to the challenges of external and other pressures of the past, could not save them from this new and overwhelming power of a greater Macedonia.[2] For Philip, the reasons for breaking the League are not hard to see; they were mainly strategic. The Chalcidians as aggressive neighbours capable of encroaching upon Macedonian territory (above, p. 176) could be forgotten now, certainly. But it was still true that for Athens, or for any other Greek power at war with him, Chalcidice with its bases and its strength for war offered the obvious alliance by means of which to carry war to Macedonia. Once the Chalcidians ceased to be his own loyal allies, they became not exactly a permanent threat of deadly proportions but a permanent nuisance liable to combine at any opportunity with any of his enemies whether Greek or Balkan. It was better to have done with this, and decisively. To destroy Olynthus itself was not necessary, once the military lesson had been given. (In a like situation later he did not judge it necessary to destroy Thebes.) Here perhaps the bonus element was too strong to be resisted; all this good land, so well sited for Macedonian settlement in some form. The squadron 'from Apollonia' the result.

How nicely calculated was the sum total of this treatment of the Chalcidian Greeks, we cannot know. But Philip will have been aware that the eyes of the Greeks abroad were on him now, and that his actions would affect Greek opinion, and (he may have hoped) Greek behaviour in the future. In the allusion of Isocrates above (something more than polite), the good Greeks now 'in that part of the world', were living happy ever after, it was only the very naughty Greeks who had been naughty once too often. This was the old method of the stick and the carrot. Philip's place in the world now, which included his place in Thessaly with its involvement in the central issues of Greek affairs, could be thought incompatible with a reputation as a sacker of Greek cities. The stick was something to have, rather than something to use, now that everybody knew that he did have it. The real question was, was the carrot a good enough carrot, was it even a real carrot at all? It consisted partly of being let off from getting the stick, and this was a real consideration certainly. But 'in that part of the world' the Greeks who now were Philip's allies were free and autonomous in a twilight world where the genuine freedom, the freedom to please themselves, had been

---

[1] For Thessaly, p. 537.
[2] On the Chalcidian institutions, see X. *HG* 5. 2. 12 ff., Larsen, *GFS* 75 ff.

extinguished. Twilight might have something to commend it, for those who feared the heat of the sun. But the Greeks who lived further afield and outside the great shadow still, though they knew of what had happened up north, went on with their own affairs in the sun, secure in the belief (if they thought of it) that 'it can't happen here.'

8. *Abdera, Maroneia, Aenus, Cardia*

Of these cities of the Thracian coast, the first three, all early members of the Second Athenian Confederacy, remained members after the war of secession (357–355).[1] Maroneia (nearly midway between the Nestus and Hebrus rivers) was still an ally of Athens in 340 probably, and perhaps did not come under Philip's control till 338.[2] If that was so, she became probably in name at least his ally then, and a member of the League of Corinth. Abdera, the largest of the three and situated only about 18 miles east of the Nestus, like Maroneia had suffered an invasion by Philip in 353 (above, pp. 265 f.), and as an ally of Athens was liable to come under pressure at any time when Philip and Athens were at war. The fact that neither orators nor historians mention Abdera either in connection with the years before the peace of 346 or with the years 345–341 (containing seven public speeches actually delivered in those years) creates a certain presumption that there was no change in her status before the new outbreak of war late in 340. The arrival in Athens of the distinguished Abderite Dioscurides with his two brothers towards midsummer 345 is suggestive but not decisive. They are exiles now and are treated as good friends of Athens, the rider to the decree proposed by the Council being proposed by Diopeithes who later led new cleruchs to the Chersonese (343) and held a Thracian command in 341.[3] Moreover the silver coinage of Abdera, after a long and not undistinguished history of about two centuries, comes to an end now, most probably in the 340s or only a year or two later.[4] This presumably means something, politically, and

[1] Tod, *GHI* no. 123, lines 87, 99, and 103. Polyaen. 4. 2. 22 shows Abdera and Maroneia as allies of Athens still in 353 (above, p. 265). [D.] 58. 37 f. alludes to the occasion when Aenus left the Athenian alliance and joined Philip (below).

[2] [D]. 12. 17 (340).

[3] *IG* ii². 1. 218 (ll. 22 ff. for the rider of Diopeithes). Beloch (3². 2. 218) did regard this as decisive.

[4] J. M. F. May, *The Coinage of Abdera* (London, 1966) 286 ff. May divided the coinage into nine periods, and his Period IX begins about 360 or a year or two earlier, and contains thirteen distinct issues. If the series began in 362, with a new issue every year, the last issue would be in 350. A new issue every year is not necessary, but May found no reason to believe the series was long drawn out or that the individual issues did not follow one another at short and regular intervals. He concludes 'We must look for the end of the Apollo-head series at some time within the years 350–345.' It could be objected that this conclusion does require very nearly a new issue every year. A new issue every other year would bring the last issue to 338. (That is where I would like to see it.)

usually it is taken to mean that Abdera has succumbed now, and is under Philip's control. Though the example of Corinth warns us not to assume that a Macedonian garrison in the citadel is sure to mean the cessation of an independent coinage, and not to make the same connection in reverse without due reserve, here in Abdera this connection in some shape or form does seem required. To infer that the coinage ended by Philip's orders, and from this to infer that Abdera became not his free ally but a subject, would be speculative certainly, and by no means sure to be right (the city at the time may have become temporarily hard up, or temporarily oligarchic with a government ready to break with traditional practices of its *demos*—and then through the years it may have found that it was getting on very well really, using the currencies of Philip and Alexander and Athens and others). However, what seems most probable is that Abdera broke with Athens and joined Philip at some time in the years 340–338, and that she became his ally in name (and consequently a member of the League of Corinth), whatever limitations to her true freedom her contiguity to the Macedonian homeland may have imposed.

The story of Aenus (at the mouth of the Hebrus) is very similar, except that the author of the speech *Against Theocrines* did have occasion to mention that 'the Aenians, they say, pay no regard to Athens', that there was 'a time when some of them were philippizing and others were atticizing', and that owing to the bungling and bullying of Theocrines and others 'they chose the least of the bad alternatives on offer . . . they preferred to accept a garrison and be subject to barbarians, abandoning you their old allies'.[1] The picture is clear enough in outline. As to the date, all the indications (as for Abdera, above) favour a date not before 340, and again the evidence of the coinage of Aenus, which terminates in this period, agrees closely enough.[2] Most probably Aenus defected from Athens during or after the final war of 340–338, and as one of Philip's nominally free allies became a member of the League of Corinth.[3]

Cardia differed from the three cities we have been considering, in that she had never been an ally of Athens in recent years. Situated at the neck of the Gallipoli peninsula (Thracian Chersonese), and its most important city, Cardia was probably alarmed when Athens gained Sestus and Crithote, Elaeus and other small cities in 365 and 364 and so came to control the peninsula itself.[4] Cardia held aloof from an Athenian

---

[1] [D.] 58. 37–8. For the date of this speech, the end of the archonship of Lyciscus (mid-343) is *terminus post quem* (cf. *RE* 2. 5 (1934) 2000 s.v. *Theokrines*).

[2] J. M. F. May, *Ainos: History and Coinage* (Oxford, 1950) 195 ff., 258 ff., dates the end of the coinage to 342/1.

[3] The garrison installed at Aenus ([D.] 58. 37) may be thought to suggest that the defection came at a time when a state of war either existed or was deemed imminent.

[4] For Cardia's position as strategic key to the Chersonese, D. 23. 182.

alliance, and is found co-operating first with Cersobleptes the Thracian king, and presently allied to Philip.[1] The alliance with Philip existed already in 346, and may go back perhaps to the time of Philip's Thracian campaign of late 352, when the eclipse of Cersobleptes, and the presence of Athenian cleruchs in the Chersonese, will have been the stimuli to Cardian policy.[2] The Cardian Apollonides, who had worked with Cersobleptes in the Pammenes affair in 353 (p. 265), came to work equally well with Philip, evidently.[3] From 346 on, Cardia remained staunchly anti-Athenian.[4] She was presumably Philip's ally and a free and autonomous city still—and the alliance paid off: it was Athens, not Cardia, whose claims in the Chersonese were ended for ever (in 338). Some of the realities of the alliance, however, had been revealed at one earlier stage in the dispute with Athens, when it had suited Philip to agree that this dispute should be settled by an arbitration, and he had told the Athenians that if the Cardians did not agree to this, he would make them.[5] However, in the relations of the small power with the great, all's well that ends well; and in 338/7 Cardia doubtless joined the other free and autonomous Greek cities as a member of the League of Corinth.

Her contribution to Philip did not end there, for already his eye for talent had discovered in the household of a leading Cardian a boy or young man (son of the house) who was to spend nearly twenty years in the royal service as surely the ablest and most eminent of all the Greek Companions, the celebrated Eumenes. His career as Alexander's Chief Secretary need not be anticipated here. But Alexander did not discover him, he inherited him; for already in 336 he had a record of seven years' service under Philip.[6] Whether or not Philip had always known (like Harold Ross) that he needed a miracle man, one to sort out the papers and keep them sorted, Theopompus at least hints plainly that this is what he did need, and it is good to know that (unlike Ross) he found him and was able to keep him, and this at just about the time perhaps when he was beginning to need him most.[7] Middle age does not improve the capacity to muddle along effectively, or the appetite for attempting it. Especially the close involvement with the affairs of Greek cities in Philip's last years will have multiplied the papers and the places, the faces and the names, into something intolerable without an efficient secretariat.

[1] For Cersobleptes, D. 23. 169, 175, 181–3 (alliance).

[2] [D.] 12. 11; D. 5. 25; 19. 174 (concerning 346). For Athenian cleruchs in the Chersonese, *IG.* ii². 1613, 297 (353/2).

[3] D. 23. 183; [D.] 7. 39.   [4] [D.] 7. 41–4; D. 8 Hypoth.; 8. 58, 64; 9. 35.

[5] [D.] 7. 41–4.

[6] Nepos, *Eum.* 1. 6. For his origins in general, ibid. 1; Plu. *Eum.* 1; 11. 2 (for his youthful and dapper appearance still in 320); cf. Berve 2 no. 317.

[7] Theopomp. *FGrH* no. 115 F 225 A. For 'miracle man', see James Thurber, *The Years with Ross* (London edn., 1959), ch. 6 'Miracle Men', and ch. 7 'More Miracle Men'. I use Thurber's phrase here because there can never have been a better.

Eumenes was quick, discreet, industrious, persuasive, good company, and a very personable young man; ambitious no doubt and fond of money and of the power which his position gave him, but capable of loyalty and too intelligent to mistake where his loyalty was to lie. Philip was lucky to have found him.

XI

THE GOVERNMENT OF THE KINGDOM

1. *King and People*[1]

THE institutions of the Macedonian kingdom before Philip's reign, in so far as the evidence allows, have been described and discussed.[2] By classical Greek standards the 'Constitution' of Macedonia was a disgrace. Here the monarchy still survived and flourished, its powers limited only modestly as yet by the rudimentary rights of an Assembly of the People, the prestige of the royal house nourished by a private mythology of its own linking it with Argos and Heracles. Here the king selected from the leading men an entourage, with all its potential for strength or dissension in the kingdom. But where is the Gerousia or an Areopagus, the corporate expression of that potential? And where are the ephors or the elected officers by any other name, who could be thought of as

[1] The copious bibliography on Macedonian king and people is assembled, and much of it discussed, by P. Briant, in his *Antigone le Borgne*, Paris (1973) especially 237–350, *Appendice à la deuxième partie . . . contribution à l'étude de l'Assemblée macédonienne*. This is the best study of the subject now, together with the essays of A. Aymard, *Études d'histoire ancienne* (Paris, 1967) 73–99 ('Le Protocol royal grec et son évolution' = *REA* 50 (1948) 232–63); 100–22 ('βασιλεὺς Μακεδόνων' = *RIDA* 4 (1950) 61–97); 143–63 ('Sur l'assemblée macédonienne' = *REA* 52 (1950) 115–37). And see R. M. Errington (cit. p. 387 n. 3 below).

As is well known, our most informative source for native Macedonian customs and institutions is Curtius Rufus, whose reliability naturally has been called in question. On this matter I agree in general with Briant (339) and Badian, 'The death of Parmenion', *TAPA* 91 (1960) 326 n. 8, in accepting this material as reliable. Though Curtius could write some miserable rubbish in (e.g.) the speeches at the trial of Philotas (below), the few sober facts about Macedonian procedures must derive from a good source probably contemporary, and themselves they are mostly innocent of anything to attract an inventor or a distorter of the truth. From Marsyas of Pella? Hammond above, p. 151. The passages are:

Curt. 10. 7. 1 ff. (election of king)
,, 6. 8. 25; 6. 11. 20; 8. 6. 28; 8. 7. 18 (treason trials)
,, 6. 11. 10 and 38; 7. 2. 1 (stoning as penalty for treason)
,, 6. 11. 20; 8. 1. 18; 8. 2. 12; 8. 8. 18 ('laws', or decisions, of Assembly; but see below, pp. 391 f.)
,, 5. 1. 42; 8. 6. 2–7; 8. 8. 3 (Royal Pages)
,, 8. 6. 6 (flogging)
,, 9. 3. 4 (baring the head when addressing the king)
,, 3. 11. 3 (king's spoils in war)
,, 4. 8. 6 (barley-meal ritual)
,, 5. 4. 3; 7. 9. 22 (burial)
,, 8. 4. 27 ff. (marriage)
,, 10. 9. 12 (purification)

[2] pp. 150 ff. above.

representatives and mouthpiece of the people, and the daily reminder to the king that he was in some sense responsible to somebody for his actions? We scan the reign of Philip in vain for any sign of these things.[1]

Nor are we justified, it seems, in blaming our defective sources of information. The Chalcidians of Olynthus, neighbours of Macedonia for more than two centuries now and distant from Pella a mere 60 miles or so across the Gulf, knew no more than we do about Macedonian officers of state or institutions. Their drafters of the treaty of alliance with Philip in 357/6 nominated 'the federal officers of the Chalcidian League' (and others) to take the oath to Philip on behalf of the Chalcidians; but the reciprocal oath of Philip to the Chalcidians is to be taken by 'Philip himself and whoever else the Chalcidians may say'.[2] This means, presumably, that the Chalcidian ambassadors were authorized to nominate whomever they thought best, when they had found Philip and could see who was around just then. For the Athenian treaty with Perdiccas II the oath had been taken by a number of the leading men of the kingdom (however nominated) starting with members of the royal family (above, p. 134). Here in 357 there is certainly no advance on this, no sign of a constitutional development in this area. At Olynthus they knew of no board of generals or ephors or archons, nor of any council of state or other institution in Macedonia that they could name, as the Athenians in a nearly contemporary treaty named 'Agelaos the archon and the polemarchs and the hipparchs and the knights and the hieromnemons and the other federal officers of the Thessalian League'.[3]

The lack of anything in Macedonia resembling a 'government' in the absence of the king is underlined perhaps by the king's evident need to appoint a deputy on occasion. Thus Perdiccas II in 432 before a campaign which would take him no further than Chalcidice and for a matter of weeks only, first 'appointed Iolaus as his deputy-ruler'. If the reign of Philip had a Thucydides, we should learn more of such occasions probably. As it is, we know only of Alexander's appointment in 340.[4] The experience of the Athenians and their embassies, especially in 346 (*annus mirabilis* for the goings-on of embassies and ambassadors to Macedonia) does not alter this impression of the monarchy. No Macedonian group or organ of government has any recorded part in all those discussions. Always it is Philip who is addressed and who replies, Philip's moods and intentions that invite hopes, fears, speculation. If Philip is away in Thrace, everything and everyone must wait till he gets back. If last-minute changes in the peace treaty are proposed as a result of the Athenian Assembly's debate, Philip's ambassadors who are present merely

---

[1] On *peliganes* ('elders') and *tagonaga* ('council of *tagoi*'?) in local government, pp. 648 f.
[2] Tod, *GHI* 158, 3–5.   [3] Tod, *GHI* 147, 23–6 (361/60).
[4] Thuc. 1. 62. 2; Plu. *Alex.* 9. 1.

say No to them (and the proposals are dropped).[1] On the Macedonian side, this was a one-man band. The ability to take his own decisions on all matters at will was counted by Demosthenes as one of the advantages that lay with Philip in his relations with the *demos* of Athens, especially in war.[2]

An autocrat, then? In practice, very largely Yes, it may be said, in the sense that the king needed no authority other than his own to replace Arybbas with Alexander on the throne of Epirus, to offer Athens a revision of the terms of her treaty of peace and alliance, or to grant a remission of taxation in Macedonia to all its citizens or to some deserving individuals among them.[3] Yet it seems clear that the Macedonians themselves would have recognized Thucydides' well-known description of the archaic 'hereditary kingships with limited prerogatives' as a fair description of their own kings.[4] Their king had to be of the Temenid house;[5] and he had to be the choice of the Macedonian people assembled for that purpose. Once chosen he was fettered by no constitutional safeguards or aids to government, except in the single sphere of jurisdiction. Trials *de capitalibus rebus* were the function of this same Macedonian Assembly.[6] The definition covers, most obviously, treason (and the only trials of which we know details were treason trials); but also presumably impiety (*asebeia*), and perhaps some categories of homicide. This, the only limitation of the king's powers that we actually know about, is a very important one, certainly. But it can hardly be seen as filling the full picture of the relationship between king and people.[7] Alexander (the Great) was reminded on one famous occasion that he was 'no Cambyses or Xerxes but the son of Philip, by descent a Heraclid and an Aeacid, sprung from forebears who came from Argos to Macedonia and then for generations ruled the Macedonians not as tyrants but by the rule of Law'

---

[1] Above, pp. 340 f.

[2] D. 18. 235; 1. 4.

[3] For Epirus, p. 505: for *epanorthosis* of the treaty of 346, p. 489: for taxation, Just. 11. 1. 10; Arr. *An.* 1. 16. 5.

[4] Thuc. 1. 13. 1.

[5] This is well shown by the choice of Philip Arrhidaeus at Babylon in 323 by the Macedonian infantry in spite of his personal disability: Curt. 10. 7. 2; 7. 14–15. On the same occasion the Macedonian cavalry, the motivation of whose leaders was more complex, still did not depart from the Temenid line in their choice of Alexander's unborn son.

[6] Curt. 6. 8. 25. The examples in Alexander's reign are well known.

[7] It is right to notice here three passages in Curtius Rufus which seem to be giving 'the Macedonians' *legislative* powers (that is, of the Assembly, presumably). A closer examination is bound to reject them. (1) Curt. 6. 11. 20, *legem Macedonum* (by which the kin of a Macedonian found guilty of treason was liable to the same penalty) is explained (and discredited) by (2) 8. 8. 18, which alludes to the same 'law' (rightly) as *istum morem*. (3) 8. 1. 18 'Ceterum Macedones . . . scivere gentis suae more ne aut pedes venaretur aut sine delectis principum atque amicorum.' The *mos* was as here described, very likely: 'Macedones . . . scivere' means here that somebody now reminded Alexander of it. This 'somebody' I take to be the circle of his close friends and associates (οἱ ἀμφ' αὐτὸν ἑταῖροι).

(οὐδὲ βίᾳ ἀλλὰ νόμῳ)[1]—where law did not mean a written constitution or the enactments of a *boule* and a *demos*, but still meant something, we must believe, and something that effectively made Philip and Alexander respectable as kings, to those who could accept kings as respectable.

The Macedonians could and did. To them, law in this context meant an unwritten pattern of behaviour in their kings which was traditional and acceptable (κατὰ τὰ πάτρια etc.). To speak of 'a contractual character' in this pattern seems admissible only in a theoretical context.[2] There was an exchange of duties which was mutually understood. Not the least of the links of inter-dependence was in the religious life of 'the Macedonians'. As befitted a people who had always lived dangerously and in a dangerous part of the world, the Macedonians propitiated every god that they knew of, and the list of their cults is impressive.[3] This sensitive area was the responsibility of the king, whose Heraclid descent in a sense marked him out for it.[4] Meanwhile the king who did all that was proper towards the gods (πατρίῳ νόμῳ etc.), and with the proper results, could please himself and make his own decisions, and the Macedonians would obey him, so long as he did not try to force them to do things which they had never done before, did not want to do now, and had no intention of doing if they could help it; things like crossing the river Hyphasis, for example, or performing an act of unseemly ceremonial obeisance to the king like a lot of fatuous Persians. In the first example the mass of the Macedonians, in the second some close associates of Alexander, objected; in each example, decisively. The Hyphasis became the eastern boundary of Alexander's empire. The Persian practice of *proskunesis* was not enforced. The Macedonian *nomos*, whatever else it was, was no mere idle form of words. The king ruled by consent.

Whether this was summarized and sanctified in the form of oaths, exchanged between people and king on his accession, as we see it in the Molossian monarchy of Epirus, is uncertain.[5] An oath of the Macedonians to the new king seems established by the known examples of 323 and 279.[6] But a reciprocal oath of the king to the people is nowhere attested, and to rely here on what they did in Epirus is unsafe, because there the community *vis-à-vis* the monarchy had more developed institutions.[7] In Epirus the king swore 'to rule according to the laws', and the

---

[1] Arr. *An.* 4. 11. 6 (reported speech of Callisthenes). This phrase is found in the epigram on the monument of the fifth-century Thessalian *tagos* Daochus of Pharsalus, set up at Delphi by his grandson Daochus in (probably) 337. (*Syll.*[3] 274, VI and VIII, and n. 8; Sordi, *LT* 114 ff.): . . . ἁπάσης / Θεσσαλίας ἄρξας οὐ βίαι ἀλλὰ νόμωι / ἑπτὰ καὶ εἴκοσι ἔτη.

[2] So Briant 322, in a context where it is justified, probably, by his preceding analysis (319–22).   [3] Above, pp. 155 f., 164.

[4] Since the illustrative evidence so much belongs to the story of Alexander, examination of it is reserved to Volume III. See meanwhile Berve 1. 85–96; Briant 326 and n. 2.

[5] Plu. *Pyrrhus* 5. 2 αὐτοὶ μὲν ἄρξειν κατὰ τοὺς νόμους, ἐκείνους δὲ τὴν βασιλείαν διαφυλάξειν κατὰ τοὺς νόμους.   [6] Curt. 10. 7. 9; Just. 24. 5. 14.   [7] Cf. Hammond, *Epirus* 525 ff.

people swore 'to defend the kingdom according to the laws'.[1] These simple propositions do seem to conform exactly to the Macedonian view of these things, and the fact that 'the laws' in Macedonia were unwritten ones (indeed maybe one ought to translate *nomous* here as 'tradition' or 'custom') does not mean that they were any the less binding, or that either party would be in any doubt as to the things that they were to do, and what not to do. The probability seems in favour of an oath sworn by the king on his accession, and an oath of this character.[2] The king–people relationship was essentially a personal one, however, in Macedonia, as appears in the 'royal style'. Though Greeks called these kings *basileus Makedonōn* when they needed to (what else should they call them?), the Macedonian kings did not call themselves *basileus* or expect to be called this by their people. Down to and including Philip, they called themselves Amyntas, Alexander, Archelaus, Philip, and nothing more, even on their coins. Alexander's conquest of the Persian empire introduced a new element, obviously; but the first king who calls himself *basileus* in Macedonia (Cassander) does so because he has no business to be there anyway. He is not a Temenid, and needs to assert himself in this way.

The king's title or 'style', it has been thought, might offer clues to the king–people relationship. This will be so, however, only if 'the Macedonians' can be shown to appear regularly as part of the royal title; and in truth 'king of the Macedonians' comes in as regular 'royal style' only with Philip V (if then). In an excellent recent article R. M. Errington shows that the single known instances of 'Amyntas son of Perdiccas' (Μακεδόνων Βασιλεύς) and of Cassander (Βασιλεὺς Μακεδόνων) are peculiar, and have special reasons; and he calls attention to the lack of any 'royal style' that can be called regular, and most of all for the kings before Alexander the Great.[3] That Philip himself would have answered to the title *basileus* cannot be doubted (though it cannot positively be proved, either).[4] But, equally clearly, he did not normally

---

[1] By 'the kingdom' I mean here, of course, not only the territorial boundaries etc. but (more) the king and his kingship.

[2] For some further discussion, see now Briant 320 and n. 8; who rightly includes the Macedonian kingship, along with the Molossian (and the Spartan) in Aristotle's category of monarchy according to the laws (*Pol.* 1285^{b}15–30).

[3] R. M. Errington, 'Macedonian Royal Style and its historical significance', *JHS* 94 (1974) 20–37. For Amyntas, son of Perdiccas, see pp. 702 ff.

[4] Nearest to proof comes the treaty document of the League of Corinth, Tod, *GHI* no. 177, 11–12, 'the kingdom of Philip and his descendants' (τὴν βασιλείαν . . . etc.). 'The kings Philip and Alexander' alluded to retrospectively by a decree of the Council of Samothrace in the reign of Lysimachus (288–281) are probably the joint kings Philip III and Alexander IV of 323–316 (J. R. McCredie, *Hesperia* 37 (1968) 220; and cf. ibid. 222). But even if the allusion is to Philip II and Alexander III acting on two separate occasions, the 'style' will be that of the 280s.

Well-informed contemporaries did of course refer to Philip as king if they had occasion (D. 1. 9; 2. 15; Arist. *Pol.* 1310^{b}39; Isoc. 5. 154 by implication).

use the title *basileus*: he normally called himself, and was called by those who had to do with him, neither 'king' nor 'king of the Macedonians', but simply 'Philip'.[1] How much significance to see in this? That 'the Macedonians' never come in here at all, not on coins, not in the official language of treaties, not as supplying the two 'new' representatives to the council of the Delphic Amphictyony, obviously is neither accidental nor uninteresting, and the significance seems underlined by those contrasting and near-contemporary Epirot coins bearing the name not 'Of Neoptolemus' but 'Of the Molossians'. The Molossians had got somewhere, as a people in relation to their kings; and some details of this can now be seen.[2] The Macedonians presumably had not: and this presumption is contradicted by nothing that we learn of Philip's life and times (or later). In Macedonia it was for the king to rule—and to remember that he was ruling free men and not slaves.

Why, then, the understatement of Philip's style? If he was king (and he was), why not say so, and be called so? This question might perhaps be very important if Philip and Macedonia were unique in this respect, but in reality this is not so; they seem to be normal, for a kingdom in this region at this time.[3] The question, then, becomes less urgent, though still not without interest. These kingdoms come to our notice, when they do come, either through their coins or through Greek channels of information, and it seems probable that we need to reckon with the Greek view of monarchy in general, as a background. In spite of some leanings towards it by some fourth-century intellectuals, the Greeks on the whole were not impressed with monarchy, and saw it as a mark of the uncivilized.[4] Neighbour monarchs in Thrace and Macedonia and the like they saw perhaps rather as in the more recent past the western world has seen the oriental potentate, a figure that need not be taken entirely

---

[1] In treaties, Tod, *GHI* no. 158 (= *Staatsv.* no. 308); no. 177. In the Amphictyonic Council's records, Tod 172, 23, 67 etc. In an official letter, [D.] 12, 'Letter of Philip', 1, probably genuine. Other purported letters of Philip beginning Βασιλεὺς Μακεδόνων Φίλιππος are agreed to be unauthentic, at D. 18. 39; 77; 157; 166; 167; T. Larsen, *P. Graec. Haunienses* 1 p. 31 col. iv, 11. 11 and 32. (Cf. L. Schlaepfer, *Untersuchungen zu den attischen Staatsurkunden und den Amphiktyonen-Beschlüsse der demosthenischen Kranzrede* (Paderborn, 1939); P. Treves, 'Les Documents apocryphes du *Pro Corona*', *Les Études classiques* 9 (1940) 138–74.) The letters of Isocrates to Philip are headed Φιλίππῳ merely (Isoc. *Epist.* 2 and 3). Cf. in general A. Aymard, *Études* 81 ff., 100 ff.

[2] Hammond, *Epirus* 525 ff., for the texts, and discussion.

[3] Cf. Tod, *GHI* no. 157, 2–4 'alliance of the Athenians with Cetriporis the Thracian . . . and with Lyppeius the Paeonian and with Grabus the Illyrian'. Cf. too Tod, no. 123, 109–10 (Alcetas, Neoptolemus); no. 151 (the 3 Odrysian kings); no. 173 (Arybbas); no. 193 (Rhebulas the Odrysian). The Odrysian Hebryzelmis is named as king of the Odrysians (no. 117, 6, 12, 21). For the Illyrian Grabus, D. M. Robinson restored Βασι]λεῖ, perhaps wrongly (*TAPA* 69 (1938) 44 ff., no. 2 = *Staatsv.* no. 307). For Straton, the king of Sidon, his royal title is retained and repeated in the Athenian treaty (Tod, no. 139, cf. Aymard, *Études* 77), in conformity probably with his own Asiatic practice.

[4] Isoc. 5. 107–8 is the classic statement of this proposition.

seriously at all times. To take themselves entirely seriously was the short way for these kings to confirm that they really were barbarians, and it seems possible that a royal house such as the Macedonian, which had been civilized for generations now, saw 'King Philip' as naïve and 'Philip' as correct. They were 'Greek' enough to forget about *basileus* now, or take it for granted.

It is interesting that Curtius Rufus, in the passage where he tells of the ancient right of the Macedonian Assembly in 'capital' trials, makes use of the Roman imperial cliché of potestas–auctoritas. (In these trials 'nihil potestas regum valebat nisi prius valuisset auctoritas'.[1]) Auctoritas is indeed a key-word, no doubt, for an understanding of how this king (in Macedonia) ruled this people. But first, who were the people, exactly? It has become customary to write of the Macedonians in political contexts as 'the people under arms' or the 'Army-Assembly', but M. Pierre Briant has shown the error of this in his excellent recent study.[2] Though the army in Asia under Alexander and on his death acted as the Assembly from time to time (for example, at the treason trial of Philotas mentioned just above), this was merely because in Asia there was no alternative.[3] But the right which it exercised on that occasion was an ancient right, as Curtius reminds us; and he adds that the right exercised here by the army (*exercitus*) was exercised in peace-time

---

[1] Curt. 6. 8. 25: whether *auctoritas* in the immediate context of the trial, or in the context of his whole reign and rule, is not immediately clear. See n. 3 below.

[2] Cited p. 383 n. 1 above: for this question, pp. 286–316 especially.

[3] Curt. 6. 8. 23–5 (the italics are mine): 'Postero die rex edixit, omnes *armati* coirent. VI milia fere *militum* venerant, praeterea *turba lixarum calonumque* impleverant regiam. Philotan armigeri agmine suo tegebant, ne ante conspici posset a *vulgo*, quam rex adlocutus *milites* esset. De capitalibus rebus vetusto Macedonum modo inquirebat ⟨rex, iudicabat⟩ *exercitus*—in pace erat *vulgi*—, et nihil potestas regum valebat, nisi prius valuisset auctoritas.' (The words rex, iudicabat supplied by the editor Hedicke are accepted as a plausible restoration, though *inquirebat exercitus*, of the manuscript, could be, perhaps, what Curtius wrote.)

I interpret the final remark, about *auctoritas*, to mean that in these trials the kings could not dictate or influence the verdict except by making out a convincing case against the accused. Interesting, obviously, are the three pairs of descriptions in military and civilian terms. But in the middle pair, *vulgo* and *milites* are virtually synonymous, I think (the soldiers being a majority in the vulgus), and it is only the last of the three that is truly significant. Here Curtius explains the 'ancient method' of trial before the army (*exercitus*), then corrects himself 'Well, in peacetime it was before the mass of the people' (*vulgus* = *plethos*). In reality it was only the unprecedented situation, with the king abroad for years in Asia, that had brought about this antithesis at all, of war and peace. To Macedonians of the past, following the 'ancient method', war and peace in this context can have made little difference. Wars were short. Treason trials need not be held on battlefields anyway, or on campaign, but more likely in Pella or Aegeae when the campaign was over. And they were held before the *plethos* (*vulgus*). Though *vulgus*, like *plethos* and similar words, is often used of a crowd of soldiers of an army, here the context makes it quite certain that Curtius was saying that this crowd was not the army, but the mass of the people.

For a different interpretation, however, see above, pp. 160 ff. On *vulgus* and *populus* in references to Macedonian assemblies, see further Briant 311–19 (with a helpful Table of Passages, 312–13).

by the mass of the people (*vulgus*). On this occasion itself the gathering included not only the 6,000 'soldiers' present but a crowd of non-combatant Macedonians ('vi milia fere militum venerant, praeterea turba lixarum calonumque impleverat regiam').[1] At this Macedonian trial, it must be certain that non-Macedonian camp-followers would not have been allowed to be present as idle spectators.[2] These were Macedonians, and even in Asia this section of the Macedonian community cannot have been a small one. *Lixae* were what we should call now 'the catering trade', and must have amounted to some hundreds at least. *Calones* were 'batmen'; one for every ten soldiers of the infantry (to take an austere view), but for the cavalry at least one for each *hetairos*.[3] The cavalry *calones*, grooms and stable men and (for the higher officers) stable-managers, masters of the skills nearest to their employers' hearts, were no riff-raff to be brushed aside, whether in Asia or in the neighbourhoods of Pella, Aegeae, or Amphipolis at home, wherever the horsey communities corresponding to Newmarket or Chantilly may be thought to have flourished. It is with some thousands of Macedonians like these, besides the poorest of the farmers and the shepherds in the 'regions' and the mountains, that one needs to reckon when making up the full tally of the Macedonian people as a whole.

The people that assembled at Pella or Aegeae to acclaim a new king or for a 'capital' trial were mostly those who lived nearest, no doubt (see p. 209 above). On the accession of Philip himself, both our sources, unsatisfactory though they are, suggest strongly enough that it is the Macedonian people, not merely the army, which sets him on the throne. Diodorus, who confuses the issue by writing of the political and the military developments of 359 in the same sentence, still allows us to see Philip addressing the Assembly, on a number of separate occasions, before he describes his intensive work on the army.[4] Justin, though he leaves much unclear, is clarity itself on the dénouement, the election of Philip as king: 'compulsus a populo regnum suscepit', where *populus* means what it says, the people, and leaves an onus of proof on any who see people and army as synonymous.[5] In the same year Argaeus, claiming

---

[1] Curt. 6. 8. 23. Cf. Briant, 338 ff.

[2] Briant however (340 f.) thinks otherwise, arguing from the use of Greek, not Macedonian dialect, by Alexander and Philotas in their speeches (Curt. 6. 9. 34–6). Whether those rhetorical details are authentic must be in some doubt. If they are, they show Greek being used so as to be understood by people who could influence the trial, not by spectators. The Greek Companions present, for example, though relatively few, were people of importance.

[3] Frontin. *Strat.* 4. 1. 6, for Philip's rule about servants (1 : 10). For *hetairoi* of the cavalry, there is no information. But Companions were not going to be up at dawn mucking out and 'doing their two', and a personal servant-groom for each cavalryman seems the bare minimum.

[4] D.S. 16. 3. 1 τοὺς Μακεδόνας ἐν συνεχέσιν ἐκκλησίαις συνέχων καὶ τῇ τοῦ λόγου δεινότητι προτρεπόμενος ἐπὶ τὴν ἀνδρείαν εὐθαρσεῖς ἐποίησε, τὰς δὲ στρατιωτικὰς τάξεις . . .

[5] Just. 7. 5. 10. (Cf. pp. 208 f. above.) On *populus* etc. in Justin in this and similar contexts, Briant 303–7, 314–16.

the throne, marched on Aegeae the ancient capital, and 'called on the people in Aegeae to accept him back from exile and become the sponsors of his reign'.[1] For him, 'the people in Aegeae' made a start, in his task of persuading the people as a whole, the Macedonians, to acclaim him now as king—in a full Assembly of the People, finally.

The electoral Assembly in 359 is not in doubt (and equally on Alexander's accession in 336).[2] In 359 other Assemblies followed, in the next few weeks or months.[3] Are we to take this as the pattern for the whole reign, the king consulting, informing, exhorting his people regularly when occasion arose, and perhaps getting their vote of approval on the more important acts of policy? The sources give no hint of this in the next twenty-three years, and in spite of all their deficiencies this silence must really be decisive. A passage of Aulus Gellius recording a decision of 'the Macedonians' in reply to Athenian ambassadors to the court of Archelaus, when they asked for the bones of Euripides for burial at Athens, does not persuade us that in the reign of Archelaus (or indeed ever) the decisions of policy were arrived at by vote of the Assembly.[4] The activity of the Assembly in the first weeks of Philip is explained by the circumstances. This was a crisis, the worst that we know of in Macedonian history so far. King and people needed to meet it together. Philip needed to establish *auctoritas*, first by words and an impact of personality, then (and soon) by deeds. The deeds began with the military training, under his own eye.[5] In this a rapport between king and people could be strengthened, and strengthened again once the victories commenced. No need for Assemblies now.

After 359 the only occasion on which one of our sources seems to show Philip addressing Macedonians *en masse* is the occasion of defeat in Thessaly by Onomarchus in 353, when casualties were heavy and Philip himself could be blamed for them, having led the army into a trap.[6] 'Philip's position now was very serious. The troops had lost heart and turned against him. He addressed them in mass meeting and restored their spirits and discipline, though not easily. Then he led them

---

[1] D.S. 16. 3. 5 παρεκάλει τοὺς ἐν ταῖς Αἰγαῖς προσδέξασθαι τὴν κάθοδον καὶ γενέσθαι τῆς αὐτοῦ βασιλείας ἀρχηγούς.

[2] D.S. 17. 2. 2 πρῶτον μὲν τὰ πλήθη οἰκείοις λόγοις παρεστήσατο πρὸς εὐνοίαν. Just. 11. 1. 8 'qui pro contione ita *vulgus omne* consolatus' (my italics).

[3] D.S. 16. 3. 1 f.

[4] *Noct. Att.* 15. 20. 9 'maximo consensu Macedonum in ea re deneganda perstiterunt.' We may be sure that Gellius did not invent this, but found it in a book, and for all we know in a very good book. But the gap between what the book said and what Gellius says here is too problematical. The source may have said (for example) that all the Macedonians had been devoted to Euripides, and Archelaus said No. In isolation (and this evidence is isolated, entirely) the passage is not acceptable. *Contra*, however, Hammond, p. 162 above; C. F. Edson, *Ancient Macedonia* 40; and (with some reserves) Briant 335 and n. 2.

[5] D.S. 17. 2. 2.

[6] See above, pp. 269 f.

home to Macedonia . . .'[1] This took place in Thessaly still, we see, the king addressing the army in the field at a time of crisis. No Assembly of the People, properly speaking, here. Indeed, on the evidence that we have, there is no reason to think that Philip was under any obligation to summon Assemblies of the People ever again in his reign, unless for trials *de capitalibus rebus* (we know of none); and it seems quite possible that he never did. The Macedonian 'freedom of speech to their kings' which Polybius two centuries later noticed as something which 'they had always had' was not (as the context shows) the *isegoria* of a democratic assembly, or of any assembly, but a more generalized freedom and habit of answering back, and letting it be known to the king, if they disliked something, that they did dislike it.[2] It was indeed another symptom, and a good one, of the character of the relationship between people and king, who reigned 'not as a tyrant but by the rule of Law'; but it tells us nothing about Assemblies, either of Philip V or Philip II. Year by year, however, in the 350s and 340s the campaigns which followed endlessly and with few intervals of peace mobilized the military levy of the year, to operate much more often than not under his personal command. Though the same soldiers did not serve every year (except the guards), all the soldiers at intervals and in course of time will have served under him, and no doubt it was through the army most of all that he came to know the people, and the people to know him. On occasion he may have found it necessary to address the army for some important purpose, as later Alexander did occasionally in Asia.[3] And at all times his main channel of liaison will have been through the corps of officers, Companions whom he knew well, just as for Alexander the great confrontation at the river Hyphasis was not with the soldiers assembled in mass but in a council of the generals and brigadiers, where it was one of the Companions (the taxiarch Coenus) who put forward the view of 'the army', which prevailed.[4]

2. Justice

The rights and the function of the Assembly of the People in 'capital' trials has been noticed. But naturally these represented only a tiny fraction of the country's legal business, about which we are in almost

---

[1] D.S. 16. 35. 2 Φίλιππος δ' εἰς τοὺς ἐσχάτους κινδύνους περικλεισθεὶς καὶ τῶν στρατιωτῶν διὰ τὴν ἀθυμίαν καταλιπόντων αὐτὸν παραθαρσύνας τὸ πλῆθος μόγις ἐποίησεν αὐτοὺς εὐπειθεῖς.

[2] Plb. 5. 27. 6 εἶχον γὰρ ἀεὶ τὴν τοιαύτην ἰσηγορίαν Μακεδόνες πρὸς τοὺς βασιλεῖς. *Isegoria* is one of the words (*demokratia* another) which Polybius used in a much more generalized sense than that of the fifth and fourth centuries. See, e.g., Plb. 2. 38. 6 and Walbank, *Commentary* ad loc. But Hammond (p. 161 above) disagrees.

[3] D.S. 17. 74. 3; Arr. *An.* 7. 8. 1. I leave out of account the conventional address before battle.

[4] Arr. *An.* 5. 25. 2; 28. 1–2; 27 (speech of Coenus).

total ignorance. We know nothing of the existence of a code of laws, or even of written laws of any kind; and the *nomos* or 'ancestral usage' of the Macedonians which we hear of (above, p. 386) may be thought much more reminiscent of law in archaic Greece than in classical Athens.[1] Yet the Macedonians for generations had not been so innocent of law as to be handicapped in their dealings with foreigners who visited the country for trade. An Athenian politician in 342 remarks that there have never been treaties defining the procedures for litigation between Athenians and Macedonians (*sumbola*); and they have got on very well without them.[2] Athenians, then, had had reasonable prospects of justice in some court or courts in Macedonia on the occasions when they had needed to sue Macedonian defendants.[3] In some way they knew (or learned) what the law was, in so far as it related to them and their concerns.

In a monarchy such as the Macedonian, it is natural to think of the king as being the supreme judge, until such time as his powers are eroded and transferred wholly or in part to organs or officers of state representing other estates of the realm. (The analogy of Sparta comes first to mind perhaps.[4]) In Macedonia one step in this direction, obviously, is to be seen in the 'capital' trials before the Assembly. But no other court is known, except a court presided over by the king himself as sole judge or by a deputy appointed by him.[5] Of the thirty-one anecdotes which survive in Plutarch's collection of *Apophthegmata Philippi*, four are concerned with Philip in his capacity of judge, and one shows him appointing a judge (and presently sacking him for an entertaining psychological reason).[6] Though the quality of the material in the anecdotes varies (in more senses than one), it will be agreed, probably, that the relatively high proportion of them devoted to this area of activity can be neither accidental nor without significance.[7] To conclude that Philip spent

[1] Cf., e.g., G. Glotz, *La Solidarité de la famille dans le droit criminel en Grèce* (Paris, 1904) 464 f.

[2] [D.] 7. 11–13 (Hegesippus). At that time Philip was proposing *sumbola*, for whatever reasons. See p. 511.

[3] The proposition of G. E. M. de Ste. Croix, *CQ* N.s. 11 (1961) 105 f., to the effect that litigation between citizens of two different governments normally must have been in a court which could enforce its decisions on the defendant (that is, in the defendant's city or country), carries conviction.

[4] Cf. Arist. *Pol.* 1285^{b}20 ff. And cf. the inscription discussed by V. Ehrenberg, 'An early source of Polis-constitution', *CQ* 37 (1943) 14 ff., where we see Dreros in Crete *c.* 600 with a single annually appointed head of state (*kosmos*) whose leading function clearly is that of judge.

[5] To see the council of the Companions as a court of justice, on the basis of Alexander's consultations before the treason trials in Asia, seems mistaken. These meetings were advisory only. See further in Volume III.

[6] Plu. *Mor.* 178 A–179 C (nos. 12, 23, 24, 25, 31).

[7] The thirty-four *Apophthegmata Alexandri* (Plu. *Mor.* 179 D–181 F) contain not one that shows him acting as judge, though Plutarch in his *Life* (23. 2) once includes 'judging' as

nearly one-sixth of his life doing this would be too simple. But to reckon it as one of his most important functions as king is legitimate, and indeed necessary, for the point of one of the anecdotes is just this—that the king *was expected* to find time for it.[1] Philip was a very good judge, and was remembered for it years and years after his death, when the Macedonians got a king who was a very bad one.[2] Though all these stories show the judgements as coming from him and him alone, it would be quite in character, one would think, for him to be supported by a group of Companions (to advise if asked, but with no part in the final judgement). Yet perhaps one of the anecdotes speaks against this. Philip dozed off once, and gave a bad judgement.[3] Companions could have come to the rescue somehow, had they been present? Or perhaps they tried, and Philip followed the natural instinct to pretend that he had not dozed off, and then had to muddle it along from there. For our present purpose this anecdote seems equivocal.

On another point, however, the same story (a witty one) is instructive. The unfortunate Machaetas on hearing the judgement given against him cried out indignantly 'I appeal!' 'Appeal?' said Philip angrily, '*Who to?*' There was no appeal from the judgement of the king, as Machaetas concedes by his reply: 'To you, your Majesty, if you will kindly keep awake and give your mind to the hearing.'[4] The final responsibility was the king's. But Greater Macedonia was a big country, and the king could not be everywhere, indeed there were times when for this purpose he could not be anywhere. It was for this, no doubt, to deputize for the king, that there existed a panel or college of judges to which on one occasion we see Philip making an appointment (κατατάξας εἰς τοὺς δικαστάς).[5] The method of individual appointment by the king shows that this was no mass panel but a select one. Probably they sat in judgement as individuals in the assize towns of the kingdom, the principal cities of Lower Macedonia and the administrative centres of the Upper cantons. The quality of these appointments was as vital to the well-being of the kingdom as the quality of the generals and other *hegemones* appointed to

one of four ways in which he might pass a typical day (. . . διημέρευε κυνηγῶν ἢ δικάζων ἢ συντάττων τι τῶν πολεμικῶν ἢ ἀναγιγνώσκων. On the analogy of (ibid. 32. 12) Ἄχρι μὲν οὖν συντάττων τι τῆς φάλαγγος ἢ παρακελευόμενος ἢ διδάσκων ἢ ἐφορῶν παρεξήλαυνεν ἄλλον ἵππον ἔχων . . . , Sintenis (unwisely) emended δικάζων to διδάσκων. For one instance of Alexander as judge, ibid. 42. 2. Naturally in Asia the army was subject to military discipline.

[1] Plu. *Mor.* 179 c (no. 31), a charming example of the Macedonian *isegoria*, on the part of an old lady with a 'case', who was not to be brushed off by Philip as he passed by saying 'No time, no time.' 'Then you've no business to be king' (καὶ μὴ βασίλευε)! (He found time, for her case, and the whole list for the day.)

[2] Plu. *Dem.* 42. 9 (where the same anecdote of Philip is told).

[3] Plu. *Mor.* 178 F–179 A (no. 24).

[4] (Philip paid the fine himself, but would not reverse his judgement.)

[5] Plu. *Mor.* 178 F (no. 23).

the military commands; and it will have been from the same class, that which supplied the retinue of Companions, that the selection was made.[1] It is always possible, one supposes, that the anecdotes of Philip as judge can have arisen from appeal cases, referred to the king after a hearing by a local *dikastes* or *dikastai*. What is clear is that the law of the land, in so large a land as Greater Macedonia, could not have been administered without some delegation; but the exact nature and extent of the delegation at this time eludes us.

3. *King and Companions*

The Companions were an ancient name and institution, the personal retinue of the Macedonian kings.[2] After Philip's death (below, p. 408) the name was applied in a wider sense by Alexander to the heavy cavalry as a whole. But here and now it is the narrower circle, of the retinue, that is to be considered. Its existence in Philip's reign became known to well-informed Athenians, and Theopompus gives an instructive insight into their recruitment 'from many places, some from Macedonia itself, others from Thessaly, others from the rest of Greece', their number 'at that time' approaching 800, some of them very rich from their landed estates.[3] Theopompus (writing as a moralist, and at his naughtiest here) adds that they were selected not for their good qualities but for their bad ones—and here the important point for our present purpose is that they were selected, and obviously by Philip himself (who else?). On this Theopompus may be judged reliable, for the very fact that

---

[1] In 187 Thessalonica had its own *dikastai*, who were not a mass panel but a very small group. (S. Pelekides, *ΑΠΟ ΤΗΝ ΠΟΛΙΤΕΙΑ ΚΑΙ ΤΗΝ ΚΟΙΝΩΝΙΑ ΤΗΣ ΑΡΧΑΙΑΣ ΘΕΣΣΑΛΟΝΙΚΗΣ* (Salonika, 1934), 6 lines 23 f. Pelekides, ibid. 17, proposed also δ[ικα]σταί for ἁ[ρμο]σταί at *IG* XI. 4. 1053, 10, of *c.* 250–230.) The same may be true of all Macedonian city or ethnic centres at that date; and it is not impossible, obviously, that the appointment of a *dikastes* by Philip himself was to a local panel not a central one, though it may be questioned whether a local appointment, even at Pella, would have achieved the anecdotic notoriety. In contemporary Greece of course the spread of democracy had made a rare bird of the magistrate who exercised individually and alone judicial powers like those of Athenian archons before Solon (Arist. *Ath. Pol.* 3. 5). The powers of the *thesmothetai* at Athens in the fourth century were nugatory. In Crete however the Gortyn Code shows *dikastai* of the standing that I have suggested as probable for the *dikastai* of Philip, whether we think of them as magistrates of his central government or of the cities or other local centres. (This 'probability' obviously must remain a matter of opinion.) At Gortyn, it is agreed, all cases were tried before a single *dikastes*, and there is no evidence for panels of judges or for trials before a jury (J. W. Headlam, 'The procedure of the Gortynian inscription', *JHS* 13 (1892/3) 48–69, especially 49; R. F. Willetts, *Aristocratic Society in Ancient Crete* (London, 1955) 206 f.). (And for Dreros, p. 393 n. 4 above.) This sort of pattern seems to me the likeliest for Macedonia at this date. For the re-emergence in Greek cities of the single *dikastes* (or the small, select panel of *dikastai*) in the third century, see W. W. Tarn and G. T. Griffith, *Hellenistic Civilisation*[3] (London, 1952) 88 ff.

[2] Above, pp. 158 ff.

[3] Isoc. 5. 19 οἱ ἀμφ' αὐτὸν ἑταῖροι; [D.] 11. 10 οἱ περὶ αὐτὸν ἑταῖροι; *FGrH* no. 115 F 224 and 225.

Greeks could be admitted, and in significant numbers, seems to prove that this was not now (and probably never had been) a closed hereditary corporation (above, p. 159).[1] The initiative lay with the king, and Philip chose to increase his retinue with Greeks. But he widened it more, and more importantly, by incorporating those vassal kingdoms of Upper Macedonia which up to now had been separate though (intermittently) dependent. Though we hear nothing of when or how this was done, the decisive event (clearly) was the defeat of Bardylis in 358 by which Philip liberated Upper Macedonia from a brutal conquest. In the joy that followed even the rulers in Upper Macedonia will have preferred incorporation to living under the Illyrians, or having them back.[2] The joy will not have lasted for ever; but the fact of incorporation is plain. No more 'kings' are heard of in Orestis, Lyncestis, Pelagonia, or the rest. The levies of Tymphaea, Lyncestis, Orestis, Elimea, are incorporated in the brigades of the Macedonian phalanx (below, pp. 426 f.). Perdiccas of Orestis, Polyperchon of Tymphaea, belonging to the local royal families, are seen holding high command under Alexander, whose list of trierarchs in 325 included (e.g.) the 'Macedonians from Orestis' Craterus and Perdiccas.[3] The high-born Leonnatus, from Lyncestis, is described there as 'of Pella'. Polemocrates of Elimea (father of Coenus) received from Philip estates in Chalcidice.[4] The 'new men' from Upper Macedonia were brought in to the Court and to the king's retinue, which came to number something approaching 800 Companions as Theopompus describes.

'New' men, 'old' men, these were the Macedonians with whom lay survival and greatness, for the kingdom and for the kings, more than with all the others. In Macedonia the king who numbered many enemies among his Companions was lost. The daily life of the king was communal to a degree hard to parallel in a modern society, and the community in which he lived moved and had his being was most often that of the Companions. Working or playing, eating or drinking, riding to the hunt, riding to the wars, he was accompanied always by a selection of 'the Companions of the retinue' (οἱ ἀμφ' αὐτὸν ἑταῖροι); and when he slept at night, in his antechamber he was guarded by a selection of the Royal Pages who were Companions' sons. This glimpse of the royal day comes of course from impressions of Alexander's way of life as we see it in Arrian and the other sources.[5] Philip's habits will have varied in some

---

[1] For Greeks, especially Arr. *Ind.* 18. 7 f.; cf. Berve 1. 31.

[2] This point of view is well expressed by C. F. Edson, 'Early Macedonia', in *AM* 43 'The princes of Upper Macedonia were soon to face the choice of remaining isolated and exposed to Illyrian assault or accepting integration into the Argead kingdom.'

[3] Arr. *Ind.* 18. 5 ἐξ 'Ορεστίδος with ibid 3 (Μακεδόνων) and ibid. 6 (Μακεδόνες).

[4] For Leonnatus above, p. 16; for Polemocrates, *Syll.*[3] 322. 5 ff.

[5] In detail, Berve 1. 11 ff., 32 ff.

particulars, but not in this particular of the ubiquity of the Companions. This is what Companions were for, as the name implies. Informal though all this intercourse was, it was 'political' too, in the sense that this king, in theory very much an autocrat so long as he continued to give 'the Macedonians' the feel that he was ruling them 'not as a tyrant but by rule of law', a king moreover with no bureaucracy of public servants to advise him on decisions, to interpret decisions to 'the Macedonians', and to execute the decisions finally, was in constant need of the Companions for just these purposes.[1] The 'advice' and the 'interpretation' can have been most often informal and through individuals or very small groups. There remains the question, whether anything constitutional can be found in this. Is there something that by any stretch of the imagination and of the English language can be called a Council?

By the standards of Greek city-state institutions, the answer must be No, categorically. Uninterested though our surviving sources are in the internal affairs of Macedonia, foreign policy (especially where it concerned Athens) was not neglected by them, and in this area a Council that had rights and powers would not have vanished from the record, if such a Council had existed. Here again the silence of the sources must be conclusive (above, pp. 384 f.). In reality there is no record of Philip's ever holding a council of any kind, formal or informal, all through his reign, though we may be sure that he did. Alexander, we find, held what could be called a council of state in 334 in Macedonia, and what could be called councils of war from time to time in Asia. Without examining these in detail now, it is necessary to summarize what they amount to. First and most significant, these councils seem to have no name.[2] *Consilio vocato* in Curtius stands for (in his Greek source) something like 'he called together his friends', or 'the most important of his friends', or (on other occasions) 'he called together the high ranking officers of the army'.[3] It is only after Alexander's death that this thing gets a name (*sunedrion*), whether because of some new development then or because of our new source, the historian Hieronymus of Cardia.[4] Arrian's 'Council of the Companions' (ἐν τῷ ξυλλόγῳ τῶν ἑταίρων) is very serviceable, but the fact that he uses it only once must mean that he did not find it standardized as a title.[5]

[1] See p. 158 above, for the *paredroi* of Alexander I.

[2] προέθηκε βουλήν . . . (D.S. 17. 16. 1, of 334) and βουλὴν προὐτίθη (Arr. *An.* 1. 29. 4) do not mean 'he held a Council (a *boule*)': cf. D. 18. 192 for the usage at its simplest, καὶ οὐδεὶς περὶ τούτου προτίθησιν οὐδαμοῦ βουλήν ('And nobody ever offers advice about that'), and LSJ⁹ s.v. βουλή (2). In the two passages cited Diodorus and Arrian use the phrase as equivalent to ἐβουλεύετο ('he took counsel' including his own view put forward), which Arrian does use as a variant on another of these 'conciliar' occasions (2. 9. 3).

[3] Curt. 4. 11. 1; Arr. *An.* 1. 25. 4 ('friends'); 5. 28. 4; D.S. 17. 16. 1 ('most important'); Arr. *An.* 2. 7. 3; 3. 9. 3 and 5 (two occasions); 5. 25. 2 (generals etc.).

[4] On *sunedrion*, see Briant 270–5.   [5] Arr. *An.* 2. 25. 2.

Nor was the composition of the councils standardized. Just as the king chose his own Companions in the first place, and appointed them to commands and offices as seemed good to him, so their corporate functioning was for him to regulate by his own choice. Philotas, the second in rank of all the generals at the time, did not attend the council as of right, and when one was summoned to deliberate on his reported treason, he was not invited.[1] In the Hyphasis crisis, three councils were held within a week, the first two attended by all the high-ranking army officers, but the third by 'the most senior of the Companions and especially those whom he could count on most'.[2] The smallest 'council' that we hear of was a duologue, when Parmenion rode up and offered advice (which was not taken).[3] The rejection of advice was not confined to this private occasion. In 334 at a full council of 'the army commanders and the most important of the Companions', Alexander gave his reasons for not accepting the proposals of the elder statesmen that the crossing to Asia should be delayed till he should have married and produced an heir.[4] At that important time it was politic and sensible, no doubt, to hear what the advisers had to say; but the decision was the king's alone.

In the light of the evidence, to write of the king's council in constitutional terms seems impossible, and to separate its functions into the political, the diplomatic, the military, the judicial, and so on, seems academic. In a council of the high army officers, for example, nearly all the high officers were Companions anyway. In a council of Companions to advise on some affair of state, it was for the king to decide which Companions should be summoned to it, the whole retinue or select personalities. In either event, and whatever the business in hand, advice was the limit of its function. In a different society, in which the king lived withdrawn and remote from all except a very few, regular council meetings could have been necessary, and those quite frequent, partly as a matter of form, and partly to preserve king and Companions from being really strangers to each other. But in Macedonia they saw each other all the time, knew each other very well (too well, even, it might seem to the fastidious). For mere communication, council meetings may even have been unnecessary, when news, views, persuasion, advice could be exchanged daily over dinner and the bottle. It may be thought that the only importance, really and truly, of a council meeting was as a mark that this matter (whatever the agenda) was of importance. Philip no doubt, like Alexander later, did hold his Council meetings from time to time as a means of concentrating the minds of his Companions, mobilizing their support, preparing their co-operation in the business in hand.

The interdependence of king and Companions is not hard to divine.

---

[1] Curt. 6. 8. 1.   [2] Arr. *An.* 5. 25. 2; 28. 2 and 4.   [3] Arr. *An.* 1. 13. 2.
[4] D.S. 17. 16. 1.

For them, wealth, fortune, fame came from him only. The estate in Chalcidice, the appointments in the army, the advancement of every kind depended on votes of no committee, council or parliament, but on his word alone. For the king, they represented his officer corps, his staff college, and his ruling class throughout the kingdom. Their strength in numbers (taking the 800 of Theopompus as a figure for 'retinue' Companions towards the end of Philip's reign) was made possible on the one hand by Philip's wealth and on the other hand by the incorporation of Upper Macedonia. Companions of the retinue through the years divided their time, no doubt, between attendance on the king and their own estates. In their own place, they and their families can be expected to have taken the main part in its government. It is impossible to think of democratic local governments in a kingdom where the national government shows no sign of democracy; and government by *peliganes* (below, p. 648) or 'elders' by some other name suggests itself as the probable pattern of rule whether in city or canton, in Pella or Pelagonia.

If this is correct, it offers scope for tensions and antagonisms, plainly, between the ruling class and the ruled, the mass of the free Macedonians. This in turn invites us to picture local situations in which the king might intervene as champion and protector of the people. And again dissatisfaction with the king himself, or with the fact of central government, obviously could arise most easily within the ruling class, where thwarted ambitions or a resentment at the dominance of Pella could take root and breed sedition. Here too king and people might need to stand together, against conspiracy in high places. It is tempting to see a pattern here, on the evidence of conspiracies in the next reign particularly; and scholars, like Oscar Wilde's witty young man, 'can resist everything except temptation'. To picture the king as surrounded by plotting malcontents and surviving only by his wits and by the support of a loyal and devoted yeomanry and peasantry might be true of some occasion, but it is unlikely to be true of all occasions. The times, the places, the personalities, were all-important; and we lack the evidence on which to generalize. A fine commander, Philotas, could be unpopular with the army in general, because he was (broadly speaking) a nasty man and one who threw his weight about and gave himself airs. A finer one (probably), Craterus, was beloved by all. Both of them were independent characters who did not knuckle under to the king (Alexander). The one made him see red, the other did not. The one came from (probably) Pella, the other from Orestis. The one commanded the Companion cavalry, the other an infantry brigade till he graduated to higher things. But even with these prominent characters the volume of what we do not know of them and their background reduces us to conjecture. For Philip's reign, with no sources comparable to the Alexander-historians, we are forced back into the area of a few inferences from fragmentary evidence and based on considerations of general probability.

First, then, Philip's organization of the army in units which were regional and in which the Upper Macedonian 'regions' corresponded also with ethnical divisions, suggests that for Philip the danger from brigades of Orestians or Lyncestians in arms and even commanded by one of their own notables was more than compensated by the advantages of this arrangement (below, pp. 426 ff.). This is not to say that separatism did not exist. In the nature of things it must have existed, and especially in the ruling class. But it was not the only thing that existed. Peace, prosperity, promotion, came from Pella now; and the king in Pella, the king who cracked the whip which kept the Illyrians where they belonged, judged evidently that he could count on the good sense of his Upper Macedonians. For more than twenty years he seems to have been right. Demosthenes could encourage his Athenian audiences by hinting at division between king and people in Macedonia, at enemies of Philip among his closest associates.[1] But even with Demosthenes it is significant that these remarks belong to the earliest of his adventures into the Macedonian question. The more he learned of it, and the more he learned to dislike Philip and what he stood for, the less he found to say about dissension inside Macedonia—indeed after 349 he says nothing of it at all. That he would have liked to say something we can be sure. Demosthenes of course could not know all that went on inside Macedonia, and his silence does not entitle us to say that Philip had no problems where his own people and his own circle were concerned. But it probably does create some sort of presumption that in the rough-and-ready Macedonian way Philip had found a formula that worked, and worked pretty well.

The most important element in it, no doubt, really was the circle of the Companions. Though we lack the details for any picture of Philip's life at court and in the field through the years (as we do see it intermittently for Alexander later), contemporary witnesses as different in temperament as Theopompus and Isocrates were aware of the importance of this circle.[2] Each of them mentions the Greek element in it, which was a new development, at least on the scale that it assumed under Philip. But it was still not on a scale that invites us to see in these Greeks a deliberate policy of Philip providing himself with a nucleus of foreigners on whose loyalty he believed he could count.[3] It was still the Macedonians themselves who were the key to the whole expansive programme

---

[1] D. 2. 21 (a rhetorical generalization); 2. 15–18 (Philip's *philotimia* a burden to the people, and prevents him from choosing good Companions); 4. 8 (enemies among his close associates). In the *First Olynthiac* when D. chose to talk of P.'s difficulties at that time, he spoke of Thessaly, Chalcidice, Paeonians, Illyrians; of domestic difficulties not at all (1. 5–6; 21–4).

[2] *FGrH* no. 115 F 225; Isoc. 5. 19.

[3] See p. 375 n. 1 above, for the proportion of Greek Companions.

of his reign. Decisive for this question must be his development of the institution of Royal Pages (*basilikoi paides*), said by Arrian to have been originated by Philip himself.[1] Though this statement may not be literally true (above, p. 168 n. 1), certainly it seems right to interpret it as meaning that Philip developed the institution as no king had done before, and on quite a big scale. In 331 we hear of fifty-one 'new boys' joining the Pages who were with Alexander already.[2] If we think of this as the normal 'intake' of three years (334–331), and of the Pages as boys aged about fourteen to eighteen, the Pages at any one time will have numbered about eighty-five. They were the sons of the leading families of the kingdom.[3] Even allowing for the abundance of brothers among Alexander's generals and officers, the age-groups of four or five years will seldom have included more than two brothers simultaneously from any one family, so that the Pages of any year may be thought to represent between sixty and seventy families. Certainly there can have been a hostage element in this, particularly for families of Upper Macedonia whose estates lay remote from the king's eye and whose habits in the past had not included a close attachment, if any, to the Court at Pella. Until their sons had all passed through and out of this establishment, any important fathers who were separatist in their views or feelings at least will have been obliged to postpone any separatist behaviour to some later, better time. This was one side of the coin.

The other side (and more optimistic) was the early introduction and attachment of these boys to the person of the king, and through them the further and future binding of their families in loyalty to the monarchy. The association of the Pages with the king was not a formality but a close one including very many of the activities of daily life.[4] Here, naturally, the personality of the king counted for much, indeed at this time if the thing on this scale was really an innovation, it counted for nearly everything. An unpleasant man as king could do himself much more harm than good, here as elsewhere. But a king who was a born leader and an attractive personality, and above all was an unparalleled success in the world, was not likely to be a failure in this. Seen at its narrowest Philip's troop of Pages was a notable preparatory school of officers and generals.[5] On a wider view, it was the system which could animate the kingdom, or galvanize an empire.

The Pages of Philip's reign included the contemporaries or near-contemporaries of Alexander, who became the great Macedonians of his

---

[1] Arr. *An.* 4. 13. 1. (So Ael. *VH* 14. 48.) Perhaps it is wrong, even, to translate Arrian's Ἐκ Φιλίππου ἦν ἤδη καθεστηκὸς . . . as 'originated'? 'Philip had established the practice . . .' better?   [2] DS. 17. 65. 1; Curt. 5. 1. 42.

[3] So described by the four historians cited in the two previous notes.

[4] For details, Berve 1. 37–9; and see p. 154 above.

[5] Curt. 8. 6. 6 'velut seminarium ducum praefectorumque'.

generation and the next, the men such as Craterus, Perdiccas, Hephaestion, Ptolemy, Seleucus. These five, named by 'the easy criterion of success', (Alexander's two best generals, his best friend and chiliarch, and the two great dynasty-founders of the Hellenistic world) represent Philip's Greater Macedonia in an interesting way: Perdiccas and Craterus from Orestis, Ptolemy from Eordaea, Hephaestion from Pella, Seleucus from Europus of Lower Macedonia. Upper Macedonia makes its mark, represented in these five to a degree which is not quite maintained in the full tally of the notables of Alexander's reign. In the picture as a whole, Pella still fills the centre, as might be expected of the capital and the cultural centre for three generations before the expansion. But with the exception of the outlying Parauaea the 'Upper' regions of the kingdom each supply their names of famous (or fairly famous) men, enough to rule out any notion that Pella and its families dominated the rest of Macedonia in the way that old-Roman families predominated in the ruling class of the middle Republic. Besides the regions, the 'new-Macedonian' cities Amphipolis and Pydna are significantly represented too, and the lesser cities of old Macedonia (Aegeae, Beroea, Europus, Alorus, and others) provide their ones and twos. Though a statistically significant record is unattainable, what does survive is suggestive of a ruling class drawn from Macedonia in its widest terms, with Pella and the old kingdom preponderant but by no means overwhelmingly so. If all the gaps in our provenances of the high-ranking Macedonians were to be filled, the ancient Aegeae and the important Pelagonia might fare better than at present, but most probably the outline suggested here would not be very radically changed.[1]

---

[1] Using as a basis Berve's list (2. 445) of the known provenances of the 'Macedonians under Alexander', I have excluded from it the very few who plainly were not of Companion class; and I have added to it (1) four recipients of proxeny etc. at Delphi, (2) (as Elimiot) the three sons of Machatas whom I identify (*pace* Berve) with the son of Derdas of the Elimiot royal house. The provenances, summarized, are as follows:

From Pella,		15
From 'Old Macedonia' excluding Pella, but including Eordaea,		13
From cities newly 'Macedonian', Amphipolis,	6	
Pydna,	4	10
From 'Upper Macedonia', Elimiotis,	3	
Orestis,	6	
Lyncestis,	4	
Tymphaea,	6	20
Pelagonia		
(Alcomenae)	1	

Of the six from Amphipolis, three are Greek Companions (the only ones whose Macedonian provenance is known).

Two Companions are doubly attested, as from a region of Macedonia and also from Pella: I count Leonnatus from Lyncestis, Aristonous from Eordaea.

The main hazard concealed inside these figures lies in the incidence of brothers already mentioned. Thus three of the four Lyncestians are the sons of Aëropus. The six Tymphaeans

The ruling class was an élite, and there are even signs suggesting that it may always have had something of an élite within the élite, and continued to do so. The wearing of the purple hat and cloak was reserved to Companions of the very highest rank or standing, and this honour was in the gift of the king.[1] Another mark of distinction was the title of Bodyguard (*somatophulax*), under Alexander a primarily honorific one carrying virtually none of the duties which go with the name, and hence (obviously) an ancient one which long ago really had carried all the duties. Traditionally seven in number, their appointment was a mark of the king's special favour, their attendance on his person was required, and they ceased to be Bodyguards if they received an appointment which made attendance impossible.[2] The king as the source and fount of all honour could give his retinue 'something to play for', evidently, in the matter of these highest preferments. Characteristically, in the whole of Philip's reign, the name of not one of his *somatophulakes* is ever vouchsafed to us.[3] But the ruling class as a whole, with its traditional name (Companions), stood much closer to the king than to the mass of the Macedonian people, and its expansion by Philip did nothing to dilute its quality or dim its distinction. In externals the court was 'Greek' in many ways, and indeed more than superficially so. This is oddly illustrated even in that lamentable party which ended in the death of Cleitus. The

are the four sons of Andromenes and a father and son. Two pairs of brothers account for four of the six Orestians, and again four of the six from Amphipolis. The Pellaeans include the four sons of Agathocles. The two from Alorus and two of the three from Mieza of 'Old Macedonia' are probably brothers.

Thus if one ceases to count heads merely, and counts families (*oikoi*) instead, the summary of figures above is changed, mostly to the detriment of 'Upper Macedonia', as follows:

From Pella			12
From 'Old Macedonia' excluding Pella but including Eordaea			11
From cities newly 'Macedonian',	Amphipolis	4	8
	Pydna	4	
From 'Upper Macedonia'	Elimiotis	1	
	Orestis	4	
	Lyncestis	2	10
	Tymphaea	2	
	Pelagonia	1	

[1] Plu. *Eum.* 8. 7, with 6. 1 (where it appears that the great Craterus would be recognizable from a distance by his hat, and that his lieutenant-general Neoptolemus, a rather distinguished brigadier under Alexander, would not be wearing the purple).

[2] Arr. *An.* 6. 28. 3–4 especially. And see Berve 1. 25–30.

[3] On the occasion of Philip's murder (D.S. 16. 93. 3; 94. 4) Pausanias the murderer, Leonnatus, Perdiccas, and Attalus are named as *somatophulakes*. Pausanias, Leonnatus, and Perdiccas are too young to have attained the distinction of the Seven (Leonnatus and Perdiccas reach it in 332/1 and 330 respectively). The only Attalus of sufficient distinction (the uncle of the young Queen Cleopatra) was not present (he was in Asia Minor with the army).

As is well known, the name itself suffers from a confusion, because it is used sometimes for the Guard detachment of the Royal Hypaspists. Cf. Berve 1. 122 f., with references; Tarn 138 ff.

last words of Cleitus were a verse or two of Euripides, well chosen but badly timed.[1] The Companions, for all their Macedonian proclivities, could see themselves as 'civilized' in a way that the people on their estates or the phalangites under their command were not. Striking evidence of this class differential shows in an incident in 318, when Eumenes of Cardia had occasion to order funeral arrangements for Macedonians killed in battle. 'He gathered up the bodies and . . . he made pyres for them, *the high officers and the common soldiers separately* (ἰδίᾳ μὲν ἡγεμόνας ἰδίᾳ δὲ τοὺς πολλούς), and he constructed two (?) mass graves (καὶ πολυάνδρια χώσας) and then went on his way.'[2] Every common soldier had a regimental officer's commission in his knapsack, as Bolon's rise from the ranks suggests; but not (one guesses) a marshal's baton, and not the entry into the circle of the retinue.[3] Inside the circle itself the members varied in status certainly, but the fixed grades seen in the Hellenistic courts later, of Friends (*philoi*) with titles indicating an ascending order of intimacy, have not yet arrived.[4]

The Companions, then, made up an aristocracy and a society which Greeks as varied in their character and attainments as Callisthenes of Olynthus, Onesicritus of Astypalaea, Eumenes of Cardia, Demaratus of Corinth were not too proud or too bored to live with, and this for years, while devoting their careers (except Demaratus) to the service of the Macedonian king. For Philip, the Companions represented the reservoir of talent, now dispersed in the cities and regions of Macedonia, now concentrated at Court or in the camp. If in this ship of state the man on the bridge was Philip, the engine-room of the ship was the Companion class, a formidable concentration of controlled power. The men (their fathers) had always been there, in the cities and regions of Macedonia. Now for the first time a king had shown them by word and by deed that the Macedonians united were invincible, and that to lead the Macedonians under his own Heraclid guidance was the destiny for them.

[1] Plu. *Alex.* 52. 8 etc.
[2] Plu. *Eum.* 9. 2; cf. 13. 5; 14. 1, for further evidence of this class distinction.
[3] Curt. 6. 11. 1 (Bolon).   [4] Further on *philoi* etc., Volume III.

XII

PHILIP AND THE ARMY

1. *Introductory*

IN Macedonia, as in archaic Greece long before, in some sense a new era may be thought to have begun when the people, as distinct from an aristocracy, became important as soldiers. Associated with this in some way, it has been thought, is the name *pezhetairoi*, Foot Companions, a name which was known to Demosthenes and his Athenian audience in 349, though (too obviously) he had no clear idea as to what it meant exactly.[1] Anaximenes of Lampsacus in his confused and confusing allusion to the origin of the Foot Companions, thought of them evidently as the whole levy of infantry from the whole country.[2] The lexicographer Harpocration, explaining the word in this same context (of Demosthenes), wrote

Anaximenes in the First Book of his *Philippica* speaking of 'Alexander' says: 'Then having trained the aristocracy as cavalry he called them Companions (*hetairoi*). The mass of the people and the foot soldiers he organized in companies and sections and the other formations and gave them the name of Foot Companions (*pezhetairoi*). In this way he intended that each class by sharing in the royal Companionship should be always exceedingly loyal.'[3]

It is natural to expect that Anaximenes here, early in his history of Philip, referred to either Alexander I or Alexander II, and described a military reform or innovation the effects of which would be visible in the army of Philip himself if we had good information about it. For the infantry, we should expect the name *pezhetairoi* to apply to the whole levy of infantry from the whole country, as indeed under Alexander the Great it does apply to all the Macedonian infantry of the phalanx in Asia.[4] But in fact our only piece of information about *pezhetairoi* in the reign of Philip shows them as something quite different. Theopompus, who actually resided at Philip's court for a time in the late 340s, described them as a Royal Guard: 'Theopompus says that picked men out of all the Macedonians, the tallest and strongest, served as the King's Guards,

---

[1] D. 2. 17. Demosthenes knows the name; but his remarks about them seem more apposite to the *hetairoi* who formed the king's circle of intimates than to a military corps.

[2] Anaximenes, *FGrH* no. 72 F 4. On this notorious passage P. A. Brunt, *JHS* 83 (1963) 40 n. 43, writes agnostically and well.

[3] Harpocrat. s.v.; (Suid. s.v.).

[4] Arr. *An.* 1. 28. 3. And see below, pp. 705 ff.

and they were called Foot Companions.'[1] This could not be more explicit, and it seems reasonably certain that Theopompus (cited here by Schol. Demosth. 2. 17) was writing of Philip's Foot Companions and not of some earlier time. On this purely factual matter Theopompus is almost sure to be right, and the probability ought to be very high that for most of Philip's reign at any rate the Foot Companions were as he described them.[2] One is driven to conclude that Anaximenes in his remarks about Companions and Foot Companions referred neither to Alexander I nor to Alexander II but to Alexander III, and that he was alluding to a change introduced by Alexander the Great whereby both these honorific names were given a wider application than hitherto. The name *pezhetairoi* itself, therefore, as a clue to developments in the army before Philip's reign or during it, does not help us. The name itself implies a relatively small *corps d'élite*, and the description of Theopompus endorses this. Under Alexander in Asia, we see, the application of the name has been widened to include all the Macedonian infantry of the phalanx, and the *corps d'élite* is now called the 'hypaspists', a name which never appears in Philip's reign or earlier. Since this account of the *pezhetairoi* is unorthodox, and since the whole question is a complicated one, further discussion of it is reserved to an Appendix.[3]

About the Macedonian infantry as a whole, the levy of the kingdom, our first real information comes to us in the Illyrian war which killed Perdiccas and brought Philip into power. In the great Illyrian victory of 360/59 more than 4,000 Macedonians were killed; implying a Macedonian army of a size now far exceeding anything we have heard of previously. In Philip's campaign against Bardylis (358) his infantry numbered 10,000, the full levy, presumably, from that part of the kingdom which was under his control at the time.[4] After this, never again in Philip's reign do we get any figures for his army which enable us to trace the growth and development of the two great arms which made it famous, the 'Companion' cavalry and the mass of infantry which we call collectively 'the phalanx' (including the Guards). On three occa-

---

[1] Theopomp. *FGrH* no. 115 F 348 Θεόπομπός φησιν ὅτι ἐκ πάντων τῶν Μακεδόνων ἐπίλεκτοι οἱ μέγιστοι καὶ ἰσχυρότατοι ἐδορυφόρουν τὸν βασιλέα καὶ ἐκαλοῦντο πεζέταιροι.

[2] The book-number of this fragment of Theopompus is not preserved. On the question of accuracy, this description obviously is in a different category from the well-known description of Philip's Companions (*hetairoi*: F 224 and 225), where Theopompus colours the facts with his own ethical judgements, and probably exaggerates them too. Milns, *Historia* 16 (1967) 511, interprets this passage (F 348) as a 'confusion' by Theopompus of *pezhetairoi* with hypaspists (the name of the Footguards under Alexander, when Theopompus perhaps wrote this). I cannot think this possible, in view of T.'s first-hand knowledge of Macedonia (cf. Speusippus, *Epist. Soc.* 30. 13). I agree that his description most probably fitted the hypaspists of Alexander (below, pp. 414 ff.). But that he could make a mistake about these names (both of them unusual, 'Macedonian', and unfamiliar to Greek readers except by hearsay) after spending months (perhaps years) at Philip's court seems incredible.

[3] Below, pp. 705 ff.　　　　　　　　　　　　　　　　　　　　　　[4] D.S. 16. 2. 5; 4. 3.

sions when a great military effort is being recorded we are given totals for his forces of cavalry and infantry; but each time we can infer that some allies were present as well as Macedonians, and for all we know there may have been some mercenaries as well—but how many allies and mercenaries we have no really reliable means of estimating.[1] It is not until we are given some more detailed figures for Alexander's army of 334 that we are on a securer basis for comparisons. These last figures will be treated on an assumption that, with some qualifications, they may represent the strength of the Macedonian army at the end of Philip's life, the product of the manpower of Philip's 'greater Macedonia'. It must be admitted that this assumption is greatly in contrast to what seems to be the assumption underlying the chapter of Diodorus in which he sketches Philip's reorganization and training of his army, a chapter which Diodorus includes in his narrative of the first year of Philip's 'reign' (359/8), and which represents the whole thing as having been completed within that single year.[2] But this is very characteristic of the internal economy of Diodorus' *History* in general, and of this Book 16 in particular; and I doubt if any reader familiar with Diodorus will quarrel with an interpretation which allows itself to spread these processes over a number of years beginning with the year 359, and indeed most probably over all Philip's years up to his death.[3] When one begins to consider the details of the army, it becomes obvious at once that these are not merely military details. In any age or land the history of a regiment is among other things a social history. In the kingdom of Macedonia a full history of the army in Philip's reign might go far to giving us a picture of the reign as a whole. As it is, the relatively few details we have, of the size

---

[1] Thessaly (352), D.S. 16. 35. 4, more than 20,000 infantry, 3,000 cavalry (Thessalian allies certainly included in these figures). Perinthus (340), D.S. 16. 74. 5, 30,000 men. (Thessalians present, D. 8. 14). Chaeronea (338), D.S. 16. 85. 5, more than 30,000 infantry, not less than 2,000 cavalry. Add Thebes (335), D.S. 17. 9. 3, more than 30,000 infantry, not less than 3,000 cavalry, 'all veterans of Philip's campaigns'. This implies that they were mostly Macedonians perhaps, and certainly they included few Greek allies or none, except probably Thessalians. But they may well have included Balkan troops, Thracians, and others: it was an officer of Thracian cavalry who raped the unfortunate Timoclea when Thebes was sacked. Plut. *Mor.* 259 E from Aristobulus (*FGrH* no. 139 F 2a).

[2] D.S. 16. 3. 1 ff.

[3] The most notable instance of this idiosyncrasy of Diodorus' method, inspired by his desperate efforts to condense a much more comprehensive source (or sources) and present it in an economical way which he felt able to control, is the notorious entry dealing with the Persian recovery of Cyprus, Phoenicia, and Egypt under the years 351/0 and 350/49: in reality these events began in 353 and ended in 342 (16. 40–51). But one remembers, too, another famous 'military reform' described by Diodorus, that by which Iphicrates produced a 'new peltast' (D.S. 15. 44. 2–4, cf. Nepos, *Iphic.* 1. 3–4). This Diodorus introduces into his narrative of Iphicrates in Egypt in the year 364; but few will believe that it happened (if it ever did happen at all) on any single occasion. J. G. P. Best in his excellent recent study (*Thracian Peltasts and their influence on Greek Warfare* (Groningen, 1969), especially 102 ff.) has shown that this 'new peltast' of Iphicrates really represents a peltast style that had existed for generations previously.

of the army, its composition and its organization, can be of an interest and importance far beyond their value to the military historian.

2. *The Cavalry*

(1) *The numbers and the name 'Companions'*

In 358 against Bardylis, the Illyrian king, Philip was able to mobilize 600 Macedonian cavalry; this at a time when much of Upper Macedonia was not yet under his control.[1] In 334 Alexander had well over 2,000 with him in Asia Minor, having left 1,500 in Europe with Antipater.[2] There are no firm figures relating to any occasion in between. Theopompus however in the famous excerpt from his 48th book on Philip's Companions (*hetairoi*) mentions that he reckoned their number 'at that time' to have been no more than 800 men; and 'that time' seems likely to have been late in Philip's reign, probably about 340.[3] The attachment of the name Companions to the Macedonian heavy cavalry as a whole was attributed by Anaximenes of Lampsacus, a contemporary of Philip II and Alexander the Great, to an Alexander. Though the general sense and probable context of the quoted passage of Anaximenes (p. 405) seems to point to Alexander I or II, and modern interpreters have followed this line (with a number of variants), the quoter himself Harpocration took it to refer to Alexander the Great, rightly as it seems.[4] It is this that best accounts for the discrepancy between the 800 Companions of Theopompus and the much larger numbers of Alexander's Companion cavalry in Asia.[5] The name itself was probably ancient, comprising originally the king's personal retinue (pp. 158f. above). Under Philip this has expanded to the number of 'not more than 800', with obvious implications for the cavalry of the army also. As for Alexander (the Great), he had not doubled or trebled the number of cavalry in the short time between his accession and his crossing to Asia; he had merely given the name Companions a wider application than before.[6] The

---

[1] D.S. 16. 4. 3, see above, p. 213.

[2] D.S. 17. 17. 4 f. (He crossed to Asia with 1,800 'Macedonians'+300 Scouts (*prodromoi*) who also were Macedonians, and was joined by an unknown number which was part of the advance force of about 10,000 men already there. See especially R. D. Milns, 'Alexander's Macedonian cavalry and Diodorus xvii. 17. 4', *JHS* 86 (1966) 167 f., where Milns's emendation of the text of Diodorus to read Θρᾷκες δὲ ⟨καὶ⟩ πρόδρομοι καὶ Παίονες carries conviction.)

The troops left with Antipater (12,000 infantry, 1,500 cavalry) are not named by Diodorus as Macedonians; but in view of Antipater's military responsibilities (illustrated at D.S. 17. 62–3), it seems certain that they were Macedonians. (On this see further Brunt, *JHS* 83 (1963) 35 ff.; Griffith, *G & R* 12 (1965) 1.)

[3] Jacoby, *FGrH* no. 115, F 224–5. The two datable allusions of Books 47 and 48 are to the year 340/39; the one such allusion of Book 46 is to 342–339; of Book 45 (one) to 343/2.

[4] Jacoby, *FGrH* no. 72 F 4. This notorious passage is discussed pp. 706 ff., Appendix 3.

[5] The best discussion of this discrepancy was perhaps by Momigliano, *FM* 8 ff. (who took Anaximenes to refer to Alexander I).

[6] So too for *pezhetairoi* and later *asthetairoi*, see pp. 705 and 709 below.

figures for his cavalry in 334 are acceptable as evidence for the last years of Philip's reign.

According to Anaximenes the Companions were drawn from 'the notables', meaning presumably the nobility and the gentry with land. These would form the nucleus of the king's court and retinue, besides being a fighting force. (It is as court and retinue rather than soldiers, that Theopompus wrote of them.) As soldiers, originally not very numerous, they could expect to fight under the personal leadership of the king, forming the élite corps of the army, the cavalry of the Royal Guard. This element of the Guard is preserved through the expansion of the corps under Philip, and can be seen clearly in Alexander's Royal Squadron of the Companions (*ile basilike*), sometimes called the *agema*.[1] Its strength of 300 (which continued as the traditional number after his death), can be thought of perhaps as a possible strength of the Companions as a fighting force, before and into Philip's early years. This Guard must certainly be included in the 600 cavalry with which he defeated the Illyrians in 358; a force small by comparison with later years, but already very effective, as the account of the battle shows.[2]

The stages by which Philip was able to expand this force into the truly formidable cavalry arm which was available to Alexander later are hidden from us almost completely. The Companions described by Theopompus were very wealthy, their wealth being in land; they were very immoral; they were associated with Philip personally, some of them non-Macedonians attracted to his court; they had no military function or significance that Theopompus chose to mention here; they were 800, Theopompus thought, not more. These people sound like an original nucleus of Macedonian grand nobility (including the minor royalties), greatly increased now by the new Macedonian prosperity and also by the recruiting from outside of Greeks of the right sort. They are Companions of the status of the traditional king's retinue consisting of the leading men, and of the four or five score of 'personal Companions' (οἱ ἀμφ' αὐτὸν ἑταῖροι etc.) who emerge from the campaigns of Alexander in Asia later. In spite of Theopompus' silence, they did have military functions, naturally. Under Alexander this inner group commanded brigades and divisions of the army; were detached as satraps or generals in charge of this or that up and down Asia; or they accompanied Alexander as the leading officers of his staff, occasionally with the title of Bodyguard (*somatophulax*).[3]

The 800 of Theopompus, then, are the Companions who supplied this top rank late in Philip's reign: they are the most important of the Macedonian notables and gentry reinforced by some Greek émigrés, and

---

[1] Arr. *An.* 2. 5. 9; 3. 1. 4; 3. 8. 1 etc. On the number 300 Tarn 162 f.
[2] D.S. 16. 4. 5 ff.; above, p. 213.   [3] On Bodyguard (*somatophulax*), p. 403.

they are men of great estates. But the notion that all the Macedonian
cavalry were inordinately rich men, in Philip's time or ever, obviously is
an implausible one. All that we need expect of them is that they were
rich enough to be cavalry men not hoplites; and this more moderate
qualification would cover a large class, larger presumably than that of
the 800, of small country gentry, who served as the troopers of the
Macedonian cavalry in general. It was on these people that the name
Companions was conferred for the first time by Alexander before he
invaded Asia. As for Philip, it looks as if he was able to develop and
expand his own force of Macedonian cavalry very notably, and comparatively early in his reign (with the reservation just expressed as to the
name Companions itself). In 352, the year of his great Thessalian victory
over Onomarchus, he is said by Diodorus to have had 3,000 cavalry
with him.[1] The figure includes certainly an unknown number of Thessalian allies (perhaps other allies as well, or mercenaries). But Thessaly
was then divided politically, Pherae and her adherents on the side of
the Phocians, and therefore cannot have provided its (later) full levy of
2,000. It seems safe to say that at least 1,500 of the 3,000 (assuming the
figure to be reliable) were Macedonians; and quite possibly something
more like 2,000 were. If these high figures are accepted, it might be
thought hard to explain why in 338 Philip's cavalry for the Chaeronea
campaign numbered only 2,000 altogether, this time with a united
Thessaly to call on (and the same possibility of other allies, and of
mercenaries).[2] But I suspect this is a problem only if one chooses to make
it one, by assuming that for every major campaign he was bound to call
out all the cavalry he had. To assume this is not necessary, and is probably mistaken. The campaign of 352 was in Thessaly, where there was
more cavalry country than anywhere else in Greece, and where 3,000
horses could be kept fed relatively easily: moreover Onomarchus had
defeated Philip heavily the year before, and it was urgently necessary to
do something special, to beat him (pp. 273 f.). The campaign of 338 was
likely to be in the north of a hostile Boeotia, where supplies had to be
carried, overland, and where most of the flat land was covered then by
Lake Copais anyway. It seems possible (probable even) that Philip
reckoned that, having regard to the terrain, if he could not beat the
Greeks with 2,000 picked Macedonian and Thessalian cavalry, he could
not beat them at all. In short, the figure 2,000 for 338 need not necessarily
throw suspicion on the figure 3,000 for 352.[3] If this is correct, the expansion of the cavalry force was well advanced already by 352.

---

[1] D.S. 16. 35. 4.   [2] D.S. 16. 85. 5.

[3] As it happens, our sources (very inadequate) for Chaeronea make no mention of the
Thessalian cavalry. If for some reason they were not present, the lower figure for the cavalry
would be explained. But I know of no good reason why they could have been absent, from

(ii) *The Squadrons (ilai)*

The name of the Royal Guard of the Companion Cavalry, 'the Royal Squadron' (*ile basilike*), suggests that the unit on which the organization of the whole cavalry force was based was the Squadron; and this is confirmed by the evidence relating to the cavalry under Alexander (for Philip's reign there is no direct evidence). From the allusions to the cavalry in the first four years of Alexander's operations in Asia, before important changes were made late in the year 330, it has been inferred (and rightly) that both tactically and administratively the Squadron was the unit that mattered. Apart from the Royal Squadron, when a Squadron of the Companion cavalry needs to be named by one or other of our sources, it is identified by the name of its commander, but occasionally also by a place-name with which that squadron was associated. The squadrons were mobilized evidently on a territorial and ethnical basis.[1] When the Companions in Asia were about 2,000 strong, the number of their squadrons, we can see, was eight. And if the Royal Squadron numbered about 300 men (above, p. 409), it looks as if the strength of the seven other squadrons was a notional 200.[2] (There were times in the early years in Asia when they were over strength.) On one occasion however (Granicus) we hear of thirteen squadrons, of which one is shown to be of Paeonians, present with Alexander as subject allies.[3] Of the twelve others, eight will be of the Companions, and the remaining four are the squadrons of the Light Cavalry, known as the Scouts (*prodromoi*), or occasionally as the Lancers (*sarissophoroi*), whose nationality has been in doubt, but who now have been firmly identified as Macedonians.[4]

Of the eight squadrons of Companion cavalry with Alexander, we learn of the territorial associations of four (perhaps five), though one of the five names defies identification. The names are: Bottiaea (Lower Macedonia, coastal); Amphipolis (annexed by Philip, 357); Apollonia (Chalcidice, annexed 348); Anthemus (northern Chalcidice, Macedonian, but in Chalcidian hands till re-annexed 348); 'Leugaian' (unidentified).[5] Striking here is the prominence of the 'new' territories,

---

this Amphictyonic campaign especially, and I consider the possibility so remote as to be negligible (see p. 596).

[1] Below, n. 5 and p. 412 n. 5.

[2] The basic text is D.S. 17. 17. 4. The best discussion now is Brunt's (loc. cit. 32–6), with bibliography.

[3] Plu. *Alex.* 16. 3; cf. Arr. *An.* 1. 14. 6 f. For the Paeonians, below, pp. 431 ff.

[4] By Brunt, loc. cit. 27; cf. Milns, loc. cit. 167. Berve 1. 129 had seen this, but Tarn 158 had dissented.

[5] (All the references in this footnote are to Arrian.) Bottiaea and Amphipolis, 1. 2. 5; Apollonia, 1. 12. 7; Anthemus and 'Leugaia', 2. 9. 3. At 3. 11. 8, all squadrons, but identified by commanders only. Cf. Berve 1. 105–7. For discussion, pp. 367 ff. above.

which in this context points clearly to a policy of settlement by Philip, whereby he introduced Companions into these areas by granting them estates on newly conquered lands (see pp. 367 ff.). Conversely, we hear less than we would wish or expect to hear of the regions of Lower and of Upper Macedonia itself, with only one squadron from the former, and none from the latter. The mysterious 'Leugaian' squadron might belong of course to either (or to neither).[1] The Royal Squadron, too, would include Companions from both Lower and Upper Macedonia if (like the infantry Royal Guard according to Theopompus) they were men 'picked from all the Macedonians'.[2] Moreover 'the cavalry from Upper Macedonia' is heard of on Alexander's Triballian campaign of 335, and in the context it seems likely that there they were not less than two squadrons present, and perhaps more than two.[3] And then there are the four squadrons of the Scouts (*prodromoi*). Though nothing at all is known of their social any more than of their local origins, it could be suggested that they were drawn perhaps from the least affluent of the Macedonian gentry, and that this could give Upper Macedonia a strong representation in these four squadrons.[4] All things considered, though our picture of the twelve squadrons is very incomplete, and though it leads to interesting and baffling questions about the units which Alexander took to Asia and those which he left at home, it still seems to establish clearly enough that Philip at his death did hand on a cavalry arm organized on a territorial basis which included the whole of Macedonia, including (prominently) the newly conquered lands in Chalcidice and in the region of Amphipolis.[5]

[1] 'Leugaian' (if the manuscript tradition has given us here what Arrian wrote), unlike the other four place-names, is in some sense an artificial or manufactured name, τὴν Λευγαίαν καλουμένην [sc. ἴλην], Arr. *An.* 2. 9. 3. On this idiom, H. W. Parke, *JHS* 64 (1944) 102, for the practice of Thucydides. If Macedonian practice was the same, Leugaia should have a literal meaning (but also of course a geographical one in this context). Is Aigaia ('of Aegeae') a possibility here? If a squadron 'of Aegeae' (Αἰγαία, Arr. *Ind.* 18. 6) used a punning nick-name Αἰγεία ('the Goats'), this might justify καλουμένη. But I see no clue to why this should ever have been corrupted to Λευγαίαν. I offer the suggestion merely as one that makes sense of a sort, in the context of Aegeae's mythology (Just. 7. 1. 7 ff.; cf. Volume I. 156). If this were acceptable, this would be the squadron of Pieria, or northern Pieria. (There could be another, based on Pydna, or Dium: for Pydna in this connection, p. 356.)

[2] Theopomp. F 348 (above, p. 405).

[3] Arr. *An.* 1. 2. 5. On Alexander's left wing, they might be thought to balance the two squadrons (named) of his right wing. But the left hand had the better opportunity of exploiting a tactical advantage here, it may seem—and Philotas, their commander, was Alexander's senior cavalry leader at this time.

[4] Brunt (loc. cit. 27 f.) showed that there is good reason to think that in the reorganization of 330 they were amalgamated with the Companions (they are never again mentioned thereafter). If this is correct, I doubt if it invalidates my conjecture about their social position (above).

[5] At Arr. *An.* 3. 16. 11 a careful reading of the whole passage (two sentences) shows that in 330 Alexander's posting the Macedonian reinforcements to their units 'by races' (κατὰ ἔθνη) applies not only to the infantry but to the cavalry also. (And cf. Curt. Ruf. 5. 2. 6

In arms and equipment the Companion cavalry did not differ, so far as we know, from the cavalry of the Greek cities.[1] We hear of them only that they had the advantage over Persian cavalry at close quarters, owing to the stoutness of their spears of cornel-wood.[2] The Scouts however (*prodromoi*) did show at least one variation in their weapons, as their alternative name shows—*sarissophoroi*, or Lancers whose lance was the *sarissa* and not the *xyston*, sometimes called simply *doru*, of the Companions. On the analogy of the infantry (below, p. 421) the cavalry *sarissa* was a longer lance, just as the infantry *sarissa* was a longer pike. But since the infantry *sarissa* needed both hands, the cavalry weapon must have been shorter than that. This still leaves the paradox that the 'light' cavalry (*prodromoi*) carried the heavier lances; but military history is not short of such anomalies. Doubtless their body-armour was lighter and less expensive than that of the Companions.

The secret of the wonderful success of the Macedonian cavalry in this generation and the next lay, no doubt, in its numbers and in the high quality of the individual horsemen. But one tactical phenomenon is noted as peculiar to the Macedonians, the wedge-shaped formation assumed on occasion by the squadrons in battle. This we see in action first with Alexander in Asia, but it was not Alexander's invention.[3] 'The "wedge formation" is said to have been invented by the Scythians and the Thracians, and then taken up by the Macedonians as more effective than the square formation because the front of the wedge tapers just as it does in the rhombus formation, of which the wedge is one-half. This made it easiest for them to break through the enemy, as well as throwing

'nam cum ante equites in suam quisque gentem discriberentur seorsus a ceteris . . .') In Macedonia itself the regions corresponded to the ethnical divisions, broadly speaking; but in the 'new' territories which supplied squadrons (Amphipolis, Apollonia), this was not so— unless Philip had made it so. It was possible for him perhaps to grant estates mainly to (say) Elimiots in the Amphipolis area, Lyncestians or Orestians at Apollonia, and so on. But such a policy would raise interesting (and unanswerable) questions as to the timing of these grants, and seems to require that they should have been nearly all simultaneous, to forestall great jealousies and dissatisfactions among and between Companions of the different *ethne*.

Even here however contradiction between the 'territorial' and the 'ethnical' is not irreconcilable—just as, in practice, it was possible to have squadrons (and brigades) that were 'ethnical' and also numerically equal, as Brunt sensibly observed (art. cit. 39–40 n. 41).

[1] There has been doubt as to whether or not they carried shields, because the monuments do not show them (cf. Launey 1. 356 and n. 4, with bibliography). However, Arr. *An.* 1. 6. 5 records what seem to be the officers of Alexander's personal staff 'taking up their shields and mounting' in order to go into action. In action, when the right hand was occupied with the weapon, the left with the reins, a shield was more bother than it was worth, one must think. In preliminaries to action and under missile fire it would be manageable, so long as it could be slung on the back before a charge brought the fighting to close quarters.

For Greek practice in general, both Snodgrass (104) and Anderson (*AGH* 142) state unequivocally that Greek cavalry carried no shields in the classical period, though Anderson finds examples earlier, mostly on vases of the sixth century (ibid. 145–7 with nn. 26, 27, 33, 34, and Pl. 29).

[2] Arr. *An.* 1. 15. 5.   [3] Arr. *An.* 5. 15. 2.

forward the officers in front of the rest. It also made for easier wheeling than in square formation, because every man kept his eyes fixed on the one leader, the *ilarch*, "as happens in the flight of cranes".[1] Thus Asclepiodotus; and Aelian adds that it was 'Philip of Macedon' who introduced the wedge formation.[2] There is no reason to doubt this, really. Though we are never given a description of the cavalry in action under Philip, as it happens we can see that in his first important battle (Bardylis), and again in his last (Chaeronea), he overcame the problem of 'breaking through' an enemy in a defensive position, the cavalry each time clinching the victory. The wedge-formation may have been among the innovations of Philip's first year.

3. *The Phalanx, including the Footguards*

(i) *The Footguards (Hypaspists, finally)*

The word phalanx is used often by Arrian (and others) describing Alexander's Macedonian infantry in action, sometimes excluding and sometimes including the units of the Royal Guard, who by that time had acquired the name 'hypaspists'.[3] Though no doubt it is right to say (as Tarn did) that there was no such formation in Alexander's army as 'the phalanx',[4] its frequent use by Arrian suggests that he used it often mainly because he found it often, presumably in Ptolemy, his most important source for military narrative. 'Phalanx' is most probably what the Macedonians themselves called their infantry of the line at this time.

As we have seen, the name *pezhetairoi* (Foot Companions) seems to have widened its meaning, from 'Royal Foot Guards' to 'Macedonian infantry of the line', only very late in Philip's reign, or most probably only after his death and under Alexander (above, pp. 405 f.). The new name 'hypaspists', attached to the corps of Alexander's Foot Guards who seem to correspond exactly to the *pezhetairoi* of Philip as Theopompus described them, never appears at all under Philip. On its first appearance in Arrian the word is used (rather oddly?) not of Alexander's Macedonians, but of the Agrianian King Langarus' Royal Guards—he joined Alexander 'with his hypaspists and the finest and best-armed of his personal troops'.[5]

---

[1] Ascl. 7. 3. [2] Ael. *Tact.* 18. 4; Arr. *Tact.* 16. 6 (= 18. 4 K.).

[3] That the Guards were included legitimately in allusions to the phalanx, is demonstrated well enough by Arrian's order of battle for Gaugamela (3. 11. 9)—'Of the phalanx of the Macedonians, next to the cavalry first came the Agema of the Hypaspists and then the rest of the Hypaspists, under Nicanor . . . next to them was the brigade of Coenus, then the brigade of Perdiccas, then Meleager's, then Polyperchon's, then Amyntas' . . . The left of the phalanx of the Macedonians was held by the brigade of Craterus . . .'

[4] Tarn 142; and now again Fox 511.

[5] Arr. *An.* 1. 5. 2: . . . μετὰ τῶν ὑπασπιστῶν ὅσους τε καλλίστους καὶ εὐοπλοτάτους ἀμφ' αὑτὸν εἶχε. A teasing point of translation seems to present itself. The position of τε warns us not to read the ὅσους . . . clause as descriptive of τῶν ὑπασπιστῶν themselves, but of some

Whenever it was precisely that the new name was given, there can be no doubt that the effective history of the corps belongs to Alexander's career and not to Philip's, and consequently what is written of them here is only what is necessary to avoid either obscurities or unnecessary gaps in the record of the infantry arm as Philip developed it.[1]

The choice of the word 'hypaspist' (meaning 'shield-bearer', a soldier's servant) to denote a Foot Guardsman is one which I have never seen explained fully, and which I can try to explain myself only with a more than customary diffidence. In this new sense it seems to be (as Kalléris proposed) a genuinely Macedonian contribution to the etymology.[2] But why were the Macedonians able to use the word naturally in the new sense? (To think of the new name as 'natural', and not as some kind of artificial or bureaucratic imposition by a Government in the modern style, seems common sense.) The essence of the pre-Macedonian usage seems to lie in the notion of service by an inferior. To explain the Macedonian 'innovation' one should look perhaps for something in the Macedonian ethos (more particularly in war) which enabled Macedonians to think of certain people who might be inferiors but still were of an honourable status. To talk of knights and squires seems inapposite here (though I think it has been done). The description could fit exactly of course the notables in relation to the king; but these were 'Companions', anyway, a description calling attention to their equality and not their subservience, and hence more complimentary. May one take a step down from there and consider the retainers of notables in relation to their great man? If for example it was Macedonian practice for the notables to go to war attended by a group of their own local people who did what they could on foot, this could provide the sort of relationship in which hypaspist could have been a name for inferiors certainly, but for men not without honour because they were the notable's own people from his own place. The name needs to have been in use in some such

other soldiers of Langarus. Yet ὅσους . . . ἀμφ' αὐτὸν εἶχε makes these 'other soldiers' a unit or units of guards or something like it—which is just what the hypaspists presumably were, too. Is Arrian writing sloppily here, or with exactitude? I do not know. (I suspect the latter, though I cannot easily say why.)

It must be certain, of course, that Arrian's source (Ptolemy?) wrote ὑπασπιστῶν here not because the guards of Langarus really had the Greek (Macedonian) name 'hypaspists' but merely because they were Guards, his troops corresponding to the Macedonian hypaspists.

[1] For an excellent discussion, R. D. Milns, 'The hypaspists of Alexander III—some Problems', *Historia* 20 (1971) 186 ff.

[2] Kalléris 271 f., who believes however that the hypaspists in Macedonia were an institution older than the *pezhetairoi*. This view does not seem to take into account Theopomp. F 348 on Philip's Royal Guard of *pezhetairoi*, not hypaspists—or the lack of any evidence that the hypaspists existed before Alexander's reign.

Milns also (loc. cit. 187) thinks of the word in this sense as likely to represent Macedonian usage, and reminds us that it is only Arrian (with his Macedonian source) who uses it regularly.

sense as this, for a relationship between a higher and a lower order which was still by no means impersonal, for it to be an acceptable new name for the Footguards of the king. The King's Own Hypaspists (*'basilikoi'*) in this way could be distinguished in an acceptable style from the Foot Companions of the phalanx in general.[1]

The hypaspists under Alexander were probably 3,000 strong.[2] The Companion cavalry were certainly 'made' by Philip; and there must be a strong presumption that the hypaspists were 'made' by him too, in the sense of his having built up his Royal Guard of infantry, under whichever name, into something big and formidable. The details have not survived. But one important point cannot be neglected, concerning their recruiting and conditions of service.

For recruiting, we are brought back again to Theopompus (F 348). He described the *pezhetairoi* of his time in Macedonia (*c.* 342) as the Royal Guards, adding that they were picked from all the Macedonians for their stature and physique. This last piece of information carries clear implications for the method of recruiting. The Macedonian infantry as a whole, we shall see, was levied (like the cavalry) on a territorial basis, and obviously it was levied for each campaign as and when it was needed; and in reality the occasions after 358 when the whole levy was needed were very few indeed—perhaps none in fact.[3] In practice, then, individual Macedonians will not have been called up to serve in the infantry every year or all the year round.[4] But the Royal Footguards as described by Theopompus were soldiers of a different sort, obviously. They were not just 'the tallest and strongest' of the levy of this year or that, who turned up when the harvest was over and expected, most years, to be home for the winter. They must have been

[1] I use 'King's Own' in the literal sense in which (as I suppose) it could have been used by the Macedonian king who first attached 'Royal' (βασιλική) to the squadron of Companion cavalry, or to the Footguards, who were in truth his personal guards. The examples of British regimental history, where a number of regiments of horse and foot, belonging neither to the Household Cavalry nor to the Brigade of Guards, have been granted the honourable 'King's Own', 'Queen's Own', 'Royal' prefixes in compliment to their distinguished service in particular wars or campaigns, are in no way comparable.

[2] There is no direct evidence for this, but the reconstruction of Beloch 3^2. 2. 330 based on Arr. *An.* 2. 8. 3–4 (with 3. 11. 10, establishing the 'brigade of Craterus') is generally accepted, and justifiably. There, the Macedonian infantry, about 12,000 in all, consists of the hypaspists and of six brigades of *pezhetairoi*; and the hypaspists are evidently about equal in strength to two brigades. Thus the 12,000 phalanx contains eight units of about 1,500 each, the hypaspists being two units. Cf. Berve 1. 125 f.

[3] The year 356 may be thought of as the year which, more than any other, could have called for the full levy in the end, with three Macedonian forces acting simultaneously, at Potidaea, at Crenides, and in the north (under Parmenion): see above, p. 246.

[4] Even in the years 342–339 when Philip is thought to have been campaigning in Thrace without a break, presumably in midwinter he will have found winter quarters for the army, when he could have made some exchanges of troops, by sending some Macedonians home and receiving new levies in their place.

men, outstanding in stature and physique, who agreed to sign on as soldiers of the Guard for a period of years, and became professionals in a way in which the other Macedonians of the levy did not.[1] This professionalism and their *esprit de corps* identified them more closely than the Macedonians of the levy with the king, and this above all when the king was a great soldier and was giving the corps (among other things) an imperishable glory. The proof of all this appears only later, at the mutiny at Opis (324). The hypaspists did not mutiny. They kept very close to Alexander as he leapt down into the crowd, and they arrested the ringleaders of the Macedonians as he pointed them out one by one.[2]

Theopompus however was describing the Footguards of Philip at a time when they were still called the Foot Companions (*pezhetairoi*). When the Footguards came to be called Hypaspists was their character changed, or only their name? Only their name, I suggest; and to this I see really no alternative. Under Alexander we see their old name *pezhetairoi* being applied to the Macedonians of the phalanx in general, and the new name 'hypaspists' to the corps of Guards whose whole performance through the years gives the impression that they were just that picked force which Theopompus had described (as *pezhetairoi*). And if Philip had built up a Royal Guard recruited in the way described, who but a fool would change it? How else has anybody ever arrived at a *corps d'élite* except by picking the best men and then keeping them together? Incidentally, the change of name itself becomes a little easier to understand, perhaps, if we can think of its happening to a corps which has already the element of professionalism which I mentioned. In a 'political' sense it is the mass of the Macedonians who gain by being included in the more complimentary name *pezhetairoi*. The Guards, receiving the less obviously honorific name of 'hypaspists', as a military unit were the best of the best, but 'politically' they could be less regarded, and a little taken for granted, just because they were in a sense professionals.

This corps, then, with its *agema* corresponding to the *agema* (Royal Squadron) of the Companion cavalry and representing the original 'bodyguard' function which still survived, made its name under Alexander. Only one other matter calls for mention here—its arms. Though it has been held that the hypaspists were a lighter infantry in some way than the other Macedonians of the phalanx, there is really

---

[1] A different relationship of the hypaspists to the king from that of the ordinary Macedonians of the levy was seen by Tarn 140 f.; and a method of filling the corps by recruiting or selection from the whole kingdom, and not on a regional basis, has been assumed by both Tarn (ibid.) and Berve, 1. 122, 126. But I know of no actual evidence for either assumption, unless Theopompus on the *pezhetairoi* of the 340s be admitted as applying to the hypaspists.

[2] Arr. *An.* 7. 8. 3.

no good evidence for this view. The question has been discussed again recently and effectively by R. D. Milns, who shows that there was no difference between the armament of hypaspists and that of the remainder of the phalanx, and that anything that can be said of the arms of the Macedonian infantry can be said of both equally.[1]

(ii) *The Macedonian infantry levy (pezhetairoi, finally)*

In his introductory chapters of Book 16 on the critical situation of the Macedonian kingdom at the time of Philip's accession Diodorus included three sentences which summarize what Philip did to improve his army. Everything that he writes here that is not pure generalization seems to apply to the Macedonian infantry primarily if not alone. Consequently it seems good to begin with a translation of the three sentences of Diodorus and a brief commentary on them.

In spite of all these horrors which could be expected, Philip viewed the prospect with equanimity. Not once but many times he got the Macedonians together in an assembly, where by his skilful and powerful speaking he rallied them and filled them with confidence for the fray. He reorganized the units of the army on a better system, equipped the troops with the arms that were needed, and continually laid on reviews and manoeuvres. He devised the compactness and the equipment of the phalanx, modelling it on the close formation of the Heroes at Troy, and in fact he was the originator of the Macedonian phalanx. In his dealings with the people he was approachable; he quite won their hearts by his bounties and his promises. And he took careful precautions to meet the various threats of the moment.

(The threats are then described briefly in succession.)[2]

Assemblies. Though the Greek word has strongly political associations, the realities here were probably as much military as political, or more so.[3] It was common form for Greek generals to make speeches to their men when they expected to go into action. Philip as a young and new king needed to make himself known and regarded by the people. Above all the people themselves, the soldiers, needed to recover their confidence, after the defeat and slaughter by the Illyrians. What was most needed was a victory—and a small victory was to be not long delayed (over Argaeus and his mercenaries). Meanwhile to hear speeches from a young king who was able to sound confident was a good start. The soldiers who heard them will have been, mostly, those who lived nearest to the capital, in coastal Macedonia and Pieria; but there may well have been a general mobilization from all the regions which Philip controlled, for his counter-attack on Paeonia came evidently within a year. Some weeks

---

[1] *Historia* 20 (1971) 187 f.   [2] D.S. 16. 3. 1–3.
[3] See above, pp. 390 f.

of intensive training can have preceded it (the 'reviews and manoeuvres'). Hard training was one of the things for which Philip evidently won a reputation later as a general—and for a tough, austere approach to the soldier's life in general and how it should be lived.[1]

'*Reorganized the units of the army*'. About the organization before Philip we know nothing, except for those few words of Anaximenes already noticed (p. 405 above). Under Alexander in Asia it can be seen that the tactical unit that mattered in the phalanx was the *taxis*, a brigade of at least 1,500 men, and that these brigades were drawn from the different regions of Macedonia.[2] Since this regional organization seems the only practical method by which the army of an extensive kingdom made up largely of regional principalities could be mobilized, it seems certain that it must have existed from the start, and that Philip made no change in it. If this was so, there was still scope for innovation perhaps in the sub-divisions of the brigades, for it would be these which could give a phalanx of infantry some flexibility, and preserve it from being monolithic. The smallest unit known in the Macedonian infantry is the dekad, and by the year 333 it had come to consist of sixteen men.[3] Presumably it had once been a unit of ten men. As to when the change was made there is no direct evidence. Anaximenes (F 4) thought of the dekad as having been invented by the Alexander who invented the name Foot Companions; but he does not tell us how many men he thought the dekad then contained. The dekad of ten men, still, perhaps may be inferred from an allusion by Frontinus to a time early in Philip's reign (*cum primum exercitum constitueret*) when he limited the number of servants to one servant for every ten soldiers of the infantry.[4] But since the purpose, obviously, of enlarging the dekad may have been to make units which would serve as files in a phalanx sixteen deep, and since Philip at Thebes will have learned everything that there was to be learned about infantry fighting in depth, it may be thought possible, even probable, that the

---

[1] Polyaen. 4. 2. 10 (long route marches with full equipment); cf. 4. 2. 1 (demotion of a mercenary officer for washing in hot water); Frontin. 4. 1. 6 (limitation of the number of soldiers' servants).

[2] For the numbers, p. 416 n. 2 above. For the regional organization, pp. 426 ff. below. The number 1,500 depends on an assumption that the six brigades together amounted to about 9,000 men (with 3,000 hypaspists). But if any Macedonians in the army already in Asia before Alexander's landing are to be added to the 9,000, the strength of each brigade will be correspondingly higher.

Recent studies (Milns, *GRBS* 6 (1966) 159 ff., Bosworth, *CQ* N.S. 23. 2 (1973) 245 ff.) have rendered the Greek *taxis* as 'battalion'. As between 'battalion' and 'brigade', obviously there is something to be said for each; but personally I prefer 'brigades', as corresponding better to the scale of Greek armies. On this scale *lochagoi* seem to correspond rather to regimental commanders, taxiarchs to 'brass-hats' or generals (e.g. the *strategoi* of Xenophon's Ten Thousand).

[3] Callisthenes (*FGrH* no. 124 F 35) described Alexander at Issus as deploying the phalanx and diminishing its depth from 32 to 16 to 8. Cf. Arr. *An.* 7. 23. 2 f. (of 324).

[4] Frontin. 4. 1. 6.

dekad of sixteen men was Philip's innovation at some time in his reign.[1]

Between the dekad and the brigade (*taxis*) the only unit which is well attested is the company (*lochos*). Its officers (*lochagoi*) make their appearance early in Alexander's career, and it must be reasonably certain that the *lochoi* were part of Philip's organization.[2] Their size can be inferred only from the status of the officers, which was quite high; perhaps about 250 men, as Milns recently has suggested.[3] Units of 500 men are attested by Curtius Rufus as the norm before Alexander created chiliarchs in 331, and officers called pentakosiarchs certainly existed in 323;[4] but they are not mentioned on the occasions (at Issus and Gaugamela) when the *lochagoi* are mentioned, and personally I would not think of their existence under Philip as a certainty, if only because tactically they seem superfluous. The phalanx in action, whatever its depth, did not cover so much ground that the *lochoi* of each *taxis* were not under close control of the taxiarch. A depth of sixteen men certainly came to be regarded as the normal, and it can be thought that Arrian's source (Ptolemy) for Alexander's innovations in his last year already regarded it as such.[5] But Callisthenes wrote of the phalanx at Issus as eight deep, and it is not certain that he was mistaken, as Polybius thought.[6] Even if he was, his writing it at all carries conviction that the phalanx could be eight deep, and sometimes was. It is not necessary to think of it as stereotyped in these early years. Sixteen deep, *lochoi* of 256 men would have formed perfect squares, on a frontage of 16 yards each.[7] Even eight deep, sixteen dekads of each company (*lochos*) would form only thirty-two files of infantry, on a front of 32 yards. Six such units, on a front of less than 200 yards, does not seem to require tactically any link in the chain of command between company (*lochagos*) and brigade (taxiarch). Tentatively it may be suggested that dekad–*lochos*–*taxis* was perhaps the organization used by Philip, and that the 500s were perhaps a later elaboration.

'*Equipped the troops with the arms that were needed*'. In the Greek cities, for the government to supply its citizens with arms at state expense was

[1] Diodorus notices the density (πυκνότητα) of the phalanx as Philip's invention (16. 3. 2). This probably implies depth as well as compactness. For discussion of *puknosis* and *sunaspismos* of phalanxes, Pritchett, *GSW* 1. 151 ff.

[2] Arr. *An.* 2. 10. 2 (Issus); 3. 9. 6 (Gaugamela). Again, Anaximenes (F 4) included the *lochos* among the innovations of his 'Alexander'.   [3] *Historia* 20 (1971) 194.

[4] Curt. Ruf. 5. 2. 3 ff.; Arr. *An.* 7. 25. 6. (For chiliarchs, see Milns, art. cit., 189 ff., with bibliography.)

[5] Arr. *An.* 7. 23. 3 f. For the later phalanx, Plb. 18. 30. 1; Arr. *TT* 5. 5; Ascl. 2. 1.

[6] Jacoby, *FGrH* no. 124 F 35, ap. Plb. 12. 19. 9; 21. 1 f.; cf. Walbank, *Commentary* II. 373, ad loc.

[7] For frontage, Plb. 18. 29. 21; cf. E. W. Marsden, *The Campaign of Gaugamela* (Liverpool, 1964) 65 f., 74. But Pritchett, *GSW* 1. 144–54, would reduce the frontage a little, for Macedonians.

not normal.[1] The citizens provided themselves with the arms and equipment that they could afford, with the result that the cavalry were always the well-to-do, and the hoplites always the men of some property, even if small. There is no reason to think that the Macedonian army in the past had not been mobilized in the same way. If so, Philip, who cannot possibly have been well off in the first years of his reign, is most unlikely to have broken with tradition by arming and equipping the army at his own (the state's) expense. The words of Diodorus mean, in fact, that Philip saw to it that the soldiers equipped themselves with what was necessary. This is important, because there is some reason to think that he may have been responsible for an important innovation in the armament of the infantry. This could be indeed Diodorus' way of recording this fact.

As is well known, the characteristic weapon of the Macedonian phalanx was the longer-than-normal pike, the *sarissa*, of up to 18 feet long.[2] But that the *sarissa* was already its weapon before Philip is in doubt: if it had been, most likely the Macedonian phalanx would have made its existence known before Philip. It is much more probable that it was the introduction of the *sarissa* and the arming of the infantry with it that represented the one material innovation which helped to make of the phalanx the formidable force which it became. The effect in action of the long pikes needs no detailed demonstration. On a closer scale, it was like the warship which out-guns an opponent, forcing it to run great risks before it can get within range to inflict damage in return. The longer and heavier pike needed both hands, and this probably imposed the need for a shield a little smaller than the conventional hoplite's, whose left hand took some of the weight of his shield by a handle close to its rim.[3] The Macedonian will have used his upper arm alone as support for his shield, his forearm thrust through an elbow-thong, and in this way will have had both hands free.[4]

---

[1] The Athenian practice (fourth century) of making a free issue of shield and spear to the ephebes when they completed their training (Arist. *Ath. Pol.* 42. 4) probably arose merely from Athens being much better off financially than most Greek cities.

[2] Thphr. *HP* 3. 12. 2; Asclep. 5. 1; Lammert, *RE* 2. IA (1920) 2515 ff. M. Andronicos, 'Sarisa', *BCH* 94 (1970) 91 ff., especially 96–107 with Plates at 99 f., shows convincingly that the metal remains (spearhead, butt-spike, and junction socket) of a great spear found at Vergina (Aegeae) belong to a *sarissa*, of a length corresponding to the 18 ft. of the literary sources cited above. The still longer *sarissa* known to Polybius (18. 29. 2; cf. Polyaen. 2. 29. 2) evidently was not yet known to Theophrastus, contemporary of Alexander the Great.

[3] The diameter of the shield was probably about 2 feet (Asclep. 5. 1). For good representations of the Greek hoplite shield, showing the handle, see (e.g.) Anderson, Pls. 2, 7, 10, 13, 14.

[4] I have not seen a representation of a Macedonian shield which illustrates this. For a brief discussion of archaeological evidence, see Pritchett, *GSW* 1. 145 ff., who inclines to a diameter of more than 2 feet (about 0·80 m), but still smaller than the hoplite shield of about 3 feet. See, e.g., the shield alongside the goddess Nike on Seleucid coins (Snodgrass, Pl. 60).

These two variants on the conventional hoplite's gear, amounting to a big increase in offensive striking power at the expense of a smaller loss in defensive cover, certainly must have come as a result of forethought and calculation, and perhaps, too, from observation of contemporary peltast infantry, some of whom (in Thrace) may have been pikemen armed with a pike longer than the ordinary hoplite's.[1] Their author had lived much with hoplites in his thoughts; perhaps (one must think) with the finest hoplites of all Greece often before his eyes, the hoplites of Boeotian Thebes. There is a third variant, however, the breastplate, which sets us on less certain ground. Twice by a fortunate accident we are given a list of the articles of a Macedonian soldier's operational gear, and from each of these lists the breastplate is missing. The second list (in date) is contained in a well-known inscription from Amphipolis which records fines or stoppages of pay for soldiers who are without articles of their arms and equipment, and lists the fines for each article: unquestionably at this date (reign of Philip V) these soldiers had no breastplates, only their officers had them; and they are certainly Macedonians, as at Amphipolis one would expect.[2] The other list is given by Polyaenus in a description of Philip II's rigorous training methods, which included very long route marches; 'fully armed, with helmets, shields, greaves, sarissas, and as well as their arms, rations, and the gear they needed from day to day'.[3] Where Polyaenus got this from we cannot know; but a source who knew about greaves obviously cannot have forgotten, merely, about breastplates (the most expensive article, except the shield, of all the articles listed in the Amphipolis inscription). Though the fact itself is surprising, in the absence of evidence to the contrary one is driven to believe that these Macedonians of Philip really did have no breastplates, for whatever reasons.[4]

The reasons must arouse curiosity, plainly. Anderson's excellent recent study of hoplite armour and weapons has shown that among the Greek armies of the fifth century there was a distinct development towards a more lightly equipped hoplite, exemplified in the conical *pilos*, often, in place of the more elaborate helmet, and especially in the *spolas* (corslet), often of leather, 'linen', or some quilted stuff, in place of the metal-plated *thorax* (cuirass).[5] The evidence of the monuments also includes hoplites who wear no body-armour at all, and Anderson calls attention to Xenophon's description of the review of the Ten Thousand, whose bronze helmets, red tunics, greaves, and shields made them a fine sight; but not (it seems) their corslets or cuirasses, of which Xenophon makes

---

[1] Best 5 ff., with Pls. 3 and 4.

[2] M. Feyel, 'Un nouveau fragment du règlement militaire trouvé à Amphipolis', *RA* 6 s. 6 2 (1935) 29 ff.

[3] Polyaen. 4. 2. 10.   [4] For further discussion, see *PCPhS* n.s. 4 (1956) 3 ff.

[5] Anderson, 25–37.

no mention.[1] Yet some of the hoplites of the Ten Thousand did wear breastplates (corslets or cuirasses), as we learn later.[2] It seems that by the fourth century the body-armour of hoplites varied quite widely, and that it was by no means uncommon for them to wear no cuirass or corslet at all.[3] Whether this development came as a result more of economic pressures, or more from military lessons learned on active service, is a matter for speculation. Obvious enough are the advantages of carrying less weight into action and (especially) on the march when action was imminent or possible. But even so it may be doubted whether a purely military choice can have opted freely for this advantage in preference to that of feeling and being safer when hoplites met hoplites in a battle of phalanxes, still more when hoplites met peltasts, archers, or slingers, and all the harassment that missiles and the fear of missiles could impose. We hear of officers equipped with breastplates when their men were not.[4] As a military proposition, officers in action led and were prominent: one infers that they needed breastplates, and that it was better to have them than not. But was it a social and economic proposition too, if (as is likely) officers were usually more prosperous citizens than their men? It seems possible that the discarding (when this happened) of this fairly expensive item of the hoplite armament in the fifth century could be a sign that the 'hoplite class' by now had come to include some who, though they were men of some property, nevertheless were relatively poor. For instance, Athenian *zeugitai* who only just qualified by census for this class, in real terms were much poorer men in the age of Pericles than men of the same census in the age of Solon.

For the Macedonians of Philip, the same factors, the military and the social and economic, may be thought to suggest an answer rather more decisive. The protection of their smaller shields was less than that of the Greek hoplite: they would seem therefore to need breastplates more. If the Macedonians of the phalanx and the hypaspists did not have them, it seems likely that it was for reasons not purely or mainly military but arising from the social and economic background, which dictated ultimately the arms of the people. In Greece the hoplite had emerged with a more advanced development of city-states, giving enough stability and prosperity to support something resembling a middle class of citizens neither too poor to supply themselves with arms nor too discontented with the government to be trusted with them. (The same criteria explain the Roman legionaries of the middle Republic.) In Greece, Aetolia as Thucydides knew it was still undeveloped, its political organization based still on the *ethnos* not on the *polis*, its citizen soldiers still light-armed

---

[1] X. *An.* 1. 2. 15 f.   [2] X. *An.* 4. 1. 18.
[3] Anderson 26–8.
[4] In the Amphipolis inscription above, p. 422 n. 2.

deliverers of missiles, not hoplites.[1] The Macedonia of Thucydides' day had been much the same in this, and two generations later it was still only in a stage of transition, with much of it still under the ethnic organization of the old principalities and only parts of it showing cities as units of administration.[2] Perhaps if Philip (or his elder brother) had been content with a force of a few thousand infantry, they could have raised a genuine hoplite force of that size. But for Philip in 359 and the years immediately following, necessity and ambition combined to impel him to raise the largest force that the country could produce, even if many of the citizens called up, probably most of them, could not equip themselves fully as hoplites. It may even have been a lack of equipment, as well as the Illyrian occupation, that limited the infantry force of 358 to 10,000. The making and issue of the right kind of pike (sarissa) and the right kind of shield to go with it, must have been organized by the government in some way, and it will have taken a little time.

Meanwhile those soldiers who could be armed were trained as phalangites, and their numbers would grow year by year. They could be made to pay for their arms, as a new and temporary tax which emergency required. But to arm the infantry on the cheap may have been a necessity, and the men who reported for duty as *psiloi* with no defensive armour may have been told that *psiloi* they could remain, for the time being, so far as breastplates were concerned. And then experience in action (against the Paeonians and the Illyrians in 358) may have shown that these semi-hoplites, trained now and disciplined in their units of the phalanx, seemed to come to no great harm, while their 'lightness' gave them more mobility and endurance. In spite of their social origins and background (that of peltasts) and in spite of the similarity of some of their arms and equipment to the peltast's, it seems more useful to call them semi-hoplites than to write (for example) 'The phalanx of these Macedonian peltasts constituted the core of the armies of Philip and Alexander',[3] a remark perceptive of origins and connections with the past, but obtuse in its indifference to Philip's own problems and the future for which he planned. It was hoplites' work, not peltasts', that he had in mind for these people. Relationships of the Macedonians of the phalanx to peltasts, whether Thracian, 'Iphicratean', or of any other kind, though interesting in many ways are not very important for the present purpose, and may be treated elsewhere.

Whatever Philip's debt to Iphicrates, his debt to Thebes has become a commonplace, and one that there is no cause to question. Those years

---

[1] Thuc. 3. 94. 4 f.; 95. 3 (ὁμόσκευοι etc.); 97. 2 f. (ψιλῶν . . . ἀκοντιστῶν . . . ἐσηκόντιζον); 98. 1 f. (ψιλοί . . . ἐσηκόντιζον etc.).

[2] Arr. *An.* 7. 9. 2, rhetoric, but not fiction.

[3] Best 142. Arrian does sometimes refer to the phalanx as 'the hoplites' (1. 1. 8; 6. 2; 21. 1; 27. 8; 28. 6 with 28. 3–4; 2. 8. 2).

spent at Thebes in his teens, so edifyingly on philosophical studies according to an ancient tradition which in terms of general probability has little
to commend it, are nowhere recorded as correspondingly seminal for
his military education; indeed Aymard who wrote with such sensible
scepticism of the one influence seemed almost equally sceptical of the
other.[1] Here, however, the general probability points the other way, and
to take account of it seems the merest common sense. Even Aymard
accepted that Philip as a hostage probably was assigned to the house of a
leading citizen, and, rejecting Epaminondas for the obvious reasons, was
prepared to believe that he lived with Pammenes as Plutarch said.[2] That
he knew Epaminondas and Pelopidas, however slightly, seems something
more than probable. Quite certainly he saw the Sacred Band and the
full phalanx of the Boeotian hoplites as they came and went about their
business and exercised on the training ground. Everything that we know
of Philip from his accession at the age of twenty-three conspires to make
us smile at the notion that his leading interest in life as a boy of fourteen
to seventeen years old was anything other than soldiers; soldiers and the
whole business of war.

It is not hard to believe that Philip at Thebes was neither of an age
nor a temperament to become a dedicated Pythagorean or indeed a
philosopher of any kind. But to observe and admire the best hoplites in
Greece, to follow the talk of generals who had led them, to understand
the tactical and strategic aims served by the striking force massed in
great depth and delivered at a decisive time and place in battle while the
weaker units of the army were held back for tasks within their powers;
to reflect that he was a hostage here at Thebes because the existence of
these hoplites had enabled a Theban general to give orders to the king
of the Macedonians—not one of these things was beyond his understanding and all but the last of them were the most congenial matters
in the world. Philip's record in battle later shows him clearly as one to
whom war was no duty merely or instrument of policy but the gateway
to one group of the major pleasures of life and its greatest thrills. Here
at Thebes in his teens, the age of plans that are partly dreams and of
obsessions that can mould a lifetime, he fed his eyes and his thoughts on
stuff that served his genius. It would be proper for a captive Macedonian
prince to promise himself that one day he would show these Thebans
something they would remember. Hoplites? Yes, even hoplites, if that
was the only thing they understood; or at least the nearest thing to a
hoplite phalanx that his country could produce.

When six years after his return from Thebes he became king, he knew
the things that he needed for the defence of the realm and the confusion

---

[1] See above, p. 205; A. Aymard, *Études d'histoire ancienne* (Paris, 1967), 435.
[2] Plu. *Pelop.* 26.

of his enemies. He was able to use freely the material he found in Macedonia, and because there was plenty of it and because he was able to train and practise it intensively through the years, he was able to produce an infantry arm both bigger and better than anything that had been seen before.

The outcome was a force decidedly mobile by Greek hoplite standards, partly because it had had harder and better training than nearly all Greek citizen armies. Yet in spite of being 'lighter' infantry its striking power as a phalanx enabled it to take its place in a line of battle against Greek hoplites and get the better of them, and to be invincible against Illyrians and Thracians. The value of an infantry training which enabled the companies and the dekads inside the phalanx to react like the cells of a living organism to special demands, is seen best in the *tour de force* of Chaeronea, Philip's controlled retreat,[1] and in the emergencies of both Issus and Gaugamela, where the phalanx advancing broke in two because its left was unable to advance as fast as its right. At Issus this was against Greek mercenaries who were fighting well, and it could have brought defeat if the brigade commanders and officers had not known how to improvise something, and if their men had not known what to do in order to survive. Though the point has been made that in the conquest of Asia the phalanx did not play a decisive role, and though its vulnerability to outflanking attacks is beyond dispute, the fact remains that neither Philip nor Alexander ever went anywhere important without it. It might not win the battles outright, but without it battles were liable to be lost almost before they were begun, as the Persian story had shown long ago.

The internal organization of the phalanx as Philip left it in the end is beyond reconstructing in detail, and its total strength leaves room for conjecture. Administratively as well as tactically the *taxis* was the unit which mattered, as is clear from a remark of Arrian about reinforcements to Alexander in 330: when they arrived at Susa they were posted to the different *taxeis* 'by races' (κατὰ ἔθνη).[2] But only once are we vouchsafed any 'ethnic' descriptions of phalanx brigades, and then only for three of Alexander's brigades (six at the time). These three were drawn respectively from Elimea, from Tymphaea, and from Orestis and Lyncestis combined.[3] These happen to be, all of them, regions of Upper Macedonia, and significance has been found in this, combined with the Companion Cavalry's regional names which are predominantly from Chalcidice and other newly conquered areas (with none from Upper Macedonia).[4] Personally I am inclined to be sceptical about this (see above, p. 411, on the cavalry), and to think that it is right to allow more

---

[1] See below, p. 600.   [2] Arr. *An.* 3. 16. 11.   [3] D.S. 17. 57. 2.
[4] Berve I. 115; Bosworth, 'PUM' 93 ff.

for accident-of-survival in these names themselves. There is great scope for accident, clearly, suggested by the regional names for the three phalanx brigades which have survived. No one can suppose that Tymphaea, the most remote of all the Macedonian 'regions' except Parauaea, could produce an infantry force equal in strength to Orestis and Lyncestis combined, which were more than twice its size and certainly not less thickly populated. The 'accident' here entails all the information, I suggest, which we do not possess, about which regions had supplied most troops to the army in the levies of the recent years before 334.

The number of phalanx brigades disposed of by Alexander in his division of forces between his own army for Asia and the army of Antipater left in Europe was probably fourteen.[1] Why Alexander took to Asia a whole brigade from Tymphaea (rather than from elsewhere) need not concern us here. What is clear is that the fourteen brigades, representing the phalanx strength at the end of Philip's reign, do offer ample scope for every region of the kingdom to be fully represented, including the more thickly populated and urbanized parts of Lower Macedonia.[2] Under Alexander in Asia two of the three brigades which can be 'located' were commanded for several years by taxiarchs (Perdiccas from Orestis and Polyperchon from Tymphaea) who were probably members of the ruling houses of these former principalities of the kingdom. On the other hand two other taxiarchs, Craterus and Amyntas, who came also from Orestis and Tymphaea respectively, commanded brigades which clearly were drawn from elsewhere.[3] This obviously was not a matter which could be subject to any rule of thumb. The gains and the disadvantages of appointing local commanders were decided by the personalities concerned, and also by the local politics which need not have remained constant over the years. Local patriotisms may have been strongest in Upper Macedonia, as Berve suggested, and they may have made for better soldiers if the local commander was right. If he was not right, they could have made for situations dangerous politically. These appointments were among the more important of a king's decisions, obviously.

In conclusion, a word on the mysterious *asthetairoi*, rescued recently

---

[1] D.S. 17. 17. 3 ff. The 12,000 Macedonian infantry with Alexander himself included the 3,000 hypaspists (p. 416 and n. 2): i.e. six phalanx brigades (9,000). The 12,000 with Antipater are sometimes assumed to include (?)3,000 hypaspists likewise (Berve 113 and 225, tentatively); but this seems improbable since hypaspists were Royal Guards and picked men. There was no royalty to guard in Macedonia; and no point in putting ideas into Antipater's head, perhaps. Antipater's 12,000 represent probably eight phalanx brigades (no hypaspists).

[2] Berve (115) thought that Alexander's three 'unlocated' brigades came from Lower Macedonia. This is perfectly possible. If it were so, there would still be the regions of Eordaea, Parauaea, Pelagonia, Amphaxitis, Mygdonia unaccounted for.

[3] Berve 1. 114 f.; 2 no. 626 (Perdiccas); 654 (Polyperchon); 446 (Craterus); 57 (Amyntas).

by A. B. Bosworth from the oblivion to which successive editors of Arrian had consigned them.[1] Bosworth did very well to remind us that in six of the nine places where the word *pezhetairoi* appears in our texts of Arrian, the manuscript reading is *asthetairoi*, and his able study established that the word (which, I think, means 'Best Companions'), was applied to three only of the six brigades of the phalanx (or perhaps to four after 330, when the number of brigades had become seven). Identifying (rightly) two of the *asthetairoi* brigades as two of the brigades known to come from Upper Macedonia, he saw this name as the distinguishing mark probably of the Upper Macedonian brigades in general, conferred on them by Philip, with interesting political implications. Unfortunately this last proposition seems to be unsound. There is good reason to think that the name was conferred first by Alexander (the Great), and first on one brigade only, later on the two (or three) others; and that it was a sort of Battle Honours rewarding distinguished service. The discussion of this in detail is best reserved for an Appendix.[2] It is still possible that all three (or four) brigades of *asthetairoi* were Upper-Macedonian—and it is certain that two of them were (including the first to win the distinction). If in truth the Upper Macedonians did predominate in what could be seen (in retrospect) as a sort of prize list for the skills of soldiering when subjected to the tests of the very highest levels, the inferences to be drawn are social and military, and they apply of course to the Macedonia of Philip and the army which was his creation. In this nation of fine soldiers the highlanders may have been in the end just that bit finer and tougher than the men of Pella and its plain or of the Pierian homeland; capable of proving themselves in the long haul 'better than the best'.

4. *Macedonian Light Infantry*

Demosthenes once, in a well-known passage, generalized about the changed character of the warfare of his day (he was speaking in 341). Decisions were no longer reached by pitched battles so much as by political warfare, and for Philip it was not so much his phalanx of hoplites (*sic*) that enabled him to go where he pleased, but more because of his light-armed troops, his cavalry, his archers, and his mercenaries— that sort of army that he had got together. (He added, then, Philip's capacity for siege warfare, and his readiness and ability to make war all the year round.)[3] Maybe this was spoken more as a politician's contribution to the morale of his audience than as a close analysis of Philip's army by a military expert; but still it has its value as a piece of impressionism,

---

[1] A. B. Bosworth, *ΑΣΘΕΤΑΙΡΟΙ*, *CQ* n.s. 23. 2 (1973) 245–53.
[2] Below, p. 709 (Appendix 3).   [3] 9. 49 f.

by a contemporary for contemporaries. Though the pitched battle and the 'phalanx of hoplites' were not as far away in 341 as Demosthenes may have hoped, these remarks probably do entitle us to conclude that well-informed Greeks at this time did see Philip's army as a well-balanced combination of arms, in which not only the cavalry but also the less spectacular auxiliaries were of importance.

Recent studies of Greek warfare have done much to illustrate this aspect of it both in the age of Thucydides and in that of Xenophon, the seventy years which preceded Philip's accession.[1] That world of hoplites (in the sense that this was the standard armament of the Greek *polis*, and that the great battles of that period were hoplite battles almost exclusively) had been subject always to occasional incursions of the more mobile styles of fighting, with results occasionally spectacular and important. The Peloponnesian War itself gave rise to interesting developments in this direction. The education as a general of Demosthenes the son of Alcisthenes has been well sketched by Best: his mauling by missile troops in Aetolia, followed by his use of similar methods himself at Olpae, in Amphilochia, and on Sphacteria, and his provision for troops of this kind in the reinforcement which he took to the Athenian army besieging Syracuse.[2] The defensive value to a hoplite army of its auxiliary corps of peltasts and slingers was exemplified by the experience of the Ten Thousand after Cunaxa; the offensive capabilities of peltasts attacking hoplites who were unsupported, by the famous victory of Iphicrates over the Spartans near Lechaeum.[3]

These obvious 'lessons' have been put in a better perspective by the recent work of Anderson and Best, whose examination in detail of some of the smaller and often indecisive campaigns recorded by Xenophon in particular, allows us to see how well these same lessons had been taken to heart by the generals of the generation of Thucydides himself, and of the one that came after it.[4] We see better now in what ways and on what scale Greek generals regularly made use of the other arms, besides the ubiquitous hoplite. The uses of cavalry must always have been plain; but so few Greek generals ever commanded cavalry of a quality or quantity that could have made it decisive. Light infantry however was not scarce, especially peltasts and especially from northern Greece or Thrace; their uses in action many and varied. Apt for ambushes where the circumstances and terrain allowed, in difficult country by seizure of a commanding position they could hinder or prevent an enemy's passage, and in the plains their presence could deter a hoplite force from scattering

---

[1] By J. K. Anderson (see List of Abbreviations), and J. G. P. Best, *Thracian Peltasts and their influence on Greek warfare* (Groningen, 1969).

[2] Cf. Best 17 ff.   [3] X. *An.* 3. 3–4; *HG.* 4. 5. 11 ff.

[4] Anderson, ch. 7 especially; Best chs. 2, 3, and 4.

to lay waste a harvest. Conversely, to meet these and other forms of harassment by light infantry, the best reply, in the absence of cavalry or in country too rugged for its use, lay in the deployment of a counter force of light infantry able to move and act on equal terms.[1] The campaigns of Xenophon already mentioned are rich in examples of operations of this kind, and illustrate well the allegory in which Iphicrates, their master exponent, is said to have likened an army's light infantry to the human hands, its cavalry to the feet, its phalanx of hoplites to the trunk with its breastplate (and the general himself to the head).[2] Xenophon himself was fully aware that the modern army (of his day), the army of Jason of a strength in hoplites and cavalry which he describes a little larger than life, was not complete without its peltast arm 'a match for the whole world'.[3]

To see these troops in action under Philip, however, and to see how he used them, whether separately in small affairs or in combination with the phalanx and the heavy cavalry in the set-piece battle, is something which we are denied, not surprisingly in view of our very defective information about the more notable arms themselves, the phalanx and the Companions and the siege-train. In reality we know almost nothing of Philip's light infantry, who, what, and how many they were, what he did with them, how and on which occasions he did it. Everything that we do know comes from our sources for the campaigns of Alexander.[4]

Alexander, we see, did have Macedonian light infantry in his army. In 335 on his campaign against Thracians and Triballians he had both slingers and archers, who probably were Macedonians since we are not told that they were anything else.[5] Slingers reappear in Asia, at Issus and at Tyre, and in those early years they are likely to have been the Macedonians.[6] Later appearances of slingers, in Bactria and at Aornos, leave open the strong possibility of Asiatic reinforcements.[7] 'The javelin-men of Balacrus' at Gaugamela were almost certainly Macedonians, as Berve inferred, since they are described thus in a context where the non-Macedonian units are given their ethnic description (Agrianians, Thracians, and so on).[8] The light infantry most in evidence in Asia however were the archers, though they were not a large force. 'The archers and the Agrianians' played a distinguished part, usually together, in the fighting of the early years. Yet together they numbered only 1,000

---

[1] Cf. e.g. (ambush) X. *HG.* 4. 8. 35 ff.; 5. 1. 10 ff.; 5. 4. 59; (difficult country) X. *HG.* 4. 3. 21 ff.; 4. 6. 7 ff.; 5. 4. 14, 36, 59; (in plain) 4. 5. 11 ff.; 5. 4. 42; (counter force) 5. 4. 14, 36, 59, etc.

[2] Plu. *Pelop.* 2. 1. [3] X. *HG.* 6. 1. 8–9 and 19.

[4] See below, pp. 440 f. for Cretan archers and others.

[5] Arr. *An.* 1. 2. 4. [6] Curt. Ruf. 3. 9. 9; D.S. 17. 42. 7.

[7] Arr. *An.* 4. 2. 3; 4. 5; 30. 1. Cf. Berve 1. 131, 152.

[8] Arr. *An.* 3. 12. 3; cf. Berve 1. 151. In Bactria (Arr. *An.* 4. 2. 3) the javelin-men there mentioned may have been reinforced by Asiatics, like the slingers (see above).

men (2,000 in the Balkan campaign of 335).[1] If the number of the archers was about 500, this means perhaps only about 200 Macedonians, since 'the archers' included a force of Cretans too, who are mentioned four times by Arrian (the Macedonians only twice).[2] If the same sort of number (or even twice as many) was left behind with Antipater, this probably gives a fair idea of the relative weakness in this arm of Macedonia itself. This suggestion is reinforced by the very fact that Cretans had been recruited at all. Berve was right to infer from the brigading together of the Macedonians and the Cretans in Alexander's army that the Cretans were very well established by 334. No other example is known of this close integration of a Macedonian with a foreign corps. Philip had recruited a force of these Cretan specialists, we may conclude, to reinforce and perhaps improve the limited resources of Macedonia here.[3]

Indeed the most significant point that emerges from a study of all these Macedonian *psiloi*, slingers and *akontistai* as well as archers, is that all three forces with Alexander were very small ones, to be thought of in hundreds of men not in thousands. (Only the archers, with the Agrianians, gain a separate place in Diodorus' 'list', at 17. 17, for the year 334.) This could be due partly to the plentiful supply, of *akontistai* at least, that could be drawn from the subjects and subject allies of Thrace and elsewhere (below, pp. 432 ff.). But partly it may be seen as an effect of the whole policy of Philip for the citizen army. If he had built up the phalanx by admitting into it Macedonians who were really quite poor and would not have qualified for the hoplite class of a Greek city, there may have been relatively few Macedonians left who were still serving as *psiloi*. In the generation of the Successors of Alexander one never hears of them at all any more.[4] There seems some reason to think that Philip, changing the army, accelerated a change in the social character of the people.

5. *Allied Troops*

To this category belong on the one hand the Balkan troops, of Thrace especially, but also of Paeonia (including the Agrianians) and of Epirus (the Molossians), and those of the Illyrians whom Philip had reduced to a dependent status; and on the other hand the Greek allies, among whom Thessaly takes a special place. All the kings and princes of the north presumably were under obligation to supply troops when required, though the details of their actual performance do not survive. For the obligation itself, the presence of these troops with Alexander in Asia

[1] D.S. 17. 17. 4; Arr. *An.* 1. 6. 6.   [2] For discussion, Berve 1. 131 f.
[3] For Cretan archers earlier, with Athens and Sparta and on the Anabasis, Thuc. 6. 43; Paus. 1. 27. 9; X. *HG.* 4. 2. 16; *An.* 1. 2. 9.
[4] Launey 1. 101–2.

provides evidence; but the size and importance of that war with its corresponding diversity of military requirements warn us against thinking of it as altogether typical. Its duration, especially, can even be thought of as transforming in a sense these northerners from the status of allies to that of mercenaries; for, unlike the Greek allies with Alexander, not one of the northerners (so far as we know) was ever discharged and sent home. Nevertheless it seems wrong to think of them as pure volunteers and mercenaries. The difference in their treatment (as compared with the Greeks) stemmed most probably from the political background as Alexander chose to interpret it, rather than from any contract of service as mercenaries. The Greek allies were his allies for the duration of the Persian war, which could be seen in 330 as terminated. If the northern kings were bound by their treaties to 'have the same friends and enemies' as the Macedonian, it was open to Alexander to decide when to send their troops back home. In a general way this kind of obligation for the northerners is suggested already by the terms of Demosthenes' reference in 349 to 'the Paeonian and the Illyrian and all that lot' as subjects (*doulous*).[1] Philip's own use of these people will have been conditioned by factors partly geographical (for Illyrian campaigns, the Paeonians and Molossians most naturally) and partly political (which Thracian allies could be used against which other Thracians?), and so on. One factor however was common to Philip's and Alexander's experience, the great value of the best of these troops for campaigns in difficult terrain and for supplying missile capacity when it was needed. Alexander's Balkan operations of 335 may be thought a pattern of many a 'lost' campaign of Philip in Thrace or in the north-west.[2] Only the Agrianians are mentioned as present with Alexander in 335; but the presence of at least one Thracian unit too can be inferred.[3] The Agrianians are mentioned repeatedly, led in one rearguard action by Alexander himself.

The allied troops from the Balkans named by Diodorus as crossing to Asia with Alexander were Odrysian and other Thracians, infantry *akontistai* (say, 3,000), and cavalry (400?); Paeonian light cavalry (200?); Agrianian infantry *akontistai* (500?); Illyrian light infantry (say, 3,000); Triballian infantry (say, 1,000).[4] The Triballians need not detain us, because they were reduced to subjection only by Alexander's visitation of 335. The Illyrians appear very little in our record, but more of them

---

[1] D. 1. 23.   [2] Arr. *An.* 1. 6. 6 ff.   [3] See p. 433 and n. 4 below.

[4] These names all appear at D.S. 17. 7. 4, included in the army list of the troops who crossed the Hellespont with Alexander in 334, infantry and cavalry, itemized in the following way: (infantry), 'Odrysians and Triballians and Illyrians, 7,000; archers and Agrianians, 1,000': (cavalry), 'Thracians and Scouts and Paeonians, 900' (accepting here the emended text proposed by R. D. Milns, see above, p. 411 n. 4).

The figures for individual units given in my text (e.g. Agrianians ?500) are estimates based on what we learn of the units in the accounts of the campaigns themselves. For full discussions, see Berve 1. 133–9, with (for cavalry) Milns, *JHS* 86 (1966) 167 f.

joined the army in Asia later. The Thracians too received substantial reinforcements, and their record in action (mostly in Arrian) is a useful one. The Paeonian light cavalry, though they were a very small corps, figure quite prominently in Alexander's early years, especially at Gaugamela. The Agrianians undoubtedly were his favourite corps of light infantry, indispensable along with the archers (Cretan and Macedonian). The Agrianian reinforcements which are attested made up a force at least 1,000 strong.[1]

The command of these non-Greek subject allies is a matter of some interest, for their loyalty and enthusiasm for Macedonian wars and objectives may have varied widely with the times and the seasons and the people themselves. For Alexander there may have been quite a strong political ('hostage') element to account for these levies, as well as the military reasons.[2] One can see some advantages, given the right personalities, in the Thracian unit led by its own prince. On the other hand these people were no doubt a rough lot if left to themselves, and as part of a Macedonian army they may have needed some integration and control, especially for administration and discipline. Perhaps this explains the organization of the Thracians, so far as we can see it in Alexander's early years. They comprised certainly three separate units at Gaugamela, one of cavalry and two of infantry; the Odrysian cavalry led by a Macedonian Agathon, infantry under Sitalces who is presumed to be a prince of the Odrysian royal family, and a second infantry unit whose commander we never learn, unless he is 'Ptolemaeus the general of the Thracians' who appears a few months later.[3] More probably, however, this Macedonian Ptolemaeus was commander of all the Thracians of the army, responsible for their discipline and administration.[4] The only other unit that we see commanded by its own prince is the squadron of Paeonian light horse, under Ariston;[5] the smallest unit of them all, this, and one which tactically was integrated closely with the Macedonian squadrons of light cavalry (*prodromoi*).[6] The commander of the Agrianians was

---

[1] The evidence on Triballians, Illyrians, Thracians, Paeonians, and Agrianians is collected and discussed by Berve 1. 133–9.

[2] Cf. Frontin. 2. 11. 3 (in an exaggerated form).

[3] Arr. *An.* 3. 12. 4–5 (cf. Berve 2 no. 673).

[4] The ilarch of Thracian cavalry at Thebes in 335 who was a Macedonian (called Alexander) does not seem a firm basis for believing that all the high officers (and not merely the commanders) of such units were Macedonians. He comes in the romantic story of Timoclea, and though the source for it is Aristobulus, the title 'ilarch' here may not be exact. Even if it is exact, the Thracian cavalry at Thebes may have consisted of one *ile* only, which would make this Alexander its unit-commander. For the story, Plu. *Mor.* 259 F; cf. 1093 c = Aristobulus F 2a (*FGrH* no. 139).

[5] Cf. Berve 2 no. 138.

[6] Arr. *An.* 1. 14. 6; 2. 9. 2; 3. 8. 1; 3. 12. 3. From 3. 8. 1 closely interpreted (ἀναλαβὼν ... καὶ τῶν προδρόμων τοὺς Παίονας ...) one could take the integration to be administrative as well as tactical.

a Macedonian Attalus.[1] For the Illyrians with Alexander there is no information.

The long duration of the service in Asia will have imposed probably some special needs. Philip's situation will have been closer to that of Alexander in his northern campaigns of 335. There the Agrianians were with him in greater strength than in Asia later, and presumably led by a Macedonian brigadier or general, while simultaneously the Agrianian king himself, Langarus, at a moment when two operations were called for, freed Alexander for the greater one by himself undertaking and carrying out the lesser. He was a personal friend, and the model client king.[2] The fact remains, however, that no client king was ever a client for choice. Intimidation had subjected them all, and might keep them subject. But any loyalty or liking for the Macedonian overlord can have come only by the personal efforts of Philip himself and his closest associates, if they took enough trouble. Macedonian commanders of Thracian or Agrianian or Illyrian units when they served with the army will have had an influence on the relations with these people only less important than that of the king himself. How did a Macedonian general converse with the Thracian or Illyrian officers of his command? Most likely in Greek, one may suppose, since even the most inland and 'continental' of these foreigners, once they moved into the great world at all, will have recognized this as the tongue which enabled them to speak and be spoken to on equal terms as necessary.

About the free Greek allies of Philip (other than Thessalians) who may have honoured their alliances by sending troops for this campaign or that, there is no information at all.

In Alexander's army in Asia later the presence of troops, both horse and foot, supplied by the Greek cities, including the very important Thessalian cavalry, can be observed in a useful way, and their standing in relation to the whole Macedonian military power assessed. Constitutionally, however, these troops were present because of their obligations to the *hegemon* of the 'League of Corinth', which began only in Philip's last years; and in practice most of them were not available to Philip as allied reinforcements earlier in his reign. The obvious exception is the Thessalians. Philip's alliances with separate Greek states probably were always defensive alliances, this being the normal form of agreement between contracting parties of equal status. This fact will have imposed some limits on the amount of use that Philip made of them; and other limits were imposed by considerations of practical and political expediency. Thus the Chalcidian League, his ally from 357/6 onwards,

---

[1] Cf. Berve 2 no. 183.

[2] Arr. *An.* 1. 6. 6 f.; cf. Berve 2. 460 (Langarus). That the connection was no new one, but a legacy from Philip, is suggested by Appian, *Illyr.* 14 (and by common sense).

may well have reinforced his armies in the wars against the coalition of the three kings against him in 356, or in operations against Athens in the years immediately following; but it would be surprising perhaps if the Chalcidians were asked to supply troops to support him in Thessaly in 353 or 352. Surprising, that is, if a 'defensive' clause in an alliance were interpreted fairly strictly, for it could hardly be claimed that the Phocians or their supporters in Thessaly had attacked either Philip or the Chalcidians, or ever would attack them; yet still not totally surprising perhaps, if Sparta is remembered, and her dismembering of the Chalcidian League in 380—for the Spartans too were among the allies of the Phocians in 353/2. Similarly in the Peloponnese in 344, his Peloponnesian allies no doubt took part, and the leading part, in the operations against Sparta then, in which Philip played only a supporting role. In 338 the positions were reversed, with Philip '*hegemon* of the Greeks' in fact, though not yet (quite) in name.[1]

Such were the political considerations that will have helped to dictate the military use which Philip was in a position to make of his Greek allies from time to time. But the rest is silence. Some 'allies' fought with him on the campaign that culminated at Chaeronea; but which, and how many, of what sort, we are not told.[2] Presumably on the occasions when they did serve they had their own regimental officers, and when a number of small units were combined the command was held by a Macedonian brigadier or general, as we see it for the cavalry and the infantry of the Greek allies in Alexander's army. There, the cavalry was commanded by Philippus son of Menelaus, later by Erigyius when Philippus was promoted to command the Thessalians.[3] The force, at least 750 strong in 333, was subdivided into squadrons (*ilai*), but the ilarch mentioned in a dedication by twenty-three cavalrymen of (presumably) Boeotian Orchomenus was evidently not himself one of the dedicators, and may have been a Macedonian (or a Boeotian of another city?).[4] The 7,000 Greek infantry were commanded by Macedonian generals Antigonus, Balacrus, and Calanus in succession.[5] They had subordinate commanders, *hegemones*, corresponding in function probably to the taxiarchs of the Macedonian phalanx. The *hegemones* attended the councils-of-war summoned by Alexander before Issus and Gaugamela and were probably though not certainly Macedonians.[6]

For the Thessalians, there is a little more evidence for their presence in armies of Philip (as Thessaly's special relationship might lead us to expect), but unfortunately not for their organization. The military strength of a united Thessaly, described by Xenophon (and perhaps a

---

[1] Below, pp. 477 f. and 615 ff.　　　[2] D.S. 16. 85. 5.
[3] Berve 2 no. 779; ibid. no. 302.　　[4] *IG* VII. 3206, = Tod 197, 3.
[5] Berve 2 nos. 87, 199, 395.　　　　[6] Arr. *An.* 2. 7. 3; 3. 9. 3.

little larger than life), was genuinely very formidable, and that not only in the famous cavalry; the infantry strength, hoplites and peltasts, among the Greek states was second only to that of Macedonia itself.[1] In the campaigns of 353 and 352 in Thessaly itself, where Philip was present by invitation of 'the Thessalians' unable to cope with the dissident Pherae and its supporters, naturally these same Thessalians will have had their own army out in what strength they could, and in the great victory of 352 it is the Thessalian cavalry (and no Macedonian corps) that is named (by a Greek source) as having won the battle.[2] How many Thessalians in the 3,000 total for Philip's cavalry on this occasion? We can only guess, within the limits of 1,000 minimum and 2,000 maximum that seem reasonable. This by its nature was a special occasion. More interesting are the years in which Thessaly was under Philip's control, if we can see what use in practice he was able to make of Thessalian arms. In the Olynthian War none, very likely; nor any, probably, for the short Thracian campaign of 346.[3] But for the march on Thermopylae in 346 and the Amphictyonic invasion of Phocis, Philip was able certainly to call out a levy of the Thessalian league as its *archon*.[4] It was not till 344, in Illyria, that he is first seen using Thessalians in a purely 'Macedonian' war (and one in which, politically, no Thessalian could be even remotely interested.)[5] They appear again in Thrace in 341.[6] By now a tighter control had been imposed on Thessaly, through the tetrarchs (pp. 533 ff.). For the Chaeronea campaign, the only clue to the

---

[1] X. *HG*. 6. 1. 9 ('cavalry 6,000, hoplites more than 10,000, peltasts any number'); 6. 1. 19 ('cavalry, including allies, more than 8,000, hoplites at least 20,000, peltasts innumerable').

[2] D.S. 16. 35. 4 f.; for the campaigns of 353 and 352, pp. 267 ff.

[3] The argument here is from silence. But the allusions of Demosthenes to Thessaly in 349 do not invite us to think of a Thessalian levy being called out for the Olynthian War; and we know that there was trouble at Pherae early in 348. (See above, pp. 319 ff.) In 346, clearly, Thessalian interests were focused on Thermopylae and the Phocians (see next note).

[4] Aeschin. 2. 132; D.S. 16. 59. 2; D. 19. 320 (ἡνίκ' ἐστασίαζε μὲν αὐτῷ τὰ Θετταλῶν, καὶ Φεραῖοι πρῶτον οὐ συνηκολούθουν). Sordi (282) drew attention to this use by Demosthenes of συνηκολούθουν, and to ἀκολουθεῖν as the *terminus technicus* for the military obligation of the allies of Sparta (X. *HG* 5. 3. 26; 6. 3. 7; 6. 5. 1).

[5] D. loc. cit., where Sordi's inference from the words quoted in the previous note is convincing, that there was an occasion, recent in 343, when the Pheraeans had demurred at the levy. More adventurous is Sordi's assigning (286 and n. 6) to the Illyrian war of 344 the Thessalian 'spoils from the Illyrians' commemorated by twelve bronze cows dedicated to Athena Itonias and by the epigram of Theodoridas (*Anth. Pal.* 9. 743). If we could be certain that this affair belongs to the reign of Philip II at all, Sordi's date for it must surely be right. But Theodoridas wrote in the second half of the third century B.C., and the sculptor whom he names, Phradmon of Argos, was a contemporary of Pheidias and Polycleitus. (For T., P. Maas, *RE* v. 1804 (1934): for P., G. Lippold, *RE* 20. 1. 739 (1941).) If Theodoridas was wrong in naming Phradmon, and if we allow that an important victory over Illyrians, to which the Thessalians could lay some claim, is most unlikely at any date before Philip II, the possibility is still very strong that this victory belongs to some later date in Thessaly's long 'Macedonian' period.

[6] D. 8. 14.

presence of Thessalians is the vague 'Philip awaited those of his allies who had not yet joined him'.[1] Yet no one can doubt that the Thessaly which was to supply Alexander with 2,000 cavalry supplied Philip also with a substantial force among the 2,000 cavalry (unnamed) attributed to him at Chaeronea.[2]

Thessaly's relationship to Philip was indeed, however, a special and in some ways an equivocal one. Demosthenes, hostile witness though he was, yet did not depart far from the truth, we must suspect, in his remarks about the financial obligations of the Thessalian *koinon* to Philip as archon, and what 'the Thessalians' thought about them: the Thessalians, like anybody else, wanted their own money raised by their own government to be spent on their own concerns and not on those of Macedonia.[3] Broadly speaking one must think of their attitude to the military obligations as being very much the same, except in so far as some individuals or even some groups in Thessaly can be seen as having identified their own interests with those of Philip to a degree which really made a difference. This is not a negligible factor, probably. Especially, Thessalians of the class that served in the cavalry may have viewed service on Macedonian campaigns in company and competition with the Macedonians of the Companion class as something congenial in itself besides offering its chances of profit or advancement, however far afield it might take them. Even the narrower view of the military obligations will have included all Amphictyonic concerns obviously, and perhaps all things that arose out of Philip's foreign policy in relation to Greece itself.[4] But significantly (perhaps) the only two occasions (apart from 346) when we actually hear of the Thessalians serving with Philip are on the Illyrian campaign of 345 and on the Thracian campaign of 341/340 which culminated in the siege of Perinthus. A war that carried Macedonian arms nearly to the Adriatic, and one that completed the subjugation of eastern Thrace, were remote indeed from Thessalian League concerns. There was opposition in Thessaly to taking part; but the opposition that we hear of was centred in Pherae, the defeated city of 352 and the city with special reasons (Pagasae and Magnesia) for dragging its feet. No feet were dragged, so far as we learn, in the great force of Thessalian cavalry that was to accompany Alexander into Asia a few years later.[5]

---

[1] D.S. 16. 85. 3.

[2] See below, pp. 599 ff., for the probable role of cavalry at Chaeronea. The figure of 2,000 for Alexander's Thessalians (not accepted by Berve 1. 140 f., following Beloch 3². 2. 324) is arrived at by accepting D.S. 17. 17. 4 (1,800), +reinforcements (200) who arrived in spring 333 (Arr. *An*. 1. 29. 4).   [3] D. 1. 22; 2. 6.

[4] Amphictyonic, D. 19. 320, for the Thessalian forces employed against the Phocians in 346.

[5] For the vote of the Thessalians to meet their obligation to Alexander on his accession, Aeschin. 3. 161 (cf. D.S. 17. 4. 1; Just. 11. 3. 2). The decision then was to march on Athens, and Alexander as *archon* of Thessaly will have been requiring them to mobilize, so as to honour their obligation to him as *hegemon* of the Greeks.

These Thessalians, with their special relationship to the king of the Macedonians, became the one corps of all the Greek allies in Asia to take rank with the Macedonians among the principal agents of the great victories.

The organization of the Thessalian cavalry with Alexander was by squadrons (*ilai*), based on the cities, as might be expected.[1] On the analogy of the 'Companions', there would be at least eight squadrons (perhaps two from each tetrarchy?). Significantly, and conforming to the new prominence of Pharsalus in the political hierarchy (noticed below, pp. 539 ff.), it was a squadron of Pharsalus that became in this mass of cavalry an equivalent to the *agema* or Royal Squadron of Companions.[2] This squadron acted as the Guards of Parmenion, the general-in-chief of what may be called the (predominantly) Greek half of Alexander's army in the great battles. The Thessalians as a whole distinguished themselves greatly, especially at Issus, where they won the 'Corps of the Day' award, the 'prize' of the Persian headquarters at Damascus.[3] Their ilarchs may be presumed to have been Thessalian nobles of the city or cities that provided the *ile* concerned; but the general in command of the whole force, as might be expected, was always a Macedonian.[4]

The Thessalians apart, however, prior to the formation of the 'League of Corinth' the role of Greek allies in Philip's wars and armies probably was always a subordinate one, except of course for those local wars in which they themselves and not Philip were really the protagonists. The 'League of Corinth' itself, in this military connection, will be considered later.[5]

6. *Mercenaries*

Since mercenaries, especially Greeks, were very plentiful in Philip's lifetime, since he was the greatest and most active general of the age, and since after his earliest years he had more money to spend on war than any other government except Persia, or the Phocians while they controlled Delphi, it could be expected that mercenaries should have had an important place in his army. Up to a point this is so; but with significant limitations. Certainly the general impression derived from passages of both Demosthenes and Diodorus, that mercenaries provided a main, if not the main, source of his military strength, is in no way confirmed by

---

[1] Arr. *An.* 2. 11. 2; D.S. 17. 21. 4; 57. 4; 60. 8.

[2] Arr. *An.* 3. 11. 10.

[3] Plu. *Alex.* 24. 2 etc., with Hamilton's note ad loc.

[4] In succession Calas (Berve 2 no. 397), Alexander the Lyncestian (Berve 1 no. 37), and Philippus (Berve 2 no. 779).

[5] In Volume III.

any details of them that have survived.[1] As it happens, there seem to be only two occasions where mercenaries can be seen to be present along with Macedonians in an army commanded by Philip himself. One was in Thessaly, at the siege of Pharcedon.[2] The other occasion appears in the story of a great fight which once broke out between Macedonians and Greek mercenaries and in which Philip himself was badly hurt. When this happened we do not know, but obviously late in his reign, for Alexander is said to have boasted years after that he had saved Philip's life then.[3] The source and the context of this tale (Curtius Rufus working up to the murder of Cleitus) do not inspire confidence, but the incident itself probably is not a pure fiction. Its scale, however, could be anything, and certainly need not have been great in order to produce the effects described: a few hundred Greeks and Macedonians could have just as good a fight in a confined space as half the phalanx and five or ten thousand Greeks in the open.

The other references to mercenaries, however (ten altogether), all are concerned either with garrisons or occupation forces (four), or else with forces sent abroad with limited objectives (as we hear of them from Demosthenes in the Peloponnese, at Megara, in Euboea and elsewhere).[4] Only once are we given a figure for their strength—1,000 mercenaries at Porthmos in Euboea.[5] But one has the impression that it is never a great army that is in question, but detachments of at the most two or three thousand men, except probably for the mercenaries included in the army of 10,000 men which Philip put into Asia Minor in 336 under

---

[1] Diodorus (16. 8. 6) adds to his brief notice of Philip's acquisition of Crenides and its mines that this gave him the wealth with which to hire many mercenaries and to bribe politicians.

The well-known allusion of Demosthenes (2. 17) to the '*xenoi* and *pezhetairoi* who surround him, with their reputation for being so marvellous and so skilled in the arts of war' is not a serious contribution (as some have taken it) to our information about two of the categories of soldiers of Philip's army. It is clear from the context, and from what follows, that Demosthenes here talks of *pezhetairoi* without knowing what they were, and that really he is commenting on *hetairoi*, the fairly close circle of nobles and friends (see pp. 395 f.). So, too, *xenoi* here means 'friends', not 'mercenaries'. (See LSJ⁹ s.v. ξένος, for ξένοι καὶ φίλοι, of which this is a variant.)

More to the point is Demosthenes (1. 22), speaking in the same year as above (349) and foreseeing a contingency in which Philip might be short of money 'and have the greatest difficulty in paying his mercenaries' (τοῖς ξένοις). As evidence that Philip did employ mercenaries this is acceptable; but no one will take it as evidence that they were the only soldiers he employed, or the most important. At this date everybody employed mercenaries, more or less. And if Demosthenes chose his word here with studied care (probably he did not), he perhaps purposely avoided the alternative ('Macedonians') which reminded of the most formidable rather than a less formidable element of Philip's military strength.

[2] Polyaen. 4. 2. 18. When Pharcedon surrendered, he sent in 'the mercenaries' not the Macedonians present, presumably to occupy it as a garrison. See p. 271 above.

[3] Curt. Ruf. 8. 1. 24. Once I wrongly associated the incident with the Chaeronea campaign because of the allusion to Chaeronea in the previous sentence (Griffith, *Mercenaries* 11).

[4] The evidence is collected and discussed by Parke 162 ff.　　　　[5] D. 9. 58.

Parmenion.[1] This last was a force of several thousands presumably, and is the most important instance known to us of Philip's using mercenaries on a fairly large scale and in the main theatre of a major war; though it may be said that this too was a campaign of limited objectives and with the field army of Macedonia and the allies still undeployed.[2]

This probably gives the clue to Philip's policy in general on this. For the great occasions he was not short of troops, both infantry and cavalry of the highest quality, mostly Macedonians, but Thessalians too for cavalry especially; Thracians, Paeonians, and others for the light-armed work; and finally hoplites and more cavalry from the Greek allies of his last years. Though mercenaries cost no more probably than citizens or allies to feed and pay (they may have cost less), when the field army was mobilized in strength there was simply no point in adding 5,000 or 10,000 mercenaries to it just in order to have more mouths to feed.[3] The same mouths were best employed in the round-the-year garrison duty or the far-flung detachments abroad, uncongenial at times to citizens and even anti-social in their effects on the country, if Macedonians were continually drained away from their homes on duties of only secondary military importance. The same pattern seems right for the Greek mercenaries with Alexander later, especially for the garrison troops and small armies of occupation, as one would expect. Apart from Alexander's 'Old Brigade' of Greek mercenaries and the two contingents of Greek cavalry, who certainly did a very good job at Gaugamela, the mercenaries in general are hardly heard of in the great battles or the spectacular feats of arms in Asia.[4] Only the Cretan archers, specialists in an arm in which Macedonia itself and the Balkans in general were not strong, allow for more interesting thoughts. That Alexander inherited them from Philip seems reasonably certain.[5] Though they were only a few hundred strong they allow us to think that Philip did pay attention to the light-armed forces of his army as he built it up. In view of the number and the variety of his campaigns, many of them against very mobile enemies in the Balkans, it would be surprising if he had not. The Balkans themselves as he subjected the neighbouring kings to his rule or suzerainty could be called on to provide troops for the most mobile section of his own army, that irregular element which Demosthenes once alluded to as something characteristic and new.[6]

[1] D.S. 16. 91. 2; 17. 7. 10; Polyaen. 5. 44. 4; E. Badian, *ASI* 40 f. There is no need to discuss here the identification (or not) of these mercenaries with the force of Greek mercenaries in Alexander's army which became known as 'the Old Brigade' (οἱ ἀρχαῖοι καλούμενοι ξένοι, Arr. *An.* 3. 12. 2). See Berve 1. 144 f. (citing earlier literature); Parke 188 f.; Griffith, *Mercenaries* 28 f. Two years' service before 334 made them 'Old' by 330, probably.

[2] See below, p. 691.

[3] For pay of mercenaries (and citizens) Griffith, *Mercenaries* 294 ff. with 271 f.

[4] See in general (and for the 'Old Brigade') the works referred to at n. 1 above.

[5] Above, p. 431.　　　　　　　　　　　　　　[6] D. 9. 49 f. See above, p. 428.

In Alexander's army later the command of mercenaries above brigade level lay always with Macedonian generals. One Greek officer is known, probably brigadier (*hegemon*), Lycidas an Aetolian.[1] Under Philip too the name of just one *hegemon* survives (Docimus of Tarentum),[2] in the anecdote of how he lost his command when Philip found him bathing in warm water.[3] The only operational news is of two important Macedonian generals, Parmenion and Eurylochus, commanding mercenaries on two separate occasions in Euboea which were really diplomatic and political interventions at Eretria backed by force;[4] and of the Macedonian general Adaeus, nicknamed Cock (*Alektruon*), who commanded mercenaries perhaps based on Philippi, and had the worst of a battle with Chares.[5]

When our sources are so short on detail (for the reign of Philip), it is impossible to reconstruct much of the organization of his mercenaries, or even of their system of command. What mercenaries liked best, no doubt, was to be left alone to organize themselves; that is, to be commanded by *xenagoi* whom they knew, and who could be thought of as being in some sense 'on their side' in relation to the employer.[6] But we may surmise that the most successful employers, and those who got the best value for their money, were perhaps those who took some trouble to intervene in the private world of these professionals, who hoped first and most, and most naturally, to survive; and having survived, hoped to make their fortune, if possible without getting hurt. The employer who knew he was always going to need some mercenaries and might just as well have some decent ones, without the continual bother of recruiting new ones every few months, needed to do two things especially, things

---

[1] *Hegemon* was equivalent in rank to taxiarch of the phalanx, ilarch of the Macedonian cavalry (Arr. *An.* 2. 7. 3; 3. 9. 3). Lycidas was appointed to command the mercenaries of the army of occupation in Egypt, but he is not called *strategos*, though his command must have been of several thousand men, as is clear from Arrian's details (3. 5. 3).

The Macedonians who led the mercenaries under Alexander were the following (the numbers in brackets after the names are those assigned to them by Berve 2 *Prosopographie*): Andromachus (75), Caranus (412), Cleander (422), Clearchus (425), Erigyius (302), Menander (501), Menedemus (504), Menidas (508), Philippus (779).

[2] Polyaen. 4. 2. 1, 'took away his *hegemonia*'.

[3] Polyaen. ibid. The inference that his command was of mercenaries seems sound (so Parke, 158).

[4] D. 9. 58; see below, p. 546. On a third occasion in Euboea (the first, chronologically) the commander Hipponicus of 1,000 mercenaries was probably at Olynthus in 348 (p. 324). Eurylochus is probably the ambassador to Athens (with Parmenion and Antipater) of 346 and the *hieromnemon* of 342 (D. 19, 2 Hypoth. 5; *Syll.*[3] 242 B 6; Berve 2 no. 324).

[5] Theopomp. *FGrH* no. 115 F 249; Heraclides F 2 (J. M. Edmonds, *FAC* 2. 530–2).

[6] For *xenagoi*, recruiting, etc., Launey 1. 30 ff.; Griffith, *Mercenaries* 254 ff.; H. Schäfer, *RE* 2 Reihe, ix. 2. 1417–19 (confined almost to Sparta only). The evidence for *xenagoi* as commanders of mercenaries is mostly of Hellenistic date. But the name, originally the title of the Spartan officers who collected the levy of Sparta's Peloponnesian allies, was already used by Xenophon (*HG.* 4. 3. 15) to describe the Spartan officer commanding *mercenaries* at Coronea (394). Demosthenes in 352 could speak of people like Charidemus (πάντες οἱ ξεναγοῦντες οὗτοι) as a well-known class.

which did not come easily to every employer, but which had the merit of being really quite likely to achieve results. The first was to pay them well, and regularly, and without trying to fiddle or diddle their pay. The second was to get them interested in what they were supposed to be doing, which was to be earning their money (as opposed to merely drawing their money) from the employer himself.

One of the silliest stories about the Achaemenid kings of Persia (and unlike many stories of these kings this one was true), tells that they were notoriously bad payers of Greeks whose services they hired.[1] These heirs of the great conquerors, having collected most of the gold and silver coin and bullion in the civilized world of that time, proceeded to deposit it in selected treasuries here and there about their Empire, where they visited it and inspected it periodically, employing meanwhile a number of trustworthy civil servants to count it regularly, and a number more to count them, and so on; till the Empire became one big bureaucratic *paradeisos*, and meanwhile the king's representatives would drive hard bargains (which they had no intention of honouring in any case, if they could avoid it) with Greeks whose services they really needed quite badly sometimes. This mistake at all events, the result (I suppose) of throwing up a well-intentioned mountain of bureaucracy to buttress the molehill of a well-intentioned house-economy-aphorism ('you can't be too careful'), Philip of all men was not likely to commit. By Greek standards rich, very rich, he still managed to leave an empty Treasury when he died; and though his detractors would tell us (according to their persuasion) that he spent all he had on drink, girls, boys, or politicians, and no doubt he really was 'a willing spender' on all these things, yet a review of his life carries instant conviction that he spent willingly on soldiers too. The Second Book of the Pseudo-Aristotelian *Economica* abounds in tales of how the captains and the kings of the Greek world (and their agents and their satraps) tried sometimes for this reason or that to cheat their soldiers out of their pay;[2] but in this rogues' gallery Philip is nowhere to be found.[3] The Macedonian name was not so universally popular in Greece that Philip's reputation as a bad payer would not have survived if it had ever existed.

The basis for thinking this is to be found in (of all writers) Theopompus; the same Theopompus who was so strong on Sin ('he was

---

[1] *Hell. Oxy.* 19. 2 (Bartoletti).

[2] Polyaen. 4. 2. 6 shows Philip temporarily embarrassed by lack of ready money to pay soldiers (described as 'the Macedonians'); but he was able to humour them, and the situation was not a serious one.

[3] I use the cliché in a purely legalistic sense and without ethical implications. Many of the 'rogues', for example, were Athenian generals, the elected and duly accredited representatives of the *demos*, which had omitted on these occasions to provide the funds needed.

against it'); and by an amusing paradox, the same Theopompus in the very same passage.[1]

When Philip came to be very rich, he did not spend his money quickly, he really hurled it and threw it away. He was quite hopeless at finance, both himself and his immediate circle. The fact was, not one of them had any idea of living an orderly life or of 'management'. For this Philip himself was to blame. He did everything on impulse, ever ready to gain wealth and to give away. Of course he was really a *soldier* ($\sigma\tau\rho\alpha\tau\iota\omega\tau\eta s$): he had no time for keeping an account of income and expenditure.

(And then begin the well-known remarks about the vices and extravagance of the *hetairoi* his Companions.) 'A soldier' here is not intended as a compliment, obviously. The profession of arms has always lent itself easily to the derogatory thoughts of superior people, and the word *stratiotes* naturally acquired unfavourable nuances, many of them deserved.[2] How many of these Theopompus had in mind when he called Philip 'a soldier', we cannot know. (All of them, perhaps.) At the very least he is implying that a king who comes into money in a great way should use it like a general (*strategos*), not like a Tommy or a G.I.[3] One sees his point—and also his limitations. In general no doubt, Philip would have done well to be more careful. But not, we may think, where his dealings with soldiers were concerned. In those matters, 'you *can* be too careful'—very much too careful, as the military and naval history of fourth-century Athens reminds us in a melancholy way. Philip may not have understood 'management' ($\sigma\omega\phi\rho\acute{o}\nu\omega s$ $o\grave{i}\kappa\epsilon\hat{i}\nu$ $o\grave{i}\kappa\acute{i}\alpha\nu$), but he understood soldiers; and here it escaped Theopompus (a self-important intellectual) that the strong element of *stratiotes* in Philip contributed something to his make-up as *strategos*.

The story of Docimus, the brigadier from Tarentum who lost his regiment, is suggestive.[4] If he was indeed a *xenagos* (as seems very probable), it suggests that he had kept his own unit, and that Philip recruited and organized his mercenaries (or some of them) in this obviously economical way. But if Docimus was not allowed to do just as he liked in his own bath, it seems unlikely that he was allowed to do it with his unit. Philip, we know, was a disciplinarian and believed in hard training, for his Macedonians. The story of Docimus shows that he believed in something not unlike it for mercenary brigadiers, and by inference for mercenaries too. This can have been a daunting discovery, perhaps

---

[1] *FGrH* no. 115 F 224.

[2] There is a little of this in Thucydides's $\pi o\lambda\grave{v} s$ $\ddot{o}\mu\iota\lambda o s$ $\kappa\alpha\grave{i}$ $\sigma\tau\rho\alpha\tau\iota\acute{\omega}\tau\eta s$ (6. 24), and much more in the soldier types of New Comedy.

[3] For this distinction, cf. Plb. 1. 84. 6; 3. 105. 9, and Walbank's *Commentary* ad loc.; also Plb. 22. 10. 4.

[4] Polyaen. 4. 2. 1 (above, p. 441). D. was a high-ranking officer (*hegemon*).

a rare one; they were in Macedonia now, no slopping around any more. It could be very unpopular, no doubt. But soldiers will put up with a lot of inhumanity, if 'the system' itself is not inhumane, and their commanders who give them the orders. Philip himself was not stand-offish; and the Macedonian generals who led mercenaries from time to time, some of them nicer some nastier than others, would rather have been leading Macedonians no doubt, but they were real soldiers themselves, and will have known, the best of them, how to get the best out of not quite first-class material. And when all was said, if the pay was good and regular, this meant that somebody was taking some trouble. As Xenophon loved to emphasize, it was the commander who took thought for his men and was seen to do so, who won their devotion.[1]

Finally, for all soldiers it was important to be on the winning side. In an earlier age, confederates who took on Sparta had been prepared to give thought and trouble to ensuring that when the day of battle dawned, it should be their allies, not themselves, who actually tangled with the formidable Lakedaimonioi.[2] As the years of Philip's reign went by, something of this aura will have begun to surround the Macedonians. On the other hand the Macedonians already may have become detested. Clearly the enemies of Macedonia, both in 339 and in 336 and later, had no difficulty in raising large armies of mercenaries to fight Philip and Alexander.[3] But if this animosity did exist, it was not powerful enough or universal enough to affect Philip as an employer. He recruited them, a few thousands as he needed them, for Megara, for Euboea, for somewhere-in-Thrace. Alexander recruited them presently, in tens of thousands, for duties in Asia.

7. *The Siege-train*

This the most important in some ways of all the military developments of Philip's reign, in the sense that its influence on the political scene is the most obvious and far-reaching, is the one on which we are the least informed. Perhaps we are unlucky, in that Diodorus already in his Book 14 had spent time and space on describing a great stride forward in siege technique made by Dionysius I of Syracuse and his engineers which enabled him to capture Motya in 397.[4] Perhaps this may have influenced him not to spend time again on Philip now in this same connection, especially with no single page here so glorious as Motya to crown it. If so, we are greatly the losers. Yet the student of Philip will not have failed to notice as one of his earliest characteristics an ability to take Greek cities in a matter of weeks or months, instead of sitting round

---

[1] e.g., X. *HG*. 5. 1. 3 f.; 13 ff. (of Teleutias, brother of Agesilaus).
[2] X. *HG*. 4. 2. 18.　　　　[3] Below, p. 591.　　　　[4] D.S. 14. 41; 42. 1.

them for months or years in Athenian style (the Athenians being the acknowledged masters among the Greeks of siege warfare). To storm a city it was necessary to be able to go through or over its wall so as to get at its defenders and overwhelm them. The defenders had many means of preventing this, and, broadly speaking, before Motya the advantage lay heavily with the defence. The new factor at Motya had been the invention of the catapult, which enabled Dionysius to direct a 'firepower' on the defence that could immobilize them enough to stop them from doing all the things they needed to do in order to survive.[1]

E. W. Marsden in his masterly study has shown that the arrival of artillery as an effective force in Greek warfare came in two stages, of which the earliest catapults at Motya represented only the first.[2] These were, in effect, composite (laminated) bows set on frames, and drawn by means of a slide in place of the unaided human arm. They outranged the handbow, and at ranges below the maximum they delivered the bolt (arrow) with a much greater force. With the example of Motya, one could have thought that the early catapult (*gastraphetes*) would have swept through Greece like the mini-skirt through the western world in modern times. But not so. It trickled in, rather, via Athens (by 371/370), via Sparta (368).[3] Indeed Aeneas Tacticus ignored it still in the 350s when he wrote his 'Manual' for defenders of cities under siege, that interesting book which was partly out of date before it was written.[4] Greek cities were short enough of capital for military expenditure; and they had lost something, too, of the avid imperialism that would have filled fifth-century Athens with catapults if they had been invented in time. The Phocians, however, in the 350s when they had occupied Delphi, could not afford not to have everything that was going. Their day of glory in Thessaly (above, p. 269) shows them with the small 'anti-personnel' stone-thrower catapults (*petroboloi*) which represented the most in this direction that the limited power of the *gastraphetes* could achieve.[5] This harrowing experience of being on the receiving end of an artillery performance is seen by Marsden as an important influence on Philip, and I dare say he is quite right.[6]

For the second stage of the catapult, the introduction of torsion to put a much greater power behind the bolt on release (or behind a stone large enough, now, to use against masonry) does seem to belong to the

---

[1] D.S. 14. 42. 1.

[2] E. W. Marsden, *Greek and Roman Artillery: Historical Development* (Oxford, 1969), especially 5–17, 48–56. My debt to Marsden in this section is very great, as will be clear.

[3] *IG* II². 1422, 8 f. (371/370); 1440, 48 (350) (Athens): Plu. *Mor.* 191 E, with X. *HG.* 7. 1. 28 ff., D.S. 15. 72. 3 f. (Sparta). Cf. Marsden 65–9 on the diffusion of artillery in general, after 397.

[4] Aen. Tact. 32. 8 mentioned catapults once, as we should say 'in a footnote'.

[5] Marsden 59.   [6] Marsden 59.

time of Philip, and probably to his later years. Nobody in antiquity actually ascribes the invention of the torsion catapult to anybody in particular. Marsden argues convincingly for Philip and Macedonia as the initiator and the place, relying mainly on two Athenian catalogue-inscriptions which list (the first, dated 338–326) at least ten 'catapults with hair-springs' (= torsion), and (the second, 330/29) eleven 'frames of the catapults from Eretria'—where the frames (πλαίσια) are accepted as torsion-catapult frames (which the technical writers later call πλίνθια).[1] The connection with Philip, as Marsden shows it, is delicate, but accept-able. The catapults 'from Eretria' are explained as booty from the occasion in 341 when the Athenians joined in expelling Philip's protégé the tyrant Clitarchus (p. 548 below). There is no other occasion of which we know that does explain them, and this explanation seems good; the tyrant's modern weapons, obtained from Philip, shared out by agree-ment between the restored *demos* of Eretria and the *demos* of Athens that had joined in the liberation?

Here, then, is the torsion-catapult in 340, the very year in which we see it, presumably, in action at the sieges of Perinthus and Byzantium, still in its experimental stages as Marsden suggests.[2] For it is not until the siege of Tyre seven years later that we find the sure indication that the experiments have come to full fruition, in the machine powerful enough to project great stones against the city walls.[3] These, evidently, were exciting years, on the drawing-boards and in the workshops some-where in Macedonia. Something of this, perhaps, came through in the contemporary garble of the Athenian theatre (in 345 probably), where (in the right mood) Macedonians and their catapults could be something to raise a laugh.[4] (No laughing matter, however, in the days after Chaeronea—until a peace had been safely negotiated.) But not a detail survives of how it was all done; only the name of Philip's chief engineer, a Thessalian Polyidus (his city unknown), and of two of his pupils Diades and Charias who made their name later with Alexander, for whom also a Macedonian Posidonius designed a famous siege-tower (*helepolis*). To infer two generations of engineers here from the master–pupil relationship, which would invite us to think of a chronological spread comparable with the active lives of (say) Plato and Aristotle, Isocrates and Ephorus, and so on, obviously would be unjustified. But it does suggest a 'school' of Polyidus in Macedonia extremely well

---

[1] *IG* II². 1467 B, col. ii 48–56; ibid. 1627 B 328–41: Marsden 56–62.
[2] D.S. 16. 74–6; cf. Marsden 59–62. [3] D.S. 17. 42. 7; 45. 2.
[4] Mnesimachus, *Philip* F 7 (J. M. Edmonds, *FAC* 2 (1959) 366–8). The date, suggested by Edmonds (ibid. ad F 8, with its allusion to, presumably, Halus), seems reasonably secure. The ten lines of F 7 describe Macedonians at dinner, swallowing swords and lighted torches for food and wine, Cretan arrow-heads and bits of spears for dessert in place of nuts, with shields and cuirasses for cushions, slings and bows for footstools, and catapults for garlands.

established for years during Philip's reign, with its ramifications in the practical field.

The record of Philip's early years, which included Amphipolis actually taken by storm after a siege (357), suggests strongly that he was giving full attention to this branch of warfare.[1] Especially, though the invention of the catapult at Syracuse did not spread quickly, it was recognized eventually as an essential aid for defenders no less than attackers of cities (this is seen most clearly at Perinthus later).[2] Catapults shooting from the towers of the walls were the best deterrents to besiegers who needed to close in with rams or ladders or for any other purpose. If cities such as Amphipolis, Potidaea, Methone, Olynthus, were liable to possess some non-torsion-catapults by this time, it can scarcely be believed that Philip began to execute designs on these places without possessing the new weapons himself. The 'machines' which he brought into action against Amphipolis need not have been catapults; for the word included rams and towers, even scaling-ladders. His 'tower' which we hear of at Methone does not prove that this must have been a tower providing the platforms for catapults; for towers had long been used for archers and slingers before catapults were invented.[3] The probability that he was using catapults in these sieges remains a general one (and strong). At Olynthus (348) it can be seen as certain, in the arrow-heads identified by their size as catapult bolts, and used here by both sides in the siege.[4] By 340 (as we have seen), Polyidus had made his break-through, and the new torsion catapults presumably were among the battery directed against Perinthus and Byzantium.

By the end of his reign (and no doubt long before it) Philip had his siege-train, a permanent and important adjunct to the field army on many (most?) of its campaigns (we see it with Alexander on the Balkan campaign of 335).[5] The men who comprised it were invaluable, certainly; but most probably we need to guard against overestimating their numbers and especially of thinking in terms of a long and 'soft' tail of 'civilians in uniform', tagging along in the rear on all occasions so as to be there on the occasion now and then when they were needed. Many hands were needed, true, in a siege, for the rams, for works of undermining, for moving up the siege-towers into position; but the hands will have been supplied by the infantry, and by any local labour on the spot.[6] Perhaps Alexander's performance once in Sogdiana may set the siege-train for us in scale and perspective. There, even the scaling-ladders had to be

---

[1] D.S. 16. 8. 2.   [2] D.S. 16. 74. 4, 75. 2 especially.

[3] D.S. 16. 8. 2 (Amphipolis); 31. 6; 34. 4 f. (Methone).

[4] D. M. Robinson, *Olynthus* 10, 382 ff., with Plates; cf. Snodgrass 116 f.

[5] Arr. *An.* 1. 6. 8.

[6] D.S. 16. 74. 2 f., for 'relays' of hands taking over in succession, to keep up the pressure. (On this phrase, R. K. Sinclair, *CQ* N.S. 10 (1960) 249 ff.)

knocked up on the spot by the infantry, so many by each company. But the catapults of course were present and ready, and the *katapelta-phetai* to fire them.[1]

The men of the siege-train itself will have been the specialists. The construction of a siege-tower needed an architect or engineer, and a team of good carpenters and joiners (not necessarily civilians?) under two or three skilled foremen. The same engineer will have designed the cata-pults, for Marsden's description leaves no room for doubt that this was a work of exceptional skill, and that the torsion-catapult in particular was an individual production. Finally the marksmen were specialists too. The early catapults (*gastraphetai*) called for considerable strength and stamina, but also, one must think, for experience and skill in sight-ing and lining up on a target. Much more so the torsion-catapult, as Marsden shows.[2] Just who these marksmen were, we do not know. As it happens, the only one of them in this period who is identified, at Athens, was a foreigner from Asia Minor, a Mysian.[3] It would be surprising if the marksmen of this generation were not, most of them, ex-bowmen (just as many of the earliest chauffeurs were ex-coachmen and ostlers). Macedonia produced its own archers, as we have seen, but not very many (pp. 430 f. above). The *katapeltaphetai* were recruited probably from the small number of specialists who had the skill and without regard to their place of origin. For their number we are to think in terms of dozens or scores rather than hundreds, and there would seem to be obvious advantages in each man's having his own machine which he would know intimately and maintain himself. This very small corps was the permanent element in the siege-train, and can be seen as the creation of Philip. We do not hear of him using it in the field, but most probably he did, since it accompanied Alexander in 335 on his Balkan campaigns, and was able at a moment's notice to open fire covering the withdrawal of a rearguard at a river crossing, with an effectiveness that argues experience.[4] When we read of Alexander later, at Tyre, collecting 'many engineers from Cyprus and all Phoenicia', we need not be surprised that they succeeded (under direction, presumably) in presenting him with many new catapults, but we can still wonder perhaps who took them over and operated them, and whether they hit anything they aimed at.[5] The scale of the targets and the length of the siege perhaps enabled them to 'come good' in the end.

Philip's failure in two great sieges, Perinthus and Byzantium, should not deceive us into underrating him as a Poliorcete. He was not in the same class as Alexander, certainly, partly because, as Marsden suggests, 'the machines' were still not fully developed. One senses, too, a different

---

[1] Arr. *An.* 4. 2. 1 and 3.   [2] Marsden 67–8.   [3] *Syll.*[3] 3. 1249.
[4] Arr. *An.* 1. 6. 8.   [5] Arr. *An.* 2. 21. 1.

mental approach, one which did not include Alexander's ferocious commitment to taking Tyre or 'the Sogdian Rock' as a personal challenge (though there were indeed impeccable political and strategic reasons for taking both). Balanced against other political reasons, the time factors and priorities elsewhere, Philip came to see that Perinthus and Byzantium after months of hard slogging had become literally more bother than they were worth, and he was able to pocket his pride and offer them a peace treaty in place of the hero's climax of fire and the sword. In purely military terms this could be seen as weak, and in political terms too, if it had encouraged Greek cities everywhere to look to their walls and their catapults and put a cheerful courage on. But in practice the effect fell far short of this, obviously. The general who could take Amphipolis and Olynthus was going to be able to take most places if he gave his mind to it. So thought the Athenians after Chaeronea, when they accepted a peace treaty which closed their future as a great power but which seemed generous and attractive in comparison with the alternative. This was no longer the age of Archidamus son of Zeuxidamus the king of the Lacedaemonians, when an unchallenged sea power and the Athens–Piraeus fortress had given the Athenians an invulnerable 'island' as the basis for their strategy and power. Now, they had the walls still and the ships (still unchallenged)—but the risk of trusting to them was too great for them to choose.

XIII

PHILIP AMONG THE GREEK STATES, 346

1. *The Delphic Amphictyony*

THERE was something to celebrate at Delphi when the Greeks gathered for the great Games and festival in the late summer of 346.[1] True, the embittered politics and the ten years of war had brought Phocis to the dust, had left the Athenians smarting still under this last humiliation, and left Sparta no better pleased to see the Boeotians relieved of their great troubles. But apart from the corresponding jubilation on the other side (of those who had cause to curse the Phocians), honest men in a hundred cities could rejoice that the god was avenged at last, that he was being honoured again after ten years with the full concourse that was his due, that peace had come to the Greeks in place of the wars that had been too much with them.

Honest men need not be simpletons, however. It did not need the honour conferred on Philip, of presiding over this renewal of the festival, to show the world who was the master now;[2] the master not as political despot but as the contriver, the artist almost, of this dénouement. The Greeks could appreciate—none better—a 'tearless battle', one which brought victory cost free to the victors.[3] But these surrenders at Thermopylae and in Phocis were something new: they were the battles which were never even joined. Statesmen up and down Greece could appraise to the full the patience, the finesse, the timing, by which Philip had ensured that the plums should drop—one, two—into his hand outstretched. But the whole Greek world, if it missed something of the method in all its detail, lost little of the whole effect. This was an amazing demonstration of power, more effective in its lesson than a storming of Thermopylae followed by an invasion of Phocis under arms succeeding where the Boeotians had failed again and again. It must be doubted whether any victory in the field can ever have delighted Philip himself so much as this chess-like combination presenting his opponents with no

---

[1] For the celebrations of Philip and his circle, D. 19. 128–30 (not without malice of course); Aeschin. 2. 162.

[2] D. 5. 22; D.S. 16. 60. 2. Philip had ended the war now as commander of the Amphictyonic forces, which made the honour closely appropriate.

[3] Plu. *Ages.* 33 (cf. D.S. 15. 72. 3), for the name given to a Spartan victory of 368.

reasonable alternative to resigning with the pieces still intact on the board.

Tearless the victory was. But the consequences reached no less far than if half the blood and tears of Greece and Macedonia had been spilt for it. Peace and alliance already made with Athens and her allies, the Phocian surrender and the gathering at Delphi gave Philip the means to exert an influence far and wide throughout Greece. The occasion itself was a *coup de théâtre*. The vehicle by which it was open to him now to further his aims, plans, a programme for the future if he had one, was the Delphic Amphictyony.

The first act, we must suppose, of the Amphictyonic Council in its first session now was to expel the Phocians from membership and to award the two Phocian votes in the Council to Philip.[1] That this was not done merely *honoris causa* goes without saying. It was done, we may be sure, after Philip had told his Thessalian friends and subjects that this was what he wanted. No doubt he informed and consulted his Boeotian allies too.[2] But the votes in the Council of the Thessalians and their *perioikoi* were twelve out of the twenty-two.[3] This initiative of Philip is not to be taken as a matter of course. It is distinctly an interesting one, when the character and venerable tradition of the Amphictyony are remembered. This was a community of 'neighbours', peoples who lived near enough to two ancient cult centres, Anthela by Thermopylae and Delphi, to develop a common attachment. 'The Ionians' were Amphictyons, but of the Ionians it was the Athenians and the Euboeans who were represented on the Council, because of their proximity. G. Daux has shown conclusively that though one of the two Dorian votes belonged to the Dorians of the Peloponnese, it was exercised always by Corinthian, Argive, Sicyonian, Epidaurian, Troezenian, Megarian, Aeginetan, Phleiasian representation, and never by a Spartan representative; nor did Daux fail to point out why—because Sparta was too far away to be a genuine 'neighbour'.[4]

The Amphictyony was a very old club, and in some ways of course a rather old-fashioned one. The membership by *ethne* belonged to an era before the fullest development of the *polis* had made it the modern power-unit of Greece.[5] The archaic membership corresponded to some religious and social needs of a neighbourhood (Central Greece).

---

[1] D.S. 16. 60. 1; D. 5. 14, with *Hypoth.* 2.   [2] D.S. 16. 59. 4; 60. 1.

[3] Twenty-two because there will not have been two Phocian hieromnemons present and voting at this meeting. For the Amphictyonic membership, see G. Daux, 'Remarques sur la composition du conseil amphictionique', *BCH* 81 (1957) 95 ff., with a definitive list, and discussion of the three lists preserved (of Aeschines, Theopompus, and Pausanias), 100 ff.

[4] Daux, loc. cit., esp. 104 ff. Sparta was enabled later to use occasionally the 'metropolitan' vote of the Dorians of Doris in central Greece.

[5] Aeschin. 2. 116; M. Sordi, *BCH* 81 (1957) 38 ff., has some interesting things to say on his. See below, pp. 465 ff.

Possessing a certain prestige and a value as an organ for publicity or propaganda, it could be used on occasion by those who wanted to play politics in it and through it. This had been done most conspicuously since 367/6 by the Boeotians, aspiring after Leuctra to a hegemony in Greece to which nothing in their past seemed to entitle them, and hoping to make of the Amphictyonic Council an organization through which they could not only control and discipline their own Central Greek allies but even come to exercise a jurisdiction which could be panhellenic or nearly so.[1] The results however were not happy. An Amphictyonic jurisdiction found itself trespassing too often on ground where other and less archaic jurisdictions existed. For the Amphictyonic Council to arraign Sparta for having seized the Cadmea of Thebes in time of peace and to fine the Spartans 1,000 talents may strike us as both spirited and just.[2] But in the eyes of the Greeks of this generation the only court competent to do this must have been a panhellenic congress of the Greek cities sitting in judgement on a breach of the *koine eirene* (the King's Peace of 386, at the time of the Cadmea incident). And in reality of course the only practical way of getting 1,000 talents (or 1 talent) out of the Spartans for their misdemeanour was by marching to Sparta with the hoplite army and trying to find it there. There is no sign that anybody ever really expected Sparta to pay this Amphictyonic fine; and Sparta never did. In the same way (though on a different plane), the condemnation to exile by the Amphictyonic Council of a citizen of a city which itself belonged to the Amphictyony (a Delphian) could be officially recorded as invalid by another city (Athens) which belonged to the Amphictyony, but which was opposed to the Boeotian-inspired political ramp which presumably had secured the condemnation.[3] This was an infringement of the autonomy of the city (Delphi), the basis of every *koine eirene* that had ever been ratified.

These incidents, and of course the final incident of the fining (excessively) of the Phocians which had brought on the Sacred War, show clearly the limitations of the Amphictyonic Council, at least in Boeotian hands, as an instrument of discipline or of political management.[4] The Greeks were not in the habit of being dictated to by this Old Boys' Club, not even Greeks who were members of it. And there were too many of the Greeks to whom, being outside the Amphictyony altogether, it was simply an irrelevance when viewed as an international force or an exponent of international law;[5] or, to be more precise, they could co-operate with Amphictyonic initiatives when these coincided with their

---

[1] See, on the whole background, Sordi, loc. cit. 40 ff., 65 ff. [2] D.S. 16. 29. 2 f.
[3] *Syll.*³ 175, 15 ff. (363/362). [4] D.S. 16. 23. 3 ff.
[5] In the Peloponnese, the Arcadians, Achaeans, Eleans: the Aetolians and all north-west Greece: to say nothing of Crete and the islands.

own interests, and could dismiss them as irrelevant when they did not.[1] As a ruler of Greece, with its archaic allocation of the Council votes to the 'neighbour' *ethne*, some of them not even free peoples but *perioikoi* and subjects of someone or other in Thessaly, no institution could be less acceptable to, or its *dogmata* less accepted by, the Greek cities in general, accustomed now to the principle that every city great or small should be free and autonomous, and to the practice of each city being represented at panhellenic congresses, each member-city represented on the Council of the Athenian Confederacy. It was not, therefore, as a means to assuming a political control over all Greece that Philip obtained now the two Phocian votes on the Amphictyonic Council. As a member now with his own votes and those of the Thessalian bloc he could produce δόγματα τῶν Ἀμφικτυόνων at will and to order. He had the power too to enforce them, as the Boeotians had not had, even all over Greece if he insisted. But this still did not make them acceptable to the Greeks. Philip knew well the recent Amphictyonic history, of strife, bungling, and failure, and he knew the political climate of contemporary Greece; he had lived through these things. The place of the Amphictyony in his plans now must have been subject to these limitations inherent in the Amphictyony itself.

There was no question of the Macedonian *ethnos* achieving membership now in place of the Phocians.[2] The Macedonians dwelling beyond the mightiest barrier of all Greece, Olympus, could hardly be called 'neighbours' (indeed they could hardly be called Greeks, unless one particularly needed to call them that for some reason).[3] To Philip himself these disqualifications did not attach quite in the same way or to the same degree. Apart from his Heraclid genealogy, as head of the Thessalian League his claim to 'neighbourship' was at least neither purely frivolous nor blatantly disreputable: it was bogus, as all neutral observers could see, but only his enemies in Greece need be disgusted by it, his friends could laugh or shrug it off.[4] It was on Philip personally

---

[1] e.g. Demosthenes (5. 18), when enumerating states hostile to Athens who might be glad to join in an 'Amphictyonic' war against her, along with five 'members' named also Megalopolis which belonged to a non-member *ethnos*, the Arcadian.

[2] Pausanias (10. 8. 2) mistakenly wrote of this occasion 'the Macedonians gained entry . . .', influenced by the usage of his contemporaries (10. 8. 4, 'The Amphictyons of my own time numbered thirty: from Nicopolis and from Macedonia and from the Thessalians . . .' etc.), of the Roman province of Macedonia.

[3] Isoc. 5. 108, οὐχ ὁμοφύλου γένους: Isocrates in this work addressed to Philip himself, naturally does not intend to be other than courteous. Yet this phrase occurs in a context where he is stressing the fundamental difference between Greeks and Macedonians: the Greeks would not tolerate monarchy. He adds (5. 107) that in this they were different from all other peoples, for whom monarchy was a necessity. He does not call the other peoples 'barbarians', but he does proceed to call the Macedonians, here, 'non-Greek'.

[4] D. 5. 14 (spoken at just this time), τοὺς συνεληλυθότας τούτους καὶ φάσκοντας Ἀμφικτύονας νῦν εἶναι . . .

and on his descendants that membership was conferred.[1] The effect was certainly to increase his stature in the eyes of the world, and his presidency at these Games heightened the effect. Demosthenes at this moment counted this among the ambitions just realized by him, along with the occupation of Thermopylae and the glory from having ended the war; and there seems no reason to quarrel with his verdict.[2]

Meanwhile the Amphictyons went to work. For the Phocians there was mercy up to a point; their lives were spared. But they must work their passage. Disarmed and dispersed from their dismantled cities into villages they were condemned to pay 60 talents a year until the account should be squared, the value of their thefts from the temple paid back in full.[3] There was a rough justice in this; and their avenging Furies, the Thessalians and Boeotians, though they were unable to have them exterminated as probably they hoped, had the satisfaction of knowing that they had reduced them to a condition of political nullity and defencelessness and to a life of hard work with heavy taxation for the foreseeable future.[4] Presumably it was Philip who told his friends that they must not press for the extreme penalty; and after this long, savage, and damaging war his treatment can be seen as lenient, though the recollection of Olynthus will warn us not to think that humanitarian motives ruled him most. The truth was that if the Phocians were exterminated Phocis itself inevitably would be occupied by its neighbours, and most of it by the Boeotians, a strategic asset to Thebes which he was not prepared to yield. It may be an accident of historiography, but it is still of interest, that Diodorus' source here, who knew about the intrinsic value of the thefts,[5] and was absolutely scandalized by their impiety, was not concerned (or not in any way that Diodorus found worth repeating) by the fact that irreplaceable objects of art had been melted down into money. Were the Greeks, then, more philistine than we might care to think? Probably. The keenest sense of period in art no doubt does belong most to ageing civilizations of failing creativity. And likely enough any Greeks who thought about it reckoned that anything Theodorus of Samos had made for Croesus 200 years ago, their own best goldsmiths could make as well or better now. Anyway, the crime of vandalism, so far as we know, was not among those for which the Phocians now were made to pay.

The friends of the Phocians came next, and those who had helped them. The Spartans were expelled along with the Phocians from the

---

[1] D.S. 16. 60. 1.	[2] D. 5. 22.

[3] D.S. 16. 60. 2; Tod, *GHI* no. 172, with commentary, especially pp. 213 f.

[4] For this sorry state of the Phocians (presumably exaggerated), D. 19. 81 and 204. For the proposal in the Amphictyonic Council to execute all the adult Phocian men, Aeschin. 2. 142. (The women and children to be enslaved, no doubt.)

[5] D.S. 16. 56. 6: 10,000 talents by this version (there were evidently more extravagant ones).

Amphictyony.[1] They certainly had been good allies, as good as their powers had allowed; and in their penalty we are to see, no doubt, the hand of the Boeotians above all. Philip could have spared them, no doubt, by directing the Thessalian bloc to vote against a Boeotian proposal. He judged that in this matter the Boeotians had better have their way.[2]

The interesting thing now is that Athens was not treated likewise. Her services to the Phocians in the war had been less than those of Sparta, but in 352 they had been decisive for the time being. Her blatantly pro-Phocian sympathies in these recent days of the invasion and surrender could be interpreted as provocative or at the least disloyal. She had sent no troops on request to join the invading army. She sent no hieromnemon to take his seat with the Amphictyonic Council, and was facing now a demand from the Council for her formal agreement to the election of Philip. She sent no *theoroi* or other representatives of the city to the Pythian festival.[3] It cannot be denied that any Amphictyon who hated Athens as the Thebans hated Sparta had ground here for proposing her expulsion: Sparta might be the worse offender because of the unpaid fine, but the Athenians compensated by their intransigence of this moment. More, any who wanted Athens humbled in war or destroyed had the train ready laid and waiting only for the match. The Council had only to fine the Athenians now a sum which they would not contemplate paying, for the *casus belli* to be complete. Demosthenes himself at this time felt obliged to warn the *demos* of the real danger, as he saw it, of an Amphictyonic War if they persisted in their nonconformity.[4]

It is true, no doubt, that the Athenians had no feud with any Amphictyonic member quite so deadly as the feud of the Thebans and Sparta. But neither the Thebans nor the Thessalians had any reason to love Athens of recent years, and the probability is that at this time they would not have been averse to participating in an Amphictyonic war against her.[5] It does seem clear that any initiative in the Council towards conciliation and a mending of the bad relations, or at least towards refusing to be provoked, must have come from Philip himself and from no one else. If this is true, it is important. It means that Philip still, even now with Thermopylae in his hands with all its consequences, had reasons to value the peace and alliance with Athens which he himself had sought in the first instance. Whatever the reasons were (and they may appear as Philip's future plans become known to us), they were still encouraging him to hope that the Athenian alliance might yet be

---

[1] Paus. 10. 8. 2. As Dorians the Spartans had belonged, though because of their geographical remoteness they had not held or shared one of the two Dorian votes.
[2] Above, pp. 342 f.   [3] D. 19. 111, 128, 181.   [4] D. 5. 14 ff., especially 18 f.
[5] D. 5. 18 f.

nourished into something serviceable. The contrast between the expulsion of Sparta and the forbearance towards Athens seems too striking to allow of any other interpretation.[1]

2. *The Greek States*

Athens, then, in this autumn of 346 Philip was treating as a new ally whom he wanted to keep: Sparta he was at no pains to conciliate or cultivate (and in this he gave pleasure incidentally to the Boeotians). What can we see, or divine, of his relations with other Greek states? One of the more sensible and practical sections of the *Philip* of Isocrates is that in which he tells Philip that he has only to gain the co-operation of the leading four Greek cities and the rest of Greece will give him no trouble.[2] 'Sensible' and 'practical' are relative terms, however, and it is certainly right to recall that Isocrates' long and blameless life (he is ninety now), though it has always been concerned with the study of contemporary politics, has never found expression in anything except words about them: Isocrates has never been obliged actually to do anything, about anything. This limited experience of life is reflected in the deceptive simplicity of his suggestions to Philip; for the political journalist all things can be simple if that is how he wants them. Thus,

What you must do, I say, is this. Without losing sight of your own personal interests, you must try to reconcile (διαλλάξαι) the cities of Argos and Sparta and Thebes and Athens: if you can get these to combine (συστῆσαι), you will easily bring peace and unity to the rest (ὁμονοεῖν ποιήσεις). They are all under the influence of those I have mentioned, and when they are frightened they run to whichever of them it may be, for support. And so, by persuading only four cities to co-operate (εὖ φρονεῖν), you will be the salvation of the rest.[3]

Q.E.D.

And yet, how did one 'reconcile' Argos and Sparta, as a matter of interest? In all their history as it is known to us, this had happened so far perhaps only once, and then by a Spartan intervention in a revolutionary situation at Argos, so as to overthrow the democracy and instal an oligarchy which would be more friendly: and it lasted about six weeks.[4] Nor was it much easier to reconcile Sparta and Thebes. Many Thebans still could remember the Spartan garrison in their Cadmea, and how it got there. Most adult Spartiates could remember Messenia as theirs, and how it was wrenched from them and given independence by

---

[1] Athens lost her προμαντεία, which was conferred on Philip (D. 19. 327).

[2] Isoc. 5. 9, with 5. 30. Among the wide literature on Isocrates, best in general is Momigliano, *FM* 183 ff.; and on his *Philip*, S. Perlman, 'Isocrates' "Philippus"—a Reinterpretation', *Historia* 6 (1957) 306–17, with bibliography (= Perlman, *PA* 103 ff.).

[3] Isoc. 5. 30; cf. 50–5 for further remarks on Sparta, Argos, and Thebes.

[4] Thuc. 5. 76–82 (418/17). Isocrates did try to meet this criticism (5. 39 ff.), but his attempt was painfully inadequate, a mere expression of wishful thinking.

the Thebans. These things were hard to forgive; and both sides knew well that they were not forgiven. Thebes and Athens could be reconciled; they had been, in the years of Spartan domination.[1] But Euboea and Oropus were living reminders of one bad turn which each owed the other, and the memory of Plataea was a third. It was going to take another real fright to reconcile these two; and where was the fright coming from? An inconvenient line of thought, this, for the political journalist addressing the descendant of Heracles, who was not supposed to be going to frighten any Greeks (any more), but only monsters and barbarians.[2]

The descendant himself (we saw) knew already that, good policy though it might be to please all the Greeks and win their trust and friendship, it simply was not possible to please all the Greeks all the time. Good friends could only be made at the expense of making some enemies. Some Greeks had got to be offended. Of the utopian *ménage à cinq* which Isocrates proffered, Philip's realistic eye had detected that there was one whose room was worth more than her company; Sparta. Only Athens would miss Sparta if she were given the old heave-ho; and Athens would not miss her much. For Thebes and Argos, this treatment of Sparta was a *sine qua non* of their own co-operation. Thebes was an ally whom Philip could not afford to take for granted. Demosthenes reminded the Athenians at this very time that these recent events had not brought unalloyed pleasure to Thebes (or to the Thessalians); and Demosthenes here seems likely to be quite right.[3] Philip had extracted the Thebans from their terrible impasse of the Phocian war and enabled them to repair the Boeotian League with the lost cities, but the war had altered their whole situation in a way which British readers at least will understand. Their own resources had been overtaxed, while their big ally had grown bigger and had taken up the dominating position in Central Greece which before had been theirs in their best days: and this in turn had cost them their power of influencing or dictating events further afield, in the Peloponnese especially. Demosthenes expressed the Theban loss in terms of prestige ($\pi\rho\grave{o}s$ $\delta\grave{\epsilon}$ $\tau\iota\mu\grave{\eta}\nu$ $\kappa\alpha\grave{\iota}$ $\delta\acute{o}\xi\alpha\nu$ $\alpha\check{\iota}\sigma\chi\iota\sigma\tau\alpha$—5. 20 f.). But it looks as if the loss was even more serious in terms of relative power, and this fact cannot have escaped the Thebans. Any who could not see it for themselves had the new set-up in the Amphictyony to spell it out for them.

As for Argos, she looks lucky, in a way, to be included in Isocrates' 'big four', for in terms of power she certainly counted for less than the others. As a candidate for reconciliation, however, Argos obviously

---

[1] As Brunt put it wittily, 'allies in perpetuity from 395 to 386 and again from 378 to 371' (*CQ* N.S. 19 (1969) 245).

[2] Isoc. 5. 109–15. [3] D. 5. 20 ff.

ranked very high, and this may have influenced Isocrates in his choice.[1] Moreover when Philip found time to read this lengthy piece, the allusions to Argos will not have bored him, for the Peloponnese now was becoming his most obvious field for 'growth'. We have seen how, in 348 before the peace of Philocrates, he had formed certain connections there already.[2] Though these cannot be assessed with any accuracy, it seems that it might be unwise to underestimate them; for Isocrates writes now of the Peloponnese in general terms which show that it was prominent in the talk and speculation of these months (summer 346).[3] An alarmist view of Philip and his plans was widespread in Greece.

Of your power they say that its increase is not meant to do Greece any good, but harm, and that you have planned to attack us all for a long time, and now you are intending ostensibly to reinforce Messene, if you succeed in settling the Phocian problem, but your real intention is to conquer the Peloponnese. You have already Thessaly and Thebes and all the Amphictyonic states ready to march with you, and Argos, Messene, Megalopolis, and many of the others are ready to join you and destroy Sparta. If you succeed in this, you will easily become master of the rest of Greece.[4]

All this Isocrates dismisses as 'rubbish', and he was vindicated by the immediate outcome. But he did not invent it, for it was both uncomplimentary to Philip and unlikely to be welcome. Those who distrusted him at this time feared the worst; and in the longer term the event was to prove them right. Though Philip made no large-scale invasion of the Peloponnese, he was to continue in the next two years the policy of infiltration, supporting the enemies of Sparta.[5] It was not the fact of his Peloponnesian ambitions, but only their timing, that his enemies now were getting wrong.

3. *Philip and Persia*

It is at this point in Philip's reign (in 346) that his name first becomes connected in our literary sources with what may be called 'a Persian policy'; or even '*the* Persian policy'. Diodorus, after describing his settlement at Delphi and his return to Macedonia in an odour of sanctity and no small glory, adds that he had done much to prepare the way for his future advancement: 'for he greatly desired to be appointed general-in-chief of the Greeks and to launch the war against Persia.'[6] Diodorus,

---

[1] The mythology, too, of the Macedonian dynasty's Argive connection will have seemed relevant (cf. Thuc. 5. 80. 2 with reference to Perdiccas in 417).

[2] D. 19. 10 f., 303 ff.; 19, 2 Hypoth. 3; Aeschin. 2. 79 See above, p. 330.

[3] From 5. 54–6 (cf. 7–8) it appears that Isocrates wrote after the Peace of Philocrates but before the settlement in Phocis. Cf. Ryder, *KE* 99.

[4] Isoc. 5. 73–5.   [5] D. 6. 15 and 25; 6, 2 Hypoth. 2. See below, p. 478.

[6] D.S. 16. 60. 4–5.

like ourselves, knew the end of Philip's story, and it is possible that this is no more than his own comment; in which case it is of no value to us. More likely, though, he found remarks to this effect in his source here, who may have been Demophilus (the son of Ephorus), who wrote the history of the Phocian war in what came to be known as Ephorus, Book 30. Failing this, the source was probably either Theopompus or a later historian who used Theopompus (e.g. Diyllus):[1] one says this because the *Philippic History* of Theopompus was a work very large, very varied, comprehensive, interesting, the standard work presumably on this period, and one which it would seem crazy for any later historian not to use as his main source. In either case, Demophilus or Theopompus, anything they wrote of Philip's state of mind in 346 is likely to have been written after 336 when they knew that he had become general-in-chief of the Greeks and had launched the war against Persia. But it is still possible for either of them to have known of Philip's real thoughts in 346 and to have recorded them accurately.

That Philip himself was aware of this 'Persian policy' at the moment when Diodorus ascribed it to him can be accepted as certain, if only because Isocrates had put it up to him in the work which we have been considering (*Philip*), written only a few weeks before. (Theopompus and Demophilus knew of the *Philip*, no doubt, by the time they wrote, too.) When Philip got his copy of the *Philip*, and when he read it, we cannot know: nor does it matter greatly. For there is nothing that encourages us to think that Isocrates was advocating here a Persian war under Philip's leadership because he knew already that Philip was thinking on these lines and would be pleased. Obviously this would be an excellent reason (among others) for a publicist to put up a policy to a man of power. But unfortunately all that we do know is that it is Isocrates himself who has been wanting a Persian war for years and years: it was as far back as 380 that he first went on record about it in the *Panegyricus*. Thus, when more than half-way through the *Philip* he comes to the point of discussing the Persian war in some detail, and writes 'concerning the invasion of Asia . . .' as of something already settled on, we are not entitled to think that Philip had already settled on it and that Isocrates knew this:[2] it is Isocrates who has settled it, and his way of referring to it here is based partly on a brief and general statement early in this work and partly (mainly) on the *Panegyricus* (to which he alludes again directly a few lines below).[3] What is interesting, however, is that the programme of a Persian war has become by this time at any rate a talking-point in some

---

[1] On sources of Diodorus 16, Hammond, *CQ* 31 (1937) 85 ff.; M. Sordi, *D.S.* 16 pp. xi ff. with bibliography. Direct use of Theopompus by Diodorus seems improbable (*contra*, C. B. Welles, *Diodorus Siculus* (Loeb, vol. 8) 4 f.).

[2] Isoc. 5. 83.

[3] Isoc. 5. 9 and 84 f. For a 'Persian plan' of Jason of Pherae, Isoc. 5. 119; X. *HG* 6. 1. 12.

Greek circles: the optimum, it was held, would be to overthrow the Persian Empire entirely, a second-best solution to annex as much territory as possible and divide Asia, 'as some say', from Cilicia up to Sinope . . .[1] Greek politicians and others have discussed these things in some detail, from a Greek point of view, which is the point of view of Isocrates himself in this connection entirely.[2] One should not make too much of this. It need not mean that politicians in cities all over Greece were talking about it: it may mean only that some people in Isocrates' own circle were talking. But at any rate these speculations did exist here and there, somewhere: to call them plans would seem academic, because no Greek who entertained them was in any position to put them into effect, now or ever. Only Philip might do it, this Isocrates took for granted.

Philip himself did not need Isocrates to instruct him about Persia: this surely does emerge from his career up to this date. If there is any king in history who less needed prompting on how and where he might expand his rule, one does not know of him. To expand was the function of any Macedonian king in this generation, and Philip, we have seen, was indefatigable in it. What makes it certain that Persia must have attracted his notice is just that nowhere else offered so great a certainty of reward that would be really worth while. To conquer half a dozen Persian satrapies of Asia Minor could bring in a gross sum in tribute approaching 2,000 talents a year,[3] more than Greece and Thrace together would yield if they were made tributary: and unlike the Greeks and Thracians the peoples of Asia Minor were quite used to paying taxes to a foreign ruler, and would give him presumably no trouble if he could once drive the Persians out. That Philip had allowed his mind to dwell on these things is something that can be thought of as a certainty. All that is in doubt is, how definite were his plans in 346.

On this we have no help from anything we know of his relations with Persia up to this time. The rumour of an embassy to the Great King in 351 (D. 4. 48), the possibility that a distinguished Persian refugee already may have settled at his court: these things are neither here nor there.[4] But what seems to have real significance in this direction is *his policy towards Athens, from 348 on*. It does seem that he abstained from exploiting to the full his military advantage over Athens after the fall of Olynthus— and it was he who had initiated the moves for peace before Olynthus fell.[5] He could probably have occupied the Chersonese any time after

---

[1] Isoc. 5. 120.   [2] Ibid. 120 f.; at 5. 9 an Athenian point of view, even.
[3] Hdt. 3. 90 gives totals for the four regions comprised by this whole area amounting to 1,760 talents.
[4] See above, p. 309: and below, pp. 485 f., for the alleged 'friendship and alliance', at some date unspecified, of Philip with Artaxerxes, recorded only by Arrian (*An.* 2. 14. 1–3) in a résumé of a letter of Darius III to Alexander. The authenticity of the letter is not above suspicion.   [5] See above, pp. 329 ff.

348: he could certainly have promoted an Amphictyonic war against Athens in September 346. It looks as if he did want Athens now as an ally. And the only purpose for which Athens was really indispensable as an ally was, for a war against Persia. The Athenian navy must be for him then, and not against him. The change of front towards Athens does seem to argue that a Persian war is something for which at any rate the preliminary foundations are being laid now. But it need not mean in itself that plans for a Persian war are far advanced, or even that Philip was committed to it now irrevocably. It was still a 'contingency plan', in the sense that an adventure into Asia became a practical possibility only if the state of Europe (Illyria and Thrace, and especially Greece) offered a basis that was secure.

Though it is understandable that in the years after 346 Philip did not advertise any intentions towards Persia (either officially or unofficially) in any way that was liable to alarm or provoke or prepare the Persian government for war, it is still surprising that the surviving public orations from Athens of the years 344, 343, and 342, and even those of early 341, all of them devoted to the foreign 'affairs' of the 340s very extensively, are quite silent on this matter. It is only the *Fourth Philippic* (of summer 341) that speaks of 'all Philip's plans against the Great King' as of something generally known, and advocates an Athenian embassy to Persia.[1] The *Letter of Philip* (summer 340) complains of the Athenian embassy, and writes of Persia in relation to Greece and Athens in terms both particular and general; but of Philip's own intentions not a word.[2] It seems certain that there was no publicity of any kind emanating from Philip earlier than Chaeronea on the subject of the Persian war. It is not the fact but the reasons for it that call for discussion.

Isocrates throws a useful light here, useful partly because we can reckon that anything Isocrates could think of in this connection, Philip will have thought of more quickly. In the *Philip* Isocrates reminded him that to invade Asia successfully it was necessary to have the Greeks either as his allies in the war or as entirely benevolent neutrals. In the years of the Spartan hegemony this condition had not been present: too many of the Greeks had seen a Persian victory as their only prospect of liberation.[3] No doubt it is with this in mind that Isocrates once reminds Philip that the Greeks will not tolerate a monarch. He puts this point with admirable

---

[1] D. 10. 32 f.

[2] [D.] 12. 6 f. The *Letter of Philip* seems to be either a genuine letter of Philip to Athens or (less likely) the composition of a writer so exceptionally well informed that we are safe in using this as the gist of a Note or Notes that Philip really did send to Athens at this time. The best studies of this question are by M. Pohlenz, 'Philipps Schreiben an Athen', *Hermes* 64 (1929) 41 ff., and by Wüst, 133–6. And see pp. 714 f.

[3] Isoc. 5. 86 ff. δεῖ γὰρ μηδὲν πρότερον πράττειν πρὶν ἂν λάβῃ τις τοὺς Ἕλληνας δυοῖν θάτερον, ἢ συναγωνιζομένους ἢ πολλὴν εὔνοιαν ἔχοντας ... ὥστε ... ῥᾴδιον καταμαθεῖν ὅτι δεῖ ... μὴ πρότερον ἐκφέρειν πρὸς τὸν βασιλέα πόλεμον πρὶν ἂν διαλλάξῃ τις τοὺς Ἕλληνας ... cf. 5. 95.

tact by turning aside into the unexceptionable area of prehistory: Philip's ancestor the first king of the Macedonians 'alone of the Greeks chose to rule over a foreign race', this 'because he knew that the Greeks were not in the habit of tolerating monarchies'.[1]

It seems that Isocrates was treading here on very delicate ground, and knew it. On the one hand, he had some good reason for fearing that Philip might try, whether sooner or later, to subject Greece or parts of it by direct rule, with the cities tributary and no longer independent. He had done this to a significant number of Greeks already: to Amphipolis and some other cities of 'the parts towards Thrace'.[2] On the other hand Thessaly was more encouraging, in appearance at least: for here he had been elected head of their League by the Thessalians themselves. Yet Thessaly was in many ways not quite Greece; with its unique complex of states, in a unique situation at the time of the election, and with a unique office vacant for Philip to fill. Could he be trusted, if he came south, to adapt his political methods so as to gain an indirect yet effective control in some way not unacceptable to most of the Greek cities and above all to the greatest of them? It looks as if Isocrates' information about Philip (no doubt they had friends or acquaintances in common) led him to believe, or at least to hope, that he was to be trusted; otherwise he would hardly have risked his own reputation by publishing this piece in his support. And especially perhaps he hoped to divert him from a close involvement in Greece into the alternative sphere of expansion, in Asia.[3]

Isocrates nowhere explains in his piece, however, by just what means, what organization, Philip was to be enabled to do what was necessary. Charitably it may be said that to explain all this here would have been premature (for he wrote before even the final collapse of Phocis).[4] But one suspects that he would have been embarrassed to know what to suggest if pressed. The panhellenic congress, the *koine eirene*, the invitation to all Greek cities great and small to join in an alliance for an offensive war against Persia: each or all of these things would be building on some part of the practice of the last generation of Greek politicians. But for

---

[1] Isoc. 5. 106–8.   [2] See above, Ch. X.

[3] This, seen by Perlman (*PA* 306 ff.) as his main theme, appears best at 5. 80, concluding the long passage (5. 73 ff.) about those who feared a sinister move by Philip into the Peloponnese, a terrible thing (so Isocrates) if it came from the descendant of Heracles 'the benefactor of all Greece'. The Greeks must be unafraid of him, as the Spartans were of their kings and as his own Companions were of Philip. 'And this *can* be achieved, if you will consent to be on the same terms with one and all, and stop having some of the cities as your friends and others as enemies, and also if you will frame your actions so as to inspire the Greeks with confidence and only the barbarians with fear.'

[4] Cf. Isoc. 5. 83 for a recognition of this: 'About the invasion of Asia, the cities which I have said you must reconcile shall hear from us the means by which they are to make war on the barbarians, when we see them on terms of peace and unity with each other.'

success these things did depend, naturally, on the realities of power, where they lay, and to whose advantage they were being exercised. How many of the Greeks would join an alliance voluntarily if they could see that the main rewards from it would go to the king of the Macedonians? Was there any alternative really to establishing a hegemony over Greece as tight as those of Sparta and Athens in the past, so that nobody would dare not to join the alliance when invited? These were questions (there were others) which Philip had to live with from now on.

4. *Stabilization or Expansion?*

This year of 346 can be thought of as a turning-point in the affairs of Philip and of the Greeks. Peace with Athens, peace in central Greece: to put it at its lowest, it was an occasion for pause and regrouping. It is of some consequence to know (yet by no means easy), just how much of a pause this was and how much it was intended to be. Crucial for this question, obviously, is the factor of *koine eirene*.[1] This settlement of 346 greatly resembles those of 386 and 362 in this at least, that it was a settlement producing a state of peace after a sufficiently long period of war. The generation including the years 386 and 362 had developed *koine eirene* as an instrument of inter-city relations, whereby all the cities subscribed to a peace treaty designed to maintain a *status quo* while guaranteeing the autonomy of every city great and small. States which for any reason refused to subscribe (because something in the terms was objectionable to them) were outside the Peace (Sparta in 362, Thebes in 371); and in favourable conditions they could be coerced into dropping their objections (Argos, Corinth, and Thebes in 386; but in 371 the coercion of Thebes produced the battle of Leuctra instead). The clause in a *koine eirene*, when there was one, which made it obligatory for all states to help a victim of aggression, was the complete protection on paper for the small and weak, and in reality it did at least give full opportunity for resistance to an aggressor to be organized, subject to the condition in practice that one or more of the strong states knew that their own interests were best served by supporting the weak in this case.

Diodorus, concluding his short account of the Amphictyonic settlement in 346, does introduce the words *koine eirene*, but in a vague and indefinite way, very different from his way of recording previous occasions on which a *koine eirene* had been formally agreed to by peace conferences of Greek states.[2] In spite of this difference some distinguished

[1] On *koine eirene* in general, Ryder, Introduction, especially p. xvi, and *passim*.

[2] D.S. 16. 60. 3 (contrast id. 15. 38. 1 f.; 45. 2; 50. 4; 51. 1; 70. 2; 76. 3; 89. 1; 94. 1). It is noteworthy that Diodorus, when recording presently the Athenian declaration of war on Philip in 340, knew perfectly well that there was no *koine eirene* in existence: οἱ Ἀθηναῖοι ἔκριναν τὸν Φίλιππον λελυκέναι τὴν πρὸς αὐτοὺς συντεθεῖσαν εἰρήνην . . . (16. 77. 1).

historians have argued that this peace of 346 was a *koine eirene*. This I have never believed; but I am spared the necessity of restating my reasons by the admirable study of T. T. B. Ryder, who discusses the question fully, and concludes that there was no *koine eirene* here.[1] I accept this conclusion and propose to consider its consequences, for the interpretation of Philip's policy.

First, it may be useful to recall how surprising, really, it would have been if the evidence had obliged us to believe that Philip did initiate or sponsor a *koine eirene* in 346. Not to overestimate the solemnity or sanctity of treaty obligations on these occasions, it cannot be denied that a *koine eirene* was a stabilizing factor in Greece, and that a state which took the lead in promoting one normally wanted a *status quo* preserved (Sparta in 371 the classic example). But all that we have seen of Philip up to now suggests just the opposite. He had never wanted Greece stabilized; very much the reverse. The division of the Greeks had been his opportunities. It may be said that anyhow no *koine eirene* yet had ever stopped wars from happening: so why should he worry? True, but a *koine eirene* still was a restraint on freedom of action, and could facilitate an organized opposition to him if he could be represented as an aggressor (Demosthenes in the next years could have used this method, had it been open to him, in building up his anti-Macedonian front). For one who meant to tighten his grip on Greece in one way or another, there was no advantage in cluttering himself up with a *koine eirene*.

It may be said, again, that Philip's past actions are no safe guide to his future intentions. Reformed poachers, let us say, do make good game-keepers. The young and grasping conqueror has settled down, perhaps, into the mature statesman, satisfied with what he holds, and content to use his power now for peaceful reconciliations and combinations in Greece on the lines adumbrated by Isocrates. The hypothesis is there; but it is not supported by what we see of Philip in action after 346. Even allowing for (perhaps) an exaggerated alarmism in Demosthenes, we shall see much of the restless *polypragmosyne* in operation south of Thermopylae that we have seen earlier in the north; of one who, if he is not precisely looking for trouble, is not missing any chances of giving it a stir wherever trouble is brewing. His interventions in the Peloponnese, at Megara, in Euboea, at Ambracia, seem to conform to this pattern.[2] They will make him some new friends, among those whom he can reinforce when they need it: they will cause some alarm to old enemies, and will make him some new enemies too. What they will not do is, convey an impression of a good genius using his power to stabilize Greece. Indeed it would have been an impolitic duplicity to become the creator and guarantor of a *koine eirene* in the full knowledge and intent of

[1] Ryder, *KE* 145 ff. [2] See below, pp. 476 ff.

subverting it himself wherever opportunities might show. Though the Greeks were less scandalized than we are by political immorality, they certainly did not either enjoy or admire it:[1] nor did it repay its per-petrators, as both Athens and Sparta had learned in their time. Philip had achieved the reputation by 346, we may surmise, of a very good friend and a very bad enemy. With its combination of the incentive and the deterrent this was no bad reputation to have, if he looked to Greece still as a field for his further expansion. With this image the Greeks had a chance of knowing where they were with him: it was best that they should.

Philip did not choose, then, the avenue via the panhellenic congress and the *koine eirene* as his approach to a presence in Greece in these next years. He chose instead the Amphictyony and its Council, as we have seen. M. Sordi in an elegant and valuable study of the political back-ground to the college of *naopoioi* at Delphi, showed that in the decade beginning with the year 367/6 there had developed a certain tension between what she comes to term 'Greece of the cities' and 'Greece of the *ethne*'.[2] This is seen in initiatives promoted, on the one hand, by pan-hellenic congresses dominated before 362 by Sparta or Athens or both, on the other hand by the Amphictyony dominated by Thebes and the Boeotians, with the Thessalians and their dependants required in support to make it effective.

The origin of this tension (which was a reality) was of course the Spartan–Theban dispute, mounting to feud, about the interpretation of the autonomy clause in the Peace of 386: by the Spartan view the central organs of government of the Boeotian League were a negation of the autonomy of the individual Boeotian cities.[3] While Sparta remained strong she pursued Thebes by every means of practice and precept, using panhellenic congresses to this end as and when she could.[4] In reaction Thebes turned to the Amphictyonic Council after Leuctra, and became able to dominate it for political ends, most importantly to bring about the condemnation of Sparta by the Council for the capture of the Cadmea; appropriately in the sense that both Thebes and Sparta were Amphic-tyonic members, but still an affair of such magnitude that no court other than a panhellenic congress could be deemed truly appropriate. Ironically, the city (Thebes) which had suffered the grossest wound to her own autonomy was unable for these political reasons to appeal to

[1] Cf., e.g., F. E. Adcock, 'Aspects of Greek diplomacy', *PCA* 21 (1924) 92 ff.

[2] M. Sordi, 'La Fondation du collège des Naopes et le renouveau politique de l'Amphictionie au IVe siècle', *BCH* 81 (1957) 38 ff.

[3] Cf. Ryder, *KE* 29, 36, 69.

[4] On the oath of Plataea and its resuscitation, cf. especially L. Robert, *Études* 307 ff.; (G. Daux, *Rev. arch.* 17 (1941) 176 ff.; id., *Studies . . . D. M. Robinson* 1. 777 ff.; Sordi, 'Naopes' 46 ff.).

the only court juridically really competent to defend just such victims of aggression, the panhellenic congress which had subscribed to the *koine eirene* known as the King's Peace or to one of its renewals.

By 346 however, this issue had receded into the background: indeed it must be thought to have done so even by 362, the year of the panhellenic congress which had made the most recent *koine eirene*, from which Sparta had remained excluded because she would not recognize Messene as a free and autonomous city.[1] Plainly, nobody in 362 was in a position to insist that the Boeotian cities swore to this peace separately: the Theban interpretation of autonomy as applied to league-members had prevailed. Whether the Thebans tried and failed to get Sparta condemned for the Cadmea crime by this same conference, is a question on which we are told nothing; but if she had been condemned we should have heard of it. It was with the Amphictyony therefore that the initiative in this matter remained, just as it was the Amphictyony (and naturally) that took up and pursued the misdemeanours of the Phocians which concerned Delphi. And now that the Phocians were done with, it was the Amphictyony that Philip, with his own two votes and those of the Thessalians and their *perioikoi*, found himself able to control as Thebes had done before.

Sordi, who believed in a *koine eirene* in 346, saw in it (incidentally) the first use to which Philip put the Amphictyony.[2] The Amphictyony, because of its unrepresentative voting arrangements, was a body neither legitimate nor appropriate for launching a *koine eirene*; but I would agree that this in itself need be no absolute bar to anyone's believing that still it might have done so. It is because it appears that no *koine eirene* was initiated at all in 346 that I rule out the Amphictyony as initiator. Secondly, Sordi saw a decisive turn of events in 346 in that Philip now, 'relying on Greece of the *ethne* and of the Amphictyony will have the

---

[1] D.S. 15. 90. 2.

[2] Sordi, 'Naopes' 38 ff., especially 74 f. Since Ryder in his study does not comment on Sordi's interpretation, perhaps I ought to say why I cannot follow her in believing in a *koine eirene* in 346 sponsored by the Amphictyonic Council.

As I see it, her elucidation of the Amphictyonic pre-history (years 367/6–357/6) does make very much more plausible the notion that a *koine eirene* could have been initiated by the Amphictyons in 346. In particular, it eases the situation, so difficult for believers in this *k.e.*, whereby in 343 the Athenians proposed the creation of a *k.e.* to be initiated by themselves (or themselves and Philip?), although there was (by this theory) a *k.e.* sponsored by the Amphictyons already in operation ([D.] 7. 30 f.). Sordi sees this situation, I conceive, as a renewal of the tension between 'Greece of the cities' and 'Greece of the *ethne*' (see above, p. 451). I agree that something of this kind could have happened. But it still seems clear to me that in reality it did not happen. To me, the allusion of Hegesippus ([D.] 7. 30 f.) shows beyond doubt that no *k.e.* of any kind existed at the time (in 343) when the Athenians were talking of initiating a new *k.e.* And the allusions of Demosthenes in September 346 show equally clearly that the Amphictyonic arrangements in preparation at that moment did not include arrangements for a *k.e.* (D. 5. 14 ff., 18 f.). For a full statement on this, see Ryder, *K.E.* 145 ff.

better of Greece of the cities and the congresses'.[1] This ideological distinction, interesting in itself, is illuminating too in so far as it summarizes approximately, (allowing for the Theban volte-face), those Greeks who were for and those who were against Philip in the war of Chaeronea presently: and Sordi concludes by describing Philip's 'League of Corinth' as the 'wise integration of the two traditional and opposed forms of panhellenism of free Greece, Amphictyony and Congress'.[2] Admirable interpretation, εἰδυίας πρὸς εἰδότας: we do have the advantage of knowing the end of the story. The interpretation could mislead, however, if it encouraged us to think of any conscious ideological alignment of the people concerned at the time: and it would mislead most of all if it gave to Philip himself even the remotest ideological interest here, or even probably any awareness that two ideologies were here at all. The contemporary Athenians seem to have left us no record of their awareness, either.[3] The contemporary Thebans and Boeotians were not prevented by any ideology from abandoning their alliance with Philip and allying themselves with Athens in 339. The *ethne* of Arcadia and Achaea, Aetolia and Acarnania, in 346 were outside the Amphictyony: some of them became allies of Philip in the next years—as did some cities, Argos, Messene, and others. The Amphictyonic Euboeans formed themselves in these same years into an ethnic *koinon* like the Boeotians—and almost simultaneously they joined the Athenian alliance. So too did the Acarnanians.[4] When all is said, the alignments noticed by Sordi had a basis primarily geographical; and above all it was by pure accident of geography that Thessaly lay next door to Macedonia, Thessaly to which Philip owed his Amphictyonic control.

Finally, one must look back to Athens; or rather to Athens as seen through Philip's eyes in September 346: his reluctant ally now, dragging her feet through the motions of her recognition of the Amphictyonic *fait accompli*. If Athens really was (as I have suggested) more important for his future plans than any other Greek state, it was his business to try to sweeten her; and thrusting the Amphictyony down her throat was about the worst way of doing this. The Athenians at this time had as much use for the Amphictyony as for a sick headache: it reminded them of the Phocians, their own humiliation, of their friends expelled (Sparta), their enemies (Thebes) not brought low as they had hoped, of the Amphictyonic rump subservient now to Philip. We have seen how on this occasion the Amphictyonic Council did not stand on its dignity or powers, and Athens was allowed to recover her poise at leisure. The

---

[1] Sordi, 'Naopes' 75.   [2] Ibid.

[3] The two passages, one of Demosthenes (19. 48–50), and one of Isocrates (5. 74 f.), cited by Sordi as significant in this connection do not seem to me to support her view strongly if at all, when they are read with close attention to their actual contexts.

[4] Euboeans, see below, p. 549: Acarnanians, Aeschin. 3. 97 f.

Council a second time may have subserved Philip's policy of conciliation, when the Delos case came to its jurisdiction. The date of this is quite uncertain, apart from some general probability that Delos might see prospects in 346, rather than later, of a successful appeal to the Amphictyony against the Athenian administration of her temple. Though the merits of the case, or of the Council as a court capable of deciding on it, escape us entirely, it can hardly be denied that Philip could certainly have procured a verdict unfavourable to Athens in this court if he had chosen. But the verdict was in favour of Athens, and probably it is right to see the influence of Philip at work here.[1]

The Council obviously was a very good means of being inside Greece, Greece north of the Isthmus, and a means of throwing in his influence when he chose. It could of course (and did) become the means of mobilizing his friends in Greece against an opposition. But to see in it now his means of controlling Greece in any sense comparable with the control exercised earlier by Sparta through panhellenic congress seems clearly premature. Most likely Philip kept still an open mind as to how in the end he would control Greece. The one thing that he of all men knew was that his control would be based ultimately on his power. His prime need always was to lose no chance of bringing Greek states individually face to face with the reality of his power, as something that could help them (at a price), or break them. In this way they could learn to know where their future lay; and Athens must learn above all. To learn the hard way was not a necessity: the choice would be hers, and theirs.

---

[1] D. 18. 134; Hyperid. *In Demad.* fr. 76 (Ox.).

XIV

EXPANSION

1. *Illyrian War* (?) *345*

A FTER nearly fourteen years Macedonia was at peace. Was the year
345 to be the first of Philip's reign (and the last) when no part
of Greece or the Balkans would hear any tramp of Macedonians
on the march?[1] To plough and to sow, to reap and to mow, and to get
in the grapes on those sunny slopes of Naoussa: for this one cycle of the
seasons the Macedonians, all of them except the household troops and
maybe a garrison here and there, might hope to be back on the land for
the whole spell. Those of them who understood the affairs of the kingdom
will have realized that this was an eminence on which they were resting
now. Macedonia had never been so great. Was this perhaps the beginning
of a new and calmer era in which some part of the nation's manpower,
deployed from time to time, would serve to hold what was won, and to
remind the world what it was to have the Macedonians as neighbours?
So it may have seemed to these sons of the soil. Only the court, probably,
knew something different. There is no need to think that the long road
from Sardis to Susa, and beyond, already was in mind. But the news of
the world came in. The gold and the silver still came out of the earth
in the region of Philippi. The king was still Philip, and at the height of
his powers. Was there unrest in the Peloponnese? Political tension in
Athens? Causes for dissatisfaction with the Illyrian neighbours of the
north-west? Were the Thracian princes up to something? Would the
Thessalians never settle down? Leaving aside the future and the greater
plans, the present was a good enough companion for a king who had
never shirked decisions or blurred priorities, who had spent so much of
his life in the saddle and was never afraid to climb back there if that
was where the news of the world and his own reactions to it directed.
This spring of 345 saw a new campaign being planned: yet another levy
of the Macedonians was warned for duty presently.

The front was beyond the western frontier, and the enemy the Illyrians,
but the occasion of this new war against them is unknown. It is six years
now at least since any Illyrian activities of Philip have been recorded.[2]

---

[1] For chronology, see below, p. 470.

[2] D. 4. 48 the most recent allusion: the allusion of D. 1. 23 (349) is to results of past
activities not to contemporary ones.

Remembering the recent record of the Illyrians against Macedonia, we can count this as stability: and we can reckon that Philip already has succeeded in establishing a good defensible frontier (pp. 652 ff. below). Since an offensive war against them did not offer material rewards either particularly rich or particularly easy, it seems right to infer that this invasion now was preventive or punitive, and was inspired by the news from those parts which was available to Philip then but is not available now to us.

Even the chronology of this war is in doubt. It seems nearly certain that Diodorus is mistaken in placing it in the year 344/3 (archonship of Lyciscus).[1] Demosthenes in his *Second Philippic*, which belongs (it is agreed) to autumn 344, makes no allusion to Philip in Illyria, though his campaign there was sensational enough to occasion a letter of Isocrates to Philip himself on the subject: Demosthenes does mention, however, recent activity of Philip in Thessaly.[2] The Illyrian campaign, then, was old news by the time Demosthenes spoke, and cannot possibly belong to the second half of 344 (Diodorus' year 344/3).[3] It seems right to date it, with Cawkwell, in 345, rather than early in 344 (where it has most often been put).[4] The spring or summer of 344 saw the developments in Thessaly and in the Peloponnese which will be discussed presently.

Isocrates writing in 346 had summarized Philip's relations with the Illyrians in the rhetorical question 'Has he not become master of the mass of the Illyrians, except those who live along the Adriatic?'[5] Hammond in his study of the Illyrians has shown that, considered in relation to the whole Illyrian *ethnos* in its widest sense, Isocrates' remark flattered Philip. But considered in relation to those Illyrians whom the Greeks of the day could be expected to know or care about, it was not an unreasonable thing to say. Hammond has identified the Illyrians of Bardylis with the Dardanians and the Illyrians of Grabus with the Grabaei, living respectively north and north-west of the Lake Lychnitis area annexed from Bardylis by Philip in 358.[6] The Dardanians in 358 had been not 'conquered', but thoroughly thrashed. The Grabaei, a lesser tribe, by Parmenion's defeat of them in 356 had been reduced to a state of dependence on Macedonia.[7] What more, if anything, was achieved in

---

[1] D.S. 16. 69. 7.   [2] D. 6. 22; Isoc. *Epist.* 2.

[3] Nor can it belong to the first half of 343: the *Embassy* speeches later in the war would surely have contained some allusion to it.

[4] Cawkwell, *CQ* (1965) 126 f. Spring 344, Beloch 3². 2. 460; so too Wüst 54 f., with a good discussion. There is nothing in Isocrates' *Second Letter* that enables the *Letter* itself to be dated: it is merely after, and soon after, the Illyrian campaign, and earlier than the *Second Philippic*.

[5] Isoc. 5. 21 (where the οὐ of 8 lines above—οὐ Θετταλοὶ μὲν . . . etc.—goes with the succeeding questions also, including this one).

[6] Hammond, *BSA* 61 (1966) 244 f., with bibliography.

[7] D.S. 16. 8. 1 ἠνάγκασε προσθέσθαι Μακεδόσι.

351, we do not know. Now, however, in 345, Philip evidently extended his reach to the Illyrians living along the Adriatic, the Ardiaei: and the Dardanians again were probably involved in this same war.

Of this war Diodorus records merely that it was against the Illyrians. Didymus in a part of his learned commentary devoted to Philip's wounds in battle, tells us that he was wounded in the right calf on a campaign 'in Illyria', while pursuing 'Pleuratus the Illyrian'.[1] Isocrates' *Second Letter*, which was evidently inspired by the news of a wound,[2] identifies this occasion in 345 with the campaign against Pleuratus: (and Hammond has identified Pleuratus securely as king of the Ardiaei).[3] Justin in his brief epitome of events gives Philip an Illyrian War between 346 and the end of 343, but the Illyrian people which Justin names is the Dardanians.[4] A question here is, whether to conflate the information from Justin with the rest, or whether to think of it as a less acceptable alternative (produced by some muddle of Justin himself?) to the circumstantial identification of this war as a war against the Ardiaeans of Pleuratus. The notion that there could have been two wars, with a Dardanian campaign in 344 or 343 succeeding the campaign against Pleuratus is not attractive, because of the silence of the *Second Philippic* and of the *Embassy* speeches.

What seems clear, however, is that the Dardanians cannot be left out of this. Hammond's identification of them as the tribe of Bardylis seems certain.[5] And he rightly reminds us that Cleitus the son of Bardylis who rose later against Alexander was at that time a client king rising in rebellion:[6] the occasion of his reduction to the status of client, therefore, will have been the war recorded here by Justin. Hammond wrote of Philip's campaign against the Dardanians (Cleitus) and that against the Ardiaei (Pleuratus) as of two separate campaigns: and the topography itself seems to demand this. What does seem likely, though, is that this was one war, against the two great tribes in coalition. Though one cannot rely heavily on the actual words of Justin, whose single clause here may be summarizing a number of chapters of Trogus, his words do suggest nothing so much as a coalition: 'Dardanos ceterosque finitimos fraude captos expugnat.'[7] 'Finitimos' could refer to 'neighbours' either of the Dardanians or of Macedonia; but in the context, since we are told of no other wars of Macedonia against her neighbours (Greeks, Thracians, or Paeonians) in these years (346/3), it ought to refer to neighbours of the Dardanians, which means other tribes of the Illyrians. In the same way 'fraude captos', which presumably alludes to something,

---

[1] Didymus, *in Dem.* 12. 64. [2] Isoc. *Epist.* 2. 1–12, especially 12.
[3] Hammond, loc. cit. 245. [4] Just. 8. 6. 3.
[5] Loc. cit. at p. 470 n. 6 above. [6] Arr. *An.* 1. 5. 1.
[7] Just. 8. 6. 3.

seems much more likely to allude to one occasion, or one nexus of events, involving all the Illyrians concerned, than to a succession of wars or campaigns in which, by a curious coincidence, not one but all of Philip's Illyrian opponents successively were lured by tricks to defeat. Justin's naming of the Dardanians too, rather than of Pleuratus and the Ardiaei, may be thought to offer some clue, if the two peoples were really acting together. The Dardanians were an important people, bordering on Macedonia and able in the past to leave their mark on Macedonian history: this is one claim to priority here. But the Ardiaei in this context were very good 'news value', because of Philip's wound, which 'made' the history books in some detail, as we see from Didymus. Justin, condensing brutally, most likely chose to name the Dardanians because it was with the Dardanians that this Illyrian section of Trogus began.

A possible reconstruction, then, is of a war of two campaigns in which the Dardanians were dealt with first, as befitted their position *vis-à-vis* Lake Lychnitis, Pelagonia, and Paeonia, their past history of conflict with Macedonia, and the likelihood that any subversion now on the Illyrian front concerned them. The trick or treachery by which Philip defeated them may have been one which enabled him to attack them separately before Pleuratus and the Ardiaei could intervene. The effect of this war was certainly to make the Dardanii dependent allies of Macedonia, their king a vassal king.[1] Any campaign against the Dardanians must have been completed before the occasion of Philip's wound received when pursuing Pleuratus. If Philip was dealing with both peoples in 345, he was able perhaps to turn on the Ardiaei after settling with the Dardanians. His defeat of Pleuratus (which led to a pursuit) was evidently only after a hard-fought battle, for it was no ordinary engagement in which 150 of the Companion cavalry were wounded.[2] Philip, wounded himself, probably did not pursue to the Adriatic, and though a treaty of peace with Pleuratus no doubt was made, there is nothing to show that the Ardiaei became subject now to Macedonia.[3] More likely, perhaps, the Ardiaei were those Illyrians (doubtless a free people, not a subject one) to whom Alexander later resorted when at loggerheads with Philip in the last year of the reign.[4] There is no question however but

---

[1] Arr. *An.* 1. 5. 6.   [2] Didymus col. 12. 65 ff.; Schol. D. 18. 67.

[3] From Arrian's wording (1. 5. 1), it seems that the Taulantii, a smaller tribe on the Adriatic in the neighbourhood of Epidamnus (hence in easier reach of Macedonia than the Ardiaei), probably were still a free people in 335: ἄγγελοι ἀφίκοντο αὐτῷ Κλεῖτόν τε τὸν Βαρδύλεω ἀφεστάναι ἀγγέλλοντες καὶ Γλαυκίαν προσκεχωρηκέναι αὐτῷ τὸν Ταυλαντίων βασιλέα. If Glaucias, too, had been a subject, Arrian probably would have joined him to Cleitus as subject of ἀφεστάναι. On these events see now Hammond, *JHS* 94 (1974) 66 ff.

[4] See below, p. 678. Alexander is not likely to have resorted to any Illyrians who were already subject to Macedonia, for obvious reasons, but to people who might not be afraid to receive him. All Illyrian kings by that time, whether subject or free, can probably be assumed unfriendly to the Macedonian government. The Taulantii, e.g., could have received

that this Illyrian war of Philip was a success. On the shortest view a coalition of tribes, if there was one, was foiled or forestalled; and the Macedonians were repaid for some hard fighting by booty from an enemy country which (unlike some) did not need the velvet glove. On the longer view, this treatment put the Illyrians where they belonged for the next eight years at least.

It is not till 337 (or 336?) that we hear of another Illyrian campaign, 'against the Illyrian king Pleurias'. The temptation to identify this Pleurias with the Ardiaean Pleuratus is too much for some; and it is true that this campaign does not appear as a regular 'entry' in the annalistic record of Diodorus, who merely alludes to it for the detail which it supplies to the story of Pausanias the murderer of Philip.[1] To identify the campaign itself with the campaign of 345 against Pleuratus (above) has become orthodox, probably; but Hammond warned against this—and incidentally the identification has very serious consequences for interpreters of the story of Philip's death.[2] But really it is quite clear that both Diodorus and Plutarch knew that this campaign belonged to the last year or so of Philip's life, and since they will have found their facts in a historian or historians who did locate the campaign annalistically, it is misspent ingenuity to assume that they must be wrong. It is ten to one that they are right.[3] In this case Pleurias will not be a king of the Ardiaei but of another Illyrian *ethnos*; Hammond's conjecture of the Autariatae, the third of Strabo's 'big three' Illyrian nations, may well be right.[4] On general grounds a demonstration in 'Illyria' before committing the main forces to Asia for several years, had everything to commend it. The record of it here is casual, but it is necessary, even to the point where, if it had not been present, it might have been necessary for us to invent it.

Meanwhile in 345 Philip could limp home with the feeling of something accomplished. The banalities of Isocrates on the subject of his wound will not have seemed worth more than the passing smile. It was not necessary, Philip could agree, to expose himself, and exchange the responsibilities of a general for a soldier's risks. But to the Macedonians themselves it was an endearing quality in a king, to join in when battle commenced. It was a rarity for the leader of victorious troops to be killed

him in 337, and still, with no contradiction in policy, have supported the Dardanians in their revolt in 335. But since the Taulantii were a smaller people and less remote than the Ardiaei, it seems more likely that it was to the latter that he went in 337.

E. Badian ('The Death of Philip', *Phoenix* 17 (1963) 244 ff.) suggests that it was to the Agrianians that Alexander went. But the Agrianians were not Illyrians, but probably a branch of the Paeonians, as Thucydides evidently counted them (2. 96. 3).

[1] D.S. 16. 93. 6 ff.

[2] Hammond, *BSA* 61 (1966) 245 and n. 27 with bibliography.

[3] D.S. 16. 93. 6 ff.; Plu. *Alex.* 10. 3.   [4] Hammond, ibid.; (Strabo, 324c, 327c).

in action, and the leader of troops such as these might well treat this as an acceptable risk. But the truth no doubt was that Philip actually enjoyed, too, the brief interludes when policy and strategy for a few minutes could be laid aside, when sword and sarissa came into their own. The number of his wounds in his lifetime needs some explanation of this sort; and for the extrovert Philip it was not the steely resolution of a Nelson submerging his nerves but something of positive enjoyment in going into action, that reduced his physical appearance in the end to something more like an old boot than a king of the Macedonians.[1]

The operations against Dardanians and Ardiaei will have consumed months rather than weeks, perhaps most of the campaigning season of 345. By the next year, recovered from his wound, he was in Thessaly, where action both military and political was called for (below, pp. 524 ff.). And meanwhile to the south events in the Peloponnese were offering him a policy decision of some importance.

2. *The Peloponnese*

Philip's earliest actual interventions with troops in the Peloponnese are still a little mysterious, because none of our sources tells us exactly what he did, and when, or for that matter just how he did it. Characteristic of our information is the casually imparted news that as early as 348 there were soldiers of Philip in a position to waylay and rob an Athenian on his way to Olympia (D. 19, 2 Hypoth. 3). In the military situation of 348 (before the fall of Thermopylae), it seems right to suppose that this was probably some landing party from a small Macedonian naval squadron. But the collapse of the Phocians and the peace of Philocrates had changed for the better this question of his access to the Peloponnese.[2] As we shall see, Philip certainly had some troops there in 344 (perhaps earlier): how did they get there? Neither Thebes nor Athens his allies were in any strong position to refuse a passage for his troops through their territory if he asked for it, however much they might have preferred to. And if the Boeotians and the Athenians consented to this, Megara and Corinth would hardly dare to refuse, though they had no alliance with

---

[1] D. 18. 67 ἑώρων δ' αὐτὸν τὸν Φίλιππον, πρὸς ὃν ἦν ἡμῖν ὁ ἀγών, ὑπὲρ ἀρχῆς καὶ δυναστείας τὸν ὀφθαλμὸν ἐκκεκομμένον, τὴν κλεῖν κατεαγότα, τὴν χεῖρα, τὸ σκέλος πεπηρωμένον, πᾶν ὅ τι βουληθείη μέρος ἡ τύχη τοῦ σώματος παρελέσθαι, τοῦτο προϊέμενον, ὥστε τῷ λοιπῷ μετὰ τιμῆς καὶ δόξης ζῆν. No doubt, Demosthenes rightly saw a determined ambition as a motive force behind Philip's deeds in war. But it seems to me to be too rational and elevated to be acceptable as the sole motive. Philip's collection of wounds was evidently thought remarkable at the time, and far exceeded Alexander's, who was himself notoriously prone to expose himself in action beyond what was prudent. The conclusion that both of them thoroughly enjoyed it seems inevitable.

[2] Cf. D. 6. 35 τίς ὁ Φωκέας πείσας καὶ Πύλας προέσθαι, ὧν καταστὰς ἐκεῖνος κύριος τῆς ἐπὶ τὴν Ἀττικὴν ὁδοῦ καὶ τῆς εἰς Πελοπόννησον κύριος γέγονεν . . .

him: in this way Macedonian troops could reach the Peloponnese overland.

All the same, it seems very improbable that this is how the Macedonians in the Peloponnese in 344 had got there, in fact.[1] If they had, it
would be most unlike Demosthenes (in the *Second Philippic*) not to
grumble about it: and there is a passage in the speech which lends itself
to the grumble ideally, if the ground for it had existed.[2] Philip did not
need to put this particular strain on the Athenian (or the Boeotian)
alliance: he had a better way now. He had no need to ask anyone's
permission to send troops through Phocis, and this gave him access to
the Gulf of Corinth at Cirrha the port of Delphi.[3] Troops bound for
Messenia could finish the journey either by sea from Cirrha all the way
or by ferry passage to an Achaean port and thence overland through
territories of states none of them unfriendly as yet. Troops for Argos
might travel direct from Macedonia by sea, securely in time of peace.
But it was this access to the Corinthian Gulf which seems the interesting
new development in the strategic situation in Greece. With the Gulf
route added to those which he could use already, there were few places
in Greece which he could not reach.

But how much, and in what senses, did he want to reach them? Most
of what we know or think we know about activities of Philip in the
Peloponnese in these years derives from allusions in speeches of Demosthenes, who was concerned always at this time to present these activities
in a sinister or alarming light. Cawkwell did well to remind us of how
unreliable he can be in contexts such as these.[4] But he may have carried
his scepticism too far by failing to allow enough for differences between
those occasions when Demosthenes alluded to events of several years
past and those when he referred to events contemporary or nearly so.
About Cardia and its status he lied in 341, though he had spoken the
truth about it in 346, when its status had been defined just recently in
the treaty (Peace of Philocrates).[5] Similarly of the Thracian forts taken
by Philip in 346, in speeches delivered in 343 or later he said repeatedly
(and mendaciously) that they had been taken after the Peace was made.[6]
About events as old as that he thought it worth while, evidently, to tell
lies calculated to stimulate hostility to Philip.

Cawkwell used these clear examples of mendacity as basis for his
contention that Demosthenes was equally unreliable in some of his

---

[1] I use 'Macedonians' here not ethnically, but to denote merely 'troops of Philip': quite
likely they were mercenaries.

[2] D. 6. 35; cf. 6. 19.

[3] Neither the Delphians themselves nor the western Locrians were in any position to say
No to the most powerful of all the Amphictyonic members.

[4] Cawkwell, 'Demosthenes' 200 ff.   [5] D. 8. 58; 9. 32 f. and 16 (341); 5. 25 (346).

[6] D. 19. 156 etc. Cawkwell, 'Demosthenes' 201.

allusions to Philip's activities in Greece after 346; that Philip in reality sent no troops into Greece earlier than 342 after it had become clear that good relations with Athens were impossible to achieve (below, pp. 494 f.); and that suggestions by Demosthenes to the contrary were based not on facts but on what it suited Demosthenes to say on those occasions, and are to be disbelieved. This view is obviously open to question on general grounds. An adviser of the people who told lies repeatedly about contemporary or recent happenings, lies which could be contradicted instantly by other speakers and which would be shown up as lies very soon by the actual course of events, was not one to win the people's confidence decisively and permanently. Yet this is just what Demosthenes did succeed in doing, to the point of retaining their confidence even after the disaster of Chaeronea, for years. Moreover it is not easy to see how Athens succeeded in 341/340 in forming a Greek alliance of states for self-defence against Philip (below, pp. 551 f.), unless these same states had come to be convinced that Philip's power really was a threat to themselves. Demosthenes cried Wolf (no man louder or clearer); but the reaction of his public both at home and abroad echoed Wolf, too, and suggests something quite other than the deserved indifference of the fable.

By Cawkwell's interpretation Philip's only 'physical intervention' (meaning with troops) in Greece between 346 and 340 was at Ambracia (343/2) and in Euboea from 342 onwards: alarming for Athens certainly, but not desperately so for Peloponnesian or Isthmus cities if his record elsewhere in the meantime had given no cause for alarm. Demosthenes does mention from time to time 'physical interventions' (i.e. troops) of Philip in Greece in the years 344 and 343; at Messene and Argos (for a war against Sparta), and at Megara, as well as in Euboea in 343. Besides the general grounds there are some particular reasons for taking these references more seriously than Cawkwell would allow.

The clear case is Messene (with Argos) (344). In the *Second Philippic* Demosthenes harking back to 346 and its aftermath said 'So they say that Philip is going to hold the Thebans in suspicion, and there are those who go round making up a story that he will fortify Elateia' (i.e. directed against Thebes). 'But Philip himself is *going to do* these things, and is going on *going to do* them, as it seems to me; but for the Messenians and the Argives he is not *going to join in* against the Spartans, he *actually is* sending mercenaries, and *is* dispatching money, and he *is* expected there in person with a great army.'[1] If these words in this context represent merely Demosthenes' own fiction and invention, then we must think of him not as a politician at all really, but as some sort of comedian or clown. Messenian and Argive ambassadors were present in Athens at

[1] D. 6. 15. My italics.

the very moment when he spoke. Let us believe by all means that he said only what suited him: the fact still remains that in this situation he had no option but to speak the truth. If the truth had not suited him, he could have kept silent about it; but what he did choose to say here has got to be the truth. That it is the truth is proved by the extract (ibid.) from his own speech made to the Messenians at Messene a few weeks or months earlier, with which he now regales the Athenian audience. In that speech he had reminded the Messenians that they were in the same position as the Olynthians in 356, and as the Thessalians in 346, occasions when these peoples had really got something tangible out of their friendship with Philip and were pleased with him.[1] These analogies do not make sense unless the Messenians too in 344 had got something tangible —the mercenaries and the money already mentioned (and the hope of Philip's support in person).

The same extract from the same speech at Messene ends with the words ' "Be on your guard," I said, "lest while you look for a way out of your war, you find a master".'[2] The natural inference from this is that Messene (and Argos) at this moment actually are at war with Sparta; they have asked for men and money from Philip, and have got some of each, and they have some hope that Philip himself will come to the Peloponnese with his Macedonians and settle with Sparta for good. This inference has not been drawn by most modern interpreters for whatever reasons. But there is external supporting evidence which suggests strongly that this is the inference which does need to be drawn. The Hypothesis to the *Second Philippic* remarks that Demosthenes in the speech undertakes to supply answers to certain ambassadors who have come, the Athenians being uncertain what answers they ought to give.

Where these ambassadors came from, and what they came for, the speech itself does not reveal; but it is possible to find this out from the *Philippic Histories*. It seems that at this time Philip sent ambassadors . . . And along with Philip the Argives and Messenians too sent ambassadors, they too protesting against the Athenians for their friendship and support of the Spartans in their attempt to enslave the Peloponnese, and for their opposition to Argos and Messene in their war for freedom.[3]

The last words (αὐτοῖς δὲ περὶ ἐλευθερίας πολεμοῦσιν ἐναντιοῦται) indicate a state of war between Argos and Messene and the Spartans; for the verb πολεμέω in Attic prose is seldom used metaphorically and in this context must mean literally 'be at war with, fight', and nothing else.[4] The value of this passage lies in its confirmation of Demosthenes' πολέμου ζητοῦντες ἀπαλλαγῆναι noticed above. This was no exaggeration of

---

[1] D. 6. 20 and 22.
[2] D. 6. 25 'οὐ φυλάξεσθ' ὅπως', ἔφην, 'μὴ πολέμου ζητοῦντες ἀπαλλαγῆναι δεσπότην εὑρήσετε;'
[3] D. 6, Hypoth. 2.   [4] LSJ⁹ s.v. πολεμέω.

Demosthenes, evidently. There was a war in the Peloponnese in this year, of consequence enough to be recorded by the standard histories. Lest it be argued that 'the *Philippic Histories*' may have derived this information from Demosthenes and Demosthenes only, it is clear that they had other sources of information too (which supplied the Hypothesis with the facts about the embassies which are not to be found in the speech itself); and it is worth remembering that 'the *Philippic Histories*' must surely include Theopompus. Contemporary and well informed, and quite likely in Macedonia at this very time, Theopompus will not have needed Demosthenes to tell him whether or not there was a war in the Peloponnese in 344.[1]

Philip's sending mercenaries, then, to the aid of Messene and Argos in their war against Sparta in 344 need not be in doubt. As to Elis, Demosthenes' allusions need not mean more than that Philip supported with money the anti-democratic faction in a *stasis*, an incident hard to place chronologically (below), but in no way improbable in itself. At Megara, Philip's alleged intervention in 343, by supplying mercenaries to Perillus, again in a *stasis*, depends solely on the word of Demosthenes, and cannot be either proved or disproved decisively (below, p. 497). In Euboea, interventions by Philip with troops are not disputed by Cawkwell, who does deny however that any took place earlier than 342.[2] A difficulty here is Demosthenes' allusion in 341 to the destruction of Porthmos the harbour of Eretria, placing it in a chronologically ordered list before the Megarian incident of 343. This seems unlikely to be wrong, of incidents so relatively recent, and with no discernible motives for reversing their order: and the fact that Demosthenes does reverse their order when alluding to the same incidents eleven years later does nothing, in my view, to undermine the probable correctness of the earlier allusion.[3] More persuasive is Cawkwell's use of the *Halonnesus* speech of 342 to discredit Demosthenes in these alarmist allusions to Porthmos and to Megara. This speech mentions neither incident, an indication (suggests Cawkwell) that the destruction of Porthmos had not yet happened, and that Philip really was not concerned in the Megara incident at all.[4] I agree that Hegesippus (if he is the author of the speech) might well have found occasion to mention both incidents if they were both genuine and recent, and that it is right to ask why he did not. The answer would seem to be that in the speech as he actually composed it, the examples

---

[1] Theopompus was certainly in Macedonia with Philip early in 342 (*Epist. Socrat.* 30. 12 = Speusippus to Philip). Jacoby, *FGrH* no. 115, prints this Libanius (*sic*) passage as F 401, in the category *Zweifelhaftes*.

[2] 'Demosthenes' 202 and n. 2.

[3] D. 10. 8 f.; 18. 71.

[4] 'Demosthenes' 202–3. Plu. *Phoc.* 15, describing the Athenian intervention at Megara, usually identified with this same occasion, also makes no mention of Philip. Plutarch's narrative is focused on Phocion of course.

which he gives of Philip's *adikia* are more narrowly defined than by Demosthenes' criterion. The passage in which Hegesippus mentions Pherae, Ambracia, and the three cities in Cassopia is concerned with attacks on cities by Philip which constituted breaches of the principle of freedom and autonomy. But in Megara and in Euboea Philip is alleged to have acted by supporting a faction or a leader inside a city, and in neither case occupied or garrisoned a city for himself: the autonomy principle was not contravened in the same way. For this reason (there may be others) the silence of Hegesippus about Megara and Euboea does not seem to me decisive. If these alleged activities of Philip were surprising in themselves, and were something that seemed irreconcilable with what we know of his career and character previously, it would be different. But as it is, it looks as if we ought to believe Demosthenes about them.

The *Second Philippic* of Demosthenes illuminates fitfully a Peloponnesian situation; the scene at the time when the speech was delivered in the year 344.[1] Allusions in the *Embassy* speech about a year later give important confirmation and some more details. Polybius throws some light on the general background of this Peloponnesian scene: and since his remarks were designed polemically, to correct what he conceived to be a false impression given by Demosthenes, they give us probably our best start. Polybius of course was fond of polemic not only for its own sake, but sometimes (as here) because his own political sympathies were engaged. The Peloponnese in the 340s was full not only of inter-city antagonisms, the legacy of Sparta's old hegemony and the more recent liberation from it, but also of the class war which simmered inside some of the cities. Both the antagonisms and the class war had lived on down the generations, even into the years of Polybius' own youth. Polybius, hardly more than Demosthenes, was the detached and impartial observer of the 340s B.C. that we might have hoped to find in the historian writing two centuries later.[2] Nor does he seem to have succeeded in bridging entirely the gap between the age of Philip V of Macedonia and that of Philip II. Himself well accustomed to the notion of a Macedonian hegemony over Greece or parts of it as something which had been

---

[1] The chronology in detail of the year 344 is very obscure. It is well discussed by Cawkwell, 'Demosthenes' 121 ff., who sees the *Second Philippic* as a speech replying to that embassy of Philip to Athens which included Python of Byzantium (below, p. 489). But the *Second Philippic* is unaware of the Persian developments which coincided with Python's embassy, and it must be a little earlier. The opening words of the Speech are: 'Whenever we hold discussions here about Philip's intrigues and acts of violence contrary to the Peace, I always observe . . .' showing that at Athens occasions for complaint and recrimination about the Peace of Philocrates were not rare at this time. The 'embassy of Python' will not have been Philip's first embassy to Athens concerned with these topics.

[2] For the 'Achaean' viewpoint of Polybius, and its occasional influence on his impartiality, see F. W. Walbank, *Historical Commentary on Polybius* 1. 12 f.

inevitable from time to time, he quite failed to enter into the minds of those earlier Greeks who faced the possibility of it for the first time. However disguised, it was a foreign rule which threatened even when it did not destroy the high first prize of the Greek political life; freedom.

Polybius, with the advantage of knowing his Peloponnesian history well (and of course knowing the end of this story as well as its beginning), was able to point out how wrong Demosthenes had been to brand as traitors to Greece those Peloponnesian politicians who co-operated with Philip. Himself he declared them statesmen of high reputation, and especially the Arcadians and Messenians, because it was they who first brought Philip into the Peloponnese, and taught Sparta a lesson, and gave peace and freedom to all the Peloponnesians. They did this, too, without making their cities subjects or dependants of Macedonia, and without making revolutions in the cities to their own advantage. In short their policy here was statesmanlike and was justified by its results (which Polybius compared favourably with the results of Demosthenes' policies for Athens). In any case the interests of Athens (as he points out) were not those of everybody else in Greece, as Demosthenes had assumed, betraying in this his ignorance and bad judgement.[1]

The passage(s) of Demosthenes which Polybius had in mind accused these political leaders in the Peloponnese (and elsewhere) of actually taking bribes from Philip: this was the 'disease' which that famous and eloquent passage of the *Embassy* speech describes.[2] It is noteworthy that Polybius never once attempted to deny explicitly that they did take money from Philip. Instead he was at some pains to define what he conceived 'traitors' to be—those who associated with the enemies of their own city to its disadvantage and to their own personal gain.[3] It is interesting, too, that he passed over in silence the party in Elis which co-operated with Philip, while defending by name the leaders in Arcadia, Messene, and Argos, as well as those in Boeotia and Thessaly, as having been called traitors unjustly. Elis, we shall see, had no cause to thank its *makedonizontes* (below, p. 499).

It is true, up to a point, to talk of a power vacuum in the Peloponnese at this time. As early as the 360s it had been shown that, speaking in terms of hegemony, neither Sparta nor Thebes nor Athens could establish themselves decisively as the leader there, and that the Peloponnesian states themselves were neither strong enough individually nor firmly enough united to form a secure bloc.[4] The Phocian War, which the Spartan king Archidamus had done something to start and more to

[1] Plb. 18. 14. 1–19.
[2] D. 19. 259 ff., with 265 ff.; cf. 18. 295, where the 'traitors' are named, in Thessaly, Arcadia, Argos, Elis, Messene, Sicyon, Corinth, Megara, Thebes, Euboea.
[3] Plb. 18. 13 and 15.
[4] See on this (e.g.) Momigliano, *FM* 76 ff.

prolong, as a means of bleeding Boeotia and so opening up the Peloponnese again to a Spartan counter-attack, had failed to achieve this
second purpose. But the indecisive Peloponnesian campaigns of 352 and
351 had shown Sparta attempting the mischief she was unable to con-
summate;[1] and the events of the next years in northern Greece had
emphasized that with Athens now Sparta's active associate and with the
Boeotians ineffective, Philip was the ally with both the power and the
will to support enemies of Sparta in the Peloponnese. Already in 346
Demosthenes could speak of Argos, Messene, Megalopolis, and some
others as ill disposed to Athens (and by inference well disposed to
Philip).[2]

The interesting inscription, too, which records the request of Messene
and Megalopolis to be admitted as members of the Delphic Amphictyony,
though it cannot be dated precisely, must surely belong to the period
between the end of the Phocian War and the time (in 344 and 343)
when those two cities can be seen to be acting as allies of Philip in fact
and probably in name (below).[3] Their leading motive in approaching
the Amphictyony, no doubt, was anti-Spartan, for Sparta's quarrel with
the Amphictyons (above, p. 452) was still unresolved. Perhaps they
could reactivate it. And anybody who disliked the Spartans was a
friend of theirs. But they might reckon, too, that membership of the
Council, if they could achieve it, might improve their access to Philip's
ear. Perhaps the likeliest dates for their application, in the absence of
any detailed information, are either in autumn 346, when Philip himself
came in as a new member in place of the Phocians, or more probably
in 344 when Philip gave them some help against Sparta, and when they
hoped for more. The application certainly failed (we never hear of them
as members hereafter), but the temporizing and diplomatic language of
the Amphictyonic reply (in the inscription), shows some concern for
retaining their goodwill, even though the Amphictyons were not prepared to include in their circle those who could not be thought of in any
real sense as 'neighbours'. Philip's voice on this will have been heard,
no doubt. He did not want to lose the Messenians and Megalopolitans
as friends; nor did he lose them in the event. If Sparta ever had agreed
to recognize Messene, this perhaps could have been taken as a symbol
of her acceptance of the new situation (since Leuctra), and perhaps
would have relaxed the Peloponnesian tension. But the Spartans presumably, apart from sentiment, could never afford to say goodbye to
Messenia, since its loss must have contributed greatly to the economic
malaise which affected their citizen body now.[4] It must have been this

---

[1] D.S. 16. 34. 3; 39. 1 ff.   [2] D. 5. 17 f.   [3] *Syll.*[3] 224; cf. Wüst 25–6.
[4] Arist. *Pol.* 1270ª10–12; 1307ª7. A. H. M. Jones's view (*Sparta* 134 f.) that losing Messenia
was no great loss to Sparta because it released her from the military strain of holding the

partly, together with some opportunism which our lack of information leaves us to guess at, that prompted the Spartan government eventually to send King Archidamus with a force to Tarentum in southern Italy, where he was to die in battle.[1] But meanwhile the Spartans pursued the quarrel with Messene; Philip's opportunity to intervene.

The occasion and causes of the outbreak of war in 344 in the Peloponnese are unknown. The only allusion to its origin in our sources is unfavourable to Sparta;[2] and even Demosthenes nowhere suggests that Philip had instigated an attack on Sparta by Messene and Argos. What is significant is that these allies turned for support against Sparta not now to Thebes (and of course not to Athens with her record of co-operation with Sparta since 369), but to Philip.[3] The scale of his support, in men and money, is not known, and may not have been very great. But he may genuinely have undertaken, as Demosthenes suggests, to follow it up by himself leading an army into the Peloponnese,[4] and very likely it was this threat which influenced the Spartans to make peace within the year. No more is heard of this war next year or later; but the Argives (and 'many of the Arcadians') are still very pleased with Philip at the time of the trial of Aeschines in 343.[5] Philip's intervention here, in fact, did have important results. For something is needed to explain the decision at Sparta which sent Archidamus overseas, first briefly to Crete and thence to Tarentum where he was to meet his death. This looks like a recognition by Archidamus and the Spartan policy-makers that the Messenian question must be shelved for the time being. And at Argos it seemed safe now to agree to send 3,000 troops and the notable general Nicostratus to Artaxerxes Ochus in response to his recruiting drive preparatory to the invasion of Egypt.[6]

The Peloponnesian tension evidently was relaxed, with effects which can be seen a year or two later (below, p. 549). The departure of Archidamus to Italy, taking with him a force raised by Sparta and presumably in part of citizens, was significant in a way that cannot have been misunderstood. This move cannot possibly have been foreseen or intended by Philip, and may even have exceeded any result that he had hoped to bring about. It might have suited him better for the tension not to be relaxed. An expedition against Sparta led by himself may have seemed his most effective way of dominating the Peloponnese with the Messenians, Argives, and Arcadians as (for the moment) well-satisfied customers.

Messenians down, seems to me unsound. It cannot have failed to aggravate the economic and social difficulties of the Spartiates, whose whole system depended on their being landed gentry, by depriving them of nearly half of their land.

[1] D.S. 16. 62. 4.

[2] D. 6, Hypoth. 2–3 (especially οὐ μὴν ἀποφήνασθαι δύνανται δίκαια πράττειν τοὺς Λακεδαιμονίους).

[3] Ibid.; cf. D. 5. 18.   [4] D. 6. 15.   [5] D. 19. 261.   [6] D.S. 16. 44. 1 ff.

The fact that Sparta made peace did not rule out such a programme even now; for it was always possible to pick a quarrel. But in the event he evidently decided not to force an issue here, and to accept the *détente*, with some short-term disadvantages, but with a substantial reputation already as an effective ally. That Messene, Argos, and some Arcadians had entered into alliances with him in this year (or earlier) seems to follow without question from the reinforcements and subsidy sent to Messene, and from the terms of Demosthenes' report in 343 of Argive and Arcadian feelings towards him.[1]

One lesson, however, from all this was that he could not afford now to undertake anything anywhere in Greece without taking into consideration what reaction might follow from his enemies. The state and the balance of political sympathies in Athens is something that we now can measure only by such indications as the trial of Aeschines, the course of negotiations about revision of the peace treaty, and so on. We must suppose that at any time after 346 Philip himself was much better informed about them than we are. But it would be a mistake, probably, to think that at every step he could reckon that he knew for sure what the Athenian reaction would be. The Athenians were his allies now, and there were influential men at Athens who saw this alliance as the basis of Athenian foreign policy for the future. There was also Demosthenes, and the irreconcilables. Philip might reckon that to support Messene and the rest against Sparta was no threat to Athens, and should not reasonably be interpreted as one. But to Demosthenes and others the Peloponnese represented the best field for Athenian diplomatic effort, the area of Greece where Athens might find the allies she needed: if Philip came to dominate the Peloponnese Athens was isolated. In this year 344 a majority of the Athenian *demos* evidently agreed with Demosthenes. The result was the Athenian embassy to Peloponnesian states, with a purpose and performance which seems to have been quite openly anti-Macedonian. Unreasonable this may well have seemed to Philip, and a subject for protest.[2] But this Athenian attitude of mind was something to be recognized and to be lived with. It was not enough to point out (as he did now) that he had not deceived Athens with false promises in 346. It was worth all his trouble now to try to convince the Athenians that his every activity in Greece was not directed against them or towards a domination by conquest, and to try to remove the ill will towards him by offering to negotiate about revision of the terms of the Peace of Philocrates. This was the constructive purpose behind a further Macedonian embassy including the celebrated Python of Byzantium which he

---

[1] D. 19. 261 Φίλιππον θαυμάζουσι καὶ χαλκοῦν ἱστᾶσι καὶ στεφανοῦσι, καὶ τὸ τελευταῖον, ἂν εἰς Πελοπόννησον ἴῃ, δέχεσθαι ταῖς πόλεσιν εἰσὶν ἐψηφισμένοι.

[2] D. 6. 20–5; 6, Hypoth. 1–2.

sent to Athens later in the year 344 and which coincided, as it chanced, with the presence of an embassy from the King of Persia.[1]

3. *The Persian Question*

In the late summer of 344 ambassadors of the Persian King Artaxerxes Ochus, who planned to invade Egypt in about fifteen months from now, approached the principal Greek cities with the aim of securing those reinforcements of Greek soldiers without which a Persian army nowadays could reckon itself no more than a second-rate military proposition.[2] We are told of the replies that the ambassadors received from Athens, Sparta, Thebes, and Argos.[3] But first it could be asked, why did the Great King not send ambassadors to Philip himself if he wanted good soldiers? That he did not, may be taken as certain, both from the silence of the record in Diodorus and from the terms in which Philip himself in the surviving *Letter* to the Athenians four years later referred to this very occasion.[4] And that the omission was not due to any mere ignorance or inadvertence of the King seems equally certain, since Philip's Macedonia by this time was already the most efficient military power in Europe, a fact which will not have escaped Persian statesmen, who from the days of the Athenian empire right through into the 350s had shown themselves always very much abreast with every change in the kaleidoscope of Greek politics and power. The presence at Philip's court of the former satrap the rebel Artabazus will not have predisposed Artaxerxes in Philip's favour;[5] but it need not have prevented him from trying to make use of him if he had thought it politic. The most likely explanation may be that already he viewed Philip with a deep suspicion, just because he had become the greatest power of the Greek area. The Macedonians were very good soldiers certainly, this had been made clear; and there were plenty of them. They were not a people to invite into Asia lightly, if at all; and especially, any invitation that might give Philip an opportunity to offer his services in person was a notion not to be entertained.

The two great monarchies were not well acquainted with each other.

---

[1] On the constructive purpose, see further, p. 489.

[2] For chronology of the Persian reconquest of Egypt, see Cawkwell, 'Demosthenes' 121 ff., 136 ff. (against the unacceptable suggestions of M. Sordi, *Kokalos* 5 (1959) 107 ff.).

[3] D.S. 16. 44. 1 f.; Philoch. F 157 (*FGrH* no. 328).

[4] [D.] 12. 6 f.

[5] D.S. 16. 52. 3 records the flight of Artabazus from his satrapy some long time (ἐν τοῖς ἐπάνω χρόνοις) before the Persian reconquest of Egypt (342, completed), and his presence at Philip's court for some time before his recall to Persia (342—D.S. ibid.). The date of his flight, as Beloch observed (3². 1. 482 n. 2) must have been before the earlier (abortive) Persian attempt to recover Egypt (351/350); that is, in 352 or 351 probably. He need not have gone then to Macedonia immediately, as Momigliano rightly warned (*FM* 123 n. 1). But his stay with Philip was known to Curtius Rufus (5. 9. 1; 6. 5. 2), and was probably not short. It seems safe to think that he was with Philip by 344.

Macedonia since Alexander I had never become important enough to be among the Aegean states that Persian kings and satraps had seen cause to cultivate as friends or circumvent as enemies. It is only the reign of Philip that brings her again into the Persian orbit, diplomatic or military. The earliest connection that can be known or suspected is not earlier than the year 351; that allusion in the *First Philippic* which records, among the rumours about Philip circulating at the time, a rumour that he had sent ambassadors to the Great King.[1] True or false? One sees no good basis for an opinion either way. But it seems safe to say that if he did send ambassadors then, nothing of any consequence resulted from it.

The well-known statement in Arrian that Philip and Artaxerxes Ochus at some time became 'friends and allies' is accepted by most modern writers; too easily, as it seems. The letter of Darius III to Alexander after the battle of Issus in which the statement occurs (twice) is not likely to have been a genuine letter of Darius;[2] and even if it is accepted as genuine, it is still necessary to question whether this piece of information in it can possibly be true. Occasions when an alliance might have been made by the two kings are, it is true, not hard to imagine. Perhaps early in Philip's reign, in 356/5 for example?[3] Perhaps in 351 when Ochus was about to try for the first time to reconquer Egypt?[4] Or in 344/3 before his second and successful attempt?[5] Or even in 342, after it?[6] Perhaps none of these occasions is impossible, and there may be others, when an alliance might have been made.

That any alliance was made, however, can be ruled out by the conspiracy of silence about it on the part of the contemporary orators which we should be obliged to assume in this case. The silence of Diodorus and Justin would not be decisive, in view of the defects in their accounts of these years. But if an alliance had been made early in Philip's reign, why did Demosthenes not mention it in the *Rhodians* speech (351/350), where he does once mention Philip and the Great King in the same breath, or in the *Second Philippic* (344) where he spoke of 'medizers' at the time of Xerxes including Philip's 'ancestor Alexander' (Alexander I)?[7] Could Isocrates merely have ignored the existence of an alliance, if any had been made before 346, in his *Philip*, so much of it devoted to advice and encouragement for an attack on Persia? We possess six speeches

---

[1] D. 4. 48.   [2] *PCPhS* 14 (1968) 33 ff.

[3] In 356/5 the relations of Persia and Athens became strained as a result of the operations of Chares in Asia Minor (cf. D.S. 16. 22. 2 etc.). Philip on his side had been at war with Athens for a year or so already, and had shown that he could look after himself very well without any help from Persia. Any initiative by Philip leading to a Persian alliance now seems improbable; but it is arguable that it would still have been good policy to accept any Persian overtures, if there were any.

[4] So Cawkwell, 'Demosthenes' 128.   [5] So Momigliano, *FM* 139 n. 1; Wüst 89 f.

[6] So Beloch 3².1. 538 n. 1.   [7] D. 15. 24; 6. 11.

belonging to the years 343–341 inclusive, just the period when the alliance, according to most theories, would have been recent and relevant. Quite apart from the relevance (which seems undeniable), is it conceivable that an orator hostile to Philip should never have used a Persian alliance as another piece of mud to throw, if an alliance and a recent one had existed? The alliance might have been a defensive one; but that would not have troubled Demosthenes (and rightly in a sense). Or it might have been a secret one (as Wüst thought).[1] Nothing could be more improbable, really, than this, in view of the situation of these alleged protagonists, to whom only an alliance that was generally known would have been of value, and who cannot possibly have either known or trusted each other in the way that is a prerequisite of pacts by secret diplomacy. And indeed in the later 340s what value was there for Philip in this alliance anyway, which could compensate him for the loss of respectability, if (as we must suppose) he had made one with no intention of observing it for very long, and this when already his hope was to become in some sense the recognized *hegemon* of all Greece and to lead the Greeks against Persia? True, there had been times in his early years when Philip had been something less than respectable in his political behaviour. Perhaps by nature he was not respectable, and never became so. Yet he had reached an eminence now, where to behave respectably was of value, and to be thought a mere political sharper was a liability. This he could see, we may be sure.[2]

In short the alliance seems to be a fiction. No such thing ever happened in reality.

There was no question, then, of any Macedonian aid to Persia in the reconquest of Egypt. The Persian requests for troops went to Greek cities, and of the four who are named in our record Sparta and Athens refused, but Thebes sent 1,000 hoplites, and Argos sent 3,000 men.[3] The decisions on this were taken presumably late in the year 344 or in the winter 344/3, and they tell us, first, that the war in the Peloponnese (above, p. 478) by now was over, whether or not by Philip's threatened intervention. The Argives felt free to commit themselves fairly heavily here in Asia, perhaps because the Spartans were committed already to sending troops abroad to Italy with Archidamus. Obviously there is room to wonder whether it is right to look for an alignment in these attitudes to Persia: the friends and allies of Philip send troops to Asia, Sparta, and Athens (the ally in name only) refuse. This has been thought, naturally, to indicate a *rapprochement* of Philip and Persia, and to support the historicity of the 'alliance' in Arrian. If one could believe in

---

[1] Wüst 91.

[2] Cawkwell, 'Demosthenes' 127–8, puts the case well, against an alliance in 343.

[3] D.S. 16. 44. 1–2.

this historicity as a possibility, even, the policy of Thebes and of Argos now might be explicable by reference to Philip's policy. But the grounds for rejecting the alliance altogether as historical fact are really very strong, and by this interpretation the reactions of Thebes and Argos to the Persian invitation must be seen in a different light.[1] It may be wrong to assume that Philip must be involved here in some way. It may be right to allow for the possibility that these were decisions taken independently in the cities, in Argos and Sparta for reasons already suggested, in Thebes continuing a tradition of good relations with Persia.[2]

Philip himself is not likely to have used his influence to promote the rehabilitation of Persia. Indeed it may not be many months after this time when his intrigue with Hermias of Atarneus began, an activity seen as sinister by the Persian government when it learned of it.[3] If already he planned to attack Persia ultimately, he would have preferred that no Greek troops went to reinforce the Persians now. But that is not to say that he tried to stop it, or that we should see the Theban reinforcement (especially) as an act of defiance or a sign of deteriorating relations of Thebes and Philip. Philip was not yet committed publicly as an enemy of Persia. The Greeks were at peace now, and were not expecting to be at war again this year or next (this much the Theban and Argive commitment now to Persia seem to show). It seems likely that Philip remained inscrutable as the Persian ambassadors went their round, and that he allowed the cities to reach their decisions without any help (or hindrance) from him. The decisions will have owed something, no doubt, to the conditions of life in these cities at this time, and to the numbers of their citizens who were not averse from finding employment in this way as soldiers. Thebes and Argos, as well as Athens, were democracies, and it may be doubted whether any democracy in these circumstances would have voted simply to send so many citizens for service in Asia by conscription. More probably they would have nominated a general (D.S. 16. 44. 1–2), and authorized him to take volunteers up to so many citizens. At Athens service in the army was not popular, and this as well as the political considerations of the moment will have been reflected in the decision of the *demos* now.

---

[1] Cawkwell ('Demosthenes' 129) though he does believe in the alliance (dating it to 351) argues rightly that the responses of Thebes, Argos, and Athens to Persia ought not to be interpreted as supporting a view that Philip himself 'was prepared to come to terms with Persia in this period'.

[2] Cawkwell's attempt ('Demosthenes' 129 f.) to explain the Theban and Argive decisions by suggesting changes in 'leadership' in Thebes and Argos at this time is laudable but very tenuous, especially for Argos. For Thebes, it is certain that a majority of Thebans did become hostile to Philip by 340/39, and a conflict of leadership between two groups in the years 346–340 can be assumed. But to interpret this decision to aid Persia as a sign that an anti-Macedonian group is in the ascendancy, still seems very hazardous.

[3] See below, pp. 518 ff.

To Philip, the action of Thebes and of Argos may have caused some irritation. But the Athenian refusal, in terms unfriendly to Persia, will have pleased him more than those others displeased him;[1] for nothing would have been more unwelcome than Athenian co-operation with Ochus, with a likelihood in consequence of Ochus' co-operation with Athens thereafter. For once the Athenians had done the right thing: so Philip may have reflected now, without letting it escape him that they had not, however, done it for the right reason. Some such equivocal view of the Athenians at this time came more easily to Philip, perhaps, than it comes to us now. He saw something of all the shades of Athenian opinion, heard something of every tone of the Athenian voice. At Athens the future just round the corner was still a matter for debate, it was not yet a crusade. This time represents for the Athenians an interval in which remembrance of things past, the impacts of the present, and some hopes or fears for the future, combined to create a period of suspense.

The interval was not a short one. If as seems likely the embassy of Hegesippus (below) returned from Macedonia in the winter, or early in the year 343, there follows a full year or more during which the attitude of the Athenian people remains open, or at least not totally committed. Open, too, stays Philip's offer of a revision of the treaty of 346 (below); as is clear from the *Halonnesus* speech of early 342.[2] It is with this background that Philip's Greek activities of the year 343 and early 342 are to be viewed. Commonly it is an Athenian viewpoint that is taken, mainly because of the insights into the Athenian scene that are given by the surviving speeches of the orators, and especially those of Demosthenes and Aeschines on the occasion of the *Embassy* trial in 343 (autumn?). That this is so is not inappropriate, for it genuinely is true that Athens has become the key to Greece in these years. But in interpreting the Athenians and their moods, there are two thoughts which we need to apply to this material as we use it. First and more obviously, our surviving speeches are preponderantly anti-Macedonian, because Philip and the Peace of 346 were neither of them generally popular, and consequently even Aeschines (for example) in his speech in his own defence was not in a position ever to expose fully and freely the views of those Athenians who did not think of Philip as a natural enemy, and who thought of the Peace and alliance of 346 as the right basis now for Athenian foreign policy. Yet that such Athenians did exist we can glimpse from the *Second Letter* of Isocrates a little earlier, and from the *Letter* of Speusippus to Philip a little later: and the acquittal of Aeschines (narrow though it was) shows that at that time and under the influence of Eubulus and his group making a great effort, it was still not quite a majority of the Athenians

---

[1] Philoch. F 157 (= Didymus, *in Demosth.* 10. 34, col. 8. 8 ff.), ὑπεροπτικώτερον ἢ ἐχρῆν etc.
[2] [D.] 7. 18 ff.

who believed that the only thing to do to Philip was to stand up and thrash him if it could be done. It was not yet a majority, in 343, who saw 'revision of the Peace' as a waste of time unless it included recovery of Amphipolis and the other slogans of the intransigents.[1]

The second thought for the interpreter of these things is, how deep was Philip's own concern for the state of public opinion at Athens and for the attitudes of the *demos* towards himself?

4. *Athens and Revision of the Treaty* (epanorthosis)

Philip's support of Messene and Argos against Sparta had enabled his opponents in Athens to represent the Peloponnese as in danger from his designs, and had led to the embassy of which Demosthenes was a member being sent to the Peloponnese in the summer of 344. Its hostile attitude to Philip and its accusations of bad faith were taken seriously by him. He not only protested at the time (the occasion which produced Demosthenes' *Second Philippic*), but he judged that the time had come for something more positive. The Athenian diplomatic campaign against him sprang evidently from a deep dissatisfaction with the terms and the results of the Peace of Philocrates. While his friends in Athens might exhort the *demos* to look to the future, his enemies had only to invite it to remember the past. He sent to Athens now a new embassy which contained the celebrated orator Python of Byzantium and which was supported by ambassadors from many of his own allies.[2] 'Let us consider, then, how this Peace may be amended': this in brief was Philip's new proposal now through Python of Byzantium. *Epanorthosis*, the word used by the Athenian politicians in this connection, no doubt was the word approved by Philip himself and used by Python when he spoke of it.[3] Exactly what Python said, and how he put it, of course we cannot know. But he conveyed to the Athenians that Philip was prepared to reopen discussion of some matters in the Peace treaty which could be thought of as being the subject of dispute. Python did not specify these matters by name in his speech. He probably covered them with some general and non-committal form of words which (as it proved) was capable of being misunderstood, particularly by those who were determined to misunderstand it.[4] What matters Philip had in mind (or some of them) we can infer perhaps only from the *Halonnesus* speech of about eighteen

---

[1] [D.] 7. 18 ff.; 23 ff.; 30 ff.

[2] Both Philip in his *Letter* of 340 ([D.] 12. 18) and Demosthenes (18. 136) speaking in 330 say 'all his allies' of this occasion; but each has his reasons for exaggeration.

[3] D. 6. 5 and 34 uses the verb twice (probably a few weeks before this occasion).

[4] [D.] 7. 19 ff. summarizes the speech of Python (nearly two years later), not necessarily accurately in all respects. He surely misreports him as saying (7. 22) 'If there is anything wrong with the terms of the Peace, then amend it; for Philip will do everything that you propose.'

months later (early 342), when they were still in dispute. Some Athenian prisoners of war of 346? The places in Thrace which, the Athenians alleged, Philip had taken after the Peace had been sworn? The boundaries of the Athenian territory in the Chersonese?[1] To be ready to discuss these things afresh now was a conciliatory gesture by Philip; a sign that he did want Athens as a real friend and ally, and a sign which he hoped would be recognized for this.

The initiative in inviting proposals for 'amendment' (*epanorthosis*) was Philip's;[2] but it was left to the Athenians to make the proposals, and it seems that at the assembly which heard Python's speech, two important proposals were drafted and passed, as the material which Athenian ambassadors were to take to Philip for his approval. The first in point of interest and practical application (though Hegesippus named it second) was that the bilateral treaty of alliance between Philip and Athens should be reinforced by means of a treaty establishing a *koine eirene* in which all Greek cities should be invited to join.[3] This, if it had come about, could have been seen as a stabilization of the *status quo* resembling that of 362 after Mantinea, and as a possible relaxer of tensions, and especially of the tension at Athens.

Though no *koine eirene* yet had absolutely put an end to aggressions by strong powers able to be aggressors (and indeed the Peace of Antalcidas had actually provided a legal framework to support Sparta in some of her worst acts of tyranny), nevertheless there was by this time some reassurance for weaker states in the accumulation of oaths in support of a situation of which they and their rights and existence were recognized to be a part. Messene was happier with the Peace of 362 than she would have been without it. The Athenians themselves and their allies in 346 would have been glad to make their peace with Philip as part of a *koine eirene* if Philip had agreed to it.[4] So now in 344 or 343 a *koine eirene* could be expected to reduce the points of possible friction. Even if the genuine realist at Athens could say always, and with some show of reason, that every movement of Philip in Greece was either directed against Athens or was to her disadvantage, yet it was of some service to get Philip's movements limited (by a *koine eirene*) to those in which he was acting only with the consent or at the invitation of the Greek cities concerned, and to rule out acts of open and direct aggression which would brand him as aggressor. For Philip to agree to limit himself in this way, by accepting a *koine eirene*, was a move which helped those Athenians who

[1] [D.] 7. 38; 36–7; 39. These last two disputes Philip offered to submit to arbitration, even in 342 when his relations with Athens had deteriorated badly.

[2] So rightly Cawkwell, 'Demosthenes' 132 n. 5, relying on [D.] 7. 18 and 26.

[3] [D.] 7. 30 ff. By this account the proposal for *koine eirene* is made by Athens not by Philip, and there seems no good reason (*pace* Cawkwell, ibid.) to doubt this.

[4] See above, p. 340.

believed already in his good intentions to reassure those Athenians who were still in doubt: the hard core of those who were firmly convinced of his bad intentions could be isolated perhaps and contained.

The second of the Athenian proposals, however, was frankly unpromising. Somebody must have persuaded the *demos*, or must have allowed it to go on believing if it believed it already, that these advances of Philip were made not from strength but from weakness. What a miscalculation—if calculation is the right word for this! On Persia, indeed, satisfactory enough (for Philip). The Athenians may well have been helped to their uncompromising reply to the ambassadors of Ochus by the knowledge that Philip's ambassadors were on the spot, and were on the point of addressing the Assembly with proposals which included *epanorthosis*.[1] But now these proposals themselves were taken up in the Assembly with a misdirected enthusiasm depressing to read of. An embassy was to be sent to Philip now to discuss *epanorthosis*. It was to include (of all people) Hegesippus, who could be counted on to be its most active member, and in the circumstances its least useful one. For the terms of reference of the embassy were discussed now and defined by the Assembly, with a result that can only be called ludicrous. Some ingenious speaker or speakers contrived to persuade the *demos* to close its eyes to its true situation of 344 (which did in truth leave much to be desired), and to re-enter its dream world of 347 and 346. The Assembly voted a *psephisma* unworthy of itself or of any sovran organ of government engaged with a problem of real life, a vote worthy only of some rhetorical school where the 'paper arguments' are encouraged to prevail.

In the Peace of Philocrates the basis of territorial demarcation was 'Each side to have what it holds' (ἔχειν ἑκατέρους ἃ ἔχουσι). The Athenian embassy to Philip now was instructed to pursue 'amendment' by proposing as a new basis 'Each side to have what belongs to them' (ἔχειν τὰ ἑαυτῶν).[2] As a slogan this was brilliant, with its transparent honesty and its appeal to the soft of heart and head. But the folly of the *demos* on this occasion lay in the failure to recognize the slogan for what it was, a rhetor's *coup* and nothing more. Instead of applauding it with the amusement it deserved and then forgetting about it, they allowed themselves to be persuaded to take it seriously at least to the point of using it (tongue in cheek?) as the basis of their reply to Philip's invitation to discuss amendment of the peace treaty.[3] Under the banner of this memorable nonsense—ἔχειν ἑκατέρους τὰ ἑαυτῶν—they instructed their ambassadors to reopen with Philip the question of the ownership of

[1] So, attractively, Cawkwell, 'Demosthenes' 133. But see above also, p. 487.
[2] [D.] 7. 18 and 26; Schol. 7. 18 and 24.
[3] Wüst (p. 73) does allow himself to question whether the *demos* can have taken it seriously, 'im guten Glauben'; but he concludes that it did.

Amphipolis, Potidaea, a score of other places lost to him in ten years of war and confirmed by them as his possessions in the Peace of Philocrates. This was magnificent, perhaps, but it was not negotiation.

Philip was a busy man; and though one may hope that the comic side of all this did not escape him entirely, he can be forgiven if he found it only moderately funny. The principal comedian, too, turned out to be not one of his favourite men.[1] Hegesippus is named by Demosthenes later as the most prominent of these ambassadors, and it was he presumably who was to blame for the bad relations which developed between them and Philip.[2] This must be counted quite an achievement in its way, for Philip must certainly have begun these negotiations hoping to attach Athens to himself more closely if he could, and he was by temperament hospitable (we have seen) and capable of taking great trouble, when he chose, to get on well with diplomatic guests. However irritated he may have been by the Athenian riposte to his proposal for 'amendment' of the treaty, and by having to listen to stale rubbish about Amphipolis, he is not likely to have lost patience quickly either with an argument or with an individual. (Demosthenes had reason to thank him for just this, in a few years time.) Most probably he met with some incivility from Hegesippus personally, and this annoyed him very much, though it cannot be seen to have affected the course of history by any influence on his decisions.[3]

If Hegesippus was a boor, and if the ancient rigmarole about Amphipolis was a bore, it was not these *longueurs* but considerations more fundamental that decided Philip now, if it was now, that in trying to win Athens to a genuine friendship and alliance he was wasting his time. This Athenian embassy was allowed to go home, most probably with something less than the customary exchange of compliments at parting. But not before the points of view had been fully exposed, and not before even the effrontery about Amphipolis had received Philip's reasoned reply. His case on Amphipolis was so good that one cannot believe that he wasted it by (for example) losing his temper. Much more likely, he reminded the Athenians at some length and with some colour of the impropriety of seeking to undo the results of a ten-years war by a bad argument, and on Amphipolis itself he produced the answer which later he summarized in his *Letter* of the year 340, a model of succinct demolition of an impertinent pretension.[4]

---

[1] That the inventor of the slogan was Hegesippus is suggested as probable by Wüst (ibid.), and I agree.   [2] D. 19. 331.

[3] Ibid. τὸν γὰρ Ἡγήσιππον ὁρᾶτε καὶ τοὺς μετ' αὐτοῦ πρέσβεις πῶς ἐδέξατο. τὰ μὲν ἄλλα σιωπῶ, ἀλλὰ Ξενοκλείδην τουτονὶ τὸν ποιητὴν ἐξεκήρυξεν, ὅτι αὐτοὺς ὑπεδέξατο πολίτας ὄντας. τοῖς μὲν γὰρ ὑπὲρ ὑμῶν λέγουσι δικαίως ὅσ' ἂν φρονῶσι τοῦτον τὸν τρόπον προσφέρεται . . .

[4] [D.] 12. 20 ff. (précis): the Athenians were not the first owners of Amphipolis, they had owned it when they did only for a very few years, and they did not own it now, as they

In that same *Letter* later Philip reminded the Athenians of this occasion, the embassy of Python in 344, when (as he wrote) he 'had meant to come to a just settlement with them to the advantage of Greece as a whole'.[1] In the *Letter*, in 340, he drew a distinction between the *demos* of Athens and its extremist advisers in 344. There is no reason why in 344 itself he need have been lacking in good information from Athens, which will have told him of the state and the strength of the political groups; and indeed on this the events themselves were eloquent enough. Though Philip by now did not lack friends in Athens who sympathized with his aims and thought them either compatible with the safety and freedom of their own city or preferable to it, this farce which developed out of the embassy of Python may have convinced him finally that there was no possibility of his friends being able to win and keep the ear of the *demos* in any way so as to dovetail the Athenian views on foreign policy with his own.[2] Philip seems right when he implied in the *Letter* that the Athenian advisers preferred war to peace, though naturally he did much less than justice to their reasons.[3] What he wrote then (in 340) he wrote in the light of the political trials of Philocrates and Aeschines in 343 and of the ever-increasing following which Demosthenes proved able to win thereafter for his policy of belligerence. Early in 343, when the embassy of Hegesippus left him after wasting his time, he could not foresee in detail how it would all turn out. But he could make a prognosis. The blow to his hopes of Python's embassy was fresh and real, carrying a message not hard to interpret. If these people could not talk sense in reply to an opening like this, then nothing, most likely, nothing on this plane of experience, was going to induce them to talk sense or to see it.

It is this indeed that seems to raise these proceedings to a level of some importance in history. Obviously, at some time between 346 and (say) 341/0 Philip's attitude to Athens changed decisively: from the new and prized ally in whom he reposed great hopes she reverted, for him, to the hostile nuisance who needed to be taught, again, that hostility did not pay. The detailed record of this change is lost. It is only from the actions of the two principals that we can try to infer their state of mind and their intentions towards each other. In Philip up to this time, since 346, we have seen some positive consideration for Athens (in the Amphictyony), which has reinforced our earlier conclusion that the

themselves had recognized by the treaty of 346: he himself had an ancestral claim to it dating back to Alexander I, he had captured it not from Athens but from the inhabitants who had thrown the Athenians out years ago, and his title to it had been recognized by Athens in 346.

[1] [D.] 12. 18 f.

[2] According to Hegesippus ([D.] 7. 23 f.), Philip's friends in Athens had told Python of Byzantium that no one would propose 'amendments' to the Peace that 'conflicted with the ψήφισμα of Philocrates that abandoned Amphipolis'.

[3] [D.] 12. 19.

Peace of 346, initiated by him in spite of his winning position in the war, was intended as a genuine reconciliation in which Athens was to be encouraged to become his ally in fact as well as in name. No acts since 346 directed against Athens can be attributed to him, except for those activities in the Peloponnese which alarmed his enemies in Athens in 344. If as seems probable these were part of a design to achieve a hegemony over Greece without conquest, we can understand and sympathize with the reactions of his enemies, Demosthenes and others, who expected the worst of him whatever he did. The two points of view were in truth irreconcilable, that of the Macedonian king promoting his own *hegemonia* and that of Athenian and Greek politicians intent on freedom, this including the freedom for their own city to have hegemony if things went well for it. But Philip did not know as yet how irreconcilable. Realist himself, he counted on realism in the Greeks too, including his enemies. How well he understood the Greek need for freedom we cannot know for certain; but at least he had dozens of Greeks among his own Companions to tell him of it, and he had Thessaly as the school in which he could practise the art of domination without conquest. With a little give and take as between realists, so he may have reckoned, a *hegemon* might hope to dominate all Greece without conquest, while the Greeks in their cities might be able to relinquish some freedom in the sphere of their foreign policy without feeling themselves 'enslaved'.

It was in this hope, one may suggest, the hope of some give and take as between realists, that Philip had framed the messages conveyed to the Athenians by Python and his colleagues. Amendment of the treaty: this to show that he was well disposed and that he was a reasonable man. A *koine eirene* in which all the Greeks could join: this proposal was acceptable to him, to reassure that there was to be no conquest, and that his activities in Greece, such as those recent ones in the Peloponnese, should not alarm Athens (or anybody else). Realists should understand that the bloodless victor of Thermopylae was at liberty to make new friends in Greece as and where he chose, while a *koine eirene*, if it came into being, gave reassurance that nobody was going to be attacked or enslaved.

To Philip, no doubt, the reply of the Athenians, the embassy of Hegesippus, seemed unrealistic, a response not to life as it was, but as the Athenians wanted it to be. It had been the same with Olynthus. The wise are those who learn from the experience of others. But the Athenians, it seemed, were not so wise: they seemed determined to learn the harder way. By the nonsense they talked now about Amphipolis they were slamming a door. The consequence of the failure of these conversations can be seen in Philip's actions in the next few months. Though he refrained from melodrama in either word or act, and indeed kept open the *koine eirene* offer for another year yet,[1] he did give up hope now, I suggest, of having Athens as his ally in any real sense in her present mood. The Athenians needed to learn, a second time, to be realists. It is in the months after the return of the embassy of Hegesippus that Philip intervenes first in Euboea and next in Megara. Viewed in relation to his plans in general, these moves may be seen as consistent with the Peloponnesian moves of 344 and of this same year 343 (at Elis), and of the moves in the north-west (Epirus etc.) a little later. The intention was, no doubt, that all these places should end up with a government friendly to himself (as Epirus did). This was the method by which he would gain control over Greece without conquest. To apply the method, though, to Euboea and Megara, in the face of Athenian susceptibilities so recently and so signally displayed, gives a clue to his intentions that is not to be missed. Euboea and Megara were close neighbours to Attica, and for the Athenians, to have them in the hands of governments allied to Philip was genuinely alarming. Philip himself most certainly must have realized this. If he had still been interested in conciliating Athens in 343, he would certainly have left Euboea and Megara alone now. That he went ahead when the opportunity offered means one of two things. Either he saw a chance of actually intimidating the Athenians by penetrating up to the frontiers of Attica; or at least he judged that the chances of conciliating them by inaction here were so poor that he had better go for the solid military and political gain of getting control in Euboea and Megara if he could. Though it was far more important to have Athens on his side than to have Euboea and Megara, it was not by conciliation, now, that this could be done. This seems the more likely interpretation of his policy here. The Athenians most probably were going to have to be taught their lesson by war, another war. This was Philip's view already now, in 343. But meanwhile he would not precipitate the war himself. He would even continue the duologue with the Athenians as and when occasion arose; and meanwhile the offer for a *koine eirene* was not withdrawn, as we shall see.

[1] Below, pp. 511 ff. Cawkwell, 'Demosthenes' 133, acutely pointed out that an allusion in Demosthenes' *Embassy* Speech (late 343) to 'the Peace' is an allusion to the *koine eirene* proposed to Philip through Python, and that ἀνώμοτον εἶναι τὴν εἰρήνην there (19. 204) implies that the proposal has not been cancelled, but is still open. I agree. (Cawkwell believed Philip to be the proposer of the *koine eirene*.)

XV

PHILIP IN GREECE
(343–342)

1. *The Incidents of 343: Elis, Euboea, Megara*

THE year 343 had begun with a turn for the worse in Macedonian–
Athenian relations, with the embassy of Hegesippus to Philip. In
Athens itself Demosthenes and his anti-Macedonian friends proceeded to improve their position, till in the second half of the year the
great attack was launched on Aeschines, whose narrow acquittal by the
jury was no encouragement to Philip if he was studying the mood of
Athens at this time. This trial had been preceded by impeachments of
Philocrates and Proxenus.[1] And the settling of new cleruchs in the
Chersonese this summer was another sign that the *demos* was taking
advice from those who counted the Macedonian danger as the first
concern of Athenian foreign policy.[2] It is against this background that
Philip's acts of opportunism in Greece in 343 are to be seen.

To describe them as this need not imply that the occasions for action
had been contrived by Philip himself, an arch-initiator of trouble.
Demosthenes of course does imply just this almost invariably by the
whole context and tenor of his allusions to these things; and occasionally
he is explicit (e.g. Μεγάροις ἐπιβουλεύειν, 19. 204). But in the single
instance (of Megara) in which he was unguarded enough to supply two
or three details, it seems to follow fairly clearly from these that 'the
trouble' at Megara was basically a domestic one, and that Philip's entry
into it was by invitation of one of the original parties to it. This is a
pattern so characteristic of Greek *stasis* as we learn of it that it is hardly
going too far to say that there is no Greek city at this time, except Athens
herself and Sparta, of which we can say confidently that it could not
occur there. General probability suggests that most Macedonian interventions in Greek affairs did begin in this way. Philip's initiative as
trouble-maker may be thought to lie in this, that by now he had advanced
himself into the position of being well known in Greece as the patron

---

[1] Philocrates, Hyperid. 30 f.; D. 19. 116 ff.; Aeschin. 2. 6. (cf. 3. 79); Proxenus, D. 19.
280 and schol.; Dinarch. 1. 63. For the timing of these prosecutions, relative to the embassy
of Hegesippus, see Cawkwell, 'Demosthenes' 126. I see no need for the prosecution of
Philocrates to have followed almost immediately on the failure of Hegesippus' mission.

[2] Philoch. F 134 (*FGrH* no. 328), 'archonship of Pythodotus' (343/2); cf. D. 8. 6; 9. 15.

whom it was worth while for anyone having trouble in his own city politics to go to for help. He had the men, he had the money; and sometimes he had the inclination.

Of the three places of which we learn from Demosthenes' *Embassy* speech in the second half of 343 about recent interventions by Philip, the action at Megara was certainly the most recent when Demosthenes spoke. Nevertheless it is convenient to consider it first, for several reasons. Elis was remote, and the trouble there was nothing new in itself; only Philip's involvement in it was new (see below, pp. 499 ff.). Euboea was (for Athens) alarmingly near. But the date of the beginning of Philip's involvement is in dispute, and since the whole story there is a long one covering events of three years, it seems good to consider it in one piece, presently. Those, however, who believe (rightly) that Philip's involvement in Euboea does antedate his involvement at Megara, keep this fact in mind while they consider the Athenian reaction to news of the trouble at Megara. This not only makes the reaction itself easier to understand; it reminds too that the Athenians twice in this summer learned of immediate neighbours on two of their frontiers who seemed in danger of coming in some sense under Philip's control.

Though the absolute date of the Megarian incident is uncertain, its date relative to the date of the trial of Aeschines is clear. It was recent, even very recent; a matter of weeks not of months.[1] It was in the third quarter of the year 343, then, almost for certain. More than once in recent months the Athenians had had disquieting news from Megara,[2] of *stasis* or something approaching it, and of a connection with Philip established by an oligarchic group. One of its leaders, Perillus, had visited Philip in Macedonia.[3] No crime in this, presumably. Yet on his return he was accused (of what?) and put on trial, and was acquitted only by the exertions of Ptoiodorus, a rich aristocrat and one of the leading men of the city. The result of this *cause célèbre* was evidently an important triumph for the oligarchs, for Ptoiodorus thereupon was able to 'send him back to Philip; and then later he returned with the mercenaries, and Ptoiodorus made cheese indoors.'[4] Demosthenes' flashing phrase illuminates an interesting underworld of intrigue (if we are guessing its meaning aright), and suggests to us perhaps a situation in

---

[1] D. 19. 294 αὐτόθι νῦν τούτων τῶν συμβεβηκότων πραγμάτων; cf. 19. 295 ἔναγχος; 19. 334 πρώην.

[2] D. 19. 87 καὶ μὴν καὶ μετὰ ταῦθ' ὁσάκις πρὸς Πορθμῷ ἢ πρὸς Μεγάροις ἀκούοντες δύναμιν Φιλίππου καὶ ξένους ἐθορυβεῖσθε, πάντες ἐπίστασθε. Here μετὰ ταῦθ' = after the Peace of Philocrates. Allowing for D.'s exaggeration, one must still reckon that Euboea (Porthmos) and Megara between them have caused scares at Athens several times in the years 346–343. For Megara, the occasion for one recent scare is known (see next note).

[3] D. 19. 294–5 (where the oligarchic character of the principals is emphasized).

[4] D. 19. 295 καὶ μετὰ ταῦθ' ὁ μὲν ἧκεν ἄγων τοὺς ξένους, ὁ δ' ἔνδον ἐτύρευε; cf. schol. ad D. ibid.

Megara reminiscent of the situation in Athens in 411 shortly before the oligarchic revolution. This was a crisis for Megara, and something decisive happened now.[1] *What* happened?

Only Plutarch tells a story, which may be this story, of an Athenian expedition to Megara at the invitation of 'the Megarians'.[2] It is obviously on an occasion of *stasis* inside the city of Megara (the message to Athens is sent secretly). Phocion at Athens, one of the generals at the time, was not unprepared for it, and knew just what to do. Since we do not know of any other *stasis*, and since we do know of the troubles involving the philo-Macedonians Perillus and Ptoiodorus (above), it seems probably right to identify Plutarch's story with this situation, as is commonly done, even though Plutarch never mentions Perillus or Philip, or indeed any other proper name except that of Phocion himself, and of the Boeotians. With Perillus recently home from Macedonia bringing a force of mercenaries, with Ptoiodorus 'making cheese indoors', it is not surprising if 'the Megarians' sent to Athens 'secretly'; and Phocion's exemplary promptitude and address in meeting the appeal suits well a situation in which the Athenians on their side were worried already about Megara and the co-operation of its oligarchs with Philip. Plutarch's summary of the result of Phocion's rebuilding of the Megarian Long Walls to Nisaea, enabling the city 'to be practically freed from anxiety about its enemies from inland and to become dependent on Athens'[3] is justified in a biographer of Phocion to whom this glimpse of Megarian history is important only on a certain scale. But Demosthenes and the Athenians could not know all along that this would be so, Long Walls or no Long Walls. Interesting, too, is Plutarch's reference to the Boeotians as the competitors whom Phocion had to beat in his race for Megara.[4] Plutarch (Boeotian though he was) will not have invented this; he found it in a source, and for all we know in a good source, for there is nothing intrinsically improbable or surprising in what he says. If Perillus found himself in sudden and urgent trouble, Boeotia was his nearest possible provider of support. Philip would have been the more reliable supporter to send to, for not all Boeotians now could be relied on to do a thing

---

[1] This is clear from the words of Demosthenes' allusion, made of course to jurors at Athens who knew the facts in full—D. 19. 294 (quoted at p. 497 n. 1 above).

[2] Plu. *Phocion* 15. Τῶν δὲ Μεγαρέων ἐπικαλουμένων κρύφα, φοβούμενος ὁ Φωκίων τοὺς Βοιωτοὺς μὴ προαισθόμενοι φθάσωσι τὴν βοήθειαν, ἐκκλησίαν συνήγαγεν ἕωθεν, καὶ προσαγγείλας τὰ παρὰ τῶν Μεγαρέων τοῖς Ἀθηναίοις, ὡς ἐπεψηφίσαντο, τῇ σάλπιγγι σημήνας εὐθὺς ἀπὸ τῆς ἐκκλησίας ἦγεν αὐτοὺς τὰ ὅπλα λαβόντας. δεξαμένων δὲ τῶν Μεγαρέων προθύμως, τήν τε Νίσαιαν ἐτείχισε, καὶ διὰ μέσου σκέλη δύο πρὸς τὸ ἐπίνειον ἀπὸ τοῦ ἄστεος ἐνέβαλε, καὶ συνῆψε τῇ θαλάττῃ τὴν πόλιν, ὥστε τῶν κατὰ γῆν πολεμίων ὀλίγον ἤδη φροντίζουσαν ἐξηρτῆσθαι τῶν Ἀθηναίων.

[3] Ibid.

[4] The reference in Demosthenes' *Conon* speech (58. 3) to an Athenian manning of the Attic fort Panactum may well refer to this occasion. Presumably the other forts of Attica were manned too as a precaution, in case the Athenian action at Megara provoked the Boeotians to war.

merely because they thought Philip would be pleased by it. But Philip was a long way off, and Phocion was expected hourly (this is the hypothetical situation set up by Plutarch): Perillus would have had to send to his friends in Thebes and hope for the best.

In the event, whatever messages for help Perillus and his friends sent out, and to whatever addressees, they did him no good. Philip's attempt on Megara, such as it was, had failed. It had worried the Athenians, and no wonder. And it will have left them aware that, given a second opportunity at Megara, Philip must be counted on, probably, as likely to worry them again.[1]

At Elis, where Philip had intervened in some way some weeks or months before the Megarian incident, events had moved similarly, up to a point.[2] Here, however, his action was confined certainly to the financial level; he provided money to the leaders of one of the factions in a serious *stasis*. The origins and the details of this story, needless to say, elude us almost entirely. Less than ten years earlier Elis had become a democracy, presumably as a result of a revolution of some kind.[3] According to the only tradition that survives (in Pausanias) she had previously enjoyed a long *eunomia*, which, in this context, means an oligarchy; and the democratic revolution evidently had to reckon with a deep-rooted opposition, which eventually turned to Philip.[4] Demosthenes gives the impression that Elis was the first Peloponnesian state where Philip's money corrupted politicians (Arcadia came later).[5] This could refer to any time after 346 (or perhaps even before it). But it was not till 343 that the counter-revolution came, and it succeeded, accompanied by slaughter of the democrats probably on a big scale.[6] 'Philip's men' were in power, and they were known already at this time to be Philip's men. They were of course primarily Elean politicians working for what they conceived

[1] Whether the mercenaries brought in by Perillus were mercenaries handed over to him by Philip, or mercenaries recruited by himself and paid with money supplied by Philip, seems of no importance either in practice or as a matter of international law. If they were Philip's originally, Perillus undoubtedly became their employer and paymaster when he took them over.

[2] That the Elis incident preceded the Megarian follows from those allusions to the latter in the *Embassy* speech of Demosthenes which speak of it as very recent, in words which are never used of Elis (or of any other event): see p. 497 n. 1 above. But it did not precede it by more than about six months at the most, because it still had not happened when the *Second Philippic* was spoken, towards the end of 344.

[3] Beloch 3². 1. 541 and n. 1 rightly pointed out that the oligarchy in control in the mid-360s was presumably still in control in 353/2, when Elis was still on the Spartan side in the Peloponnese against the Arcadians and Messenians (D. 16. 16). In 343 Demosthenes (19. 294) speaks of a democracy as just having been overthrown.

[4] Paus. 4. 28. 4; 5. 4. 9; D. 19. 294 and 260.

[5] D. 19. 260–1.

[6] Ibid. τὰς ἐν Ἤλιδι σφαγὰς πεποίηκε (the subject is not 'Philip', but the νόσημα of corruption by Philip): the σφαγαί are referred to again by Demosthenes in 341 (10. 10).

to be the best for Elis and especially for their own class and social order in Elis. They had been helped by Philip with money, and presumably they would look to him again if need be, and would co-operate with him meanwhile unless some strong reasons were against it.

One must pause, however, to reckon with the sceptics, who may object that for all this we depend too much on Demosthenes and his alarmist remarks about Philip;[1] that Diodorus, for example, who does allude once to this Elean *stasis* at a later stage (probably referring to the year 342), never mentions Philip at all, though he does mention 'the Arcadians' who helped the Eleans to repel their exiles attempting to return with a force of mercenaries.[2] The Arcadians of course were allies of Philip, it may be pointed out. But chiefly the interpretation of Diodorus here must begin with the reason why he is telling this story at all. It is not Elis, or Philip, that has prompted him, but the mercenaries of the exiles (who happen to be survivors of the Phocian War); consequently his details about Elis are only of the barest military necessities and include no political background. From Demosthenes, exaggeration certainly one can expect here; but fiction? Unlikely, on general grounds mentioned already (above, pp. 475 f.). And when Demosthenes says, as he does two years later, 'He has got hold of the important city of Elis in the Peloponnese',[3] can we believe seriously that really nothing whatever had happened at Elis to justify the remark? Something had happened there, with Philip involved in it, and the Assembly in 341 knew it, though it may be that Demosthenes has overstated Philip's part in it.[4]

Finally, it is imprudent to overlook the fact that Pausanias was in no doubt whatever of Philip's responsibility.[5] Pausanias' 'history' is very patchy of course, but evidently he is using here a tradition which accepted that Philip was behind these events in Elis, and this tradition is not at all likely itself to derive only from Demosthenes, who uttered only a dozen or two words about Elis anyhow, in an extensive corpus of speeches where these words are by no means easy to locate or remember. There was almost certainly (Pausanias reminds us here) an independent historical tradition recording Philip's involvement in the Elis affair; and no doubt this tradition was right. Elis was responsible for Olympia, and for the greatest of the 'Great Games'. Philip without doubt was the

---

[1] e.g. Cawkwell, 'Demosthenes' 203.

[2] D.S. 16. 63. 4–5, under the year 346/5, because the 'accursed' mercenaries of the Phocians are tracked along from here to their uniformly inauspicious ends.

[3] D. 9. 27 Ἦλιν ἔχει τηλικαύτην πόλιν ἐν Πελοποννήσῳ.

[4] A comparable remark, *mutatis mutandis*, might be made of Germany and Turkey in 1914. Turkey was not a member of the Triple Alliance, but if any European politician had said then 'Germany has got hold of Turkey', nobody either then or now who knew even vaguely of the money and other things poured into Turkey by Germany would complain that the remark was a fiction.

[5] Paus. 4. 28. 4; 5. 4. 9.

leading patron of this generation, for the events for horses. By Olympia's standards his wealth was inexhaustible, and so too, probably, were his enthusiasm and his knowledge of the sport. It was going to be a strange sort of government in Elis, whether of an élite or of a *demos* if it came to that, that did not keep in with Philip. As for him, he will not have underrated (perhaps the reverse) the value to himself of Olympia and its olive crown. To assess the value in numerical terms and in relation to the other ways of impressing people—the sieges, the Crocus Plain, Thermopylae, the set pieces of Isocrates and of Speusippus, the *Philippic History* of Theopompus—there is no evidence available; to guess would be invidious.

Philip had spent money here on the oligarchic leaders, who proved able to get control of Elis, and to keep it later when the exiles tried to force their way back with the mercenaries.[1] He had 'got hold of Elis', whether or not the new government entered into formal alliance with him. Elis was not to march with him in 339/8; but she did not march with the Greeks either.

Euboea, the third and the most important of the Greek areas in which Philip can be said to have intervened at this time, was an interventionist's paradise even by Greek standards, at almost any time since the great Persian Wars; containing no city of the first rank and no combination of its cities capable of presenting a united front to the world outside. In the fifth century it was predestined to be dominated by Athens in her years of empire, and in the fourth it swung between Athens and Thebes, till the rise of Philip opened new prospects for Euboean experts on foreign affairs (see above, p. 310). To suppose that Euboean politicians or peoples in any of these cities were anxious to be dominated by Philip, any more than by Athens or by Thebes, would be absurd. But our fragments of information about them in the 340s suggest that they (like Megara, and Elis) were living on the brink of *stasis*. When the contemporary Demosthenes speaks of pro-Philip and pro-Athenian parties, he is telling us nothing of what basically the parties were fighting for or about.[2] Presumably the usual elements of class warfare underlay these struggles; and it is clear that at Eretria and Oreus Philip's interventions were to the disadvantage of democracy, promoting or supporting the rule of individuals or very small groups of men whom their enemies could call 'tyrants'.[3] At Chalcis one important individual Callias evidently made contact with Philip fairly soon after the break away from

---

[1] Demosthenes later in 330 (18. 295) names three Eleans in his list of 'traitors' (Euxitheus, Cleotimus, Aristaechmus). For the exiles, p. 500 and n. 2 above.

[2] D. 9. 57 οἱ μὲν ἐφ' ὑμᾶς ἦγον τὰ πράγματα, οἱ δ' ἐπὶ Φίλιππον, of Eretria, a democracy at the time (shortly before 343).

[3] D. 9. 57 ff.

Athens in 348. Callias visited Macedonia and became very friendly with Philip, but later fell out with him. Next he turned to Thebes.[1] But in the end it was Athens, he concluded, that offered the best chances to Euboeans of controlling their own future, and his co-operation with Demosthenes in and after 341 was to make its impact on history.

But first the timing of Philip's interventions in Euboea, and their relation to his Greek policy in general and his policy towards Athens in particular, need to be examined. The Athenians could not be indifferent to the fate of Euboea, any more than they could to the fate of Megara; and Philip was well aware of this. But it did not stop him, it seems, from taking an opportunity for intervening in an open *stasis* which had broken out in Eretria in the first half of the year 343. The worsted faction evidently managed to establish and maintain itself for some time in Porthmos the port of Eretria on the Euripus, and Demosthenes in the *Embassy* speech reminds of more than one occasion when there had been a scare at Athens, of Philip's troops threatening or attacking Porthmos. In the end Philip did send 1,000 mercenaries under a certain Hipponicus: Porthmos was taken and its walls dismantled, and Clitarchus and his friends were helped to establish themselves in Eretria.[2] In the same speech Demosthenes expresses fears for Geraestus on the southern tip of Euboea, speaks of the island as 'lost to us' (ἀλλοτρίαν), and of Philip as fitting out bases in it against Athens; the language of an alarmist, but one with something to be alarmed about.[3]

---

[1] Aeschin. 3. 89 f.   [2] D. 19. 87; 9. 57 f. For the date, see next note.

[3] D. 19. 326, 334 (cf. 204); Schaefer 2. 422 f. Cawkwell, 'Demosthenes' 201 ff.; 210 ff., rejects the evidence of Demosthenes on Philip's activities in Euboea in 343, unjustifiably as I think, and maintains that Philip made no military move in Euboea before 342. Yet in the *Embassy* speech D. speaks of contemporary events, of the same year; the orator who tells lies about these things is merely making a fool of himself. Consequently, when D. says that Philip has troops in the island (19. 204), common sense obliges us to believe him; and when he says Euboea 'is lost to us' (or 'is unfriendly to us'? ἀλλοτρίαν, 19. 334), if we persist in thinking that nothing much has happened in Euboea at all, it is more likely that it is we who are misleading ourselves about this. It is possible, as Brunt suggests (*CQ* N.S. 19 (1969) 252 n. 4), that 'perhaps on publication these passages were touched up to fit events rather later than the time of delivery'; but as I see it one can only believe this here by first rejecting as unreliable the passage in the *Fourth Philippic* (of 341) which seems to place the capture of Porthmos (and consequently the establishing of Clitarchus in Eretria) not later than in the summer of 343. Both Cawkwell and Brunt do reject the passage as unreliable.

Yet the passage itself, unless we think that D. is deceiving deliberately here (which is not alleged), carries its own explanation of why its details are unlikely to be wrong merely by mistake. He was reminding the Athenians how failure to react to Philip's aggressions had led always to one aggression being succeeded by another, and he named examples in order of succession. First Serrium and Doriscus in Thrace: 'overlooking these lost us Thrace and Cersobleptes. . . . Then when he saw that he had got away with that, he destroyed Porthmos and fortified a tyranny in Euboea right opposite to Attica. When that was disregarded, he narrowly failed to capture Megara.' At the date of the speech the earliest of these events was less than six years back; Megara (in 343) was two years back; and next after Megara in the order of succession comes Oreus (342 probably), which certainly came after Porthmos (D. 9. 57–9). To believe that an orator who bothers to think out a line of argument based closely

The troubles in Euboea, at Eretria and Oreus particularly, were not to be of short duration. They offered Philip a fruitful field for intervention, and this first opportunity at Eretria he had not neglected. He cannot have supposed that the Athenians would care for none of these things. They could not live comfortably with Euboea or parts of it in Philip's hands. And the fact was that the island was a fruitful field for Athenian adventures too. Any Eretrians who had no use for Clitarchus will have turned their first thoughts to Boeotia and to Athens; and with the present political alignment they will have turned their second thoughts away from Boeotia. It had to be Athens or nothing now, together with any support that might be forthcoming from like-minded citizens of the other Euboean cities. The stage was set for a competition here, at the very least on a diplomatic level, a prospect unlikely to bring any improvement in the relations between Philip and Athens. Did Philip stumble into this situation with his eyes closed? Unlikely. Athens, unco-operative already and tossing back his olive branch as if it were a live grenade, was not offering him sufficient prospects of a reconciliation to make it worth his while to neglect useful openings in Euboea

on a succession of relatively recent events is going to produce the events in the wrong order is really more than I can do. (Incidentally, if he were being slipshod, he could be expected to put Porthmos and Oreus together because both were in Euboea, rather than get one of them wrong by sandwiching Megara in between, which is what he is alleged to have done here.) From this passage, in short, it seems certain that the capture of Porthmos was before the attempt on Megara. The attempt on Megara, we have seen, was in the summer of 343.

Why Demosthenes many years later compiled a rather similar list of acts by Philip in which he placed Porthmos after both Megara and Oreus, I do not know (18. 71). But this later list has nothing comparable to the earlier list's dependence upon certain events in the order of their occurrence; and also the later list is no less than ten years later, when all the events were ancient history. To prefer the later list to the earlier as evidence would be perverse, unless there were some compelling reason.

More important, clearly, is the silence of the *Halonnesus* speech (of spring 342) on the capture of Porthmos, as Cawkwell duly observes, finding support in this for his view that the capture of Porthmos had not yet happened (so, too, Wüst, 110; Lauffer, *RE* 22 (1953) 340 ff.). Yet the attempt on Megara certainly had happened, in 343, and the *Halonnesus* speech is equally silent about that (and about the events in Elis). The truth seems to be that the *Halonnesus* speech, at the point where it has the right opening for talking of acts of aggression, chooses to speak only of things which are (1) very recent, weeks ago rather than months ago (winter 343/2), (2) matters which are definite breaches of a city's autonomy, this being the particular point he is labouring (ἵνα δὴ αὐτόνομοι ὦσιν etc., 7. 32); at Pherae, the ending of the city's constitution and the installation of a garrison; at Ambracia, an armed attack or invasion; at the three cities of Cassopia, the ending of their freedom and their incorporation in the kingdom of Alexander of Epirus. Elis, Porthmos, Megara are not in this category, for Philip could be said to be helping *de facto* governments to overcome opposition, and certainly was acting in response to appeals.

In short, the silence of the *Halonnesus* speech, though it certainly merits consideration, does not constitute a reason for disbelieving the evidence of Demosthenes in the *Fourth Philippic* and in the *Embassy* speech. A further disadvantage of rejecting it is that, if we do, we are obliged to believe then that the three Macedonian interventions with troops at Eretria all happened in the single year 342 or the very early months of 341 (below, p. 546). This is manifestly unlikely.

merely to avoid alarming Athens. If the Athenians did not like what he did in Euboea, they could lump it.

2. *Epirus and North-west Greece*

In the winter of 343/2 Philip's immediate preoccupations in foreign affairs were with Athens and Persia. It was nearly certain by now that the Athenians could not be conciliated into being good allies. The prospect of a new war against them was not certain, but it was not remote. As for Persia, Artaxerxes Ochus was making now his great effort against Egypt. If this succeeded, the possibility of a more active Persian foreign policy in the West could not be ruled out. This was no matter of life and death, of course, for Greece, still less for Macedonia; for the limitations of Persian power were no secret now to anybody. But it was a matter of interest, obviously, as liable to introduce a factor into the Aegean balance of power which up to now Philip had not experienced directly.[1]

But meanwhile there were things nearer home that needed doing. The need may not have been urgent; and in truth we have no clue to the local motives and situations which prompted him to this priority or that. But the fact remains that from about midsummer of 342 Philip was going to be nearly three years absent for the most part from Macedonia, and this in Thrace. This may not have been all foreseen and intended beforehand. But an absence, and a long one, was intended, and must have been planned for. Operations in Thrace which were not to be terminated by the end of the campaigning season of 342 were probably foreseen now, and the orders will have been given some months ahead for a levy of troops around midsummer, and preparations for campaigns on a scale and of a duration beyond the normal. These Thracian things could perhaps bring on the war with Athens; and if they did it could not be helped. No harm, meanwhile, in making one more attempt to stabilize relations with Athens, if anybody there was in a position to talk sense about anything now (below, pp. 510 ff.). Then there was Thessaly; not a military problem, this, but one that called for his presence, to introduce and support the revival of the tetrarchs (below, pp. 533 ff.). And there was Epirus, where a demonstration in force could do what was necessary, and could lead perhaps into some useful military and diplomatic pressure on the southern neighbours of the Epirote Molossians, or further afield still if things went well. This limited operation came first: it was begun probably very early in the year 342.[2]

---

[1] See below, pp. 519 ff.

[2] Speusippus, *Epist. Socrat.* 30. 7 for the date; cf. E. Bickermann and J. Sykutris, *BVSA* 79 (1927) 7 ff., especially 29 ff. The genuineness of the *Letter* is no longer in doubt.

Arybbas the king of the Molossians had been left in 350 in a situation where one mistake was liable to be his last (above, p. 308). What mistake, if any, he had made now or recently we do not know. Perhaps some failure of will or of performance in the Illyrian war of 345, in which Philip may be expected to have looked to him as his natural ally in the West? Perhaps some more complicated delinquency in the family field, where Arybbas' niece Olympias and his nephew the young Alexander were living through eventful times at the Macedonian court. One does not necessarily accept the suggestion that Philip became Alexander's lover. Alexander had been a beautiful boy.[1] Philip and his circle were notoriously self-indulgent in the sexual appetites. The institution of the Royal Pages, serving admirable political purposes no doubt, still gave material to any who wanted to talk scandal about Philip and his friends. To say that he was his wife's brother's lover was one of the more entertaining things to say, obviously. This sort of story, coming (if it did) from this sort of source, would not carry much conviction unsupported; and it may be right to dismiss it. But it cannot be denied that Alexander of Epirus (as he is usually called) did meet with unusually favourable treatment from Philip in their political relationship. This could be because he was the alternative to Arybbas, and anybody who was not Arybbas now was a very good king of the Molossians in Philip's eyes. Or it could be for reasons we simply know nothing about. Or it could be that Philip enjoyed being generous to the young and charming Alexander; just as, later, he was to enjoy being imprudently generous to the young and (presumably) charming Cleopatra, the bride of his last years.

Very early (probably) in 342 Philip visited (or invaded?) Epirus, undoubtedly with an army though not necessarily with a large one; deposed Arybbas from the Molossian throne, replaced him with his nephew Alexander,[2] and proceeded to draw what military and diplomatic advantages he could from his position here on the north-western flank of Greece. Four relatively weak Greek cities of Cassopia, the neighbours of the Molossian kingdom on its southern frontier, were the first to feel his power. They had no means of resisting long, and were obliged to consent to being handed over to Alexander, who annexed them.[3] These places were not very important in themselves, but their

---

[1] Just. 8. 6. 4 ff.

[2] Ibid.; D.S. 16. 72. 1, under the archonship of Lyciscus at Athens (342/1). The date cannot be right, for Philip began his Thracian campaign about the beginning of this archonship, as D. 8. 2 and 35 shows, spoken in early summer 341. Philip had not yet moved into Epirus at the time of the Aeschines trial (silence of the *Embassy* speeches, late 343), but had done so recently when the *Halonnesus* speech was spoken ([D.] 7. 32, spring? 342).

Diodorus is mistaken, too, in recording Arybbas' death at this point (ibid.). For his reception at Athens, Tod no. 173.

[3] [D.] 7. 32 τὰς δ' ἐν Κασσωπίᾳ τρεῖς πόλεις, Πανδοσίαν καὶ Βούχετα καὶ Ἐλάτρειαν, Ἠλείων ἀποικίας, κατακαύσας τὴν χώραν καὶ εἰς τὰς πόλεις βιασάμενος παρέδωκεν Ἀλεξάνδρῳ

fate will not have escaped notice. They were not the first Greek cities
to lose their freedom in this way by falling into Philip's hands; but at
this time to treat them in this way may have been an act of doubtful
wisdom or value. Other Greeks observing it could draw their own conclusions.[1] Alexander and the Molossians were gratified, no doubt, but
how necessary was it to gratify them so far?

It seemed right to think (pp. 306 f. above) that in 350 Arybbas and the
Molossians were reduced to the status of a subject king and kingdom.
The evidence now in 342 suggests that this status was improved, and
presumably at this time. The bronze coinage of the Molossians (discussed above, ibid.) seems to suggest a period of subjection in which
the Molossian state ceased to coin for some years, and meanwhile the
bronze coinage of Philip himself began to circulate freely in these parts.
This period is followed by a resumption of the Molossian issues, which
continued then for a relatively long period down to their final cessation
(in 331–325), when the coinage of the Epirote Alliance took its place.
The numismatic evidence is well suited by Hammond's interpretation
which sees the years 350–342 as those of the break in the Molossian
issues, which are then resumed with the arrival of Alexander and the
expulsion of Arybbas.[2] If this is correct, it argues an improvement certainly in the status of the Molossian kingdom *vis-à-vis* Macedonia; though
to say that it proves a complete independence may be going too far.
(The Paeonian king Lyppeius must certainly be thought of as subject
to Philip by 346 and probably as early as 356, yet he seems to have
continued to coin all through his reign.[3])

τῷ κηδεστῇ τῷ ἑαυτοῦ δουλεύειν. The reading Ἐλάτρειαν for MSS. Ἐλάτειαν is supplied by
Harpocration (s.v. Ἐλάτεια). Cf. Theopomp. F 206 *FGrH* no. 115, who names four cities of
Cassopia (Bitia the fourth). It seems unlikely that Bitia escaped now (cf. id. F 207); but she
may have capitulated without any resistance at all.

[1] [D.] 7. 32. For R. M. Errington's dating of the expulsion of Arybbas and the accession
of Alexander to some year earlier than 349 (*GRBS* 16 (1975) 41–50), see above, p. 308.
Errington seems to me mistaken in his use of [D.] 7. 32, seeing it as 'totally inexplicable' and
'inconceivable' that the orator when mentioning the capture of the cities of Cassopia, should
not have mentioned the expulsion of Arybbas if it had happened recently. But a careful
reading of 7. 32 shows that the orator could not have mentioned Arybbas there without
becoming some kind of discursive Herodotean raconteur, instead of the politician making
a rather sharp point about the autonomy of Greek cities, with three apposite examples.
Arybbas was not a Greek city, and Hegesippus would have been making an ass of himself
had he brought him in here.

It is still legitimate to ask whether, if Arybbas had been expelled recently, we ought to
expect this to be mentioned somewhere in the speech, especially as he came to Athens. One
could think, Yes. Or one could think No—just because he had come to Athens and therefore
was not in any sense 'news'. One may suspect that for the average Athenian the threshold
of boredom was reached quickly, where the potentates of the north were concerned (cf.
D. 1. 13 and 23, for the patronizing tone—'Illyrians and Paeonians and Arybbas and all
that lot').

[2] Hammond, *Epirus* 541 ff.

[3] Above, p. 251.

How far is it right to read political or economic planning by Philip into the bronze coinages of the Cassopaei and Eleaei, those Epirote tribes just north of the Gulf of Ambracia who, standing outside the *koinon* of the Molossians, now (it seems) issued their own coinages by overstriking bronze coins of Philip?[1] Political ends were perhaps the more important here.[2] He had handed over the four Greek cities on the coastline of Cassopia (or three of them?) to be vassals of Alexander of Epirus. An unusual favour, this, to Alexander, though not unprecedented. (Had he not given Potidaea and Anthemus to the Chalcidian League in 356, admittedly in a situation where his expectations of quid pro quo were much more obvious than they are here?) It seems possible that he entered into a direct relationship with the Cassopaei and Eleaei now, and perhaps other Epirote tribes, in order to prevent their entering into some similar relationship with Alexander and the Molossians. Philip's second nature prevailed here over his instincts (if he had them) to give Alexander anything or everything he wanted. These two peoples, Epirote and Macedonian, had very much in common, obviously. If the Molossians might absorb other Epirote *ethne*, so might Macedonia. Parauaea had only now changed hands perhaps, and Tymphaea, now part of Macedonia, had been counted as Epirote by Hecataeus.[3] For these reasons and perhaps for others in this Molossian settlement of 342, though Alexander was certainly well treated, he was not being left with a free hand, most likely, to build up his Molossian *koinon* into a fair imitation of a great power.[4]

These are difficult questions, leaving too much to conjecture. Further afield, the reactions of neighbours to Philip's presence and activity are equally unclear in their detail, but some main lines can be suggested with confidence. The Greek city of Ambracia (colony of Corinth) clearly was not indifferent to the changes along the Gulf which bore her name. She may have had alliances with one or more of the cities or tribes concerned in them there. Anyhow she went to war with Philip now, and was invaded by him.[5] This place was an important one not only as a city which did well from a strong seaborne traffic and trade with the

---

[1] Above, pp. 306 f.

[2] Hammond, *Epirus* 541 ff., sees an economic building-up of these peoples as competitors with Ambracia in the trade with the interior.

[3] For Hecataeus as the probable source of Strabo 7. 7. 6, Hammond, *Epirus* 444 ff., 458. For the Tymphaean division of the Macedonian phalanx, D.S. 17. 57. 2. The general Polyperchon was of the princely house of Tymphaea (Berve 2, no. 654).

[4] I know of no sign later suggesting that Alexander was a vassal king. He seems to have had a perfectly free decision about his Italian enterprise in 334. No Molossian troops are recorded as having been with Alexander the Great in Asia. The Arybbas who became a distinguished officer of Alexander the Great (*somatophylax* in 331) was evidently one of those Companions who had settled in Macedonia as an individual (Berve 2, no. 156).

[5] [D.] 7. 32 (spring 342), ἐπὶ δ' Ἀμβρακίαν στρατεύεται; D. 9. 34 (341); 10. 10 (341/0).

interior, but also as a centre of communications by land. At Ambracia four roads joined; two from the north and north-west from Epirus, one from the north-east linking with Thessaly over the Pindus range and through Athamania, the fourth leading south through Amphilochia and Aetolia to Naupactus. This was a second access to the Corinthian Gulf, besides being the key to the overland entries into that interesting north-western area between Naupactus and the Gulf of Ambracia where Corinthian influence had always been strong, and still was; where Athens too had found easy alliances in her times of strength.

At Ambracia now they knew the story of Amphipolis, of Olynthus and the rest. They did not wait to measure their strength in isolation. They appealed to Corinth for support, and presumably not in vain.[1] The Acarnanians to the south of the Gulf felt themselves threatened too, and appealed to Athens. An Athenian force was sent to Acarnania (the egregious Olympiodorus of the disputed patrimony served in it, an accident to which we owe our knowledge of its existence).[2] As for Philip himself, it was not for the bright eyes of Alexander of Epirus, we may be almost sure, that he was prepared, up to a point, to quarrel with Ambracia and threaten Leucas and Acarnania.[3] This was an opportunist's probe, feeling for more soft places like the cities of Cassopia. But he did not find them here. Instead he met with a strong reaction, and one which might have led to a general war if he had persisted. For this he was still not ready. But the far-reaching views that he carried into this whole venture can be seen in the diplomatic success of his Aetolian

---

[1] This may be inferred from D. 9. 34 (spoken little more than a year later), οὐ Κορινθίων ἐπ' Ἀμβρακίαν ἐλήλυθε καὶ Λευκάδα; So Beloch 3². 1. 545 n. 5, interpreting this rightly as proof that Ambracia was still dependent on Corinth as in the fifth century (cf. Ἀχαιῶν Ναύπακτον. D. ibid.).

Cawkwell, 'Demosthenes' 205 n. 9, seems to underrate this passage when he maintains that Corinth in 342 still had no anxieties about Philip, and did not draw together with Athens before 341/0.

Wüst's (94 n. 1) explanation of it as an allusion merely to the conflicting claims to Ambracia of Corinth and of Philip, both of whom relied on mythology to support their claims, is unconvincing. It demands not only that Demosthenes knew of the *Letter* of Speusippus to Philip (below, p. 514), which is possible, but also that the citizens present in the Assembly knew of it, so as to take this point of Demosthenes instantly and without explanation. This I do not believe. It is true that there is no evidence for dating the eventual alliance of Athens and Corinth earlier than 341/0 (D. 18. 237), unless it is to be included by inference among the successes of Demosthenes 'in the Peloponnese' in 342 (Aeschin. 3. 97—a derogatory account; cf. D. 9. 72). And there may even have been local reasons why the Athenian support of the Acarnanians actually delayed an alliance with Corinth even though their interests in keeping Philip out of Greece were nearly identical. But whatever the truth about this, to suppose that the Corinthians were inactive while their colonies and dependants were under attack or threat of attack, must be thought very improbable.

[2] [D.] 48. 24 ff.; cf. 48, Hypoth. 4. I assume that the Athenian force would not have been sent had there been no appeal from Acarnania.

[3] Beloch 3². 1. 545 thought that his intention was to hand Ambracia too over to Alexander. I do not see why.

alliance.[1] The Aetolians in reality were the most formidable people of the whole north-western region of Greece, though the fact may not have been generally recognized as yet. Philip attached them firmly to himself by promising them Naupactus when he got it; Naupactus which had been held for a good many years now by the Achaeans of the northern Peloponnese, giving them a bridgehead on the northern shore of the Corinthian Gulf. He disappointed the Aetolians, no doubt, when he withdrew from Ambracia on this occasion. But he had evidently impressed them as representing their best chance of acquiring Naupactus, and they follow him presently like jackals in and through the crisis of 339 when it comes.

Meanwhile this whole affair had its repercussions further south, though neither their timing nor their violence can be measured well. The immediate reactions of Corinth and of Athens have been noticed, and their broad community of interests here. In Athens a great diplomatic activity was stirred. Demosthenes later alluded to his own mission as ambassador to Ambracia, whether during the crisis or later.[2] He claimed too that it was the activity of himself and others as ambassadors in the Peloponnese that halted Philip on this occasion, and saved both Ambracia and the Peloponnese from invasion.[3] A piece of vainglory? No doubt; yet not devoid of truth. Had there been no reaction from Athens or others, Philip doubtless would have gone forward while the going was good. Viewing all this with the advantage of hindsight, we may well say that this move to the Ambracian Gulf had been a mistake. The gain in Epirus was only peripheral, and the degree of reaction in Greece to his movements was a loss which outweighed it. A domination without conquest was going to be harder, not easier to achieve as a result of this. The criticism is probably just. But Philip himself could not know for certain what Greek reactions would be until he had tested for them. His friends in Greece would be telling him, too often, what they thought he wanted to be told, and what was likely to influence him to move in if that was going to help them. Megara seen through the eyes of Perillus looked like a push-over, till the event proved that it was no such thing. Even in Athens, where he had fewer friends than in most cities, he found now those who would tell him that he had a right to Ambracia (as to Amphipolis).[4] Politically, then, this project must be pronounced a failure, like the attempt on Megara. Militarily, it can be seen as a reconnaissance which produced reliable information as to the strength of the opposition. This was a result far from useless; especially as the signs increased that the whole decision in Greece was likely to be arrived at by a military dialogue, not a political one.

[1] D. 9. 34 οὐκ Ἀχαιῶν Ναύπακτον ὀμώμοκεν Αἰτωλοῖς παραδώσειν;
[2] D. 18. 244.   [3] D. 9. 72.   [4] Below, pp. 514 ff.

3. *Halonnesus: the Last Straw?*

Halonnesus was an island about half the size of Salamis, lying about 20 miles SSW. of Lemnos and about 40 miles NNE. of Scyros and in direct line between the two. It might be thought a useful port of call for shipping that plied between central Greece and the Hellespont, and it belonged to Athens, appropriately enough. The Athenians however made little use of it at this time, evidently, for it had been occupied by pirates. Even this did not make them throw the pirates out (they may have been tactful enough to abstain from Athenian ships and ships bound for Athens). It was Philip who threw the pirates out, presumably because they interfered with the sea traffic between Macedonia and the Cyclades or beyond, and between Central Greece and Amphipolis. Having thrown them out he occupied Halonnesus himself, so that it became an object of dispute between him and the Athenians.[1] It was a matter of no very great importance in itself. Two friendly states could have settled it amicably, and two states of neutral feelings towards each other could have settled it somehow. Between Philip and Athens in 343/2, its importance may be gauged by the fact that it gave its name to the speech which is Number 7 of the Demosthenic corpus, though the speech itself covers a whole range of topics which called for settlement if Athens and Philip were to remain at peace with each other. Great wars have been begun for poorer reasons than the material offered by Halonnesus itself; but not very many.

In the spring of 342, either while he was in Epirus or after he had moved from there into Thessaly, Philip sent a Note to the Athenians reviewing the differences outstanding between him and them, and attempting to suggest lines on which they might settle them.[2] Since the *Halonnesus* speech is concerned with advising the Athenians how to answer that Note, and alludes to it repeatedly, we can get a fair idea of what it said.

(1) *Halonnesus*. Philip claimed it as his, now, by right of conquest (from the pirates, not from Athens). But he offered it to the Athenians as a free gift. And he was willing for any remaining points at issue to go to arbitration.[3]

---

[1] [D.] 7. 2 ἔλεγε δὲ καὶ πρὸς ἡμᾶς τοιούτους λόγους, ὅτε πρὸς αὐτὸν ἐπρεσβεύσαμεν, ὡς λῃστὰς ἀφελόμενος ταύτην τὴν νῆσον κτήσαιτο, καὶ προσήκειν αὐτὴν ἑαυτοῦ εἶναι. . . . If the speaker was Hegesippus (cf. 7, *Hypoth.* 3), this reference might be to the embassy of winter 344/3 (above, p. 491). But if Halonnesus was under dispute as early as this, it is surprising indeed that Demosthenes found no occasion to mention it in the *Embassy* speech. More likely the dispute is of more recent date. The Athenians naturally will have sent an embassy when Philip took the island. If the embassy included Hegesippus again, this was too bad of them. (See above, p. 492.)

[2] [D.] 7, Hypoth. 1. See, in general, Schaefer 2. 434 ff.

[3] [D.] 7. 2–8.

(2) *A commercial treaty (sumbola).* His ambassadors who were the bearers of the Note were empowered to negotiate a treaty regulating the procedures for lawsuits to which Athenians and Macedonians were parties, whether in Macedonia or in Athens.[1] Such treaties were commonplace between Greek cities. But none had ever been found necessary before between Athens and the earlier Macedonian kings; and from the orator's treatment of this topic it appears that Philip's proposal arose, whether explicitly or not, out of the Athenian claim to Potidaea, revived under the 'amendment' (*epanorthosis*) slogan of the previous year ('each side to have what belongs to them' above, p. 491). Perhaps, for example, Philip was conceding that, if a treaty regulating *sumbola* were made now, Athenian cleruchs at Potidaea dispossessed in 356 would be entitled to claim compensation in a Macedonian court of law. This, if it were so, would be a not ungenerous concession. But of course Hegesippus was right when he reminded the Athenians that accepting this would be tantamount to recognizing Philip's right to retain Potidaea itself. Ἔχειν ἐκατέρους τὰ ἑαυτῶν would have been abandoned.

(3) *Proposal for joint action against pirates in the Aegean.* This proposal was rather explicit in form, it seems, including provision for Philip's generals or admirals with their squadron to operate together with the Athenians.[2] Not surprisingly, Hegesippus pointed out disadvantages of this, both for Athenian prestige and for the security of her allies in the islands.

(4) *Amendment of the Peace Treaty.* Philip rejected totally the ἔχειν τὰ ἑαυτῶν amendment proposed by the Athenians a year ago, and evidently he defended his right to Amphipolis in some detail.[3]

He repeated, however, his willingness to expand the 'Peace of Philocrates' into a *koine eirene* in which any of the Greek states that so wished could share.[4] This constructive proposition, acceptable to both sides, evidently remained for many months a talking point between them. But there was never a time when it was not quickly submerged in the points of contention.

(5) *Promises of favours to the Athenians, if they will be his friends.*[5] This was a delicate matter for Philip, because he was constantly being accused of having broken promises given as an inducement to making the Peace of 346.[6] But it seems that in this present Note he did undertake to 'confer

[1] [D.] 7. 9–13.
[2] [D.] 7. 14–16: ὡς κοινωνήσοντας τῆς κατὰ θάλατταν φυλακῆς (15) . . . καὶ ἀποστόλους ἀποστέλλειν βούλεται (16).
[3] [D.] 7. 18–29. See above, p. 492.
[4] [D.] 7. 30–2. There is no doubt that on this occasion Philip did renew the offer: 7. 32—τοῦτο δὲ τὸ ἐπανόρθωμα ὁμολογῶν ἐν τῇ ἐπιστολῇ, ὡς ἀκούετε, δίκαιόν τ' εἶναι καὶ δέχεσθαι . . .
[5] [D.] 7. 33–5.
[6] [D.] 7. 33; D. 6, Hypoth. 3.

great benefits on the Athenians if they would follow the advice of his friends who took his part in their speeches and if they would punish the orators who publicly maligned him'. This raises of course a crucial matter, to which we must return presently.

(6) *Outstanding points in dispute, arising out of the Peace of 346.* They were

(i) The places in Thrace which, the Athenians alleged, Philip had taken after the Peace had become valid.[1] These things Philip agreed now to submit to arbitration before an impartial court.

(ii) Certain Athenian prisoners of war, alleged not to have been restored when peace was made. Philip wrote now that he had restored all the prisoners he had had.[2]

(iii) *The boundaries of the Chersonese*; this involving also a dispute between *Athens and Cardia*.[3]

By the Peace, the Chersonese had been recognized as Athenian. But Cardia, inside the Chersonese by any interpretation of its boundaries, was Philip's ally already in 346. And as to the boundaries themselves there seems to have been genuine misunderstanding.

What Philip proposed in his Note about the boundaries, does not appear in the speech. As for Cardia, he told the Athenians that they should settle their dispute in a court of law; adding that if the Cardians refused to go into court with them, he would make them. The situation as between Athens and Cardia was as intractable as it could well be;[4] capable of solution no doubt, but only with a great amount of goodwill on both sides, and there is no sign that either side had any goodwill towards the other. Of Philip it must be said that if he erred in his reference to Cardia in the Note, he erred by being too favourable to Athens, and by paying too little heed to the freedom of action which Cardia had a right to expect as his free ally. Here he showed the cloven hoof. To say this is no anachronism, for the point would have been taken (indeed made) by every small Greek city, inured to the elastic interpretations of 'freedom' indulged in by the greater Powers, if occasion arose.

The Note, as reconstructed above, seems to set out a full and fair programme for reconciliation, if both parties had wanted this. Philip's offer of 'amendment' of the Peace, surviving still after more than a year of bad relations, seems to free him from any charge of insincerity. He was prepared to amend the Peace, not of course by abandoning its whole basis in the way the Athenians had proposed, but in some matters of detail, and even of territorial detail, as his willingness to submit certain things to arbitration shows. And he was still willing, if Athens agreed, to organize a *koine eirene*, providing those guarantees of freedom and autonomy to all cities which might have allayed the fears of conquest

---

[1] [D.] 7. 36–7.   [2] [D.] 7. 38.   [3] [D.] 7. 39–44.   [4] [D.] 7. 41 ff.

held by his opponents in Athens and elsewhere. Against this, however, must be set his activities in Greece over the last year or more, and even (in Epirus) while these negotiations were in progress, which suggested to his enemies (perhaps even to his friends) an intent to penetrate and dominate in Greece even if he did not intend to conquer. And where Athens in particular was concerned, the Halonnesus incident itself raises a question. Falling in the winter 343/2 presumably,[1] it must raise great doubts as to how much by this time Philip really wanted to be reconciled with Athens; or rather, if he did want this, how much real chance by now he thought there was of doing it. The taking of Halonnesus could not fail to antagonize most Athenians. However much trouble its pirates gave, Philip could have put up with it longer if by doing so he thought he was genuinely improving the chances of reconciliation. To seize Halonnesus at all looks like a sign that he had practically given up hope— unless he seized it simply in order to give it to the Athenians, and so influence them to becoming reconciled? This does not seem possible. He would not have spoiled this ship for the extra ha'porth of tar which 'giving it back' would have cost him.[2] All in all, it looks as if in this Note Philip tried to satisfy himself, and his friends in Athens, and anyone else in Greece whom it might concern, that he had slammed no doors; that it was still open to the Athenians to 'be reasonable', and that if they would be reasonable, he wanted and needed them as his genuine allies. But all this in the hope, rather than the expectation, of a good result.[3]

Which of their advisers would the Athenians listen to now? This was the question. Using the jury of the Aeschines trial a few months earlier as a yardstick, it is probably right to think that a considerable majority

---

[1] I use 'winter' elastically, so as to include a time late in 343, or early in 342, when conditions for navigation would allow of a Macedonian squadron conveying and landing a force on the island sufficient to deal with the pirates.

[2] [D.] 7. 5–6 for this differential (ἄν τε λάβητε ἄν τ' ἀπολάβητε), which found its way into Comedy, deservedly (Antiphanes F 169, Kock, *CAF* 2. 80 ad loc.). Philip in his Note maintained that Halonnesus was now his ([D.] 7. 2), and by modern diplomatic usage this would constitute a proof, in these circumstances, that the writer of the Note was not anxious to ingratiate himself with its recipient. A Greek rhetor, however, might reckon that to 'establish' ownership, and then to make a free gift, was conferring a greater favour than merely restoring what was the recipient's own property. (If so, a second Greek rhetor knew how to reply to that—[D.] 7. 6.) It seems more likely that Philip would be guided here by common sense and a knowledge of human nature than by values of the rhetorical schools.

[3] It seems idle to speculate (though some have done so) on what benefits Philip had in mind for the Athenians if they came to right decisions now ([D.] 7. 35). Hegesippus (ibid.) seems not too wide of the mark when he observed that Philip would not give them back their own possessions (because now they were his), and could not give them anything in Greece without upsetting some others of the Greeks: his gifts, then, must be in some better land far far away (. . . οὔτ' ἐν τῇ οἰκουμένῃ αἱ δωρειαὶ ἔσονται . . . ἀλλ' ἄλλη τις χώρα καὶ ἄλλος, ὡς ἔοικε, τόπος φανήσεται, οὗ ὑμῖν αἱ δωρειαὶ δοθήσονται. Hegesippus of course is merely being scornful, and is not thinking of Thrace, or Asia, or anywhere. I doubt very much whether Philip, either, was thinking of Thrace or Asia or anywhere specific. He was probably being polite.

of the Athenians were dissatisfied with their position in Greece as a result of the Peace of 346.[1] Few can have believed that there was any hope of turning back the clock to the good old days before Philip, of recovering Amphipolis and the other places in the north, whether by arms or by negotiation. But there was still much room for disagreement between the attitudes to Philip that could be taken up.

Demosthenes, we know, thought him not to be trusted, and very dangerous. But Isocrates saw safety and even benefit for Athens in trusting him. Isocrates would not be addressing the *demos* in this Assembly; but some of his circle might. Indeed some of them did. 'There are some who have said they consider this Note a very good one': so Hegesippus, adding that they deserved the execration of the *demos* much more than Philip himself.[2] About this very time Philip received the *Letter* of Speusippus which survives, a composition showing that the distinguished head of Plato's Academy, through his tame historian Antipater of Magnesia, had gone to no small trouble scouring the life and hard times of the god Heracles to find just those things there that might be of use to Philip at just this particular moment.[3] By a staggering coincidence they did find them; at Amphipolis, at Potidaea, at Torone, at Ambracia. At all these places, three of them so much in the news as Speusippus wrote, Heracles in his travels had found nasty men in charge and had replaced them with nice men (at Potidaea with a son of Poseidon, even). In every case, Speusippus is careful to record, these rulers received their places from Heracles as *parakatathēkē*. The places belonged to Heracles and so to his descendants (ʿΗρακλειδῶν οὖσαν, brays Speusippus, three times in fifteen lines).[4] Speusippus really has put in his thumb here, and pulled out plum after plum. What Aristotle, perhaps resident in Macedonia now, thought of this effusion, history does not record. He knew Speusippus better than we know him, and may have been waiting for it.

The main object of Speusippus in his letter, it seems, was to damage Isocrates in Philip's eyes, and to a lesser degree to damage Theopompus who was in Macedonia at this time; and since Isocrates' *Philip* (the object of attack) was some three and a half years old by now, Speusippus probably did well to add to his letter some material of topical interest smelling less of the lamp and the dust of academic vendetta. Philip

---

[1] The votes for and against Aeschines were approximately equal (he was acquitted by only thirty votes). It seems probable that many 'dissatisfied' jurors still voted for his acquittal, because he had support from Eubulus and Phocion, and because after all no clear case had been made that he had broken any law. (On the weaknesses in Demosthenes' case against him, see, e.g., Pickard-Cambridge, *Demosthenes* 317 ff.)

[2] [D.] 7. 45 ὅσοι δ' Ἀθηναῖοι ὄντες μὴ τῇ πατρίδι, ἀλλὰ Φιλίππῳ εὔνοιαν ἐνδείκνυνται . . . etc.

[3] *Epist. Socrat.* 30. (Text, translations, historical commentary, and discussion by E. Bickermann and J. Sykutris, *BVSA* 80. 3. 1928.)

[4] *Epist. Socrat.* 30. 5–7.

cared presumably as little as any other man of good sense just what Isocrates or Theopompus might once have said about Plato. But he did care about the Heracles thing in general, and in particular he may have reflected that a researcher who could find the evidence for declaring him, Philip, an Athenian citizen by virtue of his Heraclid descent, might reasonably be expected to find the evidence for anything. The researcher no doubt had been Antipater of Magnesia. But the crooked 'proof' that Philip had never attacked Olynthus (Olynthus must have attacked him) must be all Speusippus' own work.[1] Starting from an assumption that a known fact (Philip's attack on Olynthus) was really an open question, he shows that it cannot be a genuine fact, by adducing in evidence certain other facts which would speak against it if it were an open question. This is a crook writing, whether for money or merely in order to surpass Isocrates in being of use to Philip.

However that may be, we can be sure that Philip was glad enough to read that he could not possibly have attacked Olynthus, and glad that the reading public should read it too.[2] Things like the fate of Olynthus are not soon forgotten. Some Olynthian survivors lived on as Athenian citizens now, and Demosthenes made an excellent habit of reminding the world of Olynthus in all his major speeches. For the perpetrators of such things, their own continuing success and prosperity is sometimes the only real answer that can be found. Yet silence is deafening, and even in a way sub-human, like a tiger sliding away from his kill. Anything is better than silence, even a *Pravda* or a Speusippus. Good, then, to have Olynthus branded by implication as aggressor by Plato's nephew, even though no one would believe him. Good, too, to have Amphipolis named, and Chalcidice and Ambracia, as Heraclid property now being reclaimed by a true descendant, from the riff and the raff that had occupied them for all these generations. Especially good, perhaps, that the Athenian claim, 'each party to have what belongs to it' should be answered so pat by an Athenian pen. And interesting perhaps for Philip (as it is to us) to see how little it mattered to Speusippus that he was damaging the Athenian case here, such as it was.

Athenians like Speusippus were few, unquestionably. But there was a larger number, mostly of the well-to-do, who did not want another great war, and who were ready to believe something from Isocrates, and perhaps something even from Speusippus, in their writings. It was from these that the 'friends' mentioned in Philip's Note will have come, the friends whom he recommended the Athenians to choose as their advisers now,

---

[1] Ibid. This was not from historical or mythological research, it was contemporary political interpretation of an event only seven years old.

[2] This was not a purely private communication, but one intended for publication, like Isocrates' *Philip* itself (cf. Bickermann–Sykutris, loc. cit. 18 f.).

and not to listen to the other sort.[1] If Demosthenes is to be believed, Aeschines had supported Python in 344 on the occasion when 'amendment' had first come up at Athens.[2] There seems no reason to doubt this, or to doubt that Eubulus and Phocion also favoured keeping the Peace and improving relations with Philip.[3] It was a strong group, this, but probably less strong now than then. In the interval the Athenians had listened to a good deal of quarrelsome talk about Philip: and an oddity of this situation is that they seem able at this time to enjoy the luxury of being quarrelsome without any immediate danger of the quarrel changing from words to blows. Whatever the more alarmist views of Philip for the long term, there is no sign that anybody in Athens was afraid that he might strike now, if provoked too far. The speech of Hegesippus in reply to the Note is remarkable for two things really, on the one hand its treating of the points of difference as primarily matters of prestige,[4] on the other hand the complete absence of any word that failure to agree with Philip carried with it any danger to Athens. One must suppose that Hegesippus knew that his policy would lead probably to war, and that war was what he wanted. But war next year, or sometime, was what he will have had in mind; not war this year, not by a sudden bolt from the blue. The series of speeches belonging to the years 344–341 (D. 6–9) can hardly fail to leave the impartial reader surprised that a powerful king, so malevolent as Philip is depicted there, could be so slow in directing his malevolence on the city which had done little in the past except try to thwart him, and was doing the same thing now. There is no question, really, that Philip gave the Athenians all the time in the world to come round to the co-operation which was what he wanted from them.

This occasion in 342 was the last chance, however, as it proved: and this may have become clear to Philip, one judges, in the course of these negotiations; and perhaps to everybody else. The proof of this lies in the *koine eirene* proposal, acceptable in principle, it seems, to both parties, and even offering no grounds for disagreement in detail, if the silence of Hegesippus on this question is a true guide (and it ought to be). This the most important area of the programme for reconciliation, and its most constructive proposition, was common ground to both sides. Yet after this it is never heard of again. Halonnesus, Amphipolis, Doriscus, Cardia, the Chersonese—these were the names that summoned up remembrance of things past and made it a waste of time to plan for the *koine eirene* of the future. It would have to be war, it seemed. But no hurry.

---

[1] [D.] 7. 34; cf. 7. 45.   [2] D. 18. 136.
[3] Both supported Aeschines at his trial; D. 19. 290 ff. (Eubulus); Aeschin. 2. 184 (Eubulus, Phocion, and Nausicles).
[4] [D.] 7. 6–8; 43–4.

4. *Persia Again*

It was perhaps in the spring of this year 342, and it cannot have been later than midsummer, the time when Philip embarked on his long course of operations in Thrace, that Macedonia received its most distinguished literary visitor. Aristotle accepted an invitation, designed obviously to extend over some years, to take charge of the final stage of the education of Alexander, now nearly fourteen years old.[1] Philip's eye for the right move had not deserted him. He brought together the greatest intellect and the greatest practical genius alive, in this unique relationship. So we see now.

Philip himself, at this time, might have raised his eyebrows had he been told that this was what he was doing. That Alexander was full of brains and full of fire will not have escaped him. For this boy the best tutor was just good enough. But as for Aristotle, though he was known already as a distinguished man and one of the leading intellectuals of his generation, it can hardly have been recognized as yet that really he stood apart from all the rest, in a class by himself[2] (γνησιώτατος etc., D.L. 5. 1). Plato and Aristotle themselves both knew this, naturally (if we believe the anecdotes), but of the Platonic school after Plato's death, he may have ranked in the eyes of the outside world still below the older Xenocrates and Speusippus, now head of the Academy.[3] Macedonia however had its special connection with Aristotle, whose father had been court physician to Philip's father Amyntas. Though this was years ago now, and Aristotle's absence had been long, his personality probably was not one to forget, or to pass over lightly, preferring another.[4] Nor was he utterly isolated from his past during his stay in Athens, for Plato himself had had important dealings with Philip's elder brother Perdiccas, and had supplied him with one of his former pupils Euphraeus as adviser.[5] Though there is no evidence for a continuous connection of the Academy with Macedonia after Philip's accession, the letter of Speusippus to Philip (of 342) would seem an even odder production than it does seem, if really it were breaking a silence of some twenty years, or even of five years since Plato's death: more likely a connection of some sort had been kept alive, though we see, and in an interesting way, that Aristotle himself probably had not had much to do with Philip in the

---

[1] Plu. *Alex.* 7; J. R. Hamilton, *Commentary* ad loc.

[2] On Aristotle's early life and work, W. Jaeger, *Aristotle*, 2nd edn. English (Oxford, 1948) 105 ff.; I. Düring, *Aristotle in the ancient biographical tradition* (Göteborg, 1957) Part 3, esp. 272 ff., 284 ff. For a more imaginative picture, Chroust 119 f., 155 ff.

[3] The anecdotes, D.L. 4. 6; 5. 3; Quintil. 3. 1. 14.

[4] He had left Macedonia for Athens probably in 368/7, aged about seventeen (Rose, *Arist.* p. 427, line 18; cf. D.H. *Amm.* 5. 728).

[5] Speusippus, *Epist. Socr.* 30. 12; see pp. 206 f.; Caryst. Pergam. *FHG* 4. 356 F 1 ap. Athen. 11. 506 e.

years since he left the north to live in Athens.[1] A recent interpretation which makes him an agent of Philip, and as early as 348, has nothing to commend it.[2]

In 347 however Aristotle himself had moved from Athens to Assos on the south-facing coast of the Troad, to join the group of philosophers there, headed by the two former pupils of Plato, Erastus and Coriscus of Scepsis, who had become the protégés and finally the intellectual mentors of Hermias of Atarneus.[3] This interesting man, combining practical and political skills with (later in life) a willingness to listen to intellectuals and support them, and even probably to put some political theory into practice, had built up a fairly strong principality extending southwards from the Troad and having eventually Atarneus (opposite Mytilene on Lesbos) as its capital. He and Aristotle became acquainted, and a more than casual relationship developed between them. Aristotle married Pythias, the niece and adopted daughter of Hermias. In 344 he left the group at Assos to settle in Mytilene, for reasons which are in doubt, but certainly not on account of any quarrel or coolness between him and Hermias, as his reaction to Hermias' death three years later testifies. It was from Mytilene when he had been there some two years that he accepted the invitation to go to Macedonia (342).

The invitation does not absolutely require some political explanation. Philip was inviting, as it happened, the most highly qualified private tutor that any prince had ever had. Even allowing that Philip did not

[1] Euphraeus is not heard of again in Macedonia after Perdiccas' death and Philip's accession. He is next heard of in his native city Oreus in 342 as the unsuccessful leader of those who resisted Philistides and his group, who looked to Philip for support (D. 9. 59 ff.; below, pp. 546 f.). Carystius (F 2) is at variance with Demosthenes on the manner of his death in 342, and is presumably wrong.

D.L. 5. 27 lists the then surviving *Letters* of Aristotle: Letters to Philip: Letters of the Selymbrians: Letters to Alexander, four books: there follow eight more items, each named by *books*, seven of them 'one book', but 'To Antipater, nine books'.

The items of *Letters* are only the last group of this whole list of Aristotle's writings, which amount to about 150 items all told. Every one of them is named by *books*, except the two items (above) already mentioned, and the two poems, one of hexameters and one of elegiacs, which come last of all in the List. I take this to mean that the *Letters* to Philip, and the *Letters* of the Selymbrians, amounted to less than one book, and that this means really very few letters, perhaps only two or three of each.

[2] A.-H. Chroust, 'Aristotle leaves the Academy', *G & R* 14 (1967) 39–44; id., 'Aristotle's sojourn in Assos', *Historia* 21 (1972) 170–6. The hostile remarks of Demochares at Athens about Aristotle are presumably part of the attack on him in 323, twenty-five years after the events mentioned (D.L. 5. 5–6; Demochares F 2, in J. G. Baiter and H. Saupe, *Oratores Attici* 2. 341–2). Aristotle is called now the betrayer of his own city Stagira to Philip; and he is said to have assisted at the sale of the Olynthian captives in 348 by telling Philip which were the richest Olynthians. Both on chronological and other grounds Demochares is manifestly unreliable here. These things were not even plausible: in 323 (one supposes) they did not need to be.

[3] Especially Plato, *Epist.* 6 (to Erastus and Coriscus); Didymus, *in Demosth.* col. 5. 56 ff.; Jaeger, op. cit. 111 f.; Düring, op. cit. 275 f.; D. E. W. Wormell, 'The literary evidence on Hermias of Atarneus', *TCS* 5 (1935) 57 ff.

know this, he knew that he was inviting a first-rate man, and one with the earlier patronage of Amyntas to recommend him. If a savant and teacher of wide reputation in Greece was to be appointed now, this was probably the obvious appointment, if there was any such thing.[1] The attempt of A.-H. Chroust to show that, whatever the terms of Aristotle's appointment now may have been, he had very little to do with Alexander's education in reality, seems to me misguided.[2] There is no reason to doubt that he earned his money to the best of his ability; and on professional grounds the appointment was above reproach. Nevertheless a political explanation for it is forced on us, for consideration at least, by Aristotle's connection with Hermias. It is only about a year after this time (in 341) that Hermias was taken under arrest to Susa to answer charges before the Great King including charges of treasonable dealings with Philip.[3]

Whose initiative, or whose initiative most, are we to see here? About this whole situation and the importance, political and military, of northwest Asia Minor in a likely pattern of events of the not-distant future, several general propositions will probably find acceptance. Philip was interested in Asia Minor as the most profitable field for future conquests, when his position in Europe might allow of it (above, p. 460). Persia had recovered from the disorders of the last twenty years, had restored order in the West, and most recently had reconquered Egypt through the Greek general Mentor of Rhodes, who now had received a special command covering several satrapies of Asia Minor.[4] Hermias may have feared now for his own position, if he had increased his possessions by the complaisance or the weakness of the local satrap while relying on the remoteness and the preoccupations of the central government. Diodorus introduces him into his narrative as 'in revolt from the King', which may be an over-simplification, but it ought to mean that Diodorus found in his source(s) something about Hermias having acted more

---

[1] *Contra*, Chroust 125 ff. Only the fate of Aristotle's native Stagira, destroyed by Philip in the Olynthian war (above, p. 317), suggests itself as an impediment. Perhaps its restoration was offered now as an inducement. That it was restored we know, but we do not know when. Plutarch however ascribes the restoration to Philip and not to Alexander (*Alex.* 7. 3), and he seems likely to be right about this, despite the contrary tradition in Val. Max. 5. 6, ext. 5; Plin. *NH* 7. 109; D.L. 5. 4. J. R. Hamilton, *Commentary* 17, calls attention to the 'part played by Aristotle in the restoration, mentioned by Plut. *Mor.* 1126; Dio Chr. 2. 79; 47. 9; Ael. *V. H.* 3. 17; 12. 54; etc.'.

[2] A.-H. Chroust, 'Was Aristotle Preceptor of Alexander the Great?' *Cl. Folia* 18 (1964) 26–33; id. loc. cit. supra.

[3] D. 10. 32 ἔπειθ' ὁ πράττων καὶ συνειδὼς ἅπανθ' ἃ Φίλιππος κατὰ βασιλέως παρασκευάζεται, οὗτος ἀνάσπαστος γέγονε, καὶ πάσας τὰς πράξεις βασιλεὺς οὐχ ἡμῶν κατηγορούντων ἀκούσεται ... ἀλλὰ τοῦ πράξαντος αὐτοῦ καὶ διοικοῦντος, ὥστ' εἶναι πιστάς; Schol. ad loc.; Didymus 5. 16 ff., 68 ff. Callisthenes, a source favourable to Philip, seems to have introduced his name in the context of Hermias' death (Didymus 6. 55 ff.).

[4] D.S. 16. 52. 2.

independently than became a Persian vassal.[1] For Philip, if he hoped
one day to invade Asia Minor, it was valuable to acquire a good friend
there near its north-western angle, though it was by no means essential.[2]
To Hermias, if he was alarmed by the prospect of having to account for
the growth of his principality to the Great King, it was really essential to
make a military alliance powerful enough to enable him to survive, if
his explanations were not accepted. Between Hermias and Philip stood
Aristotle, the son-in-law and personal friend of the one, linked to the
other by the old family connection of patronage.

Of all the possible ways in which a political relationship between
Philip and Hermias could have developed, the two unlikeliest can be
eliminated here and now. It was not Aristotle who was the instigator and
initiator of this development. For the rest of his life, both in Macedonia
till Philip's death and in Athens after it, he had good opportunities for
playing the politician and exerting great influence, but there is no
evidence that he ever did this or tried to do it. He had better things to
do, if anyone ever had. Nor was it Philip, surely, who invited Aristotle
to come and teach Alexander mainly with the object of using him as his
agent or go-between to bring Hermias over to his side. A Persian war
was not near enough at this moment, whether it were he or Artaxerxes
that might begin it. And for that matter Hermias was not as important
as all that. The more likely sequence seems to be that Philip invited
Aristotle to Macedonia for the reasons outlined above, non-political
reasons, and that when he had settled there he did become the go-
between when Philip or Hermias became awake to the possibilities and
asked him to. And of the two it seems more probable that it was Hermias
who made the overtures through Aristotle, and Philip who responded to
them, than the other way about. It was, after all, so much more important
to Hermias, if he did fear trouble from the King and his ministers, to have
Philip behind him, than it was for Philip to win Hermias over at this
(or any) time. And if Philip had been the initiator of the negotiations
which were a contributory reason for Hermias' arrest, torture, and death,
would Aristotle have stayed on in Macedonia as though nothing had
happened? One could doubt it perhaps.

There is some ground (unfortunately not conclusive) for dating the
exchanges between them, whatever they amounted to, to the second half
of 342, when Philip was absent from Macedonia in Thrace. Theopompus
wrote a letter to Philip in which he spoke very ill of Hermias in the

---

[1] D.S. 16. 52. 5.

[2] The 'bridgehead' cliché has been much used in this context. It is really an obstacle to
our understanding, because of the inevitable associations with the opposed landings of armies
under modern conditions. There were many places where Philip could land in Asia Minor,
unopposed, and all of them in easy reach of many Greek cities, some of which could be
expected to welcome him.

present tense (i.e. before his execution).[1] Theopompus was in Macedonia in the first half of the year 342 and presumably for some long time both before and after this.[2] In the circumstances the letter is much more likely to have been a genuinely epistolary communication than a political pamphlet in epistolary form; and a genuine letter is likely to have been written at a time when Philip was abroad, and was not expected back soon. The Thracian campaign beginning in mid 342 alone suits this requirement.[3] It seems probable that in this letter Theopompus was warning Philip against Hermias at the time when their *rapprochement* was very recent. He was no lover of the Academy, and probably did not welcome the arrival of Aristotle; while Hermias, obviously, he detested, and perhaps with very good reason.[4] His own future could not be improved and might be endangered if Philip and Hermias became good friends permanently.

There is no need to think that the exchanges between Hermias and Philip were secret. Indeed to think this is impossible, since Demosthenes learned of them within a few months.[5] Mentor of Rhodes and the Persians will have heard of them, if from no other source, most likely from Mentor's brother Memnon and brother-in-law Artabazus, whose recall from their exile in Macedonia preceded the arrest of Hermias, if Diodorus is to be believed. It may be merely by bad luck that we do not learn from Didymus what actual agreement, if any, was made between them: whatever it was it did not save Hermias, and it was his unhappy end that attracted most attention. In any case an agreement between these two rulers was presumably never published on a *stele* in stone like the treaty of a city government. For Philip, this whole affair had been a waste of time, as it turned out, and with effects not merely neutral but, so far as they went, detrimental. Hermias no doubt was regarded by the Persian government as a subject who had thrown off his allegiance by entering into the unauthorized negotiation with Philip if not before, and Philip's negotiating with him will have been seen as an unfriendly act. Philip must have allowed for this in his calculations.[6] This need not mean that

---

[1] Theopomp. F 250. His death will have been some time in 341, but his arrest must have been quite early in the year, since Demosthenes knew of it (but not of his death) in the *Fourth Philippic* (probably before midsummer 341).

[2] Speusippus, *Epist. Socr.* 30. 12 takes his presence in Macedonia (in 342) for granted, and merely comments on his activities. For Philip as his patron, Sozomen, *Hist. eccl. Praef.* 5.

[3] A short absence of Philip (e.g. in Epirus winter 343/2, or even in Thessaly spring 342) cannot be ruled out of course as a possible occasion for the letter; but the long absence seems much the more probable.

[4] For the Academy, Speusippus, loc. cit. 12. For Theopomp. on Hermias, cf. also F 291 (= Didymus, *in Demosth.* 4. 66 ff.), with Jacoby ad loc. *FGrH* no. 115; Wormell, loc. cit. 65 ff.

[5] D. 10. 31 f.

[6] On those who believe in a recent treaty of friendship and alliance between Philip and

he was prepared for a war to the death with Persia now, for Persia plainly was incapable of inflicting that kind of war on any power outside Asia that was reasonably well able to look after itself, while he himself obviously was not ready to invade Asia in a war of conquest this year or next. But he may well have reckoned that, on the longer view, it was good now to advertise that he was no friend to Persia, and meanwhile to do her some harm by supporting Hermias in rebellion. In the event, the former object had been achieved, but not the latter. No great loss in this; though the outcome was aesthetically unpleasing, perhaps, to a diplomatist who is thought to have enjoyed his diplomacy.

Artaxerxes (above, p. 485), Philip's support of Hermias (my view) or intrigue with Hermias (orthodox view?) imposes fuller and more complicated explanations.

The list of Aristotle's *Letters* at D.L. 5. 27 includes the item 'To Mentor, one book'. This correspondence presumably will have concerned Hermias eventually; but also (and earlier) perhaps Memnon of Rhodes and Artabazus, refugees at Philip's court. If Aristotle corresponded about their return to Asia from their exile, it will have been before the death of Hermias, obviously. Strabo (13. 610) sketches Mentor's career with Artaxerxes Ochus—and calls him Memnon. The mistake may have arisen because Memnon's (and Artabazus') return was closely associated in time with the Hermias story which Strabo had in mind here.

XVI

THESSALY
344–342

NOTHING about Thessaly was easy, as the contemporary observers
Demosthenes and Isocrates allowed:[1] nor is it easier for us now.
These years brought important changes in the political situation,
and even in the internal organization of the country, changes by which
Philip tightened his grip. But our historical sources are so defective that
we cannot even be quite sure of what the whole substance of the changes
amounted to, let alone interpret them in detail as we should wish. One
thing can be said with confidence, however; these developments were
purely Thessalian in origin (hence partly our great ignorance about
them). There is no sign that they came about as a result of any external
pressures or influences, or were inspired by any dogmatic political programme of Philip himself. The Athenians would have liked to interfere
in Thessaly, and they tried; but they did not succeed.[2] As for Philip,
whether he had as yet (or ever) a theory about how to control Greek
states which were in a position to be controlled, can remain an open
question still. It is tempting to yield to the first impression, that his first
concern in dealing with them was to settle for something that worked.
But what perhaps is most interesting in Thessaly now is the suggestion,
which comes through rather strongly, that here after eight years as
archon of the League, he was moved to bring in something that worked
better.

As *archon* Philip must have visited Thessaly every year, most likely,
unless something very pressing prevented him; anything less would have
been imprudent. Diodorus records only one such visit in these years,
presumably an occasion when something important was done, and an
occasion for some military action, as our knowledge of Diodorus in
general would suggest, and as this passage itself does confirm by its
content.[3] After the Illyrian campaign of 345 (above), 'he passed into
Thessaly, expelled the tyrants from the cities, and so made himself
popular with the Thessalians': this, according to Diodorus, in the archonship of Lyciscus (344/3). Pompeius Trogus described, it seems, a 'subjugation' of Thessaly (and Thrace), between the Illyrian campaign and

---

[1] D. 1. 21 f.; Isoc. 5 20; *Epist.* 2. 20 (below). See above, pp. 218 ff. and 285 ff.
[2] See below, p. 537.   [3] D.S. 16. 69. 8.

the campaign of 343/2 which expelled Arybbas from Epirus.[1] The contemporary politicians add a little. Isocrates, when the news of the Illyrian compaign was fresh (345), wrote to Philip 'Your treatment of the Thessalians, at once just and advantageous, has won the approval of many: they are an awkward lot, stiff-necked and utterly unable to live at peace with one another.'[2] (It goes without saying that this is an allusion to something recent, not just a bromide compounded of ancient history.) The new developments brought Macedonian troops into Thessaly. Demosthenes in (probably) autumn 343 said 'This thing, practices like these' [i.e. corruption etc.] 'in Thessaly until just recently had ruined their position in Greece and their fair name, but now it is robbing them of their very freedom: some of them have Macedonian garrisons in their citadels.'[3] Hegesippus speaking about a year later names Pherae.[4] Demosthenes in allusions spoken in the first half of 341 refers back to an attack on the walls of Pherae and its capture by armed force.[5]

Just what went wrong in Pherae to cause this new intervention by Philip, probably we shall never know. One can think of several reasons why people at Pherae could have been disgruntled. The friends and adherents of 'the tyrants', some in exile now, the remainder discredited and debarred in practice from political careers.[6] The majority of the Pheraeans perhaps were not truly reconciled with the Thessalians of the other side in the late war, who had brought trouble on them and had got them down. Especially, the people of Pherae were never likely to learn to love Philip as their *archon*, so long as he continued to deprive them of Pagasae.[7] To Thessalians in general, on a long view, Philip's continuing occupation of Pagasae was ominous. To Pheraeans, the loss of a main source of their prosperity is likely to have been a wound which nothing short of its restoration could cure. Even the bride Nikesipolis (of Pherae) and the daughter Thessalonike had lost quickly any propaganda value they may have had in the year of victory, for Nikesipolis died very soon after her daughter's birth (probably in 351).[8] It was not easy, one suspects,

---

[1] Trogus, *Prolog.* 8, 'Ut Illyrici reges ab eo victi sunt, et Thracia atque Thessalia subactae, et rex Epiro datus Alexander eiecto Arybba, et frustra Perinthus oppugnata.' Justin, Book 8, omits the Thessalian matters described here by Trogus.

[2] Isoc. *Epist.* 2. 20. [3] D. 19. 260. [4] [D.] 7. 32.

[5] D. 8. 59 ἐκεῖνος μὲν γὰρ οὐ πολεμεῖν [sc. φήσει], ὥσπερ ... οὐδὲ Φεραίοις πρότερον, πρὸς τὰ τείχη προσβάλλων. 9. 12 καὶ μὴν καὶ Φερὰς πρώην ὡς φίλος καὶ σύμμαχος εἰς Θετταλίαν ἐλθὼν ἔχει καταλαβών.

[6] E.g. Aristomedes, Curt. 3. 9. 3; cf. Berve 2 no. 128. For him in 340, Didymus, *in Dem.* 9. 43 (= *FGrHist* no. 115 F 222). Didymus cites Theopompus from his 48th Book (= probably 340), and also (ibid.) cites a *Letter* of Philip to Athens, which is not the *Letter of Philip* which survives ([D] 12). Most probably it is the *Letter* of a few weeks later (the 'ultimate ultimatum' = October 340). Cf. Errington, 27; and below, p. 525.

[7] Magnesia, a prime source of friction in 349 (see above, pp. 320 f.) had been restored to them, presumably in 346 (D. 6. 22).

[8] St. Byz. s.v. Θεσσαλονίκη.

for Philip to find in Pherae enough good men and true to carry on the government of the city in a way that was true to him. The symptom of disaffection at this time, and the occasion for Philip's marching on Pherae, was a refusal by the city to supply troops for a campaign, presumably the Illyrian campaign of 345. The Pheraeans had done this once before, and had got away with it, in 346 at the time of the march on Thermopylae.[1] Then, a certain sweet reasonableness in Philip as *archon* was both just and expedient, the same reasonableness which had allowed him to overlook the Athenian refusal to join in the invasion of Phocis on the same campaign (the Phocians their recent allies too). Now evidently, the time had come to teach some Thessalians that they must set a limit to their 'awkwardness'. The move against Pherae is unlikely to have been long delayed, beyond what was necessary for Philip to recover from his Illyrian wound and perhaps to try to bring the Pheraean government to heel without using force. Diodorus' date 344/3 for 'expelling tyrants' may be too late, for Pherae, which more likely belongs to early 344 at the latest. (Isocrates in his *Second Letter* may be thought of as knowing of 'the troubles' in Thessaly without knowing as yet of the solutions.) It may be at this time that the flight (or expulsion) of Aristomedes of Pherae took place. This important exile is found holding a command in the army of Darius at the battle of Issus (333), and the evidence points very strongly to his being in the Persian service as early as 340.[2]

Demosthenes in 343 mentioned 'citadels' in the plural, and not Pherae alone, with Macedonian garrisons.[3] Demosthenes will not have been understating this situation; but still we ought to think of at any rate two or three other places with garrisons installed in 344 or 343. But the only one we can name is, most paradoxically, Larissa, if the identification is correct which assigns a reference by Aristotle to the collapse of 'the government of the Aleuadae under Simus', to the Simus whose name appears on coins of Larissa which belong to this time.[4] Simus was named

---

[1] D. 19. 320 (spoken late 343 and referring to 346), ἡνίκ' ἐστασίαζε μὲν αὐτῷ τὰ Θετταλῶν, καὶ Φεραῖοι πρῶτον οὐ συνηκολούθουν . . . The second occasion when the Pheraeans did not provide troops was no doubt the occasion for Philip's marching on the city, in 344.

Sordi's (*LT* 274 n. 1, 282, 360) interpretation of this allusion as being true of two occasions in 344 and 343 respectively but not true of the time to which it refers, does not convince. She brings out well, however, the significance of οὐ συνηκολούθουν, and the very probable connection here with the Illyrian campaign (ibid. 282 f., and see above, pp. 523 f.).

[2] See p. 524 n. 6 above.   [3] D. 19. 260 (quoted above, p. 524).

[4] Arist. *Pol.* 1306ᵃ26 ff. Aristotle, writing of causes of revolutions in oligarchies, names Larissa as an example of one cause at work: ἐν δὲ τῇ εἰρήνῃ διὰ τὴν ἀπιστίαν τὴν πρὸς ἀλλήλους ἐγχειρίζουσι τὴν φυλακὴν στρατιώταις καὶ ἄρχοντι μεσιδίῳ, ὃς ἐνίοτε γίνεται κύριος ἀμφοτέρων, ὅπερ συνέβη ἐν Λαρίσῃ ἐπὶ τῆς τῶν Ἀλευαδῶν ἀρχῆς τῶν περὶ Σῖμον . . .

The identification seems almost certain. Cf. Sordi, *LT* 364 ff., who seems clearly right in maintaining that Aristotle's Greek can only be referring to the fall of Simos (and not to his accession to power). For the coins, A. R. Bellinger, 'The Thessaly hoard of 1938', *Congresso Internazionale di Numismatica* (Rome, 1971); P. Gardner, *BMC Thessaly* 31 nos. 77 f.; Head

by Demosthenes later as a notable collaborator with Philip and one who was responsible for putting Thessaly in his power.[1] Aristotle seems to imply a *stasis* in Larissa originating inside the Aleuad oligarchy itself, which for fear of fighting breaking out between its own members with their armed supporters, agreed to a 'neutral *archon*' who should keep the peace with mercenaries to support him.[2] The reasons for the *stasis* may well have been partly domestic (the position of Simus himself no doubt controversial). But in view of the past association of Simus and the Aleuads with Philip, it would be surprising if the reasons were not concerned also with him at this time, and he with them.[3] Philip's position as *archon* of the League, which he owed partly to them, may have pleased some of the Aleuad group themselves less than others as time went on. His getting control of the Perrhaebian *perioikoi*, a gain for him but correspondingly a loss to Larissa, gave good public grounds to reinforce any private discontents.[4] Though the details are lacking, the tradition does preserve just enough to show that relations between Philip and the Aleuad government did deteriorate, disastrously. A 'cloak and dagger' story preserved by Polyaenus implies a situation in which Philip was anxious to weaken or remove this government without an open breach of the peace.[5] A scholiast's notes on Demosthenes tell us that the Aleuads eventually were driven out by Philip.[6] Demosthenes himself implies that Simus and his associates came to a bad end, at Philip's hands.[7] It seems most probable that the time when, according to Diodorus, 'he expelled the tyrants from the cities', was the occasion for Philip's final breach with the Aleuads. If this is correct, Larissa as well as Pherae probably is to be counted among the cities which received a Macedonian garrison then.

253, 255; F. Hermann, 'Die Silbermünzen von Larissa in Thessalien', *ZfN* 1925. 48 f. There is no means of dating the coins except relatively to other Larissaean issues (which Bellinger now does, convincingly), and by reference to the literary allusions to Simus.

[1] D. 18. 48.

[2] This is the orthodox interpretation of this passage (e.g. W. L. Newman, *The Politics of Aristotle* 4. 360 f. ad loc.), though there is some ambiguity in ἀμφοτέρων, because in the previous sentence Aristotle wrote of division between *demos* and oligarchs. But that sentence referred to wartime situations, this one refers to troubles in time of peace; and ἀπιστίαν τὴν πρὸς ἀλλήλους here is in contrast to the earlier τὴν πρὸς τὸν δῆμον ἀπιστίαν, and is not just a sloppier way of saying the same thing again. With ἀμφοτέρων Aristotle assumes, without having said it, that the oligarchs were divided into two groups.

I should not think it necessary to enlarge on this if the remarks of Polyaenus (4. 2. 19), about Philip as a supporter of popular movements in Thessaly generally, had not been referred sometimes to this date.

[3] Harpocrat. s.vv. Εὔδικος and Σῖμος, alludes to D. 18. 48, and writes merely that Eudicus was given a high office in Thessaly by Philip, and that 'Simos the Aleuad' was 'one of those who were thought to collaborate with the Macedonian'.

[4] Isoc. 5. 21; Theopomp. F 81 *FGrH.* no. 115; Str. 9. 5. 19 (440): Sordi, *LT* 252, 340 f.; see above, p. 288.

[5] Polyaen. 4. 2. 11.   [6] Schol. ad D. 1. 22; 2. 14.   [7] D. 18. 48.

No other garrisoned cities can be named. But obviously, if this could be done in Pherae and in Larissa, two of the 'big three' cities of Thessaly, it could be done anywhere, so far as the mere power to do it was concerned. There may not have been the same need, however, elsewhere. The very size and importance of Larissa and Pherae made it more necessary to Philip that they did not settle into a permanent and open opposition to him as archon. Smaller cities mattered less, and doubtless dared less, where opposition was concerned; and especially after an example had been made of the great. But this development at Pherae and Larissa shows conclusively that now if not earlier the Thessalians were brought to learn that they had elected their master as well as their *archon*. Their freedom, in the fullest sense, was gone. Their cities were autonomous, yes; in the style immortalized by the wit of the fifth-century Athenian who labelled the Peloponnesians 'autonomous in a way that suits the Lacedaemonians'.[1] For those Peloponnesians, to relinquish the alliance was something the Spartans would not allow. Their freedom of choice in the government of their own city had its resemblance to the freedom of Henry Ford's first customers: they could have any form of government they liked, so long as it was oligarchy.[2] For these Thessalians now, their elected *archon* was for life, and the only way to shorten his tenure was the way that had been found for Jason. Meanwhile Philip while he lived was showing them now (at Larissa and at Pherae) that cities and governments must not oppose him too far or too long. That he proceeded now to dictate a form of government to all cities or even to many of them, seems to go beyond the evidence we have. But since the evidence itself is equivocal, it must be looked at closely.

The important things are the two passages of Demosthenes in which he alludes to forms of government inside Thessaly, without (alas) describing them.

(1) (Spoken in ? autumn 344):

What of the Thessalians? 'Do you think,' I said, 'when he was casting out the tyrants for them and was giving Nicaea and Magnesia back to them, do you think they expected that they would get the *decadarchy* which they have now? Do you think they expected that the same Philip who restored their Amphictyonic festival would relieve them of their own revenues? Of course not. Yet that is what has happened, and is there for all to recognize.'[3]

Here is an antithesis of 'then and now'; but when was 'then', and when is 'now'? 'Then' refers to events culminating in 346, and not going beyond

---

[1] Thuc. 1. 144. 2 in a speech of Pericles. Since Thucydides used the same phrase (σφίσιν αὐτοῖς ... ἐπιτηδείως) of the same situation at 1. 19, the *mot* seems more likely to be his own than a quotation from Pericles. (Any joke worth making is worth making twice.)

[2] Thuc. 1. 19 (the exceptions to this rule are well known).

[3] D. 6. 22.

that date.[1] 'Now' is the date of the embassy in the Peloponnese as a member of which Demosthenes addressed the peoples of Messene and Argos in the terms which he recapitulates here. At the date of this speech it is still a recent embassy: some time, then, in the summer of 344.[2] By the summer of 344 something which Demosthenes calls here 'the decadarchy' has been installed in Thessaly, something which had not been there in 346. 'The decadarchy' is a notorious crux, and we shall return to it presently.

(2) (Spoken in ? May 341): 'But Thessaly, what is the state of Thessaly now? Has he not stripped them of their free institutions and their cities and set up *tetrarchies*, so that they may be his subjects not only city by city but also people by people?'[3]

It is not necessary at this moment to commit ourselves to following Demosthenes wherever the full force of his 'subjects' (δουλεύωσιν) might carry us. But one must recognize that he is alluding here to two states or conditions of Thessaly, the last state worse than the first. In the earlier condition, the Thessalians were Philip's subjects by cities (κατὰ πόλεις). In the more recent change, by setting up tetrarchies,[4] Philip in some sense stripped them altogether of their free institutions and their cities; because, presumably, each city became now subordinate to the tetrarch controlling the tetrarchy inside which, territorially, the city was included.[5] That Philip did set up tetrarchies is confirmed by Theopompus,[6] and the fact can be taken as certain. But when did he do it? And to which state or condition of Thessaly (pre-tetrarchy, or co-tetrarchy) belongs 'the decadarchy', said by Demosthenes earlier to have been in existence in the summer of 344?

But now textual criticism closes in, for *dekadarchia* is a very rare Greek noun, anyway. Though in a later, dimmer age of the language the word came to be used for the Roman decemvirate, in the hard, bright light of the fourth century and earlier, δεκαδαρχία appears in only two surviving texts. Isocrates uses it once as synonym for what Xenophon called 'decarchies', the boards of ten officials imposed by the Spartans of Lysander's day on their subject cities.[7] And Demosthenes uses it here— if Demosthenes really wrote δεκαδαρχίαν here, and not τετραρχίαν, as

---

[1] Presumably Nicaea and Magnesia were handed over as Perioecic territory to the League in the euphoria of the end of the Phocian War. See below, pp. 541, 543.

[2] D. 6. 19. For the circumstances, from which the timing can be inferred approximately, see 6. 26 and Hypothesis.

[3] D. 9. 26 (my emphasis), ἀλλὰ Θετταλία πῶς ἔχει; οὐχὶ τὰς πολιτείας καὶ τὰς πόλεις αὐτῶν παρῄρηται καὶ τετραρχίας κατέστησεν, ἵνα μὴ μόνον κατὰ πόλεις ἀλλὰ καὶ κατ' ἔθνη δουλεύωσιν; Cf. Sordi, *LT* 275 ff., for discussion of the question, one reform or two, with bibliography.

[4] This seems the most natural interpretation of the Greek.

[5] See below, pp. 533 f.

[6] Theopomp. FF 208, 209 (*FGrH* no. 115).

[7] Isoc. 4. 110 (Harpocrat. s.v.).

every textual critic beginning with Harpocration has suggested as soon as he could get his breath.[1]

The suggestion that a numeral 4 could easily be corrupted textually to 10 because copyists abbreviated it with some form of the letter Δ, which provided a standard abbreviation for 4 ultimately as we know (δ), but which earlier had provided also an abbreviation for 10 (Δ, as in the Athenian 'Tribute Lists'), was a bright and entertaining one when it was first made, and it deserved consideration. But this corruption of the text, if it ever happened, happened in antiquity before the lifetime of Harpocration, and the question was not sufficiently considered, whether in reality the ancient copyists ever did use the abbreviation which is the essential ingredient of this agreeable fairy story. The truth seems to be that most probably no copyist ever did anything of the kind. (It would have been a crazy thing to do, after all, and no employer in his senses could have allowed his copyist to do it.)

The copyists who concern us here are those of the pre-Harpocration era, and I am deeply obliged and grateful to Professor E. G. Turner for telling me what the copyists of Greek literary papyri really did when the texts which they were copying contained numerals. The answer to this question is gratifyingly simple and comprehensive. They did not abbreviate them by using any form of numeral-notation employing the letters of the alphabet: they spelt them out in full. Professor Turner reminds me that we lack evidence for the really early period of transmission, the fourth century itself. It is arguable that numerals could have been corrupted as early as this, if they were abbreviated, and if Δ (δ) in some form was genuinely an ambiguous abbreviation in the fourth century, and if the book trade was supplied by people dim enough to use an ambiguous abbreviation while knowing perfectly well that it was ambiguous and that it might be no better than an even chance whether a reader interpreted it right or wrong. This adds up to an improbability very remote indeed. It seems almost certain that our *textus receptus* here gives us the numeral that Demosthenes wrote.[2]

---

[1] Harpocration (s.v.) commented on the word, but he did not like it. He does not say that his text of D. containing the word was corrupt. His comment is (after remarks about its use by Isocrates): Φίλιππος μέντοι παρὰ Θετταλοῖς δεκαδαρχίας οὐ κατέστησεν, ὡς γέγραπται ἐν τῷ ἕκτῳ Φιλιππικῶν Δημοσθένους, ἀλλὰ τετραρχίας.

[2] See now E. G. Turner, *Greek Manuscripts of the Ancient World* (1971) 18, for the information which he kindly communicated to me by letter originally: he cites this text here in illustration. The notion that numerals in Greek texts are, of all words, peculiarly vulnerable to corruption is widely held, I believe, and deep-rooted. It may even be true. But what I am suggesting is that their abbreviation in literary papyri is not to be adduced among the reasons for it.

It will be obvious that, even if abbreviation of straight numerals in literary papyri were not almost unknown, the abbreviation in this way of a composite word such as δεκαδαρχία might still be thought a curiosity in itself. That a practice found never or rarely should be found here in the composite word seems wildly improbable.

Apart from the palaeographical improbabilities in the notion that τετραρχίαν became corrupted to δεκαδαρχίαν by the use and misuse of an abbreviation, no one will believe that Demosthenes or any other efficient orator could ever have written or uttered τετραρχίαν at all in this context of his speech of the year 344. What Philip did in Thessaly, whenever he did it, was to set up four tetrarchies, which were territorial administrative regions. Theopompus makes this clear, and nobody has ever doubted it. Moreover this was not an innovation, or something that Demosthenes could have misunderstood because (if that were so) it had come into being only recently and he did not know just how it worked or what it meant. This was no innovation but a revival of something that had once existed for generations, and that must have been known to any educated man in Greece at least in the sort of way that an educated European today knows about the ancient kingdoms of Wessex, Mercia, and the rest, or about the ancient independence of Burgundy and others of the great provinces of France, or about the component principalities that went to form the German Empire of 1871. The tetrarchs of Thessaly had been discontinued little more than 100 years before the date of this speech; and even so their replacements, the four annually elected *polemarchoi*, were a continuing reminder of the ancient political framework of the country. If Demosthenes in 344 used the singular ('the present tetrarchy', meaning 'the present system of four tetrarchs') to describe Philip's reviving the four regional officers under their ancient name, he would have been doing something which semantically and linguistically was legitimate, but which had nothing in the world to commend it, to a speaker who aimed at reminding an audience in plain terms of what Philip had really done; and especially when using the noun in the singular involved him in a needless and inevitable ambiguity, because it denoted first and most obviously a geographical part of Thessaly and not the whole of it. If Philip had revived the four ancient tetrarchies, any orator who was not a plain fool would have used 'tetrarchies' in the plural in this context if he needed to refer to them. It follows, therefore, that for this reason, too, Demosthenes really did say and write δεκαδαρχίαν here, and that our problem is to decide what he meant by it.[1]

He meant, of course, a 'Rule of Ten'. But was he applying it to the Thessalian cities individually, or to Thessaly as a whole? Linguistically either is equally possible. Perhaps one ought to say that the analogy of the Spartan decarchies, which Isocrates once preferred to call decadarchies, makes it a little more probable that Demosthenes applied the

---

[1] There is some reason, independently, to date the revival of the tetrarchs at least a year later than the summer of 344, when Demosthenes here says he talked about Thessaly to his Peloponnesian audiences. See below, p. 533.

word to *cities* here. If that were so, it would give an attractive interpretation of Demosthenes 9. 26, ἵνα μὴ μόνον κατὰ πόλεις ἀλλὰ καὶ κατ᾽ ἔθνη δουλεύωσιν: the Thessalians already were Philip's subjects 'by cities' (i.e. with a Rule of Ten installed in each city), before his setting up of the tetrarchies made them his subjects 'by peoples' also.[1] Against this is to be set Demosthenes' use of the noun in the singular here and not in the plural. He could have been using it collectively, 'the system of decadarchies'; but why should he, when the plural conveys much more effectively in this context the picture of a dozen or two cities each subjected to the ignominy of this uncivilized imposition? Though there is not the same objection on the score of an ambiguity to the singular δεκαδαρχίαν used collectively that there would be to a singular τετραρχίαν, it does represent a step away from realism and vividness, presenting the image at one remove, so to speak, from the reality of the cold and nasty facts; and consequently no decent orator is likely to have used it collectively here.

There is also the argument from silence, a very strong one. Harpocration, a learned man, evidently knew nothing of any decadarchies set up in Thessalian cities by Philip, a development so important that Theopompus in his grand-scale *Philippic History* must have recorded it, even if they lasted only for a year or two. Harpocration used the *Philippica* for as many as thirty-two of his entries. That he did not use it for this entry proves practically conclusively that Theopompus had nothing to his purpose;[2] and this in turn proves that there never were any decadarchies installed by Philip in Thessalian cities.

It ought to follow therefore that 'the decadarchy' of Demosthenes was a 'Rule of Ten' imposed on Thessaly as a whole. (And this is the natural thing which it ought to mean in this context.) It remains to ask ourselves whether we can explain the silence of Theopompus about this development. If we cannot do this, I doubt whether we can afford to entertain δεκαδαρχίαν any longer. Conversely, if a probable explanation can be found, it looks as if it ought to be the right one, if it is agreed that Demosthenes cannot have written τετραρχίαν, and that δεκαδαρχίαν can refer only to a rule imposed on Thessaly as a whole.

First, then, we must exclude any notion that *dekadarchia* here can have a constitutional significance. If a Board of ten, whether officials nominated by Philip or elected in some way by the Thessalians, had been introduced into the constitutional machinery of the Thessalian League in 344, and so as effectively to dominate it, Theopompus must have mentioned it at the appropriate time and season, and Harpocration would not have been able to make the entry (s.v.) which he did make.

---

[1] This is the interpretation favoured by Wüst and others, and by Harpocration obviously.
[2] This point was well made by Sordi, *LT* 280.

In order to meet these objections, and still to make sense, *dekadarchia* must be seen, I suggest, not as a title or a noun of factual description, but as a term of abuse. Let us suppose that by 344 Thessaly had arrived at the state in which the country, its League, its cities, in reality and in practice were being run by a small clique, of 'the friends of Philip': that these people, holding no special position in the constitution as a group though some of them might hold office incidentally in the League or in their city or both, were able to lead and dominate in the taking of decisions on policy in the League and in some of the cities; that opposition was intimidated or at least was made to know that opposition held its risks; and that finally, and probably in 344, Philip did intervene in some cities in some decisive way, as we have seen suggested by the evidence about Pherae and Larissa. In a situation such as this it would be reasonable for a political opponent to allude to this group of Philip's friends as 'the decadarchy', whether the group really consisted of ten men, or eight, or four or fourteen, or any number provided it was small. Indeed it would be very good rhetoric for a hostile orator to call them that, for it would remind an audience of 'decarchies' (still a dirty word, we may presume), and the unusual, lengthened form, with its suggestion of pomposity and consequence, allowed the speaker to linger over the sneer, and the smear. Demosthenes himself was particularly good at devizing the slightly extravagant, paradoxical word or phrase to stand out from the ordinary vocabulary of prose and to draw blood where it struck.[1] 'The decadarchy' here is one of these, most likely.

If this suggestion is right, one ought to feel some disappointment, certainly, that Harpocration, who knew his Demosthenes and his orators very well, did not realize what Demosthenes was doing here. Obviously, this interpretation did not occur to him. The words of his entry (δεκαδαρχίας οὐ κατέστησεν, ὡς γέγραπται ἐν τῷ . . . Δημοσθένους, ἀλλὰ τετραρχίας) show conclusively, even to the point of misquotation, that Harpocration followed up the association with the well-known 'decarchies', and assumed that Demosthenes was alluding to Boards of Ten in the cities, a thing which Harpocration knew he was right to contradict. It is unfortunate too that he chose to comment here on something that Demosthenes never actually wrote (the whole thing in the plural and not in the singular), while asserting that Demosthenes did write it.[2]

---

[1] e.g. Alexander 'Margites' (Aeschines 3. 160; Plu. *Dem.* 23. 2 παῖδα καὶ Μαργίτην ἀποκαλῶν αὐτόν); 'the shadow in Delphi' (5. 25); the *nosema* of bribery and corruption (19. 259).

[2] That Harpocration's text of Demosthenes contained the words τὰς καθεστώσας νῦν δεκαδαρχίας seems incredible. It is possible that our text of Harpocration is corrupt in giving δεκαδαρχίας (for -ίαν). But it seems more likely that Harpocration himself got it wrong, because he thought immediately of decarchies in the plural.

Recapitulating, the actual innovations brought by Philip into the political or constitutional arrangements inside Thessaly amounted to only one, not two : the revival of the tetrarchies. Theopompus, who wrote of Philip in Epirus in his Book 43, wrote of Philip's revival of the tetrarchs in Book 44, presumably (though not certainly) at the point where it became chronologically apposite. This would date the reform probably in the year 342.[1] Philip's Thessalian intervention of 344, though it was effective obviously, was practical and in places military, making no constitutional changes either in the League or in individual cities, except (one must suppose) those cities from which tyrants or dynasts were expelled. Philip's friends meanwhile, by 344, had become able in practice to run Thessaly : the military intervention will have removed the opposition, or important parts of it (as at Larissa). Garrisons in some cities, including Pherae certainly and Larissa probably, were a reminder of the price that was being paid for the brave new future which the association with Philip could still be expected to provide, for some.

It was in this sense, one must suspect, and not because of any constitutional changes, that Demosthenes was enabled to speak of the cities as enslaved or subject, even before the revival of the tetrarchs.[2] An observer friendly to Philip could speak of the same developments as of some kind of salutary discipline, as we have seen.[3] Viewed constitutionally, the reform which Philip did introduce in the end (? 342) was of a strictly limited significance, though it is not to be underrated. To speak of Philip as establishing or re-establishing the tetrarchies in a sense is misleading, because the four geographical divisions had never been abolished, and as administrative regions they did not need to be restored. What Philip restored was not the tetrarchies but the tetrarchs. A reform of mid fifth century had abolished these, but the four polemarchs who appear from that time evidently stood in their place, officials probably elected for one year and eponymous : an arrangement which shows that the tetrads themselves were surviving still as the constitutional and administrative organs of communication linking the individual cities the territories of which formed each tetrad, to what Aristotle evidently called ἡ κοινὴ Θετταλῶν πολίτεια, the League.[4]

---

[1] Jacoby, however, dates his Fragments 206–7 (on Epirus) to 343/2, and 208–9 (on tetrarchies) to 344, rejecting the δεκαδαρχίαν of D. 6. 22 (344) and reading τετραρχίαν there. His view that the events in Epirus and Acarnania (FF 206–7) belonged to a group of Books (38–43) on the West, producing a chronological overlap with the events in Greece itself (Books 44–5), seems to me very unlikely to be right. But those who believe that the tetrarchs date from 344 are in a difficulty here. The difficulty is removed if one recognizes that the tetrarchs are a fairly recent arrival to Demosthenes when he alluded to them early in 341 (as his words themselves imply). [2] D. 9. 26. Above, p. 528. [3] Isoc. *Epist.* 2. 20. See p. 524.

[4] Harpocrat. s.v. τετραρχία (for Aristotle). For polemarchs, G. Daux *BCH* 82, 1958, 329 ff., 'Dédicace thessalienne d'un cheval à Delphes' ; Sordi, *LT* 339 f., 344 ff. For pezarchs (sixteen in number), *IG* ii². 175 ; ix. 2. 648.

Constitutionally, the significant thing in Philip's reform of 342, as Sordi rightly emphasized (dating it earlier however), was the change in the method of appointing the four officers at the head of the tetrads. The polemarchs now were abolished in their turn, the polemarchs who had been most probably the elected representatives of their *ethnos*.[1] The tetrarchs who replaced them were appointed by Philip himself. That Demosthenes is saying this is certain, since it is by 'establishing tetrarchies', according to him, that Philip in some sense 'stripped the Thessalians of their free institutions and their cities' and thus reduced them to subjection κατ' ἔθνη.[2] Demosthenes could be lying, of course. But Theopompus used the same verb κατέστησε (καταστῆσαι) for Philip's creation of tetrarchs, and it certainly looks as if he too means their appointment by Philip; otherwise he would be recording merely a change of name from polemarchs to tetrarchs.[3] The polemarchs, though federal officers of the League, had been the elected representatives of their *tetras*, and could be thought of in some sense as guardians of the independence of their *ethnos* and of its cities, especially as against the *tagos* or *archon*, head of the federal government. The tetrarchs now appointed by Philip look back to the earlier days of the *tagos* at his more absolute. They are the servants of Philip as *archon* and of the federal government. And in their appointment in 342 at the end of a difficult time in Thessaly we are to see them most certainly as supervising agents of the *archon* in their tetrarchy, with a primary mandate to see that the cities did what the central government decided, and did not give any trouble.[4]

One of the harder things is to know just what can have been the impact of this change, and of Philip's interventions that preceded it at Pherae and Larissa and at any other cities where he had 'expelled tyrants' (Diodorus) or 'put in garrisons' (Demosthenes). The revival of the tetrarchs, an ancient office and one that was associated with an older, grander age, might be thought of as a move that could be even popular, appealing to a Thessalian sense of history and tradition. But reflection suggests that only the most naïve Thessalians are likely to have seen anything good in it, those and the Thessalians who already had become

---

[1] This is suggested by the form of their appearance in an official document, as πολέμαρχος Πελασγιωτῶν etc. *IG* ii². 175 line 6.

[2] D. 9. 26. See above, p. 528.

[3] Theopomp. F 208 (*ap.* Harpocrat. s.v. τετραρχία): ὅτι δὲ Φίλιππος καθ' ἑκάστην τούτων τῶν μοιρῶν ἄρχοντα κατέστησε δεδηλώκασιν ἄλλοι τε καὶ Θεόπομπος ἐν τῇ μδ'. id. F 209 (*ap.* Athen. 6. 55. 249 c) Φίλιππον δὲ φησὶ Θεόπομπος ... Θρασυδαῖον τὸν Θεσσαλὸν καταστῆσαι τῶν ὁμοεθνῶν τύραννον ...

[4] Theopomp. F 209 (see previous note). The passage about Thrasydaeus was evidently full of malice (the excerpt continues μικρὸν μὲν ὄντα τὴν γνώμην, κόλακα δὲ μέγιστον), but it may be presumed to be based on an actual knowledge possessed by Theopompus that the tetrarchs were really Philip's agents.

irrevocably Philip's men, whether from self-interest or for reasons of patriotism and concern for the future of their city and of the League, or often from a combination of these motives. The well-known *Stratagem* of Polyaenus which shows Philip, over a period of time and not on one occasion, getting control of Thessaly by a policy of favouring popular governments and their leaders, is not easily to be interpreted in terms of a belief in actual democracy as a solution of Thessalian problems.[1] And probably it makes better sense if its period of reference is thought of as pre-352 rather than later.[2] Garrisons do not accord well with a promotion of democracy. It might be more realistic to think of Philip as appealing to a wider circle of the well-to-do, especially perhaps in Larissa, where the downfall of Simos and his Aleuad group may well have broken a narrow monopoly of power. And it may be symptomatic that in these years after 346 it was from Pharsalus, with its tradition of a liberal oligarchy, that Philip drew his most prominent collaborators.[3] Pharsalus alone of the big three cities avoids trouble with Philip, whose determined action in her favour in reducing the perioecic Halus to submission (346) was a better augury than the friction which had developed early with Pherae over Magnesia and over Perrhaebia with Larissa. So far as can be seen, genuine democracy had never yet arrived, so as to flourish, in Thessaly, where the predominantly agricultural populations and economy did not urgently demand it. The exception may be Pherae with its important harbour Pagasae, and it seems likely, though it cannot be proved, that the succession of Pheraean tyrants based themselves on the support of a *demos* which one day might have been able to control its own destiny, given circumstances that were favourable. There is no evidence, however, that Philip ever gave them anything of the kind. The garrison of 344/3 suggests just the opposite. The possession of Pagasae was too important both to Pherae and to himself for the city to be allowed much real freedom while Pagasae remained in his own hands.

It is hard to avoid an impression that by the developments of 344–342 Philip drew a blanket of darkness and tyranny over Thessaly, effectively and finally stifling freedom. This was the impression which Demosthenes for one sought to broadcast at the time,[4] and for which later he blamed the Thessalians themselves or their leaders in retrospect, for their complaisance.[5] A striking symptom of the end of Thessalian freedom has often been seen in the cessation of Thessalian city coinages, dated to

---

[1] Polyaen. 4. 2. 19.

[2] Ibid. Φίλιππος ποθῶν κτήσασθαι Θεσσαλίαν . . . etc. ought strictly to refer to a time when Philip has not yet acquired any part of Thessaly, i.e. pre-352.

[3] See below, p. 539.

[4] D. 9. 33 (341), γράφει δὲ Θετταλοῖς ὃν χρὴ τρόπον πολιτεύεσθαι; and cf. the passages cited above, pp. 524 n. 5, 527 f.

[5] D. 18. 43 (referring to 346); 18. 64; 18. 295 (of the leaders).

this time on grounds of general probability. But a large hoard of coins which came to light in 1938 shows that this dating was incorrect. The hoard contained over 500 silver coins, 155 of them Larissean, the remainder predominantly Macedonian; but with the remarkable qualification that the earliest of the Macedonian coins were of Alexander the Great, and these not earlier than the year 325.[1] Not a single coin of Philip was present. This seems to show beyond question that Larissa continued to issue coins throughout Philip's lifetime, and probably throughout Alexander's as well (and presumably till she was prohibited by Antipater when he recovered Thessaly after the revolt in the Lamian War).[2] Why only Larissa of Thessalian cities is represented in the hoard is something of a mystery, and a deep one if considered only in the light of what is known of Philip's relations with the several cities, though less remarkable in the light of the previous history of the Thessalian city coinages in general, in which Larissa predominates throughout in a way and to a degree which has never yet been explained.[3]

The uninterrupted continuation of this city coinage represents at the least a fair façade of freedom, and one which the Thessalians themselves were bound to notice, since they used, doubtless, the coins of Larissa all over Thessaly. More gratifying perhaps to Thessalian pride, besides having some effect as propaganda on the outside world at large, will have been the seniority given to the Thessalian representatives on the Amphictyonic Council in 346 and the years that followed. As a result of this one of the two Thessalian hieromnemons always presided now.[4] This position of honour did not correspond, however, to an actual increase in Thessalian power to control the Amphictyony through its Council. On the contrary, the votes of former Thessalian *perioikoi*, the hieromnemons provided by Perrhaebians, Dolopians, Phthiotic Achaeans, Magnetes, Aenianes, and Malians, no longer could be thought of as a Thessalian bloc, now that these peoples had entered into a relationship with Philip.[5] It could be said, and probably was said, that Philip dealt with them in his capacity of *archon* of Thessaly. Honour and appearances

---

[1] A. R. Bellinger, 'The Thessaly hoard of 1938', cited at p. 525 n. 4 above.

[2] On the earlier conventional view, the hoard, buried about 250, would be consisting as to nearly three-fifths, of Macedonian coins post 325, and as to more than a quarter, of Larissa coins pre 344 or so, with a gap of nearly twenty years in which neither Larissa (Thessaly) nor Macedonia supplies a single coin, and this in a period when the Philip and then the Alexander issues were very numerous. It is surprising anyway that the hoard contains none at all of them. Really the only thing that explains it is that Thessaly (Larissa) continued its own coinage in these twenty years, and the Macedonian coins in Thessaly still were not very common.

[3] Bellinger, loc. cit.

[4] Cf. e.g. the Delphic inscription Tod 169 (346–344), lines 23 ff., Ἀναλώματα ἐπὶ Δαμοξένου ἄρχοντος, ὀπωρινᾶς πυλαίας, ἱερομναμονεόντων τῶν μετὰ Κοττύφου καὶ Κολοσίμμου, . . . Cottyphus and Colosimmus were the two Thessalian hieromnemons (Tod 172, l. 22).

[5] For the list, Tod 172, lines 27 ff.

were saved by this explanation. The reality still was that these hieromnemons now were in Philip's pocket, instead of getting their orders or suggestions from Thessalian politicians as heretofore. No less, the Thessalian hieromnemons themselves, Pharsalians for some years without interruption, were men who (as the events of 339 showed) were entirely 'reliable'.[1] This equivocal situation, irritating to us when hot for certainty, was good for Philip certainly; and even for the Thessalian public it was better than one which plainly underlined the limitations on their freedom. In this way the Thessalian League still had a foreign policy, in contrast to the members of the Delian Confederacy in its later years. To have a foreign policy probably was then, as it certainly is to us, one of the criteria by which we recognize freedom; and it was better all round to seem free than to be openly repressed.

The most telling sign, though, that Thessaly as a free country was not a total illusion comes to us from the mouth of Demosthenes himself, this Demosthenes who talked (naturally) of Thessalian subjection when it suited him. Many years later (in 330) Demosthenes included Thessaly among the names of places which he had visited with some success as an ambassador of Athens.[2] The date of this embassy is not known; but on general grounds it is almost certain to have been later than 346, in the years when Demosthenes had arrived at the position of recognized protagonist of anti-Macedonian policy at Athens. It belongs in any case to the period when Philip already was *archon* of Thessaly. The embassy headed by Aristodemus to 'Thessaly and Magnesia', too, belongs most probably to the year 343/2.[3] The spurious letter of Philip to the Athenians which appears in our text of Demosthenes' *On the Crown* alludes to an Athenian embassy in Thessaly in what seems to be the year 339.[4] If we have preconceived notions that the Thessalian League and its component cities have become pure puppets controlled by strings from Philip's fingers, this information about the Athenian embassies cannot fail to surprise us greatly. Any Athenian ambassadors in these years must have addressed their Thessalian audiences in terms which Philip will have judged inflammatory or worse. Their object was to make trouble for Philip in Thessaly, and if possible to undermine the loyalty of the Thessalians to their *archon*. Aeschines alleged that the activities of Aristodemus and his colleagues was a breach of the treaty of 346 (Peace of Philocrates).[5] Nevertheless these embassies were allowed in; they said their pieces, presumably to the League Council; and if the exact words of Demosthenes are to be believed, Philip here in Thessaly, no less than in Ambracia and in the other places mentioned, sent his own representatives to say whatever was appropriate on his side of the

---

[1] See below, pp. 585 ff.   [2] D. 18. 244.   [3] Aeschin. 3. 83. and schol.
[4] D. 18. 166.   [5] Aeschin. 3. 83.

argument.[1] This was a debate. It looked like freedom. In Ambracia and Byzantium, where (according to Demosthenes) the same or similar debates took place, it was freedom. In Illyria and in Thrace the kings whom Demosthenes visited were by now (in every case probably) vassal kings of Philip. If Philip's ambassadors were present on these occasions (as Demosthenes implies), whatever they said in public they will have reminded them how they had come to be his allies; after being at war with him and being beaten.

Considerations not very different from these can have influenced the Thessalians now, too; for they had all seen the power of Macedonia in action, against the Phocians to their benefit, and since then against some of their own number. For a Thessalian who simply would not put up with Macedonian domination, the danger and difficulties of resistance now were very great. It is not surprising if the majority were content to accept the situation, free as they were to all appearances in their cities and their *koinon*, except where a tetrarch or a garrison might recall them on occasion to the reality. And of course the fund of goodwill and popularity which Philip had enjoyed in 352 need not have been dissipated. Philip was personally a very likeable man, and quite probably even after the various acts of 'discipline' already mentioned, he still was popular with many or even with most. Though there was no room now for dynastic ambitions of Aleuads in Larissa or of the tyrants' family in Pherae, there were evidently assured careers for those Thessalian political leaders who could contrive to be friends of Philip and still command the support of their own people. There is neither evidence nor probability that Philip appointed personally any of the League's officers other than the new tetrarchs when he reintroduced them in 343/2. One ought to presume that the two hieromnemons, the representatives of all Thessaly in the Amphictyony, were still elected in the same way as before, though we are told nothing of who had elected them, or how they did it. That the hieromnemons after 346 were men known to be friends of Philip is obviously no accident. But I doubt if it ought to be interpreted, either, as a proof that the elections cannot have been free, but depended merely on Philip's word or nod. There is no obvious reason why at this time the friends of Philip should not have commended themselves to the electorate, whatever that was, as being the best men for the job. The most prominent enemies of Philip by this time had been driven out of business, notably at Pherae and Larissa. Only a genuine and widespread opposi-

---

[1] See p. 537 n. 2 above. Whether the messengers of the *archon* of the League to its Council were genuinely to be called 'ambassadors', as Demosthenes calls them here, or not seems to me questionable. I cannot answer the question really; but my guess is that they were not. (I should think it possible that Philip himself could not have answered the question either.)

If they genuinely were 'ambassadors', the independent status of the League would be affirmed by this.

tion in the cities to Macedonian domination could have thrown up new anti-Macedonian leaders to risk their future in the highest offices; and the whole story of the sixteen years beginning in 358 suggests that this opposition, except in Pherae, never had existed.

No doubt it is, now, the deficiencies of leadership at Pherae and Larissa, after the recent troubles, that led to the prominence of Pharsalians in the highest offices of the League. Pharsalus is named by Aristotle as an example of the good and stable oligarchy (in contrast to Larissa, where the oligarchy destroyed itself).[1] For Larissa, he had the recent events in mind (see above, p. 525). Since he has contemporary Pharsalus in mind, too, his allusion is the more useful to us.[2] Sordi was right, very likely, in suggesting that the stability of this Pharsalian oligarchy in the past, and its survival through the 350s and 340s when first Pherae and later Larissa lost their leading citizens by war and *stasis*, left Pharsalus as the only one of the big three cities with an experienced and strong ruling class.[3] Some of its leading members in these years became hieromnemons of Thessaly in the Amphictyony, others became tetrarchs by Philip's appointment. Cottyphus and Colosimmus, hieromnemons in the late 340s and to 339 inclusive, Daochus and Thrasydaeus, tetrarchs from 343/2 and hieromnemons from 338, all probably Pharsalians, were the leading men of Thessaly at this time, traitors according to Demosthenes. That they promoted their own careers is true, no doubt; that they stabilized oligarchy in Pharsalus by working in with Philip, true likewise; and *douloi* you could call the Thessalians now, if you were in the mood, since ultimately they could and would be stopped from acting in any way so as to displease Philip.[4] Yet Thessaly now had peace, with its cornucopia of blessings,[5] after a punishing generation or more of wars civil and external, and it was no foreign conqueror who held their future in his hands, but their own *archon* of their own choice. If politics is the art of choosing correctly between evils, who is to say that the friends of Philip in Thessaly were choosing wrong?

As for benefits from colonization, either by Macedonians in Thessaly or by Thessalians abroad, there seems to be no real evidence for either. Only the name Philippopolis (or Philippi) suggests something of the kind, if it is right to see these names in Thessaly as meaning the same (or thereabouts) as they mean when we see them in Thrace. Stephanus, s.v.

[1] Arist. *Pol.* 5. 5. 7. 1306ᵃ10 ff. (Pharsalus): ibid. 27 ff. (Larissa), see above, p. 525 n. 4.
[2] Ibid. 1306ᵃ9 ff. ὁμονοοῦσα δὲ ὀλιγαρχία οὐκ εὐδιάφθορος ἐξ αὐτῆς· σημεῖον δὲ ἡ ἐν Φαρσάλῳ πολιτεία, ἐκεῖνοι γὰρ ὀλίγοι ὄντες πολλῶν κύριοί εἰσι διὰ τὸ χρῆσθαι σφίσιν αὐτοῖς καλῶς.
[3] Sordi, *LT* 288 ff.　　　　　　　[4] D. 18. 295 ἕως δούλους ἐποίησαν.
[5] *Syll.*³ 274. vi (cf. P. de la Coste Messelière, *BCH* 73 (1949) 201 ff.), from the 'monument of Daochus' at Delphi, has lines about 'Daochus I', the fifth-century *tagos*, which might apply equally to Thessaly under a *pax Macedonica*: πολλῆι δὲ καὶ ἀγλαοκάρπωι | εἰρήνηι πλούτωι τε ἔβρυε Θεσσαλία. The monument was set up by 'Daochus II', who became tetrarch in 342, and hieromnemon in 338.

Philippi, writes first of the former Crenides and quotes verbatim from Artemidorus of Philip's arrival there as a saviour and his naming the place Philippi. Then he adds (no longer quoting): 'The name Philippi was given too (ἐκλήθησαν Φίλιπποι) to Thebes of Thessaly [= Phthiotic Thebes] and Gomphi of Thesprotia [*sic*].' It is perhaps significant that of these two places he does not say that Philip named them, or founded (or refounded) them, as he does say it of Crenides–Philippi (above), and of Philippopolis in Thrace (s.v.). But Gomphi, in western Thessaly on an important route to Ambracia, does show a Philip-connection in its coinage, on which appears the name not Philippi indeed but Philippopolis.[1] To explain this, however, is not easy, for these coins are too late in date for Philip's lifetime, and are thought to belong to the period of Demetrius I (say, 302–286). Nor did they last for very long, it seems. They were replaced, without change of types, by the former city-name (Gompheōn). Altogether, it seems hazardous to claim that there must be some initiative by Philip himself to explain the name on the coins. It is best left open to the city itself, too, to have done something complimentary with its coins; but in either case the occasion for the issue escapes us. As for Thebes of Phthiotis, there is no confirmation from elsewhere of the lexicographer's 'Philippi', for her. This city of course had an interesting position, about 8 miles south of Pherae, 8 miles west of Pagasae, and the same distance north of the battlefield of the Crocus Plain. At that time (in 352) it will certainly have been in the hands of Pherae, and Philip is almost sure to have come to Thebes as a liberator. It seems possible that the city could have paid Philip the compliment of naming itself Philippi now, and of keeping the name for long enough at any rate for it to leave the mark on the tradition which Stephanus could still find and preserve.[2]

It remains to think of the Thessalian *perioikis*. As we have seen, it was part of the traditional function of the *tagos* to be able to dominate the *perioikoi* more tightly than the cities individually could count on doing.[3] In this sense, Philip's taking over control in Magnesia and Perrhaebia, in 352 and soon after, could be seen as part of the strong hand to be expected by the Thessalians themselves of an *archon* with the whole country behind him. The *perioikoi* had always been numbered among the Amphictyons, sending their hieromnemons to the Council, where their votes presumably strengthened the hand of this or that Thessalian city or bloc which dominated at the time this or that of the neighbouring *ethne* (Perrhaebia for Larissa, Magnesia for Pherae, and so on). Of the

---

[1] P. Gardner, *BMC Thessaly* pp. xxxv and 19 and Pl. III. 2.

[2] It is a curiosity of these three places reported by Stephanus as being renamed Philippi, that they all had names in a plural form to begin with.

[3] pp. 290 ff. above.

twenty-four Amphictyonic votes, Thessaly itself had only two, but her *perioikoi* (Perrhaebians, Dolopians, Phthiotic Achaeans, Magnesians, Aenianes, and Malians) had no fewer than ten.[1] For control of the Council, control over the Thessalian *perioikoi* was almost all that was necessary.

This was a good political reason for achieving it. But when the archonship of Thessaly came to be vested in the person of a king of Macedonia some obvious geographical factors presented themselves more urgently still. His own communications with Thessaly were vulnerable to interference by the northern *perioikoi* if they were unfriendly, the coast route via Tempe by the Magnetes, the inland route via Oloosson by the Perrhaebians. It is this, no doubt, that most of all explains his precautions in Magnesia in the years between 352 and 349, the building of forts implying some military occupation.[2] By 346 evidently he felt secure here, enough to 'give back Magnesia' in some sense to the Thessalians themselves, whatever this may mean.[3] The phrase belongs to Demosthenes, who would much rather have been able to talk of Magnesia as still in Philip's power: it alludes therefore to a genuine concession of some kind, perhaps a withdrawal from the forts, and very likely a clarification of Magnesia's position, as subject to the League and not to Philip separately. If this were so, as *archon* of the League his effective control of Magnesia need not have been weakened. In Perrhaebia his control is illustrated, and apparently at so early a date as 352, by his appointment of the Thessalian Agathocles as governor (whatever his title).[4] This was perhaps a military precaution corresponding to the forts in Magnesia, and perhaps not a permanency. But Isocrates writing in 346 could write of the Magnesians and Perrhaebians (along with the Paeonians) unequivocally as 'subjects' of Philip, and there seems no reason to question this as a practical summary, though it need not be juridically correct.[5] Strabo, too, wrote of the Perrhaebians as 'subject and paying taxes to Larissa till Philip took over those parts'.[6] Though one cannot be certain, it seems likely that this means that they ceased to be subjects of Larissa and became subjects of Philip as *archon* of Thessaly. If this interpretation

---

[1] For the list, see, e.g., Tod 172 lines 21 ff. [2] See above, p. 292.

[3] D. 6. 22 ὅτ' αὐτοῖς . . . πάλιν Νίκαιαν καὶ Μαγνησίαν ἐδίδου.

[4] Theopomp. F 81 (*FGrH* no. 115); in his 9th Book, which appears to contains events of 353 and 352, ἀπέστειλε διαφθεροῦντα Περραιβοὺς καὶ τῶν ἐκεῖ πραγμάτων ἐπιμελησόμενον.

[5] Isoc. 5. 21 Μάγνητας δὲ καὶ Περραιβοὺς καὶ Παίονας κατέστραπται καὶ πάντας ὑπηκόους αὐτοὺς εἴληφεν.

[6] Str. 9. 440 οὗτοι [= Λαρισαῖοι] δ' οὖν κατεῖχον τέως τὴν Περραιβίαν καὶ φόρους ἐπράττοντο, ἕως Φίλιππος κατέστη κύριος τῶν τόπων.

That Perrhaebia was never mentioned, along with Magnesia, by Demosthenes as a matter for dispute between Philip and the Thessalians may be due to his having been initially on excellent terms with the rulers of Larissa, who may have refrained from making a public issue of it in the years 352–346.

is right, each of the two great cities lost their *perioikoi* to their *archon* and the federal government. When they elected Philip *archon*, in this respect they saddled themselves with another Jason.

Similarly, for the route southwards into Central Greece, it was important that the Phthiotic Achaeans, the Aenianes, and the Malians and the rest could be counted on always to help and not to hinder. The Achaean city Halus already (in 346) had been disciplined, and at that time had been returned to Pharsalus its normal overlord.[1] There is no absolute need, obviously, for all the perioecic *ethne* to enter into the same relationship with Philip. A local context or environment could easily dictate a different treatment for one or other, as indeed we have just seen, comparing the treatment of Halus with that of the Perrhaebians and Magnetes. All the same, though nothing is heard of any change in the status of Halus itself, there are some small signs that most of these *perioikoi* were not assigned to any Thessalian city as subjects, but became subject to Philip himself, presumably in his capacity as *archon* of Thessaly. Their position had always been prone to anomaly, since there had been many years in which some of them had been tribute-paying subjects of Larissa or Pherae or Pharsalus, and yet simultaneously they had been Amphictyons, with their votes on the Council, giving the appearance of freedom. Their Amphictyonic membership (continued now) is no criterion of their true status: it tells us neither whether they were subject or free, nor, if they were subject, whom they were subject to.

The same limitation (to look forward now) may be deemed to inhibit any use of their membership of the League of Corinth from 338/7 onwards, for drawing inferences as to their true status. Just as their Amphictyonic votes were useful to their overlord if they had one, so in the sunedrion of Corinth it was an advantage to Philip to augment the vote of the Thessalian bloc by giving separate votes to the *perioikoi* even if they were his tribute-paying subjects.[2] (Corinth presumably had her votes in the sunedrion even though the Macedonian garrison held her Acrocorinthus, the sign of subjection to the Greek world and of freedom gone.) It was not part of Philip's policy, obviously, to split hairs about freedom and true status of Greek states in his power, any more than it has been Russian policy since 1945 to do anything other than pretend, for the purposes of international law, that her satellites have been free and sovereign states.

This, however, does not relieve historians of a duty to split hairs if any can be found worth splitting. One occasion may be thought to provide a clue here, the occasion at Thebes in the autumn of 339 when

---

[1] [D.] 11. 1; D. 19, 2 Hypoth. 7; 19. 36; cf. Sordi, *LT* 362 f.

[2] Tod 177 lines 32 ff., where the names of Malians, Dolopians, and Perrhaebians are preserved.

ambassadors of Philip and of some of his allies sought to divert the Boeotians from their collision course which they were setting now in company with Athens and her Greek alliance. Several ancient sources record a pair of Thessalian ambassadors here, as well as Philip's own pair; appropriately of course, since in the forefront of this crisis was a triangular dispute about Nicaea (see below).[1] One ancient source (Philochorus) records, besides the Thessalians, ambassadors from the Aenianes, Aetolians, Dolopians, and Phthiotic Achaeans as being present.[2] The Aetolians need not concern us now of course, except in so far as they remind us that genuinely free allies (as they were) could have their reasons for being exceedingly anxious to oblige. The Aenianes, Dolopians, and Phthiotic Achaeans no doubt were told by Philip to send embassies to Thebes, and whether these were all the *perioikoi* who got this order, or who obeyed it, we cannot be quite certain; but it seems likely that Philochorus here, since he troubled to name these, would have added any other names if he had known of any. These three were in fact among the *perioikoi* who were nearest to Nicaea. Probably Philip was organizing now a display of unanimity on the subject of this disputed place, his friends protesting just as he protested himself against the Boeotian seizure of it by force (below, pp. 589 f.). However this may be, it seems undeniable that his ability to command their support speaks a little in favour of their being subject to him as *archon* of Thessaly and not the subjects of any Thessalian city individually.

If this is correct, the revenue from the taxes paid to the *archon* by these and others of the *perioikoi* will have been a useful acquisition. More important, though, the strategic value of having these peoples under direct control. And strategically Nicaea itself occupied nearly the highest place in the scale of importance, because of its proximity to Thermopylae. Nicaea was a small city of the eastern Locrians, and as such had never been numbered among the Thessalian *perioikoi*.[3] The Boeotians probably got control of it in their expansive years of the 360s.[4] But in

---

[1] D. 18. 211; Plu. *Demosth.* 18 (= Marsyas F 20 (*FGrH* nos. 135–6)); Theopomp. F 328 (*FGrH* no. 115).   [2] Philoch. F 56 (*FGrH* no. 328).

[3] *Pace* D. 6. 22, ὅτε ... πάλιν Νίκαιαν καὶ Μαγνησίαν ἐδίδου [sc. Θετταλοῖς]. See pp. 587 f. below.

[4] Aeschin. 3. 140 ἐπειδὴ Φίλιππος αὐτῶν [sc. Βοιωτῶν] ἀφελόμενος ... Θετταλοῖς παρέδωκε. Aeschines referred to the year 346, when Philip took Nicaea from Phalaecus; but he evidently believed it had belonged to the Boeotians before the Phocians took it from them, and he was probably right. So Westlake 134.

A similar history probably explains the allusion by Demosthenes to the Malian Echinus ('Echinus which belonged to the Thebans' D. 9. 34), on the coast-road which ran close to the northern shore of the Malian Gulf. Though Phthiotic Thebes was much nearer than Boeotian Thebes to Echinus, there can be no question that it was to Boeotian Thebes that Demosthenes was alluding. The date of Philip's laying hands on it is thought to be 341, but the occasion is unknown; probably a reply to the depredations of Callias of Chalcis (see pp. 552 f.: cf. Wüst 120 f.).

the Sacred War it fell into the hands of the Phocians, and was one of the strong points by virtue of which Phalaecus in 347/6 had commanded Thermopylae and the main route south.[1] When Phalaecus surrendered his position to Philip in 346, the key to Central Greece, Philip will not have needed any reminder that Nicaea must never get into wrong hands again. Consequently, when we are told that he thereupon 'gave it to the Thessalians', we can be sure that whatever he did he was not really letting this place out of his own control.[2] He was *archon* of the Thessalians, commander-in-chief of their army. If Nicaea was always garrisoned after Phalaecus abandoned it (as I judge that it certainly was), and if now by Thessalian troops, their commander would be nominated by Philip, who was in a position too to ensure that the troops themselves and their officers included none who were untrustworthy. Thermopylae was a prize when it was won; and a prize it remained, not to be fooled about with. To control it as *archon* of Thessaly and not as king of the Macedonians was not to control it any less effectively. It was presumably a source of interest and pleasure to the Thessalians that Nicaea was to be administered now through their own organs of government. A source of deep dissatisfaction, however, to the Boeotians, with their claim to it, and their knowledge of what Thermopylae meant. 'Giving Nicaea to the Thessalians' was, among other things, a formidable diplomatic wedge driven between the two strongest peoples of northern and central Greece. Here was a quarrel between them which could be made to last for ever, if the need should arise.

---

[1] Aeschin. 2. 132, 138.

[2] D. 6. 22; Aeschin. 3. 140. Each orator introduces, apparently, his own inaccuracy, which does not invalidate however the statement that 'he gave it to the Thessalians'. Demosthenes wrote 'When he gave Nicaea and Magnesia back [sc. to the Thessalians]', where πάλιν referring to Magnesia is right, but referring to Nicaea is wrong, so far as we know. Aeschines wrote 'When Philip had taken Nicaea from them [sc. the Boeotians] and given it to the Thessalians . . .'; Philip certainly took Nicaea from Phalaecus and the Phocians. Aeschines meant, no doubt, that the Boeotians had had it before the Phocians took it, and they regarded it as theirs.

XVII

POLEMOS APOLEMOS[1]
(342–340)

1. *Euboea*

FROM about midsummer of 342, for two years or nearly, the first aims and energies of Macedonia were to be directed to the east, to Thrace, to the important Greek cities of the Sea of Marmara, Propontis, and the Bosphorus, to the northern nations up to the Danube. Philip in person will have had with him an important part of the Macedonian army for these campaigns. Antipater, it is thought, was left in effect in charge of the kingdom, as adviser to the young Alexander as regent. Its security in a narrow sense cannot have been seriously in question, since Philip so recently had dealt severely with the western Illyrians. All the more interesting, then, that Parmenion did not accompany Philip into Thrace, Parmenion his best and most experienced general.[2] Parmenion was left behind, we must surmise, in order to meet any emergency that might arise from among the states of Greece, where Philip's relations with the Athenians had reached a point at which an outbreak of war was not impossible or even unlikely; and with Athens no longer entirely isolated (as in 346), an Athenian war would be inevitably, in some sense, a general war. Ironically, the presence of Parmenion in Greece (not in Thrace) is made known to us in a campaign of the year 342/1 which, though a minor operation in itself, was part of a series which becomes too important to be dismissed as merely a sideshow, and which unquestionably had the effect of making the outbreak of the Athenian war more likely and its proportions more serious.[3] The theatre was Euboea.

The whole train of events in Euboea, and their chronology, remains one of the more elusive forays of Philip's policy in Greece, even after the masterly study of them by Professor Brunt.[4] In view of their contribution in sum to the breakdown of the peace, it would be good to know for sure

---

[1] I hope this title does not give offence because I use the phrase in a sense that differs from that both of A. *Pr.* 904 and of Eur. *HF* 1133.

[2] Plu. *Mor.* 177 c, for Philip's own opinion of Parmenion, as his only general. For the evidence that Parmenion was left behind, below, p. 546 and n. 3.

[3] On the chronology, below, p. 546.

[4] P. A. Brunt, 'Euboea in the time of Philip II', *CQ* N.S. 19 (1969) 245 f.

how closely the events in Euboea which ran concurrently with Philip's campaigns in Thrace in 342 and 341 were followed and directed by Philip himself. It seems possible, for example, that requests for troops from Macedonia by leaders in Euboean cities were answered by Antipater without the long delay of communicating with Philip in eastern Thrace. If this was done, Antipater will have followed a line of policy laid down by Philip before he left Macedonia. Indeed it seems that no new situation arose in Euboea after midsummer 342 (Philip's departure into Thrace), apart from the novelties in detail which inspired the actual requests for troops which were made. Already in 343 Philip had sent 1,000 mercenaries to Eretria to help Clitarchus (above, pp. 502 f.). In the view of Demosthenes, already at that time he had been bent on making trouble in Euboea, trouble for Athens. On a cooler view, he had certainly not been neglecting the opportunities of supporting the Euboean leaders at Eretria and probably elsewhere who could be looked to to support him in return. It is presumably a continuance and extension of this policy that is to be seen in the Macedonian interventions of 342, whether they were made before or after the moment when Philip himself moved east into Thrace.

Early in 341 Demosthenes knew of three occasions when mercenaries from Macedonia had made an appearance at Eretria, with the effect of overthrowing a democracy there and confirming Clitarchus and his associates in their seizure of power.[1] The first of these occasions had been in 343 (the incident at Porthmos, above, p. 502). The other two occasions belong to the year 342, and most probably to the second half of the year when Philip was already absent in Thrace;[2] and it was the last of these expeditions that was commanded by Parmenion. Why so distinguished a commander needed to take the field we are not told; but it seems likely that this force may have combined an objective at Eretria with another at Oreus. In this same year, a somewhat similar pattern of events was completed at Oreus, with a force from Macedonia arriving to enable Philistides and others to overthrow democracy and take control.[3] In both these cities we see a disturbed political scene, of *stasis*

---

[1] D. 9. 57 f.; cf. 9. 27, 66.

[2] This follows from D. 8. 35–6, if the time sequence in this passage is reliable. The date of the speech is spring 341, and the allusions here are to events fresh enough to make unprofitable any falsification by manipulating their order, which shows (and this is Demosthenes' point) that it is while Philip has been active in Thrace that the Athenians have remained inactive while two tyrannies have been established in Euboea: . . . δέκα μῆνας ἀπογενομένου τἀνθρώπου . . . οὔτε τὴν Εὔβοιαν ἠλευθερώσατε οὔτε . . . ἀλλ' ἐκεῖνος μὲν ὑμῶν οἴκοι μενόντων . . . δύ' ἐν Εὐβοίᾳ κατέστησε τυράννους . . . ὑμεῖς δ' οὐδὲ ταῦτ' ἀπελύσασθε . . . ἀλλ' εἰάκατε. The οὐδὲ ταῦτ' refers clearly to something fresh that has happened during the 'ten months', and makes it impossible for δύ' ἐν Εὐβοίᾳ κατέστησε τυράννους to refer to action by Philip before the 'ten months'.

[3] D. 9. 59 ff., especially 61; cf. 9. 12. For Euphraeus the democratic leader, Carystius

leading to a foreign intervention. Of the origins of the *stasis* we know nothing, and presumably Philip was not concerned in them. His moment came when somebody needed help, and asked for it. The inter-city relations of the Euboean cities, too, would surely tell us more if we knew about them. Some years back (in 346) there had been a proposal from Chalcis to create a Euboean League. This may well not have commended itself to many Euboeans of the other cities, if they saw it as a move to promote a hegemony for Chalcis.[1] It is significant that Demosthenes at the time (early 341) when he spoke of Eretria and Oreus as under tyrannies enjoying Macedonian support, evidently counted Chalcis as reliably anti-Macedonian.[2] More, by 341 it was recognized in Chalcis that what had been done already in Euboea, at Eretria and Oreus, was a threat to freedom.

The Chalcidian leader Callias, who had played an important part in the secession of Euboea from Athens in 348, had some personal knowledge of Philip and Macedonia, having spent some time there at court, on a visit which was not just a brief one.[3] Almost all that we know of Callias comes to us from Aeschines, who disapproved of him strongly, and who is not necessarily reliable when he tells us that after becoming one of Philip's Companions, Callias disgraced himself in some way and had to leave the country.[4] If Callias had hoped to gain Philip's support for the Euboean League project, he may well have found him unsympathetic, for a strong and united Euboea which could look after itself was in some ways an unpromising proposition, for Philip. Conversely, if Callias aimed to keep Euboea independent and to keep foreigners out wherever they might come from, his association with Philip may have taught him to beware of the Macedonians no less than of the traditional exploiters of Euboea, Athens, and Thebes.[5] According to Aeschines it was to Thebes that he turned when he had fallen out with Philip; but with no better result. The fault lay with Callias, Aeschines implies; but at Thebes, too, a divided Euboea subservient to Boeotia was traditionally the thing to work for, and it may well have

---

Pergamenus *ap.* Athen. 11. 506 e, 508 d (= *FHG* 4. 1–2); [Plato], *Ep.* 5; Suid. s.v. *Euphraios*; above, pp. 206 f.

It is only Carystius who names Parmenion as concerned in the events at Oreus. He says that Parmenion put Euphraeus to death, contradicting Demosthenes' account of Euphraeus' suicide in prison. Demosthenes ought to be right about this. But Carystius' mistake would be understandable if the collapse of the *demos* at Oreus had been completed by the mercenaries from Macedonia with Parmenion in command. Brunt (art. cit. 252) suggests this tentatively, and I think rightly.

[1] Aeschin. 3. 89 Καλλίας ὁ Χαλκιδεὺς . . . Εὐβοϊκὸν μὲν τῷ λόγῳ συνέδριον εἰς Χαλκίδα συνάγων, ἰσχυρὰν δὲ τὴν Εὔβοιαν ἐφ' ὑμᾶς ἔργῳ κατασκευάζων . . .

[2] D. 8. 18; 9. 74.   [3] Aeschin. 3. 86 ff.

[4] Aeschin. 3. 89 f.

[5] On Callias in general, Brunt, art. cit. 253 f.

been the policies of Callias, as well as his face, that did not fit.[1] That he should have looked to Philip first (and to Thebes second) to guarantee his future was entirely natural in one who had been a leader of the movement against Athens in 348. For Philip, Callias when he arrived in Macedonia must have seemed just the kind of young man he most liked to see arriving in Macedonia; ambitious, an enemy of Athens, sure to come in useful some day. One must suspect in Callias a rare independence that declined to be merely useful, or to subordinate the interests of Chalcis or Euboea to the tramp of big battalions. His actual alarm for Chalcis and Euboea, which led him to turn about, towards the old enemy, and seek an alliance with Athens, can be seen (from its timing) to have been inspired by those movements supported by Philip in Eretria and Oreus which developed in the year 342 (above).

It was in May, probably, of 341 that his ambassadors were in Athens and succeeded in negotiating a defensive alliance in the usual form as between contracting parties who were of equal status.[2] The motives of Callias, according to Aeschines, were those of sheer terror: the armies of Macedonia and of the Thebans were actually on the march against him.[3] How and where these armies were occupying themselves when in the month of June a combined force from Chalcis, Athens, and Megara liberated Oreus from the rule of Philistides,[4] Aeschines did not trouble himself to explain. (He was speaking, after all, eleven years after the event, and there is a limit to the trouble a self-respecting orator need take to lend verisimilitude to a lie at such long range.) Aeschines' tale about the armies is fiction. In real life, the Macedonians had not moved, and the Boeotian hoplites were busy with their harvest, we may be sure. Nor was there any intervention from the north or the west when later in the year the Athenians under Phocion (and with Chalcis no doubt in support) liberated Eretria and expelled Clitarchus.[5] For a man who had started in a blue funk Callias came through this summer remarkably well. Aeschines had been *proxenos* of both Philistides and Clitarchus, and his sympathies both in Euboea and further afield in Macedonia did not allow him later an objective appreciation of what Callias really achieved, more especially as he had achieved it mainly by co-operating with the arch-enemy Demosthenes.[6]

For this defensive alliance of Athens and Chalcis was a much more

---

[1] His father, Mnesarchus, had turned against the Boeotians in 357 when Euboea reverted from the Boeotian to the Athenian alliance: cf. Brunt, art. cit. 248, 253.

[2] Aeschin. 3. 92 βοηθεῖν μὲν Χαλκιδεῦσι . . . καὶ Χαλκιδέας βοηθεῖν, ἐάν τις ἴῃ ἐπ᾽ Ἀθηναίους.

[3] Aeschin. 3. 91 τηλικαῦται δυνάμεις ἐπ᾽ αὐτὸν ἐπεστράτευον, ἥ τε Φιλίππου καὶ Θηβαίων.

[4] Philoch. F 159 (*FGrH* no. 328); schol. ad Aeschin. 3. 85 (month Skirophorion); Charax *FGrH* no. 103 F 19 (Megarians); cf. *FGrH* 3 b. Suppl. p. 535.

[5] Philoch. FF 160–1 ἐπὶ τούτου . . . This should mean in or about August 341. For discussion, Brunt, art. cit. (and below, p. 549 n. 3).

[6] D. 18. 82 (*proxenos*); Aeschin. 3. 91–105.

potent diplomatic weapon than its name discloses. Its potency derived in part from the community of interests, with a view to the immediate future. Both Chalcis and Athens were determined to free Euboea from the governments which they saw as in some sense the agents of Macedonia now. Unlike so many defensive alliances in Greece which never led to any action even when one of the parties was attacked, this one led immediately to the preventive, pre-emptive blows which freed Oreus and Eretria. (This naughty animal, even before anyone had attacked it, defended itself by taking an offensive.) The priority of Oreus as a target may have owed something to the state of things inside this city and inside Eretria. But it was good policy to take Oreus first, the more easily reached by Macedonian troops via the Gulf of Pagasae or the Malian Gulf; and with Oreus taken the Macedonians might need Boeotian co-operation if they were to reinforce Eretria at all.[1] But also, for the longer term, the urgency of the Athenian desire for action here led the *demos* to accept a more liberal view of their future relations with Euboea than any they had adopted in the past. They accepted, in effect, the proposals of Callias for a Euboean League, and they made the alliance with Chalcis in the first place, and with the other Euboeans presently, without obliging the Euboean cities whether individually or collectively to become members of the Athenian Confederacy. For this, it seems, Demosthenes was largely responsible.[2] The sacrifice was well conceived, judging by results.

Callias himself emerges as a powerful advocate for Greek unity to resist Macedonian aggressions. Although, with Philip far away in eastern Thrace, there came no quick reply from Macedonia to the strokes at Oreus and Eretria, Callias judged presumably that Philip would react when he was free, and that something like a general war was to be expected. Late in this same year (341) it was Callias who together with Demosthenes visited the Peloponnese and laid the foundations of the Hellenic alliance which, led by Athens, was to defend Greek freedom.[3] Our information about it consists of a report by Aeschines eleven

---

[1] These points are well made by Brunt, art. cit. 261–3.   [2] Aeschin. 3. 91–4.

[3] That Callias was associated in some way with Demosthenes on the Peloponnesian visits seems to follow from his addressing the Athenian assembly on the subject. Demosthenes followed him immediately as a speaker on the same occasion, if Aeschines is to be believed (3. 95–9).

The dating of the missions to the Peloponnese follows from the date fixed for a conference of the new allies in Athens. 16 Anthesterion mentioned by Aeschines (3. 98) can only be February/March of the year 340. It is reasonable to think of an interval of some weeks, but not of some months, between the fixing of the date of this conference and the conference itself (so Brunt rightly, art. cit. 256 ff.). The ambassadors will have been in the Peloponnese, then, very late in the year 341.

Brunt (ibid.) has argued convincingly for placing all these Euboean developments in the year 341, against Cawkwell ('Demosthenes' 210 ff.). The remaining difficulties, about the position of Clitarchus of Eretria who, if all Aeschines' facts about him are sound, will have

years later of a report made by Demosthenes to the Athenian Assembly at the time; and since Aeschines was concerned to represent Demosthenes as an irresponsible liar and magnifier of his own achievements, we should be wrong to accept what he tells us literally. Demosthenes did not say 'All the Peloponnesians are in the bag' (πάντας μὲν Πελοποννησίους ὑπάρχειν), we probably ought to conclude. He may have reported promises of war contributions sufficient to finance a fleet of 100 ships and a large force of mercenaries. And his alleged report of a mere 2,000 citizen hoplites promised from the Peloponnese, and another 2,000 from Acarnania, is moderate enough to make one think that this bit very likely may be true.[1] In the same way Aeschines' report of Callias' report, which was confined to enumerating financial undertakings from Megara and Achaea and from the Euboeans themselves, contains nothing that is impossible or improbable.[2] When allowance is made for Aeschines and his context, it seems that these missions to the Peloponnese had returned with some genuine success to their credit. Some Peloponnesians now were prepared to join an alliance to be led by Athens and directed expressly against Philip. Yet only three years before (*Second Philippic*) Athens had been friendless in the Peloponnese, except for Sparta. The change is great.

It is hard to avoid concluding that Philip's own actions had been in part responsible for it, perhaps largely so.[3] Allowance should be made for the relaxing of tension in the Peloponnese as a result of Sparta's temporary quiescence, signalized by the absence of King Archidamus in Italy. Messene could feel safe enough now to conclude an alliance with Athens though she was already an ally of Philip.[4] Argos and the Arcadians may have approximated to this same position. But there were Peloponnesian states that by now had been given cause not merely for neutrality but for a positive hostility to Philip. His threat to Ambracia had alienated Corinth, his Aetolian alliance with its contingency clause about Naupactus had alienated the Achaeans.[5] Particularly illuminating are the consequences of his aid to Perillus and the enemies of democracy at Megara,[6] which turned the Megarian *demos* to Athens, and evidently not in mere gratitude for Phocion's support in 343, but with a lively sense that Philip was an enemy to be not only resisted but forestalled.

joined the alliance briefly before being overthrown by the allies themselves (Athens and Chalcis) cannot all be resolved by any interpretation. Personally, I think that some of Aeschines' facts about him are not sound, and that his expulsion from Eretria probably preceded Eretria's joining the alliance. (In the context Aeschines has a good enough reason for representing it otherwise.)

[1] Aeschin. 3. 91–4.　　　　　　　　　　　　　　　　　　　　　　　　　[2] Ibid.

[3] So Brunt, art. cit. 261. 'Philip's interventions in Euboea in 342 were gravely misjudged, for they consolidated much of Greek opinion against him . . .'

[4] Above, pp. 482 f.　　　　　　[5] Above, p. 509.　　　　　　[6] Above, pp. 497 ff.

Nothing but this can explain the association of Megara with Athens and Chalcis in the Oreus campaign of June 341.[1] So too in Euboea. The interventions at Eretria and Oreus had alarmed Chalcis to the point of driving her into the arms of Athens. (Both Megara and Chalcis had a recent record of hostility to Athens, which makes this the more striking.)

Finally, the Peloponnesian embassies of Demosthenes and Callias of Chalcis in late 341 suggest that the developments in Euboea had not passed unnoticed in the Peloponnese. That Demosthenes may have magnified the success of his mission there is likely enough. But Aeschines' attempt to reduce it in retrospect *ad absurdum* does not carry conviction.[2] The conference of allies fixed for 16 Anthesterion of 340 probably did take place, though Aeschines as good as says that it did not.[3] It may easily not have met on the date which Demosthenes originally announced for it: it may have been postponed in fact, like many another conference. But the anecdote in Plutarch which has as its setting just such a conference as this, one which meets before war has been declared and at which it is relevant to talk about fixing rates of contributions in money, presumably is of the conference organized by Demosthenes, and presumably it did meet at some date in the year 340, before the occasion in April when Demosthenes was 'crowned' for his good services.[4] Philip meanwhile was attacking first Perinthus (July), then Byzantium. The smaller states of Greece no longer could look instinctively to him as supporter and perhaps saviour in a time of trouble: some of them at least had come to view him with a profound suspicion.

Not only the smaller states of course. The Athenians, with their obvious interest in Euboea, showed by their prompt and effective support of Chalcis both that they had appreciated the Euboean situation correctly and that they had shed some doubts and hesitations in their attitude to Philip in general. It is from Hegesippus and Demosthenes now that they are taking their advice. There was to be no co-operation, no learning to live with Philip. But Thebes, too, was an interested party. A Euboea dominated by Philip was no more comfortable for the Boeotians than for Athens. And wherever in these recent years Philip had moved in a way suggesting that he aimed to penetrate, or dominate, or control, whether in Euboea or in the Peloponnese or in north-west Greece via Ambracia, always these were regions where in the recent past the Boeotians had exercised hegemony or had tried to. The Acarnanians who had been their allies in the 360s and had lent some support in the Sacred War, now when they were nervous of Philip turned to Athens for alliance, not to Thebes whom now they had no choice but to identify

---

[1] Above, p. 548.
[2] For the actual support forthcoming in 339/8, D. 18. 237; Plu. *Mor.* 845 A.
[3] Aeschin. 3. 98 f.   [4] D. 18. 83; Plu. *Dem.* 17. 3.

with the enemy.¹ To those Theban leaders who retained the big ideas, each move of Philip came as a constriction and a prevention; Euboea, because it came nearest home, a particularly sharp turn of the screw. The *Schadenfreude* of those Arcadians and others in Sparta's great days who had rejoiced (as Xenophon describes) in reverses of the *hegemon* may be our guide perhaps to the feelings of these Boeotians when Philip had paused before Ambracia, still more when his puppets tumbled in Euboea. What Callias could do, others could do too.

Finally, to return to the question already anticipated in part (above), why did the puppets tumble, in Euboea? Or, having tumbled (as puppets sometimes will), why were they not straightened and replaced by the controlling hand? To point to these Euboean experiences as a sign and a proof that still, after eighteen years as sovereign, Philip could and did delegate nothing of any consequence, is probably too easy an answer to this question; and he had never been one of those great ones who never for one instant must be seen to lose face. On the contrary, whether in diplomacy or in the field he had shown himself capable of accepting reverses, and of exercising great patience, even for years, before returning to settle a score.² One cannot call it impossible, then, for Philip to have received in Pella the news of Oreus and Eretria, and still to have held his hand, if it had seemed to him that next year, or some time, was better than this year for invading Euboea, with the likelihood of open war with Athens and her allies. As it was, however, he received the news far away in Thrace, and with a time-lag that may have been considerable. Meanwhile it was for Antipater to decide, presumably, whether immediate action was called for, whether to send in Parmenion again if Parmenion was still at home and not abroad. Evidently he decided not. And in view of the general situation in Greece it is not difficult to appreciate that Antipater may have recognized that this was a decision for the *maestro*. This was not a war to be begun 'by accident', as Aristotle might have said.³ With Diopeithes sowing *casus belli* in and round the Chersonese with a prodigal hand, with Amphictyons un-furnished as yet with even the smallest scrap of trouble or contention from which to weave an Amphictyonic war, it was not for Antipater to start a general war because of Oreus or Eretria or both together.

Less easy to understand, perhaps, is the inactivity in Macedonia which seems to have permitted attacks executed by Callias of Chalcis

---

¹ Above, p. 508, for Athens–Acarnania alliance. For 360s, X. *HG*. 6. 5. 23; for Sacred War, Tod 160 (Alyzea).

² Thermopylae and Ambracia spring to mind, and (for diplomacy) his overtures to Athens for peace in 348, so tardily taken up. Within the next eighteen months from now, Perinthus and Byzantium were to give him the opportunity of showing that he had not lost the capacity for cutting losses and giving an enemy best.

³ e.g. Arist. *Pol.* 2. 1274ᵃ12, οὐ κατὰ . . . προαίρεσιν ἀλλὰ μᾶλλον ἀπὸ συμπτώματος.

on allies of Philip in the Gulf of Pagasae. (The recapture of Halonnesus by a force from the neighbouring island of Peparethos can be seen as part of the same strategy.) We learn of these attacks from the '*Letter of Philip*' ([D.] 12), and unfortunately from the only passage in the *Letter*, perhaps, which calls for the comment that Philip really cannot have written what we read now in this text—if his purpose was to write seriously and effectively. 'Callias, then, your agent and general, captured all the inhabited cities on the Gulf of Pagasae, though they were at peace with you by the terms of the treaty, and though they were my allies. He also sold as enemies all whom he took at sea who were bound for Macedonia.'[1] The information about prisoners is above suspicion, and the odd description of Callias himself seems even an interesting mark of authenticity: to call the Chalcidian leader and new ally of Athens an Athenian general (which of course he was not) was a very good way, rhetorically speaking, of blaming the Athenians for supporting and using him against Philip, and the effective and unusual phrase ὁ παρ᾽ ὑμῶν στρατηγός carries conviction as being much more likely to be Philip's own than that of a literary composer of the *Letter*.[2]

The statement however that Callias had taken all the cities of the Gulf of Pagasae is simply unbelievable. These cities included Pagasae itself, a major fortress. Callias could only have taken it and them by a long campaign. And if he had taken them, what had he done with them? The *Letter* neither asks for them back nor mentions the second long campaign which would have been needed to win them back if Callias meant to hold them. It is incredible that nothing of all this can be found in our surviving accounts of the events leading up to the outbreak of war. Personally I am not going to believe that Callias had taken all or any of the cities on the Gulf of Pagasae. I believe (on the evidence of this passage) that he had done something to them, or to some of them. And if pushed to say what I think he did to them, I think he most probably plundered or ravaged them.[3]

---

[1] [D.] 12. 5. (For Halonnesus, 12. 12 ff.)

[2] If I am right in translating 'your agent and general', the phrase besides being effective is accurate enough, in view of the Athenian ships furnished to Callias for these acts of war. On the authenticity of the *Letter*, see below, pp. 714 ff.

[3] The most obvious ways of accounting for this unconvincing information about Callias seem to be three: (1) It derives from a literary composer of the *Letter*, who made a bad mistake here. If so, it seems to be the only really bad mistake he did make, for no other allusion in the *Letter* causes such difficulty. (It would be possible, I suppose, to think of this one sentence as an interpolation; but this seems very improbable.) (2) Philip wrote the *Letter*, and wrote this sentence, although it was untrue. If he did, it was childish, ineffective, and out of keeping with the rest of the *Letter*, which consists of complaints founded on genuine facts. I consider this explanation so unlikely as to be hardly worth considering. (3) The writer of the *Letter*, whether Philip or another, did not write exactly what we read now in our text. For a historian to emend his way out of a difficulty is often a counsel of despair, unless the text really invites it urgently. Yet the whole of our difficulty here does arise from one word only in this text,

These acts of war by Callias, and the capture of Halonnesus too, were the acts of enemies who were no longer in doubt that war was inevitable, and were wasting no time in making some quick profit. That there was any deep political plan in intimidating the cities of the Gulf of Pagasae seems unlikely, for there can have been no hope of detaching these people from Philip now even if they had wanted to be detached. But one political bonus which can hardly have been foreseen may have been helped to accrue from acting boldly in these waters. The Boeotians had an interest not indeed in the Gulf of Pagasae but in the region immediately adjacent to it on the south. The energy and nerve of Callias, meeting as he did no immediate reply, may have encouraged them to act boldly too (below, p. 587). As for the inactivity of the Macedonian command under Callias' pinpricks, it seems inexplicable except by the reasons suggested already. Neither Antipater nor Parmenion nor even the young Alexander was going to start this war 'by accident'. There were reasons enough now for going to war, but for this war Philip might want a Cause; and if so only he had better choose it, and frame it, and name it.

2. *Philip in Thrace, 342–340*

Philip's Thracian campaign of 346 had been short, sharp, and for the moment decisive. What occasioned it is unknown; presumably some disturbance of the *status quo* by Cersobleptes. Philip's objectives however were limited, and evidently he was confident of achieving them, and quickly, since he counted on being back home in Macedonia in time to swear the oath to the treaty with Athens when the Athenian ambassadors should have returned.[1] Nevertheless he covered a lot of ground. Of the

the verb ἔλαβεν. It is the *taking* of a number of cities in these circumstances that goes beyond what is credible. It goes beyond, too, the writer's own comment on it in the sentence that follows. He writes (addressing the Athenians) 'In fact I do not know what you can find to do that is fresh, if you declare that you are at war with me. When we were openly at war you sent out privateers and you sold travellers making for Macedonia, you supported my enemies, you did damage to my territory' (ibid. 5). To accept the negative supplied by Richards ('When we were *not* openly at war . . .) makes no difference to this: the Athenians never had taken any city belonging to Philip or one of his allies in the previous war: if Callias had taken cities now, the complaint could (doubtless would) have been put even more strongly.

What the sense seems to require here is τὰς μὲν πόλεις . . . ἦγεν καὶ ἔφερεν ἁπάσας, or . . . ἐλῄστευεν ἁπάσας or something of the sort. Ἐλῄϊζεν ἁπάσας suggests itself as the verbform which perhaps could have been corrupted to ἔλαβεν most easily; but ἐλῃΐζετο seems to be the usual form (ἐλῄϊζεν at Thuc. 4. 41. 2, all manuscripts, and at 3. 85. 2, some manuscripts: see LSJ⁹ s.v.). Or, if the true reading was ἔφερεν καὶ ἦγεν (or vice versa), and one of the two verbs fell out, the survivor perhaps could have been 'corrected' to ἔλαβεν. Whatever the details of the text's history, I do suspect that what this writer originally wrote here amounts to his saying that Callias *ravaged* all the cities of the Gulf of Pagasae.

[1] See above, p. 341.

Thracian places mentioned repeatedly by Demosthenes in later years as having been taken by Philip after the date when the Athenians swore to the Peace in Athens, Serrium and Doriscus were on the coast between Maroneia and Aenus, but Hieron Oros was beyond the Hebrus and north of the Chersonese, and Ganos was east of the Chersonese on the Propontis coast (Sea of Marmara).[1] Philip counted no doubt on Cersobleptes submitting when he realized that any chances of support from Athens were at an end.

At Athens itself this campaign left a legacy of grievances, arising from the unfortunate timing of some of Philip's captures in relation to the ratification of the peace-treaty (above), and also from the feud with Cardia, Philip's ally now and determined to maintain her independence of Athens in face of the Athenian claim to own everything and everybody inside the Chersonese. Philip's proposal or promise to construct a canal across the neck of the Chersonese from Pteleum to the spot on the northern coast known as White Beach (Leuke Akte), dates from the time of his conversations with the second Athenian embassy of 346, and is mentioned later (by Demosthenes) in bad company, along with the other baits for the gullible (in Euboea, Boeotia, and the rest) with which these ambassadors had misled the Athenian *demos* at that time.[2] Nevertheless the proposal was probably a serious one, and remained open and subject to discussion for some long time, for Hegesippus could allude to it four years later in a way that shows that it was well known to everybody.[3] For the Greeks in the Chersonese the canal would have served some purpose of demarcation and perhaps of defence, *vis-à-vis* the kingdom of Cersobleptes, but perhaps at the expense of some economic disadvantages from the opening of the new route into the Propontis. For Philip himself the new route offered strategic advantages sufficient to explain his making the proposition and his keeping it open: the canal would have done away with his naval embarrassments of the year 340 (below, p. 567). In all this Cersobleptes presumably was not consulted.

The years 342–340 are thought of as those of Philip's 'final conquest' of Thrace. This was certainly the time (the only time) when he can be said to have concentrated on Thrace in some way that gave it a priority in his plans, though in the end one can see that this clearly is something less than a total conquest; and the recently found site and remains of the next generation's Seuthopolis remind us how far the conquest was from being final.[4] But Philip's performance here is still impressive.

---

[1] [D.] 7. 36 f.; D. 8. 64; 9. 15 f.; 19. 156 etc.; 18. 27; Aeschin. 2. 89 f. and schol. 3. 82; cf. Schaefer 2. 246 f.; U. Kahrstedt, *Beiträge zur Geschichte der thrakischen Chersones* (Baden-Baden, 1954) 36 n. 101.

[2] D. 6. 30; [D.] 7. 39.   [3] [D.] 7. 39.

[4] H. Bengtson, 'Neues zur Geschichte des Hellenismus in Thrakien', *Historia* 11 (1962) 18 ff.

Thrace was a geographical expression covering a much greater area than Macedonia itself. No Thracian ever unified it or ruled it all. The Odrysian king who prospered occasionally, the Sitalces, the Seuthes, or the Cotys, could make himself obeyed 'from Mt. Haemus and Rhodope to the sea', and respected from the Strymon to the Danube.[1] It was the Odrysian Cersobleptes who in this generation would have succeeded, no doubt, in reassembling that divided kingdom if he had not had to count Philip among his competitors in the power struggle of this area. One says this because of his capacity for survival, suggesting a resilience and ability above the average. We do not know what had prompted Philip's campaigns against him of 352 and of 346. Though he had certainly become (by 346) in status a vassal king, the repeated recourse to war must mean that he was not one for the quiet life (*asphalōs douleuein!*), but was still *polypragmon* when the occasion allowed it. He is sure to have been the chief of 'the Thracian kings' whom Demosthenes commemorates as among those with whom he had been a success as an ambassador.[2] In 342 according to Diodorus (who alone offers an explanation here) it was attacks by him on the Greek cities 'on the Hellespont' that provided Philip with the occasion for mounting this big Thracian affair.[3]

The explanation itself carries some conviction, as reproducing a Macedonian 'official' view of these things; but also as a reminder of the classic relationship of Greek city and Thracian overlord, with the annual tribute payments in acknowledgement of the privilege of being allowed to farm, to trade, and indeed to exist, without being harassed or exterminated (this year) by the local warriors.[4] But the limits of the explanation are plain when we recall how this Thracian affair all ended, with the leading Greek cities of the area (Byzantium and Perinthus) themselves at war with Philip, and with no signs of their having been 'saved' by him from Cersobleptes or anyone else. That Philip did become the ally of some Greek cities we know (below), and also of important kings. But as to the purpose of this whole exercise, it probably is right not to be satisfied with the purely local and ephemeral explanation, still less with the Athenocentric explanation of Demosthenes, adapted sometimes and expanded by some modern interpreters. It was not Thrace itself that interested Philip, Demosthenes seems to be saying, but Thrace as a step towards conquering Athens.[5] Yet Philip seems so determined to take his

[1] Thuc. 2. 96, for the realm and influence of Sitalces; cf. Str. 7 F 48. See in general J. Wiesner, *Die Thraker* (Stuttgart, 1963), esp. 116 ff., 135 ff.; G. Kazarow, *RE* 6A (1937) s.v. *Thrakien*, esp. 423 ff.; Berve 1. 227 f.

[2] D. 18. 244. The context, with Demosthenes competing against ambassadors from Philip, dates the occasion before the outbreak of this war.

[3] D.S. 16. 71. 1.

[4] Cf. (e.g.) Tod 151. 4 ff., 10 ff., 15 (τὸμ φόρον τὸμ πάτριον): the date, 357. (For the 'revenues' of the Scythian king Atheas, below, p. 561.)

[5] D. 8. 44 f.

time over Athens, even as late as in 339, that really it is not convincing to think of him in 342 as using Thrace as a means of intimidating Athens after diplomacy has failed. It seems better to see Thrace more as a problem in its own right, and with strategic implications of a more general and long-range character than those which concerned Athens especially.

Philip will not have meant to take three years over all this when he began it in 342;[1] but the scale of operations, and some aspects of his methods, especially some city-foundations now, do seem to distinguish this from any earlier campaign series in this area. Though the echoes of this campaign seem to have resounded afar, with impact on the Getae north of the Haemus range and even on the Scythians settled now south of the Danube delta, the plan itself was confined, so far as we know, to the area south of Haemus, with the Odrysians the main target.[2] The plan was probably a radical one, however, for in its first months Philip is described as 'campaigning in the interior, in upper Thrace, against the king of the Odrysians'.[3] He did not return to Macedonia for the winter, but still there after more than ten months, he is mentioned already in connection with one of the places (Cabyle), which presently becomes known as one of his new colonies in Thrace.[4] Cabyle is indeed in 'upper Thrace', not far south of Haemus, on a tributary of the upper Hebrus river, on which is situated the better-known colony Philippopolis itself (the modern Plovdiv).[5] In occupying these places, and perhaps others in the same locality, and spending incidentally a hellish Thracian winter doing it (as Demosthenes expresses it graphically), Philip was going to the heart of the matter of Cersobleptes and his kingdom.[6] Probably the city of Apollonia, on the Black Sea coast on the latitude of Philippopolis and Cabyle, was a Greek city that had suffered from Cersobleptes (as Diodorus suggested that some did). Apollonia evidently became Philip's new ally now, for it was 'through Apollonia' that Atheas the Scythian king made his appeal to Philip presently.[7]

In this year (342) or the next, Cersobleptes was driven out of his kingdom. So likewise was Teres, son of Amadocus (above, p. 282), and what became of them we do not know.[8] Nor is it clear in detail what became of their kingdoms. Diodorus writing of the Thracians as 'conquered' (καταπολεμηθεῖσι), and 'commanded to pay tithes to the

---

[1] His wintering in Thrace (342/1) was due in part to an illness, perhaps (D. 8. 35).
[2] D.S. 16. 71. 1.   [3] D. 8, Hypoth. 3.
[4] D. 8. 44 (10. 15: the passages are almost identical).
[5] *RE* 19 (1937) 2244 f. (C. M. Danoff); cf. G. Mihailov *IGBR* 3. 1 (1961) 19–20.
[6] D. 8. 44 (ἐν τῷ βαράθρῳ χειμάζειν). Beroe (Beroea) with its good Macedonian name, lay between Cabyle and Philippopolis, and may perhaps be another foundation of Philip (*RE* 3. 1. 306, s.v. *Beroia* (3), 1897). The site of Bine (or Binae) is not identified (cf. *EM* s.v. *Βίνη*; Theophr. *De lapid.* 12 and 15, *Binai*).
[7] Just. 9. 2. 1 (and cf. in general D.S. 16. 71. 2).
[8] [D.] 12. 8–10.

Macedonians', invites us to think of a Thrace organized now as a province, 'policed' by the cities newly founded (D.S. ibid.), and perhaps
put under the charge of a 'General over Thrace' (στρατηγὸς ἐπὶ Θρᾴκης),
though to be sure we hear of this General only in Alexander's reign for
the first time.[1] Fire and sword had their part in all this, and the Odrysians
will have suffered quite severely in this war (D.S. ibid). They were not
the only ones, however. The Maedi of Rhodope 'revolted', and were
chastised by Alexander in his first independent command, probably in
340.[2] To the north-east of them the Tetrachoritae had to face at one
time both Antipater and Parmenion together. Presumably they were
brought to heel, but we have no details.[3] The colony Alexandropolis
belongs to the occasion of Alexander's command, as Plutarch records it,
and the objections to this are unconvincing.[4] In a later generation, for
Alexander to have founded a city bearing his own name in his father's
lifetime would have been a declaration of independence and an act of
rebellion, as Tarn observed, and concluded therefore that this was
a military colony (not a city) which Alexander settled, and that it took
its name from him later. But in this generation Philip was not observing
precedents or protocol, he was creating them. Philippi is the first city
we know to bear its founder's name, and Philippopolis the second.
Alexandropolis probably was founded in the territory of the Maedi on
Philip's instructions when he got the welcome news of Alexander's
successful command. The name was an agreeable *stephanos* for Alexander.
The new foundation need not be thought of as something less than a *polis*.
Its name calls it a *polis*, and the two details transmitted by Plutarch
about its population can be taken as characteristic, probably, of any of
the new foundations in Thrace.

The details are (1) He drove out the barbarians (the site was a *polis*
of the Maedi); (2) He settled in it a mixed population (συμμίκτους κατοι-
κίσας). This 'mixed' character has been taken to denote a military
colony rather than a *polis* foundation, but I do not know why.[5] All these
colonies were liable to have 'mixed' populations, some of it drawn from
the army on the spot perhaps. The unfavourable tradition which
associated the nickname Poneropolis with Philippopolis (and with
Cabyle), and which made the obvious kind of fun of the name Bine(or-ae)
is not to be taken over-seriously, or explained in terms which presuppose
a prison population like our own, and penal servitude as a regular part

---

[1] D.S. 16. 71. 1–2; cf. Arr. *An.* 7. 9. 3, 'Philip added most of Thrace to Macedonia'.
For the 'General', D.S. 17. 62. 5 (cf. Berve 1. 228; Bengtson, *Strategie* 1. 38 ff.).

[2] Plu. *Alex.* 9. 1. The date follows from the fact that early in 339 Alexander was sent for
by Philip to join him on his campaign to the Danube. (Just. 9. 1. 8).

[3] Theopomp. F 217 (*FGrH* no. 115); Polyaen. 4. 4. 1; cf. Oberhummer, *RE* 3. 1 (1897)
329–30 s.v. *Bessoi*.

[4] Tarn, *Alexander* 2. 248 f., 242.   [5] Ibid. 249.

of the system.[1] When Theopompus wrote that 'he brought together there those with a reputation as rogues, informers, false-witnesses, prosecutors, and rogues of all sorts to the number of 2,000', perhaps the figure 2,000 is the most useful thing he is telling us. The scale of these foundations was not very large. They were replacing existing Thracian centres, the old inhabitants having no place in them (so at Alexandropolis above). One of their functions was as garrison towns in areas which had given trouble, one group (earlier) in the Strymon area of Parorbelia and perhaps including Heraclea Sintica,[2] now the upper-Hebrus group as detailed above. In these places unwilling or disloyal settlers could be a dangerous proposition, and consequently in this connection one will be selective in accepting what Justin writes (and overwrites) about the sheeplike transfers of populations which he inserts in the years 346–343.[3]

It was something big that Philip was doing in Thrace in 342–340, but still it fell short, probably, of forming Thrace into his first satrapy.[4] Still in 335 there are 'the autonomous Thracians' of the Haemus region or to the north of it.[5] Even the Odrysians, still after Philip has finished with them, have their Sitalces and their Seuthes to show that the kingdom or kingdoms were never suppressed.[6] Basically, it was a question now of putting the fear of God into the Odrysians and any others who needed it; and of keeping it there more effectively than before, it might be hoped, if several new cities provided 'a presence'. Whether the government itself was given a 'presence' in the person of a *strategos* now may be left an open question. More likely perhaps the first appointment was by Alexander.

These activities were all (so far as we know) to the south of the Haemus, and north of it (as we have seen) there was still a people or peoples who could be called 'the autonomous Thracians'; and the powerful Triballians too still kept their independence (below, p. 583). But there were also strong kings now, reigning in the country between Haemus and the Danube, who judged it expedient to compromise their independence if

---

[1] Theopomp. F 110 (*FGrH* no. 115); Plin. *NH* 4. 41; Str. 7. 320.

[2] Str. 7. 36. See p. 656 below. [3] Just. 8. 5. 7–6. 2.

[4] The Persian connection has been made often, and most recently by D. Kienast, *Philipp II von Makedonien und das Reich der Achaimeniden* (1973) 249 f., with bibliography (= *Abhandlungen der Marburger gelehrten Gesellschaft* 6 (1971)).

[5] Arr. *An.* 1. 1. 6. Alexander's march north over Haemus was barred by τῶν τε †ἐμπόρων† πολλοὶ ὡπλισμένοι καὶ οἱ Θρᾷκες οἱ αὐτόνομοι παρεσκευασμένοι εἴργειν τοῦ πρόσω etc. The reading ἐμπόρων is certainly corrupt, for obvious reasons. Arrian may have written a proper name here, but none offers itself that is palaeographically plausible in the context. Best of the conjectures are ἐγχωρίων (Gronovius), or ὁμόρων (Krüger). But we are still left in need of a proper name, for them, whoever they were. Some tribe such as the Treres of Thuc. 2. 96. 4 might come to mind (cf. J. Keil, *RE* 6A (1937) 2291 s.v. *Treres*). Theopompus wrote of them (as Trares), but unfortunately no context either chronological or topographical can be supplied (*FGrH* no. 115 F 378).

[6] For Seuthes, especially Tod 193. 1; Berve 2 no. 702. For Sitalces, Berve 2 no. 712.

need be, in order to have Philip as friend and not foe. The well-known story of Philip's sixth marriage, to Meda, daughter of Cothelas, king of the Getae, shows Cothelas anxious for Philip's favour, and there is some reason to think that this was due not to a mere distant view of his successes or news of his reputation, but to a practical experience of him in action.[1] The story in Jordanes of Philip attacking the Greek city of Odessus at a time when it was held by 'the Goths', and of how the Goths saved themselves by a musical exercise of their priests which impressed the Macedonians, may be thought a challenge to our credulity.[2] But as it happens Theopompus, too, is quoted as alluding to (presumably) the same musical performance. He calls these 'Goths' *Getae*; and as a well-informed contemporary he is to be taken seriously.[3] He warns us that in Jordanes the juxtaposition of the marriage story and the music story is no accident: they both belong to the history of Philip's dealings with Cothelas, king of the Getae. Here indeed is another Greek city being rescued from the classic situation with its local Thracian king. Cothelas had seen the Macedonian arms at close quarters, it seems, before he capitulated and made a treaty with Philip which included his daughter's hand.[4]

An interesting variation on this theme is provided by Atheas, king of those Scythians who were fairly recent arrivals south of the Danube in the Dobruja. On Philip's relations with Atheas we are relatively well informed thanks mainly to Justin who gave a section to them, the material deriving ultimately, no doubt, from Theopompus.[5] The variation here lies in the fact that it is not Atheas now who bullies Greek cities, it is Greek cities who are bullying him. Philip 'rescues' Atheas from (it seems) the Greek city of Istria (or Istros). And Atheas has trouble too from (it seems) the Byzantians, who are 'doing harm to his revenues'.[6] There

---

[1] For the marriage, Satyrus F 5 *FHG* 3. 161; Jordanes, *Getica* 10. 65.

[2] Jordanes, loc. cit., 'qua tempestate [the occasion of the marriage with Meda] Dio storico dicente Philippus inopiam pecuniae passus Odyssitanam Maesiae civitatem instructis copiis vastare deliberat, quae tunc propter viciniam Thomes Gothis erat subiecta. unde et sacerdotes Gothorum illi qui pii vocabantur subito patefactis portis cum citharis et vestibus candidis obviam egressi patriis diis, ut sibi propitii Macedonas repellerent, voce supplici modulantes. quos Macedones sic fiducialiter sibi occurrere contuentes stupescunt et, si dici fas est, ab inermibus terrentur armati. nec mora soluta acie quam ad bellandum construxerant non tantum ab urbis excidio abstinuerunt, verum etiam et quos foris fuerant iure belli adepti reddiderunt, foedereque inito ad sua reversi sunt.'

[3] Theopomp. F 217, *FGrH* no. 115. Θεόπομπος δ' ἐν τεσσαρακοστῆι ἑκτῆι τῶν Ἱστοριῶν "Γέται" φησί "κιθάρας ἔχοντες καὶ κιθαρίζοντες τὰς ἐπικηρυκείας ποιοῦνται."

[4] V. Iliescu, 'Geten oder Skythen? Zu Iord. *Get.* 10. 65', *Eos* 56 (1966), 316–30, tries to show that the 'Goths' of Jordanes were Scythians, of the kingdom of Atheas (below). But on this Theopompus seems decisive.

[5] Just. 9. 1. 9–3. 3; A. Momigliano, 'Dalla spedizione scitica di Filippo alla spedizione scitica di Dario', *Athenaeum* n.s. 11 (1933) 336–49; P. Alexandrescu, 'Ataias', *St. Clasice* 9 (1967) 85–91; V. Iliescu, 'Le problème des rapports Scytho-Byzantins du ive siècle av. N.È.', *Historia* 20 (1971) 172–85.   [6] Just. 9. 2. 1 ff.; Clem. Alex. *Strom.* 5. 31. 3.

are elements of paradox in both these bullies in this context, and consequently their appearance here has been contested; they are said to be textual corruptions. But in reality they seem to be nothing of the sort. They are here to be explained, not explained away.

It was 'the warfare of the Histriani', writes Justin, that made Atheas turn to Philip for help.[1] Let us admit that there is a suggestion in this of 'Man bites dog'. But in our utter ignorance of Istria and what went on inside it at this time, we really cannot call it impossible for the Istriani to have been so effective in war. But then another detail comes to light—they had a king: can we believe in a 'king of the Histriani' in 342?[2] Taking it quite literally, no, probably we cannot. But allowing ourselves to translate *rex* as 'tyrant', we have then a rather plausible situation: it is just the city with an efficient tyrant which could make itself formidable to the Scythian king who ought by rights to have been doing the terrorizing himself. Istria/Istros was on the Dobruja coast exactly in the area occupied by the kingdom of Atheas. It cannot be right, methodologically, to see *Histrianorum* as a corruption of (e.g.) *Triballorum* (as has been done), and Momigliano rightly offered an interpretation that retained the Istrians at all costs, and indeed linked them with the other Greek enemies of Atheas, the Byzantians.[3]

To the Byzantians Atheas is said to have written 'Do not do harm to my revenues, unless you want my horses to drink your water.' V. Iliescu has written convincingly on these revenues, warning against our endowing Atheas with a sophisticated modern economy, and reminding us that in this Scythian–Greek context, 'revenues' certainly meant the tribute payable by Greek cities to Scythian king.[4] He pointed out the impossibility (on geographical grounds) that Byzantium ever paid tribute to Atheas, and he concluded from this that 'the *demos* of the Byzantians' has got into this text as a corruption of some similar name. On the first point all will agree with him, but his inference from it was neither necessary nor convincing.[5] The most natural interepretation of 'Do no harm to my revenues', as Iliescu said, is 'Do not stop paying your tribute'. But since this is inadmissible here (Byzantium paid no tribute to him, ever), it is right to try other possibilities before emending 'Byzantians' out of the text. For example, 'Do not do harm to my revenues—by supporting Istria which is refusing to pay its tribute'?[6] This would seem

---

[1] Just. 9. 2. 1 'Erat eo tempore rex Scytharum Atheas, qui cum bello Histrianorum premeretur, auxilium a Philippo per Apollonienses petit . . .'   [2] Just. 9. 2. 2.

[3] A. Momigliano, loc. cit. 343 ff.   [4] V. Iliescu, *Historia* 20 (1971) 172–85.

[5] He restores ingeniously Βιζωνιτῶν for Βυζαντίων. Bizone was an unimportant city of the Dobruja, rightly situated for paying a tribute to Atheas. But what seems grossly improbable is that a letter from Atheas to Bizone should ever have survived for quotation. For Bizone, *RE* 3. 1. 551 (Brandis, 1897). In antiquity, Bizone was not 'news'; Byzantium sometimes was.

[6] So, approximately, P. Nicorescu, 'La campagne de Philippe de 339', *Dacia* 2 (1935) 24 f.

good sense, explaining a grievance of Atheas against the geographically remote Byzantium without presupposing an economic (commercial?) competition between them which would be unlikely for the Scythians of this date. It also brings together the two Greek cities, Istria and Byzantium, who most notably depart from the pattern which Diodorus led us to expect, of Philip the protector of Greek cities against Thracian kings.

Unfortunately the lack of a firm chronology is a great hindrance here, for Philip's entering into alliance with Atheas obviously carries with it implications for his attitude at the time to Istria and to Byzantium. Spring or early summer of the year 340 seems the most probable occasion for the appeal for help by Atheas and the actual sending of help by Philip.[1] If this is right, Philip's move here may be seen perhaps as a symptom of bad relations with Byzantium, but hardly as a cause of them (below). As for Atheas, he was probably a very old man now,[2] and according to Justin (ibid.) he gave some undertaking about adopting Philip into the succession to his kingdom. In this way, becoming Philip's ally he seems to become in some sense a vassal king and to enter into subjection. Not every *i* was dotted or every *t* crossed, however. Above all, the pressures and realities of power in this part of the world were unstable, and for Atheas, as we shall see, they came to allow of a wide discrepancy between his view and Philip's of the sanctity of their treaty and the validity of his own obligations (p. 582).

If the interpretation offered here of Philip's dealings with Istria (via Atheas) is accepted, it shows him (as we might expect) unconcerned about any principles of politics or policy at stake. To champion Greek cities in this part of the world was very good, very often. But the main thing was to champion somebody, the one who needed it. The effect of this opportunism, as a shock to Greek public opinion in the Black Sea itself will not have been great, probably. Whether or not they read Isocrates here, with his suggestion of the Heracles figure, benefactor of the Greek race, they will all have heard of Olynthus, and will have been under no illusions that merely as Greeks they could count on special treatment from Philip always. All of them alike now were liable to see him at close quarters. All were maritime cities, their economic life owing much to their trading relations with the Thracian interior. In so far as Philip's conquest of Thrace guaranteed peace and stability,

---

[1] Just. 9. 2. 1 f. 'Erat eo tempore rex Scytharum Atheas, qui cum bello Histrianorum premeretur, auxilium a Philippo per Apollonienses petit, in successionem eum regni Scythiae adoptaturus.' The use of Apollonia as intermediary suggests that no alliance of the two kings existed as yet. Philip's successes of 342 and 341 will have spread his reputation abroad. His sending of the *auxilium* was, most likely, before the siege of Perinthus became necessary; and this date just leaves time for the further developments outlined by Justin which come to a head while the siege of Byzantium is still on. (Below, p. 582.)

[2] Lucian, *Macrob.* 10.

they were gainers, and especially any who were freed now from danegeld obligations to a Thracian king. There is no evidence that any cities became tributary to Philip now, or lost their independence.

On the longer term however Philip must always have been recognized as a potential threat to political freedom. Like the Olynthians before them these Greeks had every reason to reckon that he was 'too great' for their own safety, perhaps even for their survival.[1] Byzantium especially, with her wide interests and connections in the Black Sea, will have seen these all coming to depend too much on the goodwill of the too powerful ally (as the Istria connection illustrates, if it can be relied on). The risks incurred by breaking with Philip could be frightful, of course; and Athens was still deeply mistrusted because of the past. But Athens seemed on the point of fighting Philip now, and there might never be another time like the present. For Philip, the nearer he and Athens came to war, the more important it became that Byzantium should be a loyal ally. Diopeithes now (and Demosthenes) seemed to be bringing it very near.[2]

Though we are told nothing of the particular reasons, we can see that by 341 (spring) the relations of Philip and Byzantium had become strained. It was 'about the time of the incursion by Diopeithes' (as Philip was to complain later) that 'the triremes of the Byzantians and of the pirates' were allowed to put in at Thasos (ally of Athens), a breach of the treaty of Philocrates.[3] For this incident to be genuinely a breach of the treaty, the Byzantians need to be either at war with Philip already, which we know they were not (below), or else they need to have acted as pirates themselves. Speculation about details is idle; but Philip seems to claim here that the Byzantians had acted like pirates, and that he had suffered by it. The allusions of Demosthenes to Byzantium just a few weeks after this incident, equivocal and tantalizing though they are, do allow us to infer that there was some trouble between Byzantium and Philip, though it took some months for it to drive the Byzantians into accepting the alliance with Athens which Demosthenes in person urged upon them in the autumn.[4] At the root of the trouble is likely to have

[1] Above, p. 297 etc.   [2] Cf. D. 8. 14–16; Plu. *Phoc.* 14. 2 f.
[3] [D.] 12. 2 f.

[4] D. 18. 302. At 8. 14 (spring 341), D. speaks of the possibility of Philip's attacking Byzantium, and at 9. 35 (early summer 341) he puts the odd rhetorical question 'Is he not now marching against the Byzantians who are his allies?' Professor Brunt has suggested to me as a general proposition that the editing for publication by Demosthenes of his speeches is something for which we need to allow more than is commonly done. These two allusions to Byzantium might seem good candidates for belonging to an editorial touching-up, to insert here a notable piece of political foresight. Yet the explanation of these passages by Wüst (124 f.) is ingenious and carries conviction. Spoken genuinely in 341, they could be very effective as suggesting that Philip's final campaigns subjugating eastern Thrace were directed against Byzantium in effect (this adding something in each context to Demosthenes' argument), and especially at 9. 35 the oxymoron πορεύεται ἐπὶ συμμάχους is a fine rhetorical stroke of exaggeration.

been a Byzantian refusal or reluctance to co-operate actively in Philip's reduction of eastern Thrace. If their alliance with him was a defensive one (as is likely), they would have been justified in a refusal. But Philip, who will have known something of the true state of opinions and feeling inside Byzantium, may well have had good reason to judge that in this important place, able to affect all his future plans concerning Athens, Thrace, Persia, 'he that is not with us is against us'—and that this was a bad risk to take.

Finally, Philip had no reason to hope or think that what he was doing in Thrace was going to improve his relations with Athens. The Athenians were always sensitive about the Chersonese, and at this time they had reinforced it recently with additional cleruchs, and their general Diopeithes, who had led the cleruchs, held command there in 342 and 341.[1] Though clearly he had no instructions from the *demos* positively to pick a quarrel with Philip, his business was to look after the cleruchs, and this at once caused more friction with Cardia, who as an independent ally of Philip was not taking any instructions from Athens on this or any other matter. Diopeithes like most Athenian generals was kept very short of money, and he was very energetic in raising money locally by his own methods.[2] Cardia, her long dispute with Athens still unresolved (above, p. 512), felt herself threatened now, and both sought and received protection from Philip in the shape of a garrison, though not before he had first tried once again to bring Athens and Cardia together in a court of law.[3] Diopeithes however next attacked also Crobyle and Tiristasis, neighbouring coastal towns of Thrace in territory which was now Philip's, and plundered them thoroughly, selling the captives into slavery.[4] He even extorted a ransom from Philip's ambassador Amphilochus who visited him to negotiate about these prisoners.[5] By this time Philip himself was at the wars again, in upper Thrace (spring 341). Diopeithes could wait of course, Athens could wait. But meanwhile Philip sent to Athens what evidently was a firm and uncompromising diplomatic Note, complaining of Diopeithes and his flagrant acts of war, and warning the Athenians that he was prepared if necessary to invade the Chersonese (presumably in aid of Cardia his hard-pressed ally).[6] This is the situation to which the *Chersonese* speech of Demosthenes was addressed (D. 8), in terms not less uncompromising than Philip's

[1] Philoch. *FGrH* no. 328 F (year 343/2); D. 8. 6; 9. 15; cf. Schaefer 2. 451.

[2] D. 8. 21 ff.; 26 ff.

[3] D. 8. 58 and 64 and Hypoth. 2 f.; [D.] 12. 11; schol. Aeschin. 3. 83.

[4] [D.] 12. 3; D. 8, Hypoth. 2 f. These places were a few miles east of Cardia, in the kingdom till recently of Cersobleptes no doubt.

[5] [D.] 12. 3.

[6] D. 8. 16. 'And indeed it is far from certain that he will *not* attack the Chersonese. On the contrary, if we are to go by his own Note here, he says that he will retaliate against our people in the Chersonese (ἀμυνεῖσθαί φησι τοὺς ἐν Χερρονήσῳ)'; cf. D. 8, Hypoth.

own.[1] Demosthenes saw the problem as a strategic one mainly, how to contain Philip's growth in Thrace and maintain the Athenian position there. He seems surprisingly unafraid of the risk of immediate war, if Athens shows herself intransigent. Some others of the Athenian politicians were nervous of it, obviously; or they hoped to be able to continue to live with Philip, and would rather recall Diopeithes than risk the good relations or the hope of good relations with him.[2]

Why, one wonders, was Demosthenes so unconcerned? Is it a measure of what Philip's own personality and 'personal touch' meant to the world around him? Away for nearly a year, sending in a deputy to preside over the Pythian Festival of 342.[3] Even with Antipater and Parmenion both of them 'at home' meanwhile, and able to take good care of Euboea as the events of that summer (342) have suggested, still it was not the same thing as having the great man on the spot. And while this was still so, for Demosthenes and Diopeithes it was all right to be confident: there would be no general war this year. For Demosthenes too, as it happened, there was a good time coming: did he know by now that it was coming, perhaps? Good news from Euboea now (Chalcis), from where a few months earlier all news had been bad (pp. 501 ff.). Through this summer (341) Oreus and Eretria were to come in; the Euboean confederacy with Callias to the fore as a man of parts and of action; next the diplomatic successes in the Peloponnese; the comings together of the Hellenic League. Of this flow into prosperity a high-water-mark was to appear with the *stephanos* voted for Demosthenes in spring of 340. The confident tone of the *Chersonese* speech is that of a man who senses already a turning of the tide, and it communicated itself to the *demos*. Diopeithes was not recalled, or reprimanded, or prosecuted. The *Third Philippic* and then the *Fourth Philippic* (about midsummer 341) do not represent replies to new initiatives of Philip, they are initiatives on their own. Demosthenes prepares his public for the general war—his general war as much as anybody's, by now. Let Athens remember her grievances, and her apprehensions. Let the Greeks be warned before it was too late. Let allies be brought together, everywhere in Greece; and

---

[1] For the date and composition of D. 8 (and D. 10), I follow S. G. Daitz 'The "De Chersoneso" and the "Philippica quarta" ', *CP* 52 (1957) 145 ff., who argues convincingly the view advanced by C. D. Adams, 'Speeches VIII and X of the Demosthenic Corpus', *CP* 33 (1938) 129 ff., concerning the long 'parallel passages' which are found in both speeches. These 'passages' were composed evidently for D. 10, spoken in about midsummer 341. D. 8 (without 'the passages') was spoken in spring 341, and was published later with 'the passages' added.

Of the references in these speeches to recent events (where the 'speak-date' is important or interesting), only one comes from 'the passages' (D. 10. 15 = 8. 44—with a particularly clear indication, as it happens, that D. 10. 15 is its true and original home).

[2] D. 8. 4 ff.; 27 ff.; 52 ff. (10. 55 ff.); 67 (10. 69 f.).

[3] D. 9. 32.

the Persians especially.[1] Let the *demos* be jollied along, even, just a little, now that it was beginning to get the hang of things and to know good advice when it saw it. Even the Theoric Fund could be accorded a few not-ungracious words, conceding the necessity that the poor must live, somehow.[2] For Philip the conference of the Greek allies at Athens in February (340), the *stephanos* awarded to Demosthenes a few weeks later were clear enough as messages.[3] The ending of the Peace was not certain, but it was probable now. It was time to finish off in Thrace in expectation that he would be marching against Athens itself next. This meant making sure that Byzantium and any other dissatisfied customers stopped making trouble and toed the line now.

3. *Perinthus and Byzantium: the Athenian reaction*

While Philip campaigned in Thrace, his relations with Athens did not stand still. How could they, with Cardia and the Chersonese still unsettled (above, p. 512)? It was this that led to the acts of war between Athenian cleruchs and Cardia, reinforcements to Cardia supplied by Philip, plundering forays by the Athenian general Diopeithes into the neighbouring Thrace which was Philip's territory now; all this by the early months of 341.[4] Later in the year the Athenians were sending their ambassadors to Persia,[5] and were meeting with successes in Euboea (above, p. 549). Over the winter (341/0) Greece was astir, and in March the Greek alliance of Demosthenes was born (p. 551). Descending from the sublime to the ridiculous, Halonnesus was lost to Philip, Athenian allies (and agents) the Peparethians having seized it (this in spring 340 probably).[6] There seem to be many reasons here why two states which have come to distrust each other should now go to war.

However, the Greeks (like ourselves) had a great capacity for not resorting to open war before it suited them, and in this matter at least the 'Greekness' of Philip has never been in dispute.[7] He replied to the depredations of Diopeithes (and to the boorish and insulting treatment by the Athenians of a herald and an ambassador), not with a declaration of war or reprisals in kind, but with a Note (or Notes).[8] And the Athenians, while they listened to Demosthenes and more and more agreed with him (pp. 565 f.), did not come quickly to the sticking-place. Even when Philip himself violates the Chersonese itself by invasion (we shall see), an Athenian admiral cruises offshore like a sheep-dog on guard, looking a match for half a pack of wolves; but prudently unsure

---

[1] For Persia, pp. 519 f. above.   [2] D. 10. 35 ff.   [3] Aeschin. 3. 98; D. 18. 83.
[4] D. 8, Hypoth. 2 f.; D. 8. 58 (= 10. 60); 9. 35; [D.] 12. 3 and 11; cf. Schaefer 2². 451 ff.
[5] D. 10. 34 f.; [D.] 12. 6.   [6] [D.] 12. 12–15.
[7] For the general proposition, the *locus classicus*, I suppose, is Thuc. 5 *passim*.
[8] D. 8, Hypoth. 3.

whether or not he hears his master's voice (below). Evidently not, it transpires; not yet. Philip thereupon gives himself the trouble of justifying his action and of reminding the Athenians that he left the place just as he found it: this in the Note written between the time of his quitting the Chersonese and the time of his besieging Perinthus—or at latest in the very early day of the siege; the Note in which he details his grounds for grievance against Athens (*enklemata*)—eleven of them, counting the more general ones—and concluding 'It is you who are the aggressors! As for me, the more punctilious I am, the worse it makes you: there's nothing you will not do to hurt me! I shall defend myself with a good cause, the gods my witnesses as I deal with your case!'[1]

This reads like Philip's ultimatum to Athens in the most literal and genuine sense of the word, and it has sometimes been called that. But incorrectly, because of the still more ultimate ultimatum that we hear of, sent some weeks later from Byzantium; because, too, of the self-justification about the Chersonese invasion, and because we cannot help remembering how unintelligent it would be to force Athens into defending Perinthus while there was a chance that she might be neutral still.[2] War was not declared for two or three months yet, and though the ultimate wagging of the beard fell to Philip's ambassador at Athens on positively his last appearance (as has been said), it was the Athenians who had the satisfaction of making the actual declaration of war, tearing down the *stele* which bore the text of the Peace of Philocrates.

It is not easy to be sure just what Philip (or what the *demos*) was waiting for, all this time, amounting to two years in sum (or not much less), during which everybody knew that, barring accidents, the pin-pricks and the little wars were going to stop some day soon; *der Tag* (under whatever name or *aitia* or *prophasis*) was coming.

Philip's campaign of the year 340 shows well the uses and the limitations of sea power at this time. By now he had mobilized his fleet. Its strength is not known, but it may have been the biggest naval force he ever produced. Even so, it was inferior, evidently, to the Athenian strength in these waters (forty ships?), as its behaviour shows.[3] But since

---

[1] [D.] 12. 23 ('Philip's *Letter*'): the dating follows from the fact that nothing later than the Chersonese invasion is mentioned in it. (Ibid. 16 f.)

[2] For the ultimate ultimatum, [D.] 11, Hypoth. ('Reply to the *Letter* of Philip'). In the words of the Hypothesis, there is nothing to prevent the letter that it mentions from being identical with [D.] 12: ὁ Φίλιππος πρὸς τοὺς Ἀθηναίους πέπομφεν ἐπιστολήν, κατηγορῶν αὐτῶν καὶ πόλεμον προκηρύττων ἄντικρυς. But the Reply ([D.] 11) to this *Letter* is addressed to a situation some weeks later than that of [D.] 12. Whereas in the latter the siege of Perinthus is not even mentioned as begun, in [D.] 11 Perinthus can be spoken of as 'saved' and Byzantium now is under siege or threatened ([D.] 11. 4).

[3] The squadron of Chares later in this campaign was of 40 ships, before the arrival of Phocion's squadron (Hesych. Miles. 26 = *FHG* 4. 151; see below, p. 575). But this was in

his object now, besides supporting Cardia, was to put pressure on Byzantium and Perinthus, the allies whose loyalty he could no longer count on,[1] he judged it necessary to introduce his ships through the Dardanelles into the Sea of Marmara, and to risk their being attacked by the Athenian fleet, in the hope that, if they were not attacked or if they survived, their presence would be a strong inducement to the Byzantians and the Perinthians to reconsider their position. The cities would be facing also his army at their gates, unchallengeably strong by land.

The ancient commentator saw this expedition as directed really against Athens; and though his explanation was based partly (not exclusively) on Athenian sources, it is hard to fault this interpretation of the high strategy here.[2] The allies Byzantium and Perinthus were proving unsatisfactory perhaps, and needed correction. But

the war of Athens against the Macedonian was kindled because of various provocations offered by Philip while still proffering peace, and especially because of his campaign against Byzantium and Perinthus. He had two motives for wanting to win over the cities: to cut off the Athenian corn supply, and to deprive Athens of the cities which would give them naval bases for the war against him . . .[3]

Though this is written with hindsight (Philip did attack the corn fleet: war was declared), nevertheless these developments (in September) followed closely enough on the start of this campaign (after midsummer) to make this interpretation plausible.[4] Only, without its over-simplifications.

autumn already. Whether it was as big as 40 ships some months earlier is uncertain. Chares held a command in this area as early as February of this year 340 (*Syll.*³ 255).

[1] D.S. 16. 74. 2 (Perinthus); [D.] 12. 2 and 16; D. 18. 87 ff., 240 f. (Byzantium); [D.] 12. 11 (Cardia). See above, pp. 563 f.

[2] Didymus 10. 34 ff. (going on to cite Philochorus; but also Theopompus).

Diodorus (16. 77. 2) and Justin (9. 1. 1 f.) make the attack on Byzantium the proximate cause of the outbreak of war between Philip and Athens, and Diodorus does not even mention Philip's capture of the Athenian corn fleet (below). Wüst (134 ff.) was undoubtedly right (as against Momigliano, *RIL* 65 (1932) 565 ff.) in explaining this by the small scale of Diodorus' history and not by a 'pro-Macedonian' source here. (Demosthenes himself could omit to mention the corn-fleet incident when it suited him; see D. 18. 87 and below, p. 575 n. 1.)

[3] Didymus 10. 34 ff.

[4] Philochorus, F 53–4 (*FGrH* no. 328), quoted by D.H. *Amm.* 11, makes the attack on Perinthus the first event of the year 340/39 (Θεόφραστος Ἁλαιεύς. ἐπὶ τούτου Φίλιππος τὸ μὲν πρῶτον ἀναπλεύσας Περίνθῳ προσέβαλεν . . .). Violence is done to Philochorus by the interpretation of these events which makes Philip attack Perinthus in spring, and explains Philochorus as alluding to a moment when Philip brought his fleet into action after midsummer. (So, e.g. Wüst 127 n. 3, with earlier bibliography. Kromayer, *AS* 1. 172 ff. preferred the later date.) Philochorus may have been wrong, but obviously what he meant was that the attack on Perinthus (with a fleet) began after midsummer. It made better sense to attack Perinthus with the fleet than without it, and to attack when the Etesian winds had set in, making any quick reinforcements from Athens impossible. (For Philip's practice, noted by Demosthenes ten years before this, D. 4. 31, 'He waits for the Etesian winds or for

Experience had shown that to deny Athens absolutely her corn supply by this route it was necessary to destroy the Athenian navy or totally prevent it from operating in these waters. To command the bases of the European shore was one thing; but the Asiatic shore was not in Philip's power to dispose of, and here Persia might have other plans. In reality by this campaign Philip was threatening the corn supply, he was bringing the Athenians face to face with the difficulties they might have in getting the corn through, if for example Persia as well as Philip were to deny them bases for their squadrons. It was a threat, and in an area where the Athenians were very sensitive to threats. But with Athenian naval power immeasurably superior and with Persian policy still inscrutable, it fell so far short of being decisive that it seems right not to interpret it at once as the sign that Philip meant war with Athens now, and this as its first act, but to allow still for the possibility that he meant it as the final deterrent from war. This could be a shaking of the fist, still, not yet the blow itself.

Let us beware, however, of making too much of the difficulty of knowing just when, how, and why Philip decided to cross a Rubicon in his relations with Athens. Our own hindsight, which knows of 'the last days of Greek freedom', is liable to feel cheated if it cannot relive a final moment of high and grand decision, irrevocable, irreversible. Demosthenes, too, like that historic crew of the *Paralus* which 'was always chasing oligarchy even when there wasn't any there', was a professional inventor of Rubicons for Philip, hoping rightly to produce the Athenians in the end as jumpy as himself and ready to fight for their lives. But Philip himself will have been much more relaxed in his mood and in his whole outlook on Athens and the prospect of a new war with her. Once he had spent eleven years at war with Athens, without being obliged to lose any sleep over it so far as we can see. Months, even years of 'war with Athens' could go by without any serious blow being offered or exchanged at all. Moreover, however much some Athenians might see him as a malevolent figure of doom and destruction, Philip did have the advantage over all his contemporaries in knowing the exact truth about this. He knew that he had no intention of destroying Athens even if he did go to war with her.[1] For him therefore, nothing could be more

the winter and attacks then, when we could not possibly get to the spot'; and in this very context just a year ago D. 8. 14 'If then he waits for the Etesian winds and then attacks Byzantium . . .'. The season of the winds began after the summer solstice but not long after, and their effect on this voyage from Athens was well known: Arist. *Meteor.* 2. 361^{b}35–362^a; Hp. *Aer.* 10. 26 ff.; Hdt. 6. 139. 4; 140. 1.) If this is right, the siege of Perinthus could have been begun in July, but not earlier. It seems that Philip had not yet invested Byzantium when the corn fleet assembled in the Bosporus in September (below, p. 575).

[1] This is, surely, a legitimate inference from his whole treatment of Athens from 348 on, as we have seen.

revocable or reversible than the declaration of war, or the act of war without the formality of a declaration.

It may be this partly, and not only the Athenian intransigence or his own loss of patience, that explains an appearance almost of *insouciance* in his actions of the year 340; the touch of ruthlessness alternating or even combined with the letter of justification; and in the end even the act of provocation which proved 'decisive' (the capture of the Athenian transports), undertaken by him perhaps less with a view to a 'decision' than as a means of cheering up his own army which rather badly needed it at that moment (below). Philip was not much aware of Rubicons at this time—and perhaps not enough aware of a Chaeronea round the corner, though it has been well suggested that his 'Letters' to Athens of this year, clearly a waste of time as weapons of persuasion at Athens, were designed mainly as exercises in propaganda addressed to the Greek cities in general, and especially the cities of the new 'Greek alliance'. To depict Athens as aggressor was to remind her allies (new and old) that they were in no way bound to come to her aid ($\beta o\eta\theta\epsilon\hat{\iota}\nu$) : the normal requirement of the defensive alliance.[1] War with Athens was more of a diplomatic than a military problem really, for Philip, in the sense that when all was said and done it was the Athenians who were going to be required to supply the backbone of the Greek fleet in the Persian war in a year or two's time. They must not be damaged in any way that would make that impossible.

Meanwhile, he needed his fleet at Perinthus, if he could get it there. The presence of an Athenian squadron under Chares in the neighbourhood of the Hellespont made this a problem, if Chares were to act as aggressively as Diopeithes recently. When an army and a naval squadron advance in co-operation, we are accustomed to think of the ships as protecting the soldiers and adding to their strength. Ancient conditions did produce often enough situations when this was so; but this was not one of them. Philip and his troops were not really vulnerable themselves to anything that the Athenians or anyone else operating by sea could do to them, and were quite capable of looking after themselves.[2] It was his ships that were vulnerable, if the Athenians decided to attack them. Philip could not protect them from the attack if it came; he could only protect them from its full consequences perhaps, by keeping pace on the march with the progress of the fleet and by holding his troops in readiness for an occasion when, if the ships were attacked, they could be beached or run aground with a good chance of being saved from capture or total

---

[1] This point is made by Wüst 132.

[2] Supply by sea for the army was the easiest way, no doubt, for operations against Perinthus or Byzantium. But it cannot have been essential, since Philip was accustomed to a problem of supply on campaigns inland, constantly.

loss. It was for this that Philip moved to Cardia near the neck of the Gallipoli peninsula, and invaded with his army the Athenian territory of the Chersonese itself. This act of war he justified, no doubt, by the provocations of Diopeithes on the one plane and the need to protect Cardia his ally, and on the other plane by the military necessity. (In any case the fleet might have had some trouble in making the long haul round the peninsula and up the Dardanelles as far as Cardia before putting in at least for rest and water.)[1]

The Athenians did not attack. Chares, their commander, will surely have known that he could count on the support of the orators and the *demos* at home.[2] But with war still undeclared he may have been guided by his purely military appraisal on the spot. If he judged Philip's counter-measure likely to be effective if put to the test, better not to test it. In political terms, even the Athenian 'war party' were not anxious to start this war 'by accident', most probably. The pattern that favoured them and which they favoured was one which would culminate in a tableau where Athena *soteira* was starting forward to the rescue of a victim on the point of being dispatched. The victim had much better be somebody else, not a bunch of Athenian cleruchs. The squadron was allowed to complete its passage of the Hellespont unopposed, and to continue on course up the Propontis. Philip accompanied it and withdrew from the Chersonese, having done, as he said, no harm there. The prime objective now was Byzantium, no doubt. But Perinthus came first, as they marched and sailed, a city less important for its own sake, but not one to leave behind hostile and in league with Athens. Since the Perinthians remained intransigent and prepared to face everything that the Macedonians could do to them, Philip was obliged to pause here, and bring them to heel. A siege of Byzantium was likely to be tough. A siege of Perinthus meanwhile could be a useful exercise, not least perhaps for its effect on the will to resist of the Byzantians themselves.

The siege of Perinthus (begun in ? July) evoked from Diodorus about the best piece of narrative in his Sixteenth Book, derived most probably from Ephorus who had recognized it evidently as one of the great passages of arms even in this age of soldiers and soldiery.[3] Perinthus was not a great city, but it was well defended both by nature and by the works of man—and now by its citizens and by allies who served them well.

---

[1] This reconstruction of Philip's movements and their motives is based on the allusion at [D.] 12. 16. For Diopeithes, [D.] 12. 3; for Cardia, [D.] 12. 11.

[2] [D.] 12. 16.

[3] D.S. 16. 76. 5; cf. Hammond, 'SD', esp. 86 f. (for Ephorus). When I call a piece of narrative by Diodorus good, I mean that it is well furnished with details from a source reasonably well informed, not that it is a good piece of writing. For the date, see above, p. 568 n. 4.

Momigliano (*RIL* 1932. 541 ff.) saw Duris as the likely source of Diodorus here.

It was built on a headland approached by a neck only about a furlong wide, so that attacks by land were confined to this narrow front. There is no word of Philip's being able to use his fleet for landings on the promontory inside the isthmus wall. Nor could the fleet make its base in the bay itself, close enough to the city harbour to establish a blockade. All through the siege reinforcements of men, arms and supplies seem to have reached the defenders at will.[1] But the Macedonians had a great superiority in numbers and in 'firepower'. On the evidence as we have it, this is the first great siege of the Macedonian era. None of Philip's earlier sieges is described by Diodorus, and we are left wondering whether this is in some sense accidental, or whether Diodorus' source(s) left him in no doubt that here was something special and probably new; for the writer bent always on economizing on space, Perinthus, no other, was the siege to describe in detail.[2] This may well have been so. E. W. Marsden's cautious conclusions as to the probable time and place of the invention of the torsion catapult (above, pp. 445 f.) led him to think that its first appearance was here at Perinthus, where he notes in Diodorus the presence of the arrow-shooting catapults (16. 74. 4 ὀξυβελεῖς; in bureaucrats' jargon 'anti-personnel'), and the absence of the more massive stone-shooters (effective also against masonry), which do not appear till Halicarnassus six years later.[3] The new weapon outranged the non-torsion catapult and was more lethal at moderate ranges—and Philip probably had many more of the new than Perinthus could muster of the old. With this advantage he could hope to overcome the handicap of his defective naval power. A series of frontal assaults on the isthmus wall with his battalions relieving each other in relays and keeping up the attacks by night at times as well as by day, would end by breaking and taking this wall, not exactly quickly or cheaply perhaps, but without too great a loss of time and lives.[4]

The Macedonians tried all they knew. They had their artillery, plenty of it. They had rams to batter down selected bits of the wall. They had sappers to tunnel under it and cause other bits to collapse. They had scaling-ladders on which to go over it wherever and whenever their

---

[1] D.S. 16. 74. 4; 75. 1–2; 76. 3. Shortage of food at 75. 1; but still reinforcements come in after this.

[2] Athenaeus Mechanicus (Wescher p. 10. 5 ff.), summarizing technical progress in the fourth century, names as landmarks Dionysius of Syracuse and Philip at Byzantium. If we had a description of the siege of Byzantium we might agree. (Or did he name Byzantium merely as the more famous place? I think so.)

[3] E. W. Marsden, *Greek and Roman Artillery: Historical Development* (Oxford, 1969) 58–70.

[4] On 'relays', R. K. Sinclair, *CQ* N.s. 10 (1960) 249 ff. If Diodorus did sometimes use this phrase conventionally, meaning merely to convey that this was a big and exciting siege (so Sinclair), it must still be true that relays were used often in sieges wherever the besieger had greatly superior numbers (so again Sinclair), and that these conditions were most clearly present at Perinthus (D.S. 16. 74. 5, 30,000 men for Philip's army).

infantry could get there. By building high towers of over 100 feet they were able to shoot down on the defenders and so immobilize them at critical times and places. And by sheer weight of numbers they were able to keep on doing these things until the defence could no longer resist everywhere. The wall was breached, the ladders were brought up and set, the Macedonians poured through and over and in. They were brought up short by the second wall which the Perinthians had been building under cover of the first. The same processes had to begin again, less easily now because access to the second wall was impeded by the presence of the first. Time and toil, the determination of the general and the guts of the men, brought the Macedonians through the second wall too by the same methods. They were inside the city. But still the city had not fallen. Facing them now were the houses, high buildings rising in tiers up the hill and pierced only by the steep and narrow streets, easily blocked by men determined to fight on. Hope had been kept alive by the help freely given by their friends. Byzantium had supplied artillery, arms and supplies, and finally picked officers and troops.[1] This was to be expected. An unlooked-for bonus, and one of great significance, was the decision of the Persian government to reinforce Perinthus liberally. 'The satraps of the maritime provinces' sent money and mercenaries on a big scale, besides ammunition and corn and other supplies.[2] The Athenians however did not participate in the defence, though the presence of an Athenian squadron in these waters may have deterred Philip from committing his own fleet to anything that might put it in a trap which it only needed the Athenians to close.

Philip, then, found the Perinthians defending their houses and streets with the same skill and valour as their walls. They could be overcome perhaps, but slowly, and up hill all the way. It was a situation such as makes soldiers curse their general and look to him to use his brains instead. Philip used his brains. He withdrew half of his army from their positions at Perinthus and marched swiftly on Byzantium, the fleet presumably in support. The Byzantians were heavily committed at Perinthus now, and had left themselves short of artillery at home. Philip hoped no doubt that the shock of his arrival might bring the city over, especially if he had friends and agents inside, a likely thing in view of the

---

[1] D.S. 16. 74. 4; 75. 2.

[2] D.S. 16. 75. 1 f.; [D.] 11. 5; Arr. *An.* 2. 14. 5; Paus. 1. 29. 10. (For Persian subsidies to Diopeithes, presumably in the previous year, Arist. *Rhet.* 2. 1386ᵃ13.) I do not see why the Persian aid to Perinthus is called sometimes 'unofficial' (e.g. by Wüst 130, 143). It was supplied by the satraps nearest to the scene (e.g. by Arsites satrap of Hellespontine Phrygia, Paus. 1. 29. 10), but there is no reason to doubt that it was authorized by the king himself: [D.] 11. 5–6 οἱ κατὰ τὴν Ἀσίαν σατράπαι καθεστῶτες ἔναγχος μὲν ξένους [μισθοφόρους] εἰσπέμψαντες ἐκώλυσαν ἐκπολιορκηθῆναι Πέρινθον, νῦν δὲ τῆς ἔχθρας αὐτοῖς ἐνεστώσης καὶ τοῦ κινδύνου πλησίον ὄντος, εἰ χειρωθήσεται Βυζάντιον, οὐ μόνον αὐτοὶ προθύμως συμπολεμήσουσιν, ἀλλὰ καὶ βασιλέα [Περσῶν] χρήματα χορηγεῖν ἡμῖν προτρέψονται . . .

alliance of recent years.[1] But at Byzantium too, as it proved, there was no quick road to victory. This was to be another siege, not a storm. Indeed he was obliged to invest Selymbria too, no great city but important now on his communications between the two halves of his divided army, and as a naval base for any fleet (his own, the Byzantian, the Athenian) in the approach to the Bosporus.[2]

What is the place of Athens in relation to this move against Byzantium? The question has its bearing both on the politics and the strategy. Demosthenes told the Athenians ten years later that Philip's attack and siege followed a refusal by the Byzantians to 'take part in the war against

[1] Suid. s.v. *Leon* (= *FGrH*, no. 132 T. 1). The anecdote suggesting that the portly peripatetic Leon was prepared to betray his city to Philip for money is probably unreliable, and even Philip's quoted remark 'If I had given Leon all the money he was asking for, I should have taken Byzantium at first blow' is impossible to reconcile with Plutarch's allusion to Leon's co-operation with Phocion, a fellow pupil of Plato (Plu. *Phoc.* 14).

[2] The reliability of the evidence for a 'siege of Selymbria' has not yet been generally accepted; but it seems to me established by Pohlenz and Wüst (M. Pohlenz, 'Der Ausbruch des zweiten Krieges zwischen Philipp und Athen', *NQG* 1924. 38 ff.; cf. *Hermes* 1929. 59; Wüst 129 ff. and especially 136 ff., Pickard-Cambridge 356 n. 7). The siege is not mentioned by contemporary orators, or by any surviving historical writer, but only by the writer of the long Hypothesis (if that describes it rightly) to [D.] 11 (Πρὸς τὴν ἐπιστολὴν τὴν Φιλίππου), by the compiler of the documents (recognized as spurious) quoted in Demosthenes *On the Crown* (D. 18. 77 f., cf. 73 f.), and by the scholiast commenting on D. 18. 76 (Dindorf 8. 289). (The 'Hypothesis' can be found at Dindorf 8. 209.) Not to recapitulate now the excellent work of Pohlenz and Wüst, I give the main reasons which seem to me to make it very highly improbable that the siege of Selymbria *in toto* is a scholiasts' fiction. I follow Wüst (and Pohlenz) in accepting (from the writer of the Hypothesis) the synchronism of a siege of Selymbria and the capture of Athenian ships, and in not accepting the additional details supplied by the *Crown* documents and the scholiast (see further p. 577 n. 2 below).

(1) No commentator is likely to have invented this siege if it never happened, or to have produced it by a confusion with the more important Perinthus or the more important still Byzantium. The same must be true of historians, even bad ones, and true more obviously still of contemporary orators (to name the material which scholiasts used).

(2) As I suggested in my text above, even if nobody had ever mentioned Selymbria for us at all, we should still have been bound to conclude that when Philip moved on Byzantium from Perinthus, he must have either occupied Selymbria or besieged it if it refused to admit him.

(3) We learn of the siege of Selymbria only incidentally: it was while Philip was doing this that he captured Athenian ships (*ploia*). *Ploia* usually means merchant ships not warships; but here it does not refer to the great haul of corn-ships, but apparently to a section of the squadron of Chares which was detailed to convoy them. Though I do not believe that Philip captured Athenian triremes now or their 'nauarch', and still less that he gave them back to Athens (D. 18. 77 ff. and Schol.), obviously Philip's charge that the convoy squadron had had designs on the siege of Selymbria (schol. [D.] 11. 1) was a plausible one (it could even have been true). True or false, it will have added something to the fury of the Athenian *demos*.

(4) In the list of Aristotle's writings at D.L. 5. 27 (see above, p. 518 n. 1) among the *Letters* appears the extraordinary item 'Letters of the Selymbrians'. (No other such item, of a composition addressed to Aristotle, appears in the whole List or in the List of Hesychius, V. Rose, *Aristotelis Fragmenta* 11 ff.) Obviously one cannot speculate far, on the business of the Selymbrians with Aristotle. It is surprising to find this not very important city in correspondence with him, its letters preserved (or if not preserved, 'reconstructed'). Perhaps this fact does lend support to the tradition which shows Selymbria in a serious crisis.

Athens' as he asked. If this were true, it would be important, telling us that Philip thought of himself as already at war with Athens before the start of this whole campaign including the attack on Perinthus.[1] But it cannot be true, because it is contradicted by the course of the campaign itself; by Philip's explanation to the Athenians of why he had been obliged to enter their territory in the Chersonese, by Chares' failure to attack Philip's fleet with his own, by the Athenian failure to give direct military or naval help to Perinthus. Demosthenes identified the Byzantian cause with the Athenian ten years later (when these discrepancies could escape notice), because his own policy had been aimed to attach Byzantium to Athens. But in reality 'the war against Athens' was still cold war, and not yet irreversible. In the first weeks of the siege of Perinthus (July–August?) Philip's *Letter* went to Athens, and the Athenians refrained from helping Perinthus, for the reasons suggested above.[2]

But still by the Sea of Marmara and on it, the men on the spot watched each other with due suspicion. Philip had not dared to bring his squadron past Chares through the Hellespont without the army's protection. And as the summer drew on Chares had it among his orders to concentrate the corn ships as they arrived from South Russia and see them safely through into the Aegean. As they came into the Bosporus he gathered them in to Hieron on the Asiatic side some 7 miles from the northern entry and about 17 from the strait separating Calchedon and Byzantium. It was a wise precaution, for Philip by now had decided to move from Perinthus on Byzantium. By the time the corn fleet was assembled he was besieging Selymbria some 40 miles west of Byzantium on the European coast, and part of his forces probably had invaded the territory of Byzantium and were laying it waste.[3] His fleet probably hugged the European shore, friendly territory except for Byzantium itself. It was not a good moment, this, for Chares to have left his squadron in order to confer with Persian commanders, admirable though the concept of a concerted strategy must seem. He was away for some time, evidently. Not once but

---

[1] This is evidently what Demosthenes did mean, 18. 87, βουλόμενος τῆς σιτοπομπίας κύριος γενέσθαι, παρελθὼν ἐπὶ Θράκης Βυζαντίους συμμάχους ὄντας αὐτῷ τὸ μὲν πρῶτον ἠξίου συμπολεμεῖν τὸν πρὸς ἡμᾶς πόλεμον, ὡς δ' οὐκ ἤθελον, οὐδ' ἐπὶ τούτοις ἔφασαν τὴν συμμαχίαν ποιεῖσθαι, λέγοντες ἀληθῆ, χάρακα βαλόμενος πρὸς τῇ πόλει . . . ἐπολιόρκει. Once the Byzantians had reinforced Perinthus, Philip would no longer be asking for their help against Athens or anybody else.

[2] Demosthenes knew very well of course when 'the war against Athens' genuinely did begin: 18. 72 'It was Philip who broke the peace *when he captured the merchantmen*; not Athens, Aeschines.'

[3] Devastation is recorded only in the (spurious) 'Decree of the Byzantians' interpolated at D. 18. 90. That the siege of Byzantium itself had not yet begun follows from the synchronization of the capture of the Athenian ships with the siege of Selymbria, if that is accepted (p. 574 n. 2 above). No writer could ever have synchronized it with a siege of Selymbria if a siege of Byzantium also was on at this time. (Justin however (9. 1. 6) does put the capture of the ships after a long siege of Byzantium.)

twice the Macedonians approached the assembled merchant shipping with orders to seize it and bring it away. First Philip's squadron was foiled by the Athenian warships which interposed. Then he landed troops on the Asiatic shore, and it was through these that the corn fleet was captured, in an operation which must have been a truly unconventional and remarkable one: not one detail of it has come down to us.[1]

The haul amounted to 230 vessels, fifty of which Philip released (those which were owned by non-Athenians presumably).[2] The value of these prizes to him is said to have come to 700 talents, and the figure may not be too high.[3] It was a heavy blow, this, to the Athenian economy and morale; and this is what it was meant to be, no doubt. It was also, as

---

[1] Philoch. F 162 Φίλιππος δὲ αἰσθόμενος οὐ παρόντα τὸν Χάρητα τὸ μὲν πρῶτον ἐπειρᾶτο πέμψαι τὰς ναῦς τὰ πλοῖα καταγαγεῖν· οὐ δυνάμενος δὲ βιάσασθαι στρατιώτας διεβίβασεν εἰς τὸ πέραν ἐφ᾽ Ἱερὸν καὶ τῶν πλοίων ἐκυρίευσεν.

Hieron seems to have been the regular rendezvous where the corn fleet awaited its escort of triremes on occasions when escort was needed: cf. [D.] 35. 10; 50. 17 ff., where the squadron of Timomachus spent forty-five days at Hieron before it finally got under way. For the site etc., Dion. Byz. frs. 3 and 58 (*GGM* 2. 2. 12 f., 75 f.); Plb. 4. 50. 2.

How did soldiers after a landing succeed in taking possession of a great argosy of merchantmen which a squadron of warships had failed to take, prevented by (presumably) a superior squadron? I suppose that the merchantmen lay at anchor, and that the Athenian triremes were beached, or anchored close inshore; that the naval crews camped (or were billeted?) near their triremes, and that most of the merchant seamen were on shore too, since that is where sailors mostly like to be. The attack itself very likely was timed to coincide with one of the preoccupations of the nautical day; a mealtime, or better still the hours of darkness when all good sailors were asleep. And when it came, it must have landed out of sight, and it must have concentrated first on driving the Athenians away from their triremes, over which a section of the Macedonians would need to mount guard while the remainder made prisoners of all the merchant seamen they could lay their hands on, and seized all the dinghies in which they had come ashore. Using these they could take over the merchant ships one by one, a slow business, which would become easy if the Macedonian triremes could be timed to appear and take over now, with the Athenian warships immobilized. The Macedonians on guard over the shore had to be taken off last. They could not take away the Athenian triremes because they were too few to row them; and they could not set fire to them because their guard duty needed full concentration in the face of an enemy whose crews may have included several hundred hoplites (the *epibatai* of each ship).

But still the mystery remains, How did the Macedonians make their landing undetected, and achieve surprise, as one supposes they must? (This is the baffling feature of Lysander's surprise move at Aegospotami, too, in broad daylight—an operation which Philip may have studied; X. *HG* 2. 1. 23 ff., esp. 27 f.) And the second mystery, How did all this keep out of Polyaenus' book of *Stratagems*? One could believe that no Athenian might ever bring himself to commit to paper some lamentable fiasco of this sort; but Theopompus would have enjoyed it. I give it up.

[2] Philoch. F 162; Theopomp. F 295 *FGrH* no. 115 (= Didymus 10. 35 ff.).

[3] Philoch. F 162. The hulls themselves he used, according to Philoch., as timber for his siege train (πρὸς τὰ μηχανώματα), and this may be true for some if not all. The cargoes, of corn and hides, were quite valuable, but most of the 'much money' which Philoch. records as falling into his hands came probably from the sale or ransom of his prisoners. If 1,000 prisoners were taken, and 100 of them were sea-captains or owners of ships (who were more likely perhaps than ordinary seamen to be taken on board), the sale or ransom money could have amounted to 300–400 talents. See, for finance by plundering in general, A. H. Jackson, 'Plundering in War and other Depredations in Greek History, from 800 B.C. to 146 B.C.', Unpublished Dissertation, Cambridge, 1970, 102 ff. and ch. 3.

it proved, the act which prompted the Athenians to vote, on the motion of Demosthenes, 'to destroy the record of the treaty of peace and alliance with Philip', or as we say, to declare war.[1] That Philip was prepared for this must be obvious, and it is natural to think of it as the only possible result he can have counted on. But the tradition which made Philip's capture of shipping coincide in time with a siege of Selymbria is still of interest here (see p. 574 n. 2).[2] Wüst's interpretation of it as a Macedonian version of the corn-fleet operations, providing a red herring and some kind of apologia, seems most probably right. As for the grand act of piracy itself, Philip's decision on this may well have been for reasons local and military rather than diplomatic and replying to something that the Athenians had done or not done. The setback at Perinthus was thwarting Philip's policy and damaging his prestige, and his naval inferiority was handicapping him now. It seems likely that this particularly drastic *coup* by an amphibious operation which may have been

[1] D. 18. 72 and schol. 18. 139; Philoch. F 55. This Athenian version is doubtless correct, as Momigliano saw (*FM* 153 n.): D.S. 16. 77. 2 and Just. 9. 1. 1 f. make Philip's attack on Byzantium the occasion for the Athenians to declare war, and D.S. omits the seizure of the corn fleet, a version less discreditable to Philip.

[2] Schol. [D.] 11. 1 (Dindorf 8. 209, referred to below as the 'Hypothesis'); D. 18. 73 f., 77 f., and schol. (Dindorf 8. 289).

For a good evaluation of this material in general, P. L. Schläpfer, *Untersuchungen z. d. Attischen Staatsurkunden u. d. Amphiktyonenbeschlüssen d. Demosthenischen Kranzrede* (Paderborn, 1939), especially 56 ff., 241 ff. Unfortunately the interpolated *Letter* of Philip is not examined in detail by Schläpfer of course, though he suggests at 73 f. that it is by the same hand(s) as the Decree, which is certainly very probable; and since Selymbria is mentioned only in the *Letter*, the Hypothesis, and the scholion to 18. 76, but not in the Decree, Schläpfer does not pronounce on this historical point.

He puts this Decree (of D. 18. 73 f.) in his lowest category, of those which he considers to be the product largely of 'free invention', 'für deren Komposition keine Quellen oder nur sehr ungenügende Andeutungen vorhanden waren und die infolgedessen zum Grossteil Phantasieprodukte sind'. He thinks of the compiler(s) as belonging to an Athenian rhetorical school (second–first century), and shows that where the material is 'good' it can be found in Demosthenes himself. Where the material is 'bad' it is horrid, as in the latter part of Philip's interpolated *Letter* (18. 78). But the allusion in the 'Letter' to Selymbria and its connection with the capture of Athenian ships has close verbal affinities both with the scholion to 18. 76 and with the 'Hypothesis' to [D.] 11, showing that this is not free invention. Either all three derive from a common source (not Demosthenes, or any surviving writer), or two of them derive from the earliest of the three (presumably the 'Hypothesis'). That the 'Hypothesis' invented a siege of Selymbria I still see as an impossibility or nearly (above, p. 574 n. 2).

(The verbal affinity mentioned above is as follows: (1) 'Hypothesis' to [D.] 11 (Dindorf 8. 209). καὶ ὑπονοήσας Φίλιππος μὴ ἐπὶ σιτηγίᾳ πεπομφέναι τὰ πλοῖα, ἀλλ᾽ ἐπὶ συμμαχίᾳ Σηλυμβριανῶν, ἔλαβε ταῦτα τὰ πλοῖα, καὶ γέγραφεν Ἀθηναίοις ἐπιστολήν, αἰτιώμενος ὅτι βοηθοῖεν Σηλυμβριανοῖς οὐ συμπεριειλημμένοις ταῖς συνθήκαις, καὶ παρ᾽ αὐτοῖς εἶναι τὸ λελύσθαι τὴν εἰρήνην, ἀπειλῶν τε ἀμυνεῖσθαι αὐτοὺς παντὶ σθένει.

(2) Schol. ad D. 18. 76 (Dindorf 8. 289 f.), almost identical, except ἀφῖχθαι (for πεπομφέναι), τῇ εἰρήνῃ (for ταῖς συνθήκαις), κατέσχεν αὐτά τε καὶ τὸν ναύαρχον (for ἔλαβε ταῦτα τὰ πλοῖα), and an εἰ μὴ . . . clause following παντὶ σθένει.

(3) *Letter* (18. 77) εἰ οἴεσθ᾽ ἐμὲ λανθάνειν ὅτι ἐξαπεστάλη ταῦτα τὰ πλοῖα πρόφασιν μὲν ὡς τὸν σῖτον παραπέμψοντα . . . βοηθήσοντα δὲ Σηλυμβριανοῖς τοῖς ὑπ᾽ ἐμοῦ μὲν πολιορκουμένοις, οὐ συμπεριειλημμένοις δὲ ἐν ταῖς τῆς φιλίας κοινῇ κειμέναις ἡμῖν συνθήκαις.)

technically something of a *tour de force* was designed to show the Athenians (and the world) that the master of Thrace could still make life very uncomfortable for those whose lives depended on the passage of the Bosporus, naval power or no naval power.[1] Also the financial aspect of these sieges should not be underrated, probably. Philip's resources by now raised him above the level of living from hand to mouth; but still it was disagreeable to undergo these expensive operations for months with no return, and the corn fleet represented prize money on a scale which not only was very healthy for the treasury but also could be a real sweetener for the army (which by now was badly needing it?).[2]

Demosthenes and his supporters controlled the Assembly at Athens now, and the Athenians had good reason to be in a rage, and to declare war.[3] Seen from Philip's side, to be at war with Athens openly now was a thing which would need to be attended to, in due time; but it is remarkable how little difference it seems to have made to his immediate plans. Just as, in the previous war, he had gone about his business in Thrace, Illyria, Thessaly, Chalcidice, all without regard to Athens except in so far as the Athenians might choose to concern themselves in any of these theatres, so now he continued with his operations against Byzantium (and Perinthus); he did not return, himself, to Macedonia or Thessaly or the Amphictyony to concert arrangements to meet the new situation; he did not hurry to conclude his pacification of eastern Thrace, where one final campaign still claimed his attention; and meanwhile the prize money from the corn fleet was serving good ends, both for his own treasury and perhaps to provide payments to his troops caught up in these two strenuous sieges with hope deferred of the cities to sack.

It was probably very soon after the capture of the corn fleet that the siege itself of Byzantium began. No account of it survives, only isolated details which enable us to see that it was a full-scale affair lasting some months at least, that is, from about October of 340 to probably spring of 339.[4] If Philip had hoped for treachery from inside, he was to be disappointed.[5] We hear of Philip's siege-train, of damage to the walls, of

---

[1] This point is well made by Wüst 131 f.

[2] Cf. Just. 9. 15, 'Igitur Philippus longa obsidionis mora exhaustus pecuniae commercium de piratica mutuatur.'

[3] The trierarchic reform proposed and carried through by Demosthenes is a good sign of this; D. 18. 102 ff.

[4] Precise indications of time are lacking. The Athenian declaration of war will have been in October, and it was followed up by a decision to send out another squadron, under Phocion. It has been supposed often that this reinforcement was in spring 339, but it seems much more likely that it was sent without delay, as Wüst rightly saw (p. 141). The end of the siege can be dated only by general probability, and earliest spring seems likely, since Philip planned to campaign now far to the north, and he needed to extricate himself first (the fleet, especially, had to be got through both of the narrow straits in order to get home).

[5] One of his hopes may have lain in Leon; whom he tried to corrupt, without success. Suid. s.v. *Leon* 265; see above, p. 574 n. 1.

a surprise assault on a very wet night when dogs of the city gave the alarm, of a naval defeat for Philip's squadron, of Chares with forty ships based on the coast opposite near Calchedon, of the popular and trusted Phocion arriving with reinforcements and of the Athenians thereafter based on the city and harbour itself.[1] The city's old allies Rhodes, Chios, and Cos did their duty in support; so, we know, did Tenedos, and doubtless other Athenian allies of the Confederacy.[2] No word, however, of Persian aid to Byzantium. This is surprising on a first view, and political implications have been sought, and found.[3] But none really makes sense here. The Persian government had committed itself at Perinthus, and clearly had a common interest with Athens (now openly at war) to thwart Philip in this area in every way possible. A mistrust of Athens (or a cynic might add, of Chares ?) simply does not carry conviction in this situation. Nor does the classic doctrine of 'exhausting both sides' (τρίβειν ἀμφοτέρους). Probably the reasons for the Persian inaction were not political at all but purely practical, because of the time of year. If military aid was in question, October was an unpromising month in which to start collecting another force of mercenaries (the first had gone across to Perinthus a few weeks earlier). If Philip had not withdrawn from Byzantium quite early in the following year, one could have expected confidently to find Persia again numbered among the defenders of Greek freedom here.[4]

In the end Philip had to make up his mind to cut his losses at Byzantium and Perinthus. Coolness at the one and heroism at the other, together with the still imperfect development of his own siege apparatus, left the balance of advantage still with the defence. Like a good professional he accepted this—and probably he took some trouble to cover with some political decencies the mess made by these military reverses. Diodorus records that 'he raised the sieges of the cities and he made the peace with the Athenians and with the other Greeks who were at war with him.'[5]

---

[1] D. 18. 87; Just. 9. 1. 2 and 5; Hesych. Miles. 26–7 (*FHG* 4. 151); Plu. *Phoc.* 14. 2–3. Frontin. 1. 3. 4. Dionys. Byz. fr. 66 (*GGM* 2. 92 f.) adds nothing reliable, except the quoted epitaph of the wife of Chares from a stone on the promontory Bos near Calchedon, one couplet of which could scarcely have been composed thus unless Chares had really engaged Philip's squadron in a way which could be thought of as a victory.

> Εὐνέτις ἦν [δὲ] Χάρητος, ἔπλων δ' ὅτε πλῶεν ἐκεῖνος,
> τῇδε Φιλιππείων ἀντίπαλος σκαφέων.

[2] D.S. 16. 76. 3; Tod, *GHI* 175 (Tenedos), esp. line 10 βεβοηθήκασι.

[3] See especially Wüst 143, on the well-known story of the Persian embassy received by the young Alexander in Philip's absence; Plu. *Mor.* 342 B–C; *Alex.* 5. 1; cf. 9. 1; J. R. Hamilton, *Commentary* 13 and 23. The historical value of this anecdote has been questioned (e.g. by P. Treves, *Athenaeum* 1936. 199). I am prepared to believe that there was such an embassy, and this is the most probable time for it.

[4] Cf. [D.] 11. 5–6, quoted at p. 573 n. 2 above.

[5] D.S. 16. 77. 3 διόπερ ὁ Φίλιππος καταπλαγεὶς τῇ συνδρομῇ τῶν Ἑλλήνων τήν τε πολιορκίαν τῶν πόλεων ἔλυσε καὶ πρὸς Ἀθηναίους καὶ τοὺς ἄλλους Ἕλληνας τοὺς ἐναντιουμένους συνέθετο

Polemos Apolemos

For Athens, this is obviously unacceptable; and for Byzantium and Perinthus hardly less so, because Demosthenes tells us that Byzantium was still at Athens' side through the war that follows, and because Perinthus is associated with Byzantium in *stephanoi* conferred on Athens by the two cities in grateful recognition of her services to them.[1] Diodorus has made some muddle here; but I suppose that he made it out of something in his source(s), and did not invent it out of his own head. There probably were peace negotiations,[2] in which Philip hoped to renew his old relations with Perinthus and Byzantium, and not merely withdraw his armies, beaten off. Perhaps (and this would better explain Diodorus, without exonerating him), Philip did really make treaties of peace with somebody; with the Rhodians for example, and Chios and Cos. These off-shore islands of Asia Minor might have been well satisfied to keep out of a war to save Athens in mainland Greece.

It remained only to extract his fleet from its awkward and now useless situation, imprisoned in the Black Sea by the Athenian fleet in the Bosporus. Two *Stratagems* recorded by Frontinus and Polyaenus are concerned with this withdrawal of the fleet, and though both timing and topography are obscure, probably the fleet did escape by a stratagem executed while peace negotiations were on.[3] Why the Athenian fleet did not pursue it and bring it to battle as it made its way along the Sea of Marmara, through the Dardanelles, and back to its home bases, remains a mystery. Perhaps when it did slip through the Bosporus it was able to get such a good start that it could not be caught. Philip did invade the Chersonese when he raised the siege of Byzantium, and it has been suggested that he was repeating now in reverse the operation by which he had got the fleet through the Dardanelles eighteen months earlier.[4]

τὴν εἰρήνην. Wüst (145 and n. 2) interprets this, together with 84. 1, as *koine eirene* propaganda designed to isolate Athens, but this is not convincing.

[1] D. 18. 230 ἀντὶ δὲ τοῦ τὸν Ἑλλήσποντον ἔχειν Φίλιππον λαβόντα Βυζάντιον, συμπολεμεῖν τοὺς Βυζαντίους μεθ' ἡμῶν πρὸς ἐκεῖνον. This could be a lie, just possibly (spoken nine years later). But the *stephanoi* support it, D. 18. 89. (The ψήφισμα Βυζαντίων interpolated 18. 90–1 is not authentic.)

[2] Frontin. 1. 4. 13 A, an obscure story, refers evidently to peace negotiations in this context, and according to this story they were protracted.

[3] Ibid. 13 and 13 A. For 13 A, see the previous footnote. The other anecdote (1. 4. 13) is basically the same story in a different setting as Polyaenus 4. 2. 8, where it is told of Philip's deception of Chares and Proxenus the generals covering Amphissa early in 338: a false dispatch to Antipater, telling of rebellion in Thrace which demands Philip's presence, is allowed to fall into Athenian hands. Even Chares would not have fallen for this if the same thing had happened to another Athenian general (presumably Phocion) the year before. But I see no way of knowing which of the two occasions is authentic, if either is.

Very attractive, certainly, is Hammond's interpretation (*HG*² 567) which takes both as authentic. This makes Philip so brilliant and amusing that I cannot quite believe it, much as I want to. The more I think of it (obviously), the more I want to.

[4] By Wüst (142 and n. 5) who rightly pointed out that all the evidence for this invasion of the Chersonese puts it unequivocally after the Athenian declaration of war. D. 18. 139,

But that operation had succeeded only because Athens was not yet at war with him, and Chares then had refrained from attacking ships which he could not be sure of destroying anyway, if they ran for the shore held by the Macedonian army. Now that they were at war, the Athenians could have driven the enemy ashore even if they failed to destroy them, and could have harassed them all the way home. Perhaps they did this; but at all events an Athenian naval victory is something that Demosthenes in the *Crown* would not have passed over, and there can be no doubt that most of Philip's squadron did escape.[1] The capture of some ships by Phocion and raiding attacks by him on a Macedonian-held coast belong probably to the later stages of this voyage home.[2]

4. *Philip's Scythian Expedition*

Philip's sangfroid in relation to the new war in Greece was almost certainly not a pose, merely. He continued to besiege Byzantium and Perinthus so long as he thought there might be some prospect of taking them soon, and while the winter lasted. It was a genuine need to move elsewhere, most probably, that led him to abandon the siege of Byzantium. But when he did move it was still not towards Greece. Though it might be tempting to interpret his northern campaign of 339 as mainly a demonstration, a gesture even, timed to proclaim that to him at least Greece was not a matter of first importance, what we learn from the north itself suggests that there really was a crisis there, and one which called for Philip's presence in person. Diodorus could omit it from his record altogether, because it was an episode and a diversion, with no bearing on the developing crisis in Greece except that it delayed Philip's personal intervention there.[3] But the terms in which Justin describes the events in the north allow us to see that though this was a thing that Philip could have left unsettled without immediate danger to his kingdom or to his rear while he turned to Greece, yet it could not be left unsettled for all time. Thrace was newly pacified; but the overlord of Thrace had just been defied successfully by Perinthus and Byzantium. The army, too, needed to stretch its legs, to give somebody a hiding, to

---

ἀλλ' ἐπειδὴ φανερῶς ἤδη τὰ πλοῖ' ἐσεσύλητο, Χερρόνησος ἐπορθεῖτο, ἐπὶ τὴν Ἀττικὴν ἐπορεύεθ' ἄνθρωπος . . . Cf. Just. 9. 1. 6 f. (same order); Porphyrius Tyr. (*FHG* 3. 692 ff.); Syncellus 263 c (ed. Dindorf p. 501). Justin (loc. cit.) implies that he attacked the Chersonese with a picked force while the siege still continued ('deinde ne unius urbis oppugnatione tantus exercitus teneretur, profectus cum fortissimis multas Chersonesi urbes expugnat').

[1] D. 18. 87 ff. is the *locus* where a naval victory would have been commemorated appropriately.

[2] Plu. *Phoc.* 14. 5.

[3] Diodorus was acutely embarrassed, no doubt, in the composition of this part of his 16th Book, by the coincidence of the stirring events in Sicily (Timoleon) with the outbreak of the war in Greece. Something had to go.

fill its pockets, after the frustrations of those two sieges. Victory and the Macedonian name needed to ring through Thrace once more, before Philip led the men first into Greece and next into Asia.

Atheas the Scythian king had chosen this time to declare his independence, principally (as Justin tells us) because the recent death of the king of the Histriani his enemy had made Philip's aid to him no longer necessary; but the resistance of Perinthus and Byzantium may have helped him to make up his mind, too.[1] At the time when Philip had sent the troops to support him, his status may have been left unclear, as suggested above.[2] This latest news decided Philip that he had better clarify it. He sent to Atheas demanding a payment towards the cost of besieging Byzantium (the siege was still on).[3] Atheas by his reply repudiated all notions of obligation towards Philip, and thus convinced him that now was the time to make Atheas recognize his suzerainty, or to crush him if he refused. This was the warning conveyed by the message that he had vowed to set up a statue to Heracles by the mouth of the Danube; that he was coming to do this now, and that he expected no opposition.[4] But Atheas was not to be intimidated.[5]

The details of this campaign may well have been interesting, but they are not recorded. This was a very mobile enemy, and one not without striking power, from the mounted archers. The quality and the numbers of their horses must have impressed Philip deeply; after the victory he had 20,000 well-bred mares sent to Macedonia to breed from, according to Justin.[6] But the victory itself was evidently complete, since 20,000

[1] Just. 9. 2. 1 ff. Cf. P. Alexandrescu, 'Ataias', *Stud. Clas.* 9 (1967) 85 ff. (See above, p. 562).

[2] Ibid.

[3] Just. 9. 2. 5 ff. 'legatos ad Ateam mittit impensae obsidionis portionem petentes, ne inopia deserere bellum cogatur.'

[4] 9. 2. 10–11 'vovisse se statuam Herculi, ad quam in ostio Histri ponendam se venire, pacatum accessum ad religionem dei petens, amicus ipse Scythis venturus.' The interpretation in my text seems preferable to that of Justin or his source, who takes the message for a stratagem of war ('quo securiores faceret', ibid.).

[5] 9. 2. 12 f.

[6] 9. 2. 16. If this is true, and the whole truth, it seems an oddity, because in modern times improvements in breeds of horses have always been made, I think, by importing stallions of superior quality. Whether or not the qualities of a breed are transmitted more consistently or effectively to individual foals by the mare or by the stallion, it is certain that whereas each mare can have only one foal each year, a stallion can sire dozens or scores. If Philip hoped to improve the Macedonian and Thessalian stock by cross-breeding with the Scythian, the economical way would have been to import a few dozen stallions. To import thousands of mares seems pointless, unless it was thought that it was by the mares that the characteristics of the stock were transmitted best. But most likely the importing of 20,000 mares signifies that he intended them to replace the home-bred stock altogether for some purposes (presumably for cavalry mounts), and if this were so he will have imported some Scythian stallions too at the same time. To writers not much interested in horses, the great number of the mares will have been the impressive thing.

It is not certain that these horses ever reached Macedonia, of course. They may have been intercepted by the Triballians (below).

women and children were made captive after it, as well as great flocks and herds. 'Cum virtute et animo praestarent Scythae, astu Philippi vincuntur.' Some Greek writer anxious to disparage the Macedonians presumably lies behind Justin's summary here. Since the Macedonians of this generation had never given anyone any reason to doubt their courage in battle, probably the value of this remark, if it has any, lies in the tail. It would not be surprising if Philip was able in some way to outgeneral Atheas, who was killed in the battle. Any Scythians who remained south of the Danube were left in no doubt that now they were Philip's vassals, whether or no the symbolic statue to Heracles was really set up and left in place.

And so, at last, the Macedonians turned for home. It was a long march, its first stages through unknown mountains and an unconquered people.[1] The Triballians ought to have been sufficiently impressed by the fate of Atheas and his people to know what to do now. Politeness, hospitality even, and a formality of paying homage, suggest themselves as the expedients for seeing these uncomfortable conquerors off the premises and back to their homeland, never (it might be hoped) to come again. The Triballians, simple folk, saw their duty differently. Armed foreigners entering their territory were enemies, merely; and if they entered encumbered by 20,000 captive women and children, by great flocks and herds, and perhaps by 20,000 well-bred mares into the bargain, they were an enemy sure of the welcome they deserved. They got it. Philip was warned, by the Triballian offer to allow him safe passage on payment of a part of his great booty; but pride and policy rejected the offer, naturally. The passage itself, however, was no easy matter. It came to a battle, and in the battle Philip had his horse killed under him by the same spear which first had gone through his own thigh. Probably his horse rolled on him too, for there was a moment when he was taken for dead. From Justin's synopsis one suspects that the Macedonians found themselves fighting for their lives. They came through, but they had had to break away from their captives and their herds and leave them in Triballian hands.[2] This was a score to be settled another day—when the settler, as it proved, was to be not Philip but Alexander, who probably was present on this occasion.[3]

Meanwhile this army, this general, after three years was home from the wars (about midsummer probably, 339); not without glory certainly and with much solid gain from the Thracian province annexed and established. They had had to work for this, and not all their work had

---

[1] On the locality, Nicorescu, 'La campagne de Philippe en 339', *Dacia* (1925) 51 ff.; Columba, 'Le sedi dei Triballi', *Stud. stor. per l'Antichità* (1910) 203 ff.

[2] Just. 9. 3. 1–3.

[3] Just. 9. 1. 8 'filiumque Alexandrum, decem et octo annos natum, ut sub militia patris tirocinii rudimenta deponeret, ad se arcessit' (at or near the end of the siege of Byzantium).

shown a profit; and most recently they had known frustrations of a damaging and irritating kind. Nor had they come home to peace and ease. Philip and Athens already were at war. An Amphictyonic war had been declared against Amphissa. A new crisis was at hand for the future of Macedonian policy in Greece. The resilience and the resources in depth of Macedonia in fighting men are well illustrated here. Not all the Macedonians who had just served in Thrace need be the same Macedonians who were to be called up for service in Greece in November: perhaps, even, few of them were the same.[1] It was the same Philip, however, who nursed his wound through late summer and autumn, while catching up with whatever arrears of decisions and administration his long absence from the kingdom had accumulated.[2] Not to name the innumerable questions concerned with justice and the government as it affected the Macedonian people and especially its notables, and the questions raised by embassies from the frontier kings and from Greek cities, there was Thessaly in particular and the duties of its *archon*, there was the acute diplomatic problem of Thebes and Nicaea (below, p. 587), there was the Amphictyony and its war with Amphissa (below, pp. 586 ff.), there was the war with Athens already declared, there was the Getic princess whom he brought home now, a symbol of prestige maybe to the public in general but an interesting addition to the life of the Court and its neighbourhood. It was no rest cure, this, for Philip, even though seen now in a remote perspective it gives the appearance of a lull before a storm.

[1] See *G & R* (1965) 129 ff. for an estimate of the Macedonian army strength, based on the numbers recorded for Alexander's army in 334 (D.S. 17. 17. 3–5), of about 30,000 Macedonian infantry of expeditionary force quality. The army at Perinthus was 30,000 (D.S. 16. 74. 5), at Chaeronea more than 30,000 infantry (D.S. 16. 85. 5); but in each case some allies must have been present, surely. (D.S. ibid. The presence of the Thessalian cavalry at Chaeronea seems a certainty, on general grounds.) If only one-third of the Perinthus army were allies, and if the 'Guards' troops served in both campaigns, there would be scope for releasing most of the Macedonian levy that had served in Thrace, and calling up fresh Macedonians for Greece.

[2] It is commonly assumed that Philip himself was absent from Macedonia for three years, from about midsummer of 342 to the summer of 339; but I do not know of anything that makes this certain, and there are obvious reasons that make it improbable. We know that he did not return to Macedonia between summer 342 and spring 341 (D. 8. 2), and since that brings us to the start of a campaigning season, we are safe in keeping him in Thrace till its end. We know too that he did not return to Macedonia in winter 340/39, once the season of sieges had begun. There remains the winter of 341/0, with no clue as to his whereabouts. I would count it as nearly certain that he did return to Macedonia then, merely because his presence must have been needed after an absence of eighteen months or nearly.

For the army in Thrace, there is no need, obviously, for any of its units to serve the whole three years there without going home, though quite likely the units of the Guards, horse and foot, did do this. We hear of the army being heavily reinforced in eastern Thrace in spring 341 (D. 8. 14; D.S. 16. 74 for 340) and this could include some replacement of troops who had gone home for the winter.

XVIII

THE AMPHICTYONIC WAR

1. *Amphissa*

SINCE 346 the Amphictyony had provided much of the basis for Philip's standing in Greece, and it was natural that if another great war threatened, the Amphictyony might be closely concerned. Demosthenes in 346 had been nervous of an Amphictyonic war against Athens, and this could happen again:[1] with Philip's control of the voting-power among the hieromnemons of the Amphictyonic Council, it could be made to happen. The 'Amphissa case' which developed in the twelve months immediately before Philip's arrival in Greece with an army in November 339 looks as if it was designed originally to bring to bear on the Athenians first the threat and if necessary the reality of the Amphictyonic war before which in the end her hostility to Philip must yield. The bare facts about the Amphissa case are known and are not in dispute.[2] There has always been great uncertainty, however, about their dating, important obviously for a full interpretation. The account which follows reverts to the chronology of Beloch, and reserves for an Appendix (p. 717) some reasons for being able to follow it confidently.

The regular autumn Pylaea of the Amphictyons in October 340 fell a few weeks after Philip's capture in the Bosporus of the Athenian corn fleet assembled there, the incident which led the Athenians to declare war on him (above, pp. 575 ff.). When the hieromnemons met, the Locrians of Amphissa launched an unexpected attack on Athens for having set up irregularly in the rebuilt temple their ancient trophy of gilded shields, spoils 'from the Medes and the Thebans when they fought against the Greeks', as the inscription uncompromisingly recorded. The Amphisseans proposed that Athens should be fined 50 talents.[3] As a guide to the motives which inspired this attack, it would be helpful to know (which we do not) how recently the Athenians had set up the shields. According to Aeschines the Amphisseans were acting as agents of the Thebans, and he makes no suggestion that Philip was behind their action.[4] But Aeschines by 330 was a committed pro-Macedonian, and would be

---

[1] D. 5. 14 ff., 19, 25; above, p. 347.

[2] From Aeschines and Demosthenes. The condensed narrative of Diodorus does not find room to mention Amphissa at all, and leaves the capture of Elateia unexplained.

[3] Aeschin. 3. 116.　　　　　　　　　　　　　　　　　　　　　[4] Ibid.

likely to omit whatever he knew of machinations instigated by or for Philip against Athens in 340. Demosthenes names Aeschines, not Amphissa, as the agent of Philip on this occasion, and he need not be taken altogether seriously, for obvious reasons.[1] In reality, the issue raised by the Amphisseans (and diverted by Aeschines) suited the interests of Philip quite peculiarly well. Not only did it start a dispute which could end in an Amphictyonic war being declared on Athens, but it had chosen a matter on which Thebes and Athens were irrevocably on opposite sides. If an Amphictyonic war did develop from this issue, the Boeotians would be marching with the Amphictyons. The timing, especially, of this incident reinforces strongly the suggestion that it was designed as Philip's riposte to the recent Athenian declaration of war.

The story is well known of how Aeschines, present at Delphi as one of the Athenian *pylagori*, used the best form of defence by attacking the Amphisseans, and of how the hieromnemons of the Council, simple folk and unused to oratory as Demosthenes cattily put it later, fell under the spell of an hour or two's fast talking, even to the point of diverting their inquisition away from Athens and on to the Amphisseans themselves, accused by Aeschines of working some parts of the land of the Sacred Plain, and of making money from harbour dues levied on goods which passed through the interdicted ancient harbour of Cirrha. Next morning the Council made a tour of inspection of the Crisa Plain and the harbour, and they did not like what they saw. Less still however did the Amphisseans like them, poking about in the Plain. They came down through the olive groves in full force and under arms. They seized some of the hieromnemons, and the party as a whole had to run for it, back to Delphi up the steep; they made it, but only just. Blood pressures will have been high among the shorter-winded of the hieromnemons, and it says much for the influence of the Boeotians, who certainly will have defended and excused Amphissa to the best of their powers, that nothing precipitate was decided against her on the spot. But an extraordinary meeting of the Council was summoned, to meet at the Gates (Anthela, by Thermopylae), presumably at an early date.[2]

At this meeting, Amphissa (supported by the Boeotians still) having offered no conciliation, became the object of an Amphictyonic war. The Thessalian Cottyphus, who presided over the Council, was appointed to command the army, and a date no doubt was fixed for mobilization, as soon as spring made a campaign feasible in the neighbourhood of Parnassus. We are not told of any fighting, which really could only have developed if the Boeotians had joined Amphissa in the field against Cottyphus. Terms were imposed on Amphissa, including the punishment

---

[1] D. 18. 147 ff. [2] Aeschin. 3. 116–24; D. 18. 149–51.

by exile of the leaders responsible for the sacrilege and outrage, and the recall from exile of those who had unsuccessfully opposed them. Amphissa was fined also, and was given till the autumn Pylaea to pay, an interval of six months if these terms were ratified at the regular spring Pylaea of 339 as seems likely (below, p. 719).[1]

Athens, like the Boeotians, had sent no representative to the extraordinary Council meeting, for reasons which are obvious, and which were given to the *demos* by Demosthenes.[2] To punish the insolence of Amphissa was one thing. But to make an open enemy of Thebes was another, at this moment when Athens and Philip were at war, and when the whole future depended on Philip's not being able to use Boeotia as a friendly corridor for an invasion of Attica. Already, we see, Thebes has become the key both to this immediate situation in the Amphictyony and to the much wider and more serious situation involving Athens and her Greek alliance. For Thebes to support Amphissa was natural, from the traditional patron–client relationship of the Boeotians and the Locrians, and because Amphissa's original move which started this dispute had been a pro-Theban one. But that is not to say that the Boeotians were committed from the start to support Amphissa to all lengths and against their own true interests. It was open to them to advise the Amphisseans to pay their fine by the autumn Pylaea and reckon that they had got off lightly (which is probably the truth—though to be sure we do not know the amount of the fine).[3] Amphissa however did not pay the fine by the autumn Pylaea, and in the summer months meanwhile she evidently reverted to intransigence, recalling from exile the leaders recently banished because Cottyphus had demanded it, and banishing in turn moderates who had come in when the extremists went out.[4] This hardening at Amphissa can only mean that the Boeotians were behind them and were dictating the hard line now. The mood of the Boeotians is shown beyond all possibility of doubt by a really sensational move. In this summer they marched on Nicaea, commanding Thermopylae, expelled the Macedonian garrison there, and occupied the place themselves.[5]

Their immediate object is plain. By holding Nicaea they intended to ensure that neither Cottyphus nor any other Amphictyonic general should lead a second expedition south of Thermopylae against Amphissa. But the further implications are remarkable. They show a determination at Thebes to push this Amphictyonic nonsense to the point of an open breach with Philip and beyond. A second expedition against Amphissa,

[1] Aeschin. 3. 128 f.; D. 18. 151.   [2] Aeschin. 3. 125–8.
[3] Aeschin. 3. 128 (where μάλα μετρίως seems a not unfair comment).
[4] Aeschin. 3. 129.
[5] Didymus col. 11. 26 ff. (Philoch. *FGrH* no. 328 F 56. 6).

if it came to that, was going to be led most probably by Philip (this could be foreseen). The Boeotians were determined to keep the Macedonians out of Greece, allies or not. Unless Philip should bring himself to turn a blind eye to this quite extraordinary and unprovoked act of hostility, the Boeotians (and this means the Thebans of course) were burning their boats at Nicaea. To explain the decision more is needed than the exigencies of the local 'Amphissa case', more even than the long-standing dissatisfaction with Philip's award of Nicaea to the Thessalians in 346. One must think, really, that a majority at Thebes had come to see that only by keeping Philip out of Greece was there any hope of the Boeotians being able to continue to live (politically) in the style to which they felt themselves entitled; and that to co-operate with Philip, for example in invading Attica and laying Athens low, would be an act of self-destruction, reducing themselves to impotence along with Greece as a whole, all alike in the Macedonian grip. It is really now in this summer of 339 while Philip was still in the far north 'among the Scythians' that the future alignment at Chaeronea was settled—unless the Boeotians should flinch and draw back when the moment of truth arrived.

And meanwhile the Amphissa case smouldered on. At the autumn Pylaea the time was up, the fine was not paid, and the hieromnemons knew that they had the Boeotians (and Athens) as well as Amphissa to reckon with.[1] Philip's attitude and wishes will have been made clear through his own pair of hieromnemons if not earlier. In terms of power the Amphictyons were not capable now of coercing Amphissa if the Boeotians and Athenians supported her, without the Macedonian army. And now that the Boeotians could close Thermopylae, could the Macedonians and Thessalians reach Amphissa anyway? Seen through an Amphictyon's eye now, this matter was not purely and simply one of doing what Philip said because that was what one was there for. The naked truth was clothed, here, with the best of practical reasons in a most satisfactory way: if Philip did not coerce Amphissa, Amphissa could not be coerced. The hieromnemons cast their votes, to mobilize a second army against Amphissa, and to make Philip its commander (*hegemon*).[2] This must correspond to Philip's own intention and request. But to close the Amphissa case was not, any more, just a formality or a few days' route-march for an Amphictyonic army. As a military operation it needed a general now, and a plan. As a political operation it was bringing Philip to the crisis of his whole policy in Greece, where he needed to settle quickly with Athens, but needed and hoped to localize the conflict.

[1] Aeschin. 3. 129; D. 18. 151–2 (where the military effort now needed is brought out though Boeotia and Athens are not named).
[2] Aeschin. and D. locc. citt.

2. *Elateia: the Winter Campaign*

The Amphictyonic war against Amphissa was Philip's opportunity to penetrate into the heart of Greece. It was probably in November that he moved south with an army drawn from Macedonia only and unsupported as yet by levies from Thessaly and from the other Amphictyonic states; for his arrival near the centre of things came evidently as a surprise. Nicaea, commanding Thermopylae, was in the hands of the Boeotians, and the holding of Thermopylae had kept Philip out of Greece in 352 and until 346. It seems that strategists in Thebes and Athens counted on it to keep him out now. But this overlooked a radical change. Then, the Phocians had been capable of looking after the alternative by-pass routes. Now, nobody was looking after them. This obtuseness reflects badly on the amateurishness, relatively speaking, of the Greek military thinking (and practice), for which the responsibility lies primarily at Thebes, though Athens too, obviously, cannot be left out. That Demosthenes knew nothing useful about a particular military situation will surprise nobody; but generals like Phocion and Charidemus (even Chares) must have known. However, Philip by-passed the garrison of Nicaea with no trouble, and left it there without even bothering about it as a threat to his communications. (For this, it needed to be strongly reinforced, probably.) He marched first on Cytinium in Doris on the direct road to Amphissa, and then without delay turned eastward and seized Elateia on the edge of the Cephissus valley which runs down through Phocis and into Boeotia through the narrow neck of Parapotamii. It was the capture of Elateia that advertised that his intentions went beyond his commission from the Amphictyons. It was at Athens and Boeotia that this thrust was aimed.

The Athenians were impressed as they were meant to be, and as Demosthenes later described.[1] Counting Thebes as their enemy from force of habit and by a failing to keep abreast with the latest political currents there, they reckoned that Philip at Elateia was no more than two days' march or three through Boeotia to the borders of Attica.[2] This, too, was Philip's hope. But he knew, as Demosthenes knew, that his Boeotian allies were deeply divided now in their views and sympathies towards himself. For him therefore, Cytinium and Elateia became now the springboards for a political offensive, not for a swift march on Athens. To send ambassadors to Thebes was the first move.

The Boeotians were his allies, but they had behaved recently like enemies, in their taking of Nicaea. And in the Amphictyonic dispute they were aligned with the delinquent Amphissa in opposition to the majority which had brought on the war. If there was fighting to be done now, it

---

[1] D. 18. 169 ff.; cf. Diod. 16. 84. 2 ff.   [2] D. 18. 169 ff.

was important to remove the Boeotians from the opposition before it began. Philip's ambassadors Amyntas and Clearchus were supported by ambassadors from Thessaly and from three more of the northern Amphictyonic states and from Aetolia; a reminder, this, of Philip's power and the solidarity of his northern allies.[1] The Boeotians were being threatened now; but they were being given the chance to move out of danger without loss of face. The armies at Cytinium and Elateia were very close, but they had paused when they could have come right on. Nicaea now must be surrendered by the Boeotians (this was part of the message); but Philip undertook that it should revert not to himself nor to the Thessalians (to whom it had been assigned in 346) but to the Epicnemidian Locrians in whose territory it lay.[2] Finally as to the war against Athens, the Boeotians were invited to join Philip in invading Attica, or, if they preferred, to give him free passage while remaining neutral: the alternative, if they refused, would be a war in Boeotia.[3] The warning was clear, to stand by the old friends and keep out of trouble. But by this time the Athenian embassy headed by Demosthenes was in Thebes waiting to be heard. The Athenian army was mobilized and ready to march in. The terms of alliance offered by Demosthenes were exceptionally favourable.[4] And (to face the naked facts), to stand with Athens offered the chance to loosen this grip on northern Greece which had reduced Boeotia from the politics of hegemony to the politics of survival. The majority at Thebes voted for the alliance with Athens; and with a promptitude unexampled by Greek armies in November, the Athenians had marched north, the positions covering both Boeotia and Amphissa had been occupied, and a winter campaign had begun.

It was rare (for all I know, unique) for Greeks to begin the operations of a major war at this season of the year, and their strategic decisions taken now took Philip himself by surprise. (This at least seems implied by the events that follow.) If Philip had reacted to the rebuff at Thebes by advancing immediately one day's march from Elateia and Cytinium and seizing Parapotamii and the pass at the modern Gravia which commands the descent to Amphissa, he would have saved himself an immense amount of time, thought, and trouble. That he did not advance is not likely to have been through sheer obtuseness or inertia, for these faults would be uncharacteristic to say the least. More likely

---

[1] D.S. 16. 84. 5; Plu. *Demosth.* 18. 1 f.; D. 18. 211. Wüst's reference (157) to the 'gewissen panhellenischen Anstrich' conferred by these ambassadors seems unworthy of him; they were really a bunch of backwoodsmen from the north, well known to be in Philip's pocket. Diodorus' (16. 85. 3 f.) naming of Python of Byzantium as Philip's leading ambassador must be a mistake, since his quotation from D. 18. 136 refers to a much earlier occasion (see above, p. 489).

[2] Didymus col. 11. 37 ff.   [3] D. 18. 213.

[4] But cf. D. J. Mosley, 'Athens' Alliance with Thebes 339 B.C.', *Historia* 20 (1971) 508–10.

he persuaded himself that there was still something here for the politician, that Thebes and Athens might still be prised apart, that the Boeotians had not really said their last word. If so, he soon realized his mistake, when 10,000 mercenaries under the Theban Proxenus (with Chares representing Athens) had occupied the Gravia pass, and when Parapotamii was held by a strong force of the Boeotian and Athenian citizen levies.[1] Between and behind the two the great befriending hulk of Parnassus barred the way.

The Greek positions here were in the role which had been that of Thermopylae in the past. While they were held, Boeotia and Attica were safe from invasion; Amphissa was covered too; and Philip was barred from access to the Corinthian Gulf which could lead to his rousing his allies in the Peloponnese. The Greeks lacked the confidence to push forward from Parapotamii, seek out Philip and his main force, and destroy it; no doubt they were right in this. But a strategy of defence based on these positions was sound. So long as the allies were willing and able to maintain considerable forces here indefinitely, they were achieving their immediate object, and were laying on Philip the onus of regaining his mobility in some way. There was no future in trying to force these strong points direct. Only by taking some risk, or by producing something special in generalship, could he undo this barrier at one point or the other. This was not the way he can have planned to pass this winter, one feels. Most probably he sent some part of his army home, and if so the Greeks will have done the same. But allusions of Demosthenes to 'the winter battle' and 'the battle by the river' (the Cephissus, at Parapotamii?) do something to recapture what must have been a very uncomfortable Phocian winter indeed for all concerned. Philip will have probed and tested and tried this and that like the soldier that he was, and the Greeks to their credit were not caught napping.[2]

Meanwhile, looking forward, he sent word to the cities of the Peloponnese that were his allies, and claimed their support now. These people, Argos, Messene, the Arcadians, probably Elis, cannot possibly have been indifferent to what was going on north of the Isthmus. In their Peloponnesian world the balance was a delicate thing, and since Leuctra (371) external interventions had affected it easily and often. With Thebes weakened by the Phocian struggle, alliances with Philip had been the obvious insurance against a Spartan revival. But even Laconophobes knew that the one thing fatal for all Greeks was to get all Greece dominated by one military power and only one. Hence the reinsurance of alliances with Athens; a means of serving notice, really, that in the event of a war between Philip and Athens, these doubly allied states (Messene certainly, and probably the Arcadians, above,

---

[1] Polyaen. 4. 2. 8 and 14; Aeschin. 3. 146; Dinarch. 1. 74.   [2] D. 18. 216.

p. 550) hoped to be able to remain neutral. It is significant that on this occasion Philip's messages to the Peloponnesians stressed the Amphictyonic crisis and not his own quarrel with Athens (and Thebes).[1] This was undoubtedly the best thing he could do. Though these Peloponnesians cared relatively little, probably, for the Amphictyons and their troubles, they cared only too much for the survival of the traditional seats of power in Greece. It was not healthy for these smaller states that Athens and Thebes should be extinguished; and in the event they left the Amphictyons to sort themselves out by themselves. No Peloponnesians joined Philip north of the Isthmus.

In the theatre of war itself of course, beggars could not be choosers. In those lovely landscapes of east Locris and Phocis Philip was not popular, for obvious reasons. His awarding Nicaea now to the Locrians has been represented as an astute political move to win them over, but this seems to overrate their importance. Even if they did hate Philip they were too weak to act accordingly, and most likely the Nicaea award represents a saving of face for the Boeotians, who would have resented much more being told to give it back to the Thessalians, or to Philip himself. As for the Phocians, they had been reduced to the depths, politically, and would clutch at any hand that would help them out. Both Elateia and Parapotamii formerly had been Phocian cities, and the land of Phocis was straddled now by the two armies in their winter positions. The Phocians themselves hated the Thebans the worst of their former enemies, but they hated the Thessalians little less and they had no cause to love Philip either. The accident of the war settling in their territory did give them, however, an obvious chance of improving themselves in ways forbidden by the peace treaty of 346. According to Pausanias it was the Athenians and the Thebans who refounded their cities, apart from any which were too weak and poverty-stricken (of which Parapotamii itself seems to have been one): and the Phocians (he continues) fought with the Greek allies at Chaeronea.[2]

This no doubt is what the Phocians themselves chose to remember of these things in later generations, when the glories of the Greek tradition became linked not with their times of co-operation with Macedonian kings but with their briefer outbreaks of resistance. But obviously it cannot be the whole story, here. The Phocians as a whole came out of

---

[1] D. 18. 156, 158.

[2] Paus. 10 3. 3 f.; 33. 8 (Parapotamii). I am not persuaded (*contra*, F. Schober, *RE* 20. 1. 490 (1941) s.v. Phokis) that the naming by Demosthenes of Elateia in 344 (6. 14), or by Aeschines in 343 (2. 142) of 'ambassadors from the Phocian cities' is evidence for thinking that already the dispersal of the Phocians into villages had been ended or modified. Nor does the existence of a Phocian archon in 342/1 (*Syll.*[3] 231. 3 f.) signify anything decisive here; for the Phocians must have had a government of some kind even if they were in villages, if only to organize the taxation by means of which the fine could be paid.

this war with a much improved status, their Amphictyonic fine reduced from 60 talents a year to 10 talents, their cities restored, their entry into the 'League of Corinth' presently approved, in short with the stigma of their defeat and subjection more or less wiped out.[1] But it was Philip through the Amphictyony, and not the Greek allies, who must have brought this about, and the records of Delphi and Elateia preserve just enough to suggest the process and its timing.[2] In reality, both Philip and the allies this winter did what they could with those of the Phocians who had passed under their control. Thus Ambrossus was refortified by the Thebans.[3] But Lilaea on the northern foot of Parnassus, and a place which the Greeks really needed to hold, somehow managed to keep out of their hands and to be with the winner.[4] No doubt at Chaeronea some Phocians fought with the allies and some with Philip, who was content thereafter to be magnanimous to all the Phocians alike, reckoning (rightly) that those who had fought against him had had no option.

Meanwhile winter merged into spring. The campaign had become an institution, almost; the last weapon, this, in Philip's armoury. With unerring judgement he directed it against the mercenaries covering Amphissa; for Chares at least was a general who talked too much and thought too little,[5] and after so many months perhaps he and Proxenus could conceivably believe, if they were told it, that Philip had decided to give up and go home. It was the old trick, but it served. The false dispatch was allowed to fall into their hands: Thrace in rebellion, Philip summoned home.[6] What more could wishful thinking want? The word came that the Macedonians were indeed on the move withdrawing from Cytinium. Good generals might have thought it their duty to move forward, to observe, keep contact, and especially to do all in their power

[1] *Syll.*[3] 232, with 230 C 20–7; 260 b 8 ('League of Corinth'). On the Phocian revival, see especially G. Glotz, 'Philippe et la surprise d'Élatée', *BCH* 33 (1909) 526 ff.

[2] See previous note. In spring 338 the Phocians paid to Delphi a half-yearly instalment of 30 talents for the last time. Their next payment is of 10 talents, spring 337, and thereafter they pay 10 talents annually in spring. The change was authorized presumably by the Amphictyonic Council of spring 338, which probably sanctioned formally now (and retrospectively) the restoration of Phocian cities and *koinon* by Philip over the winter; cf. Glotz, art. cit. 536.

[3] Paus. 10. 36. 3 f.; 4. 31. 5.

[4] *Syll.*[3] 232. 15; a Lilaean is among the five Phocian 'witnesses' named, together with three Elateians, in the record of payment to Delphi of spring 338. In the same record Elateia supplies two of the four Phocian archons (232. 3 ff.); which attaches these people firmly to the 'Macedonian' side.

Paus. (10. 33. 3) does not say which side 'restored' Lilaea, though one must agree with Glotz (loc. cit. 540) that he implies in the context that it was the allies. I suppose Lilaea might even have changed hands during the winter.

[5] The anecdote at Plu. *Pelop.* 2. 4 f. suggests that this opinion of Chares was held by some at least of his Athenian contemporaries (it is attributed to Timotheus). The mercenaries will have been in the pass covering Amphissa perhaps four months.

[6] Polyaen. 4. 2. 8. And see p. 580 n. 3.

to see to it that not all of them got home alive. Not Proxenus and Chares however. The Macedonians turned again, and moving by night reached the Gravia pass, made the ascent, and fell on the mercenaries with their guards relaxed. The pass and the camp were theirs, and next Amphissa itself. In one night and one day the Amphictyonic war was at an end, and the war against the Greek allies, shaken out of its stalemate, moved into its next and last phase.

Yet the contrast is striking between the quickness of this blow at the Gravia pass and the slowness of the follow-up. It was not till the beginning of August that the final decision came (at Chaeronea). During all this summer Philip seems strangely inactive. Probably he took Naupactus now, but if he did, a few days will have sufficed.[1] It seems most probable that he paused long and deliberately before going forward to the military exploitation of the victory, because he hoped still to avoid altogether the purely military decision by trial of strength. At the same time (and really now is the only time that makes sense) he opened peace negotiations. Once he was 'about to send embassies', according to Aeschines, and further fragments of information show that he did send embassies in reality, certainly to Thebes but also, it seems, to Athens.[2] Aeschines explained that Philip had not underrated the Greeks, and had had no wish to risk his all on the hazard of one short day. This seems not uncharacteristic, and in truth may well have been in Philip's mind, among other things. Yet he had just won an important success, and he had no real cause to think, viewing the whole record, that a great battle with the Greeks would end in his own defeat, a thing which he had experienced only once in his life, and that in a very unusual situation. It seems likely that the assessment which led him to negotiate was not purely or mainly a military one.

For the strategy of the present campaign, of course it was right, elementary good sense, to work again on Thebes especially. Without the Boeotians, Athens and her Greek alliance had no real chance of defending Attica or anywhere else. What new terms, if any, he offered at Thebes we do not know; but Amphissa, the Theban protégé, had been spared a characteristic Amphictyonic vengeance.[3] Most telling, no doubt, was

---

[1] Theopomp. F. 235; Str. 9. 427. There is no indication as to date. The capture is commonly placed here rather than later, I presume, because there was really much more spare time for it before Chaeronea, than after.

[2] Aeschin. 3. 149–51; Plu. *Phoc.* 16. 1 f.; *Demosth.* 18. There is no reason to doubt the accuracy of Aeschines' 'embassies' in the plural; and if this is right, it is really very hard to see where a second embassy would go to, if not to Athens.

Plutarch here (*Phoc.* 16. 1 f.) clearly thought that he knew of an occasion when Philip offered peace to Athens before Chaeronea (... ἔπειθε τὸν δῆμον εἰρηνικῶς ἔχοντος τοῦ Φιλίππου καὶ φοβουμένου τὸν κίνδυνον ἰσχυρῶς δέχεσθαι τὰς διαλύσεις).

[3] According to Str. 9. 427 Amphissa was destroyed. But this seems disproved by D.S. 18. 38. 2 (321). So Wüst 163.

the fact that the Boeotians faced now a military situation which had changed for the worse. Their own country would be invaded this summer unless they either made peace or fought for their lives to prevent it. All this was taken very seriously now at Thebes. To say that it was touch and go with the alliance might be to say more than we really know. But obviously Demosthenes at Athens was obliged to take it very seriously too, and to make his appeal at Thebes in very striking and effective terms.[1] The Boeotians did decide to stand by the alliance, rightly of course if it was right to make it in the first place. It was now (unless it was earlier as a stimulus to these negotiations) that Philip sent his raiding parties by the mountain routes through into Boeotia in the rear of the Greek army in the north.[2] If the Greeks would not make peace, they must stand and fight now.

When all is said, however, these strategical considerations probably took second place to a political aim. If he really did send an embassy to Athens now as well as to Thebes (and most probably he did),[3] to suppose that he meant nothing by it, or that he was only pretending to want peace, is unconvincing. If he was insincere, what was gained by the pretence? The rational inference from this evidence seems to be that his aims were, in order of preference, first and best, peace with both Boeotia and Athens, which meant the end of the whole war. Next best, if Athens was intransigent, peace with Boeotia, making his military task relatively easy. Third, and worst, no peace at all, but a military decision with the full strength of the Greek alliance against him. Remembering how rare it must be in the history of Greek warfare for peace to be proposed by a commander or a government after winning a victory which obviously has improved the chances of a more decisive victory, one ignores this incident at one's peril. It looks as if Philip genuinely did not want to fight the battle of Chaeronea. And there is no good reason to think this was because he thought he might lose it. His reasons came from his thoughts of the future. These were not Olynthians any longer that he was fighting, enemies who were expendable. They were the people without whose co-operation or acquiescence his greatest plans for the future could not be begun, let alone consummated. They could see now, no one could fail to see, that they stood right on the brink of getting badly hurt. Perhaps, and if they chose that way, only by being badly hurt would they agree to toe his line. But it was still the best policy not to spill their blood, unless they insisted.[4]

---

[1] Aeschin. 3. 148 ff.   [2] Polyaen. 4. 2. 14.

[3] See above, p. 594 n. 2.

[4] For the well-known 'Amphictyonic' coinage which once was attributed to this time and crisis (see, e.g. Wüst 161 f.), but now is dated firmly to 335, see below, p. 622.

3. *Chaeronea*[1]

The fall of Amphissa and the turning of the Greek defensive screen did not itself make the battle of Chaeronea inevitable. The Greeks reacted by falling back from their main position at Parapotamii into the Cephissus valley some 5 miles to the south, where they barred Philip from invading Boeotia by this route. But now that he had broken through to the Corinthian Gulf, he could invade if he chose by the route skirting the southern faces of Helicon and entering Boeotia via Thisbe and Thespiae. If he did that, however, the Greeks on interior lines could meet him quickly in the south, and meanwhile for Philip to rely on supplies reaching him by his route of entry might have been too optimistic. The intermediate mountain routes (used by his raiders recently?) were uninviting for the grand army, especially with a siege train, and especially if it should need to be supplied from outside Boeotia for any length of time.[2]

In reality, then, the battle was fought near Chaeronea because both Philip and the Greek command were content to seek a decision now in one great trial of strength. The Greeks may have been obliged to listen too much to the Theban generals, who will have been influenced by the recent raids into Boeotia (above); but also they must certainly have had a financial problem, of paying a large force for a long campaign. They were able to see the plain of Chaeronea, just wide enough to give scope for a great hoplite army but not so wide as to put a big premium on superior cavalry, as a position which gave them a reasonable chance of victory. Certainly the natural features gave their flanks some security against the formidable cavalry of Macedonia and Thessaly.[3] Hindsight suggests that there was no basic unsoundness in the Greek strategy here. They could perhaps have won this battle if they had had a great tactician in command. But where to find him among the generals available to the allies in August of 338?[4] They really needed the Corinthian Timoleon; and he, unfortunately, at this moment was otherwise engaged.

Philip when he viewed the Greek position at Chaeronea reckoned that it gave him a reasonable chance of victory. This was no Thermopylae. For cavalry such as Greece had never yet seen, and 2,000 of them, this Cephissus valley, dead flat or nearly, offered an arena too good to be

---

[1] The study of J. Kromayer (*AS* 1. 127 ff.; for the battle, 158–69), for all its thoroughness in topographical and other matters, reconstructs the battle itself in a way that seems wholly unconvincing. My account owes most to N. G. L. Hammond 'The two battles of Chaeronea (338 B.C. and 86 B.C.)', *Klio* 31 (1938) 186 ff. (esp. 186–8, 210–18) = *StGH* 534 ff., and to W. K. Pritchett, 'Observations on Chaeroneia', *AJA* 62 (1958) 307 ff.

[2] On these routes, Kromayer, *AS* 147 and n. 4, 156 f.

[3] There is no ancient evidence that Thessalians fought in this battle at all; but it would be very remarkable if they did not.

[4] The date was 7 Metageitnion (Plu. *Camill.* 19. 7), most probably 2 August ; cf. Kromayer, *AS* 1. 185.

missed. The river running down its northern edge, the irregular hills all along the south, might be thought of as safeguards by the Greek generals fearful for the flanks of their hoplite phalanx; and safe they might be when battle commenced and so long as the Greek phalanx kept its station. But if the battle could become mobile, even a little, then even

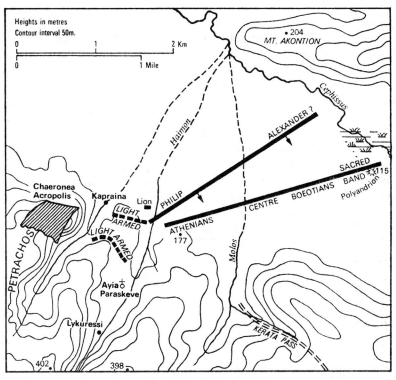

MAP 7. CHAERONEA

small gaps in the hedge of hoplite spears might be exploited to give cavalry its chances of decisive blows.

The battle itself, the great set-piece battle of Greeks against Macedonians which this master of war had worked so hard not to have, and which ought to tell us so much of the quality and character of the men and the generals, tells us very little that we can trust absolutely, and indeed shows the surviving Greek historical tradition at its most poverty-stricken. For Diodorus, in a chapter and a half of journalese the topography does not exist, and he does not even allow us to know which wing of the Macedonian army was which: Philip had superiority in numbers as well as in generalship; the young Alexander led a decisive attack;

but Philip himself, not to be outdone, contributed notably to the victory.[1] For Justin (in a single sentence) the Greeks had much the bigger army, the Macedonians much the better.[2] Plutarch adds some details on Alexander's part, and especially he names two or three local features of his own native landscape which are invaluable. Pausanias tells about the Lion of Chaeronea and the dead whom it commemorated.[3] 'Stratagems' of Polyaenus show that the victory was thought by some at least to have been due in part to an interesting and sophisticated tactical performance by those of the Macedonians who were under Philip's personal command; but this is hard to understand fully, or even to accept at all, unless it can be linked reliably to the topography of this quite small plain of Chaeronea, its river Cephissus and one tributary of it (Haemon), and the mountain features of the plain's southern fringe. (See Map overleaf.) Finally, however, the excavation by G. Sotiriades of one of the two notable mass-graves situated one at each extremity of the battlefield threw some valuable light. The mound at the northern extremity was shown to be a *polyandrion* of Macedonians burnt in one great pyre, and is generally accepted as marking the area where the Macedonians (of Alexander's wing) suffered their severest losses, especially against the Theban 'Sacred Band'.[4] This pinpoints for us the position of the Greek right wing, its flank resting on the Cephissus and its fringe of marsh. The other *polyandrion* is marked by the Lion of Chaeronea itself, which was thought by Pausanias to stand over a common grave of the Thebans.[5] The Lion bore no inscription when Pausanias saw it, and his story has not been accepted by all modern interpreters, though the excavation by P. Stamatakes in 1880 on the whole supported rather than undermined it.[6] The burial of the Thebans at the end of the battlefield furthest from where they had fallen remains unexplained, however;[7] and by this

---

[1] D.S. 16. 85. 5 ff., and 86.   [2] Just. 9. 3.   [3] See below, nn. 5–7.

[4] G. Sotiriades, *MDAI(A)* 28 (1903) 301–30. 'Das Schlachtfeld von Chäronea', *MDAI(A)* 30 (1905) 113–20. Cf. Plu. *Alex.* 9. 3, with id. *Pelop.* 18. 7.

[5] Paus. 9. 40. 10; cf. Str. 9. 2. 37 (414) who writes merely 'Here may be seen a public tomb [tombs?] of those who fell in the battle' (ταφὴ τῶν πεσόντων . . . δημοσία).

[6] The *polyandrion* was found to contain 254 skeletons buried in rows (not cremated like the Macedonians). The number approximates nearly enough to the traditional 300 of the 'Sacred Band', who were said to have fought and died to a man. (If all fell where they fought, some few must have been badly wounded, not dead.)

[7] After the battle the bodies and the territory were in Macedonian control, and there was delay in handing over the Theban dead for burial (below, p. 610). Meanwhile the Macedonian funeral pyre will have been built and fired. Though modern sentiment might prefer that the enemies should lie near to each other in death, I doubt if either Macedonians or Thebans would have preferred it. The Lion is by the roadside close to Chaeronea itself, at the farthest point on the battlefield from the pyre of the Macedonians, and this choice may have been quite deliberate.

Hammond (*StGH* 554 f.) noted the difficulty of believing that Thebes, treated so roughly by Philip in the peace treaty after this battle (below, pp. 610 f.) and destroyed by Alexander less than three years after it, was ever allowed to erect the Lion as a monument over the

interpretation the Lion and its dead do not help us to reconstruct the order of battle or its course.

It is the firm identification by Hammond (supported by Pritchett) of the stream called Haemon that enables us to be reasonably sure of the position taken up by the Greeks when they deployed into line of battle. The Haemon, Plutarch thought, must have been filled with blood and bodies in the battle.[1] The Greek right, near the Macedonian *polyandrion* and the Cephissus, can never have got anywhere near the Haemon (or either of the other two tributaries of the Cephissus which cross the plain). Only the Greek left (the Athenians) can have been within reach of the Haemon near to where it enters the plain from the south. The Greeks evidently took up a position which gave them the best chance, if defeated, of falling back on to their route of escape, the hill road which gave access via the Kerata pass to central Boeotia opposite Lake Copais.[2] Here they stood, then, the Thebans and Boeotians on the right, the Athenians on the left, their allies in the centre between them. But where was their cavalry? They were not deficient in cavalry; but in face of the exceptionally strong Macedonian and Thessalian horse it cannot have been easy to know where to station their own and how to use it. On this there is no information.[3]

Philip was probably outnumbered, but not very seriously.[4] Of his battle order we are told nothing at all, and of his plan hardly more. We know only that Alexander commanded on the left, opposite the Thebans and Boeotians, and that Philip himself was on the right facing the Athenians.[5] His problem was to defeat this large force of Greek

dead of the Sacred Band. There is force in the objection, certainly (*contra*, W. K. Pritchett, *AJA* (1958) 311). Yet the Sacred Band will have been drawn from just that class of Thebans who formed the government of the city in defeat, believers in oligarchy or aristocratic rule and willing to collaborate with Philip. I think it probable that the Thebans of the ruling oligarchy got on well enough with the Macedonians to come to an arrangement with Philip about the honouring of the Sacred Band. Incidentally, as a band of lovers, besides being heroes, they may have made a claim on his sympathy and generosity (whatever the value of the anecdote at Plu. *Pelop.* 18. 7 which suggests this).

[1] Plu. *Demosth.* 19. 2; Hammond, *StGH* 540 ff.; Pritchett, loc. cit. 309.

[2] Hammond, *StGH* 539 (Plu. *Mor.* 849 A implies that the Athenians who escaped did use this route).

[3] See next note.

[4] D.S. 16. 85. 5 gives Philip's army as more than 30,000 infantry, 2,000 cavalry. (For the Greek army he gives no total.) J. Kromayer (1. 195) reckons the Greek cavalry at 2,000 too. This may be an over-estimate, but it cannot be a very serious one, for the Greeks knew that they were up against cavalry of unusual strength and quality, and must have done their utmost (cf. Plu. *Dem.* 17. 3, 2,000 *mercenary* cavalry; but I doubt this). Kromayer's estimate of about 35,000 for the Greek infantry cannot be far wrong, with Athens and Boeotia supplying at least 20,000 between them. The total of Greek hoplites must have been over 25,000 and might be about 30,000. Of Philip's 30,000 infantry at least 20,000 will have been Macedonians of the phalanx or the hypaspists. There were 24,000 of expeditionary force quality available to Alexander in 334 (D.S. 17. 17. 4).

[5] Plu. *Alex.* 9. 3 (Alexander); Polyaen. 4. 2. 2 and 7 (Philip).

hoplites, of whom the Boeotians were very good indeed, and the rest certainly were not negligible. His own Macedonians of the phalanx and the hypaspists were outnumbered and had less protective armour; but with their long spears, their toughness, their training, experience, and *savoir faire*, probably they could be trusted to look after themselves and get the better of the Greek hoplites, if they could contain the Boeotians. They might not be able to beat them decisively, however. For this he must have relied on the cavalry. The story of the battle, if it had come down to us, would have told, presumably, how, where, and when the decisive blows by the cavalry were delivered; especially, how the Greek hoplite phalanx, which began by presenting an unbroken wall of spears and which could not be outflanked, was induced in some way to break formation and offer a gap or gaps which could give a cavalry charge its point of entry.

As it is, we are left to reconstruct the course of the battle from two pieces of information, and two only. (1) Alexander 'is said to have been the first to assault the Sacred Band of the Thebans'.[1] (2) Philip himself, facing the Athenians, directed a controlled retirement of his own phalanx on this (his right) wing, till a moment arrived when he could halt and counter-attack, with devastating effect.[2] We do not know the relation in time between these two things. All we can say is that an 'assault' on the Sacred Band is a thing that really cannot have come about very early in the battle; for the Thebans could not be outflanked, and in order to be assaulted by (presumably) cavalry, they needed first to be isolated in some way, or attacked in rear by a force which had broken through the Greek lines elsewhere. Diodorus, in his description which seems inspired more by rhetoric and 'theatre' than by a method of genuine narrative, makes Alexander 'the first to break the enemy's formation', and makes Philip's local success (which he allows to have been decisive) come later.[3] But I am not persuaded that this is a reliable story, or that if Alexander's break-through did come first, it was necessarily the Sacred Band who were his first victims. More likely, in fact, they were his last.

Philip's own manœuvre obviously is crucial; so much so that the actual words of Polyaenus become essential. Of the two *Stratagems*, one is more generalized, and consequently less valuable. 'Philip at Chaeronea realising that the Athenians were impetuous and short of training while his Macedonians were highly trained and disciplined, prolonged the battle and thus soon exhausted the Athenians and made them easy

---

[1] Plu. *Alex.* 9. 3.

[2] Polyaen. 4. 2. 2 and 7.

[3] D.S. 16. 86. 3–4 πρῶτος τὸ συνεχὲς τῆς τῶν πολεμίων τάξεως ἔρρηξε [sc. Ἀλέξανδρος] . . . μετὰ δὲ ταῦτα καὶ ὁ βασιλεὺς . . . αἴτιος ἐγένετο τῆς νίκης.

game.'[1] The other *Stratagem* seeks an effect partly by quoting what purport to be remarks of Philip and the Athenian general Stratocles in action. If the story is reliable at all (obviously, the source for it could be Theopompus here—but it could be anybody else!), it shows the Athenians thinking they are winning, and it shows Philip directing a preconcerted plan with unconcern and sang-froid.

Philip when he went into action against the Athenians at Chaeronea gave ground and retired. The Athenian general Stratocles yelled 'On! On! On! To Macedonia!' [or some such thing], and kept pressing forward. 'The Athenians have no idea how to win a battle', said Philip as he withdrew contracting his phalanx behind its wall of spears. Soon when he got to higher ground, he spoke a word to the men, then turned and charged the Athenians and fighting like a hero overcame them.[2]

One can sympathize with Pritchett (for example) in his reluctance to take every detail of this story seriously.[3] Especially, the detail of 'higher ground' presents great difficulties, because higher ground in any meaningful sense really can only mean, here, the ground rising into the hills at the southern edge of the plain. This leads to Kromayer's reconstruction of the battle which did make Philip withdraw the Macedonian right wing on to the foot-hills in a way which looks impossible both because of the length and duration of this Macedonian retreat while still under pressure from the Athenians (a most difficult operation, this, as Hammond appreciated well, and one which only a very cool general in close control of very experienced battalions of infantry could even think of attempting), and also because of the bizarre situation of the divided Macedonian army at the finish.[4] Hammond has shown the impossibility of Kromayer's interpretation, and has argued that Philip's retreat was only to the

---

[1] Polyaen. 4. 2. 7. Frontinus 2. 1. 9, based on the same source material as Polyaenus here, clearly understands the 'drawing out' of the battle in terms of time, not space. We ought therefore to suppose that Polyaenus too thought in the same terms. His actual words might be thought equivocal, and indeed they have been interpreted in both ways: γιγνώσκων τοὺς μὲν Ἀθηναίους ὀξεῖς καὶ ἀγυμνάστους τοὺς δὲ Μακεδόνας ἠσκηκότας καὶ γεγυμνασμένους, ἐπὶ πολὺ τὴν παράταξιν ἐκτείνας ταχέως παρέλυσε τοὺς Ἀθηναίους καὶ εὐχειρώτους ἐποίησε [there is a v.l. τὸν χρόνον τῆς παρατάξεως ἐκτείνας]. But the point of the anecdote is that the Athenians were quick off the mark but lacked steadiness and staying-power, and the apparent contradiction between ἐκτείνας ἐπὶ πολύ and ταχέως is no real contradiction at all. Speed is a relative matter, and ταχέως here need not approximate to εὐθύς, since very good sense comes from interpreting it as (e.g.) οὐ διὰ πολλοῦ. Παράταξιν can be either 'battle-formation' (which suits a 'space' interpretation) or merely 'battle', synonym of μάχη as often in post-classical writers. I would translate 'by prolonging the battle he soon exhausted the Athenians . . .' etc. (So Kromayer 168 n. 3; *contra*, Hammond 543 f., relying especially on the technical military sense of παράταξιν ἐκτείνας 'extend the line', cf. LSJ⁹ s.v. παράταξις.)

[2] Polyaen. 4. 2. 2.

[3] I am inclined to agree with Pritchett (art. cit. 310) that this anecdote has a character in which the 'higher ground' may well be adding a touch of verisimilitude without necessarily being accurate description.

[4] J. Kromayer, *AS* i. 167.

Haemon stream, the bank of which represented the 'higher ground'.[1]
Though this last point seems open to doubt, the direction and the extent
of the retreat must have been as Hammond outlined it. For the Haemon
really was a natural limit to the retreat which simply could not be
ignored. To try to retreat deliberately through and over the Haemon
with the enemy actually in contact would seem another impossibility.
The Macedonians had to halt at the Haemon, and this is where they did
halt (as Hammond suggested, for other reasons).[2]

This controlled retreat of the Macedonian right under Philip's direction, if one can accept the tradition preserved by Polyaenus, led to the
counter-attack, whether this fell (as Polyaenus has it) upon the Athenians
of the Greek left themselves, or whether (by Hammond's interpretation)
it fell on the Boeotians of the Greek right, left isolated in the end as the
Athenians advanced and the centre followed them extending all the time
until a gap or gaps appeared in the Greek phalanx line. That this extension was the object of Philip's withdrawal seems something more than
probable; and it seems implicit in such a plan that the Macedonian and
Thessalian cavalry should be used to take the fullest advantage of the
openings when they appeared. And when they did appear, the units of
the Greek phalanx on the move and stretched to their limits may have
invited more than one counter charge, of which Alexander's may have
been the first. But without knowing where the cavalry forces were
stationed at the outset and what their movements were, I do not see how
to pursue this any further.[3] The Macedonian blows however were heavy

[1] Hammond, *StGH* 544 f. estimated the distance of this retreat at about 150 metres, and
its duration in time at about half an hour, and thought that anything longer, for this
operation, was impracticable. I agree. (*Contra*, Pritchett, 310.)

[2] If the Haemon's bed was not significantly different in Plutarch's day from what it had
been more than 400 years earlier, Plutarch's thinking of it as being filled with bodies (and
blood) tells us that it was a distinct channel through which even in August no phalanx was
going to move slowly backwards with impunity, the enemy following at no more than a
pike's distance away. This was obviously the line where the Macedonians needed to halt,
listen to Philip's words, and wipe the Athenians up.

[3] The conventional positions for Philip's cavalry would have been on the wings, of course,
and the Greek cavalry, though inferior, would serve its best purpose in the wings too, trying
to deny the enemy a completely free hand. But since the Cephissus gave a real guarantee
against outflanking, the Greeks may have 'anchored' the Boeotians, their best infantry,
close to the river. In that case, the Macedonian cavalry, unable to ride round the flank
whatever happened, could have been stationed more profitably not on the extreme left
wing, but nearer the left-centre of the Macedonian line: outside them on their left would be
several *taxeis* of the Macedonian phalanx, with the task of containing so far as possible the
dangerous deep formation of the Boeotian hoplites. If these Macedonians gave ground (as
well they might), and if the Boeotians advanced more, or more quickly, than the Greek
allies of the centre, this could give the Macedonian cavalry their opportunity to get at the
Boeotians on an inside exposed flank: this after they had first disposed of any Greek cavalry
that tried to get in their way.

On the Macedonian right flank, the terrain of the extremity became unsuitable for cavalry
because of the hills, and this ground no doubt was exploited by light-armed troops of both
sides as Hammond has suggested (*StGH* 543 f. and fig. 23). The line of the modern road

and effective. A thousand Athenians were killed and 2,000 taken prisoner. The Boeotians lost heavily in dead and prisoners. The Achaeans, too, probably suffered in the centre of the Greek line.[1] But there seems to have been no classical pursuit *à outrance*, perhaps because the near-by hills enabled men who threw away their arms to save themselves. Perhaps, too, Philip even in the heat and glow of victory was able to look beyond the day and towards the morrow.[2]

where it skirts these hills on the southern edge of the plain may be taken as marking roughly where cavalry terrain begins. But Philip's retreat before the Athenians, as described by Polyaenus, seems to be essentially an infantry operation. If the object of the retreat was to draw the enemy into an extended line which might break eventually into gaps, it might have been good policy for Philip to station his second striking force of cavalry (Thessalians?) behind his original phalanx-line and in a central position, since he could not know in advance just where the gap(s) might appear. And his own withdrawal to the Haemon of the phalanx troops of his right wing could have made deliberately a big gap in his own front line, which would open, to the cavalry behind, their way of getting at the enemy without riding through or over their own infantry in front.

There is not however one particle of concrete evidence to support these suggestions, which are purely speculative.

[1] D.S. 16. 86. 6 (Athenians and Boeotians) ; Paus. 7. 6. 5 (Achaeans).
[2] As Hammond (e.g.) suggested (*StGH* 551 and n. 2).

XIX

PEACE IN GREECE

1. *The treaties with the Defeated States*[1]

AFTER the battle, the Greek fugitives came together near Lebadeia some 10 miles to the south; but this army had been beaten too badly to fight again.[2] They had not lost a battle, they had lost the war. Philip did not move in next day or next week and cut them to pieces. He owed it to himself as a general to do this, and as a statesman to do nothing of the kind. The Greek alliance was not going to raise a second army to face the same treatment, and each ally now was looking after himself. The immediate reaction of the different cities to the news varied, no doubt. At Athens, after the first shock the *demos* rallied to the stirring words of Hyperides, and was ready for desperate measures in order to survive.[3] At Corinth too the citizens were ready for self-defence.[4] At Thebes, where opposition to the war had been strong from the start, the seeds of a revolution developed, perhaps very quickly.[5] The only one of our sources which describes in general terms the behaviour of the Greeks at this time writes that 'they surrendered to him city by city in terror'.[6] The character of Aelian's summary here does not inspire the confidence that could accept it literally. Its over-simplification submerges who knows what agonies of indecision and contested decision in this city or that. But in the end (and this means in a few weeks, not more), probably it is true that the Greek governments individually did approach Philip to sue for peace, and with no reasonable option really but to accept the terms that he offered.

[1] See here the careful study of Carl Roebuck, 'The settlements of Philip II with the Greek states in 338 B.C.', *CP* 43 (1948) 73 ff.

[2] Plu. *Mor.* 849 A; Lycurg. fr. 76 *ap.* Harpocrat. s.v. Lysicles.

[3] Lycurg., *In Leocr.* 16; 36 f.; 39 ff.; 52. D. 18. 114; 117; 195; 248; Hyp. fr. 27–32 Ox. Suid. s.v. ἀπεψηφισμένοι. Cf. Schaefer, 3. 5 ff.

[4] Lucian, *Hist. Scrib.* 3. See below, p. 613 n. 3.   [5] See below, p. 610.

[6] Aelian, *VH* 6. 1. Ἐπεὶ τὴν ἐν Χαιρωνείᾳ μάχην ἐνίκησεν ὁ Φίλιππος, ἐπὶ τῷ πραχθέντι αὐτός τε ᾖρτο καὶ οἱ Μακεδόνες πάντες. οἱ δὲ Ἕλληνες δεινῶς αὐτὸν κατέπτηξαν καὶ ἑαυτοὺς κατὰ πόλεις ἐνεχείρισαν αὐτῷ φέροντες. καὶ τοῦτό γε ἔδρασαν Θηβαῖοι καὶ Μεγαρεῖς καὶ Κορίνθιοι καὶ Ἀχαιοὶ καὶ Ἠλεῖοι καὶ Εὐβοεῖς ⟨καὶ⟩ οἱ ἐν τῇ Ἀκτῇ πάντες.

The list of names is correct in excluding Athens (because of its different treatment), incorrect in including Elis and 'all those in (Argolid) Akte'. The naïve and uncritical character of the entry, quoted here complete, is obvious. It concludes with the comment 'Philip did not keep his undertakings to them however. He reduced them all to subjection unjustly and unlawfully.'

It is easy, perhaps, to call Hyperides the last of the Athenians (for they did not in the end fight to the death), and to conclude that the *demos* as a whole was no longer the *demos* which had had to be starved into surrender by Sparta; for after Chaeronea no one went hungry or was likely to, the sea belonged still to Athens, and it was open to the Athenians to stand up and defend their walls like anybody else.[1] But to argue in this way would be a failure to understand. For all we know, the Athenians would have cried 'No surrender' and fought on, if the alternative had been bad enough. That it was not, may be set to the credit of Philip's political sense and sensibility. For Athens there was to be no question of surrendering or not surrendering. This was a moment for negotiation; and it was Philip who began it.

It began, as the story goes, in a characteristic storm of wine on the evening of the great day itself. The swords and *sarissas* were laid by, the sweat after some fashion was washed off. It was time to eat and drink, and drink again. Δημοσθένης Δημοσθένους Παιανιεὺς τάδ᾽ εἶπεν.[2] To the drunk everything said is witty, if one means to be witty. But this is rather witty, by sober standards (one hopes the story is true). From wit to insult is a short step however, for the inebriated especially. The winner strolled among the losers, the Athenian prisoners of war, and spoke to them in words which were no advertisement for alcohol. One of them took his life in his hands. It was the politician Demades, unwashed, unfed, with more than 1,000 of his fellow citizens on his mind perhaps (they lay dead on the field of battle). 'Agamemnon', he said, '. . . Thersites'.[3] Philip was not too drunk for those names to register. He did not hurl himself on Demades; he pulled himself together (not the easiest thing). Demades had spoiled his evening; but in a sense he had made his day.[4]

---

[1] On the uninterrupted corn-supply, D. 18. 89. The Athenian walls, with their vast perimeter (Thuc. 2. 13. 7), had never been 'modernized' to meet the recent advances in siegecraft. By modernization I do not mean the strengthening which would enable walls to withstand bombardment with great stones from *petroboloi* (which we first hear of in use at Tyre in 332), but the addition of towers and emplacements to hold the arrow-firing catapults which were becoming recognized as the best defence against the corresponding artillery of a besieger, under cover of which he hoped to work on the wall at close quarters, with rams especially. (On these developments in general, see E. W. Marsden, *Greek and Roman Artillery: Historical Development* (Oxford, 1969) 56–62, 68 ff., 105, 113 ff., 126 ff.) The Athenians after this war was over evidently recognized the need to look to their walls: Aeschin. 3. 27 ff.; *IG* ii². 244 (337/6); cf. F. G. Maier, *Griech. Mauerbauinschriften* i (Heidelberg, 1959) 40.

[2] Plu. *Demosth.* 20. 3 (iambic tetrameter catalectic, they tell me).

[3] D.S. 16. 87. 1 ff. Theopompus is suggested as the source of this material (Wüst 167 n. 2; Laqueur, *RE* 5. 2186, *et al.*). Very likely he is the ultimate source, but 87. 3 (τέλος δ᾽ ὑπὸ τοῦ Δημάδου καθομιληθέντα ταῖς Ἀττικαῖς χάρισι . . .) suggests an Athenian intermediary used by Diodorus here (Diyllus? Cf. Hammond, 'SD' 89 f.).

[4] Justin's (9. 4. 1) summary of Philip's use of victory is hardly credible as it stands. 'Huius victoriae callide dissimulata laetitia. Denique non solita sacra Philippus illa die fecit, non in convivio risit, non ludos inter epulas adhibuit, non coronas aut unguenta sumpsit, et quantum in illo fuit, ita vicit ut victorem nemo sentiret.' Even as a summary of Philip's considered attitude and policy after the event, this picture must be thought overdrawn.

For whatever the truth of the anecdote, there is no doubt that the accommodation with Athens after Chaeronea does deserve to be called (as Schaefer called it) the peace of Demades.[1] It was Demades whom Philip sent off to Athens with friendly messages about the Athenian dead and prisoners; and no doubt he had convinced Demades personally that he intended Athens to survive, and in conditions that the Athenians could be invited to tolerate. Of this Demades evidently managed to convince the *demos*. The ambassadors whom it elected now, including three figures known to be congenial to Philip (Phocion, Aeschines, and Demades himself) were instructed to negotiate for the recovery of the prisoners, but presumably were empowered, too, to discuss terms of peace.[2] The reception of the terms at Athens was prepared by Philip's prompt release of the prisoners, and without ransom, an act of largesse which was felt directly by hundreds of Athenian families.[3] Hundreds more were thankful for the return of the bones of the men who had fallen in the battle, conveyed to Athens with honour by no less a personage than the crown prince Alexander accompanied by Antipater and Alcimachus.[4] And meanwhile the Macedonians stayed where they were: the soil of Attica was not invaded.[5]

The terms of Philip's treaty with Athens are nowhere recorded for us in set form. They have been pieced together satisfactorily from isolated bits of information and by inferences drawn partly from these bits and partly from some significant silences, and from the political behaviour of Athens in the years immediately following 338.[6] In a word, in this treaty Athens was dealt with as a defeated enemy, but not as a conquered one. No Macedonians did enter Attica (it is one of the curiosities of Philip's career that so far as we know he never in his life set foot in Athens himself).[7] The political life of Athens went on untouched:

---

[1] Schaefer 3. 18 ff.; cf. also P. Treves, 'Demade', *Athenaeum* 1933. 105 ff. Demosthenes himself has (of 338) οὐδὲ Δημάδην, ἄρτι πεποιηκότα τὴν εἰρήνην (18. 285).

[2] Aeschin. 3. 227; Suid. s.v. *Demades*, 3; D. 18. 282 ff.; Nepos, *Phoc.* 1. 3. For Philip's hospitable reception of the embassy, Theopomp. F 236; Plu. *Mor.* 715 c. Schaefer 3. 22 f. (followed by Roebuck 81) seems to put too much weight on the Suidas entry (καὶ πρεσβευτὴς ὑπὲρ τῶν αἰχμαλώτων ἀπεστάλη) and too little on Aeschines (ἀλλ' ὑπὲρ τῆς σωτηρίας τῆς πόλεως ἐπρεσβεύομεν). There is nothing improbable in what Aeschines said.

[3] The number of the Athenian prisoners was 2,000, according to Diodorus 16. 86. 5; cf. D.S. 16. 87. 5; Just. 9. 4. 4; Plb. 5. 10. 1–5; [Demades] ὑπὲρ τῶν δώδεκ. 9–10; D. *Epist.* 3. 11 f.

[4] Plb. 5. 10. 4 f.; Plu. *Dem.* 22; Just. 9. 4. 5. And see p. 610 n. 1 below.

[5] It was at this time, no doubt, that (as Aeschines put it, 3. 131) 'the conqueror refrained from invading the territory of the defeated because the omens were unfavourable.' 'The omens' etc., according to Aeschines, is what Demosthenes had said of Philip at the time, and Aeschines implies that it was nonsense (or worse). But 'the omens' etc. could easily be the authentic reason which Philip did give to his Macedonians for not invading Attica, as they hoped and expected.

[6] Schaefer 3. 25 ff. is still indispensable. And see the references at p. 605 n. 1 above.

[7] The argument from silence on this seems practically conclusive.

democracy, Demosthenes, everything was still there, unchanged except in so far as the *demos* might decide to change something itself. In the next few months Athens became the place of refuge for political refugees from other cities less fortunate or favoured.[1] So far the treaty carried the imprint not of a dictated peace but of an instrument negotiated between contracting parties of equal status.

One of the two parties, however, did happen to have lost a war, and this fact naturally was reflected in the terms of the treaty concerned with territorial possessions and accessories of power. Of the important Athenian possessions overseas, there is evidence that no change was made in the Athenian possession of Lemnos, Imbros, Scyros, and Samos, or in the special position of Athens in Delos.[2] But this list does contain one vital omission—the Thracian Chersonese. There is no positive evidence on what happened to the Chersonese now and to its Athenian cleruchs. But no Athenian connection with the Chersonese is ever recorded again from this time on, and the generally held view, that Athens lost it by this treaty, undoubtedly must be right. Strategically this loss was a shrewd if obvious blow to Athenian power, influence, and even security. For Philip, the Athenian presence in this area had so much potential for nuisance (in Thrace, *vis-à-vis* Cardia, with Byzantium and the other Greek cities), that its continuance could fairly be called intolerable. For Athens, depending on corn from south Russia in order to live, and on the Black Sea trade in general in order to live well, to lose the Chersonese was not automatically a death-blow, nor did it lay her helpless at Philip's feet. But it did impair the ability to use her fleet in the area 'to keep the Hellespont open', and it will have acted as a standing discouragement to the Athenians from going to war with Philip again or making preparations to go to war.[3]

Effective, too, in the same direction was the termination of the Athenian Confederacy. That it did terminate now we are told by Pausanias, and there is no reason to disbelieve it.[4] Its value to Athens in terms of power since 355, though much reduced, had not been negligible. And it was a relic of hegemony, important not only symbolically or sentimentally but as a matter of practical reality especially in the diplomatic field: to have permanent allies everywhere, or anywhere, was to extend legitimate 'Athenian interests' in a way and to a degree that asked for trouble, in a world where a new hegemony now was being installed.

---

[1] *Syll.*³ 259 (Acarnanians); Hyp. 4. 31 f. Budé (*In Athenogenem*, Troezenians). Cf. Roebuck 83.

[2] D.S. 18. 56. 7 f.; and cf. *Ath. Pol.* 61. 6; 62. 2; Plu. *Alex.* 28. 2. *IG* ii². 1652, 20 ff.; cf. Laidlaw, *History of Delos* 86.

[3] See above, pp. 567 ff. for naval power and bases in the area. The lack of the Chersonese did not inhibit Athens from initiating the Lamian War in 323, however.

[4] Paus. 1. 25. 3.

One territorial detail shows finesse, and is significant beyond its intrinsic value: the detachment of Oropus from Boeotia and its return to Athens.[1] It seems an unnecessary interference, in the sense that if Philip had left Oropus alone, no one could possibly have felt surprise, either then or now. To leave it alone may have been more than his professionalism as a diplomatist could endure. This small adjustment, which could not fail to make trouble for somebody else for the whole of the foreseeable future—no professional could neglect this and still feel that he had done his duty. But more important, it shows Philip thinking still in these terms, of this pair of incompatible allies whose alliance (painfully achieved) had forced him to 'stake all on the hazard of one day'. The Greek unity of Isocrates (*homonoia*) was to be won by 'reconciling' the four big cities: to reopen this old sore was the exact opposite.[2] With the gadfly of Oropus to prevent it, these yoke-fellows would not soon come together again.[3] At the moment they were powerless anyway; but life is long and full of surprises, and for the professional it is always good to take pains.

Philip's treaty with Athens is said to have provided for 'friendship and alliance' between them (φιλίαν τε καὶ συμμαχίαν).[4] Since the Athenians had been allies of Philip since 346, till they quarrelled with him, there is nothing surprising in the statement, *a priori*. For Athens, it must be probable that the treaty of alliance was renewed in 338; and there is no reason why this should not be true of all Greek allies of Philip (including the Boeotians) who had 'defected' in the recent war. The suggestion that Philip at this time in his dealings with the individual Greek states made a treaty of alliance with every one of them separately, is less easy to maintain.[5] This view is attractive if one thinks that Philip's arrangements presently with the Greeks collectively (in the 'League of Corinth') did not include any provisions for alliance (see below, pp. 626 ff.): consequently, the occasional reference to the Greeks as 'allies' after the foundation of the League of Corinth would be well explained if individually they had all become allies by separate treaties. It is not impossible that this was so; but it is improbable. It seems to introduce a uniformity and a system into things which in reality had had no occasion to become systematized in this way. As these things actually happened, Philip was making treaties with a number of cities in the autumn of 338, but not with all cities. There was no need to make treaties now with states that had been his allies and had honoured the

---

[1] Paus. 1. 34. 1.

[2] Isoc. 5. 30; see above, p. 456.

[3] See below, p. 611 n. 5 (for year 322).

[4] D.S. 16. 87. 3; cf. perhaps Plb. 5. 10. 5 (but in a rhetorical and unreliable context, καταπληξάμενος τῇ μεγαλοψυχίᾳ πρὸς πᾶν ἑτοίμους αὐτοὺς ἔσχε συναγωνιστὰς ἀντὶ πολεμίων).

[5] So Hampl, *GS* 52 ff.

alliance, fighting with him in the recent war. Of the states which had fought against him, some were allies who had defected (Athens and Boeotia *imprimis*), others had never been his allies at all. There were also many small Greek states which had managed to remain neutral through all these things. To suppose that all states now were roped in, to make separate alliances, seems to demand something of bureaucracy and *dirigisme* in this settlement of Greece for which really there is neither evidence nor probability. The criterion of common sense is against it: that amount of fuss and bother was simply not worth the trouble. Collectively, 'the Greeks' could be corralled in another way.

This other way was through the medium of a *koine eirene*, and it will be considered presently (pp. 623 ff. below, 'The League of Corinth'). It has been suggested, however, that Philip's separate peace treaty with Athens, and perhaps with other states, contained a clause binding (or allowing?) them in advance to adhere to the collective arrangement which he had in mind and which was to follow soon.[1] Plutarch wrote 'After the defeat . . . Phocion considered that Philip's lenient treatment of Athens ought to be accepted; but when Demades proposed that Athens should join the League of Corinth, Phocion was against their joining until they knew what Philip would require of the Greeks.'[2] Here 'Philip's lenient treatment' refers obviously to his separate treaty of peace with Athens. But it is an open question whether we are to consider this as accepted and settled before Demades made his proposal concerning the League of Corinth, or whether an adherence to the League of Corinth is part of the separate treaty which is not yet accepted and ratified. The former alternative seems by far the more probable. To object to a single 'collective' clause in a peace treaty in other respects acceptable seems hardly practical or practicable at that stage, and Phocion of all men would have known this. It was probably not till all the separate treaties had been concluded that Philip put forward any formal proposals to the cities, for inaugurating the League of Corinth. His intentions may well have been an open secret, but that is another matter.

Philip's terms for Athens were indeed 'lenient', more so than most Athenians can have hoped for. Though the honours paid to Philip and Alexander at Athens at this time (and to Antipater also and Alcimachus) are not to be taken as reflecting any genuine affection or admiration of the *demos* for the great Macedonians, there is no reason to doubt that the return of the prisoners and the dead was appreciated, and that the

---

[1] Roebuck 81 n. 57; Schaefer 3². 29 no. 3.
[2] Plu. *Phoc.* 16. 4 (discussed in detail below, p. 632). Δημάδου δὲ γράψαντος ὅπως ἡ πόλις μετέχοι τῆς κοινῆς εἰρήνης καὶ τοῦ συνεδρίου τοῖς ῞Ελλησιν, οὐκ εἴα πρὸ τοῦ γνῶναι τίνα Φίλιππος αὐτῷ γενέσθαι παρὰ τῶν ῾Ελλήνων ἀξιώσει.

character of the treaty itself came as a great relief.[1] This was peace
without dishonour, when the expectation had been for unconditional
surrender after a siege. To Thebes and the Boeotians he showed a different
face. No question here of friendly gestures concerning the prisoners and
the dead of Chaeronea. The Boeotians were required to ransom their
prisoners, and even (if the story can be believed) to pay to recover their
dead for burial.[2] The Macedonian army seems to have stayed in Boeotia
for some weeks after the battle. It would have been easy to move in on
Thebes, and Philip no doubt was ready to do this, had the Boeotians not
shown themselves realistic. His terms were designed to break Boeotia as
a military power; and this meant breaking Thebes. (This last fact made
them, incidentally, much more acceptable to many Boeotians of the
other cities.[3]) A Macedonian garrison was to occupy the Cadmea.[4]
Whether or not this was represented as a temporary measure (it lasted
in fact for about two and a half years, till the 'revolt' of 335), the truth
may have been that Philip saw Thebes, because of its military potential,
as a place where he was not prepared to have a government in charge
that was not friendly to himself. Thebes was the seat of government of
the Boeotian League, and the government at this time was democratic,
by direct assembly, a method which had enabled the Thebans themselves
to exert that preponderance which we observe when we see them in
action.[5] Only with a garrison could the government now be kept in
reliable hands. But Philip did what he could, too, to see that the reliable
hands had every chance. In the treaty of peace itself provision was

---

[1] For the honours paid at Athens, especially Schaefer 3². 31–3.

The proposal by Demades to deify Philip (Apsines 1. 470) is not commonly accepted as
historical; nor do I accept it myself. (And see p. 692.) For grant of citizenship to Philip,
Plu. *Dem.* 22. 3. For his statue in the *agora*, Paus. 1. 9. 4. For Demades in general in this
connection, [Demad.] ὑπὲρ τῶν δώδεκ. 9 ff.; 26 ff.; cf. D. 18. 320; Arr. *An.* 1. 1. 3.

For grant of citizenship to Alexander, Aristid. *Panath.* 178. 16. For *proxenia* (probably) to
Alcimachus, Tod 180 (cf. Hyperid. F 77 Oxford, *ap.* Harp. s.v. Ἀλκίμαχος). For *proxenia* to
(perhaps) Antipater, Tod 181 (the name of the honorand is lost; cf. Hyperid. loc. cit.).

[2] Just. 9. 4. 6. On the prisoners, the *Anonymi Philippica* of P. Ryl. 3. 490. 45–60 may have
recorded a more favourable treatment, but the text depends heavily on restoration.

[3] Roebuck (79) seems wrong in suggesting that Philip treated first with the city of Thebes,
and only later, when a government favourable to himself had been installed at Thebes,
with the Boeotian League as a whole. This would certainly have been incorrect procedure,
and besides would have sacrificed the advantage of dealing from the start with some Boeotians
who were not averse from seeing Thebes put down. That Justin wrote *Thebanorum* in connection with the prisoners and the dead is not important. He does the same at 9. 3. 5, of their
alliance with Athens. Diodorus however correctly wrote 'Boeotians' repeatedly in his account
of the alliance, the campaign, and finally this treaty of peace (16. 84–7; εἰς δὲ τὰς Θήβας
φρουρὰν ἐγκαταστήσαντα συγχωρῆσαι τὴν εἰρήνην τοῖς Βοιωτοῖς, 87. 3).

[4] D.S. 16. 87. 3; Paus. 9. 1. 8; 6. 5; Arr. *An.* 17. 1. Roebuck (80 and n. 44) rightly notes
Wüst's error (169) in linking the garrison not to this separate peace but to the 'League of
Corinth' arrangements later.

[5] Larsen, *GFS* 175, 178. For League assembly and trials at Thebes, see especially D.S.
15. 52. 1; 71. 7; 78. 4; 79. 5; 80. 2 with 81. 1; Plu. *Pelop.* 25.

made, probably, for the return of exiles.[1] Justin's account of this is hard to take literally, with its implication of hundreds of exiles returning to Thebes itself (we know of no reasons for so many). But taken as referring to Boeotian exiles, this is good sense of course, since there were undoubtedly some thousands of Boeotian exiles from the 'destroyed' cities (see below). In the same way an oligarchic Council of 300, created now and packed with the former exiles, makes sense as a Boeotian institution, and one which could supersede the predominantly Theban *demos* which had been the League's organ of government. Whether Philip himself intervened to bring about the change, as Justin says he did, and the persecution of political undesirables that preceded and followed it, might be thought doubtful; except that his reported gift of a Boeotian estate to Demades does something to confirm it.[2]

There is no doubt that the Boeotian League continued to exist and was not dissolved by Philip's treaty now,[3] and one reason for this has been suggested already. The existence of the Boeotian state as a whole had some effect of neutralizing its Theban core which was the real danger. Especially, this treaty 'restored' the three cities which had been destroyed, Orchomenus, Plataea, and Thespiae.[4] These people were healthily hostile to Thebes, and could be relied on to pull their weight. (They did, with a vengeance, in 335 the year of crisis.[5]) Significant, no doubt, is the representation of Boeotia at the Delphic meeting of *naopoioi* held in autumn 338, after Chaeronea, by delegates from Tanagra and Thespiae, but not (as in the previous autumn) from Thebes.[6] The loss now of Oropus and of Nicaea (above, pp. 608, 592) will have had some impact certainly, but more at Thebes than elsewhere, and anti-Theban politicians will have made the best of it.

In these treaties, the contrasting treatment of Athens and Thebes is very marked in several ways, but most of all by the garrison in the Theban Cadmea. It is important to know whether, on the subject of garrisons, Philip had any general policy, and, if so, whether it is Thebes now or Athens that is to be thought of as the exception. An anecdote makes this

---

[1] Just. 9. 4. 7 f. 'Principes civitatis [= Thebanorum, above] alios securi percussit, alios in exilium redegit, bonaque omnium occupavit. Pulsos deinde per iniuriam in patriam restituit. Ex horum numero trecentos exules iudices rectoresque civitati dedit.'

[2] Suid. s.v. *Demades* (3).

[3] Arr. *An.* 1. 7. 11 (Theban Boeotarchs).

[4] D.S. 17. 13. 5 (all three cities); Paus. 9. 1. 8; 37. 5; 4. 27. 10 (Orchomenus and Plataea). For Thespiae see also *Anth. Pal.* 6. 344 (cavalry with Alexander), and Dio Chrys. 37. 42. 466 (statue to Philip); and n. 6 below (*naopoioi*).

[5] D.S. 17. 13. 5. Significantly, the Boeotians are found in action with Macedonia and against Athens at the start of the Lamian War in 322 (Hyperid. 6. 11).

[6] E. Bourguet, *Fouilles de Delphes* 3. 5, 175 f. No. 48. 8 ff.; No. 47. 72; P. Cloché, *BCH* 40 (1916) 125; Roebuck 80.

clear: Philip was setting his face (even with an epigram) against controlling Greece by garrisons.[1] But is the anecdote reliable? Yes, it would seem. A policy of garrisoning even a dozen of the most important Greek cities, but excluding Athens, would be remarkable indeed. In the unrest which greeted Philip's death presently, we could count on detecting a garrison policy had it been present, in allusions to talk of 'expelling the garrisons' and so on.[2] In fact, two garrisons are attacked, at Ambracia in 336 and at Thebes the year after; and for only one other city, Corinth, is a garrison ever attested.[3] It seems almost certain that Thebes, Ambracia, and Corinth were singled out by Philip as exceptions to a general policy of not enforcing 'discipline' on the Greeks by means of garrisons; and that these very likely were the only exceptions.

The motives for choosing them, obviously, were mainly strategic. Corinth needs no explanation. Ambracia in general terms was a point of entry and control for north-west Greece; and in particular for the area which forms a wedge between the two powers recently in receipt of solid benefits from Philip, Alexander, king of the Molossians and the Aetolian League.[4] Firm friends, these, and allies for the foreseeable future? So it might be hoped. But Philip will have learned that to the

---

[1] Plu. *Mor.* 177 c Ἐπεὶ δὲ νικήσαντι τοὺς Ἕλληνας αὐτῷ συνεβούλευον ἔνιοι φρουραῖς τὰς πόλεις κατέχειν, ἔφη μᾶλλον πολὺν χρόνον ἐθέλειν χρηστὸς ἢ δεσπότης ὀλίγον καλεῖσθαι.

[2] D.S. 17. 3 and 4, with its fairly full account of the reactions in Greece to Philip's death, is silent on garrisons, apart from its mention of the two individual cases at Ambracia (expulsion) and at Thebes (talk of expulsion), 17. 3. 3.

[3] Ambracia, D.S. 17. 3. 3; Thebes, Arr. *An.* 1. 7. 1, D.S. 17. 8. 7, etc.; Corinth, Plu. *Arat.* 23; cf. Dinarch. 1. 18; perhaps Plb. 38. 3. 3 (but no firm link with this occasion). Plutarch's story of Aratus, after his great capture of Acrocorinthus, restoring to the Corinthians the keys of their city-gates 'for the first time since the days of Philip' (τότε πρῶτον ἀπὸ τῶν Φιλιππικῶν καιρῶν), vague and anecdotic though it is, obviously preserves what was popularly believed by the contemporaries of Aratus; and this is the kind of matter about which the victims of a tyranny are not likely to have made mistakes. Dinarchus makes it practically certain that the garrison was there in 335, when ambassadors from Thebes to Arcadia reached only with difficulty, and 'by sea', the Arcadian army which had 'arrived at the Isthmus' (but obviously had not committed itself to pushing north of Corinth; if they had, the Thebans would have reached them easily, without needing a boat). Since we need to know whether Corinth was garrisoned by Philip or not, I give the passage in full. (That Corinth was garrisoned first by Alexander, in 336, can be ruled out, I am sure, by the silence of Diodorus and Arrian on so striking a move at so critical a time; Arr. *An.* 1. 1. 2; Diod. 17. 4. 3–9.) Dinarch. 1. 18 καὶ Ἀρκάδων ἡκόντων εἰς Ἰσθμὸν καὶ τὴν μὲν παρὰ Ἀντιπάτρου πρεσβείαν ἄπρακτον ἀποστειλάντων τὴν δὲ τῶν Θηβαίων τῶν ταλαιπώρων προσδεξαμένων, οἳ κατὰ θάλατταν μόλις ἀφίκοντο πρὸς ἐκείνους ἱκετηρίαν ἔχοντες καὶ κηρύκεια . . .

The physical difficulty of arriving can be explained only by a military control of Corinth and its two harbours by the Macedonians.

Chalcis is often named as a fourth city garrisoned by Philip, but I know of no evidence which shows this plainly, and the evidence for the survival there of Callias for some years speaks strongly against it. (Below, p. 614 and n. 2.) Plb. 38. 3. 3 alludes to the later cliché of Chalcis as one of the 'Fetters of Greece', and is valueless for close dating. Str. 10. 1. 8 (447) suggests to me that Chalcis was certainly in Macedonian hands in 334 (cf. perhaps Arr. *An.* 2. 2. 4), and that the garrison probably was installed either then or (more probably) in 335 after the rising at Thebes.   [4] Cf. Roebuck 76.

young and the enterprising (and both these powers were this) gratitude can be brief and the need for it a source of irritation and an odious constraint. Epirus and Aetolia were to carve their names deep in the Macedonian record of the next generations. While there is no need to credit Philip with clairvoyance, there is no need, equally, to deny him some judgement in a field which made up the most important part of his life. (Alexander of Epirus of course he knew very well.[1]) Thebes, too, he knew as he knew no other Greek city, from the inside. By Macedonian standards, it may be that Boeotia still contained more first-rate soldiers than the rest of Greece put together. The function of these people was to dominate Central Greece if they were free to do so, and they would not put up indefinitely with being told that they must not. At Thebes the friends of Philip must be in charge. They were not very many: the Theban *demos* did not like them very much, and it would like them less and less every day that they were in charge. For Philip, as for Phoebidas, 'no more nonsense from Thebes' meant holding the Cadmea with a garrison. There was no other way.

Besides the question of garrisons, there are two other topics which need to be looked at in terms of general policy, to determine whether or not Philip in 338 was acting in a way that deserves that name. (1) Did he systematically exert pressure to promote revolutions in the cities of Greece so as to install governments favourable to himself? (2) Were federal states acceptable to him, or did he insist on dealing whenever possible with the individual cities?

Athens and Boeotia, again, present the contrast. In the one, the most scrupulous refraining from interference, exemplified by the Athenian help given to political refugees from elsewhere, and by the free choice of Demosthenes to pronounce the *epitaphios* over the dead of Chaeronea; in Boeotia, as we saw, a change of government with savage persecution of anti-Macedonians, whether by Philip himself or by the Boeotian politicians who were his agents. But on this matter as a whole no such clear conclusion appears as that which offered itself for the garrison question. There is positive evidence for a change of government in Acarnania and at Troezen, and probably at Ambracia, all of them places which had joined the Greek alliance of Demosthenes.[2] The same thing has been asserted of Corinth and Megara, and of Euboea, but on evidence which seems insufficient.[3] In Euboea indeed it seems clear that at Oreus the

---

[1] See above, p. 505.

[2] Acarnania, D.S. 17. 3. 3; *Syll.*[3] 259 (refugees at Athens, June 337). Troezen, Lycurg. *In Leocr.* 42; Hyp. 4 (*In Athenog.*) 29–35 Budé; cf. Roebuck 83. Ambracia, D.S. 17. 3. 3, where a restoration of democracy on Philip's death makes it probable that there had been an overthrow of democracy in 338/7.

[3] Roebuck 83 (Corinth and Megara), and 82 n. 67 (Euboea), relying (for Corinth and Megara) on a literal interpretation of Aelian, *VH* 6. 1, where C. and M. are among the allies

democracy survived for some considerable time after Chaeronea (long enough for a debt of a talent to be repaid to Demosthenes over a period out of the public revenues); and also that the formerly anti-Macedonian leader Callias of Chalcis was still able to exert influence there in this same period.[1] An expulsion of Callias may have been inferred too easily, from the grant of Athenian citizenship which had been made to him by the year 330. But Aeschines at that time spoke of the grant as of a recent one ('whom Demosthenes now for money dares to propose for enrolment as citizens', 3. 85), and the fact that shortly before 330 he was on good terms with Olympias speaks strongly against his ever having been a victim of Macedonian reprisals.[2] In any case if he was expelled it was not by or through Philip in 338, and his survival then represents a rather notable instance of *laissez-faire* on Philip's part. In Achaea, too, almost certainly there was no change after Chaeronea in the democratic governments which had brought the League into the Greek alliance, and which had further reason for hostility in the loss of Naupactus, awarded by Philip to the Aetolians now as he had promised.[3]

There is certainly not enough evidence here to support a view that Philip put on pressure systematically to ensure friendly governments in all the states that had fought against him. It seems right to think that pressures originated inside the states themselves, and occasionally, where a discredited regime was insecure, resulted in a political revolution by which a group favourable to Philip came to power. In states where it never came to a change of constitution, a change of faces among the leading politicians is to be expected, as leaders discredited by defeat took back seats and the *makedonizontes* came into their own. And in the states which had been neutral in the war or had fought as allies of Philip, the pressures resulting from defeat will not have operated at all, but only the more general incentives to conform and to co-operate with the winners.

said to have 'surrendered' to Philip after Chaeronea (on which however, see above, p. 604). Since there is evidence that the first reaction at Corinth was to prepare to defend the city (above, p. 604 n. 4), Roebuck infers that the 'surrender' came as a result of a change of government. But if, as I have suggested above, Aelian's reported 'surrenders' represent an over-simplification, I cannot think of them as sound support for inferring changes of government. *Si vis pacem para bellum* is an elementary axiom, and especially for the defeated. But when the Corinthians learned that Boeotia and Athens were making peace, they had really no option but to do the same, even when Philip's terms included the garrison.

[1] Aeschin. 3. 103–5.

[2] Hyp. 5 (*In Demosth.*) 20 Budé. Aeschines' (3. 87) reference to Callias' brother Taurosthenes is taken most naturally, certainly, to imply that T. was resident in Athens in 330, though it still makes good sense as referring to a well-known visiting politician—ὅ τ' ἀδελφὸς αὐτοῦ Ταυροσθένης, ὁ νυνὶ πάντας δεξιούμενος καὶ προσγελῶν . . . Roebuck 82, followed Schaefer (3². 195 n. 5) in believing that Callias was expelled from Chalcis in 338; but Berve showed a prudent caution on this (2 no. 399).

[3] [D.] 17. 10; Str. 9. 427; Theopomp. *FGrH* 115 F 235. (See above, p. 509.)

About federations, and Philip's attitude towards them, the evidence seems unequivocal. (The Phocians in 346 are a special case, clearly, and to take account of it in the present context would be misleading.) The continuance of the Boeotian League after 338 is certain, and one can see the local reasons which recommended it.[1] But the continuance of the Achaean League certainly, and of the Euboean League also, both of them members of the defeated Greek alliance, suggests strongly that Philip was not on the look-out for opportunities to break up federations, and probably had no objection to them at all on general grounds.[2] What he objected to was a federation which was dangerous in terms of military power, as Boeotia could be dangerous when it was dominated by Thebes. But there is no sign at all that presently the 'autonomy clause' of the League of Corinth (below, p. 625) was ever interpreted by Philip or anybody else in any way remotely resembling the Spartan interpretation of the corresponding autonomy clause of the Peace of Antalcidas, as a means of breaking up federations which were hostile or potentially so. Relevant here, one must think, is the difference in the scale of power, as between Sparta then and Macedonia now. Philip could afford to let the Greeks please themselves about federations, because with one exception even the strongest of them represented no danger to him. He only drew the line at Thebes: a federation dominated by Thebes would not do. Whether, as has been inferred, he had a positive preference for federations, as a stabilising factor in Greece or as a creative political expedient, seems much more doubtful.[3]

The individual treaties of peace with the cities which had fought against him were made with little delay, it seems, in the weeks after Chaeronea. The Pythian Festival was held, and in the autumn the *naopoioi* met at Delphi, including representatives of most of the states aligned against Philip in the war, their presence a sign that the peace was restored.[4] The time was drawing near when all the Greek states might be invited to assemble in conference and hear plans for the future. But there was still one important area of Greece where Philip needed to be surer of support than he could feel as yet—the Peloponnese.

[1] Above, p. 611 and n. 3.
[2] Achaea, Hyperid. 5. 18; Euboea, Aeschin. 3. 103–5 (see above, pp. 613 f.), where I take the ability of Callias of Chalcis to influence policy in Oreus as proof that the federal state continued to exist after Chaeronea. Roebuck 82 and n. 65 concluded rightly that this League did survive, on general grounds and because there is no evidence for its dissolution (*contra*, Wüst 174).
That the Leagues of Aetolia (Philip's ally in the war) and Arcadia (a neutral) continued, goes without saying, and is attested.
[3] Inference by (e.g.) Roebuck 90 and 82 n. 65.
[4] P. Cloché, 'Les Naopes de Delphes et la politique hellénique de 356 à 327 av. J.-C.', *BCH* 40 (1916), especially 119 ff.

No Peloponnesian state had fought with him in the war. The Isthmus states and others of the northern Peloponnese had joined the Greek alliance against him, and those states which had entered into alliance with him earlier had remained neutral. So, too, had Sparta, that unfriendly neighbour of his friends and allies in Arcadia and Messenia, Argos and Elis, all of whom had territorial claims still against her. To appear in the Peloponnese as a champion, to supply the leadership which the Boeotians had been able to offer on occasion in the past, this followed among the natural consequences of Chaeronea.

According to tradition favourable to Philip, it was by invitation that he moved into the Peloponnese in the late autumn of 338.[1] There is no need to doubt this, for he had good friends among the politicians of Argos, Arcadia, and Messenia, and those who had worked against them earlier could not work against them now.[2] Presumably he allowed it to be known that he was prepared to rectify legitimate grievances against Sparta. At Argos he was received with acclaim, and doubtless in Arcadia too.[3] Argos and Messene, Megalopolis and Tegea, all had territorial claims to press, for the Laconian frontiers in all these quarters were drawn still very favourably to Sparta. The exact course of the diplomatic exchanges which led up to a state of war with Sparta would certainly be interesting if we could know them. But our evidence consists only of the allusions of Polybius (pro-Macedonian in their contexts); the well-known poem of Isyllus (pro-Spartan) inscribed on a big *stele* in the Asclepieum at Epidaurus; and a small handful of 'Spartan sayings' linked to this occasion, some more reliably some less so.[4] The result is obscurity of the most profound, as to how, in detail, Philip conducted this offensive which began with diplomacy and ended in military action. That it did come to war, an invasion of Spartan territory and laying it waste, is certain.[5] But the anecdotes which report or imply negotiations, including one story of a top-level meeting *à deux* of Philip and the Spartan king Agis, suggest that Philip's intention was to achieve the objectives without war, by presenting demands on Sparta which the Spartans would agree to concede because they had not the means to resist.[6] The version

[1] Plb. 9. 33. 8 f. (speech of Lyciscus at Sparta in 210).

[2] For these politicians, D. 18. 295; Plb. 18. 14.

[3] Plu. *Mor.* 760 A–B (Argos). In Arcadia his visitation was commemorated in the place-name Philip's Camp at Nestane near Mantinea and a spring there called Philippion (Paus. 8. 7. 4).

[4] The attribution of two of the 'Sayings' to Archidamus, at a date (after Chaeronea) when he was in Italy (and probably dead by now), does not necessarily discredit the circumstances which gave rise to them (Plu. *Mor.* 218 E, F).

[5] *IG* iv². 1. 58 f.; Plb. 9. 28. 6 f.; 33. 8; Paus. 3. 24. 6; 5. 4. 9; 7. 10. 3; Plu. *Mor.* 235 B, 53; Stobaeus, *Flor.* 7. 59.

[6] The remark of Agis deserves to be authentic, and perhaps may be so. Plu. *Mor.* 216 B 16, 'When Philip said "What! Have you come all alone?" "Yes", said Agis, "just like you".' ("τί τοῦτο; μόνος ἥκεις;" "καὶ γὰρ πρὸς ἕνα.") Plu. *Mor.* 219 F; 235 A, 53; Stobaeus, *Flor.*

of Isyllus, that he intended to overthrow the Spartan monarchy, cannot possibly be true—because there was nothing to stop his doing it if he really had intended that. (And in what sense Asclepius could be thought of as having 'saved' Sparta in this crisis, as Isyllus celebrates it, is wholly obscure.[1]) The demands on Sparta were territorial, and probably only territorial.[2] The Spartans were expected to give way to them; but they refused, even though a refusal was not really feasible for them.[3] Their territory was invaded by Philip and his troops, with the Peloponnesian allies in support.[4] Once again the great mystery of Sparta was enacted here and now: we hear of no rising of helots, *perioikoi*, or 'inferiors' of any description. The Lacedaemonians stood ready to die for their country; but Philip did not require it of them. He occupied, with his allies, those frontier districts which had given the Spartans their easy access to central and western Peloponnese, detaching them now from Sparta, and 'restoring' them to their claimants, to Argos Thyreatis and the eastern Cynuria, to Tegea Sciritis and Caryae, to Megalopolis Belbinatis, to Messene Denthaliatis and South-east Messenia on the Gulf of Kalamata.[5]

The frontiers of the Dorian states were a matter of ancient history reaching back into mythology, the original division of the Peloponnese among the sons of Heracles. The claims and the counter-claims had passed from generation to generation; but recent studies had been made of them by (among others) Aristotle; and his *Dikaiomata* included the material on which decision of these and other Greek frontier problems could be based.[6] The decisions now were Philip's.[7] They were recognized

---

7. 59 have the anecdotes which imply demands on Sparta by Philip. For further discussion, Roebuck 87 n. 104.

[1] *IG* iv². 1. 57 ff., 68 ff., 74 ff. On Isyllus in general, U. v. Wilamowitz-Moellendorff, *Philolog. Untersuchungen* (Berlin, 1886); R. Herzog, *Die Wunderheilungen von Epidaurus* 41 ff. (*Philologus* Suppl. 22. 3, 1931).

[2] This is to be inferred from the fact that the territorial changes are the only known results of the invasion. It is probably right to connect (so Roebuck 87) an anecdote of King Agis with the territorial demands (Plu. *Mor.* 216 A 14), 'Philip will make Greece inaccessible to us' (λέγοντος δέ τινος ὅτι Φίλιππος αὐτοῖς ἀνεπίβατον τὴν Ἑλλάδα ποιήσει . . .).

[3] Plu. *Mor.* 235 A, B 53: the anecdote of Eudamidas (220 F 4) deciding against war with Macedonia though the citizens were in favour of it, which is placed here by Roebuck 87 n. 106, seems to require really that Eudamidas was king at the time (i.e. *post* 330).

[4] Oddly, only the Eleans are recorded as taking the field (Paus. 5. 4. 9), the only one of these allies who is not recorded as getting some territory now from Sparta. That the other allies marched too cannot be in doubt.

[5] Plb. 9. 28. 7 (general). For Argos, Paus. 8. 35. 4; Liv. 38. 34. 3; Theopomp. F 238. Aristot. fr. 611 (Rose) = *Vita Marciana* 4, καὶ τὰ γεγραμμένα αὐτῷ Δικαιώματα Ἑλληνίδων πόλεων ἐξ ὧν Φίλιππος τὰς φιλονεικίας τῶν Ἑλλήνων διέλυσεν, ὡς μεγαλοφρονῆσαί ποτε καὶ εἰπεῖν Ὥρισα γῆν Πέλοπος. γέγραπται δ' αὐτῷ καὶ ἡ τῶν πολιτειῶν ἱστορία ὕστερον. Cf. Ingemar Düring, *Aristotle in the Ancient Biographical Tradition* (Göteborg, 1957) 97 and 107.

[6] N. 5 supra. Roebuck 92; Momigliano, *FM* 133 f. (n. 2).

[7] The speaker at Plb. 9. 26. 7 (Chlaineas) makes Philip responsible. His opponent, Lyciscus (9. 33. 11 f.) denies this, and gives the responsibility to the 'court of all the Greeks'

by Sparta in the sense that the Spartans from now on respected the new frontiers because they had no choice. Probably they were forced now to swear to a treaty accepting them, as the alternative to being wiped out.[1] But this was rough and ready work really, campaign law; and Philip judged that something more seemly was needed if these new frontier-labels were to stick. A congress of all the Greeks should recognize formally this new partition of the Peloponnese by the new Heraclid.[2]

Philip's presence in the Peloponnese at the end of this year 338, and his action against Sparta, were a demonstration that his power now did not stop short at the Isthmus but was capable of dominating all Greece. Inside the Peloponnese itself he went to the heart of things, Sparta and the attitudes to Sparta of her neighbours. By the territorial changes to Sparta's disadvantage he strengthened Argos, Arcadia, and Messene, no one of whom was in a position to develop a hegemony in the Peloponnese as a whole.[3] Nor was Sparta herself utterly or permanently crippled, as the event was to show. Philip's treatment of Sparta is among the most entertaining of his political essays. He invaded Laconia at a time when he was on the point of inviting all the Greeks to join in an organization of states under his own leadership (below, pp. 624 ff.). But Sparta, when the time came, was not required to join; this is clear.[4] To allow this anomaly seems to show in Philip (besides a pleasing indifference to uniformity for its own sake) a just political realism, for Sparta after the recent treatment could never have joined willingly, and would have been of all his Greek collaborators the most untrustworthy. Moreover the leaving of Sparta in isolation was calculated to be salutary in its effects on the Peloponnesians her neighbours. His own prestige in the Peloponnese stood high.[5] Argos, Arcadia, and Messene had good and solid cause for satisfaction with him as their ally and champion. But so, he might reflect, had had Olynthus and the Chalcidians in 356. This is where Sparta

which Philip established. But no such court existed until what we call the 'League of Corinth' had been formed (below). It seems probable that the decisions were taken by Philip on the spot and immediately, and that they were presented later to the 'court of all the Greeks' to be publicized, confirmed, and in some sense guaranteed there.

[1] I say this merely because it seems unlikely that Philip would have withdrawn from Laconia without making the Spartans swear to a treaty. It was an elementary precaution. Justin 9. 5. 3 does not contradict this, in my opinion ('Soli Lacedaemonii et regem et leges contempserunt, servitutem non pacem rati, quae non ipsis civitatibus conveniret, sed a victore ferretur'). Cf. Hampl, *GS* 49 ff.; Treves, loc. cit. 105.

[2] Plb. 9. 33. 12; 5. 10. 1 ff. I agree with Treves (loc. cit., p. 105) that this Polybian version is unreliable in its implication that Sparta agreed (under compulsion) to accept the decision of the Greeks, and still more that the governing decision was not Philip's but that of κοινὸν ἐκ πάντων τῶν Ἑλλήνων . . . κριτήριον.

[3] By 'Arcadia' here and elsewhere, I mean the Arcadian League, which in my view had reunited (probably in 361) and comprised now all or most of the Arcadian cities.

[4] Sparta was compelled to join finally by Alexander in 331; Curtius Rufus 7. 4. 39.

[5] For his statue at Elis, Paus. 6. 11. 1; *stoa* at Megalopolis, id. 7. 30. 6; 36. 1; cf. Plb. 18. 14 for the Megalopolitan favourable view of Philip.

could come in useful. While Sparta survived, she took first place in the attentions of Argos, Arcadia, and Messene, and she concentrated their minds wonderfully. A risk, no doubt, to leave Sparta free and embittered; ready to work with Persia, no doubt, in the coming Persian war. But a risk evidently which he preferred to take, following the instinct which told him that most of the Greeks would co-operate with him best if they had something on their minds, something to suggest to them that he and they might be necessary to each other still.

In these ways the one-time leaders of Greece were disabled, now, from becoming leaders again. The garrison at Thebes, the ring of anti-Spartans round Sparta, reduced the two genuinely military powers to impotence. Athens, genuinely a great power still by sea, presented no military threat in Greece, and on her record of recent years seemed most unlikely to be able to organize others so as to threaten Philip's hold. The Athenian navy itself presumably could have been destroyed after Chaeronea. If Philip had been implacable and had put Athens under siege, the navy could have been among the first victims of an unconditional surrender. The conclusion is unavoidable that he wanted the Athenian navy to survive, and the presumption must be that he recognized his own need of it, for a war against Persia.

This would seem, indeed, the overriding reason for his whole policy towards Athens. Troublesome, intransigent, unreliable, tedious—all this and more the Athenians had shown themselves in their attitudes to him. But whether they liked it or not, and whether he liked them or not, they had got to take their part in the Greek fleet which would be needed to deal with the Persian naval effort and counter-attack which could be expected. Reason enough for hoping to keep the Athenians sweet, by the display of magnanimity after the jolt of defeat. Other reasons too have been suggested: the importance to the Macedonian economy of Athens as the centre of commercial enterprise: the veneration for Athens as the centre of the Greek intellectual world.[1] For the first of these, quantitatively there is no way of assessing its importance. The revenues of Macedonia and of cities and kings now subjects or subject-allies of Philip will have been improved by peace and a flourishing trade; and incidentally the Athenian navy provided the best deterrent to piracy, that arch-enemy of prosperity through trade. Yet if Athens had been destroyed or crippled, it is hard to believe that her place as the centre of commercial enterprise would not have been filled in a few years by Corinth, Rhodes, and other maritime cities. The trade of the Aegean generally speaking was supplying its inhabitants with things that were necessities, and if Athenians had become unable to provide the shipping and the capital, it seems unlikely that the whole system would thereupon

[1] So, e.g., Roebuck 80 f.; Wüst 169 f.

have collapsed. It would have faltered, then readjusted itself and resumed, as other Greeks stepped in to promote it. It seems doubtful if trade can have influenced Philip much, if at all, in the framing of his foreign policy in general or his favourable treatment of Athens in particular.

And Athens as the intellectual capital of the Greek world? One has seen that Philip was not exactly a philistine. Certainly there is no evidence of his personal devotion to any area of literature or the arts that can be compared (for example) to Alexander's famous love of Homer. But there is no need, either, to dismiss his known connection with literary figures as purely utilitarian on both sides. Orators, historians, actors, philosophers addressed themselves to him. Were they all in it simply for the money? Was his time (and money) spent on them merely for the prestige or the propaganda? The men themselves are shadowy figures for us, mostly, one or two of them (whose personality can still make some impression) somewhat unpleasing.[1] The greatest mind of the day, however, and one which gives an impression of suffering neither fools nor knaves gladly, was able evidently to put up with Philip. Aristotle did not absolutely need to settle in Macedonia so far as we know, though to be sure there was a family connection which favoured it. When he got there he stayed much longer than he need have done had he found it uncongenial. Probably Aristotle found Philip sufficiently serious (*spoudaios*) to be worth while, and he did not leave Macedonia for Athens while Philip was alive. Theophrastus was with him in Macedonia in these years.[2]

Whether Aristotle thought of Athens as his intellectual and spiritual home, we have no means of knowing, still less whether Philip was captivated by it in this way, or in any way. One thing however suggests that he was not. To talk with men who had talked with Plato, to tread where Socrates, Sophocles, Thucydides had trod, to see the gleaming columns of the age of Pericles, these are wishes which even an idle curiosity might have indulged. Philip, however, did not bother to visit Athens, ever. He was a busy man, a king. But kings can find time for the things that are near their hearts. Philip, one must think, had never succumbed to the spell of the Athenian past. The present and the future were enough. One can see good political and diplomatic reasons for not visiting Athens at the time when the peace treaty was made (338) or near it. But at some later occasion those same feelings of delicacy might have been overcome in some way that paid Athens a compliment, it might be thought, at some great day of the Dionysia (for example), when the king might have stayed on to address the Assembly after the holiday

[1] I think especially of Speusippus and probably Callisthenes and Theopompus.
[2] See Appendix 6, p. 720.

was over. But Philip never came, for whatever reasons. Perhaps he could not be sure of his reception, and preferred not to risk a fiasco or worse.

Whether this failure to pay homage to the Athens revered by the literate of many generations was based on political tact or (more likely) on lack of inclination, the amount of harm that it did, to Philip himself or to anybody, was probably small or none. The Athenians themselves did not think very much of Aristotle, or Speusippus, or Isocrates, who were none of them good democrats anyway. In political terms the men of consequence now were Phocion and Demades, men who had decided that they could 'makedonize' now without disgrace, and who needed to be able to appear before the *demos* still and command a hearing, and still to command the reluctant respect of the irreconcilables, of Demosthenes and Lycurgus if not of Hyperides. This most of all is what the separate treaty with Athens of 338 was designed to bring about. Peace without dishonour was the setting in which the Athenians, guided by their wiser counsellors, might salvage their pride, turn away from acts or thoughts of disloyalty, and lend their necessary support on the element which was truly their own, the sea, in its Aegean and eastern waters.

Finally, in this time when it was a question of preparing and mobilizing Greek opinion to cope with a new era, it may be right to count the Delphic Amphictyony, too, among Philip's assets; but it would be unwise to overrate it, and to see the hand of Philip in everything done at Delphi is probably mistaken. The risks are well illustrated by the evidence about the new board of Treasurers (*tamiai*) created by the Amphictyons at Delphi in autumn 337.[1] The Thessalians Thrasydaeus and Daochus, the hieromnemons who appear in the text of the decree (by Bourguet's restoration, line 2) are easily seen as stooges of Philip, who may in truth have initiated this innovation himself, as Bourguet tentatively suggested.[2] But if he did, it is not easy to see high-level political or other reasons for it that are convincing. The reasons seem likely to be merely administrative, giving a tighter and more responsible control in a period of greater activity. This was a matter of running Delphi (and Anthela), and getting the temple rebuilt. Since 366 the financial administration of Delphi had been in the hands of the board of *naopoioi*, responsible to the Council of Amphictyons itself (the hieromnemons). The *naopoioi* were numerous, supplied by subscriber-states, fewer than half of which were member states of the Amphictyony. The new treasurers, corresponding exactly to the hieromnemons themselves in their number and their places of origin, did not supersede the *naopoioi*, but controlled them now. One can see

---

[1] *Syll.*³ 249 A. For the date, P. de la Coste-Messelière, *BCH* 73 (1949) 201 ff., esp. 235–43.

[2] E. Bourguet, *L'Administration financière du sanctuaire pythique* (Paris, 1905) 110 ff.; cf. P. Cloché, *BCH* 40 (1916) 119–28; 44 (1920) 317 ff.

'politics' in this (the Treasurers being all from member-states, a closer corporation); but it cannot have been 'politics' that really mattered to anybody deeply, because the change was only one of detail not of principle. The final control, before the change and after it, was always with the hieromnemons.[1]

For the wider issues too, Delphi with its panhellenic gatherings is apt to give us perhaps a cosy feeling about the Greeks that might be misleading. In reality there was something equivocal in the whole ethnic set-up of the Amphictyons, their majority so blatantly made up of Macedonian 'clients' (above, p. 451). Moreover their time-serving performance in the Amphissa dispute in 339 presumably was recognized by most of Greece as only just not disreputable.[2] These toadies could be the framers and fixers again one day, as they had been then; and this thought will have set limits on their value as genuine promoters of reconciliation. It may even seem that a *hegemon* of true political tact and sensitivity might reckon that the best thing that he could do with the Amphictyony at this juncture was to forget about it, and hope that everyone else would do the same.

For this reason the well-known issue from Delphi of the coinage bearing the inscription ΑΜΦΙΚΤΙΟΝΩΝ should be interpreted, probably, with some reserve.[3] The issue, which began in the autumn of 336 a few weeks after Philip's death, certainly can be accepted as something that he must have known about and authorized; but whether it can be seen as any part of his own propaganda seems more doubtful. It was quite a modest affair anyway, lasting only about two years, and amounting to no more than 200 talents in total; its object, to provide out of the miscellaneous subscriptions of the Greeks in coins of various standards and denominations, a silver currency from which to meet the expenses of rebuilding the temple at Delphi.[4] The point has been made that these coins, unlike the normal Delphic issues, are fairly high denominations, which ought to mean that they were not intended primarily for local building workers or small people on the spot, but for bigger-scale finance dealing with contractors or merchants supplying materials in bulk.[5] They would tend to have a wider circulation, through the hands of more important people. But what exactly were they supposed to be saying to these people? Apollo at the *omphalos*, Demeter at Anthela, the divine pair of

---

[1] On this see Sordi, *Naopes* 54 ff.

[2] Demosthenes would not agree to the Delphic oracle being consulted, reckoning the Pythia a philippizer; Aeschin. 3. 130 and schol.; Plu. *Dem.* 19. 1; 20. 1. Parke and Wormell 1. 237; 2 no. 265.

[3] On the date, see p. 595 n. 4 above. For interpretation, E. J. P. Raven, 'The Amphictyonic coinage of Delphi, 336–4 B.C.', *NC* 65. 10 (1950) 1 ff.; Perlman, 'Coins' 57 ff.

[4] Raven. art. cit. 9.

[5] Perlman, 'Coins' 60. Of the twenty-three surviving coins twenty are staters. The discovery of one small hoard could change this picture completely, of course.

the obverses and reverses, were unimpeachably in place here; but they were not in any sense news. Only the legend was new, the grander 'Amphictyons' for the customary 'Delphians'. And of course the fund itself was something, the fund which contained now (say) 200 talents for this purpose; for though it might be chickenfeed to the Great King, and though Philip would spend 200 talents several times in a single year, to an association of Greek states this was real money, even something perhaps to be a little grand about. As a political message, the name Amphictyons was equivocal in the ways already suggested; and the more sophisticated the addressee, the less liable to be receptive of suggestions that Amphictyons were different now from what they always had been. But at least their fund was all right, and their money was good (while it lasted), and it may be on this prosaic level that the legend on the coins is to be read, like the small flourish on some signature that signs a bill.[1]

2. The 'League of Corinth'

Philip's 'League of Corinth', as it is most often called, has been the subject of closer study than any other topic of his life and times. History has gained, naturally, from the devotion, learning, penetration, and judgement of the scholars and historians who have contributed.[2] It has gained most, undoubtedly, from those who came to it with the widest areas of vision, understanding best the whole record of Greek institutions and inter-state relations, the Greek gropings towards Panhellenism, the whole background, social and economic, intellectual and moral, of fourth-century Greece. Yet, surprisingly perhaps, there may be something still to be said. For what has been rare has been the vision that saw this phenomenon not as a piece of Greek history merely, but as Macedonian history too. The battle of Chaeronea had not changed Philip from being a Macedonian king, and to forget about Macedonia now is like explaining the Book of Genesis without bothering about God.

History has needed here its own *Makedonizontes*. The 'pure-Greek' historian with his accumulated preoccupations, especially if he has become excited in some way about the Greek city in development or in decline, can make some strange remarks about the League of Corinth

---

[1] Perlman ('Coins') saw the legend 'Amphictyons' as reminiscent of the Greek federal coinages (Euboeans, Chalcidians, Boeotians, etc.), and suggestive perhaps of free institutions inside a corporation; but I am not altogether persuaded that the phoney freedom of this time was really a propaganda asset at all. It will be agreed, of course, that if these coins were designed to give a message to the Greeks, Philip did well to allow no hint of his own hegemony to appear on them.

[2] Cf. Schmitt, *Staatsv.* 3, no. 403 for an excellent summary (pp. 12–14), and bibliography (14), as well as the collected *Testimonia* (4 ff.). Of the latter, the important *IG* ɪɪ/ɪɪɪ². 236 (= *Syll.*³ 1. 260 = Tod. 177) is perhaps most easily accessible to most English readers as Tod 177, and I therefore continue to refer to it thus.

without even being aware that he has propounded a paradox. Thus, 'an instrument for leadership and the attempted unification of Greece by Macedonian kings'. Or 'When that was done, the organization had advanced far along the road towards federation and, given time and opportunity, might well have reached the goal.' But whose goal? Not Philip's and Alexander's, whose 'organization' was in question here. And why would Macedonian kings try to 'unify' Greece, when everything they had seen for themselves, or read, or heard, told them unmistakably that if Greece ever *were* unified it would be no place any more for Macedonian kings? One can imagine the great man's amused reply—"*Καθ' ἓν οἱ Ἕλληνες; οὐ μὰ Δία, ἀλλὰ καθ' ἕνα ἕκαστον.*" ('The Greeks all together? Not likely! Altogether separately, you mean.')

Larsen, the author of the two remarks just quoted about unification and about federation,[1] has been signally successful in interpreting the League in a way which illuminates its interest for the student of what may be called the collective institutions of the Greeks. He notices, too, as 'disastrous in the long run . . . the absorption of the kings in larger problems'.[2] This point has always been taken, in so far as its reference is to Alexander. But in Philip too, it is unreasonable to look for the motives and behaviour of a man primarily concerned with the Greeks and their problems for their own sake. His formation of the League was linked very closely in time with the publication of his plans for a Persian war.[3] Isocrates in 346 had known that a precondition of invading Asia was to be able to count on a strict neutrality of the Greeks, and preferably on their active co-operation:[4] and Philip was at least as good a strategist as Isocrates. It is natural now to think of the League of Corinth as primarily an item in his strategy, and a means to his end. If it was also an interesting and promising experiment in politics or government, this comes in the nature of a bonus, for the Greeks then and for us now. It reflects, too, on Philip's ability to produce something serviceable (notable, even?) as a *parergon*, when much of his mind was on something (to him) more important.

Late in the year (338) the cities and the *ethne* received their invitations to the great peace conference at Corinth, the first of its kind for twenty-four years, and doubtless the greatest in its size and scope that Greece had seen. A new *koine eirene* was to be established. The cities and the *ethne* were invited now to send their delegates to a Council of representatives (*sunedrion*), the powers and functions of which, presumably, cannot

[1] Larsen 47. The interesting article of H. Kelsen, 'Aristotle and Hellenic–Macedonian policy', *Internat. Journ. Ethics* 48 (1937–8) 1–64, (esp. 52–64), is written with a good appreciation of the true context.

[2] Larsen, *RG* 49.

[3] Plu. *Phoc.* 16. 4 is especially important for this. See below, p. 632.

[4] Isoc. 5. 86 ff. Above, p. 456.

have been defined as yet.[1] They are in part implied and summarized in the oath which the cities and the *ethne* swore after the close of the first meeting, where evidently a detailed treaty was drawn up. In it the *koine eirene* was proclaimed, to include probably all the states of Greece except Sparta,[2] and all the Greek cities of the Aegean except those which were under Persian rule.[3] All were to be free and autonomous, their forms of government of this moment guaranteed against subversion, their territory guaranteed against aggression.[4] All bound themselves by oath to join in military action against any breaker of this Peace in the future.[5]

All this was unexceptionable; the more so because much of it was not unfamiliar. These were the principles which had underlain the *koine eirene* treaties of the 370s and 360s, the treaties which had never been kept for very long.[6] Those failures (if it is right to call them that) had not discredited the whole idea of *koine eirene* for ever. The Athenians had been prepared to revert to it in 346 when it suited them, and again in 344/3 (above, pp. 340 and 490). Philip offered it now afresh, and with it some innovations written in to this treaty with the object of making it effective and lasting. In the first place the oath of the Greeks included a clause naming Philip as the opposite party with whom this contract was being made, and also an undertaking not to subvert the kingdom of Philip and his descendants.[7] This Peace was designed to last, evidently, sponsored by kings of Macedonia for the foreseeable future. Secondly, it was supported by institutions. The new *sunedrion* is named in the oath as something that will always be there, able at any time to make decisions if the Peace should be endangered.[8] Likewise 'the Hegemon' will always

---

[1] Plu. *Phoc.* 16. 4. The distribution of votes among the states cannot have been fixed yet, either, as Larsen points out (*RG* 49).

[2] Arr. *An.* 1. 16. 7; Just. 9. 5. 3.

[3] Melos and Cimolos presumably were members presently when their dispute reached the *sunedrion* for adjudication (Tod 2. 179): Chios almost certainly a member in 332 (though this has been contested), when Chiot exiles were to be subject to the *sunedrion*'s jurisdiction (Tod, 192, 11–16).

As to the cities under Persian rule, I know of no ancient evidence either that they were or were not eligible to be included in this Peace now. But we can be certain in effect that they were not invited to join, because if they had been, this would have been a clear *casus belli*, which could not have failed to appear somewhere at one of the relevant occasions in the surviving accounts of the actual beginning of the war in 336 or (more certain still) in 334. Their relationship to the 'League of Corinth' in and after 334 when they were liberated will be discussed later (in Volume III).

[4] Tod 177, 5–15; [D.] 17. 8, 10, 15 f. That this speech Περὶ τῶν συνθηκῶν τῶν πρὸς Ἀλέξανδρον may be used safely as evidence for the content of Philip's treaty is commonly agreed: cf. e.g. Ryder, *KE* 150 f.

[5] Tod 177, 18 ff.

[6] Cf. Ryder, *KE* chs. 4 and 5; Appendices 2, 3, 4, 7, and 8.

[7] Tod 177, 5 f., 11 f. Presumably Philip himself took a reciprocal oath, as is implied in the alleged breaches by Alexander or his representatives of this or that clause of the treaty. [D.] 17. 4, 6, 10, 16, 19, 26.

[8] Cf. D.S. 17. 4. 9 οἱ συνεδρεύειν εἰωθότες (336).

be there. Philip is not named in the oath as the Hegemon. It was not necessary to name him.[1]

The official title of the sponsor of this Peace was *hegemon*, beyond doubt.[2] The word has been associated hitherto with alliances, and can be thought to support a view that this organization is another alliance. But the official description of the Greek states whom we describe most conveniently as 'members of the League' was 'those who participate in the *koine eirene*' (οἱ μετέχοντες τῆς κοινῆς εἰρήνης) or some other equivalent periphrasis.[3] It is this that makes it certain that 'the League' (as we call it) in its inception was not an alliance or symmachy comparable with Sparta's Peloponnesian League, the Delian League of Athens, or the Second Athenian Confederacy.[4] This fact may have some importance which is not purely academic. The controversy about it among modern writers stems from our lack of a truly satisfactory record in any surviving ancient writer of the details of how the *koine eirene* came into being, and how, within a very short time after (time to be measured in weeks rather than in months), these same Greeks who had just joined the organization for preserving the *koine eirene* (which we call the 'League of Corinth') were organized by Philip for the war against Persia which he proclaimed now as his immediate intention.[5]

Diodorus, with an ineptitude remarkable even for him, records how 'the *sunedrion* was summoned' to hear Philip's plans for the Persian war, without having recorded that a *sunedrion* had been created (i.e. that the 'League of Corinth' for *koine eirene* had been formed).[6] Justin gives us an account which makes sense, but which is so brief and 'telescoped' that it can be interpreted as a record of the formation of an offensive and defensive alliance, an old-style symmachy indeed. Thus,

ibi [sc. at Corinth] pacis legem universam Graeciae pro meritis singularum civitatum statuit, consiliumque omnium veluti unum senatum ex omnibus legit ... Auxilia deinde singularum civitatum describuntur, sive adiuvandus ea manu rex oppugnante aliquo foret seu duce illo bellum inferendum. Neque enim dubium erat imperium Persarum his apparatibus peti.[7]

---

[1] He had probably been named as *hegemon* in one of the (lost) clauses of the treaty which preceded the oath which survives. The view of Heuss (*Hermes* 73 (1938) 171 ff.) that because he was not named as Hegemon in the oath, he was not *hegemon* of the Peace at all, is not convincing.

[2] For a full discussion, Bengtson, *Strategie* 1². 3 ff.; Ryder, *KE* 154 f.

[3] e.g. Tod 192, 11 ff., [D.] 17. 6, 10, 15, 16, 30.

[4] This was seen by Schwahn, Hampl, and Heuss in the 1930s, and seems to me to be clearly established now afresh by Ryder (*KE* 150 ff.), who cites the earlier bibliography.

[5] Plu. *Phoc.* 16. 4 is the important text which, by a lucky chance, preserves for us the close timing of this sequence of events.

[6] D.S. 16. 89. 3. This prompted Wilcken and others to postulate the loss of a sizeable piece of Diodorus' text, which is supposed to have fallen out of its place between 89. 2 and 89. 3 of our text as it stands. It is charitable to think this; but not necessary.

[7] Just. 9. 5. 2 ff.

In the first sentence the *koine eirene* is recorded (*pacis legem universam*), and the forming of the *sunedrion* (*consilium* etc.). This describes a meeting which corresponds exactly to the meeting to which Plutarch alluded in the *Phocion* (16. 4) passage quoted above. It ought to be (and no doubt it is) the treaty drafted at this meeting which is summarized in the oath of the Greeks which is preserved (Tod 177). The military obligations (*auxilia*) of Justin's second sentence could perfectly well have been detailed at the same meeting and in the same treaty and without thereby making the treaty *ipso facto* an alliance; because the treaty clearly did contain a clause or clauses providing for military aid to victims of aggression by breakers of the *koine eirene*.[1] But what cannot possibly belong to the same treaty are the occasions for the use of the *auxilia*, if these be interpreted (as seems natural) as Justin's way of recording 'offensive and defensive alliance'. The oath speaks of *koine eirene*, and hypothetical breaches of it: it says nothing of *summachia* in any form.[2] The speech of 330 ([D.] 17, see p. 625 n. 4 above) knows nothing of any *summachia* either. Either Justin or Pompeius Trogus or the Greek source(s) of Trogus must have misunderstood something in the terms of this treaty; and most probably what was misunderstood was the detailed provisions in the text (now lost) that preceded the (surviving) oath, about the Hegemon's rights of requiring an army of the Greeks to be mobilized.[3] If Justin is recording an alliance-treaty here, then he must be disbelieved, unless further evidence can be found in support.

Support was found by Larsen in an inscription (*post* 164) recording, as part of a judgement passed by a special court of law on the ancient territorial dispute between Sparta and Megalopolis, a reference back to previous judgements on the same dispute—'in order that . . . the judgements given previously in ⟨courts of⟩ *the Greeks and allies* may be valid and intact for all time'.[4] It is suggested that the occasion alluded to here was identical with the occasion alluded to by Polybius referring to this same dispute and its settlement by Philip's initiative 'not by violence . . . but by means of the Court of all the Greeks which he had established'.[5]

---

[1] Tod 177, 18 ff.

[2] Contrast the oaths in alliance-treaties, e.g. Tod 111, 23 ff. (Amyntas and Chalcidian League, *c.* 393), Ὅρκος συμμαχίης etc.; Tod 147 (361/0—headed Συμμαχία Ἀθηναίων καὶ Θετταλῶν . . .), 16 and 26 βοηθήσω παντὶ σθένει κατὰ τὸ δυνατόν etc., 42 Τὴν δὲ συμμαχίαν τήνδε ἀναγράψαι etc.; Tod 157, 39 ff. (356).

[3] If the misinterpretation belongs to Justin himself (which seems most probable), it could well have arisen by his compressing into this sentence also some provisions for Philip's mobilizing a Greek army for the Persian war, which would belong properly to his next sentence.

[4] *Syll.*³ 665. 19–20 ἵνα . . . αἵ τ' ἐν τοῖς Ἕλλησιν καὶ συμμάχοις γεγενημέναι πρότερον κρίσεις βέβαιαι καὶ ἀκήρατοι διαμένωσιν εἰς τὸν αἰεὶ χρόνον; cf. Larsen, *RG* 52.

[5] C. Roebuck, *CP* 43 (1948) 91 ff.; Plb. 9. 33 . . . ἀλλὰ κοινὸν ἐκ πάντων τῶν Ἑλλήνων καθίσας κριτήριον. Cf. Liv. 38. 34. 8 'quod agrum restitutum Megalopolitanis dicit ex decreto vetere Achaeorum quod factum erat Philippo Amyntae filio regnante . . .' (where it is

If this is accepted, then 'the Greeks' at this time were 'allies'. But the suggestion is really not acceptable, because this allusion is to 'the previous judgements', in the plural; and it means what it says, because the drafters of this document were quite capable of writing 'judgement' in the singular when they meant that, as we can see when they do write this very thing repeatedly.[1] The drafters were alluding here to all the occasions when this dispute had come to judgement; and of course for a long period much nearer to their own time 'the Greeks' had been the allies of Macedonian kings (the 'Hellenic league' of Antigonus Doson comes especially to mind). This inscription does not require us to believe that 'the Greeks' of Philip's 'League' of 338/7 were 'allies'.

But there was still (and is still) the Persian war to be considered. Justin's summary of the proceedings at Corinth passes from *koine eirene* and *sunedrion* to *auxilia*, and concludes 'For it was clear that the objective of all this preparation (implied by *auxilia*) 'was the Persian empire.' Plutarch's anecdote about Phocion shows the Athenians, on the proposal of Demades, agreeing to 'join in the *koine eirene* and the *sunedrion*' at a moment when they still did not know to what if any military or naval obligations this was committing them. Even Diodorus in his defective account shows by implication that the *sunedrion* was formed first, then on some later occasion it met and 'the Greeks elected Philip supreme commander of Greece' for the Persian war.[2] Though this actual title must be a matter for doubt (see below), this same duality of function, Hegemon of the Greeks (i.e. for the *koine eirene*) and supreme commander of Greece against Persia, is suggested by Diodorus' account of Alexander's succession to these functions after Philip's death: and again the second title is conferred on Alexander by the *sunedrion*, which as Hegemon he had summoned for the purpose.[3]

It may be said, and rightly, that once the Greeks had committed themselves to fighting under Philip's command in his war with Persia, they had become his allies in effect and in reality, whatever their status *de jure* might be. It is a question merely whether, when they elected him commander against Persia, they also contracted a second treaty with him, a treaty of alliance, either an *ad hoc* alliance with Persia named as the objective or an alliance on more general terms. The Greeks (other than mercenaries) who fought with Alexander in Asia are called 'allies' occasionally by Arrian, who also feeds modern controversy by his πρὸ τῆς εἰρήνης τε καὶ τῆς ξυμμαχίας τῆς πρὸς Μακεδόνας γενομένης, where τε καί and the repetition of the article τῆς, it is claimed, denote the *two*

supposed that Livy wrote Achaeorum for Graecorum anachronistically). On the Polybius passage, see above, pp. 617 f.

[1] *Syll.*[3] 2. 665, 15, 16, 23, 42.   [2] Just. 9. 5. 5; Plu. *Phoc.* 16. 4; D.S. 16. 89. 3.
[3] D.S. 17. 4. 1, 2, 6, and especially 9.

treaties governing the status of the Greeks, the *koine eirene* treaty and the alliance treaty.[1] This seems to demand too much exactitude of Arrian, who was not thinking in strict 'constitutional' terms here, as is shown by his reference to 'the Macedonians' instead of to 'Philip'. That he did imply that there was an alliance, whenever it may have been made, is not to be ignored. But much more telling, one would think, is the language used by Alexander's secretariat in the well-known edict relating to Chios, composed while the Persian war was still being fought. The clause relating to certain delinquents who are 'to become exiles from *all the cities which share in the Peace*' should be read alongside a corresponding clause in the Decree of Aristoteles on the formation of the second Athenian Confederacy in 378/7. There, the (hypothetical) delinquents may 'become exiles from all territories controlled by Athens and *the allies*': the words σύμμαχοι and συμμαχία, occur six times in the twenty adjacent lines.[2] In the Chios edict the exiles are to be tried 'in the *sunedrion* of the Greeks', the organ of the League of Corinth. Yet it was this same *sunedrion* which had nominated Alexander to the command against Persia, and had renewed an alliance with him, if any alliance ever existed. It would have been correct (and natural) to refer to 'all the allies' or 'all the cities of the alliance' in this context; but Alexander's secretariat chose to write 'all the cities which share in the Peace'. This seems to me conclusive. Even when Philip was elected to the 'Persian' command (and later Alexander), no treaty of alliance was made.

By the interpretation suggested here, then, Philip made no new treaty with the Greeks which defined their reciprocal obligations relative to the Persian war. No symmachy was created, either temporary and for a limited end, or general and permanent. He merely told the *sunedrion* of his plans, doubtless with all the propaganda and encouragement that seemed appropriate, and the *sunedrion* agreed then that the states should supply whatever quota of their obligations in troops or ships the Hegemon might name. If this view of affairs is right, it will seem improbable that any special title was conferred on Philip on this occasion (or any other) to signify a new or special relationship. As is well known, a Greek tradition did exist presently, accepted by Diodorus and by an anonymous

---

[1] Arr. 3. 24. 5; cf. 1. 9. 9 (operation against Thebes); 24. 3; 3. 19. 5; cf. D.S. 17. 63. 1 (the equivocal παρὰ τῶν συμμαχούντων Ἑλλήνων of Antipater in Greece). Cf. Ryder, *KE* 157 ff. for good discussion of this question, with bibliography.

[2] Tod 2. 192, 14–15 (Chios); 123, 41 ff., esp. 57 ff. In case it should be thought unsound to use the Decree of Aristoteles for this purpose, just because it was concerned with the actual formation of the alliance (and consequently perhaps preoccupied with it in an untypical way), the decree of Hegesippus about Eretria twenty-one years later serves my purpose just as well: Tod 2. 154, 9 ff. ἐὰν δέ τις τοῦ λοιποῦ χρόνου ἐπιστρατεύσῃ ἐπὶ Ἐρετρίαν ἢ ἐπ' ἄλλην τινὰ τῶν συμμαχίδων πόλεων, Ἀθηναίων ἢ τῶν συμμάχων τῶν Ἀθηναίων, θανατὸν αὐτοῦ κατεγνῶσθαι . . . καὶ εἶναι τὰ χρήματα αὐτοῦ ἀγώγιμα ἐξ ἁπασῶν τῶν πόλεων τῶν συμμαχίδων· ἐὰν δέ τις ἀφέληται πόλις, ὀφείλειν τῷ κοινῷ τῷ τῶν συμμάχων.

late chronographer, that the *sunedrion* elected Philip now, and Alexander later, '*strategos autokrator* for the Persian war'.[1] Unfortunately the source of Diodorus here is uncertain, as indeed is the source of Arrian when he uses the title *hegemon* (once *hegemon autokrator*) of Alexander in relation to the Persian war. But for Arrian, it seems, there is some positive reason for thinking that he used in one instance a good source, and consequently his title is to be preferred.[2] Philip was *hegemon*. He had sponsored the *koine eirene* and was in charge of it: in this sense it was not incorrect to call him (as writers did call him, including Diodorus) *hegemon* of Greece or of the Greeks.[3] He was still *hegemon*, and probably nothing more, when, fortified by the vote of the *sunedrion*, he led the Greeks into the Persian war. *Autokrator*, when in this connection it is added to his title (whether *hegemon* or *strategos*) need not be an invention.[4] It could preserve, perhaps, the substance of a vote of the *sunedrion* granting Philip (and Alexander) the full powers of military and diplomatic decision (meaning, decision on the spot without the necessity of referring back to the *sunedrion*), which plainly were necessary (no less) for the commander in Asia. In this case *autokrator* would be neither meaningless nor purely honorific, but would be stating the facts of the case; just as the same word stated similar facts when it was used occasionally of Athenian generals or ambassadors to whom the same powers had been voted by the Assembly at Athens.[5]

---

[1] D.S. 16. 60. 5; 89. 3; 17. 4. 9; *P. Oxy.* 1. 12 col. III. 9 ff. Cf. M. Scheele, Στρατηγὸς Αὐτοκράτωρ (Diss. Leipzig, 1932) 12 ff.; A. Momigliano, *RFIC* 12 (1934) 500; Bengtson, *Strategie* 1². 4 ff. (a good summary, though I disagree with its conclusion).

[2] Arr. 1. 1. 2; 2. 14. 4; 7. 9. 5 (ἡγεμὼν αὐτοκράτωρ). Unfortunately not one of these appearances of ἡγεμών comes in a passage of straight narrative and consequently with a probability that Arrian found the title in Ptolemy: whatever title Ptolemy used in these contexts surely must have been correct. The first reference is to a passage of cursory résumé of acts by which Alexander secured his 'succession' to Philip in Greece in 336, the second to a letter of Alexander, the third to a speech of Alexander. This makes the question of Arrian's sources *a priori* problematical. The letter, as it happens, is a notable 'problem'. L. Pearson (*Historia* 3 (1955) 448 ff., 'The diary and letters of Alexander the Great') thought it certainly 'Ptolemaic'; and I have argued elsewhere that it gives the gist of Alexander's actual letter on the occasion, derived by Arrian presumably from Ptolemy (*PCPhS* 14 (1968) 33 ff., 'The letter of Darius at Arrian 2. 14'). Arrian certainly introduced his own words in one instance even where he purported to be quoting from a letter verbatim (ibid. 33–5). But it would be surprising if he changed a title reported by Ptolemy as part of Alexander's text. To me therefore the appearance of *hegemon* in this letter establishes it pretty firmly as the correct title. But this does depend on being able to believe that the letter in Arrian is Alexander's letter derived via Ptolemy, or something close to that.

The speech (at Opis, Arr. *An.* 7. 9 ff.) is no less of a problem, and few have followed Kornemann (*Alexandergeschichte des K. Ptolemaios* 158 ff.) in seeing Ptolemy as its ultimate source (see Bengtson, *Strategie* 1². 8, for discussion, with bibliography). Of itself certainly it adds no support to *hegemon* as the correct title, which must rely on the letter (above).

[3] D.S. 16. 64. 3; 91. 1; 17. 3. 204; 4. 1–2 and 6. Cf. Ryder, *KE* 155 f.

[4] Bengtson, *Strategie* 1². 6 ff.

[5] e.g. Thuc. 6. 26. 1 (the generals sent to Sicily in 415) cf. 6. 72. 5 (Syracuse); Andoc. 3. 6 (ambassadors 421), 3. 33 f. (392/1); 39 (Sparta), cf. Thuc. 5. 27. 2 (Argos). See further U. Kahrstedt, *Untersuchungen zur Magistratur in Athen* (Stuttgart, 1936) 235.

Hegemon then, or *hegemon autokrator*, he was to lead the Greeks into the Persian war. Was it good logic, it may be asked, or good law, to require the Greek states to join in what was really an attack on the Persian empire, merely as part of their treaty obligations to the *hegemon* of the *koine eirene*? As to the legal question, perhaps it was not very difficult. True, the Great King could not be thought or said to have broken the *koine eirene* or to have done any harm to any of those who were included in it.[1] He could be said, however, to be preventing the Greek cities of Asia from enjoying the autonomy which now had come to be accepted and assumed as the right of all cities of Greece and the Aegean great and small; and in practice, though not in law, this might justify an attack.[2] But all that we are told of propaganda now by Philip through his friends in Greece, is of a war of retribution on the Persians for their crimes against the Greek holy places in 480. This was complimentary to Athens, certainly (whose temples had suffered most). But whether it can have kindled real feeling in Greeks at this date, even in Athenians, seems very doubtful.[3]

The practical considerations no doubt were the most important, and not only for Philip himself. How were they viewed by 'the Greeks'? In what may be called 'government circles' (in the democracies, the orators and the men of affairs; in oligarchies, the men in control), there is unlikely to have been much real enthusiasm for a Persian war, because no Greek city or league or *ethnos* was likely to gain directly from it if it were a success: in political terms it would be the Hegemon who gained. Provinces in Asia, if they were annexed, would swell the power and the revenues of Philip, not of any Greek government. Anti-Macedonians, too, will have seen any weakening of Persia as a dimming of their own prospects of liberation. Meanwhile the war was going to involve the Greeks in some military and naval effort. We have seen already that their

[1] The Persian aid to Perinthus had harmed Philip, no doubt (above, p. 573); but it had helped Perinthus, now a member of the League probably (though we do not know this). The siege of Perinthus, and the occasion for it, was not a fruitful source of either inspiration or legal comfort to Hegemon and League members now. It was best forgotten.

[2] There is no evidence that Philip (or Alexander) did use this as a *casus belli*. We are told however that Alexander's first act when he was in a position to 'liberate' the Greek cities in Asia was to declare them autonomous (Arr. *An.* 1. 18. 1–2 καὶ τὰς μὲν ὀλιγαρχίας πανταχοῦ καταλύειν ἐκέλευσε, δημοκρατίας δὲ ἐγκαθιστάναι, καὶ τοὺς νόμους τοὺς σφῶν ἑκάστοις ἀποδοῦναι, καὶ τοὺς φόρους ἀνεῖναι ὅσους τοῖς βαρβάροις ἀπέφερον).

[3] D.S. 16. 89. 2. It is in this context that the 'Congress Decree' attributed by Plutarch to Pericles (Plu. *Per.* 17), is attributed now by A. B. Bosworth to this propaganda of or for Philip ('The Congress Decree: another hypothesis', *Historia* 20 (1971) 600–16). But as I suggest briefly elsewhere (*Historia*, 27 (1978) 218), Pericles can have meant very little to anybody in 338/7, and Philip's panhellenic congress summoned with propaganda talk about the temples could not have been helped in any way whatever by inventing a tale that Pericles too had talked about these same temples while summoning a panhellenic congress long long ago—and then it never happened because Sparta had spoiled it. Not even Antipater of Magnesia could have thought this worth while (p. 514 above).

oath of the *koine eirene* treaty bound them to supply troops for an army
on occasions when the *sunedrion* and the *hegemon* judged that the Peace
had been broken.[1] At some stage, perhaps at this stage of Philip's communication to the *sunedrion* of his Persian plan (or perhaps earlier), the
extent of these obligations was defined.[2] We are given no details, apart
from Justin's total of 200,000 infantry, 15,000 cavalry; which few have
ever accepted (and rightly). The strength of Alexander's Greek 'allied'
troops in Asia later (except the Thessalians) was surprisingly small,
though the strength of his Greek fleet was not.[3] The only practical method
of assessing the individual states for their military or naval contributions
was to make the assessments proportional to their actual resources, which
means the number and character of their citizen populations.[4] That this
was done may be taken as certain, though the attempts that have been
made to reconstruct the asssessments in detail inevitably have been too
insecurely based to be really satisfactory.[5]

The only insight that we are given into the reaction inside a particular
city to this aspect of the 'League of Corinth', the military or naval
obligations, concerns (predictably) Athens.

When Demades drafted a proposal that Athens should join in the *koine
eirene* and the Greek *sunedrion*, Phocion spoke against their joining before they
knew what Philip would actually require the Greeks to do for him. In the
circumstances Phocion's view was overruled, and presently he found the
Athenians wishing they hadn't joined, because now they had to supply Philip
with triremes and cavalry. 'This is just what I was afraid of when I advised
against it', he said. 'But now since you did agree to join . . .'[6]

Plutarch does not tell us, as it happens, whether the plan for the Persian
war was known as yet to the Athenians or not. With the Athenians,
doubtless, the news of the plan will have made little difference to their
attitude to Philip, which was not quite typical of Greek attitudes in
general. In the history of the next years everything shows the Athenians
willing to wound even when they were afraid to strike. They were not

---

[1] Tod 177, 18 ff.

[2] Just. 9. 5. 4 f.; Plu. *Phoc.* 16. 4; D.S. 16. 89. 3; Tod 183 (fragment, from Athens, of a
treaty or some other arrangement with Alexander, containing details of military administration). Justin implies (see above, p. 626) that the obligations were defined before the Persian
plan was made known officially.

[3] D.S. 17. 17. 4; Arr. *An.* 1. 11. 6; 18. 4. For discussions, Berve 1. 139 ff.; 159 ff.; Schwahn
31 ff.

[4] Larsen, *CP* 20 (1925) 319; cf. Schwahn 4 ff.

[5] In the fragmentary Tod 2. 177, 25 ff., the basis for any reconstructions, the list of names
of states followed by numerals is so defective that there are only three instances in which both
the name and the numeral survive. See especially, Schwahn, op. cit. 2 ff., 16 ff., 22 ff.;
a 'reconstructed' army-and-navy list at 25; W. W. Tarn, *CR* 45 (1931) 88 (critical review
of Schwahn). For a good short summary, Tod, commentary to 177, pp. 230 f. See, further
below, p. 635 n. 8.

[6] Plu. *Phoc.* 16. 4.

reconciled to defeat and its consequences; which made *mnesikakia* into a virtue. In inter-state politics, when the stakes have been high, who wants to be a good loser? Not the ex-*hegemones* of Greece certainly (Athens and Thebes), whatever a Demades or a Phocion or an Isocrates might advise from their different angles. The new *hegemon* need be under no illusions about this (he was not).

In the other states of Greece there need not have been the same intransigence on these grounds. True, there were other grounds, and especially that feeling for a freedom and autonomy that were not words graven on a stone but the realities that enabled free and autonomous communities genuinely to please themselves. But doubtless there were, too, for many of the Greeks some greater or smaller compensations in the new regime. For the smaller states in general, and for states in particular which had suffered in the past from Sparta or Thebes or Athens, there was real advantage in a *koine eirene* sponsored and guaranteed by a *hegemon* of real power. And the Persian War? Even if Greek 'governments' saw no advantages from it for their own people in terms of political power, individual Greeks may well have seen it as offering to some a military career, to more a military livelihood. This was at least the right sort of war, a war in which some cities could be sacked, some countrysides stripped, some prisoners sold or ransomed; some provinces, even, occupied in the end, in which, just as Isocrates had said, new Greek cities could be founded, with farms and estates for the new citizens.[1] Thereafter as a neighbour there would always be a Persia, with her satrapies good for plunder, as the Athenians and their allies had found them in the early years of the Delian Confederacy. Persia, too, was a refuge now, and always would be, for those who had fallen from power, or safety, in revolutions some of them recent; or for that matter for any who decided now or later not to stomach any longer the stink of Macedonians or of those who collaborated with them. The Persian war, for a number of individuals in Greece, was not too bad a proposition, most likely. This fact was to be reflected in the numbers of Greeks who did go to Asia when they had no obligation to go, as mercenaries and volunteers in the armies of both Alexander and of Darius; and still when the war proper was over they went among the reinforcements raised by Alexander's recruiting officers and by his satraps on their own account.[2]

Finally, how important was it that this Peace should be kept, unbroken? The Greek experience, of the 370s and 360s, suggests that the Greeks themselves recognized the advantages of peace in a general way, but easily found reasons why their own special cases could be promoted

[1] Isoc. 5. 120 f.
[2] See e.g. Parke 177 ff., 186 ff.; Griffith, *Mercenaries* 12 ff.; Berve 1. 144 ff.

better by war. This is true most obviously of states with pretensions to
hegemony, but not exclusively of these. Philip now with his superior
power could afford perhaps to be indifferent whether the Greeks were
at peace or at war, so long as they did not combine to make war against
him. But his position as *hegemon* of the Peace involved his own prestige,
and perhaps his popularity with the smaller states; and especially his
projected war against Persia made it really necessary that the Peace
should be kept. A new outbreak of war in Greece could be seen as
Persia's opportunity now, just as it had been in the past. It was with this
in mind, most probably, that those clauses were written in to the *koine
eirene* treaty which were designed to prevent revolutionary outbreaks in
the cities, or the harbouring of exiles who might return to their own
places and overthrow governments there by force.[1] Greek history is full of
such incidents, among the concomitants and often among the origins of
its innumerable wars. Also in the *koine eirene* treaty was a clause designed
to safeguard the free use of the sea: any interference with shipping made
the interferer the 'enemy of all the states that share in the Peace'.[2]
Piracy, or aid to pirates, or any unfair interference with normal use of
narrow waters (such as Bosporus and Hellespont) represented another
fertile source of disputes leading to wars, and fully justified this general
interdiction, with its reminder of the sanctions that lay behind it.

The suggestion that the treaty also limited the right of entry into the
harbour of another state to entry by one warship only, seems impossible
to maintain in the light of the Piraeus incident later described by the
orator of Demosthenes 17.[3] The more natural inference from this
description is that the treaty prohibited *any* entry into harbours by
warships without prior consent.

It remains to consider briefly the institutions of the League of Corinth,
designed to enable it to function through the years—years in which the
hegemon himself was liable to be abroad in Asia for longish periods at
a stretch. One turns back, here, to the inscription recording the oath of
the Greeks (Tod 177), and also to the Epidaurian inscription relating to
the Hellenic League as revived by Demetrius in 302 (*IG* iv². 1. 68).
This League of Demetrius, unlike Philip's 'League of Corinth', was not
formed to promote and preserve a *koine eirene* but to create an alliance
through which the Greeks should take the right side in a great war just

---

[1] [D.] 17. 15–16.
[2] [D.] 17. 19.
[3] [D.] 17. 26 ff. *Contra*, G. Cawkwell, 'A note on Ps. Demosthenes 17. 20', *Phoenix* 15
(1961) 75 f. This limitation may well have been normal practice at this date, as it was in the
fifth century (so Cawkwell, loc. cit., with references).

approaching its climax.¹ It was not intended however that the new League should terminate when the war ended. The arrangements made for the future sessions of its *sunedrion* show that it was to be permanent, and two details of these arrangements which recall known details of corresponding features of Philip's League reinforce the probability, which would be strong in any case on general grounds, that the institutions and procedures of Philip's League formed the basis of the new League's arrangements too.² It has seemed safe to use this inscription as evidence for the 'League of Corinth' except if it suggests something inappropriate to the conditions or circumstances of the earlier occasion.³

The *sunedrion*, the only known deliberative body of the League, meeting normally once a year on the Festival occasions, had the supreme power of decision.⁴ The *hegemon* was its supreme executive officer, with the right also to summon extraordinary meetings at need and doubtless to introduce whatever business he pleased.⁵ Delegates were sent to the *sunedrion* by 'constituencies' comprising cities or *ethne* sometimes individually, sometimes in small groups, the groups consisting of states of modest size who were neighbours. The allocation of the voting power in the *sunedrion* departed from the normal Greek principle of one vote for each state great or small.⁶ Here each delegate had one vote, but the number of delegates supplied by each 'constituency' varied according to its size.⁷ The number of delegates may have been about 100 altogether, and it may be that the 'constituency' method of producing them was introduced partly to prevent the *sunedrion* becoming tiresomely large.⁸ Since the decisions voted by the *sunedrion* were final and decisive (above), the delegates were 'true representatives and not mere ambassadors':⁹ there

---

¹ *IG* IV². 1. 68. 12 ff.

² The two details which correspond are: (1) Normal times and places for sessions of the Synedrion (the Great Games): *IG* IV². 2. 68, 70 ff.; cf. (in Alexander's reign), Curt. Rufus 4. 5. 11 (Isthmia, 332), Aeschin. 3. 254 (Pythia, 330); perhaps D.S. 17. 109. 1, 18. 8. 21 (Olympia, 324). (2) The general ἐπὶ τῆς κοινῆς φυλακῆς καταλελειμμένῳ, *IG* IV². 2. 68 f., 71 f.; cf. (in Alexander's reign) οἱ ἐπὶ τῇ κοινῇ φυλακῇ τεταγμένοι of Tod 182, 13; [D.] 17. 15 (on which see below, pp. 639 ff.).

³ The *summachia* of the revived League is the notable instance of this. The validity of the method I propose is, I think, generally accepted (cf. e.g. Larsen, *RG* 54).

⁴ *IG* IV². 1. 68. 73 f. τὰ δὲ δόξαντα τοῖς συνέδροις [κύρια] εἶναι; cf. Tod 177, 20 f.

⁵ *IG* IV². 1. 68. 67 ff. Cf. Philip's introduction of the Persian War business; Alexander and Thebes; Antipater and Sparta.

⁶ See below, p. 637.

⁷ This seems to follow from the provision for a quorum, *IG* IV². 1. 68. 74 f., χρηματιζόντωσαν δὲ ὑπ[ὲρ] ἥμισυ γινόμενοι, ἂν δ' ἐλάττους συνέλθ[ωσιν], μὴ χρηματίζειν. If the 'constituencies' had been allowed to send an indefinite number of delegates, while their voting power was fixed and limited, it would have been difficult and tedious to determine whether a true quorum, in terms of voting power, was present or not, and to control the actual voting process properly.

⁸ The estimate (Schwahn's) is acceptable if allowance is made for possibilities of error which could add up to 10–15 per cent. The 'one state one vote' principle could have produced a *sunedrion* of several hundred votes. ⁹ So rightly Larsen, *RG* 59.

was a prohibition on their being called to account for their voting in their states after the event.[1] The conduct of the *sunedrion* in session was presided over by five presidents (*proedroi*) chosen by lot from among the delegates themselves, no state to provide more than one *proedros* at any one time.[2] The *proedroi* were responsible for convening the *sunedrion*, for preparing its agenda, for putting the motions to the vote, and for keeping a clear record of the decisions. They had a secretariat to help them in these things.[3]

The question of the judicial powers of the *sunedrion* is one that in the main can be reserved for discussion later, since the evidence for it all dates from the reign of Alexander.[4] Relevant here and now, however, is whether, or how far, judicial powers were assigned or defined at all for the *sunedrion* at its foundation, or whether these powers accrued to it empirically and through the years. (What can be taken as certain is that no separate court of justice was established, other than the *sunedrion* itself.[5]) Though no certain answer can be given, it is indisputable that the primary function of the *sunedrion*, to preserve the *koine eirene*, itself conferred on it something of the character of a court of justice from the very start, since any and every inter-state dispute that ever came to its notice inevitably threw up its plaintiff and its defendant, addressing the *sunedroi* like dicasts. So obvious a contingency may not have called for lengthy legislation or definition, which in any case could not be divorced entirely from political implications. Elaborate fuss about this could be construed as something that detracted from the freedom of the cities as individuals. On the other hand to produce something about this could be defended, as a charter protecting the cities against arbitrary decisions or pressures by the *hegemon* or his agents. Precedent undoubtedly suggested that something should be said of what should be done 'If anyone does break the peace . . .'.[6] At the most serious level, this meant military

---

[1] *IG* iv². 1. 68. 75 f.

[2] Ibid. 69 ff., 76 ff., 81 ff. In 302, these presidents-by-lot were to operate 'when the war is over' (line 77). For the duration of the war the presidents were to be appointed by the kings, most probably (but the text fails here: line 91 ἕως ἂν ὁ κοινὸς πόλεμος λυθ[ῆι], προεδρεύειν [ἀεὶ τοὺς π]αρ[ὰ] τῶν βασιλέων). It seems right to think of the presidents-by-lot here as the 'normal' procedure for which there was precedent.

For a president appointed by the king in war, see the dispatch of Adeimantus to Demetrius, as interpreted by L. Robert, *Hellenica* 2 (1946) 15–33.   [3] *IG* iv². 1. 76 ff.

[4] Except perhaps for the Melos/Cimolos arbitration case (Tod 179—'after 338 B.C.').

[5] The argument from silence must be decisive here, since the 'cases' which presently do go to the *sunedrion* would not have gone to it if a separate Court of Justice had existed for the purpose. The Delphic Amphictyony, which once was thought to be linked in some way with the 'League of Corinth' in this connection (cf. Ryder, *KE* 161 f. for discussion of the passages D. 18. 322; Paus. 7. 10. 10; Aeschin. 3. 254), obviously was not its regular 'court'. (It always had assumed powers of jurisdiction within its own competence, and it did not lose them now.)

[6] I am thinking especially of the 'judicial' clauses of the Decree of Aristoteles (Tod 2. 123). See Larsen, *RG* 62–5, for a good summary.

sanctions as the oath shows (Tod 177, 18 ff.). But it would be sensible to think, too, in terms of breaches which had not attained (yet) to the most serious level, and to make provision for disputes to be brought to the *sunedrion* for a ruling.[1] Sensible, too, to define the position of individuals (not states) who might be judged to have proved themselves enemies of the Peace and hence malefactors. On the whole it seems probable that the treaty did contain a clause or clauses defining, perhaps in rather general terms, powers of the *sunedrion* to give judgement on cases in both these categories (which need not be the only ones, of course).

To the interesting features of this *sunedrion* and its working, for the history of institutions, full justice has been done by the modern interpreters, and notably by Larsen.[2] In principle the method of representation according to size and population, the method practised in the ethnic confederacies of Boeotia (before 386) and Arcadia, was an advance, no doubt, on the method of the great alliances of Sparta and Athens in the fifth century and even of contemporary Athens in the fourth;[3] and probably it was recognized as such.[4] In practice too the method as applied at this moment seems fair, and not merely a means of gerrymandering to suit the Macedonian interest.[5] It produced a *sunedrion* manageable in size and representative in character, with the important qualification that prominent anti-Macedonians were very unlikely to be elected to it.[6] As to its quality, the same reservation is important, if

---

[1] It can be argued that the Melos/Cimolos case proves that this was so. 'On paper' it does prove it; but obviously the possibility cannot be ruled out that the Melians and Cimolians merely went to the *sunedrion* because it was a body capable in practice of doing something for them, even if it had nothing in its constitution which legally empowered it to act. The weakness of 'arbitration clauses' in Greek treaties up to this time must have been, always, the difficulty of finding a third party as arbitrator acceptable to both the principals in dispute.   [2] Larsen, *RG* ch. III, esp. 53 ff.

[3] Boeotia, *Hell. Oxy.* 16. 2–4 (ed. Bartoletti); Arcadia, Tod 2. 132, for the *damiourgoi* elected obviously on this principle. For Second Athenian Confederacy, the 'one city one vote' method seems almost certain, though it has been contested (e.g. by Schwahn 47, U. Kahrstedt, *RE* 4A, 1334): Larsen, *RG* 54 ff. writes very well on this.

[4] Larsen, *RG* 56, sees it as 'more than a mechanical reform', tending to replace the idea of an assembly of separate states by one of an assembly of the Hellenes, and even 'subtly tending to foster national consciousness and to create a national federal state'. This seems to go beyond what is probable, for the reason I have given already (p. 624 above).

[5] Our only evidence is the list of names of states which follows the oath of the Greeks at Tod 177, 25 ff. Each name or group of names was followed by a numeral, the largest surviving numeral being Δ—10—for the largest Greek *ethnos*, the Thessalians. The list is so fragmentary that the only other instances of both name and numeral surviving are Phocians 3 : Locrians 3. The *perioikoi* of Thessaly formed separate 'constituencies'; which might seem to favour Macedonian interests, since this area was firmly in the Macedonian grip politically. If each city of Central Greece, the Peloponnese, and the Aegean had had a separate vote, they would have outnumbered the individual cities of the northern, 'Macedonian' area, no doubt. But the smallest cities everywhere might have tended to vote pro-Macedonian anyway, for protection against their large neighbours (Thebes, Sparta, Athens etc.). Most likely the method actually used was intended both to look fair and be fair.

[6] See below, p. 644 (for Demosthenes, possibly).

in practice many of the cities and *ethne* were unable to entrust their vital interests here to some of their best politicians.[1] Its procedures, in so far as we are allowed to see them, are irreproachable, with the *hegemon* discreetly excluded and the presidency decently in the hands of its member-*proedroi*. Its supreme competence to make the decisions, without which the *hegemon* himself would make no move, was exemplary.

All these things the Greeks could accept as a civilized way of running this organization for maintaining the *koine eirene*. The institutions in their detail are quite likely to have been the work of Aristotle. For Philip, the problem was there and the expert was there, at his court or in the country near by: that he did not think to bring the two together is inconceivable, and there seems no reason for Aristotle to refuse. Philip himself hoped to please the Greeks, no doubt, with the new institutions, just as he had refrained from demanding alliance of them and had contented himself as *hegemon* of a *koine eirene*, less demanding and less reminiscent of past hegemonies or tyrannies, more public-serving in its prospectus, and well attuned to the political thought of this generation. His conciliatory mood need not be in doubt. But it need not be pressed too far. Philip was not stupid, or devoid of tact when he chose, and he could see a symbol by bright Mediterranean sunlight as well as the next man. If his only thought, or even his first thought, had been to please the Greeks, he would not have invited them to meet him at Corinth, one of the three cities of Greece (so far as we know) where a Macedonian garrison was installed. This Peace, this *sunedrion*, this piece of *politeia* from Aristotle's workshop (if it was his) might be offered with the velvet glove; but there was no mistaking the steel underneath.

The 'League of Corinth' is our name for this thing, not Philip's name for it, or the name used by the Greeks themselves either then or later. It is worth while to make this point again, because modern interpreters can still be misled by the 'accident' of the modern name, even when their eyes are open wide to it. Thus the South Stoa of the Agora of Corinth itself, built in the third quarter of the fourth century, it is thought, 'probably . . . as a gigantic hostelry', is interpreted as a sign that Corinth has become in 338/7 in some sense a capital city or headquarters of the 'League' with which our nomenclature endows her;[2] this despite Philip's garrison on the Acrocorinthus, which alone is enough to prick any

---

[1] The only *sunedros* that I know of is Polyeuctus, the minor Athenian politician against whose action of impeachment Euxenippus was defended by Hyperides at some date in the years 330–324 (Hyp. 3. 20). (Cf. G. Colin, *Hyperide: Discours*, Budé edition pp. 145 ff.) Hyp. 3. 20, criticizing Polyeuctus for never having made anti-Macedonian speeches in 'the *sunedrion* of the Greeks', only makes sense if he had had the opportunities regularly, i.e. as *sunedros*: so Wilamowitz, *Hermes* 58 (1923) 66; cf. in general H. Schaefer, *RE* 21. 2. 1620–1 (1952) s.v. *Polyeuktos* (5).

[2] O. Broneer, *Corinth* (Princeton, 1954) 1. 4. 98, esp. 94 ff.

bubbles of this kind; and despite the fact that the only meetings of Philip's organization that we know of which were held at Corinth were the extraordinary meetings concerned with its first foundation and with the recognition of Alexander as Philip's successor, and that our only evidence on the regular meetings suggests strongly that these were held at Olympia, Delphi, Nemea, and the Isthmus coinciding with the Festivals; and despite the fact that our only evidence which names a place where records of decisions taken at meetings were to be published, names not Corinth but Pydna.[1] Corinth's prolific silver coinage, too, in the years after 338, has been linked with the 'League of Corinth' and 'Philip's propaganda', though in what sense 'Pegasi', associated with Corinth for generations past, could be thought to advance the name and fame of Philip and Alexander now, it is not easy to see. The truth seems to be that Corinth, while garrisoned still by the Macedonian kings, became very prosperous from the trade with Sicily as a result of the great revival there initiated by Timoleon, and the 'propaganda' of the Pegasi celebrated (incidentally) the successes and triumphs of the city of Corinth in fields mercantile, cultural, and even politico-moral, where Philip's garrison was unable to stop the Corinthians from minding their own business in ways that brought them both profit and prestige.[2]

There is still one more 'institution' of the League to be considered, the mysterious 'Defence Officers' of the Demosthenic speech who appear also in the fragmentary inscription of ? 336/5 (Tod 183), οἱ ἐπὶ τῆς κοινῆς φυλακῆς τεταγμένοι. 'Mysterious' is no merely conventional epithet, for there is deep mystery here, miching mallecho even, one might surmise if one were in that kind of mood. These officers had some functions, of which by happy accident we have come to know two; but they had no title, only a descriptive paraphrase. That this oddity is just an accident seems out of the question, for the Greek vocabulary was particularly rich in its variety of names for officials and magistrates of every kind; and no Greek, I suppose, knew them all better than Aristotle. Why then did he, or somebody, choose to call the engine-driver 'the man who makes the wheels go round'?

Perhaps their two functions that are known to us may help—though one of them is banal enough. Among their duties was the duty of having important documents suitably inscribed and set up in the temple of

---

[1] For the 'regular' meetings, above, p. 635; for Pydna, below, pp. 640, 643.

[2] For a discussion of the Pegasi and their implications, see R. J. A. Talbert, *Timoleon and the revival of Greek Sicily* (1974) 161–70. I accept the interpretation which Talbert tentatively offers.

Corinth will have prospered, too, as a garrison town, and a recruiting centre from time to time, as M. Thompson suggested ('A Hoard of Gold Coins of Philip and Alexander from Corinth', *AJA* 74 (1970) 349: fifty-one coins, forty-one of them Philip's, date of burial 'ca. 327 B.C.'). As to the owner of that hoard speculation is idle; but no doubt what had brought the gold into Corinth was the Macedonian expenditure military or political.

Athena at (of all places) Pydna.¹ A matter of administrative routine: the safety of the realm could survive without this. The administrative historian may be glad to notice where in this matter the duties of the *sunedrion's proedroi* ended and where those of our officers began: the first were responsible for making and keeping a true copy of its decrees,² but it was these officers who were responsible for publishing them if they were to be published. Can they have run an office at Pydna, with a clerk or two and their stonemason round the corner? Can they even have resided at Pydna themselves permanently (Pydna giving good access from Macedonia to Thessaly by land and to the rest of Greece and the Aegean by sea, as well as to the *hegemon* in the north)?³ There need be no end, almost, to speculation at this level of bureaucracy. Better to leave Pydna and turn to higher things?

The Demosthenic speech offers this:

More absurd still! The treaty says that the *sunedrion* and the Defence Officers (τοὺς συνεδρεύοντας καὶ τοὺς ἐπὶ τῇ κοινῇ φυλακῇ τεταγμένους) are to ensure that in the states participating in the Peace there be no acts bringing death or exile contrary to the laws of those states, no confiscation of property, no redistribution of land, no cancellation of debts, no freeing of slaves for revolutionary ends. But they, far from preventing any of these things, actually contribute towards bringing them about.⁴

This is a very different matter from what we have just been considering. The clause of the treaty quoted or summarized here is presumably part of the section summarized more briefly still by the oath of the Greeks '(I will not subvert) the governments in existence in the individual states at the time when I swore the oaths concerning the Peace.'⁵ Here the Defence Officers are admitted to the highest level of political responsibility. They (with the *sunedrion*) are made responsible for maintaining the political *status quo* in every state of Greece. This genuinely is 'defence' (φυλακή), and no mistake. It gave to these officers (with the *sunedrion*) the duty of exercising a supervision over the internal affairs of every Greek state, with the object of preventing any outbreak of *stasis*, one of the most potent promoters of war in the Greek world. One could suggest that officers with this among their duties may easily have been empowered also (with the *sunedrion*) 'to ensure that no state participating in the peace takes up arms against any other'. This would make them (with the *sunedrion*) virtually the supervisors of the Peace in general and the controllers of Greece. Even without the second and hypothetical duty, they

---

¹ Tod 183, 12 ff.   ² *IG* IV². 1. 68. 80 f.

³ Pydna, a delightful spot now (and then too, I am sure), can never have been the hub of the universe, and important officials or politicians no doubt would have preferred to reside in Pella, or Corinth, or Athens. A. Wilhelm (*SAWW* 10 (1917) 48) did suggest Pydna as the headquarters of these officers.   ⁴ [D.] 17. 15.

⁵ Tod 2. 177, 10 ff.; cf. [D.] 17. 10, 4 and 7 f., 16, referring to other parts of the same section.

are still (with the *sunedrion*) set to exercise very great powers of super-vision, and especially in those delicate areas of action in which each state was most liable to consider its autonomy infringed if officers of the League should intervene.

A sentence of Curtius Rufus associates the Defence Officers, it seems, with Antipater in 333 when he and they receive 600 talents sent over by Alexander from Asia Minor: 'ad Antipatrum *et eos qui Graecas urbes tuebantur*' seems to translate οἱ ἐπὶ τῆς κοινῆς φυλακῆς τεταγμένοι.[1] If this is right, 'defence' includes straight military defence (as should be ex-pected, probably), for this is in the context of the Persian naval counter-attack, with the 'Antipater etc.' clause sandwiched between two sentences concerned with the defence of the Hellespont.[2] And A. J. Heisserer points out acutely that Arrian covering this same ground names a subordinate commander of Antipater in words which suggest that this Proteas son of Andronicus was indeed a Defence Officer himself: ἐν δὲ τούτῳ Πρωτέας ὁ Ἀνδρονίκου ἐτύγχανε μὲν ξυναγαγὼν ἐξ Εὐβοίας τε καὶ Πελοποννήσου ναῦς μακρὰς ὑπὸ Ἀντιπάτρου τεταγμένος, ὡς εἶναί τινα ταῖς τε νήσοις φυλακὴν καὶ αὐτῇ τῇ Ἑλλάδι, εἰ καθάπερ ἐξηγγέλλετο, ἐπιπλέοιεν οἱ βάρβαροι.[3] At first sight the word-association of τεταγμένος . . . φυλακήν seems quite conclusive. But next one realizes that these are, undeniably, the first and best words for saying this thing in Greek (that Antipater appointed somebody, for a purpose of protection or defence) and that probably one will use these two words here for this, whether or not the man appointed was one who happened to have these same two words as part of an official title. Arrian's use of them here could be 'accidental', in fact, and personally I see it as a nice linguistic point, whether he uses them by association or by accident. Though I cannot feel confident, I think it perhaps was by association, and that we are making the acquaintance here (thanks to A. J. Heisserer) of one of the Defence Officers.[4] Another of them, as Bengtson suggested, may have been the

---

[1] Curt. Ruf. 3. 1. 20.

[2] Ibid. 19–20 'Cum deinde Dareum ubicumque esset occupare statuisset, ut a tergo tuta relinqueret Amphoterum classi ad oram Hellesponti, copiis autem praefecit Hegelochum, Lesbum et Chium Coumque praesidiis hostium liberaturos. His talenta ad belli usum quingenta attributa, ad Antipatrum et eos qui Graecas urbes tuebantur DC missa, ex foedere naves sociis imperatae, quae Hellesponto praesiderent.'

[3] Arr. *An.* 2. 2. 4; cf. A. J. Heisserer, 'Alexander's Letter to the Chians', *Historia* 22 (1973) 196 f.

[4] If Proteas was not a Defence Officer, Arrian (or his source) would use τάσσω as the first and best word for Antipater's giving him this job; but he need not have chosen to use the participle of the perfect tense. He could have written as easily ταχθείς; perhaps more easily, since this was a once-for-all job, of collecting ships, not a continuing one. That he wrote τεταγμένος is some support for 'association', perhaps—especially if Arrian's source described him as (e.g.) τῶν ἐπὶ τῇ κοινῇ φυλακῇ τεταγμένων.

For Proteas, see Berve 2 no. 664, and no. 665 perhaps. The brilliance of his little *coup* at Siphnos (Arr. *An.* 2. 2. 5) explains probably why Arrian recorded, among important naval

Macedonian Corragus who was defeated in the Peloponnese by Agis III of Sparta in 331, having been directed there by Antipater.[1]

Whatever the extent of the powers and duties of the Defence Officers, they operated with the *sunedrion* (ἐπιμελεῖσθαι τοὺς συνεδρεύοντας καὶ τοὺς ἐπὶ τῇ κοινῇ φυλακῇ τεταγμένους . . .). This was the saving clause, for constitutional lawyers and for those who believed in freedom. The Officers could never act without a vote of the *sunedrion*, and the *sunedrion* was composed of delegates of the cities and *ethne* on a fair system of representation. Moreover the *sunedrion* was named first the Officers second, as was right and proper ([D.] 17. 15). These were comforting thoughts perhaps. But second thoughts brought less of comfort. Who were these Officers, anyway? From where did they come? By whom chosen or appointed? And what was really their relationship to the *sunedrion* when it met and between its meetings? To take the last question first, there can be no doubt that initiatives were supplied by the Officers for the *sunedrion*, and not by the *sunedrion* for the Officers. Their duty was to supervise Greece through the years and all the year round. If they saw something wrong, it was they who needed to start something, and presumably by first telling the *hegemon* or his representative. Could the matter wait till the next annual meeting of the *sunedrion*, or was it necessary to summon an extraordinary meeting? The decision would be the *hegemon*'s, but in reaching it he would rely greatly on the information and counsel of these Officers. When the *sunedrion* did meet, its *proedroi* formally presented the business and presided; but it was the Officers who knew the business, and knew what the *hegemon* wanted done (if he was not present himself). The real *probouleusis* for all important business of the *sunedrion* will have been the work of these Officers and of the *hegemon*. In this sense, one wonders whether their missing name or title would not have been most naturally *probouloi*. The name and the office were well known to Aristotle, and to most Greeks no doubt. But *probouloi* were oligarchs, always.[2] ('Perhaps we won't call them *Probouloi*

---

reinforcements to Alexander besieging Tyre, the personal arrival of Proteas 'flying his flag on a single pentekonter from Macedonia' (id. 2. 20. 2). If Arrian thought of him as a celebrity, this perhaps is an encouragement to identify this Proteas (Berve no. 664) with the Proteas (no. 665) who (with no patronymic) figures in anecdotes as a boon-companion of Alexander from this time on (Plu. *Alex*. 39. 4 etc., see Hamilton, *Commentary* ad loc.). But after Tyre Arrian never mentions a Proteas again.

[1] Aeschin. 3. 165 and schol.; *Acad. Philosoph. Index Herculanensis* col. 11. 33; 12. 43 (pp. 30, 32) ed. S. Mekler; Bengtson, *Strategie* 1. 50 and n. 4.

[2] For *probouloi* in general, Arist. *Pol.* 4. 1298ᵇ26 ff. (ἐν δὲ ταῖς ὀλιγαρχίαις . . .); 1299ᵇ31 ff. (οἷον ἡ τῶν προβούλων [sc. ἀρχή], αὕτη γὰρ οὐ δημοκρατική, βουλὴ δὲ δημοτικόν . . .); 1322ᵇ17 ff. (καλεῖται δὲ ἔνθα μὲν ἐν πρόβουλοι διὰ τὸ προβουλεύειν, ὅπου δὲ πλῆθός ἐστι, βουλὴ μᾶλλον).

So Aristotle. The interesting discussions of Françoise Rusé, 'La fonction des *probouloi* dans le monde grec antique', in *Mélanges d'histoire ancienne offerts à William Seston* (Paris, 1974), 443–62, warn against over-simplification here; but they do not alter the picture so far as Aristotle's own notions (over-simplified or not) of *probouloi* as oligarchic are concerned.

after all, my dear Aristotle? Better not, perhaps?' The point could be made, and taken.)

In any case, *probouleusis* for the *sunedrion* was not the sum of their functions. They were the supervisors of the Peace in Greece, most likely, investigators if need be and fact-finders, reporters to the *hegemon* of anything serious enough to warrant report. They were the *hegemon*'s main link with the *sunedrion*, perhaps with the Greek states individually and the Greeks in general. Philip had entertained enough embassies from Greek cities in his reign to have learned that, now that he had acquired a formal and permanent responsibility as *hegemon*, he could look forward to having clusters of Greek ambassadors on his back for the rest of his days unless he did something to stop it. This board of Officers may represent his procedure for dealing with his Greek affairs now. Perhaps the notion of an office in Pydna is not so preposterous after all. For this purpose the great thing about Pydna was that it was not Pella (or Aegeae, or wherever in the north Philip might find himself from time to time)? Greeks in their hordes could descend on Pydna from the south or the sea; but few need be allowed any further.

If these suggestions are accepted, they carry implications for the identity of the Officers themselves, what kind of men they were likely to be, and by whom chosen and appointed. The qualities that most suggest themselves as necessary are reliability (to the *hegemon*), political intelligence and experience, congeniality (to the Greeks); the first most likely to be found among Macedonians, the last among Greeks, if there were any Greeks sufficiently detached from internal Greek problems and controversies. If they were to be any real use, to rely on annual elections of these officers by the *sunedrion* or any other voting system of the Greeks would defeat the purpose. Men of the right qualities were relatively few, anyway, and men of the wrong qualities were a waste of time, or worse. Though there might be attractions (for window-dressing) in a Board composed partly of elected Greeks and partly of appointments by the *hegemon*, it may be significant that these Officers do not appear at all in the Epidaurus inscription relating to the League of 302. There, the descriptive phrase about 'Defence' is attached to a general, a general appointed by the kings (Antigonus and Demetrius)—τοῖς συνέδροις καὶ [τῷ στρατη]γῷ τῷ ὑπὸ τῶν βασιλέων ἐπὶ τῆς κοινῆς φυλακῆς καταλελειμμένῳ.[1] This change may be due entirely to the state of war in Greece in 302. But it is not clear that it must be due to that; for this was a time of liberation, too, and of enthusiasm for democracies restored after the garrisons and restricted governments of Cassander, a moment in which a board of officers, even a board which looked more 'liberal' than Philip's,

---

[1] *IG* iv². 1. 68 f.: the restoration [στρατη]γῷ is ensured by οἱ πρόεδροι καὶ ὁ βασιλεὺς ἢ ὁ ὑπὸ τῶν βασιλέων ἀποδεδειγμένος στρ[ατ]ηγός, 71 f.

would not have been out of place.[1] It seems possible that the change now, to a general, may be telling us something about Philip's appointments, by implication. Demetrius did not control Macedonia in 302, and relatively few high-ranking Macedonians were at his disposal. As a practical matter, it was easier for him to find one general than to find a board of officers. This appointment by Demetrius does seem to make it more probable that it was Philip who as *hegemon* appointed the members of the original board; and also that these members were mostly Macedonians (for Proteas, and Corragus, pp. 641 f. above). The number of Greeks who both could and would serve on it, and whose qualities he could trust, was so very small: the Demaratus of Corinth, the Python of Byzantium, the Phocion or Demades of Athens, the small handful of prominent Thessalians such as Cottyphus.[2] There might have been one of these perhaps, or two, on Philip's board, which probably was small, very small; some three or four or five men who, Macedonian or Greek, were committed now to the Macedonian regime in Greece and were devoted to Philip whether as king or *hegemon*.

What is the significance, if any, of the strange Peace-Defender (εἰρηνο-φύλαξ) of Aeschines 3. 159 (describing Demosthenes)? 'But when Athens became a safe place to be in, to everyone's surprise, and this brought him back, in the early days he was still a bundle of nerves, and he would come crawling up to the platform, and bid you elect him Defender of the Peace.'[3] Aeschines alludes evidently to a time not long after the separate peace with Philip was made in 338, and obviously one should consider whether he may be alluding to an office (χειροτονεῖν) connected with the *koine eirene* organization. In spite of the etymological link, one must think that the election at Athens of one of the Defence Officers cannot possibly have been in question, for the reasons given above. That the allusion is to the election of the Athenian *sunedroi* of the new *sunedrion* seems not impossible. If that were so, I suspect that εἰρηνοφύλακα is Aeschines' ironical quotation or parody of some grandiloquent description used by Demosthenes himself. However, if Demosthenes really did offer himself as a candidate to be a *sunedros*, there was really no chance

---

[1] For these developments, E. Will, *Hist. politique du monde hellénistique* 1. 59 ff., 66 ff., with bibliography.

[2] This is not to suggest that any particular one of these men did serve on it. Phocion (e.g.) obviously did not: if he had, he would not have been able to remain in Athens through the anti-Macedonian war-fever of 323/2—and Plutarch most probably would have learned of it.

[3] Aeschin. 3. 159 καταγαγούσης δ' αὐτὸν εἰς τὴν πόλιν τῆς ἀπροσδοκήτου σωτηρίας . . . παριὼν ἡμιθνὴς ἐπὶ τὸ βῆμα, εἰρηνοφύλακα ὑμᾶς αὐτὸν ἐκέλευε χειροτονεῖν. See above p. 638 n. 1 for the Athenian *sunedros* Polyeuctus. See now T. T. B. Ryder, 'Demosthenes and Philip's Peace of 338/7 B.C.', *CQ* N.S. 26 (1976) 85 ff., where this passage is discussed fully. I am most grateful to Dr. Ryder for letting me see his article before it was published, and I am encouraged to find that we agree on this.

whatever of his being elected, as Aeschines' next words show—'But you would not even let the name of Demosthenes as proposer head your decrees on this matter; you made Nausicles do it.' At this time the *demos* was listening to Demades and Phocion (and perhaps Aeschines himself), and was being careful.

I have spent time and space on this (perhaps too much) because I have not seen these officers of Defence fully explained elsewhere.[1] My own explanation makes them a key, indispensable to Philip's whole organization of the League and to its purposes. The League as a whole was designed, naturally, to be attractive, or not unattractive, to those who had accepted the invitation to 'share in the Common Peace and the *sunedrion*'. It proclaimed them autonomous, and it gave them the institutions which were not incompatible with autonomy. It gave them an assured Peace now, an end to the wars between the states and the revolutions inside them. It offered a share in a glorious war against Persia, a war of revenge. But the fine words and the fair names could not deceive the Greeks into believing that they really were free. The League was preserving the decencies of life, but it was not altering its facts. The Greeks knew that they had not dared to refuse to 'share in the Common Peace and the *sunedrion*', and were not daring to refuse to join in the Persian war.[2] Was this freedom? They knew that now they could not change the forms of government in their own states without breaking their oath to the *hegemon*. The Thessalians by this interpretation were 'free and autonomous': they were numbered among 'those who share in the Peace'. But Philip was *archon* of Thessaly, and in reality his word in Thessaly was law. Was this autonomy? The Greeks knew all this, and Philip knew that they knew. Hence the Defence Officers. It was not for a whim or an ideal, out of concern for the Greeks themselves or a sense of obligation to contribute to the history of their institutions, or to exercise Aristotle or gratify Isocrates, that he was giving the Greeks peace and 'the League of Corinth'.[3] He positively needed that Greece

---

[1] Explanations which see in them merely the *hegemon* or his representative(s) (J. Kaerst, *Rhein. Mus.* 52 (1897) 531 ff.), or the commanders of the garrisons in Greece (Wilcken, *SDAW* 1922. 139 f., followed by Berve 1. 230, Bengtson, *Strategie* 1. 50), seem to take no account of the inscription Tod, *GHI* 183, with its allusion to the Temple of Athena at Pydna. Bengtson (1. 50) writes well though very briefly of them as Antipater's agents.

[2] Cf. [D]. 17. 30.

[3] Isocrates' *Epistle* 3, if genuine, was written after Chaeronea but before the settlement at Corinth. Apart from its much discussed allusion to Philip as a future candidate for the final honour of becoming a god, which I take to be a literary extravagance by way of compliment and no more (οὐδὲν γὰρ ἔσται λοιπὸν ἔτι πλὴν θεὸν γενέσθαι), the letter adds nothing to the earlier counsel of Isocrates in the *Philip* of 346, which it very briefly recapitulates. For a good short analysis, with bibliography, see J. P. V. D. Balsdon, *Historia* 1 (1950) 366 f. and n. 24. Though I can see no really decisive argument either for its genuineness or for the reverse, personally I think the letter probably is genuine. If so, it tells us that Isocrates at ninety-eight was able still to summarize sensibly what he had said when he was eighty-nine;

should give no trouble, that the Greeks should not delay or divert him from his Persian plans, and should co-operate with him by land and sea in so far as they could be trusted. For these ends the Defence Officers were of great use from the start, and would be of greater importance still when he was across the sea in Asia himself. Greece and the Greeks needed constant attention. These were the men who could attend to them. The *sunedroi* when they met at Corinth had only to cast their eyes up to the citadel to be reminded. There on the Acrocorinthus, a flash in the sun or a silhouette against the sky, the soldiers of the garrison went through their duties of the day, the living mockery of any notion that the Greeks were free.

but it cannot be thought likely to have influenced Philip at all now, or even to have been of any value to him. Not many Greeks can have cared what Isocrates thought or advised about all this; and not one can have changed his own mind because of it.

XX

INTERNAL ORGANIZATION OF MACEDONIA AND OF MACEDONIAN CONQUESTS IN THE BALKANS

1. *Internal Organization of Macedonia*

THE organization of the Macedonian kingdom in the time of Philip seems not to have been fully understood by those who have written on the subject, although the evidence has generally been available. The essential point to grasp is that within the geographical area which we call Macedonia a free man might have had as many as three citizenships: for example, he might have been a 'Macedon', an 'Elimeotes', and a citizen of the town Aeane, or again 'Macedon', 'Orestes', and 'Battynaeus'. In practice, since the 'Macedones' were an élite group, as we have seen (p. 164 above), most free men had only the second and third forms of citizenship, namely that of a tribal state, e.g. the Elimeotae, and that of a town, or that of a lesser tribal state, e.g. the Geneatae. This system seems strange to those who are familiar only with the Greek city-state; but there is an exact parallel in the Molossian state *c.* 370–368, when inscriptions show an individual to have been a 'Molossos', and 'Arctan', and a citizen of the town Eurymenae (*Eph. Arch.* 1956. 1; see *Epirus* 525 f.).[1]

Let us begin with the élite citizens, the 'Macedones'. Many of Alexander's trierarchs in 326 were contrasted as 'Macedones' with 'Hellenes' and 'Persae', and each 'Macedon' was listed by the district or town of which he had citizenship. There were nine Μακεδόνες Πελλαῖοι; three Μακεδόνες ἐξ Ἀμφιπόλεως; two Μακεδόνες Ὀρέσται; two Μακεδόνες Ἐορδαῖοι; two Μακεδόνες ἐκ Πύδνης; one Μακεδὼν Στυμφαῖος; and so on (Arr. *Ind.* 18. 3–6). There are, of course, earlier examples of this kind of definition: Ptolemy Alorites was a citizen of Alorus, and Alexander Lyncestes was a Macedon, who hailed Alexander as king in 336 and was tried in the Assembly of the Macedones. As we have seen (p. 163 above), Macedonian citizenship was in the gift of the king.[2] Nearchus, for instance,

---

[1] In this section I have been much helped by conversations with C. F. Edson. Hampl 78–82 argued that Macedonian towns and districts had no form of citizenship.

[2] It should be noted too that he withheld it in some cases. Thus Eumenes of Cardia, who served both Philip and Alexander as a *grammateus*, was a Companion (Arr. *An.* 7. 4. 6) but not a Macedon (*Ind.* 18. 7, where he was listed as a Greek). When Alexander made Persians

was a Cretan by origin; he was given not only Macedonian citizenship but also the citizenship of Amphipolis, where 'he resided' (Arr. *Ind.* 18. 10). Similarly in the time of Philip two Athenians were given grants of land at Pella and Beroea, where they married very well and presumably were made Macedones, so that they became respectively Μακεδὼν Πελλαῖος and Μακεδὼν Βεροιαῖος (Ps.-Aeschin. *Letter* 12, 8).[1] Thus all 'Macedones', whatever their origin, were registered as citizens also of a tribal state and/or of a town. Numerous cases are known from inscriptions: for example, *c.* 346 Μακεδόσι ἐκ Πέλλης (*SGDI* 2. 2759), late in the fourth century Μαχάτας Σαββαταρᾶ Εὐρωπαῖος Μακεδών (*BCH* 20 (1896) 73), *c.* 298/7 Πολυδάμας [Ἀν]ταίου Ἐρεθούσιος Μακεδών (*Fouilles de Delphes* 3. 1, n. to no. 187), and *c.* 275–250 Μακεδὼν Ἐλειμιώτης ἐκ Πυθείου (*BCH* 21 (1897) 112).

The citizenship of a town was a political reality. Each *polis* had its territory; for instance, Strabo 7 fr. 20 mentioned ἡ Πελλαία (sc. γῆ) in a confused passage (see Volume I. 143). When a king endowed a man with an estate as a 'Macedon' within the territory of Pella or Beroea, for instance, then the man became a Μακεδὼν Πελλαῖος or a Μακεδὼν Βεροιαῖος. Each *polis* had its own finances; for example, soon after 323 Aegeae (restored), Edessa, Atalante, and Europus made their own contributions of money to Asclepius at Epidaurus (*IG* IV no. 617, 17). No doubt each raised taxes and paid dues to the king. Each, we may assume, trained its own levy as a home guard, and each contributed its quota of 'Macedones' to serve in the king's army; Amphipolis, for example, and Apollonia (whether in Mygdonia or Chalcidice) each contributed a squadron of Companion cavalry to Alexander's army. It is obvious that decisions in these matters were taken by the citizens in some form of Council and/or Assembly (such as we find in later inscriptions),[2] and that they were implemented by executive officers, some being called perhaps πολιτάρχαι as in later inscriptions.

One term for Councillors in a Macedonian town goes back to the time of Philip and probably much earlier: πελιγᾶνες. Hesychius preserved the name for Councillors in Seleucid Syria, which perpetuated the use of Macedonian terms as well as place-names: πελιγᾶνες· οἱ ἔνδοξοι, παρὰ δὲ Σύροις οἱ βουλευταί. He was proved correct by an inscription[3] found at Lattakia, the ancient Laodicea, founded by Seleucus I: δεδόχθαι τοῖς πελιγᾶσι. Strabo 7 fr. 2 takes us back to Macedonia by saying that the Macedones call 'those in positions of honour πελιγόνας, as in the case of

'Companions' but not 'Macedones' (7. 8. 2 and 7. 11. 3–6), he had a precedent in the actions of Philip.

[1] The letter is not genuine but the persons mentioned seem to be historical.
[2] See Volume I. 86 f., 114, and 120.
[3] *Syria* 23 (1942–3) 21 f.; see Kalléris 242 f.

the γέροντας at Sparta and Massalia', and he goes on to explain that the word was derived from the word for γέροντας among the Thesproti and the Molossi, which was πέλιοι. Thus in Macedonia the form πελιγάν was West Greek and probably derived, like the word itself, from the Molossian group of tribes to which most of the tribes of Upper Macedonia belonged (see Volume I. 91 and *Epirus* 460 f.); it was in use probably in south-western Macedonian towns. The form πελιγών may have been used in Pelagonian towns where *Pelagón* and *Erigón* are similar, or/and in other towns.[1] Hesychius has preserved another 'Macedonian office: ταγόναγα' which is plausibly explained by Kalléris as an archaic Greek word meaning 'leadership of magistrates'. The word *tagos* and the Doric form -αγα suggest that the term was used in a town of Pieria, where the influence of Thessaly was most likely to have penetrated.

We must remember that most of the towns in Lower Macedonia had had a long history before Philip came to the throne. 'Ichnaei' and 'Letaei' were issuing coins in their own name in the late sixth century, when the king of Macedon had no coinage. Hecataeus and Herodotus mentioned many native towns, as compared with Greek cities, in the area. Macedonians in the fourth century were as proud of their town, as Athenians were of their deme; a stele at Pella had the inscription Ἄρχων Φιλίσκου Ληταῖος (*BS* 4 (1963) 162), and a trierarch of Alexander Archon, son of Cleinus (Arr. *An.* 8. 18. 3 giving Cleinias), praised his home town in a verse inscription Πέλλα τε ἀείμναστον πατρὶς ἔ[χουσα κλέος] (*SEG* 18 (1962) 222 в). Again, in the third century the epigrammatist Poseidippus of Pella wanted appreciation by the 'Macedones' but boasted that he was a man of Pella Πελλαῖον γένος ἁμόν (D. L. Page, *Greek Literary Papyri* 473 no. 114. 16). But in one vital particular the Macedonian town differed from the Greek *polis*. It administered its affairs only up to a point, as any borough or *municipium* may do within a kingdom, but it was not independent.

The districts were of different kinds (see Map 9). In Lower Macedonia some districts were mentioned in connection only with the king's army; thus Anthemus provided one squadron of Companion cavalry and Bottiaea another. It seems that the chief administrative units in the plain were the towns, and that the territories of the towns and the estates of the king covered the whole of the coastal plain. Inland, however, citizenship was primarily by district. There were many Μακεδόνες Ἐορδαῖοι; town-citizenships developed later there than in Lower Macedonia, and one inscription of Roman date may indicate such

---

[1] The Macedonian personal name 'Pelignas' (Athen. 14. 659 f) may be of the same derivation; indeed it may be a cult title. The word 'Adeiganes' in Plb. 5. 54. 10 has been emended to 'Peliganes' by P. Roussel, but it may be a genuine word in the vocabulary of western Macedonia.

a citizenship, Ἐορδαῖος Κραννέστης (*SEG* 1. 292).[1] The citizenship 'Eordaeus' postulates the existence of a self-administering community, analogous to the town-community in Lower Macedonia, and this community had existed presumably since the latter part of the sixth century, when the area had been repeopled by the conquering Macedones. Different from the Eordaei and many centuries older were the self-governing tribes (*ethne*) in the rest of Upper Macedonia: Elimeotae, Tymphaei, Orestae, Lyncestae, and Pelagones. That each tribe had its own monarch was noted by Thucydides (2. 99. 2). However, the monarch was not an absolute despot but the head of a tribal state which had its own organs of administration. This is attested for the tribal state of the Molossians, to which the tribal states of Upper Macedonia were closely related (see Volume I. 111 and 119); for inscriptions of the 360s mention the king as head of the Molossian state, called τὸ κοινὸν τῶν Μολοσσῶν, and *prostates*, *grammateus*, ten *damiorgi*, and fifteen *synarchontes* as its officials. Indeed the tribal state of the Orestae belonged for some years after 370 or so to the Molossian state, and it was then called τὸ κοινὸν τῶν Ὀρεστῶν in accordance with Molossian usage. It is probable that all Macedonian tribal states were called *koina* in the reign of Philip, although inscriptions with this term are known only from the Roman period.[2] Another point of similarity between the tribal states of Upper Macedonia and their counterparts in Epirus was the fact that they consisted of constituent tribes (see Volume I. 88, 114, and 120).

That the tribal states of Upper Macedonia had a strong individuality and a desire for independence is obvious from their history between 483 and 359. Philip welded them into his kingdom. While he abolished the monarchies, he incorporated some members of the ruling house into his Companions and he placed their sons among the Royal Pages. Becoming resident in a town of Lower Macedonia they were given not only the Macedonian citizenship but also a town-citizenship. Thus if a member of the Lyncestid royal house such as Alexander Lyncestes resided at Pella, he might have been described as Λυγκηστὴς ἐκ Πέλλης Μακεδών. Thus Aristonous came from Pella (Arr. *An.* 6. 28. 4) and was also 'Eordaios' (*Ind.* 18. 5). Indeed some of Alexander's senior officers were members of the royal houses—Polyperchon (Tymphaea), Perdiccas son of Orontes (Orestis), and Leonnatus son of Eunous (Lyncus)—and they were 'Macedones' and one, Leonnatus, was a citizen of Pella. But the tribal states continued in existence, administering their own affairs and maintaining their identity and self-respect. They certainly

---

[1] The stone carrying this inscription was seen at Monastir by Dimitsas (*BCH* 4. 101); it was brought there presumably from Eordaea.

[2] See Volume I. 111 f. and 119 f.

organized and trained their own men for defence against the Illyrians and the Dardanians. In addition they provided troops for the king's army; for instance, at Gaugamela Alexander had phalanx-brigades of Tymphaei, Elimeotae, and Orestae–Lyncestae (D.S. 17. 57. 2). Thus Philip chose deliberately to encourage local loyalties and arranged his army on the territorial system.

At the head of this complex state stood the king, defined in 359/8 or a following year as 'Amyntas, son of Perdiccas, king of Macedones' Ἀ[μ]ύντας Π[ερ]δί[κ]κα [Μα]κεδόνων βασιλεύ[ς] (*IG* vii. 3055).[1] He claimed suzerainty over the tribes of Upper Macedonia, as his predecessors had done, naming them e.g. 'Lyncestae Macedones' in the manner recorded by Thucydides (2. 99. 2 and 10; 4. 83. 1), even if they had thrown off their allegiance. But in a juridical sense 'Macedones' proper in 359/8 were the 10,000 or so men who held Macedonian citizenship from the king, served in his army and formed the Assembly of Macedones. They were a small proportion of the adult men in the kingdom. The king's government was economical in the extreme. The towns were self-administering, and the tribal states ran their own affairs, so that they were in routine matters 'allied with' as well as 'subject to' the Macedones

---

[1] Aristotle, *Politics* 1310[b]39, used the same terms. The dating of the inscription is controversial. In a persuasive article in *JHS* 91 (1971) 15 f. J. R. Ellis has argued for a date after the death of Philip and seen in the title a claim to the throne by Amyntas. However, the difficulty is that it is not Amyntas himself but the authorities in charge of the oracle at Lebadea who are describing Amyntas as 'king of the Macedones'; and if he was never in fact king but was merely hatching a plot in Boeotia, I cannot conceive that the authorities would have committed themselves publicly in a list of eminent people who had consulted the oracle. The evidence of the inscription that Amyntas *was* king seems to me superior to statements in later writers, such as Diodorus and Justin, however we interpret them. No weight can be laid on the phrase παρέλαβε τὴν βασιλείαν which Diodorus used at 16. 2. 4 of both Ptolemy Alorites and Philip; for as Ptolemy was certainly regent, Philip may equally well have been regent in 359. The reckoning of Philip's reign at twenty-four years, i.e. 359–336, is not decisive because the reckoning of Aëropus' reign included the years of his regency (see p. 168 above and Beloch, *GG*[2] 3. 2. 55 and 60); indeed Satyrus in Athen. 13. 557 b gave twenty-two years, i.e. 357–336, which Beloch boldly emended to twenty-four. As heir and as king Amyntas was a mere child, as Justin 7. 5 emphasized correctly ('parvulus quidem filius' and 'in exspectatione infantis'), and the sentence 'Philippus diu non regem sed tutorem pupilli egit' referred to two eventful years; one should not use the rhetorical 'diu' to overthrow the whole sentence. When the Assembly at Oropus granted proxeny to this same Amyntas, he was described as 'Amyntas son of Perdiccas a Macedon' (*IG* vii. 4251). I infer from this that, whereas Amyntas had been king at the time of the Lebadean inscription, he was not king at the time of the Oropian inscription, which has to be dated before the cession of Oropus to Athens in 338 and cannot therefore be associated with any plot by Amyntas after the death of Philip. Rather proxeny was granted to Amyntas, one imagines, because he held a high position in Philip's entourage and had perhaps acted as an envoy of Philip in negotiations with the city. Two such phases in the life of Amyntas are what we are led by Justin to expect. If Ellis is right in attributing a plot to Amyntas and other Macedonians in Boeotia after the death of Philip, it belonged to a third phase and does not discredit what Justin said of the first phase. We do not know, of course, why Amyntas was taken as a child king to the oracle at Lebadea; all we can say is that it was presumably before summer 356, when the Phocian War started (*StGH* 533). But for another view, pp. 208 f.

in the words of Thucydides (2. 99. 2). He and the chosen Companions who formed his advisory Council were free to concentrate on the Macedones proper and the main problems of the state of Macedon, τὸ κοινὸν τῶν Μακεδόνων as it was called in Arr. *An.* 7. 9. 5.

So far we have considered only those districts which spoke Greek as their native language. The eastern part of Philip's enlarged kingdom spoke Paeonian and Thracian. It seems that each tribe retained its identity, managed its internal affairs, and paid financial dues to Philip. When the king of the Paeones 'was compelled to side with the Macedones' (D.S. 16. 22. 3), he was left to rule his own state and indeed to issue his own coinage, and Paeonian cavalry served under Alexander in Asia. The Bisaltae retained their identity as a tribal state from Alexander I to Perseus, and they were evidently trained to defend themselves against their Thracian neighbours; for they were described as 'fortissimi viri' in 168, when Perseus asked them to fight for Macedon (Livy 44. 45. 8 and 45. 30. 3). The towns of Crestonia, Mygdonia, and the Strymon basin were fully established in the time of Herodotus, and their populations were predominantly of Paeonian and Thracian origin. They were incorporated into the Macedonian system as self-governing boroughs. Language seems not to have caused any difficulty. It is likely that more Greek was spoken in these areas than in the remote parts of the Athos peninsula (Thuc. 4. 109. 4).

2. *Territories Added by Philip and the Frontiers of his Kingdom*

In the west (see Map 9), when Philip defeated Bardylis, he forced Orestis to change its allegiance from the Molossian state to the Macedonian state, and he freed Lyncus and Pelagonia from Illyrian occupation. He was now at the confines of Macedonia as they had been set by the most ambitious of his predecessors, and the line of the frontier lay along the massive range of Mt. Peristeri, which can be crossed only by the pass of Diavat in the north and the pass of Pisodherion in the south (see Volume I. 42 and 99). Yet Philip advanced beyond that range and even beyond the next great range, formed by Mt. Petrina and Mt. Plakenska, and 'made all the inhabitants as far as Lake Lychnitis his subjects' (D.S. 16. 8. 1, based on Ephorus). The new frontier ran probably from the hill of St. Erasmus, which commands the narrow entry by the eastern shore of the lake; then along its eastern shore; and then along the ridge of Mt. Petrina and Mt. That to the watershed with the river Haliacmon. Philip now had defence in depth. Anyone attacking from the west had to force the entry by St. Erasmus, then the pass of Pylon on Mt. Petrina, and then the Diavat pass; or if he attacked farther south, the narrow entry of Grykë e Ujkut by Tren[1] and the Pisodherion pass. The extra-ordinary strength of this frontier is clear from Plate III.

It is most probable that the inner part of the fortifications on the hill of St. Erasmus[2] was built early in the reign of Philip (see Map 8). They consist of a 2 m wide wall, built in polygonal style; a tower of small proportions, which protects a narrow and simple straight entry, 1·50 to 2 m wide; and a bastion. The circuit was only some 150 m and

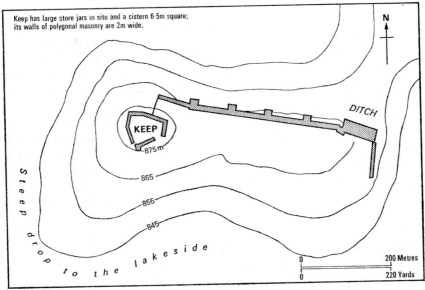

Keep has large store jars in situ and a cistern 6·5m square; its walls of polygonal masonry are 2m wide.

N

DITCH

KEEP

875m

865

855

845

S t e e p   d r o p   t o   t h e   l a k e s i d e

0   200 Metres
0   220 Yards

MAP 8. THE FORTIFICATIONS OF ST. ERASMUS BY LAKE LYCHNITIS

there was no layer of habitation inside it, but large *pithoi* for stores had been sunk in the ground. A date after 360 suits the polygonal style (see *Epirus* 713), and the site was appropriate for a garrison in time of danger. The outer fortifications are much more substantial: a curtain wall 3 m wide and 240 m long, four large towers projecting 7 m and made in roughly ashlar style, and a large bastion with a trench in front at the weakest point. The change in scale and style shows that the outer fortifications should be dated later than the inner part; they belong to the Hellenistic period on the analogy of fortifications in Epirus. The excavator, W. Unverzagt, proposed to relate all the fortifications to one period only, namely that of the Trebenishte burials in the late archaic period, and he made an analogy with the fortifications at Heuneburg

---

[1] For this area see *JHS* 94 (1974) 66 f.
[2] The excavations were reported in *Germania* 32 (1954) 19 f.; see also *ŽA* 3 (1953) 260 fig. 3.

the Danube. However, there is no sign of any walled site north of Ambracia in the archaic period, and the analogy with Heuneburg is too distant to be relevant. In fact the fortified site called Trebenisko Kale is close to the Trebenishte cemetery; it has been excavated and is of the Hellenistic period. In 1968 I walked from Ochrid past the hill of St. Erasmus and the village of Gorenzi, visited Trebenisko Kale, and returned by the village of Trebenishte; it was clear that the hill of St. Erasmus controlled the route from the north towards the town of Ochrid.

By advancing his frontier Philip acquired the eastern side of Lake Lychnitis, including the already important town Lychnidus, the basin of Lake Prespa, and the basin of Lake Ventrok (also called Little Prespa), all of which had rich fisheries, fertile agricultural land, summer pastures, and extensive forests. Silver was mined already at Damastium, and there are copper deposits on the western side of Lake Ventrok.[1] In antiquity these territories were named from north to south as follows: Atintania, of which the eponym Atintan was added to the sons of Macedon (probably by Theagenes; see p. 34 above); Strymepalis, probably the basin of Prespa; and Eordaea, the basin of Ventrok, from which the river Eordaïcus then flowed into the plain of Poloskë through the Grykë e Ujkut.[2] This Eordaea was one of the four districts so named according to Stephanus Byzantinus; one was the original one by Lake Begorritis (it has dropped out of his text); another that in Mygdonia to which the surviving Eordi fled (Thuc. 2. 99. 5); one in 'Iberia', convincingly emended to 'Illyria'; and the last in Thrace. As the river Eordaïcus was mentioned in connection with the campaign of 335, it is clear that Philip introduced its name and that of Eordaea. Thus it is apparent that when Philip extended his kingdom he used names of the homeland for similar areas—a practice followed by Alexander and the Successors in Asia.

In order to hold the extensive areas which were adjacent to the Illyrians and the Dardanians, Philip planted towns and made fortified points, such as we have seen at St. Erasmus. Otherwise he would soon have lost them. In the *First Philippic* 48, delivered *c.* 350, Demosthenes mentioned rumours at Athens about the activities of Philip, and one was that he 'was fortifying towns among Illyrians'—not of course towns in Illyrian occupation, but towns captured in what Demosthenes chose still to call Illyria. The names of two towns in 'Illyria' have come down to us through St. Byz. Ἄστραια, πόλις Ἰλλυρίας, who cites from Hadrianus, *Alexandrias* 1, οἱ δ' ἔχον Ἀστραιάν τε Δόβηρά τε. The name Astraea was native to the marshy plain of Lower Macedonia (see Volume I. 143), and Doberus to southern Paeonia near Valandovo (see Volume I. 200). It is

---

[1] *AE* 1932. 113.   [2] See Volume I. 46 and *JHS* 94 (1974) 74.

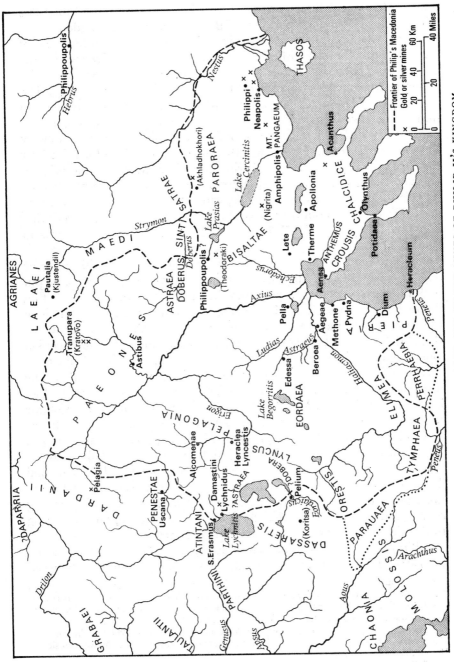

MAP 9. THE FRONTIERS AND THE GOLD AND SILVER MINES OF PHILIP II'S KINGDOM

most probable that these two towns were founded by Philip in the years which followed the incorporation of these areas into the kingdom.[1]

In 199, when Sulpicius marched into the plain at the southern end of Lake Ochrid, 'he established a base near Lyncus (*ad Lyncum*) by the river Bevus [now Molca; see Volume I. 64] and from there sent parties to forage among the granaries of the Dassaretii' (Livy 31. 33. 5). The main plain of Dassaretis lay to his south; therefore Lyncus was close to him on the east. It appears then that the region of the two Prespa lakes had been added to Lyncus for administrative purposes presumably by Philip, and the reason for this was that anyone going from the lakes over the Diavat pass and the Pisodherion pass descended into the original Lyncus.[2] Similarly, when Philip annexed part at least of Perrhaebia, he included it in an enlarged Elimeotis, which thus came to contain within itself the strategic Volustana pass (Volume I. 117 f. and the inscription Μακεδὼν Ἐλειμιώτης ἐκ Πυθείου, which suggests that Pythion was in Elimeotis).[3]

Philip extended his frontiers to the east and to the north with the same objectives in view (see Map 9). When he advanced to the Nestus, he put both the narrows at Amphipolis and the narrow pass of Rendina within the realm, and these gave him defence in depth. His frontier ran along the Nestus river and then along the ridge of Mt. Orbelus as far as the Rupel defile of the Strymon. As we have seen, Philip left the Paeonian kingdom intact, including the Strumitsa valley. The frontier of Macedon then ran from the Strymon across to Mt. Cercine and then along the watershed between the Strymon and the Axius. Here too Philip had an inner line of defence in Mt. Orbelus, west of the Rupel defile (see Volume I. 200). The northern limit of the kingdom was set probably at the Kačanik pass north of Skopje and at the Preševo pass above Kumanovo. If these passes were carried by invaders from the north, Philip had the defile of Demir Kapu as a second line of defence. The Paeonian and Thracian tribes of these regions were not reduced to serfdom or broken up. Rather they were incorporated into the kingdom as self-governing *ethne*, arranging their own affairs and their own defence, and rendering to the king of Macedon such tribute and such service as he required.[4]

Philip planted cities in the eastern areas, as in the west. One bearing his name, Philippoupolis, was in the important passage-way between

---

[1] In Volume I. 201 n. 5 I thought Stephanus had put 'Illyrias' in error for 'Makedonias', but since then I have visited the area and realized how much territory Philip annexed.

[2] In the Roman period the area of Lake Little Prespa belonged to Orestis, which was no doubt rewarded in this way for its defection to Rome.

[3] Hampl 37 n. 3 attributed to Philip the annexation of Pythion. When Philip annexed Parauaea *c.* 350, he weakened his frontier somewhat; for Parauaea is on the western side of the Pindus range (see *Epirus* 680).

[4] I disagree here with I. L. Merker in *BS* 6 (1965) 44 'this subjection did not mean that ˀaionia was incorporated into the Macedonian kingdom.'

the Bisaltae and Mt. Orbelus (see Volume I. 199 f.). The name Astraea near the Strumitsa valley was probably that of another city founded by Philip, a twin to that in the western Eordaea. In the catchment area of the Axius Philip surely strengthened the Macedonian element in the strategic district north of the Demir Kapu, known then as Emathia and now as Kavadarci or Tikvetch (see Volume I. 173). Colonies of Greek-speaking settlers, i.e. citizens of Macedonian towns, have been inferred from Greek inscriptions of later date to have existed in the vicinity of Sveti Nikola and Kratovo (see Volume I. 204), and it is probable that Philip made a start in these cases.

The languages of the inland peoples between the Axius and the Nestus were Paeonian, Bisaltic, and Thracian. There is no indication that these peoples acquired more knowledge of Greek than was necessary for co-existence with the Greek-speaking Macedonians in matters of commerce and administration. Their forces were a part of the kingdom's defence force; but very few of them ever had the privilege of fighting in the field army of the king.

3. Military Security, Economic Development, and Unity under the King

A discussion of the sources of Arrian will be given in Volume III. The speech at Opis has been a centre of controversy e.g. between Tarn 2. 286 who regarded it as 'certainly, in substance, genuine' and F. R. Wüst in *Historia* 2 (1953–4) 177 f. who thought it a later rhetorical composition, based probably on Clitarchus. My concern is with 7. 9. 1–5, which Wüst held to be a rhetorical *topos* on primitivism, such as was composed by sophists, Plato, and the school of Aristotle. In fact, however, it is specific in detail and particular to the Macedonians; of course it is rhetorical in expression but it is not made up of rhetorical generalizations at all. The source behind this section of the speech seems to me to have had a Macedonian viewpoint and a knowledge of the conditions of life in Macedonia in the time of Philip. In this section I shall use excerpts from the speech as starting-points for discussion.

'Philip made you leaders (ἡγεμόνας) instead of slaves and subjects of the very barbarians who used to pillage and carry off your persons and property' (Arr. *An.* 7. 9. 3). In the decades before 360 the constant threat to life, limb, and property came from the Balkan peoples—Illyrians, Dardanians, Paeonians, and Thracians; and it was against these that the Macedonians had to fight for survival in the opening years of Philip's reign. The Greek hoplites or the Greek mercenaries of Thebes, Athens, and Chalcidice were less of a menace; they entered the coastal plain only rarely and Upper Macedonia not at all. The Balkan peoples came to slaughter and loot, especially in Upper Macedonia, and carried off great numbers of prisoners and stock, whereas the Greek powers were usually concerned to apply political pressure on the king. Thus when Philip reconstituted and re-equipped the field army of the Macedones in 359–8, he had the Illyrians and Dardanians primarily in mind; for the forces of Bardylis had just killed 4,000 Macedonian soldiers and were occupying a considerable part of (Upper) Macedonia (D.S. 16. 2. 5 and 4. 4). He designed the phalanx formation, the long pike (*sarissa*), and the 'Macedonian' shield in order to counter the tactics and the armament of the Balkan peoples, not those of Greek hoplites. The heavy cavalry of Macedon had been superior always to Balkan cavalry, as was shown in 429. What Philip did was to create an infantry force of a quality superior to that of any of the Balkan peoples.

Philip gave first priority to the extension of his frontiers. As we have seen, those which he established on the west and on the east of his kingdom had very great natural strength. However, the few passes through them had to be safeguarded. The name Parembole near the Diavat pass was probably that of a permanent encampment for Macedonian troops, and it is likely that towns near the passes, such as Astraea, if it was near the Grykë e Ujkut, or Arethusa near the Rendina pass, were expected to have their levy on the alert. But if Balkan raiders succeeded in breaking through, they would move with great rapidity (see pp. 128 f. above), and it was therefore essential for Philip to have a field force at a central point, which could move with speed to any threatened area. Both cavalry and infantry were trained with this aim, and there is no doubt that Philip improved and extended the system of royal roads which Archelaus had started. Certainly after 356 Macedonia enjoyed a security from attack by land as never before, and this position was maintained for a long time by his successors. Attack by sea was possible at first because Philip never had more than a small fleet by Aegean standards, but he achieved comparative security in 348 when he had the whole of the north-western Aegean coast under his control.

As soon as he felt secure against his Balkan neighbours, Philip embarked on a social and economic revolution. As we have seen (p. 95 above) life in Upper Macedonia was still mainly pastoral, and the people were in part nomadic, because each autumn the flocks were driven down from the mountain pastures of Grammus and Pindus, for instance, to the low-lying pastures on the coast, and vice versa in the spring. When transhumance is practised on a large scale, it is necessary to keep a large proportion of the coastal lands under grass. On the other hand if the coastal lands are given over to agriculture, the transhumance of sheep has to be drastically reduced. The change from transhumance to agriculture has been achieved in Albania during the twenty-five years after

1945. The first step was to control the floods which used to cover the whole of the coastal plain (the Myzeqijë), from the mouth of the Shkumbi to the mouth of the Semeni every spring and autumn; for these floods were beneficial to pasturelands but fatal to agriculture. The next step was to cut down trees and scrub and drain the fenlands, which were extremely fertile. Productivity increased rapidly, and the population has doubled since 1945. Towns have developed, communications have improved, and the contrast between countryman and townsman and especially between shepherd and tiller of the soil has begun to disappear, particularly in dress.[1] It is clear from the following sentences in Arrian 7. 9. 2–3 that something similar happened in Philip's Macedonia.

Philip found you nomadic and lacking in resources, the majority of you wearing sheepskins and pasturing your few sheep on the mountains, and fighting for these unsuccessfully against Illyrians and Triballians and the neighbouring Thracians. He gave you cloaks to wear instead of sheepskins, brought you down from the mountains to the plains, made you worthy opponents of the adjacent barbarians, so that you relied on your own courage rather than on natural strongholds for your survival; he made you into inhabitants of towns and into an orderly people by introducing good laws and a good way of life.

The change from nomadic pastoralism to a settled agricultural life was possible only if it was accompanied by the control of floods and the draining of deforested fenlands. We have evidence that during the reign of Philip and probably during the early years flood-control, deforestation, and draining were carried out on a large scale in the extensive plain of Philippi. Theophrastus, *CP* 5. 14. 5, mentioned that under the control of the Thracians the plain was forested and waterlogged, and he described the change which came about when Philip held it; 'when the water had been drained off, the land mostly dried out, and the whole territory brought under cultivation' (ἐπεὶ καταποθεὶς ἐξήρανται τὸ πλεῖστον, ἥ τε χώρα πᾶσα κάτεργος γέγονεν), the climate altered and new flora developed. As Philip took over the plain in 356 and Theophrastus visited the area probably in 336, when he was with Aristotle in Macedonia, there had been time for new flora and fauna to become established. What Philip did for Philippi, he certainly did for the coastal plain of the Thermaic Gulf, which was subject to immense floods then, as in Turkish times (see Volume I. 142–9). This important development may have been inspired by his familiarity with the drainage of Lake Copaïs and with intensive agriculture in Boeotia, when he was there as a hostage. One effect of controlling the waters of the Axius and the Haliacmon was the provision

[1] I write here from personal experience, having travelled in Albania in 1930–9 and again in 1972.

of an all-weather waterway, an *anaplous*, from the Gulf to Pella (see Map 16 in Volume I. 150). The transhumance of sheep declined correspondingly in Lower Macedonia. However, it was still practised in parts of the kingdom, e.g. in Tymphaea, which has superb alpine pastures and extensive forests,[1] and Tymphaea supplied a phalanx-brigade in 331.

Security from invasion and draining of fenlands gave a great impetus to agriculture not only in Lower Macedonia but also in Upper Macedonia, where many areas were liable to flooding, e.g. in the basin of the upper Erigon in Pelagonia and Lyncus. In later times Roman writers commented on the industry of the farmers, for instance in the lowlands between the Peneus and the Axius, which were worked by 'permultos Gallos et Illyrios, impigros cultores' (Livy 45. 30. 5). In Philip's reign too there were many free peasants of Illyrian, Paeonian, and Thracian descent in the kingdom, and it was probably these who laid the foundations of Macedonia's agricultural prosperity. Stock-breeding played an important part in the economy. Paeonian cattle and Macedonian horses were particularly famous, and Philip sent back 20,000 brood mares from Scythia in 339/8 (Just. 9. 2 fin.).[2] As confidence grew, men put capital into viticulture and arboriculture. Crestonia, Bisaltia, and Amphipolis, areas in which the bulk of the population was of Thracian descent, yielded particularly fine harvests of figs, grapes, and olives during the reign of Philip, which was marked by spring seasons of unusual mildness (*FGrH* 115 F 230). Cereals too must have flourished then as now in the great plains and the partly continental climate of Macedonia; indeed ears of wheat and other cereals appear as emblems on some of the coins of Philip.

The extension of the kingdom and the change from pastoralism to agriculture in many areas led to a redistribution of population which was directed by the king both for purposes of defence and for the economic development of his resources. 'He brought you down from the mountains to the plains . . . made you into inhabitants of towns', a change which is familiar to anyone who has known north Greece and Albania over the last forty years. Philip moved more quickly. On defeating Bardylis in 358 he probably founded Heraclea Lyncestis, named after his ancestor Heracles, who figured prominently on his coinage—'probably', because we have to emend the founder's name in Stephanus Byzantinus to 'Philip son of Amyntas' from 'Amyntas son of Philip', which is a misnomer. On capturing Crenides from the Thasians in 356 he renamed it Philippi and 'increased it with a great number of settlers'

---

[1] The western part of Tymphaea is occupied by Vlach villages, which obtain their living from sheep and timber (see Volume I, Map 2).

[2] Presumably some Scythian stallions too; for if he had planned cross-breeding, he would have used Macedonian mares, one imagines.

(D.S. 16. 3. 7 and 9. 6). He may have done the same for Damastium, another mining town, which lay east of Lychnidus. We have seen that he probably founded Astraea and Dobera in the western Eordaea, and another Astraea in the Strumitsa valley. Philippoupolis in the valley between Bisaltia and Mt. Orbelus was named after him; and he probably strengthened the Macedonian town by Demir Kapu and planted other settlements in Tikvetch. For these towns he needed different kinds of settlers: at Heraclea Lyncestis a considerable number of Macedones and then a greater number of selected Lyncestae; at towns near the frontier a majority perhaps of Macedonians from Lower Macedonia and an admixture of local people; and at mining towns few Macedonians and many miners and traders. He made changes also on the coast. The territory of Methone was 'divided up among the Macedones' by Philip in 354 (D.S. 16. 34. 5); land in the vicinity of Potidaea was distributed to Macedones in the same way (*Syll.*³ 1. 332); and many Macedones were settled in the region of Amphipolis, which was able to provide a squadron of Companion cavalry. Great estates were given too to his 800 Companions, who derived more income from their lands than the richest 10,000 landowners in Greece according to Theopompus (*FGrH* 115 F 217). At a humbler level 20,000 women and boys were brought from Scythia in 339/8 (Just. 9. 2 fin.); and 'more than 10,000 Sarnousii' from Sarnous in Illyria, perhaps near the territory of the Penestae (Polyaen. 4. 2. 12; St. Byz. s.v. *Sarnous*).

Philip was not the first Macedonian king to move people at will. Alexander I, and his father Amyntas I, must have done so during the expansion of the kingdom and the settlement of areas such as Eordaea, from which the original inhabitants were expelled; and later, when territory was given to the Chalcidians to use,[1] the existing Macedonian population must have been removed and resettled by the king. Philip, however, did it to an unparalleled extent.[2] The clearest statement of his policy is in Justin 8. 5. 7 and 8. 6. 1–2, where Justin was abridging a much fuller account, derived ultimately perhaps from Theopompus:

When Philip returned to his kingdom [in 346], he moved peoples and cities at his pleasure, wherever he thought a district should be repeopled or

---

[1] e.g. in Thuc. 1. 58. 2 the evacuees were given land to cultivate, *nemesthai*.

[2] J. R. Ellis has discussed the policy of Philip in *Mak.* 9 (1969) 9–17 'Population-Transplants by Philip II'. He is closer to my view than is A. B. Bosworth in *CQ* 23 (1973) 250, who holds, I think mistakenly, that there was only 'a redistribution within existing settlements', and that new settlements were made only in Thrace. But Bosworth runs counter to the evidence of Justin; Philip returned 'in regnum' to carry out the movements of population (8. 5. 7) and it was only 'compositis ordinatisque Macedoniae rebus' that Philip turned to the Dardanii and other neighbours 'finitimos' (8. 6. 2), and express mention was made of planting people at the frontiers 'in finibus ipsis' (8. 6. 1). Justin maintained a clear distinction between the kingdom and the empire. What Philip did in Thrace was merely an extension of what he did in Macedonia.

depopulated, even as shepherds move their flocks now to winter, now to summer pastures . . .

. . . some peoples he placed facing his enemies on the very frontiers; others he settled in the furthest parts of the kingdom; and some peoples whom he had captured in war were divided up and sent to supplement the populations of the towns. So from many tribes and races he formed one kingdom and one people.

The new towns and the enlarged towns were important for the development of agriculture and commerce, and they contributed to the development of communications. In some places they were of military value. They brought people of different origins together and created a form of culture which was based on contemporary Greek culture but remained specifically Macedonian in colouring; for Philip produced 'an orderly people by introducing good laws and a good way of life'. Whatever else Philip achieved, he gave to the people of his enlarged kingdom freedom from fear and want, and a promise of security and prosperity for the future. These were major factors in enabling him to form 'one kingdom and one people' out of 'many tribes and races'.

National unity sprang in part from the womb of prosperity. As forests were cut down, e.g. at Philippi, more timber was exported. As more land was brought under cultivation, Macedonia became self-supporting in foodstuffs and probably had a surplus of cereals for export. Chalcidice too was rich in cereals, olives, and fruit. 'Philip developed the commerce of your country by taking over the most conveniently placed towns on the coast, and he enabled you to work the mines in security' (Arr. *An.* 7. 9. 3). After 348 he traded directly with states in the Aegean and towards the end of his reign with states in the Black Sea, as well as overland with Central Europe. His policy in regard to the Greek cities on his coast was eclectic: for instance, he destroyed Galepsus and its neighbour Apollonia (Str. 7 frs. 33 and 35 fin.) and he favoured the growth of Neapolis, Amphipolis, and Pella, 'hitherto a small place' (Str. 7 fr. 23). We gain the impression of a well-planned economy. It was the same with the mines. Those at Crenides–Philippi were 'trivial and insignificant' until Philip increased their output so much 'by his installations that they could yield a return of more than 1,000 talents a year, and by amassing capital reserves from them he advanced the kingdom of Macedon to a leading position more and more as his wealth grew' (D.S. 16. 8. 7). Other mines of gold, silver, copper, and iron were no doubt developed with equal enterprise and efficiency.

The coinage of Philip (see Plate II) has not yet been the subject of a special study,[1] unlike that of Damastium, for instance. Here we can

---

[1] It has been reported that G. Le Rider of the Cabinet des Médailles in Paris is undertaking this study (*AJA* 74 (1970) 348 n. 10); it will be most valuable. I am using the list of Philip's coins in Gaebler, and the article of A. B. West, 'The early diplomacy of Philip II of Macedonia

draw only the general outlines although even these may be upset by a detailed study of die sequences. In 356 to 348 his coinage rivalled that of the Chalcidian League, and in 348 to 336 his coinage became the strongest currency in Europe. Departing from the practice of his predecessors since Archelaus, he adopted the Attic standard in gold and the Thracian standard in silver, thus exploiting the key position which his kingdom held between the Mediterranean basin and Central Europe. The volume of Macedonia's trade is shown by the very wide distribution of his coins, particularly those in gold called *Philippeioi*. In the words of C. T. Seltman[1] 'the *Philippeioi* quickly overspread the Greek world and were as popular in the West as in Greece proper and the Near East. Hoards have been found in northern Greece, Corinth, and the Peloponnese, in South Russia, near Constantinople, in Asia Minor, Cyprus, Syria, and Egypt, as well as in South Italy, and particularly in Sicily.' To these we may add the Balkan countries, Switzerland, France, and Germany, where the coins were much imitated. His silver coins have been found in hoards in Greece, Bulgaria, Rumania, and Sicily but not in Asia. Philip realized the potential which had been suggested by the Thraco-Macedonian coinages of the archaic period.

There are probably no coins of Amyntas IV during the period of Philip's regency.[2] Philip began to coin in 356, and his use of the Thasian obverse marks a continuity between the Thasian coinage of Crenides and those of Crenides–Philippi and his own self, the former inscribed ΦΙΛΙΠΠΩΝ and the latter ΦΙΛΙΠΠΟΥ.

The Thasian gold staters had the head of a young Heracles with a lionskin / ΘΑΣΙΟΝ ΗΠΕΙΡΟ with either tripod, laurel-branch, and cantharus or club and bow. The gold staters of Philippi had the same obverse and a tripod with the name of the town ΦΙΛΙΠΠΩΝ on the reverse; there was a *protome* of a horse as a lesser emblem. The silver coins of Philippi, ranging from the tetradrachms to hemidrachms, used the same devices as the gold coins, but had as lesser emblems a dolphin, an axe, and an ear of corn—the last two probably celebrating the deforestation and the agricultural development in the plain of Philippi. The bronze coins of Philippi had the same obverse as the gold and silver coins, and the tripod on the reverse; but they had other emblems too, such as a crescent moon and a bow and quiver.

Philip's own coins, all inscribed ΦΙΛΙΠΠΟΥ, had the same obverse,

---

illustrated by his coins', *NC* 3 (1923) 169–210, which was based more on the supposed plans of Philip than on a detailed study of the coins. West's conclusions have been challenged recently by A. R. Bellinger, 'Philippi in Macedonia', *ANSMusN* 2. 29 f.

[1] *Greek Coins* (London, 1933) 201. See also L. R. Laing, *Coins and Archaeology* (London 1969) 123.

[2] It has been suggested that some coins attributed to Amyntas III may be those of Amyntas IV; there is no proof either way.

i.e. the head of a young Heracles with a lionskin, and were issued in gold, silver, and bronze, presumably from Pella, where Strabo said the mint was 'in early times' (7 fr. 20 τὸ τῆς Μακεδονίας χρηματιστήριον).[1] They started probably at the same time as the staters of Philippi in 356. On the reverse of the gold pieces (half-staters, quarter-staters, and eighths of a stater) he had a springing lion, or a club and bow (as on the Thasian coins), or the foreleg of what was probably a goat, or a cantharus (as on the Thasian coins), or a trident. On the reverse of the silver didrachms and octobols he had a racehorse with a naked jockey, celebrating the victory of the horse at the Olympic Games of 356. On the reverse of the larger bronze pieces the same racehorse and jockey appeared; and a thunderbolt or a club with a spearhead and a crescent moon on the smaller coins. Another lesser emblem was a curry-comb, alluding no doubt to his victory with the racehorse. Links between Philip and his predecessors, including his father Amyntas III, are to be seen in the head of Heracles, his club, the springing lion, the thunderbolt, and the foreleg of the goat if that is what is represented.

In 359 to 356 the magnificent coinage of the Chalcidian League was not challenged by Macedon, and the silver coinages of Damastium and Daparria far inland adopted the devices of the Chalcidian League (see pp. 189 f. and 191 above).[2] The Chalcidians coined in gold, silver, and bronze with the artistically superb head of Apollo, laureate / cithara; this Apollo was short-haired until the latest issues, ending in 348, when he was long-haired. Philip issued silver tetrobols with the head of Apollo, short-haired and laureate / a racehorse ridden by a naked jockey. As the reverse commemorated the victory of the racehorse at Olympia in 356, we infer that the tetrobols were issued soon after 356 in imitation of Chalcidian coins, which had an established reputation. When Olynthus fell and Chalcidian coinage ceased in 348, Philip struck gold staters with the head of Apollo, long-haired and laureate / a two-horse chariot at the gallop. In the other issues of gold staters Apollo was short-haired. We may conjecture, then, that Philip used the current obverse of the Chalcidian coins for his first instalment of gold staters. These famous coins, the so-called *Philippeioi*, were mentioned in D.S. 16. 8. 7, a chapter which I have argued was based on Ephorus,[3] as indicative of the wealth which enabled Philip to raise a large force of mercenaries and bribe politicians in Greek states. Now the victory of the two-horse chariot, evidently at Olympia,[4] did not occur in 356 (for Plutarch, *Alex.* 3, would

---

[1] Numismatists generally regard Pella as the chief mint of Philip; e.g. M. Thompson in *AJA* 74 (1970) 343 f. for gold coins late in his reign.

[2] For Damastium and Daparria see J. M. F. May, *The Coinage of Damastion* 47 and 165.

[3] In *CQ* 31 (1937) 81 f. and 85.

[4] He had more than one victory with a chariot at Olympia and recorded them on his coins according to Plu. *Alex.* 4. 9.

have mentioned the double, if it had coincided with the victory of the racehorse) but in 352 or 348. It would be appropriate for the victory to be commemorated shortly after the event, and we may therefore put the victory and the issue with the long-haired Apollo late in 348. The subsequent staters and the smaller gold pieces, a twelfth of a stater, had the short-haired Apollo; and the latter had on the reverse a thunderbolt and a lion-head, repeating motifs from his earlier coinage.

The largest silver coins of Philip, tetradrachms, had the head of Zeus, laureate—unparalleled in earlier Macedonian coinage— / a bearded rider with *kausia* or *petasus*, tunic, and cloak on a high-stepping horse—reminiscent of the much earlier rider so dressed and mounted but holding two spears.[1] Some tetradrachms had the same head of Zeus on the obverse but a racehorse ridden by a naked jockey on the reverse. The head of Zeus on these fine tetradrachms advertised the connection of Macedon, the eponym of the Macedones, and of Heracles, ancestor of the royal house, with Zeus, the supreme god of the Hellenes. Some of Philip's silver tetrobols had the head of a young man, clean shaven— a device introduced by Archelaus and used by Aëropus, Pausanias, and Alexander II— / a racehorse ridden by a naked jockey; and some bronze pieces had the same obverse and reverse as the silver tetrobols. We put the start of these issues soon after 356. The device of the head of a young man, clean shaven, was used on silver diobols with either a *protome* of a prancing horse or the head of a bridled horse on the reverse. Lastly, some silver tetrobols had the head and shoulders of Artemis, facing, on the obverse, a device unknown on earlier Macedonian coins but occurring on silver coins of Orthagoria near Maroneia;[2] it is probable then that, repeating what he had done at Philippi and in Chalcidice in 348, Philip adopted the device of Orthagoria, and that he allowed her to continue coining (as in the case of Philippi). Gaebler attributed the coins of Orthagoria to the mid-fourth century and later years. Some of the lesser emblems on all the issues in this paragraph were the same as in issues which we described earlier; others were new, namely palm-branch, bee, grasshopper, ear of wheat, and—on the Artemis issue only—the *protome* of a Pegasus.

The excavation of Olynthus produced one silver coin and thirty-seven bronze coins attributable to the reign of Philip before 348, when the city was made desolate.[3] Four bronze pieces had the head of a young Heracles / the racehorse with the naked jockey; two had the same head / thunderbolt; thirty-one had the head of a young man, clean shaven / the racehorse with the naked jockey; and the one silver tetrobol had the same obverse and reverse as the thirty-one bronze pieces. We can thus

---

[1] G. xxviii. 4 and xxx. 37 and 38.   [2] G. xviii. 23 and xxxi. 3.
[3] *Olynthus* 9. 233 f. and 327 f.

conclude that between 356 and 348 Philip's favourite device on bronze coins was the head of the young man, clean shaven (a traditional Macedonian emblem), and that there were fewer bronze coins with the head of Heracles. As bronze coins were for local circulation, this indicates that within Macedonia more importance was attached to the cult of the young god, represented by the head of the young man, than to that of Heracles, who was connected with Macedonia only through the royal house (see Arr. *An.* 4. 10. 6). The same conclusion is reached when we consider the coins found in the excavation of near-by Mecyberna, where the corresponding figures for bronze pieces were two, five, and sixty-one; there were no silver pieces of Philip.[1] There were three bronze coins of Philippi at Olynthus and four at Mecyberna. At the other end of the time scale we have to note that some of the coinages introduced by Philip were issued again after he was dead.[2]

Before we consider the final problem, that of the date of the introduction of the head of Zeus on the silver tetradrachms (Philip's largest coins in this metal), we must relate his coinages to the accessibility of precious ores.[3] In 359 to early 357 he had access to only small amounts of gold near Kilkis and Lete. On acquiring control of Amphipolis in autumn 357 he added gold at Nigrita and silver at Theodoraki in Bisaltia. The next step, to Crenides–Philippi early in 356, gave him a great quantity of gold and silver on Mt. Pangaeum and by Philippi. Meanwhile in the north-west the silver mines of Damastium came within the enlarged kingdom after his victory over Bardylis in 358; as we shall see, he allowed Damastium to continue coining. Gold and silver ores at Kratovo and elsewhere in Paeonia were used by the Paeonian kings, and after the victory of Philip in 356 the mines were left in Lycceus' hands. The deposits of gold and silver at Akhladhokhori were probably under the control of Berisades and his sons until late in the 350s. The next accession on a grand scale was that of the gold and silver at Stratoniki, which provided the Chalcidian League with its prolific coinage in both metals. After 348 Philip had great quantities of gold and silver at his disposal. As regards copper for coining in bronze there were considerable deposits in western Macedonia, which were available from the beginning; also some at Kilkis; and late in 357 at Theodoraki. A further accession of copper followed the defeat of the Chalcidian League in 348.

It is clear from the finds at Olynthus and Mecyberna that Philip coined considerably in bronze from 356, when he first began to issue coins in his own name, down to 349. When he gained control of gold and silver in the region of Bisaltia, Amphipolis, and Philippi, he issued from 356 onwards gold coins from half-staters downwards and silver didrachms

---

[1] *Olynthus* 9. 253 f. See Bellinger, loc. cit., for a hoard of bronze pieces at Drama.
[2] e.g. *AJA* 74. 349 and *Olynthus* 3. 82.   [3] See Volume I Map I, and above, p. 70.

and octobols with the device which the Thasians had made familiar at Crenides–Philippi, the head of a young Heracles with a lionskin. From the same time there were silver tetrobols with the head of a young man, clean shaven / racehorse and jockey. It is interesting that the devices on the gold and silver coinages of this period, 356–348, were all used also on bronze coins. When he gained control of Chalcidice, he issued the gold staters, the so-called *Philippeioi*, with the head of a long-haired Apollo in 348 as in the last issues of the Chalcidians; thereafter Apollo was short-haired. Just as he issued now larger gold coins than in the past, so too he issued silver tetradrachms for the first time.[1] For the large accession of silver enabled him in late 348 or a subsequent year to issue the very striking tetradrachms with the head of Zeus. He chose this device probably because his aim was to bring the Greeks and the Macedonians into a state of peace and amity under the auspices of Zeus, the supreme god of both peoples. It should be noted that the devices on the gold *Philippeioi* and the silver tetradrachms were not reproduced on bronze coins; this suggests that after 348 Philip made relatively little use of bronze in his minting. Smaller denominations in gold[2] and in silver of the period 356–348 were minted also for the rest of his reign; this is apparent from the summary of starts in the various denominations.

Date of start	Gold Stater	Gold half to twelfth	Silver Tetra-drachm	Didrachm	Octobol	Tetrobol	Bronze Diobol
356–		x		x	x	x	
348–	x		x			x	x

It is not clear whether Philip's version of the Orthagoria tetrobol with the head and shoulders of Artemis should be placed before or after 348.

It has been suggested that Philip himself was portrayed as the head of the young man, clean shaven, as the bearded rider, and even as the head of Zeus.[3] I see no case for the first and third suggestions; but the bearded rider with hat, tunic, and cloak seems to be a revival of the figure which we suggested was a representation of Alexander I. It is possible that Philip wished to show himself after 348 as a mediator between Macedonians and Greeks on the reverse of the Zeus coins.[4]

[1] Seltman, following West and others, attributed the silver tetradrachms to Philip's 'first' coinage; but it seems unlikely that he had such large resources of silver at the start.

[2] Philip probably ceased coining in gold with the head of the young Heracles when his gold *Philippeioi* became established; for there are none of the former in the hoard of gold coins buried at Corinth soon after 329/8 (*AJA* 74. 343 f.).

[3] The first and third were favoured by Kleiner in *AM* 63/64 (1938/9) 39 f.; and the second by Seltman, op. cit. 199.

[4] It is remarkable that the head of Zeus had not been used before on coins of the Macedonian kings, and it may be that Philip wished to stress the common derivation of Macedones and Hellenes through their eponymous ancestors from Zeus.

In 358 Philip annexed the territory within which one at least of the silver mines controlled by Damastium was situated. He allowed the 'Damastini' to continue issuing their fine coinage, mainly of tetradrachms, with their established and well-known emblems (as he was to do at Crenides–Philippi in 356). As we have seen, the coinage of Damastium was used mainly for trade westwards and northwards,[1] and it suited Philip to favour such trade in the Balkans. Ingots of silver were also exported from Damastium, and it has been noted that in the latter half of the fourth century, when the so-called Asiatic fibulae, Blinkenberg's class XII, were particularly popular throughout Yugoslavia, most of them were made in silver.[2] It is probable that Damastium supplied silver to Epidamnus, whose prolific coinage was current throughout the Balkans and in Sicily and Italy at this time. A hoard at the site of Rhizon in the Gulf of Kotor contained some 300 coins, of which two-thirds were tetradrachms of Damastine and related coinages and one-third staters of Corinth and her colonies, including Epidamnus for the period *c.* 360–330.[3] No doubt a tax in silver ore was paid to Philip as king of Macedon, and we have conclusive evidence that at Damastium and at Philippi Philip's officials were in charge of the mints for some years between 358 and 345 approximately. The names or the monograms of Heracleidas and Cephisophon appeared sometimes together, sometimes singly, on the coins both of Damastium and Philippi during the period of Philip's reign, and there is no doubt that the link between the two mining towns was forged by Philip.[4] Heracleidas, too, was a name appropriate to the royal house of Macedon and to that of Lyncus. Three Companions of Alexander were so named, and a prominent Macedon of Pella carried that name *c.* 200 B.C. (*SEG* 24. 539).

---

[1] So too the coinage of the Paeonian kings; cf. I. L. Merker in *BS* 6. 54 'quite clearly Paionia's trade was with the north.'

[2] Blinkenberg in *Lindiaka* 5. 229.   [3] See *Epirus* 541 with references.

[4] May, *Damastion* 105, wrote as follows. 'The sudden appearance of the names of Herakleidas and Kephisophon, at first to the total exclusion of that of the Damastini, shows that there must have been considerable changes at the mines at the beginning of the period of Group VII', i.e. after *c.* 365–360 on his dating of the groups. The first coins of the new group were a shade lighter than their predecessors, and they carried on the reverse HPAKΛEIΔO and KH and a knife (a new emblem); and they were followed at once, as a linked die shows, by coins with ΔAMAΣTINΩN and KHΦI on the reverse (May 83 f.). Some coins of Philippi carried the letters HPA and KH (May 109, citing Babelon 2. 4. 750 no. 1186, Pl. 324, 18 and p. 751). Another monogram in common was ΔH. That the appearance of these names at the same period at places so far apart as Damastium and Philippi should be a freak of chance is incredible, *pace* May who wrote 'to see in them proof of Macedonian control at Damastium would be quite unjustified.' This surely is to close one's eyes to the evidence.

A. R. Bellinger, 'Philippi in Macedonia', *ANSMusN* 2. 29 f., recorded the abbreviation HPA on a silver tetradrachm of Philippi, the last according to his arrangement. He does not refer to the same name at Damastium. His theory that Philippi and Damastium, having the same standard, were to compete for influence in the Paeonian region (p. 35) seems unlikely; rather the co-ordination was due to the influence of Philip.

Lycceus, who succeeded Agis as king of the Paeonians in 359/8, issued a fine silver coinage of tetradrachms, drachms, and tetrobols, which were at first of the same standard as the coins of Damastium.[1] Later Damastium and Lycceus used a lighter version of the standard, probably at a time when they were both within the kingdom of Philip. The tetradrachms have a head of Apollo, named *Derronaios* on one coin / Heracles wrestling with a lion, or a portrait of the king's head with the same reverse, or a head of Zeus with the same reverse. The drachms have a female head or a head of Apollo / a lion about to spring or standing. The tetrobols have a head of Apollo or a portrait of the king's head / a horse grazing. Emblems are Heracles' club, bow, and quiver, and also a flower like that on a coin of the Derrones.[2] The king was probably honouring Paeonian deities, who were sometimes equated then as now, with Greek gods, and depicting the lions and the horses of his own country; at the same time he shared with the king of Macedon a devotion to the cult of Heracles. The originality of his coin-types and the self-portrait show that Lycceus had a high degree of independence. He minted his coins, probably at Astibus, from silver mined at Kratovo, resuming the practice of the Derrones (see p. 79 above). He died shortly after Philip.

A coinage was issued by the Pelagitaes or Pelagiteis throughout the reign of Philip and probably down to *c.* 280 in the form of tetradrachms, drachms, and tetrobols, which became increasingly barbaric in style and lettering.[3] The earliest tetradrachm had a head of Apollo / a round shield, called 'Macedonian' by numismatists but probably common to the peoples of the Central Balkans. At the same period the drachm had a female head / a portable ingot, and the tetrobol a head of Apollo / a tripod. The types are close to those of Daparria and Damastium, and the standard was that of Damastium. A knife, which was the Illyrian weapon *par excellence*, appeared on a coin in the time of Philip. Once again a mining area was exporting bullion both in ingots and in coinage. It is probable that the Pelagiteis were in Polog, the high flat country of Tetovo, where there are deposits of silver; for the name Pelagia would suit the flat area, just as Pelagonia fitted the flat plain of the upper Erigon. Also May held on stylistic grounds that this coinage, being closely related to the coinages of Damastium, Daparria, and Paeonia, came from a region 'not far from the northwestern borders of Paeonia'.[4] If so, the Pelagiteis lay just outside the frontier of Macedonia as we have drawn it.

Two other coinages,[5] which were related to the coinage of Damastium but were more barbarous, appeared *c.* 350–340. The tetradrachms of

[1] G. 199 f., xxxvii. 1–14. [2] G. xxvii. 26. [3] See May, *Damastion* 169 f.
[4] Ibid. 172. [5] Ibid. 192 and 197.

the 'Tenestini' have Damastine types and came presumably from another mining area, perhaps in the Kossovo district. Three coins with the same relationship to Damastium bear the name 'Darado', ΔΑΡΑΔΟ, not dissimilar from 'Derdas', which is the name perhaps of a Dardanian or Illyrian dynast in the Metohija, where there are also deposits of silver. All these coinages appeared as a result of the quickening of trade which resulted from the growth and expansion of the Macedonian state.

The first sign of great wealth according to Aristotle (*Rhet.* 1. 5. 7) was 'an abundance of coinage', and Philip's Macedon certainly had that. Another was the maintaining of a large professional army. When Diodorus, drawing probably on Ephorus at 16. 8. 7, connected the abundant coinage of Philip with the growth of his power, he made the point that 'Philip organized a remarkable force of paid troops' (μισθο-φόρων τε δύναμιν ἀξιόλογον συνεστήσατο). The word μισθοφόρων, both here and in another Ephorean passage of Diodorus 16, namely 75. 2 at Perin-thus, referred not to national troops, paid though these were, but to mercenaries of whatever race, such as those engaged by Dionysius and the Phocian commanders. It is probable that Ephorus (if he was the source) had in mind not only Greek mercenaries, of whom Philip had a few specialist groups, such as the Cretan archers, but also Thracians and Illyrians who served Philip but were in receipt of pay. Otherwise the passage is difficult to explain. However, the main point is that after 348 Philip was able financially to maintain a large army for a campaign of considerable duration, whether in the Balkans or in Greece. For example, the 30,000 men he had at Perinthus (D.S. 16. 74. 6) probably included many Thracian troops; on the other hand, the slightly larger army at Chaeronea seems to have been composed of Macedonians alone.[1] It is clear that the army of Macedones proper trebled in size between 358 and 338. This remarkable increase is an indication not only of the king's resources but also of wealth in private hands; for the cavalry and the infantry were landholders, and the amount or the value of land in the hands of the Macedones must have trebled in those twenty years. As we have seen, Theopompus was amazed by the wealth of Philip's 800 Companions and by the lavishness of Philip's gifts. Very large sums were available evidently for the building of new towns and for the fortification and embellishment of old towns, such as Edessa, which were equipped with fine walls and gateways (see Volume 1. 165).

The great wealth of Philip was acknowledged also by Theopompus. But with typical malice Theopompus described Philip as profligate and incompetent, without of course explaining how such a person could have raised his state from poverty to affluence. 'Philip being the worst manager in the world—not only himself but also his entourage—threw it away

[1] See *StGH* 546.

rather than spent it rapidly . . . and being a soldier he was too busy to calculate income and expenditure' (*FGrH* 115 F 217). So wrote an armchair historian, and later Hellenistic writers were delighted to describe Alexander as one who inherited a tiny, bankrupt, or indebted treasury according to taste.[1] But a state which could maintain the campaigns against Perinthus and Byzantium, Atheas of Scythia, and the Greeks in 340–338, and send a fleet and a vanguard of not less than 10,000 men into Asia in 336 was very far from being financially debilitated. Philip certainly practised a 'rolling economy' whereby the profits of one campaign or enterprise might pay for the mounting of another, and the income from one developed area might be spent on developing another area; but he left to his successor a kingdom richly endowed with capital resources for the first time in its history.

The Macedonian state derived its unity primarily from the king. He decided who were to be 'Macedones', and Philip certainly gave the franchise to many who were Greeks by origin, as Archelaus and others had done before him. He decided what land they and their families should possess, what taxes they should pay and what services they should render (*Syll.*[3] 1. 332; Arr. *An.* 7. 10. 4). Within the army he decided the rank of every man from the highest officer, ἡγεμών, to the lowest soldier; promotion depended on him, and a man could rise from the bottom to the top with his favour (as Bolon did, Curt. 6. 11. 1); and all matters of pay and bounty were in his hands.[2] The king was traditionally regarded with veneration by the Macedones; and as a successful commander and generous benefactor Philip was particularly loved by his contemporaries as we learn repeatedly from the account of Arrian. But more than loyalty to the king was involved. Every Macedonian was deeply attached to his own town or his own district. The territorial organization within the army fostered this local loyalty, and each regiment and unit strove to attain the highest honours in battle. The cavalry squadrons and the infantry phalanx excelled as a result not only of their spirit but also of intensive training; each man depended on the co-operation of his neighbour in action, and each unit depended on the co-ordinated movement of other units, as was demonstrated so clearly on the battlefield of Chaeronea. The morale of the army which Philip led almost always to victory with a minimum of casualties was similar to that of the Spartiates at their acme. But there was a significant difference. The Spartiates were engaged in holding down a multitude of serfs and underprivileged persons. The Macedones were the élite members of a free society which shared in the benefits of military security and economic prosperity.

---

[1] Bellinger, loc. cit. 36 f., lists the passages and comments on them.

[2] Philip gave large bounties for gallantry in action, ἀνδραγαθία; see D.S. 16. 53. 3, 75. 3–4 and 86. 6.

4. *The Organization of the Balkan Empire*

Pursuit by the cavalry was a feature of Philip's Balkan campaigns. The object was usually to destroy not the infantry, who took to the hills and escaped, but the cavalry, who constituted the ruling class, whether the enemy was Illyrian, Paeonian, Dardanian, or Thracian. In the course of the long pursuit Philip and his Companions demonstrated beyond dispute their superiority over that ruling class and their right to displace them. But Philip's intention was not in fact to do that; he preferred the co-operation of the survivors, and if they were prepared to give it he used them to administer their own country. Paeonia is an excellent example of his method. In 358 he defeated the Paeonians in battle and 'compelled the tribe to obey the Macedones'; again in 356 he defeated them and 'compelled them to take the side of the Macedones' (D.S. 16. 4. 2 and 22. 3; cf. Isoc. 5. 21); and it was characteristic of their situation that the Paeonian king was allowed to keep his mines and coin in his own name, and that he and his nobles fought as a cavalry unit probably for Philip and certainly for Alexander. Beyond the boundaries of the kingdom Philip seems to have left Langarus, king of the Agrianes, in a position almost of independence; for in 335 Alexander treated him apparently as an equal and offered him not only great gifts but also the hand of his half-sister. Langarus certainly managed his own kingdom and raised his own troops, including a select regiment of what Arrian called 'hypaspists' (1. 5. 2). Within the kingdom he allowed the right of coinage to Philippi and to Damastium, which flourished under his favour, and outside the kingdom Daparria, Pelagia, and Orthagoria were treated in the same manner.

In his wars Philip acquired spoils and booty, for instance from Illyrians and Scythians, or from Methone and Olynthus.[1] We do not hear of any slaughter of adult males in a captured town, such as Athens committed *c.* 353 at Sestus (D.S. 16. 34. 3). Where an alliance was broken unilaterally, as by the Chalcidians, or a community revolted, as Methone or a town of the Maedi, the people were deported, or put to forced labour (Aeschin. 2. 156) or in the case of Olynthus sold into slavery (D.S. 16. 53. 3). By the standards of his contemporaries both in the Balkans and in Greece Philip practised clemency and did not engender the excessive hatreds which were a mark of inter-state relations among so many Greek city-states. This enlightened policy made reconciliation possible and might lead to what Isocrates called *homonoia*. When he defeated a Balkan people in war, he usually imposed the payment of tribute (D.S. 16. 71. 2), but not universally; for we read in Arrian of 'the

[1] D.S. 16. 69. 7; Just. 9. 2 fin.; D.S. 16. 31. 6 and 16. 53. 3.

autonomous Thracians', who seem to have been like 'the autonomous allies' of Athens, not tribute-paying.[1] As in Macedonia itself, there were probably grades of privilege among the Balkan tribes: some equal allies, some allowed to coin, some subject to tribute and others not, and so on. Apart from the over-all control by Philip or his deputy on occasion there seems to have been no imposition of governors or inspectors or magistrates in the manner of imperial Athens or Sparta and no imposition of 'democracy' or 'oligarchy'.[2] It is only in the coinage of Philippi and Damastium that we see signs of Macedonian officials. Philip left tribes and cities to govern themselves as in the past, and he abstained from creating any form of bureaucracy at any level.

Philip brought to an end the intertribal warfare which had torn the Balkans for many generations, and he imposed a peace from which prosperity grew. His regime was particularly beneficial to the agricultural workers, who had been despised and maltreated as Herodotus had noted (5. 6. 2), and now the settled conditions were favourable to commerce and urban development. In Thrace, for example, 'Philip founded important towns in appropriate places and put an end to the unruly ways of the Thracians' (D.S. 16. 71. 2 ἔπαυσε τοῦ θράσους τοὺς Θρᾷκας). The population of the new towns was what Plutarch called 'mixed': it included Macedonians, Greeks, and the leading local people, and it resulted in a fusion of ideas and cultures. In particular the new towns such as Philippoupolis at Plovdiv[3] promoted agriculture and trade. It is probable that large areas of land were reclaimed and brought into cultivation, as in Macedonia; some were royal domains and others were given by Philip to his friends ([D.] 7. 39–41). Peaceful conditions in the hinterland were welcomed by the Greek cities on the coasts of the Adriatic, the Aegean, and the Black Sea, and many of them 'gladly entered into the alliance of Philip' (D.S. loc. cit.). Military roads were built for the rapid movement of troops, especially cavalry,[4] and in his

---

[1] Hdt. 7. 111. 1 called the Satrae, alone among the Thracians, *eleutheroi* because they had never been conquered. Since Philip was said to have subdued all Thrace and was friendly with the king of the Getae on the Danube, it seems that the 'so-called autonomous Thracians' of Mount Haemus (Arr. 1. 1. 5) were subject to Philip but chose to resist Alexander in 335.

[2] The worst that Demosthenes said of Philip's actions in Thrace was that he set up some of the kings there and deposed others (*Olynth.* 1. 13); cf. Isoc. 5. 21. The picture which Hampl 41 f. drew of a uniform imperial unit of Thrace east of the Nestus—'einem grossem einheitlichen Verwaltungsbezirk'—seems to me mistaken.

[3] No town could have been better sited than this; for it has defensible rock-outcrops, commands the route by the Hebrus, and controls the great and fertile plain of central Thrace. Theopompus gave the number of Philip's settlers as 2,000 and the nickname of the city as Poneropolis (*FGrH* 115 F 110 and Pliny, *NH* 4. 18).

[4] Albanian archaeologists have discovered traces of the predecessor of the Roman Via Egnatia in the region of the upper Shkumbi valley; it was a narrow paved way, suitable for cavalry, and its original construction may go back to the time of Philip (see my article in *JRS* 64 (1974) 192).

last years Philip used the waterways which bounded his Balkan empire on the coasts of the Aegean and the Black Sea.

Resistance was inevitable. We hear of a revolt by some of the Maedi, which was put down by Alexander, and the assassination of Philip was followed by risings of Illyrians, Triballians, and 'the autonomous Thracians' of Mt. Haemus. The surprising thing is that it was so limited. There is no sign that Philip held down his empire by planting garrisons at strategic places; indeed when Alexander asserted his authority in the Balkan empire in 335 he did not go to relieve or make contact with any Macedonian garrisons at all. It is probable that the Balkan peoples provided contingents for many campaigns of Philip. As Justin put it (2. 1. 1), 'in exercitu Philippi . . . variae gentes erant.' For example, the army of 30,000 men with which Philip attacked Perinthus is likely to have included a large number of Thracian troops; and his army against Atheas may have been strengthened by Thracian peoples south of the Danube who had every reason to fear the Scythians. Illyrians and Thracians were recruited in considerable numbers to serve under Alexander in Asia, and the commander of one Thracian unit, Sitalces, a member of the Odrysian royal house, held a high position among the officers of Alexander. Co-operation with Philip was certainly developing in the Balkan empire, as it did so remarkably in Thessaly, and the reason for it was that Philip created conditions of life in the Balkans which many men thought were worth defending.

XXI

DECLINE AND FALL
(337–336)

IN spite of the able studies of modern interpreters, some of them
recent, Philip's last year and his end are still in part at least an
enigma. Through the years of his rise and glory, defective though our
sources so often are, an impression still survives of the king who knows
what he is doing, plans where he is going, adapts his moves and himself
to present needs; and all this with his feet most firmly on the ground,
his eyes alert and not overmuch preoccupied with the stars, his head
safely clear of the clouds—except those passing clouds from the wine he
loved now and then. But now at the end something new. His death scene
itself could be seen as an example of 'tragic history' as it came to be
written.[1] But in the events that lead up to it, too, this king and unifier
of the Macedonians, conqueror of Thrace and subjugator of the neighbouring kingdoms, this reconciler-conqueror-manipulator of the Greeks
who prepares now to stride from Europe over to Asia and who meets
instead the assassin's short-sword in his ribs—this is not a plan any more,
it is a destiny.

The Macedonian *ethos* still kept something in it from the heroic age.
Philip himself nearly died under the walls of Methone like many a Greek
and Trojan under the walls of Troy, and a dozen times he could have
ended his life as a soldier in some Thracian or Greek or Illyrian *aristeia*
which the surviving tradition implies only in some easy generalization
or in the tally of his wounds. Some few of the old Achaean heroes became
embalmed in the Greek mythology as tragic heroes. If Philip ever likened
himself to great ones of the past, it will not have been to one of these.
Or to Odysseus? Perhaps yes. To a realist's eye even the great ancestor
Heracles left something to be desired, if only in the ratio of brain to
brawn.[2] A misty, idealized Heracles as seen through the ageing eyes of

---

[1] Especially, D.S. 16. 91–4. Diodorus 'went to town' on this piece of writing, with results
which few will commend. The description contains (*inter alia*) a wealth of detail which invites
us to think of an eye-witness as its ultimate source (Theopompus? Anaximenes? Marsyas
of Pella?) Yet not every detail may be trustworthy. For example, there was another version
current too, perhaps, of what became of the assassin (*P. Oxy.* 1798 = *FGrH* 148. 1; Just.
9. 7. 10; cf. Bosworth, 'PUM' 93 ff.). And the 'Celtic sword' with which he was stabbed
betrays a Hellenistic writer as the immediate source of Diodorus.

[2] Cf. e.g. D.S. 16. 95. 2–4, for the tradition that Philip himself was prouder of his own
political than military skills. There seems no reason to doubt this.

Isocrates and given to the Greek world in page upon page of periodic prose was a Benefactor figure well worth bringing to the notice of any who could be bothered with him.[1] In this last year, the year of *koine eirene* in Greece and of preparation for the Persian crusade, many a Greek can have seen in Philip (or pretended to see) just such a benefactor and saviour as Isocrates had outlined. The more of this kind of thing the better, no doubt, even to the point of an apotheosis of Philip himself (so some have thought).[2] But this was the year, too, of the new and more sinister signs. The Heracles of *Alcestis* may always have been discernible in Philip's make-up; and the Heracles of *Trachiniae*.[3] But something now, too, of *Hercules Furens*? The children of Philip were not all babes and young things for the slaughter. The chief of them was Alexander, not the young man upon whom a prudent father would draw his sword, however provoked. A time came, however, when Philip did just this. *Quem Iuppiter vult perdere, dementat prius*?

Philip's murder in 336 by one of his own circle on an occasion of great glory and when he was soon to lead the grand army of the Macedonians and his Greek allies into Asia, was selected by Aristotle in his *Politics* as an example of a monarch murdered for a private revenge.[4] But though the assassin Pausanias did have, indisputably, a powerful grievance of his own, other interpreters, both among Aristotle's contemporaries and later, have not hesitated to make this a political murder, and to make of Pausanias not a principal, but an agent of conspiracy in high places to ensure the succession of Alexander to the throne.[5] The stage was set for this violent act by Philip's marriage in 337 to Cleopatra, a daughter of a great Macedonian family. A feud between the murderer Pausanias and Cleopatra's uncle Attalus, a powerful figure in Philip's *entourage*, provides the connection between private and public life which obviously cannot be ignored. But it is Philip's marriage itself that prompts the search for more radical explanations. Philip's sexual prowess, like his record in battle, had always approximated to the heroic, but it did not escape the observant that he used marriage no less than war as an instrument of policy. As Athenaeus put it amusingly, 'Philip of Macedon did not actually take wives with him to the wars, as Darius did . . . but Philip was always getting married in the course of a war. In his reign of twenty-two years, as Satyrus says in his *Life*, he married Audata . . . Phila . . . Nikesipolis . . . Philinna . . . Olympias . . . Meda . . . Cleopatra. . . .'[6]

Most of the 'marriages' were of short duration. Three of them most

---

[1] Isoc. 5. 109 ff.　　　　　　　　　　　　　　　　　　[2] Below, pp. 682, 692 f.

[3] See especially, G. Murray, *Greek Studies* 113 ff., for *Trachiniae*: for *Alcestis*, Theopomp. (*FGrH* 115 F 225, 236); cf. D. 2. 18–19.

[4] Arist. *Pol.* 5. 1311ᵃ25 ff.–1311ᵇ3. And see below, pp. 689 f.

[5] See especially Badian 244 ff.

[6] Athen. 13. 557 d (= Satyrus, *FHG* 3. 161 F 5); cf. Beloch 3². 2. 68 ff.

probably were before his marriage to Olympias the Molossian princess who became his official queen, and presently (356) the mother of Alexander. Three of them, however, undoubtedly were after his marriage to Olympias. The Thessalian Nikesipolis in 352 and the Getic princess Meda in 339 seem to have had no influence on public affairs in Macedonia, whatever their impact on Philip's family life and his relations with Olympias. They were married 'in the course of a war', and any political advantages to be gained from them were concerned with Philip's public relations with new allies or subjects in Thessaly and Thrace respectively. But Cleopatra was different, as was seen by Satyrus (and doubtless by his source). She was not married 'in the course of war'. She was a Macedonian of high birth, and Philip 'fell in love with her' (only of her did Satyrus record this, in the excerpt which Athenaeus gives us).[1] And though she was not the first new wife to be brought home to the palace and to Olympias, she was the first to supplant Olympias. By bringing Cleopatra into the palace Philip threw his whole life into confusion, as Satyrus had put it.[2]

Philip cannot have intended this, obviously; but we are sadly in the dark as to what he really did intend. His relations with Olympias had long since deteriorated, it is said (plausibly enough).[3] And that Olympias herself was unpopular with the Macedonians seems quite likely, though we are not actually told so.[4] To repudiate or put away Olympias and make Cleopatra his queen might well correspond with Philip's own desires, even though Olympias' brother Alexander of Epirus was an important client-ally and neighbour, and to alienate him was impolitic, at this time especially when the invasion of Asia Minor was being planned. More impolitic still, however, to alienate the family and connections of Cleopatra by making her his mistress. But most impolitic of all, to alienate Alexander the crown prince, whose birth, education, and attainments had marked him out unmistakably as first in order of succession to the throne, as Philip himself had recognized most clearly by duties and honours assigned to him in recent years. To marry Cleopatra while still not breaking with Olympias was not the happiest of arrangements, obviously, but it seemed better, one must suppose, than any of the alternatives that were feasible at the time. This, anyway, is what did happen. Cleopatra was married. Olympias was still around. And Alexander was still putting up with it, until the occasion of the party at which Cleopatra's uncle Attalus in his cups so far forgot discretion as to invite the Macedonians to pray for a legitimate heir to the throne

---

[1] *Athen.* loc. cit. So Plu. *Alex.* 9. 6.   [2] *Athen.* loc. cit.

[3] Plu. *Alex.* 9. 3; cf. 2. 4 ff.; 3. 1, with Hamilton's *Commentary* ad loc. pp. 4 f. The 'dramatic date' of the story of Olympias and the snake is pre-Methone (354, when Philip lost his eye): Parke and Wormell 1. 240; 2 no. 269.

[4] It is implied in the insulting words of Attalus (below, see next note).

from the union of Philip and Cleopatra.[1] In the brawl that followed, Philip was not sober enough to emerge with credit (or even with the last word). He had been provoked by Alexander into making a great fool of himself in public. To draw the sword on one's son is one thing, but to fall flat on one's face while plunging about among the couches in order to get at him is quite another. Alexander did well, probably, to leave home without delay, taking his mother with him. They went first to Epirus, where Olympias stayed at her brother's court. Alexander himself moved on into Illyrian territory, and remained there for some little time.[2] This bitter quarrel was quicker kindled than quenched.

Whether Alexander was 'exiled' on this occasion by Philip seems open to doubt.[3] The actual words of Plutarch imply that he (with Olympias) left Macedonia on his own initiative, and in the end was persuaded with difficulty to return. But Plutarch also writes then that Philip 'brought him back' (κατήγαγεν, used of restoring exiles). And obviously his returning only after persuasion is not incompatible with his being formally an exile, now formally restored: for was it safe to return? On any reckoning this must have been his first concern, and it will have been of this that Demaratus the Corinthian, well known and trusted by both father and son, succeeded in convincing him. It had been Demaratus who had 'brought Philip to his senses' by speaking freely and in a context that underlined the political danger as well as the ethical squalor of this quarrel.[4] Philip must have been alive to the danger as soon as he sobered up on the morning after. But he had lost his temper and had lost 'face'. It was intolerable now to take the swift initiative for a reconciliation which was necessary. Cleopatra will not have made it any easier for him, and Attalus and all their friends will have had his ear. He needed a good and candid friend to tell him what he must do, and among the courtiers after the quarrel it is not surprising perhaps that the good friend in the end had to be a Greek and not one of the leading Macedonians (who had to go on living in the place anyway).

Alexander, then, returned to Macedonia (Olympias did not return, and perhaps there was no question of it). The court, however, was divided now by the great quarrel;[5] and Philip himself was divided. Cleopatra

---

[1] Plu. *Alex*. 9. 7.

[2] Plu. *Alex*. 9. 11. To which Illyrian kingdom is unknown. Badian (244 n. 8) suggested, to Langarus the Agrianian king. But the Agrianians were not Illyrians (Thuc. 2. 96. 3; Appian, *Illyr*. 14).

[3] *Pace* Badian, art. cit., whose interpretation is based on reasonable inference from what Plutarch wrote, and I should accept it, if I could rid myself of doubt as to whether Philip when sober, whatever he might have said or done when drunk, deliberately created for himself so dangerous an 'exile' at so inopportune a time. He refrained from this a little later, when he did 'exile' a group of Alexander's friends (below, p. 680).

[4] Plu. *Alex*. 9. 12.

[5] It is the great service of Badian that he succeeded in representing this division so vividly.

and her friends doubtless wanted Alexander out of the way. The good of the realm required a secure succession to the throne in the person of a prince of quite unusual talents. Philip himself is said to have taken the greatest pride and pleasure in Alexander's promise and performance as a boy and as recently as the victory at Chaeronea.[1] No other prince of the royal house could replace him (and of course any candidate, had there been one, would have been as unwelcome as Alexander himself to Cleopatra and her circle). But the difficulties of this horrible mess are illustrated in Plutarch's account of the overtures made by Pixodarus the dynast of Caria who hoped to arrange a marriage of his eldest daughter to Alexander's half-brother Arrhidaeus.[2]

Badian indeed has made the great quarrel of 337 a point of no return, after which Alexander's position was always insecure and in need of a desperate remedy.[3] For this view the strongest support comes from the Pixodarus story, which does indeed show Philip and Alexander still estranged though outwardly and formally reconciled: this in the sense that they seem to have had no free discussion of the Carian marriage proposition until discussion was made absolutely necessary because of Alexander's secret intervention counter to Philip's own plan. It was possible therefore for Alexander's friends (and Olympias—by letters presumably, if Plutarch is right on this) to play on his resentment to the point even of convincing him (or not dissuading him?) that Philip now was grooming the half-brother Arrhidaeus as heir to the throne.[4] That this was true is manifestly unlikely unless, again, we think of Philip now as having lost every vestige of political sense; because Arrhidaeus, though in age he was probably Alexander's senior by a few months, was of unsound mind, and therefore as an heir to the throne a mere hostage to fortune at any time, let alone at this time.[5] The first duke of Wellington doubtless would have said to Alexander 'Sir, if you believe that you will believe anything'— and this approximately, in words more numerous and less well chosen, is what Plutarch does record Philip as saying to him in the end.[6] But he

---

[1] Plu. *Alex.* 6. 8; 9. 1 and 3.   [2] Plu. *Alex.* 10. 1 ff.

[3] Badian 245.

[4] Plu. *Alex.* 10. 1: for the doubt as to the complicity of Olympias, Hamilton, *Commentary* p. 25.

[5] For the probable date of Arrhidaeus' birth, Beloch 3². 2. 69. The dating of C. Ehrhardt (*CQ* N.S. 17 (1967) 297), which makes him at least three years younger than Alexander, though it is accepted by Hamilton (*Commentary* p. 25), seems to me very improbable (see *CQ* N.S. 20 (1970) 69 ff.).

[6] Plu. *Alex.* 10. 3. Badian, art. cit., did not think much of the explanation attributed to Philip here. I see nothing strange, or even inexact, in his describing a proposed marriage of Alexander to Pixodarus' daughter as a *mésalliance* (though it is expressed in more rhetorical terms). This Pixodarus story is serviceable in another respect also. Alexander's being able to believe that Philip intended to make Arrhidaeus his heir now shows conclusively that he was not simultaneously intending to make as his heir his nephew Amyntas son of Perdiccas, as some believe (while believing also in the Pixodarus story itself).

said it too late, much too late, and only after losing his temper a second time now, on learning of Alexander's secret emissary sent to Pixodarus on his own account.

The sending of this emissary (the tragic actor Thessalus) is a striking indication of the estrangement, as Badian rightly emphasized. Philip's order for the summary arrest of Thessalus, and the exile of the group of Alexander's friends who had aided him in this piece of folly (five are named) shows well that he was really furious again, and this time without being drunk (so far as we know).[1] He had some reason for anger, for this meddling had the effect of losing altogether the co-operation of Pixodarus, who evidently revised his estimate of the power and prospects of Philip in the light of this chaos in his court and family, and decided to remain a loyal vassal of Persia.[2] Yet even this new quarrel of father and son has its paradox. Alexander's friends were punished and removed from the scene, but he himself was not. Philip's rebuke and reproach to him (about the *mésalliance*) itself was a reassurance that he was heir to the throne; and even if this was insincere (so Badian), the fact was beyond dispute, that he had given Philip a good reason now for getting rid of him if he wanted—and he had not wanted. On the contrary, it was not Alexander who was removed now, or next, it was his arch-enemy Attalus. A few months or weeks later (in spring 336), when Philip sent Parmenion to Asia Minor with an advance force to establish a bridgehead for the invasion, Attalus accompanied Parmenion, presumably as second in command.[3]

The significance of this incident should not be lost. Parmenion was more than capable of commanding this force, with two or three brigadiers subordinate to him, not one of whom need have been Attalus the uncle of the young queen, the man who had insulted Alexander publicly, the man whose presence at Court when Alexander returned can only have been a constant cause of tension. It looks as if this appointment to the army of Asia Minor was a way of kicking Attalus upstairs (and not very far upstairs, at that). One could suspect, even, that the finest hour of Attalus was already in the past. It was after all only through Cleopatra,

---

[1] For the names, Plu. *Alex.* 10. 4; Arr. *An.* 3. 6. 5.

[2] Badian, loc. cit., makes this point convincingly.

[3] D.S. 17. 2. 4 (cf. 5. 1 f.) names 'Attalus with Parmenion' as commanding this force. If this were accurate, it would suggest an interesting 'demotion' of Parmenion, who presumably would resent it. Attalus at some time married a daughter of Parmenion, and Curtius 6. 9. 17 implies clearly that it was at this time (after the great quarrel scene). Badian makes much of this. Yet this passage of Curtius is very vulnerable to exactly the same source-criticism that Badian himself accepts as valid for D.S. 16. 93. 9 (see p. 684 n. 4 below); and personally I am inclined to think that Attalus could have become Parmenion's son-in-law at any date between (say) 346 and 336, and that to trust Curtius for fixing it in 337/6 is unsafe.

Equally unsafe, however, to trust Diodorus here for a demotion of Parmenion. He was much more interested here in Attalus than in Parmenion, and consequently put him first.

presumably, that he had ever come right to the top; and if Cleopatra's power over Philip declined Attalus ceased to be indispensable if he ever had been. The marriage was about a year old now, Cleopatra had recently borne a daughter to Philip.[1] She was the queen certainly; but was she still the face that had launched him into impolitic decisions? In Philip's marriages, the record suggests, time did not stand still. In the past (before 337), though 'marriages' had been frequent, nothing suggests that Philip had ever been dominated by a woman. Only Cleopatra may have infatuated him to the point of risking everything for her hand. If so, the infatuation need not have lasted for ever, and one supposes that it did not.

Speculation unfortunately is not confined to the area of Philip's feelings for Cleopatra. In the spring of 336 when Parmenion crossed to Asia Philip himself intended to follow with the main army in a matter of weeks, or months at the most. He must have had a plan for the government of Macedonia and supervision of Greece in his absence; but we do not know what it was. In the late 340s when he campaigned in Thrace, Antipater had been left, in effect, in charge of Macedonia. Antipater was to be left again in the same capacity by Alexander in 334. In the years of Philip's reign as a whole, Antipater alone emerges as a figure of distinction comparable to that of Parmenion, the leading general. On the evidence we have, we are bound to think of either Parmenion, or Antipater, or Alexander, as destined in Philip's plan for the office over Macedonia and Greece when he himself would be in Asia. Yet it is not easy to imagine a full-scale invasion of Asia Minor being undertaken without Parmenion—or without Alexander. Antipater seems the obvious choice for the home command. For the sake of peace and quiet it would have been wise to keep Attalus and Alexander apart still, by sending Attalus home when the main army arrived in Asia.

One detail of Philip's preparations we are informed about, and that an important one; his arrangements for Olympias. She could be counted

---

[1] Satyrus, *FHG* 3. 161 F 5; Just. 9. 7. 12. The date of the marriage is uncertain: it cannot have been earlier than near the end of the year 338. Uncertain too is the date of Philip's death, in the summer of 336. There was a version of the Cleopatra story that gave her a son, Caranus; and according to Diodorus this son was born only a few days before Philip was murdered (D.S. 17. 2. 3; Just. 9. 7. 3; 11. 2. 3. But Just. 9. 7.12 speaks only of a daughter). The time (say, eighteen months, maximum, perhaps much less) hardly allows Cleopatra two children, as Beloch pointed out (3². 2. 71–2), adding rightly that no version gave her two, but alternative versions gave her a daughter or a son. (R. L. Fox 18 believes in two children, however.)

I follow Beloch in preferring the 'daughter' version on the ground that Satyrus, careful as a rule and with a pronounced interest in this topic, preferred it. I would add that the 'son' version is so obviously the more interesting, exciting, and significant that, if it were true, the 'daughter' version could never have started. The 'daughter' version, therefore, I take to be true, and the 'son' version an improvement on it, because it was more exciting that way.

on to be up to no good, and at present she was in Epirus, where her brother Alexander, in spite of past benefits from Philip (to whom he owed his kingdom), still might be seduced into thoughts above his station.[1] Family pride could resent the repudiation of his sister, and could even prompt him to attack Macedonia in Philip's absence if the time seemed ripe for ending his status as a dependant or for adding to his own kingdom. Philip hoped now to win him over by honouring him highly. He offered him the hand in marriage of his daughter Cleopatra.[2] The relationships are full of interest here, for Olympias was this Cleopatra's mother, and Alexander of Epirus was her uncle. Are we to think that Philip, who knew his daughter, knew that she would not be dominated by her mother, but in fact could be relied on to influence her husband against her? If he was right in this, he was doing here the very best that he could to guard against troubles from this quarter. The marriage was fixed to be celebrated in early summer, at Aegeae, and with all the magnificence that seemed required not so much by the importance of the bridegroom or of the bride, or even of the diplomatic *coup* which had brought about their union, as by the opportunity that it offered to Philip of displaying himself to his own people and his vassals and to the whole of Greece in all his power and glory.[3]

One detail especially from the splendid scene described by Diodorus has attracted comment, up to and beyond what it deserves. To entertain the guests Philip had organized a great Festival of the Arts, as well as all the banqueting late into the night that could be expected of him.[4] The formal opening of the Festival was the occasion chosen by his murderer for his murder. But it had been chosen, too, by Philip himself for a singularly 'tragic' *coup de théâtre*. The people had filled the theatre at Aegeae even before dawn, and at daybreak the official *cortège* brought in the superb images of the Twelve Gods designed and executed for the occasion. And with them came a thirteenth image, of Philip himself: the king enthroned as one of the company with the Twelve Gods.[5] An apotheosis? An unprecedented claim to divinity made by a king of divine descent (from Heracles) aware of all the heroes who had been 'heroized' in the past

---

[1] For his earlier relations with Philip, above, pp. 306, 505.

[2] D.S. 17. 91. 4.

[3] D.S. 16. 91. 6; 92. 1 (with reference to Greece only, characteristically). Cf. 16. 91. 2 for his consultation of the Delphic oracle, for 'victory over the King of Persia'. (Parke and Wormell 1. 238; 2 no. 266.)

[4] D.S. 16. 91. 2 and 92. 5.

[5] My text here is a close paraphrase of the text of D.S. 16. 92. 5; cf. 16. 95. 1 . . . τὸ μὲν πλῆθος ἔτι νυκτὸς οὔσης συνέτρεχεν εἰς τὸ θέατρον, ἅμα δ' ἡμέρᾳ τῆς πομπῆς γινομένης σὺν ταῖς ἄλλαις ταῖς μεγαλοπρεπέσι κατασκευαῖς εἴδωλα τῶν δώδεκα θεῶν ἐπόμπευε ταῖς τε δημιουργίαις περιττῶς εἰργασμένα καὶ τῇ λαμπρότητι τοῦ πλούτου θαυμαστῶς κεκοσμημένα· σὺν δὲ τούτοις αὐτοῦ τοῦ Φιλίππου τρισκαιδέκατον ἐπόμπευε θεοπρεπὲς εἴδωλον, σύνθρονον ἑαυτὸν ἀποδεικνύντος τοῦ βασιλέως τοῖς δώδεκα θεοῖς.

and of the great ones (himself among them) whom the Greeks themselves from time to time in this city or that, quick to acclaim greatness and to honour benefactors, had greeted as in some sense super-human, and had associated in some sense with the established deities of the place.[1] The idea is striking and interesting, obviously; but probably it is not historical. Philip was not claiming here to be a god, any more than the people of Ephesus a few weeks before this had been honouring him as a god when they had put his statue in the temple of their own Artemis there; or any more than the contemporary Thespiaeans were honouring as a goddess their local girl who had made good, the celebrated and desirable Phryne, one of the top two or three *hetairai* of this generation, when they set her statue in their temple between the cult-figures of Aphrodite and Eros.[2] The Ephesians and the Thespiaeans were acclaiming Success, and a Benefactor of themselves.

Philip himself, then, was not claiming to be a god; he was merely claiming to be (say) by far the most important person present, the most important man alive in the world at that moment, the greatest king that Macedonia had ever had or that the Greeks had ever seen or were ever likely to see. This was enough, it may be said. Tributes and compliments paid to a benefactor by a grateful and admiring public might be acceptable, though even here the wise man would want to beware of the extravagant. But there was something alarming here in the vast compliment paid by himself to himself. The tribute paid to him recently by the Ephesians he was paying now to himself, by introducing his statue into the company of the Twelve Gods. It was a very unwise thing to do. Those masters of understatement the English ruling class of the imperial era would have called it bad form. No Greek (or Macedonian) on mature reflection could possibly think of it as anything less than *hubris* of an alarming order. But mature reflection was just the thing for which no time was given now. Like something in a moralist's cautionary tale this

---

[1] For the historical examples, starting with Lysander at Samos, C. Habicht, *Gottmenschentum und griechische Städte*, *Zetemata* 14 (2nd edn. Munich, 1970) 3 ff.; F. Täger, *Charisma* 1. 150 ff. (Stuttgart, 1957). For Zeus Philippios at Eresus, *c.* 340, Tod 191, 4 ff., and p. 720 below.

[2] See A. D. Nock, 'Σύνναος Θεός', *Essays on Religion and the Ancient World* 1. 237 ff. and 204 (= *HSCP* 41 (1930) 1 ff.) for the crucial distinction between ἄγαλμα (cult statue) and εἰκών (statue not designed to be the object of cult); cf. Habicht, op. cit. 245, who now accepts the application of this to Ephesus (Arr. *An.* 1. 17. 11; below, p. 692). The εἴδωλα ... εἴδωλον of Diodorus, loc. cit., is non-committal, as to this. His σύνθρονον etc. is highly suggestive, intentionally (for its contribution to the great *peripeteia* and paradoxology of this piece of writing), just as Plutarch, also in search of paradox though more briefly, calls Phryne σύνναος ... καὶ συνίερος. (For Phryne, Plu. *Mor.* 753 F; Alciphron, *Epist.* 4. 1.) Nock's comment (loc. cit. 247 = 57 n. 1) on their 'loose use of epithets of this type' seems fully justified. So too his comment (ibid.) on the absence of any indication of cult in the Philippeum building at Olympia, where the statues in gold and ivory of Amyntas and Eurydice, Philip and Olympias, and Alexander were εἰκόνες not ἀγάλματα (Paus. 5. 20. 10).

nemesis trod swiftly, instantly on the heels. Almost before he could know what had hit him, this perpetrator of *hubris* had been struck down.

The great day had collapsed into confusion; and confusion in some degree still reigns. The detailed story of Diodorus suggests so many questions. So few of the questions can be answered with any confidence. What was the motive of Pausanias? Was he a lone assassin and a principal, or was he the agent of a conspiracy, and had he accomplices? These questions lead on to others.

The story of Pausanias as we have it is an excerpt from the sex life of the Macedonian court, where such things went on not (one supposes) every day; but where such things could happen, and without the life of the court or the nation being shattered by the scandal.[1] The young Pausanias had quarrelled violently with another young Pausanias (the two young men were rivals for Philip's favours at the time), and had insulted him deeply. Not long after, the insulted threw his life away in battle defending Philip's person, but not before he had confided in Attalus (his protector in some sense) the uncle of Cleopatra, the young queen. Attalus held Pausanias responsible for this death, and he made him pay for it, by inviting him to dinner, making him dead drunk, and handing him over to the sexual appetites of his stable lads. Pausanias went to Philip for redress; Philip would take no action against Attalus. It was a very bad business, obviously. But to bring Attalus to trial and condemn him would make it a worse business, he judged. Though we cannot know his reasons precisely, politics not justice were his guide. Meanwhile Pausanias should be soothed and appeased: he was made one of the officers of the king's Guards.[2]

The most significant detail in this story is that which dates the death of 'the other' Pausanias to Philip's Illyrian campaign 'against Pleurias'.[3] To identify this with the campaign of 345 against Pleuratus is by no means the certainty that many have thought it (above, p. 473). The identification makes the grievance of Pausanias about nine years old when he took action on it; and in fact discredits it, as a motive that can have mattered. Moreover the identification makes Diodorus here contradict himself a few lines later on this very question of chronology, when he explains Philip's complaisance by reference to the situation of 337 after the royal marriage.[4] Diodorus is capable of a 'mistake' like this,

[1] D.S. 16. 93–4; Just. 9. 6. 4 ff. and 14; Plu. *Alex.* 10. 6.

[2] D.S. 16. 93. 9; *somatophulax* here presumably not in its specialized sense (see above, p. 403).

[3] D.S. 16. 93. 6.

[4] At D.S. 16. 93. 6 the 'Illyrian' detail is unnecessary and unaccountable, and therefore authentic; at 93. 8–9 comes the detail linking the story to the situation at court after Philip's marriage to Cleopatra.

certainly. But Plutarch makes just the same 'mistake' here, of seeing the whole Pausanias story in the context of 337, and the probability is that this is because his source(s) (and Diodorus') put it there; that there is no 'mistake' at all in fact, except by refusing to believe that Pleurias and Pleuratus could be two different kings (like Edward and Edmund). In short, the grievance of Pausanias was nearer to nine months old than nine years old when he took matters into his own hands.[1] As to his psychological history we can only guess. A puzzling summary of a conversation with 'the sophist Hermocrates', though it could be recalled (or invented) later as relevant and significant, without its context cannot be seen as good evidence for conspiracy.[2] It tells us that Pausanias wanted to be famous, and it may suggest an obsession with his disgrace and the denial of justice, a 'wrath of Pausanias' that took on Homeric and Achillean proportions. Even so, some explanation of his final flinging off of the mask that lays the whole onus of decision on Pausanias himself may seem less probable than one that allows him to be guided or prompted to it by advisers who knew his story and knew the man—and who when the time came recognized him as their man now. The story of Pausanias almost asks to be interpreted by a rationale which makes him the agent of one or more of those great ones of the kingdom in 336 who had come to prefer Philip's room to his company.[3] And the rationalist interpreters poured in almost from the moment when Philip himself hit the floor. The Macedonian 'establishment' itself led the way. The official interpretation saw 'the sons of Aëropus' as having been in some sense behind Pausanias, and two of the three sons were quickly put to death.[4] The 'establishment' itself however consisted at this moment of Alexander, supported and sponsored by Antipater, and with Olympias, when the news from Aegeae reached her, making the journey of return from Epirus as fast as the horses could travel. The names of the new king and of the queen mother, it need hardly be said, were not spared by the contemporary rationalist interpreters: and to their names that of Antipater has been added in recent times.[5] *Cui bono?* The question released the tongues of contemporary scandal and sensationalism; but it still compels the impartial historian to explore.

Olympias, however, should be exonerated immediately, it seems, from suspicion of having used Pausanias as her agent to murder Philip. She had the motives and the character, no doubt, but she had not the opportunity, having been out of the country and in Epirus for the best

---

[1] Plu. *Alex.* 10. 4.   [2] D.S. 16. 94. 1 f.
[3] This was seen and expressed most clearly perhaps by Beloch, 3². 1. 606 f.
[4] Arr. *An.* 1. 25. 1 ff., etc.
[5] The ancient evidence for Antipater's support of Alexander is not strong, but in view of the record both before and after it does not really need to be (Ps.-Callisthenes 1. 26, accepted by Badian 248, rightly in my opinion).

part of a year up to Philip's death. To recruit and prepare as assassin such a man as Pausanias by means of letters or confidential messengers seems to strain credulity too far. Her unseemly joy after the event and her characteristic vengeance on the young queen Cleopatra and her baby daughter did her reputation no good then or now, but they do not make her Philip's murderess or the instigator and employer of his assassin.[1]

Alexander himself remains under suspicion; and recently reasons have been advanced for suspecting Antipater also. These views are open, however, to serious objections, and rely very greatly on their ability to convince us that Alexander (and Antipater) found themselves in 336 in a situation which called for the truly desperate remedy of Philip's death by assassination. Beloch presented Alexander's position as undermined by Philip's marriage, with the likelihood that Cleopatra would have sons in due course, endangering Alexander's succession to the throne. Beloch also saw a large following in Macedonia for Amyntas, Philip's nephew, as candidate now for the throne which had eluded him in 359. For this last there is really no evidence except that *after* the murder Macedonia was said by Plutarch to be 'unsound (*hupoulos*, literally "festering")' and 'looking to Amyntas and the sons of Aëropus', and that Alexander did put Amyntas to death.[2] Plutarch's sources of information for the rotten state of Macedonia are unknown, and it seems possible that the information itself is really inference from the fact that Amyntas and two of the three Lyncestian brothers, the sons of Aëropus, were in fact put to death by Alexander in the first months of his reign. The sons of Aëropus cannot have been candidates for the throne of Macedonia, and probably fell under suspicion as known associates of Pausanias the murderer.[3] In any case Plutarch's remark occurs in a rhetorical exercise concerned at that moment with making the most of Alexander's difficulties at the time of his accession. Plutarch says nothing of it in his more sober *Life*, and the extent of any Macedonian support for Amyntas as king, either before Philip's death or after it, is obviously a matter for scepticism. Philip had been content not to bother about Amyntas for all these years. He must have known Amyntas very well indeed—just as he knew Alexander very well indeed. It seems highly improbable that after twenty years he began thinking of Amyntas as a suitable alternative to Alexander as his successor, even when he quarrelled seriously with Alexander himself. Indeed Alexander's deluded fear of Arrhidaeus as Philip's intended heir proves that Amyntas at any rate was not that,

---

[1] *Contra*, Beloch 3². 1. 606 f., who saw Olympias as the prime mover, without however meeting the practical difficulties. Badian (249 n. 25) rightly exonerates her.

[2] Plu. *Mor.* 327 c, justly evaluated by Badian 249 n. 26.

[3] Arr. *An.* 1. 25. 1 ff., etc.; Cf. Berve 2 no. 37. Arrian describes them as 'Heromenes and Arrhabaeus who had a part in the murder of Philip', reproducing here probably what was the official Macedonian version.

and of course Philip's giving one of his daughters in marriage to Amyntas need not mean that he had anything of the sort in mind. It may be added that at this time Queen Cleopatra and her friends and family would not have welcomed an advancement of Amyntas any more than they welcomed the presence of Alexander himself as heir apparent.[1]

As to the threat to Alexander from Cleopatra and her sons as yet unborn, it was real, certainly, and especially if Alexander and Philip continued to quarrel through the years; but it was not immediate or urgent. The trouble that Philip had taken in order to make up the great quarrel showed clearly that he did look to Alexander still to succeed him (above, p. 680). And indeed it did not take a Macedonian king of Philip's perception to know that to disturb the existing situation now would be something more than imprudent; it would have been plain imbecility. It was one thing to have underrated the effects and consequences of the rash marriage, when wishful thinking was disposed to minimize them anyway. But now in the light of the great quarrel the consequences were clear. To ignore them, or exacerbate them by cobbling up a new plan for the succession which would eliminate Alexander, preparatory to launching the great invasion of Asia Minor and a war likely to go on for years, would have been one of the most obtuse essays in statecraft in recorded history. What Philip really did in 336, we may think, was to try to convince Alexander by all the means in his power that on his side the reconciliation was genuine; and this in all sincerity.

In short, Alexander was not seriously or immediately threatened by the new marriage and the group at Court that supported it. This is clear from the ease with which he was acclaimed king by the Macedonian assembly.[2] The absence of Attalus in Asia Minor, and the presence of Antipater supporting Alexander, explain something of this, no doubt, but they cannot explain everything. Though the Macedonian people were not highly developed as a political instrument or engine, the events of only thirteen years later show that when the succession was genuinely in doubt they were capable both of showing a mind of their own and of coming to terms with propositions put to them by their superiors whether acting as one group or more than one. In 336 neither Attalus and the group round the young queen, nor Amyntas nor the sons of Aëropus,

[1] The connection between Amyntas and Cleopatra's group seen by Badian (245) and Bosworth, 'PUM', 103, via Philotas (son of Parmenion), whose sister was wife of Attalus, while Philotas himself was said later to have been friendly with Amyntas, does not carry conviction. (Cf. Curt. 6. 9. 17; 10. 24, for the allegations against Philotas in this connection at his trial in 330.) If Philotas had been against Alexander at the time of the quarrel, he would never have been promoted to his high command in 334. (See below, p. 688.)

[2] For a different view, Bosworth, 'PUM' 102 ff., who makes much of Alexander's difficulties at this time, though he allows that the single sentence of Plutarch (*Mor.* 327 c) 'is the sole evidence that Alexander's accession was a stormy period at home'.

nor any other leader or group of nobles, had support among the Macedonians which has left any trace in the record of these events (except for
the remark of Plutarch, above), a record which, though its survival has
been haphazard and defective, cannot have been a purely perfunctory
one at the time, for this was not a dull story about dull people; on the
contrary, how Alexander became king is something that every scribbler
will have attended to. All that we are told is that he succeeded to the
throne unopposed—and then got rid of his enemies.[1]

The exciting suggestions of a power struggle at Court in Philip's last
year in which Antipater was a loser and Parmenion a gainer by reason
of his being father-in-law of Attalus the young queen's uncle, seem
insecurely based.[2] There was no 'set-back' for Antipater in Parmenion's
being given the command in Asia in spring 336, for Parmenion had been
holding important and sometimes independent commands throughout
Philip's reign from 356 onwards, and was indisputably his senior
general (indeed his only general, as Philip is reported to have said in one
of the wittier *mots* attributed to him).[3] Nor did Alexander's succession
with Antipater's support, and the swift elimination of Attalus put to
death in Asia Minor, affect Parmenion's position adversely. As Diodorus
puts it, the death of Attalus ended any danger of disloyalty from the
Macedonian troops in Asia, 'Parmenion being on the closest possible
terms with Alexander'.[4] That Diodorus is reliable here is clear from what
follows. A few months later Parmenion is recorded as having offered
Alexander some sound advice before the invasion of Asia began;[5] and
when it did begin, Parmenion held the most important command in the
army, his son Philotas held the second-most-important command, and
his son Nicanor the third-most-important command. In short, there had
been room for both Antipater and Parmenion in the highest circle for
twenty years at least, and there still was room for them both now.

The interesting views of A. B. Bosworth ('PUM'), with Philip's last
year and last marriage as the occasion for a power-struggle in which the
nobility of Upper Macedonia (or some of it) sought to reject a domination
by Pella and the Old Kingdom (represented now by Cleopatra and
Attalus and their faction), though they are based on some general
considerations that are persuasive, still lack the positive evidence to
carry conviction. In truth we do not really know from which region of

---

[1] D.S. 17. 2. 1 ff.; Plu. *Alex.* 11. 1; Just. 11. 1, and 2. 1–3.

[2] Badian 247 ff. For the date of Parmenion's daughter's marriage (uncertain), see above,
p. 680 n. 3.

[3] Plut. *Mor.* 177 c 2. For Parmenion in general, p. 545 above.

[4] D.S. 17. 5. 2.

[5] D.S. 17. 16. 2 (the advice to marry and produce an heir, suggestive of the close and
intimate adviser, not merely of the speaker at some council of war. Antipater is associated
with Parmenion in the same advice on this occasion).

Macedonia Cleopatra and Attalus did come.[1] Though Pausanias (from Orestis) and the sons of Aëropus (from Lyncestis) were Upper Macedonian, so too was Perdiccas (also from Orestis), in command of the guards who caught and slew Pausanias on the spot.[2] In Philip's reign in general, some tensions between 'Upper' cantons and the centre are to be suspected certainly, even though the evidence is lacking; but as yet they cannot be thought to impose a pattern on the events of this last year.[3]

Philip's last marriage had been a disaster, and its effects most probably would not have died away even if Pausanias had not struck when he did strike. But the evidence does not compel us or even invite us to think of Alexander (or Antipater) as the principal then, and Pausanias as his tool.[4] Two further considerations seem to be strongly against this. First, the occasion of the murder. Though this point has been obscured (as it seems) by all the sensational circumstances and the absorbing political consequences, the fact remains that this murder on this occasion was (literally) a bloody disgrace, and one that made Macedonia and the Macedonians and the Macedonian royal house and all the pretensions to being civilized people, a laughing-stock. The Macedonian royalty always had murdered one another when necessary, and perhaps they always would; but for the crown prince or his sponsor (Antipater) to choose to have the king, his father, murdered at the time and place where all the Greeks were assembled by invitation to witness and applaud their *hegemon* in his glory, seems incredible. (Again, 'Sir, if you believe that, you will believe anything.')

Finally, the evidence of Aristotle, from which we began. Though we cannot be quite certain, most likely Aristotle did know the truth about the murder. It was, he implied, for private revenge, and unpolitical.[5] Though the modern critic needs to recall that Aristotle's connection with Alexander may have impelled him to write what was not true here to serve Alexander's interests (and his own), he needs to remember too that this same piece of source-criticism was open to every one of Aristotle's readers at that time—as Aristotle knew very well.

[1] Bosworth cites the incendiary remark of Cleopatra's uncle Attalus, "*νῦν μέντοι γνήσιοι*", ἔφη, "*καὶ οὐ νόθοι βασιλεῖς γεννηθήσονται*", with the comment 'The reference to legitimate heirs must mean that Cleopatra came from Lower Macedon.' But really all that it must mean is that she did not come from the Molossi like Olympias; she was a Macedonian, whether from Pella or from one of the upper cantons, which were undeniably Macedonian now for these twenty years, whatever some of them might have been in the past.

[2] D.S. 16. 94. 4 (for Perdiccas and his guards). Named with Perdiccas here are also Leonnatus (from Orestis; Berve 2 no. 466) and Attalus (from Tymphaea, Berve 2 no. 181).

[3] For Upper Macedonia in general, see also pp. 649 ff. above.

[4] Mine is, broadly speaking, the view argued at great length by K. Kraft, *Der 'rationale' Alexander*, Frankfurter Althistorische Studien 5 (1971) 11–42; but the argumentation is of so variable a quality that I do not propose to discuss or cite it for each point in turn. Cf. the review of E. Badian, *Gnomon* 47 (1975) 48–58.   [5] Arist. *Pol.* 5. 1311^{a}25–1311^{b}3.

The context itself of his remark warns us to be careful about it. Aristotle had no need to mention Philip's murder at all here (or anywhere). All he needed was an example of a monarch killed for private and not for political motives. Presumably he knew of a dozen or two examples, and he chose Philip and Pausanias as one example out of ten that he actually set down here, because it was fresh and famous and therefore a particularly good one for his purpose—so long as it was true, and everybody knew it was true. To suppose that Aristotle chose to use this small opportunity for inserting an untrue 'example' to serve Alexander's interests, and one which (if it was untrue) would not deceive anybody anyway coming from his pen, is to think him capable of a ludicrous little exercise that would brand him as a simpleton. One does not see him as a simpleton (or as a crook either, for that matter). The sensible inference from what he writes here seems to be that not only was this true but that nobody seriously thought anything different, at the time when he wrote. If this had been a controversial matter still and if Alexander's guilt was widely believed in, for Aristotle to go out of his way to choose this particular 'example' would have been crass and inept beyond all belief. Malice, naturally, had made Olympias and Alexander guilty of the murder which had served their interests so well. But by the time Aristotle wrote this in the *Politics*, nobody that mattered believed this any more, if they ever had. It was accepted that Pausanias had been nobody's tool.

Though this conclusion is less exciting, it seems more convincing even as to the murder itself, which, when all is said, was among other things a piece of exhibitionism by the murderer more suggestive of a solitary (and perhaps deranged) obsession than of an agent's crime planned by those whose first consideration was that the attempt should not fail. (This attempt itself cannot have had more than about an even chance of succeeding?) As for the sons of Aëropus, they were probably close associates of Pausanias, and suspect on that account. One of them, Alexander, saved himself by instantly saluting the new king (and presumably because he was well known and trusted by him and was Antipater's son-in-law). But the fate of his brothers, which he need not have seen in just the same light as Alexander who ordered it, may have undermined his loyalty and made him the target for the Persian approach to him that we hear of later.[1]

Pausanias himself, when he struck Philip down, turned and raced for his horse near by, but he was overtaken and killed instantly by the guards; this according to Diodorus, with circumstantial detail that would be utterly convincing if it were not contradicted by the other surviving version of this scene, which shows him arrested now and put to death

[1] Arr. *An.* 1. 25. 1 ff.; cf. Berve no. 37.

later by the Macedonians presumably after trial.[1] Bosworth after an excellent analysis of these sources concluded that 'the manner of his death must remain a mystery', and so far as the source-criticism can take us, this seems right.[2] However, if a subjective intuition is allowed here, based on one's sense of what those people in that situation are most likely to have done, there can be little doubt really that Diodorus somehow or other had got it right. For the Macedonian guards were not like London policemen armed with truncheons, a book of rules, and the knowledge that the eyes of four or five societies for safeguarding civil liberties were upon them. They had just seen a sword drawn and plunged into the king. Their reaction can be imagined, swift and violent, like hounds closing in for a kill; when they caught Pausanias they stabbed him through and through (συνεκέντησαν). If they did do this, it was not because of an order from some officer, a conspirator making sure that Pausanias should tell no tales and name no names (as the higher criticism has suggested). What officer on earth could have stopped them, excited and enraged, taking blood for blood by instinct and plunging their weapons home the more furiously because they were too late?

To call the death of Philip untimely would be no more than a superficial truth. For his aims and plans, he had been cut off from fulfilling them. The war was already begun in Asia, where the troops under Parmenion had made an auspicious start, by winning Ephesus.[3] Rich and easy conquests in Asia Minor could be predicted for the king of the Macedonians and the *hegemon* of the Greeks; and the conquests themselves, the final reward for all the years of diplomatic and military endeavour and hard work, might even open a new future for Greece, if this outward move should bring benefits and a community of interests between allies and *hegemon* that could gloss over the recent past, reshape the present, and reorientate the future. The programme of Isocrates, or something reminiscent of it, might have been realised.

In this sense, then, Philip had come to an untimely end. Yet those who have followed his career closely may find themselves wondering whether after all he had not lived long enough; whether perhaps the signs do not suggest that the great man was past his best now and was losing his grip. In Macedonia itself when he married Cleopatra he had sown the wind, and hereafter he must go on reaping the whirlwind; a bad prospect for an ageing king.[4] At Aegeae at the wedding festival he had presumed too far on his good fortune. Even in Greece, at Olympia, his Philippeum

---

[1] References at p. 675 n. 1 above.   [2] Bosworth, 'PUM' 93-6.

[3] D.S. 16. 91. 2; Arr. *An.* 1. 17. 10 f.; cf. E. Badian, *ASI* 40.

[4] He is forty-six or forty-seven now; not yet an old man, but old enough to be well past his best, especially if he did drink too much and too often, as he probably did.

may be thought to strike a jarring note; and though its completion doubtless was left for Alexander, the idea of it, its planning and presumably the choice or negotiation of its site, was Philip's. As a building it must have been attractive, arresting even, and relatively modest in scale. It's position, however, was far from modest, right next to the Prytaneum. It was the only new building inside the precinct for many years. Whatever exactly its function was to be, it stood greatly in contrast to the Treasuries of Greek states, aligned discreetly outside. In spite of Philip's distinguished local record as a winning owner, and his political standing as *hegemon* of the Greeks, this *tholos* in this place seems self-assertive in a way that a truer judgement might have seen as unnecessary and unpleasing: Philip's own judgement indeed in his earlier years. Is the Philippeum perhaps another sign that age and alcohol were catching up with him?

What was the function of the Philippeum, anyway? And how far (if at all) are we to see any claim by Philip to divinity, among the instances and incidents suggesting that contemporaries here and there, for this reason or for that, were ready to treat him as divine whether he claimed it or not? As to the incidents in Greek cities, there is really little to be said, it seems. As Lysander had found, one of the Greek reactions to extreme political pressures was the extravagant gratitude and admiration paid to the charismatic liberator-figure or to the benefactor whose support in a revolutionary crisis had been decisive.[1] At Amphipolis (359–357), at Ephesus (336), at Eresus (340/39 probably), Philip had entered a local scene as in some sense a liberator.[2] At Ephesus the politicians newly in power honoured him highly with a statue placed in the temple of Artemis, associating him in this way with the goddess though not as a sharer in her cult.[3] At Eresus they honoured him by naming cult statues of Zeus 'patron of Philip' (Philippios).[4] At Amphipolis 'they sacrificed to him as a god', according to the rhetor Aelius Aristides writing 500 years later.[5] Not everyone believes Aristides on this; but he is telling us no more than we knew already of Lysander, years before, and of Alexander a few years after this; and it tells us nothing

---

[1] For Lysander at Samos (and elsewhere?), C. Habicht, *Gottmenschentum*[2] (1970) 3–7.

[2] The late story (Apsines, *Rhet. Graec.* 1 p. 221 ed. Spengel-Hammer) that at Athens Demades proposed to recognize Philip 'as thirteenth god', and to make a temple for him, is accepted by nobody, I think. (Cf. Schaefer 3[2]. 32 n. 1; Habicht 13.) Nor can Clement of Alexandria (*Protr.* 4. 54 p. 16) be thought to allude to a deification νῦν μὲν τὸν Μακεδόνα τὸν ἐκ Πέλλης τὸν Ἀμύντου Φίλιππον ἐν Κυνοσάργει νομοθετοῦντες [ἀγωνοθετοῦντες?] προσκυνεῖν. Cf. Schaefer, loc. cit.

[3] Arr. *An.* 1. 17. 10 f., explained by Nock (above, p. 683 n. 2). Habicht, op. cit. 14 n. 3, disagrees on sharing, persuaded by σύνθρονον etc. of D.S. 16. 92. 5; 95. 1 (Aegeae).

[4] Tod 191. 1 ff. and 43 ff. (= *OGIS* 8a); Habicht, op. cit. 14.

[5] Aelius Aristides 38. 715 D, with Habicht, op. cit. 11–13. When Philip withdrew the garrison in 359, enthusiasts may have greeted the liberation with three cheers (and more) for the liberator.

of any initiative by Philip himself. The enthusiasts were capable of anything; why stop them? (So too, one supposes, with 'the temple of Amyntas' at Pydna, commemorating who knows what act of benefaction by Philip's father to those grateful Greeks.[1])

Very different, however, the acts of worship or the cult established as a matter of duty, something expected and required by Philip as his due. But do we know of any such? One category suggests itself, that which belongs to the new cities of which Philip himself was the founder. As *ktistes* and *oikistes* he could look to be worshipped with a hero cult in perpetuity, and we are perhaps entitled to think that now this was being done, in the new cities whether of Greek or Macedonian population, though no clear instance of it has come to light.[2] Nor (what is more surprising) do we hear anything of Alexander in Asia being worshipped in this way in any of his new foundations. One can see, though, how in Macedonia this worship could spread with a spread of urbanization, even to the point of giving a rather ridiculous picture of the king in the end being worshipped as a god by most of the Macedonians as a result of a lengthy and piecemeal process of local government reform. There is no sign that this, or anything like it, did happen. Nor is there any basis really for taking Amyntas' temple at Pydna as an indication that it was normal for the Macedonians to worship their kings after they were dead. Pydna was a Greek city, and is not evidence for what was normal in a Macedonian city or *ethnos*. For that matter this was not normal in the Greek city, it was something special and prompted, we may be sure, by special merits.

It is a pity that the Philippeum cannot tell us more than it does of Philip's self-estimation or claim to recognition at the end of his life. That the building was Philip's plan, as Pausanias says, can be accepted. But it cannot possibly have been completed by Philip, and we cannot be sure that what we learn of it did correspond to his own intentions. It contained (in the end) chryselephantine statues of the Macedonian royal family; Amyntas III and Eurydice, Philip and Olympias, Alexander.[3] Olympias cannot have been in Philip's own scheme of things in 337/6. Perhaps the family gathering had been his idea; but surely in a somewhat different form.[4] The chryselephantine statues are a bold

---

[1] Schol. D. 1. 5 (a temple, 'the Amynteum'); Aelius Aristides, loc. cit. ('the temple of his father').

[2] For Philippi 'das alles ist ganz unsicher' is the just comment of Habicht (16) on the tentative identification by Ch. Picard (*Rev. arch.* 5. 6, 11 (1938) 334 f.) of the priest by whom is dated a then (and still?) unpublished inscription found at Philippi, as eponymous priest of Philip the founder. Picard suggested that the small building in or by which the inscription was found was Philip's *heróon*.   [3] Paus. 5. 20. 9.

[4] R. L. Fox (504) suggests that Eurydice here may be not Philip's mother but his wife Cleopatra, who was named as Eurydice by Arrian (*An.* 3. 6. 5). But I cannot see either Philip or Alexander approving a family group which included both Olympias and Cleopatra.

stroke, whether of Philip or of Alexander. This expensive material was usually for the gods. (But Phryne had one at Thespiae—and at Delphi!¹) Are we to think of the Philippeum as a *heröon* of the Macedonian royal family? Or as a 'temple of Philip' as E. N. Gardiner called it firmly?² There are objections, from the building itself.³ The fact of its being a *tholos* cannot be decisive, though A. W. Lawrence came near to pronouncing that *tholoi* in general were not temples. This *tholos*, however, faced south (a *heröon* should face west). It contained no cult-statue (*agalma*); no altar (*bōmos*); no hearth (*eschara*); no *bōmos* adjacent or attached and obviously designed to serve it (as had the temple of Hera, for example, here at Olympia).⁴ Though the precinct at Olympia was not short of *bōmoi* (Pausanias lists about seventy), one would suppose that a temple really needed 'its own'. In short the Philippeum, as executed, does not carry conviction as a temple or a *heröon* instantly, if at all.

As a secular building, however, with a political background, it seems to make some sense. At this date only someone very important could think of building inside the precinct at all, and the Philippeum is sited at the only place where there was room for a new building. That this place was next to the Prytaneum was an additional recommendation— for someone very important. The patron who used the Philippeum on his visits to Olympia was assuming tacitly that he was himself always the most important person present, that everyone would look for him—in the best place. As the local headquarters of a *hegemon* the Philippeum seems to answer very well really, and it is not necessary to see it also as the headquarters of a new god. Its particular local appeal was sporting and 'epinician' (for Philip was a notable owner of winners here)—and this was probably not negligible, up and down Greece, especially among the noble and the well-to-do who knew and appreciated the form at Olympia most, and objected least to this new success story and its fancy new building here, and who were the most frequent visitors anyway. To these people the Philippeum represented the hospitable, bonhomous, free-spending patron. In the area of high politics it represented the Hegemon, whom hardly any Greeks positively wanted and welcomed for his own sake, though not a few looked to him for safety from their enemies, and needed him quite badly.

These last were the people who in their own cities would pay the extravagant compliment to the benefactor king, even to the point of

¹ Plu. *Mor.* 336 C–D, 401 D, 753 F; Paus. 10. 15. 1. See in general, K. Scott, 'The significance of statues in precious metals in Emperor Worship', *TAPA* 62 (1931) 101 ff.
² *Olympia* 134.   ³ See especially *RE* 18. 1 (1939) 105 s.v. *Olympia*.
⁴ On *tholoi*, A. W. Lawrence, *Greek Architecture*² (London, 1967) 185. For relationship between altar and cult-statue, W. H. Plommer, *Ancient and Classical Architecture* (London, 1956) 116–18.

treating him as a god, like Lysander before him and Alexander presently. For the benefactor to pay himself the same compliment, by building his own temple in the greatest assembly-place of the Greeks, is a wide step forward and beyond the limits of 'thinking like a mortal' (θνητὰ φρονεῖν). In sheer self-assertion, too, this seems to surpass the mere request or order to the Greek cities later by Alexander, to treat him as a god, if Alexander did indeed request or order that. For all Alexander's notorious religiosity, this anecdote in the tradition is thought nowadays hardly respectable, by many.[1] To accept that Philip in his last year expected and indeed arranged for himself to be worshipped widely at Olympia in a temple of his own providing, seems to be imposing a strain on the credulity which only the final scene of all, at Aegeae, might enable it to bear. Any who see Philip's 'thirteenth statue' at Aegeae as his own claim to receive worship on a par with the Twelve Gods will easily see the Philippeum perhaps as his temple (and himself as the first god to build and pay for his own?).[2]

But in truth the 'thirteenth statue' need not, indeed should not, mean all that. It was a claim not to worship but to homage.[3] Even in that context it was an indiscretion; for in the best circles homage is not claimed, it is merely given. In the context of Olympia the Philippeum was something of an indiscretion too perhaps, even on the purely secular interpretation of it offered here. Insufferable as a temple (which on this view it was not), as a *hegemon*'s headquarters it was a bit heavy-handed, probably.[4] Only as the gift of the good patron and owner-competitor could it be seen as unexceptionable, the reminder of those good winners, and more to come (so they could all suppose). But 'the god' had other ideas.

> τῶν δ' ἀδοκήτων πόρον ηὗρε θεός·
> τοιόνδ' ἀπέβη τόδε πρᾶγμα.

This was more than untimely, it was tragic, in some sense or other. The true tragic hero is (deep down) a professional loser, and that Philip emphatically was not, any more than was Julius Caesar. These were lucky leaders, all their lives; lucky so often that when they play their 'double or quits' act once too often, we feel almost cheated. We do not much remember Caesar's last silly mistake, with Brutus and his mob, we choose to think of him passing coolly from the night life to the Senate

---

[1] Ael. *VH* 2. 19 (= Plu. *Mor.* 219 A). The wide modern literature on the subject will be considered in Volume III.

[2] For the scene at Aegeae, above p. 682.

[3] The distinction is Nock's (*Essays* 1. 241 = *HSCP* 41 (1930) 50).

[4] If Philip had been worshipped at Olympia in the 330s and 320s, I should have expected some speech of some orator in these years to have passed comment on it that would have earned survival.

to be viceroy to be c.-in-c., making mistakes all the time and always picking them up before they hit the ground.

So (or somewhat so) with Philip. An egregious Frederick William (but how much more entertaining?) to Alexander's Frederick (only Greater).[1] A good and interesting general, and a marvellous soldier in the field, and above all in the height and heat of action. Yet prouder to win by 'politics' than by war. A temperament like this should have been born poor, to show what it could really do; in Athens, to out-Themistocles Themistocles, or (better) in Sparta, to out-Brasidas Brasidas. But Philip was born a king, and made himself a plutocrat before he was thirty. ἀργύρου πηγή τις αὐτοῖς ἐστι, θησαυρὸς χθονός.[2] And to 'silver', add gold. (Think of a number: double it: multiply it by 5 or 6 and so on.) It was too easy, for a king like Philip, in a geographical expression like Greece. No wonder he is remembered most of all (apart from his son of course!) not for his own victories, or even for his *sarissas* or his torsion-catapults, but for his *Philippeioi* ('Philips').

Demosthenes had told us so—before it had happened, too, as well as after. These irresistible objects the 'Philips' found Demosthenes himself immovable (and all honour to him for it); but not every politician was a Demosthenes. This was honour in a Greek politician, to take money only for doing what you thought right and meant to do anyway (as Demosthenes himself from Persia). The Phocion was a rare bird indeed, who took money from nobody, on principle; a little embarrassing really, irritating even, to the benefactors themselves, who liked Phocion so well, and who would far rather have set him up for life than any number of the creepy-crawlies whom they did find themselves endowing.

Yet not all creepy-crawlies, either? Philip's hegemony, Philip as *hegemon*, commanded just enough consensus to survive while all went well, from the Demades and the Daochus, the Cottyphus and the Demaratus, multiplied through every city of the Aegean, who recognized that when the best has gone, unattainable, life can still go on (must still go on, the simpler-minded might say), with the second-best. (Does the road wind down hill all the way? Yes, to the very end.) Demosthenes took poison rather than be tried and executed, or become a fugitive with a price on his head. (He was an old man: one must draw the line somewhere, and men of sense will applaud him.) But Demosthenes had got himself trapped by his own intransigence and reputation. Those who had compromised in good time, and with Philip rather than with the next generation of tougher (nastier?) Macedonians, had not too bad a bargain: the *hegemon* who was good company (great company, even) and who had a fair amount of decency and magnanimity to appeal to in case of need,

---

[1] A comparison first made long ago, and often since.
[2] Aesch. *Pers.* 239. 'They have, you may say, a fountain of silver, a treasury of the earth.'

not to mention the 'fountain of silver' (and gold,) helping himself to the 'Philips' from the inexhaustible vaults of the Earth itself. Even the Athenian proud of his autochthonous descent from the soil of Attica which made him superior to ordinary Greeks, let alone to 'a bloody Macedonian, from a country that in the past never produced even a slave who was any good',[1] even the proud Athenian when he laid his own well-tried, well-used, archaic-looking 'Owls' alongside the new 'Philips' might feel obliged to allow that the *hegemon* had got something here. Whichever the god (of the obverse), Heracles or old-style Apollo, or new-style Apollo (long-haired) and brand-new Zeus, these gods in gold and in silver, with their glamorous assortment of fun and games (on reverse) made more noise in the world, certainly, than any coinage since the fabulous Syracusan and other Siceliot issues of the fifth century, some of those for no particular reason that we know of, except a felicitous coincidence of plenty of money (the winner's) and plenty of talent (in the master-goldsmiths of that era).

Philip was lucky in his artists as in most other things.[2] His horse-and-jockey (a useful-looking sprinter by our present-day criteria of conformation) will remind the twentieth-century observer of Diomedes or Delirium or Deep Diver, or a score of other 5-furlong champions. The boy jockey looks slight, certainly, for so big a horse (can he be safe?). Jockeys are not put up in order to be safe, we remind ourselves: the boy has his prize of olive. The horses of the *biga* team are superb (surely), and the driver shows them the whip with all the fidelity, even if without the magical combination of tenseness and nonchalance, of the *quadriga*-driver of the great Syracusan decadrachms, or the rather morose confidence of the driver from Messana poking at his pair of mules. Philip's attractive adult horseman (in a hat) is thought to be a portrait of himself. I do not know if this can be proved or disproved, but if it is not true, perhaps it deserves to be. (And see p. 667.)

Though Philip's Apollo obverses have attracted the most attention (because of the obvious Chalcidian connection), the most important story, if we are looking for a story from the coins, might yet come, some day, from the Zeus heads, the genuine novelty of his reign. For me as an ignoramus, Zeus on coins stands (first) for Elis and Olympia, and if I felt competent to read the tea-leaves, I think I should be seeing a dark stranger and at least four legs (perhaps eight; or can it be sixteen?), and certainly a pair of wheels—until I can see nothing for dust any more. A Peloponnesian connection, starting *when* in his reign? The sooner it could be shown to start, the more interesting it would be, obviously.

---

[1] D. 6. 31.

[2] The coin-types mentioned here are discussed more professionally by Hammond, pp. 663 ff.

I began by warning (in the context of Thessaly, p. 219) that it cannot be sound method to look at 359 through the eyes of 340 or even 350 (but rather of 370). Here, on the Peloponnese, the same warning leads us back to the years in Thebes. This is where the teenage Philip first opened the form-book; and what he found there was (much of it) concerned with the Peloponnesian politics leading up to Mantinea (of 362). He learned there never, never to have an obol on Sparta, but always to be at the beck of any Peloponnesian who wanted to kick Sparta behind and then run away. Elis, Arcadia, Messenia, Argos: and Olympia the focus of 'Peloponnese for the Peloponnesians', no less than Delphi presently as focus of freedom-loving Amphictyons hoping to get Thebes off their backs. As a kite for a future *hegemon* to fly, this (more than presentable) head of Zeus shows promise—especially if he is still a new boy, or a fairly new boy, when he first begins to fly it. The mid 360s brought a spectacular head-of-Zeus on the Arcadian silver, as well as good contemporary examples of the long-established series at Elis.[1] These are striking coins by any standard (the Arcadian particularly), and Philip in his 'formative years' could have been impressed. When he came into the money himself, and wanted to impress Peloponnesians, and to remind them that any Peloponnesian who kicked Sparta behind and ran away was a very good friend of his, Zeus and no other clearly was the god through whom to appeal to all the finest instincts of these brave fellows.

[1] See Head 445 and 422–4; and (for fine pictures), G. K. Jenkins, *Ancient Greek Coinage* (London, 1972), Pls. 244 (Arcadia) and 246 (Elis); C. M. Kraay and M. Hirmer, *Greek Coins* (London, 1966), Pls. 562–8.

APPENDIX 1

The Half-brothers of Philip

PHILIP's three half-brothers, sons of Amyntas III from another wife Gygaea, are not heard of as contestants for the throne in the troubled years of the 360s. Writing of Philip's reign, however, Justin does indicate that Philip found something to fear from them: one of them he put to death, and the other two fled the kingdom. The two extracts from Justin (below) both refer to the same trio of brothers, clearly, and it is assumed that he named the eldest of them first, and that it was the eldest (Archelaus) whom Philip put to death. The date of this needs to be established.

> Justin 7. 4. 5 (of Amyntas III): '. . . qui ex Eurydice tres filios sustulit, Alexandrum, Perdiccam et Philippum, ex Gygaea autem Archelaum, Arridaeum, Menelaum.'

> id. 8. 3. 10 (of Philip): 'Post haec Olynthios adgreditur; receperant enim per misericordiam post caedem unius duos fratres eius, quos Philippus ex noverca genitos veluti participes regni interficere gestiebat.'

In the second of the two passages Justin clearly intended to record the reason for Philip's attack on 'the Olynthians' (Chalcidian League) in 349—because they had given refuge to Philip's two fugitive half-brothers. It is natural to think that Justin thought that they had given refuge recently; and we have seen (above, p. 315) that there is compelling reason to believe that this indeed was so. It is natural, too, to think that the events which forced the brothers to flee from Macedonia—events which had culminated in Philip's putting Archelaus to death—also must have happened recently. These members of the royal house had brought suspicion on themselves. Philip did not make a habit of killing those who by birth and blood stood closest to the throne merely because of the relationship (his nephew Amyntas though next of kin to Perdiccas III lived safe and sound all through his reign). The implication is that Archelaus became suspected of subversion and was executed for treason, and that the brothers Arrhidaeus and Menelaus were involved too, but had managed to escape. An exciting story, probably. It is strange that Diodorus has not a word to say of it when he begins his brief notice of the Olynthian war.[1] It is more than strange, it is astonishing, that Demosthenes in this same year 349 in the three *Olynthiac* speeches never thinks to mention these recent happenings at Pella. In the *First Olynthiac* when he talked of Philip's difficulties at the time, he spoke only of Thessaly, Chalcidice, Paeonians, Illyrians; and of troubles in Macedonia not at all. In the *Second Olynthiac* he alleged that the Macedonians were dissatisfied with Philip, the people because

---

[1] D.S. 16. 53. 2.

his campaigns wore them out and interfered with their normal livelihood, the
circle of his Companions because he took all the glory for himself (and some
of them because he promoted a dissolute way of life).[1] But tame stuff, this,
if in reality he could have reminded them that only a few months before
Philip had had to put his own half-brother to death for treason, and that the
refugees Arrhidaeus and Menelaus were what this Olynthian war was all about
anyway. On reflection it seems evident that, though the coming of the refugees
to Olynthus was probably recent, their flight from Macedonia and the execution of Archelaus was certainly not recent. It must have happened years
before, and in circumstances which did not allow Demosthenes to make
political capital out of it. Both inferences seem justified. Mere remoteness in
time, by itself, need not have kept Demosthenes silent on the death of Archelaus,
if he had been able to use it (even falsely) as a sign of Philip's insecurity. One
can think this confidently just because the presence of Arrhidaeus and Menelaus
at Olynthus as a *casus belli* makes it certain that their whole history cannot
have escaped his attention.

Further reflection suggests that the ten years of Philip's reign before the
year 349 contain only one occasion which satisfies these two conditions (it
must be long before 349; and it must be of no use to Demosthenes when making
the point which we are considering). The occasion of course is the very beginning of the reign, the first few weeks or months when Philip was ringed by
enemies and claimants to the throne in the way that Diodorus briefly describes.[2]
If Archelaus conspired and was executed *then*, not even a Demosthenes could
transform it into a sign of Philip's insecurity in 349 without making himself
ridiculous. Theopompus probably did write of Archelaus in connection with
Argaeus and Pausanias the other two claimants to the throne in 359; and the
fact that Diodorus did not write of him in that same connection is not decisive.[3]
The orthodox view which places the Archelaus affair in 359, though it has
been contested recently, seems likely to be right.[4]

As to the details obviously it is idle to speculate at length. Presumably
Archelaus was dissatisfied with the choice by the Macedonians of Philip in

---

[1] D. 1. 5–6; 2. 15–18 (generalized at 2. 21). The allegation in the *First Philippic* 4. 8
(of 351 probably), that Philip had enemies even among his intimates, is ruled out by its
date from any consideration in connection with Olynthus in 349. But it remains true that if
Demosthenes had known of names inside the royal family which were significant in 351,
undoubtedly he would have named them.

[2] D.S. 16. 2. 4–6; 3. 3–6.

[3] *FGrH* 115 F 29, where the emendation of the text supplying Ἀρχέλαον for the manuscripts
ἀγγέλαον and ἀγέλαον is generally accepted. But the lexicographer's citation is too brief to
allow us to see what Theopompus was saying (Harpocration s.v. Ἀργαῖος· περὶ τούτου καὶ
Θεόπομπος ἐν α′ τῶν Φιλιππικῶν λέγει· τὸν Ἀρχέλαον καλοῦσι καὶ Ἀργαῖον καὶ Παυσανίαν).
And cf. Hammond, p. 175 above, who proposes τὸν Ἀρχελάου καλοῦσι . . . etc.

For a good discussion of this, and of the whole problem of Archelaus and his brothers,
J. R. Ellis, 'The step-brothers of Philip II', *Historia* 22 (1973) 350–4. On Diodorus, Ellis
points out (and I agree) that his source (Ephorus?) was well informed on the situation in
Macedonia in 359, and Ellis legitimately uses the silence of Diodorus in support of his view
that the Archelaus affair belongs not to 359 but later. But the silence of Demosthenes (above),
who might have found good material in the Archelaus affair if it had happened later, seems
to me to outweigh that of Diodorus here.

[4] *Contra*, J. R. Ellis (see previous note).

359, and allowed this to be seen. In the climate of that critical year a disaffected prince of the royal house was a dangerous liability, and Philip acted against him, presumably by a charge of treason before the Macedonians. His two brothers fled the country, but what became of them then for nearly ten years we cannot know. Finally they came to Olynthus, where their presence provoked the breach between Philip and the Chalcidian League, and the Olynthian War of 349.

APPENDIX 2

Amyntas, the Son of Perdiccas

WRITING of Philip's accession in 359 (p. 208), I have departed from the orthodox view which sees him elected then not as king but as regent for his young nephew Amyntas, and which prefers in effect the testimony of Justin on this (if that is indeed what Justin did intend to record) to that of Diodorus.[1] The orthodox view starts off with two quite serious disadvantages: (1) (the lesser) we never learn when Philip was elected king, if it was not in 359; (2) in the desperate circumstances of 359, self-evidently there was something unrealistic in electing an infant king when it was open to the people to elect the man on whom their hopes of survival really depended. That is not to say that it cannot have happened, for history is full of people doing silly things. But people in desperate trouble are less likely to do them than other people, and the improbability here ought to seem quite strong. The orthodox view, then, needs some really strong grounds for believing that in 359 Amyntas became king and Philip became regent; and needless to say it has grounds that must be admitted as perfectly respectable.

First, the authority of Diodorus (using Ephorus?) can be undermined, when he says that Philip reigned for twenty-four years (= 359–36).[2] Satyrus wrote of twenty-two years as the duration of his reign.[3] It can be argued that the source of Satyrus knew of a regency (and knew that it lasted about two years); a substantial point, though not by itself a decisive one. The real basis of the orthodox view is that inscription of Lebadeia in northern Boeotia which records the names and the contributions in money of visitors to the oracle of Trophonius in its cave there. 'Amyntas, son of Perdiccas, king of the Macedonians' at line 8 is an entry to catch the eye; for though the story of this stone itself is a melancholy one, and the entry as I quote it above has not been recovered easily, I accept that this message is what the stone did once hold (and perhaps still does after a fashion, if only one knew where to find it again).[4] Its importance is self-explanatory. There was a time, it seems, when this young Amyntas was known abroad as king of the Macedonians. The presumption follows that the time must have been in that period when Philip was regent; and if so Justin's account of what happened in 359 is vindicated.

Though this inscription ought really to settle the matter (it might be thought), the difficulties of interpreting it satisfactorily are very great. The numismatic evidence lends no support for a reign of Amyntas IV. The literary sources are silent on it. There is no suggestion that Philip, when his activities came to

---

[1] Just. 7. 4. 5; 8. 3. 10; D.S. 16. 1. 3; 2. 1 ff. And see p. 209 nn. 1, 2. J. R. Ellis, *JHS* 91 (1971) 15 ff., does not accept the regency. But see Hammond, above, p. 651.

[2] D.S. 16. 1. 3.

[3] *FHG* 3. 161 F 5 (Athen. 13. 557 b); so too Suid. s.v. *Karanos*. And see p. 209 n. 2.

[4] *IG* VII. 3055 (undated). The history of the stone (now lost) is summarized by Ellis, art. cit. 16 f.

be mentioned, was ever anything other than king; and Demosthenes especially, it may be thought, missed some chances here, if in reality Philip had become king by displacing his nephew on the throne. Those who believe in a regency make it a short one, three years at the very most: the refounding of Crenides, for example, under his own name (Philippi) in 356 must surely have been done by Philip as king. Amyntas, therefore, must have visited Lebadeia and consulted the oracle of Trophonius as a boy, and perhaps quite a small boy; for he cannot have been more than eleven or twelve years old in 356, and he may have been much less.[1] There is something distinctly improbable in this. The alternative (suggested by J. R. Ellis) is that the visit of Amyntas to this oracle was in 336/5, in the brief period after Philip's death when Amyntas could be seen as Alexander's rival for the Macedonian throne.[2] But this seems even more improbable, for it would have been a wild imprudence if these Boeotians had committed themselves gratuitously to this Amyntas then, by naming him as 'king of the Macedonians'. This title itself, too (we remind ourselves), was not used normally by the king himself at this time: we have no evidence of Philip's ever having used it (see pp. 387 f.). It's use here by Greeks at Lebadeia is itself an oddity, and to explain it in terms of some kind of political emphasis is only to underline the extreme imprudence of these little people, if they really were choosing to be politically emphatic about this of all things.

In short, though this inscription of Lebadeia ought to be decisive, personally I do not trust it, and I am not convinced that its description of Amyntas as 'king of the Macedonians' is literally correct. I am prepared to believe that these people at Lebadeia, who did not have royal princes visiting their cave and oracle every day, may have been a little over-excited by the experience, and may have allowed this to pass into their record of it. *Ἀμύντας Περδίκκα Μακεδόνων βασιλεύς*: 'Amyntas, son of Perdiccas, prince of the Macedonian royal house'. This seems a possible interpretation;[3] preferable to one that insists that *basileus* must mean 'king' here as it normally does, with all the attendant improbabilities that here ensue.

In the years 355–346 northern Boeotia became an unhealthy area for visitors, some parts of it for much of the time under Phocian control. The visit of Amyntas to the oracle at Lebadeia will have been in the years 346–339, perhaps breaking a journey to or from Thebes on some diplomatic mission or errand in pursuit of good relations. To the same period (and perhaps with the same implications) must belong the connection of Amyntas with

---

[1] On the age of Amyntas in 359, Ellis, art. cit. 18.   [2] Ellis, art. cit. 18–21.

[3] I am encouraged to find now that R. M. Errington reaches a not dissimilar conclusion in his recent article 'Macedonian "Royal Style" and its historical significance' (*JHS* 94 (1974), especially 25–8). Errington, not questioning that this Amyntas was or had been king, but concerned with the oddities of his title here, concludes 'I . . . prefer to envisage the Lebadeians so describing Amyntas simply because they wanted a famous name to head their list.'

Errington also makes the interesting suggestion (loc. cit. 26 and 28) that Amyntas II, whose patronymic is nowhere attested, perhaps cannot be excluded as a possible candidate for identification with Amyntas Perdikka of this inscription. If this could only be true, all our troubles would be over. But I fear that Aelian *VH* 12. 43 makes it only too probable that the father of Amyntas II was Menelaus. (So Hammond, p. 169 above.)

Oropus which led to his receiving proxeny honours there.[1] It could just be significant, too, that both these places, Lebadeia and Oropus, contain the sites of peculiarly interesting hero-cults with chthonic associations.[2] Can this Amyntas have become some kind of an expert on religion, a *mantis* even, or a student-*mantis*? This could be his private and personal interest in life, or one of them. Or it could be part of his duty as a royal prince, perhaps. The king as priest in Macedonia had a heavy programme of sacrifices all the time, and a deputy on occasions will have been necessary.[3] Remembering Alexander's ferocious devotion to duty in the matter of religious observance, one could not easily find room for two royal princes as king's deputy in this matter. But before (say) 340 when Alexander became sixteen, Amyntas might have done a useful job on this. However that may be, in due time Amyntas received the hand in marriage of Philip's daughter Cynane (her mother the Illyrian Audata).[4] Whether he is the Amyntas who led the vitally important embassy which Philip sent to Thebes immediately after he occupied Elateia in 339, we do not know. The royal prince, and with some Boeotian connections, was a good choice perhaps for the occasion; strongly supported by colleagues including the important Daochus of Pharsalus.[5] As a soldier, however, nothing is heard of him in campaigns of Philip's later years. So far as we know, he led a blameless and undistinguished life all through Philip's reign. It was not till Alexander came to the throne that his troubles began—and ended.[6]

[1] *IG* VII. 4251, = Tod, *GHI* 164A. The decree belongs certainly to the period of Oropus' independence from Athens, which ended in 338 after Chaeronea. For this reason the dating of it by Ellis (art. cit. 21) 'probably in mid-335' cannot be accepted. (Cf. Tod, loc. cit.; *SEG* 25. 482. Mr. A. G. Woodhead kindly tells me now that in his opinion the lettering of this inscription suggests on balance a date not much later than 350.)

[2] On Trophonius and Amphiaraus in this sense, see A. D. Nock, 'The cult of heroes' 1, *Essays* 2 (1972) 578.

[3] On Arrhidaeus (later Philip III) as deputy for Alexander the Great, Curt. Ruf. 10. 7. 2, *sacrorum caerimoniarumque consors modo*; and cf. the important observations of P. Briant, *Antigone le Borgne* 323–7, esp. 326 n. 2.

[4] Satyrus, *FHG* 3. 161 F 5.   [5] Plu. *Demosth.* 18. 1 f.

[6] Amyntas at Oropus on this occasion was associated with Amyntas, son of Antiochus (*IG* VII. 4250, a proxeny decree which is the 'twin' of *IG* VII. 4251 above), who fled from Alexander to Persia in 335; and perhaps also with Aristomedes of Pherae, another refugee to Persia (B. Ch. Petrakos, *Ὁ Ὠρωπὸς καὶ τὸ ἱερὸν τοῦ Ἀμφιαράου* (Athens, 1968) 25 and 174). This association clearly is of great importance for the first months of Alexander's reign, and it will be discussed in that connection. For Philip's reign, these inscriptions show that the two Amyntases (and perhaps Aristomedes) were associates in or before 338; but to try to interpret their association in or before 338 in the light of their behaviour after 336 would be unwise, for obvious reasons. (Aristomedes had deserted perhaps by 340 already, see p. 525.) Especially, to see them as a group whom Philip in or before 338 needed to beware of (as Alexander thought he did, in 336/5), and consequently to see their honours at Oropus as a sign of Boeotian hostility to Philip, would be quite unjustified. The reasons for the proxeny decrees are unknown. They may represent thanks for benefactions received. J. J. Coulton's interesting suggestions for connecting the Amyntases with the building of the *stoa* of the Amphiareion at Oropus, which belongs probably to this period, were prompted by features suggesting a Macedonian architect (*BSA* 63 (1968) 169 ff.; conclusions at 180–3).

R. M. Errington's suggestion (art. cit. 27) that Amyntas was perhaps the bearer to the Oropians of the news of Philip's decision to restore them to Athens (338), and was rewarded by them with this proxeny decree, does not convince me. An envoy of this rank for this purpose seems out of all proportion, to a city which was being treated here as a chattel.

APPENDIX 3

The *pezhetairoi*[1]

1. *Anaximenes F 4 and Theopompus F 348*

THE date of the origin of the *pezhetairoi* is important enough to justify a thought as to our two sources. On a general view they could be counted as about equal in value. Both were contemporaries of Philip and Alexander (the Great), both knew Macedonia well.[2] (Demosthenes, though his allusion to *pezhetairoi* in 349 establishes that they existed then, tells us nothing of their origin or composition. His remarks that follow are interesting and even amusing, but as historical commentary they suffer from the disadvantage of commenting on a different word—*hetairoi*—from the word which they purport to illuminate.[3])

Anaximenes gains in value here from being quoted verbatim: we do at least know what he wrote, if our text is sound. What Theopompus wrote we know only from the paraphrase or précis of the scholiast who used him to explain Philip's *pezhetairoi* mentioned by Demosthenes: 'Theopompus says that picked men out of all the Macedonians, the tallest and strongest, served as the King's Guards, and they were called Foot Companions.'[4] According to Anaximenes it was 'the mass of the Macedonians and the infantry' who were called Foot Companions, when 'Alexander' had given them that name. If Anaximenes meant Alexander I or II, before Philip, could the apparent

---

[1] I have profited greatly from a close reading and discussion of this Appendix by Professor R. D. Milns and by Mr. A. G. Woodhead. To both of them I owe thanks on a wider front than the particular points for which I make acknowledgement in footnotes.

[2] Anaximenes is said to have been one of Alexander's tutors, perhaps wrongly (*FGrH* 72 T. 1; cf. T. 6, = Paus. 6. 18. 3).

[3] D. 2. 17. It is hard to believe that he expected his charming aside 'My informant, a man quite incapable of telling a lie', to be received with utter and unmoved solemnity.

[4] For the Greek, p. 406 n. 1 above, *FGrH* no. 115 F 348. I take this remark as a true description of the King's Guards as Theopompus himself knew them in Macedonia in the late 340s, including their name *pezhetairoi*. If he referred here to an earlier period of Macedonian history, and if in his own time *pezhetairoi* already had come to mean all the infantry of the phalanx, he must have gone on to mention this change, and in that case the scholiast, seeking to explain *pezhetairoi in Demosthenes*, would have found the 'new' meaning and would have reported it instead of (or as well as) the 'old' meaning.

Nor do I see it as possible that in the late 340s all the infantry of the phalanx already were called *pezhetairoi*, and the King's Guards also were called *pezhetairoi*. Clearly the whole sense of what Theopompus wrote was that the King's Guards were very special soldiers, and they had a special name. It is presumably from Theopompus, directly or indirectly, that the *EM* entry gets its facts (as opposed to its 'theory'): s.v., 658. 39–50; ibid. 699. 47–8: πεζεταίρους εἶναί φασιν ἀπὸ ὁδοιπορικῶν ἔργων ἑταίρους γεγονότας· οἱ δέ, τοὺς περὶ τὸ σῶμα τοῦ Φιλίππου φρουρούς. Ἦσαν δὲ οὗτοι καὶ πρῶτοι καὶ ἰσχυροί· ἀπὸ μεταφορᾶς τῶν πεζῶν. Πέζαι γὰρ λέγονται αἱ ᾦαι τῶν ἱματίων· etc.

Elsewhere (F 213) Theopompus adapts this word perhaps satirically against the Athenian general Chares, whose 'guards' (he says) were a bevy of girls—ὅς γε περιήγετο στρατευόμενος αὐλητρίδας καὶ ψαλτρίας καὶ πεζὰς ἑταίρας . . .

contradiction in Theopompus be explained by a scholiast's inept paraphrase? Is it possible that the real sense of what Theopompus wrote was that the King's Guards were a picked force, chosen for their physique from all the Foot Companions, who were the infantry levy of all the Macedonians? I judge that this is possible, but only just. The scholiast's aim here, after all, was to explain the word *pezhetairoi*. He turned for his explanation to Theopompus, who, whatever he did really write here, was writing of a plain matter of fact which cannot have been hard to follow or understand. A scholiast who could get this wrong could get anything wrong. But the scholiast who knew that Theopompus offered support for one of the alternative explanations of a word which had become a textual *crux* was capable, surely, of reporting him correctly.[1] In short, the possibility that Theopompus is misreported here seems remote enough to be negligible.

For Theopompus, then, the Foot Companions of Philip are a *corps d'élite*: in the 340s (and probably the late 340s when Theopompus was in Macedonia), the name had not yet been given to the Macedonian infantry levy as a whole. Since all modern interpreters disbelieve Theopompus and prefer to rely on Anaximenes, it is lucky that we are given one glimpse of the *pezhetairoi* in action at a time when they were a force such as Theopompus, and not Anaximenes, describes. Some Macedonian king or general, we are told, 'invaded Illyria at the head of the troops known as the *pezhetairoi*, a picked corps'.[2] Yet Anaximenes undeniably gives the impression that his 'Alexander' was a king of the past, not of the present, a king who seems almost to be creating a Macedonian army for the first time. 'Then having trained the upper class as cavalry he called them Companions (*hetairoi*). The mass of the people and the foot soldiers he organized in companies and sections and the other formations, and gave them the name Foot Companions (*pezhetairoi*). In this way he intended that each class by sharing in the royal Companionship should be always exceedingly loyal.'[3] The essential comment to be made on this piece of writing is that some of it is nonsense, to whichever Alexander it may be referring, Alexander I, II, or III. No Alexander 'trained the upper

---

[1] Dindorf 8. 96. Only two manuscripts preserve the Theopompus reference, which resolves the small controversy suggested by the scholia of BSTCEV.

[2] *EM* loc. cit. Between the lemma and the entry quoted at p. 705 n. 4 above is the following quotation: καὶ τῶν Μακεδόνων τοὺς πεζεταίρους μὲν καλουμένους ὄντας δὲ ἀπολέκτους ἔχων ἐνέβαλεν εἰς τὴν Ἰλλυρίδα. See further p. 709.

[3] Anaximenes F 4, ἔπειτα τοὺς μὲν ἐνδοξοτάτους ἱππεύειν συνεθίσας ἑταίρους προσηγόρευσε, τοὺς δὲ πλείστους καὶ τοὺς πεζοὺς εἰς λόχους καὶ δεκάδας καὶ τὰς ἄλλας ἀρχὰς διελὼν πεζεταίρους ὠνόμασεν, ὅπως ἑκάτεροι μετέχοντες τῆς βασιλικῆς ἑταιρίας προθυμότατοι διατελῶσιν ὄντες. Momigliano's (*FM* 8 f.) proposal to emend the text by deleting (as a gloss) καὶ τοὺς πεζοὺς so as to improve both the sense and the grammar seems unpromising. Πλειστούς and πεζούς are synonyms here, and though the second is not necessary for the sense, it is necessary for the rhetoric, in order to prepare the way for πεζεταίρους, the interesting Macedonian word destined to keep the lexicographers busy. (For much the same synonyms, without the same banality, cf. the πολὺς ὅμιλος καὶ στρατιώτης of Thucydides 6. 24. 3.) For the ancient lexicography of πεζέταιροι (πεζέτεροι, πεζαίτεροι), see (besides Harp. s.v. and Suid. s.v. who quote Anaximenes), Hsch. s.v., Phot. s.v., *EM* 658 and 699. I hope I am right in ignoring those ancient scholars who derived the word from the sole or instep of the foot (πέζα), or from the border of a garment (again πέζα), and in sticking to the obvious derivation from 'infantry'.

class as cavalry'. Like other nobles they had known all about horses and *were* cavalry, for generations before Alexander I. In the same way 'the mass of the people and the foot soldiers' were foot soldiers, as he himself writes, already. If they were foot soldiers, they were organized already in companies, like any other infantry there has ever been. Alexander I or II or III may have reorganized them in some way; but that is not what Anaximenes wrote. For him, 'his' Alexander virtually created the Macedonian army, horse and foot at one and the same time. To write this is to write nonsense.

It is this that discourages me from taking this passage altogether seriously, let alone accepting it as literally true. Nonsense when applied to any King Alexander, it is contradicted, on *pezhetairoi*, by Theopompus if it is applied to Alexander I or II. The fact that it seems to be the worst nonsense of all when applied to Alexander III (where the Theopompus contradiction on *pezhetairoi* need not operate) does not prevent me from thinking that Anaximenes perhaps was writing of Alexander III after all. A writer capable of stuff like this perhaps was capable of a rather unusual silliness. Anaximenes was (among other things) an orator, and in the view of one ancient critic a second- or third-rate one. To Dionysius of Halicarnassus he seemed a 'jack of all trades, master of none', with pretensions to being what we should call an all-rounder in literature; historian, literary critic, and orator, 'yet first-rate in none of these categories, but feeble and unconvincing'.[1] If Anaximenes wanted to say (for example) that Alexander the Great widened the application of the existing name Companions to include all the Macedonian heavy cavalry, and that of the existing name Foot Companions to include all the Macedonian infantry of the phalanx, could he have embellished these two facts with cliché nonsense so as to produce what he is quoted as having written here? Though it may seem a hard thing to say, I suspect that he could.

My suspicion is strengthened by the character of the lexicographer's entry itself here.[2] His mentioning the First Book of the *Philippic History* as the source of the quotation invites us first to think of one of the Alexanders before Philip as the Alexander of whom he wrote here, and perhaps to overlook a second and much more decisive clue to identification, namely that Harpocration did not think it necessary to specify which Alexander. This was not by accident or by ignorance, or by negligence.[3] Clearly it ought to mean that Harpocration knew that Anaximenes meant Alexander the Great, the only Alexander whose name by itself was sufficient identification.[4] It would seem that we are positively

---

[1] Dion. Hal. *De Isaeo* 19. (= *FGrH* no. 72 T. 13).   [2] Harp. s.v. πεζέταιροι.

[3] Harpocration knew his Alexanders: s.v. *Alexandros*, he names four whom he found in the oratorical Corpus which was his field; Alexander I and II of Macedonia, Alexander of Pherae, Alexander of Epirus. In a case where a confusion of identity was possible, he took trouble to prevent it: e.g. s.v. Nikanor, 'There were three Nikanors, the son of Balakros, the son of Parmenion, and Nikanor of Stagira, to whom the orator would be referring here.'

[4] Comparably, Harp. s.v. *Philippoi*, names as founder of the city 'Philip, king of the Macedonians', no further identification needed.

Milns reminds me that Harpocration was not interested in Alexander here, but in defining *pezhetairoi*. I accept this as a possible reason but not as a certainty. If he knew that Anaximenes referred to an earlier Alexander, it really was incumbent on him to say so: to his public 'Alexander', alone, meant Alexander the Great.

obliged to connect this piece of information with Alexander the Great, unless there are compelling reasons to the contrary. The reasons already suggested (above) do not seem to me decisive.

More persuasive is the objection (of Milns) that if it was Alexander the Great who did something new to the 'Companion' names, it is surprising that none of the surviving Alexander-historians tells us so. I agree, they ought to have told us. But remembering their silence on Alexander's deification by Greek cities (a much more spectacular development), I do not take their silence on this as proof that Anaximenes was referring to an earlier king, especially if, as I am suggesting, this was only a change concerning names (and not new institutions), the widening of two existing names to cover groups not covered by them before. The thing itself had some importance and significance, but as a Macedonian thing and not a Greek one. I see the silence of the sources as surprising, but not astonishing. Weighing against it the advantages of the interpretation of Anaximenes already suggested, I still prefer the latter.

To accept that Anaximenes was writing here of Alexander the Great removes the contradictory element from what Theopompus tells us of *pezhetairoi* (and even of *hetairoi* too, perhaps). If allowance is made for some extravagance in Anaximenes (as suggested above), the two sources can be seen perhaps as complementary. Theopompus described the *pezhetairoi* of Philip as a royal guard and a *corps d'élite*; and he thought of the *hetairoi* as numbering not more than 800 men 'at that time', probably about 340.[1] The phrase 'at that time', to whatever date it refers, shows that Theopompus knew that at some later time the number was greater (or less). Anaximenes said that Alexander (the Great) gave the name *hetairoi* to 'the upper class' (τοὺς ἐνδοξοτάτους)—and we see that in Asia presently some 2,000 Macedonian cavalry do bear the name: he said that Alexander gave the name *pezhetairoi* to 'the mass of the Macedonians and the infantry'—and in Asia the name belongs either to the infantry of the phalanx as a whole or to a large part of it.[2] There is at least a sequence of development here that makes sense. If what Alexander really did was to widen greatly the restricted circles covered hitherto by these honorific names, so as to include now all the soldiers of the two classes concerned, this in itself was a fairly striking exercise in public relations, and one that even justified the claim made for it by Anaximenes ('in order that both classes by sharing in the royal Companionship should be always exceedingly loyal'). This version of what Alexander really did does not justify, certainly, the absurd details of Anaximenes about training the upper class as cavalry and organizing the infantry in their units; but perhaps it does help a little to explain his extravagance, if it is indeed right to think of him as a writer who was really not very strong in the head.[3]

Finally, fascinating is the fragment of the historian (unnamed), from a narrative passage evidently (concerning an unnamed king or general), which

---

[1] F 225. See above, p. 409. [2] For whole or part, below, p. 710.

[3] See, besides Dionysius (above), *FGrH* 72 T. 25 (cf. T. 12). 'Theocritus [of Chios] when Anaximenes began to speak said "Now for a river of words, and a water-drop of sense." ' Ibid. T. 27, for an unflattering remark of Alexander to Anaximenes.

does introduce the *pezhetairoi* as the force which Theopompus described, and not as the force which we see with Alexander in Asia. The *EM* entry already noticed (p. 705 n. 4), after the lemma quotes thus: 'At the head of the Macedonian "Foot-Guards", a picked force, he invaded Illyria.'[1] And what Macedonian king or general before Philip 'invaded Illyria'? Alexander the Great himself, moreover, did not 'invade Illyria'. In fact, this ought to be Philip, in the quotation (and the historian, obviously, may well be Theopompus). And the occasion ought to be either in 345, the invasion in which Philip was seriously wounded, or in 337 (or 336), the occasion which saw the start of the story of the two Pausaniases, which ended in Philip's murder (p. 684). Whichever the occasion (and especially if the later is preferred), this bit of information, if it is accepted, does give serious support to a view that the Alexander of the Anaximenes fragment can only be Alexander III.

2. *pezhetairoi* and *asthetairoi*

The foregoing pages have suggested that Alexander (the Great) inaugurated his command of the Macedonian army by conferring the honorific title of Companions on all the Macedonian cavalry units except the light cavalry (*prodromoi*), and that of Foot Companions on a mass of the Macedonian infantry of the phalanx. On *a* mass, or on *the* mass? Our acquaintance with the *pezhetairoi* of Alexander in Asia comes entirely from Arrian, and the text of Arrian in all our editions contains the word *pezhetairoi* eight times, providing the evidence for believing that all the Macedonians of the phalanx, except the hypaspists the *corps d'élite*, were known now as *pezhetairoi*. Recently however A. B. Bosworth in an important article has pointed out that six out of the eight appearances of *pezhetairoi* in the text of Arrian are the result of emendation.[2] In these six instances the manuscripts have *asthetairoi* (or *asthetheroi*), words unattested elsewhere and rejected by the editors as corrupt. Bosworth shows beyond all doubt that the editors have been mistaken. Apart from the gross improbability of a scribal corruption repeated six times in favour of the

---

[1] *EM* p. 699. 47–8 καὶ τῶν Μακεδόνων τοὺς πεζεταίρους μὲν καλουμένους ὄντας δὲ ἀπολέκτους ἔχων ἐνέβαλεν εἰς τὴν Ἰλλυρίδα. Bosworth's interpretation of this (art. cit. at my next note 245 n. 5) ignores Theopomp. F 348.

[2] A. B. Bosworth, *ΑΣΘΕΤΑΙΡΟΙ, CQ* N.S. 23 (1973) 245–53. Arr. *An*. 1. 28. 3 (MSS. πεζ.); 2. 23. 2; 4. 23. 1; 5. 22. 6; 6. 6. 1; 6. 21. 3; 7. 2. 1 (MSS. πεζ.); 7. 11. 3. The reference at Arr. 7. 2. 1 was not noticed by Bosworth, and my thanks are due to Professor Milns for drawing my attention to it. Here the manuscripts have πεζεταίροις, with no alternatives. As it happens, however, this reference is in a different category from all the others, because it comes not in a piece of military narrative but in the anecdote (λέγεται) of Alexander meeting the philosopher Diogenes at the Isthmus (Corinth)—ἐν Ἰσθμῷ ἐντυχὼν τῷ Διογένει κατακειμένῳ ἐν ἡλίῳ, ἐπιστὰς ξὺν τοῖς ὑπασπισταῖς καὶ τοῖς πεζεταίροις καὶ ἐρόμενος εἴ του δέοιτο κτλ. There is nothing here for us, I think. Whatever Arrian's source (Onesicritus?), this is a *raconteur* playing with words, his mind on the paradox and the parable of the Sage and the Warrior King rather than on any niceties of the Macedonian military vocabulary. His 'hypaspists and foot-companions' nearly corresponds to our 'horse, foot, and guns' (meaning 'the lot'). For the present purpose this is a 'rogue' reference, and I propose to ignore it. (It was taken seriously, however, in this connection by D. G. Hogarth, *JPhilol*. 17 (1888) 11 f., as Milns reminds me.)

same unknown form, decisive is the passage where the manuscripts give *pezhetairoi* and *asthetairoi* side by side as two components of a list, and where the emendation of *asthetairoi* to *pezhetairoi* produces a nonsense in the modern text.[1] Thanks to Bosworth (and I do thank him), I accept it as a certainty now that the phalanx in Asia contained (apart from the hypaspists) some brigades of *pezhetairoi* and some of *asthetairoi* (whatever the word may mean).

Bosworth's detailed examination of the five passages in Arrian containing *asthetairoi* (alone) establishes that the word refers never to the whole of the Macedonian phalanx, but covers about half of it, probably three of its six brigades (later perhaps four out of seven).[2] Does *pezhetairoi*, then, comprise the whole of the phalanx, or only the remaining part of it? A sixth passage of Arrian, that which contains *pezhetairoi* and *asthetairoi* together, as separate components of a list, seems to require the second alternative. But there is also one appearance of *pezhetairoi* in Arrian, the only one (apart from the list just mentioned) where the word appears as the manuscript reading, which certainly refers to the whole phalanx of six battalions, and not to a part of it.[3] There is inconsistency here, as compared with the 'list'. One factor not to be overlooked is the difference in date of the two points of reference, the one in 334/3 the other in 324. We do not know yet when the first *asthetairoi* were created, and this factor may be decisive (see below). Two possible explanations of the inconsistency seem possible. By the first, *pezhetairoi* would have applied to the whole phalanx, but some battalions of it had also the special name *asthetairoi* which applied to them only (and which Arrian found in Ptolemy, who followed the Macedonian usage). Alternatively, the passage which (alone of all the passages) names *pezhetairoi* only, and referring certainly to the whole phalanx, is incomplete and incorrect: there, Arrian (Ptolemy), ought to have written (see below, n. 3) '. . . he had the hypaspists, and next, to them the ⟨*asthetairoi* and the⟩ *pezhetairoi* extending right up to the left wing . . .'.[4] Bosworth favours the former alternative (without mentioning the

---

[1] Arr. *An.* 7. 11. 3: the solution of recent editors has been to expel καὶ ἀσθέταιροι ἄλλοι from the text altogether, as a gloss (a very strange one, as Bosworth observes, loc. cit. 246).

[2] Bosworth, loc. cit. 245–50. (He prefers 'battalion' as translation for *taxis*.) For the seventh brigade, added probably in 330, see especially R. D. Milns, 'Alexander's Seventh Phalanx Battalion', *GRBS* 7 (1966) 159–66.

[3] Arr. *An.* 1. 28. 3, describing the attack on the Pisidians, at a time when the only known absentees from Alexander's army were the Greek allies, detached under Parmenion, and the newly married Macedonians sent home on leave for the winter (*An.* 1. 24. 1 and 3). 'Alexander deployed the phalanx of the Macedonians like this: On the right, where he was himself, he had the hypaspists, and next to them the *pezhetairoi* whom he extended right along to the left wing, the brigades under their generals of that particular day.' This description obviously cannot refer to only three brigades, and must include all six. The odd (unparalleled) phrase about the generals, suggestive of a rotation of commanders among the brigades (rather than a rotating order of precedence, as in, e.g., Robson's Loeb translation) arises really, I take it, from an oddity (also unparalleled) of Alexander's situation of the moment. Either two or three of the six regular generals, as it happened, also were on leave, being themselves newly married. (Arr. *An.* 1. 24. 1; cf. Berve, 1. 114 for brigade commanders.) Ptolemy's record or memory (or patience) may have failed him, as to the temporary substitutes.

[4] It is not hard to see that Ptolemy perhaps could have written that, and that the three words could have fallen out through an oversight of Arrian, or of a copyist.

second), and I am inclined to follow him in this, both on general grounds and for a particular reason which will appear presently.[1]

Bosworth succeeds in identifying two of the *asthetairoi* brigades of the phalanx, the brigade of Coenus and that of Polyperchon, and he observes that each of them is a brigade from Upper Macedonia, that of Coenus from Elimiotis, and Polyperchon's from Tymphaea. He conjectures plausibly that the third *asthetairos* brigade was that of Perdiccas, from Orestis and Lyncestis, and he sees this name as the distinguishing mark, in the phalanx, of the units of Upper Macedonia as opposed to those of the Old Kingdom or Macedonia of the Plain. In search of the name's meaning and derivation he suggests an original ἀσισθέταιροι from ἄσιστα a by-form of ἄγχιστα—'most closely related companions'. ' "Closest in kin companions" would have encapsulated nicely both their Macedonian nationality and their previous independence of the central monarchy.'[2] There is something very attractive in these suggestions. Personally I prefer an alternative original ἀρισθέταιροι ('best companions'), supported by the shortened forms of some Thessalian proper-names (Astoboulos, etc.).[3] This was considered by Bosworth but rejected by him on grounds that seem in the one instance insufficient and in the other instance valid only if his 'Upper Macedonian' suggestion is first accepted.[4] Further examination of the *asthetairoi* passages in Arrian leads me to question or qualify the Upper Macedonian connection.

The first reference of Arrian to *asthetairoi* (at the siege of Tyre, early 332) reads 'the brigade of Coenus, the *asthetairoi* (ἡ Κοίνου τάξις οἱ ἀσθέταιροι καλούμενοι), not *of* the *asthetairoi* (τῶν ἀσθεταίρων καλουμένων) as we ought to expect if there were three such brigades at the time.[5] If Arrian is writing here with exactitude, he is telling us that here and now, at Tyre, the brigade of Coenus is the *only* brigade of *asthetairoi*. Opinions vary as to Arrian's *akribeia* as a military historian (and doubtless his performance itself varies from time to time). But a second detail suggests to me that in this instance he perhaps is being absolutely exact. Comparing Alexander's battle-order for Granicus (334) and for Issus (333) (and Gaugamela 331), we see that the brigade of Coenus has won promotion at Issus (and keeps it at Gaugamela). The order

---

[1] Bosworth, loc. cit. 247: 'Πεζέταιροι, it seems, designates the whole six phalanx battalions.' The fact that this explanation is 'untidy', leaving the three regiments with both names applicable to them, need not count against it perhaps. There is a close parallel in the popular (though not the official) nomenclature of the British Brigade of Household Cavalry. To the general public they are all Horse Guards (and their haunt is Horse Guards Parade). But the name of only one of the three regiments is Royal Horse Guards. The other two regiments, 1st and 2nd Life Guards, are Horse Guards popularly none the less, though Life Guards (1st or 2nd) to the discriminating.

[2] Loc. cit. 251.

[3] Cited by Bosworth, loc. cit. 251 n. 3: Astoboulos, *IG* ix. 2. 414 b 3; Astodamos, ibid. 536, 10; Astokleas, ibid. 506, 5; 580. 6; Astomachos, ibid. 234, 13; 281, 3. There are many more (see ibid. Index, p. 288).

[4] Bosworth (loc. cit.), 'there is no reason why Philip should have used this peculiarly Thessalian contraction.' But common factors in the Thessalian and Macedonian dialects are not to be ruled out: see on *tagonaga*, p. 649 above. I do not see *asthetairos* as a word coined now by the king, but as a word in current use, for 'best friends'.

[5] Arr. *An.* 2. 23. 2. Cf. 6. 6. 1 καὶ τῶν ἀσθεταίρων καλουμένων τὴν Πείθωνος τάξιν.

of the brigades, reading from the right (the position of honour or seniority, next to the hypaspists) is: at Granicus, 1 Perdiccas 2 Coenus: at Issus (and Gaugamela), 1 Coenus 2 Perdiccas. And at Tyre itself, the brigade of Coenus is the only brigade selected (along with hypaspists) for service in the ship-borne assault which did carry the city.[1] Something has happened, in the first year in Asia, to bring the brigade of Coenus to the top. Perhaps it distinguished itself at Granicus or at Halicarnassus: perhaps it was always the smartest and the best on the job: perhaps at this time Alexander liked Coenus best. What-ever the reasons, this brigade, and if Arrian is being exact this brigade only, by 332 has been honoured with the name *asthetairoi*, 'best Companions'; and on this interpretation the name was honouring their performance, and without reference to their Elimiote origin. It is a battle honour, making them (by a modern usage) 'King's Own'.

On this interpretation still, after Gaugamela perhaps, and certainly by the time of the invasion of India, the same honour has been extended to two more brigades (one of them Polyperchon's), or perhaps to three more, if the number of brigades now has risen to seven (as seems probable).[2] If distinguished service was the criterion for the brigade of Coenus, the same criterion cer-tainly must have obtained for the others too. I see support for the inter-pretation in the coincidence (which does need explaining) that on the three occasions in India where the army is divided and Alexander has about half of it under his personal command, his 'half' of the phalanx is, each time, 'the *asthetairoi*', along with his favourite hypaspists.[3] On another occasion, when only one phalanx battalion is included in his own personal command, it is a brigade of the *aesthetairoi*.[4] This almost seems to bring the *asthetairoi* in these years inside that charmed inner circle of the king's special favourites, so familiar to readers of Arrian, 'the hypaspists, the archers and the Agrianians . . .'). The 'coincidence' of his repeatedly commanding *asthetairoi* himself ceases to be remarkable, for no student of Alexander will be surprised if, when he divided his forces, he took it for granted that for his own command the best was just good enough. Finally, this reconstruction of how the *asthetairoi* came into existence, piecemeal and beginning with the brigade of Coenus in 334 or 333, virtually removes any inconsistency from that use by Arrian of the name *pezhetairoi* covering all six brigades of the phalanx in winter 334/3 (above, p. 710). If the brigade of Coenus were already *asthetairoi* then (uncertain; the award could have come after Issus, autumn 333), they were still the only *asthetairoi*, one brigade out of the six, and Arrian's (or Ptolemy's) failing to name them separately would not be surprising.

Recapitulating: the Alexander of Anaximenes (F 4) who extended the name *pezhetairoi* to 'the mass and the infantry of the Macedonians' was Alexander the Great. (Presumably it was now, too, that the *pezhetairoi* of Philip, the royal guard and the *corps d'élite*, were named hypaspists.) In Asia from the start the six brigades of the phalanx were *pezhetairoi*. Whether the eight brigades that

---

[1] Arr. *An.* 2. 23. 2; 24. 3.
[2] See on this, Bosworth, loc. cit. 247 and n. 2, with bibliography.
[3] Arr. *An.* 4. 23. 1; 5. 22. 6; 6. 21. 3; cf. Bosworth, loc. cit. 247–9.
[4] Ibid. 6. 6. 1.

remained in Macedonia under Antipater were *pezhetairoi* too, is a matter for inference. Perhaps not, since the name, interesting and glamorous as it is, did not survive in the tradition beyond Alexander's own lifetime to be borne by Macedonians of Antipater, Cassander, or the Antigonids, so far as we know. In Asia Alexander found occasion to reward distinguished service by conferring on a whole brigade battle honours in the form of the more select name *asthetairoi*, until as time went on half the brigades (or perhaps four out of seven) had achieved this distinction, which carried with it the likelihood of their being kept most often under the king's personal command. This development belongs to military history, and can tell us little of the social, ethnical, or political development of the Macedonian people directly. The fact that certainly two and perhaps three of the three or four *asthetairoi* brigades were levies from four or more *ethne* of Upper Macedonia is to be seen as an 'accident', in the sense that they had been awarded this status not because they came from Elimea or Orestis but because they had distinguished themselves in action. The inference that perhaps the uplands of Upper Macedonia did produce the very best and toughest soldiers, the 'Highland Divisions' of the army, is legitimate, and not surprising.

Asthetairoi is a welcome addition to our Macedonian military vocabulary. To feel disappointment if it is not also a political or social master-key is natural, but to grumble about it would be ungrateful as well as unrewarding.[1]

Epilogue

I suggested above (p. 711) that it was the brigade of Coenus that first became *asthetairoi*, a reward for distinguished service in 334 or 333. It is entertaining to notice how nearly the brigade of Perdiccas (No. 1 at Granicus but No. 2 at Issus and Gaugamela) may have come to winning the new *asthetairos* name. At the siege of Halicarnassus (334), on one occasion two soldiers of this brigade, not drunk perhaps but having drink taken, began an impromptu assault alone, which drew more of the brigade in, and brought about some fierce fighting in which 'the city narrowly escaped being taken' (Arr. *An.* 1. 21. 1–4). If only it had been taken, this, surely, would have been *asthetairos*-worthy. (As it was, the two heroes had called attention, perhaps prematurely, to a weakened section of the city wall which Alexander did try hard to exploit now, but in vain: ibid. 5–6; 22. 1–3.)

---

[1] Mr. Woodhead points out to me a difficulty in Arr. *An.* 7. 11. 3, the passage about the filling of the famous Macedonian units with Persians, with 'a Persian *agema*, and Persian *pezhetairoi*, and *asthetairoi* as well' . . . etc. Could Alexander give a 'battle honours' name to a Persian unit of new recruits? Logically of course he could not: the difficulty must be allowed. The circumstances however, with Alexander in a towering rage, may be thought to condone the anomaly; or even to suggest it as one that Alexander enjoyed, a form of punishment for the mutinous Macedonians.

APPENDIX 4

Afterthoughts on the *Letter of Philip*

FOR the final outbreak of war between Philip and Athens, important sources obviously are [D.] 11 and 12. [D.] 11 *Reply to the Letter of Philip* was accepted in antiquity by some as Demosthenes' 'reply' to an ultimatum of Philip; but nobody now accepts it as genuine. Didymus (*in Dem.* 11. 7) wrote that this speech appeared complete and almost word for word in the 7th Book of the *Philippica* of Anaximenes, who was believed by many to be its compiler. Compilation is the word, for it includes a number of short excerpts or reminiscences of passages from speeches of Demosthenes (one of them the *Crown*, of 330). Anaximenes can be accepted as author (so Jacoby, *FGrH* no. 72 F 11, and J.'s commentary ad loc. p. 108). P. Wendland, *Anaximenes von Lampsakos* (1905) 5–12, examines the passages.

[D.] 12 (*Letter of Philip*) was attributed by Wendland to Anaximenes also (op. cit. 13 ff.). Momigliano concurred.[1] But this view relied over-much on a belief that there was only one *Letter* of Philip surviving in antiquity, and that therefore citations or allusions to it which do not correspond with our *Letter* ([D.] 12) count strongly against the genuineness of [D.] 12.[2] The survival of two *Letters* seems certain (above, p. 567), and the arguments of Pohlenz reinforced by Wüst carry conviction that [D.] 12 is not a composition of Anaximenes for his *History* but is basically the Note which Philip really sent on this occasion.[3] If this is so it gains greatly in interest of course, as our only example of something that can be thought of as in some sense Philip's composition. Those who accept the *Letter* as 'genuine' can still see it, if they choose, as the work of an orator from the school of Isocrates acting as Philip's 'speech-writer' here. As a composition it certainly is a disappointingly 'rhetorical' work, and does perhaps encourage the thought that Philip may have got an orator to write it for him. (Python of Byzantium perhaps, or even the young Eumenes of Cardia?[4])

Against that, we remember that Philip himself was a very good orator.[5] He had not studied under Isocrates; but really anybody could write something like Isocrates if he abandoned his mind to it. I mentioned earlier an oddity in the manner of referring to Callias of Chalcis in this *Letter* ('your general, Callias'), which to me suggests an idiosyncratic (and authentic) touch (p. 553). (Idiosyncratic certainly, but less encouraging, is the patent

---

[1] 'Due problemi storiografici, I Anassimene e la lettera di Filippo', *RIL* 65 (1932) 565 ff.; cf. P. Treves, *Athenaeum* 14 (1936) 199–200.

[2] Did. *In Dem.* 10. 24; 9. 43; D. 18. 76. The first reference ought to correspond exactly with [D.] 12. 23, but does not.

[3] Wüst 133 ff.; M. Pohlenz, 'Philipps Schreiben an Athen', *Hermes* 64 (1929) 41 ff.

[4] For Python, p. 489; for Eumenes, p. 381.

[5] p. 337 above.

error by which the writer names a Thracian king Sitalces when all the attendant circumstances show that he must mean Cotys (Cotys II, father of Cersobleptes).)[1] This ought to be the error of a not-very-good compiler: as an error of Philip, very surprising, and as an error of the rather unusually skilful compiler that we recognize as author here if the author is not Philip, hardly less surprising.) Very interesting is the closing sentence of the whole piece, quite unrhetorical. In the place where every rhetor wants to leave something memorable, this writer says, with a rather woolly clumsiness that baffles me a little, 'with the gods my witness I will deal with your case' (διαλήψομαι περὶ τῶν καθ' ὑμᾶς). One feels that nobody writing this for money would have dared to leave it like that: this must be the great man himself writing?[2] Whatever exactly he means (see below, n. 2), it would have been cleaner to write περὶ ὑμῶν, rather than the shuffling περὶ τῶν καθ' ὑμᾶς. (But perhaps cleanness here could be too brusque?) One other clause in the piece makes me wonder ([D.] 12. 20): 'It is easy for me to stop their mouths (and it would cost very little), and *to make them speak* panegyrics in my honour' (. . . καὶ ποιῆσαι λέγειν ἐπαίνους ὑπὲρ ἡμῶν). The accusative and infinitive construction (sc. αὐτοὺς λέγειν etc.) after ποιῆσαι is good for poets at any time, it seems, and (one would think) very good for the ordinary man in his daily conversation; but it is no favourite of the orators (I have not found an instance of it).[3] To me it suggests the king doing it himself here, not the rhetor doing it for him.

More important, obviously, would be matters of substance (if any) in the *Letter* which could be seen as the personal offerings of Philip himself. One passage especially could be of interest in this way, [D.] 12. 19–20. The writer has mentioned as one of his complaints (*enklemata*) that the Athenians had rejected his conciliatory proposals for a just settlement of Greece (ibid. 18). He goes on

The *demos* was the gainer from the proposals; but they did not suit the politicians (τοῖς λέγουσιν). I am told by those who know your system of government well that for the orators peace means war, and war means peace. They either support the generals or they attack them, but either way they make something out of them; and also by abusing publicly the most distinguished of the citizens . . . they win a reputation with the mob for being great democrats. Now it is easy for me to stop their mouths (and it would cost very little), and to make them speak panegyrics in my honour. But I should be ashamed if I were seen purchasing my good relations with you from these people. Why, to cap everything, they even try to dispute with me about Amphipolis . . .

[1] [D.] 12. 9.

[2] I cannot translate it as easily as I ought, or without recourse to the lexicon; LSJ[9] s.v. διαλαμβάνω III. 7 'state distinctly', Philip. ap. D. 12. 23! The verb is rich in alternatives, but this category is the only attested use of it followed not by a direct object but by περί. And apart from 'Philip' here, the only attested user is the grammarian Apollonius Dyscolus (2nd cent. A.D.), who uses it indeed constantly, to mean simply 'discuss', 'deal with': see R. Schneider and G. Uhlig, *Grammatici Graeci* 2. 2/3 (1910) *Index vocab.* p. 188. (In the *Epitaphios* attributed to Demosthenes—[D.] 60. 13—διαλαβεῖν means something quite different, to 'take apart' (sc. τὸν λόγον?) = 'digress'.)

Philip ends his *Letter*, then, 'I will deal with the things in relation to you.' (For καθ' ὑμᾶς, cf. LSJ[9] s.v. κατά B. IV. 2, τὸ κατ' ἐμέ etc. 'so far as I am concerned', D. 18. 247, Hdt. 7. 158 etc.). I do not know why LSJ[9] makes it 'I will state distinctly'.

[3] LSJ[9] s.v. ποιεῖν, A. II. 2. For conversational use, Socrates at Pl. *Theaet.* 149 A ὅτι ἀτο-πώτατός εἰμι—καὶ ποιῶ τοὺς ἀνθρώπους ἀπορεῖν. Cf. X. *Cyr.* 2. 2. 13; 4. 5. 48.

That paradox about war and peace had been used by Isocrates addressing Philip in 346, and in just this context to which Philip alludes now, the politicians who are hostile to him.[1] A nice compliment to Isocrates, perhaps, to borrow one of his better things. Yet there seems little to commend in the sentiment itself, as here developed. From every angle, it seems an error of taste and judgement, like that of the last German Emperor when he brushed aside as 'a scrap of paper' a treaty signed by several Great Powers. It was not good to call in question the *politeia* of the great and proud democracy. It was indiscreet to make the (well-justified) criticism of the relations between orators and generals. To tell the Athenians that their politicians could be bought, and bought cheaply, was itself a cheap sneer; and one very damaging to those who *had* been bought already. These unfortunates may be pardoned for thinking that with a friend like Philip they did not need an enemy. The object in making this remark, I suppose, was to encourage the demos to suspect most of its politicians now, and especially perhaps some who really were quite above suspicion.[2]

Really, this point made by Philip against the politicians at Athens is something of a disappointment. It is 'dirty', and probably that need not surprise us. But it is not very clever either; or it is clever in a small way and without regard to a longer term. It suggests Philip as a terror to his friends in Greece as well as to his enemies. How old a friend had one to be, to be confident that one would not be exposed or let down if it suited the patron better?

However, with this single exception the *Letter* is well designed and well executed for the purpose in hand. If Philip wrote it himself, we can recognize him as something more than just competent in the art of communication in this form. He is particularly good on Amphipolis (20 ff.), a topic where his case is incontrovertible, and he does not spoil it by including anything from the pitiful contribution of Speusippus and Antipater of Magnesia (p. 514).

---

[1] Isoc. 5. 73 f.

[2] An example, the anecdote told of Leon of Byzantium (Suid. s.v. *Leon* 265), containing a quotation from a letter of Philip to the Byzantians 'If I were giving Leon all the money he asked for, I should have taken Byzantium at the first blow.' Though Leon had opposed Philip, he could not face the *demos*, according to this story, but committed suicide. Yet the Suidas entry includes a book on Alexander and his times among his publications. The anecdote is unreliable, obviously, but we cannot know that it is totally fictitious.

APPENDIX 5

Chronological note on the Amphissa case, 340/39

Wüst's pages on the chronology of the fourth Sacred War are a model of lucidity in their statement of the alternatives. Did the Amphissa case first erupt at the autumn Pylaea of 340 or at the spring Pylaea of 339?[1] If at the former, was Philip elected to the command against Amphissa at the spring or the autumn Pylaea of 339? The timing of the other incidents in the story follows from the answers to these questions, and especially the first.

Beloch had made a good case for the autumn Pylaea of 340 as the occasion for the 'eruption'. But Wüst offered an elegant refutation of the technical argument (concerning the election date of the Athenian officials of whom Aeschines was one, the *pylagori*) on which Beloch's case partly depended.[2] Moreover one of the consequences of beginning the sequence of the story in autumn 340 is that the extraordinary meeting of the Amphictyonic Council, made necessary by the events at and after the 'eruption' meeting, must be put probably in winter 340/39, *fairly soon* after the 'eruption' meeting.[3] At this extraordinary meeting the Council voted for military action against Amphissa, and elected Cottyphus to command it 'because Philip was not at home in Macedonia, nor in Greece, but was so far away among the Scythians'.[4] Philip did not begin his Scythian campaign against Atheas before (we must suppose) spring of 339, and up to then was still in the neighbourhood of Byzantium. If Aeschines is reporting accurately here, his report points to summer 339 as the date of Cottyphus' election as general, and probably to the spring Pylaea as the date of the 'eruption' meeting.

But elegant though Wüst's demonstration was, the truth seems to me that the conclusion to which it led him was almost certainly wrong, and that Beloch's dates were almost certainly right. For the plain fact is that the incidents themselves of the whole story do require a full twelve months in which they can happen, and not less than twelve. The few details of the story that we possess come to us from Aeschines, and there is no reason at all to disbelieve in them.[5] The expedition led by Cottyphus did take place. Amphissa

[1] The Athenian 'archonship of Theophrastus' (Aeschin. 3. 115) allows for either.

[2] Beloch 3². 2. 295; so, too, Momigliano, *FM* 155); *contra*, Wüst 153 ff. Since the technical argument has become irrelevant, thanks to Wüst, I do not reproduce it here.

[3] Aeschines (3. 124) said of the extraordinary meeting that 'the Council was instructed to meet at Thermopylae on a date fixed in advance of the next regular meeting' πρὸ τῆς ἐπιούσης πυλαίας ἐν ῥητῷ χρόνῳ εἰς Πύλας. Violence had been offered to Council members, and tempers were running high at the time of this decision; it seems very unlikely that the matter was being simply shelved for some months.

[4] Ibid. 128.

[5] The discrepancy between Aeschines and Demosthenes in their accounts of the action taken by Cottyphus is more apparent than real. According to Aeschines there was an expedition, and it imposed terms on Amphissa (3. 129). According to Demosthenes, the expedition

was in some way brought to terms. A fine was imposed, and she was given time in which to pay it. She agreed to exile the leaders responsible for the recent actions against the Council, and to recall others who had opposed them and had been driven out. It was when Amphissa had failed to fulfil the terms, as Aeschines puts it 'a long time after', that Philip was elected to lead a second expedition (the army with which he seized Cytinium and Elateia in autumn 339).[1] Aeschines certainly had an interest in emphasizing this 'long time', because it helped to disconnect him personally from having been responsible for Philip's arrival in Greece. But this does not throw doubt on his details about Amphissa during this interval. There had been time for Amphissa to default and to be seen to default in the payment of her fine by the final date; and also for her to recall from exile the leaders expelled by Cottyphus, and to exile in turn their opponents who had been recalled then. A matter of months is needed, a good many months, to make any sense of this at all. It would be satisfactory, for example, to think that the fine on Amphissa was ratified at the spring Pylaea at the end of a short campaign by Cottyphus, and that Amphissa was given six months in which to pay the fine, by the autumn Pylaea.

In short, there is a contradiction here between Aeschines when he tells of these details which require a lapse of many months between the expedition of Cottyphus and the election of Philip to lead the second expedition, and Aeschines when he said that Cottyphus had been appointed to command the first expedition because Philip already was 'among the Scythians' (i.e. in summer 339). If this last detail is correct, then the other details about Amphissa's treatment by Cottyphus are an invention or a mistake, because the timing simply would not allow for the interval of months which is required. If the details about Amphissa are correct, then the detail about 'the Scythians' is wrong. If a choice must be made between these two things (and it must), there seems no room for doubt or even hesitation. The detail about 'the Scythians' is, in itself, extraneous and an accident. In the lawcourt at Athens in the year 330 it did not matter to anybody whether on that occasion nine years earlier Philip had been among the Scythians or the Illyrians, outside Byzantium or in bed nursing his thigh run through by a Triballian spear. All that mattered was that he had been out of reach then, and could not be chosen to command an Amphictyonic army. If Aeschines made a mistake about this after nine years, it would be neither very reprehensible nor very surprising (as Beloch rightly saw). The details about Amphissa, on the other hand, are

was a fiasco: 'some of the Amphictyons never arrived, and those who arrived got nothing done' (18. 151). The Boeotians and the Athenians absented themselves from Cottyphus. And a hostile critic could say not unfairly that those who came accomplished nothing, since Aeschines himself shows (ibid.) that Amphissa did not fulfil the terms imposed, and a second expedition (Philip's) had to be voted later.

Demosthenes' information that Philip's election to command the second expedition was 'at the next Pylaea' (after the expedition of Cottyphus) does not prevent our thinking that Cottyphus' terms to Amphissa were ratified at the spring Pylaea (though the expedition itself was just before it), and that Philip's election was at the autumn Pylaea of 339: this against Aeschines 3. 128 f. (on which, below, here).

[1] Aeschin. 3. 129.

crucial for the whole story, in fact they are the story, at this point of it. They contain nothing in any way improbable, and there must be a strong presumption that they are right.

If we discard, then, Aeschines' detail about the Scythians, a table of the events of the Amphissa story comes out as follows:

Autumn Pylaea 340
October/November
	(1) Amphissa's charge against Athens
	(2) Aeschines' counter-charge against
	     Amphissa
	(3) Violence in the Sacred Plain etc.
	(4) Decision to hold an extraordinary
	     Council meeting
		Philip at
		Byzantium; his
		seizure of Athenian
		corn fleet is recent
		(September); Athens
		has declared war
		on him

Extraordinary meeting of Council December/January	Decision to use an army against Amphissa: election of Cottyphus to command	Philip at Byzantium
Spring 339	Cottyphus' expedition against Amphissa	Philip leaves Byzantium, for 'Scythia'
Spring Pylaea 339 April/May	Amphissa fined: payment by autumn Pylaea?	Philip in 'Scythia'
Summer 339	Thebans occupy Nicaea	Philip in 'Scythia'
Autumn Pylaea 339 October/November	Amphissa's fine still unpaid. Decision for a second expedition: Philip to command	Philip back in Macedonia
November 339		Philip seizes Cytinium and Elateia

Since there have been writers who thought that Philip's election as general to lead the second expedition against Amphissa was at the spring Pylaea of 339, one must point out briefly the consequences of this view.[1] One needs to believe either that Philip's expedition to the Danube ('Scythians') began in late autumn 340, went on through the winter, and enabled him to be back in Macedonia by April 339; or that the Amphictyons elected him to the command when he was still in 'Scythia', in spite of the fact that this was a command which needed to produce some visible results quickly, since the previous expedition had failed to produce any. The former alternative would imply one of the most improbable stories in the history of Greek warfare. The second would imply that the Amphictyons were not quite right in the head. However much they may have wanted to oblige Philip, to do it in so inept and transparent a way would go beyond what is possible κατὰ τὸ ἀνθρώπινον; and if it had been done thus some trace of the ribaldry that greeted it must surely have come down to us.

[1] Kromayer, *AS* 182 f.; Pickard-Cambridge, *Demosthenes* 363 and 390 and *CAH* 6. 256; and others.

APPENDIX 6

Philip's intervention at Eresus

THE inscription of Eresus through which we learn that altars to Zeus Philippios were set up there does not tell us why they were set up, or when.[1] The only other evidence connecting Philip with Eresus (indirectly) is that concerning Aristotle's pupil Theophrastus, who is said to have been on good terms with Philip, and to have had an important part in the overthrow of tyranny at Eresus his native city.[2] The inscription itself is concerned retrospectively with a tyranny of three brothers, Hermon, Heraeus, and Apollodorus.[3] The altars to Zeus Philippios, whatever precisely they may mean in terms of honour and recognition of benefits received, mean obviously something of very great local importance, and the inference no doubt is justified that Philip had been in some sense a liberator here. This looks like another of the cities where he had been able to intervene by sending troops or money or both in support of revolutionaries who in this instance were able to overthrow the government. But when, and in what circumstances, remains open to conjecture.

H. Pistorius, who considered this question in detail, found three occasions in Philip's reign where an intervention could be thought possible.[4] (1) In 350, as part of the activities by sea alluded to in general terms by Demosthenes in the *First Philippic* (which he dated to spring 349);[5] (2) in 343, as part of the activities at sea alluded to in the *Halonnesus* speech;[6] (3) in 340 in connection with the Perinthus and Byzantium operations and the renewal of war with Athens. Any date much later than 340 becomes very difficult to accept, because by 336 (Alexander's succession as *hegemon* of the Greeks) a second tyranny already had established itself at Eresus.[7]

[1] Tod 191, 4 f. On Zeus Philippios, see p. 692.

[2] Plu. *Mor.* 1126 A; ibid. 1097 B; Aelian *VH* 4. 19. Plutarch gives to Theophrastus the same order of credit and responsibility as to Plato and Aristotle, as philosophers who once did something worth while in practical terms; Plato at Syracuse (fall of Dionysius II), Aristotle at Stagira (its restoration). If it is right to think of the same kind of responsibility in all three cases, it was responsibility by influence, on Dion to attempt Syracuse, on Philip to agree to the restoration of Stagira, and (for Theophrastus) on Philip to promote in some way the liberation of Eresus.

The allusion of Aelian (loc. cit.) to Theophrastus connects him with Philip only in the most general way—καὶ Πλάτωνα δὲ ἐτίμησε καὶ Θεόφραστον—concluding a short passage on Philip's open-handed support of Aristotle. But Theophrastus' local knowledge of Macedonia and his property at Stagira are generally accepted as good evidence for his having moved to Macedonia from Mytilene with Aristotle in 343. (Cf. O. Regenbogen, *RE* Suppl. VII (1940) 1357 f.; W. Jaeger, *Aristotle* (2nd edn., trans. R. Robinson, Oxford, 1950) 115 f. n. 1.)

[3] Tod 191, 35 ff., 137 ff.

[4] H. Pistorius, *Beiträge zur Geschichte von Lesbos im vierten Jahrhundert v. Chr.* (Bonn, 1913) 60 ff., 120 ff.

[5] D. 4. 34.   [6] [D.] 7. 15.

[7] [D.] 17. 7. The tyranny of Agonippus and Eurysilaus (Tod 191 ,1 ff., 127 ff.).

Pistorius favoured 343; but there is an objection both to that date and to the earlier one that seems insuperable. The Athenian concern with the cities of Lesbos, former members of the Confederacy (Mytilene rejoined in 346) was such that Demosthenes must have commented on an intervention by Philip at Eresus in the *First Philippic* if it had already happened, or in an *Olynthiac* speech if it happened a little later. Likewise the silence of the *Halonnesus* speech and of Demosthenes in the three speeches (8, 9, and 10) of 341, really guarantees that Philip had taken no action at Eresus in 343.

In the same way *polypragmosyne* in Lesbos in the time leading up to the embassies and the Peace of 346, or in the time leading up to the trial of Aeschines (345–343) could not possibly have been overlooked by Demosthenes speaking in 346 (D. 5) or 344 (D. 6) or (especially) at the trial itself in 343 (D. 19). Philip's intervention, in fact, came most probably in 340 or 339: with no contemporary speeches surviving, the greater events have squeezed it out of our very defective historical record.

The importance of Lesbos to Philip, for the war against Persia, is obvious. No one will be surprised if his sense of priorities invited him to give time and money (and perhaps troops) to a small adventure at Eresus even if it came when he was greatly preoccupied elsewhere.

SOME DATES IN THE REIGN OF
PHILIP II

359	Spring or early summer	Defeat and death of Perdiccas III : Illyrians in Upper Macedonia.
	Summer	Philip becomes King. ? His marriage with Phila.
		Athenian intervention : Philip defeats Argaeus : treaty with Athens.
	359–8	Training of the army.
358	Spring	Philip invades Paeonia, defeats Lyppeius.
	? Early summer	Philip defeats Illyrians (Bardylis) : recovers Upper Macedonia and extends frontier with Bardylis.
	? Summer	Marriage with Audata. ? Founding of Heraclea Lyncestis.
	Autumn or winter	Philip in Thessaly (Larissa) : ? marriage with Philinna.
357	Early summer	Beginning of Athenian 'War of the Allies' : Philip attacks Amphipolis.
	Summer	Chalcidian alliance with Illyrians (Grabus), and approach to Athens (rejected). (Athenians defeated by 'Allies' at Chios.)
	? Autumn	Philip takes Amphipolis : Philip's marriage with Olympias.
	? Winter	Philip takes Pydna : Philip's alliance with Chalcidian League.
356	? Spring	Coalition of Illyrians (Grabus), Paeonia, and Cetriporis (W. Odrysians) : Philip attacks and besieges Potidaea.
	? Early summer	Philip detaches Parmenion against Illyrians (Grabus) : occupies Crenides attacked by Thracians (Cersobleptes).
	c. 20 July	Birth of Alexander the Great.
	? 26 July	Athens joins coalition (above).
	August/September	Philip takes Potidaea : Parmenion's victory over Grabus.
	? End of August	Philip's racehorse wins at Olympia.
	(? September	First fighting near Delphi in the 'Sacred War'.)
	Autumn	(Athenians defeated by 'Allies' at Embata.)

355	? Spring	? Philip invades Paeonia and makes Lyppeius his vassal.
	Summer	(Athenians end 'War of the Allies', disastrously.)
		? Philip in Thessaly.
	Autumn Pylaea at Delphi	Amphictyons declare 'Sacred War' against Phocians.
	? Late autumn	Philip attacks (? or threatens) Methone.
354	Spring or summer	Philip takes Methone.
	Summer	(Sacred War: battle of Neon in Phocis.)
353	? Spring	? Alliance of Philip with Boeotian League.
		Philip supports Pammenes in Thrace.
	Summer and autumn	Philip in Thessaly: victory over Phayllus: defeated twice by Onomarchus.
352	Spring and early summer	Philip in Thessaly (Onomarchus in Boeotia): battle of Crocus Plain: capture of Pherae, then of Pagasae.
	Summer	Philip's election as *archon* of Thessalian League: his marriage with Nikesipolis.
		Chalcidian League makes separate peace with Athens.
		? Philip wins at Olympia with chariot.
	August	Philip threatens Thermopylae, defended by troops of Athens, Sparta, and Achaea.
	Autumn	Philip in Thrace: advances on Chersonese.
	November	Philip at Heraion Teichos: is taken ill.
351	? Early	Philip invades Chalcidice, intimidates 'Olynthus'.
		Philip puts pressure on Arybbas (Epirus).
		First Philippic of Demosthenes.
350	? Winter	Philip's half-brothers settle at Olynthus.
349	Summer	Philip invades Chalcidice.
		Alliance of Chalcidian League with Athens.
	Autumn	First Athenian reinforcement to Olynthus (Chares).
348	February	'Rising' against Athens in Euboea.
	Spring	Second Athenian reinforcement to Olynthus (Charidemus).
		Philip in Thessaly, expels 'Peitholaus' from Pherae.
	Early summer	Philip in Chalcidice; attacks Olynthus.
	Summer (and autumn)	Philip's peace overtures to Athens.
	September	Fall of Olynthus.

348/7	Winter	Athenian attempts to form a Greek alliance against Philip.
347		*Stasis* in Phocis: Phalaecus loses command.
346	January	Phalaecus regains command in Phocis.
	February	Athenian embassy to Philip.
	March	Philip invades Thrace (Cersobleptes).
	April (18 and 19 Elaphebolion)	Athenian Assembly, on peace.
	(24 Elaphebolion)	Philip takes Hieron Oros.
	May (3 Mounychion)	Second embassy leaves Athens for Macedonia.
	June (*c.* 23 Thargelion)	Philip arrives back in Pella.
	July (13 Skirophorion)	Philip at Thermopylae.
	(23 Skirophorion)	Surrender of Phocians to Philip.
	August–September	Amphictyonic Council at Delphi. Philip presides over Pythia.
345	? Spring	Appeal of Delos to the Amphictyony.
	? Summer	Philip in Illyria: campaign against Ardiaei: Isocrates' 2nd Letter to Philip.
	? Autumn	Applications of Messene and Megalopolis to join the Amphictyony.
344		Philip in Thessaly: trouble with Pherae, and others: the 'dekadarchy' of Demosthenes (6. 22).
	Summer	Philip supports Messene and Argos in war against Sparta: Demosthenes in Peloponnese as ambassador.
	Autumn	Embassies at Athens, from Philip and from Messene and Argos: *Second Philippic* of Demosthenes
	Winter 344/3	Persian embassy at Athens (also at Thebes, Sparta, and Argos): Embassy of Philip at Athens, including Python of Byzantium: treaty revision (*epanorthosis*) discussed.
343	Spring	Athenian embassy to Philip (Hegesippus).
	Summer	Philip supports oligarchs at Elis, Perillus at Megara.
		Athenian cleruchs to Chersonese under Diopeithes.
		Philip has troops in Euboea (Porthmos).
	September	Phocians pay first instalment of their fine at Delphi.
	? Autumn	Trial of Aeschines at Athens.

	Winter 343/2	Philip in Epirus.
		Persian reconquest of Egypt.
		Demosthenes ambassador in the Peloponnese and at Ambracia.
342	Early spring	Philip threatens Ambracia: Athenian troops to Acarnania.
	Spring	Philip in Thessaly: Revival of tetrarchs.
		The Halonnesus dispute: Philip's ambassadors at Athens: Speech of Hegesippus ([D.] 7).
		Philip's intervention in Euboea: Hipponicus helps 'tyrants' at Eretria.
	? July	Philip's series of campaigns in Thrace begins.
	Summer	Eurylochus at Eretria in Euboea.
	September	Antipater represents Philip at Pythian Games.
	Autumn	Friction between Cardia and Athenian cleruchs in Chersonese.
		Parmenion at Oreus in Euboea.
	Winter 342/1	Philip winters in Thrace.
341	Very early	Philip supports Cardia with troops.
		Diopeithes raids Macedonian territory in Thrace.
		Alliance of Athens with Chalcis.
	Spring	Callias of Chalcis raids Gulf of Pagasae with Athenian ships.
		Demosthenes' *Chersonese* speech (D. 8).
	Summer	Demosthenes' *Third Philippic* (D. 9).
		Demosthenes' *Fourth Philippic* (D. 10).
		Philip deposes Cersobleptes and Teres.
		Philip's alliance with Cothelas, king of the Getae, and marriage with his daughter.
	? Summer–autumn	Founding of Philippoupolis (Plovdiv), and other cities of Thrace.
	Autumn	Athenian embassies to Persia, and to Byzantium and other cities.
	Winter	Demosthenes and Callias of Chalcis in Peloponnese.
340	March: (16 Anthesterion)	Foundation meeting at Athens of Demosthenes' Greek Alliance.
		? Philip's alliance with Atheas, king of the Dobruja Scythians.
	June–July	Philip invades Chersonese supporting his fleet.

	July	Philip begins siege of Perinthus.
	September	Philip attacks Byzantium.
		His capture of the Athenian corn fleet.
	October	Athenian declaration of war.
	Autumn Pylaea	At Delphi Amphissa dispute breaks out.
	Winter	Amphictyons declare war on Amphissa.
339	Spring	Philip retires from Byzantium.
	Spring Pylaea	Amphictyons fine Amphissa.
	Early Summer	Philip's Scythian campaign against Atheas. Thebans occupy Nicaea.
	Late Summer	Philip's return to Macedonia.
	Autumn Pylaea	Amphictyons appoint Philip to command against Amphissa.
	November	Philip captures Elateia.
338	Spring	Philip's defeat of Chares and Proxenus: capture of Amphissa.
	Summer	Capture of Naupactus.
	22 August	Battle of Chaeronea.
		Peace with Boeotia and Athens and other Greek states.
	Autumn	Philip in Peloponnese.
337	Early	Formation of 'League of Corinth'.
	? Spring or summer	Philip's marriage with Cleopatra.
336	? Spring	? An Illyrian campaign of Philip (against Pleurias).
		Advance force under Parmenion invades Asia Minor.
	? July	Philip assassinated at Aegeae.

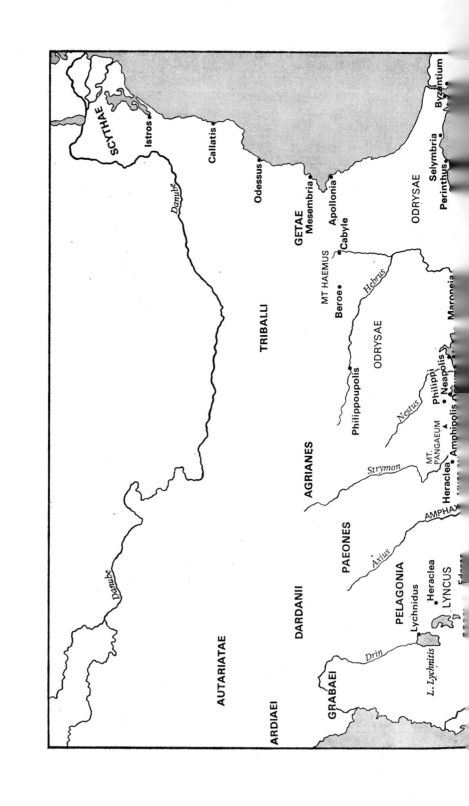

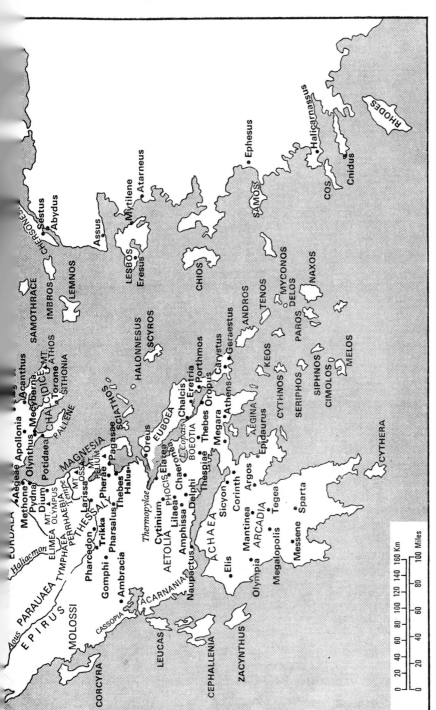

MAP 10. MACEDONIA AND ADJACENT AREAS

GENERAL INDEX

Iatrocles, 329, 337
Ichnae *and* Ichnaei, Maps 3 and 4
Idomenae, 128 n. 1.
ile, of Amphipolis, 352 f., 367, 411, 648; of Anthemus, 367, 369 f., 374, 411, 649; of Apollonia, 367 ff., 374, 378, 411; of Bottiaea, 367 f., 411, 649; 'Leugaian', 367, 411 f.; of Greek allies, 435; of Thessalians, 438
ile basilike, royal squadron, 367, 409, 411 f.
Ilium, 20, 25, 33, 38
Illyria, Illyris, 10, 14 f., 24, 35, 70, 81, 158, 223 n. 3, 306, 437, 709
Illyrian language, 43
Illyrians, 6, 9, 15, 52 f., 141 f., 147, 165 f., 172 f., 179, 181, 183, 185, 188, 191, 199 f., 208, 209 n. 1, 210 f., 213 f., 215 f., 220, 246 f., 251, 304 ff., 396, 406, 418, 424; in Philip's army?, 431 f., 434, 670, 674; an I. war (345), 469 ff.; 654, 658, 672
Imbros, Map 10; 232, 311, 331, 607
Imphees, 22
India, 46, 159
Inglis, 71, 116
Ingots, 74, 92, 189, 190 n. 3, 191 f.
Iolaus, 42, 123, 134, 384
Iollas, 42
Ionia, 94
Ionian Gulf, 91
Ionian Revolt, 87
Ionians, 451
Ionic dialect, 48, 75
Ipek, 190
Iphicrates, 177, 184, 195, 199, 204, 233, 407 n. 3, 424, 429 f.
Iraq, 74, 78
Iron, 71, 140, 143, 157
Irras, *see* Sirras
isegoria of Macedonians, 161, 392, 394 n. 1
Ismenias, 171
Isocrates, 14, 205; on Thessaly, 221, 223, 288, 524, 541; *Epist.* 6, 228 n. 2; 254, 277, 329, 350; on Amphipolis, 352; on 'cities of the north', 223 n. 2, 377 f.; on Companions, 400; on Macedonians, 453 n. 2; his *Philip*, 456 ff., (on Persia) 459–62, 464, 485; on monarchy, 461 f.; on Illyrians, 470 f.; *Epist.* 2, 488; trusted Philip, 514; 515, 528, 530, 608, 621, 624, 633; *Epist.* 3, 645 and n. 3; 672, 676, 714, 716
Issus, battle of, 420, 426, 430, 711 ff.
Istros *and* Istria, 560 ff.
Isyllus, 616 f.
Italy, 87, 668
Ivy, 110

Jason of Pherae, 179 f., 181, 260, 262, 288, 290 ff.; sons of, 291; 311, 430
Javelin, 53 n. 1, 71
Javelin-men, see *akontistai*
Jordanes on 'the Goths' at Odessus, 560
Jordania, 69 n. 4, 74 f., 77, 87 f., 91
Judge, the king as, in Macedonia, 393 ff.
Justin, 208, 220 f., 222–6, 285; mistaken on Arybbas?, 306 n. 4; on Philip's election, 390, 651 n. 1; on Illyrians, 471 f.; on population transfers, 559; on Scythians, 560 ff.; on Byzantium, 568 n. 2; on Atheas, 582 f.; 598, 605 n. 4; on 'League of Corinth', 626 ff., 632; 699, 702

Kabul, 88
Kačanik, 94, 190, 656
Kačanj, 142
Kalamaria 93 n. 2
Kalamata, Gulf of, 617
Kalamitsa, 97 n. 3
Kalamoto, 194, n. 2
Kara Burun, 63, 140
Karaburnu Megalo, 116
Karaburnu Mikro, 97, 144
Karaorman, 95, 111, 158
Karatove, 190, 192
Karvale, N., 97 n. 3
katapontismos, 276 f.
Kavadarci, 139, 145, 657
Kavalla, 69 n. 4, 71 n. 5, 75, 97 n. 3, 158 n. 1, 234
Keos, Map 10
Kepia, 158 n. 1
Kerata, pass, 599
Khortiatis, Mt., 10, 197
Kilkis, 70, 73, 138 n. 2, 666
Kirli Dirven, pass, 129, 131
Kithas, *see* Scithae
Kitsevo, 92, 141
Kjustendil, Map 9; 70 f., 80, 82, 111, 114, 190
Klodones, 51
Knife on coins, 669
Koine, standard Greek, 49
Koine Eirene, 216 f.; proposed (346), 340; 452, 462; no *KE* in 346, 483 ff.; proposed (344/3), 490 ff., 511 f.; in 'League of Corinth', 624 ff., 634, 636
Korčula, 190
Koritsa *or* Korcë, Map 9; 53 n. 1, 92, 191
Kossovo, 70 f., 91 f., 172, 191
Kotor, 190, 668
Koufalia, 79
Kozani, 95 f., 143 f., 164 n. 2, 165, 196
Kratovo, Map 9; 70 f., 73, 75, 79, 82, 94 n. 5, 111, 138 n. 2, 657, 666 f., 669

PLATE I. THRACO-MACEDONIAN SILVER COINS (*see table on p.* 80)

a. Tynteni, Æ triple stater; Oxford, see Kraay, *Greek Coins and History* VI 7 (p. 74)

b. Ichnaei, Æ hemi-stater; Cambridge, G XIV 13 (p. 77)

c. Derrones, overweight (41·12 gm); Oxford, G XXV 15 (p. 76)

d. Derrones, overweight (40·46 gm); London, G XXV 16 (p. 76)

e. Laeaei, overweight (32·08 gm); London, G XXV 19 (p. 79)

f. Letaei, Æ stater; Oxford, like G XIV 17 (p. 77)

g. Orrescii, Æ triple stater; London, G XVIII 2 (p. 78)

h. Orrescii, Æ stater; Oxford, G XVIII 13 (p. 78)

i. Edones, Getas king of, Æ triple stater; London, G XXVII 29 (p. 78)

j. Ichnaei, Æ stater; London, G XIV 12 (p. 77)

k. Goat with Æ, Æ stater; London, like G V 29 (p. 84)

l. Goat with ΛΑ, Æ stater; London, like G V 25 (p. 84)

m. Goose and salamander, Β diobol; Oxford, like G XXVII 19 (p. 81)

n. Bisaltici, Β octobol; Cambridge, like G XII 9 (p. 77)

o. Ox with sun/Pegasus, Β tetrobol; Oxford, like G XXVII 27 (p. 113)

G = Gaebler

PLATE II. THRACO-MACEDONIAN SILVER COINS (*continued*)

p. Alexander I, octodrachm; Oxford, like G XXVIII 1 (p. 84)

q. Alexander I, tetradrachm; Oxford, like G XXVIII 20 (p. 109)

r. Alexander I, tetrobol; Oxford, G XXVIII 23 (p. 107)

s. Perdiccas II, tetrobol; Oxford, like G XXIX 2 (p. 120)

t. Pegasus, tetradrachm; Oxford, like G XXVI 23 (p. 113)

u. Docimus, tetrobol; Oxford, like G XXVII 33 (p. 110)

v. Archelaus I, didrachm; London, like G XXIX 11 (p. 138)

w. Amyntas III, didrachm; Oxford, like G XXX 6 (p. 180)

x. Chalcidian League, tetradrachm; London, G XVII 10 (p. 189)

y. Damastini, drachm (2·72 gm); Oxford, May XII 17a (p. 189)

z. Damastini, 'Heracleido-Keph', tetradrachm; Oxford, May IV 51a (p. 668)

aa. Philip II, tetradrachm; Oxford, like G XXX 42 (p. 665)

bb. Philip II, tetradrachm; Oxford, like G XXX 37 (p. 665)

cc. Pelagia, drachm of *z* standard above; Oxford, May X 2 (p. 669)

c.

f.

i.

l.

o.

b.

e.

h.

k.

n.

a.

d.

g.

j.

m.

r.

u.

x.

aa.

cc.

q.

t.

w.

z.

bb.

p.

s.

v.

y.

PLATE III.

The western frontier area of Philip
II, seen from the satellite. Lakes
from west to east are Ochrid,
Large Prespa, Little Prespa and
Ostrovo, and further south Kas-
toria and Ioannina; in the south-
west the sea shows by Corcyra.
Photo NASA

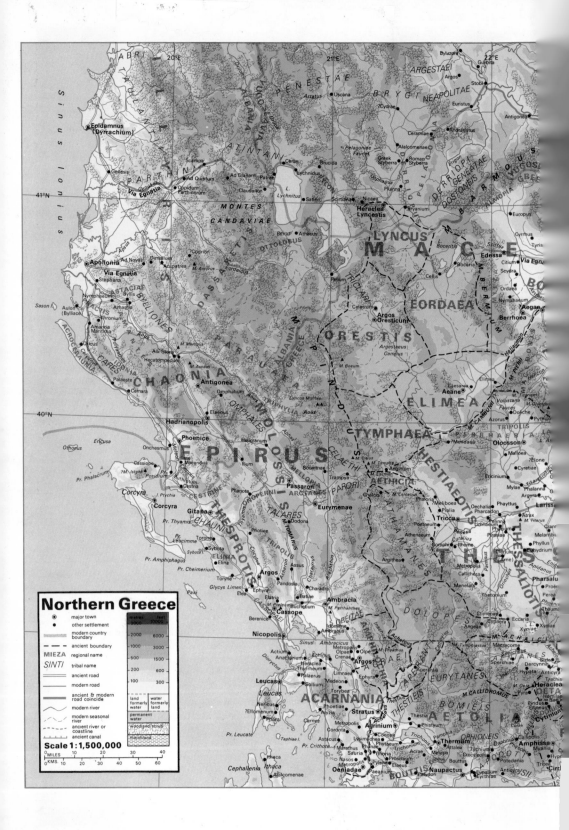

Northern Greece

⊛	major town	
•	other settlement	
	modern country boundary	
	ancient boundary	
MIEZA	regional name	
SINTI	tribal name	
	ancient road	
	modern road	
	ancient & modern road coincide	
	modern river	
	modern seasonal river	
	ancient river or coastline	
	ancient canal	

	metres	feet
	6000	18000
	2000	6000
	1000	3000
	500	1500
	200	600
	100	300

land formerly water · water formerly land
permanent water
woodland/scrub
marshland

Scale 1:1,500,000

MILES 10   20   30   40
KMS. 10 20 30 40 50 60